An Historical Dictionary of German Figurative Usage

By KEITH SPALDING

PROFESSOR EMERITUS OF GERMAN, UNIVERSITY COLLEGE OF NORTH WALES, BANGOR

WITH ASSISTANCE FROM
GERHARD MÜLLER-SCHWEFE

PROFESSOR EMERITUS OF ENGLISH,
UNIVERSITY OF TÜBINGEN

Fascicle 51

streng – tauschen

BLACKWELL PUBLISHERS · OXFORD

KEY TO PRINCIPAL ABBREVIATIONS

a.	archaic
Adolphi	O. Adolphi, *Das große Buch der Fliegenden Worte, etc.*, Berlin n.d.
Ahd. Gl.	*Die Althochdeutschen Glossen*, ges. und bearb. von E. Steinmeyer u. Eduard Sievers, Berlin 1879—98.
Bav.	Bavaria, Bavarian
bot.	botanical term
Büchmann	G. Büchmann, *Geflügelte Worte*, 27th ed., ergänzt von A. Langen, Berlin 1915.
c.	century
Car.	Carinthia, Carinthian
cf.	compare
cl.	cliché
Cod.	codex
coll.	in colloquial use
comm.	used in language of commerce
dial.	dialect expression
Dornseiff	F. Dornseiff, *Der deutsche Wortschatz nach Sachgruppen*, Berlin und Leipzig 1934.
dt.	deutsch
DWb	*Deutsches Wörterbuch von Jacob Grimm und Wilhelm Grimm*, Leipzig 1854ff.
e.l.	earliest locus or earliest loci
etw.	etwas
Fast. Sp.	Fastnachtspiele, usually quoted after *Fastnachtspiele aus dem 15. Jahrhundert*, herausgeg. v. Keller, Stuttgart 1853.
Fick	F. C. A. Fick, *Vergleichendes Wörterbuch der indogermanischen Sprachen*, 3rd ed. Göttingen 1874.
f.r.by	first recorded by
gen.	general
Götze	A. Götze, *Frühneuhochdeutsches Glossar*, 2nd ed., Bonn 1920.
Graff	E. G. Graff, *Althochdeutscher Sprachschatz*, Berlin 1834—42.
Hirt, *Etym.*	H. Hirt, *Etymologie der neuhochdeutschen Sprache*, 2nd ed., München 1925.
Hirt, *Gesch.*	H. Hirt, *Geschichte der deutschen Sprache*, 2nd ed., München 1925.
hunt.	word or expression used by huntsmen
jem.	jemand (nom. or acc.)

© *Basil Blackwell Ltd., 1992 ISBN 0 631 181482*
Typeset by Hope Services, Abingdon
Printed and bound by Whitstable Litho Printers Ltd., Whitstable, Kent.

Begierden . . . zu widerstehen . . . Der Streit der Urstoffe, ihr Streben gleichsam einander aufzulösen oder von sich zu stoßen'.

im Streit liegen to be in conflict or at variance; this can be used with ref. to people who are at war or at loggerheads and with ref. to abstracts which are in conflict, at least since the 17th c., e.g. Opitz 2,257: '*die Element selbst vollführen ihren Streit*', Gellert, *Nov.* 1,206: '*unsre Begierden stehen sehr oft mit unsern Pflichten im Streit*' (also Goethe, *Dicht.u. Wahrh.* 10); cf. similar *im Widerstreit liegen, sein, sich befinden,* figur. in non-mil. contexts with ref. to persons or abstracts since the 18th c., e.g. Mendelssohn, *Ges.Schr.* 1,71: '*die Punkte der Übereinstimmung und des Widerstreits dieser beiden Lehrgebäude*', Goethe 28,109 (W.) or 23,216 (W.).

mit sich selbst ~ (or *im Streit liegen*) to quarrel or argue with oneself; since OHG, e.g. Notker 1,288; cf. Goethe 2,145 (W.): '*ein edles Herz . . . das . . . bald mit sich selbst und bald mit Zauberschatten streitet*', also 10,237 (W.): '. . . *und stritt mit meinem tiefsten Sein*'.

die streitende Kirche (relig.) the Church Militant; translates *ecclesia militans* (contrasted with *ecclesia triumphans*); since MHG; cf. Jung-Stilling, *Werke* [edit. Grollm.] 1,157: '. . . *ein Reich gegründet, welches bis zu seiner* [i.e. Christ's] *Zukunft . . . die streitende Kirche genannt wird*'.

ohne Streit (a.) incontestably, undeniably; since MHG, e.g. *Iwein* 3027: '*sô was her Iwein âne strît ein degen*', still in Lessing, *Sinnged.* 1,124 as *ohne Streit,* but now a. and *unstreitig,* recorded by Steinbach [1734], has displaced it.

bloß keinen Streit (nicht) vermeiden! (joc.coll.) why fight? nonsensical remark made to lower the temperature between two people who are on the point of coming to blows; since ca. 1920.

der Streitpunkt point in dispute, question at issue; since the 17th c., e.g. (DWb) Hartknoch, *Pr.Kirch.* 48 [1684], f.r.b. Aler, *Dict.* 2,1852a [1727]; also as *ein strittiger Punkt; strittig* appeared in dictionaries in the 17th c., e.g. Kramer [1678] and Stieler [1691]; similarly, *ein umstrittener Punkt; umstritten* = 'contested, disputed.' is not yet listed in Adelung.

die Streitschrift polemical pamphlet (or treatise); since the 16th c., e.g. (DWb) Spangenberg, *Jagteuffel* 04b [1562], f.r.b. Kramer, *Teutsch-ital.* 1024a [1678].

streitlustig quarrelsome, pugnacious, fond of quarrelling; since late in the 18th c., e.g. J.J.Engel, *Schr.* 2,234 [1801]: '. . . *der immer Streitlustige . . .*'; not yet in Adelung who listed *streitmüthig* (now obs.) in this sense, but Campe [1810] recorded *streitlustig.* Much older is *streitsüchtig,* since the 17th c., f.r.b. Kramer [1719].

der Wortstreit altercation, dispute; beginnings in MHG, e.g. Wolfr.v.E., *Parz.* 258: '*ir bêder strît der worte*', then as a compound, e.g. *Passional* [edit. K.] 611: '. . . *heten manigen wortstrit,* f.r.b. Calepinus

1517b [1598]. The secondary meaning, i.e. 'quarrel about (or the meaning of) words' arose in the 18th c., e.g. Chr. Wolff, *Menschl.Verstand* 166 [1713]; cf. Goethe, *Faust I,* 1997: '*mit Worten läßt sich trefflich streiten*'.

jem.m etw. streitig machen to contest or dispute sb.'s right to sth.; since the 16th c., f.r.b. Faber, *Thes.* 929b [1587], e.g. Wieland 2,44 or 12,3; also used sometimes in reflex. locutions, e.g. Goethe 9,363 (W.): '*beide machen sich die Ehre streitig, uns zu unterjochen*'.

weit vom Streit macht alte Kriegsleut (prov.) if you keep out of the firing-line, you will live long; recorded. as prov. since the 17th c., e.g. Lehman, 480 [1640]; cf. the entry on *Fernkämpfer* on p. 764.

← See also under *abstreiten, anspinnen* (for *ein Streit spinnt sich an*), *Bart* (for *um des Kaisers Bart streiten*), *beilegen* (for *einen Streit beilegen*), *bestreiten, dritte* (for *wenn zwei sich streiten, lacht der Dritte*), *Esel* (for *ein Streit um des Esels Schatten*), *Geschmack* (for *über den Geschmack läßt sich nicht streiten*), *Hahn* (for *Streithahn*), *Hammel* (for *Streithammel*), *Kost* (for *die Kosten bestreiten müssen*) and *Zaun* (for *einen Streit vom Zaun brechen*).

streng: strong, severe, strict

streng (1) strong, great, mighty; belongs to the sense 'harsh, hard arduous' which could easily come to describe magnitude; extended to abstracts since MHG, e.g. '*strengiu arbeit*' (*Parz.* 285), '*strengiu nôt*' (*Parz.* 296), f.r.b, Maaler [1561]: '*das streng reden*'; cf. Gryphius, *Trauersp.* 185: '*die strenge Macht der stolzen Lieb*', Goethe, *Die guten Weiber:* '. . . *hätte sie alle Anlagen zum strengen Geize gehabt*'.

streng (2) exact, consistent, determined; belongs to the sense 'harsh, hard' (e.g. Luther 15,302 (Weimar): '*eyn strenge hart weltlich regiment*') which was extended to 'strict, severe', as in *strenge Regel* (current since MHG) and compounds which describe strict adherence or strong convictions such as *strenggläubig* (e.g. Goethe 7,122 (W.)), *strengkatholisch,strengkirchlich,* etc. (all since the 19th c.). An off-shoot from this is *strenggenommen* = 'strictly speaking' and 'actually, in actual fact, really' (since the 19th c.).

die strengen Künste (obs.) the crafts; describing the work of artisans as opposed to those of artists; e.g. Goethe, *Wanderj.* 3,12: '. . . *werden die Handwerke . . . durch die Bezeichnung strenge Künste von den "freien" entschieden getrennt*'. Now obs.

streng (3) (coll.) (adv.) definitely; in the sense of 'very much (so)'; 20th c. coll. in such compounds as *strengverheiratet* = 'very much married, not a free agent, kept on a short lead by his wife'; similarly *strengverlobt* = 'engaged without any hope of escape or of forming other relationships'.

drakonische Strenge draconic severity; a ref. to Drako, renowned for the severity of the laws which he imposed on Athens (ca. 621 B.C.); the adj. entered French as *draconique* in the 16th c., Engl.

in the 18th c. ('draconic' recorded since 1708); in German only since ca. 1800 (cf. Feldmann in *ZfdW.* 12,71).

strenge Herren regieren nicht lang (prov.) strict masters do not hold sway for long; mostly used with ref. to the weather, esp. heavy downpours or violent storms assumed to be of short duration; at least since the 17th c., e.g. (R.P.) Moscherosch, *Philander* 212 [1677].

←See also under *anstrengen, halten* (for *wir hielten strenge darüber*), *rechnen* (for *strenge Rechnung, gute Freunde*) and *Schule* (for *dir war das Unglück eine strenge Schule*).

Stresemann

er trug einen ~ (coll.) her wore a formal suit (black jacket, grey waistcoat and black grey-striped trousers); after Gustav Stresemann, German Chancellor (1923) and later Foreign Minister who was usually seen in this suit; since ca. 1925.

streuen: strew, scatter

jem. streut etw. (lit.) sb. throws, casts, scatters or spreads sth.; figur. since MHG, e.g. Bertold, *Dt. Predigten* 411: '*an allen sînen stricken, die er . . . gestreuwet allen unsern sachen*', sometimes with ref. to sowing, as in Luther Bible transl. Matth. 25,24: '*. . . vnd samlest, da du nicht gestrawet hast*', but also in many special locutions, e.g. *jem.m Dornen auf den Weg* ~ = 'to cause sb. difficulties or pain, make life hard for sb.' (cf. Steinbach's recording [1734]: '*einem was in den Weeg streuen*'), e.g. Klinger, *Werke* 4,97 and 8,129 (cf. also the entries on *Dornenbahn, Dornenweg, auf Dornen wandern* and *dornenvoller Weg* on p. 487), *Hindernisse* ~, as in Goethe, *Tasso* 1,4, *Licht* ~, as in Gotter 1,341: '*Licht streust du auf Dunkelheiten*', *Taten* ~ (poet.) = 'to sow acts, perform deeds', as in Kleist, *Werke* [edit. Schmidt] 4,9: '*Taten in die offenen Furchen streun*' (cf. Schiller 1,145 (S.): '*nur in die Furche der Zeit bedenkst du dich Taten zu streuen*' and the entry on p. 883), *Töne* ~ (poet.), as in Stifter, *Sämtl.W.* 1,146 on a zither player: '*. . . streute er gleichsam noch ein paar Hände voll Töne . . . über den See*', *jem.m Weihrauch* ~ = 'to praise sb., show one's veneration for sb.', since the 18th c., also with ref. to abstracts when it can mean 'to extol sth.', e.g. Gottsched, *Dt. Schaubühne* 1,277 [1741]: '*. . . deren sklavische Gefälligkeit allen Ausschweifungen Weihrauch streuet*'; also with ref. to scattering sugar over sth., as in Weise, *Polit. Red.* 132 [1677]: '*. . . an statt des Zuckers . . ., welcher auf die Rede gestreuet wird*'; also in compounds, e.g. *niederstreuen*, as in Arndt, *Ged.* 432 [1840]: '*dann streust du bunte Himmelsblumen nieder*'.

etw. streut etw. (lit.) sth. scatters, spreads, emits sth.; since MHG, e.g. (B.-M.-Z.) Megenberg, *B.d.Nat.* 346,2P: '*ain rôsenpoum der seinen smack . . . umb sich sträwt*', Luther Bible transl. Prov. 15,7: '*der weisen mund strewet guten rat*' (in A.V. 'the lips of the wise disperse knowledge'), often with ref. to the Sun, e.g. Megenberg, *B.d.Nat.*

3,14: '*diu sunne sträwet irn schein auf andren dinch*', Luther 30,3,576 (Weimar): '*. . . die liebe sonne . . . strewet yhren reichen schein*'; cf. also (DWb) Grob, *Dicht.Vers.* 102 [1678]: '*. . .daß der tau die perlen streuet*', Henrici, *Ernsth . . . . Ged.* 1,16 (1727): '*. . daß das Hertz dir süße Wünsche streut*', Ramler, *Einleit.i.d.sch.Wiss.* 2,172 [1758] on Homer: '*. . . keine kleinen verstohlnen Metaphern, die einen unzeitigen Glantz streun*'.

weitgestreut widely scattered or dispersed; a modern word (not even listed in *DWb.* [1955]), but now frequent in figur. use; cf. also modern *Streubesitz* = 'estate or holding consisting of dispersed fields, woods, etc.' (19th c.).

etw. verstreuen (1) (obs.) to waste, dissipate sth.; mainly with ref. to money or possessions, f.r.b. Kramer [1702]: '*das Geld, sein Gütlein verstreuen*'; occasionally with ref. to abstracts, e.g. Gutzkow, *R.v.G.* 1,334: '*. . . daß er seine Jugend verstreut, verzettelt hatte*'; now obs.

etw. verstreuen (2) to disperse, scatter sth.; figur. since Early NHG, e.g. Luther Bible transl. Psalm 1,4: '*. . . die gottlosen . . . . wie spreu, die der wind verstreuet*', Klopstock, *Zürcher See:* '*schön ist, Mutter Natur, deiner Erfindung Pracht auf die Fluren verstreut*'; also used with ref. to the spreading of rumours for 'to circulate, spread, disseminate', mainly in 18th c., now obs. (see the entry under *ausstreuen*); *verstreut* = 'dispersed, scattered', current since Early NHG (e.g. Fischart) is still alive.

Leute verstreuen to disperse people; in Early NHG both the simplex ~, e.g. Luther Bible transl. Neh. 1,8: '*so wil ich euch unter die völker strewen*' and *verstreuen* could be used in this sense, e.g. Luther Bible transl. Deuter. 30,3: '*. . . aus allen völkern, dahin dich der herr dein gott verstreuet hat*'; hence also *weit verstreut*, e.g. Denis, *Lied. Sin.* 221 [1772]: '*. . . ferne . . . von der Donau weit verstreut*'.

Menschen zerstreuen to scatter people; since Early NHG, e.g. Luther Bible transl. 1 Sam. 11,11: '*. . . wurden also zustrewet, das ir nicht zween mit einander blieben*' (also Deuter. 4,27); also in reflex. use, as in Schiller, *Räuber* 4,5: '*zerstreut euch im Wald*'.

etw. zerstreuen (a.) to distract sth.; in the sense of 'turning away (sb.'s mind, thoughts, etc.) from sth.' since MHG, esp. in the language of the Mystics (Seuse, Tauler) and in Luther 22,77 (Weimar): '*das man . . . das herz zusamen halte, das es nicht zurstrewet werde*'; now a., if not obs.

etw. zerstreuen to dispel sth.; figur. since Early NHG, mainly with such abstracts Zweifel, Unmut, Unbehagen; e.g. *Ldb.d. Hätzlerin* 1,5,39: '*. . . und alles mein laid zersträen*'; with ref. to Unmut in H. Sachs [edit. K.] 11,464, with *Zweifel* in Wieland, *Agathon* 1,33.

zerstreut distracted, absent-minded; derived from the previous entry under influence of French *distrait*; since early in the 18th c., recorded by Frisch [1741] for '*égaré*'.

jem. zerstreuen to divert, amuse sb.; since the 18th c.; frequent in the reflex., e.g. (DWb) C.F.Richter, *Adel d.Seele* 147 [1739]: '. . . *vielerlei Wege . . . in denen sie sich zerstreuen und ihr Vergnügen suchen*'. Hence *Zerstreuung*, since the 18th c. for 'diversion, pastime, amusement' (note that in the 19th c. *Zerstreuung* could still be used for 'spreading', e.g. Bismarck, *Pol.Reden* [edit. K.] 4,145: '*die Zerstreuung falscher Kriegsgerüchte*', where *die Verbreitung* or *das Ausstreuen* would now be used).

die Streusiedlung scattered settlement or housing estate; 20th c.

das Streuungsmaß (statistics) measure of scatter (which describes the deviation from the mean value); derived from ~ = 'to scatter' with ref. to grapeshot; 20th c.; hence also *Streuungskoeffizient*.

← See also under *Auge* (for *jem.m Sand in die Augen streuen*), *ausstreuen*, *bestreuen*, *Blume* (for *jem.m Blumen auf den Weg streuen*), *Büchse* (for *des Heiligen Römischen Reiches Streusandbüchse*), *einstreuen*, *Erbse* (for *jem.m Erbsen auf die Stiegen streuen*), *gelb* (for *gelbe Schatten streuen*), *Hand* (for *die Götter ihre Gaben streun*), *Professor* (for *ein zerstreuter Professor*), *Punkt* (for *Streusand drauf*), *Rose* (for *Rosen streuen*), *Saat* (for *Saaten in die Zukunft streun*), *Same* (for *Samen streuen*), *Sand* (for *Sandmann hat Sand in die Augen gestreut*), *Schwanz* (for *Salz auf den Schwanz streuen*) and *Wind* (for *etw. in den Wind streuen* and *in alle Winde verstreut*).

Strich: line

der ~ (1) path, way, route; also 'march'; since MHG, e.g. ~ *eines Flusses* = 'course of a river', as in Rud.v.Ems, *Weltchron.* 4863 and *seinen* ~ *nehmen* = 'to follow one's or its path', *ibid.* 22380, also with ref. to mil. movements = 'to march, travel, advance', still in modern period. e.g. Mörike, *N*.308: '*wir rasteten nach einem ermüdenden Strich*'. It is this meaning which led to *in einem* ~ = 'in one move, at one go, without a break', since the 18th c., recorded by Campe, who listed '*in einem Striche weg arbeiten, lesen, schreiben*, etc.', e.g. Lessing [edit. L.-M.] 18,101 '. . . *unmöglich wäre, in einem Striche an der nehmlichen Sache zu arbeiten*'. Hence also for 'way of life, path that one pursues', since MHG, e.g. *Meier Helmbr.* 1456: '*hin fuor er sînen alten strich*', Schiller, *Tell* 2,2: '. . . *den gleichen Strich unwandelbar befolgen*'. Adelung quoted from Gryphius (no details): '*ich bin dem geilen Sündenstrich wie eine Hündinn nachgerennet*'.

der ~ (2) established, prescribed or habitual route; derived from ~ (1); for 'route laid down' (e.g. in mil.sense) since the 18th c., for 'beat' (of a prostitute) since the 17th c., e.g. Logau, *Sinnged.* 598 (cf. also Schmeller's recording of '*Strich eines Bettelmönches*'); hence *auf den* ~ *gehen* = 'to walk the streets (for prostitution)', since the 18th c. (cf. *Finkenstrich* on p. 795 and *Schnepfenstrich* on p. 2167). A new (20th c.) compound is *Strichjunge*

(sl.) = 'male prostitute' (sometimes also used for 'poof').

der ~ (3) area, territory; since MHG, e.g. Rud.v.Ems, *Weltchron.* 1877, Luther 10,1,1,545 (Weimar): '*Sanct Paulus . . . hatt denselben strich der lincken seytten des mehriss bepredigt*', Haller, *Vers. schw.Ged.* 41 [1753]: '*ein Strich von grünen Thälern*', Wieland 29,197: '*in gewissen Strichen des Erdbodens*'; frequent in compounds such as *Erdstrich*, *Himmelsstrich*, *Landstrich* (cf. also ~ *Landes*, as in Schiller, *Kab.u.L.* 5,2).

der ~ (4) (obs.) distance; this is an extension of ~ (3) taken as a measure of distance; still recorded by Adelung: '*es ist noch ein guter Strich dahin, eine gute Strecke*'; now obs.

der ~ (5) word; cf. Engl. 'stroke'; in images taken from the strokes in painting or drawing, e.g. *mit einigen wenigen Strichen etw. umreißen* = 'to describe or outline sth. in a few words'; since the 19th c.

der ~ (6) manner of playing a string instrument; cf. Engl. 'stroke' used in this sense; f.r.b. Kramer [1702]: '*er hat einen frischen, kecken, manierlichen, freyen Strich*'. ~ can also mean 'sound produced by a string instrument' (an extension of 'action of playing a string instrument'); 19th c.

der ~ (7) cut, sth. cut out or deleted; refers to the deleting stroke of the pen through sth. in a text, e.g. *die Striche betrafen Dinge, die dem Zensor nicht gefielen*; 19th c. For other phrases concerning crossing-out strokes see below and under *durchstreichen* on p. 532.

er ist nur (noch) ein ~ (coll.) he is very thin, looks emaciated; since the 19th c., also in the comparison *er ist dünn wie ein* ~.

einen ~ *haben* (coll.) to be drunk; also used for 'he is not quite right in the head'; cf. similar use of *Hieb* and *Stich*; 18th c. coll.; Campe [1810] recorded: '*uneigentlich sagt man im Holsteinschen, einen Strich haben, für, halb berauscht sein*', e.g. Immermann, *Münchh.* 2,275. The meaning 'deranged' was only recorded towards the end of the 19th c., e.g. by Heyne.

jem. auf dem ~ *haben* (coll.) to have it in for sb.; assumed to be derived from hunt. jargon with ~ being the sight of the gun (cf. *jem. aufs Korn nehmen* on p. 1531), although it has also been suggested that the phrase could belong to ~ (2) and could mean that sb. wanted by the police had entered their 'beat' (i.e. the territory which they regularly patrol); since the 19th c., e.g. Gutzkow, *R.v.G.* 2,290.

es geht jem.m gegen den ~ (coll.) it goes against the grain; since the 2nd half of the 18th c., e.g. Lichtenberg, *Verm.Schr.* 2,169, Tieck, *Ges.Nov.* 1,120 or *Nov.Kr.* 2,71 [1831]. Bismarck used it in *Reden* 7,394: '*ich habe noch andere Konzessionen gemacht, die mir sehr gegen den Strich gingen*'. Nietzsche in *Werke*, 4,329 used '*wider den Strich denken*', which he explained as '*nicht den Gedanken zu folgen, die sich ihm von innen her anbieten'*.

keinen ~ tun (coll.) to do not one stroke of work; since the 18th c., e.g. (DWb) Bothe, *Zuv.Beschr.* 2,177 [1752]: *'du sollst keinen Strich mehr thun . . .'*. Campe's [1810] entry on this suggests that he believed that *~ auf einer Geige* explained the origin of the idiom, but examples in *DWb*. make it clear that 'strokes' in the performance of work are meant.

weder ~ noch Stich halten (coll.) to fail every test, be totally inadequate; also in the positive version *~ und Probe halten* = 'to stand all tests', e.g. F.K.Moser, *Ges.Schr.* 1,436 [1763]; derived from the practice of testing the purity of metals by rubbing them against a *Probierstein* (see p. 1907); cf. Decimator, *Hochzeitpred.* R4b [1601]: *'. . . alle lehr auf den probestein göttliches wortes thun, helt sie den strich, das ist, kömpt sie mit gottes wort uberein, so ist sie anzunehmen'*; sometimes as *Stich, Strich und Probe halten*, as in Petri, D.Dt.Weißh. [1605]; see also under *Stich* for *etw. hält Stich* and *stichhaltig*.

den rechten ~ halten (coll.) to follow the right course, do what is expected of one; belongs to *~* (1); since the 19th c., recorded e.g. by Wander [1876].

er kann den ~ nicht halten (coll.) he is drunk; ref. to the straight line drawn on the ground or the line between floor-boards to test sb.'s sobriety; recorded by Wander [1876].

~ für ~ stroke for stroke, line for line, in every detail; usually with such adjectives as *gleich* or *identisch*; refers to lines or strokes in drawing and painting; since the 19th c., e.g. Freiligrath 1,79.

nach ~ und Faden thoroughly; refers to weaving where *Striche* in the texture in both directions (called *Kette* and *Einschlag*) must be perfect; hence *ein Gewebe nach ~ und Faden prüfen*; this was extended to other spheres with *prüfen* or *untersuchen* and later used for 'thoroughly', e.g. *jem. nach ~ und Faden verprügeln*; since the 19th c.

jem.m einen ~ durch die Rechnung machen to foil sb.'s plans, queer sb.'s pitch; the entry on p. 1957 needs correction. The phrase has been current since MHG, e.1. Oswald v. Wolkenstein [edit. Schatz] 92,18: *'all meiner sünd ain grosser kranz; die rechnung mir gepirt. doch wil es got der ainig man, so wirt mir pald ain strich dadurch getan'* (cf. also Luther 32,103 (Weimar): *'mit dem spruch mache ich ein strich durch das register, da ynnen meine sunde sind angeschrieben'*). The notion of 'thwarting' or 'cancelling' can also be expressed without *Rechnung*, e.g. Bürger, *Frau Schnips*: *'. . . zog den Strich durch ihr Schlaraffenleben'*.

einen ~ erleiden (obs.) to suffer a setback; presumably a shorter version of *~ durch die Rechnung* (see above) or phrases with *Querstrich* (see below); Goethe used it in 31,218 (W.); now obs.

auf dem ~ sein (regional coll.) to be fit, feel fine; recorded for some areas (esp. in N. and E.) since

the 19th c. (cf. *DWb*. X,.3,1525 [1957]); hence *er ist wieder auf seinen ~ gekommen* (coll.) = 'he is well (or his own self) again', recorded by Wander [1876]. Now obs.

unterm ~ sein (coll.) to be (or feel) below par, (with ref. to things) to be unsatisfactory or insufficient; this is a ref. to the line on the glass which shows the correct measure (*Eichstrich*); if the contents do not reach that line, the quantity is insufficient; since the 19th c. Keller in *Ges. Werke* 2,129 [1889] used it in its phys. sense: *'er zog von einem Wirtshaus ins andere, um nachzusehen, wo das Getränke unter dem Strich blieb'*.

unterm ~ (print.) in the non-news section of the paper, in the feuilleton part; newspapers at one time drew a thick line under the top section with items of news, and opinions, entertaining items, etc. appeared below that line; since the 19th c., e.g. (Sa.E.) Herrig 63,249: *'deßhalb verweise ich die ganze Notiz unter den Strich'*. Occasionally in extended figur. sense, e.g. *Gegenwart* 18,20b: *'. . . außerhalb der engeren Regierung gelassen . . . und nicht zum Kabinett gehören. Sie stehen so zu sagen unter dem Strich'*.

einen ~unter etw. (or *darunter* or *drunter*) *ziehen* (or *machen*) to make a clean break with sth., to let bygones be bygones; since the 18th c., e.g. Goethe IV,7,250 (W.) with ref. to Lavater: *'ich habe auch unter seine Existenz einen großen Strich gemacht und weis nun, was mir per saldo von ihm übrig bleibt'*; hence coll. *~ drunter!* = 'forget it!'.

der Strichbube (coll., a.) pimp; f.r.b. Sanders, *Erg.Wb.* [1885]; now a. or obs. The usual coll. term is *Louis*, f.r.b. Sanders [1963].

strichweise arbeiten to work intermittently, in fits and starts; since the 19th c., f.r.b. Campe [1810].

Abstriche machen to make cuts or deductions; can be used in the financial sense, but also for other deductions, e.g. not accepting the whole of sb.'s statement, curtailing one's plans, reducing one's expectations; since the 2nd half of the 19th c., not yet listed in *DWb*. [1854], but recorded by Sanders [1865], e.1. (Sa.) *Nat.Ztg.* 17,15.

der Bindestrich (lit.) connecting link; in its original sense = 'hyphen' (for which Stieler [1691] listed *Mittelstrich*); recent in figur. use.

einen Querstrich durch etw. machen to thwart sth.; esp. with ref. to *Rechnung*, f.r.b. Möller, *Teutsch-Schwed. Wb.* [1782], e.g. Lessing 1,304: *'. . . daß uns das Glück einen solchen Querstrich machte'*.

← See also under *anstreichen* (for *Anstrich*), *Feder* (for *Federstrich*), *Fink* (for *Finkenstrich*), *Gedanke* (for *Gedankenstrich*), *Pinsel* (for *Pinselstrich*), *quer* (for *Querstrich*), *rechnen* (for *jem.m einen Strich durch die Rechnung machen*), *Schluß* (for *den Schlußstrich ziehen*) and *Schnepfe* (for *Schnepfenstrich*).

Strick: rope

der ~ (1) (lit.) fetter; since OHG, e.g. Notker (edit. P.) 2,53,25: *'des tiêueles striccha'* and 2,48,2: *'diê striccha des tôdes furefiêngen mih'*, Gottsched,

Dt.Schaub. 2,59; '*ich selbst zerreiß hiemit des Eides Band und Stricke*', Goethe 5,42 (W.): '*Stricke, die den hohen Schwung der Seele fesselten*', *Götz* 2,3: '. . . *warf ich ihm ein Seil um den Hals, aus zwey mächtigen Stricken Weibergunst und Schmeicheley gedreht*'; hence also *in Stricken (und Banden) liegen* (lit.) = 'to be in chains, confined, held in bondage', e.g. Raabe, *Sämtl. Werke* 2,5,245: '*in diesem in Stricken und Banden liegenden Menschenleben*', and *jem. am* ~ (or *in seinen Stricken*) *haben* = 'to have sb. in one's power', e.g. Lessing [edit. L.-M.] 2,24: '. . . *daß ihn nicht das verdammte Mädel* . . . *in ihren Stricken hat*'; see also under *Horn* for similar *jem.m. das Seil über die Hörner werfen*.

der ~ (2) trap; figur. since MHG, e.g. Berth.v. Regensburg 410,2;: '*lât iuch den tiuvel niht vâhen in sinem stricke der unkiusche*'; hence *in Stricke fallen*, e.g. Luther 10,1,2,370 (Weimar): '*die da reych werden wöllen, die fallen in versuchung und stricke*' (cf. Lehman, *Flor.pol.* 3,231 [1662]: '*mancher in den Strick selbst fällt, den er andern hat gestellt*', similarly worded already in MHG, e.g. in *Jüng.Titurel* 3934); hence *der Fallstrick*, figur. since Early NHG, e.g. in Luther Bible transl. Luke 21,35 (where the A.V. uses 'snare'); in modern period often in *jem.m Fallstricke legen* = 'to set a trap for sb.', e.g. Liscov, *Schriften* 616 [1739].

der ~ (3) (lit.) falsehood, deception, evil machination; since MHG, e.g. Seuse, *Dt.Schr.* [edit. B.] 380: '*dü welt ist vol striken, falschheit und untrüwen*', Luther 23,283 (Weimar): '*das sie eitel stricke müssen schreiben*'; hence in linguistic contexts used for 'sophistry, fallacy', f.r.b. *Voc.theut.* ff4a [1482].

der ~ (4) hanging, the rope; same extension as in Engl.; since the 16th c. in such phrases as *den* ~ *verdienen*, f.r.b. Kramer [1702], *der* ~ *erwartet ihn, darauf steht der* ~ , etc., e.g. Fischart, *Garg.* (repr.) 316: '*es belangt jhnen nicht zum glück, sondern zum strick*', Goethe, *Ben.Cell.* 2,10: '*er* . . . *rettete seinen Schreiber von dem Strick*'.

der ~ (5) rogue, rascal; an extension from 'rope' to 'sb. who deserves the rope', often in *Galgenstrick*, for which see under *Galgen* on p. 900; *Galgenstrick* was f.r.b. Stieler [1691], but Schmeller found an earlier *Strickbub* for 'rogue, criminal' in a vocabulary of 1618. ~ is sometimes used half-affectionately, since Early NHG, e.g. Fischart, *Werke* [edit. Hauffen] 2,36: '. . . *kleiner strick* . . . *wir wöllens deim vatter sagen*'.

jem.m einen ~ *aus etw. drehen* (coll.) to use sth. (e.g. sb.'s statement or action) as a way to trip sb. up, give sb.'s statement an interpretation which will harm him; *drehen* here used for 'twisting' or 'turning' (see the entry on *Bolzen* on p. 372). ~ can be interpreted as *Fallstrick* (perhaps in hunt. contexts) or as ~ (4). The phrase is modern, older in the regions than in the standard language, not yet listed in *DWb.* [1860] or Heyne [1895]. Hence also *sich selber einen* ~ *drehen* = 'to harm oneself'.

alle Stricke spannen to make every effort, use all means at one's disposal; since the 19th c., e.g. Droste-Hülshoff, *Br.* [edit.Sch.] 180; cf. the saying: *er hat schon an allen Stricken gezogen und keinen zerrissen* = 'he has tried all sorts of jobs (ventures, etc.) and got nowhere', f.r.b. Wander [1876].

das Gestrick (lit.) tissue, web; pejor., belongs to ~ (3); e.g. Rückert, *Werke* 7,222: '*durchs verwirrte Truggestrick*'.

alles war nach dem gleichen Strickmuster (gemacht) (coll.) everything followed the same pattern, was modelled as before; *Strickmuster* = 'knitting pattern' was f.r.b. Campe [1810]. The phrase is recent.

etw. stricken (lit.) to compose or produce sth.; cf. Engl. 'to weave a tale'; modern; usually with ref. to literary products, with allusion to 'knitting' and somewhat contemptuous, e.g. Gutzkow, *R.v.G.* 5,122 [1850]: '*die Thatsachen sind wahr, aber ihre Verknüpfung haben Frauenhände gestrickt*' or L.Schücking, *Br.* [edit. Muschler] 175 (1843]: '. . . *abscheulich schlechte Novellen, so recht gestrickte Damenarbeiten*'; cf. similar *ein Seil spinnen* (under *Seil*).

etw. entstricken (lit.) to disentangle sth.; since the 18th c., e.g. Schlegel, transl. of Shakespeare *Richard II*, 4,1: '*entstrick das Gewebe verworrener Thorheit*' (where the original runs: 'must I ravel out my weaved-up folly'); also reflex. *sich entstricken* = 'to free itself or oneself', since the 18th c., but now rare.

jem. umstricken to ensnare or entangle sb.; since the 17th c., e.g. Gryphius, *Trauersp.* [edit. P.] 587: '. . . *wie von Kindheit an mich Angst* . . . *umstricket*' (with *Irrtümer* in Goethe 46,11 (W.)), J.N.Götz, *Verm.Ged.* 2,197 [1785]: '*umstrickt mit Banden ihrer Liebe* . . . *denk ich nur sie*'; figur. *Umstrickung* followed, recorded by Adelung.

etw. verstricken (lit.) to entwine things, tie sth. up; since MHG, e.g. Gottfr.v.Str., *Tristan* 16499: '*ir ouge und ir herze enein mit blicken sô verstricken*', also pejor. for 'to ensnare, entangle', as in Luther 28,477 (Weimar): '*ire gewissen* . . . *zu verstricken*'; cf. also (Sp.) Keller, *Salander* 215: '. . . *den Brüdergreisen* . . . *die Haare zu verstricken als Gläubiger und Schuldner*'.

jem. (in etw.) verstricken to entangle or involve sb. in sth.; since Early NHG, e.g. Fischart, *Ehzuchtb.* 130: '. . . *weiber, welche* . . . *die männer zu verstricken unterstehn*' (where it is the same as *bestricken*, which see on p. 288); later and in lit. usage also with abstracts, e.g. Schiller, *Jungfr.v.O.* 1772: '*verstrickend ist der Lüge trüglich Wort*'. Frequent in *in die Schlingen von etw. verstrickt sein*. See also under *Netz* for *das Schuldennetz zerreißen, in welchem er verstrickt war*. Hence *die Verstrickung*, since Early NHG (e.g. Fischart, *Ehzuchtb.* 212), often with ref. to figur. *Netz*.

sich in etw. verstricken to become entangled or caught in sth.; f.r.b. Stieler [1691]: '*er hat sich muthwillig in noht verstricket*', e.g. Luther Bible transl. Prov. 29.96 (where the A.V. translated:

'there is a snare'). See also under *Netz* for *sich im eignen Netz verstricken*.

an etw. weiterstricken (lit.) to pursue sth. further, continue with sth.; *stricken* here in the sense of 'writing, composing' (see above); very recent, e.g. *er strickt an diesem Thema* (*Problem*, etc.) *weiter*.

je fauler ~ , *je größer Glück* (prov.) the more knave the better luck; in this form in Sanders [1865], Simrock [1846] has it as *je ärger* ~ , *je besser Glück*. In Engl. recorded since the 17th c.

man zerreißt den ~ , *wo er am dünnsten ist* (prov.) the thread breaks where it is weakest; in this wording f.r.b. Simrock [1846], but there are older forms, e.g. *wenn der* ~ *am dünnsten ist, so bricht er* (as in Petri [1605]); in Engl. recorded since the 17th c.

← See also under *bestricken*, *Galgen* (for *Galgenstrick* and *im Hause des Gehängten spricht man nicht vom Strick*), *Netz* (for *zum Strick und Netz werden*) and *Strang* (for *wenn alle Stricke reißen*).

striegeln: groom with a currycomb

jem. ~ (1) (coll., obs.) to scold, reprimand sb.; since the 18th c., recorded by Adelung, e.g. Lichtenberg 1,274 or C.F.Bardt, *Leben* 125 [1790].

jem. ~ (2) (coll.) to treat sb. roughly, inconsiderately or despotically; since the 18th c., f.r.b. Frisch [1741]: '*die Bauren strigeln = vexare rusticos*'; now *schikanieren* might be preferred.

gestriegelt und gebügelt (coll.) spick and span, dolled-up; also *gestriegelt* on its own = 'as neat as a bandbox'; cf. also Auerbach, *Schatzk.d.Gev.* 325 [1857]: '*das Soldatenleben striegelt und putzt den Mann*'. See also under *schniegeln* for a similar idiom.

Strippe: strip, strap

jem. an die ~ *nehmen* (coll.) to keep sb. under tight control; also as *jem. an der* ~ *haben* (coll.); since the 19th c. The opposite is *jem. von der* ~ *lassen* (coll.) = 'to leave sb. free to do what he likes'; since early in the 20th c.

es regnet Strippen (regional coll.) it is raining hard; recorded since the 19th c., but only for some areas (others prefer *Bindfäden*, for which see under *binden*).

eine ~ (regional coll.) a glass of spirits (ordered together with *Weißbier*); mainly in Berlin, f.r.b. *D.richt. Berliner* [1882]. The same dictionary also recorded *besoffen wie eine Sackstrippe* = 'dead drunk'.

die Quasselstrippe (1) (coll.) talkative person; variants are *Quasselkopf* and *Quasselmeier* (both since the 19th c.) and *Quasseltüte* (only since 2nd half of the 20th c.).

die Quasselstrippe (2) (coll.) telephone; ~ for 'telephone' arose late in the 19th c.; the compound was formed roughly at the same time.

← See also under *hängen* (for *an der Strippe hängen*).

Stroh: straw

auf dem ~ *liegen* (a.) to live in poverty, exist in wretched conditions; s.e. and very old; cf. *das* ~ *der Armut* (lit.) = 'the wretched living conditions of the poor'; in some areas used for 'to be dead', in Bav. for 'to be in childbed' (cf. Engl.obs. 'in the straw = in childbed'); cf. also Frisius [1556]: '*einen ins strouw trincken = einen truncken und voll machen*', *jem. aufs* ~ *bringen* = 'to impoverish sb.', since Early NHG. All the phrases in which ~ = 'bed' are now a. or obs.

brennen wie ~ to flare up quickly and be consumed rapidly; since MHG, e.g. Freidank, *Bescheid.* 121 also in comparisons, e.g. Alberus, *Fabeln* (repr.) 146: '. . . *das wie stroh ein gantze stadt brennt liechter loh*', Luther Bible transl. Joel 2,5: '*wie eine flamme loddert im stro*', Isaiah 5,24: '*wie des fewrs flamme stroh verzehret*' (in both cases the A.V. has 'stubble').

dumm wie ~ (coll.) very stupid; the notion of uselessness associated with ~ led in the 17th c. to *Strohkopf* = 'blockhead' and ~ *im Kopf haben*; *dumm wie* ~ appeared late in the 18th c., e.g. Forster, *Br.* 2,655.

gelb wie ~ , *strohgelb* straw-coloured; since the 17th c., f.r.b. Kramer [1702] (Stieler [1691] recorded the noun *Strohfarbe*); *strohfarben* appeared in the 18th c., *strohfarbig* only in the 19th c.

Geld haben wie ~ (coll.) to have loads of money; 19th c. coll., e.g. (Sa.) Klencke, *D.dt.Gespenst* 1,39 [1846].

das ist leeres ~ trash, valueless stuff (or statement); ~ for 'sth. of no value' was much used in Early NHG (Luther, Fischart); *leeres* ~ became general in the 17th c., e.g. (DWb) Chr. Weise, *Polit.Red.* 69 [1677]: '*die Musen haben ihn mit leerem Stroh gespeiset*', Ruge, *Briefw. u.Tageb.* 2,122: '. . . *das leere Stroh von Zschokke – keine gute Lectüre*', still in Th.Mann, *Lotte i.W.* 107 [1946].

~ *dreschen* (coll.,a.) to pass one's time in useless pursuits; a shortened form of the previous entry. Goethe used it in *Werke* IV,3,89 (W.): '*die Liebe giebt mir alles und wo die nicht ist, dresch ich Stroh*'; usually, however, with ref. to idle or wasteful talk, e.g. Freytag, *Br.a.s.Gattin* 566: '. . . . *fuhr in die Sitzung, Stroh gedroschen bis nach 5 Uhr*'.

es schmeckt wie ~ (coll.) it is utterly tasteless, tastes of nothing; recorded since the 19th c., e.g. by Sanders [1865].

das ist nicht von ~ (coll. obs.) that is not to be sneezed at, of considerable value; since the 19th c.

ich bin nicht von ~ (coll.) I am not made of stone, I have feelings, too; since the 18th c., e.g. Thümmel, *Reise* 10,118 [1791]: '. . . *ich bin ja nicht von Stroh!*'; usually with ref. to sexual temptation.

trocken wie ~ , *strohtrocken* very dry and tasteless, stale; with ref. to stale food, old bread, etc., but also with abstracts, e.g. Jung-Stilling, *S.Schr.* 6,279: '*unsere heutige strohtrockene Moral*', Feuchtwanger, *Füchse i.W.* 469: '*wie strohtrocken . . . war das Schreiben abgefaßt*'.

er hat Korn im ~ (coll., obs.) there is much to

him; at least since the 18th c.; it can refer to intelligence, but also to financial wealth, e.g. Bürger, *Frau Schnips*: '*Frau Schnipsen hatte Korn im Stroh*'; cf. the prov. *viel ~ , wenig Korn* = 'there is little of substance in it', recorded since the 17th c. for *Korn* = 'sth. of value' see p. 1532.

der Strohbaß (coll.) rough, unmelodic bass voice; since the 18th c., e.1. (DWb) Mattheson, *Crit. Musica* 1,112 [1722].

strohblond flaxen; since late in the 19th c., e.g. (DWb) Kahlenberg, *Eva S.* [1901].

das Strohfeuer strong passion, enthusiasm or infatuation which passes very quickly; cf. French *cela se passe comme un feu de paille*; comparisons of the type *es verraucht wie ein Strohfeuer*, as in Harsdörffer, *Teutsche Secret.* 2,565 [1659], could easily lead to the now current meaning which was f.r.b. Kramer [1702].

das Strohgewicht (boxing) bantamweight; classification of boxers weighing not more than 53.5 kg; modern (not listed in *DWb.* [1957]).

keinen Strohhalm wert (coll.) not worth a straw; since Early NHG, e.g. Luther 30,1,213 (Weimar); in Engl. since the 13th c.; cf. French *cela ne vaut pas un fêtu*.

nicht eine Strohhalmbreite (coll.) not an inch; beginnings in Early NHG, e.g. Luther 52,685 (Weimar): '. . . *eines strohalms breyt . . .*', Bismarck, *Reden* 14,334: '. . . *nicht um eines Strohhalms Breite . . .*'.

die Bäume wurden umgeknickt wie Strohhalme trees snapped in two like straws; in hyperbolic descriptions of storms; since the 19th c.

der Strohmann (1) (coll.) man of straw, ineffectual person, sb. without backbone or lacking virility; term of contempt since the 18th c., e.g. Goethe, *Werther* I. Either a transfer from the phys. meaning of *Strohmann* = 'scarecrow' (often made of straw), or with allusion to the weakness of straw.

der Strohmann (2) (coll.) dummy, (mere) figurehead; a transl. of French *homme de paille*; 19th c., e.g. (Heyne) '*er ist bei dem Geschäft nur Strohmann, hinter ihm steht ein anderer*'. The statement in *Trübner* that it is a term coined in the *Gründerzeit* (1870 onwards) is wrong, since earlier instances of use have been found. The feminine *Strohfrau* is very recent (2nd half 20th c.).

der Strohmann (3) (cardplayers' jargon) dummy; recorded since the 19th c. (e.g. by Heyne [1895]); the usual term is *der Blinde*.

der Strohmann (4) (cardplayers' jargon) substitute who has taken the place of a regular partner in a game; 20th c.

heiliger (allmächtiger, gerechter) Strohsack! (coll.) good heavens! exclamation of astonishment or (unpleasant) surprise; recorded for many regions from early in the 19th c. onwards; perhaps euphemistic corruption of sth. drastic (*Sakrament? Hodensack?*).

die Strohwitwe (coll.) grass widow; the term appears with ~ , *Heu* or 'grass' in most Germanic languages; it refers to the bed of straw, grass or hay on which a woman is left on her own (cf. Frau Marthens complaint about her husband in Goethe, *Faust I*, 2867: '*geht da stracks in die Welt hinein und läßt mich auf dem Stroh allein*'); f.r.b. Amaranthes, *Fr.-Lex.* [1715]. The older meanings 'girl with an illegitimate child deserted by her lover' and 'woman of easy virtue' are obs. The masculine form *Strohwitwer*, although derived from the feminine, was recorded by Kramer [1702] who surprisingly did not list *Strohwitwe*; e.g. Bismarck, letter to Gerlach 193: '. . . *die Rückkehr meiner Frau . . . hinausgeschoben, und ich noch immer Strohwittwer*'.

← See also under *Bart* (for *jem.m einen ströhernen Bart drehen*), *Bohne* (for *grob wie Bohnenstroh* and *dumm wie Bohnenstroh*), *dreschen* (for *leeres Stroh dreschen*), *ertrinken* (for *der Ertrinkende klammert sich an einen Strohhalm*), *Hafer* (for *so glücklich wie eine Gans im Haferstroh* and *so dumm wie Haferstroh*), *Licht* (for *wie nasses Stroh sein*) and *stolpern* (for *über einen Strohhalm stolpern*).

Strolch: tramp, vagabond

ein kleiner ~ (coll.) little scamp or rascal; ~ , current since the 17th c., e.g. Grimmelshausen, *Simpliz. Continuatio* [edit. K.] 2,291, may have started as a cant term, though some scholars derive it from Ital. *astrologo*; in modern coll. use for 'boy', e.g. Th.Mann 7,280 (*Kön.Hoh.*), also affectionately, as is the case with *Stromer*.

der Sittenstrolch (coll.) sex fiend, beast; term of condemnation for sb. who abuses women and children; 20th c. coll. (at first mainly in press jargon).

der Straßenstrolch (sl.) reckless driver; since 2nd half of the 20th c.; if the driver owns a very expensive car, the sl. term *Stromlinienstrolch* is used.

die Strolchenfahrt (coll., Swiss) joy ride by a (juvenile) thief in a stolen car; since the fifties of the 20th c.

Strom: stream, river

der ~ (lit.) the river, stream; personalized as a powerful and dangerous force in lit. since the 17th c., called *wütend* (e.g. Wieland 1,1,138 [Acad. Edit.]), *ungetreu* (e.g. Lessing [edit. L.-M.] 3,11, 189), *hartnäckig* (e.g. Opitz, *Teutsche Poem.* 180), but *wild* already in MHG. Since the 18th c. also regarded as beneficent or worthy of admiration and called *prächtig, freudig, schön* or *fruchtbar*; cf. also Novalis, *Schr.* [edit. Minor] 4,169: '*die Ströme sind die Augen einer Landschaft*'.

wie ein ~ like a stream; comparisons appeared in Early NHG, e.g. Fischart, *Nachtrab* [edit. K.] 81,3112: '. . . *laufft zu das volck gleich wie ein strom*', Gottsched, *Ged.* 228: '. . . *Thränen . . . die Strömen gleich hervorgedrungen*'; also with abstracts, such as *Äußerung, Gefühl, Empfindung*, etc.; since the 18th c.; cf. also Bismarck, *Ged.u. Erinn.* 2,104:

'*der deutschnationale Aufschwung . . . ., vergleichbar einem Strome, der die Schleusen bricht*'.

ein ~ (or *Ströme*) *von* . . . (1) streams of . . . .; with ref. to blood since MHG, often with such verbs as *fließen* and *vergießen*, with ref. to lava since the 17th c., to tears since the 18th c. In the 17th c. *~* (or *Ströme*) *von Menschen, Volk, Truppen*, etc. appeared in lit., with abstracts general since the 18th c., e.g. Klopstock, *Über Spr.u.D.* 1,47: '*in . . . Strömen des Beifalls*'; an early example of a compound is *Geldstrom* used by Luther [edit. Dietz] 2,61b: '*. . . wo der gelltstrom hin gefuret wird*'; hence also *stromweis* (earlier *strömenweise* or *strömeweis*) = 'in streams', e.g. Schiller, *Räuber* 1,1.

ein ~ (or *Ströme*) *von* . . . (2) floods of . . .; with ref. to abstracts seen as 'flowing' from above or from one person to another; at first mostly in relig. contexts, e.g. with ref. to divine grace, since MHG, as in *Minnes.* [edit.v.d.Hagen] 3,61a: '*aller guete voller vluete vloz in gnaden stramen*', also to love, e.g. Rückert, *Ged.* 347: '*der Strom der Liebe . . . wie er meine Brust durchflutet!*', sympathy, affection, etc., e.g. Zschokke, *Alamontade* 1,2: '*jeder gab sich dem Strom durch einander wogender Empfindungen hin*', but also with ref. to undesirable emotions and passions such as *Ehrgeiz, Schwärmerei, Angst*, etc., frequent since the 18th c., e.g. (Sp.) Trenck, *Lebensgesch.* 1,129: '*. . . sich dem Strom der Eigenmacht, des Fanatismus und der Unwissenheit stolz entgegenzustellen*'; sometimes the river image is evoked, as in Goethe IV,14,34 (W.): '*der Strom des Interesses, der Leidenschaft, findet sein Bette schon gegraben*'. Other images suggest 'drinking', e.g. Jung-Stilling, *Sämtl.Schr.* 2,32: '*ich trinke Ströme voller Seeligkeit*'. There are numerous compounds, e.g. Haller, 71: '*des Jähzorns Feuerströme*', Alexis, *Hosen d.H.v.B.* 1,1,235: '*es pulste ihm wie ein Feuerstrom durch die Adern*', E.Th.A. Hoffmann, *S.W.* [edit.Gr.] 2,59: '*ein Glutstrom brauste durch meine Adern*'; Fouqué in *Ged.* 1,184 used *Gnadenstrom* and Goethe and Jean Paul used *Freudenstrom*.

ein ~ von . . . (3) a stream or flood of . . ., the course taken by sth.; beginnings in Early NHG, e.g. (DWb) Keisersberg, *Granatapfel Hld* [1510]: '*. . . so du . . . die stromen deines contemplierens . . . bestät hast*', Goethe 46,93 (W.): '*deutsche Philologen . . . die den Strom solcher Kenntnisse auch zu den Weltleuten leiteten*'; sometimes with ref. to sth. abstract which turns into a flood, as in (Sp.) Keller, *Salander* 186: '*. . . hatte zu besagter Fest- und Wanderfreude . . . beigetragen . . . dann begann der wachsende Strom ihn stutzig zu machen*', also in such phrases as *der gewaltige ~ technischer Entwicklungen*; cf. also such poetic images as A.Zweig, *Nov. um Claudia* 224: '*Menschenstimmen machten den Saal erbrausen . . . ein lobsingender Strom*', Huch, *Pitt u. Fox* 69: '*. . . war ihr, als rinne ein geheimer, stiller Strom durch sie beide*' (which may also contain an allusion to *~* = 'electric current'). Frequent in compounds since the 18th c., particularly in *Rede-*

strom, Gedankenstrom, Wortstrom; Campe [1808] recorded *Gedankenstrom* with an example from Herder (no details); cf. also modern *Schicksalsstrom des Lebens* and *Bewußtseinsstrom* (lit.) = 'stream of consciousness' (and its derivatives such as *Bewußtseinsstromroman*), a loan from Engl.

der ~ der Dichtung (lit.) the river or stream of poetry; here the rush and power of poetic outpourings are alluded to; since the 18th c., e.g. Hagedorn, *Vers.ein.Ged.* (repr.) 36 addressing *Poesie*: '*du bist ein Strom, der ungehemmt schnellt, einbricht, stürzt und überschwemmt*'; cf. Goethe 21,291 (W.) on Shakespeare: '*der Strom jenes großen Genies*'.

der ~ der Zeit (lit.) the flow or passage of time; as a comparison already in Luther Bible transl. Psalm 90,5: '*du lässest sie dahin fahren wie einen Strom*'; figur. since the 18th c., e.g. Gottsched, *Neueste Ged.* 29 [1750]: '*auch wenn der Zeiten Strom ihn mit dahingerissen*'; similarly, also since the 18th c., *~ des Lebens*, as in *sich vom ~ des Lebens treiben lassen* or *sich dem ~ des Lebens überlassen* and such images as Novalis, *Schr.* [edit. Minor] 3,201: '*alles Leben ist ein ununterbrochener Strom*'; cf. also Winckelmann, *Sämtl.W.* 10,65 and *Schicksalsstrom des Lebens* (above). See also under *Fluß* for similar phrases.

in Strömen in vast quantities; usually in phys. sense with ref. to rain or blood, more hyperbolic with ref. to tears, sweat, wine, etc.; figur. since the 17th c., e.g. E.v.Kleist, *Werke* [edit. Sauer] 1,235: '*oft trinket der Mensch die Lust in Strömen und dürstet*'; *in vollen Strömen* arose at the same time, e.g. Wieland 1,1,51,600 (Acad.Edit.): '*. . . .und ungemischte Lust in vollen Strömen trinkt*'.

in einem ~ (lit., rare) without a break, uninterruptedly; with stressed *einem*; since the 18th c., e.g. Herder [edit. S.] 3,98; now usually *in einem Zuge*.

dem ~ folgen to follow the crowd, fall in with the general trend; since the 18th c., e.g. (Sp.) Trenck, *Lebensgesch.* 2,92: '*. . . kein anderes Mittel, als dem Strome zu folgen*'; cf. Gutzkow, *Uriel Ac.* 2,7: '*ins Allgemeine möcht' ich gerne tauchen und mit dem großen Strom des Lebens gehn*'.

sich auf den ~ setzen or *schwingen* (sl.) to take a tram or trolley-bus; *~* here = 'electric current', extended to the electrically-propelled vehicle; recent sl.

strömen (1) (intrans.) to flow; first with ref. to *Blut* (17th c.), since the 18th c. to *Tränen*, then increasingly to other liquids, e.g. Stolberg, *Ges.W.* 4,58: '*nur Wein soll heute strömen*'; with ref. to *Regen* only since late in the 18th c. (not yet listed by Adelung, even in his 2nd edit., but recorded by Campe [1810], e.g. *der Regen strömt, im strömenden Regen* (cf. also *es regnet in Strömen*); since the 18th c. also in lit. with ref. to *Licht, Luft, Duft, Feuer*, e.g. Klopstock, *Od.* 2,247: '*tief in dem Herzen fließt, da strömet die Quelle der Freude*', Goethe 49,102 (W.):

'*Feuer strömt aus den Augen*', (DWb) Ebert, *Ep.u. Ged.* 134 [1789]: '. . . *Ergetzen, das immerfort von Brust zu Brust elektrisch strömet*'. Also since the 18th c. with ref. to streams of people, e.g. Goethe 33,206 (W.): '. . . *Emigrirten, die . . . nach Deutschland strömten*', also since the 19th c. with ref. to objects which arrive in a constant stream, as in Ranke, *Werke* 1,180: '*in sein Haus . . . strömten die Geschenke*'. There are several compounds, e.g. *entgegenströmen*, as in Schiller, *Räuber* 4,1, *fortströmen* for 'to continue to flow', as in Lichtenberg 8,300 and for 'to flow along, rush away', as in *die fortströmende Zeit* (recorded in *DWb.* [1878]), *hineinströmen*, as in Bürger, 115a: '. . . *strömte Wohlgeruch hinein*' (in coll. use as *reinströmen*), *hinströmen*, as in Schiller, *Jungfr.v.O.* 3,11, and *nachströmen*, as in Alxinger, *Doolin* 249 [1797]: '*Lob strömt ihrer Rede nach*'. For *überströmen* and *verströmen* see separate entries below.

strömen (2) (intrans., lit.) to issue, gush or rush out; since the 18th c., e.g. *Klänge, Reden, Gesänge, Klagen strömen*, often with mention of the organ which produces this flow, e.g. Lessing [edit. L.-M.] 2,361: '. . . *die von der Zunge des Pöbels strömt*' (also in *von den Lippen, aus der Kehle, aus dem Munde strömen*); cf. also Freytag, *Erinn.* 242: '*die Gedanken strömten ihm voll und gleichmäßig aus der Feder*', and such compounds as *aufströmen* (lit., rare), as in Nicolai 8,16: '*es strömet . . . das Blut mir in dem Busen auf und nieder*', *herströmen*, as in Gotter, 1,455: '*von allen Enden herströmend*' and *hervorströmen*, as in Haller, *Rest.d.Staats.* 2,92: '*das Geld strömt aus allen Cassen und Winkeln hervor*'. Worth noting is the locution *die Augen strömen von Tränen*, a case of linguistic confusion, *Begriffstauschung*, since it is the tears which flow and not the eyes; current since the 18th c., e.g. Goethe, *Wahlverw.* 2,6: '*ihre Augen strömten von Thränen*' (surprisingly not recorded in *DWb.* [1942]).

etw. (in etw.) strömen (lit., obs.) to pour sth. (into sth.); since the 18th c., e.g. Bürger, 12a: '*du strömst in die Adern reines Blut*', Heinse, *Hild.* 1,10: '. . . *strömte er seine Gefühle in die Saiten*'; cf. Rahel, *Buch d.And.* 2,304 [1834]: '. . . *in den gesundheitsströmendsten Abend*'. Such usage is obs.; purely poet. and unusual is Goethe's '*dich strömt mein Lied*' in *Wanderers Sturmlied*. In compounds such transitive use still occurs, though confined to lit., e.g. *einströmen*, as in (Sa.) *seine Begeistrung strömte uns Muth ein*, *umströmen*, as in Voß 1,8: '*Schauer der Wonn' umströmt' ihm das Herz*', also *ausströmen* (see p. 164) and *überströmen* and *verströmen* (see below).

etw. überströmt etw. (1) sth. floods or covers sth.; with abstracts since the 18th c., e.g. Klopstock, *Oden* 1,109: '*siegswerthe Röthen überströmten flammend die Wang*'.

etw. überströmt etw. (2) (lit., obs.) sth. exceeds sth., goes beyond sth.; e.g. (DWb) Ötker, *Lebenserinn.* 2,28: '. . . *Beredsamkeit, die . . . das richtige Maß überströmte*'.

überströmen (intrans.) to overflow; since the 17th c., f.r.b. Stieler, [1691], e.g. Geßner 2,60: '*alles überströmt im vollen Segen*'; frequent in pres. participle *überströmend* since the 18th c., e.g. Keller 4,55: '*aus überströmendem Herzen*'. The noun *Überströmung*, used by Lessing [edit. M.] 9,301: '. . . *mit welcher Überströmung des Herzens*', is obs.

verströmen (lit.) to cease to flow, vanish; since the 18th c., when Klopstock used it with *Duft*, Jean Paul with *Töne* (for 'fade away'), also with ref. to time, e.g. in Jean Paul, where *verrinnen* would now be used.

etw. verströmen to spread, send out sth.; figur. since the 19th c., e.g. Hebbel 6,316: '. . . *verströmt sie . . . flammenheißen Duft*'. C.F.Meyer in *J.Jen.* 129 used *sein Leben für etw. verströmen*.

die Strömung current, trend, drift, tendency; originally with ref. to the current of a river, since last quarter of the 18th c., figur. since the 19th c., e.g. Goethe 42,2,563 (W.): '*standhaft muß man seine Stellung zu behaupten suchen, bis die Strömung vorüber gegangen ist*', also Bismarck, *Reden* 4,218, Freytag, *Erinn.* 197, Keller, *Salander* 61. Hence *die Gegenströmung* = 'reaction', as in Freytag, *Bilder* 2,144 [1859], although it can also mean 'drift in the opposite direction'. Sometimes the same as *Rückstrom*, which is now mainly used for 'flow or stream (of people or traffic) back (e.g. from holidays or into town from the countryside)'.

die Entwicklungen wurden zu Stromschnellen (lit.) the developments became rapids; since the 19th c., e.g. Gutzkow, *Ges.W.* 3,378: '*Geselligkeit, die . . . ein Strudel, ein Wirbel, eine fortreißende Stromschnelle werden kann*', Werfel, *Nicht d. Mörder* 180: '*diese Stromschnelle der Gedanken*'.

es geht mir alles wider den ~ (coll.) nothing works out for me as planned, everything goes against me; f.r.b. Kritzinger [1742].

viele Bäche machen einen ~ (prov.) many drops make a flow, many a little makes a mickle; in German at least since the 16th c., f.r.b. Eyering, *Prov.* [1604].

← See also under *anbrausen* (for *anströmen*), *ausströmen, beströmen, durchströmen, einströmen, entströmen, fließen* (for *dahinfließen wie ein Strom* and *Strom der Folgerungen*), *mahlen* (for *Mahlstrom*), *Meer* (for *ganze Ströme und Meers voll Unglück*), *regen* (for *in Strömen herniederregnen*), *schwimmen* (for *gegen den Strom schwimmen, im Strom der Dinge fortschwimmen* and *dem Strom nachschwimmen*) and *Strolch* (for *Stromlinienstrolch*).

strotzen: bulge, protrude

von (or *vor*) *etw.* ~ to be over-full of sth., brimming with sth., teeming with sth.; in phys. sense since OHG, at first mainly with ref. to breasts and udders; since the 18th c. with ref. to persons who are 'full of (or burst with) sth.', e.g. *von Gesundheit, Kraft*, etc. ~, e.g. Nicolai, *Nothanker* 1,177 [1773]: '. . . *Landmädchen . . . , die vor Gesundheit strotzten'*, with ref. to abstracts since the 19th c., e.g. *etw. strotzt von Widersprüchen, Fehlern*, etc. The sense of 'to be full of sth.' could easily lead to 'to be full of oneself, proud, conceited', which explains ~ = 'to strut (about proudly)', since the 18th c., cf. Ludwig [1716]: *'strotzig einhergehen'*; also (since the 18th c.) in compounds, e.g. J.Möser, *Phant.* 3,18: '. . . *wie frech sie daher strotzte'*; *aufstrotzen, einherstrotzen* and *entgegenstrotzen* also occur, but all are rare now.

strotzend (lit.) boastful, conceited; since the 18th c., recorded by Adelung who quoted *'strotzende Beredsamkeit'* from Gellert (no details).

strotzig (coll., a.) obstreperous, refractory; since the 17th c., e.g. Freytag, *Erinn.* 292: *'er blieb strotzig'*; Goethe IV,3,16,11 (W.) used *'strozzlich'* for 'arrogant'.

Strudel: whirlpool

der ~ (lit.) whirlpool; figur. since the 16th c., e.g. in *der* ~ *der Zeit, des Lebens*, e.g. Ense, *B.* 3,129: *'in dem Strudel jener Zerstörung fortgerissen'* (see also the example in Gutzkow quoted under *Strom*); frequent in compounds, e.g. Pfeffel, *Pr.* 8,151: *'ich woge in einem Wonnestrudel'*, Thümmel 2,275: *'in einen Zauberstrudel gerathen'*, Goethe, *Faust I*, 643: *'wenn Glück auf Glück im Zeitenstrudel scheitert'* (Goethe also used *Zeitstrudel*, e.g. in IV,39,216 (W.)). Since the notion of noise has always been present in the term, it can be used like *Trubel* for 'bustle, hubbub, tumult, hurly-burly', esp. in Alemannic areas, e.g. Gotthelf, *Uli* 1,299: *'während dem Hochzeitsstrudel'*.

etw. strudelt in jem.m (lit.) sth. swirls in sb.; since the 18th c., e.g. Kinkel, *E.* 24: *'Gefühle* . . ., *die in ihm gestrudelt'*; cf. also Wieland 17,22: *'meine* . . . *Seele kochte und strudelte von* . . . *Verlangen'*, and Möser, *Ph.* 4,106: *'ihre Worte strudeln, wo sie nur fließen sollten'*.

strudeln (coll.) to work sloppily, skimp one's work; same as regional coll. *hudeln* (see p. 1376); f.r.b. Frisius [1556], e.g. Goethe 19,119 (W.): '. . . *daß ich nicht so strudele und sudele wie sonst'*; hence *Strudler* (coll.) = 'botcher, bungler', frequent in Goethe, e.g. IV,21,170 (W.), *Strudelei* = 'negligent work, hasty performance, careless behaviour', recorded since 1762 and *Gestrudel*, f.r.b. Krämer [1702].

der ~ (gastr.) strudel; recorded since the 17th c.; mainly used for pastry where the word refers to circular shape or the fact that the dough was rolled (e.g. *Apfelstrudel*), but now (in some regions) also for dishes which to the eye do not suggest anything circular (perhaps a ref. to the circular whipping action).

Struktur: structure

die ~ structure; figur. only since the 19th c., e.g. with ref. to writings, as in Hegel, *Ästhet.* X, pref. xiii [1835]: '. . . *in der innern Struktur der* . . . *Sätze'*, Freytag, *Verm. Aufs.* 1,113 [1851] on a novella: *'Struktur der Handlung'*; with ref. to people and society only since the 20th c., e.g. (S.-B.) *Sociologica* 14 [1955]: *'Divergenz zwischen dem Menschen als psychologisches Wesen – "Persönlichkeitsstruktur" – und der objektiven Einrichtung – "institutionelle Struktur" – der Welt'*.

Strumpf: stump; stocking

auf den ~ *kommen* (coll.) to get into a difficult situation; ~ here = 'candle-end, small remainder of a candle'; since the 17th c., now probably only in some regions. Hence also *ein Strümpfchen* (coll.) = 'a tiny amount', as in Corvinus (= Amaranthes), 632 [1720]: *'du willst mir nur ein Strümpfchen Zeit* . . . *gönnen'*.

einen ~ *zusammenreden* (coll.) to talk a lot of nonsense; ~ in some regions can mean 'stupid talk' (esp. in the S. and in Austria), as in Auerbach, *Schr.* 16,128, but also 'stupid fellow' (e.g. in Saxony), recorded since the 18th c. The locution belongs to an extensive group in which sb.'s remarks are compared to sth. of little value (see entries under *Blech, Kohl* and *Makulator*).

auf (or *in*) *dem* ~ *sein* (regional coll.) to be well-off; also used for 'to be fit (again)'; origin is doubtful. It has been suggested that it refers to not being in bed (any longer) and able again to put on stockings for going out, but others have pointed to the fact that the wearing of stockings could indicate wealth and that *auf die Strümpfe kommen* = 'to become wealthy' should be seen as the starting-point; since late in the 18th c., e.g. Bürger [edit. Str.] 3,34, Reuter, *Briefe* (edit. W.) 64, Mörike, *Werke* 1,191: '. . . *schon wieder auf den Strümpfen und getrosten Muts'*, Mügge, *Romane* 3,6,156 [1862]: '. . . *immer noch munter auf seinen Strümpfen'*; cf. also regional coll. *ein vollgefressener* = 'a paunchy chap'; in some areas also used for 'to be in a good mood, fine spirits' (esp. in Alemannic regions). It also occurs in the negative *nicht auf dem* ~ *sein* = 'to be sick', recorded by Heyne [1895], e.g. Gotthelf, *Uli* 2,30: *'ob krank oder sonst nicht recht im Strumpf'*.

jem.m auf die Strümpfe helfen (coll.) to help sb. to regain financial or phys. health; for origin see previous entry; current since early in the 19th c., e.g. Heine [edit. Elster] 1,312; cf. also Raabe, *Fab.u.Seb.* 1 [1881]: '. . . *der würde die schöne deutsche Literatur endlich auf den Strumpf gebracht haben'*.

sich auf die Strümpfe machen (coll.) to get going, push off; since the 18th c., e.g. H.v.Kleist [edit. Schm.] 1,250. Chamisso, *Werke* 5,126 [1836]. See also under *Socke* (p. 2269) for another version of this phrase.

etw. in den ~ *tun* (coll.) to save up, put sth. by; refers to the custom of putting one's savings in stockings (mentioned in lit. since the 17th c.); hence *der Sparstrumpf*; the phrase has been recorded for several regions since the 19th c., e.g. by Albrecht for Leipzig [1881], e.g. Werfel, *Nicht der Mörder* 237 [1920]: '. . . *darauf bedacht* . . . *etwas in den Strumpf zu tun'*.

das ist aus dem ~ geschüttelt (coll.) that did not require much thought or effort; e.g. Droste-Hülshoff, *Briefe* 14 on examples in a handbook: '*sie sind aus . . . dem Strumpf geschüttelt*'. See also under *Ärmel* for the much more frequently used *etw. aus dem Ärmel schütteln.*

jem.m ein Loch in den ~ reden (coll.) to weary sb. with incessant talk; cf. Engl. 'to talk the hind leg off a donkey'; e.g. Löns, *Dahinten i.d.H.* 49 [1910]: '*die redet einem ein Loch in den Strumpf, und wenn man Kniestiefel anhat*'; cf. *jem.m ein Loch in den Bauch reden* (p. 1626) and the version with *Kind* on p. 1466.

deine Strümpfe haben Hunger (coll.) you have holes in your stockings; since early in the 20th c.; a little older is *du wächst wohl durch die Strümpfe?* (since 2nd half 19th c.).

das ist so egal wie zwei Strümpfe (coll.) that comes to the same thing; since the middle of the 19th .

er hat dicke Strümpfe an (coll.) he can't hear you; frequently also used for 'he does not want to hear you'; recorded since the 2nd half of the 19th c.; e.g. by Albrecht for Leipzig [1881]; a variant dating from the same period is *er hat zwei Paar Strümpfe an.*

deine Strümpfe ziehen Wasser (coll.) your stockings hang down; since the 19th c., recorded e.g. by Müller-Fraureuth [1914].

der ~ (vulgar) penis; modern sl., cf. similar *Schlauch* (p. 2130); therefore also *den ~ auswinden* (vulg.) = to urinate' (since ca. 1930). Since the 1st half of the 20th c. *~* has also been in use for 'condom'.

der Wadenstrümpfler (polit.hist.) member of the *Freisinnige Vereinigung*, so called because *Wadenstrümpfe* were worn at court and its wearers were considered 'upper-class' (contrast: *Wasserstiefler* for 'member of the *Freisinnige Volkspartei*', considered 'lower-class'); for details see Ladendorf, *Hist. Schlagwb.* 323 [1906].

der Strumpfwein (joc.coll.) sour wine: so called because it is alleged to close the holes in one's stockings by contraction; recorded since the 19th c., e.g. by Wander [1876], where the joc. variant *Strumpfschließungsbeglücker* is also mentioned.

← See also under *blau* (for *Blaustrumpf*), *Familie* (for *Familienstrumpf*), *Kartoffel* (for *eine Kartoffel im Strumpf*), *Kopf* (for *abhauen Ast und Strumpf*) and *Stiel* (for *mit Strumpf und Stiel*).

Strunk: stalk, stump

ein kleiner ~ (coll.) a (nice) little boy; usually in affectionate sense, e.g. G.Hauptmann, *Gab.Sch. Flucht* III [1912] about a child: '*es ist ein entzückender kleiner Strunk*'; cf. similar *Bengel* on p. 252.

Stube: room which is or can be heated

mit jem.m die ~ kehren (coll.) to treat sb. despotically or contemptuously; literally 'to use sb. like a broom with which to sweep the floor'; cf. Engl. 'to wipe the floor with sb.'; since Early

NHG, e.g. Luther 34,1,64 (Weimar); cf. the prov. *die ~ mit dem Weibe fegen, um das Geld für Besen zu sparen*', used by Keisersberg in *Narrenschiff* 72 [1511].

eine ~ voll Kinder haben (coll.) to have many children; cf. Engl. 'to have a house full of . . .'; since Early NHG; extended to things or abstracts for 'a lot of . . .', e.g. Mörike, *Schr.* 2,92: '. . . *gab es Gelächter einer Stuben voll*'.

die ~ ist nicht gekehrt (coll.) be careful about what you say; warning that there are listeners within earshot; only in some regions; modern.

immer rein (or *rin*) *in die gute ~* (coll.) come in! since the 19th c., popularized by the song hit '*kommen Sie rein in die gute Stube*' (1870s).

die gute ~ Deutschlands (cl.) the Black Forest; mainly used in propaganda by travel agents; since ca. 1960.

Stuben- . . . (pejor.) bookish . . ., unrealistic . . ., unwordly . . .; with ref. to views or statements stemming from sb. who has no real knowledge or practical experience; frequent since the 18th c., when Adelung recorded *Stubengelehrte*, e.g. Herder [edit. S.] 5,105: '. . . *keinen . . . abstrakten Stubenphilosophen*', Lichtenberg, *Aphor.* 3,77: '. . . *wurde Professor . . . spitzte Stubenmaximen zu*', W.H.Riehl, *D.dt.Arb.* 112: '*ein rechter Stubenmoralist*'; others are *Stubentheorie, Stubenpolitiker* (which can be used like *Stammtischpolitiker*, for which see under *Tisch*) and *Stubengelehrter* = 'armchair scholar'. The earliest instance appears to be *Stubenspeculation*, used by Paracelsus, *Op.* 1,270c [1616]; cf. also Harnisch, *Mein Lebensm.* 45: '*es giebt zwei Schulen, die Stubenschulen und die Lebensschulen*'.

stubenfarbig pasty, pale; since the 19th c., e.g. Seidel, *Lebr.H.* 22 [1882]; cf. similar *stubenbleich*, as in Gutzkow, *R.v.G.* 9,352. Adelung recorded '*stubensiech aussehen*'.

stubenrein (1) (coll.) clean, unobjectionable; derived from the sense 'house-trained' with ref. to a dog; mainly used with ref. to jokes; since late in the 19th c., e.g. Wolzogen, *Erzketzer* 362 [1911].

stubenrein (2) (coll.) clean, free from taint; mainly in polit. contexts for 'staunch, reliable'; 20th c. coll.

← See also under *Fenster* (for *die Stube zum Fenster hinausschmeißen*), *gut* (for *das gute Zimmer*, where *die gute Stube* should have been added), *hocken* (for *Stubenhocker*), *hüten* (for *Stubenhüter*, where *die Stube hüten*, as used by Goethe, might have been included), *Kind* (for *er hat keine gute Kinderstube gehabt* and other phrases), *ober* (for *das Oberstübchen*) and *Pflug* (for *die Stube auf und ab pflügen*).

Stüber: see *Nase*.

Stück: piece

das ~ (1) part; figur. with ref. to parts of writing, documents, treaties, speeches, prayers; since MHG, e.g. Luther 7,351 (Weimar): '*die puß hat drey stuck'*, transl. Apocrypha 1 Macc. 8,26: *'und sollen die Juden solche stücke trewlich halten'* (where the A.V. has 'keep their covenants'); therefore also = 'passage' (in a book), e.g. *er las mir ein ~ vor*.

das ~ (2) thing, item; since Late MHG, e.g. Franck, *Turkey* D3a: *'yn essen und trincken, hauß-halten und anderen stücken'*, Petri,165a: *'gedenck der vier letzten stück, des todts, des gerichts, der helle und des himmels'*. It therefore corresponds also to Engl. 'matter', as in *'in Stücken der Kunst'*, e.g. Winckel-mann [in Justi 1,185], now obs., and to Engl. 'regard', 'respect', since Early NHG, e.g. *in einem ~ =* 'in one respect', e.g. Luther 46,435 (Weimar), *in keinem ~ =* 'in no respect', e.g. Luther 6,581 (Weimar), *in jedem ~ =* 'in every respect', e.g. v.König, *Ged.* 59: *'er ist in jedem Stück ein Meister seiner Kunst'*.

das ~ (3) story, event; close to the previous entry; since Late MHG, e.g. *Dt.Städtechron.* 5,53: *'die geschicht und stuck, die hiernach geschrieben stand'*; obs. in this sense, but partly alive in some locutions (see under *stark* for *ein starkes ~*) and in the diminutive *Stückchen*, as in Schiller, *Räuber* 1,2: *'ein Stückchen aus meinen Bubenjahren'*, where it often means 'anecdote'; cf. also Goethe IV,3,87 (W.): *'die erzählten einander Stückgen'*.

das ~ (4) piece, piece of writing or music, play; with ref. to poems already in Early NHG, e.g. H. Sachs [edit. G.] 18,1; since the 18th c. for all kinds of 'pieces of writing', essays, articles, plays, compositions, operas; f.r.b. Kramer [1702]: *'ein Stück auf der Schaubühne'*, e.g. Goethe, *Lehrj.* 3,2: *'das Stück war in fünf Acten geschrieben'*. Hence *Aktenstück* = 'document' (used by Goethe), *Dek-lamierstück* = 'drama with more speech than action', e.g. Tieck, *Ges.Nov.* 1,11, *Familienstück* = 'domestic tragedy', e.g. Wieland 34,237, *Fest-stück* = 'play for a festival', e.g. Goethe, *Anmerk. über Ram.N.*, where Goethe also used *Theaterstück* and *Schubladenstück* = 'play in which the different scenes lack cohesion'. Elsewhere he also used *Fratzenstück* = 'farce', *Gaststück* = 'play in which guest artists appear' and *Schicksalsstück* = 'fate tragedy'; a modern compound is *Zeitstück* = 'topical drama'. In the field of music there are among others *Instrumentalstück*, *Konzertstück* and *Musik-stück* (since the 18th c.).

das ~ (5) painting, etching, drawing, piece of sculpture; since the 16th c., e.g. Dürer, *Tagebuch* [edit. L.]68: *'17 geäzter stuck'*, Goethe IV,9,31 (W.): *'. . . wünsche, daß Sie für diese Dame einige recht schöne Stücke machen'*. It is assumed that this sense is derived from *~ Arbeit* (cf. Schiller, *Kab.u.L.* 1,2: *'das verhunzte Stück Arbeit'*). There are many compounds, most of them describing the subject of the painting, drawing, etc., such as *Landschaftsstück*, *Portraitstück*; cf. also Wieland 23,332: *'das Gemälde ist sein Lieblingsstück'*.

das ~ (6) (coll.) person (pejor. or abusive); used

in reinforcements of abuse or condemnation since Early NHG. It can stand as an intensifier before a noun, at first often in the genitive, e.g. *ein ~ Schelms, ein ~ Weibs*, later in the nominative, f.r.b. Kramer [1702]: *'ein Stück Esel'*. It can also be used on its own as a term of abuse (since Early NHG), now only in some regions, e.g. for 'good-for-nothing' in Swabia, for 'disreputable woman' in Lower Franconia, for 'wicked person' in Saxony and Thuringia, usually, however, with an adjective. Stieler [1691] recorded *'loses Stück = mala femina'*, e.g. Sturz 2,194: *'ein leichtfertiges Stück'* and in coll. it is now in frequent use: *du dummes, eitles, verrücktes*, etc. *~* (also in compounds, e.g. *er ist ein Miststück*). Sometimes this pejor. *~* means no more than 'some', e.g. Seume, *Spazierg.* 1,43: *'ein Stück von Geistlichkeit* [= 'some priest'] *hatte Lunte gerochen'*. In the modern period *~* with ref. to persons has a wide range. It can express mild contempt, e.g. *ein ~ Poet* = 'something of a poet', as in Freiligrath, *Sämtl.W.* 6,294, make a general statement, as in Storm, *Werke* 5,154 (*Doppelgänger*): *'. . . ein Stück von einem Träumer'*, express a degree of pity, e.g. *du ~ Unglück* = 'you wretch' (first in Berlin, since ca. 1840), also *er ist ein Stückchen Malheur* = 'he fails in whatever he attempts' (= *Versager*), since the beginning of the 20th c. In *ein ~ Beamter* = 'some minor official' contempt and resentment can combine. Quite vague is such usage as *'ein Stück Landsmann von mir'* in Freytag, *Verl.Hand.* 2,28, which one might render with 'sort of a compatriot of mine'. See also the prov. *je ärger das ~, je größer das Glück'* = 'the more knave, the better luck', f.r.b. Simrock [1846] (the Engl. version recorded since the 17th c.)

das ~ (7) stretch, distance; since the 18th c., as in *ein gutes ~ Weg* = 'a fair distance, a considerable stretch of road', but now also in extended sense, where no phys. distance is implied, e.g. *eine Idee ein gutes ~ weiterentwickeln*.

das ~ (8) part; used with ref. to time; since the 17th c., e.g. Goethe II,11,184 (W.): *'. . . ein gut Stück des Octobers'*; not in general use now.

das ~ (9) piece, part, portion; figur. with ref. to persons or abstracts; this appears to be older in prov. than in general use, e.g. Lehman,218: *'vor ein gut Stück am Menschen muß man fünf böse abrechnen'*, or (Wander): *'jeder bekommt sein Stück, es sei Glück oder Unglück'*; literary examples appear in the 19th c., e.g. Uhland, *Ich hatt' einen Kame-raden: '. . . als wär's ein Stück von mir'*, Raabe, *Hungerpastor* XIV [1863] used *jem.m ein ~ Sorge aus dem Tornister nehmen*. Cf. also such locutions as *ein ~ Vergangenheit wird in diesem Buch lebendig* or *dieser Schreibtisch ist ein ~ Heimat für ihn*.

Stücker drei (*hundert*, etc.) (coll.) about three, a hundred, etc.; linguistically a contraction with *Stück oder drei* leading to *Stücker drei*; since the 18th c., occasionally in lit., e.g. Rahel, *B.d.Andenk.* 2,124 [1834]: *'ein Stücker sechs bis acht weibliche*

Domestiken', Kürnberger, *Amerikam.* 101: '*ein
Stücker hundert Menschen . . . sind hier im Handge-
menge*'.

er ist unser bestes ~ (joc.coll.) he is a darling, a
poppet, sb. we could not do without; 20th c. coll.;
now also in wider contexts, e.g. *sie geht zu ihrem
besten* ~ = 'she is joining her husband (friend,
lover)'.

ein böses ~ (a.) a misdeed, reprehensible action,
instance of bad behaviour; since Early NGH, e.g.
Luther Bible transl. Deuter. 19,20: '*solche böse
stücke*' (in A.V. 'any such evil'), Jerem. 5,28: '*sie
gehen mit bösen stücken um*' (in A.V. 'they overpass
the deeds of the wicked'); Goethe still used it in
Rein. Fuchs 1.

jem.s ~ *Brot* sb.'s livelihood; at least since the
18th c., e.g. Iffland, *Spieler* 2,1: '. . . *hätte er mich
noch um mein Stückchen Brot gebracht*'. Cf. also
Schubart, *S.Ged.* 3,132.

ein ~ *Brot* (cant) booty or haul of a thief; f.r.b.
Ostwald, *Rinnsteinspr.* 150 [190;6]; hence *ein* ~
Brot verdienen (cant) = 'to steal'.

ein hübsches (*schönes, stattliches*, etc.) ~ *Geld*
(coll.) a tidy sum, a considerable amount of money;
since the 17th c. (Moscherosch, Gryphius, Grimmelshausen, Schupp), f.r.b. Kramer [1702], e.g.
Hebel 3,39: '*ein hübsches Stück Geld*'.

an einem ~ (coll.) continuously, without a break
or interruption; since Early NHG; assumed to be
derived from the image of a bale of cloth; e.g.
Wieland, *Luc.* 1,378; Wieland 13,109 also used '*in
einem Stück fort*'; cf. also modern sl. *er hat's am* ~
= 'he rattles on and one, talks endlessly', since
early in the 20th c.

auf dem ~ *ergriffen werden* (coll.,obs.) to be
caught *in flagrante delicto*; e.g. Bahrdt, *Gesch.m.
Lebens* 4,262 [1790ff]; presumably derived from
böses ~ (see above); now obs.

aus einem ~ *sein* to be of one piece, harmonize in
all its parts; beginnings in MHG, when *an* was
used, e.g. Wolfram, *Parz.* 127,3: '*daz doch an eime
stücke erschein*'; later with *aus*, as in *mit etw. aus
einem* ~ *sein*, e.g. Wieland 23,225, or Ramler,
Schön. Wiss. 2,198: '*das ganze Werk ist von einer
Natur und aus einem Stücke*', Häusser, *Dt.Gesch.*
3,168 [1855]: '. . . . *bei dem Leben und Denken aus
einem Stücke sei*'.

jem. wie ein ~ *Dreck behandeln* (coll.) to treat sb.
like (a piece of) dirt; modern coll.

er würde sich eher in Stücke reißen lassen als . . .
he would sooner be torn limb from limb than
. . .; hyperbole of strong refusal; modern.

auf seinem ~ *stehen* (obs.) to stick to one's
statement or opinion; still in use in the 18th c., e.g.
M.Claudius, *Asmus* 3,104: '*also muß man nicht auf
seinem Stück stehen . . .*'; now obs.

das ~ *hat ausgespielt* (coll.) it's all over, the
matter is over and done with; cf. French *tirez le
rideau, la farce est jouée*; recorded since the 19th c.

das Brautstück (obs.) present given by the
bridegroom to his bride's female relatives; not
recorded by Adelung or Campe, but Campe
recorded *Bräutigamsgabe* for the present handed by
the bridegroom to the bride's parents (supposed to
be a relic of the *Kaufpreis*); in lit. since the 19th c.,
e.g. Freytag, *Bilder a. d.V.* 1,294; now probably
obs.

das Erbstück heirloom, sth. or sb. inherited; in
phys. sense for 'inherited object' since Early NHG;
figur. with ref. to persons since the 18th c., e.g.
(Sa.) O.Müller, *Stadtsch.* 1,141 [1856]: '*die alte
Köchin Gertrud, ein Erbstück aus dem Weidenhof*'
(also in Hebel 3,33), also extended to abstracts,
e.g. (Sa.) Wackernagel, *Dt.Lesebuch* 4,405 [1847]:
'*der . . . Bürgerverstand . . . ist das Erbstück unsrer
Nation*'.

das Hauptstück principal piece, chief item; since
Early NHG in many contexts, at first mainly in
relig. sphere, e.g. Luther, *S.W.* 63,139: '. . . *das
hauptstück . . ., das Christus unser heil ist*' (*DWb*.
surprisingly missed examples of such usage and
stated '*erst aus jüngerer Zeit bezeugt*'); often used for
'article of faith'; with ref. to lit. 'pieces' frequent
since the 18th c., e.g. Lessing 4,177.

das Kopfstück coin with the portrait of the
sovereign on one side; since the 17th c., e.g.
Schuppius,226. Adelung mentioned that in French
such coins were called *gros testons*, in Lat. *testones*
or *grossi capitones*. In various trades *Kopfstück* is
used for the upper part of things, e.g. doors, walls
or flutes (where it means *Mundstück*).

jem.m ein Kopfstück geben (coll.,obs.) to hit sb.
on the head, give sb. a box on the ear; f.r.b. Campe
[1808]; cf. *Kopfnuß* listed under *Nuß* (p. 1796).

das Leibstück favourite play; since the 18th c.,
e.g. Goethe (in Merck, *Briefe* 2,164); same as
Lieblingsstück, for which see above under ~ (5).

das Musterstück model, paragon; with ref. to
objects since the 18th c., frequent in Goethe's
writings; then also for 'exemplary piece' e.g.
of writing, same as *Musterbeispiel*, e.g. (*DWb*)
'*Musterstücke deutscher Prosa*'; cf. similar compounds listed on p. 1728.

das Schelmenstück nasty prank, dirty trick; same
as *Schelmenstreich* (see *Streich* (3)); Adelung recorded
it as *Schelmstück*.

das Wagestück daring deed, hazardous enterprise;
since Early NHG, e.g. Fischart, *Gl.Schiff* 173;
Schiller used both *Wagstück* (e.g. *Fiesco* 4,6) and
Wagestück, Goethe the latter, e.g. *Lehrj.* 8,7: '*in der
Liebe ist alles Wagestück*'.

das Zugstück (coll.) box-office draw, popular
play; so called because it 'pulls in' the public in
large numbers; 20th c. coll.

Stück-. . . piece-. . ., partial . . ., interrupted . . .;
there are many compounds, but few which are
strictly figur. The main ones are *Stückarbeit*, in
original sense = 'piece-work' (usually now *Accord-
arbeit*), but also figur. for 'work done with pauses
in between', e.g. Alexis, *Andalusien* 224 [1842]:

'. . . *das Treppensteigen ist jetzt nicht mehr eine so saure Stückarbeit für mich*'; *Stückrechnung* (econ.) = 'partial account, bank statement for a limited period', modern (see also under *Stumpf* for similar *Stumpfrechnung*); *Stückwerk*, first used for 'piece-work' (14th c.), changed its meaning when Luther, translating *ex parte* in 1 Cor. 13,9, used it to express the notion of 'fragmentary state, scrappiness': '*denn unser wissen ist stückwerck*' (in A.V. 'we know in part'), and this is now its chief meaning.

das Stückchen (also *Stücklein, Stückelchen*, etc.) little piece, a bit of . . .; this can occur as a diminutive for many meanings of ~ , e.g. with ref. to distance, as in Goethe 15,109 (W.): '*ein Stückchen Welt durchwandre . .*', to time, as in Goethe IV,1,186 (W.): '. . . . *noch ein Stückgen Februar im Käfig zubringen*', to abstracts, as in Heine [edit. Elster] 3,351: '*ich gönne . . . Platen sein Stückchen Ruhm*', to persons, as in Holtei, *Erz.Schr.* 12,34: '*wie wohl ich auch ein Stückchen Musickus bin*', to writings, e.g. (DWb) Forster 5,6: '. . . *wagte, ein sehr mittelmäßiges Stückchen drucken zu lassen*', to music, as in (DWb) Voigtländer, *Od.u.Lied.* 62 [1642]: '. . . *und höret ein liebliches stückgen darein*', to anecdotes, as in (DWb) Weise, *Kl.Leute* 83 [1675]: '. . . *ein lustig Stückgen erzehlen*'. The same applies, esp. in the regions, to *Stücklein, Stückle, Stückel*; Luther 26,604 (Weimar) used *stücklin*, but also *stucklein*, e.g. in 6,5 (Weimar).

zerstückeln to dismember, dissect; figur. since the 18th c., e.g. Goethe 3,95 (W.): '. . . *keine Macht zerstückelt geprägte Form, die lebend sich entwickelt*'; cf. also Goethe 22,110 (W.): '*das Zerstückelte unsres Daseins*'. Now also used for 'to analyse'; figur. *Zerstückelung* since the 18th c., e.g. Goethe 27,67 (W.): '*solcher vielfacher Zerstreuung, ja Zerstückelung meines Wesens*'. The verb is a diminutive derivation from *zerstücken*, but *zerstücken*, both in phys. and figur. senses is now hardly used. It occurs in lit., e.g. Goethe, *Faust* 1,3385: '*mein armer Sinn ist mir zerstückt*'.

← See also under *abfangen* (for *ein Stück Wild*), *brechen* (for *in Stücke brechen* and *Bruchstück*), *Bube* (for *Bubenstück*), *Fleisch* (for *ein schlimmes Stück Fleisch* and *ein Stück Weiberfleisch*), *frei* (for *aus freien Stücken*), *Frühstück, Gegenstück, Gold* (for *Goldstück*), *gut* (for *das gut Latein zerstücken*), *halten* (for *große Stücke auf jem. halten*), *Herz* (for *Herzstück*), *Knie* (for *Kniestück*), *Kunst* (for *das ist kein Kunststück*), *Meister* (for *Meisterstück*), *Mund* (for *ein gutes Mundstück haben*), *Museum* (for *er ist ein Museumsstück*), *Nacht* (for *Nachtstück*), *Pfaffe* (for *Pfaffenstück*), *rühren* (for *Rührstück*), *schauen* (for *Schaustück*), *schmücken* (for *Schmuckstück* (1) and (2)), *Seife* (for *müde wie ein Stückchen Seife*) and *stark* (for *ein starkes Stück*).

Student: student

ein ewiger ~ (coll.) perpetual student, student who continues endlessly with his studies without presenting himself for examinations. Modern coll.

Although usually pejor. the locution can occur in a neutral or even positive sense, e.g. Gutzkow, *R.v.G.* 1,332 [1850]: '. . . *gehört zu einer gewissen Klasse von Gelehrten, die man "ewige Studenten" nennen möchte*'.

← See also under *Futter* (for *Studentenfutter*).

studieren: study

etw. ~ to look (critically or out of interest) at sth., peruse or examine sth.; since the 18th c., e.g. Schiller, *Anmut* [1793]: '. . . *kann man . . . die falsche Würde studieren*', Goethe IV,39 (W.): '. . . *soeben studire ich Deine Briefe . . .*'. Also now coll. *er studiert jetzt die Zeitung*, where it means no more than 'to read'.

an etw. ~ to explore sth., try to make sense of sth., consider sth. (carefully); since Early NHG, e.g. Luther 18,502 or 32,65 (Weimar), e.g. (S.-B.) Platter, 146 [1612]: '*doran hatt er ettlich tag gstudiert*', Hebel 3,478: '*wir haben immer dran studiert*'; now little recorded, but there is still coll. *an etw. herumstudieren*.

auf etw. ~ to plan sth., consider sth. with a definitive objective in mind; since MHG, e.g. (S.-B.) *Hausball* 19 [1781]: '*denn jeder studirte auf ein neues Schelmstück*'. It can also mean 'to prepare oneself (mentally) for sth.', as in Schiller, *Macbeth* 1,7: '*er starb, wie Einer, der aufs Sterben studirte*' (where Shakespeare wrote: 'he died as one that had been studied in his death', which Dorothea Tieck rendered with '*er starb wie einer, der sich auf den Tod geübt*').

studiert (pejor.) studied, forced, unnatural, artificial; since the 18th c., e.g. Wieland, *Danischm.* 25: '*Zwang einer studierten Anständigkeit*'; *anstudiert* and *einstudiert* can in some contexts express the same notion. Cf. also the opposite, e.g. Wieland 15,1: '*die Grazie tanzt nach unstudierten Gesetzen*'.

jem.m etw. anstudieren (obs.) to ponder on sth. which one will address to sb.; e.g. Gutzkow, *Zaub. v.Rom* 3,173 [1858]: '*sonst studiert er Jedem . . . eine Frage an*'; now obs.

etw. durchstudieren to explore (or read) sth. thoroughly (and from beginning to end); at least since the 18th c., e.g. Goethe, *Faust I*, 2012; '*Ihr durchstudiert die groß' und kleine Welt*', Schiller, *Picc.* 4,7: '*Hat Er's durchstudiert?*'; cf. also Herder's remark: '*der Leser liest Kritiken, um keine Bücher durchzustudieren*'.

sich in etw. hineinstudieren to immerse oneself (or land) in sth. through long studies (or much pondering); since the 18th c., e.g. Lessing 7,453: '. . . *sich tief in den Irrthum hineinstudieren*'; cf. also non-reflex. use as in Goethe's '*ich studierte das Stück ganz in mich hinein*'.

ins Studium der Zeitung (des Fahrplans, etc.) *vertieft sein* to be immersed in the (study of) newspaper (timetable, etc.); here in the wider sense of 'perusing' sth. (see *etw. studieren*, above), where no more than 'reading' is implied; modern.

daran (or *dabei*) *kann man seine Studien machen*

(coll.) that gives one sth. to think about, that allows one to make interesting observations; in professional sense since at least the 19th c., in wider coll. sense modern.

← See also under *ausstudieren*, *Bauch* (for *ein voller Bauch studiert nicht gern*), *probieren* (for *Probieren geht über Studieren*) and *rollen* (for *eine Rolle einstudieren*).

Stufe: step, grade

die ~ (1) step; with allusion to steps of a ladder or staircase; since the 17th c., e.g. Lohenstein, *Soph.* 129 [1680], Goethe 24,50 (W.): '*aller Anfang ist leicht, und die letzten Stufen werden am schwersten und seltensten erstiegen*', often in *die höchste ~* , cf. Goethe 22,119 (W.): '*seine Recitation(stieg) . . . zu einer hohen Stufe von Wahrheit, Freiheit und Offenheit*'.

die ~ (2) grade, degree, stage, rank; derived from the extended sense of Lat. *gradus*; since Early NHG, e.g. Luther 32,137 (Weimar): '*wenn du zum andern stuffen des glaubens kompst*', often with allusion to climbing or struggling up towards sth. higher, including particularly the notion of development, e.g. Lessing [edit. L.-M.] 10,83: '*ob man auf dieser ersten Stuffe der Weisheit stehe*', Gottsched, *Beob.* 142: '*Freundschaft . . . hat verschiedene Stufen der Vertraulichkeit*', Goethe 41,2,12 (W.): '*die Stufen der Cultur betreffend*', Goethe 25,221 (W.) '*die Stufen von Lehrling, Gesell und Meister müssen aufs strengste beobachtet werden*'; cf. the saying in Wander [1876]: '*eine Stufe hinauf soll man den Freund und eine Stufe hinab die Frau wählen*'; hence *Stufen bilden, durchmachen, erklimmen*, etc., *durch Stufen nach und nach geschehen* (hence also *stufenweise*, since the 17th c.); very frequent in compounds, e.g. *Bildungsstufe* = 'stage or degree of culture', as in Goethe, *Dicht.u.Wahrh.* 3,12: '*das deserted village von Goldsmith mußte jederman auf jener Bildungsstufe höchlich zusagen*', *Ehrenstufe*, f.r.b. Kramer [1702], apparently the first recorded compound, *Entwicklungsstufe* = 'stage of development', since the 19th c., recorded in *DWb.* [1862], e.g. (Sa.) Scherr, *Blücher* 1,296 [1862], *Farbenstufe* = 'nuance (of colour)', still missing in *DWb.* [1862], recorded by Sanders [1865], *Tonstufe* = 'pitch', also 'degree', since the 18th c., recorded by Campe [1810], e.g. Koch, *Handbuch . . . Harmonie* 33 [1811]; often in econ. contexts, e.g. *Gehaltsstufe* = 'salary grade (bracket or level)', *Preisstufe* = 'price level or bracket', modern; also since the 20th c. with ref. to grades in schools, e.g. *Oberstufe*, *Mittelstufe*, *Unterstufe*. For the action of placing sb. (or sth.) in a certain category, rank or bracket *Stufung* is used, only in compounds such as *Rückstufung* = 'downward adjustment (in salary award or tax assessment)', *Umstufung* = 'regrading, reclassification', etc.; modern.

etw. stufen to grade, gradate or graduate sth.; in general = 'to produce a step-like arrangement', hence sometimes in the comparison *gestuft wie eine*

Treppe; since the 18th c., e.g. Goethe 31,106 (W.): '*. . . Bilder, wie sie der Mahler durch Lasiren auseinander gestuft hätte*', 3,86 (W.): '*Glieder an Glieder gestuft*'; cf. also *stufenförmig*, since the 18th c. and older *stufenweis* (since the 17th c.).

jem. or *etw. einstufen* to rate, grade, classify sb. or sth.; a modern word, still missing in *DWb.* [1862], even in Heyne [1895], listed without examples in Sanders [1865]; hence *Einstufung*, since late in the 19th c.

← See also under *abstufen*, *Keller* (for *eingelegte Kellerstufen*), *Leiter* for *Stufenleiter*), *Schatten* (for *Schattenstufe*) and *Schwund* (for *Schwundstufe*).

Stuhl: stool, chair

der ~ throne; both in relig. and secular contexts, since Gothic, OHG, OS, frequent since MHG, e.g. *Kaiserchron.* 4987, Bible transl. 1 Kings 2,19; then extended to any 'seat' of office or authority, e.g. Luther Bible transl. Matth. 19,28: '*da des menschen son wird sitzen auff dem stuel seiner herrligkeit, werdet jr auch sitzen auff zwelff stuelen vnd richten . . .*'; still in modern period, e.g. Zschokke, *Ausgew. Schr.* 1,28 [1824]: '*die von ihren Stühlen gestoßenen Beamten . . .*', Heine [edit. Elster] 3,346: '*. . . am Tage des Gerichts . . . werde ich . . . vor den Stuhl der Allmacht treten*'.

der Lehrstuhl chair (at a university); specialization of the previous entry; since MHG (cf. Diefenbach, *Gloss.* 106a and 80a under *cathedra*); Stieler [1691] has: '*Lesestul sive Lehrstul*', e.g. Jean Paul 31,3: '*von dem "Armesünderstuhl" des historischen Lehrstuhles aufspringen*'. Sometimes in cases where the meanings of 'university chair' and 'throne, seat of authority' can both apply, e.g. Fichte 8,37: '*. . . auch Kanten von dem hohen Stuhle, der ihm als dem ersten Philosophen Deutschlands gesetzt wurde, herunterzustoßen*'.

der Meister vom ~ Master of the Lodge; title in Freemasonry; in lit. since the 18th c., often in Goethe, e.g. IV,30,112 (W.); also in the 18th c. transferred to men of distinction in their field, e.g. Herder [edit. S.] 17,130.

mit etw. nicht zu Stuhle kommen können (coll.) to fail to manage sth.; originally a ref. to *~* = 'bowel movement', but since the 19th c. in wider sense (where the original connotation is totally forgotten), e.g. Raabe, *Horacker* 60 [1876]: '*. . . auf daß wir endlich mit Horacker zu Stuhle kommen*' (= 'get somewhere, settle sth.').

jem.m den ~ vor die Tür setzen to throw sb. out, dismiss sb.; originally a phrase in law (cf. Grimm, *Rechtsalterth.* 1,261, older edit. 189), in general use for 'to eject' since the 16th c., e.g. Gellert 3,195, Alexis, *Hosen d.H.v.Br.* 2,3,151.

zwischen zwei Stühlen sitzen to fall between two stools; cf. French *assis entre deux selles le cul à terre*; since the 11th c. in Lat. form *labitur enitens sellis haerere duabus sedibus in mediis homo saepe resedit in imis* (cf. *Haupts Zs.* 6,305, *Germania* 18,324), f.r.b. Tunnicius [1295] in LG, then in MHG, e.g.

Minnes [edit. v.d.Hagen] 1,307, also used by
Luther 19,304 (Weimar): '*also sitzt er zwischen
zweyen stulen nidder, das er keins krieget*', f.r.b.
Henisch [1616]; also with *fallen* instead of *sitzen*,
e.g. G.Keller 2,161: '*nehmen wir uns in acht, daß
wir nicht zwischen zwei Stühle fallen*'.

auf zwei Stühlen sitzen (coll.) to sit on the fence,
try to agree with both sides in an argument;
cf. Lat. *duabus sedere sellis* (which occurs in
Macrobius). German recordings are late, e.g.
Eiselein [1838].

in einem (stressed) *Stuhle stehen mit jem.m* (coll.,
a.) to get on well with sb., be in agreement with
sb.; probably derived from *Kirchenstuhl*, i.e. share
a pew with sb., have the same faith; still recorded
in the 19th c., now a., if not obs.

sich einen ~ im Himmel verdienen wollen (coll.) to
try to secure a place in heaven; since the 17th c.,
f.r.b. Kramer [1702], now a., though probably still
alive in some regions (I have heard it used with
Platz instead of ~).

der Glockenstuhl belfry; one of the many tech.
compounds for erections in or on which sth. sits
(e.g. *Dachstuhl*); as ~ already in the 16th c. (cf.
Goethe 1,204 (W.): '*das Kind es denkt, die Glocke
hängt da droben auf dem Stuhle*', later as a compound.

der Großvaterstuhl (coll.) easy-chair with head-
rests in the top corners; since the 18th c., e.g.
Kortum, *Jobsiade* 221 [1799]: '. . . *im Großvaterstuhl
fast den ganzen Tag sitzen*'.

← See also under *arm* (for *Armesünderstühlchen*),
fallen (for *zwischen Stuhl und Bank fallen*), *Frosch*
(for *setz den Frosch auf goldnen Stuhl, er hüpft doch
wieder in den Pfuhl*), *Gewitter* (for *das Gewitter im
Nachtstuhl*), *hauen* (for *das haut mich vom Stuhl*),
heilig (for *der Heilige Stuhl*), *rasieren* (for *Rasierstuhl-
platz*), *reißen* (for *das reißt einen vom Stuhl*), *richten*
(for *Richterstuhl*) and *Sorge* (for *Sorgenstuhl*).

stülpen: put on or over; turn up
den Pelion auf den Ossa ~ (obs.) to heap Pelion
upon Ossa, to add one difficulty (disaster, misfortune, embarrassement, etc.) to another; a ref. to
the giants who wanted to scale the seat of the Gods
by piling Mount Pelion upon Mount Ossa (in
Thessaly), as told by Homer in *Od.*XI,315; hence
den Pelion auf den Ossa ~ wollen = 'to want to
undertake an enterprise of gigantic proportions, to
be unreasonably ambitious; still in Heine, *Reis.*
4,139, now obs.

(sich) ein Glas hinter die Binde ~ (coll.,a.) to
down a quick one; since the 19th c., e.g. (T.)
v.Lauff, *Frau Aleit* 294 [1905].

etw. (einer Sache) überstülpen (lit.) to invest sth.
with sth. else, impose sth. on sth.; not yet figur. in
19th c. dictionaries, but now in frequent use, e.g.
*einer unbedeutenden Sache eine größere Bedeutung
überstülpen, man kann einer Gesellschaft keine neue
Kunstform überstülpen* (cf. similar locutions with the
simplex, e.g. *über manches Kunstlose läßt sich eine
Aura von Kunst stülpen*).

etw. umstülpen to turn sth. upside down, stand
sth. on its head; not listed at all in Adelung, only in
phys. sense in Campe, though in use since the
16th c., e.g. (DWb) *Staatspapiere z.Gesch. Karls V*,
259, where '*umbgestulbt*' occurs. Heine [edit. E.]
7,108 used '. . . *einer umgestülpten Weltordnung*',
Raabe, *Hungerpastor* 2,31 [1864] has '*ich stülpe
meinen Gedächtniskasten um*'; *umstulpen* also occurs,
e.g. (DWb) Wackernell, *Beda Weber* 298 [1903].

jem. umstülpen to change sb. fundamentally;
modern, e.g. F.Bonn, *Ges.W.* 1,414 [1911]: '*du
hast mich ganz umgestülpt, – ich erkenne mich selbst
nicht wieder*'.

einer Sache etw. aufstülpen to pop sth. over sth.
else; some dictionaries class *aufstülpen* = 'to turn
up', esp. in *aufgestülpte Nase* = 'turned-up nose'
(e.g. Raabe 1,1,432) as figur., although this is
debatable. Really figur. use is rare, but can occur,
e.g. *einer delikaten Sache eine Schutzglocke aufstülpen*.

← See also under *Pfannkuchen* (for *wenn's
Pfannkuchen regnet, ist mein Faß umgestülpt*).

stumm: mute, silent
stumm (lit.) mute, dumb; in lit. with ref. to
abstracts since the 17th c., e.g. Wieland 20,135:
'*die Sinne werden stummer*', Goethe 2,325 (W.): '*ich
vernahm sein stummes Flehn*', Storm, *S.Werke* [edit.
K.] 1,156 [1859]: '. . . *hing stumm die Finsternis in
Halm und Zweigen*', Vischer, *Auch Einer* 2,422:
'. . . *mit dem stummen Brüten in der Luft*' (cf. the
oxymoron in Chamisso 4,70: '*was redet dieser Stein
mit stummem Munde?*'); sometimes = 'secret', also
since the 17th c., e.g. Hoffmannswaldau-Neukirch,
Ged. 2,89: '*ich brenn in einer stummen Glut*'. In
poetry *stumme Nacht* can stand for 'death', e.g.
Goethe 10,258 (W.).

~ für etw. sein (lit.) to refuse to react to sth., take
no interest in sth., be unreceptive; since the
18th c., e.g. Kretschmann, *S.Werke* 5,43 [1784ff]:
'*bist du für Lieder stumm, bist du für Bitten taub?*',
Pfeffel, *Pros.Vers.* 2,27 [1810]: '*mein für die Freude
stummes Herz*'.

~ vor etw. sein to be speechless with sth. (rage,
surprise, etc.); since MHG, e.g. (L.) *Rosengarten* C
140:':'*vor zorn stumb*'; also *~ vor Staunen*, e.g.
Schiller, *Jungfr.v.O.* 1,9.

~ wie . . . as mute or silent as . . .; in many
comparisons, at first mainly with *Fisch*, f.r.b.
Tappius, 141b [1545], sometimes with mention of
particular kinds of fish, e.g. *~ wie ein Karpfen*, e.g.
Wieland, *Sylph.* 5,4, *~ wie ein Hecht*, e.g. J.G.Kohl,
Reisen in Engl.u.Wales 3,184 [1841]; *~ wie ein
Block, ein Ölgötze, ein Stock* also occur.

das muß einem Stummen den Mund öffnen (coll.)
that is extraordinary, unbelievable; recorded since
the 19th c.; cf. Eiselein, 583 [1838]: '*eher werden
die Stummen reden* . . .' with ref. to an unlikely
event.

jem. ~ machen (sl.) to silence sb. (by using
violence); modern sl.

stumme Buchstaben silent letters; since the 16th c. and still in general use for letters which are written but not pronounced.

stumme Laute (or *Buchstaben*) (ling.,a.) *mutae*; comprizing labials, dentals and gutturals; in use since the 16th c., recorded by Tappius; now unusual if not obs.

stumme Münzen coins without inscription; e.g. v. Schrötter, *Wb.d. Münzkunde* 669 [1930]: '*die mittelalterlichen stummen Münzen sind solche, die Trugschrift oder gar keine Umschrift haben*'; also called *schriftlose* or *anepigraphe Münzen*.

jem.m keine stumme Rede geben (regional coll.) to say not one word in reply; recorded e.g. by Fischer for Swabia.

stumme Sänger (mil.sl.) lice; f.r.b. Imme, *Soldatenspr.* 94; now obs.

stummes Spiel mime; at least since the 18th c., e.g. Lessing 4,254; cf. also Schiller, *D.Carlos* 1,5: '*seiner Liebe stumme Mienensprache*'; hence also *stumme Rolle* for 'non-speaking part in a play'.

stumme Sünden (theol.) execrable sins; called ~ , because they are unmentionable; Luther used the term in Apocr. transl. Wisd. of Sol. 14,26 (where the A.V. has 'defiling of souls'); it corresponds to lat. *nefandum*, and became a general term for sexual perversions, unchastity, particularly sodomy and homosexuality; Luther also used the term in 30,2,142 (Weimar); Stieler [1691] recorded '*Geheimsünden alias stumme Sünden*'; in later periods masturbation was sometimes counted as one of the *stumme Sünden*.

stummer Wein stum, must; cf. French *vin muet*; recorded since the 16th c.; e.g. Schwan 3,1022b [1787]: '*stummer Wein, den man nicht gären läßt, sondern süß in Fässern behält*'; cf. Adelung: '*. . . nennt man auch den Wein stumm, wenn er so geschwefelt ist, daß er darüber den Geist verloren hat*', to which Campe [1810] added: '*. . . und daher nicht redselig macht*' (which certainly is not the correct explanation of the term).

ein stummer Zeuge a silent witness; figur. with ref. to objects which 'witness' an event; e.g. (Sp.) Zschokke, *Alamontade* 2,9 [1802]: '*der Kranz und der schmale Theil des . . . Hauses . . . sollten nun . . . wieder die stummen Zeugen meiner Liebe . . . werden*'.

stummberedt (lit.) silently eloquent; since late in the 18th c., e.g. Tieck, *Schr.* 5,354: '*im stummberedten Schweigen*'; a variant is *stummberedsam*, which Gutzkow used in *Zaub.v.Rom* 7,204.

etw. verstummt (lit.) sth. becomes silent; with abstracts since MHG, e.g. Minnes. [edit. v.d.Hagen] 2,378b: '*diu kerge an werdekeit ist gar verstummet*', e.g. Günther, *Ged.* 570: '*ein wahrer Schmerz verstummt und sagt nicht, was man fühlet*', Schiller, *Jungfr.v.O.* 699: '*. . . Stimme der Gerechtigkeit? Sie ist verstummt vor der Partheien Wuth*'. Unusual now is Goethe, *Tasso* 1544: '*mir verstummt die Lippe*'. The noun *die Verstummung* has been current since Early NHG, e.g. Klopstock, *Briefe* 41: '*. . . die*

Verstummung der Liebe'; now a.

jem. verstummen (obs.) to silence sb.; from MHG until the 19th c., still Tieck, *Schriften* 1,352: '*. . . bis ich verstummt der Christen hündisch Bellen*'; now obs.

← See also under *betrügen* (for *ein schön Weib ist ein stummer Betrug*), *Bild* (for *stumm wie eine Bildsäule*), *dienen* for *stummer Diener*), *Fisch* (for *stumm wie ein Fisch*), *Grab* (for *stumm wie das Grab*), *Poesie* (for *stumme Poesie*), *Portier* (for *stummer Portier*) and *Stimme* (for *stumme Stimme*).

Stummel: stump, stub

ein kleiner ~ (coll.) a tiny chap; recorded for several regions since the 19th c.; also applied (sometimes affectionately) to little boys. Synonymous *Stümpchen* dates back (regionally) to the 17th c., *Stumpax* or *Stümpax* to the 18th c.; Gotthelf, *Uli* 1,32 used *Stimps* for this.

meine ~ (coll.) my poor old legs; mainly in complaints by old people; f.r.b. Campe [1810].

der ~ (vulg.) penis; in sl. since the 19th c. and *Stump* in this sense has also been current since the 19th c.

stümmeln: reduce in size

etw. verstümmeln (formerly also *stümmeln*) to mutilate or dismember sth., make sth. unusable; since MHG, when with ref. to abstracts it could also mean 'to reduce, diminish', e.g. Luther Apocr. transl. Ecclesiasticus 35,14: '*verstumpel deine gabe nicht*' (cf. also 2 Macc. 7,5: '*als er nun so zustümpelt war*'), Luther, *Werke* 29,176 (Weimar): '*du grober esel, verstummel myr nicht das sacrament*'. The verb has a wide range; it can mean 'castrate', as in Gutzkow, *Zaub.* 8,193, 'corrupt', as in Harsdörffer, *Secret.* 1 Hh VIIa [1656]: '*. . . die teutsche sprache . . . verstimmelt und unterdruckt wurde*', 'to garble' (with ref. to messages) or 'to mutilate', e.g. Börne 7,37: '*der Staat ist das Bett des Procrustes, worin man den Menschen ausreckt oder verstümmelt, bis er hinein paßt*'; Herder 2,263 has *jem.s Seele verstümmeln* and Schiller used *an etw.* ~ for 'to lop off parts of sth.', which is now obs.; the noun *Verstümmelung* has been current since the 17th c.

Stump: push, shove

einen ~ *kriegen* (regional coll.) to be told off; also used for 'to be given a rude reply'; recorded for several regions since the 19th c.; cf. also Aler 2,1860a [1727]: '*einem Stümp geben = deludere, aliquem rejicere*'.

Stümper: see *stumpf.*

stumpf: blunt

stumpf dull, undefined, stolid, insensitive; figur. at first with ref. to colour, e.g. Megenberg, *B.d. Natur* 438: '*ainer stumpfen varb*' or the senses, e.g. *stumpfes Gesicht, stumpfes Auge, stumpfer Blick*, Gottfr.v.Straßb., *Tristan* 4666: '*die stumpfe sinne triegent*', Wieland, *Idris* 1,87: '*stumpf an innern Sinnen*', Logau 3,10,29: '*Phyllis war von stumpfen ohren*', Goethe, *Ital. Reise* 1: '*ich habe mich . . .*

ganz stumpf gearbeitet'. – Over the centuries ~ has been used for practically everything that could be described as 'not sharp, pointed, acute, clear, bright, clear, sensitive', but many of the older meanings such as 'brusque, unfriendly, sudden(ly), incomplete, faulty, clumsy' had become obs. or at least rare by the 18th c. Still current are 'indistinct' with ref. to pictures or speech, as in Goethe II,2,39 (W.), 'hazy, subdued' with ref. to light, as in Th.Mann, *Königl. Hoh.* 1: '. . . *in einer stumpfen . . . Beleuchtung'*, 'heavy, dull-sounding' with ref. to music, 'dull', also 'unpleasantly mild' or 'sultry' with ref. to the weather, as in Werfel, *Abitur.* 301, 'witless, dull' with ref. to intelligence, as in Mommsen, *Röm.Gesch.* 5,40: *'von trägem Körper und stumpfem Geist'*, 'tired, worn-out', as in Hebbel, *Werke* [edit. W.] 8,335: *'da die jüngeren Kräfte die stumpfen des Alters verdrängen'*, 'lifeless, dull, lacking vivacity', as in Goethe IV,3,217 (W.): '. . . *Sie für meine stumpfe Gesellschaft . . . zu entschädigen'*. Recently the old meaning expressing the notion of 'useless, defunct' has led to coll. ~ = 'bad, insignificant, uninteresting' (since the middle of the 20th c.).

die Stumpfheit dullness, clumsiness, stupidity, lassitude; following the adjective from the 16th c. onwards, but in regular use only since the 18th c., recorded by Heynatz and Campe, e.g. Klinger, *Werke* 9,288: *'die Stumpfheit und Armuth ihres Geistes'*, Lavater, *Physiog.Fr.* 2,130: *'daß die Stutznasen . . . auch Stumpfheit und Dummheit bezeichnen'*, Nietzsche 1,532: *'an sich selber durch Ekel und Stumpfheit zu grunde gehen'*; often in *in Stumpfheit versinken* and *mit Stumpfheit geschlagen sein*; since the 18th c.

mit stumpfem Besen kehren (coll., a.?) to take ineffective measures, deal in half measures, pursue an inadequate policy; e.g. Hohberg, *Georgica* 3,44a; now probably a. or obs.; cf. Goethe 3,324 (W.): *'Besen werden immer stumpf gekehrt und Jungen immer geboren'*. See also under *Eisen* for *mit eisernem Besen kehren*.

ein stumpfer Reim rhyme ending in one syllable; first used as a techn. term in the rules of the *Meistersinger* (16th c.), with *klingend* as the opposite; f.r.b. Schottel [1663]; displaced by *männlicher Reim* (under French influence) in the course of the 17th c., but *stumpfer Vers* is still used in some works on prosody. See also under *klingen* for *klingender Reim*.

eine stumpfe Wunde (or *Verletzung*) (med.) a wound from which no blood has issued; e.g. (DWb) v.Alten 2,330: *'als Ursachen treten . . . stumpfe Verletzungen . . . hervor'*.

er ist stumpfer als eine Mörserkeule (coll.,1.) he is incredibly stupid, as daft as a brush; recorded in Wander [1876], now probably obs.

der Stumpfsinn (1) dullness (of mind), insensitivity, feeblemindedness, hebetude; derived from the adjective *stumpfsinnig* (first recorded in the 15th c.,

but rarely used until the 18th c.) late in the 18th c., e.g. Wieland 18,209: '. . . *seinen Stumpfsinn für alles Schöne und Gute'*, Ense, *T.* 3,264: '. . . *aus dem Stumpfsinn in Irrsinn übergegangen'*.

der Stumpfsinn (2) apathy, indifference; since early in the 19th c., e.g. Tieck, *A.* 2,85: '. . . *versank ich in einen betäubenden Stumpfsinn'*.

der Stumpfsinn (3) (coll.) tediousness, monotony; describes dull conditions (not related to persons); only since the 20th c., but *stumpfsinnig* for 'boring' since late in the 19th c.

der Stümper (1) wretched creature; since the 15th c. (cf. Diefenbach-Wülcker, 869), e.g. Schottel [1663]: '*Stümper = miserae fortunae aut tenuis conditionis homo, der abgestumpfet und stumpf geworden ist'*; still used in commiseration: *er ist ein armer Stümper* = 'he is a poor wretch'.

der Stümper (2) bungler, duffer; f.r.b. Frisch [1741] who defined it *'opifex artis suae ignarus'*, e.g. Schiller, *Räuber* 4,2: *'der ist ein Stümper, der sein Werk nur auf die Hälfte bringt, und dann weg geht'*; hence *stümperhaft*, e.g. Wieland, *Agathod.* 3,1 and *Stümperei*. There is also a verb *stümpern*, since the 17th c., e.g. Goethe, *Wahlverw.* 1,18: *'ich pfusche, ich stümpere nur in den meisten Dingen'*, occasionally even in transitive use, e.g. C.F.Meyer, *Nov.* 2,99: *'diese verpfuschte Riesin, die Gott Vater stümperte'*. There are also several compounds, e.g. (Sp.) Brod, *Leben m.e.Göttin* 183: *'schablonenhafte Stümperpsychologie'*.

← See also under *Nagel* (for *sich mit stumpfen Nägeln wehren*).

Stumpf: see *Rumpf* and *Stiel*.

Stunde: hour

die ~ (1) time (in a general sense, not as a measure); in many locutions, some since OHG, most of them since MHG, but all of them now unusual or obs., e.g. *zu allen stunden* = 'always', since MHG, e.g. *Nibelungenl.* 663, also as *alle ~*, since Early NHG, e.g. Luther Bible transl. 1 Cor. 15,30 (now usually *zu jeder Zeit* or *jeden Augenblick*), *auf die ~* = 'punctually, at the agreed time', as in Goethe, *Egmont* 2, *bis auf diese ~* = 'until or up to now', e.g. Luther Bible transl. 1 Cor. 4,11 (now usually *bis jetzt*), also as *bis diese ~* (obs.), as still in Lessing 10,230, *von Stund an* (or *ab*) (obs.) = 'from now on', e.g. Luther Bible transl. John 19,27 (now usually *von jetzt an*), *zu der ~* = 'now, immediately, at this moment', e.g. Luther Bible transl. Matth. 10,19 (now usually *jetzt* or *sofort*), but also = 'at that particular time', since Early NHG and still in the 18th c., e.g. Goethe, *Wirkung in die Ferne* 9: *'neben der Königin schlürft zur Stund Sorbett die schönste der Frauen'* (now displaced by *im gleichen* or *in diesem Augenblick*, *zur gleichen Zeit*), *es ist an der ~* (a.) = 'it is the right or appropriate time' (now *es ist an der Zeit*), *unter Stunden* = 'sometimes, occasionally', still listed as current in coll. use by Adelung, but now obs. (displaced by *bisweilen, gelegentlich*), *zu Stunden* (obs.) = 'for a very long time', still used by Lessing, *Oden, Der Tod eines Freundes*: '*sie steht, ein Marmorbild, zu Stunden unverrücket*' (displaced by *stundenlang*), *Tag und ~* = 'the whole time, the entire period', since the 18th c., e.g. Goethe, *Wanderj.* 2,4, now obs. (now *die ganze Zeit* would be used).

die ~ (2) time, moment, period; since Early NHG in many locutions, e.g. Lehman, 830: '*mancher ist zur vnglückhafften stund geboren, da Mars vnd Venus einander den rucken gewandt*' (cf. Lessing 11,101: '*zu einer unglücklichen Stunde geboren*'), Goethe, *Wanderj.* 3,6: '*sie hatte . . . ihre schöne Stunde*', Adelung: '*keine gesunde Stunde haben = ununterbrochen krank sein*'.

die ~ (3) time (seen as a person or a moving object); since Early NHG, e.g. Goethe, *Herm. u. Dor.* 5: '*so wie es die Stunden gebieten*' (cf. Schiller, *M. Stuart* 3,3: '*das Gesetz der Stunde*'), Schiller, *Wall. Tod* 5,3: '*ihn besiegen die gewaltgen Stunden*' (and *die ~ pocht* in the same scene); very frequent with verbs of motion, e.g. Luther Bible transl. John 2,4: '*meine stunde ist noch nicht komen*', Petri [1605]: '*eine stund geht nach der andern hin*', *Buch d. Liebe* 284 [1587]: '*und nähet die stunde seines todes*', Goethe, *Wanderj.* 1,7: '*wie schmerzlich die Stunde des Abschieds herannaht*', also with *vorüberziehen* (e.g. Schiller, *Räuber* 5,1), *sich dehnen, heranrücken, schleichen* or *verrinnen*.

die ~ (4) lesson; established in the modern sense of *Unterrichtsstunde* since the 18th c. (but in religious contexts for hours spent in devotion and discussion on relig. subjects since the 16th c.), hence still in Swabia *in die Stund gehen* = 'to attend a gathering of the Pietists'; e.g. Wieland, *N. Amad.* 3,24: '*das hatt er wahrlich nicht in seinen Stunden gehört*'. In the sence of '(university) lecture' since early in the 18th c. Hence *Stunden geben, bekommen, nehmen* since the 18th c., followed in the 19th c. by many compounds such as *Privatstunde, Nachhilfestunde, Deutschstunde*, etc.

die Stunden (lit., obs.) the Hours; in Classical mythology term for the divinities who preside over the changes of the seasons; translation of Lat. *horae*; cf. Milton, *Comus* 986: 'the rosy-bosomed Hours'; in German mainly in the 18th c., e.g. Wieland, *Aur. u. Cef.* 25: '*die Stunden, die ihre* [i.e. Aurora's] *Zofen sind*', Schiller, *Eleus. Fest*: '*die leichtgeschürzten Stunden*'.

jem. s ~ sb.'s (moment of) death; since Early NHG, e.g. Luther, *S. W.* 60,169 (as '*seliges fröhliches stündlin*'), also Apocr. transl. Ecclesiasticus 11,19 (as '*stündlein*'), Goethe, *Götz* 5: '*meine Stunde ist kommen*'. Equally old are the compounds *Todesstunde* (used by Luther) and *Sterbestunde*, e.g. Olearius, *Pers. Baumg.* 65a [1696]. Still in use in *sein leztes Stündlein ist gekommen* and in the prov. *jedem schlägt seine ~* 'we all must die (some time)'.

ihre ~ (euphem.) (the time of) her confinement; in general use since the 19th c., e.g. (Sa.) Baggesen, *Poet. W.* 1,87 [1839]. It is also called *die schwere ~*, e.g. Auerbach, *N. Leb.* 1,308 [1852].

die blaue ~ (coll.) dusk; since the 19th c.; for the figur. use of *blau* for 'hazy' see p. 334.

Aktivist der ersten ~ (polit., obs.) politically active person who dedicated himself to the establishment of the DDR in its earliest period; since the fifties of the 20th c., now obs.

in einer guten ~ (a.?) at a suitable time; since MHG, e.g. *Edelstein* 61,18, Geßner 4,10: '*es sei in einer guten Stunde geredet*'; for this use of *gut* see *gut* (8) on p. 1179; Goethe used *die rechte ~*, e.g. in *Herm. u. Dor.* 4; cf. also *es ist an der ~* (e.g. Goethe, *Ital. Reise* II) and the opposite '*jetzo ist nicht die Stunde*' in Schiller, *M. Stuart* 3,3.

Stunden schieben (sl.) to work overtime; since the middle of the 20th c.; for this use of *schieben* see p. 2103.

die trockene ~ (mil. sl.) instruction period; refers to its dullness; since the 2nd quarter of the 20th c.

etw. stunden to grant a delay of payment, defer a demand for payment; in LG since the 15th c. in general sense of 'to defer', then in HG, mainly with ref. to *Geld* or *Schuld*, f.r.b. Schottel [1663]; since the late 18th c. also in non-monetary contexts for 'to grant a respite', e.g. (DWb) Krug, *Lebensreise* 179 [1825]: '*unerbittlich kommt der Tod . . . keinem mag er stunden*'; cf. also Gutzkow, *Zaub. v. R.* 9,411 [1858]: '*Paula . . . zahlte die lang gestundete Schuld der Ehe*'.

stündlich (1) everlasting(ly), present the whole time; f.r.b. Stieler [1691], e.g. Goethe 24,303 (W.).

stündlich (2) constant(ly), incessantly repeated; since the 17th c., e.g. Hagedorn, *Fab.* 2,46.

stündlich (3) at any time (now), at any moment; e.g. Goethe, *Wahlverw.* 1,2: '*stündlich soll mir eine Antwort kommen*'; now usually *jeden Augenblick*.

stundenlang mit wachsender Begeisterung (sl.) for ever and ever with growing enthusiasm, again and again; particularly in hyperbolic expressions of annoyance, e.g. *den könnte* (or *möchte*) *ich stundenlang mit wachsender Begeisterung ohrfeigen*; since early in the 20th c., but *stundenlang* since late in the 17th c., f.r.b. Kramer [1702].

ich zähle nur die heitern Stunden, sagte die Sonnenuhr I only count the bright hours, said the sundial; recorded since the 19th c., e.g. by Wander [1876].

er weiß, was die ~ geschlagen hat (prov. expr.) he has comprehended the true state of affairs, knows what is being played. Beginnings in the 17th c., see examples on p. 2121.

alle Stunden ein anderes Gesicht machen (prov. expr.) to have constantly changing moods, to be never the same for long; recorded since the 19th c., e.g. by Wander [1876].

keine Stunden sind an einen Stock gebunden (prov.) time flies, you cannot stop the clock; in this form f.r.b. Petri [1605], in singular in Henisch [1616], with *Stecken* in Lehman [1640].

besser eine ~ zu früh als eine Minute zu spät (prov.) better one hour too early than one minute too late; in this form only recorded since the 19th c., e.g. by Wander [1876].

die Polizeistunde closing-time (in public houses); since the 19th c., e.g. Auerbach, *Ges.Schr.* 18,153; formerly called *die Bürgerstunde*.

← See also under *elf* (for *in der elften Stunde*), *geben* (for *Stunden geben*), *Gebot* (for *das Gebot der Stunde*), *Geist* (for *Geisterstunde*), *Gespenst* (for *Gespensterstunde*), *Glück* (for *dem Glücklichen schlägt keine Stunde*), *Gold* (for *goldene Stunden*), *Gunst* (for *die Gunst der Stunde*), *nehmen* (for *jede Stunde nehmen*), *Null* (for *die Stunde Null*), *Pan* (for *die Stunde des großen Pan*), *regieren* (for *Mars regiert die Stunde*), *ruhen* (for *ruhige Stunde*), *Schaf* (for *Schäferstunde*), *schlagen* (for *eine geschlagene Stunde, die Stunde schlägt jem.m* and *Stundenschlag*), *schwach* (for *schwache Stunde*), *schwer* (for *die schwere Stunde*), *Stern* (for *die Sternstunde*), *zählen* (for *seine Stunden sind gezählt*) and *zwölf* (for *in der zwölften Stunde*).

Stunk: see *stinken*.

stupfen: push

ein Stupfer mit einem Zaunpfahl (coll.) a very strong hint; at least since the 19th c., e.g. Kürnberger, *Amerikamüde* 220 [1855]. See also under *Pfahl* for *jem.m mit dem Zaunpfahl winken*.

jem. stüpfen (regional coll.) to drive or urge sb. on; mainly in Alemannic areas,, e.g. Gotthelf, *Geld u. Geist* 70.

stupsen: push

jem. mit der Nase auf etw. ~ (coll.) to draw sb.'s attention forcefully to sth., make sth. very obvious to sb.; *~* is a LG variant of *stupfen* (see previous entry); current since the 19th c.; see also under *Nase* for *jem. mit der Nase auf etw. stoßen*.

stur: heavy, strong

stur immobile, ponderous, clumsy; in OHG in phys. sense for 'heavy, strong', then in LG regions; in the South later, since the 19th c. in many extended meanings (as listed above), since the 20th c. mainly pejor. for 'dull' (with ref. to situations), 'mulish' (with ref. to persons) and 'monotonous' (e.g. with ref. to occupations), e.g. *ein sturer Bock* (coll.) = 'a mule, obstinate fellow'.

Sturm: storm

der ~ (1) storm; personified with many verbs, e.g. *der ~ erhebt sich*, e.g. Luther Bible transl. Acts 14,5, *heult*, e.g. Gotter 2,510, *jagt* (*die Wolken*), e.g. (DWb) Withof, *Acad.Ged.* 1,258 [1782], *legt sich*, e.g. Bode, transl. of Fielding, *Tom* 3,250 [1786], *schweigt*, e.g. E.v.Kleist 2,23 [1760], *tobt*, e.g. Geibel, Juniuslieder 2,35, also *der ~ brüllt, pfeift, geht* (*wieder weg*), etc.

der ~ (2) storm, assault; at first only with ref. to phys. fighting (e.g. *Annolied* 127), frequent since MHG, e.g. Hartm.v.Aue, *Greg.* 1990; sometimes in alliterating combination with *Streit*. Hence *ein ~ auf etw.* = 'an attack or assault on sth.', in phys.

and figur. senses still today, *etw.* (or *jem.*) *im ~ nehmen* = 'to take sth. (or sb.) by storm', general since the 18th c., *gegen etw. ~ laufen* = 'to make an assault on sth.', in phys. sense since Early NHG, figur. since the 17th c., e.g. Hippel, *Lebensläufe* 1,242 [1778]: '*ich bin deinetwegen beym lieben Gott Sturm gelaufen*', *~ schlagen* = 'to raise the alarm', derived from phys. *zum ~ die Glocke schlagen*, since Early NHG, also in humorous figur. contexts, e.g. Fischart, *Garg.* (repr.) 25: '*wann die freßglock im magen sturm schlegt . . .*'. The range of *~* (2) is very extensive and comprises 'attack, rebellion, war, unrest, opposition, trouble' (as early as in the OHG period *sturma* = *seditiones* has been recorded) and the numerous compounds reflect this variety, though most of them are no older than the 18th c., e.g. *Ansturm*, since the 19th c., *Gedankensturm*, since the 19th c. (but *~ von Gedanken* earlier, e.g. Schiller, *Tell* 1,2), *Hauptsturm*, e.g. Lessing 10,48, *Reformsturm* and *Reformationssturm*, both since the 19th c., *Tatensturm*, e.g. Goethe, *Faust I*, 501, *Wörtersturm*, e.g. Jahn, *Merke z.dt. V.* 45 [1833]. *Gestürm* can also be used, e.g. Görres, *Hl.Allianz* 14 [1822]. Cf. also *die Sturmglocke(n) läuten* = 'to sound the alarm', figur. since the 18th c., and numerous compounds with-*stürmer*, e.g. *Maschinenstürmer* = 'Luddite' or *Barrikadenstürmer* = 'fighter against the barricades', figur. often for 'rebel, fighter against the established order', e.g. *eine fanatische Gruppe von intellektuellen Barrikadenstürmern* (modern). Closely related to this is *der ~*, a revolutionary movement of artists and writers, founded by Herwarth Walden in Berlin [1910], which published a journal entitled *der ~* . The adherents of this movement were called *Sturmkünstler* or *Sturmdichter*. Lastly, *Sturmabteilung* (mil.) = 'assault party', e.l. of 1906 in *DWb.*, and *Sturmtrupp* (mil.) = 'assault detachment', e.l. of 1917 in *DWb.*, acquired wider currency in 1921, when the National Socialists adopted these terms for their uniformed militant members.

der ~ (3) (lit.) storm, inner disquiet or turmoil, raging excitement; with ref. to emotions since MHG, e.g. Heinr.v.Neustadt, *Apollon.* 15684: '*min hertze leydet grossen sturm*'; in many compounds, e.g. *Beifallssturm*, as in Hackländer, *D.Dt.* 1,89, *Fiebersturm*, *Freudensturm*, *Gefühlssturm*, *Gemütssturm*, *Jubelsturm*, *Lachsturm*, *Liebessturm*, *Sorgensturm*, *Verzweiflungsturm*, *Wirbelsturm* (*von Gefühlen*), *Wonnensturm* or *Zornsturm*, all lit. and only current since the 19th c. The derivative *der Stürmer*, however, for 'hot-head, fanatic, impetuous person' established itself much earlier, as borne out by *Kirchenstürmer*, used by Fischart, *Bien.* 10a [1588]. *Stürmer* for 'fanatic' occurs in Ense, *Biogr.D.* 3,300 [1824], and the numerous compounds, such as *Glaubensstürmer*, *Herzensstürmer*, *Regelstürmer*, *Religionsstürmer* or *Weltenstürmer* only arose in the 19th c., though *Stürmerei* can be found in Lavater, *Phys.Fr.* 1,220 [1775]. Most of the compounds with -*stürmer* and -*stürmerei* do not differ semantically from those listed under ~ (2). The same applies to the large number of participial compounds such as *sturmdurchbraust, -durchrast, -durchtost, -durchwühlt, -erfüllt, -erkrankt, -gebrochen, -gedämpft, -gehetzt, -gequält, -geschüttelt, -gestählt, -umsaust, -umtobt, -verschlagen, -verweht, -zerstört* or *-zerwühlt*, all lit., of which only a few appeared late in the 18th c., the majority in the 19th c.

der ~ (4) rush, run, push forward; modern in such locutions as *ein* ~ *auf die Banken* = 'a run on the banks', *ein* ~ *auf die vorderen Sitze* = 'a rush towards the front seats', also in compounds, e.g. *Schaltersturm* = 'rush towards the counters (in shops, banks, stations)' and similar *Kassensturm*. See also *etw. stürmen* below.

der ~ (5) (sport) the forward line of players (in football); 20th c., hence also *Stürmer* for '(player in a) forward (position)', and the compounds *Mittelstürmer, Außenstürmer*.

der ~ *und Drang* (lit.) *Sturm und Drang*, Storm and Stress; lit. movement (ca. 1771–1786); term coined by Christoph Kaufmann as a suggested title for Klinger's play *Wirrwarr* [1776], f.r.b. J.Richter [1781]; extended in 19th c. to emotional ferment, e.g. Raabe, *Hungerpastor* XXX: '*ich habe alle Begeisterung, Sturm und Drang, so der Mensch fühlen kann, in meinem Herzen gefühlt*'; hence also *der Stürmer* (obs.) for a revolutionary enthusiast, a *Kraftkerl* of the period, as used by Klinger, *D.leidende Weib* 3,1 [1775]: '*du Stürmer du! Da stellt er sich vor einen hin, redt kein Wort, und redt doch tausendmal mehr als die andern alle*'. Details in *ZfdW.* 6,114; 9,290; 10,230 and 14,18.

der ~ *im Wasserglas* a storm in a teacup; coined by Montesquieu in connexion with the unrest in San Marino which he called *une tempête dans un verre d'eau*. Cicero in *De legib.* 3,16 used similar *excitare fluctus in simpulo* (= 'create a storm in a ladle') quoting Gratidius, and a closely related comparison was used by Athenaeus in *Deipnos* VIII,19. In German general since the 19th c., e.g. Treitschke, *Dt.Gesch.* 3,287 (or 473).

der Stürmer (obs.) a kind of tricorn hat; worn by soldiers and in the 19th c. by students, e.g. Ense, *D.* 1,11: '*ein Student zu Halle mit Kanonen und Stürmer*'. Note that *Sturmhut* is used for a different kind of headgear, mainly for the oilskin hat worn by sailors in stormy weather. – For other meanings of *Stürmer* see under ~ (2) and (3) and ~ *und Drang*.

stürmen (1) to rage, be furious, excited; derived from the noun in OHG period (e.g. Notker, *Ps.* 45,4: '*wanda gentes sturmdon sô sie novam doctrinam gehôrton*'), e.g. Goethe, *Dicht.u.Wahrh.* 14: '*sein Betragen war . . . wenn es nicht innerlich stürmte, gemäßigt*', Arndt, *Ged.* 150 [1840]: '*was stürmst du, Herz, und bist so wild?*'.

stürmen (2) to rush forward; describes rapid movement in general, but also when an attack is implied; fully established by the Early NHG period, e.g. Luther Bible transl. Acts 19,29: '*sie stürmeten aber einmütiglich zu dem schawplatz*'; current in many compounds since the 18th c., e.g. *gegen etw. anstürmen*, as in Goethe, *Farbenlehre* 3 (Bacon v.V.), *jem.m nachstürmen* = 'to rush after sb.', as in Goethe, *Camp.i.Fr.* (Nov. 1792), and in many others since the 18th c., e.g. *hervor-, herbei-, herein-, hinauf-, hinausstürmen*.

auf jem. stürmen (lit.,a.) to entreat sb., try with great urgency to influence sb. in a certain way, e.g. Wieland, *Urtheil d. Paris* 66: '*weil alle stürmend in ihn dringen*'; cf. also Trenck, *Lebensgesch.* 51: '*nun stürmten auf einmal alle Leidenschaften über mich her*'.

etw. stürmen to storm or make an attack on sth.; in phys. sense since MHG, e.g. Stricker (in Wackern., *Leseb.* 1,864): '*sit der kreftige wint daz* (i.e. house) *stürmet*'; in modern times in wider sense, e.g. Bismarck, *Reden* 5,57: '*Arbeiter, die in einem Aufstande . . . einen Bäckerladen stürmen*'. Very rare, if not obs., is *jem.* (aus etw.) *stürmen*, as in Geibel, *Ges.Werke* 1,219: '*der Glöckner, der aus ihrer Ruh die Völker stürmt*'.

stürmisch (1) rebellious; since Early NHG, e.g. Luther 18,68 (Weimar), where '*sturmischem . . . geyste*' occurs; now rare.

stürmisch (2) stormy, tumultuous, wild, frenzied; since Early NHG; used with ref. to persons, e.g. *stürmischer Liebhaber*, as in Lessing [edit. L.-M.] 2,255, or to abstracts (since the 17th c.), e.g. *stürmische Angst, stürmischer Jubel*, e.g. Bismarck, *Ged.u.Erinn.* 2,184: '*stürmische Entwicklung unsrer Politik*'; also in hyperbolic locutions, e.g. *stürmische Nachfrage* (econ.) = 'very strong demand' (modern).

sturmbewegt (lit.) agitated, highly excited; figur. since the 2nd half of 18th c., e.g. Körner [edit. Hempel] 3,146: '*in meines Herzens sturmbewegten Wellen*'; *sturmerregt* (lit.) also occurs.

in (or *mit*) *Sturmeseile* (lit.) at great speed, in great haste; since early in the 19th c., e.g. Uhland, *Ged.* 6; there is also synonymous *im Sturmflug* (lit.), since late in the 18th c., sometimes as *mit Sturmesflug*, e.g. (DWb) Kind, *Ged.* 5,125: '*. . . enteilt Lothar mit Sturmesflug*'.

sturmfest impregnable, resisting all attacks; in mil. contexts since the 17th c., in phys. sense also applied to buildings = 'stormproof', figur. with ref. to women since the 18th c., e.g. Lenz [edit. Tieck] 1,274.

sturmfrei safe from trouble or disturbance; originally applied to impregnable fortresses, f.r.b. Schottel [1663], then coll., esp. among students for lodgings where one was not disturbed, usually in *sturmfreie Bude* (since late in the 19th c.); for *Bude* see p. 420.

sturmreif allowing for a successful assault; an earlier term for this was *sturmbar* (now *erstürmbar*); since the 19th c.

im Sturmschritt at the double; first in mil.

contexts, general since the 19th c. also in non-mil. contexts, e.g. Platen 4,320 or Ense, *B.* 3,518. Strauß chose it as the title for one of his polkas.

der Sturmvogel (1) (zool.) petrel (Order of *Procellarliformes*); since the 18th c., e.g. Forster, *R.* 1,39.

der Sturmvogel (2) (lit.) harbinger of troubled times; cf. F. Schlegel, *Dt.Museum* 1,132 [1812]: '*die kleinen Sturmvögel . . . weissagen die Stürme*'; from there extended to harbinger, e.g. Treitschke, *Hist.u.pol.Aufs.* 2,427: '*. . . Hungerjahre, die Sturmvögel aller Revolutionen*'.

nicht so stürmisch! (coll.) hold your horses! take it easy! in lit. contexts since the 18th c., e.g. Schiller, *Räuber* 2,1; now loosely used when restraining an impetuous person.

ist der ~ vorbei, wirft man's Gebetbuch weg (prov.) once on shore we pray no more; the German form recorded since the 19th c., e.g. Wander [1876].

← See also under *beschwören* (for *den Sturm beschwören*), *bestürmen*, *Bild* (for *Bildersturm* and its derivatives), *durchstürmen*, *einstürmen*, *entstürmen*, *erobern* (for *im Sturm erobern*), *erstürmen*, *Himmel* (for *Himmelstürmer* and derivatives), *kühl* (for *ein kaltes Stürmen*) and *ruhen* (for *die Ruhe vor dem Sturm*).

stürzen: turn over; fall

etw. ~ , also *ausstürzen* to pour (out) sth., spill or shed sth.; in Early NHG with ref. to blood, e.g. Luther 32,383 (Weimar), where '*blut zu stortzen*' occurs, then with ref. to tears, both obs. now, but *etw. ~* in the sense of 'pouring out' survives in some lit. images, e.g. Stifter [edit. Sauer] 1,80: '*Beethoven aber stürzt gleich einen Wolkenbruch von Juwelen über das Volk*'; *hinabstürzen* can also occur in such cases.

← See also under *ausstürzen*.

jem. etw. ~ (stud.sl., obs.) to call sb. (insultingly) sth.; derived from the sense in the previous entry (cf.Engl. 'to pour insults'); for stud.sl. f.r.b. *Göttinger Student* [1813], hence *Beleidigungen ~ =* 'to call sb. names', e.g. *jem. einen dummen Jungen ~ =* 'to call sb. a stupid boy', f.r.b. *Leben auf Univ.* [1822], e.g. Immermann [edit. B.] 20,75, now obs.; hence *der Sturz* (sl., obs.) = 'insult', f.r.b. *D.flotte Bursch* [1831].

jem. (or *etw.*) *~* to depose sb., deprive sb. (or sth.) of office or power; since Early NHG, e.g. Luther 23,525 (Weimar): '*. . . noch sturtzt die könige*'; hence also *einen Minister ~ =* 'to force or bring about the resignation of a minister', *die Regierung ~ =* 'to overthrow or bring down the government'; also with abstracts, e.g. Luther 8,218b (Jena): '*dieser spruch, der das pabstthum zu grund störtzet*' (and in his Bible transl. Prov. 29,23), Goethe, *Gespr.* [edit. Biederm.] 3,147: '*. . . Jugend, welche das Alter zu stürzen kommt*', Tieck, *Werke* [edit. B.] 1,98: '*als das . . . Christentum den heidnischen Götzendienst stürzte*'.

jem. in etw. ~ to plunge, push, drive sb. into sth.; since Early NHG, e.g. *jem. ins Unglück ~* (H.Sachs), *ins Verderben ~* (Moscherosch), even *in Träume ~* , as in Goethe 42,2,191 (W.), *in Schulden, Unkosten*, etc. *~* (since the 19th c.). Even abstracts could be 'thrown' into sth., e.g. Luther 32,384 (Weimar): '*stürtze alle jr anschlege jn abgrundt der helle*', but this is now unusual, as are such cases as Adelung: '*die lange Weile stürzt uns in eine gedankenlose Unthätigkeit*'. Reflexive use has been current since Early NHG, e.g. *sich in Schulden, Gefahren ~*.

stürzen (1) (intrans.) to rush, move rapidly, dash; originally *~* denoted involuntary falling, frequent in simplex and compounds since MHG, then transferred to rapid movement, making it synonymous with *stürmen*, e.g. *herstürzen, hereinstürzen, wegstürzen*, since the beginning of the 19th c. in a departure from the original sense even for movement upwards, as in *hinaufstürzen*, e.g. Arnim [edit. Gr.] 3,448 or Raabe, *Sämtl.W.* 2,3,387: '*. . . stürzte ich die Stufen hinauf*'; also in reflex. locutions, e.g. *sich auf etw. ~ =* 'to pounce on sth.', and in compounds, e.g. *sich über etw. herstürzen*, as in Heine, *Lut.* 2,133. Hence *der Sturz* = 'rush, sudden movement', but only since the 18th c., e.g. *ein Sturz auf die Feinde*, as in Gleim, *Sämtl. W.* 4,125, *vom Sturz der Empfindungen fortgerissen*, as in Vischer, *Ästhetik* 3,798 (cf. also Goethe 16,374 (W.)), but now very rare, displaced in many contexts by *Sturm*.

stürzen (2) (intrans.) to fall, drop, collapse; since OHG, e.g. Notker 2,378: '*sturze in den dot*', Luther Bible transl. Jerem. 50,32: '*der stolze soll stürtzen*', Goethe, 41,2,47 (W.): '*welch ein Jammer stürzt auf dich?*'; often = 'to perish, decay', as in Schiller, *Tell* 4,2: '*das Alte stürzt, es ändert sich die Zeit*'. There are many compounds. Campe [1808] quoted from Tiedge (no details): '*wie ein Blitz aus heitrer Bläue stürzt herein sein Mißgeschick*' (which could also have found its place under *~* (1) above) and from Meißner (no details): '*jetzt stürzen eine Menge Unglücksfälle über dich her*', similarly *hervorstürzen*, recorded by Campe, *niederstürzen*, as in Klopstock, *M.* 2,25: '*Paradies . . . du bist niedergestürzt in den Wassern*' and *zusammenstürzen*, since the 18th c., e.g. Goethe 24.29 (W.) (cf. Forster, *Ges. W.* 3,113: '*Zusammensturz politischer Formen*'), but *ab-, fort-* and *wegstürzen* only in phys. contexts; hence *der Sturz* = 'fall, collapse, reduction', general since the 18th c., in compounds since the 19th c., e.g. *Kassensturz, Preissturz, Temperatursturz*.

sich in etw. einstürzen (a.) to plunge into sth., immerse oneself in sth.; in phys. sense since the 17th c., figur. since the 18th c., but then usually as (*sich*) *in etw. hineinstürzen*, e.g. Schiller, *M. Stuart* 1,7: '*den Abgrund saht ihr . . . und, treu gewarnet, stürtzet ihr hinein*'; *reinstürzen* (coll.) also occurs.

← See also under *einstürmen* (for *etw. stürzt auf jem. ein*), *einstürzen* (for *etw. einstürzen, etw. zum*

Einsturz bringen and *eingestürzt*) and *Himmel* (for *wenn der Himmel einstürzt, so sind alle Spatzen tot*).

sich überstürzen to act rashly, rush into things; figur. since the 19th c., e.g. Nietzsche 4,330, also with ref. to abstracts, e.g. Bernhardt, *Gesch. d.Wald.* 3,10 [1872]: '*die Ereignisse überstürzten sich*'; hence *überstürzt* = 'hasty, rash' (also adverbially), since Early NHG.

jem. überstürzen (regional) to rush sb., urge sb. to hurry; mainly in Alemannic regions, e.g. Gotthelf, *Ges. Schr.* 3,303.

etw. umstürzen to overthrow, topple, subvert sth.; since Early NHG, e.g. H.Sachs [edit. K.] 9,242: '. . . *umbgestürtzt die regiment*', Bismarck, *Ged.u.Erinn.* 1,63: '*Vorwürfe sind nicht das Mittel, einen umgestürzten Thron wider aufzurichten*'; *jem. umstürzen*, still used by Lessing [edit. L.-M.] 10,254, is now rare. The noun *Umsturz* only established itself in the 18th c., e.g. Gottsched, *Anmuth.Gel.* 4,10 [1751], but *Umstürzung* has been current since the 16th c., e.g. (DWb) Hedio, *Chron.Germ.* 102a [1530]: '*umbsturtzung der warheit*'.

aus allen Himmeln ~ to be very surprised; also used with ref. to sudden disillusionment; biblical in origin (from Isaiah 14,12: '*wie bist du vom Himmel gefallen, du schöner Morgenstern!*'); see also under *fallen* for *aus allen Himmeln fallen*.

ein Sturzbach von Tränen (lit.) a flood of tears; since the 19th c., e.g. Heine [edit. E.] 1,361; cf. Freiligrath, *Ges. Dicht.* 5,28: '*ihrer Thränen wilde Sturzflut*'.

ein (kaltes) Sturzbad (lit.) a cold shower; figur. for sth. which brings sudden sobering or disappointment; since the 19th c., e.g. (DWb) Arnim [edit. Grimm] 8,45 or Gutzkow, *Ges.W.* 1,162. Some authors have used *Sturzbach* (see above) in the same sense, e.g. Laube, *Ges.Schr.* 2,137 or Rosegger, *Schr.* 1,7,365. See also under *Dusche* (p. 538).

eine Sturzflut (lit.) a torrent; figur. with such nouns as *Beschimpfungen, Flüchen*, etc.; modern; see also under *Sturzbach* (above).

die Sturzwelle (lit.) roller, heavy sea; figur. since the 19th c., e.g. (DWb) Fontane 1,1,100: '*die wendische Invasion habe nur den Charakter einer Sturzwelle gehabt*'.

← See also under *ausstürzen, bestürzen* and *entstürzen*.

Stute: mare

die ~ (regional coll. or vulg.) woman, wench; term of contempt since Early NHG, now still current in some regions, esp. in Alemannic and Austro-Bav. areas for 'women of easy virtue' (Vinna) or in derogatory refs. to women, e.g. *eine faule* ~.

← See also under *Füllen* (for *Füllen schlagen oft ihre Stuten mit Fersen*).

stützen: support, prop up

etw. or *jem.* ~ to support, uphold, back up sth. or sb.; figur. since the 17th c. (but in LG since the

14th c.), e.g. Gryphius, *Trauersp.* [edit. P.] 36: '*da must ein Held das Reich, das schon erkrachte, stützen*', also reflex., e.g. Goethe 9,418 (W.): '*wer stützt uns, wenn wir uns in unserm Jammer nicht auf einander stützen?*'; also *etw. mit etw.* ~ = 'to support sth. (abstract) with sth. else', f.r.b. Kramer [1702]: '*seine Meinung mit guten Beweißgründen stützen*'; similarly, *etw. auf etw. anderes* ~ = 'to base, found sth. on sth. else', since the 17th c. In the 20th c. (ca. 1930) the locution was extended to the economic field: *die Währung* ~ = 'to back (or buttress) the currency'.

etw. stützt sich auf etw. sth. is based on or rests on sth.; since the 17th c., e.g. Dietr.v.d. Werder, *Bußpsalmen* B4b [1632]: '*du bist der unsichtbare grund drauf unser erden kreiß sich stützet*', Gottsched, *Vers.crit.Dichtk.* 308 [1751]: '*laßt einmal . . . sehen, worauf sich eure Tugend stützt*'; often also with ref. to work deriving its validity from work done by others, hence also *jem. stützt sich auf etw.* = 'sb. bases or rests (his claims, position, etc.) on sth.'; cf. also the unusual image in Börne, *Ges.Schr.* 4,65: '*der liebende Mann hat sein ganzes Daseyn auf das Herz eines Weibes gestützt*'.

die Stütze support, prop, pillar; derived from the verb, figur. since Early NHG, e.g. Franck, *Germ. chron.* 56 [1538]: '. . . *den trewen helden und stützen des reichs*', Herder [edit. S.] 17,31: '. . . *Voltaire als die letzte Stütze des Geschmacks . . .*', Fontane 1,6,84: '*ich . . . bin eine Stütze von Land und Thron*'; hence *eine Stütze an jem.m haben* = 'to have sb. as a support or sb. to lean on', f.r.b. Frisius, *Dict.* 591a [1556]; frequent in *Stütze des Alters*, e.g. Petri, *D.T.Weish.* 2, LlG [1604]: '*kinder und kindes kinder sind stützen und stebe deß alters*'; since the 20th c. also *die Stütze der Hausfrau* = 'domestic help', partly euphem., partly joc. The title of Ibsen's play *Die Stützen der Gesellschaft* [1877] led to its use as a cl., often iron. or sarcastic with ref. to the rotten condition of 'pillars of society'. Among the compounds *Gedächtnisstütze* = 'memory aid, mnemonic' is probably most used; Adelung did not record it (even in the 2nd edit.), but Campe listed *gedächtnisstützend* with an example from Herder (without mentioning the noun).

der Stützpunkt base, strongpoint; since early in the 19th c., mainly in mil. contexts, but also in wider sense for 'sth. which gives one support or supports one's assertion', e.g. (DWb) Schelling 2,3,37: '. . . *dieses Besondere . . . an den Dingen ist der eigentliche Stützpunkt der Wissenschaft*'.

das Stützwort (ling.) prop word; 20th c.

jem. or *etw. unterstützen* to support sb. or sth.; since Early NHG; *Unterstützung* established itself in the 18th c., first in general sense of 'support', but later increasingly with ref. to financial help given by the community or the State, current in many compounds such as *Armen-, Kranken-, Wöchnerinnenunterstützung* (since last quarter of the 19th c.) and *Unterstützungsempfänger* (20th c.).

← See also under *Rohr* (for *sich auf ein schwaches Rohr stützen*).

stutzen: (1) stop abruptly; push; stand upright

etw. stutzt (lit.) sth. comes to a halt, is brought to a stand-still; with abstracts since the 17th c., e.g. (DWb) Fleming, *Dt.Ged.* 1,459: '*mein gedächtnüß stutzt*', Triller, *Poet.Betr.* 4,287 [1750]: '*hier stutzt und stocket mein Verstand*' (also used by Schiller with *Scharfsinn*).

jem. stutzt sb. is surprised, taken aback, is puzzled by sth.; also with ref. to a feeling of suspicion; since Early NHG when locutions with *stutzig* also arose, e.g. *stutzig werden*, e.g. Goethe 22,34 (W.) and *jem.* ~ *machen*, still used by Goethe IV,17, 225 (W.), led to *jem. stutzig machen*, since the 17th c., f.r.b. Stieler [1691]; cf. Kant (Acad.Edit.) 1,7,255: '*einem Schreck ähnlich ist das Auffallende, was stutzig (noch nicht bestürzt) macht*'.

stutzen (obs.) to show off, strut about with a superior air; since Early NHG; at first with ref. to one's posture in riding (upright body and thrown-back head), then to walking in an ostentatious manner and showy clothing, also in compounds such as *einherstutzen, herumstutzen*, pejor. suggesting that the aim is to draw attention to oneself; now obs., but see the derivatives below.

der Stutzer (a.) dandy, fop; from the previous entry, since the 17th c., e.g. Goethe 37,43 (W.), still in use in 19th c. lit. (Brentano, Laube, Gutzkow, Holtei), now a., as are the derivatives *Stutzerei, stutzerhaft* and *Stutzertum*. Same as *Geck* and regional *Gigerl*, which are still in use. – Note that *Stutzer* (obs.) = 'drinking glass' and 'short overcoat for men' belong to *stutzen* (2).

begriffsstutzig (Austrian *begriffsstützig*) slow in the up-take; not yet in *DWb.* [1854], but Sanders [1865] lists it with a *locus* from *Gartenlaube* 9,410b [1862]; hence *Begriffsstutzigkeit* (late 19th c.).

stutzen: (2) cut, trim, prune

etw. ~ (1) (a.) to embellish sth.; derived from the activities of the barber: *die Haare* or *den Bart* ~ (since Early NHG), but for wider 'to improve the appearance of sth.' only since the 18th c., e.g. Goethe 16,109 (W.) and even further extended in Goethe IV,29,106 (W.); also in compounds such as *zurechtstutzen, zustutzen*, as in Goethe 27,348 (W.). These two compounds are still in use, but the simplex in its figur. sense is a. or obs.

← See also under *aufstutzen*.

etw. ~ (2) to curtail, clip, pare, prune sth.; figur. since the 17th c., sometimes with allusion to the pruning of trees, e.g. Rückert 3,51: '. . . *daß er nie die kühnen Ranken stutzte meinem Jugendmut*'; cf. *etw. in ungestutzter Form nachdrucken* = 'to reprint sth. in an unabbreviated form' (19th c.); now *ungekürzt* would be preferred.

jem.m die Flügel ~ to clip sb.'s wings; of Classical origin: '*pinnas incidere alicui*', as in Cicero, *Att.* 4,2,3; in German since the 17th c.; Kramer [1702] recorded it with *Federn*.

← See also under *beschneiden*.

stutzig (regional coll. or obs.) obstinate, pig-headed; belongs to ~ = 'to stand upright and buck'; since Early NHG, e.g. H.Sachs [edit. K.] 11,336 (as *stutzig*); now only in some regions; cf. prov. *stutzig wie ein roter Esel*, recorded by Wander [1876], which makes less sense than *stutzig wie ein Ackergaul*, as in Melchior Liebig, *Geistl.Trostb*. Bla [1586].

Suade: see *Schwarte*.

subaltern: subordinate

subaltern (lit.) inferior, without independent judgment; since the middle of the 18th c., e.g. (S.-B.) Herder, *Br.* 356: '*er ist subaltern an Dienst und Charakter*', Friedell, *Kulturgesch.* 1,351: '*der subalterne Tretmühlenfleiß des Kanzlisten*'; also used as a noun pejor. for 'underling'; hence *Subalternität*, since the 18th c.

Subjekt: subject

ein gemeines ~ (coll.) a common individual, coarse character; pejor. since the 19th c., e.g. Holtei, *Schneider* 2,313 [1854]: '. . . . *daß . . . er ein gefährliches Subjekt sei*', Freytag, *Soll u.H.* 2,343: '*er ist ein verächtliches Subjekt*'.

sublimieren: sublimate

etw. ~ (psych. and med.) to sublimate sth.; extension from 'to refine sth., raise sth. to a higher level', current since the 18th c.; in the 20th c. taken over by psychologists for 'to transfer an urge to a higher form of expression', e.g. (S.-B.) Bauer, *Verbr.* 110 [1957]: '*die sublimierende Wirkung einer künstlichen Welt*'; hence *Sublimation* and *Sublimierung*; cf. Jalliger, *Seelenleben* 79 [1924]: '*die Psycho-analyse hat die Höherentwicklung und Umgestaltung der rohen Triebstrebungen in feinere (sublimere) als Sublimierung bezeichnet*'.

subtrahieren: subtract

etw. ~ (lit.) to deduct or take away sth.; from math. language transferred to other contexts in the 20th c., e.g. *von diesem angeblich wahren Bericht muß man viel Erfundenes* ~.

suchen: seek

etw. ~ to seek, try to obtain, find, bring about or secure sth.; since OHG, in locutions with many abstracts, e.g. *Ausflüchte* ~, as in Luther 20,569 (Weimar), *eine Ausrede* ~, as in Goethe 24,45 (W.). In OHG *Frieden* ~, *Ruhe* ~ and *Trost* ~ have been recorded, in MHG *Gnade, Hilfe, Huld* and *Rat* ~ came into use, and in Early NHG the list of locutions grew considerably. At the same time *nach etw.* ~ established itself. An abstract, too, can be described as 'seeking' or 'striving to obtain' sth., since Early NHG, e.g. (DWb) Paracelsus, *Opera* 2,72 [1616]: '*ein jegliche kunst, die da mehr suchet, die ist falsch*'. Even the reflex. verb can be used in lit. contexts, e.g. Bettina, *Günderode* 1,14: '*große Gedanken . . . suchen sich ihren Ausdruck*'; cf. also Goethe 4,291 (W.): '*lasset ewige Harmonien bald sich suchen, bald sich fliehen*'.

~ *zu* . . . (plus infinitive) to strive, attempt, seek

to . . . ; here Lat. *quaerere* was of influence (see examples in OHG quoted in *DWb.*); general since Early NHG and used by Luther Bible transl. John 8,40 or Luke 11,54 (where the A.V. also has 'to seek'); Frisch [1741] listed this with two meanings, a.) = '*conari, sich unterstehen, etwas zu thun*', b.) = '*tentare, probieren ob es angeht*'; both are still alive.

er hat hier nichts zu ~ he has no business to be here; this belongs to ~ = 'to plan, intend to do', as in Lessing [edit. L.-M.] 2,69: '*was suchst du damit, daß du dem Theophan dieses sagst?*' (also *ibid.* 2,153); this usage is obs., but the locution under discussion retains part of this meaning.

das Weite ~ to run away, flee, make oneself scarce; also sometimes *die Weite ~*, e.g. Görres, *Briefe* 3,28: '. . . habe ich . . . die Weite suchen müssen', but *das Weite* is preferred, e.g. (DWb) A.U.v. Braunschweig, *Octavia* 2,1195; cf. Goethe 24,158 (W.): '*er wollte das Freie suchen*'; in Early NHG *die Luft* (or *die Flucht*) *~* also occurred, now obs.

etw. sucht seinesgleichen sth. is unrivalled, there is nothing to be compared with it; cf. Engl. 'sth. is yet to seek'; since the 18th c., e.g. Goethe 24,248 (W.) on the Jews: '*an Zähheit sucht es seines gleichen*'.

etw. an jem. ~ (obs.) to request sth. from sb.; current in Early NHG and still used by Goethe, e.g. 36,25 (W.), but already in Early NHG increasingly displaced by *jem. um etw. ansuchen*, e.g. Luther 1,134b (Jena): '*wollest auch Hansen . . . und andere ansuchen und des . . . erinnern*'. This led to the noun *das Ansuchen* = 'request, application for sth.' (in Luther still as *ein Ansuchen tun*, now *vorbringen, unterbreiten*, etc.). Frisch [1741] recorded '*Ansuchung thun*', which is now obs.; cf. similar *das Gesuch*, originally a masculine noun meaning 'claim', 'usage', even 'profit' (under influence of Lat. *quaestus*), then = *Ansuchen* or *Ersuchen*, since Early NHG.

etw. an jem.m ~ (obs.) to expect sth. from sb.; since Early NHG, e.g. Luther Bible transl. 1 Cor. 4,2: '*nu suchet man nicht mehr an den haushaltern, denn das sie trew erfunden werden*' (where the A.V. has 'required'); now displaced by *von jem.m. erwarten*.

das hätte ich nicht hinter ihm gesucht I would not have expected that from him, I would not have thought him capable of that; this belongs to ~ = 'to expect to find', since Early NHG (often also with *in* or *bei*), e.g. Tappius, *Adag.* v7 [1545]: '*ei, wer solt das hinder dem bauren gesucht haben*'; cf. also modern coll. *hinter allem etw. ~* = 'to be suspicious of everything, always expect or impute sth. bad'.

da haben sich Zwei gesucht und gefunden (coll.) they were made for each other; modern coll., also used ironically with ref. to two people who are incompatible.

gesucht (1) much wanted, in great demand, sought-after; this originated in comm. jargon, current since the 17th c. (cf. Schirmer, *Wb. d. Kaufmannsspr.* 74 [1911]), e.g. *ein sehr gesuchter Artikel.*

gesucht (2) artificial, put on for show; it is generally assumed that this is derived from *weit gesucht* (= *weit hergeholt*), f.r.b. Kramer [1702].

jem. (or *etw.*) *aufsuchen* to visit sb. (or sth.); in Frisch [1741] still only with ref. to actual 'seeking', 'searching'; since the 18th c. in modern extended sense.

etw. aussuchen to select sth.; originally = 'to search through things', since Early NHG, then with the notion of picking out what one wants since the 18th c.; hence *ausgesucht* = 'choice, excellent, select', recorded by Steinbach [1734], used with ref. to things, e.g. Goethe, *Wahlverw.* 1,6: '*sie solle in Kleidern reicher und mehr ausgesucht erscheinen*' and to abstracts, e.g. *jem. mit ausgesuchter Höflichkeit behandeln*. In a purely phys. sense *ausgesucht* can also be used with ref. to things which are left over after the best items have been removed.

jem. um etw. ersuchen to request sth. from sb., to ask sb. for sth.; *ersuchen* had a variety of meanings, such as 'to examine, test, explore, investigate' (e.g. Luther 2,66a (Jena) and Bible transl. 1 Sam. 13,14); Luther also used it for 'to visit', e.g. 2,455b (Jena); all are obs., but in the 15th c. the now current meaning established itself, including the locution with *um*, e.g. Luther Bible transl. 2 Sam. 12,16. Hence the noun *das Ersuchen* = 'request, demand', which appeared in the 18th c. (in 1741 Frisch only listed *die Ersuchung*).

etw. (or *jem.*) *untersuchen* to examine or investigate sth. (or sb.); only since Late MHG (in Engl. since OE); the original notion is that of 'searching by turning upside-down (a pile of things)'; recorded since MHG period for 'to investigate, explore', but only since Early NHG with ref. to abstracts, e.g. Schiller, *Wall.Tod* 960: '*hab ich des Menschen Kern erst untersucht, so weiß ich . . .*'; since the 17th c. with ref. to scientific investigation; hence *die Untersuchung*, since MHG, with ref. to abstracts since Early NHG.

etw. versuchen (1) to try or attempt sth.; developed from 'to seek to experience sth.'; since MHG, often in *sein Glück versuchen* = 'to try one's luck', later expanded in *sein Glück bei jem.m. versuchen*, as in Goethe 22,61 (W.); also with dependent clauses since MHG, e.g. *versuchen, ob . . .* , later (since 16th c.) with the infinitive *versuchen, zu*, as in Goethe, *Faust, Zueignung* 3: '*versuch ich wohl, euch diesmal festzuhalten?*'.

etw. versuchen (2) to test sth., put sth. to the test; since MHG, oft in past participle *versucht* (where influence of Lat. *expertus* may be assumed), e.g. Freidank, *Besch.* 95.18: '*gewisse friunt, versuochtiu swert . . .*', still in Kant [edit. H.] 1,99: '*versuchte Vernunft*' (where *erprobt* or *bewährt* would now be used). Into this group also belongs *etw. versuchen* with ref. to tasting sth., since MHG, with abstracts since Early NHG.

jem. versuchen (1) to tempt sb., seek to lead sb. astray; biblical (Matth. 4,1 or Luke 4.12); also extended to 'to seduce sb.', f.r.b. Kramer [1702], where *verleiten* would now be used, e.g. Schlegel, transl. of Shakespeare, *Richard III*, 4,2: '*weißt du mir keinen, den bestechend Gold wohl zu verschwieg'nem Todeswerk versuchte?*'. Abstracts, too, can be seen as tempters, e.g. Lessing, *Nathan* 4,652: '*noch hat mich nie die Eitelkeit versucht . . .*' Still alive in *versucht sein, etw. zu tun* and in *in Versuchung geraten* = 'to feel tempted'; cf. *führe uns nicht in Versuchung* = 'lead us not into temptation'.

jem. versuchen (2) (obs.) to put sb. to the test, try sb. (out); biblical, current since MHG (e.g. Hartm. v.Aue, *Arm.Heinr.* 1362), also in Luther Bible transl. 2 Cor. 13,5: '*versuchet euch selbs, ob jr im glauben seid*' (where the A.V. puts 'examine'); cf. Schlegel's transl. of Hamlet 3,2: 'and who in want a hollow friend doth try directly seasons him his enemy' with '*und wer in Not versucht den falschen Freund, verwandelt ihn sogleich in einen Feind*'; cf. also related (still current) *es mit etw. versuchen* = 'to give sth. a try', also with ref. to persons *es mit jem.m versuchen* = 'to try sb. out, give sb. a chance to prove himself'.

sich versuchen an etw. to test one's skill (strength, etc.) on sth.; since Early NHG, f.r.b. Alberus, e.g. Luther 10,3,215 (Weimar): '*. . . darwidder lauffen und sich versuchen an dem felß*', Goethe, *Was wir bringen* 115: '*die Jugend . . . versucht sich weit umher, versucht sich viel*'.

einen Versuchsballon steigen lassen (coll.) to fly a kite; modern in figur. sense.

gesucht wie der Pelz in Sommer (prov.expr.) not wanted at all, entirely superfluous; recorded since the 19th c., e.g. by Eiselein [1838].

suche, so wirst du finden (prov.) seek and you shall find; international, with examples both in Classical lit., e.g. *si acum quaereres, acum invenisses* (Plautus) or *quaere et invenies* and in the Bible (Matth. 7,7); recorded as prov. since the 17th c., e.g. by Henisch [1616].

niemand sucht den andern hinterm Ofen, er habe denn selbst dahinter gesteckt (prov.) no one will another in the oven seek, except that he himself have been there before; international, e.g. Italian *se la madre non fosse mai stata nel forno non vi cerbarebbe la figlia*; in German f.r.b. Franck [1541]. The prov. also exists with *Sack* instead of *Ofen*.

← See also under *besuchen*, *Flucht* (for *sucht den ruhenden Pol in der Erscheinungen Flucht*), *gleich* (for *gleich suchet sich, gleich findet sich*), *halten* (for *Halt suchen*), *Handel* (for *Händel suchen*), *Heim* (for *jem. heimsuchen*), *Heu* (for *das hätt ich mit der Heugabel nicht in ihm gesucht*), *Laterne* (for *das muß man mit der Laterne suchen*), *Licht* (for *das Licht am hellen Mittag suchen*), *Maus* (for *Mäuse suchen*), *nachsuchen*, *Nadel* (for *etw. wie eine Nadel/Stecknadel suchen*), *Pfennig* (for *mancher sucht einen Pfennig . . .*), *Pferd* (for *ein Pferd suchen und darauf sitzen*) and *Sack* (for *den fünften Zipfel am Sack suchen*).

Sucht: sickness

die ~ craze, mania, greed (for sth.); originally = 'sickness', a meaning now no longer in use except in compounds such as *Gelbsucht*, *Schwindsucht* and the now only dialectal *Fallsucht* or *fallende* ~ = 'epilepsy'; influenced by wrong association with *suchen*; in medical contexts used for 'addiction' (to drink, drugs, etc.), but only established in this sense since the 20th c. Transfer to diseases of the mind, crazes, manias began as early as in OHG and led to many compounds, some derived from adjectival locutions, e.g. *sehnende* ~, as in Walther v.d.Vog. 54,346 ('*seneder sûhte*'), which led to *Sehnsucht*, the only compound which is not essentially pejor. In Early NHG period *Eifersucht* arose, e.g. H.Sachs [edit. G.] 3,63 and Luther 1,363a (Jena) used *blutsüchtig*, followed by many others in the 17th c., which describe a blameworthy or unreasonable craving for sth., e.g. *Geldsucht* (as in Dannhauer, *Catech.* 1,169 [1657]) *Ehrsucht* (as in Stieler, *Geh.Venus* 27) and *Rachsucht* (f.r.b. Stieler [1691]). In the 18th c. the list grew, e.g. *Gewinnsucht* (Lessing 11,182), *Herrschsucht* (Wieland 36,226), *Lobsucht* (Jean Paul), *Großmannssucht* (Schiller, also Gutzkow, *R.v.G.* 1,217) and *Selbstsucht* as an alternative to *Egoismus* (in use since 1759, as detailed in Heyne 3,584); Adelung also mentioned *Spielsucht*, *Tadelsucht* and *Zanksucht* as current. More recent are *Habsucht* and *Ichsucht* (e.g. Gutzkow, *R.v.G.* 9,375). The adjective *süchtig* (at first *suchtig*) arose in the MHG period. The verb *suchten*, still recorded by Campe [1810] for '*eine Sucht haben, Sucht empfinden*', as well as for '*seufzen, vor Verlangen*', is obs.

Sud: boiled liquid, broth

der ~ (pejor.) dirty liquid, filthy puddle, mud; derived from *sieden*; extended in modern times, e.g. Freytag, *Ges.W.* 11,234: '*. . . holte sie den kleinen Purzel . . . , welcher dort jämmerlich im Sude lag*'.

Sudel: (1) puddle, swamp

der ~ (coll.) filthy liquid, ditch-water; influenced by *Sudel* (2) and therefore used for 'filth' in some areas, but in the 19th c. also for 'filthy liquid', e.g. R.Wagner, *Ges.Schr.* 6,89: '*deinen Sudel sauf allein*'.

sudeln to do messy work, deal with sth. filthy, muck about; e.g. Goethe 3,22: '*das Mischen, Sudeln und Manschen ist dem Menschen angeboren*'; this was extended to mean 'to work in a negligent or untidy fashion', since Early NHG, e.g. Brant, *Narrensch.* 50 [1494], and then particularised with ref. to writing, hence = 'to write negligently or messily, jot things down (in no particular order), scribble'. In the 18th c. nouns became current, e.g. *der Sudel* = 'rough draft, jottings', e.g. Wieland (in Merck, *Briefw.* 2.81): '*wenn Sie es haben abschreiben lassen, bitte ich mir den Sudel wieder zurück'* (also in plural, as in Lessing 12,409: *'meine Sudeln'*, who also used *das Gesudel*, e.g. *Werke* 12,449), also *die Sudelei*, recorded by Adelung. Compounds began in Early NHG, e.g. *Sudelpapier*, f.r.b. Maaler, *Sudelbuch* = 'note pad', recorded by Adelung. *Sudler* developed from 'incompetent worker, botcher', current since Early NHG, e.g. Luther 6,220a (Jena), to 'scribbler, bad writer'. There are also verbal compounds, e.g. *etw. hinsudeln* or *zusammensudeln*, e.g. Schiller, *Räuber*, 1,2.

← See also under *besudeln*.

sudeln

sudeln (coll.) to cook, boil; belong to *sieden*, but contaminated by *sudeln* (see above) so that the notion of 'filth' entered into the meaning. In this way *Sudelkoch*, originally a mil. term for 'cook', became a pejor. term, e.g. Fischart, *Garg.* (repr.) 66, later – as in the case of *Sudel* (see above) extended to bad writers (since the 18th c.); cf. also Goethe, *Faust I*, 2341: *'die Sudelköcherei'* with ref. to the concocting of the elixir of youth in the witch's kitchen. Adelung recorded *Sudelkoch* only as *'ein ungeschickter Koch, welcher schmutzig und unreinlich mit den Speisen umgehet, welche er bereitet'*, but Campe [1810] added: *'uneigentlich nennt man Schriftsteller Sudelköche, welche schmuzige Arbeiten liefern'* (for which he also recorded *Sudler*). Adjectives are *sudelhaftig* and *sudelig* = 'dirty, messy', both coll.

Süden: see *Obst*.

Suff: boozing, intoxication

sich dem stillen ~ ergeben (coll.) to tipple on the sly, become a silent drinker; mainly with ref. to habitual drinkers who imbibe in silence (as opposed to riotous drunkards); since the 19th c., f.r.b. Hügel, *Wiener Dial.* 161 with the gloss: *'er trinkt viel, ohne dabei zu sprechen'*, e.g. Holtei, *Erz. Schr.* 22,209: *'. . . Großvater . . . hat sich dem stillen Suff ergeben'*.

Suhle: muddy, swampy place

sich in etw. suhlen (lit.) to wallow in sth. dirty; *suhlen* originally in hunt. jargon only referred to animals wallowing in mud; transferred in modern period, e.g. *sich in Obszönitäten suhlen* = 'to wallow in (or enjoy using) obscene language'.

Suite: suite

Suiten reißen (stud.sl.,obs.) to indulge in pranks, have fun; since the 18th c., derived from 'row of carriages on an excursion into the country', which became 'get-together for which carriages are used' (hence also in stud.sl. used for 'journey, party, duel'), f.r.b. *Bemerk.e.Akadem.* [1795]: *'Suiten reißen = lustig und übermüthig sein'*, e.g. Goethe 27,115 (W.); hence *Suitier* = 'fun-loving chap, happy-go-lucky fellow', but also used for 'lady-killer, philanderer', e.g. Goethe, *Wanderj.* 3,8, *suitisieren*, etc.; all obs.

← See also under *alt* (for *alter Schwede*).

Sultan: sultan

wie ein ~ like a sultan; a ref. to polygamy; e.g. Lenz, *Ged.* [edit. W.] 206: *'gleich einem Sultan . . . im Arm paradiesischer Schönen'*; cf. *~* (cant) = 'bigamist', f.r.b. Ostwald, *Rinnsteinspr.* 151.

die Sultanine sultana; taken over from Near Eastern countries where *sultane* was used for 'imperial, princely' and used with ref to valuable coins, precious textiles and superior kinds of fruit, including the largest of the raisins; modern (in Engl. since 1841, in German even later).

Sülze: jellied meat, aspic

sülzen (coll.) to talk rubbish or tommyrot; since *~* consists of little bits in sth. insubstantial, a pejor. verb could easily arise (cf. similar *quatschen* and *Quark reden*, p. 1925); hence also *Sülzkopf* (coll.) = 'driveller, twaddler'; both 20th c. coll.

Summe: sum

die ~ (1) (lit.) the highest possible entity; since MHG, e.g. Konr.v.Würzb., *Gold.Schm.* 1236: *'ein summe ob allen summen der hôhen saelikeit dû bist'*; cf. 19th c. *Summität* = 'illustrious personage', e.g. (S.-B.) Curtius, *Lebenserinn.* 3,203 [1866]: *'. . . alle Summitäten der Neuzeit kennen gelernt'*.

die ~ (2) the sum total, the end result; from math. language transferred to other spheres, since Early NHG, f.r.b. Maaler, e.g. *die ~ ziehen* = 'to tot up' (e.g. the various experiences), e.g. Schiller, *Wall.Tod* 1,7.

die ~ (3) the important thing or point; since Early NHG, e.g. Luther 12,37 (Weimar); he also used *die Hauptsumme* = 'the chief point', e.g. 10,3,366 (Weimar): *'darumb ist das die hauptsumme . . .'*.

sich summieren to add up to a (considerable) total; removed from strictly math. contexts, e.g. Goethe, *Geschwister*: *'am Ende summirt sichs doch'*.

← See also under *quer* (for *Quersumme*).

Sumpf: swamp

der ~ swamp, squalor, corruption, morass, sink; since OHG, esp. with ref. to sin, e.g. Otfrid [edit. E.] 5,23,110: *'in suntono sunfin'*; in compounds since MHG, e.g. Berth. v. Regensb. 337, 20: *'in dem stinkenden hellensumpf'*. There are many locutions, e.g. *jem. in den ~ ziehen*, as in Schiller, *Räuber* 4,8, *im ~ der Ausschweifungen, Laster versinken* (recorded by Campe), *einen ~ trockenlegen* = 'to end an immoral condition, reform society', a ref. to the draining of marshes (sometimes with allusion to the Pontine marshes), modern, *in einen ~ von Faulheit* (or *Trägheit*) *geraten* (cf. Bettine, *Günderode* 1,372 [1840]: *'alles . . . steckt doch im Sumpf der Dummheit'*). See also under *Morast*, *Pfuhl* and *Schlamm* for similar locutions.

sumpfen (coll.) to drink a lot, (also) to go on a pub-crawl, live it up, burn the candle at both ends; from stud.sl. (but Kluge called it *'modern'* and produced no early recordings), then general coll. Hence *herumsumpfen* (coll.) = 'to spend much time drinking, pub-crawl' and *versumpfen* (coll.) = 'to become a drunkard', also *Sumpferei* = 'drinking orgy' and *Budensumpf* (stud.sl.) = 'boozing party in sb.'s digs'.

zu etw. versumpfen to deteriorate into sth., go to the bad; since the 19th c., e.g. Heine 7,195: *'ihre Geisteswelt versumpfte zu einem. . . . Aberglauben'*; hence *die Versumpfung*, e.g. Gutzkow, *Werke* 2,426: *'moralische Versumpfung'*.

die Sumpfblüte (lit.) sth. (or sb.) that flourishes in an immoral or decaying society; since 2nd half of 20th c.

das Sumpfhuhn (coll.) pub-crawler, habitual drinker; 20th c. coll., e.g. Wolzogen, *Norddt. Gesch.* 78 [1924].

Sums: hum

viel ~ (or *Gesumme* or *Gesums*) *um etw. machen* (coll.) to make a great fuss about sth., much ado about nothing; recorded for several regions since the 19th c.; derived by back formation from *sumsen* = 'to hum'; hence also *Sumserei* (coll.) = 'empty prattle, worthless talk'; cf. also *sumsen* (regional coll.) = 'to put oneself out, go to much trouble' (= *Umstände machen*).

Sünde: sin

die ~ (personified) sin (seen as a person); e.g. Luther Bible transl. Gen. 4,7: *'so ruget die sünde fur der thür'* (where the A.V. has 'sin lieth at the door'), Schiller, *Räuber* 4,5: *'worüber die Sünde roth wird'*. Sometimes in mod.lit. also for 'sinful person, sinner', as in C.F. Meyer [edit. K.] 3,421 or Stifter 2,77.

in ~ leben (a.) to live in sin, cohabit without being married; now a. due to changing moral attitudes; the same is true of *Kind der ~* = 'illegitimate child'.

eine ~ wider den heiligen Geist a very grave sin, a violation of a generally accepted principle; the phrase has a long history in religious contexts. It is derived from Mark 3,29 and was first recorded as *~ in den Heiligen Geist* (a wording also used by Luther). It chiefly meant 'denial of God's grace', but in wider sense also 'denial of God's existence'. The use of *gegen* or *wider* established itself gradually (to be found as early as in Luther 2,61 (Weimar)). Transfer to secular contexts took place in the 18th c., e.g. Goethe IV,17,14 (W.).

es wäre eine ~ . . . it would be a shame; *~* here stripped of its religious sense and reduced to no more than 'the wrong thing to do, a mistake'; also used with the notion of regret and meaning 'it would be a pity'; both since the 18th c. (but *sündigen* in this wider sense is older; see below); e.g. Goethe 3,335 (W.): *'das ist eine von den alten Sünden, sie meinen: rechnen das sei erfinden'*. Similarly, *es ist eine ~, wie er . . .* = 'it is quite wrong of him to . . .', where *~* = 'unjust or inappropriate action', often applied to the breaking of rules, principles, requirements, e.g. in art, language use, etc.

in der ~ Maienblüte (lit.) at the blossoming time of (his, her, its) sinfulness, in the heyday of sinning; since the 18th c., either as *in der Sündenblüte*, e.g. Fontane 1,2,27 or *in der Sünden Blüte*, as in Schlegel's transl. of Shakespeare, *Hamlet* 1,5: *'in meiner Sünden Blüte hingerafft'* (where the original has 'cut off even in the blossoms of my sin') and in *Hamlet* 3,3 in the fuller form *'in seiner Sünden Maienblüte'* (in the original 'with all his crimes broad blown, as flush as May'); also in ironic contexts, e.g. Raabe, *Abu Telfan* 60 [1870]: *'die Mama hatte den Papa nicht in seiner Sünden Maienblüthe geheiratet'*.

etw. hassen wie die ~ to hate sth. like poison; at least since the 18th c., e.g. Goethe, *Gespr.* (edit. B.) 8,140: *'ich hasse alle Pfuscherei wie die Sünde'*; cf. the comparisons *häßlich wie die ~* = 'as ugly as sin', e.g. Grimm, *Kinder- u. Hausm.* 2,237, and *schlecht wie die ~* = 'as wicked as sin'.

diese ~ vergibt dir der Küster (regional coll.) that is not an unpardonable sin; meaning 'you do not trouble to see a priest about absolution, the verger can do it for you'; modern.

eine ~ wert sein (coll.) to be worth sinning for, to be irresistible; Wander [1876] recorded it with the gloss that the remark is used with ref. to a very attractive woman, but it is in wider use; sometimes it can also be a comment on sth. or sb. of great value, e.g. Hügel, *Wiener Dial.* 161: *'der Mann da is a Sünd werth'*.

für meine Sünden (coll.) as a punishment for my sins; the phrase had its beginning in relig. usage with ref. to penitence, e.g. Wolfr.v.E., *Willehalm* 217 or *Parz.* 251; in loose usage, as in Engl. coll. 'for my sins', where no real 'sins' are in the mind of the speaker since the 18th c., e.g. Goethe 9,67 (W.): *'für meine Sünden mußt ich mich . . . mit einem Vieh verbinden'*.

die Erbsünde original sin; attributed to wordings used by St. Augustine; current since Early NHG, e.g. Keisersberg, *Christl.Kön.* aa2a [1514]; hence *Erbsünder* and *erbsündig*, also since Early NHG.

die Unterlassungssünde sin of omission; reflects biblical sayings on omitting to do what one should have done; f.r.b. Dannhawer, *Cat. m.* 1,284 [1642], e.g. Lessing [edit. M.] 8,40. Surprisingly, it is classified as *'umgangssprachlich'* in recent *Duden* editions; cf. also *Unterlassungsschuld* (which is modern).

Sünden- . . . sinful . . . , wicked . . . , . . . of sin; in many compounds since the 16th c., first in such which express the notion of moral failings or depravity (the same as in the adjective *sündlich*) e.g. *Sündengreuel, -laster, -fehler, -schuld*, often with ref. to sexual misbehaviour, e.g. *Sündenhaus* = 'brothel', *Sündengewerbe*, etc. Man's sinful inclinations or behaviour are referred to when Luther 34,1,56 (Weimar) calls the hand of a thief *sündefaust*; other compounds of this type are *Sündensinn, -herz, -wille*. Adelung recorded only *Sündenübel*, but Campe [1810] listed 45, including some in which the second part of the compound is used in its figur. sense, e.g. *Sündendeckel, Sündengift, Sündenheer, Sündenhöhle, Sündenknecht, Sündenlast, Sündennest, Sündenpfuhl, Sündensklave, Sündensold, Sündenstrich, Sündentrieb, Sündenvater* (both for 'Satan' and for 'sinner'), *Sündenverzeichnis* and *Sündenweg*. More recent are the (adjectival and noun) compounds, recorded for many regions since the 19th c. which describe an excessive amount of sth., e.g. *das kostet ein Sündengeld, das ist sündenteuer, sündenschade, er ist sündendumm.*

sündig (coll.,a.), *sündhaft* (coll.) wickedly, frightfully; used both as an adj. or an adverb, as *sündig* since the 18th c., e.g. Goethe 32,18 (W.): '*sündiger Überfluß*', now a. and displaced by *sündhaft* (earlier *sündlich*), generally used as an adverb, since the 19th c., e.g. *sündhaft dumm, sündhaft teuer.*

gegen etw. sündigen to contravene or violate sth.; with ref. to rules, established practice, etc. since the 17th c., e.g. (DWb) Bellin, *Rechtschreib.* 113 [1657] on sb.'s grammatical mistake: '. . . *dagegen sündigt Lobwasser*', Schopenhauer [edit. G.] 2,131: '*eine Regel, gegen welche . . . bisweilen gesündigt wird*'.

sündigen (coll.) to indulge oneself, do sth. which one knows to be wrong or harmful; beginnings in 18th c. *sündigen* = 'to commit an error, make a *faux pas*', since the 19th c. with the notion of deriving pleasure from sth. which one considers as (mildly) wrong or selfish, e.g. Stifter, *Briefw.* 3,29: '*ich sündigte daher durch Zugabe von ein paar Tagen*', lastly with ref. to self-indulgence, e.g. *heute sündige ich und trinke ein Glas mehr.*

sich versündigen to sin (against sb. or sth.), cause some harm; at first usually with *gegen Gott* (still alive in *versündige dich nicht* = 'don't blaspheme'), but then also with ref. to persons with *an*, since Early NHG, e.g. Luther 34,1,494 (Weimar): '. . . *die sich an uns versündigen*', Lessing 18,15: '. . . *daß ich mich auch wohl mit meinen Augen da könnte versündigt haben*', also with abstracts, e.g. Fontane, *Werke* 6,10: '. . . *als ob das Gesetz sich gegen euch versündige*'. Furthest removed from the original sense in such locutions as *versündige dich nicht an deiner Gesundheit* = 'don't abuse your health', modern; the noun *Versündigung* in non-relig. sense since the 18th c.

die Sündermiene shame-faced (or guilty) expression; since the 19th c., e.g. Herwegh, *Ged.e.Leb.* 9 (1841).

wer sich der ~ (or *des Frevels*) *rühmt, sündigt doppelt* (or *zwiefach*) (prov.) if you boast about your wrongdoing, you sin twice; recorded by Simrock [1846]; sometimes also as *wer mit seinen Sünden Staat macht, sündigt doppelt.*

ein Kuß in Ehren ist keine Sünd (prov.) a kiss in all propriety is no sin; recorded by Simrock [1846], who also listed *Lieben ist nicht Sünd und Küssen macht kein Kind.* See also under *Ehre* for *ein Küßchen in Ehren kann niemand verwehren.*

← See also under *abbüßen* (for *da kannst du deine Sünden daran abbüßen*), *alt* (for *alter Sünder*), *arm* (for *armer Sünder* and compounds), *beladen* (for *beladen mit Sünden*), *Bock* (for *Sündenbock*), *dumm* (for *dumm wie die Sünde*), *entbinden* (for *die Seele von der Sünde entbinden*), *fallen* (for *in Sünde fallen* and *Sündenfall*), *fliehen* (for *vor der Sünde fliehen*), *frei* (for *von der Sünde frei*), *Nacht* (for *der Sünde Nacht*), *Pfuhl* (for *Pfuhl aller Sünden* and *Sündenpfuhl*), *Register* (for *Sündenregister*), *rot* (for *wenn eure Sünde gleich blutrot ist*), *Schande* (for *es ist eine Sünde und Schande* and *in Sünde und Schande leben*), *Schlamm* (for *Schlamm der Sünden*), *Schleim* (for *der Sünden Schleim*), *Schoß* (for *Schoßsünde*), *schwer* (for *schwere Sünde* and *Schwere der Sünde*), *Sintflut* (for *Sündflut*), *Stein* (for *wer unter euch ohne Sünde ist . . .*), *stumm* (for *stumme Sünden*), *Sumpf* (for *Sumpf der Sünden*) and *Vater* (for *Sündenvater*).

Superlativ: superlative

der ~ (lit.) the highest form, the finest specimen of the species; originally a linguistic term, figur. since the 17th c. in such locutions as *nach dem ~ streben* = 'to try to reach the peak, achieve perfection', *etw. im ~ besitzen* = 'to possess sth. in its highest form', Zschokke, *Schr.* 18,103: '*ein Banquier ist in der Handelswelt allezeit ein Superlativus*', Rosegger, *Schr.* II,11,146: '*Wien . . . die eigentliche Heimat des Superlativs*'; as an adjective for 'highest in quantity or quality' since the 18th c.

Suppe: soup

die ~ (a. or regional) meal, food; a case of the particular standing for the general and also in use for a meal which does not include soup; since Early NHG, e.g. *jem. zur ~ laden* = 'to invite sb. to a meal', f.r.b. Corvinus [1646], even *für einen Löffel ~* (cf. *auf ein Glas Wein, für ein Butterbrot*), e.g. Brentano, *Ges.Schr.* 5,111; still in the regions for special meals, e.g. *Brautsuppe* = 'meal after the wedding', *Taufsuppe, Totensuppe*, also (in Bav.) *Elternsuppe* = 'meal taken by a newly-wed couple at the parents' home on the first Sunday after the wedding'. Other examples are: Wieland (in *Briefw.* Merck 1,107): '*wenn ich mich durch feiste Hofsuppen verleiten ließe*', Niemeyer, *Beob.* 2,345: '*scherzend nennt man die zurückkommenden Artikel Krebse und den Leipziger Buchhändlerschmaus am Ende der Messe die Krebssuppe*'.

in der ~ sitzen (coll.) to be in the soup, in (a lot of) trouble; since Early NHG, e.g. Schade, *Sat.u.Pasq.* 1,59,153 [1524]: '*er hat uns recht in der suppen lassen stan*'; similarly, *in der ~ stecken*, e.g. Luther 28,486 (Weimar), *in die ~ geraten*, e.g. (DWb) J. Kraus, *Luther* 7 [1719], *in eine ~ kommen*, e.g. Brentano, *Ges.Schr.* 4,233 [1852] and *jem. in die* (or *eine*) *~ bringen, führen, ziehen* (all since Early NHG).

die rote ~ (vulg.) blood; since Early NHG; in some regions still used for 'blood', also for 'nosebleeding', and in some Swiss dialects *sie ist in die Suppen kommen* = 'she has her period'.

blinde ~ (joc.coll.) soup without fat content; an allusion to *Fettauge* (see p. 114); since the 19th c.

(*dicke*) ~ (coll.) thick fog; modern coll. (esp. among sailors and airmen); cf. Engl. coll. 'pea-souper'.

jem.m die ~ *versalzen* (coll.) to queer sb.'s pitch, put a spoke in sb.'s wheel; current since the 16th c., also in phrases with *einsalzen*; see also *jem.m etw. versalzen* on p. 2053; cf. also Börne 4,127: '*wir wollen eine Suppe zusammen essen, die gesalzen sein soll*' to be understood as a threat that during the next meeting unpleasantries will be exchanged.

die ~ *ausessen müssen* (coll.) to have to bear the consequences of one's actions; see the entries on *ausessen* (p. 127), *ausfressen* (p. 130) and the prov. *was man in die* ~ *gebrockt hat, muß man auch ausessen*, recorded by Dove, *Polit.Sprichw.* [1872] and by Lohrengel, *Altes Gold* [1860] as *wer die* ~ *eingebrockt hat, muß sie auch ausessen*.

es hat ihm in die ~ *geregnet* (coll.) his plans have been foiled, sb. has queered his pitch; at least since the 19th c., e.g. Raabe, *Hungerpastor* XIV.

die Grundsuppe (obs.) lees, filthy sediment; the word has had several meanings in its long history (since Early NHG). It could describe the 'deposit, settlings' at the bottom of a vessel (also in ships' bottoms); Luther used it figur. in 15,184 (Weimar) for 'filthy place of origin', but also in 7,441 (Weimar) for 'the base part of human nature'. It was still used in the 19th c., e.g. Raabe, *Uns.Herrg. Kanzl.* 377: '*bei . . . dem Zeisigbauer sei aber die Grundsuppe des Übels zusammengeflossen*'; now obs.

die Spitalsuppe (obs.) poor broth; in wider sense 'sth. which provides little sustenance' and therefore = *Bettelsuppe*, for which see p. 298; so called because beggars used to receive it at the doors of monastery kitchens; still in use in the 19th c., e.g. Gutzkow, *R.v.G.* 3,302 or Gotthelf, *Uli d.K.* 253; a regional variant is *Spittelsuppe*, which Heine [edit. E.] 6,51 used: '*die magersten Spittelsuppen der christlichen Barmherzigkeit*'; both compounds are now only current in some regions.

das Suppengrün (sl.) bouquet, bunch of flowers; mainly used among school children and students; since early in the 20th c.

jem.m ein welsch Süpplein geben (prov.expr., obs.?) to poison sb.; since Early NHG, e.g. Keisersberg, *Narrenschiff* 54; variants are *venediger Süpplein* and *spanisches Süpplein*; cf. *Giftsüpplein* in Fischart, *Bien.* 45a; cf. also French *servir un plat d'Espagne*.

die ~ *ist versalzen – die Köchin ist verliebt* (prov. expr.) the cook must be in love – there is too much salt in the soup; recorded since the 19th c., e.g. by Simrock [1846].

ein Kuß ohne Bart ist wie eine ~ *ohne Salz* (joc. prov.expr.) a kiss from a man without a beard is like soup without salt; recorded since the 19th c., e.g. by Sanders [1865].

jeder kocht (or *siedet*) *sich seine* ~ (or *sein Süppchen*) (prov.) everybody looks after number one, does what is to his greatest advantage;

recorded since the 19th c., e.g. by Wander [1876]; hence also *seine eigne* ~ *kochen* (coll.) = 'to look after one's own interests' and *sein Süppchen am Feuer anderer Leute kochen* = 'to gain benefits or advantages at other people's expense'.

es gibt keine teuerere ~ *als die man umsonst bekommt* (prov.) what one gets for nothing can turn out to have been very expensive; used as a caution about accepting gifts; f.r.b. Franck [1541].

man muß sich nicht an fremden Suppen den Mund verbrennen (prov.) scald not your lips in another man's pottage; recorded since the 19th c., e.g. by Wander [1876]. The Engl. version has been recorded since the 16th c.

← See also under *betteln* (for *Bettelsuppe*), *Brocken* (for *er kann 'was in die Suppe brocken*), *einbrocken* (for *jem.m eine schöne Suppe einbrocken*), *fett* (for *das macht die Suppe nicht fett* and *die Suppe bei jem.m verschütten*), *fressen* (for *etw. in jeder Suppe zu fressen kriegen*), *Haar* (for *ein Haar in der Suppe finden*), *Kaspar* (for *der Suppenkasper*), *kochen* (for *jem.m ein Süppchen kochen*), *Prügel* (for *jem.m Prügelsuppe geben*), *Salz* (for *er verdient nicht das Salz in der Suppe*), *sieden* (for *das schönste Geld siedet noch keine Suppe*) and *spucken* (for *jem.m in die Suppe spucken*). See also under *Peter* (for *er will Peterlein auf allen Suppen sein*, where it should have been stated that *Schnittlauch* can also be used instead of *Peterlein*).

Surrogat: substitute

das ~ inferior substitute, emergency stop-gap or surrogate; as 'substitute' current since the 18th c., f.r.b. Kinderling [1795]; at that time still neutral and usable with positive adjectives, e.g. Goethe IV,28,30 (W.): '. . . *erfreuliche Surrogate der Originale*', but gradually pejor., as in Goethe 48,186 (W.): '*der Humor ist eins der Elemente des Genies, aber sobald er vorwaltet, nur ein Surrogat desselben*'; now usually pejor., e.g. *zu Surrogaten wie Drogen und Alkohol flüchten*.

Susanne: Susanna

eine keusche ~ (coll.) a prude; refers to ~ in the Apocrypha, *The Story of Susanna*, whose chastity was proved by Daniel; now becoming a.

der Susannenbruder (obs.) old lecher; a ref. to the Elders in the story of ~ (see above); f.r.b. Corvinus, *Fons lat.* [1660], still in Ludwig's dictionary of 1716 and glossed with '*alter Hurenhengst*', and still used by Goethe IV,40,257 (W.). Now obs.

der Susannist (obs.) lecher, rake, voluptuary; since the 17th c. and still in occasional use in the 19th c., e.g. (DWb) Ayrenhoff, *Werke* 4,275 [1814]: '*Ihr kommt Beyde in wahre Susannistenhände*'; now obs.

. . . *-suse* (coll.,pejor.) . . . woman, . . . girl; in pejor. compounds in which the first part describes the woman's weakness, e.g. a woman who weeps at the slightest mishap or has a whining voice can be called *Flennsuse, Heulsuse* or *Tränensuse* (still listed in Kapeller, *Schimpflexikon* [1964]), a woman who moves slowly or appears half-asleep most of the time is called *Transuse*. For a similar type of compound see *Heulliese* on p. 1319.

süß: pleasant; sweet

süß, also *süßlich* (pejor.) sugary, honeyed; this pejor. meaning usually containing the notions of insincerity or hypocrisy, sometimes that of affectation, can be seen as the only extension of the original meaning since ~ has had a wide range of meanings since its OHG beginnings (with indications that even its IE root covered many aspects of pleasantness), such as 'pleasant, delightful, charming, sweet, fragrant, dulcet', esp. since the 8th and 9th c. lit. the non-phys. meanings occur more frequently than 'sweet' in its phys. sense; cf. the detailed notes on ~ by Theodor Kochs in *DWb*. X,4,12871 [1942]. The pejor. sense appeared in the 17th c., e.g. (DWb) Paracelsus, *Op*. [edit. H] 1,303 [1616]: '*ein süß geschwätz*', where ~ stand for 'attractive-sounding but insincere'. It can also be used for 'effeminate, affected, unmanly', as in Goethe 9,51 (W.): '*die süßen Herrn*' (also in Kant 7,421); *süßlich* has also been used for pejor. 'sugary, insincerely friendly' since the 2nd half of the 18th c. A verb *süßeln* = 'to flatter, be sycophantic' and also = 'to behave in an affected manner', both since the 18th c., is now rare if not obs. The abstract *Süßigkeit* could at one time be used with ref. to persons, e.g. Luther 4,81 (Jena): '*Gott ist nichts denn eitel süßigkeit und güte*', but has become the concrete 'sweet, sweetmeat, confection'.

das süße Nichtstun (lit.) *il dolce far niente*; taken over at first in its Ital. form towards the end of the 18th c. (cf. Feldmann in *ZfdW*. 9,298 on *il divino far niente* and similar phrases), e.g. Lichtenberg, *Aphor*. 5,94 [1798]: '*das dolce far niente*', later in German form. Cf. the similar (recent) loan *das süße Leben* from Ital. *la dolce vita*.

← See also under *Bein* (for *je näher dem Bein, je süßer das Fleisch*), *bitter* (for *bittersüß*), *Frucht* (for *verbotene Frucht schmeckt süß*), *Galle* (for *dem wird das Leben süß gemacht und dem vergällt*), *Honig* (for *süß wie Honig* and *honigsüß*), *Kern* (for *Maria grozer süeze ein kern*), *Maul* (for *ein süßes Maul machen* and *jem.m das Maul süß machen*), *Rache* (for *Rache ist süß*), *raspeln* (for *Süßholz raspeln*), *Sacharin* (for *sacharinsüß*) and *sauer* (for *nichts Süßes und nichts Saures* and *sauersüß*).

swing

swingen (sl.) to indulge (or participate) in group sex; a strange development of the Engl. term which in German at first only referred to playing music or dancing in a certain style; since the 2nd half of the 20th c. in the sl. sense which is essentially euphem. The noun is *Swinging* and a participant is called *Swinger*.

Sybaris: Sybaris

der Sybarit (lit.) sybarite, epicurean, luxury-loving high liver; from the Greek city of Sybaris whose inhabitants were noted for luxurious living and gourmandizing; in German general since the 18th c.; Campe [1813] glossed it with '*Lüstling oder Wollüstling*' (today *Schlemmer* would suggest itself as an alternative), the adj. *sybaritisch* he wanted to see replaced by '*üppig, wollüstig, schwelgerisch*'.

Sylphe: sylph

der (also *die*) ~ (lit.) sylph, spirit of the air; in German in use (generally in the pl.) since Paracelsus [1590], who also called them '*lufftleut*' (Campe rendered ~ with *Luftgeist*), but general only since Pope, *Rape of the Lock* [1712], f.r.b. Amaranthes, *Frauenz.-Lex*. [1773], often used by Wieland, e.g. *Oberon* 10,15. In comparisons such as *leise wie ein* ~ *schleichen, leicht wie ein* ~ *schweben, unhörbar wie ein* ~ since the 19th c.; hence *sylphenhaft* = 'butterfly-like', since butterflies have been associated with or even called *Sylphen* since the 18th. c.

die Sylphide (lit.) female sylph; taken over from Engl. through Pope, e.g. Gottschedin, *Popens Lockenraub* 13 [1744]: '*hört . . . o ihr Sylphen und Sylphiden*', Goethe 49,322 (W.): '*. . . sind Sylphiden in der Luft*'; since the 19th c. applied to beautiful (graceful, delicate, fairy-like) girls, e.g. Pückler, *Briefw.u.Tageb*. 3,108; hence *sylphidenähnlich*. Some authors have used *Sylphin* instead of *Sylphide* and the adj. *sylphisch*.

Symbiose: symbiosis

die ~ (lit.) symbiosis; originally a biological term for the 'living-together of organisms in a mutually advantageous relationship' (still missing even in this sense in *DWb*. [1942]); since early in the 20th c. figur. for 'mutually beneficial coexistence in a close relationship', e.g. ~ *von Vernunft und Freiheit*; often in *eine* ~ *eingehen*.

Symbol: symbol

das Symbolum (obs.) motto, devise, slogan; since the 17th c., derived from the religious meaning of ~ = 'confession of faith'; still in use in the 19th c., e.g. O. Ludwig 5,147 (on Schiller): '*. . . selbst seinem Symbolum, der Schönheit um jeden Preis, wird er oft untreu*'; now obs.

Symmetrie: symmetry

voll ~ full of harmony (and equipoise); transfer from the phys. and geometric areas to other aspects, e.g. Wiechert, *Einfaches Leben* 126: '*das Pflanzenreich (ist) voller Symmetrie und Gesetz*', or *soziale* ~ = 'balance (or equity) created by allocating sth. to both sides of society' (esp. with ref. to employers and workers), coined ca. 1965, e.g. *F.A.Z.* of 25.8.1971.

sympathetisch: sympathetic

sympathetisch (a.) sympathetic, exercising mysterious power, producing mysterious effects; Campe [1813] glossed it with '*geheimkräftig oder geheimwirkend*'; since the 18th c., esp. in *sympathetische Mittel*, e.g. Droste-Hülshoff, *Ges.Schr.* 2,361 on popular superstitions: '*. . . äußert sich . . . vorzugsweise in sympathetischen Mitteln*'; cf. Herder [edit. S.] 1,212: '*dies hat wie der Mond eine* *sympathetische Einwirkung auf leere Köpfe'*, Goethe 19,81 (W.): *'ein geheimer, sympathetischer Zug hatte mich hier so oft gehalten, ehe ich noch Lotten kannte'*; still in the 19th c. in *sympathetische Tinte* = 'sympathetic ink', which Campe glossed with *'geheime oder Wundertinte'* (cf. Bailey's definition in 1721: 'Sympathetick inks are such as can be made to appear or disappear, by the Application of something that seems to work by Sympathy'), and in *sympathetische Kuren*, as in Fontane, *Ges.W.* 1,6,314: *'sie . . . quacksalberte nicht bloß, sondern machte auch sympathetische Kuren'*. – Note that ~ for 'sympathetic' in the present-day sense, still current in the 19th c., is now obs.

Symphonie: see *Simfonie*.

Symptom: symptom

das ~ symptom, sign, indication; sometimes also pejor. for 'bad sign, omen'; the medical term was transferred to other areas in the 18th c., e.g. (S.-B.) Mendelssohn, *Philos. Schr.* II,29 [1761]: *'die Bewegungen, durch welche sich das Mitleiden zu erkennen giebt, sind von einfachen Symptomen der Liebe . . . unterschieden'*, Goethe 17,178 (W.): *'in allem beobachtete sie nichts als Symptome, ob Eduard wohl bald erwartet werde . . .'*; hence *symptomatisch*, since the middle of the 18th c., f.r.b. Heinsius [1822] for *'anzeigend'*, e.g. *es ist von symptomatischer Bedeutung* or *das ist symptomatisch für ihn* = 'that is typical of him'.

synchronisieren: synchronise

Dinge (abstracts) ~ to bring things into conformity or harmony; originally only used with ref. to time, but since ca. 1920 in wider sense for many kinds of harmonisation (= *Abstimmung*), e.g. *sie synchronisierten ihre Meinungen, synchronisierter Fortschritt* or in the econ. sphere, as in Schumpeter, *Wirtsch. Entw.* 49 [1926]: *'. . . keine Lücke zwischen Aufwendung und Bedürfnisbefriedigung . . . Die beiden werden, nach Clarks zutreffendem Ausdruck, von selbst "synchronisiert"'*.

Syndrom: syndrome

das ~ (lit.) syndrom; current in medical sense since the 18th c. for the 'coming-together of several symptoms in a diseased organism'; in ca. middle of the 20th c. transferred to the presence of a number of phenomena which indicate a certain (sociological) condition (not connected with disease), usually in compounds. The *DWb.* [1942] does not list the word.

Syrup: see *Sirup*.

systematisch: systematic

systematisch (pejor.) systematic, habitual (or consistent); originally = 'planned, following a system or established method'; since the middle of the 19th c. pejor., usually in adverbial locutions, e.g. (S.-B.) Rochlitz, *Gauner* 5 [1846]: *'. . . übten das Verbrechen systematisch im Großen aus'*, *durch sein Rauchen ruiniert er systematisch seine Lunge*. The pejor. use of Engl. 'systematic' has been recorded since 1803, a good deal earlier than the German extension.

← See also under *Lawine* (for *Lawinensystem*).

Szene: scene

die ~ (1) stage (figur.), centre or prominent point of some event; transfer from the theatre to real life, e.g. *die* ~ *betreten* or *auf die* ~ *treten* = 'to come onto the stage', or *die* ~ *beherrschen* = 'to dominate proceedings, exert a strong influence on the course of events'; Fontane used the locution in the poem *Die Alten und die Jungen*: *'sie beherrschen die Szene, sie sind dran!'*.

die ~ (2) the scene, scenery; a landscape (or a view of it) compared to scenery in the theatre; since the 18th c., e.g. Zachariä, *Tagesz.* II,22 [1756] on a sunrise: *'prächtige Scene, wer kann dich beschreiben?'*, Wieland, *Agathon* 2,26 [1773]: *'. . . die mannigfaltigen Scenen der Natur . . .'*.

die ~ (3) scene, picture of conditions or events; since the 18th c., e.g. (S.-B.) transl. of Smollet, *Pereg. P.* 1,10 [1785]: *'Eintritt in eine Scene des Lebens, worauf er ganz fremd war'*, La Roche, *Frl.v.St.* 63 [1771]: *'Scenen des Landlebens'*; now frequent in such locutions as *die politische* ~ and in numerous compounds, such as *Hochschulszene, Rauschmittelszene, Wahlkampfszene*, also *Rührszene*, where the Engl. equivalent would be 'situation'. Recent editions of *Duden* call this usage coll., which seems a debatable classification.

die ~ (4) scene, loud or violent quarrel; since the 18th c., e.g. Goethe 20,174 (W.): *'er . . . fürchtete eine leidenschaftliche Scene'*; frequent in *eine* ~ *machen* = 'to make a scene', since the 19th c., e.g. Eckstein, *Hartwig* 377 [1895].

hinter der ~ behind the scenes; since the 19th c.

← See also under *Kulisse* (for *hinter den Kulissen*)

etw. in ~ *setzen* to engineer sth., produce a situation artificially, stage sth.; since the 19th c., e.g. Tieck, *Krit.Schr.* 4,96 [1826] or Polenz, *Grabenhäger* 2,101 [1887]: *'das Schweinepack von Gegnern behauptet . . . , unsere ganze Geschichte wäre künstlich in Scene gesetzt'*; similarly the intrans. *in* ~ *gehen* = 'to be performed', also without ref. to the theatre, and modern *etw. inszenieren* (formerly *szenieren*).

sich in ~ *setzen* to put oneself into limelight, draw attention to oneself; in wider sense also 'to show off'; since the 19th c., e.g. Stahr, *Nach fünf Jahren* 1,232 [1857]: *'. . . Widerwille gegen allen Charlatanismus des Sichselbstinscenesetzens'* (similarly in Gutzkow, *Longinus* 88 [1878].

der Szenenwechsel (lit.) change of scene (place, domicile); transfer from the language of the theatre, since the 19th c., e.g. *der häufige Szenenwechsel in seinem Werdegang*.

Szepter: see *Zepter*.

Szylla: Scylla

zwischen ~ *und Charybdis* (prov.expr.) between Scylla and Charybdis, between the devil and the deep sea; refers to the monster with twelve feet, six heads and three rows of teeth in each head which lurked on one side of the Straits of Messina snatching sailors from passing ships and Charybdis, a dangerous whirlpool on the other side of the Straits (in Homer, *Od.* 12, 85–110); in prov. use in many languages, in Engl. since the 16th c. (cf. *Oxf.*,568), used by Shakespeare in *Merchant of Venice* 3,5, in German lit. at least since the 18th c.

der ~ entfliehen und in die Charybdis fallen (prov.) to fall from Scylla into Charybdis, from the frying-pan into the fire; in Lat. form *incidis in Scyllam cupiens vitare Charybdim* by Ph. Gualtier, *Alexandreis* 5,301, frequent in German since the 18th c., recorded by Sutor, *Chaos* [1716], e.g. Lessing 8,324: '*aus Scylla in Charybdis gestürzt*'; cf. J.v. Müller 7,259: '. . . *zwischen Scylla und Charybdis durchgesteuert*' (also Goethe's humorous plural: '*wenn ihr auch Cyclopen, Sirenen und Scyllen in die Klauen fielet*').

Tabak: see *stark*.

Tabernakel: tabernacle

das ~ (regional coll.) the head; since tabernacles and some relig. statues have a roof, the term came to be applied to 'head' (cf. the entry on *Dach* on p. 442); since the 18th c., e.g. Bürger, 48a: '. . . *weil nun der letzte Ärger ihr noch spuckt*' im *Tabernakel . . .*'. Küpper's dating is wrong.

Tablett: tray, salver

das kommt nicht aufs ~ (coll.) that is out of the question; belongs to *Tapet* (which see). Modern.

Tablette: tablet

Tabletten- . . . tablet- . . . , pill- . . . ; in compounds with a pejor. flavour since the middle of the 20th c., e.g. *Tablettensucht* = 'addiction to pills' (and the adj. *tablettensüchtig*), *Tabletteninflation* = 'excessive increase of pills for all kinds of ailments'.

tabu: taboo

das ist ~ (coll.) don't touch that, don't mention that; *~*, a loan from Engl., has been gradually extended from 'prohibited by (relig.) tradition' to 'to be avoided, left untouched'; general since the 1st quarter of the 20th c.; hence also *etw. mit einem Tabu belegen* (frequent since ca. 1930), *ein Tabu brechen* or *übertreten, sich in die Tabu-Zone verirren* = 'to stray into an area (subject, etc.) which is taboo', *die Tabuschranke durchbrechen*, etc. and the verbs *etw. tabuieren* (now usually *tabuisieren*), in original sense since the middle of the 19th c., in extended sense since early in the 20th c.; around 1960 *etw. enttabuieren* (more frequently *enttabuisieren*) established themselves.

tabula rasa

~ machen to make a clean sweep, remove everything or everybody; *~* contains the notions of thoroughness and/or ruthlessness; of Classical origin (mainly Aristotle, but also Plato in *Theaitet* 191c8); in German since the 18th c. via Engl. and French; first used for the impressionless mind of a newly-born, also for a mind not yet affected by experiences (cf. *unbeschriebenes Blatt*, which has been discussed

on p. 332) and in wider sense for 'nothingness, complete emptiness'; cf. Goltz, *Buch d. Kindh.* 108 [1847]: '*eine Kinderseele ist keine tabula rasa*'. Late in the 19th c. under influence of French *faire table rase* the locution with *machen* arose; hence also such compounds as *Tabula-rasa-Lösung* (middle of 20th c.).

Tacheles

~ reden (coll.) to come to the point, get down to brass tacks; with such subsidiary meanings as 'to come clean, confess' and (more recently) 'to get down to discussing finance'. Yiddish *tachlis* = 'aim, purpose' entered German coll. at the beginning of the 20th c., in wider senses since ca. 1920.

Tadel: see *Ritter*.

Tafel: tablet, board, panel; table, meal.

die ~ (1) (lit.) table, tablet; figur. with abstracts since Early NHG, e.g. Luther, Bible transl. Jerem. 17,1: '*die sunde Juda ist . . . auf die tafel jres hertzen gegraben*' (where the A.V. used 'table' and modern Engl. Bibles have 'tablet'), but also used for 'tablet' = 'law, prescription' with ref. to the bibl. tablets (Exod. 24,12), e.g. Klinger 6,307: '*die Tafeln der Sittlichkeit*', Schiller, *D.Carlos* 1,2: '*die Tafeln der Natur und Roms Gesetze . . .*', Wieland, *Herm.* 1,142: '*die heiligen Tafeln des ewigen Schicksals*'.

die ~ (2) meal, banquet; the meaning 'table' (for a meal) led naturally to the extension to 'meal'; in German since the 17th c., recorded by Steinbach [1734], further extended in metaphors, e.g. Auerbach, *Ges. Schr.* 16,215: '. . . *Festwein auf der reichen Tafel unsers Lebens*'; since the 17th c. also in compounds such as *Tafelfreund, Tafelgast, Tafelgesellschaft* (although *Tisch* is now preferred in such compounds), but still in *Tafelfreude* = 'pleasure of the table', since the 18th c., recorded by Campe (cf. also Wieland, *Idris* 1,64: '*ihre Tafellust zu mehren*'); hence also *tafeln* = 'to eat' (now lit. or stilted), since MHG, e.g. *Das Buch Jüdel* [edit. Hahn] 331: '*daz man tavelte in der stat*'.

die ~ (3) table, index, register; mainly in compounds such as *Ahnentafel* = 'genealogical table, family tree', recorded since the 18th c., e.g. by Adelung, *Logarithmentafel*, f.r.b. Campe [1813], but as *logarithmische Tabelle* already in the 17th c.

Tafel- . . . (geogr.) table- . . . ; in geogr. compounds, e.g. *Tafelberg* = 'table mountain', recorded since the 18th c., *Tafelland* = 'plateau'; cf. Herder, *Id.* 2,13: '*auf dieser großen . . . Tafel der Tartarei*', but *Tafelland* was not listed by Adelung and Campe.

die Liedertafel choral society, (male) choir; coined by C.F. Zelter who in 1808 called his choir *Liedertafel* in an allusion to the Round Table of King Arthur, describing it as '*gesanglichen Tischverein*'.

der Tafelaufsatz (joc.coll.) distinguished guest at a dinner table; compared to the ornamental 'centre piece' on a festive table, invited (chiefly) in order to impress the other guests; 20th c. coll.

die Tafelrunde group of guests assembled for a meal; since Early MHG (*tavelrunde*) taken over from French *table ronde*, used in courtly epics, revived in the 18th c. by Wieland, e.g. in *Oberon* 5,40. Goethe still used it with ref. to a round table for a meal, but since the 19th c. chiefly with ref. to people seated around it.

das Tafeltuch entzweischneiden to sever all connexions, terminate one's friendship; since the 19th c., best known through Uhland, *Die Schlacht bei Reutlingen*: '*da faßt der Greis ein Messer und spricht kein Wort dabei und schneidet zwischen beiden das Tafeltuch entzwei*'; see also *etw. zerschneiden* on p. 2164.

← See also under *aufheben* (for *die Tafel aufheben*), *offen* (for *offne Tafel halten*) and *rund* (for *Rundtafel*).

Tag: day

der ~ (1) (personified) the day; personified since MHG, at first mainly with ref. to 'light', e.g. *Iwein* 672: '*begunde liehten der tac*' (also with *erleuchten*); very frequent with ref. to its growth and progress, e.g. Fischart, *Pract.* 22: '*der tag wächst*', Aler, 1871a: '*der tag streckt sich*' (similarly later with *sich dehnen*), and since the 18th c. in many poetic images, e.g. Uz 1,50: '*der junge Tag erwacht*' (also in Schiller, *Räuber* 4,1), Bürger, 72b: '*heiter lacht ein blauer Tag*', Schiller, *Räuber* 2,3: '. . . *Kluft . . . wo der Tag vor meiner Schande zurücktritt*', Fiesco 4,12: '*hinter dem Rücken des verschämten Tags*', Goethe, *Zueignung*: '*der junge Tag erhob sich mit Entzücken*', Lenau 1,296: '*jubelnd ist der Tag erschienen, schwingt den Goldpokal der Sonne*', Mörike, *Ged.* 2: '*es träumt der Tag, nun sei die Nacht entflohn*'; cf. also Goethe, *Wanderj.* 2,12: '*bald nahm mich der gewöhnliche Tag* (= 'the routine occupations of the day') *mit sich fort*'.

der ~ (2) time, period, moment; a vague time indication in many locutions. Kramer [1702] listed: '*Tag und Nacht studieren*' (= 'all the time, continuously'), '*den lieben langen Tag müssig gehen*' (= 'to be lazy all day long'), '*das geschieht nicht alle Tage*' (= 'that does not happen every day'), '*alle Tage in Freuden leben*' (= 'to enjoy oneself all the time'), '*ein Kleid für alle Tage*' (= 'a dress for everyday use'), '*sich gute Tage machen, schaffen*' (see below), '*das hab ich meine Tage nicht gesehen*' (= 'never in my life have I seen that'), '*seine Tage beschließen*' (='to end one's life'), '*was der Tag mit sich bringt*' (='what occurs in the course of time or of the day'), '*er starb bey seinen besten Tagen*' (= 'he died in the prime of life'), '*Jahr und Tag*' (see p. 1405), '*dieser Tage*' (= 'one of these days, recently'). Adelung [1780] added: '*von Tag zu Tag warten*' (='to wait from one day to the next'), '*Tag für Tag*' (= 'every day'), '*morgen des Tages*' (= 'tomorrow'), which is now obs., '*in meinen alten Tagen*' (= 'in my old age'), '*auf seine alten Tage*' (= 'at his advanced age'), '*heut zu Tage*' (= 'nowadays'), '*nächster Tage*' (= 'in a few days, soon'). For some of these and others falling into the same category see below.

← See also under *einst* (for *einst wird kommen der Tag*), *ewig* (for *ewig und drei Tage*), *fordern* (for *die Forderung des Tages*), *hell* (for *die helle Wahrheit an den Tag bringen*), *kommen* (for *kommt der Tag, so bringt der Tag*), *Nacht* (for *über Tag und Nacht* and other phrases), *neigen* (for *meine Tage gehen zur Neige*), *nimmer* (for *der Nimmerstag*), *Ring* (for *sich goldene Tage versprechen*), *Sonne* (for *Sonnentag* and *die Sonne bringt es an den Tag*), *Sonntag* (for *es ist nicht Sonntag alle Tage*) and *Stunde* (for *Tag und Stunde*).

der ~ (3) (mining) daylight, surface (as opposed to underground); in lit. since Early NHG, recorded by Frisch [1741]; used mainly in *am Tage* = 'on the surface', *unter ~* = 'below ground', and in many compounds, e.g. *Tagarbeiter* = 'surface worker' (although in other contexts it can also mean 'labourer paid by the day', same as the more usual *Taglöhner*), *Tagebau* or *Tagbau* = 'opencast mining' (as opposed to *Grubenbau*), also called *Tagbergwerk*, f.r.b. Jacobsson 7,511a.

der ~ (4) (mainly lit.) the fateful day, the moment ordained by fate; mainly with ref. to death; since Early NHG, e.g. Luther Bible transl. Ezek. 21,29: '. . . *erschlagenen . . . welchen ir tag kam*', Schiller, *Kab.u.L.* 2,3: '*sie alle erlebten ihren Tag*', *Räuber* 1,2: '*jeden ereilet endlich sein Tag*'.

mein ~ (*nicht*) (coll.) ever, never; in such locutions as *das hätte ich mein ~ nicht vermutet* = 'I would never have thought that possible (or expected that to happen)'; sometimes without the negation, e.g. Grillparzer 7,13: '*hätt ich mein Tag geglaubt, daß so was Sünde!*'

der ~ ist unser (lit. or a.) victory is ours, we have carried (or won) the day; at least since the 18th c., e.g. Schiller, *Jungfr.v.O.* 3,7.

seinen ~ leben (a.) to pass one's time, spend one's life; e.g. Ranke, *Päpste* 1,276; '*hier lebte der Papst seinen Tag und vergaß die übrige Welt*'.

Tages- . . . (poet.) . . . of light; mainly in poet. terms for the Sun, e.g. *Tagesfackel*, recorded by Campe [1810], who also listed *Tagesflamme* (citing Jean Paul), *Tagesgestirn* (19th c.), *Tageskerze*, as in Opitz 1,125 [1644] and *Tageskönigin*, used by Freiligrath.

. . . *Tage* times, periods, moments; the same in essence as *~* (2), but used in the plural and always with qualifying adjectives; since Early NGH, e.g. Luther Bible transl. Ecclesiastes 12,1: '*ehe denn die bösen tage kommen*', H. Sachs, *Fast.Sp.* 1,121: '*du fürest . . . klag und hast doch gute faule tag*'; hence *sich gute Tage machen* = 'to enjoy oneself, have a good time', current since Early NHG, e.g. Luther, *101.Psalm* . . . Qa: '. . . *verderbte natur, die gute tage nicht tragen kan*' (cf. Goethe, *Sprichwörtlich*: '*alles in der Welt läßt sich ertragen, nur nicht eine Reihe von schönen Tagen*'), Wieland 18,45: '*sich gute Tage machen*'. The earliest of such locutions refers to age and occurs in OHG, e.g. (DWb) Otfrid, *An Hartmut* 79: '*thô er zên altên dagon quam*', frequent since MHG, e.g. Wittenweiler, *Ring* 19: '*sie sei schön und junger tagen*', H. Sachs 9,438: '*in meinen jungen tagen*', f.r.b. Maaler [1561]: '*in seinen besten tagen sein*'.

am ~ liegen to be evident, public knowledge, obvious to everybody; derived from ~ (3) but without a conscious ref. to mining; general since Early NHG, e.g. Luther 1,156b (Jena): '*es ist am tage*', Schiller, *Phaedra* 4,2: '*deines Weiberhasses verhaßte Quelle liegt nunmehr am Tag*', *D.Carlos* 2,10: '*es ist am Tag. Er wird erhört. Sie liebt!*'; similarly intrans. *zu Tage kommen* or *treten*, *an den ~ kommen* and reflex. *sich zu Tage drängen*. Transitive versions are *etw. an den ~ legen* = 'to make sth. public, expose sth. to the light of day', with *bringen* f.r.b. Maaler [1561]: '*an tag bringen*', in Bismarck, *Reden* 14,57 as *zu Tage bringen*, with *geben* in Luther 4,259a (Jena), also *etw. ans Tageslicht bringen* (cf. phrases under *Licht* (4) on p. 1616) and *etw. zu Tage fördern* (modern). – Note that *etw. an den ~ geben* = 'to publish sth.', used with ref. to books in Luther 3,465a (Jena), is obs. (but in the 18th c. Günther still used *am ~ sein* for 'to be available in published form').

etw. in den ~ hinein tun to do sth. without due thought or consideration; this also is related to ~ (3), here = 'open air', 'empty space' (in phys. sense used in building and architecture) and therefore similar to *ins Blaue* (see p. 335), also *ins Gelage* (see p. 969); since the 18th c., e.g. Lessing 11,222: '. . . *so in den Tag hinein schreiben*', Goethe, *Dicht.u.Wahrh*. 13: '*wie doch so vieles grundlos . . . in den Tag hineingesagt wurde*'.

in den ~ hinein leben to live without a care for the next day; cf. Latin *in diem vivere*, French *vivre du jour*; here ~ is assumed to refer to 'day in the calendar'; f.r.b. Mathesy [1554].

es wird ~ (coll.) I am beginning to understand; ~ here a ref. to the light which the day brings, similar to *mir geht ein Licht auf* (see p. 86); since the 18th c., frequent in Goethe, e.g. Immermann, *Münchh*. 1,279: '*hui . . . es wird Tag!*'.

der Jüngste ~ the Day of Judgment; since Early NHG with ref. to biblical language (e.g. John 6,39 and 11,24), chosen by Luther, where the A.V. puts 'the last day' (*jüngster ~* for 'last day' had been current in non-relig. contexts since MHG); cf. also Schiller, *Räuber* 5.1: '*Konterfei vom jüngsten Tage*'. In lit. *~ des Gerichts* and *der ~ der Tage* also occur for 'Day of Judgment'.

der Mann des Tages the outstanding personality of the day, today's hero; modern; see under *Held* (for *Held des Tages*) and under *Löwe* (for *Löwe des Tages*); cf. also *Tagesheld*, as in Heine 14,271: '*mein erstes . . . Zusammentreffen mit dem damaligen Tageshelden*'.

~ machen (a.) to get up; since the 18th c. in lit., e.g. Lessing, *Em.Gal.* 1,1: '*ich habe zu früh Tag gemacht*'; now a. or obs.

wirken, so lange es ~ ist (bibl.) to work as long as there is an opportunity to be active; from Luther's transl. of John 9,4: '*jch mus wircken die werck . . . so lange es tag ist*' (where the A.V. has 'I must work the works . . . while it is day').

es ist klar wie der ~ it is evident, obvious, as clear as daylight; at least since the 18th c., e.g. Schiller, *M.Stuart* 4,5: '*sein Verbrechen ist klar wie der Tag*'.

ja, guten ~ ! (coll.) no such hope, that is not likely (to occur); ironic expression of greeting sth. which is not likely to occur; e.g. (Sa.) Burmann, *Fabeln* 161 [1773]; cf. similar *prost Mahlzeit*, discussed under *Mahl* (p. 1645).

dem ~ (or *der Zeit*) *dienen* to fall in with the current trend, conform with prevailing views and attitudes, be a time-server; usually pejor. (criticising lack of independent thinking); hence *Tagdiener* = 'time-server', since the 19th c., f.r.b. Sanders, e.g. Auerbach, *Schrift u. Volk* 9 [1846]: '*vergängliche Tagdiener*'; surprisingly, not recorded in *DWb.* [1935]; now a. or obs.

es ist noch früh am ~ (coll.) it is early days yet; note of caution suggesting that things may change (with ~ not taken literally); modern, but *früh am ~* in the literal sense has been recorded since Henisch [1616].

sie hat ihre Tage (euphem.) she has her period; recorded since the 19th c.; the period is also called *die kritischen Tage* (since early in the 20th c.); since the 19th c. *die roten Tage* (vulg.) has also been in use.

er hat heute seinen großen ~ (coll.) today he has his big day, it is a specially important day for him today; modern; cf. *groß* (3) on p. 1150.

sich einen guten ~ machen (coll.) to take one's ease for the day, enjoy oneself; in essence the same as *es sich gut sein lassen*, listed on p. 1179.

er hat seinen guten ~ (coll.) he is in a good mood today, today he is affable and approachable; modern.

am hellichten ~ (regional coll.) in broad daylight; see *hell* (3) on p. 1285; influenced by (or a contraction of) *am hellen lichten ~* (cf. *am hellen Tage*, as in Schiller, *Jungfr.v.O.* 5,1); recorded since the 19th c., e.g. Heyse, *Ges.Werke* 8,283: '*am hellichten Tage*'. Cf. also *am hohen Tage* (obs.), as in the Bible (e.g. Luther's transl. of Jerem. 6,4), indicating midday when the Sun is high in the sky. Campe [1810] still recorded '*es ist schon hoch am Tage . . . wenn es gegen Mittag ist*'.

ein (richtiges) Tagblatt (or *Tageblatt*) (coll.) a gossip, sb. who always has all the latest news; recorded since the 2nd half of the 19th c., e.g. by Albrecht for Leipzig [1881].

die Tagesberühmtheit ephemeral fame; since the 19th c., also applied to the person enjoying temporary fame (see also below for *Eintagsfliege*).

die Tagesfrage the problem, question or subject of discussion of the day; since the 19th c., e.g. Heine 10,184; *Tagesgeschichte* can also be used, e.g. Thümmel, *Reise*, 7,307 [1802], as well as *Tagesgeschehen* (missing in *DWb.* [1935]).

das Tagesgespräch, also Taggespräch the talk or
subject of conversation of the day; since the 19th
c., e.g. Heine 8,351; also applied to persons: er ist
das Tagesgespräch des ganzen Dorfes.

die Tageslast the burdens of the day; since the
18th c., e.g. Brockes 1,125; cf. figur. Last on
p. 1586, and the 19th c. adjectives tagesmatt and
tagesmüde = 'tired from the exertions of the day';
Platen 2,245 used tagmüde.

die Tagesphrase topical phrase, expression in
vogue; since the 19th c., e.g. Freytag, Ges.W.
15,131.

taghell (as) light as day; since the 18th c., e.g.
Schiller, Glocke: 'taghell ist die Nacht gelichtet'.
Goethe used tagklar (see also above on the com-
parison with klar). The noun die Taghelle was f.r.b.
Campe [1810].

das Taglied or Tagelied (lit.hist.) morning song of
the watchman; also used for the song of lovers
parting at daybreak; current since MHG (tageliet),
now only used in historical accounts of the genre.

schuften (sich abarbeiten, abrackern, etc.) wie ein
Taglöhner to work like a slave (horse, etc.); in
comparisons since the 18th c., e.g. Schiller, Räuber
4,2 (with abarbeiten), Moltke 4,194 (with schanzen
und graben).

der Tagstern (a.) the morning star; current since
MHG, revived in the 19th c. (in lit.), but now a. or
obs., displaced by Morgenstern.

tagtäglich usual, common, routine; originally
and mainly an intensified täglich = 'all the time',
f.r.b. Stieler [1691]; then extended to mean 'occurring daily, regularly recurring', since the 18th c.,
e.g. tagtägliche Arbeiten (as in Goethe, Hör-,
Schreib- u. Druckfehler), sometimes coming close to
'humdrum, commonplace, dull', and in this pejor.
sense also used by Goethe, e.g. in D.dt. Gil Blas.

der Tagwähler (obs.) superstitious person who
chooses certain days for particular occupations or
abtains from some activities on others; this old
superstition, alive in antiquity among Jews and
Greeks, is mentioned in the Bible, e.g. Luther's
transl. Deuter. 18,10: 'das nicht unter dir funden
werde . . . ein tageweler', also in verse 14 (in A.V. in
both cases 'observer of times' is used), also Isaiah
2,6 (where the A.V. has 'soothsayer'); Kramer
[1702] recorded it as Tagewähler; Herder (quoted
by Campe) still used Tagewählerin.

tagen (1) (lit.) to become bright, shine; extension
from phys. 'to become daylight'; in lit. since
MHG, e.g. Minnes. Frühl. 130: 'sô tagt ez in dem
herzen min', Schiller, Tell 1,4: 'und hell in deiner
Nacht soll es dir tagen'; also with abstracts where
the notion 'to appear' is added to that of 'shining',
e.g. Gotter 1,431: 'die Ewigkeit vor meinen Blicken
tagt', Göckingk 2,204: 'eh die Vernunft in diesen
Köpfen tagt'; hence also es tagt ihm (or bei ihm) = 'it
becomes clear to him, he is beginning to understand', cf. Engl. 'it dawns on him', f.r.b. Campe
[1810]: 'es fängt an zu tagen in seinem Kopfe' (cf.

coll. es wird ~ bei ihm); in essence the same as es
leuchtet ihm ein (see p. 583).

tagen (2) to meet in conference, hold a meeting;
originally a legal term which could be used transitively for 'to summon sb. (to appear on a certain
day)' and intrans. for 'to hold a session'; current
since MHG, later also used for 'to negotiate,
confer' (e.g. H. Sachs 5,272); by the 18th c. used
for 'to meet for discussion', e.g. Schiller, Tell 2,2;
hence die Tagung = 'conference', in this sense only
since the 19th c.

tagen (3) (coll.) to have a party, have an
enjoyable time; e.g. wir tagten fröhlich bis an den
frühen Morgen; 20th c. coll.

mein Lebtag all my life; this can mean 'all my
past life', but also 'in my life to come', as in
Schiller, Räuber 4,3: 'das soll mir mein Tag des
Lebens eine Warnung sein' (where mein Lebtag could
also have been used); Lebtag for 'life, duration of
one's life' arose in Early NHG, also (since the 16th
c.) for 'all one's life, throughout one's life', f.r.b.
Maaler [1561], e.g. Weckherlin, 813; '. . . der
seinen lebtag nichts gethan'; frequent also in the
negative, e.g. Goethe, Götz 1 (Bisch.Pal.): 'das hab
ich mein Lebtag nicht gehört'.

sein Lebtag nicht . . . (coll.) never in a thousand
years; since the 17th c.; Kramer [1702] recorded:
'das ist sein lebtag kein gold'.

der unsinnige Pfinztag (regional coll.,a.) the last
Thursday before Easter, Maundy Thursday; Pfinztag for 'Thursday', derived from the Greek for
'five', was in general use in MHG, recorded by
Stieler [1691]; it is still alive in some Austro-Bav.
and Swiss dialects. The last Thursday before
Easter was called unsinnig (also fett), because
people indulged (excessively) in luxuries and pleasures which were forbidden from the next day
onward; Spindler, Vogelhändler 1,326 [1841] mentions der unsinnige Pfinztag as still current; now a.,
if not obs.

die Eintagsfliege (coll.) ephemeral phenomenon,
sth. that will not endure, also sb. enjoying temporary fame; in zool. sense = 'day-fly, ephemera';
figur. since the end of the 18th c., used by Jean
Paul, e.g. Dämm. 11 or Siebenk. 3,577; cf. similar
Tagesberühmtheit listed above.

kein ~ ohne Linie (prov.expr.) no day without a
line (having been written, drawn or composed); of
Classical origin (cf. Pliny 35,10,36), attributed to
the painter Apelles; sometimes quoted in its Lat.
form nulla dies sine linea, e.g. by Schiller in a letter
to Goethe.

ein jeder ~ hat seine Plag (prov.) every day brings
some kind of trouble; based on Matth. 6,34, in
Luther's transl. 'es ist gnug, das ein jglicher tag sein
eigen plage habe'; the prov. has been listed by
Henisch [1616] and Lehman [1640].

jeden ~ lernt man etw. Neues (prov.) you learn
sth. new every day; modern in this form, but there
are old prov. with nie auslernen or nie aufhören zu

lernen, e.g. Lehman, 496 [1640]: '*wer außgelehrt will seyn, der muß in Grab liegen*'; see also the prov. under *Kuh* (p. 1563).

oft ist ein ~ besser als ein ganzes Jahr (prov.) oft times one day is better than sometimes a whole year; in Engl. since the 15th c. (cf. *Oxf.* 130); in German at first usually as *ein ~ kann bringen, was ein Jahr nicht bringen mag* (or *weigert*), recorded for LG by Tunnicius, for HG by Petri [1605]: '*ein tag liehet wol, das ein gantz jahr wegert*', also in Lehman, 704 [1640].

wenn die Tage langen, dann kommt erst der Winter gegangen (prov.) as the day lengthens the cold strengthens; in Engl. since the 17th c., but in German apparently only recorded since the 19th c., e.g. by Simrock [1846].

← See also under *Abend* (for *noch nicht aller Tage Abend* and *man soll den Tag nicht vor dem Abend loben*), *all* (for *Alltagsmensch* and other compounds), *anbrechen* (for *der Tag bricht an*), *Aranjuez* (for *die schönen Tage von Aranjuez*), *betagt, beten* (for *ums tägliche Brot beten*), *blau* (for *blauen Montag machen*), *Brot* (for *das tägliche Brot* and *Tagesbrot*), *Damaskus* (for *seinen Tag von Damaskus erleben*), *Dieb* (for *Tagdieb*), *drei* (for *aussehen wie drei Tage Regenwetter* and *dreitägiger Gast ist eine Last*), *dunkel* (for *ein dunkler zerrissener Tag*), *erwachen* (for *der Tag erwacht*), *Feier* (for *zur Feier des Tages*), *Gesicht* (for *Feiertagsgesicht*), *gestern* (for *den gestrigen Tag suchen*), *Held* (for *der Held des Tages*), *heute* (for *heutigstägig*), *Hund* (for *Hundstage*), *Jahr* (for *seit Jahr und Tag*), *Jahrmarkt* (for *es ist nicht alle Tage Jahrmarkt*), *jung* (for *den jungen Tag ansingen*), *Kalender* (for *einen Tag rot im Kalender anstreichen*), *lang* (for *der lange Tag*), *Licht* (for *dem Tag ein Licht anzünden* and *des Tages verbergen sie sich*), *lieb* (for *den lieben langen Tag*), *Loch* (for *ein Loch in den Tag brennen/schlafen*), *Löwe* (for *der Löwe des Tages*), *Mittag, morgen* (for *morgen ist auch ein Tag*), *Nacht* (for *Tag und Nacht, über Tag und Nacht, die Nacht zum Tag machen* and *je dunkler die Nacht, je schöner der Tag*), *ordnen* (for *Tagesordnung*), *reiben* (for *tägliche Reibereien*), *Reihe* (for *nur nicht eine Reihe von schönen Tagen*), *Reise* (for *die Tagereise*), *Rom* (for *Rom ist nicht an einem Tag erbaut*), *Rose* (for *Rosentag*), *rot* (for *die Festtage rot gedruckt*), *schwarz* (for *der schwarze Tag*), *stehen* (for *soviel von etw. verstehen wie die Krähe vom Sonntag*), *Stich* (for *Stichtag*), *Topf* (for *täglicher Eintopf*), *Traum* (for *Tagtraum*), *Tür* (for *Tag der offenen Tür*) and *viel* (for *er redet viel, wenn der Tag lang ist*).

Taifun: typhoon

der ~ (polit.) typhoon, violent storm, stormy time; esp. in journalese and in polit. contexts; frequent since ca. 1950.

Taille: waist

jem.s Taillenweite prüfen (sl.) to embrace sb.; since ca. 1930.

per ~ gehen (regional coll.) to go (out) without an overcoat; in some regions, esp. Berlin.

das ist genau meine Taillenweite (sl.) that suits me to a t; since ca. 1940.

← See also under *Wespe* (for *Wespentaille*).

takeln: see *abgetakelt* and *auftakeln*.

Takt: time, measure, metre

der ~ (lit.) even rhythm, (life of) harmonious existence; since the 18th c., e.g. Moritz, *A.Reiser* (repr.) 50: '*auch das . . . Leben des Handwerksmannes hat seine Einschnitte und Perioden, wodurch ein gewisser Takt und Harmonie hineingebracht wird*' (Schiller, too, used ~ with ref. to 'harmony' in the mind).

nach ~ und Noten (coll.) thoroughly, properly, soundly; a ref. to strict adherence to prescribed metre; modern; see also under *Note* (p. 1793).

aus dem ~ kommen to be put out of one's stride; from mus. 'to be off-beat'; since the 18th c.; hence also *jem. aus dem ~ bringen* = 'to disconcert sb., put sb. out of his stride', and *sich nicht aus dem ~ bringen lassen* = 'to remain unperturbed, to go on steadily (in spite of diversions, interruptions, etc.)'; modern.

den ~ angeben to lead, dominate the proceedings; this arose later than *den Ton angeben*, for which see p. 41; *den ~ geben* in the mus. sense has been recorded since the 18th c.

jem.m den ~ schlagen (coll.) to thrash sb.; coll. (since 1st quarter of 20th c.).

ein paar Takte (coll.) a little; mainly with such verbs as *ausruhen, rasten, einhalten, warten*; since the 1st half of the 20th c.

ein paar Takte mit jem.m reden (coll.) to have a few serious words with sb. (by way of reproach, reprimand, not with ref. to friendly talk); 20th c. coll.

nicht taktfest (coll.) susceptible, of delicate health; e.g. *nicht takfest auf der Brust*, recorded by Heyne [1895]. The locution can also mean 'not firmly grounded, weak, shaky (with ref. to knowledge)' e.g. (S.-B.) *Dt.Bibl.* 4 [1770]: '*in Schlüssen ist der Verfasser wahrhaftig nicht taktfest*'.

← See also under *Auftakt* and *fest* (for *taktfest*).

Taktik: tactics

die ~ tactics; originally a mil. term, f.r.b. Sperander [1728]; later in the 18th c. used in extended sense for other kinds of planned procedure, e.g. Goethe-Schiller, *Briefw.* IV,306. Since the 20th c. (2nd half) also in numerous compounds, e.g. *Verschleppungstaktik* (also *Verzögerungstaktik*) = 'tactics of procrastination or delay' *Drucktaktik* = 'tactics of (applying) pressure'. Hence *Taktiker* and *taktisch*, in wider sense since early in the 20th c., also *taktieren* = 'to proceed tactically (or cleverly)'.

die ~ der verbrannten Erde scorched-earth policy; 20th c. mil. term for deliberate destruction when retreating from an area.

← See also under *Salami* (for *Salamitaktik*).

Tal: valley

das ~ (+ abstract) (lit.) valley, vale; ~ can be

treated as an area or place in a general sense divorced from its geogr. denotation, as can be *Feld* (see p. 757), *Gefilde* (see p. 940), *Grund* (see p. 1159) or *Reich* (see p. 1972); since MHG, e.g. Luther Bible transl. Psalm 23,4: '*ob ich schon wandert ym finstern tal*', Minnes. 3,29a: '*diu werlt ein sündig tal*'; after that in many locutions with abstracts, e.g. Gryphius, *Lyr.Ged.* 391: '*das elend hier im thal der thränen*', Klopstock, *Od.* 1,134: '*durch das dunkle Thal des Todes*', Tiedge, *Werke* 2,28: '*der Strom durchs Thal der Zeit*'. There are many compounds, e.g. '*in seiner Wollust Blumenthal*' (Klopstock), '*von einem irdischen Katzen-Jammerthal*' (Heine), *Dornen-, Erden-, Freuden-, Friedens-, Tränen-, Wonnetal* (in poetry since the 18th c.).

zu ~ (a.) down(wards); since OHG *ze tale* (cf. Graff 5,396), sometimes (since MHG) as *gegen thal*; e.g. *die Sonne geht zu* ~, as in Kinkel, *Ged.* 34,109 [1850]; cf. also *es geht mit ihm talab*, as recorded by Wander [1876] for 'he is sinking, approaching death' (cf. Engl. 'downhill' with ref. to state of health).

etw. ist in einem ~ sth. has sunk to a low level, dropped to a low point (e.g. on a graph); e.g. *die Kurswerte befinden sich in einem* ~; modern.

die Talfahrt (coll.) drop, ·decline, fall; ~ in its original sense (since the 19th c.) meant 'journey downwards (e.g. on a river)'; since the 20th c. used for 'downward journey on a mountain railway, ski-lift or on skis'; since ca. 1970, when Karl Schiller, the *Bundeswirtschaftsminister*, used or coined it with ref. to the fall of currencies, in general use now with ref. to the rapid decline in values (of shares, properties, etc.); later also in sport for the 'drop' of a team into the lower reaches of the results table.

die Talsohle ist erreicht the lowest point has been reached; often with ref. to economic conditions; 20th c.; see also p. 2270.

← See also under *Berg* (for *Berge ins Tal ziehen, je höher Berg, je tiefer Tal, Berg und Tal kommen nicht zusammen, aber Menschen* and *wer nicht auf den Berg kann, soll im Tal bleiben*), *Jammer* (for *Jammertal*) and *Sohle* (for *Talsohle*).

Talar: see *Staub*.

Talent: talent

das ~ talent, talented person; starting as a term for sth. of a certain weight (and monetary value) ~ came to describe a 'natural gift', first in Lat. form *talentum* (17th c.); only since the 18th c. applied to a person with talent (cf. analogous development of *Genie* and *Kopf*); e.g. Platen 3,347: '*manch großes Talent trat später hervor*'; frequent in Goethe who even combined the two meanings in one sentence: '*wer mit einem Talente zu einem Talente geboren ist*'.

nun steh ich da mit meinem ~ (coll.) now I'm flummoxed; ironic confession that all one's intelligence has proved of no avail; first in the farce *Berlin bei Nacht* by Kalisch [1850]. See also under *Hals* for similar *dann steh' ich da mit meinem gewaschenen Hals*.

Taler: taler, dollar

ein paar ~ (coll.) a small sum; ~ here not taken literally; general since the 18th c., but older since in prov. ~ often stands for 'money' (unspecified). Often also in diminutive *Tälerchen*.

der Kirchentaler (coll., obs.) small coin, penny; so called because it is considered to be only suitable for use in church to put into the offertory box; recorded since the 19th c., e.g. in *DWb.* [1873]. Now obs.

← See also under *hecken* (for *Hecketaler*) and under *Pfennig* (for *wer den Pfennig nicht ehrt, ist den Taler nicht wert* and *der ungerechte Pfennig verzehrt den gerechten Taler*).

Talk: tallow, suet

der ~ (also *Talg*) (regional coll.) stupid or immature fellow; since the 19th c. in some regions, e.g. Auerbach, *Ges.Schr.* 2,110; '*o du Talk! Geschieht dir recht*'; probably by comparison with 'senseless and unfeeling lump'. Hetzel [1896] recorded: '*talket = dumm, plump*'.

Talmi: pinchbeck

Talmi- ... false ... , fake ... , imitation- ... ; from ~ = 'pinchbeck, talmi gold', invented by the Frenchman Tallois, consisting of a mixture of copper and tin brushed over (under pressure) with gold, which was called *Tallois-demi-or*, in the trade *Tal.mi.or* which was shortened to ~; since ca. 1870. Soon used for things or persons which are 'false, impure, faked', e.g. (H.) *Grenzboten* 36 [1884]; '*gesegnet war Österreich von jeher mit echten und talmi-Edelleuten*'. Applied to shoddy goods since ca. 1900.

Tambour: *drum*

der ~ (a.) drummer; first as *Tambourer* (as suggested by Wolfr.v.Esch., *Parz.* 19,9, where *tamburr* occurs, assumed to stand for *tamburer*). The Persian term reached Germany via France. Of French origin are also the other meanings of ~, which denote 'drum-like' things, esp. the 'tambour-frame, embroidery ring', e.g. Wieland 10,168, and the protective wooden structure in front of doors of big buildings (e.g. cathedrals), used by Goethe in *Ital. Reise* (22.11.1786).

Tand: trifle, trash

der ~ (lit.) trash, junk; originally a comm. term derived from Lat. *tantum* (still alive in some regions) ~ became 'merchandise of little value', and as early as in the MHG period acquired a figur. meaning 'idle talk, nonsense', f.r.b. Maaler [1561]: '*alter weyber Tannt oder märe* ... *Tantmär = unnütz vnnd leychtfertigs geschwätz*', in Schottel [1663] for 'figment, imagined thing', e.g. Zwingli 2,4: '*so ich nicht meinen tand red, sondern Gottes wort*'; for this pejor. sense cf. also Schiller, *M. Stuart* 4,9: '*vom Tand der Erdengröße fern*' or *Picc.* 3,2: '*der Dienst, die Waffen sind nur eitler Tand*'. The lit. compounds *Erden-, Flitter-, Kindertand*, etc. are now little used.

tändeln to dally, trifle; sometimes in erotic

contexts = 'to flirt'; e.g. Schiller, *Kab.u.L.* 2,3: *'flatterhafte Pariserinnen tändelten mit dem furchtbaren Zepter'*, Hölty, 47 on a breeze: *'. . . tändelt durch das Thal'*. Frequent in compounds which all contain the notion of 'playful or wasteful frivolous activity', e.g. *durchtandeln* or *-tändeln*, as in Goethe, *Urworte.Orphisch*: *'es ist ein Tand und wird so durchgetandelt'*, *hintändeln*, as in Goethe, *Triumph d.Empfinds.* 4: *'hintändelnd ihre Jugend'*, *hinwegtändeln*, as in Wieland 5,153 (missing in *DWb.*), all rarely used now, but still in current use in *vertändeln* = 'to dissipate or lose through carelessness or frivolity', e.g. Goethe IV,3,258 (W.): *'ich vertändle viel von meinem Einkommen'*, Raabe, *Abu Telf.* 2,154: *'wir vertändelten unsere besten Gefühle'*, or = 'to waste', as in Wieland 3,75 (Acad.Edit.): *'. . . vertändelt ihr unbrauchbares Leben'* (also Schiller, *D.Carlos* 2,9 or Goethe, *Clavigo* 1). Adelung recorded an example of reflex. use: *'sich auf eine leichtsinnige und unbedachtsame Art zur Ehe versprechen'*.

Tandem: tandem
Tandem- . . . coupled, (operating) in tandem; with ref. to things which have two (or more) sources of energy with allusion to the 'tandem (-cycle)'; since the middle of the 20th c., e.g. *Süddt.Ztg.* (Dec. 1953): *'"Tandem-Verfahren", bei dem Windflügel, Pumpe und E-Motor ein geschlossenes Ganze bilden'*; also occasionally for 'couple of people who share responsibility or authority', in sl. for '(married) couple of actors', since ca. 1970.

Tangente: tangent
die ~ ring-road; a kind of bypass, called ~, because it 'touches' the outskirts of a conurbation; since the middle of the 20th c. in the jargon of town-planners.
Tangenten zu etw. haben (lit.) to have points of contact with sth.; since the 2nd half of the 20th c., e.g. (S.-B.) *Stuttgt.Ztg.* (1.2.1968): *'. . . Probleme . . . , die eindeutige Tangenten zur politischen Situation des Tages haben'*.
tangieren to touch, concern, affect; in figur. sense since the middle of the 19th c., e.g. (S.-B.) Fontane-Lipel, *Briefw.* 2,10 [1852]: *'. . . wird die wahre Bildung . . . von all dem modischen Plunder nicht tangiert'*, or *diese Bestimmung tangiert mich nicht* = 'this regulation does not affect me'.

Tango: tango
die Tangobeleuchtung (coll.) dim lighting; 20th c. coll.
ein Tangojüngling (coll.obs.) a dandy; also sometimes used for 'gigolo', or even 'spiv'; 20th c. coll.

Tank: tank
frische Luft tanken (coll.) to get a breath of fresh air; transfer from the language of motorists (cf. similar Engl. 'to recharge one's batteries'); also in *neue Kräfte tanken*, e.g. *Die Welt* (21/22.8.1988); hence also *seelisches Auftanken*. 20th c.
zuviel tanken (sl.) to drink too much, go over the limit; e.g. *heute hat er aber ganz gehörig getankt* =

'today he has had more than a few (drinks)'; 20th c. sl.; hence also *die Tankstelle* (joc.sl.) = 'pub' (since 1st half of 20th c.).

Tanne: fir
schlank wie eine ~ as slender as a young sapling; since the 18th c., e.g. Göckingk, *Lieb.* 108.
nach Tannenholz riechen (coll.,a.) to have one foot in the grave, be near death; recorded since the 19th c., e.g. by Wander [1876].
← See also under *Apfel* (for *Tannapfel*).

Tantalus: Tantalus
Tantalusqualen ausstehen (or *leiden*) to suffer like Tantalus, experience torments over sth. desired but unattainable; a ref. to ~, son of Zeus and the nymph Pluto who revealed the secrets of the gods to mankind and was flung into Hades where he stood in water which receded when he wanted to drink and had fruit above his head which moved out of reach when he stretched out for it; recorded since the 19th c., but probably older as suggested by Goethe's *'dieses tantalische Streben nach ewig fliehendem Genuß'* and the verb. *jem. tantalisieren* = 'to torment sb.', as used in Wieland 24,167. For the origin of the story of ~ see Homer, *Od.* 11,582–92.
das Tantal (also *Tantalum*) tantalum; a rare heavy element, found in 1802 by Ekeberg who named it after ~ (see entry above), because this element can stand in acid without being affected by it; f.r.b. Oken, *Allg. Naturgesch.* 1,122 [1833]. when H. Rose in 1840 looked for a name for another element which had been found in Bavaria, he called it *Niobium* after the daughter of ~, because the two elements are related in some respects.

Tante: aunt
die ~ (coll.) some woman, that female; used (vaguely and rather disrespectfully) when referring to a woman with whom one deals on an impersonal basis, e.g. *die* ~ *am Bankschalter war heute ganz freundlich* or *wann kommt die* ~ *wieder, die für das Rote Kreuz Geld sammelt?* 20th c. coll.
eine . . . -tante (coll.) a female addict to sth.; mainly in *Kaffeetante* = 'coffee addict' (cf. similar use of *Schwester* discussed on p. 2218) or *Spieltante* for a woman who is very fond of card games; modern coll.
~ *Klara* (col..) charwoman; a pun on *klar machen*; since early in the 20th c. The same pun is present when the Sun is jocularly referred to as ~ *Klara* (cf. *sonnenklar*, p. 2276); also current since the beginning of the 20th c.
~ *Rosa* (or *die rote* ~) (vulg.) period, menstruation; since early in the 20th c. Similarly, *die* ~ *aus Amerika zu Besuch haben* which dates from the same period.
der Tante-Emma-Laden (coll.) small shop which has not been modernised and is run by (elderly) people who do not wish to change; since the 2nd half of the 20th c.; also applied contemptuously to

other establishments which have not kept up with the times.

tantenhaft prudish, spinsterish, governess-like in behaviour; also sometimes for 'holding old-fashioned views' or for 'officious, fussy'; since the 18th c.; Goethe used it in *Dicht.u.Wahrh.* 1,3, Heine in *Reis.* 1,219, Gutzkow in *R.v.G.* 3,203; cf. also Holtei, *Nobl.* 1,67: '*in alttantenhafter Nachgiebigkeit*'; there is also *Tantenhaftigkeit* (rare), e.g. L. Diefenbach, *Nov.* 143 [1856]. The adjective *tantlich* is rare, but was used e.g. by Gotthelf, *Schuldenb.* 54.

meine ~, *deine* ~ lansquenet; a card game, formerly called *Landsknecht*, a term still used by Hauff in *Lichtenstein* 3,1, because it was popular among soldiers (current since the 16th c.), entered Engl. via French. In the game a pack of cards is turned over one by one between two single cards (placed face upwards), on which one can place bets, which are won when a turned-up card has the same value as the one on which one has put one's stake; recorded under its modern name since the 19th c., e.g. by Sanders [1865]; cf. Wander's quotation from *Bresl.Ztg.* 305 [1865] of Bismarck commenting on the take-over of Rechberg's office by Mensdorff: '*Rechberg oder Mensdorff, d.i. meine Tante, deine Tante*'.

die Kummerkastentante (coll.) the agony aunt; since the 2nd half of the 20th c.

dann nicht, liebe ~, *gehn wir zum* (or *heiraten wir den*) *Onkel* (joc.coll.) all right – let's forget about it, very well – if you don't want to, there's no more to be said about it; originated in Berlin (middle of 19th c.).

wenn die ~ *Räder hätte, wäre sie ein Omnibus* if my aunt had been a man, she'd be my uncle; used facetiously, when sb. makes inane suppositions 'if . . .' or 'if only . . .'; this arose earlier than stated by Küpper, who mentions 1900ff as the time of its first appearance. It was recorded by Wander [1876], who also listed variants, e.g. *wenn die* ~ *einen Pint* (= 'penis') *hätte, wäre sie mein Onkel*, or more delicately, *wenn die* ~ *ein Onkel wäre, hätte sie etwas mehr*. The Engl. version has been in print since 1813.

← See also under *Meier* (for *zu Tante Meier gehen*).

Tanz: dance

der ~ (1) (coll.) row, rumpus, fuss, to-do, quarrel; used for 'war, battle' since the 14th c. and still alive in coll. locutions, e.g. G. Keller, *Sinngedicht (Geisterseher)* on participation in fighting: '. . . *der . . . stürmte . . . mit seiner Muskete von Schlacht zu Schlacht, und erst auf Leipzigs Feldern kam ich zum Tanze*'; cf. Adelung' recording: '*mit an den Tanz müssen, figürlich, mit daran müssen*'; then (18th c.) in milder sense for 'dispute, argument', as in Lessing 10,170: '. . . *drei Sätze, um welche der Herr Pastor den Tanz mit mir angefangen*', also for domestic 'quarrel', e.g. Wagner, *Kindermörd.* (repr.)

28: '*wenn dein Vater . . . dich so . . . sieht, so geht der Tanz wieder von vornen an*'; also for 'disagreeable event, unpleasantness', e.g. Schiller, *Räuber* 3,2: '*genug dießmal für den Tanz dacht ich*' and *da haben wir den* ~ *!*, same as the locution with *Bescherung* (see p. 267), also used by Schiller.

der ~ (2) (lit.) dance; with ref. to rhythmic movements by objects since the Baroque, e.g. Weckherlin, 373: '*der sternen danz*', Schiller, *Räuber* 5,7: '*so manchen Tanz darf die Erde um die Sonne thun*' (cf. also Herder, *Krit.Wälder* 1,15); hence also ~ *der Planeten*; in frequent use with ref. to waves, clouds, leaves in the wind, even extended to abstracts, e.g. Lenau 1,62: '*der wilde Tanz der Zeit*'.

neue Tänze (coll., pejor.) newfangled notions, innovations (esp. such, of which one disapproves); since the 2nd half of the 19th c.

ein ~ *auf dem Vulkan* (cl.) a dance on the edge of a vulcano; taken over from French *nous dansons sur un volcan*, first said by Salvandy, French Ambassador in Naples, on June 5, 1830 commenting at a ball on the dangerous situation which led to the fall of the Bourbons in the July Revolution. The remark was taken up by the French press and soon acquired international currency (cf. Büchmann, *Gefl.Worte*).

tanzen (1) to dance; figur. when applied to objects and abstracts; since Early NHG, first with ref. to fate or luck, then to waves, sunbeams, stars, e.g. Lenz 1,97: '*ihr Sterne, die ihr fröhlich über meinem Schmerz daher tanzt*', Kotzebue, *DramSp.* 1,256: '*die Sphären tanzen und musicieren, und selbst die Sonne tanzt am Ostertage*' (cf. *Sphärentanz*, as used by Goethe 4,133 (W.)), also Göckingk, *Lieb.* 76: '*wie tanzt mein Herz vor Freuden!*', Wieland 14,195: '*neue Aussichten tanzten vor ihrer Stirn*', Platen 2,31; '*durch die Bäume tanzen Lichter rosenroth*'. When one's vision becomes blurred through excitement, things 'dance' before us, e.g. Uhland, *Ged.* 123: '*Allen tanzt es vor den Augen*' or (Sp.) Huch, *Pitt u. Fox* 244: '*die Buchstaben tanzten auf und nieder*'.

tanzen (2) to go, move (about); in locutions of various kinds, e.g. Wieland, *Luc.* 5,62: '*wir tanzen, wie das Sprichwort sagt, im Finstern*', Schiller, *Räuber* 2,3 (with allusion to *nach jem.s Pfeife tanzen*): '. . . *nach Kanonen-Musik zu tanzen*', Heyne [1895]: '*er muß ins Gefängnis tanzen*'. Frequent in compounds, e.g. *antanzen* (coll.) = 'to come, appear', as in *er soll morgen in meiner Sprechstunde antanzen, auftanzen* = 'to flicker or spurt upwards', esp. with ref. to flames, e.g. W. Humboldt 3,36: '*hebt sich . . . auftanzend die lodernde Flamme*' (similarly in Bürger, 60a with *emportanzen*), *herabtanzen* (coll.) = 'to come down', as in Schiller, *Räuber* 2,3: '*der Kutscher . . . mußte vom Bock herabtanzen*', *hintanzen*, as in Gerstäcker, *Flatb.* 150: '*das Kanoe tanzte nur so über das Wasser hin*'. – Goethe, when quoting Lat. *hic Rhodus, hic salta* = 'show what you can do' (from Aesop, *Fable* 203) in German, put *'hier ist Rhodus, tanze!'* where *springen* is the preferred verb.

sich um etw. tanzen (obs.) to forfeit or lose sth. (through carelessness, etc.); 18th c., e.g. Kosegarten, *D.* 3,61, also Wieland 5,188; now obs.

er läßt sich auf dem Kopf (herum) tanzen (coll.) he lets people get away with too much, is too lenient or tolerant; cf. the similar phrase with *Nase* (p. 1762).

vom ~ zum Rosenkranz gehen (regional coll.) to leave worldly pleasures abruptly and turn to religion; in some (mainly Catholic) regions.

Tanzbeine haben (coll.) to be a good (or passionate) dancer; since the middle of the 19th c.

der Tanzboden (mil.sl.) exercize (or parade) ground; since the thirties of the 20th c.

die Tanzplatte (sl.) bald head; since early in the 20th c.

← See also under *Affe* (for *Affentanz*), *anbrausen* (for *angetanzt kommen*), *Bär* (for *Tanzbär*), *Bein* (for *das Tanzbein schwingen*), *Ei* (for *Eiertanz*), *Esel* (for *wenn's dem Esel zu wohl ist, geht er aufs Eis tanzen*), *essen* (for *vor Essens wird kein Tanz*), *Gold* (for *Tanz um das goldene Kalb*), *Hexe* (for *Hexentanz*), *Hochzeit* (for *man kann nicht auf allen Hochzeiten tanzen*), *Nase* (for *ich lasse mir nicht auf der Nase tanzen*), *Not* (for *Not lehrt ein alt Weib tanzen*), *Pfeife* (for *nach jem.s Pfeife tanzen*), *Reihe* (for *aus der Reihe tanzen*), *Schuhe* (for *es gehört mehr zum Tanz als ein paar Schuhe*), *Seil* (for *auf dem Seil tanzen, den Seiltänzer springen lehren, Tanzseil, Seiltanz* and derivatives), *Veit* (for *Veitstanz*) and *Wut* (for *Tanzwut*).

Tapet: carpet

etw. aufs ~ bringen to bring a subject up; cf. Engl. 'on the carpet'; also used with *kommen* and *sein*; since the 17th c., e.g. Stieler, *Zeitungsl.* 315 [1697], Lessing 1,275, Wieland 1,190, Schiller, *Räuber* 1,2: *'wie wär's, wenn wir . . . das Königreich wieder aufs Tapet brächten?'*; more recent is *das steht nicht auf dem ~* = 'that is not the point at issue'. See also under *Tablett* and *Trapez* for modern corrupt forms of this idiom.

als Tapete dienen (coll.) to be a wallflower, find no dancing partner; sometimes in the form *die Wand tapezieren*; also used for 'to be a silent witness (or an actor with a non-speaking part)'; modern.

die Tapeten wechseln (coll.) to have a change of scenery or surroundings, move to another place (i.e. new house or different place of work); since ca. 1960, also in the noun *Tapetenwechsel* = 'change of surroundings'; hence also *andere Tapeten sehen wollen* (coll.).

die Tapetenflunder (sl.) bed-bug; modern sl.

etw. mit etw. tapezieren to adorn or decorate sth. with sth. else; since the 18th c., e.g. Schiller, *Kab.u.L.* 2,1: *'soll ich meine Zimmer mit diesem Volk tapezieren?'*; *austapezieren* is also used, e.g.

G. Keller, *Seldw.* 2,282: *'das Gebäude seiner Rede tapezierte er schließlich mit tausend Verslein . . . aus'*.

Tapfe: footprint

in jem.s Tapfen wandeln (lit.,obs.) to follow in sb.'s footsteps; obs., since the locution with *Fußstapfen* (see p. 893) proved stronger; cf. Goethe, *Iphig.* 2,1 [1781]: *'die Tapfen unsrer Anherrn neben uns'*, which he changed six years later to *'der Ahnherrn Tritte'*.

tapfer: compact, massive, stocky

tapfer (adv.,coll.) thoroughly, properly, amply, very much; sometimes coming close to Engl. 'bravely'. The phys. meanings led to figur. 'considerable, valuable, weighty' in Early NHG, as in Luther 6,383a (Jena): *'tapfere, klare sprüche der heiligen schrift'* (now obs.), then adverbially for 'properly, very much' since Early NHG, influenced by Lat. *fortiter*, as in Luther's *'tapfer sündigen'* for *fortiter peccare*, f.r.b. Maaler [1561]: *'dapfer und redlich liegen = ampliter mentire'*, Goethe, *Faust I*, 3577: *'wie konnt' ich sonst so tapfer schmälen'*, Freytag, *Erinn.* 236: *'ich habe . . . tapfer darüber geschrieben'*; still in *er hat sich ~ geschlagen* = 'he gave a good account of himself', *greif ~ zu!* = 'help yourself properly!'; often with the notion of rapidity, current since the 17th c., recorded by Kramer [1702]: *'komm tapfer! = vieni presto!'*, e.g. (DWb) Pauli, 107b: *'. . . so ich dapfer fahr'* or Auerbach, *Ges.Schr.* 1,452: *'hernach muß ich tapfer machen* [= 'hurry up'], *daß ich wieder heim komm'*.

Tappe: paw

laß deine Tappen weg! (coll.) don't touch it! keep your fingers off it!; transfer from animal to human contexts; cf. coll. *tappen* = 'to grope, paw', since Early NHG, e.g. S. Franck, 51: *'weder vom wein noch vom tappen der weiber sich enthalten'*, *Tapper* = 'groper', *Tapperei* = 'groping' and *tappig* = 'fond (or in the habit) of pawing people', for which Kramer [1702] recorded *zutäppisch*.

tappen to walk unsteadily, move about clumsily, fumble, grope (for sth. to hold on to); here the clumsiness of an animal's paw is referred to; since Early NHG, e.g. Luther Bible transl. Isaiah 59,10: *'wir tappen als die keine augen haben'*, and at the same time in figur. use, e.g. Luther 6,517a (Jena): *'die blinde vernunft tappet in gottes sachen'*, Goethe, *Das Göttliche* 26: *'auch so das Glück tappt unter die Menge'*, Lessing 10,222: *'die tappende Neugier der Sterblichen'*, Fichte 8,366: *'das Phantasieren . . . ist ein blindes Tappen, dessen Grund dem Tapper ewig verborgen bleibt'* (cf. also Fichte 7,402: *'ein blindes empirisches Zutappen'*); frequent in compounds. Kramer [1702] recorded *'hinan-, hinauf-, hinaus-, hineintappen etc.'*, also the unusual *fehltappen*, but the most frequently used compound is *herumtappen* (missing in *DWb*.), e.g. Wieland 24,125 (Goethe to Zelter 6,115 has *'die liebe Jugend tastet und tappt umher'*); also usual is *in eine Falle hineintappen* (used by Goethe), less usual is *nachtappen* = 'to limp behind'. The noun *Tapp(e)s* = 'clumsy person' is coll. (but occurs in Heine's and Immermann's writings), but the adjective *täppisch* (sometimes *tappig*, *täppig*, formerly *tappicht*) = 'clumsy' has been current since Early NHG, f.r.b. Stieler [1691]; *tappeln* = 'to walk clumsily, stagger', current since Early NHG, survives only in some regions.

sich vertappen (obs.) to misappropriate, steal sth.; e.g. (Sa.) Rank, *Schön Minnele* 39 [1853]: '*da vertappte sich seine Hand im Haufen Gold*'; probably rare even then, since unrecorded in Adelung and Campe; now obs., displaced by *sich (an etw.) vergreifen*.

← See also under *blind* (for *im Blinden tappen*), *ertappen* and *finster* (for *im Finstern tappen*).

Tarantel: tarantula
aufspringen wie von einer ~ gestochen to jump up as if bitten (or stung) by sth.; cf. French *être piqué de la tarentule*; recorded by Heyne [1895], e.g. C.F. Meyer, *J. Jen.* 260, but probably current since at least the 18th c., as indicated by many allusions to it by Jean Paul (e.g. *Hesp.* 2,91).

Tarif: tariff, rate
das kann man nicht zum Nulltariff haben (coll.) that cannot be had for nothing, that has to be paid for; originally applied to free fare on public transport, then extended to other areas; 20th c. coll.

tarnen: hide
etw. ~ to hide, screen, mask, cover up sth.; *~* = 'to hide' is old (cf. *Tarnkappe*, which was fully established in MHG, e.g. *Nibelungenl.* 97 and came to be understood again when mediaeval epics were republished in the 18th c.), but the verb fell into disuse and was only revived when a German alternative was required for *camouflieren* (mil.), taken over from French *camouflage*. After World War I Karl Ammon suggested ~ [1921] (cf. *Muttersprache* 44,331 [1929], 50,418 [1935] and 51,315 [1936], but even in 1935 the *DWb.* did not yet list the term. The noun *Tarnung* followed, and in the 2nd half of the 20th c. compounds established themselves, e.g. *Tarnorganisation* = 'cover organisation (which hides the true aims of its originators)' or *Tarnscheinwerfer* (tech.) = 'masked headlight'. Hence now also *enttarnen* = 'to reveal the true nature of sth., bring out what sb. has tried to hide'.

Tartuffe
ein ~ (lit.) a hypocrite; allusion to Molière's play of that name [1664]; now usually spelt *Tartüff*; hence also *Tartüfferie* = 'hypocrisy'. In Engl. both terms were also taken over, soon after the appearance of the play.

Tarzan
der ~ (coll.) heavy lorry with a mounted crane; a ref. to ~ in the books by Edgar Rice Burroughs (on the world market since 1914) and their film versions; since the thirties of the 20th c. At the same time a very strong and hairy man came to be called in joc.coll. *ein ~*.

Tasche: bag; pocket
die ~ (1) (vulg. or regional coll.) woman, wench; here the development follows the same route as in several other cases where an object becomes the name for a part of an animal body, is then transferred to the human body and lastly extended to a person (see similar cases discussed under *Maus, Muschel* – where due to a printer's error the head word *Muschel* in the middle of the left-hand column of p. 1725 has been omitted –, *Pflaume, Schwanz*, also as a partial parallel *Fotze* and *Maul*). In the case of ~, the meaning 'vulva (of an animal)' became 'human vulva', e.g. *Fast.Sp.* 729 and 756, and then 'woman'. The last stage was reached as early as in MHG, e.g. Oswald v. Wolkenstein, 46: '*get, ir faule tasch! die schüssel wasch!*', also in compounds such as *lüppertesche* = 'sorceress' (cf. Lexer 1990), *klappertesche* and *vlattertasche*. Later examples are *Plappertasche* and *Plaudertasche*, both recorded by Stieler [1691]. There is also *Taschenmacher* (Bav.) = 'father of daughters (and no sons)', recorded by Schmeller. Frisch [1741] has *Maultasche*, which he glossed: '*die lezte Erbin der Grafschafft Tyrol, wegen der großen Lippen*'. He also recorded: '*Tasche, Täsche, Täschel = vulva, im Oberrheinischen Ländern, als zu Straßburg etc.*'. This is still true in Alemannic areas, and Gotthelf frequently used *Täsche* or *Tätsch*.

die ~ (2) purse, money; in many idioms, e.g. *jem.m auf der ~ liegen* (coll.) = 'to live off sb.', used esp. with ref. to young people who are supported by their parents, e.g. *er liegt seinen Eltern noch immer auf der ~*, *aus der eignen ~ etw. bezahlen* = 'to pay for sth. out of one's own pocket', since the 19th c., e.g. Bismarck, *Reden* 1,139: '*diese Servitutberechtigungen . . . aus seiner Tasche abzufinden*', *in die eigne ~ arbeiten* (coll.) = 'to line one's own pocket' (1st half 20th c.), *sich in die eigne ~ lügen* (coll.) = 'to fool oneself' (1st half 20th c.), *die Taschen fegen* (cant) = 'to pick pockets, steal', in cant since early in the 19th c. (cf. *jem.m den Beutel fegen* on p. 748, and *jem.s ~ leeren* also exists); *die Taschen nach links drehen* (sl.) = 'to show that one has no money' (since early in the 20th c.), *jem.m in die ~ arbeiten* (coll.) = 'to help sb. to line his pockets, assist sb. to make a secret or illegal profit' (20th c.), *die Hand auf der ~ halten* (coll.) = 'to be miserly, reluctant to pay' (20th c.), *sich die Taschen füllen lassen* (coll.) = 'to take as much as one can get, allow oneself to be bribed' (20th c.), *sie hat ihn lieb auf der Seite, wo seine ~ hängt* (prov.expr.) = 'she loves him for his money, is affectionate as long as he is generous to her', recorded by Simrock [1846]; frequent also in coll. or sl. in idioms which describe sb.'s attitude towards money, e.g. *große* (or *weite*) *Taschen haben* = 'to expect presents or bribes' (19th c.), *offene* (or *weite*) *Taschen haben* = 'to be venal, bribable' (since the middle of the 19th c.), *zugenähte Taschen haben* = 'to be miserly (20th c. sl., but with *zugeknöpft* much older, e.g. Goethe 2,292 (W.): '*Mann mit zugeknöpften Taschen* . . .'; cf. *den Knopf auf dem Beutel haben* on p. 1506.

die ~ (3) pocket; in various idioms describing a.) deception by slight of hand as practiced by *Taschenspieler*, f.r.b. Stieler [1691]: '*aus der Tasche spielen*', e.g. Olearius, *Pers.Reis.* 4,32: '*Gaukler, die aus der Taschen spielten*'; hence *Taschenspieler* (also recorded by Stieler); cf. Goethe, *Faust* 2267: '*ach das sind Taschenspielersachen*', b.) 'possession', e.g. *er hat es schon in der* ~ = 'he has it in his pocket, it (i.e. the appointment, title, pass in an examination, etc.) is already his', e.g. Börne 2,333: '. . . *hat gut fragen, wer die Antwort schon in der Tasche trägt*', c.) 'domination', e.g. *jem. in der* ~ *haben*, as in Gutzkow, *Blasedow* 1,228.

die ~ (4) (coll. or vulg.) mouth; at least since the 17th c. when Stieler recorded: '*einem eins auf die Tasche geben = colaphum alicui infringere*', e.g. Gryphius, *P.Squentz* (repr.) 22: '*so werd ich euch schlagen auff die Taschen*'; Adelung recorded it as '*eine nur in den niedrigen Sprecharten im verächtlichen Verstande übliche Bedeutung: Halt die Tasche!*'.

die ~ (5) pocket, bag, pouch; with ref. to sth. which encloses sth. else so that it appears tucked away as if in a bag; mainly in compounds, e.g. *Bruttasche* (zool.) ~ 'nidamental bag' (19th c.) *Öltasche* ~ 'oil pocket' (in the crust of the earth) (20th c.); in cookery for slits in meat into which some stuffing is put; see also *Maultasche* (1) below.

die ~ (6) (vulg.) the behind; euphem. substitute for *Arsch*; mainly in *leck mich in der* ~ ! (cf. entries under *einladen* and *lecken*). Recordings or printed instances are difficult to find, but Röhrich, *Sprichw. Redens.* 1059 [1973] has listed it as well as the similar phrase *er kann mir in die* ~ *steigen*.

eine Faust in der ~ *machen* to fume inwardly; cf. the entry under *Faust* (p. 741); cf. also Freytag, *Ges.W.* 11,283: '*wir haben lange genug die Fäuste in der Tasche gehabt*'.

etw. kennen wie seine eigne ~ (or *Westentasche*) to know sth. inside out; cf. French *connaître quelque chose comme sa poche*; since the 19th c., e.g. Hackländer, *Dunkle Stunde* 1,45 [1863] or Keller, *Nachlaß* 47: '. . . *der die Schweiz wie seine eigene Tasche gekannt*'.

er hat das Maul nicht in der ~ (coll.) he is not tongue-tied, stuck for a reply, knows how to speak up for himself; recorded since the 19th c., e.g. Auerbach, *Ges.Schr.* 1,180.

faß mal einem nackten Mann in die ~ (sl.) it is stupid to expect anything from sb. who has nothing; originally a Berlin phrase, but then general (cf. the old prov. on p. 1747: *der Nackte ist schlecht zu berauben*).

ohne ~ *baden* (sl.) to bathe in the nude; in sl. since the middle of the 20th c.

etw. in die ~ *stecken* (coll.) to give sth. up, set sth. aside; the usual meanings of this phrase have been given on p. 2340; since the 19th c., however,

also in another sense of 'pocketing', e.g. Mommsen, *Auch e.W.* 18 with ref. to leaving his title out of account: '*dann stecke ich den Professor in die Tasche* . . .'.

er hat einen toten Vogel in der ~ (coll.) he stinks; modern.

. . . *im* (or *in*) *Taschenformat* (coll.) pocket-size . . . , . . . in miniature; a ref. to books which fit a pocket (e.g. Lessing 7,490), but since the 18th c. also figur., e.g. Claudius 5,52 on a church: '*sie ist nicht so in Taschenformat, wie die Kirchlein, die bei euch . . . stehen*', Wassermann, *Maurizius* 140: '. . . *daß sie den damals Vierzehnjährigen den Sherlock Holmes in Taschenformat nannten*'; intensified as *im Westentaschenformat*, e.g. (Duden) *ein Politiker im Westentaschenformat*.

das Taschengeld pocket money; since the 18th c., e.g. Schiller, *Räuber* 1,1: '*ein hübsches Taschengeld*' (ironic); metaph. in Goethe, *Br.* 167 (W.): '*wenn sie [i.e. Lotte] auch die Taschengelder ihrer Empfindung . . . nicht an mich wenden wollte*'. Often in belittling remarks such as *nur ein Taschengeld* = 'a trifling sum, a mere bagatelle'.

die Taschenmäuse (sl.) fluff in one's pocket; 20th c. sl.

zusammenklappen wie ein Taschenmesser (coll.) to go to pieces, collapse, pass out; since the 17th c., e.g. Philander, *Lugd.* 3,81 (with *zusammenfallen*).

zutunlich wie ein Taschenmesser (coll.) very amenable, easy to get on with; a pun with *zutun* (coll.) = 'to close' and *zutunlich* = 'amenable', here joc. taken as 'closable'; recorded since the 19th c. For another pun with *Taschenmesser* see under *Messer*.

ich muß mir einen Knoten ins Taschentuch machen (coll.) I must try to remember that; though this can sometimes be used in its phys. sense by making a knot in one's handkerchief as an *aide-mémoire*, it can occur figur.

der Taschenkrebs (zool.) the common crab (*Cancer pagurus*); so called because of its purse-like shape; recorded since the 18th c., e.g. by Frisch [1741].

die Maultasche (1) filled pastry square; recorded since the 19th c.; cf. *Mundtasche* for '*gefülltes Gebäck aus Blätterteig*' in Scheibler, *Kochb.* 441 [1855].

die Maultasche (2) (coll.) gossip, garrulous person; recorded by Campe [1809] and equated with *Plaudertasche*.

← See also under *Tatsch* for another meaning of *Maultasche*.

die Meertasche (zool.) a jellyfish; recorded by Campe [1809] for *Medusa marsupialis*; because of purse-like appearance.

die Pilgertasche nehmen (lit.,a.) to become a pilgrim; used in this sense by Schiller, but then also to be found in wider sense of going on a walking-tour.

die Schmiertasche (coll., obs.) flatterer; recorded by Campe [1810] as used for *Schmeichler* in some LG regions.

← See also under *Auge* (for *die Augen in der Tasche haben*), *blind* (for *blinde Tasche* and *er trägt lauter blinde Taschen am Rock*), *einstecken* (for *in die Tasche stecken*), *füllen* (for *sich die Taschen füllen*), *greifen* (for *tief in die Tasche greifen*), *Messer* (for *einschnappen wie ein Taschenmesser*), *plaudern* (for *Plaudertasche*), *Spiel* (for *Taschenspiel* and derivatives) and *stecken* (for *etw. in die eigne Tasche stecken* and *die Hände in die Tasche stecken*).

Tasse: cup

die ~ (sl.) person; always with a pejorative adjective, e.g. *dämliche, müde, trübe* ~; first in mil.sl. (1st quarter of the 20th c.), then (since middle of the c.) in general sl.

er hat nicht alle Tassen im Schrank or *Spind* (sl.) he is not quite right in the head; this arose through ~ (sl.) = 'skull', current in sl. since the twenties of the 20th c., cf. also synon. *seine* ~ *hat einen Sprung* (sl.) and the similar *er hat nicht alle im Koffer* (20th c. sl.).

hoch die Tassen! (sl.) cheers! bottoms up! first in Berlin (ca. 1920), then general, often with joc. addition *in Afrika ist Muttertag*.

tasten: feel, grope

tasten to probe, grope; 18th c., very frequent in Goethe, e.g. to Zelter, 769: '*die liebe Jugend tastet und tappt umher . . .* ', *Wanderj.* 3,14: '*ängstlich tastendes Versuchen*', Gutzkow, *R.v.G.* 9,498: '*. . . daß Dieser Das sicher besaß, was tastend er selber suchte*'; hence in compounds, esp. *herumtasten*, e.g. Goethe, *Wanderj.*2,9: '*der Bauende soll nicht herumtasten und versuchen*'.

tastbar (rare) palpable, tangible; since the 18th c., e.g. Herder, *Plastik* 1,3: '*tastbare Wahrheit*', hence also *bis zur Tastbarkeit wahr* (19th c.); now rare, but the negative *unantastbar* = 'irreproachable, inviolable' has been in frequent use since the 18th c., f.r.b. Campe [1810], e.g. Goethe 41,2,115 (W.)

(mächtig) in die Tasten greifen (sl.) to show off, give oneself airs; derived from the activity of a pianist; since early in the 20th c.

die Tastatur (sl.) nervous system; since the middle of the 20th c.; hence *jem.m auf die Tastatur fallen* (sl.) = 'to get on sb.'s nerves'. In obscene use there is *Tastatur* = 'vulva' (middle of the 20th c.).

der Tastenlöwe (coll., obs.) Franz Liszt; term of admiration for the pianist and composer in use in the 19th c.; see also Heine's remarks quoted on p. 1635.

← See also under *antasten, betasten, blind* (for *ein Blinder hätte es mit den Händen tasten köhnnen*), *durchtanzen* (for *sich durchtasten*) and *ertasten*.

Tat: action, activity

die ~ (personified, lit., rare) the deed, action; occasionally in lit. since the 18th c., e.g. *die* ~ *ist stumm*, as in Schiller, *Wall.Lager* 6, or (a marginal case) *die werdende* ~ in Klopstock, *Od.* 1,92; cf. also Langbein, *Ged*, 1,128 [1854]: '*ihn umschirmt sein Thatenchor*' or Klopstock, *Od.* 1,219: '*tatenumgeben*'.

den (guten) Willen für die ~ *annehmen* to take the (good) intention for the deed; since Early NHG, e.g. Waldis, *Es.* 41,74: '*er nam den willen für die that*', in similar phrasing in Lessing (letter of 1778).

ein Mann der ~ a man of action; at least since the 18th c., also in compounds as *Tatmensch*, in Jean Paul, *Nachdämm.* 107 as '*Thatenmensch*'; Goethe used '*Thatmann*', e.g. in *Noten z. Diwan* (*Israel i.d.Wüste*).

in der ~ indeed; gradual change from 'in (or through) the (phys.) deed', as in Early NHG, e.g. H. Sachs 13,62: '*das solt du in der that erfaren*', then (as in Engl.) as a formula of confirmation or emphatic statement, established by the 18th c., e.g. Lessing, *Em.Gal.* 1,4.

tat- . . . or *taten-* . . . (lit.) . . . in (or for) deeds or action; in some compounds several of which have a figur. component, e.g. *tatenarm* = 'with no accomplishments or deeds to its name', as in Treitschke 1,520, *Tatendrang* (also *Tätigkeitsdrang*) = 'eagerness for action' (also since the 19th c. and used by Treitschke). Others, all dating from the 19th c., are *Tatenlust, Tatenscheu* (also *tatenscheu*) and *Tatsucht* (= *Tatendrang*), used by Heine. A special case is *es ist tatkundig* (regional coll.) = 'it is a well-known fact (that) . . .', since the 18th c. current in the S., recorded by Heynatz, probably obs. by now.

Tatsache a matter of fact; loan transl. of the Engl. phrase (which itself was a loan from Lat. *res facti*), current since the 18th c., first used by J.J. Spalding [1756] according to Heynatz, as stated by Lessing 11,645. Although Goethe, Wieland, Schiller and Kant used *Tatsache*, Adelung rejected it as '*unschicklich*'; Campe [1810] set his objections aside; hence *tatsächlich*, f.r.b. Heynatz 2,467, used now both for 'indeed' and 'in reality'.

nach der ~ *weiß jeder guten Rat* (prov.) if things were to be done twice, all would be wise; cf. French *après coup tout le monde sait être sage*; for Engl. recorded since the 17th c.; earlier in German, e.g. Franck [1541]: '*nach der that wer findt nit rath?*'; in modern form since the 19th c., recorded e.g. by Eiselein [1838].

← See also under *Durst* (for *Tatendurst*), *Fluch* (for *Fluch der bösen Tat*), *frisch* (for *auf frischer Tat*), *nackt* (for *die nackte Tatsache*), *Rat* (for *mit Rat und Tat*) and *retten* (for *die rettende Tat*).

Tatar: Tartar

die Tatarennachricht false report; also used for 'scare story'; derived from the fact that a Tartar in September 1854 sent a report to newspapers in Bukarest asserting that Sewastopol on the Crimea had been taken by British and French forces (but S. was only taken in September 1855); this led to the compound; e.l. of 1865 in Wander [1876].

das Tatarbeefsteak steak tartare, raw minced steak; the Tartars are said to have prepared their meat by placing the raw meat under the saddle; 19th c.

die Tatarsoße sauce tartare; a slightly modified loan from French *sauce tartare*; 19th c.

tattern: tremble

den Tatterich (regionally *Datterich*) *haben* (coll.) to have shaky hands; mainly with ref. to trembling fingers due to intoxication, but also when trembling with cold; from ~ = 'to tremble', current since Early NHG; e.g. (Kl.-St.) Fallada, *Wolf* 1,380: '*vom Saufen hab ich doch noch nie 'nen Tatterich gekriegt*'. The drunkard in E.E. Niebergall's comedy in Darmstadt dialect [1841] is called *Der Datterich*.

ein Tatterich (regional coll.) a (shaky) old man; in the 19th c. recorded as *(alter) Tatter* or *Tatterer* or *Tattergreis*, now mainly as *Tatterich* (20th c.).

Tattersall

das ~ riding school, manege; also used for firms which organise auctions and events associated with equestrian sports; named after the horseman Richard Tattersall (1724–1795) whose equestrian school and auction rooms existed in London from 1773 to 1936; the German term established itself in the 19th c.

Tatze: paw

die ~ (1) (coll.) (strong or brutal) hand; cf. Engl. coll. 'paw'; since MHG; Goethe 27,87 (W.) used it: '*Gottsched . . . gab mit seiner Tatze dem armen Menschen eine Ohrfeige*', Wieland 18,88 (with ref. to a hermit): '*. . . bekreuzigt sich mit beiden Tatzen*', Weiße, *Kom.Op.* 3,137: '*kein schwarzer Mann kneipt uns mit rauhen Tatzen*'; now only in occasional (sometimes joc.) coll. use; cf. also Heine 19,180: '*die liebefrommen Tätzchen*' (ironic).

die ~ (2) (regional coll.) slap on the hand (e.g. with a ruler); since the 19th c., e.g. Spindler, *V.* 1,319 or Auerbach, *Barf.* 4.

← See also under *Bär* (for *Bärentatzen*).

Tau (1)

der ~ (1) (lit.) dew; since MHG figur. in several contexts, e.g. '*der minne tou*' in Konr.v.Würzb., *Engelh.* 3263, often with ref. to divine grace, e.g. Keisersberg, *Pred.* 76b: '*der himelische taw der gnaden*', but also with ref. to other blessings, e.g. (DWb) Logau 2, *Zugabe* 201: '*des friedens thaw feuchtet wieder unser aw*', F. Schlegel, *Ged.* 81: '*wenn süßer Rede Thau uns netzet milde*', Fallmerayer, *Fr.a.d.Or.* 2,49 [1845]: '*wo die . . . Gottesfurcht der . . . Zaren den Thau ihres Geldes über alle Konvente . . . niederträufeln läßt*'; sometimes with the added notion of sweetness, as in *Honigtau*, current since the Baroque. There are numerous poet. comparisons, e.g. biblical instances, such as Deuter. 32,2: '*meine rede fließe wie thaw*', Psalm 110,3: '*deine kinder werden dir geborn wie der thaw aus der morgenröte*' (in Luther's version, rendered quite differently in the A.V.), Hosea 14,6: '*ich wil Israel wie ein thaw sein*'.

der ~ (2) (lit.) liquid; with ref. to wine (or nectar), also water, at least since the 18th c., e.g. Wieland 20,94: '*saugt . . . den süßen Thau des Zauberbechers ein*'; Schiller used '*des Nektars . . .*

Thau'; for 'water' in F. Schlegel, *Jon* 5 [1803]: '*Castiliens silberklarer Thau . . . am Felsenborn geschöpft*'.

der ~ *der Augen* (lit.) tears; since MHG, e.g. Wolfr.v.E., *Willehalm* 268: '*. . . mit dem herzen touwe, der ûzer brust durch d'ougen vloz*', Goethe, *Tasso* 2,1: '*. . . trocknete dein Blick den Thau von meinen Augenlidern ab*', (Sp.) Zschokke, *Alamontade* 1,9: '*In Roderichs Augen funkelte der Thau einer Thräne*'. There are several compounds such as *Augentau* (but in MHG *ougen saf* or *ougen regen*), *Tränentau* (since the Baroque), *Zährentau*, e.g. Matthisson, *Schr.* 1,41 [1825] and *Tautropfen*, e.g. Thümmel, *Reise* 7,381 [1802]: '*. . . ein Thautropfen, der . . . aus den Augen . . . herab fiel*'; cf. also *Freudentau* = 'tears of joy', as in Körner 2,132.

der rote ~ (lit.) blood; since MHG, e.g. Konr.v. Würzb., *Troj.Kr.* 23333: '*. . . geroetet vil gar mit bluotes touwe*'; cf. also *roter Saft* on p. 2043.

vor ~ *und Tag* very early in the morning; old in dialects of the N., in lit. (mainly N. authors) since the 19th c., e.g. Reuter or P. Heyse.

taufrisch fresh as dew, dewy; since the 19th c. (still missing in Campe [1810]); the negative *nicht (ganz) taufrisch* can be used now in a coll. euphemism for 'stale' or 'rather old'.

ein Tautropfen (lit.) a tiny drop; e.g. Schiller, *Kab.u.L.* 1,3: '*dieser kurze Thautropfe Zeit*'.

das Tauwetter (lit.) time of thaw, gentle climate (after harsh conditions); figur. since the 18th c., e.g. (DWb) Börne 2,81: '*das Thauwetter ihrer warmen Stimme . . .*'. Now also in polit. or econ. contexts.

tauen (1) (poet.) to send sth. (abstract) into (or onto) sb.; since the Baroque, e.g. J.E. Schlegel, *Ästh.u.dram.Schr.* (repr.) 73: '*der vom Himmel thauende Honig des Schlummers*', Hippel 7,144: '*Gott ließ Fassung auf deine Seele thauen*'; hence also since the Baroque for 'to flow, run', also as *herniedertauen*, as in W.v. Humboldt, *Sonette* 234: '*. . . hernieder aus der Liebe goldner Schaale . . . Perlen thauen*'.

tauen (2) (lit.) to shed tears; cf. ~ *der Augen*; in lit. use since the 18th c., e.g. Uz 2,20: '*erröthend thauten ihr die Wangen*'; hence *die Augen tauen machen* (lit.) = 'to bring tears to sb.'s eyes, as in Schlegel transl. of Shakespeare, *Hamlet* 2,2.

← See also under *auftauen, betauen* (also for *Gnadentau*) and *Mehltau*.

Tau (2) rope

das Tauziehen tug-of-war; figur. with ref. to struggles by opposing forces since the 20th c. (not yet recorded in *DWb.* [1935]).

← See also under *schleppen* (for *jem. ins Schlepptau nehmen*, p. 2137, where regrettably due to a printer's error the head word *schleppen* is missing).

taub: without sensual perception; deaf

taub (1) (lit.) empty hollow, without substance; with abstracts since MHG, e.g. *Minnes.* 2,395b: '*toup lob wil vil vallen*', and still in modern period, e.g. Immermann, *M.* 4,181: *'taube Redeblume'*, *taube Phrasen, tauber Manierismus*.

taub (2) empty, barren, without substance or value; since MHG in many contexts, but all relating to objects, e.g. Gottfr.v.Str., *Tristan* 2505: *'ein toup gevilde'* (= 'empty or barren landscape') *'toup loup'* (= 'dead or withered leaves'); *taube Ähren* are empty ears of corn. (f.r.b. Stieler [1691]), *taube Nuß* is a nut without kernel, *taubes Ei* is an empty egg-shell (f.r.b. Stieler), *taube Nessel* is a nettle which does not sting (now also as a compound *Taubnessel*), *taube Blüte* is a seedless blossom (cf. *taubes Gras* in Hebel 2,2), *taubes Salz* has no savour. In geology *tauber Berg* and *taubes Gestein* describe the absence of exploitable minerals (since Early NHG). Out of this group only *taube Nuß* has come to be used in idioms, e.g. G. Keller, *Nachlaß* 291: *'so leer . . . wie eine taube Nuß'* and *keine taube Nuß wert sein* (or *um etw. geben*), for which see under *Nuß* (p. 1797).

taub (3) (regional) stupid, dull, dumb; transfer from sensual to mental perception; f.r.b. Maaler [1561]: *'taub und unsinnig sein = insanire'*; this has survived in some regions, both as ~ in Bav., recorded by Schmeller 1,579 [1872] and as *dof* in the N., first in Berlin, then general (as low coll. even in the S., 20th c.).

taub (4) deafening, stunning, stupifying; since the 17th c., e.g. E.v.Kleist, *Ciss.u.Paches* 3,53: *'tauber Lärm'*, Tieck, *Schr.* 7,295: *'ein tauber Schmerz'*; now unusual, displaced by *betäubend*.

taub (5) unfeeling, unresponsive; mainly lit., e.g. Schiller, *Räuber* 4,5: *'. . . hab ichs tauben Felsenwänden zugewinselt'*, Goethe, *Iphig.* 1707: *'die taube Noth'*, *Nat.Tochter* 3,4: *'Liebe selbst ist in der Ferne taub'*. Closely related to this is ~ = 'benumbed, dazed', since the 18th c., e.g. Adelung's recording *'taubes Hinbrüten'* or Knebel, *Lit.Nachl.* 3,11 [1835]: *'das Neujahrsbetteln macht mir den Kopf so taub'*, and also *taube Füße = eingeschlafene Füße* = 'feet which have gone to sleep' (since the 19th c.).

~ *für etw. sein* to be deaf to sth., refuse to listen to sth.; since MHG, e.g. *Eraclius* [edit. Graef] 3028: *'er was maneger rede toup'*, also in Brockes, Lessing, Wieland or Goethe, *Faust II*, 4814: *'. . . und fürs Kommando bleibt man taub'*; cf. also *mit Taubheit geschlagen sein*, which can refer to the affliction of deafness but also to refusal to listen; cf. Wieland, 3,75: *'Taubheit gegen die Stimme aller Pflichten'*.

der ist sehr ~, *der nicht hören will* (prov.) none so deaf as they that will not hear; late in German (not even in Simrock [1846], but in various forms in Wander [1876]); the Engl. version has been recorded since the 16th c.

← See also under *betäuben*, *Glück* (for *taubstumm*), *Nuß* (for *taube Nuß*), *Ohr* (for *tauben Ohren predigen*), *Stock* (for *stocktaub*) and *stumm* (for *für Bitten taub*).

Taube: pigeon, dove

meine ~ my dove, darling, love; due to its occurrence as a term of endearment in the Bible (Song of Songs 5,2: *'meine taube'*) and its general reputation as a gentle, affectionate and faithful creature (e.g. Matth. 10,16:*'seid . . . on falsch wie die tauben'*) and one that is alleged to show no anger, because it has no gall-bladder (cf. Megenberg, *Buch d.Nat.* 179: *'diu taub . . . ist ân gallen'*), ~ has been current as a term of affection since OHG, e.g. Williram 38,2: *'mîn tûba, mîn scôna'*, often in the diminutive *mein Täubchen*, e.g. Weiße, *Kom.Op.* 3,275 [1768] or Goethe, *Zauberflöte* 2: *'bist du denn nicht mein süßes Täubchen?'*.

sanft, fromm, unschuldig wie eine ~ as gentle, kind, innocent as a dove; in many comparisons, even in mediaeval descriptions of the Virgin Mary, also in compounds (see *taubenartig, taubenfromm, taubenrein* below), e.g. *taubensanft* and *Taubensanftheit* (18th c.), also *ein Taubenherz haben*, e.g. Günther, *Ged.* 1042 [1735], *Taubeneinfalt*, f.r.b. Campe [1810], e.g. Merck (to Herder in *Briefw.* 2,14) and (M.T.) Schiller, *Picc.* 3,8: *'mit Löwenmuth den Taubensinn bewaffnen'*.

← See also under *Galle* (for *eine Taube ohne Galle*) and *rein* (for *rein wie eine Taube*).

Taubenaugen haben to have eyes full of innocence (and kindness); of biblical origin: Song of Songs 1,15: *'deine Augen sind wie Taubenaugen'*; in lit. since MHG, e.g. Grimmelshausen, *Simplic.* 1,28: *'ich aber hatte Taubenaugen'* (also Stolberg 3,43); also *Taubenblick* for an innocent (but warm) look, in lit. since the 18th c., not yet in Adelung, but listed by Campe [1810] with a quotation from Benzel-Sternau.

der Taubendreck (coll.) small matter, trifle, bagatelle; figur. in *sich streiten um einen Taubendreck*, since Early NHG, e.g. Franck, *Sprichw.* [1541]: *'zanken umb einen taubendreck'*.

jem.m den Taubendruck geben (regional coll.) to give sb. the *coup de grâce*, final blow; ref. to the slight pressure needed to kill a pigeon; listed by Campe [1810] as Swiss referring to the recording by Stalder; e.g. Gotthelf, *Schuldenbauer* 387.

taubenfromm (lit.) as kind and gentle as a dove; since the 18th c., e.g. Göckingk 3,34 or Geibel 7,99: *'. . . sich noch so taubenfromm gebärden'*; cf. also *taubenartig* mentioned below under *taubengrau*.

taubengrau dove-grey, pale bluish grey; since Early NHG, e.g. Fischart, *Garg.* 153b, surprisingly missing in Adelung and Campe, but still in current use, as in *Taubenhalsfarbe*, f.r.b. Stieler [1691]; *taubenartig* can also be used, though it usually refers to sb.'s character, e.g. Klinger, *Theater* 2,185: *'so wie du bist, keusch und rein und so taubenartig'*.

der Taubenhals (zool.) the butterfly *Sphinx statites*; f.r.b. Nemnich 3,590 [1793ff].

das Taubenhaus, der Taubenschlag dovecote; figur. with ref. to the constant coming and going in a dovecote, since Early NHG, e.g. H. Sachs, *Fab*, 2,104: '*dein hertz das ist ein taubenhauß, ein lieb fleugt ein, die ander auß*' (similarly in Gotthelf, *Uli d.Kn.* 288); more frequently now with *Taubenschlag*, e.g. *es geht zu wie in einem Taubenschlag* = 'there is constant movement in and out, to and fro', e.g. Zelter (to Goethe, 415).

taubenrein immaculate; since Early NHG, e.g. Luther, *Tischr.* 374a; cf. also Luther 4,54b (Jena): '*daher ein sprichwort ist, es ist so rein als hettens die tauben erlesen*'.

die Friedenstaube the dove of peace; since the 2nd half of the 18th c., e.l. (T.) Weiße, *Kinderfreund* 7,234 [1777]. Goethe used '*die Friedenstaube der Entsühnung*' in *Noten z. Diwan*.

die Kammertaube (coll., obs.) chambermaid; *DWb.* V, 130 [1873] has an example of 1658; now obs., but *Kammerkätzchen* still exists, for which see under *Katze*.

die Meertaube (zool.) a spine-covered fish (*Diodon hystrix*); f.r.b. *Vocabularius optimus* 40 [1495]: '*turtur = mertub*'; in modern form since Nemnich 2,1420 [1793ff]. In Campe [1809] it is listed as *Meertaube* with the remark that by Müller it is recorded as *Stacheltaube* (*Diodon echinatus*).

die Turteltaube turtle-dove; since OHG used figur. in several contexts, e.g. as 'bringer of Spring' (derived from the Song of Songs), as a symbol of purity, chastity and faithfulness (same as ~) and then since MHG period (first in the *Physiologus*) with ref. to faithful widowhood (as also in Shakespeare, *Winter's Tale* 5,3), e.g. Günther, *Ged.* 817 [1746]: '*sie sitzt in Einsamkeit bey ihres Gattens Raube* [= 'death'] *und seufzt und weint nach Art der Turtel-Taube*'; hence also in many comparisons since MHG, e.g. *Von dem jungesten tage* 77 [13th c.]: '. . . *turteltuben glich: einvaltig, senfte, minneclich*', Wieland, *Sämtl. Werke* 22,269: '*so lebten sie . . . wie fromme Turteltauben*'. Frequent also as a term of endearment, e.g. Joh.v.Tepl, *Ackermann a.B.* [edit. Spalding] 3,8, and in descriptions of affectionate lovers, general since the 18th c.

die Tauben (polit. coll.) the doves; with ref. to people who advocate conciliatory measures, a development from *Friedenstaube* (which see above), but historically a loan from Engl.; antonym *die Falken* = 'hawks'.

die gebratenen Tauben (*Hühner, Schnepfen*) *fliegen einem nicht ins Maul* (prov.) he that gapes until he be fed may well gape until he be dead; old and widespread (in Classical lit. in Telekleides); Luther 12,635 (Weimar) has it with *Tauben*, French has it with *alouettes*, Lehman [1640] with *Lerchen*. See also the entries under *fliegen* and *Schlaraffe*.

wo Tauben sind, fliegen Tauben zu (prov.) to him that hath shall be given; cf. French *où il y a un pigeon, pigeon y vient*; Luther used it (cf. *Sprichw.-Slg.* [edit. Thiele], No. 242), f.r.b. Petri [1605].

← See also under *Eule* (for *Adler brüten keine Tauben, eine Krähe heckt keine Turteltaube* and *keine*

Taube heckt einen Sperber), *Galle* (for *eine Taube ohne Galle*), *girren* (for *girren wie eine Taube*), *Katze* (for *abziehen wie eine Katze vom Taubenschlag*), *rein* (for *rein wie eine Taube*) and *Schnabel* (for *sie schnäbeln sich wie die Tauben*).

tauchen: dip; dive

etw. in etw. anderes ~ to dip sth. into or immerse sth. in sth. else; general since the 18th c., e.g. W. Humboldt 4,350: '*das was in uns strebet, in Leben selbst das Lebenlose tauchet*', Schiller, *Phaedra* 4,6: '*ins Blut der Unschuld will ich . . . die Mörderhände tauchen*', Uhland, 392: '*dein Name sei . . . in ewge Nacht getaucht*' or *der Mond tauchte die Landschaft in ein silbernes Licht*; also reflex., e.g. Wieland, *Ob.* 3,61: '*wo sich in eine See der Liebe die Seele taucht*'; cf. also (Sp.) Huch, *Pitt u. Fox* 238: '. . . *dessen Gedanken er, getaucht in die Farbe seiner eigenen Sprache, wiederholte*' or Gutzkow, *R.v.G.* 8,464: '*jetzt ist mein ganzes Dasein in Verklärung getaucht*'; *eintauchen* can also be used in such contexts.

die Sonne taucht ins Meer the Sun sinks into the sea; this intrans. 'dipping into sth. or immersing sth. (or oneself) in sth.' can also occur with ref. to 'going back to sth.', e.g. *in die Geschichte der Ahnen* ~, or to 'entering into sth. (so as to explore it or participate in it)', e.g. (Sp.) Gutzkow, *Uriel A.*2,7: '*ins Allgemeine möcht ich gerne tauchen und mit dem großen Strom des Lebens gehn*' or (Sp.) Werfel, *Abiturient.* 17: '*Sebastian tauchte in die reiche Maskengarderobe seiner sozialen Richtererfahrung*', Wieland, *Wasserkufe* 231: '*indeß . . . sein Blick mit Lüsternheit in jede Schüssel taucht*', or to 'penetrating sth.', e.g. (Sp.) Zschokke, *Alamontade* 1,7 [1802]: '*man muß aber seine Worte zwei- und dreimal hören, um ganz in ihren Sinn zu tauchen*'; also in compounds, e.g. *emportauchen*, as in Chamisso, 3,5: '*sein Bild taucht aus dem tiefsten Dunkel nur heller empor*'; Goethe used *hervortauchen* for 'to emerge', for which *aus etw.* ~ also occurs.

auf Tauchstation gehen (sl.) to go into hiding; 20th c. sl.

untertauchen (intrans.) to disappear (from view); figur. at least since the 18th c., e.g. Goethe 30,226 (W.): '*das habe ich abgelehnt und bin ganz entschieden wieder untergetaucht*'; often with the notion of 'hiding (from pursuers)', e.g. (Sp.) *Die Zeit* (30.3. 1962): '*die andern tauchten meist im Frühjahr 1945 mit falschen Ausweisen unter*'. In sl. there is *auf Tauchstation gehen*, derived from submarine warfare.

~ See also under *auftauchen* and *eintauchen*.

taufen: baptize

etw. ~ to baptize, give a name to sth.; simple transfer from persons to things or abstracts; since Early NHG, e.g. Luther 6,166a (Jena) for the title of a book, 6,319a (Jena) for the name of a town, also 6,84a: '*eine glocke teuffen*' (cf. Schiller, *Glocke* 399), with ref. to an abstract in Keisersberg, *Seelenparad.* preface 3b; cf. *jem. umtaufen* = 'to give sb. a new name', since the 18th c., e.g. Musäus, *Ph.* 4,10.

den Wein ~ (coll.) to add water to (or adulterate) the wine; since Early NHG, e.g. Bebel, *Facetiae* 81a [1589]: '*er wolt lieber trinken ein jüdischen* [= *verschnittenen*] *wein weder ein getauften*'.

eine richtige Taufe bekommen, tüchtig getauft werden (coll.) to get a thorough soaking; probably old, but lit. instances only since the 19th c., e.g. Uhland 2,147.

die getaufte Welt (lit.) Christendom; since the 18th c., e.g. Schiller, *D. Carlos* 1,6.

die Feuertaufe baptism of fire; of biblical origin (cf. Matth. 3,10) and used by Klopstock in *Mess.* in its religious sense: '*die Feuertaufe des heiligen Geistes*'; since the 19th c. also applied to a soldier's experience of being under fire for the first time; cf. Scherr, *Blücher* 1,247: '. . . *erhielt die Unabhängigkeit der Amerikaner auf Bunkershill ihre Blut- und Feuertaufe*'.

die Korntaufe (regional, obs.) the spraying of corn seeds in the field with holy water; recorded by Campe, now obs.

die Linientaufe, also *Äquatortaufe* or *Matrosentaufe* crossing-the-line ceremony; in German since the 17th c. (Gottschald in *Trübner* [1955] states that the custom was first mentioned in 1605), e.g. Schnabel, *Insel Fels.* 1,89: '. . . *so oft wir an diesen Ort* [i.e. the Equator] *kämen, die Ceremonie der Tauffe bei den Neulingen zu beobachten*'.

er hat vor der Taufe geniest (prov. expr.) he is too clever by half, a real Mr. know-all; usually pejor. or ironic; f.r.b. Simrock [1846]; the same as *superklug*.

← See also under *heben* (for *etw. aus der Taufe heben*), *Maus* (for *naß wie eine getaufte Maus*) and *Spree* (for *er ist mit Spreewasser getauft*).

taugen: be suitable, of use

ein Taugenichts a good-for-nothing; cf. French *vaurien*; this belongs to the group of so-called *Wahlspruchwörter* which proclaim sb.'s motto or slogan, such as *Gernegroß* (see p. 992), *Guckindiewelt* (p. 1169), *Haberecht* (see p. 1192), *Springinsfeld* (see p. 2316), *Störenfried* (see p. 2380), *Tunichtgut* (see p. 1180) and *Wagehals* (see p. 1206), derived from *ich tauge nicht*; since Early NHG, e.g. Waldis, *Esop* 4,68 as *tügenicht*, then usually as *Taugenicht* and in this form recorded by Frisch [1741] and still used by Goethe, *R. Fuchs* 5; now *Taugenichts*, f.r.b. Stieler [1691]; cf. Eichendorff's story *Aus dem Leben eines Taugenichts*.

taumeln: stagger

taumeln (lit.) to stagger, sway, reel; figur. in lit. when it refers to emotional unsteadiness or inner turmoil rather than phys. 'staggering'; since the 18th c., e.g. Klopstock 8,231: '*deine Cherusker taumeln heute vor Stolz*' (also *Mess.* 2,641), Goethe, *Faust I*, 3249: '*so tauml' ich von Begierde zu Genuß*'; there are many compounds, e.g. *entgegentaumeln*, as in Hagedorn 3,50 or Gotter 3,436, *forttaumeln*, as in Gutzkow, *R.v.G.* 6,21; even an abstract can be the subject,

e.g. (Sa.) Beck, *Heim.* 118: '*da taumeln sie frisch empor, die wühlenden Sorgen*'. The noun *Taumel* can describe a trancelike state, ecstasy or (non-phys.) intoxication, frequent since the 18th c., also in compounds, e.g. *Freudentaumel*; Goethe used *Jugendtaumel* in *Wahlverw.* 2,5 and *Wonnetaumel* in 16,91 (W.).

tauschen: exchange

etw. ~ to exchange things; with ref. to abstracts since the 18th c., mainly in *Blicke, Grüße, Küsse* ~; in other cases (*Gespräche, Reden*, etc.) *austauschen* has proved stronger.

jem.m etw. abtauschen (a.) to take sth. away from sb.; since the 18th c. with abstracts, e.g. Müllner, *Dram.W.* 2,52 [1828]: '*mit der Schrift . . . tauscht er mir die Ruhe ab*' (where *wegnehmen* would now be used).

der Abtausch (sport) exchange (e.g. of blows in boxing); also as *Schlagabtausch*; both appeared in the 20th c., but cf. Freytag, *Ges.Werke* 9,161: '*sie . . . tauschten blitzschnelle Schläge*'.

etw. für etw. anderes eintauschen to acquire sth. by way of exchange; since the 18th c. in figur. contexts, e.g. Gotter 1,442: '*Kenntnisse tauscht ich für Gefühle . . . ein*'; Campe listed it with ref. to *Namen*, quoting Wieland.

etw. umtauschen to change or exchange sth.; now in general use only with ref. to things, but in the 18th c. Goethe could write: '*wir tauschten sonderbar die Pflichten um*' and Herder 15,68: '*mit jedem Alter tauschtest du dich um*' and even in the 19th c. Eichendorff, *S.W.* 3,32 wrote: '*die Bauernburschen . . . waren nun auf einmal wie umgetauscht*'; *umtauschen* was also in the 18th c. used with ref. to exchanging views, displaced by *austauschen*: cf. Wieland 19,315: '. . . *traulichen Umtausch der Gedanken*'.

etw. vertauschen (1) (a.) to change sth.; since the 18th c., e.g. Herder 20,243: '*unsre Natur aber können wir nie vertauschen*' (where *ändern* would now be used).

etw. vertauschen (2) to confuse or mix up sth. with sth. else; since the 18th c., recorded by Adelung, often used with ref. to words or concepts.

etw. vertauschen (3) to exchange sth. (for sth. else); in lit. since the 19th c. with ref. to a change in life-style, e.g. (Duden) *er vertauschte die Kanzel mit dem Ministersessel*; in the 18th c. ~ was sufficient, e.g. Wieland, *Ob.* 9,23: '*tauscht er Pilgerstab und Kleid mit einem Sklavenwamms*'.

ein Tausch ist kein Raub (prov.) exchange is no robbery; in Engl. since the 16th c., in German f.r.b. Pistorius 10,56 [1714].

wer Lust hat zu ~ *hat Lust zu betrügen* (prov.) people who like to barter also like to cheat; in this form recorded by Simrock [1846], but earlier in Stieler [1691] as: '*wer gerne tauschet, betreugt gern*'. The shortest version is *tauschen ist täuschen*.

← See also under *austauschen* and *Rolle* (for *die Rollen tauschen* or *vertauschen*).

KEY TO PRINCIPAL ABBREVIATIONS

jem.m	jemandem (dat.)
Kluge	F. Kluge, *Etymologisches Wörterbuch der deutschen Sprache*, 11th ed., Berlin und Leipzig 1934.
Lehman	C. Lehman, *Florilegium Politicum*, etc., Frankfurt 1640.
Lexer	M. Lexer, *Mittelhochdeutsches Handwörterbuch*, Leipzig 1872–8.
LG	Low German
Lipperheide	F. Freih. v. Lipperheide, *Spruchwörterbuch*, 2nd ed., München 1909.
MHG	Middle High German
mil.	military
M. Latin	medieval Latin
N.	Northern Germany
NED	*Oxford English Dictionary, A New English Dictionary on Historical Principles*, Edited by Sir James Murray, Henry Bradley, W. A. Craigie and C. T. Onions. Oxford 1884–1928.
NHG	New High German
NW	North-Western Germany
obs.	obsolete
OE	Old English
offic.	in civil service language
OHG	Old High German
ON	Old Norse
OS	Old Saxon
Oxf.	*The Oxford Dictionary of English Proverbs*, compiled by W. G. Smith, Oxford, 1935.
p.	page
poet.	used mainly in poetic language
pop.	popular
pop. etym.	popular etymology
prov.	proverb, proverbial
sb.	somebody
Schmeller	J. A. Schmeller, *Bayerisches Wörterbuch*, Stuttgart 1827–37.
Schulz-Basler	G. Schulz und O. Basler, *Deutsches Fremdwörterbuch*, Strassburg und Berlin 1913ff.
s.e.	self-explanatory
sl.	slang
S. Singer	S. Singer, *Sprichwörter des Mittelalters*, Bern 1944–7.
sth.	something
SW.	South-Western Germany
Trübner	*Trübners Deutsches Wörterbuch*, herausg. v. A. Götze, Berlin 1939ff.
v.	verse, verses
vulg.	in vulgar use (obscene terms are included under this heading, but specially marked as such)
Waag	A. Waag, *Die Bedeutungsentwicklung unseres Wortschatzes*, 5th ed., Lahr 1926.
Wb.	Wörterbuch
Weigand	F. L. K. Weigand, *Deutsches Wörterbuch*, 5th ed., Gießen 1909–10.
Weist.	Weistümer; usually the collection by J. Grimm, Göttingen 1840–69 is referred to; Österr. is appended to the Austrian collections.
Westph.	Westphalia, Westphalian
zool.	zoological term.

Where later editions than those cited above have been quoted (especially in the cases of Büchmann, Dornseiff and Kluge), details of the editions used are given in the text.

The abbreviations for journals mostly follow the accepted practice (*MLR* for *Modern Language Review*, *MLN* for *Modern Language Notes*, *IF* for *Indogermanische Forschungen*, etc.), only some long titles have been still further abbreviated though still left recognizable (e.g. *Z.f.d.W.* for *Zeitschrift für deutsche Wortforschung*, *Z.f.d.U.* for *Zeitschrift für den deutschen Unterricht*, *Z.f.r.P.* for *Zeitschrift für romanische Philologie*, etc.). Other works, referred to or quoted have been mentioned in abbreviated but recognizable form. It is intended to give a comprehensive list of them when the dictionary is completed. From Fasc. 9 Goethe (W.) = Weimar edition, Schiller (S.) = Säkularausgabe.

ISBN 0 631 181482

An Historical Dictionary of German Figurative Usage

By KEITH SPALDING

PROFESSOR EMERITUS OF GERMAN, UNIVERSITY COLLEGE OF NORTH WALES, BANGOR

WITH ASSISTANCE FROM
GERHARD MÜLLER-SCHWEFE

PROFESSOR EMERITUS OF ENGLISH,

UNIVERSITY OF TÜBINGEN

Fascicle 52

täuschen – Trommel

BLACKWELL PUBLISHERS · OXFORD

KEY TO PRINCIPAL ABBREVIATIONS

a.	archaic
Adolphi	O. Adolphi, *Das große Buch der Fliegenden Worte, etc.*, Berlin n.d.
Ahd. Gl.	*Die Althochdeutschen Glossen*, ges. und bearb. von E. Steinmeyer u. Eduard Sievers, Berlin 1879—98.
Bav.	Bavaria, Bavarian
bot.	botanical term
Büchmann	G. Büchmann, *Geflügelte Worte*, 27th ed., ergänzt von A. Langen, Berlin 1915.
c.	century
Car.	Carinthia, Carinthian
cf.	compare
cl.	cliché
Cod.	codex
coll.	in colloquial use
comm.	used in language of commerce
dial.	dialect expression
Dornseiff	F. Dornseiff, *Der deutsche Wortschatz nach Sachgruppen*, Berlin und Leipzig 1934.
dt.	deutsch
DWb	*Deutsches Wörterbuch von Jacob Grimm und Wilhelm Grimm*, Leipzig 1854ff.
e.l.	earliest locus or earliest loci
etw.	*etwas*
Fast. Sp.	Fastnachtspiele, usually quoted after *Fastnachtspiele aus dem 15. Jahrbundert*, herausg. v. Keller, Stuttgart 1853.
Fick	F. C. A. Fick, *Vergleichendes Wörterbuch der indogermanischen Sprachen*, 3rd ed. Göttingen 1874.
f.r.b.	first recorded by
gen.	general
Götze	A. Götze, *Frühneuhochdeutsches Glossar*, 2nd ed., Bonn 1920.
Graff	E. G. Graff, *Althochdeutscher Sprachschatz*, Berlin 1834—42.
Hirt, *Etym.*	H. Hirt, *Etymologie der neuhochdeutschen Sprache*, 2nd ed., München 1925.
Hirt, *Gesch.*	H. Hirt, *Geschichte der deutschen Sprache*, 2nd ed., München 1925.
hunt.	word or expression used by huntsmen
jem.	jemand (nom. or acc.)

© *Basil Blackwell Ltd., 1993 ISBN 0 631 188223*
Typeset by Hope Services, Abingdon
Printed and bound by Whitstable Litho Ltd., Whitstable, Kent.

täuschen: deceive

sich mit etw. ~ (obs.), *sich über etw. hinwegtäuschen* to be (deliberately) blind to sth., delude oneself as to sth., make light of sth.; an off-shoot from 'to deceive oneself, be mistaken'; since the 18th c., also non-reflex., as in (DWb) Thümmel, *Reise* 9,274: '*ich täuschte unterdeß meine Ungeduld mit Besichtigung des Ortes*'; now obs., displaced by (*sich*) *über etw. hinwegtäuschen*; Herder, *Ph.* 13,158 used *hintäuschen*.

jem. enttäuschen to disappoint sb.; only since late in the 18th c., when W.v.Humboldt (in *Werke* 3,208) was unaware of its existence: '*uns Deutschen fehlt es an einem Worte für das Zurückkommen von einer Täuschung oder Verblendung, span. desengannar, frz. désabuser*', but Goethe used it in *Dicht.u.Wahrh.* 2,10, where *entteuscht* (in this spelling!) still means 'to be disabused, undeceived', and this is listed in Campe [1807] as *enttäuschen*, but still only for 'disabuse'. Two questions arise: where did Goethe hear or find the word which is not listed in any 18th c. dictionary known to me, and when and where did the new sense 'to disappoint' arise? It is still missing in Lloyd-Noehden [1827], even in Elwell [1851], but Hilpert [1845] and Meißner [1856] listed the new meaning. Paul [1896] recorded it with the remark '*junges Wort*'.

etw. vortäuschen to feign or simulate sth. (e.g. an illness); since Early NHG, e.g. Luther 8,192 (Weimar); Kramer [1702] did not record it, nor *Vortäuschung* which appeared much later; often now in *unter Vortäuschung* (also *Vorspiegelung*) *falscher Tatsachen* (jur.) = 'under false pretences'; see also p. 2295.

← See also under *tauschen* (for *tauschen ist täuschen*).

tausend: thousand

tausendmal a thousand times; hyperbole (as in *Dutzend* and *hundert*); since OHG, e.g. Otfrid 4,17 in many hyperbolic statements, e.g. Lessing 12,480: *jem.m ~ Glück wünschen*, Goethe, *Stella* 3: '*ich sollte . . . der gnädigen Frau tausend Segen wünschen*', Nicolai 2,49: '*tausend Dank dafür!*'; in the *Sturm und Drang* period very much used (e.g. Schiller 3,6ff (S.)), also Goethe, *Faust I*, 1053: '*ich habe selbst den Gift an Tausende gegeben*'; intensified as *tausend tausend* (since MHG), *~ und aber ~*, e.g. Goethe, *St.-Rochus-Fest zu B.* or *~ und ~*, as in Goethe, *Egmont* 1, or *vieltausendmal*, as in Luther Bible transl. Gen. 24,60; cf. also *zu Tausenden* = 'in vast numbers', as in Goethe, *Faust II*, 6598 or Schiller, *D.Carlos* 5,5, and hyperbolic locutions of the type *in ~ Ängsten schweben, in ~ Nöten sein*.

ein Wort (or *eins*) *für ~* (a.) to mention but one instance, without enumerating all the arguments, in one word; since the 18th c., e.g. Goethe, *Werther* (May 9), also Weiße, *Kom.Op.* 5,234.

~ gegen eins wetten (coll.) to lay any odds; since the 18th c., e.g. Göckingk 1,122.

voll wie ~ Mann (coll.) dead drunk; modern.

nicht um ~ Taler! (coll.) not for a mint of money! not if you paid me . . . ; strong refusal; modern.

er ist einer von ~ (coll.) he is an exceptional person, one in a thousand; at least since the 17th c., as suggested by Kramer [1702]: '*auserwehlter Freund unter Tausenden, Tausendfreund*'.

das weiß der Tausendste nicht hardly anybody knows that; since the 17th c.; Kramer [1702] recorded: '*das weiß der Tausende nicht*'.

ei (or *was*) *der Tausend!* (coll.) good grief! heavens! would you believe it! exclamation of surprise or annoyance; *der Tausend* is the devil, older form *Daus* (for which see the notes on p. 457). There are many versions, esp. in curses, e.g. *Schocktausend*, as in Lessing 1,222, *Mordtausend*, as in Müllner 7,254, *~ Sakerment*, as in Schiller, *Räuber* 2,3, *~ noch einmal*, as in Keller, *Gr.Heinr.* 4,238, *ei der ~*, as in Immermann, *Münchhausen* 1,114.

der Tausendkünstler the devil; explained in *Vita S.Salabergae* (in *Germ.* 10,100) as '*cuius mille nocendi artes sunt*'; cf. also the lines in H.Sachs (quoted by Campe) put into the mouth of the devil: '*ich bin ein tausend listig geist, der alle heimlich anschleg weiß*'. Luther used the word, as *tausendkünstler* in 8,351b (Jena), as *tausendkünstner* in 3,384a (Jena); a forerunner was MHG *tûsentlisteler*, as used by Berth.v.Regensburg [edit. Pfeiffer] 1,408. Later the word came to be used in secular contexts for a 'Jack of all trades, person versed in many things', f.r.b. Stieler [1691], e.g. Möser, *Phant.* 1,168.

der Tausendfüßler (zool.) millipede; general since the 18th c., at first also as *Tausendfuß* and *Tausendfüßer*. Adelung recorded it as *Tausendfuß*.

der Tausendsas(s)a devil of a fellow; mainly as a term of praise (similar to the later meaning of *Tausendkünstler*), but sometimes slightly pejor.; since the 18th c., e.g. Schiller, *Kab.u.L.* 1,1.

der Glaube vom tausendjährigen (or *ans tausendjährige*) *Reich* chiliasm; the belief that Christ will reign in bodily presence on earth for a thousand years is old in the history of the church, considered a heresy in the early church and condemned by the Pope in the 4th c.; Kramer (1702) recorded it. The belief had a non-religious revival among followers of Hitler in the thirties of the 20th c.

← See also under *Daus, deutsch* (for *tausend Deutscher*), *hundert* (for *hunderttausend, vom Hundertsten ins Tausendste gehen* and variants), *Kraut* (for *Tausendguldenkräutel*), *Mord* (for *Mord-Tausend Sapperment*) and *Sakrament* (for *Tausendsakrament*).

Tedeum

man darf noch kein ~ singen (a.) one cannot start thanking God yet, we are not out of the wood yet; recorded by Wander [1876], now a.

Tee: tea

laß dir ~ kochen (coll.) you ought to take sth. for that; meaning: 'you must be ill to suggest that'; modern coll.

auf den ~ kommen (sl.) to come to grief, have bad luck; first in stud.sl., f.r.b. *Bem. eines Akadem.* [1795]; still alive in recent sl., also in *seinen ~ haben* (or *kriegen*) = 'to be sacked, fail, be in the soup'.

im ~ sein (sl.) to be drunk; since the 19th c.; some scholars have suggested that this does not belong to ~, but arose as an abbreviation of *Tran*, with the letter T used euphemistically (cf. euphem. *er hat T.B.* = 'he has tuberculosis').

Augen wie Teetassen (coll.) very big eyes; first used by H.Chr. Andersen in *Der Soldat und das Feuerzeug*, which then became a coll. comparison in the 2nd half of the 19th c.

Teekessel spielen to play a party game in which the participants have to guess homonyms and their meanings, since the 19th c.(?), not yet recorded in 1890 when Lexer compiled the entry on ~ in *DWb.* XI,1.

← See also under *abwarten* (for *abwarten und Tee trinken*) and *Kessel* (for *Teekessel*).

Teer: tar

die Teerjacke (coll.) sailor, Jack tar; from Engl. since 1848 with misunderstood Engl. 'Jack'; e.g. Gerstäcker, *Verhängnisse* 1,23 [1871]: '*es waren lauter richtige und echte Teerjacken*'.

← See also under *Sache* (for *Teerbüchse*).

Teich: pond

der große ~ (coll.) the big pond, the Atlantic Ocean; taken over from Engl., esp. by emigrants to America (from middle of 19th c. onwards); in lit. since the 2nd half of the 19th c., e.g. L.Schücking in *Gartenlaube* 222 [1881].

das ist in den ~ gegangen (sl.) that has gone wrong or phut; since early in the 20th c.; same as *ist baden gegangen* (modern sl.).

da warst du noch im großen ~ (coll.) at that time you were not born yet; an allusion to the fiction that babies are brought by the stork who fishes them out of a pond; since early in the 20th c.

über den großen ~ gehen (mil.sl.) to be killed; a modern version of old phrases in which 'crossing a river' describes 'death', as in Gk. myths about Styx and later locutions referring to the river Jordan; since the 2nd World War.

Teig: dough

er ist aus keinem andern ~ gebacken als wir (prov. expr.) he is no better than we are; French uses 'flour' in the saying '*gens de même farine*'. There are numerous phrases of this group, beginning in the 16th c., e.g. Dedekind-Scheidt, *Grobianus* 334 [1551]; variants are *wir sind alle aus einem ~ gebacken, der ist von beßrem Teige* (or *nicht vom besten Teige*), etc., listed in Wander [1876].

der Teigaffe (regional coll.) clumsy fellow, numskull; in some areas also used for 'coward'; recorded since the 19th c.

← See also under *Affe* (for *Teigaffe* = 'baker').

teigig spongy, dough-like; figur. when used with ref. e.g. to skin; modern.

← See also under *kneten* (for *etw. aus dem Teig kneten*).

Teil: part

er hat sein(en) ~ (bekommen) or coll. *er hat sein ~ weg* he has had his due, got what was coming to him; ~ here = 'share', general since MHG, e.g. Walther v.d.V. 66,32, also in the Bible, Luther's transl. Jerem. 13,25: '*das sol dein lon sein und dein teil, das ich dir zugemessen habe*'; Stieler [1691] recorded: '*er hat sein teil*', Kramer [1702]: '*er hat seinen Theil bekommen*' and '*einem jeden seinen bescheidnen Theil geben*'; cf. Voß, *Od.* 22,54: '*doch nun hat er sein Theil dahin*', Petri [1605] listed as prov. '*jeder hat sein bescheiden theil*'; cf. *zuteil werden* = 'to be allotted, to receive', since OHG, later also *jem.m etw. zuteil werden lassen* = 'to grant, give, allot sth. to sb.'; cf. also *sein ~ zu tragen haben* = 'to have to bear (or put up with) one's lot'. Closely related is *jem.m sein(en) ~ geben* (coll.) = 'to tell sb. (bluntly) what one thinks of him'; cf. Engl. 'to let sb. have what was coming to him'; modern.

er hat sein ~ (coll.) he is drunk; since the 18th c., e.g. Lichtenberg 3,75.

das bessere ~ erwählen to make the better choice; biblical, derived from Luther Bible transl. Luke 10,42: '*Maria hat das gute teil erwelet*'; in use since MHG, e.g. (DWb) H.v.Neustadt, *von gottes zukunft* 3058, Schiller, *M.Stuart* 5,6 (with '*beßre*'); Goethe used '*beste*', as did Wieland in *Ob.* 5,62.

der ~ part, party (in legal sense), part, side (in general contexts); translates Lat. *pars*; general since Early NHG, e.g. Luther, *Tischr.* 1,95, sometimes as *die (streitenden) Teile* = 'the opposing sides (or parties)', e.g. Aler, 1889b: '*man soll beide Theile anhören*', which renders the Lat. saying *audiatur et altera pars*; also (since Early NHG) extended to 'part, side, partner', e.g. in marriage (recorded since 1444), as in Goethe, *Wanderj.* 2,12, or in friendship. This meaning of 'person' in the legal sense led to *ich zu mein ~* = 'I for my part', since Early NHG, e.g. H.Sachs 17.157, now obs., displaced by *ich für mein ~*, since the 17th c., f.r.b. Stieler [1691], e.g. Lessing 12,269; hence *meinesteils*, etc.

sich sein ~ denken to have one's own (private) opinion about sth.; modern, e.g. Holtei, *Ob.Bote* 1,125 [1854]: '*mein Theil dacht' ich mir freilich dabei*'.

etw. teilen (1) to divide sth., part or split things; the phys. sense of 'dividing', current since OHG, could be extended to abstracts or to things which are not strictly 'divided' but 'separated' (in a wide sense), e.g. *der Adler teilt die Lüfte, das Schiff teilt die Wellen*, (cf. Engl. 'cleave') f.r.b. Maaler [1561]: '*mit farben theilen = variare*', current since MHG with ref. to clothing in varied colours, e.g. Wolfr.v.E., *Parz.* 235,13; Luther used it reflex. in his Bible transl. 2 Kings 2,8: '*das wasser teilt sich auf beide seiten*' (in A.V.: '. . . smote the waters, and they were divided hither and thither'); cf.

modern *die Kosten teilen* = 'to share the cost', which belongs to the old math. sense of 'to divide', *geteilter Meinung sein* = 'to be of different opinions', from the sense 'to keep separate', in figur. sense current since Early NHG, e.g. Luther 6,56a (Jena); cf. also Schiller, *Lied an die Freude: 'was die Mode streng getheilt'*.

etw. teilen (2) to share sth. (with sb.) sympathize (with sb.) about sth.; the concepts of 'dividing' and 'sharing' are so closely related that the extension is s.e. It occurred both in *teilnehmen*, current since OHG (as *teil neman*, but only used for sharing or participating in material contexts), and in *teilen*, but both only became 'to sympathize' in the 18th c. (not yet recorded in Frisch [1741]), mainly in *jem.s Freude, Leid, Trauer teilen*, e.g. Tiedge, *Urania* 95: *'getheilte Freud' ist doppelte Freude, getheilter Schmerz ist halber Schmerz'*; in extended sense also in *jem.s Ansichten teilen* = 'to share sb.'s opinion', *mit jem.m Tisch und Bett teilen* = 'to cohabit with sb.'; cf. also Goethe, *Faust I*, 1238: *'soll ich mit dir das Zimmer teilen, Pudel . . .'*. Hence *die Teilnahme*, e.g. Goethe, *Wahlv.* 1,1, also *innerliche Teilnahme*, as in Goethe to Zelter 466, and *Anteilnehmung*, since the 18th c., e.g. Heinse, *Ard.* 2,40 (also Goethe to Fr.v.Stein 3,319), later *Anteilnahme*, e.g. Gutzkow, *R.v.G.* 3,233. See also under *Anteil*. Note that *teilhaben an etw.* = 'to share in sth.' goes back to OHG, e.g. Notker 121,3. This could also mean 'to be responsible for sth.', f.r.b. Stieler [1691], e.g. Klopstock, *Mess.* 4,530 (still used by Goethe and Schiller), so that *Teilhaber*, which now only means 'partner' or 'joint owner', could also mean 'sb. responsible for sth., cause of sth.', still used by Campe [1810], now obs.

jem. beteiligen (econ.) to give sb. a share or interest (in sth.); since the 18th c.; Campe [1807] considered it an Upper German substitute for foreign *interessieren*.

sich an etw. beteiligen to take part or share in sth.; since the 19th c., often = *teilnehmen*.

sein Geld einteilen to manage carefully, live economically; extension from the original sense 'to divide one's money into (appropriate) parts' with the added notion of 'care, economy', with ellipsis of *gut, sorgfältig, sparsam* or a similar adverb; recorded since the 19th c.

etw. mitteilen (1) (obs.) to give sth.; used with ref. to alms since Early NHG, f.r.b. *voc.inc.theut.* N8a [1485], e.g. Luther Bible transl. Hebr. 13,16: *'wol zu thun vnd mit zu teilen vergesset nicht, denn solche opffer gefallen Gott wol'*. Goethe still used *mitteilen* in this sense in *Wahlv.* 2,5. Now obs. Note that *teilen* was in Early NHG considered sufficient to render 'to share out', e.g. Luther Bible transl. 1 Tim. 2,15.

etw. mitteilen (2) to communicate, impart sth.; from the above since the 18th c., e.g. Lessing 10,310: *'dieser mitgetheilte, nicht erworbene Begriff'*; hence *die Mitteilung*, also since the 18th c.

etw. verteilen to distribute or disperse sth.; with abstracts since the 18th c., e.g. Lessing 17,80: *'der wahre Dichter vertheilt das Mitleiden durch sein ganzes Trauerspiel'* or *seine Sympathie unter beide Parteien verteilen*.

sich verteilen (1) to be spread or dispersed; phys. since Early NHG, figur. with ref. to abstracts or groups of people since early in the 19th c. (still missing in Adelung and Campe), e.g. Bettina, *Frühl.* 472.

sich verteilen (2) to misdeal, make a mistake in dealing cards; Campe listed this, referring to it as a (Swiss) regional term recorded by Stalder. Now it is little used, displaced by *sich vergeben*.

ich kann mich nicht zerteilen (coll.) I cannot be in two places at the same time. Modern coll.

einer Sache teilhaftig werden (or *sein*) to partake of sth., share in sth.; in wider sense 'to enjoy sth.', esp. in relig. contexts, e.g. with ref. to divine grace; since MHG, frequent in Luther's Bible transl., e.g. Romans 15,27 or 1 Cor. 9,10; now becoming a.

das Erbteil inheritance, inherited feature or characteristic; since the 18th c., e.g. Hagedorn 2,107: *'. . . wie seit Evens Näscherei der Weiber Erbtheil Leiden sei'*.

der Gegenteil (legal, obs.) the opponent, the opposing party; since MHG, still recorded as current by Adelung, now displaced by *Gegner* or *Gegenpartei*.

das Gegenteil the opposite; used with ref. to persons, things (when it is the same as *Gegenstück*, for which see p. 943) or abstracts, e.g. *die Idee verkehrt sich in ihr Gegenteil, ins Gegenteil umschlagen*. Often in the strong rejection *ganz im Gegenteil* = 'the very opposite is true'; hence *gegenteilig*, of which Adelung maintained that it only existed in Upper German (now it is general) and *gegenteils* (adv.) = 'on the contrary', since the 17th c., recorded by Kramer [1702], e.g. (Adelung) Hagedorn (no details): *'. . . die war der Maus gewogen, ihr waren gegentheils die Vögel ganz verhaßt'*, now obs., displaced by *im Gegenteil* or *dagegen*.

der Nachteil disadvantage; formed as the antonym to *Vorteil*; since the 15th c., hence *zum Nachteil gereichen, Nachteile bringen*, etc.; *nachteilig* was f.r.b. Maaler [1561]; from this *benachteiligen* was derived in the modern period (whereas *bevorteilen* was derived from the noun *Vorteil*).

sich ein Urteil bilden to form an opinion; *Urteil* began as 'judgement' and 'sentence (issued by a judge)', since OHG; since MHG also for 'expressed opinion', e.g. *Myst.* [edit. Pfeiffer] 1,318, also 'decision about sth.', e.g. *das Urteil des Paris* (since the 18th c.), or Goethe IV,11,100 (W.): *'Willkürlichkeit im Urteil'*, also used for 'discernment', e.g. Goethe 7,118 (W.): *'es ist nicht möglich, weniger . . . Urteil zu zeigen als diese . . . Männer'*; hence *urteilsfähig* (18th c.), f.r.b. Campe, and *Urteilsfähigkeit*, e.g. Herder [edit. S.] 22,93; cf. *sich kein*

Urteil erlauben = 'to be in no position to express an opinion' (19th c.), also *sich selbst sein Urteil sprechen* = 'to be condemned by one's own words'. The verb *urteilen* has been current since OHG, e.g. Kramer [1702]: '*er urtheilet davon wie ein Blinder von Farben*'; etw. *verurteilen* = 'to condemn sth.' arose in MHG and *Verurteilung* has been recorded since Early NHG, when *Vorurteil* = 'prejudice' also arose, f.r.b. Hulsius [1616], perhaps formed as a transl. of Lat. *praejudicium* (although *DWb*. 12,2,1857 [1951] suggests other possibilities); hence *vorurteilsfrei* = 'unprejudiced', since the 18th c. (sometimes, as in Campe, without the *s*) and *vorurteilen* = 'to prejudge', f.r.b. Hulsius.

der Vorteil advantage; since MHG, often as a neuter noun, as in Luther 18,360 (Weimar), but as a masc. in Maaler [1561]; derived from 'superiority in a contest'; since the 18th c. also used for 'material gain', recorded by Adelung, now a.; cf. also prov. '*es ist kein nachteyl on ein vorteyl*', recorded by Franck [1541], and *kleine Vorteile machen langsam reich* similar to Engl. prov. 'light gains make a heavy purse'.

der Weltteil or *Erdteil* continent; *Weltteil* was f.r.b. Kramer [1678], *Erdteil* came later; the cl. *der schwarze Erdteil* for 'Africa' is modern.

etw. auf Teilstrecke kaufen (coll.) to buy sth. in instalments; joc. transfer from the system of buying journeys on public transport; 20th c. coll.

viele Teile, schmale Brocken (prov.) if you have to share with many, the portions are small; mainly in wider sense with ref. to estates divided on sb.'s death; f.r.b. Simrock [1846].

← See also under *Anteil*, *Bruder* (for *brüderlich teilen*), *einnehmen* (for *wer austeilen will, muß auch einnehmen*), *ersehen* (for *seinen Vorteil ersehen*), *erteilen*, *fallen* (for *das Urteil ist gefallen*), *fällen* (for *ein Urteil fällen*), *Fett* (for ironic *Teil*), *Gewitter* (for *Gewitterverteiler*), *Gold* (for *sein Teil denken*), *Hinterkastell* (for *Hinterteil*) and *Nase* (for *beim Austeilen der Nasen . . .*), also under *Geschmack* (for *Beurteilung* and *urteilen*), *gießen* (for *den ewigern Teil erwählen*) and *Grenze* (for *seinen Vorteil wahren*).

Telegramm: telegram

im Telegrammstil in telegram style or in telegraphese, in a wording reduced to bare essentials; ~ was coined by the American P. Smith in 1852, used in German since the middle of the 'sixties; *Telegrammstil* followed in the 20th c.

telegraphieren: telegraph

er lügt wie telegraphiert (coll., obs.) he is a terrible liar; coined by Bismarck (13.2.1869): '*es wird vielleicht dahin kommen zu sagen: er lügt wie telegraphiert*', made up as a variant of *er lügt wie gedruckt*, for which see p. 505.

etw. ~ (coll.) to indicate or intimate sth. without words; describes communication by glances or messages conveyed under the table; since early in the 20th c.

er ist so dünn wie eine Telegraphenstange (coll.) he is (as thin as) a bean-pole; 20th c. coll. See also under *Bohne* (p. 370).

Teleskop: telescope

das ~, also *der Teleskopfisch* (zool.) telescope goldfish (*Carassius auratus auratus*); so called because of its protruding eyes; f.r.b. Sanders [1871]; cf. *Teleskopenaugen haben*.

das ~ (zool.) the snail *Trochus telescopium*; f.r.b. Nemnich.

das ~, also *Telescopium* (astron.) a constellation named by La Caille [1792], who in his observations on Table Mountain added a number of new terms to the list of recently-discovered constellations; cf. Scherer, *Gestirnnamen bei den indogerm. Völkern* 192 [1953].

Teller: plate

der ~ der Hand, *der Handteller* the palm; Adelung recorded both terms (note that in MHG *tisch der hand* was used); e.g. G.Keller, *Gr. Heinrich* 3,177.

die ~ (pl) *des Schwarzwilds* (hunt.) the ears of a wild boar; recorded since the 19th c., but not yet in Campe [1810].

tellerförmig plate-shaped; recorded as *tellerformig* by Kramer [1702].

tellergroß as big as a plate; in lit. mainly with ref. to the eyes, since the 18th c., e.g. Bürger, 151 [1778]: '. . . *schwarzer Hund . . . mit Feueraugen, tellergros*', G.Hauptmann, *Schluck u. Jau* 3: '. . . *tellergroße Augen*'.

die Tellerkröte (zool., obs.) tortoise; f.r.b. Frisius, now obs., displaced by *Schildkröte*.

der Tellerlecker (obs.) flatterer; also used for 'parasite'; since Early NHG, used by Luther, but still to be found in Grillparzer, though *Speichellecker* displaced it long ago (see p. 1598). Keller in *Seldw.* 1,159 used *Tellerleckerei* for *Naschsucht*.

die Tellermütze flat cap, beret; f.r.b. Stieler [1691]; now *Tellerkappe* is also used. Similarly, because of its shape: *die Tellermine* (mil.) = 'antitank mine' (20th c.).

die Tellerschnecke (zool.) pond snail, planorbis; f.r.b. Nemnich.

← See also under *bunt* (for *der bunte Teller*) and *präsentieren* (for *auf dem Präsentierteller sitzen*).

Tempel: temple

der ~ (lit.) temple, sanctuary, hall, palace; the originally relig. term used in secular contexts; at first still with ref. to God, as in Luther Bible transl. 1 Cor. 3,16: '*das jr gottes tempel seid*', but since the 18th c. secular with abstracts, e.g. Wieland 4,56: '*Tempel der Sinnlichkeit*', Klopstock 12,135: '*Tempel der Wahrheit*', Goethe, *Faust I*, 1992: '*zum Tempel der Gewißheit*'. Since the 18th c. also in many compounds, e.g. *Ehrentempel* in Hagedorn 1,84, *Musentempel*, often used as a cl. for 'theatre', e.g. Wieland 3,24; cf. also Uhland, 185: '*unsres deutschen Liedertempels Pfleger*'.

jem. zum ~ hinausjagen (coll.) to throw sb. out (of the house); use of ~ here with allusion to the

Bible (John 2,15 or Mark 11,15); for the phrase without ~ see p. 1330.

tempeln (obs.) to pile up, place one above the other; f.r.b. *Brem.Wb.* 5,52 as '*up tempeln*'; in lit. also in compounds such as *auftempeln* or *emportempeln*, still recorded by Campe [1810] and used in the 19th c., but now obs.

← See also under *Gerümpel* (for *Lebenstempel*), *Götze* (for *einen Götzentempel aufrichten*) and *Mammon* (for *Mammonstempel*).

Temperament: temperament

voll ~ full of spirits, vivacity, fire, fervour; ~ began as 'right mixture' (from Lat. *temperamentum*), was then applied to the fluids in the human body, and this led to 'disposition'; only since the 18th c. for 'passion, excitability, fire, fervour', sometimes with the notion of sensual 'fervour', as in Schiller, *Kab.u.L.* 2,3: '*es ist Temperament, Hang zum Vergnügen*'; often with adjectives such as *warm*, *heiß*, *hitzig* (Goethe used it with *hitzig* and with *leicht*), but *voll(er)* ~ or *temperamentvoll* only since the 19th c.; Sanders [1865] recorded *sie hat viel ~*, which he glossed with '*Trieb zur Sinnlichkeit*', but *viel* can be omitted without loss of meaning; current phrases with ~ are: *sein ~ ging mit ihm durch, er konnte sein ~ nicht zügeln, sein ~ riß alle mit*; cf. also Auerbach, *Tagebuch aus Wien* 139 [1849]: '*Wien hat weit mehr politisches Temperament als politischen Charakter*'; frequent compounds are *Temperamentsausbruch* and *Temperamentsache* = 'a matter of temperament'.

← See also under *leicht* (for *das warmblütige* and *das leichtblütige Temperament*).

temperieren: moderate

temperiert (lit.) moderate, controlled; ~ was derived from Lat. *temperare* in the 13th c., e.g. Reinbot v. Durne, *Hg. Georg* 5333, when it meant 'to produce the appropriate relationship'; in Early NHG this led to 'to moderate', as in Luther, *S.W.* 56,125: '*sauer getemperiert mit süßem*', still in modern period for 'restrained, controlled, moderated', e.g. Wassermann, *Maurizius* 212: '*außer der . . . temperierten Zärtlichkeit*'. In music ~ came to mean 'to produce an equal temperament' (by dividing the octave into twelve equal half-notes), since the 18th c., hence *wohltemperiert*, as in J.S. Bach, *Das wohltemperierte Clavier*. – *Temperanz* = 'moderation' was loaned from Engl. in the 19th c. and led to *Temperenzler* = 'teetotaller', which is now becoming a.

Tempo: time, (right) moment

das ~ speed; ~, taken over from Ital. in the 16th c. referred first to 'time, right moment' which led to 'favourable time, appropriate measure' and then developed its special significance in musical contexts (early in the 18th c.); only since the 19th c. extended and generalized to mean 'speed', e.g. Goethe 33,8 (W.); coll. in *aufs ~ drücken* = 'to increase speed', *~ hinter etw. machen* = 'to hasten

sth.' (20th c .), also in compounds such as *Zeitlupentempo, Zeitraffertempo*.

← See also under *hundert* (for *etw. im Hundertkilometertempo erledigen*) and *Schnecke* (for *im Schneckentempo*).

Tendenz: tendency

die geheime ~ (rare) the secret intention; modern, e.g. Wassermann, *Maurizius* 137: '*voll der geheimen Tendenz*', where *Absicht* would generally be used, but the notion of '(hidden) intention' is still present in the adjective *tendenziös* (at least in some contexts).

← See also under *oben* (for *Tendenz nach oben*).

Tenor: tenor

den ersten ~ (or *die Rolle des ersten Tenors*) *spielen* to play the principal part, play first fiddle; since the 19th c., e.g. (S.-B.) Szavardy, *Paris* 1,253 [1852]: '. . . *vertritt der Hauptredacteur . . . die Stelle des ersten Tenors*'; cf. Dombrowski, *System* III,40 [1920]: '*in einer badischen Nachwahl ging er . . . siegend durchs Ziel . . . Ein Heldentenor war er nicht*'. See also under *Geige* for similar *die erste Geige spielen*.

← See also under *kastrieren* (for *Kastratentenor*).

Teppich: carpet

der ~ (lit.) carpet; in comparisons as early as in the Bible, e.g. Psalm 104,2: '*du breitest aus den himel wie einen teppich*' (where the A.V. uses 'curtain'); since the 18th c. frequent in lit. images, e.g. Klinger, *Gesch.e.Teutsch.* 184 [1798]: '*Teppich der Nacht*', Schiller, *M.Stuart* 3,1: '*auf dem grünen Teppich der Wiesen*', and in numerous compounds, e.g. *Blumenteppich* as in Forster, *It.* 1,159, *Moosteppich*, as in Vischer, *Ästh.* 2,92, *Schneeteppich*, as in Kohl, *Alpenreisen* 3,2 [1841], *Wiesenteppich*, as in Boree, *Dor u.d.S.* 214. Schiller used *Farbenteppich* with ref. to the rainbow, Heine, *Rom.* 73 has: '. . . *webt emsig seines Liedes Riesenteppich*'. Sometimes the old meaning 'curtain' comes to the fore, as in Goethe, *Egmont* 4: '*die Religion . . . sei nur ein prächtiger Teppich, hinter dem man jeden gefährlichen Anschlag nur desto leichter ausdenkt*'. The verbs *überteppichen* and *umteppichen*, still to be found in 19th c. lit., are obs.

mit jem.m auf den breiten ~ *treten* (a.) to get married to sb.; a ref. to the carpet in front of the altar on which bride and bridegroom stand; recorded by Adelung, now a.

den roten ~ *ausrollen* (coll.) to prepare for the arrival of an important visitor; 20th c. coll.

etw. auf den ~ *bringen* (coll.) to bring a matter up for discussion or settlement, put sth. on the agenda; since the 19th c., also the opposite *es soll unterm* ~ *bleiben* = 'it is to remain undiscussed or unmentioned'; cf. Engl. 'to sweep sth. under the carpet'.

der Flickenteppich rag rug; figur. for 'patchwork'; modern, e.g. with ref. to the map of the old German Empire with its numerous states, principalities, Free Cities, etc., but also with ref. to works of literature with many not closely related parts.

der Ölteppich oil slick; since 2nd half of the 20th c., e.g. *Verwendung von Mikroorganismen zum Abbau eines Ölteppichs.*

bleib auf dem ~ ! (coll.) be reasonable! control yourself! keep your shirt on! meaning 'deal (calmly) with the matter, keep to the point at issue'; 20th c. coll.

etw. unter den ~ kehren (or *fegen*) (coll.) to sweep sth. under the carpet; 20th c. coll. (under Engl. influence?).

der kommt bei mir nicht auf den ~ (sl.) I will not see him; in wider sense 'he will not get anything from me'; since the middle of the 20th c.

verhandeln (or *feilschen*) *wie ein Teppichhändler* (coll.) to argue fiercely or tenaciously about the price; since the 2nd half of the 20th c.

← See also under *Tapet* for related phrases.

Termin: time limit, fixed time

den ~ schmeißen (sl.) to achieve sth. within the allotted time, manage to finish in time; 2nd half of 20th c. sl.

das paßt nicht in meinen Terminkalender (coll.) that does not fit in with my plans; literally: 'it does not fit into my book of appointments', but then used in wider sense for plans, ideas, etc.; 20th c. coll.

← See also under *stopfen* (for *ich habe jetzt einen vollgestopften Terminkalender*).

Terrain: terrain, ground

das ~ sondieren to reconnoitre, explore the lie of the land; originally a mil. locution; since the 18th c. extended to other contexts; similarly: *an ~ gewinnen* = 'to gain ground' (e.g. in a debate), *auf einem ~ nicht bewandert sein* = 'to be unfamiliar with an area, a subject-matter, etc.'; 19th c.

terra incognita

das ist ~ für ihn he does not know anything about that; originally *~* meant 'unexplored territory', then in 19th c. extended to sth. about which one has no knowledge, unfamiliar ground.

Terrier: see *Pudel.*

Terror: terror

in dem Haus gibt es immer ~ (coll.) in that house they are always quarrelling, at each others' throats; 20th c. coll.

~ machen (sl.) to cause trouble, rebel (unreasonably), make difficulties or a fuss; since the 2nd half of the 20th c., often in *mach keinen ~ !* = 'take this calmly, be sensible about this!'.

jem. terrorisieren to intimidate, bully, harass sb.; originally 'to terrorize, ill-treat through acts of terrorism', then extended to acts which are much less serious; 20th c.

Testament: last will and testament

sein ~ his legacy, what he has left to posterity; not strictly correct use of *~*, since it is not the last will but the legacy left behind (through sb.'s achievements, etc.) that is really meant (*Erbe* or

Hinterlassenschaft would be correct); *DWb.* [1935] does not list this usage, but it is now recorded, e.g. in *Duden.*

der kann sein ~ machen (coll.) he is dangerously ill, on his last legs; at least since the 19th c., in Eiselein [1838] listed as '*er kann sein Testament machen, wenn er will*'; now more loosely = 'he had better prepare himself for sth. nasty to come his way'.

← See also under *Gewalt* (for *ein Testament machen*).

teuer: brave; excellent; expensive

er wird sein Leben so ~ wie möglich verkaufen he will sell his life as dearly as possible, defend himself fiercely (to the end); Adelung recorded it with *Haut*, Campe with *Leben.*

← See also under *anschließen* (for *ans Vaterland, ans teure, schließ dich an*), *Auge* (for *nicht zu teuer mit dem Tod gebüßt*), *bezahlen* (for *etw. teuer bezahlen*), *bitten* (for *Bittkauf, teurer Kauf*), *erkaufen* (for *das ist teuer erkauft*), *Haut* (for *seine Haut teuer verkaufen*), *hoch* (for *hoch und teuer schwören*), *Honig* (for *das ist teurer Honig, den man aus Dornen lecken muß*), *kommen* (for *teuer zu stehen kommen*), *Mauer* (for *Maurerschweiß ist teuer*), *Pflaster* (for *ein teures Pflaster*), *Rat* (for *da ist guter Rat teuer*), *schenken* (for *es ist mir geschenkt zu teuer*), *Schiff* (for *teure Schiffe bleiben am Rande*), *Spaß* (for *ein teurer Spaß*), *Sünde* (for *sündhaft teuer*) and *Suppe* (for *es gibt keine teurere Suppe als die man umsonst bekommt*).

Teufel: devil

ein ~ a devil, devilish individual, real devil, devil incarnate; e.g. Wieland, *Klelia* 2,193: '*du selber bist ein Teufel oder Engel*'; Luther 6,117a (Jena) used it as a term of abuse for Papists, Mendelssohn 4,2,349 for literary critics; also in milder sense for 'little devil, holy terror, mischief-maker', esp. when applied to young people, also in expressions of pity such as *ein armer ~* = 'a poor devil', general since Early NHG, see p. 73,, used ironically in Goethe, *Faust I*, 1675, and with contempt in *dummer ~*, closely associated with the figure of fun in dramas of the 17th c.; hence also *den ~ im Leib haben*, since Early NHG, e.g. (*DWb*) Ettner, *Unw.Doctor* 785.

← See also under *braten* (for *Teufelsbraten*), *Engel* (for *junger Engel, alter Teufel*), *Leib* (for *leibhaftiger Teufel*), *Mensch* (for *ein Teufel in Menschengestalt* and *eingemenschter Teufel*), *Nacken* (for *jem.m den Teufel auf den Nacken setzen*). See also under *Satan* for similar locutions.

des Teufels sein to be possessed (by the devil), to be mad; since MHG, also sometimes as *einen ~ im Kopf haben*, e.g. Weiße, *Kom.Op.* 3,180: '. . . daß meine Frau einen verwetterten Hochmuthsteufel im Kopfe hat'.

← See also under *backen* (for *den Teufel im Nacken haben*), *besessen* (for *vom Teufel besessen*), *Donner* (for *daß dich der Teufel . . .*), *fahren* (for *zum*

Teufel fahren), *glotzen* (for *der Teufel glotzt jem.m aus den Augen* and *teuflisch glotzen*), *holen* (for *hol mich der Teufel*), *Nase* (for *der Teufel sitzt in jem.m*), *reiten* (for *der Teufel reitet jem.*), *schwarz* (for *jem. zum Teufel jagen*) and *Sibylle* (for *vom Teufel selbst bestellt sein*).

zum ~ ! damn it! hell! old curse; similar curses are *in Teufels Namen*, current since Early NHG, *der ~ !*, e.g. Lessing 1,322: '*der Teufel! das verschnupft*', *zum ~ noch einmal*, as in G.Keller, *Gr. Heinr.* 4,255. Earlier *was teufels* was used, current since MHG, e.g. Veldeke, *En.* 302,36, but this gave way in the 17th c. to *was ~*, e.g. Chamisso 4,85: '*was Teufel ficht uns Alexander an?*' and *was zum ~*, f.r.b. Stieler [1691]. *~* on its own can be inserted as a curse, e.g. Schiller, *Turandot* 3,4: '*wie Teufel kamt ihr zu dem Narrenstreich?*', Lenz 2,99: '*wo Teufel kommen Sie denn nun hieher?*'; in some dialects *was Teufels* is still used, e.g. Gotthelf, *U.* 2,141.
← See also under *Galeere* (for *was zum Teufel*).

beim ~ ! (coll.) truly! really! strong affirmation; since the 18th c., but not yet listed in Kramer [1702], e.g. Schiller, *Räuber* 4,5. See also below under *das weiß der ~*.

den ~ (kümmert er sich) (coll.) the devil (he cares); emphatic negation; cf. the negative sense of Engl. 'the devil' and 'damn all'; since MHG, e.g. *Nibelungenl.* 1993: '*ir habet den tiuvel getân*' (also 6993: '*ja bringe ich iu den tiuvel, sprach aber Hagene*'), e.g. Goethe, *Pater Brey* 77: '*. . . kennt den Teufel* (= 'not at all') *der Männer Ränken*', Ense, *T* 1,111: '*er weiß den Teufel* (= 'nothing') *davon*', G.Keller, *Gr. Heinr.* 4,240, where *sich den ~ um etw. kümmern* occurs.

das weiß der ~ (coll.) nobody knows that; negation as in the previous entry; recorded by Campe, but presumably much older. Note, however, that *weiß der ~* (coll.) can also be a strong affirmation = 'truly, really, as everybody knows', as in Schiller, *Wall.Tod* 5,2.

kein ~ (coll.) nobody; since Early NHG, e.g. Fischart, 371a: '*. . . verrosten, das sie kein teufel im fegfeur erpanzerfegen könte*', Müller 5,177: '*niemand anwortet dort, kein Teufel hört mich hier*', Jean Paul 3,43: '*im Grunde fragt kein Teufel Viel nach meinem Siechthum*'.

. . . wie der (or *ein*) *~* like the devil, madly, furiously; in many comparisons, often simply added as an intensifier, when it means 'enormously, tremendously, terribly'; sometimes with ref. to speed (*rasch, flink wie der ~, er fährt in seinem Wagen wie der ~*), or to character (*falsch, verschlagen, listig wie der ~*), or astonishing achievements, e.g. Rabener 4,30: '*saufen kann er wie ein Teufel*', G.Keller, *Gr.Heinr.* 2,337: '*er könne nähen wie der Teufel*'. Kramer [1702] listed: '*es stinckt wie der Teufel, er schreyet, tobet, wütet wie der Teufel, er ist schlimm wie der Teufel, das ist schwer etc. wie der Teufel*'.

← See also under *Abschied* (for *Abschied nehmen wie der Teufel*), *aussein* (for *auf etw. aus sein wie der Teufel auf eine arme Seele*; see also under *Seele*), *Feld* (for *wie ein Feld voll Teufel aussehen*), *schwarz* (for *schwarz wie der Teufel*) and *stinken* (for *mit Gestank scheiden wie der Teufel*).

es ist zum ~ gegangen (coll.) it is kaput, broken, gone to pieces; with ref. to abstracts 'it has failed, come to nothing, gone phut'; in this particular coll. sense since the 18th c., e.g. Klinger, *Theater* 1,247: '*unser ganzes Projekt . . . ist zum Teufel*', Goethe, *Faust I*,3700: '*zum Teufel erst das Instrument*'. Hence also *der ~ hat's gesehen* = 'it has gone wrong, failed, miscarried', as in Schiller, *Räuber* 2,3. For a similar emphatic statement of failure see p. 74 for *es ist im Arsch*.

← See also under *Graus* (for *kein Teufel hat kein Schwänzerl mehr*).

auf ~ komm heraus (coll.) like mad, very much, to the utmost; meaning 'madly or wickedly enough to provoke the devil to come and fetch the sinner', the kind of provocation which is also alluded to in *den ~ an die Wand malen* (which see under *malen*); since early in the 18th c., at first in the N.

das ist (eben) der ~ mit. . . . (coll.) that's the trouble with . . . ; used for 'difficulty, problem' since Early NHG, e.g. Luther, *S.W.* 60,120: '*ei, das müßte der teufel sein, das du solltest fromm und gerecht sein*'; later more loosely for 'trouble, drawback'; cf. *der ~ steckt im Detail* = 'it is the particulars, the details which constitute the problem', since the 20th c., but not yet in Schulz, *Fremdwb.* [1913].

Teufels-. . . (1) damned . . . , damnable . . . ; in many compounds since Early NHG (Luther used many for things or people whom he considered execrable), e.g. *Teufelsbetrug* = 'damnable deception', f.r.b. Ludwig [1716], *Teufelsgedanke* = 'devil-inspired idea', f.r.b. Kramer [1702], *Teufelsgeld* = 'money acquired with the help of the devil' (since Early NHG) and 'damned, accursed money' (since the 17th c.), *Teufelsglück* = 'the devil's (own) luck', f.r.b. Stieler [1691], also in the prov. *Teufelskinder haben Teufelsglück* = 'the devil's child the devil's luck' (recorded for Engl. since the 17th c.), *Teufelskind* = 'progeny of the devil', since Early NHG, e.g. Luther 6,47b (Jena), also as a term of abuse for 'wicked child' (since Early NHG), *Teufelskopf* = *Teufelskind*, also used by Luther as a term of abuse in *Werke* 3,93a (Jena), *Teufelskunst* = 'black magic, devilry', since Early NHG (cf. also Schiller, *Wall. Tod* 5,2 on Wallenstein: '*er ist gefroren, mit der Teufelskunst behaftet, sein Leib ist undurchdringlich*'), *Teufelsmesse* = 'black mass', a modern compound, still missing in *DWb.* [1935] but surely older, *Teufelspakt* = 'pact with the devil', recorded since the 18th c., e.g. by Zedler, *Teufelsreich* = 'realm or province of the devil', e.g. Luther 6,491a (Jena) on the papacy, f.r.b. Stieler, *Teufelsstreich* = 'wicked prank or trick', e.g. Schiller, *Fiesco* 3,7: *'was will mir mein Geiz für einen Teufelsstreich spielen!'*, *Teufelswerk* = 'work of the devil', since Early NHG, f.r.b. Stieler.

← See also under *Braut* (for *die Braut des Teufels*), *Dank* (for *des Teufels Dank*), *Finger* (for *Teufelsfinger*), *Gewitter* (for *Teufelsbraut*), *Grille* (for *Teufelsgrillen*). *Kreis* (for *Teufelskreis*), *Küche* (for *des Teufels Küche*) and *stief-* (for *die Stiefmutter des Teufels Unterfutter*).

Teufels- . . . (2) confounded . . . , terrible . . . ; in compounds which either express a high degree of sth. or are used in irritation about sth.; examples are *er hat Teufelsangst* = 'he is dead scared' (see p. 1364 for similar terms with *Hölle*), *Teufelsding* = 'damned thing or business or state of affairs', e.g. Goethe, *Br.* 2,65 (W.): '. . . *ein Teufelsding, wenn man alles in sich selbst sagen muß'*, *Teufelsgeschichte* = 'confounded affair', recorded since the 19th c., *Teufelslärm* = 'damned row', e.g. Immermann, *Schr.* 4,427 (and similar *Teufelskrach, Teufelsradau*). In angry refs. to people *Teufelsmann, Teufelsleute, Teufelspack, Teufelsvolk* have occurred since Early NHG (Stieler [1691] recorded *Teufelsrotte* and *Teufelsvolk*). Other compounds of this type are *Teufelsrätsel* = 'confounded riddle', e.g. H.v.Kleist [edit. H.] 1,218, *Teufelswirtschaft* = 'damned business or goings-on', e.g. Freytag, *Ges.W.* 15,135 on the Frankfurt Parliament: *'die ganze Teufelswirthschaft in Frankfurt ist ihm nicht recht'*, *Teufelszeug* = 'damned stuff or contraption', since the 18th c., e.g. A.Zweig, *Beil* 612; cf. also such instances as *teufelsteuer* = 'damned expensive, as in Pestalozzi 1,46, *teufelstoll* = ' completely mad', as in Jean Paul, *Uns. Loge* 1,87, or *teufelsweit* = 'damned far', f.r.b. Stieler [1691].

← See also under *Gewalt* (for *mit Teufels Gewalt*) and *Gezücht* (for *Teufelsgezücht*).

Teufels- . . . (3) amazing . . . , extraordinary . . . ; in compounds which express a degree of admiration, sometimes also used affectionately. The chief examples are *Teufelsbursche, – junge, -kerl* = 'devil of a fellow', current since the 17th c., *Teufelskerl* recorded by Stieler [1691] and used by Goethe in *Mitschuld.* 3,9, *Teufelsweib* = '(quite) some woman' (modern in this sense, but since the 17th c. as a term of abuse). G.Keller in *Gr.Heinr.* 2,171 and 2,233 used *Teufelsbuben* and *Teufelskerl*. In some of the early dictionaries it is difficult to ascertain whether in the listed compounds irritation or admiration are to be expressed.

der Teufelsbolzen (regional zool.) long-tailed titmouse (*Aegithalos caudatus*); f.r.b. Nemnich with the old Lat. name *Orites caudatus*. *Teufelsbolzen* is also used in some areas for 'dragon-fly' and was used in pl for 'matches' (displaced by *Streichhölzer*), esp. when used as tokens in gambling (cf. Freytag, *Ges.W.* 4,457).

der Teufelsdreck (chem.) asafoetida; since Early NHG, e.g. Luther 4,531a (Jena); Jacobsson recorded

Teufelsdreck with the gloss *'das stinkende Bergtheer, merde de diable'*; it was also called *Teufelskoth*, e.g. Logau 2,9,49.

die Teufelsfarbe (obs.) indigo; known by that name since the 16th c., when it acquired its bad reputation because it was alleged that it weakened the fibre of textiles (cf. *Zs.f.dt. Phil.* 20,491), still in use in the 18th c., e.g. Möser 1,205, now obs.

der Teufelsmaler (regional, obs.?) itinerant painter who did simple painting jobs in villages on furniture or the outside of houses; still in use in the 19th c., strangely missing in *DWb.* [1935].

die Teufelsnadel (zool.) blue darter (the fish *Boleosoma*); so called because of its rapid movements; others have recorded *Teufelsnadel* for 'dragon-fly' (see the entry on *Teufelsbolzen* above; cf. Oken 5,1496 [1833ff]).

die Teufelsnatter (zool.) the snake *Coluber melanis*; f.r.b. Nemnich [1793ff]; Campe [1810] added its other name *Teufelsschlange*.

der Teufelsrochen (zool.) manta ray, devil-fish (*Manta birostris*); recorded since the 19th c.

. . .-teufel sb. who pursues sth. fanatically or is mad about sth.; often coming close to 'maniac', but sometimes the second part stands for 'devil' and the first part of the compound is a mere intensifier, e.g. *Erzteufel* = 'devil incarnate', as used by Luther 1,124a (Jena). Other examples are *Arbeitsteufel* = 'mania for work', as in *den Arbeitsteufel im Leib haben*, e.g. Gotthelf, *Schuldenb.* 399 [1852], *Hausteufel* = 'domestic tyrant', f.r.b. Stieler [1691], e.g. Auerbach, *Jos.* 49 [1860], cf. also Auerbach, *Gv.* 333: *'es steckt in jedem Menschen ein kleiner Kommandierteufel'*, and *Waldteufel* (obs.) = 'satyr', since the 18th c., but also recorded for a species of monkey, and (by Adelung) for the butterfly *Papilio nymphalis Semele*.

← See also under *fegen* (for *Fegteufel*, to which one could add synonymous *Putzteufel*), *Feld* (for *Feldteufel*) and *Spiel* (for *Spielteufel*).

der Meerteufel (zool.) coot (*Fulica atra*); in some dictionaries as *Fulica aterrima*; the more usual names are *Bläßhuhn* and *schwarzes Wasserhuhn*.

den (or *die Rolle des*) *Advokaten des Teufels spielen* to act the part of devil's advocate; less used than the Lat. form *advocatus diaboli*. In the procedure for canonization or beatification in the Roman Catholic Church a priest termed *advocatus diaboli* had to put forward arguments against proceeding further; in modern period extended to a person who in the course of a debate puts forward arguments which help the opposing side, though or even if he does not himself believe in them.

des Teufels Paternoster beten (obs.) to curse; in Engl. 'pattering the devil's paternoster' has been in use since the 14th c. (Chaucer used a similar wording); for German recorded by Wander [1876], but earlier *loci* have eluded me.

dem hat der ~ ein Ei in die Wirtschaft gelegt sb. or sth. has messed up his affairs; Engl. has no direct parallels, but such phrases as 'the devil has cast a bone' (cf. Oxford 139), 'the devil sets his foot or casts his club on sth.' (cf. Oxford 142) express the same notion; used by Schiller in *Kab.u.L.* 2,4, recorded since the 19th c., e.g. Kinkel, *Erz.* 87: '*da legte auf einmal der Teufel ein Ei in die Wirthschaft*'.

der ist dem ~ aus der Bleiche gelaufen (coll.) he is dirty (or black) all over; at least since the 18th c., recorded by Campe [1810]; also applied to people with a dark complexion, mentioned by Eiselein [1838]; now obs.

der ~ bleicht seine Großmutter (regional coll.) sunshine and showers are following each other in quick succession; current since the 18th c., recorded by Campe [1810].

der fängt den ~ auf freiem Felde (coll.) he is a resolute and plucky fellow (and quick to act); also can contain the notion of being afraid of nothing; recorded by Franck [1541] and in dialect dictionaries since the 19th c., e.g. by Schmeller for Bav.; a Franconian variant is *mit dem kann man den ~ auf freiem Feld fangen*, in other areas *er fing den ~ auf der Heide* (where *fing = würde fangen*) is used.

der ist dem ~ vom Karren gefallen (regional coll.) he is a nasty customer, a criminal type; recorded since the 19th c., e.g. by Sanders [1865]; Gotthelf used the phrase in *Schuldenb.* 66 and *Uli* 44; variants are: *der ist dem ~ aus der Butte gesprungen* (Austria), *aus der Hölle gelaufen* (recorded by Klix [1863]), *ins Garn gefallen*, e.g. Mathesius, *Post.* 79a [1567].

er fürchtet sich davor wie der ~ vorm Weihwasser (coll.) he is dead scared of it; the devil's fear of holy water has been mentioned in lit. since the MHG period, e.g. Hugo v. Trimberg, *Renner* 11309; cf. also the Engl. prov. the devil loves no holy water, current since the 16th c. (cf. Oxf. 141); cf. also the entry in Kramer [1702]: '*ein Teufel, der kein Weihwasser förchtet, d.i. ein schön und geiles Weibsbild*'.

dem ~ den Weihkessel nachwerfen (coll.) to throw good money after bad, increase one's losses or damage unnecessarily; at least since the 19th c., e.g. G.Keller, *Salander* 56: '. . . hatte so viel gekostet, daß Salander sich scheute, dem Teufel noch den Weihkessel nachzuwerfen, wie er sagte'.

für Geld kann man den ~ tanzen sehen (coll.) one can get everything for money; recorded since the 19th c., e.g. by Sanders [1865].

es träumt ihm vom ~ (coll.) he has a bad conscience, he is plagued by remorse; recorded since the 19th c., e.g. by Eiselein [1838].

hat der ~ X geholt, mag er auch Y haben (regional coll.) since the devil has taken X (= since X has gone phut), he may as well have Y; in very many forms in the regions and presumably very old but not recorded (to my knowledge) before the 19th c., e.g. Müller-Fraureuth [1911] listed for Saxony: *hat der ~ den Sack geholt, mag er auch noch das Bändel*

holen and *hat der ~ die Kuh gelangt, kann er den Schwanz auch kriegen* and Fischer listed for Swabia: *hat der ~ den Gaul geholt, so soll er auch den Zaum haben*.

der ~ prügelt sein Weib (coll.) when it rains if sun is shining, devil is beating wife; in Engl. since the 18th c., in German probably old as well, but I have only found it recorded in dialect dictionaries, e.g. in Fischer for Swabia.

der ~ schläft nicht the devil is never asleep, we are always in mortal danger; Luther 7,285a (Jena) has it as '*der teuffel schleft nicht*', Grimmelshausen, *Simpliz.* 2,484 as '*der Teufel feiert nicht*'; it has become a much-used saying among huntsmen and members of rifle associations as a word of warning when handling loaded guns (recorded in this context by Hetzel [1896]).

die Teufelei (1) damnable behaviour, devilry; since Early NHG, e.g. Luther, *Wider H.Worst* (repr.) 24; Kramer [1702] recorded '*allerhand Teufeleyen anfangen*' and '*Teufeley treiben*', Frisch [1741] listed it for '*opera diabolica*'. It could also be used for 'sorcery', e.g. Nicolai 5,101: '. . . daß Circe selbst, mit ihr verglichen, von Teufeleien kaum das Abece verstand'.

die Teufelei (2) unpleasant business, trouble; usually the same as *Teufelsgeschichte* (which see above); since the 17th c., recorded by Kramer: '*es ist lauter Teufeley mit solchen Sachen*', following Stieler [1691] who had '*es ist wol eine rechte Teufeley mit dieser Sache*'; now unusual and *etwas Verteufeltes* would be used instead.

teuflisch devilish; frequent since MHG (*tiuvelisch*, also *tiuvelhaft* and *tiuvelhaftec*) for 'wicked' or 'possessed by the devil', e.g. *Passional* 285,5: '*der tuvelhafte man*', also used as an adverb, e.g. *Nibelungenl.* 2167: '*tievellîchen gelogen*', as *tufelhafftig* in Keisersberg, *Post.* 127. Stieler [1691] recorded *teufelhaft, teufelhaftig* and *teufelisch*, as well as *teufelscher Betrug*. Coll. use in emphatic speech = 'very much' (cf. Engl. 'hellish') is old, though at first it still denoted cruelty or wickedness (e.g. Kramer [1702] listed '*einen teufelisch brügeln*'), since the 18th c. used for emphasis, e.g. *man muß teuflisch aufpassen, es ist ein teuflisch weiter Weg*.

die Teufelin she-devil; since MHG (*tiuvelinne*); in modern period sometimes for 'vamp', but also for 'hateful woman' (e.g. Platen 2,251 referring to Catherine the Great) or (admiringly) for a 'woman-virtuoso' (e.g. Heine, *Lut.* 2,297).

teufeln (regional) to find fault with people, call people names; recorded e.g. for Saxony by Müller-Fraureuth [1911]. He also listed *jem.m etw. teufeln* for 'to refuse to give sb. what he wants'.

verteufelt damned, accursed; since Early NHG, e.g. Luther 28,324 (Weimar); the range of the term is wide and comprises 'damned, desperate, possessed by the devil', also 'cunning, sly, highly skilled', often in irritated refs. to a person, as in Goethe 43,159 (W.): '*läßt sich doch der verteufelte Benvenuto auch gar nichts sagen*', also adverbially in coll. use, as in Schiller, *Br.* 3,68: '*es ist eine verteufelt schwere Aufgabe*' (Schiller in *Räuber* 2,3 also used *teufelmäßig*).

etw. verteufeln (1) (obs. or regional) to ruin sth. (deliberately), mess up sth. (through lack of skill); occasionally in lit. since the 19th c., but mainly in dialects of the S., where it can also mean 'to waste (e.g. one's money, but also one's life by sinful living)'; cf. also intrans. *verteufeln* = 'to despair', as in *es ist zum Verteufeln*, e.g. (*DWb*) Handel-Mazzetti, *J.u.Mar.* 1,206 (where some regions would use *es ist zum Teufelholen*).

etw. verteufeln (2) to disparage, decry sth. present sth. (or sb.) in a bad light; only since the 20th c.; hence *die Verteufelung* = 'disparagement' (but for the 18th c. *Verteufelung* is recorded as 'changing into a devil, becoming a devil').

jem. verteufeln (regional) to slander sb., give sb. a bad name; recorded for some regions, e.g. for Saxony by Müller-Fraureuth [1911]; cf. synonymous *den ~ von jem.m sagen*, as in (*DWb*) *Briefe d.Herz. Elis.Charl. (1676–1706)* [edit. Holland] 446.

jem.m den ~ im Glas zeigen (regional) to frighten sb.; *Glas* could be a mirror, but Fischer who recorded the phrase for Swabia suggests that *der Cartesische ~* is meant, recorded by Adelung: '*der Cartesianische Teufel, oder Teufelchen, gläserne hohle Figuren, welche sich, so wie man will, im Wasser untertauchen, und wieder hervor kommen*'.

er hat mit dem ~ Kuhdreck gedroschen (regional) he has freckles all over his face; recorded in this form for Swabia by Fischer; a variant, current in many areas is: *bei ihm hat der ~ durchs Sieb geschissen* (recorded since the 19th c.).

← See also under *Erbse* (for *der Teufel hat Erbsen gedroschen*).

der ~ (tech., coll.) willow, teaser, devil (for treatment of wool); recorded since the 19th c., e.g. Karmarsch, *Mech.* 2,680 [1837]; usually called *Reißwolf*.

der Feuerteufel (also *Speiteufel* or *Sprühteufel*) fireworks; terms for figures made of moist powder which sparkle when set alight; recorded since the 19th c., when *DWb.* [1862] listed *Feuerteufel* and Sanders [1865] all three terms. Seidel used *Sprühteufel* in *Leb. Hühnchen* 1,46 [1881], and P. Keller in *Hubertus* 270 [1918] employed it in a metaphor: '*sie war lustig und lebhaft, aber kein quecksilbriger Sprühteufel*'.

. . . sagte der ~ . . . (prov.expr.) *. . .* quoth the devil *. . .* ; sayings of this type occur in Engl., too, but few have been recorded (*Oxford Dict. of Engl. Prov.* only lists: 'like will to like, quoth the devil to the collier' with an e.l. of 1568), whereas German examples are very numerous. Hetzel [1896] listed: '*gleich und gleich gesellt sich gern, sagte der Teufel zum Kohlenbrenner, als er merkte, daß sie alle beide schwarz waren; wo man singt, da laß dich ruhig*

nieder, sagte der Teufel und setzte sich auf einen Bienenschwarm; so kommt Gottes Wort in Schwung, sagte der Teufel, da schmiß er seiner Großmutter die Bibel an den Kopf; wie die Welt doch auf- und niedergeht, sagte der Teufel, als er auf einem Brunnenschwengel saß; Sorte zu Sorte, sagte der Teufel, da gab er einen Pfaffen und ein altes Weib zusammen; ich kann damit nicht fertig werden, sagte der Teufel, da sollte er über seine Großmutter weinen; das Alter geht voraus, sagte der Teufel und schmiß seine Großmutter die Treppe hinunter; das wollen wir stehen lassen, sagte der Teufel und ging am Kreuze vorbei, ohne es weiter zu beachten; jeder nach seinem Magen, sagte der Teufel, da aß er Torf mit Teer; viel Geschrei und wenig Wolle, sagte der Teufel, da schor er ein Schwein; einfach aber niedlich, sagte der Teufel und strich sich den Schwanz grün an, etc.etc.'. Fischer in his *Schwäb.Wb.* listed among others '*besser etwas als nichts, hat der Teufel gesagt und die Rührmilch mit der Heugabel gefressen*'. See also under *best* (for *das Beste ist in der Mitte, sagte der Teufel, da ging er zwischen zwei Pfaffen*).

wenn der ~ krank wird, will er ein Mönch werden (prov.) the devil was sick, the devil a monk would be; the devil was well, the devil a monk was he; in both languages this goes back to M.Lat. *aegrotavit daemon, monachus tunc esse volebat; daemon convaluit, daemon ut ante fuit*; in Engl. recorded since the 16th c., but late in German, listed in Simrock [1846].

wenn man den ~ nennt, kommt er gerennt (prov.) the devil is never nearer than when we are talking of him; proverbs concerning the naming or calling of the devil, current since Early NHG, are very numerous (cf. the lists in Wander [1876]), mainly in such wordings as *dem ~ darf man nicht rufen, er kommt von selbst*, f.r.b. Pistorius [1716]. The earliest recording is Franck [1541]: '*wo man dess teufels gedenckt, da will er seyn*'. Engl. versions have been recorded since the 17th c. (cf. *Oxf.* 140). In modern usage the prov. corresponds to Engl. 'talk of the devil' (see the entry under *Esel*).

wenn der ~ will probieren, so kann er auch die Schrift zitieren (prov.) the devil can cite Scripture for his purpose; recorded in this form since Eiselein [1839], but in essence surely older; cf. Luther 15,591 (Weimar): '*unsere widersacher zyttyerent disen text auch*'.

der ~ scheißt immer nur auf große Haufen (prov.) the devil always tips at the biggest ruck; in German recorded since early in the 16th c. (for Engl. only since the 19th c., cf. *Oxf.* 138). The meaning is the same as in *wo Tauben sind, fliegen Tauben zu*, for which see under *Taube*.

← See also under *abschwatzen* (for *dem Teufel ein Ohr abschwatzen*), *abschwören* (for *dem Teufel ein Bein abschwören*), *Apotheke* (for *der Teufel traue dem Apotheker*), *arm* (for *an armer Leute Hoffahrt wischt der Teufel den Arsch*), *austreiben* (for *den Teufel mit Beelzebub austreiben* and *jem.m den Hochmuts-/ Hoffahrtsteufel austreiben*), *bauen* (for *. . . baut der*

Teufel eine Kapelle), *Beichte* (for *selbst wenn der Teufel Beichte säße*), *Bein* (for *dem Teufel ein Bein brechen*), *blau* (for *blaue Teufel*), *Eichhorn* (for *weismachen, der Teufel wär' ein Eichhörnchen*), *Fliege* (for *in der Not frißt der Teufel Fliegen*), *Galopp* (for *den hat der Teufel im Galopp verloren*), *Gebet* (for *des Teufels Gebetbuch*), *Gevatter* (for *den Teufel zum Gevatter nehmen*), *Großmutter* (for *des Teufels Großmutter*), *halb* (for *Halbteufel*), *Kerze* (for *dem Teufel eine Kerze anzünden*), *Kirche* (for the same as under *bauen*), *los* (for *der Teufel ist los*), *malen* (for *den Teufel an die Wand malen*), *müßig* (for *Müßiggang ist des Teufels Ruhebank*), *Patsch* (for *der Teufel kehrt auch seinen Freunden den Rücken zu*), *Pferd* (for *des Teufels Reitpferd*), *plagen* (for *sich mit dem Teufel plagen*), *scheren* (for *scher dich zum Teufel*), *Schwanz* (for *der Teufel hat seinen Schwanz dabei*) and *Stelze* (for *und wenn der Teufel auf Stelzen ginge*).

← For locutions in which the devil is referred to in other terms or euphemisms see under *Bock*, *bös*, *dieser*, *Henker*, *Kuckuck* and *Satan*, also under *Gott* (for *Gottseibeiuns*).

Text: text

der ∼ subject, topic, theme; an off-shoot from the original meaning, since late in the 17th c., e.g. Stoppe, *Ged.* 1,209 [1728]: '*die Ehen sind ein Text, worüber jeder Narr sich seine Glossen macht*' or Goethe 48,160 (W.); 'subject' is also meant in the locution *zu tief* (or *weit*) *in den* ∼ *kommen* (or *geraten*) = 'to pursue a subject too far or in too much detail', e.g. Lessing, *D.alte Jungfer* 1,1 [1740], Goethe, *Werther* 1: '*bei diesem Anlaß kam er sehr tief in Text*' (now a.); similarly *bleib beim* ∼ ! = 'stick to the subject'. The opposite is *vom* ∼ *schweifen*, as in Scheidt, *Grobianus* 7 [1551], where, however, Scheidt used ∼ in its original meaning.

weiter im ∼ ! go on! continue! beginnings in Early NHG, e.g. Fischart, *Garg.* (repr.) 77: '*item ferner im text*', also Wieland 8,252.

jem.m den ∼ *lesen* (coll.) to read sb. the riot act, give sb. a telling-off; ∼ here is a relevant passage in the Bible to serve as admonition or reproof, e.g. from Leviticus (cf. *jem.m die Leviten lesen* on p. 1615, also *jem.m die Epistel lesen* on p. 663); current since Early NHG, e.g. Scheidt, *Grobianus* (repr.) 4717 [1551], also Lessing 12,299 or Wieland 10,114; now dropping out of use.

aus dem ∼ *kommen* to lose one's thread; general only since the 19th c.; the same applies to the transitive *jem. aus dem* ∼ *bringen* = 'to make sb. lose his thread', e.g. (Sp.) Zschokke, *Alamontade* 1,5 [1802]: '. . . *bringe die geschicktesten Heidenbekehrer aus dem Text*'.

sich seinen ∼ *zu etw. machen* (coll.) to interpret sth. in one's own way, draw one's own conclusions from sth.; modern, e.g. (Sp.) Brod, *Leben m.e. Göttin* 195: '*dazu macht sich doch jeder seinen Text*'. Since ∼ and *Glosse* are closely connected, it is not surprising that similar locutions exist with *Glosse*

(see p. 1083), and in the phrase with ∼ one also has a critical or unpleasant interpretation in mind.

← See also under *klar* (for *Klartext*) and *Melodie* (for *er weiß die Melodie, aber nicht den Text*).

Theater: theatre

das ∼ (1) (lecture-) theatre; first in the medical faculty and in Lat. form *theatrum anatomicum* (e.g. Haller, *Tagebücher 1723–27*, 58), later for any lecture-room with seating arranged as in an amphitheatre (or *amphitheatralisch*, current since the 18th c.).

das ∼ (2) (lit.) theatre, scene, stage; used for a place in which sth. is offered to public view; since the 17th c., often at first in Lat. form, e.g. *theatrum mundi*, in German as ∼ *der Welt*, e.g. Lauremberg, *Scherzged.* 17 [1652], Hegel, *Orient.Welt* 270 [1822]: '*das dritte Theater der Geschichte sind die Stromebenen des Oxus*' (also Goethe 17,112 (W)), Uhland, *Ged*, VII: '*auf dem kritischen Theater hat er uns (Gedichte) zur Schau gestellt*'. In compounds also since the 17th c., e.g. *Kriegstheater* = 'theatre of war', used by Goethe, *Welttheater*, e.g. Heinse, *Ardingh.* 1,68; cf. also (S.-B.) *Süddt.Ztg.* (21.7.1953): '"*Theatrum Europeaum*" *oder auch* "*Großes Welttheater*" *nannten sich die Chroniken der Barockzeit*'.

jem.m (ein) ∼ *vorspielen* (coll.) to put on an act to sb.; since early in the 20th c., e.g. (S.-B.) Wittek, *Bewährung* 120 [1937]: '*er hatte sie alle angeführt, hatte ihnen Theater vorgespielt*'; hence also *sich selber* ∼ *vorspielen*, e.g. Görlitz, *Gesch. Generalstab* 112 [1967]; cf. also the sense 'pretense, sham', as in Hilty, *Neue Briefe* 72 [1906]: '*es ist in den menschlichen Dingen ungemein viel bloßes "Theater"*'; hence also *Theatralik*, pejor. for 'pose' (since early in the 20th c.); *theatralisch* has been current since the 18th c., first for 'pertaining to the theatre, histrionic', then (mainly pejor.) for 'showy, affected, melodramatic, bombastic'. See also under *spielen* (p. 2300).

mach kein ∼ ! (coll.) don't make a fuss; since the 1st half of the 20th c.; hence also *ohne viel* ∼ (coll.) = 'without much ado'; it can be intensified as *Affentheater*, e.g. (S.-B.) Welk, *Hoher Befehl* 94 [1957]: '*das Ganze hier ist Theater, Herr Konsul, und heute ist es sogar Affentheater*'. – See also under *Affe* (p. 25). In coll. usage ∼ can also mean 'trouble', e.g. *mit ihm hat man immer ein* ∼, or 'row, rumpus', e.g. *wenn er betrunken nach Hause kommt, gibt es immer ein* ∼.

zum ∼ *gehen* (coll.) to go on the stage, become an actor; modern; cf. also *sie ist vom* ∼ (coll.) = 'she is an actress', since the middle of the 19th c.

Theater-. . . theatre-. . . ; there are several compounds with a figur. component, such as *theaterbesessen* = 'stage-struck' (modern), *Theaterblut*, as in *Theaterblut rollt in seinen Adern* = 'the theatre is in his blood', Th.Mann 6,387 (*Faustus*): '*es fehlte ihr . . . an komödiantischem Instinkt, an dem, was man Theaterblut nenne*', *Theaterdonner* = 'promise of sth. important which turns out to be a damp squib' (cf. similar *Theaterfeuer*, which Schiller used in *Räuber* 1,2), *Theatereffekt* = 'stage or theatrical effect' (19th c.), *Theaterfimmel* (sl.) = 'theatre mania' (20th c.), *Theaterhase* (sl.) = 'expert in matters of the theatre' (20th c.) and *Theaterklatsch* (coll.) = 'green-room gossip'.

der Theatercoup sensational or scandalous event; at first (since 2nd half 19th c.) as a loan (as in Engl.) from French *coup de théâtre* = 'abrupt and unexpected change in the plot'; later (mainly in politics) for an event which causes (or was intended to cause) a sensation, e.g. (S.-B.) Hesselmeyer, *Hannibals Alpenübergang* 6 [1906]: '. . . in diesem strategischen Alpenübergang Napoleons lediglich den großartigen Theatercoup eines politisierenden Generals zu erblicken'.

← See also under *auffliegen* (for *das Theater ist aufgeflogen*), *Mark* (for *das Theater entnerven . . .*) and *Stück* (for *Theaterstück*).

Theke: counter
unter der ~ (coll.) under the counter; ~ has only been in use since ca. 1850 (not even listed yet in Heyne [1895]); the phrase refers to sales of prohibited goods or scarce goods reserved for special customers; current since the middle of the 20th c.

Thema: theme, subject
~ (*Nummer*) *eins* (sl.) sex, erotics; since 1st World War and probably of mil.sl. origin; the locution was soon extended to ~ *eins-zwei* (sl.) = 'sex and booze', ~ *eins-zwei-drei* (sl.) = 'sex, booze and food'; cf. also ~ *null* (sl.) = 'sth. one cannot talk about' and *das ist für mich kein* ~ (coll.) = 'that does not concern (or interest) me'; since the fifties of the 20th c.

← See also under *abspringen* (for *von einem Thema abspringen*), *anschneiden* (for *ein Thema anschneiden*) and *berühren* (for *ein Thema berühren*).

Theorie: see *grau*.

Thermometer: thermometer
das ~ (1) (lit.) indicator; though now a neuter noun, in the past and still in some regions treated as masculine; in lit. figur. use since the 18th c., e.g. Moser, *Patr.Arch.* 1,503 [1784]: '. . . Magen ist oft der Thermometer des Verstandes mancher Hofleute*', Devrient, *F.* II,278 [1839]: '*das Gesicht eines Kaufmannes . . . ist der Thermometer seines Kredites*', Steinmann, *Rothschild* 1,28 [1857]: '*Herr v. Roths-child ist in der That der beste politische Thermometer, ich will nicht sagen Wetterfrosch*', Pfleiderer, *Erinn.* 55 [1890]: '*wie hoch . . . der Gemüthsthermometer . . . gestiegen war*'.

der ~ (2) (cant) bottle of spirits; in the sl. of the criminal underworld (20th c.).

Thespis: Thespis
der Thespiskarren (theatr. jargon) travelling theatre; named after Thespis, Greek author of tragedies (ca. 540 B.C.), who, according to Horace in *Ars poetica* travelled about in a cart; used among actors since the 19th c.; cf. Dryden, prologue to *Sophon-isba*: 'Thespis, the first professor of our art, at country wakes sang ballads from a cart'.

Thomas: Thomas
ein ungläubiger ~ (coll.) a doubting Thomas; biblical, referring to John 20,24–29; as a phrase current since the 16th c., e.g. Franck, *Sprüchw.* [1541]: '*der ungleubig sant Thomas*'.

Thron: throne
den ~ *besteigen* to ascend the throne, begin to rule (as king); since MHG ~ has been used in many locutions in the extended sense of 'rule, authority, royal power', e.g. *Passional* 118,69: '*sitzen in des gewaldes trône*', Luther Aprocr. transl. 1 Macc. 10,52: '. . . sitze auf dem königlich thron'; other locutions are *den* ~ *besteigen*, as in Roth, *Radetzkymarsch* 258, *jem. auf den* ~ *erheben*, as in Gutzkow, *Uriel Ac.* 1,1, *sich des Throns bemächtigen*, as in Schiller, *Fiesco* 2,8, *dem* ~ *dienen*, as in Schiller, *Picc.* 2,7, *den* ~ *würdig erfüllen*, as in Wieland 5,198. In relig. language with ref. to God's throne, e.g. Luther Apocr. transl. Ecclesiasticus 1,8: '*der auf seinem thron sitzet, ein herrschender gott*' (cf. Schiller, *Kab.u.L.* 2,5: '*des Weltrichters Thron*'); cf. also Schiller, *D.Carlos* 1,5: '. . . mein . . . , mir zugesprochen von zwei großen Thronen'. Occasionally, since the 18th c., in lit. metaphors, e.g. Schiller, *Kab.u.L.* 4,8: '*von allen Thronen meines Stolzes herabgestürzt*'.

jem. vom ~ *stoßen* (lit.) to deprive sb. of his power, dethrone sb.; also with ref. to abstracts, e.g. Th. Mann 12,831: '. . . ein . . . Reaktionär, die die Vernunft von ihrem Throne stieß'; cf. recent coll. (sport) *eine Mannschaft vom* ~ *kippen* = 'to topple a team off its leading position in the table'.

sein ~ *wackelt* (coll.) his leading position is in danger; since the 19th c., e.g. Scherr, *Gr.* 2,56: '*die wackelnde Throne und Thrönchen*'; cf. such lit. locutions as in Hebel 3,86: '*die alten Königsthronen schwanken*'.

. . . *-thron* (lit.) seat of . . .; in many lit. compounds, e.g. *Felsenthron*, as in Heine 15,125 with ref. to Montblanc: '. . . auf dem Felsenthron sitzend*', *Richterthron*, used by Schiller and by Platen, or joc. *Pädagogenthron* for 'teacher's desk', as in Pfeffel, *Poet.Vers.* 3,8 [1789].

der ~ (coll.) lavatory-seat, chamber-pot, throne; since the 19th c.; hence also *Thronsaal* (joc.coll.) = 'lavatory'.

thronen (1) to sit (in majesty, often ironic); the verb is not mentioned in Kramer [1702] in any sense, but made its appearance early in the 18th c., e.g. Hagedorn 3,89: '*wie thront auf Moos und Rasen der Hirt*', A. Zweig, *Grischa* 174: '*Pont, der im Dienstzimmer seiner Registratur hinter seinem Schreibtisch thronte*'; also with abstracts, e.g. Gutzkow, *R.v.G.* 6,83: '*die Weisheit soll die Klugheit zu ihrer Dienerin haben, jene thront, diese regiert*'; cf. also *auf* (sometimes *von*) *etw. thronen*, e.g. Seume, *Ged.* 71 [1804]: '*die Anmuth thront von ihrer heitern Stirne*'.

thronen (2) to sit above (or dominate) its surroundings; since the 19th c., e.g. Kinkel, *Ged.* 374 [1850]: '*Sphären, wo die Weltseele thront*', Renn, *Kindheit* 276: '*oben thronte breit und massig das Schloß*'.

← See also under *anfallen* (for *der angefallene Thron*), *entthronen*, *Granit* (for *der Thron ruht auf den granitnen Pfeilern . . .*), *Roman* (for *der Romantiker auf dem Thron*), *schaukeln* (for *Menschen bald auf schwanken Thronen schaukeln*), *schlafen* (for *auf dem Thron schlafen*), *setzen* (for *jem. auf den Thron setzen*), *stürzen* (for *der umgestürzte Thron*) and *stützen* (for *Stütze des Throns*).

Thusnelda

seine ~ (coll.) his sweetheart, girlfriend; probably first in schoolboy's jargon, since Kleist's *Hermannsschlacht*, where they would learn about Hermann's wife *~*, was required reading in many schools; since late in the 19th or early in the 20th c., now general coll., e.g. M.Walser, *Halbzeit* 579: '. . . *der fährt jetzt mit seiner neuen Thusnelda im sündigen Süden herum*'.

Tick: touch

einen ~ haben to have a crotchet, fad, kink, peculiarity; influenced by French *tic*; since the 18th c., e.g. Goethe, *Farbenlehre* 5 (*Akad.Gött.*): '*Kästner . . . hat als Mathematiker den besondern Tick, die Physiker anzufeinden*'; also used for an utterance produced by such a kink, e.g. Seume, *Spaz.* 2,17: '*weil er . . . einen etwas bösartigen Tik gegen die Insel äußere*', and lastly for 'trick', e.g. G.Keller, *Werke* 1,387: '. . . *ein einfacher Tick, dessen Verständnis ihnen . . . durch Zufall gekommen*'. There is also *auf jem. einen ~ haben* (coll.) = 'to bear sb. a grudge' and lastly there is *~* (coll.) = 'tiny amount, bit, shade', as in *das ist einen ~ besser als früher*. It is difficult to decide whether anything in this group is truly figur. or merely an extension of regional locutions influenced by French in parts.

jem. ticken (coll.,obs.) to tease sb.; derived from the original sense 'to touch', used by Goethe in *Die Fischerin*, recorded by Adelung, but then extended to 'to tease', also 'to strike (lightly)', f.r.b. Campe [1810], now obs.

ticken (intrans.) (coll.) to react; modern, e.g. *nicht jeder tickt gleich schnell*; hence also *bei dir tickt es wohl nicht ganz richtig* = 'you must be off your rocker'; in coll. use *ticken* can also mean 'to grasp, comprehend', e.g. *er hat's getickt* = 'he has got it, caught on, the penny has dropped'.

tief: deep

tief (1) deep, low; setting aside *~* = 'deep, extending far (inwards or downwards)', current since MHG, e.g. *Nibelungenl.* 869: '*riten si . . . in einen tiefen walt*' or ibid. 1309: '. . . *mantel tief unde wît*' as remaining on the phys. level (even if slightly extended), one of the first figur. senses appears to be 'deep, low' with ref. to sounds, since Early NHG, e.g. Luther Bible transl. Isaiah 33,19: '*volk von tiefer sprache, die man nicht vernemen kan*'

(where the A.V. puts 'of a deeper speech'), hence *tiefer Glockenton, er hat einen tiefen Baß*, etc.

tief (2) deep, dark; with ref. to colours, e.g. *ein tiefes Blau*, Geibel 1,45: '*der Wald scheint tiefer heut zu grünen*'; Kramer [1702] recorded '*tiefe Farben*'; Jean Paul, *Titan* 1,15 has the compound *tiefblau*. *~* can also be used for the absence of colour; since Early NHG, e.g. Luther Apocr. transl. Wisd. of Sol. 17,21: '*uber diesen stund ein tiefe nacht*' (where the Engl. version has 'heavy night'), Schiller, *Demtr.* 1,118: '*in tiefer Mitternacht*', Goethe, *Faust* 11499: '*die Nacht scheint tiefer tief hereinzudringen*', also *tiefes Dunkel, tiefe Finsternis*.

tief (3) deep, strong, penetrating, profound; beginnings in OHG, then frequent with ref. to both phys. and mental conditions as an adjective and an adverb, e.g. *tiefer Schlaf* (as in Luther Bible transl. Gen. 2,21) or Goethe, *Faust I*, 3507: '*doch meine Mutter schläft nicht tief*', often with ref. to deeply-felt emotions such as *tiefes Elend, tiefe Not, tiefe Trauer, tiefe Teilnahme* (but also *tiefe Gleichgültigkeit*, as in Wieland, *Agathon* 7,6). Steinbach [1734] recorded '*sich etwas tief zu Herzen gehen lassen*'; cf. also Goethe, *Iphig.* 1,2: '*er . . . fühlt es tief*' (hence also *im Tiefsten*, as in Goethe, *Tasso* 2,1), Klopstock 1,27: '*mich scheucht ein trüber Gedanke . . . tief in die Melancholei*', Heine, *Rom.* 69: '. . . *leerten sie den Kelch . . . tiefsten Leidens*', Lessing, *Nathan* 5,3: '*sollte . . . in mir der Christ noch tiefer nisten als in ihm der Jude?*'. Compounds are numerous, and most of them established themselves in the 18th c., e.g. *tiefanbetend* (Klopstock, *Oden* 1,124), *tiefbeklommen* (Bürger, 193b), *tiefbetrübt* (Bürger, 120), *tiefgebeugt* (Gotter 2,413), *tiefgefühlt* (Thümmel, *Reise* 3,99; cf. also *tieffühlend*, which Goethe used), *tiefgeprüft* (W.v.Humboldt, *Sonette* 97), *tiefgerührt* (Haller [edit. Hirzel] 155). Goethe also used *tiefrührend* and *tiefschmerzlich*.

tief (4) deep, profound; with ref. to intellect, wisdom, exploration, knowledge, etc.; since OHG, used by Luther in his Bible transl., e.g. Job 11,8 or Psalm 92,6: '*herr, . . . deine gedanken sind so seer tief*', Schiller, *Wall.Lager* 9: '*er denkt gar zu tiefe Sachen*', *ein tiefer Sinn liegt in etw.* (where Schiller used '*ein hoher Sinn*' in the same sense), Ense, *T.* 1,364: '*Gervinus ist nicht oberflächlich, aber auch nicht tief*'; cf. also *ein tiefes Geheimnis* = 'a deep secret', where 'profound' and 'deeply-buried' combined to some extent, f.r.b. Kramer [1702]: '*die allertiefeste Geheimnüssen*', e.g. J.Böhme, *Morgenr.* 3,29: '*hie merke die tieffe geheimnis*'. Many compound nouns and adjectives belong under this heading, e.g. *tiefbedacht* (Kirchhof, *Mil.Disc.* 265), *tiefdenkend* (recorded by Frisch [1741], e.g. Kant 10,228), *tieferforscht* (Dach [edit. Öst.] 713), *tiefgedacht* (Klopstock 10,184), *tiefgelehrt* (Fischart, *Bien.* 73b [1580]), *tiefsichtig* (Luther 1,212a (Jena)), *tiefsinnig* (f.r.b. Stieler [1691]), which led to *Tiefsinnigkeit*, f.r.b. Kramer [1702], and in the 18th c. to *Tiefsinn*, soon used in two senses, both for 'profundity, depth of thought' and 'melancholy, moroseness' (for which *Tiefsinnigkeit* could also be used in the 18th c., now rare in this sense).

tief (5) (adv.) very (much); used as an intensifier since Early NHG, e.g. Luther 1,86b (Jena): '*die so tief blind sind*'; now mainly in compounds, since the 18th c., e.g. *tieferkrankt* (Goethe, *Nat. Tochter* 4,2), *tiefverstummt* (Herder, *Cid* 33), *tiefgestirnt* (Geibel 2,7); often in *etw. aufs tiefste bedauern* = 'to regret sth. profoundly'. In many cases it is difficult to decide whether the compound expresses an emphatic statement or belongs to ~ (3) or (4).

das ist wie im tiefsten Mittelalter that is as bad as sth. in the Dark Ages; modern.

. . . -*tief* (lit.) deep in . . . , as deep as . . . ; the earliest examples are contracted comparisons, e.g. *hölltief*, as in Fischart, *Bien.* 174b (now *höllentief*, cf. also *Höllentiefe*, as in Lenau, *A.* 120), *abgrundtief*, as in Heine, *Rom.* 241 and *Reis.* 2,174, *meertief*, as in Kürnberger, *Am.* 500: '*meertief erlogen*'. Others contain different meanings of ~, e.g. *gedankentief*, as in Keller, *Gr.Heinr.* 3,255 (cf. *Gedankentiefe* in Ense, *D.* 2,327), *grundtief* as in Gervinus, *Lit.* 5,403, *seelentief*, since the 19th c., e.g. Holtei, *Mensch.* 1,163.

untief shallow; in figur. use since the 18th c., e.g. Herder [edit. S.] 5,639. The noun *die Untiefe*, also current figur. since the 18th c., is ambiguous. It can mean 'shallowness', e.g. Humboldt, *En.* 33 or Immermann, *Münchh.* 1m36, but also 'great depth, deep abyss'. Jean Paul used *Untiefe* in both senses, Goethe apparently only for 'great depth'.

er ist in einem seelischen Tief he is in a state of depression; transfer from meteorological 'low pressure area or condition'; 20th c.

der Tiefgang (lit.) depth; originally a mar. term for 'draught', and still only in this sense in *DWb.* [1935], but since ca. 1950 used to indicate depth, profundity or deep significance, e.g. in a person or a work of literature.

die Tiefenpsychologie (psych.) depth psychology; since early in the 20th c., e.g. (S.-B.) *Imago* 1,489 [1912]; cf. *Tiefenheini* (sl.) = 'psychiatrist', also used for 'opinion-pollster', only since the 2nd half of the 20th c.

der Tiefpunkt low(est) point, nadir; in math. = 'minimum', but now figur. in many contexts. Not listed at all in *DWb.* [1935], but frequent since ca. middle of the 20th c.

der Tiefstand low (level), nadir; a 20th c. word not yet listed in *DWb.* [1935], which also does not record *tiefstehend* = 'low, inferior'.

die Tiefstapelei understatement, undervaluing oneself, reticence to impress; also used for 'presenting things as less severe, important, dangerous, etc. than they appear to be'; formed in the twenties of the 20th c. as an antonym to *Hochstapelei* = 'swindling, confidence trick(ery)'; hence also *tiefstapeln* = 'to understate' and *Tiefstapler*.

der Tiefschlag (sl.) unfair blow; from the language of boxing; since ca. 1920.

das läßt ~ *blicken* (coll.) that is very revealing; since ca. 1870, reputedly given wider currency through its use in a speech in the *Reichstag* by Adolf Sabor (17.12.1884); a joc. off-shoot in sl. is *das Kleid läßt* ~ *blicken* = 'the décolleté is very deep' (only since 2nd half of 20th c.).

er hat einen tiefen Griff in eine fremde Kasse getan (coll.) he has misappropriated (a considerable amount of) money; 20th c. euphem. coll.

er hat ihn ~ *hineingeritten* (coll.) he has put him into deep trouble, brought him into a very awkward situation; since the 19th c., e.g. (Sa.) Lewald, *Ferd.* 3,187: '*sie haben uns verdammt tief hineingeritten mit ihren Kongressen . . .*'.

etw. vertiefen to deepen, heighten sth.; figur. since the 18th c., e.g. *einen Eindruck vertiefen* = 'to strengthen or deepen an impression'; the noun *Vertiefung* = 'heightening, increase' followed in the 19th c. Transitive *jem. vertiefen* = 'to plunge sb. into melancholy', used by Klopstock, *Od.* 1,83, is obs.

sich vertiefen to plunge into sth., become engrossed in sth.; the sense of entering deeply, immersing oneself began in Early NHG, e.g. Zwingli, *Dt.Schr.* 1,100: '*sich . . . in Gott vertiefen*', Luther 8,174b (Jena): '*. . . noch im irrthum verteufft*'; mainly now in *in etw. vertieft sein*, f.r.b. Kramer [1702], e.g. Hebel 3,299: '*er war so vertieft in seinen Gedanken und in seiner Arbeit*', but usually with the accusative as in Schiller, *Räuber* 1,2: '*in ein Buch vertieft*'; hence *die Vertiefung* = 'absorption', f.r.b. Stieler [1691], e.g. Goethe 42,3,176 (W.).

← See also under *Auge* (for *jem.m zu tief ins Auge sehen*), *beugen* (for *tiefgebeugt*), *bewegen* (for *tiefbewegt*), *Blick* (for *ein tiefer Blick*), *dringen* (for *tiefdringend*), *durchwühlen* (for *das tiefe Herz durchwühlen*), *eingraben* (for *sich tief ins Gedächtnis eingraben*), *Gedanke* (for *tief in Gedanken*), *Glas* (for *zu tief ins Glas geguckt haben*), *greifen* (for *tief greifen* and *tief in die Tasche greifen*), *Grund* (for *im tiefsten Grund*), *haben* (for *tiefsinniger Kopf*), *hoch* (for *wer hoch steigt, wird tief fallen*), *Höhe* (for *die Höhen und Tiefen des Lebens*), *Kluft* (for *tiefe Kluft*), *Knie* (for *knietief*), *Kreide* (for *tief in der Kreide sein*), *Nacht* (for *tiefe Nacht* and *tief in süßem Schlummer*), *nisten* (for *im tiefen Herzen nisten*), *Patsch* (for *tief in die Patsche bringen*), *Schacht* (for *die innere Welt, der tiefe Schacht*), *schlafen* (for *tiefgeprägte Bilder*), *Seele* (for *in tiefster Seele*), *senken* (for *je tiefer der Winter sich senkte*), *sinken* (for *ich bin so tief gesunken*), *stecken* (for *tief in der Arbeit stecken*), *still* (for *stille Wasser sind tief*) and *studieren* (for *sich tief in den Irrtum hineinstudieren*).

Tiegel: pan, pot

der ~ (lit.) crucible; figur. since MHG, e.g. Gottfr.v. Str., *Tristan* 4890: '*diu mînen wort muoz er mir lân durch den vil liehten tegel gân der camênischen sinne*', Heinr.v. Müglin, *Schr.* 461: '*ûz sînes herzen tegel'*, still in modern period, e.g. Kinkel, *Erz.* 432 [1849]: '. . . *was noch trüb im Tiegel des menschlichen Geistes kocht und brodelt'*.

← See also under *schmelzen* (for *Schmelztiegel*).

zwei Dinge in einen ~ *werfen* to lump together two things which ought to be kept separate; e.g. (Sp.) G.Keller, *Salander* 201 (*Topf* is the preferred noun in most regions).

aus einem ~ *mit jem.m geschmolzen sein* (obs.) to bear a strong likeness to sb.; since the 19th c., e.g. Gutzkow, *R.v.G.* 1,245; now obs.

er malt schwarz und weiß aus einem ~ (prov.expr.) he blows hot and cold out of the same mouth; f.r.b. Simrock [1846]. See also under *blasen* for a similar locution.

Tier: animal

er ist ein ~ he is a beast, brute, animal; used as a term of abuse for human beings, e.g. Wieland 1,48: '*du unvernünftiges Thier*' (ibid. 24,259: '*menschliche Thiere zu Menschen bilden*'), Schiller, *D.Carlos* 5,3: '. . . *macht mich zur Furie, zum Thier*', G.Hauptmann, *Sonnaufg.*III: '. . . *Trunkenbold von Vater . . . ein Tier*'; hence also *das* ~ *in jem.m wecken* = 'to bring out or rouse sb.'s animal instincts', e.g. Eichendorff 3,338: '. . . *hüte dich, das wilde Thier zu wecken in deiner Brust*', and *sich tierisch benehmen* = 'to behave in a bestial manner (or like an animal)', since MHG, f.r.b. Dasypodius [1556], e.g. Keisersberg, *Irrig Schaf* 6b [1514].

das ~ (lit.) the beast; in literature used with ref. to abstracts (as in the case of *Untier*, which see below), since the 17th c., e.g. (*DWb*) Weckherlin [edit. G.] 44: '*die misgunst, das arge thier*', Schiller, *Fiesco* 1,7: '. . . *der Fuß des trägen vielbeinigten Thieres Republik zu sein*' (in *Räuber* 1,2 Schiller calls the gallow '*das dreibeinige Thier*').

. . . *-tier* . . . creature; in several, often abusive, compounds, e.g. *Halbtier*, as in Wieland 9,188: '*eine Herde roher ungebildeter Halbthiere durch Kultur . . . zu veredeln*' (in its phys. sense *Halbtier* is also used for 'centaur', e.g. by Goethe), *Trampeltier* = 'bumpkin, clod' (in original sense = 'camel'), also non-pejor. *Arbeitstier* = 'work horse, workaholic', modern, but cf. *Fast.Sp.* 875: '*ein arbeitseligs thier*'; cf. also Keisersberg, *Narrensch.* 128b [1516]: '*ein mensch ist ein gesellig thier*' = 'man is a social animal' (after Aristotle, *Polit.* 1,1,9). There is also *Wundertier* = 'astonishing creature', but also pejor. 'freak', since the 18th c., e.g. Hagedorn 2,112 or Wieland 17,118: '*man beschrieb ihr das philosophische Wunderthier als ungewöhnlich scheu und störrig*'.

ein armes ~ (coll.) a poor creature; in expressions of pity since the 18th c.; cf. also *ein gutes* ~ (coll.) for a person who is good-natured but rather stupid (or at least naive).

das arme ~ *haben* (regional coll.) to be depressed, down in the dumps; mainly in the Rheinland and parts of the N.; recorded since the 19th c. It is not clear whether a particular animal is meant, but some scholars have suggested that it is a ref. to the cat, because of *Katerstimmung* (see p. 1446) and *Katzenjammer* (see p. 1407); Engl. coll. has the 'black dog' (much used e.g. by Churchill).

ein großes ~ (coll.) big shot; since the 17th c., e.g. (*DWb*) *Wolgeplagter Priester* 97 [1691]: '*ein junger prediger dünkt sich ein gewaltig thier zu sein, wenn er in ein ampt kommt*', Günther, 196 [1735]: '*ein groß und vornehm Thier zu werden*'. The term could also be used (in the 17th c.) for an illustrious but emptyheaded person and for sb. who gives himself airs, but since the 18th c. in the modern sense; *hoch* can also be used; cf. also *das höchste* ~ (sl.) = 'the boss, chief (of an organisation or a deputation)'; *berühmtes* ~ occurs in sl. for 'famous person'.

das Gewohnheitstier creature of habit; since the 18th c. both as ~ *der Gewohnheit*, as in Seume, *Spaz.* 2: '. . . *daß der Mensch ein Thier der Gewohnheit ist*', and as a compound, e.g. in Pestalozzi, *Lienhard* 4,90.

← See also under *Gewohnheit*.

das Untier monster, wild animal, dangerous beast; since MHG, e.g. Seuse, *Dt.Schr.* [edit. B] 450 with ref. to a person; with ref. to abstracts since the 16th c., applied to sin, war, luxury, hunger, e.g. (*DWb*) Tschudi, *Chron.* 1,79 [16th c., Klopstock, *Od.* 2,84, Herder [edit. S.] 26,431 or Immermann [edit.B.] 16,334: '*Hunger, du Unthier, laß vom Nagen ab*'.

das ist Tierquälerei (joc.coll.) that is cruelty to dumb animals; joc. extension to human beings (20th c.) of a term coined early in the 19th c.

das ~ *mit zwei Rücken spielen* (obscene) to make the beast with two backs; cf. French *faire la bête à deux dos*; Shakespeare used the phrase in *Othello* 1,1,117; in German at least since the 16th c., e.g. Fischart, *Geschichtsklitt.* (where it occurs with '*des thiers* . . .').

mit tierischem Ernst (coll.) with awful seriousness; expresses the notion of unimaginative, humourless determination; 20th c. coll. (not yet listed in *DWb.* [1935]).

← See also under *Bauer* (for *der Bauer und sein Stier sind ein Tier*), *belegen* (for *ein Tier belegen*), *eingießen* (for *Eingußtierchen*), *faul* (for *Faultier*), *Getier*, *König* (for *der Löwe der König der Tiere*), *Kreuz* (for *Tiere kreuzen*), *Müller* (for *Müllertier*), *Murmeltier*, *Muskel* (for *Muskeltier*), *Opfer* (for *Opfertier* and *Schlachttier*), *Pläsier* (for *jedem Tierchen sein Pläsierchen*) and *Reich* (for *Tierreich*).

Tiger: tiger

der ~ brute, beast, cruel person; since the 17th c., e.g. Ziegler, *Banise* 266; in the feminine in Schiller, *Turandot* 1,1. Hence in many compounds describing brutality or cruelty, such as *Tigergeist*, as in Lenau 2,201, *Tigerherz*, f.r.b. Stieler [1691], *Tigerseele*, used by Herder and Wieland, and *Tigertat*, as in Bürger, 102a. – Note that *tigern* (coll.) = 'to go for a (long) walk, march' does not belong to ~, but is of Hebrew origin (*thigar* =

'move from place to place as a commercial traveller') and entered coll. usage from cant in the 19th c.

Tiger-. . . (zool.) spotted . . . ; in many animal names. Frisch [1741] recorded *Tigerhund* and *Tigerpferd*, Nemnich *Tigerraupe, -spinne, -tute* and *-zunge*; others were listed by Oken, e.g. *Tigermotte, -muschel* and *-schlange.*

getigert spotted; since the 18th c., used e.g. by Goethe in *Morphologie. Beiträge zur Optik*; often in descriptions of horses (e.g. in Wieland 15,21), but also of minerals, textiles and with ref. to freckles, e.g. v.Horn, *Schmiedj.* 47 [1852]: '*mit Sommerflecken getigert*'.

der Papiertiger paper tiger; coined in figur. sense by Mao Tse-Tung in August 1946, when he used the term with ref. to reactionaries. The word was adopted by the press, at first in Engl. and USA, in German papers since 1962. For details see A.D.Nunn, *Politische Schlagwörter in Deutschland seit 1945*, 156 [1974].

tilgen: see *vertilgen.*

tingieren: colour

tingiert (rare) coloured; with ref. to abstracts since the 18th c., e.g. (S.-B.) Wieland 19,295: '. . . *von einer* . . . *mit etwas schwarzer Galle tingierten Sinnesart*'.

die Tinktur (lit.) superficial covering, thin layer of sth.; *Tinktur* developed from phys. 'colouring' to 'colouring water', which became 'tincture'; figur. in the sense of *Anstrich* (see p. 63) since the 18th c., e.g. *Tinktur von Größe, von Neuheit, von Gelehrsamkeit*, e.g. (S.-B.) Wölfling, *Reise* 1,275 [1795]: '. . . *mehr oberflächliche Tinctur als solide Kenntnisse*'.

Tinte: colour, ink

die ~ (lit.) colour, tint, hue; from the language of painting, since the 18th c., e.g. Bode, *Yor.Empf.* 2,77 [1768]: '*die Sonne warf eine so warme Tinte auf die Wangen*' (Goethe used '*in der blauen Tinte des Morgens*'), fully figur. in such cases as Knigge, *Umgang* 2,90: '*da werden die sanftern Tinten in den Charakter eingetragen*'. Cf. also Wieland *Hor.Br.* 2,47: '*eine schöne Mitteltinte zwischen Erniedrigung und Gleichheit*'.

in der ~ *sitzen* (coll.) to be in trouble, in a pickle, in the soup; since Early NHG, e.g. Keisersberg, *Post.* 61: '*ir stecken mit mir in der dinten*' and *Narrensch.* 130d [1520]: '*du steckst mitten in der tincten*'; still in many locutions, such as *in die* ~ *kommen* (or *geraten), jem.m aus der* ~ *helfen, jem. in die* ~ *führen* (*bringen, reiten*).

die rote ~ (coll.,obs.) blood; e.g. (*DWb*) Soltau, *Histor. Volkslieder* 2,473 [1826]: '. . . *daß ihnen die rothe Tinte lief über den dünnen Leib*'.

so klar wie dicke ~ (coll.) as clear as mud, obvious; ironic, general since the 19th c.; Schopenhauer maintained that the phrase was derived from French *c'est clair comme la bouteille à l'encre.*

du hast wohl ~ *gesoffen?* (vulg.) you must be mad; general since the 19th c., used by Keller in *Ges.W.* 5,148 (*Mißbr.Liebesbr.*). It is claimed by

some scholars that ~ in this phrase refers to *vino tinto*, the effects of which on the brain would have been experienced by German soldiers fighting in Spain.

mit roter ~ *schreiben* (econ.jargon) to be in financial trouble; a ref. to the debit entries in a balance sheet printed in red; since the 1st half of the 20th c. (see also a similar entry under *rot*).

darüber ist schon viel ~ *verspritzt* (or *vergossen*) *worden* much that has been inconclusive has been written about that, much ink has been spilt over this; at least since the 18th c.; cf. also Goethe, *Lehrj.* 8,9: '*wo man am wenigsten Dinte und Feder sparen soll*', Lichtenberg, *Schr.* 3,49: '*für jeden Dürftigen sein Blut oder wenigstens seine Dinte zu verspritzen*', also *ibid.* 2,76: '*er kann die Dinte nicht halten*' = 'he writes too much'.

das steckt noch im Tintenfaß (coll.) that has not yet been written; recorded since the 19th c., e.g. by Heyne [1895].

der Tintenfisch (zool.) cuttlefish, octopus; f.r.b. Henisch [1616]: '*dintenfisch, blackfisch, sepia coligo*'.

der Tintenklecker (coll.) wretched scribbler, inferior writer; f.r.b. Stieler [1691]. There are several variants; Weise, *Erzn.* 410 [1673] used *Dintenlecker*, Jean Paul, *Flegelj.* 4,81 *Dintenmann*; in the derogatory sense *Tintenfresser* also occurs, recorded by Stieler; cf. also '*tintenklecksendes Säkulum*' in Schiller, *Räuber* 1,2.

← See also under *Klecks* (for *Dintenklecker* and *Dintenkleckser*).

der Tintenscheißer (vulg.) clerk, teacher, official; cf. French *chieur d'encre*; in vulg. sl. (especially among juveniles) since the 19th c. The word started as an abusive term for 'scholar, academic' (beginnings in the 15th c.) and then came to be used for 'writer' before it acquired its variety of meanings.

tintenschwarz as black as ink; f.r.b. Henisch [1616].

← See also under *Kuli* (for *Tintenkuli*) and *sympathetisch* (for *sympathetische Tinte*).

tippen: touch lightly

an etw. ~ (1) to touch on sth. (e.g. a subject in a conversation); 20th c. (not even listed in *DWb* [1935]).

← See also under *antippen.*

an etw. ~ (2) (coll.) to attack sth., cast doubts on sth.; 20th c., e.g. Kant, *Aula* 71: '*den wollten sie sehen, der daran tippen mochte*'; hence *daran ist nicht zu* ~ (coll.) = 'that is a hard fact, is incontrovertible'.

der Tips (regional coll.) (state of) slight intoxication; recorded since the 19th c., first by Stalder [1806] for Switzerland, then by Campe [1810]; hence *tipseln* (coll.) = 'to booze' and *betipst* (coll.) = '(slightly) drunk', recorded by Sanders [1865], now obs. or regional.

danebentippen (coll.) to make a wrong guess; 20th c. coll. for 'to fail in one's bet' and in wider sense for 'to make a wrong assumption'. This belongs to *auf etw.* ~ which is not derived from ~, but is a loan from Engl. 'to tip', though cross-influences between the two may be assumed. The meaning 'to type' also arose through Engl. influence.

Tiroler: see *Salon*.

Tisch: table

der ~ (1) the (people sitting at a) table; beginnings in MHG, e.g. *Nibelungenl.* 559,2: '*der künig wolde gân ze tische mit den gesten*' (though this could also be taken as belonging to ~ (2)), Luther 1,191a (Jena): '. . . *der einen tisch vol armer leut speiset*', Musäus, *M.* 5,94: '. . . *wobei der volle Tisch das Ohr spitzte*', Waldau, *N.* 3,201: '. . . *das Gelächter des ganzen Tisches*'; hence also *der Kopf des Tisches* = 'head of the table', used not only for the place but also for the person occupying it.

der ~ (2) meal; since Early NHG, e.g. in biblical language, as in Psalm 78,19: '. . . *einen Tisch bereiten in der Wüste*', Ecclesiasticus 29,29: '. . . *köstlicher Tisch unter den Fremden*' (in the Engl. version 'delicate fare in another man's house'); *trockener* ~ for a meal without wine occurs in Mathesius, *Luther* 68a [1576]; often in compounds such as *Bürgertisch* = 'plain fare, good home cooking', *Festtisch* = 'festive meal', *Hausmannstisch* = 'ordinary or plain fare', *Werktagstisch* = 'weekday fare', etc., e.g. Rückert, *Rost* 27a: '*des Löwen Mittagstisch war mit der Kuh berathen . . .*'; there is also *Freitisch* = 'free board' (cf. the notes on *frei* on pp. 844 and 846).

der ~ (3) conference (or negotiating) table; in many locutions, modern, not yet listed in *DWb.* [1935], although most of them have been current since the 19th c., e.g. *das bleibt auf dem* ~ = 'that remains unresolved, to be dealt with another time', *es kommt auf den* ~ = 'it will (or must) be discussed', *etw. vom* ~ *bringen* = 'to settle sth., consider sth. as no longer requiring negotiations or debate' (20th c.), hence elliptic *das ist vom* ~ (coll.) = 'that's settled, subject closed', already in the 18th c. as *untern* ~ *damit*, as in Bürger [edit. B.] 479b: '*untern Tisch mit dieser klassischen Kleinelei!*', and similar *etw. vom* ~ *nehmen* (coll.) = 'to discuss sth. no further, remove sth. from the agenda', *etw. unter den* ~ *fegen* (or *kehren*) = 'to sweep sth. under the table (or carpet)', (*mit der Faust*) *auf den* ~ *hauen* (coll.) = 'to take a hard line, put forward one's views in a violent manner'. One may also include a phrase like *mit dem setze ich mich nicht an einen* ~ = 'I will not get round the table with him, refuse to deal with him' (though this can also refer to refusing to have a meal with sb.); cf. also the metaphor in Börne 5,116: '*die tausend Schmarotzer am Staatstische*'.

← See also under *fallen* (for *unter den Tisch fallen*), *grün* (for *am grünen Tisch*) and *rund* (for *der runde Tisch*).

der ~ (4) counter; in comm. contexts since OHG, also in the Bible, e.g. Luther Bible transl. Matth. 21,12: '*Jhesus . . . sties umb der wechsler*

tische'; figur. in modern phrases such as *ich zahle bar auf den* ~ = 'I pay cash down', *etw. auf den* ~ *legen* = 'to lay out a sum of money', also 'to put sth. (e.g. an offer) on the table'.

← See also under *Laden* (for *unterm Ladentisch gekauft*).

der ~ *des Herrn* (relig.) the table of the Lord, altar; general since the Middle Ages; cf. French *la sainte table* and parallels in many Western languages; MHG had *ze gotes tische*, as in *Minnes.* 3,44a; the Bible has it in Malachi 1,7, Goethe, *Dicht.u. Wahrheit* 7: '. . . *ging am andern Tag mit den Eltern zu dem Tische des Herrn*', where it refers to the partaking of the Lord's Supper.

Trennung (or *Scheidung*) *von* ~ *und Bett* (jur.) separation from bed and board; ~ *und Bett* in phrases relating to married life has been current since Early NHG, e.g. H.Sachs 16,283, with ref. to divorce since the 16th c.; *Scheidung von* ~ *und Bett* was f.r.b. Frisch [1741] for '*separatio a thoro et mensa*'.

jem. über den ~ *ziehen* (coll.) to get the better of sb., outmanoeuvre sb.; taken from the act of pulling sb. across a table for phys. punishment; since early in the 20th c.

es geht über ~ *und Bänke* (coll.) things have got out of hand; it can also mean that everything is at sixes and sevens and can refer to high jinks; assumed to refer to the behaviour of mice when no people or cats are about; since the 19th c.

reinen ~ *machen* (coll.) to make a clean sweep, clear things up, sort things out; ultimately derived from Lat. *tabula rasa* (for which see p. 2425), in this form since the 18th c., e.g. (Sa.) Scherr, *Bl.* 1,196; cf. also the partly-phys. example in a letter to Lessing [1774]: '. . . *damit ich heute oder morgen wenigstens reinen Tisch verlasse*'. In some dialects the phrase can mean 'to spend all one has'.

das Tischleindeckdich means through which one is able to lead an easy life; at first a ref. to a 'magic table' which supplies all one's needs (a notion current since Classical times, Büchmann refers to instances in Krates and Athenaeus), in German through a fairytale by the Brothers Grimm.

es ist abgetischt the meal is over; also sometimes in wider sense for 'it is too late to deal with that now'; since the 18th c., e.g. Wieland 11,86. There is also coll. *er hat alles abgetischt* = 'he has eaten the lot', as in (Sa.) Kohl, *R.i.Südrußland* 1,17 [1841], but this is obs.

übertischt (obs.) overloaded with dishes; with ref. to a dining table in Goethe 14,12 (W.).

der Stammtisch regulars' table in a public house; also used for the people who regularly sit at it; recorded since the 19th c. (but not yet in Sanders [1865]).

Stammtisch-. . . (pejor.) bar-room . . . , bar-parlour . . . ; in compounds with ref. to opinionated statements or claims made in a pub, such as *Stammtischgeschwätz, -stratege, -philister, -politik*.

ein armer ~ *ist bald gedeckt* (prov.) a poor man's table is soon spread; in Engl. recorded since the 17th c., much later in German, recorded by Wander [1876].

← See also under *auftischen, biegen* (for *der Tisch bog sich*), *decken* (for *du findest deinen Tisch überall gedeckt*), *Fuß* (for *die Füße unter jem.s Tisch haben* or *strecken*), *Katze* (for *Katzentisch* and its diminutives and for *wenn die Katze aus dem Haus ist, tanzen die Mäuse auf dem Tisch*), *Nachtisch, rücken* (for *jem.m den Tisch rücken* and *den Tisch rücken*) and *saufen* (for *jem. unter den Tisch saufen*).

Titan: Titan
der ~ (1) giant, person of enormous physique; a ref. to the children of Uranus and Gaea in Greek mythology who were of gigantic size and strength; in lit. since the 18th c., e.g. Hölderlin, *Hyperion* 1,40.

der ~ (2) titan, outstanding personality; since the 18th c., sometimes with allusion to the mythological meaning of ~ used for 'rebel against the existing order'; *titanenhaft* and *titanisch*, also *Titanentum* both for 'rebellion against the universe' and for 'possession of greatness or enormous power', e.g. Auerbach, *Leb.* 1,245. The feminine *Titanide*, originally the term for a sister of a titan (cf. Ramler, *Mythol.* 2,400 [1790]), came to be used for 'very remarkable woman' in the 19th c. The adjective *titanesk* = 'distorted through exaggeration, unbelievably enormous' is a recent pejor. formation.

Titel: title
der ~ (1) (obs.) pretext; ~ (jur.) = 'section or paragraph of a law or regulation' led to 'reason, justification', also 'right to sth.' (since Early NHG), when used unjustifiably to 'pretext', e.g. Wieland, *Gold.Sp.* 2,16: '. . . *damit das Volk . . . unter allen nur ersinnlichen Titeln belastet worden war*'.

der ~ (2) (obs.) pact, written contract; still in Goethe, *Faust* 11613, now obs.

der ~ (3) term of abuse; the meaning 'term of address', as in Gellert, *Betschw.* 1,7: '*mit der Madame verschonen Sie mich. Solche weltliche Titel kann ich nicht leiden*' could lead easily to 'term of abuse', as in Wieland, *Att.* 2,2,193; the verb *betiteln* in this sense followed, and in the 20th c. *titulieren* arose, though in its non-pejor. sense it has been current since MHG.

der ~ (4) name, label; since Early NHG, later in the phrase *unter dem* ~ *von* used with ref. to abstracts, e.g. Wieland, *Gold.Sp.* 1,7: '*das Laster . . . unter dem Titel des Verdienstes*'.

← See also under *betiteln, Mittel* (for *ein Titel ohne Mittel* and related proverbs) and *Narr* (for *Betitelung*).

titschen: see *austitschen*.
Titte: female breast, nipple
schwach auf der ~ *sein* (regional, vulg.) to be short of money; first recorded for Berlin (early in the 20th c.); cf. *schwach auf der Brust sein* on p. 413.

das schmeckt wie ~ *mit Ei* (vulg.sl.) that tastes very good; 20th c. sl.

← See also under *Land* (for *andere Mädchen, andere Titten*).

Titus: Titus
der Tituskopf (obs.) head with curly hair cut short; refers to the appearance of Talma [1791], when he played ~ in *Brutus* by Voltaire; in German lit. since Jean Paul, *Katz.Bad.* 177 [1809]; Naumann in *ZfdW.* 7,260 has given details on origin and popularity of the *coiffure à la Titus*. Cf. similar *Schwedenkopf* on p. 2208.

toben: rage
der Sturm tobt the storm rages; ~ originally referred to turmoil, agitation, wild behaviour, etc. in human beings, also in lit. for immoral, criminal behaviour, as in Goethe, *Faust I*,1052: '. . . *haben wir . . . weit schlimmer als die Pest getobt*'; then transferred to natural phenomena, since MHG, e.g. Gottfr.v.Str., *Tristan* 11699: '*in den tobenden wilden sê*', also Luther Bible transl. Jer. 5,22 and Psalm 77,17, Schiller, *Jungfr.v.O.* 5,1: '*wie eine losgelaßne Hölle tobt der Sturm*'. See also under *Hölle* (p. 1363).

← See also under *brausen* (for *Tobsucht*) and *durchtoben*.

Tobias: Tobit
~ *sechs Vers drei* (obs.) said to sb. who yawns without holding a hand before his mouth; a ref. to the Book of Tobit in the Apocrypha, where chapt. 6,3 runs: '*o herr, er will mich fressen!*'; probably older than the 19th c. recordings suggest; now obs.

der Tobiasfisch (zool., regional) sand launce (*Ammodytes tobianus*), recorded by Adelung who added '*im gemeinen Leben Tobies, Tobieschen*'; officially called *kleiner Sandaal*.

Tochter: daughter
Tochter (1) female inhabitant; since the Middle Ages, also in the Bible, e.g. Gen. 34,11: '*sie ging heraus, die Töchter des Landes zu sehen*', Schiller, *Kab.u.L.* 2,3: '*die freigeborne Tochter des freiesten Volkes*'; still used for 'woman' in such (somewhat stilted) locutions as *die berühmteste Tochter dieser Stadt* or *die Töchter dieser Gegend haben blonde Haare*.

die ~ (2) (regional, mainly Swiss) girl; also used for 'maid (servant)' and in the compound *Saaltochter* = 'waitress'. The first girls' schools were founded by Usteri in Switzerland [1773]. He called them *Töchterschulen*, and this Swiss usage then entered standard German (from 1792 onwards); cf. also *meine* ~, used by Catholic priests when addressing a female member of their congregation.

die ~ (3) (lit.) daughter, off-spring; personification, current since Classical lit., e.g. *veritas temporis filia*, recorded in German since Early NHG, e.g. Franck [1541]: '*die wahrheit ist der zeit tochter*', Haller [edit. H.] 224: '*der Höchste schützt die Eh, die Tochter seiner Liebe'*, Kant [edit. R.-S.] 1,200: '*weil die Bewunderung eine Tochter der Unwissenheit ist*' (cf. Forster's transl. of *Die Ruinen* by Volney, 32: '*Gierigkeit, die Tochter und Gefährtin der Unwissenheit*'), Schiller, *Glocke* 164 with ref. to fire: '*die freie Tochter der Natur*'. Adelung recorded '*die Musik ist eine Tochter des Vergnügens*'. Flowers have been called *Töchter des Mais* since the 18th c., e.g. by Chr. Stolberg.

die ~(4) (econ.) subsidiary firm; short for *Tochtergesellschaft*; only since the 2nd half of the 19th c.; before then *Filiale* was used, which entered German from Lat. in the 16th c., at first as *Filial = Tochterkirche*, in econ. contexts only since the 19th c. One can, however, also assume influence of biblical usage, e.g. Numbers 21,25: '*Israel wohnete . . . zu Hesbon und allen ihren Töchtern*' (where the A.V. has 'in all the villages thereof'), where ~ = '*Tochterstadt*'.

Tochter-. . . subsidiary . . . , derivative . . . ; since the 19th c. in econ. contexts (see above), but also in ling. contexts, esp. in *Tochtersprache*, e.g. *die romanischen Sprachen sind Tochtersprachen des Lateinischen*.

. . .-tochter (poet). daughter; in poetry in several compounds, e.g. *Felsentochter* for *Quellennymphe* in Bürger, 27a, *Himmelstochter* for 'goddess', used by Schiller, *Glocke* 301, also by Wieland (cf. Schiller's '*Tochter aus Elysium*' in *An die Freude*).

mit einer ~ zwei Eidame machen (prov.) to promise the same thing to two persons; current since OHG, recorded since the Middle Ages (Tappius, Franck), commented on by Erasmus; parallels in many languages, e.g. French *faire d'une fille deux gendres*.

die ~ frißt die Mutter (prov., a.) the interest swallows up the capital; recorded since Early NHG; *Mutter* here = 'loaned sum', ~ = the interest which eventually amounts to more than the borrowed sum and, if interest has not been paid, is bound to lead to the loss of the surety given for the original loan.

mit der Mutter soll beginnen, wer die ~ will gewinnen (prov.) he that would the daughter win must with the mother first begin; in many versions recorded since the 17th c. (also in Engl.), e.g. Pistorius 6,53; Eiselein [1838] recorded '*wenn du willst die Tochter han, fange mit der Mutter an*'; cf. French *il faut amadouer la poule pour avoir les poussins*.

← See also under *Eva* (for *Evastochter*), *fortgeben* (for *eine Tochter fortgeben*), *Herz* (for *Herzenstochter*), *hoch* (for *höhere Töchterschule*), *Müller* (for *Müllerstochter*), *Muschel* (for *Muscheltochter*, p. 1725, where unfortunately the head-word is missing), *Pastor* (for *unter uns Pastorentöchtern* or *Pfarrerstöchtern*), *Seil* (for *des Seilers Tochter heiraten müssen*), *sitzen* (for *ungeratene Tochter*) and *Sohn* (for *verheirate deine Tochter, wenn du kannst*).

Tod: death

der ~ (personified) Death; death has been seen as a person since the earliest periods of the language (the most extensive list of instances can be found in *DWb.* XI,1,1,597ff [1935]); *der ~* is called *Bruder des Schlafs*, e.g. by Herder 11,444, also *Schwester des Schlafs*, e.g. by Teichner, *des Teufels Bruder*, e.g. by Ayrer. He has *Arme*, e.g. Chamisso 4,296, indeed is *tausendarmig*, as in Schiller, *Räuber* 1,2, has *Hände*, e.g. Goethe, *Clavigo* 4: '*die kalte Hand des Todes*', *blutige Nägel*, e.g. Lessing 8,245, *Klauen, Zähne, Rachen*, the last very frequent since the 17th c. (Gryphius, Lessing, Schiller), though he is also called *stumm* and *blind*. He is equipped with every deadly weapon, e.g. a *Speer*, as in Hugo v. Trimberg, *Renner* 21508, a *Bogen*, as in H.Sachs 1,472, *Messer, Beil*, or is equipped with a *Stachel*, e.g. Luther Bible transl. 1 Cor. 15,55. He wields a scythe (cf. Böhm, *Altdt. Liederb.* No. 650: '*es ist ein Schnitter, heißt der Tod*'), but also uses *Bande, Netz* and *Strick* (e.g. Konr.v.Würzb., *Trojanerkr.* 12178), he hunts man down, jumps on his victim's back (cf. *Minnes.Frühl.* 116,15: '*swie mir der tôt vast ûf dem rugge waere*'), but he can also be a friend (see the entry on *Freund Hein/Hain* on p. 853). He has a house (often = 'the grave', as in Schiller, *Braut v.M.* 4,9), hence *des Todes Pforte, Schwelle, Tor*, as in Schiller, *Br.v.M.* 4,9: '*zu des Todes traurigen Thoren*'. He has servants, as in *des Todes Heer, Boten, Gesinde*, but also comes in person, as in *der ~ sitzt vor der Tür, klopft an, steigt ein, rückt am jem.s Seite, sitzt jem.m im Genick*; he can also be sent for, e.g. *Nibelungenl.* 486,6: '*ich habe gesant nâch tôde*', invited or challenged; one fights or wrestles with him, e.g. *Nibelungenl.* 939,2: '*dô rang er mit dem tôde*', Neidhart 5,3: '*ein altiu mit dem tôde vaht*', also Luther Bible transl. Luke 22,44.

← See also under *Auge* (for *den Tod vor Augen haben*), *Fazit* (for *der Tod, das letzte Fazit aller Zahlen*), *Fiedel* (for *Fiedler Tod*), *Geselle* (for *der Tod ein rascher Gesell*), *Gevatter* (for *Gevatter Tod*), *gut* (for *er ist gut nach dem Tod schicken*), *mähen* (for *des Todes Sense*), *Pfeil* (for *Pfeile des Todes*), *Schippe* (for *dem Tod von der Schippe springen*), *Sichel* (for *die Sichel des Todes*) and *Streich* (for *des Todes Streichen erliegen*).

Tode (lit.) death-bringers, deadly things; in lit. since the 18th c., e.g. E.Kleist 1,5: '*zehntausend Tode laßt ihr . . . auf die Brüder fliegen*', also with abstracts, e.g. Rückert (in *Guttenbergs Album* 106): '*die Kritik und die Politik . . . die beiden Tode der Poesie*'; cf. also the hyperbolical plural, as in Luther 1,426b (Jena): '*hundert töde leiden*' = 'to suffer a hundred agonies'.

etw. ist der ~ für etw. anderes (lit.) sth. is fatal to sth. else; with abstracts since MHG, e.g. Walther v.d. V. 97,38: '*ein missevallen daz ist mîner fröiden tôt*', Stolberg 13,81: '*das Zaudern ist der Thaten Tod*', (Sa.) *Mißtrauen ist der ~ aller Freundschaft*.

etw. ist der ~ für jem. sth. is a bitter blow or terrible experience for sb.; general since the 18th c., e.g. Stilling 4,176: '*dieser Gedanke war Mord und Tod für ihn*', but the phrase can, of course, also be taken literally as 'proving fatal', e.g. Wieland 34,15: '. . . . *wo jeder Mißtritt Tod war*'; cf. also hyperbolical *sein Lebenswandel ist mein* ~ = 'his way of life will be the death of me, will bring me to an early grave, is a nail to my coffin'.

etw. für (or *auf* or *in*) *den* ~ *nicht leiden können* (coll.) to hate sth. like poison; the prepositions vary, *in* is used by Goethe in *Wahlverw.* 2,5, *auf* by Schiller in *Räuber* 2,3 (with *hassen*), *für* by Auerbach in *Ges.Schr.* 1,26 (with *nicht ausstehen können*); Campe [1810] recorded it with *bis in den* ~ (*zuwider*). *Teufel* can be used instead of ~, e.g. Osmin's aria in Mozart's *Entführung*, act 1.

ich will des Todes sein, wenn . . . (a.) I'll be damned, if I . . . : general in the 18th c., e.g. Sturz 2,200; cf. also *tausend Tode will ich lieber sterben als* . . . = 'I'd rather die than . . .'. On the other hand, *es soll mein* ~ *sein* could be used as a strong affirmation = 'truly, really, on my word of honour'; all these phrases are now a., if not obs.

← See also under *Kind* (for *ein Kind des Todes sein*).

auf den ~ *krank sein* (*liegen*, etc.) to be fatally (or terminally) ill; current since Early NHG, which makes Lessing's remarks in *Werke* 11,619: '*an dem Tode liegen, wofür wir itzt sehr abgeschmackt sagen: auf den Tod liegen*' quite inappropriate; now *sterbenskrank* (see p. 2364) is preferred. Both locutions can also be used with ref. to things or abstracts.

zu ~ or *zum Tode* . . . very much, extremely; *zum* ~ at first meant 'fatally, mortally', e.g. H. Sachs 11,246: '*sein krankeit ist nit zum todt*' = 'his illness is not fatal'; since Early NHG increasingly used in hyperbolical statements, f.r.b. Rädlein, 879b: '*sich zu tod arbeiten*', e.g. Keisersberg, *Omeis* 56a: '. . . *ich würde mich zu tod schammen*', Goethe, *Egmont* 3: '*zum Tode betrübt*' (which goes back to -partly phys. – *bis an den* ~, as in Luther Bible transl. Matth. 26,38: '*meine seele ist betrübet bis an den tod*'), Schiller, *Kab.u.L.* 5,5: '*zu Tode weinen*' (also *Fiesco* 1,5 with *zappeln*). In modern times *zu* ~ is still current in *sich zu* ~ *schämen* or *langweilen*, also in *zu* ~ *betrübt*, but in many cases compounds with the adjective *tot* have arisen, e.g. *sich totärgern, totlachen, totschaffen*. The locution with the genitive *des Todes* = 'very much' (still in Lessing 7,145), e.g. *sich des Todes verwundern* = 'to be extremely surprised', as in Schnabel, *Felsenb.* 4,85 is obs. The same applies to the locutions with *in*, as in Körner, 228b: '. . . *ist mir in Tod fatal*', or the fuller *bis in den* ~.

Tod! (coll.) death and destruction! hell! in exclamations of anger, exasperation, disappointment, etc., also as a curse, e.g. Goethe, *Faust I*, 518: '*o Tod! ich kenn's – das ist mein Famulus*'. There are several other exclamations with ~, e.g. ~ *und Teufel!*, ~ *und Verderben!*

← See also under *Gift* (for *Gift und Tod!*)

der ~ *ist mir übers Grab gelaufen* (coll.) I feel a cold shiver running down my spine; at least since the 18th c., recorded by Campe [1810]. See also the entry under *Grab* (p. 1119) with *etw.* instead of ~.

Leben und ~ life-and-death; in several locutions, e.g. *um Leben und* ~ *spielen*, as in Goethe, *Clavigo* 2, *auf Leben und* ~ *kämpfen* = 'to be engaged in a life and death struggle'; cf. Musäus, *M.* 2,118: '*auf Leben und Tod mit Einem anbinden*'.

der bürgerliche ~ (jur.) loss of civil rights; modern.

Tod(es)-. . . (1) fatal . . . , mortal . . . , deadly . . . , . . . of death; in very many compounds, e.g. *Todesangst* = 'agony, mortal dread' (cf. also *todesbang* in Hölderlin, *Hyp.* 1,124), *Todesbote* = 'messenger from death', e.g. Butschky, *Patm.* 48: '*krankheiten des leibes als todesbohten*', also Goethe, *Iphig.* 3,1, *toderweckt* = 'raised from the dead', e.g. Klopstock, *Mess.* 19,445, *Todfeind* = 'mortal enemy', since MHG (*tôtvîent*), figur. with ref. to abstracts since the 17th c., *Todesgefahr* = 'mortal danger', since Early NHG, *Todsünde* = 'mortal sin', since MHG, recorded since 1482, *Todesurteil* = 'sentence of death', in figur. contexts since the 18th c., e.g. Hölderlin, *Hyp.* 2,92; cf. also in *Todesnöten sein* = 'to be in dire distress'.

← See also under *Engel* (for *Todesengel*), *fallen* (for *Todesfall*), *Geschöpf* (for *Todesgestalt*), *Kampf* (for *Todeskampf*), *Kandidat* (for *Todeskandidat*), *klappern* (for *bitterer Todestanz*), *Schlange* (for *Todesschlange*), *setzen* (for *jem.m den Todesstoß versetzen*) and *Stunde* (for *Todesstunde*).

Tod(es-. . . (2) very . . . , exceedingly . . . ; in many compounds since the 17th c. (Kramer [1702] listed *todmüd*), e.g. *todbang*, also *todesbang* = 'very much afraid' (18th c), *todesblaß* = 'very or deathly pale' (since the 18th c., when *todbleich* and *todesbleich* also appeared), *todesmatt* = 'very tired, exhausted', e.g. Schiller, *Fiesco* 5,13 or Grillparzer 4,241, *todstill* = 'very still or calm', esp. in mar. contexts since the 18th c. Others are recent additions, such as *todtraurig* = 'extremely sad' and *todunglücklich* = 'very unlucky or miserable'.

tödlich very, exceedingly; originally used for 'mortal, liable to die', then describing sth. which leads to death, recorded by Maaler [1561], frequently used in the Bible (e.g. Psalm 7,14, Mark 16,18); then used as an intensifier, since the 18th c.; e.g. '*tödlich langweilig*' for 'terribly boring' in Wieland 7,169 (in *Idris* 3,110 he also used '*tödlich lange Stunden*').

umsonst ist der ~ (*und der kost's Leben*) (prov.) everything costs money except death (and that costs you your life); prov. only since the 19th c., recorded by Simrock [1846] and in dialect dictionaries for many regions; there are variants esp. in the addition, e.g. . . . . *aber er kostet Leute* (listed by Simrock) or *umsonst ist der* ~ *auch nicht, denn*

Priester und Küster wollen auch ihr Teil; some areas have *umsonst ist nicht einmal der* ~.

← See also under *Auge* (for *etw. mit dem Tode büßen*), *aussehen* (for *aussehen wie der Tod von Ypern/Basel/Lübeck*), *blaß* (for *im Tod erblassen*), *bleich* (for *des Todes verbleichen*), *Bote* (for *Boten des Todes*), *Brot* (for *des Einen Tod ist des Andern Brot*), *entgegengehen* (for *dem Tod entgegengehen*), *feucht* (for *einen feuchten Tod finden*), *geben* (for *sich den Tod geben*), *gerade* (for *gerade wie der Tod*), *Gesicht* (for *dem Tod ins Gesicht treten*), *Hauch* (for *zu Tode vergiften*), *hetzen* (for *etw. zu Tode hetzen*), *Hund* (for *viele Hunde sind des Hasen Tod*), *jagen* (for *jem. in den Tod jagen*), *Kammer* (for *des Todes Kammer*), *Kraut* (for *gegen den Tod ist kein Kraut gewachsen*), *Nacht* (for *die Nacht des Todes*), *Schatten* (for *der Tod umschattet ihn*), *schwarz* (for *der schwarze Tod*), *Spaß* (for *einen Spaß zu Tode hetzen*), *studieren* (for *sich auf den Tod üben*) and *Tal* (for *das dunkle Tal des Todes*).

Tohuwabohu: tohu bohu

ein richtiges ~ terrible disorder, confusion, hubbub; biblical, from Gen. 1,2, where in Hebrew it means 'barren and empty'; in extended sense recorded since the 19th c., e.g. Sanders [1871].

Toleranz: tolerance

die ~ (tech.) tolerance, allowable variation or margin; this began as a term with ref. to coinage in the 1st half of the 19th c., f.r.b. Heyse [1838] describing the allowable deviation from prescribed content and weight of a coin (also called *Remedium*); transferred to wider technological contexts in the 1st decade of the 20th c.; frequent now also in *Toleranzgrenze* = 'limit of what is (legally) permitted', only since the 2nd half of the 20th c.

toll: raving mad, crazy, frantic

toll (1) wild, unruly, unorthodox; it can include the notion of irresponsibility; since Early NHG, e.g. Goethe, *Faust I*, 2337: *'das tolle Zauberwesen'*, also *Gespr.* [edit. Bied.] 911: *'man muß oft etwas Tolles unternehmen, um nur wieder eine Zeit lang leben zu können'*; also his *'die genialisch tolle Lebensweise unserer kleinen Gesellschaft'* can find a place here. Sometimes the use of ~ can come close to 'odd, strange, droll', at least since the 18th c.

toll (2) (coll.) splendid, terrific, jolly; used as a term of approval, originally Upper German only (beginnings in MHG period), since the 19th c. recorded for many areas (esp. Bav., Austria and Switzerland), now general coll., e.g. *tolles Wetter* = 'gorgeous weather', *tolle Sache* = 'marvellous thing', *tolle Frau* = 'fantastic woman'. – Note that in *es kommt noch toller* (coll.) the negative sense usually predominates so that it means 'there's worse to come'.

wie ~ like mad; in many contexts at least since the 18th c.

bist du ~ ? are you mad? rhetorical question expressing doubts about sb.'s sanity, e.g. Schiller, *Räuber* 2,3 (or 2,16) and *Wall. Tod* 3,4.

es ist um ~ *zu werden* (coll.) it is enough to drive you mad; since the 18th c., e.g. Körner, *Zriny* 3,1; cf. also *jem.m den Kopf* ~ *machen*, frequently used by Goethe; Klinger, *Theater* 2,368: *'es wird mir toll ums Herz'*.

~ *nach* . . . very eager or mad for sth.; modern, but old in compounds, of which *mannstoll* appears to have been the first (as *mannes tol* in *Liedersaal* [edit. Laßberg 2,587, as *manntoll* in Rabener, *Sat.* 3,187 [1751], as *männertoll* in Thümmel 6,242) meaning 'nymphomaniac'. Others expressing infatuation with or mania for sth. or sb. followed, such as *liebestoll*, as in Gutzkow, *Z.* 4,352; cf. also Heine, *Sal.* 1,119: *'der übertolle Freiheitsrausch'*.

~ *vor* . . . mad with . . . ; expressing violent emotion; f.r.b. Stieler [1691]: *'tollwerden von zorn'*, later mainly with *vor*, e.g. Grimm, *M.* 194: *'toll und blind vor Wuth'*.

. . .*-toll* (coll.) very wild or uncontrolled; a ref. to rabies and mentioning animals which can have rabies, hence *fuchstoll*, as in Immermann, *M.* 1,183, *hundstoll*, as in Immermann, *M.* 2,265, *wolfstoll*, as in Alexis, *Hosen d.H.v.B.* 1,1,30. Refs. to *toller Hund* are old, e.g. Kirchhof, *Wendunm.* 268b, Arnim, *Schaub.* 1,60: '. . . *wenn mich kein toller Hund gebissen hat'*.

sich ~ *und voll saufen* (coll.) to drink to excess, get hopelessly drunk; since Early NHG, e.g. H.Sachs, *Fab.* 2,34, Luther 1,298b (Jena): '. . . *das die Deutschen nit alletzeit tol und vol sein'*; cf. also H.Sachs 19,133: *'den tollen macht der wein noch töller'*, which is derived from Ecclesiasticus 31,37: *'die trunkenheit nacht einen tollen narren noch töller'*.

er reitet ein tolles Pferd (prov.exprs., obs.) he has embarked on a very dangerous undertaking; recorded since the 18th c., e.g. by Frisch [1741], now obs.

er muß Tollbeeren gegessen haben (coll.,a.?) he must be off his head; *Tollbeere* = 'deadly nightshade' has been recorded since the 18th c. The phrase may now be obs.

tolldreist as bold as brass, madly reckless; modern, f.r.b. Campe [1810].

tollkühn foolhardy, rash, dare-devil; since early NHG, recorded by Henisch [1616], e.g. Goethe, *Nat. Tochter* 3,2: '. . . *von der Wuth tollkühner Reiterei . . . abzustehen'*. Hence *Tollkühnheit*, recorded since the 17th c.

tollen to romp, gambole, frolic; since the 15th c., e.g. Luther, *Streitschr.* (repr.) 2,112 [1521]; now more frequently in compounds such as *sich austollen* (coll.) = 'to have a good romp' (esp. with ref. to children), *herumtollen* also *umhertollen* = 'to romp about', e.g. L.Büchner, *Leben* 186 [1861]: *'wann sie mit den Kindern herumtollte'*. Goethe used *tollern*, a form which is now obs. (as is 18th c. *tollieren*).

← See also under *Haus* (for *Tollhaus*), *Kopf* (for *Tollkopf*) and *Roß* (for *das tolle Roß*).

Tolpatsch

der ~ clumsy fellow; derived from Hungarian *talpas* = 'flatfooted', which became a derogatory term for 'infantry soldier', because they wore flat textile soles fastened with string instead of boots, e.g. Gleim, *Werke* 4,243: '*der ist . . . ein Hottentott, ein Talpatsch, ein Pandur*'; then since the 18th c. used for 'clumsy person', probably influenced by *Tölpel* (see below) and *(herum)patschen*; the adjective is *tolpatschig* (since the 18th c.). The meaning 'galosh, overshoe', still recorded by Adelung, is obs.

Tölpel

der ~ stupid or uncouth or clumsy person; originally *Dörfer* = 'rustic, peasant', reflecting contempt for villagers (cf. Engl. 'boor'); since Early NHG, e.g. Luther 8,175b (Jena): '*grobe tölpel*'; hence *tölpisch* (since Early NHG, used by Fischart) and *tölpelhaft* (since the 18th c., used by Wieland, Goethe, Fichte). ~ can also be used for 'fool, sb. who has been taken in by sth.', as in Börne, *Frz.* 43: '*ein Tölpel des Patriotismus*'. See the next entry.

jem. über den ~ *werfen* (or *stoßen*) (obs.) to fool sb. or get the better of sth. There is extensive literature about this phrase (listed in *DWb.* [1935]), but there is now general agreement that at one time in Early NHG two words collided and came to be confused. They were *dorpel* = 'threshold' and *dörpel*, which later became ~, so that the phrase, still used by Lessing 1,246, meant originally 'to throw sb. out, treat sb. with contempt', which led to 'getting the better of sb.'; now obs., displaced by *jem. übertölpeln* (since Early NHG, used e.g. by H.Sachs), which is still current, whereas *betölpeln*, still recorded in *DWb.* [1854], has dropped out of use.

Tomate: tomato

sie wurde rot wie eine ~ (coll.) she turned crimson; since the 1st half of the 20th c.

du treulose ~ (coll.) you faithless creature, a fine friend you are! current since ca. 1920. It may, according to some, refer to the disappointment over the unreliability of the Italians in the 1st World War, according to others, to the initial failures experienced by gardeners who tried to make money by growing tomatoes at the end of 19th c. Others have put forward that '*perfides Albion*' and 'Tommy' together might suggest an anglophobe origin. To me it seems more likely that the rapid deterioration of ripe tomatoes, which finds expression in the sl. phrase *mit Tomaten handeln* = 'to be mistaken, calculate wrongly', could have led to its description as *treulos*.

hast du Tomaten auf den Augen? (sl.) did you not notice it? where have you had your eyes? in sl. or brusque coll. since the 2nd half of the 20th c.

er hat Tomaten unter den Augen (coll.) he looks tired, has deep shadows under his eyes; since 2nd half of the 20th c.

Tommy

ein ~ (coll.) a British soldier; taken over from Engl. and used in World Wars I and II.

Ton: (1) sound, tone, tune, nuance

der . . . . ~ the . . . tone, sound or shade; used with ref. to speech, music or painting with a wide variety of descriptive adjectives, with *süß* already in MHG (where *süz gedoene* also occurred), e.g. Hagedorn, *Od.* 1,6. Equally old is *großer* ~, since MHG for 'loud noise' (cf. Franck, *Sprichw.* [1541]: '*leere fässer geben grossen thon*'); others are *heller* ~, f.r.b. Steinbach [1734], *fremder* ~, as in Goethe, *Wahlverw.* 2,3, *rauher* ~, recorded by Campe, *schläfriger* ~, as in Freiligrath 6,175, *sonniger* ~, as in Goethe, *Dicht.u.Wahrh.* 3. *Töne* can be called *dünn, freundlich, gebrochen, hohl, hölzern, schneidend* or *trocken*. Even *nasser* ~ can occur, as in W.Müller, *Ged.* (repr.) 22: '*der Bach . . . mit seiner Leichenred' im nassen Ton*'; Goethe IV,38,118 (W.) used '*panische Töne*'; cf. also Wieland 13,193: '*der naserümpfende Ton, womit er . . . zu sprechen pflegte*'.

← See also under *fallen* (for *fallender Ton*), *Gold* (for *goldne Töne*), *hoch* (for *der hohe Ton*), *rauh* (for *dort herrscht ein rauher aber herzlicher Ton*) and *scharf* (for *scharfe Töne*).

. . . -ton . . . sound, . . . way of speaking; in descriptions of sb.'s voice, intonation or general way of speaking; e.g. *im Kanzelton* = 'in the kind of voice used in the pulpit', e.g. Schnabel, *Ins.Fels.* 2,433, *Katheterton* = 'professorial or schoolmasterly way of speaking' (similarly *Professorenton*). The group can be extended *ad lib.*; frequent since the 18th c., e.g. Klopstock, *Od.* 2,71: '. . . *Ausländertöne nachzustammeln*', Wieland, *Hor.Br.* 2,216: '*ein jedes Werk . . . hat seinen eigenen Farbenton und Stil*', Schütze, *Hamb. Theat.-Gesch.* 210 [1794]: '. . . *von dem steifen Haupt- und Staatsaktionston*', Knebel, *Lit. Nachlaß* 3,54: '. . . *dem der Herrscher- und Posaunenton in Weimar auch nicht gefällt*', Wieland, *Luc.* 6,424: '*Jammerton*' (similarly *Freudenton, Jubel-, Klage-, Reue-, Schmeichelton*, etc.), Salis, *Ged.* 10 [1839]: '*Klag' ist ein Mißton im Chore der Sphären*'; also with ref. to colours, e.g. Spielhagen, *Pr.* 6,202: '*der Sammetton des dunklen Teints*'.

← See also under *Flöte* (for *in Flötentönen* and *jem.m Flötentöne beibringen*), *gleiten* (for *Silberton der Stimme*), *Grab* (for *Nacht- und Gräberton*), *Kaserne* (for *Kasernenhofton*), *Mißton* (also for *Mißgetön*) and *Posaune* (for *Posaunenton*).

der ~ (personified, lit.) (1) sound; in wider contexts = 'music' seen as capable of movement or action, since the 18th c., often in Goethe's writings where such phrases as *der* ~ *entwindet sich dem Worte* (Diwan 12,9) and *zu den heiligen Tönen, die jetzt meine ganze Seel' umfassen* (*Faust I*, 1202) occur; cf. also Wieland, *Att.* 3,3,113: '*Rouladen . . . wodurch ein Ton in eine Menge anderer sich schnell um ihn herumdrehender Tönchen gleichsam gebrochen wird*', Platen 1,127: '*drängt auch hier von ferne dein*

Ton zu mir sich her'.

← See also under *glühen* (for *alle Töne schwinden*).

der ~ (a.) (2) song, verse, poem; this stems from *Meistersinger* nomenclature and its pedantic rules and classifications. It has survived in lit., often in the diminutive *Tönchen* = 'little song', even 'story', e.g. Voß, *Ar.* 1,239: *'kein alter Verseler hier tont sein Tönchen'*, J.G.Müller, *Lind.* 1,14: *'wenn ich dir das Döhnchen* [= 'story, anecdote'] *erzähle'*.

der gute ~ the *bon ton*, good manners; in wider sense = 'the done thing (in polite society)'; from French in the 18th c., given wider currency by v.Knigge in *Über den Umgang mit Menschen* [1788]; e.g. Schiller, *Fiesco* 2,2: *'der Mann, der in den Assembleen des guten Tons gelitten wird'*, G.Keller, *Sinnged.* 34: *'. . . in die Stadt gebracht, wo sie die sogenannte feinere Sitte und die Führung eines Hauswesens von gutem Ton erlernen sollte'*. Close to this is *~* for 'appropriate way of speaking', as in *sich im ~ vergreifen*, as in (Sp.) G.Keller, *Salander* 74 or *den rechten ~ nicht finden können*, as in Huch, *Pitt u. Fox* 20. Cf. Adelung: *'endlich kommt er in den Ton . . . , figürlich, er kommt auf die Spur, er spricht wie er sprechen sollte'*.

den ~ auf etw. legen to stress sth.; with ref. to syllables or words since the 18th c., recorded e.g. by Adelung; since the 19th c. in wider contexts for 'to stress sth., attach special importance to sth.'; hence also *etw. hat den ~* (ling.) = 'sth. bears the stress, is accented'.

jem. aus dem ~ bringen (a.) to disturb sb., trouble sb.'s composure; also in the intransitive *den ~ verlieren* = 'to become confused or upset', both still recorded in the 19th c. (e.g. by Wander [1876]), but now a. Similar *jem. um den ~ bringen* = 'to damage sb.'s reputation or belittle sb.'s value', which could also be used with ref. to abstracts, e.g. (DWb) J.Möser 2,72: *'. . . alle Freuden um ihren Ton gebracht'*, is obs.

hat der aber einen ~ am Leibe! (coll.) the language that man uses! modern; for phrases of this type and their origin see p. 1603.

davon hat er keinen ~ gesagt (coll.) he never mentioned that at all; modern coll.

hast du da noch Töne? (coll.) that takes your breath away; rhetorical question expressing amazement; since late in the 19th c.

red' doch keine Töne (sl.) don't beat about the bush, don't mince matters, get to the point; 20th c. sl., probably of stud. or juvenile origin.

im Brustton der Überzeugung (cl.) in a confident voice full of conviction; 20th c. cl.

etw. tönen (lit.) to speak, sing, proclaim, chant sth.; frequent in lit. since the 18th c., e.g. Geßner 1,10: *'ihr Lied tönte des Schaffenden Lob'*, Goethe, *Faust I*, 243: *'Die Sonne tönt nach alter Weise in Brudersphären Wettgesang'*, *Iphig.* 5,3: *'die heil'ge Lippe tönt ein wildes Lied'*; also in intrans. locutions, e.g. Wieland 15,4: *'für euch tönt meine Leier nicht'* or 21,148: *'das tönt ja beinah wie Eifersucht'*. There

are many compounds, e.g. Tieck, *Novellenkr.* 3,21: *'Klage . . . die Dantes Erbitterung vielfach austönt'*, Kosegarten, *Poesien* 2,322 [1798]: *'melodischer nun tönet mein Leben dahin'* (Lessing 7,71 used *dahertönen*), Hagedorn 3,127: *'Der Zimbeln Klang durchtönt den Jubel der Mänaden'*, Geßner, *Schr.* 1,11 [1762]: *'von jeder Flur wird dann Lob und Dank zu dir emporgetönt'*, Wieland 9,14: *'mit einem Tone . . . der alle empfindsamen Saiten seines Herzens mittönen machte'*, Ense, *Denkwürd.* 2,48 [1837]: *'die aus der innersten Seele herauftönende Stimme'*, Forster, *Briefw.* 1,89 [1829]: *'der . . . Zwiespalt mißtönte durch sein ganzes Leben'*, Hölderlin, *Hyp.* 1,131: *'. . . die Freude. Laß sie nachtönen in dir'*, Tieck, *Novellen* 1,51: *'der Enthusiasmus übertönt die Einsicht'*, Auerbach, *Neues Leben* 2,106 [1852]: *'so umtönte Heiterkeit alles Thun Eugens'*, Herder, *Phil.* 4,133: *'. . . daß die ganze Erde ihr wie ein harmonisches Saitenspiel zutönet'*. – At the end of the 19th c. a school of lyrical poets proclaiming a new way of expressing feelings called themselves *Neutöner*.

etw. tönt aus etw. (lit.) sth. rings out of sth., can be discerned in sth.; *ertönen* (as in Klopstock, *M.* 20, 471) *in etw.* is preferred in such contexts now.

einen tönen (sl.) to have a quick one, take an (alcoholic) drink; belongs to the group of verbs which associate a noise with drinking, e.g. *einen blasen, gluckern, gurgeln, pfeifen, schmettern* or *zwitschern*.

. . . -tönend (lit.) . . . -sounding; in such lit. compounds as *gleichtönend* (e.g. *gleichtönende Seelen* for 'souls in agreement' in Schiller, cf. also Goethe 40,337 (W.)), but *gleichtönig* only since the 19th c., *hochtönend* = 'bombastic', e.g. Wieland 13,135: *'. . . Sinn in dem hochtönenden Unsinn zu finden'*, Bürger, 180b: *'das Volle, Langtönende unsrer Sprache'*, Klopstock, *Mess.* 8,85: *'im silbertönenden Flug'*.

die Tonkunst music; coined in the 17th c., f.r.b. Stieler [1691], who also listed *Tonkünstler* for *'musicus, philomusus, cantor, musicae peritus'*.

die Tonleiter scale; translates Lat. *scala*; since the 1st half of the 18th c., recorded by Adelung.

tonlos toneless, tuneless; since the 18th c. also in wider senses for 'emitting no sound or remaining without response', e.g. (DWb) Bismarck, *Br.a. s. Braut u. Gattin* 86: *'die Saiten meiner Seele werden schlaff und tonlos'* or for 'flat, in a flat voice', e.g. *matt und tonlos, heiser und tonlos*, and this can be extended even to writings, as in Herder 16,216: *'die Strophe ziehet sich . . . tonlos und matt dahin'*. In ling. contexts *tonlos* = 'unstressed, unaccented'. The recording in Campe [1810] appears to be the first.

die Tonmalerei onomatopoeia; in music also = 'tone painting'; since late in the 18th c., f.r.b. Campe. A 'tone-poem' can also be called *Tonmalerei*; general only since the 19th c., and this applies also to *Tonmaler* and *tonmalend*.

die Tonsilbe (ling.) the stressed syllable; since the

18th c., recorded by Adelung [1780].

der ~ macht die Musik (prov. expr.) it's not what you say but the way that you say it (that matters or that I object to); either from Ital. *è il tono che fa la musica* or from French *c'est le ton qui fait la musique*; modern.

wer singt im alten ~ , *bekommt den alten Lohn* (prov.) unless you bring sth. new you will not receive any rewards; recorded by Simrock [1846].

Untertöne undertones; in figur. (as opposed to musical) sense with ref. to abstracts since the beginning of the 20th c.

Zwischentöne overtones; with ref. to music and painting since the 18th c., e.g. Herder [edit. S.] 22,71: figur. with allusion to sound in Herder 7,122; since the middle of the 19th c. frequent with ref. to abstracts (not yet mentioned in *DWb.* [1954]), e.g. (Sa.) König, *K.Jer.Karn.* 3,244 [1855]: *'mit einem Zwischenton von Rührung und Verwarnung'* (still with sound association, but approaching modern usage).

← See also under *ändern* (for *seinen Ton* or *seine Tonart ändern*), *angeben* (for *den Ton angeben*), *betonen* (also for *betönt*), *Bild* (for *Tonbild*), *Einklang* (for *rein gestimmter Ton*), *eintönig*, *glucken* (for *reine Töne*), *hoch* (for *jem. in den höchsten Tönen loben*), *hochtönend*, *Kaskade* (for *Tonkaskade*), *Pfeife* (for *aus andern Tönen pfeifen*), *rein* (for *jeder Ton perlenrein*), *Saite* (for *den Ton angeben*), *schleifen* (for *Töne schleifen*), *schwingen* (for *große Töne schwingen*), *Simphonie* (for *Tonreihe*) and *streuen* (for *Hände voll Tönen streuen*).

Ton: (2) clay

aus ~ sein (lit., bibl.) to be human or made of mortal clay; biblical, derived from Gen. 2,7 where Luther used *~* (or *than*, as in *Brief.* 2,442: *'wir sein than'*), Wieland, *Gandalin* 6,162: *'du bist aus Thon gebildet wie jeder Erdensohn'*; Uz (repr.) 188 used *'beseelter Thon'*; strange is Schiller's *'ein Weib aus Thon gewoben'*.

jem. zertreten wie ~ (lit.) to smash sb. to pulp; occasionally in lit., e.g. (Sp.) Gutzkow, *Uriel Ac.* 4,6: *'ich glaub' an einen Gott . . . , der seinen Feind zertritt wie Ton'*.

← See also under *Koloß* (for *ein Koloß auf tönernen Füßen*).

Tonne: drum; tonne

eine ~ (coll.) a barrel of a man; esp. with ref. to a corpulent drinker, when *Biertonne* is used, f.r.b. *DWb.* [1860]; cf. Schlegel's transl. of Shakespeare, *King Henry IV*, 1,2,4: *'eine Tonne von einem Mann'*. *~* for 'fat man or woman' was f.r.b. Vulpius, *Glossarium* 131 [1788].

das wiegt eine ~ (coll.) that weighs a ton; hyperbole; cf. similar exaggeration in Gellert, *Betschw.* 3,8: *'ein so steinreicher Mann, der fast eine Tonne Goldes im Vermögen hat'* or Fontane, *Wander.* 1,331 [1883]: *'. . . eine Tonne Geld gekostet'*.

seine ~ wälzen (lit., a.) to ride one's hobby-horse, pursue one's favourite activities; taken over

from French *rouler son tonneau*, since the 18th c.; Goethe used the phrase in IV,10,303, and IV,11,134 (W.). Now a.

dem Walfisch eine ~ zuwerfen or *vorwerfen* (obs.) to (try to) avert a danger, divert sb.'s anger away from oneself; since Early NHG (cf. Fischart, *Garg.* 346: '. . . *spilt wie der walfisch mit den tonnen*'), explained in Rabner, *Sat.* 2,16 [1755]: '. . . *Tonnen bei den Walfischen . . . welche man ihnen vorwirft, damit sie das Schiff in Ruhe lassen*', e.g. Lessing, *Dram.* 101: '. . . *eine Tonne für unsere kritische Walfische!*', Kleist, *Hint.Schr.* [edit. Tieck] 2,351: *'du wirfst dem Walfisch, wie das Sprichwort sagt, zum Spielen eine Tonne vor'*; now obs.

das Tonnengewölbe (archit.) barrel-vault; since the 18th c., recorded by Hübner [1708].

die Tonnenschnecke (zool.) helmet tun shell; this is a shell of the Doliidae family and therefore not the same as *Tonne*, which Nemnich recorded for *Buccina ampulacea*, sometimes called *Trompetenschnecke* = 'great triton, sea trumpet (*Tritonium tritonis*)'.

← See also under *Glück* (for *weil das Glück aus seiner Tonnen die Geschicke blind verstreut*) and *Pulver* (for *auf einer Pulvertonne sitzen*).

Tonti

die Tontine (a.) tontine; a group pension plan devised by Lorenzo Tonti (ca. 1653) to which members contribute annually and receive an annuity; as members die, these annuities increase until the last survivor claims the total capital; figur. in Börne 2,209: *'Schwärmerei ist eine Tontine, der Antheil der Verstorbenen fällt den Überlebenden zu'*; now a.

Topf: pot

der ~ (coll.) head; in many phrases, *aus hohlem ~ reden* = 'to talk nonsense', current since the 16th c., *der beinerne ~*, as in Auerbach, *Dicht.* 2,107, also *das ist* (or *wurde*) *nicht in seinem ~ gekocht* = 'that was not thought up, worked out, instigated, etc. by him', e.g. Wieland, *Luc.* 6,26; cf. Engl. coll. 'crackpot'.

alles in einen ~ werfen (coll.) to put everything together (whether it fits or not); already in the 17th c. in the phrase *'in einem Topf kochen'*, as in Weise, *Hauptverderber* 85 [1671], in modern wording used by Schiller (letter to Goethe, 1795) or Bismarck, *Reden* 4,134 (or 1,164): *'in Bauerndörfern sollten die Bauernhöfe alle in einen Topf geworfen werden'*.

den ~ aufdecken (coll.) to reveal the state of affairs, expose what is going on; modern, e.g. v.Horn, *Rh.D.* 2,156.

in alle Töpfe gucken (coll.) to be very curious; sometimes *alle* with the notion of being anxious about what is going to happen; hence also *das Topfgucken*, as in G.Hauptmann, *Biberpelz* 1 or *ewige Topfguckerei*, as in G.Keller, *Nachlaß* 9. Cf. also *seine Nase in alle Töpfe stecken*, a variant of idioms listed under *Nase*.

der ~ kann ohne Holz nicht kochen (coll.) without fuel the pot will not boil; at least since the 18th c., when Wieland used it in *Perv.* 1,137.

die Sache ist noch nicht in dem ~, *in dem sie kochen soll* (coll.) this is not ready yet (for publication, for setting in train, etc.); since the 18th c., e.g. K.Lessing, *R.Frau* 38 [2nd half of 18th c.], recorded as prov. by Simrock [1846].

bei Tisch und ~ at the dining-table or in the kitchen; e.g. Goethe, *Camp.i.Fr.* (24.7.1792).

der Tod im ~ *!* (obs.) what a terrible meal! of biblical origin, derived from 2 Kings 4,40, still recorded in the 19th c., now obs.

der ~ *kocht über* (coll.) things are going wrong; cf. Fr. *le pot s'enfuit*; modern.

pack (or *faß*) *den* ~ *am Henkel!* (coll.) make a proper job of it, tackle it the right way; modern coll.

der tägliche Eintopf (coll.) the usual uninteresting mixture, the same old stew; modern coll., pejor.; hence also *eintopfartig* with ref. to mixtures which are made up of things which ought to have been kept separate; modern.

der ~ *mit dem Riß ist im Hause der älteste gewiß* (prov.) cracked pots last longest; international and old; cf. French *les pots fêlés sont ceux qui durent le plus*; also as *gesprungene Töpfe dauern am längsten*; Wander [1876] recorded both forms. Often used with ref. to people in delicate health who survive their more robust contemporaries.

der schwarze ~ *heißt den schwarzen Kessel Zigeuner* (prov.) the pot calling the kettle black; cf. French *la pelle se moque du fourgon*; Simrock [1846] recorded it also as *der* ~ *verweist es dem Kessel, daß er schwarz ist.*

die leeren Töpfe klingen am hellsten (prov.) empty pots make most noise; Binder [1861] referred to Lat. *vasa vacua plurimum sonant*; Klix [1863] recorded it; cf. similar phrases under *Tonne*.

kleine Töpfe haben auch Ohren (prov.) little pitchers have great (or wide) ears; in Engl. recorded since the 16th c., for LG first in Tunnicius, 268 [1515]: '*kleine potte hebben ôk twe oren*'; in modern wording recorded by Simrock [1846].

kleine Töpfe kochen leicht über (prov.) a little pot is soon hot; in Engl. recorded since the 16th c.; meaning: small persons are inclined to be irascible. Simrock [1846] recorded it.

es ist kein ~ *so schief, er findet seinen Deckel* (prov.) even the ugliest find a partner; often used as a comment on married people who differ very much in appearance; international, e.g. French *il n'y a si laid pot qui ne trouve son couvercle*; for German recorded by Simrock [1846]. A different view is taken by another prov., f.r.b. Petri [1605]: *auf einen schiefen* ~ *gehört ein schiefer Deckel.*

wenn der ~ *brodelt, brodelt auch die Freundschaft* (prov.) friendship lasts as long as the hospitality lasts; also as *so lange der* ~ *siedet, so lange dauert die Freundschaft*; f.r.b. Petri [1605]; cf. French *à table bien servie beaucoup d'amis.*

wenn's Brei regnet, hat er keinen ~ (prov. expr.) he is never in the right place at the right time; recorded by Simrock [1846]. Wander [1876] also *wenn du den Brei gegessen hast, so nimm auch den* ~ and *er will in einem* ~ *zwei Brei kochen.*

← See also under *Ägypten* (for *sich nach den Fleischtöpfen Ägyptens sehnen*), *aufdeckeln* (for *jem.m das Töpfchen aufdeckeln*), *aussehen* (for *aussehen wie ein Topf voll Mäuse*), *Brei* (for *wenn es Brei regnet, hab' ich keinen Topf*), *Gesicht* (for *ein Gesicht machen wie ein Topf voll Teufel*), *Glück* (for *Glückstopf*), *Götze* (for *des Glückes Rad ist oft eine Töpferscheibe*), *Kessel* (for *der Kessel schilt den Ofentopf*), *Mus* (for *er kommt aus dem Mustopf*), *Nudel* (for *voll wie ein Nudeltopf*), *Ohr* (for *an Ohren faßt man Töpfe und leere Köpfe*), *pissen* (for *sie pissen alle in einen Topf*), *Riese* (for *Riesentopf*) and *sauer* (for *Sauertopf* and *sauertöpfig*).

Tor: (1) fool

ein weiser ~ (lit., obs.) a fool who considers himself clever; in 18th c. lit., e.g. Wieland 15,144.

eine reiner ~ (ironic) an adult who has preserved the ideals of his youth; the mediaeval *tumber tôre*, as in Wolfr.v.Eschenbach's *Parz.* was taken up by Richard Wagner as *reiner* ~; now in ironic (or pitying) use for 'naive idealist'.

← See also under *alt* (for *Alter schützt vor Torheit nicht*), *betören*, *Grab* (for *Grab menschlicher Torheit*), *Grenze* (for *grenzt an die Torheit Land*), *grob* (for *grobe Torheit*), *puffen* (for *verliebter Tor*) and *Schelle* (for *schellenlauter Tor*).

Tor: (2) door

das ~ (lit.) entrance, gate, portal; early figur. instances in the Bible, where *des Todes* ~ occurs, e.g. in Job 38,17: '*haben sich dir des Todes Tore je aufgetan, oder hast du gesehen die Tore der Finsternis?*' (also Psalm 9,14), also in modern literature, e.g. Lessing 4,280: '*das trieb den Tag in sein östliches Thor zurück*', E.Th.A. Hoffmann, *Ausgew.W.* 7,149: '*das Thor der Poesie . . . weit geöffnet*', Schiller, *Wall.Tod* 3,18: '*weit offen ließ ich des Gedankens Thore*'. Figur. use of non-religious ~ occurred as early as in MHG poetry, e.g. Walther v.d.V. 20,31: '*mir ist verspart der saelden tor*'.

einer Sache Tür und ~ *öffnen* to open the door to sth., give free access to sth., allow sth. to enter, infiltrate, etc.; since the 17th c., e.g. Lohenstein, *Arm.* 1,22a: '*zu dem hätte ihre eigene zwytracht den Römern thür und tor aufgesperret*', Herder, *Ph.* 17,199: '*aller Unordnung Thür und Thor öffnen*'; cf. also phys. *dem Feind die Tore öffnen* = 'to surrender the city to the enemy', as in Mommsen, *Röm.Gesch.* 1,615 [1856].

das Eiserne ~ (geogr.) the Iron Gate (near Orsova); e.g. (Sa.) Daniel, *Geogr.* 239: '. . . *die Strom-Enge, welche die Türken . . . eisernes Tor nennen*'; whilst this refers to the Iron Gate near Orsova, it should be noted that the expression is also used for other narrows and passes in the Near East.

ein ~ schießen (sport) to score a goal; 20th c.

← See also under *fünf* (for *fünf Minuten vor Torschluß*), *Hannibal* (for *Hannibal ist vor den Toren*), *Kuh* (for *etw. anstarren wie die Kuh ein neues Tor*), *Morgen* (for *Morgentor der Zukunft*) and *Schluß* (for *Torschlußpanik*).

Tornister: see *Marschall*.

Torpedo: torpedo

etw. torpedieren to torpedo, frustrate or destroy sth.; figur. mainly in polit. contexts, also as *einen ~ loslassen*, and *Torpedierung*, all three since ca. 1930.

Torso: torso

(nur) ein ~ (lit.) a (mere) torso, sth. incomplete or fragmentary; figur. since the 19th c., e.g. (DWb) Löben, *Lotosblätter* 1,89 [1817]: '*die Welt, die uns umgibt, ist ein großer Torso, an dem wir alle studieren*'; often in *es bleibt ein ~* = 'it remains unfinished'.

Torte: see *Spiegel*.

Tortur: torture

die ~ torture; figur. in wider sense of 'painful or cruel experience'; since the 2nd half of the 18th c., e.g. Schubart, *Originalien* 34 [1780]: '*iche habe die Kassentortur der Leichtgläubigen, die Lotterie, ziehen sehen*'; often in *etw. ist eine für jem.* = 'sth. is (sheer) torture for sb.', since the 19th c.

tot: dead

tot (1) dead, lifeless; with ref. to plants as early as Late MHG, e.g. Megenberg, 288: '*die toten pluomen*', Stieler [1691] recorded it with ref. to *Baum*, then in wider sense for objects which were not alive at any time, e.g. *die tote Schöpfung* = 'inanimate nature', e.g. Herder, *Ebr. Poesie* 1,165, Daumer, *Hafis* 1,69 [1846]: '*so beseelt wie tote Klötze . . .*', Auerbach, *Dt.Abende* 248 [1851]: '*. . . bist ein Kerl . . . und fürchtest dich vor einer toten Flinte*', Schiller 16,259 (S.): '*der todte Buchstabe der Natur . . .*' (he also used *tote Güter* and *totes unfruchtbares Gold*), *M.Stuart* 5,7: '*das Wort ist tot, der Glaube macht lebendig*'. Such locutions as *toter Glaube* or *totes Symbol* could be included here but with equal justification be listed under *tot* (3). Stieler listed *toter Glaube* and interpreted *~* as 'sterilis'; cf. also Kramer's [1702] recording: '*geistlich/sittlich todt seyn*'.

tot (2) dead, silent, soundless; cf. Engl. 'dead silence'; since the 18th c., e.g. Goethe 11,58 (W.): '*seh ich nicht . . . an dem todten Stillschweigen eurer Freunde, daß . . .*' (he also used *toter Kummer* for 'silent sorrow'). At the same time *totenstill* and *Totenstille* arose, e.g. Schiller, *D.Carlos* 4,22: '*. . . ist todtenstill, man hört sie Athem holen*', Hölderlin, *Hyp.* 1, 92: '*die Todtenstille der Nacht*'. Cf. also *tote Leitung* (tech.) for 'dead (electric or telephone) line'.

tot (3) dead, dull, showing no spirit or liveliness; beginnings in the 17th c. (Kramer recorded *tote Farben* in 1702), in many contexts, e.g. *tote Augen*, recorded by Adelung, *tote Straße* = 'empty street', also *totes Geschäft* (comm.) = 'business without customers' (modern).

tot (4) dead, having no energy, producing no results; e.g. *toter Weg* = 'water-course that flows under a mill-wheel without setting it in motion', *toter Gang* (of a machine), *tote Kraft*, etc. Campe [1810] and Karmarsch 3,39 [1854] listed many special tech. locutions which all express the same notion; *totes Kapital* = 'dead capital, barren money, money bearing no interest', general since the 18th c. (used by Goethe).

tot (5) dead, extinct; e.g. *tote Sprache* = 'dead language', since the 17th c., f.r.b. Kramer [1702]: '*eine nicht mehr übliche (todte) Sprach*'; close to *~* = 'finished', as in *er ist ein toter Mann* = 'he is finished (e.g. as a financier, politician)', modern; cf. also *das ist ~ und begraben* = 'that is dead and buried' and *für mich ist er ~* = 'he does not exist for me anymore'; in phys. contexts there is *tote Asche* = 'cold ashes', recorded by Kramer; Adelung also listed a related *~* in legal contexts: '*die Handschrift soll todt und ab seyn*'.

tot (6) undecided, without a result; mainly in *totes Rennen* = 'dead heat', since the 2nd half of the 19th c., e.g. (Sa.) *Nat.Ztg.* 11,248.

tot (7) (coll.) dead beat, exhausted, fagged; e.g. *ich bin ganz ~*; modern, but *todmüd* has been current at least since the 17th c., recorded by Kramer in 1702.

~ für etw. sein to be insensitive to sth.; since the 18th c., e.g. Gotter 1,113: '*tot ist er für der Schöpfung Pracht*', Nicolai 1,27: '*tot für jede Freude*'; an early (slightly different) forerunner was *~ an etw. sein* in MHG for 'to be deprived or bereft of sth.', e.g. *MSH* 1,71a: '*an fröuden tôt*', Konr.v. Würzburg, *Troj.* 14873 and 22,351, now obs.

mehr ~ als lebendig more dead than alive, totally exhausted; recorded by Kramer [1702], Goethe used it, also Platen, 348: '*ich war mehr tot als lebendig, da er diese Worte sprach*' (which comes close to 'near fainting'); quite different is *lebendig ~*, as in 1 Tim. 5,6: '*welche aber in wollüsten lebet, die ist lebendig tod*'; Kramer recorded: '*lebendig-todt = vivente-ò vivo morto*'.

der tote Arm the dead (stagnant, standing) arm (or branch) of a river or brook; modern (not mentioned yet in Kramer or Adelung).

totenblaß, totenbleich deathly pale; at least since the 17th c., recorded by Kramer [1702] as '*todtblaß, todtbleich*'; he also listed '*todtfarb werden*'.

bürgerlich ~ (jur.) officially dead: Sanders [1865] glossed it: '*ein Verschollener ist bürgerlich tot, in Bezug auf seine bürgerlichen Rechte*'.

tote Glieder numb, benumbed, dead limbs; at least since the 17th c., when Stieler [1691] recorded '*todt glieder*', e.g. Auerbach, *Ges.Schr.* 5,198: '*. . . was ich für todte Finger hab*'.

das ist tote Hose (sl.) that does no good, leads to nothing; when applied to a person = 'he is a dull dog'; sl. of the 2nd half of the 20th c.

tote Kolumnentitel (also *tote Marginalien*) (print.)

entries in headings or text in the margin which consist only of numbers; recorded since the 19th c., e.g. Frank, *Buchdruckerkunst* 71 [1856].

der tote Mann exhausted pit, worked-out part of a mine; a volcano which is extinct is also called ~.

den toten Mann machen (coll.) to float motionless on water; modern.

das Tote Meer (geogr.) the Dead Sea; in German since Late MHG, e.g. Megenberg, 101 [1482].

der tote Punkt (1) dead stop, deadlock, standstill; modern, often with ref. to negotiations, e.g. *die Verhandlungen waren an einem toten Punkt angelangt*; modern.

der tote Punkt (2) low point; with ref. to energy or stamina; e.g. *der Redner suchte seinen toten Punkt zu überwinden*; modern.

der tote Winkel blind spot, area which cannot be seen; first in mil. jargon for 'area which gun-fire cannot reach' = 'dead angle'; then extended, e.g. by motorists with ref. to the area which they cannot see in their mirror. – Quite different is *der tote Winkel* = 'forsaken place, village in which nothing happens', as used by Goethe in *Scherz, List u. Rache* 3.

der tote Zeuge (jur.) silent witness, *corpus delicti* which constitutes a silent witness; since MHG.

. . .wie . . . like dead, as if dead; as *alse ein tôte* as early as in MHG, e.g. Gottfr.v.Str., *Tristan* 11695 (cf. Schiller, *Räuber* 4,5: 'ins Leichentuch gewickelt wie ein Toder'); often now in *daliegen, umfallen* or *schlafen wie* ~, e.g. G.Hauptmann, *Fuhrm.H.* 5 [1898]; *für* ~ = 'for dead, believed to be dead' has been current since MHG, e.g. *Iwein* 5049: 'für tôdt liegen', Goethe, *Nat. Tochter* 1,4: 'für todt hob man mich auf'.

sich tot- . . . to . . . oneself to death; hyperbole with many verbs, since the 17th c., when Logau 3,7,80 used *sich totsaufen*; Goethe in *Wanderj.* 3,8 used *sich totlachen* (cf. Lat. *emori risu*); frequent in *sich totschaffen* = 'to work oneself to death'. In the 20th c. *sich totlaufen* was added to this group; it is different because the subject is not a human being but an abstract (first a machine which has 'stopped running'), e.g. *diese Methode hat sich totgelaufen* meaning that it has run its course and has reached its end. Hence also *es ist zum Totlachen*, since the 18th c. In modern coll. there is also *es ist zum Totschießen* = 'it is too funny for words', recorded by Wander [1876]. Non-reflex. locutions belonging under this heading are old, e.g. Petri in his prov. collection of 1605: 'besser todt geschlaffen, den todt gelauffen'.

← See also under *arg* (for *sich totärgern*).

es hat sich mal einer totgemischt (joc. coll.) when will you stop shuffling these cards? joc. extension of the pattern of the previous entry, current among card-players since the beginning of the 20th c.

. . .-tot dead, stone-dead; in intensifying compounds; examples are *leichentot*, as in Heine, *Sal.* 1,306, *starrtot*, as in J.G. Müller, *Lind.* 2,409,

steintot, as in Abr. a Sta.Clara, *Etw.f.A.* 1,527.

← See also under *Maus* (for *mausetot*) and *rein* (for *er ist rein tot*).

er ist nicht totzukriegen (coll.) (1) he is indestructible, in amazingly robust health; since the 19th c.

er ist nicht totzukriegen (coll.) (2) he is unbeatable, nobody gets him down or gets the better of him; since the 19th c.

jem. totmachen (coll.) to knock sb. out, ruin sb.; esp. in comm. contexts, since the 19th c., e.g. Freytag, *Soll u. Haben* 2,360.

jem. mundtot machen to silence sb., stop sb. (by force or tricks) from speaking, defending himself, etc.; a case of pop.etym., since *mundtot* does not belong to *Mund* = 'mouth', but to *Mund/Munt* (jur.obs.) = 'legal protection'; f.r.b. Schottel [1663], e.g. (Sa.) Stahr, *Nach 5 Jahren* 1,224 [1857]: 'das Leben des französischen Geistes ist freilich mundtot in der Presse . . .'; often in *ich lasse mich nicht mundtot machen* = 'I will not be gagged, I insist on speaking out'.

die Zeit totschlagen (coll.) to kill time, spend one's time in useless occupations; there are 18th c. idioms which use *töten* in this context, e.g. Körner, *Braut* 2: 'die langen Stunden tödten'; the coll. variant with *totschlagen* appeared in the 19th c., e.g. (Sp.) Werfel, *Abitur.* 49: '. . . lange Nächte mit philosophischen Gesprächen totgeschlagen'.

selbst wenn du mich totschlägst (coll.) I really do not know (or have) it; since the 19th c. in strong denials of being able to respond; cf. similar *ich will (auf der Stelle)* ~ *umfallen, wenn . . .* = 'may I be struck dead, if . . .', used as a strong assertion.

sich für jem. totschlagen lassen (coll.) to be sb.'s supporter through thick and thin; since the 18th c., e.g. Klinger 3,36. There is also *sich für etw. totschlagen lassen* (coll.) = 'to be absolutely convinced of sth.'; *für* is the correct preposition now, but *DWb.* listed it as *sich auf etw. totschlagen lassen*, adducing an example from Jean Paul, *Tit.* 2,20. There is also *eher laß ich mich totschlagen, als daß . . . .* (coll.) = 'I'd sooner die than . . .'.

der Totschläger life-preserver; transfer from the person = 'homicide' (current since MHG) to the tool used; 20th c. (not yet listed in *DWb.* [1913]).

etw. totschweigen to hush sth. up; since the 17th c., f.r.b. Schottel [1663]; with ref. to persons it can mean 'to ignore'.

einer Sache das Totenglocklein läuten to sound the death-knell for sth.; modern in the extended sense of 'declaring sth. to be dead or moribund'.

der Totentanz (lit.) dance of death; originally (14th c.) an allegorical picture or sculpture in which death plays the fiddle to doomed humans dancing to his tune; now figur. to describe sth. abstract tumbling, swerving or sliding to its death (which includes the notion of helplessness among the participants), e.g. *der Totentanz der langen Verhandlungen.*

der Totenvogel (zool., coll.) little owlet (*Athene noctua*); an old term to which superstitions concerning an impending death are attached. The standard term is *Steinkauz*. *Totenvogel* is also used for some other owls, also some moths and butterflies (listed in Campe [1810]).

etw. tötet (*jem.* or *etw.*) sth. kills or destroys (sb. or sth.); figur.when the subject is an abstract, since MHG, e.g.*MSH* 1,341a: '*diu milte kan vor got die sünde toeten*'; frequent in the Bible, e.g. Job 5,2: '*den albernen tödtet der eifer*' (also Rom. 7,11 and Ecclesiasticus 30,25), Leisewitz, *Jul.v.T.* 2,5: '*der Staat tötet die Freiheit*' (cf. also Goethe, *Laune d.V.* 8: '. . . *wird jede Lust getödtet*').

etw. töten (1) to destroy, annihilate sth.; also often = 'to overcome sth.'; mainly biblical, e.g. Col. 3,5: '*so tödtet nu ewre glieder, die auf erden sind, hurerey, vnreinigkeit . . .*'.

etw. töten (2) (jur.) to set sth. aside, rescind sth.; since MHG; Adelung recorded '*einen Contract tödten*'.

etw. töten (3) (stud. sl., a.) to drink what is left in the glass; since the 19th c., e.g. (Sa.) Waldau, *Natur* 2,122 [1850]: '*er tödtete, wie er es nannte, seinen Rest*'.

Quecksilber töten (chem.) to deaden mercury; since Late MHG, e.g. Megenberg, 477, and still in use; 'to deaden' is also used with ref. to colours: *Farben töten*, and in various trades *töten* is used for 'to reduce lustre', 'to make sth. ineffectual'; cf. also *dieser Teil des Gemäldes tötet den Rest*. In modern coll. there is also *eine Zigarette* (or *Zigarre*) *töten* = 'to extinguish, kill a cigarette (or cigar)', e.g. Werfel, *Abitur*. 9.

tötend killing, destroying; modern in phys. contexts such as *ein schmerztötendes Mittel* (where older dictionaries only have *schmerzstillendes Mittel*), but earlier in figur. contexts, e.g. Lessing, *Miss S.S.* 5,11: '*bei diesem tödtenden* [='devastating'] *Anblick*', J.J.Engel, *Schr.* 7,319 [1801]: '*tötend* [= 'most wounding'] '*wird diese Nichtbeachtung*'.

totenhaft (lit.) death-like, deathly; since the 18th c. (Goethe used it), e.g. Mörike, *N.* 283: '*die todtenhafte Stille*'.

'*Laß die Toten ihre Toten begraben*' let the dead bury their dead; quotation from Matth. 8,22.

von den Toten soll man nur Gutes reden (prov.) speak well of the dead; old and international, e.g. Lat. *de mortuis nil nisi bene*.

← See also under *Bart* (for *den toten Löwen kann jeder Hase am Bart zupfen*), *Baum* (for *Totenbaum*), *Buchstabe* (for *der Buchstabe tötet*), *drohen* (for *droht, macht dich nicht tot*), *ertöten, erwecken* (for *von den Toten erwecken*), *Furz* (for *wer sich von Drohungen töten läßt*), *Geißel* (for *er geißelt einen Toten*), *Gerücht* (for *das Gerücht tötet den Mann*), *Gleis* (for *auf dem toten Gleis sein*), *Hand* (for *die tote Hand*), *heute* (for *heute rot, morgen tot*), *Hund* (for *besser ein lebendiger Hund als ein toter Löwe*), *Jude* (for *toter Jude*), *Kind* (for *ein totgeborenes Kind*), *Löwe* (for *ist der Löwe tot, ist er der Hasen Spott*), *Masse* (for *lieber scheintot im Massengrab* – where *scheintot* has been misprinted), *Maus* (for *mausetot*), *Mord* (for *das gibt Mord und Totschlag*), *Nerv* (for *den Nerv töten*), *neun* (for *Neuntöter*), *Ratte* (for *verliebt wie eine tote Ratte*), *rot* (for *lieber rot als tot*) and *Schmied* (for *Totenschmied* and *Totenuhr*).

Tour: turn, route, tour

in einer ~ (1) at a stretch; refers to doing at least two things in one trip; since the 19th c., e.g. (S.-B.) Holtei, *Schneider* 2,5 [1854]: '. . . *werden in einer Tour mit der Eisenbahn . . . von Hamburg absausen, um in Berlin zu arbeiten*'. Whilst this retains its phys. basis, it could easily lead to the next:

in einer ~ (2) (coll.) incessantly, continually; since early in the 20th c., e.g. *er redet in einer ~* = 'he never stops talking'.

auf Touren kommen (coll.) to get going at full speed, get into one's stride; 20th c. coll., hence also *auf vollen Touren laufen* (coll.) = 'to go full blast, be in full swing'.

jem. auf Touren bringen (coll.) to get sb. going, urge sb. on; also used for 'to make sb. mad, infuriate sb.'; both 20th c. coll.

auf diese ~ (coll.) in this manner or way; under the influence of French *tour* German *~* in the 17th c. acquired such meanings as 'skilful behaviour', 'trick' and this led in the 18th c. to the meanings 'manner', 'way of behaving', f.r.b. Hübner, *Ztglex.* 467 [1763], e.g. Wieland, *Gesch.d.Gel.* 48 [1757]: '. . . *bedienten sich die Päpste eines sehr politischen Tours*'; since early in the 20th c. frequent in *auf die . . . ~*, e.g. *Lok.Anz.* of 1.1.1933: '*nu machen Sie bloß nicht auf "vornehme Tour"*'. In coll. or near-sl. idioms now with many adjectives, e.g. *auf die alte, bequeme, billige, faule, feine, harte, milde ~*, all describing either a mode of behaviour or a condition one finds oneself confronted with, e.g. Fallada, *Wolf* 1,327: '*mich kannst du nicht auf die süße Tour* [= 'through flattery'] *kriegen*'; an off-shoot from this sense is *für dich ist die ~ gelaufen* (coll.) = 'that has gone wrong for you'; hence also *jem.m die ~ vermasseln* (coll.) = 'to queer sb.'s pitch, spoil things for sb.'.

← See also under *krumm* (for *etw. auf die krumme Tour machen*).

er hat wieder einmal seine ~ (coll.) he has one of his fits (of anger) again, he is in a bad mood again; 20th c. coll.

außer der ~ gehen (coll.) to do sth. irregular, inappropriate or unscheduled; derived from *~* = 'turn', as in *die ~ ist an ihm* = 'it is his turn', current since the 18th c.; now used in several contexts, also euphem. with ref. to marital infidelity, since the 20th c.; hence *außertourlich* = 'unscheduled', since late in the 19th c.

die Ochsentour (joc. coll.) the slow and unexciting career of a civil servant (in which every stage is fixed beforehand and dependent on seniority);

coined by Bismarck in 1893 (Klemm 2,94): *'ein preußischer, in der Ochsentour großgewordener Regierungsbeamter'*. See also under *Ochs* for *Ochsentrott*.

← See also under *Hochtouren* and *spritzen* (for *Spritztour*).

Trabant: soldier; companion

der ~ (1) associate (who does not enjoy full independence); ~ was taken over from Czech and first used for 'foot-soldier'; with ref. to supporting troops or servants figur. as early as in the 17th c., e.g. (S.B.) Suter, *Lustg.* 73 [1665]: *'ein Soldat sagte,die Läuse wären seine Trabanten'*, Voß II,114 [1802]: *'doch um den Aufsatz standen französische Frücht' und Salat, als Trabanten des Bratens'*, Steinmann, *Rothschild* 1,26 [1857]: *'. . . nur eine Macht . . . und das ist Rothschild; und seine Trabanten sind ein Dutzend anderer Bankierhäuser'*.

der ~ (2) (astron.) moon, satellite; when the moons of Jupiter and Saturn were discovered (1609 and 1655), scholars called them in Lat. *satellites*, but from the 1st half of the 18th c. onward the terms *Mond*, *Trabant* and *Satellit* came to be used without clear distinction. Then the planets came to be called *Trabanten* of the Sun, e.g. Lichtenberg, *Verm.Schr.* 4,253. Since early in the 19th c. minor intellectual or artistic 'stars' can be called *Trabanten* of some greater luminary, e.g. (DWb) Bremser, *Parömien* 122 [1802]: *'jeder dieser neuen Planeten am gelehrten Horizonte hat nun auch wieder seine Trabanten'*; with ref. to abstracts in Börne, *Ges.Schr.* 3,253: *'die Eitelkeit ist der Mond dieser Erde, der Ehre kühler und kleiner Trabant'*.

der ~ (3) (regional coll.) chap, fellow, (undesirable) companion, hanger-on; a vague term used in some regions as a term of contempt for 'disagreeable person' (mainly in Alemannic areas), 'stupid person' (esp. in Vienna, hence also in Nestroy 2,160). When applied to small children, it usually occurs in the plural and can be used affectionately.

Trabanten-. . . satellite-. . . ; since the 19th c. in compounds which are synonymous with *Satelliten-*compounds (which see on p. 2058), e.g. *Trabantenstaat*, as in Treitschke, *Dt.Gesch.* 1,231: *'die "Sonnennation" Frankreich umgeben von Trabantenstaaten'*.

traben: trot

traben to trot along, move at a leisurely pace; figur. since Early NHG, e.g. Luther 5,255a (Jena): *'Epikureer, welche nicht traben, sondern zur höllen zurennen'*; frequent in compounds, most of which remain on a phys. level. Exceptions are *dahertraben*, as in Wieland, *Luc.* 4,132: *'. . . wo seine Imagination wie auf einem allzu mutigen Pferde dahertrabt'* and *vortraben*, current since Early NHG, e.g. Luther 34,1,554 (Weimar), e.g. Gellert 1,292 (or 1,272 in 1839 edit.): *'der Leichtsinn trat sein Amt mit Eifer an, das Amt, der Liebe vorzutraben'*; *hoch* ~ = 'to be conceited, give oneself airs' has become obs. as a verb, but is still alive in the adjective *hochtrabend*, which see on p. 1354.

. . . *-trab* . . . *-trot*, . . . *-pace*; in compounds describing kinds of movement, e.g. Heine, *Tr.* 92: *'im Eselstrab'*, Kohl, *Alpenreisen* 1,235 [1831]: *'im Gänsetrab'* (the preferred form is *Gänsemarsch*, which see on p. 908), Heine, *Börn.* 266: *'die kurzen Sätze, der kleine Hundetrab'*. A special case is *der Vortrab* = 'advance-guard, vanguard, forerunner', figur. since Early NHG, when Fischart called the dawn *'der sonne vortrab'* (cf. also Luther 5,533a (Jena): *'. . . diese zeichen als seine vordraber'*).

← See also under *Hund* (for *Hundetrab*) and *Nachtrab*.

sich in starken Trab setzen to take energetic steps forward; since the 19th c., e.g. (Sa.) Ense, *Biogr.D.* 3,63 [1824]; similarly *jem. auf Trab bringen* = 'to make sb. bestir himself', also *mach ein bißchen Trab* (coll.) = 'get a move on!'.

Tracht

die ~ (lit.) load, large amount; the meaning 'load, amount that one can carry' could, like *Bürde* or *Last*, be used with ref. to abstracts; general only since the 19th c., e.g. Lenau [edit.B.] 124 on a poet: *'. . . taumelt heim mit seiner Tracht unsterblicher Gedanken'*.

← See also under *besehen* (for *eine Tracht Prügel besehen*).

die ~ (2) (obs.) course (of a meal); refers to 'amount that is carried to the table' which led to 'course'; since MHG, e.g. Freidank 15,16: *'ein hôchgezît dâ man siben trahte gît'*; still current in the 18th c., e.g. Goethe, *Ben.Cell.* 3,5; then displaced by *Gang*.

trächtig mit (or *von*) *etw. sein* (lit.) to be pregnant with sth.; figur. since the 18th c., e.g. Klopstock, *Oden* 2,82: *'. . . Krieg, der beinah stets trächtig . . . Seuche dann warf'*, Goethe, *Kenner u. Enthus.*: *'mein Busen war . . . von hundert Welten trächtig'*; cf. also Th.Mann, *Buddenbr.* 251: *'schwer und trächtig hing der dunkelgraue Himmel hernieder'*; then in compounds which originally expressed the notion of 'destined or likely to produce sth.', e.g. *unglücksträchtig*, as used by Goethe, now often meaning no more than 'full of', e.g. *fehlerträchtig*, *symbolträchtig*, and in the 20th c. extended in nouns such as *Geschichtsträchtigkeit*.

träge: lazy, idle

träge slow, sluggish; originally a description of phys. movement, but since MHG extended to mental disposition, as in Megenberg, *B.d.Nat.* 119: *'die traegen schuoler'* and used with ref. to abstracts, e.g. Schaidenraißer, *Od.* 31b [1537]: *'. . . mit . . . trägem . . . gemüt . . .'*, Hagedorn, *Fab.* 2,47: *'ein greises Weib . . . von trägem Dienst'*, Göckingk, *Lied.zw.L.* 136: *'des Herzens träge Mühle'*, Schiller, *D.Carl.* 5,11: *'meiner Jahre trägen Lauf'* (with *Farbe* in *Räuber* 2,2); cf. also H.Sachs [edit. Keller] 9,14: *'treger marckt wird offt gut'* (where *flau* would now be preferred); *Trägheit* followed, f.r.b. Maaler [1561].

← See also under *Geist* (for *Geistesträgheit*),

Gewohnheit (for *Gewohnheit beruht auf Trägheit*) and *Sumpf* (for *Sumpf von Trägheit*).

tragen: carry, bear

etw. ~ (1) to bear, suffer, endure, feel sth.; with abstracts since MHG, e.g. Wolfr.v.E., *Parz.* 26,29: *'jâmer tragen'*. The range of ~ in this sense contracted and only a few locutions such as *Leid* ~, *Bedenken* ~, as in Lessing, *Minna* 4,6: *'kein Bedenken tragen'*, *eine Neigung in sich* ~, as in Wieland 32,204: *'. . . daß er eine geheime Neigung zu Veränderungen in sich trüge'*, *Sorge* ~, *die Verantwortung* ~ are still in current use; many others are now a. or obs., e.g. *Ekel vor etw.* ~, *Freundschaft für jem.* ~, *Gefallen an jem.m* ~, all three recorded as current by Adelung, *Feindschaft wider jem.* ~, as in Luther Bible transl. Ezek, 35,5 (for MHG *jem.m feintschaft* ~ is recorded), *jem.m Haß* ~, since MHG and still used by Ense, *Tagebücher* 1,63, *Liebe jem.m* (or *zu jem.m*) ~ (in MHG as *minne zuo einem* ~), *Scham* ~, as still in Geibel 1,236.

← See also under *Joch* (for *ein schweres Joch tragen*), *Kreuz* (for *sein Kreuz tragen müssen*), *Leid* (for *um jem. Leid tragen*), *Kost* (for *die Kosten tragen*), *packen* (for *einen Packen tragen müssen*), *Rechnung* (for *einer Sache Rechnung tragen*), *Schicksal* (for *Ehrfurcht tragen*), *Schuld* (for *die Schuld tragen*) and *Sorge* (for *Sorge tragen*).

etw. ~ (2) (lit.) to carry sth. or take sth. somewhere; with ref. to abstracts which are seen as being 'transported' or 'conveyed' somewhere, e.g. *sein Gebet vor Gott* ~ (since MHG), *Krieg in ein Land* ~, *die Revolution in das Nachbarland* ~, *jem.m etw. zu Ohren* ~ (since MHG, still used by Schiller). Frequent in compounds, e.g. with *davontragen*, e.g. *den Sieg davontragen* (cf. Hagedorn, *Od.* 2,9: *'ein luftiger Chamäleon trägt stets das Kanzleramt davon'*) and the elliptical *es davontragen*, where *es* stands for *den Sieg*, corresponding to French *l'emporter* = 'to win, prove stronger', as in Alexis, *Hosen d.H.v.B.* 2,1,160: *'die Dominikaner haben's davongetragen über die Augustiner'* (now obs.), also *etw. hineintragen*, as in Ranke, *Werke* 1,304: *'. . . in die Schrift etwas hinein zu tragen, was nicht darin liege'*, *herumtragen*, as in Häußer, *D.Gesch.* 3,106: *'die neuen Kriegsprojekte, die man geflissentlich herumtrug'* (cf. also *Klatschereien, Gerüchte*, etc. *herumtragen*) and many more.

← See also under *Athen* (for *Eulen nach Athen tragen*), *Fackel* (for *die Fackel vor jem.m tragen*), *Grab* (for *etw. zu Grabe tragen*), *Haut* (for *seine Haut zu Markte tragen*), *Holz* (for *Holz hinzutragen* and *Holz in den Wald tragen*), *Hund* (for *Hunde tragen müssen*), *Kranz* (for *den Siegerkranz davontragen*), *Kirche* (for *die Kirche ums Dorf tragen*), *Licht* (for *etw. im wahren Licht vortragen*), *Markt* (for *etw. zu Markte tragen*), *schauen* (for *etw. zur Schau tragen*) and *Scherflein* (for *sein Scherflein beitragen*).

etw. ~ (3) to hold, carry, wear, possess sth., have sth. on or in oneself; in idioms since MHG, e.g. *J.Tit.* 6166 on the Grail: *'dâ von er diese*

heilikeit sô tragte', Wolfr.v.E., *Parz.* 656,28: *'diu truoc den minneclîchsten lîp'* or 313, 29: *'Cundrî truoc ôren als ein ber'*, also *einen Namen* ~ (e.g. *Parz.* 627,16), *Sünde* ~, e.g. Kramer's recording from the Bible (John 1,29): *'sihe, das ist Gottes Lamb welchs der Welt Sünde tregt'*, Gellert, *Zärtl. Schw.* 1,8: *'du trägst dein gutes Herz in den Augen und auf der Zunge'*; also in legal language mainly with the notion of 'possessing', as in Adelung's recording *'kraft meines tragenden Amtes'* (now obs.).

← See under *Fessel* (for *die Fessel der Liebe tragen*), *Fuchs* (for *einen Fuchsbalg tragen*), *Geweih* (for *ein Geweih tragen*), *Gürtel* (for *ein Kind unter dem Gürtel tragen*), *Hand* (for *das Herz in der Hand tragen*), *Himmel* (for *seinen Himmel in der Brust tragen*), *Hut* (for *den Hut in Händen tragen*), *Kain* (for *das Kainsmal tragen*), *Kopf* (for *den Kopf hoch tragen*), *Kranz* (for *keinen Kranz mehr tragen*), *Krone* (for *die Krone tragen*), *Mantel* (for *den Mantel auf beiden Schultern tragen*), *Marschall* (for *den Marschallsstab im Tornister tragen*), *Maske* (for *eine Maske tragen*), *Nacken* (for *den Nacken aufrecht tragen*), *Narbe* (for *Narben tragen*), *Pelz* (for *noch den alten Pelz tragen*), *Rücken* (for *die Hände auf dem Rücken tragen*) and *scheu* (for *Scheuklappen tragen*).

jem. ~ (1) (obs.) to suffer sb., bear with sb.; since Early NHG, e.g. Luther Bible transl. 2 Tim. 2,24: *'. . . der die bösen tragen kan mit sanftmut'*; now obs., displaced by *ertragen*; cf. the related *sich mit jem.m vertragen*.

jem. ~ (2) to carry, hold, convey sb.; in many figur. locutions, e.g. Logau, *Sinnged.* [edit E.] 244: *'die mutter trägt im hertzen die kinder immerdar'*, also *einen Schalk im Busen tragen* (see p. 2075), Schiller, *Räuber* 2,2: *'dieser Blick hätt' euch über die Sterne getragen'*.

← See also under *Hand* (for *jem. auf Händen tragen*).

jem. ~ (3) (a.) to support sb.; in wider sense also 'to sustain sb.'; since MHG, e.g.Tauler, *Pred.* 24.3: *'dis sint minnecliche menschen,su tragent alle die welt'*, also in Luther Bible transl. 1 Thess. 5.14: *'traget die schwachen'*; with *einander* since Late MHG and still in Goethe, e.g. *Lehrj.* 4,15: *'(die Schauspieler) waren einander nicht gleich, aber sie hielten und trugen sich wechselweise'* (also *'doch blieben wir immer gute Gesellen, wir trugen ein ander vor wie nach'*); now a., if not obs.

sich mit etw. ~ to have sth. in mind, consider or contemplate sth.; beginnings (without *mit*) in Early NHG, e.g. Waldis, *Esop* 1,3,4: *'dazu sich trug jr mut und sinn'*, Günther, *Ged.* 146: *'man hört sich . . . im Tempel mit den Seufzern tragen'*, Schiller, *Kab.u. L.* 3,4: *'mit frechen thörichten Wünschen hat sich mein Busen getragen'*; now becoming unusual except in *sich mit dem Gedanken, der Hoffnung* ~.

etw. trägt etw. (1) sth. carries or bears sth. (or sb.); since MHG, often at first with allusion to the soil 'bearing' or plants 'bearing fruit', e.g. Konr.v.

Würzburg, *Troj.* 6831: '*sîn herze truoc der êren bleter*', Mathesius, *Sar.* 182b: '*Adam ist . . . ein vater aller bösen buben, so diese erde getragen und noch treget*' (with *Erdboden* in Goethe 22,30 (W.)); cf. also Luther 10,3,172 (Weimar): '*das wort gottes ist ein grundt, der do ewiglich erhelt und tregt*', where *tregt* here may mean 'sustains' or 'brings forth fruit'. Cf. also Fallada, *Wolf* 1,428: '*die Welle des Glücks trägt uns*', with which compare Kramer's [1702] entry: '*der reitet sanft, dem* (sic!) *die Gnade Gottes trägt*'.

← See also under *Maus* (for *das kann eine Maus am Schwanz forttragen*) and *Mücke* (for *nicht so viel wie eine Mücke am Schwanz wegträgt*).

etw. trägt etw. (2) sth. yields or produces sth.; also derived from the tree/fruit image; frequent in comm. contexts, since Early NHG, e.g. Luther Bible transl. Luke 19,18: '*dein pfund hat fünff pfund getragen*' (where in verse 16 '*erworben*' is used); still general in *das Kapital trägt Zinsen* and in such negative locutions as *das trägt die Kosten nicht* = 'that does not cover the costs involved'.

etw. trägt etw. (3) sth. bears sth.; with ref. to the character or aspects of phenomena or persons since the 18th c., e.g. *etw. trägt den Keim des Verfalls in sich*, also *jetzt trägt die Sache ein ganz anderes Gesicht* or *eine gute Handlung trägt ihren Lohn in sich*; current since the 19th c. (not recorded by Adelung or Campe); before then *haben* or *führen* were used.

← See also under *Gepräge* (for *das Gepräge von etw. tragen*), *Spur* (for *die Spuren von etw. tragen*) and *Stempel* (for *den Stempel von etw. tragen*).

etw. trägt (4) sth. carries, reaches or extends (into the distance); in essence an elliptic locution with ellipsis of *die Kugel* or *den Blick*; since the 17th c.; Kramer [1702] recorded: '*die Pistolen (Augen) tragen nicht so weit*', e.g. Schiller, *Tell* 2,2: '*die Luft ist rein und trägt den Schall so weit*'; hence also *sie hat eine tragende Stimme* = 'her voice carries well; cf. also the related locution in Chamisso 4,159: '*des Meisters Pfeife war's, vom Wind getragen . . .*'. ~ in the sense 'to carry, support' occurs in such cases as *meine Knie ~ mich nicht mehr* (which Goethe used).

sich ~ to appear, present oneself; at first mainly with ref. to outward appearance, clothing, e.g. Wieland, *H.B.* 1,298: '*. . . der . . . aus eitler Hoffahrt sich über sein Vermögen trägt*', then also with ref. to the 'carriage' of the body (cf. similar Engl. 'to deport oneself'), e.g. Sanders, *Wb.* [1865]: '*ein Soldat darf sich nicht so schlottrig tragen*'. Goethe still used the noun, e.g. *Dicht.u.Wahrh.* 2,9: '*. . . der an meinen Tritten und Schritten . . . an meinem Tragen und Behaben noch manches ausbesserte*'; now obs.

tragbar bearable, endurable; figur. since MHG, e.g. Gottfr.v.Str., *Tristan* 12412 (with *swaere*) and 18444 (with *nôt*); later with ref. to demands, taxes, etc., esp. in polit. contexts; recently also with ref. to persons for 'acceptable, unobjectionable'; the noun *Tragbarkeit* was f.r.b. Kramer [1702].

tragend (1) (lit.) chief, dominant; presumably derived from ~ = '*innehaben, besitzen*' (for which see above under *etw.* ~ (3)); e.g. *er spielt die tragende Rolle in diesem Drama*.

tragend (2) (lit.) basic, fundamental; modern, e.g. *das tragende Motiv in diesem Buch ist . . .*'.

gut tragend (comm.) profitable, lucrative; derived from *etw. trägt etw.* (2) above; e.g. *er hat eine gut tragende Stellung*; now a., displaced by *einträglich* (for which see p. 608).

hochtragend (a.) conceited, proud; since Early NHG, e.g. Luther 1,363a (Jena), but before then MHG had *hôhe* ~ = 'to be proud', but also 'to be in a superior position (and show it)'; still used in the 19th c., e.g. Keller, *Gr.Heinr.* 4,178: '*hochtragisch siehts aus; er wollte sagen: hochtragend oder hochstelzig*'; now a. if not obs.

getragen (mus.) measured, slow, solemn; derived from Italian *portar la voce* (also Fr. *port de voix*), recorded since early in the 18th c.; e.g. Mendel 1,267 [1870]: '*appoggiato heißt eigentlich angelehnt, dann aber auch gehalten, getragen*'; hence *Getragenheit* since the 19th c., which can also be extended to lit. contexts, e.g. Ad.Müller, *Bereds.* 155 [1816]: '*es ist ein gewisser Kothurn, eine edle Getragenheit in der Schreibart*'.

etw. davontragen to get, catch, sustain sth.; with ref. to unpleasant experiences, first with ref. to such abstracts as *Schimpf, Schande, Schaden*, at least since the 18th c., later mainly with ref. to illness, e.g. *von diesem Marsch im Regen hat er eine Erkältung davongetragen*. For the positive sense, e.g. *den Sieg davontragen* see above under *etw.* ~ (2).

jem. emportragen (lit.) to raise, lift, elevate sb.; figur. with ref. to persons favoured by superiors or by fate since Early NHG, e.g. Schiller, *Wallenstein* prol. 99: '*von der Zeiten Gunst emporgetragen*'; now a., if not obs.

sich von etw. forttragen lassen (lit., rare) to get carried away by sth.; current in the 19th c., now unusual, displaced by *sich fortreißen* or *hinreißen lassen*.

jem. hinaustragen to take sb. to his grave, bury sb.; Goethe used '*bis man dich trägt hinaus*' with ellipsis of *tot*; cf. *jem. für tot hinaustragen*, as in Wieland 22,19. Cf. also *jem.* (or *etw.*) *in die Ferne hinaustragen* (lit.) = 'to take sb. (or sth.) abroad', as in *seine Wanderlust trug ihn über die Alpen hinaus*.

etw. in etw. anderes hineintragen (lit.) to introduce sth. into sth. else, bring about sth. in sth. else; figur. in cases where abstracts are concerned, e.g. *der gute Ton soll Wohlbehagen in das gesellschaftliche Leben hineintragen*; modern.

etw. mittragen (lit.) to share responsibility for sth. or costs, burdens, etc. of sth.; Goethe used it with *Kriegslasten*. Sometimes now also in present participle *mittragend* for 'accompanying, associated, inherent', e.g. *das die moderne Welt mittragende Verlangen nach Originalität*; cf. also *mittragende Rolle* with ref. to theatrical performances (cf. entry under *tragend* (1) above).

etw. übertragen (1) (obs.) to bear, suffer sth.; since Early NHG, still used by Goethe, e.g. IV,14,206 (W.): '*wir wollen die unvermeidlichen Folgen zu übertragen suchen*'; now obs., displaced by *ertragen*. Hence *Übertragung* (obs.) = 'bearing (of suffering)' and 'toleration', recorded by Kramer [1702].

etw. übertragen (2) to transfer sth.; in many contexts, e.g.in comm. usage, e.g. Ludwig, *Teutsch-engl.Lex.* 2072 [1716]: '*die Posten aus dem Journal ins Hauptbuch übertragen*', with ref. to 'translating', f.r.b. Stieler [1691]: '*etwas aus dem Lateinischen ins Deutsche übertragen*' or 'semantic change', since the 18th c., often in *im übertragenen Sinn gebraucht* = 'used in its figurative meaning'; sometimes also used with ref. to infection, as in Schopenhauer [edit. Gr.] 3,303: '*es kommen Fälle vor von übertragenen Krankheiten*'. In the 17th c. still frequently treated as a separable verb with *übergetragen* as the past participle, even still in Lessing, Wieland and Goethe. Herder 15,477 even wrote '*indessen war und blieb dieses nur eine übergetragene Bedeutung*'; occasional instances in 19th c. lit., e.g. Raabe, *Hungerpastor* 1,24, now a. The noun *Übertragung* = 'transfer' with ref. to translating, infecting or giving a figur. meaning general since the 18th c. (Kramer [1702] recorded it).

etw. vortragen to recite, deliver or perform sth., lecture on sth.; also in wider sense for 'to state, propose, submit, present, contend'; figur. since Early NHG (in its development influenced by the noun *Vortrag*), e.g. Joh.v.Tepl, *Ackermann a.B.* 22: '*gaukelweise traget ir mir vor*', Fischart [edit. Hauffen] 3,62: '*ich könnte . . . noch vil hundert exempel vortragen*', Goethe IV,42,104 (W.): '*die Lehre vom Licht . . . wie sie . . . Professor Fries in Jena vorträgt*'; f.r.b. Hulsius-Ravellus [1616], cf. also Kramer [1702]: '*eine Sache schriftlich vortragen*'. The noun *der Vortrag* = 'presentation, proposition, lecture, declaration', e.l. (DWb) Zinkgref, *Apophth.* 1,33 [1628]. – In some central and Eastern regions there is also *Vortrag* (vulg.) = 'bosom', with which one can compare Engl. coll. 'she carries all before her'. The adjective *vorträglich* = 'useful, salutory', current since MHG, died out in the 19th c. (Wieland and Schubart still used it in letters).

etw. weitertragen to pass sth. on, spread sth.; esp. with ref. to gossip, news, etc.; since the 18th c., usually the same as *etw. verbreiten*.

etw. zusammentragen to collect sth., compile sth.; since Early NHG, e.g. Luther 18,27 (Weimar), Goethe 11,5,1 (W.); strangely missing in Adelung.

sich zutragen to happen, occur; in this figur. sense since Early NHG; Kramer [1702] recorded: '*gestern hat sich etwas merckwürdiges zugetragen*'.

zuträglich beneficial, wholesome, salutory, salubrious; since Early NHG. Adelung explained: '*es ist von dem Neutro einem zutragen, ihm wohl bekommen, ihm heilsam, nützlich seyn, welches aber*

im Hochdeutschen längst veraltet ist'. Kramer recorded it and referred also to synonymous *vorträglich*, for which see above. He did not record the noun *Zuträglichkeit*, but Adelung did.

der Träger bearer, holder, representative, supporter, upholder; figur. since OHG period; in many contexts since Early MHG, later also with ref. to abstracts used for 'vehicle', e.g. *die Sprache ist der Träger des Gedankens*; very frequent in compounds, e.g. *Beiträger* = 'contributor (to a collection)' (18th c.), *Gewaltträger* which Adelung recorded as Upper German for 'plenipotentiary', *Schleppenträger* = 'follower, sycophant' (19th c.), but cf. earlier *Schweifträger* used by Wieland 9,145: '. . . *der Schweifträger eines Andern zu sein*'), *Würdenträger* = 'dignitary, high official' (19th c.), *Zusammenträger* (a.) = 'compiler', used e.g. by Lessing.

die Tragweite (lit.) consequence, importance; originally denoting the distance covered by a projectile (influenced by French *portée*); figur. since the 19th c. and at first rejected by many when it became an overused term in politics during the 1848 debates; now used esp. in *es ist von großer Tragweite* = 'it is a matter of great moment'.

← See also under *abtragen*, *Achsel* (for *auf beiden Achseln tragen* and *Achselträger*), *antragen*, *auftragen* (also for *Auftrag*), *austragen*, *Bart* (for *einen Bart tragen*), *beitragen* (also for *Beitrag*), *betragen* (also for *Betrag*), *eintragen* (also for *Eintrag*), *entgegentragen*, *ertragen*, *Esel* (for *es gibt viele Esel, die nicht Säcke tragen*), *Fahne* (for *jem.m etw. antragen*), *Fittich* (for *auf Dichterfittichen emportragen*), *forttragen*, *Frucht* (for *Frucht tragen*), *Fuß* (for *wohin der Fuß trägt*), *Geschichte* (for *Geschichtenträger*), *gleich* (for *an gleicher Bürde trägt sich niemand müde*), *Grab* (for *das Grab im Schoß tragen*), *Hand* (for *das Herz in der Hand tragen*), *herantragen*, *herumtragen*, *hinübertragen*, *Kranz* (for *den Siegeskranz davontragen*), *Markt* (for *nichts davontragen*), *nachtragen*, *packen* (for *Pack verträgt sich*), *Sack* (for *Sackträger*), *Schleppe* (for *Schleppenträger*), *Schulter* (for *auf beiden Schultern tragen*), *schwarz* (for *kann man getrost nach Hause tragen*) and *vertragen*.

tragisch: tragic

etw. ~ nehmen to take sth. too seriously, to let sth. upset one; transferred from theatrical contexts in the 18th c.; with *nehmen* since the 19th c., e.g. Freytag, *Soll u.H.* 1,224 [1855]; also as *etw. von der tragischen Seite nehmen*; similarly, *mach doch keine* (or *nicht gleich eine*) *Tragödie daraus*, e.g. (S.-B.) Heuß-Knapp, *Münsterturm* 15 [1934]: '*mir sind Menschen immer unverständlich, die aus ihrer Schulzeit eine Tragödie machen*'.

← See also under *Stiefel* (for *der tragische Stiefel*).

trainieren: train

sein Gedächtnis ~ to train one's memory; extension from phys. 'training' (loan from Engl.) to mental contexts; since the 19th c., e.g. (S.-B.) *Dt.Dichtung* 17,232 [1855]: '*ich war gezwungen, mein Gedächtnis zu trainieren'.*

Traktat: tractate, tract

das Traktätchen (pejor.) religious pamphlet, edifying tract; diminutive originally used for 'small publication, short tract' (15th c.); since the 19th c. used mainly pejor. or mockingly.

traktieren: treat

jem. mit etw. ~ (a.) to regale sb. with sth. (agreeable); ~ was mainly used with ref. to '(bad) treatment', also for 'dealing with sth.', as in Wieland, *H.B.* 2,182: *'traktierte er die Sache nicht bloß als ein Knabenspiel'* and for 'to negotiate', as in *mit jem.m über etw.* ~ (used by Schiller); these meanings are now obs.; with ref. to regaling sb. with food, drink, etc. since Early NHG, e.g. Waldis, *Esop* 4,75, now rarely used, displaced by such verbs as *bewirten*.

trampeln: trample, stamp, clump

der Trampel (coll.) bumpkin, clod; derived from the verb; since the 19th c. used as a term of contempt in many regions. *Trampeltier*, originally = 'Bactrian camel' is used in the same pejor. sense for clumsy people, esp. women; recorded since the 19th c.

auf etw. ~ to stamp or trample on sth., deal roughly with sth., treat sth. with contempt (or smash it in anger); figur. since the 18th c. (Schiller in Fiesco used *auf den Gesetzen* ~); hence also *etw. niedertrampeln*, e.g. (Sp.) Boree, *Dor u.d.Sept.* 105: '. . . daß wir unser Gewissen niedergetrampelt haben', and *auf jem.m herumtrampeln*, as in Auerbach, *Schr.* 13,106: *'so lang man einen für gutmütig hält, trampelt ein jedes auf ihm herum'* or Hauptmann, *Biberpelz* 56: *'uff 'm Koppe rum trampeln laß ich mir nich!'*.

der Trampelpfad (lit., rare) sth. made unattractive through over-use; *Trampelpfad* in phys. sense = 'beaten track (esp. through rough country)'; occasionally figur., as in Dieter Wellershoff (in pref. to his essays on *Trivialliteratur*): *'das Triviale ist ein ausgetretener Trampelpfad'*; cf. also figur. *auf ausgetrampelten Wegen etw. tun* = 'to do sth. by methods which have too often been used in the past' (20th c.).

Tran: fish-oil, blubber

im ~ *sein* (1) (coll.) to be drunk; since the 19th c.,e.g. Heine 1,21: *'wenn er im Thran ist, hält er den Himmel für ein blaues Kamisol'*.

im ~ *sein* (2) (coll.) to be absent-minded, inattentive, half asleep; modern coll., recorded since the 19th c.

die Tranfunsel (1) (coll.) miserable lamp, poor light; 20th c. coll.; cf. also G.Keller, *L.v.Seldw.* 1,18: *'das armselige Thranlämpchen'*.

die Transfunsel (2) (coll.) dim-wit, slow-coach; 20th c. coll.

tranig (coll.) slow, ponderous; 20th c. coll.

← See also under *Susanne* (for *Transuse*).

Träne: tear

die ~ (1) (poet.) pearl of dew; in poetic images since the 18th c., e.g. Matthisson, *A.*11,27: '. . . *bis*

ein . . . Zephir deinen Busen aufküßt und Aurorens frühe Thränen, gleich Perlen ihn umschimmern', also Jean Paul 21,144; cf. also Louise Büchner, *Leb.* 67 [1861]: *'ein eigenthümliches Getränk . . . Hippokras oder poetische Brautthränen genannt, stehet [in Holland] stets bereit, um die Besuchenden [der Braut] zu bewirthen'*. This must be old, since Kramer [1702] recorded: *'Brautthränen = lagrime da sposa . . . per la verginità agonizzante'*.

die ~ (2) (a. or regional) tiny quantity of a liquid; e.g. Hackländer, *Erl.* 1,75: *'nachdem er in die Tasse nur eine Thräne Rahm geträufelt'*; Stalder [1806–12] recorded it for Switzerland in the diminutive: *'ein Thränlein Wein'*. Granules of some chemicals are also called *Tränen* in the trade; f.r.b. Karmarsch 2,626 [1854].

die ~ (3) (tech.) tear-shaped faults in glass; recorded since the 19th c., e.g. by Sanders [1865].

jem.s Tränen trocknen to still sb.'s misery; e.g. Schiller, *Kab.u.L.* 2,2: *'ich habe sie alle getrocknet die Thränen des Landes'*; cf. also Goethe, *Prometheus*: *'hast du die Thränen gestillet je des Geängsteten?'*; with *abwaschen* since Early NHG, e.g. Luther Bible transl. Revel. 7,17: *'Gott wird abwasschen alle threnen von jren augen'*.

einer Sache keine Tränen nachweinen to shed no tears over (the loss of) sth.; modern, not yet listed in *DWb.* [1889]; similarly, *die Sache ist keine* ~ *wert*.

Christi Tränen lachryma Christi; wine from the slopes of Mount Vesuvius; e.g. G.Keller, *Werke* 10,22: *'süß und selig ist zu trinken, was man Christi Thränen nennt'*; the Lat. term is more usual.

bei ihr sitzen die Tränen locker (coll.) she is easily reduced to tears, weeps much and often; 20th c. coll.

mit einer ~ *im Knopfloch* (coll.) with pretended sympathy, in hypocritical (or even mocking) commiseration; first in juvenile sl. late in the 19th c.; cf. the standard *Heucheltränen*, recorded by Kramer [1702].

auf die Tränendrüse drücken (coll.) to make sb. weep; used with ref. to sentimental plays, books, etc. since late in the 19th c.; cf. *Tränen melken* (sl.) for 'to use sentimental or moving language which produces tears; 20th c. sl.

die Tränenpumpe (unusual) tear-jerker, sentimental drama; Heine used the expression in 1822; not in general use (locutions with *pressen* and its compounds are more usual).

tränen (1) (poet.) to weep, shed tears; figur. with abstracts as the subject, e.g. Goethe 3,51: *'wie Zweifel oft das Haupt hing, Treue thränte'*; cf. also *etw. betränen* (lit.) = 'to weep over sth.' (since MHG as *betrehenen*), f.r.b. Henisch [1616], now obs., displaced by *Tränen vergießen um etw.* (or *jem.*), current since Early NHG, e.g. Luther Bible transl. Isaiah 16,9; very unusual now is *etw. betränen* = 'to cover or moisten sth. with tears', as in Klopstock, *Mess.* 20,61: *'ein bethränter Pfad'*.

tränen (2) to emit moisture; with ref. to plants, esp. vines: *die Rebe tränt*, f.r.b. Stieler [1691].

tränen (3) (tech.) to leak; with ref. to barrels, etc.; modern.

von (or *vor*) *etw. tränen* to shed tears of sth.; Goethe used '*wo jedes Auge von Entzücken thränt*'; *vor* can also be used, e.g. Tieck, transl. of *Cymb.* 4,7: '*die Augen thränen ihm vor Lachen*'; cf. also Voß, *Landl.* 3.41: '*vor Wehmuth thränet das Elfenbein*'.

← See also under *ablocken* (for *jem.m Tränen ablocken*), *absetzen* (for *es setzt Tränen ab*), *auflösen* (for *sich in Tränen auflösen*), *ausheben* (for *jem.m Tränen ausheben*), *auspressen* (for *jem.m Tränen auspressen*), *Bach* (for *Bäche von Tränen* and *Tränenbäche*), *baden* (for *in Tränen gebadet*), *Blut* (for *blutige Tränen weinen*), *einschlucken* (for *seine Tränen einschlucken*), *entladen* (for *sich in Tränen entladen*), *fließen* (for *sein Auge fließt von Tränen*), *Flut* (for *Flut von Tränen*, *Tränenflut* and *Tränenfluß*), *glühen* (for *die Brust glüht jem.m von Tränen*), *Gold* (for *goldne Tränen*), *Hügel* (for *eine Träne rollt herab*), *Kanne* (for *die Tränenkanne*), *Krokodil* (for *Krokodilstränen*), *Mai* (for *Tränen, die den Mai von seinen Wangen ätzen*), *Perle* (for *Tränen perlen in den Augen*), *Quelle* (for *der Tränen Quell*), *Rettich* (for *es gäbe viele Tränen, wenn man alle Rettiche schaben wollte*), *schleichen* (for *eine Träne schleicht sich aus ihrem Auge*), *Schleier* (for *Auge durch Tränen verschleiert*), *schwemmen* (for *Tränen schwemmen etw. weg*), *schwimmen* (for *das Herz schwimmt in Tränen*), *Strom* (for *die Augen strömten von Tränen*), *stürzen* (for *ein Sturzbach von Tränen*), *Susanne* (for *Tränensuse*), *Tal* (for *Tränental*) and *Tau* (for *der Tau einer Träne*).

Trank: drink

der ~ (lit.) drink, beverage, potion; figur. in lit. since Early NHG, e.g. (DWb) Dannhawer, *Catechismusm.* 1,1: '[*Christus*] *rufft . . . hie ist ein edler tranck, wolt ir trincken?*', Herder [edit. S.] 27,29: '*alles Bittere wird zum süßen Trank der Lippe des Weisen*', Wieland 27,205: '*das Vergnügen ist ein zu berauschender Trank*', Storm 2,299: '*Frauenliebe ist ein süßer Trank*'; also frequent in comparisons since Early NHG, e.g. (DWb) *Offenb.d.hl. Brigitte* 5 [1502]: '*. . . meine wort . . . ersetigend als ein gutes tranck*', also in many compounds, e.g. *Gifttrank*, as in Schiller, *Räuber* 4,4: '*ich muß den Gifttrank dieser Seligkeit vollends ausschlürfen*', *Henkertrank*, as in Haller, 142: '*die Unsterblichkeit wird ihm zum Henkertrank*', *Himmelstrank*, as in Rist, *Parnaß* 660 [1652]: '*ich schmeckte lauter nichts als süßen Himmelstrank*'. See also under *Trunk*.

Tränke: see *Pferd*

tränken: still thirst, give to drink

jem. ~ (lit.) to still sb.'s thirst; figur. since Early NHG, e.g. Luther Bible transl. Psalm 36,9: '*du trenkest sie mit wollust als mit einem strom*', Ecclesiasticus 15,3: '*. . . wird jn trenken mit wasser der weisheit*' (also Revel. 14,8), Heine, *Rom.* 169: '*ich ward getränkt mit Bitternissen*'.

etw. ~ (lit.) to feed sth.; since Early NHG, e.g. Luther Bible transl. Pslam 65,11: '*du trenkest seine furchen*', Ecclesiasticus 39,27: '*. . . sein segen . . . trenkt die erde*', Seume, *Ged.* 66 (or 53): '*Ruhe jeder Leidenschaft tränkt das Herz mit Götterkraft*'.

getränkt (lit.) steeped in, full of, imbued with sth.; in compounds with abstracts since the 18th c., e.g. Heine, *Lied.* 324: '*mit solcher feuergetränkten Riesenfeder*', Spielhagen, *Hoh.* 1,260: '*des Vaters leidenschaftgetränkte Seele*'.

← See also under *durchtränken*, *eintränken* and *ertränken*.

Transfusion: transfusion

die ~ (lit.) transfusion; the term is of recent origin, not even listed in DWb. [1933]; transferred from med. contexts to other areas around the middle of the 20th c., sometimes in the compound *Bluttransfusion*, e.g. (S.-B.) *Süddt.Ztg.* [21.12.50]: '*im ökonomischen Bereich war die Marshallhilfe die Bluttransfusion . . .*'; in the simplex in Adorno, *Noten* 89 [1958].

← See also under *greis* (for *eine Transfusion parodieren*).

transparent: transparent

transparent (lit.) clear, evident, intelligible, clearly defined; from phys. 'transparent' with ref. to materials extended in the 19th c., e.g. Keller, *Ges.W.* 1,272 [1889]: '*. . . Unterschied zwischen einem transparenten scharfen und einem rußigen stumpfen Vortrage nicht recht begriff*'; since the 1st half of the 20th c. often in *etw.* ~ *machen* for *erhellen, einleuchtend machen*; hence *die Transparenz*, since the middle of the 20th c.

transportieren: transport

jem. (or *etw.*) *transportiert jem.* (lit.) sb. (or sth.) transports, conveys sb. (e.g. into a different world); only since the 2nd half of the 20th c.; also occasionally with abstracts, *etw. transportiert etw. anderes*, e.g. *etw. transportiert Gefühle in ein ästhetisches Erleben*.

jem. ~ to move sb. (by force) somewhere else; since the 18th c., e.g. Kortum, *Jobsiade* 3,78 [1799]: '*man transportierte ihn . . . weil er zu laut wurde, vor die Thür*'; usually the same as *an die Luft setzen* (see p. 1638) or *hinauswerfen* (see p. 1332); *hinaustransportieren* can also be used.

Traube: grape

die Trauben (lit., obs.) children; based on Psalm 128,3 and used by Luther; still in the 19th c., e.g. Schubart (in a letter, in D.F. Strauß 8,171): '*empfiehl mich deiner Frau und ihren Trauben*'.

eine ~ *von* . . . a bunch or cluster of . . .; with ref. to things and people; first in comparisons, e.g. (DWb) Heyden, *Plinius* 195 [1565]: '*. . . hangen stetts an einnander wie die beer an einem trauben*'; much later also *eine* ~ *von Menschen*. Since the 17th c. also used with ref. to a swarm of bees that has collected in one place, f.r.b. Orsäus, *Nomencl.* 204 [1623], e.g. Bürger, *Il.* 6,121: '[*Bienen*] *schwirren wie in Trauben auf des Lenzes Blüthen*'.

Meertrauben (also *Seetrauben*) (obs.) raisins; since MHG, f.r.b. Dasypodius, e.g. Ryff, *Spiegel* 243a [1574]: '*Meerträubel oder Rosinen*'.

die Trauben sind ihm zu sauer (prov. expr.) these are sour grapes to him; based on Aesop's fable of the fox and grapes; in German since the 13th c., e.g. Goethe IV,1,226 (W.): '*die Trauben sind sauer, sagte der Fuchs*'. Also in phrases with *hoch*, e.g. Eyering, *Prov.cop.* 1,262 [1601]: '*gleich wie der fuchs auf etwan sprach dem die trauben hingen zu hoch*', (Sp.) Adorno, *Wörter aus der Fremde* (in *Akzente* 177 [1959]: '. . . Seelenzustand der Zornigen, denen irgendwelche Trauben zu hoch hängen*'.

← See also under *Blut* (for *Traubenblut*), *Dorn* (for *Dornen tragen keine Trauben*), *Fuchs* (for *er macht es wie der Fuchs mit den Trauben*) and *Jungfer* (for *Jungferntraube*).

trauen: trust; wed

sich mit etw. ~ (lit.) to become united with sth.; belongs to ~ = 'to unite in marriage' (current since MHG); figur. in lit. since the 18th c., e.g. Schiller, *Fant. an Laura*: '*wenn mit Ewigkeit die Zeit sich traut*'; also in non-reflex. locutions, e.g. Lessing 5,346: '*Ewigkeit,die ohne Ziel uns aufs Neue treuen will*'.

trau, schau, wem (prov. expr.) make sure you know with whom you are dealing; international advice of caution (versions from many countries listed in Wander 4,1289 [1876]); in German since MHG, e.g. Vintler, 7333: '*lueg wem du traust vnd in wen*', f.r.b. Petri [1605].

wer nicht traut, dem ist nicht zu ~ (prov.) people who do not trust are likely to be untrustworthy; in this wording f.r.b. Simrock [1846], but there are older warnings of this type, e.g.Lehman [1640]: '*wer niemand trawt ist gemeinniglich selbst vntrew*'.

← See also under *Apotheke* (for *der Teufel traue dem Apotheker*), *Ecke* (for *jem.m nicht um die Ecke trauen*), *Friede* (for *dem Frieden nicht trauen*) and *Ohr* (for *seinen Ohren/Augen nicht trauen*).

trauern: mourn

etw. trauert (lit.) sth. mourns or bemoans (the loss of) sth.; figur. when things or abstracts are seen as 'mourning'; since the 16th c., e.g. Sebiz, *Feldbau* 54 [1579]: '. . . die herbstzeit, darin dem gras all fräud und mut vergehet, fahet an zu trauern*', Schiller, *Räuber* 3,2: '*traure mit mir, Natur*', Sturz, *Schr.* 2,67: '. . . kehrte der Frühling . . . zu der trauernden Erde zurück*'; also in compounds, e.g. Mörike, *N.* 451:'. . . trauret ringsumher der Wald mich an*', Geßner 1,78: '*die Blumen . . . trauerten ihrer Verwesung entgegen*', Wieland 11,6: '*mittrauernd murren die Wellen empor*', Schiller, *Leichenfant.* 5: '*Sterne trauern bleich herab*', Kosegarten, *Po.* 2,75: '*wenn wehmüthiges Gefühl aus dem Spätroth niedertrauert*'.

Trauer-. . . (coll.) wretched . . . , miserable . . . , morose . . . ; in coll. compounds since 2nd half of 19th c., e.g. *Trauerkloß* = 'disgruntled individual', *Trauerklotz* = 'dull or rejected person', *Trauerweide* = 'sad creature' with allusion to the tree and its drooping branches.

die ganze Sache ist ein Trauerspiel (coll.) the whole affair is a deplorable business, it is all quite pathetic; modern coll.

einer Sache nachtrauern to bemoan or feel sad about (the loss of) sth.; ~ alone sufficed, e.g. Goethe 1,381 ,(W.): '*traure das verlorne Glück*' (or 1,56: '*traur ich ums verlorne Glück*'); the compound since the 18th c., but not yet recorded by Kramer [1702] or Adelung (even in the 2nd edit.); Campe listed it.

← See also under *Hof* (for *Hoftrauer haben*), *Rand* (for *Trauerränder haben*) and *Stimme* (for *jem. traurig stimmen*).

Traufe: see *Regen*

träufeln: drip; trickle

etw. träufelt (also *träuft*) sth. drips or trickles; figur. with abstracts as the subject since the 18th c. (older dictionaries only quote examples with *triefen*), e.g. Herder, *Zur Rel.u.Theol.* [edit. Müller] 7,96: '*sein Urtheilsspruch träufelte auf sein Volk wie Thau*', also *ibid.* 9,38, Stolberg, *Schausp.* 1,14 [1787]: '*der Thränen jede träufelt Fluch auf mich*'; also transitive *jem.m etw.* ~, as in Heinse, *Ardingh.* 1,119: '*er träufelt ihr mit der Stimme des lebendigsten Gefühls ins Ohr*' (with ellipsis of *Worte*). There are several lit. compounds, e.g. Klopstock, *Messias* 13,678: '*mit jedem Tropfen Zeit . . . der in das Meer hinträuft der Vergangenheit*', Chamisso 4,173: '*endlich träufelt Schlummer auf ihn nieder*'; similarly *herabträufeln* or *herunterträufeln* (Goethe used *herunterträufen*, left unrecorded in *DWb.* [1877]), also *jem.m etw. einträufeln* or *einträufen* = 'to infuse sth. into sb.', figur. with abstracts, e.g. *jem.m einen Verdacht einträufeln* = 'to fill sb. (little by little or subtly) with suspicion'; much more recent is *etw. von sich abträufen lassen* (cf. Engl. idioms with 'like water off a duck's back'), as in P.Heyse, *N.N.* 3,147.

Schulden einträufeln (obs.) to pay off one's debts little by little; recorded by Rädlein [1711], now obs. (coll. *abstottern* might now be used).

← See also under *beträufen*.

Traum: dream

der ~ (1) (poet.) dream; occasionally in poet. transfers, since the 18th c., e.g. Jean Paul [edit. H.] 45,429: '*die Wolken sind die Träume des Himmels*', Eichendorff, *Sämtl.W.* 1,561: '*in Träumen rauschts der Hain*'.

der ~ (2) (personified) dream; seen sometimes as a person, particularly with verbs of motion, e.g. with *umtanzen* in Goethe 4,101 (W.), with *umziehen* in Droste-Hülshoff, *W.* [edit. Sch.] 2,339: '. . . ein süßer Traum umzieht sein Haupt*'.

der ~ (3) dream; with ref. to illusion, selfdeception, unjustified fear, etc.; general since Early NHG, e.g. Luther 32,446 (Weimar), hence also *etw. Traumhaftes* = 'sth. that could never happen', as in Hofmannsthal, *Erzählung* 31, frequent in compounds, e.g. Goethe 10,274 (W.): '*nun ists nicht mehr ein kranker Grillentraum*',

Gutzkow, *Zaub.v.R.* 1,352 [1853]: '*der Gaukeltraum ihres Lebens war zu Ende*'; since the 19th c. also often with ref. to untenable hypotheses, theories, etc. General in verbal form since the 17th c., e.g. *du träumst* = 'you are under an illusion', or *du träumst wohl?* = 'you cannot be serious, you must be dreaming'.

← See also under *Fieber* (for *Fiebertraumgeschwätz*).

der ~ (4) dream, wish, hope, sth. longed for; close to ~ (3) but seen from its positive side, current at least since the 15th c., e.g. S.Brant [edit.Z.] 50: '. . . *Narren . . . sie gehen um mit süßen träumen*' (cf. Luther's use of '*ein gülden traum*'), Herder [edit. S.] 15,309: '*er lebt vom süßen Traum des . . . geistigen Wahnes*'. Hence also in verbal form *von etw. träumen* = 'to desire or long for sth.', e.g. Langbein 31,92: '. . . *Erben, die . . . von Goldbergen träumen*'; hence such locutions as *die Frau seiner Träume* = 'the woman of his dreams' (joc. coll. *der* ~ *seiner schlaflosen Nächte*), Wieland 23,297: '*wachend und im Schlaf ist Rezia sein Traum*'. There are very many compounds of the type *die Blütenträume von einst* = 'the optimistic hopes of one's youth' or with ~ as the first component, e.g. *mein Traumauto* = 'the car I have always wanted', or *die Traumfabrik* (coll., slightly pejor., coined by Hugo von Hofmannsthal) = 'the film industry' (often = 'Hollywood'), also *der amerikanische* ~ (see the entry on p. 32). Hence also the modern expression of disappointment or return to reality: *der* ~ *ist aus* = 'that is gone for ever, a thing of the past'.

← See also under *Frühling* (for *Frühlingstraum*), *glühen* (for *goldne Träume*), *Gold* (for *goldne Träume*), *Land* (for *Land der Träume* and *das Land seiner Träume*), *Reich* (for *Reich der Träume*) and *Rose* (for *der Zukunft Rosenträume*).

der ~ (5) (coll.) dream; term of admiration for sth. extremely attractive; modern; e.g. *sein neues Auto ist ein* ~ = 'his new car is fabulous'; hence also *ein* ~ *von . . .* = 'a dream of . . .', e.g. *es ist ein* ~ *von einem Haus* = 'it is a marvellous house'. Also in adjectival form: *es ist traumhaft schön* (modern).

ich denke nicht im ~ *daran* I wouldn't dream of it; current since MHG, e.g. *Renner* 7010, Luther, *Urth.d.Theol.* (repr.) 51, Opitz 2,45 (or 3,31); also with *einfallen*, e.g. Gottsched, *D.Neueste* 4,387 [1751], Mörike, *N.* 495, formerly also with *beifallen*, as in Müllner, *Dram.W.* 2,13 [1828] or with *beikommen*, as in Stifter, *Sämtl.W.* 3,194. See also under *Schlaf* for similar idioms.

jem.m aus dem ~ *helfen* (obs. or regional) to enlighten sb., make sb. aware of the real state of affairs; belongs to ~ (3), frequent in the 17th c., still used by Lessing 13,323, Schiller, *Neffe als Onkel* 3,6, also by Goethe, now obs., except in some regions.

wie ein ~ (poet.) like a dream; since the 18th c. in poet. images, e.g. Novalis 1,71 on the moon: '*selbst wie ein Traum der Sonne lag er über der in sich*

gekehrten Traumwelt', Droste-Hülshoff, *W.* [edit. Sch.] 2,320: '*da bebt's . . . hervor blaß wie ein Traum mit ungewissem Tritte*', Keller, *Ges.W.* 1,196: '. . . *lag . . . so fern wie ein Traum*'.

nichts als (or *nur*) *ein* ~ nothing but a dream, a mere illusion; since MHG, e.g. U.v.Winterstetten, *Lied.* 32,15: '*sost mîn sorge gar ein troum*', or Neidhart 46,20.

etw. geschieht wie im ~ (1) sth. happens as if in a dream; refers to sth. unreal; also as *es ist wie im* ~ = 'it seems quite unreal'.

etw. geschieht wie im ~ (2) sth. happens in a flash, disappears immediately; a ref. to shortness, hence often in *vergehen wie im* ~ = 'to pass quickly'; beginnings in MHG, e.g. (DWb) Reinfried 368; cf. also Goethe IV,1,236 (W.): '. . . *vergessen wie ein Traum*'.

der Alptraum nightmare; 19th c. coinage (Adelung, even in his 2nd edit., only recorded *das Alpdrücken*), e.g. Alexis, *Neap.* 128: '*die schwere Kette von Alpträumen*'; cf. Lichtwer, *Schr.* 136: '. . . *hatt' ihm nicht vom Alp geträumt*', publ. in 1825, but written in the 18th c. (Lichtwer died in 1783).

das Tagträumen day-dreaming, reverie; modern (not yet in Campe [1810]); Keller in *Leute v.Seldw.* 1,96 used *Tagtraum*; around the same time *Tagträumer* and *Tagträumerei* arose; cf. also *mit offenen Augen träumen* (modern).

traumverloren or *traumversunken sein* to be lost in dreams, to be sunk in reveries; modern; in essence the same as *ganz im* ~ *sein*, as e.g. in Goethe IV,3,106 (W.): '*er war ganz im Traum, da ich ihms sagte*'; hence also *träume nicht!* (coll.) = 'pay attention!'; modern.

etw. träumt (poet.) sth. dreams; figur. with abstracts since the 18th c., e.g. Mörike 1,24: '*es träumt der Tag, nun sei die Nacht entflohn*' (also in phys. contexts *ibid.* 1,109: '*noch träumen Wald und Wiesen*', Voß 3,216: '*wir leben nicht, uns träumet des Daseins dunkler Traum*'.

sich etw. nicht träumen lassen not to expect sth. (even in one's wildest dreams); general since the 18th c., e.g. Lessing, *Gal.* 2,10: '*des Marchese Marinelli Freundschaft hätte ich mir nie träumen lassen*'.

etw. austräumen to continue dreaming sth. to the end; since the 18th c., e.g. Wieland 10,54. In lit. sometimes as *er hat den* ~ *des Lebens ausgeträumt*; also in intrans. locutions for 'to finish dreaming', as in Arnim, *Schaub.* 2,216 on the end of the year's hibernation: '*es hat das Jahr nun ausgeträumt*'.

sich etw. austräumen to visualize or wish for sth. in one's (day-)dreams; since the 2nd half of the 18th c., e.g.Fouqué, *Dram.Dicht.* 1,10 [1813], not yet listed in *DWb*. [1854]. Herder and Lichtenberg used (*sich*) *etw. beträumen* in this sense (now obs.). Much older and still current is *etw. erträumen*, frequent in Luther, e.g. pref. Ezekiel: '*das ertreumen sie selbs*'; often with abstracts in the past participle for 'desired in one's dreams', e.g. *erträumte Macht*,

Krone. Heine, *Sal.* 1,304 used *sich in etw. hinein-träumen* (cf. also Heine, *Reis.* 3,177: '*wir haben Alles mitgeträumt*'). When in one's day-dreams one changes things, *umträumen* can be used, e.g. (Sa.) J.König-Rumohr, *Kochk.* 2,85 [1822]: '. . . *daß der richtige Idealismus nicht darin bestehe, daß man die wirklichen Dinge der Welt umträume*'. *Jem.m etw. vorträumen* has been current since the 18th c., e.g. Wieland 32,234.

etw. verträumen (1) to pass or spend sth. dreaming; since the 17th c., f.r.b. Stieler [1691], e.g. Goethe, *Mitschuld.* 501: '*wie süs verträumt ich nicht die jugendlichen Stunden einst in Sophiens Arm*'.

etw. verträumen (2) to miss sth. through dreaming; since the 18th c., e.g. Schiller, *Äneide* 335: '. . . *den verheißnen Thron im Arm der Lust verträumet*'. Close to this is *etw. verträumen* = 'to eliminate sth. by pleasant thoughts, get over sth. painful', e.g. Herder 23,336: '. . . *vor süßen Zaubereien der Bürger seinen Gram verträumet*'.

verträumt dreamy, sleepy; figur. since the 19th c. with ref. to persons, e.g. *ein verträumtes Kind* and to things which look 'sleepy' or 'secluded', e.g. *eine verträumte Gegend*.

← See also under *ausgehen* (for *mein Traum geht aus*), *austräumen, durchträumen, Ferkel* (for *wenn das Ferkel träumt . . .*), *greifen* (for *Greiflichkeit eines Traumes*), *Morgen* (for *Morgentraum*), *Schaum* (for *Träume sind Schäume*), *Spiegel* (for *Träume spiegeln sich in etw. hinein*) and *Stück* (for *ein Stück von einem Träumer*).

treffen: touch, reach, meet

jem. ~ to hit, meet sb.; in several contexts, early with ref. to (figur.) missiles, since MHG, e.g. (DWb) Lampr.v.Regensb., *Syon* 3741: '*wer hât mich aber troffen nû? . . . hast mich verwunt mit der minne*', Goethe 2,128 (W.): '. . . *trifft mit der Liebe Gewalt nun Philomene das Herz*', often with the weapon named, e.g. Goethe, *Iphig.* 4,1 on the lie: '*sie kehrt, ein . . . Pfeil . . . sich zurück, und trifft den Schützen*', Schiller, *Spaz.* 17: '*glühend trifft mich der Sonne Pfeil*', *Braut v.Mess.* 1542: '*der Liebe heilger Götterstrahl, der in die Seele schlägt und trifft und zündet*', Platen, *Sonette* 43: '*wann . . . mich solch ein Schlag aus blauer Luft getroffen*'. Kramer [1702] recorded: '*vom Blitz, Wetter getroffen*', Goethe 24,92 (W.): '*er stand wie vom Blitz getroffen*'. It is also used with ref. to 'stroke' (in medical sense) since Early NHG; a curse, judgment, reproof or bad luck can also 'hit' sb. (beginnings in Late MHG; cf. also Gerstenberg, *Ugolino* 260: '*wenn das Schwert ihn . . . nicht erreichen kann, so treff ihn das Gebet meiner Seele in der Todesstunde*', Luther Bible transl. Prov. 26,2: '*ein unverdient fluch trifft nicht*' (also Deuter. 31.17 or Job 4,5), Goethe, *Ep.Erw.* 1,1: '*der Segen trifft, wenn Fluch uns nie erreicht*'. Close to this are the meanings 'to harm, hurt, afflict sb. (by design or accident)', since Early NHG, e.g. Luther Bible transl. Job 3,25: '*das ich sorgete, hat mich troffen*', frequent in *der Verlust hat*

ihn schwer getroffen, and 'to reach, meet up with', as in *das Gericht wird ihn* ~, e.g. Mommsen, *Röm.Gesch.* 2,49: '*strengere Behandlung . . . traf . . . Theben*', Graf Pocci, *Lust.Kom.* 234: '*wer nicht gehorcht, den trifft alsbald der Tod*'.

← See also under *Keule* (for *es traf ihn wie ein Keulenschlag*), *Los* (for *jem. trifft das Los*), *Reihe* (for *die Reihe trifft jem.*) and *Schlag* (for *der Schlag, der ihn traf*).

etw. ~ (1) to hit (upon) sth.; figur. with abstracts since Early NHG, e.g. *die rechte Rede* ~, as in Job 32,11, or *ein Rätsel* ~ = 'to solve a riddle', as in Judges, 14,18, *den richtigen Ton* ~ = 'to find the right tone' (both in singing and with ref. to manner of speaking), *die Lösung* ~ = 'to hit upon the solution', *das Richtige* ~ = 'to find or hit upon the right way, thing, etc.', also 'to guess correctly, make the proper reply or remark' (cf. Lessing 5,60: '*der Verfasser, welcher . . . Blößen unserer Systematiker glücklich trifft*'; hence also *etw. gut* ~ = 'to give a correct picture of sth.' (e.g. the likeness in a painting, at least since the 17th c., used by Grimmelshausen or by Lessing 7,97, or now also in photography), and further with *es* for 'to find what one wanted, to have made a fortunate choice', e.g. *mit diesem Hotel hat er es gut getroffen* = 'he was lucky in hitting upon or finding this hotel'; hence (*gut*) *getroffen!* = 'you have hit upon it, a palpable hit!', recorded by Adelung [1780], e.g. Schiller, *Turandot* 2,4 or Goethe, *Was wir br.* 9: '*das trifft vollkommen*'.

← See also under *Nadel* (for *etw. mit der Nadel treffen*), *Nagel* (for *den Nagel auf den Kopf treffen*), *nah* (for *nah schießen hilft nichts, es gilt treffen*), *Nerv* (for *den Nerv treffen*), *Pflock* (for *das Pflöckchen treffen*) and *Punkt* (for *den rechten Punkt nicht treffen*).

etw. ~ (2) to make, effect, conclude sth.; with abstracts where nothing phys. is 'hit' or 'met'; beginnings in Late MHG, where *einen Frieden* ~ = 'to make or negotiate a peace' occurred (still recorded by Adelung [1780], but now obs.); mainly in *ein Abkommen mit jem.m* ~ = 'to enter into an agreement with sb.', *Anordnungen* ~ = 'to give orders', *eine Entscheidung* ~ = 'to make, reach, come to a decision', *Maßnahmen* or *Anstalten* ~ = 'to take measures', as in Schiller, *Kab.u.L.* 3,1, *eine Auswahl* ~ = 'to make a choice', *ein Bündnis* ~ = 'to form an alliance', f.r.b. Stieler [1691], *eine Wahl* ~, as in Schiller, *Picc.* 2,2. Adelung even recorded *eine Heurath* ~ = 'to marry', which is obs.

← See also under *anstellen* (for *Anstalten treffen*).

auf etw. ~ to come up against or meet sth.; with ref. to abstracts since the 18th c., e.g. *auf Widerstand* ~ = 'to meet with opposition', as in Mommsen 3,24. In the case of *auf jem.* ~ the sense is mainly 'to meet sb.', as in Wieland, *Klel.* 4,201: '*so traf er unterwegs auf ihn*', it can, however, also mean 'to be directed against sb., be meant to apply to sb.', e.g. *was er gesagt hat, trifft nicht auf uns* (since the 19th c.).

← See also under *betreffen* (also for *Betreff* and *betroffen*).

auf eins ~, *zusammentreffen* to agree, harmonize; beginnings in Early NHG, f.r.b. Maaler [1561]: '*in sitten und pärden einem gleich sein und wol zesamen träffen*'; with *auf eins* in Schiller, *Räuber* 1,2:'; cf. also Ranke, *Werke* 1,174: '*seine Reime . . . treffen in glücklichem Wohllaut zusammen*' or Goethe 4,170 (W.): '*denn das ist Gottes wahre Gift, wenn die Blüth' zur Blüthe trifft*'.

es traf sich, daß . . . it so happened (by chance) that . . . ; often with *gut* or *erwünscht*; since the 18th c.

treffend apposite, to the point; at first only in the sense of 'scoring a hit' (phys. and figur.), but since 2nd half of the 18th c. mainly with ref. to remarks, judgments, e.g. Bürger [edit. B.] 1,153: '*im Ausdruck treffend*', Bräker, *S.Schr.* 2,289: '*mit lauter treffendem Witz*', Goethe 22,103 (W.): '*seine Urtheile waren . . . treffend, ohne lieblos zu sein*'. The notion of 'agreeing' or 'conforming' can also be present, e.g. Schiller, *Räuber* 2,1: '*wie treffend die Stimmungen des Geistes mit den Bewegungen der Maschine zusammen lauten*'; cf. also *treffsicher* = 'accurate, precise', modern.

das Treffen encounter, fight; at first only in mil. contexts, e.g. Luther, Apocr. transl. 2 Macc. 15,20: '*da es nu gelten solt zum treffen*', f.r.b. Stieler [1691]; figur. in *etw.* (e.g. *gute Argumente*) *ins Treffen führen*, since the 18th c., e.g. Schiller, *Räuber* 1,2.

der Treffer hit, win; first in shooting, then with ref. to lotteries, figur., often with mention of *Lostopf*, as in Goethe 8,261 (W.) or *Lotto*, as in Schiller or *Los*, as in Klinger; hence *einen großen Treffer haben* (or *machen*) = 'to have a great piece of luck'; Hügel [1873] recorded for Vienna *einen Treffer machen* = 'to make a good choice'.

trefflich excellent(ly), splendid(ly); since Late MHG, in the beginning also in the sense of 'considerable', as in Luther Bible transl. Zech. 11,13: '*eine treffliche summa*' (where the A.V. puts 'a goodly price'); also as an adverb, f.r.b. Maaler [1561]: '*träffenlich große hitz, träffenliche schöne*', Goethe 14,93 (W.): '*mit Worten läßt sich trefflich streiten*'; hence *vortrefflich*, originally = 'superior', then 'excellent', current since the 12th c. (*vür-trefliche*), f.r.b. Hulsius [1618], who also recorded *Vortrefflichkeit*.

zutreffen to hold or come true, to be or prove correct; current since the 16th c., also figur., e.g. (DWb) Wicelius, *Annot.* 60a [1536]: '. . . *das ihr warsagerei nimmer zutraf*', Goethe 22,306 (W.): '*dies alles traf bei mir weder nahe noch fern zu*'. Cf. also *zutreffendenfalls*, on questionnaires = 'if applicable' (20th c.).

das ist Treff (coll., obs.) that is a piece of luck; recorded by Wander [1876].

jem.m einen Treff geben (regional coll.) to hit sb.; f.r.b. Klein [1792]; cf. also *er hat seinen Treff bekommen* = 'he has had his share or what was coming to him', f.r.b. Eiselein [1838].

wer sich getroffen fühlt, der meldet sich (prov.) let him, whom the cap fits, wear it; f.r.b. Simrock [1846], but in other wordings much older, e.g. Pistorius [1716]: '*wer getroffen wird, der regt sich*'; cf. also '*dein getroffenes Gewissen*' in Schiller, *Räuber* 4,2.

← See also under *ausspeien* (for *man kann nicht ausspeien, ohne . . . zu treffen*), *blau* and *schießen* (for *mancher schießt ins Blaue und trifft ins Schwarze*), *eintreffen*, *Esel* (for *den Sack schlagen und auf den Esel treffen wollen*), *Fliege* (for *zwei Fliegen auf einen Schlag treffen*), *Fuchs* (for *ein nicht beabsichtigter Treffer*), *Hintertreffen* (for *ins Hintertreffen geraten*), *Kegel* (for *er will immer elf Kegel treffen*), *Los* (for *jem. trifft das Los*) and *schwarz* (for *ins Schwarze treffen*).

treiben: drive, move, push

jem. ~ to drive or push sb., urge sb. on, chase sb.; frequent since Early NHG, e.g. Luther 8,823a (Jena) and in his Bible transl. Romans 8,14. There are numerous locutions, e.g. *jem. aus dem Paradies* ~, since MHG, later with figur. *Paradies*, *jem. ins Bockshorn* ~, since the 16th c., *jem. in die Flucht* ~ (loan from Lat. *in fugam conicere*, since Early NHG), *jem. ins Elend* ~, as in Zinkgref, *Apophth.* 27 [1628], with which cf. Goethe 3,6 (W.): '*mich trieb dein Geschlecht in die Ferne*', *jem zum Äußersten* ~ = 'to drive sb. to extremes', since the 18th c., *jem. zum Wahnsinn* ~ = 'to drive sb. mad' (cf. also Kleist, *Verlob.in St.Dom.*: '*der Wahnsinn der Frei-heit . . . trieb die Neger . . . die Ketten zu brechen*'). An abstract (emotion or experience) can be the subject, since the 16th c. with *Angst*, later also with *Liebe, Sehnsucht*, etc., e.g. Schiller, *Br.v.Mess.* 373 '*uns aber treibt das verworrene Streben blind und sinnlos durchs wüste Leben*', Goethe, *Tasso* 4,4: '*die Hast . . . die dich übel treibt*', or the urge can be expressed by *es* in *es treibt mich . . .* = 'I feel an urge to . . .', as in Hebel 3,90; see also under *forttreiben* below. When the sense is 'to chase away', *vertreiben* is now preferred (current since OHG), e.g. Jean Paul: '*die Erinnerung ist das einzige Paradies, aus welchem wir nicht vertrieben werden können*'.

← See also under *Bär* (for *den Bären treiben*), *Bock* (for *als ich den Brutus trieb aus Rom*), *eng* (for *jem. in die Enge treiben*), *hetzen* (for *die Sehnsucht trieb und hetzte mich*) and *Paar* (for *zu Paaren treiben*).

etw. ~ (1) to do, pursue, engage in sth., go in for sth., carry on with sth.; since OHG, e.g. Notker, *Ps.* 81,2, also in the Bible, e.g. 1 Tim. 3,3: '. . . *nicht vnehrliche hantierung treiben*', *Unzucht* ~, as in 2 Cor. 12,21, *Mutwillen* ~, as in Ecclesiasticus 26,13, *Alfanzereien* ~ = 'to play the fool', frequent in Luther, still used by Lessing, now a. if not obs., *Spott* ~ = 'to mock, scoff, ridicule', as in Schiller,

Räuber 5,1, *Scherz* ~, as in Schiller, *Glocke* 366: '. . . *und treiben mit Entsetzen Scherz*', *ein Handwerk* ~, as in Schiller, *Kab.u.L.* 3,6, *Handel* ~, as in Hauff 3,53, *unnützes Zeug* ~, as in Eichendorff, *Taugen*. 6. Sometimes *es* replaces the noun, as in *es bunt* ~ or *es zu grob* ~, for which see under *bunt* and *grob*.

← See also under *bauen* (for *Raubbau treiben*), *schinden* (for *mit jem.m Schindluder treiben*), *Spaß* (for *seinen Spaß treiben*) and *Strauß* (for *Vogel-Strauß-Politik treiben*).

etw. ~ (2) to put forth, sprout sth.; image taken from plant growth; general in figur. use since the 18th c. (but not yet in Kramer [1702]), e.g. Schiller, *D.Carlos* 2,15: '*zu jenem Ideale, das . . . verschwenderisch Blüthen treibt*', Chamisso 4,135: '*mein alter Stamm treibt fürder keine Zweige*'.

etw. ~ (3) to send or bring sth. somewhere; general since the 18th c. in such locutions as *jem.m die Schamröte ins Gesicht* ~, *jem.m Schweiß* or *Angsttropfen auf die Stirn* ~, as in Iffland, *Bewußts.* 3,7, *die Preise in die Höhe* ~, hence also *Preistreiberei* = 'forcing up of prices'; cf. also *den Fuchs aus dem Bau* ~, as used by Bismarck in *Briefe an Gerlach* 71 [1896].

← See also under *Haar* (for *die Haare zu Berg treiben*) and *Höhe* (for *etw. in die Höhe treiben*).

etw. ~ (4) to chase sth. (away); figur. since Early NHG, e.g. Luther Apocr. transl. Wisdom of Sol. 17,8: '*die furcht und schrecken von den kranken seelen zu treiben*', Ecclesiasticus 30, 24: '*treibe trawrigkeit weit fern von dir*'; now compounds such as *forttreiben, vertreiben* and *wegtreiben* are preferred.

etw. ~ (5) to push (or propel) sth.; figur. since the 18th c., e.g. Wieland, *Musarion* 3,105: '*man treibt in einem Ritterbuch die Tugend kaum so weit*', Jean Paul, *Lit.Nachl.* 4,23: '*der Mensch denkt, er sei das Wasser, das die Räder der Schöpfung treibt*'; now often in such locutions as *den Vergleich zu weit* ~; cf. also Schiller, *Räuber* 1,1: '*die Pulse des Weltzirkels zu treiben*'.

treiben (1) (intrans.) to ferment, expand; first in chem. contexts (16th c.); figur. since the 18th c., e.g. Goethe 8,200 (W.): '*damals kocht' es und trieb*', Heine [edit. E.] 1,17: '*was treibt und tobt mein tolles Blut?*'.

treiben (2) (intrans.) to move quickly, rush along; through comparison with wind and water; figur. since the 17th c., e.g. Chr.v.Schallenberg [edit. Kurd] 160: '*die lieb ist eben wie das meer, heut ists still, morgen tuet es . . . treiben*', Schiller, *Wall. Tod* 3,18: '*weg treibt . . . der wilde Strom in grausamer Zerstörung*'; often with allusion to ships and in compounds, e.g. Wieland, *S.Werke* 8,94: '*ich trieb lange ohne Mast und Segel in der Welt umher*'; cf. also Storm, *Werke* 4,132: '*dann trieben die Beiden weiter durch die wimmelnde Menschenfluth der großen Stadt*'.

← See also under *Hafen* (for *in den Hafen treiben*).

treiben (3) (intrans.) to grow; image taken from plant life; general since the 18th c., e.g. Chamisso, *Werke* 3,180: '*die Kinder treiben und gedeihen*'; cf. Jean Paul, *S.Werke* 22,224: '*seine treibende Seele, die in die Erde und den Himmel hineinwachsen wollte*'.

etw. . . . *-treiben* to drive sth. (in certain ways or directions); in compounds in many different contexts; many have been dealt with previously (see list below); others are *etw.* (or *jem.*) *forttreiben*, in various contexts, e.g. 'to continue practicing or devoting oneself to sth.', or 'to drive sth. or sb. away', e.g. Goethe, *Diwan* (*Anklage*): '*gränzenlos vom eigensinn'gen Lieben wird er in die Öde fortgetrieben*' or Schiller, *Jungfr.v.O.* 3,4: '*es treibt mich fort*', *etw. hintertreiben* = 'to thwart, foil, obstruct sth.', f.r.b. Stieler [1691], e.g. Gryphius 1,323: '. . . *sich eußerstes bemüht, den streich zu hintertreiben*' (Schuppius, 420 used '*hintertreiben und widerlegen*'), *etw. übertreiben* = 'to exaggerate sth.', f.r.b. Kramer [1702], e.g. Goethe, *Faust I*, 1734: '*wie magst du deine Rednerei nur gleich so hitzig übertreiben*', *etw. untertreiben* = 'to understate sth.', in this sense only introduced in the 2nd half of the 20th c. as an antonym to *übertreiben* (still missing in *DWb.* [1936]), *etw. vorantreiben* = 'to further, promote sth.', figur. only since the 20th c. (before then *vor sich* ~ was used, e.g. Gryphius, *Kath.* 16: '*der . . . ist hiermit selbst bemüht und treibt das werck vor sich*'), *etw. zurücktreiben* = 'to drive, send sth. back', e.g. Wieland, *Luc.* 4,101: '*das wolle . . . Apollo auf die Häupter unsrer Feinde zurücktreiben*'; cf. also Wieland 22,249: '. . . *genöthigt, mit dem Strom des allgemeinen Enthusiasmus fortzutreiben*', Schiller, *Tell* 4,3: '*jeder treibt sich an dem Andern rasch und fremd vorüber*'.

← See also under *abtreiben, antreiben, auftreiben, austreiben, beitreiben, betreiben, durchtreiben, eintreiben, Gift* (for *alle Sünde austreiben*), *Gilde* (for *vertriebene Fürsten*), *Grille* (for *Grillen vertreiben*), *hervortreiben, hinauftreiben, hineintreiben* and *Ring* (for *sich im Ring herumtreiben*).

es mit jem.m ~ (sl.) to have intimate relations with sb.; since (at least) the 19th c.; similarly, *sein Spiel mit jem.m* ~, used euphemistically for which see *Spiel* (5) on p. 2297.

der Treiber (1) oppressor; since Early NHG, e.g. Luther Bible transl. Isaiah 16,4; sometimes used for sth. that roughly corresponds to Engl. 'slave-driver', e.g. Fallada, *Bauern* 308.

der Treiber (2) stimulator, inciter; since Early NHG, e.g. Luther Bible transl. 2 Chron. 34,13: '*treiber zu allerlei erbeit*' (on which Adelung commented: '*im Hochdeutschen ungewöhnlich*'). Goethe used it in its feminine form in *Meine Göttin*: '*die edle Treiberin, Trösterin, Hoffnung*'.

← See also under *quer* (for *Quertreiber* and *Quertreiberei*).

die Treiberei machinations, hostile interference; an offspring from *Treiberei* = 'gossip, tale-bearing', current since the 17th c., but now obsolete; according to Heyne [1895] it was introduced in its new meaning as a replacement for *Chikanen*; since the 19th c., e.g. Oken, *Nat. Gesch.* 1,21 [1833], Reventlow, *Von Potsdam* 121 [1940]: '*man denke auch an die konfessionellen-politischen Treibereien*'. Following *Treiber* (1), *Treiberei* can also mean 'constant pushing or urging on, slave-driving'.

er ist die treibende Kraft (lit.) he is the prime mover; derived from its tech. sense in the 19th c., e.g. Häußer, *Dt.Gesch.* 3.,108: '*die treibende Kraft der Coalition*'; cf. similar *das treibende Motiv* = 'the prime or principal motif', as in Moltke 1,122.

die Treibhauspflanze delicate creature; in this figur. sense since early in the 19th c.

← See also under *Gewächs* (for *Treibhausgewächs*).

die Treibjagd hunt; in original hunt. sense = 'battue'; figur. since the 18th c., first as *das Treibjagen*, then in the 19th c. as *Treibjagd* for 'hunting down of sb. by several people', now often with ref. to combined action by the police.

der Schweinetreiber (or *Farkentreiber*) (coll., obs.) slow-coach, ship (or vehicle) which moves very slowly or falls behind; f.r.b. Sanders [1865], both missing in *DWb*. Kluge, *Seemannsspr.* 246 [1911] recorded *Farkentreiber* for '*schlechtester Segler (der am meisten zurückbleibt, wenn mehrere Schiffe zusammen segeln)*'.

der Zeitvertreib pastime, amusement to kill time; since MHG (*zîtvertrîb*); this was followed in the 17th c. by *Zeitvertreiber* for the abstract as well as for the person who helps one to pass the time, f.r.b. Stieler [1691], e.g. Günther, *Ged.* 630: '*wer mag wohl, werthes Kind, dein Zeitvertreiber seyn?*'. Some 17th c. authors, e.g. Moscherosch in *Ges.* 65 [1642] used the noun also for 'clown, entertainer', now obs. The abstract *Zeitvertreibung* (since the 16th c.) is now unusual.

← See also under *Gewicht* (for *das Uhrwerk der Welt treiben*), *Keil* (for *ein Keil treibe den andern*), *Kessel* (for *Kesseltreiben*), *Sand* (for *Treibsand*), *Strom* (for *sich treiben lassen*), *Trieb* and *tun* (for *Tun und Treiben*).

trennen: separate, divide, sever

etw. von etw. anderem ~ to keep sth. separate from sth. else; with ref. to abstracts since Early NHG, e.g. Luther 20,345 (Weimar): '*trennt und sondert die götliche natur von der menschlichen*', but in modern sense of 'distinguishing' only since the 18th c., e.g. Chr. Wolff, *Vern.Ged.v.Gott* 156 [1720]: '*Begriffe, die entweder getrennet oder verknüpfet werden*', Goethe, *Faust II*, 4: '. . . *verstehen sie vom Sein den Schein zu trennen*'. Hence *die Trennung* = 'separation, split, schism', f.r.b. Stieler [1691], with ref. to religion f.r.b. Steinbach [1734]. Also in compounds such as *Kirchentrennung* with ref. to the Reformation (same as *Kirchenspaltung*), used by Schiller.

jem. von jem.m ~ to separate sb. from sb.; at first in Early NHG in relig. contexts with ref. to

separation from God, e.g. H.Sachs 1,356, then also in secular contexts, e.g. (DWb) Barth, *Weiberspiegel* Hib [1505]: '*der jetzige könig hat sich . . . unterstande, mich von meinem manne zutrennen*', Schiller, *D.Carlos* 2,12: '*man trennt mich von der Person der Königin*', Grillparzer [edit.Sauer] 10,88: '*nicht Menschen Macht, nicht Kerker, nicht der Tod kann vom Geliebten die Geliebte trennen*'; frequent with ref. to divorce.

← See also under *Tisch* (for *Trennung von Tisch und Bett*).

etw. trennt jem. von etw. (lit.) sth. separates sb. from sth.; since the 18th c., both with ref. to time, e.g. *ein ganzes Jahrhundert trennt uns von jenen Ereignissen* (used by Schiller) and other abstracts, e.g. Schiller, *Braut v.M.* 571: '*auch kein Geheimnis trenn uns ferner mehr*'. Cf. also *uns trennen Welten voneinander* = 'we are worlds apart' and *unsere Wege trennen sich hier* = 'this is where our roads part'.

etw. trennt etw. anderes (poet.) sth. cuts or pierces sth. else; in poetry sometimes with ref. to air or water since Early NHG, e.g. (DWb) H.Sachs [edit. Lit.Verein] 188,84: '*die wolcken trennt seins glantzes glitzen mit eim großen hagel und blitzen*', Lenz [edit.Weinh.] 20: '*Schluchzen und Seufzen trennt die nachhallende Luft*', Goethe 1,269 (W.): '*strebe, mächtiger Kiel, trenne die schäumende Fluth*'.

sich ~ to separate, come apart; mainly lit. when figur. with abstracts, e.g. Bürger, *Lenore* on death: '*wann Leib und Seel sich trennen*'. There is also *sich von etw.* ~ = 'to abandon sth., take leave from sth.', and with abstracts for 'to become separate entities', where Kant 3,280 used *sich abtrennen*: '*Metaphysik trennt sich gänzlich vom Fortgang der Erfahrung ab*'.

ein Band ~ (lit.) to sever a bond, destroy a union; since the 17th c., e.g. Gottsched, *Ged.* 1,166 [1751]: '*(die Vaterhand) selber jedes Eheband zu trennen wie zu knüpfen pfleget*', Schiller, *Punschlied*: '*das Band der Elemente trennt ihr herrschendes Gebot*'.

Getrenntheit der Meinungen (lit.) difference of opinion; since the 19th c., e.g. Gervinus, *Kath.* 7 (with *Urtheil*); cf. also Ense, *Gal.* 2,215; '*ein schaudervolles Sinnbild der Getrenntheit unserer Seelen*'; cf. also *das sind zwei getrennte Begriffe* = 'these are two different concepts.'

etw. zertrennen to disrupt or dismember sth.; at first with the original image of 'ripping apart', e.g. Luther 7,164a (Jena): '*denn lügen und untreu "zurtrennet" erstlich die herzen, wenn die herzen "zertrennet" sind*'. Luther 8,145a (Jena) also used *unzertrennt*; *unzertrennlich* was f.r.b. Frisius [1556].

einen Trennungsstrich ziehen to make clear distinction, draw a definite line; derived in the 20th c. from the orthographic *Trennungsstrich* = 'hyphen' (= *Bindestrich*); e.g. (T.) Sluyterman v.v. Langeweyde, *Die Herzen* 230 [1940] with ref. to wearing a white collar: '. . . *zog einen Trennungsstrich zwischen ihm und dem Arbeiter im blauen Kittel'*.

eine Trennwand errichten (lit.) to put up a dividing wall, create sth. which separates people; modern (Schiller and Wieland used figur. *Scheidewand* for this); also the opposite *die Trennwand niederreißen*; cf. also *die Trennwand zwischen diesen beiden Begriffen ist dünn geworden*.

Treppe: stairs

die ~ (lit.) stairs or steps; in the beginning often = *Stufe* (which see) with ref. to difficult ascent, as in Luther 16,531 (Weimar): '*das was eine hohe treppen an Christus hinan*'; cf. also Fouqué, *Zauberring* 1,47: '*was unsern Wünschen unersteigbare Klippen sind, werden jenem* (i.e. misfortune) *bequeme Treppen*'. Since the 18th c. also for 'way or chance of approach', as in *eine ~ zu jem.m finden*, used by Jean Paul, *Werke* [edit. H.] 15–18, 327.

du hast Treppen (coll.) your hair has been cut unevenly (producing steps); modern coll.

ein Treppenwitz der Weltgeschichte an irony (or paradox) of history; usually in the sense of 'sth. cruelly ironic'; coined by W.L. Hertslet (creating a variant to *Humor der Weltgeschichte*, which first occurred in *Kladderadatsch* 162 [1863]) for the title of his book [1882], which became very popular and gave the locution immediate currency.

die Wendeltreppe (lit.) spiral staircase; in its phys. sense in use since the 16th c.; figur. in Jean Paul, *Werke* [edit. H.] 15–18,73, also Perthes, *Leb.* 2,179 on Steffen's writings: '*so eine unendliche Wendeltreppe ohne Ausruher läßt den geistlichen Athem mir bald ausgehen*'.

treppenförmig stepped, terraced; since the 18th c., similarly *treppenartig* and *treppenähnlich*, both in lit. since the 19th c.

← See also under *hinauffallen* (for *die Treppe hinauffallen*), *Hintertreppe* (for *Hintertreppenwitz*), *oben* (for *wer oben wohnen will, muß Treppen steigen*), *schleichen* (for *Schleichtreppe*), *Stück* (for *das Treppensteigen ist saure Arbeit*) and *Teufel* (for *das Alter geht voraus, sagte der Teufel und schmiß seine Großmutter die Treppe hinunter*).

treten: tread, step, kick

jem. ~ to ill-treat, oppress sb.; since OHG, at first in biblical contexts, then in general use (though not much in the 20th c.); e.g. Varnhagen v. Ense, *Tagebücher* 6,179: '*der König . . . tritt das Volk, wie er nur kann*', Arim [edit. Gr.] 18,354: '*arm Leut tritt jedermann*'; cf. also *dem muß ich mal ins Kreuz ~* (coll.) = 'I shall have to cut him down to size, tell him a few home-truths'; 20th c.

← See also under *Fuß* (for *jem. mit Füßen* or *unter die Füße treten*), *Ochs* (for *der schwarze Ochs hat ihn getreten*) and *Staub* (for *jem. in den Staub treten*).

auf jem. ~ to ill-treat sb., hurt sb. (deliberately); same as the transitive locution above; in early periods often in religious contexts, e.g. Luther 29,263 (Weimar): '*tritt auf den teuffel*'; now rare.

auf etw. ~ to treat sth.with contempt, step on

sth. in anger or fear; since Early NHG.

← See also under *Auge* and *Huhn* (for *jem.m auf die Hühneraugen treten*), *Fuß* (for *jem.m auf den Fuß treten*), *Nacken* (for *auf jem.s Nacken treten*), *Pinsel* (for *auf den Pinsel treten*), *Pudding* (for *bei ihm tritt man auf Pudding*), *Schlips* (for *jem.m auf den Schlips treten*) and *Schwanz* (for *dem Teufel auf den Schwanz treten*).

aus etw. ~ (lit.) to come out of sth., emerge from sth.; in lit. with abstracts since the 18th c., e.g. Schiller, *Picc.* 5.1: '*glänzend werden wir den Reinen aus diesem schwarzen Argwohn treten sehen*'.

← See also under *Schatten* (for *aus dem Schatten heraustreten*).

in etw. ~ (1) to step or move into sth., enter sth.; general since Early NHG in many contexts, where concrete nouns occur in figur. locutions.

← See under *Bach* (for *in den Bach treten*), *Bresche* (for *für jem. in die Bresche treten*), *fett* (for *bei jem.m ins Fettnäpfchen treten*), *Fuß* (for *in jem.s Fußstapfen treten*), *Hahn* (for *ihm hat der Hahn ins Gesicht getreten*), *Napf* (for *ins Näpfchen treten*), *Pfanne* (for *in eine Pfanne treten*), *Reihe* (for *in eine Reihe treten*), *reißen* (for *in den Riß treten*), *Schranke* (for *für jem. in die Schranken treten*), *Schuh* (for *in jem.s Schuhe treten*) and *Spur* (for *in jem.s Spuren treten*).

in etw. ~ (2) to move into sth., enter sth.; with ref. to abstracts of various kinds; since MHG, e.g. Wolfr. v.Eschenbach, *Parz.* 654,25: '*Gâwân ûz sorge in fröude trat*', also in Luther Bible transl. 2 Chron. 15,12: '*sie tratten in den bund*', Schiller, *Räuber* (2nd pref.): '*der Verirrte tritt wieder in das Geleise der Gesetze*'. From the 17th c. onward with such abstracts as *Amt*, *Ehestand*, *Orden*, recorded by Kramer [1702], in the 19th c. frequent in *in Verbindung ~* (e.g. Ranke, *Werke* 1,192), in *Erscheinung ~*, *in seine Rechte ~* (both used by Goethe), *in Beziehung ~*, *in einen Gegensatz ~*, *in Verkehr ~*, all now considered somewhat stilted (except in locutions with *Streik*, for which see p. 2392), but in chem. contexts it is still usual to speak of *in Verbindung ~*, e.g. *der Sauerstoff tritt in Verbindung mit dem Kalium*.

← See also under *Licht* (for *in das Licht treten*), *Mittel* (for *ins Mittel treten*) and *rechnen* (for *in Rechnung treten*).

in etw. ~ (3) to move into sth.; in locutions which refer to movements in time, e.g. *die Sonne tritt aus dem Zeichen des Widders in das des Stiers* = 'the Sun moves from Ram to Taurus in the zodiac', recorded by Kramer [1702], *der Hirsch tritt in die Brunft* = 'the stag has entered the rutting-season', also in Kramer.

neben etw. ~ to join sth., become associated with sth.; since the 19th c., e.g. Vischer, *Ästh.* 2,46: '*neben die Reihe von Erscheinungen tritt nun noch die Stufenleiter . . .*'; also *neben jem. ~*, as in (T.) Drost, *Barockmalerei* 80 [1926]: '*Abraham Janssens tritt fast ebenbürtig neben Rubens*'.

unter die Waffen ~ (a.) to join the armed forces; since the 18th c. (?), not yet in Kramer [1702]; now a., displaced by *ins Gewehr* ~ = 'to take up arms' (though *ans Gewehr* and *unters Gewehr* ~ also occur).

zu jem.m ~ (a.) to come to sb.'s assistance, support sb.; since Early NHG, e.g. Luther Bible transl. Psalm 94,16: '*wer tritt zu mir, wider die ubelthetter?*'; now unusual, *beistehen* is preferred.

zwischen zwei Menschen ~ to come or step between two people, disturb the union of two people; general since the 19th c., e.g. Freytag, *Soll u.H.* 1,485 [1855]: '*er fühlte, daß etwas zwischen ihn und seine Liebsten getreten war*'.

jem. ~ (stud. sl., obs.) to dun sb.; also = 'to challenge sb.'; f.r.b. Vollmann [1846]; it can refer to demanding payment and to challenging to a duel; still in Spielhagen, *Probl.Nat.* 7,335 [1861]; now obs., as is *Tretbrief* = 'dunning letter'; in coll. usage, however, one can still say *man muß ihn immer* ~, *daß er es tut*, where ~ = *drängen*.

etw. tritt jem.m vor Augen sth. comes into (or rises in) sb.'s mind; similar to *vor Augen haben* or *kommen* (see p. 118).

etw. tritt jem.m ans Herz sth. moves or disturbs sb.; mainly in lit., since the 18th c., e.g. Gellert 4,209: '*itzt tritt mirs recht ans Herz*', Schiller, *Phaedra* 5,6: '*es trat uns Allen eiskalt bis an das Herz hinan*'; cf. also *ich glaub' mich tritt ein Pferd* = 'that leaves me speechless'; late 20th c. coll.

die Kelter ~ to get on with one's task, carry on with the work in hand; image taken from wine-making; in phys. sense recorded by Kramer [1702], figur. since the 18th c., e.g. Goethe IV,35,198 (W.): '*leider muß ich die Kelter alleine treten, denn jedermann hat für sich und mit sich zu thun*'.

etw. platt ~ (coll.) to overwork sth., make sth. uninteresting through too much use; 20th c. coll.

← See also under *breit* (for *etw. breittreten*).

einen Weg, Pfad, Steig, etc. ~ (lit., a.) to follow a certain path, course, etc.; only in lit., mainly in the 18th c., e.g. Goethe, *Iphig.* 2,1: '*es ist der Weg des Todes, den wir treten*', Brachvogel, *Narc.* 50: '*ist das so wunderbar, daß ich das Pflaster von Paris trete?*'; cf. also *ein breitgetretener Pfad, eine tiefgetretene Spur* (Schiller); displaced by *betreten*, but still in use when 'creating a path through constant walking along a certain line' is meant, as in Uhland, 11: '*mein ist der unfruchtbare Weg, den Sorg' und Mühe trat*'.

← See also under *Pflaster* (for *Pflastertreter*).

die Treter (coll.) shoes, boots; in cant as *Trederikken* as early as 1841, as *Treter* since early in the 20th c., also in mil. sl., then in ordinary coll.

dazwischentreten to step between enemies, combattants or disputants; figur. with ref. to interfering or mediating since the 17th c., f.r.b. Stieler [1691], e.g. Häußer, *Dt.Gesch.* 3,16: '*Massenbach trat auch hier wieder hemmend dazwischen*'; earlier is *sich*

dazwischenlegen, f.r.b. Maaler [1561].

aus etw. heraustreten to leave (or desert) sth.); modern, e.g. (T.) Christoffel, *Welt d.gr.Maler* 68 [1938]: '*Rembrandt begehrte keineswegs, aus seinem handwerklichen Lebenskreis herauszutreten*'. Equally modern is reflex. *aus sich heraustreten* = 'to show one's true feelings, reveal one's innermost thoughts', as in (T.) E.Zahn, *Was d.L. zerbricht* 275 [1918]: '*er war ohnehin ein Mensch, der nicht so leicht aus sich heraustrat*'.

← See also under *Schatten* (for *aus dem Schatten heraustreten*).

etw. übertreten to infringe, transgress, trespass on sth.; translates Lat. *transgredi*, current since MHG, then in the Bible, e.g. Luther transl. of Matth. 15,2: '*warumb vbertretten deine jünger der eltesten aufsetze?*', also Luther 24,209 (Weimar); hence *Übertreter* = 'transgressor', f.r.b. *voc. theut.* hh7a [1482] and *Übertretung*, also recorded since the 15th c.

zu jem.m übertreten to join sb.; often in mil. contexts for going over to the enemy; f.r.b. Steinbach [1734].

zu etw. übertreten to go over or convert to sth.; general since the 18th c., e.g. *zum katholischen Glauben übertreten*, as in Miller, *Siegwart* 1,55 [1777].

jem. vertreten (1) (a.) to stand up for sb.; esp. with ref. to defending sb. in court; since Early NHG, e.g. H.Sachs [edit. K.] 1,433; '*der vertritt uns vor dem gericht*'; with ref. to 'assisting' also in the Bible, e.g. Psalm 119,122: '*vertrit du deinen knecht und tröste in, das mir die stolzen nicht gewalt tun*'; now a. Hence *Vertreter* = 'protector' since Early NHG, now a. except in legal contexts for 'advocate, champion', as in Schaubart, *Ged.* 1,195: '*und du, Vertreter, rede laut, wenn uns der Richter droht*'.

jem. vertreten (2) to represent sb., deputize for sb.; since Early NHG, f.r.b. Schönsleder [1618]; extended to representing a constituency, a firm, group, etc.; hence *der Vertreter*, e.g. Klopstock, *Od.* 2,88: '*wenn der Vertreter des Volkes . . . blutet*', modern in comm. sense, also used in med. contexts for 'locum tenens', also with ref. to abstracts, e.g. *er ist ein typischer Vertreter dieser Anschauung* = 'typical representative, exponent of . . .' (modern); hence also *die Vertretung übernehmen* = 'to take the place of sb., act as a substitute for sb.', and *vertretungsweise* (adv.) = 'by proxy', modern, e.g. Th.Mann, *Buddenbrooks* 2,519.

etw. vertreten to stand by sth., defend sth., answer for sth.; since MHG, f.r.b. Schottel [1663], e.g. Tieck, *Schr.* 2,193: '*den Mord will ich vor Gott dem Herrn vertreten*', still frequent in *eine Ansicht vertreten*; hence *Vertreter* = 'defender of sth.' (e.g. of an opinion), since the 17th c., and modern *vertretbar* = 'justifiable'.

jem.m den Weg vertreten to block sb.'s path, obstruct sb.; since the 17th c., e.g. Lohenstein,

Armin. 2,992b.

sich (die Füße) vertreten to stretch one's legs, move about after having sat for a long time; since the 16th c., e.g. Brockes, *Ird.Vergn.* 2,191: '*als ich jüngst, mich etwas zu vertreten, mich auf das Feld begab*'; there is also *den Fuß vertreten* = 'to sprain one's foot', but see its extended use listed under *Kuh*: *die Kuh hat vier Beine und vertritt sich doch.*

zurücktreten to come back, return; frequent still in 18th and 19th c., e.g. Goethe IV,1,128 (W.): '*ein zurücktretendes Übel ist das gefährlichste*', (Sp.) Zschokke, *Lebensgesch.Umr.* 41: '*je mehr die kleinen Völkerschaften . . . in die ehemalige Bundesschaft zurückgetreten waren*'; now unusual, displaced by *zurückkehren.*

etw. tritt zurück sth. becomes less visible, stands in the background; since the 18th c.; also with abstracts for 'to become less prominent' (19th c.).

von etw. zurücktreten to cancel sth. (e.g. a previous agreement); f.r.b. Kramer [1702]; also = 'to resign from sth.', e.g. *ins Privatleben zurücktreten* (after public service), but older with ref. to 'standing back, going away', as in Luther 10,3,12 (Weimar). For *Rücktritt* see under *Tritt.*

zusammentreten to convene, assemble; since Early NHG, e.g. Luther 9,199 (Weimar), Goethe 45,65 (W.): '*wo Menschen in Gesellschaft zusammentreten*'.

mit etw. zusammentreten to combine or come together with sth.; since the 18th c., often in phys.or chem. contexts, e.g. Goethe II,4,367 (W.), but also sometimes with abstracts.

etw. zusammentreten to smash sth.; early recordings, e.g. Adelung, only list this for 'treading or kicking things into one heap', but now usually for 'to smash' = *niedertreten* = 'to stamp on sth., smash sth. to smithereens'.

← See also under *abtreten* (also for *Abtritt*), *antreten* (also for *Antritt*), *auftreten* (also for *Auftritt*), *Auge* (for *jem.m unter die Augen treten* and *einer Pfütze ein Auge austreten*), *austreten, beitreten* (also for *Beitritt*), *betreten* (also for *Betretung* and *unbetreten sein*), *Brücke* (for *jem.m die Brücke treten*), *Dorn* (for *den Blumenpfad der Lust betreten*), *eintreten, fehl-* (for *fehltreten* and *Fehltritt*), *herantreten, hervortreten, Kot* (for *etw. in den Kot treten*), *krumm* (for *auch ein Wurm krümmt sich, wenn er getreten wird*), *kurz* (for *kurztreten*), *leise* (for *Leisetreter*), *link* (for *Vertretungsstaat*), *Mühle* (for *Tretmühle*), *nachtreten, nahe* (for *jem.m nahe treten* and *jem.m zu nahe treten*), *Orden* (for *in den Orden der Pantoffelhelden eintreten*), *Pfad* (for *einen Pfad treten* and *ausgetretene Pfade verlassen*), *Stelle* (for *auf der Stelle treten*), *subaltern* (for *Tretmühlenfleiß*), *Tag* (for *der Tag tritt zurück* and *zutage treten*) and *Tritt.*

treu: faithful, true, devoted, staunch

treu (1) faithful, true; with abstracts since MHG, e.g. Frauenlob [edit. Ettm.] 370,11: '*min triuwer muot*', f.r.b. *Voc.theut.* [1482]: '*trewes gemut*', often with *Herz* (also in Frauenlob), also since the 15th c. in *treuer Rat* = 'valuable (and well-meant) advice';

later also used in *treue Worte* (e.g. Goethe IV.8,213 (W.)), *treuer Dank, treue Grüße*, where the notion of 'affection' also enters into the term, e.g. Goethe 2,185 (W.).

treu (2) faithful, trusted, reliable; lit. rather than general with ref. to things, since the 18th c., e.g. A.W.Schlegel (in *Athen.* 2,276): '. . . faßt den treuen Degen*', Hebbel [edit.W.] 4,153: '*mein treuer Schild*'; not yet recorded by Adelung and Campe who only noted that ~ can also be applied to animals; such usage has been current since the 16th c.; the opposite *untreu* or *ungetreu* can be traced back further, e.g. Stumpf, *Schw.Chron.* 392a [1606]: '*ein untreuw wasser*', Lessing 2,198: '*die ungetreuen Ström' hinüber*'.

treu (3) faithful, rendering or depicting sth. exactly; since the 18th c., recorded by Adelung, e.g. *ein treuer Abdruck, ein treuer Bericht, eine treue Übersetzung, der Natur treues Bild*; very frequent now in compounds, usually with *getreu*, e.g. *naturgetreu* (as in Börne 1,213), *sinngetreu* (opposite *sinnentstellend*), *werkgetreu* = 'true to the original'. The noun *Treue* in this sense also since the 18th c., e.g. Lessing 4,13: '. . . durch allzugroße Treue ihren Lesern die Röthe ins Gesicht treiben*'.

treu (4) faithful (to sth.); with ref. to standing by sth. devotedly or courageously; often in compounds, e.g. *verfassungstreu*, as in Mommsen, *Röm.Gesch.* 3,287 [1854]. This can be intensified in various ways, e.g. *felsentreu*, as in Rückert 1,88: '*o Glück der felsentreuen Brust*', *festgetreu*, as in Chamisso 5,202: '*festgetreue Freunde*'; cf. also Heine 18,294: '*mit pudeltreuem Gemüthe*'.

treu (5) (lit., rare) exact, accurate; derived from ~ = 'true' (in the sense of *wahr*, already to be found in Gothic); in modern use since the 18th c., frequent in Goethe who used *treue Kenntnis* (in IV, 42,213 (W.)), *treues Aufmerken* (in 28,63 (W.)), *treues Auge* (in 24,370 (W.)), also in use for the result of having *treue Augen* or *treue Kenntnis* in *treuer Abriß* (in IV,36,26 (w.)), *treues Tagbuch* (in IV,8,23 (W.)), also adverbially, e.g. Goethe 16,126 (W.): '. . . erzählt das eben fix und treu . . .'; in the 19th c. still in *treues Bild, treuer Spiegel*, even for persons, e.g. Bauernfeld, *Ges.Schr.* 1,15: '*das muß man sagen, einen treuen Spiegel hab ich an meinem Bedienten!*'; now rare (*echt, wahr* or *genau* are preferred).

meiner Treu! (a.) on my honour, upon my word, truly! since Early NHG, as *auf meine Treu* (e.g. H.Sachs, *Fab.* 2,360: '*auf mein trew!*') or *bei meiner Treu* (e.g. Wieland 11,172) or *meiner Treu* (even *mein Treu*), now a.

einer Sache ~ *bleiben* to remain true to sth., hold on to sth.; also as *einer Sache die Treue halten*; with such abstracts as *Glaube, Grundsatz, Prinzip*, etc.; in earlier periods mostly as *getreu* (MHG *getriuwe*); with *bleiben* or *halten* general since the 16th c., e.g. Petri, *D.Teutsch.Weish.* [1604]: '*bleib trew in deinem christenthumb*'; *sich selbst* ~ *bleiben* became general in the 18th c. (Herder, Goethe, Schiller).

ein treues Gedächtnis a reliable memory; recorded since the 18th c.; cf. also Gellert 9,16: '*mein Gedächtnis ist mir sehr untreu*'; *gutes Gedächtnis* is now preferred.

zu treuer Hand in confidence, in trust; this arose through confirmation of an agreement by a handshake; since Late MHG, f.r.b. Frisius [1556]. Luther used '*zu trewer hand*' (in 15,34 (Weimar)) for 'in safe keeping' (cf. Maaler's recording '*zu trüwen handen gestelt*'), but the phrase also occurs as early as in the 15th c. with ref. to 'guardianship, wardship'. It must be even older, since Haltaus has traced *Treuhänder* back to 1283, which first meant 'guardian', later 'trustee, custodian, fiduciary'. Modern is *Treuhandgesellschaft*.

die Treue (personified) Fidelity; e.g. Herder, *Z.Litt.* 3,158: '*Liebe schwärmt auf allen Wegen, Treue wohnt für sich allein*'; often in proverbs with *Treu und Glauben*, e.g. Eyering, *Prov.cop.* [1601]: '*traw, glaub sind aus der welt gezogen*'; cf. Goethe 8,72 (W.): '*Treu und Glaube, du hast mich wieder betrogen*'.

auf Treu und Glauben in good faith; first in relig. contexts, then secular, since Early NHG, e.g. Schaidenreißer, *Odyssea* 65b [1538]: '*sie versprachens bei glauben und treuen*'; frequent in *Treu und Glauben halten* = 'to remain honest and true', f.r.b. Maaler [1561], e.g. Goethe 8,187 (W.): '*ich weiß wohl, daß Politik selten Treu und Glauben halten kann*', also *auf Treu und Glauben etwas annehmen*, as in Goethe 27,96 (W.).

Treu und Glauben erfordern . . . (legal) current morality or concepts of justice demand . . . ; with ref. to decisions in which the letter of the law can be set aside because its application would strike people as unjust and running counter to what in law is called *Verkehrssitte*, influenced by legal Lat. *bona fides*.

treuherzig guileless, simple; for 'faithful, reliable', also 'friendly', then also seen as 'trusting too much because of being good-natured' (since the 17th c., e.g. Grimmelshausen [edit. K.] 3,428), hence (by the 18th c.) 'naive', even 'simple'; now also, more explicit, in 20th c. pejor. coll. *treudoof*.

etw. betreuen to look after sth., attend to sth.; also with the notion of 'being in charge' for 'to supervise, handle, manage sth.'; a modern word, still missing in *DWb.* [1854] and all the 19th c. dictionaries I have consulted.

etw. veruntreuen to misappropriate sth.; Frisch [1741] in listing it described it as a euphemism for *stehlen*.

← See also under *brechen* (for *die Treue brechen*), *Eckart* (for *ein getreuer Eckart*), *Fahne* (for *treuer Untertan*), *Gold* (for *treu wie Gold*), *halten* (for *seine Getreuen, getreulich zu jem.m halten* and *Treu und Glauben halten*), *Hund* (for *treu wie ein Hund* and *Hundetreue*), *Muschel* (for *Muttertreue*, where the headword *Muschel* is regrettably missing), *Nibe-*

lungen (for *Nibelungentreue*), *Pudel* (for *treu wie ein Pudel* and *pudeltreu*), *stürzen* (for *treu gewarnet*) and *stützen* (for *treuer Held*).

Tribunal: tribunal

das ~ (lit.) tribunal, judgment seat: figur. since the 18th c., e.g. *jem. vor das* ~ *ziehen* = 'to force sb. to submit to judgment'; Schiller used *das innere* ~ for 'conscience' and *das* ~ *des Verstandes*; cf. also *das* ~ *der Geschichte* = 'the judgment of history', as in J.v. Müller 6,457 [1810].

Tribut: tribute

jem.m (or *einer Sache*) ~ *zollen* (lit.) to pay tribute to sb. (or sth.), acknowledge the merits of sb. (or sth.); since the 18th c., e.g. Kant (Acad.Edit.) 5,77: '*Achtung ist ein Tribut, den wir dem Verdienst nicht verweigern können*'.

den ~ *der Natur zahlen* (lit.) to die; since the 16th c., e.g. Bode, transl. of *Tristram S.* 5,32 [1774]: '*Sterben ist der große, der Natur schuldige Zoll und Tribut*'; also sometimes with ref. to illness, as in Goethe IV, 29,277 (W.).

Trichter: funnel

der ~ (1) funnel through which knowledge is poured into sb.; since early in the 16th c., e.g. Franck II,107b [1541], Fischart, *Bien.* 39a: '*gleichsam mit einem trechter eingegossen . . .*', Abr. a S. Clara, *Etw.f.Alle* 1,264: '*. . . kleine trachter . . . wodurch man könnte einem strohkopf die wissenschaft eingießen*'; often in *Nürnberger* ~, a ref. to the title of a book by Harsdörffer (Nürnberg, 1647), which claimed to teach poetry in six lessons (but earlier was *Der hebraische Trächter, die sprach leicht einzugießen* by W.Schickhardt (Tübingen, 1627)), e.g. Hebel 8,216: '*. . . denn der Nürnberger Trichter ist schon vor dem siebenjährigen Krieg zerbrochen*'; hence also *hier hilft kein Nürnberger Trichter* (prov. expr.) = 'he is too stupid to learn', recorded by Wander [1875].

der ~ (2) (med.) *infundibulum cerebri*; name for a passage in the brain; recorded by Bock, *Anatom.* 517 [1838], but as early as in the 16th c. it was compared to a funnel by Ryff, *Anatomi* M1a [1541]. Bock also recorded ~ for the cavity of the cochlear turn in the ear.

der ~ (3) (archit.) funnel-shaped lecture theatre; e.g. Goethe, *Ital.Reise* I: '*in einem hohen spitzen Trichter sind die Zuhörer über einander geschichtet*'. According to Zuccalmagno-Waldbrühl (in Brugger, *Dt.Eiche* [1850]) the pointed top section of a steeple is also referred to by architects as *der* ~.

der ~ (4) (zool.) limpet; ~ is used for some limpets such as *Patella graeca* and *Patella nimbosa*; recorded by Nemnich. The coral *Mandrepora crater* is also called ~.

der ~ (5) crater; recorded by Eggers for the crater made by an exploding projectile [1757], by Campe [1810] for the crater of a volcano; current compounds are *Bombentrichter* and *Granattrichter*, since the 19th c.

Trichter-. . . funnel-shaped . . .; in many

compounds and in many contexts, mainly since the 19th c. (Adelung mentioned only one plant under this heading, Campe a few plants and animals and one tech. compound). The chief ones now are *Trichterbrust* (med.) 'funnel-chest', *Trichtergewölbe* (archit.) = 'fan vaulting', *Trichterlautsprecher* = 'cone speaker' and *Trichtermündung* (geogr.) = 'estuary'.

auf den ~ kommen (coll.) to discover or understand sth., be on the right track; as early as in the 17th c. as *sich auf dem ~ finden*, e.g. (DWb) B.v.d. Sohle, *Don Kichote* 19 [1648], now with *kommen*, e.g. G.Hauptmann, *Der rote Hahn* IV [1901].,

jem. auf den ~ bringen (coll.) to start sb. off on the right foot, give sb. a clue; since the 18th c., e.g. Musäus, *Physiog.Reisen* 2,82 [1778].

auf dem ~ sein (coll.) to have arrived at a solution, be in the picture; since the 18th c. and still today, e.g. (T.) Schröer. *Mannesehre* 352 [1931].

jem. in den ~ jagen (regional coll.) to corner sb., drive sb. to the wall; recorded for Swabia by Fischer; same as *jem. in die Enge treiben*.

← See also under *eintrichtern*.

Trieb: driving force; germinating power; young shoot

der ~ (1) impulse, urge, desire to be active; since Early NHG, f.r.b. Maaler [1561]; in Schottel [1663] glossed with *instinctus*; e.g. Hagedorn, *Poet.W.* 2,72 [1757]: '*da wollte die Vernunft und selbst die Triebe wollten, daß wir gesellig sein*', Wieland 9,185: '*zur ungebundensten Befriedigung jedes thierischen Triebes*' or 27,54: '*dieser stolze, wunderbare Trieb nach dem Unendlichen*', Schiller, *Braut v.M.* 2078: '*Trieb des Bluts*', *Glocke* 316: '*Trieb zum Vaterlande*', Arndt, 368: '*Lieb* ist . . . *die Mutter aller milden Triebe*'.

der ~ (2) (lit.) shoot; image derived from plants, figur. since the 18th c., e.g. Wieland, *Ob.* 6,43 on an old man: '. . . *schien vor hohem Muth zu schwellen . . . es war der letzte Trieb von einem dürren Holz*', Freiligrath 2,124 (or 3,52): '*der Knospe Deutschland regt sich's . . . ein alter Trieb, doch immer muthig keimend*'.

der ~ (3) (obs.) flock, crowd; a ref. to *~* = 'herd, flock'; figur. occasionally in the 18th c., e.g. Schiller, *Eberh.d.Gr.*: '*um ihn her der Helden Trieb*'; now obs.

das Getriebe (1) the wheels, the machinery; figur. since the 18th c., e.g. Thümmel, *D.heil.K.* 45: '*wann das Getriebe der Lebensquelle dir trocken blieb*', Goethe, *Was wir bringen* (Forts.): '*denn stockt einmal der ernsten Kunst Getriebe, dann wirkt Natur mit ihrem eignen Triebe*', Gutzkow, *R.v.G.* 1,164: '*Ehrgeiz ist die Achse des ganzen Getriebs*'.

das Getriebe (2) fuss, bustle, commotion; since the 18th c., e.g. (DWb) Baggesen, *Ad.u.Eva* 10: '*das Leben . . . scheint mir ein stetes Treiben und Getriebe*', Rückert, 88: '*das verworrene Getriebe der Zeit*'.

Umtriebe (pejor.) machinations, subversive activities, intrigues; since the 17th c., e.g. Moscherosch, *Phil.* 1,233 [1650]; since the 19th c. generally in polit. contexts, e.g. *demagogische Umtriebe*; hence *umtriebig*, also *umtrieberisch* (since the 19th c.), now also in a noun *Umtriebigkeit* (20th c.). *Umtrieber* and *Umtriebler* (19th c.) are now rarely heard.

← See also under *antreiben* (for *Antrieb*), *auftreiben* (for *Auftrieb*), *befriedigen* (for *einen Trieb befriedigen*), *betreiben* (for *Betrieb* and *auf seinen Betrieb*), *bezähmen* (for *Triebe bezähmen*), *Feder* (for *die Triebfeder*), *Frühling* (for *Frühlingstrieb*), *gelten* (for *der Geltungstriebwagen*), *groß* (for *Triebe . . . die vergnügen*), *hoch* (for *Hochbetrieb*), *Johann* (for *Johannistrieb*), *Not* (for *der Not gehorchend, nicht dem eignen Triebe*), *Sand* (for *Sand im Getriebe*), *selbst* (for *Selbsterhaltungstrieb*), *sublimieren* (for *rohe Triebstrebungen*) and *Sünde* (for *Sündentrieb*).

triefen: drip, trickle

von etw. ~ (lit.) to be full of or rich in sth.; beginnings in Early NHG with a phys. basis, e.g. in the Bible, Joel 3,23: '. . . *werden die Berge von süßem Wein triefen*', then extended since the 18th c., e.g. H.v.Kleist [edit. S.] 2,212: '. . . *deren junge Seele . . . von . . . Schönheit gänzlich triefte*', Seume 2,219: '*jeder Fußtritt triefe von Segen*'; sometimes expressing disgust at a superfluity of sth., e.g. Laube, *Ges.Schr.* 15,65: '*er triefte von Kenntnissen*', Bismarck, *Ged.u.Errinn.* 1,279. '*wenngleich ihr Adreßentwurf von Loyalitätsversicherungen trieft*'.

trillen: see *drillen*.

trinken: drink

etw. ~ (lit.) to drink in, enjoy, absorb sth.; since Early NHG, e.g. Luther Bible transl. Job 34,7: '*Hiob, der da spötterei trinkt wie wasser*', Goethe, *Schatzgräber* 33: '*trinke Muth des reinen Lebens*', Schiller, *An die Freude*: '*in der Traube goldnem Blut trinken Sanftmuth Kannibalen, die Verzweiflung Heldenmuth*', Heine, *Lied.* 118: '*dort wollen wir . . . Liebe und Ruhe trinken*', Daumer, *Hafis* 1,210: '*ich möchte wohl ein Spiegel sein . . . um jene reine Wohlgestalt . . . zu trinken*'.

von etw. ~ (lit.) to drink, taste, imbibe sth.; with ref. to abstracts since Early NHG, e.g. Luther Bible transl. Prov. 4,17: '*vom wein des frevels trinken*', Job 21,26: '*vom grimm des allmächtigen trinken*', Schiller, *Semele* 116: '*die Tochter Kadmus trinkt vom Lethe nicht*'; cf. also Keller, *Abendlied*.

aus etw. ~ (lit.) to drink from or out of sth.; in images since the 18th c., e.g. Göckingk 3,103: '. . . *trinkt er aus der Sorgen Schale*', Klinger, *Seidenwurm* 114 [1780]: '*mein Ohr spitzt sich, aus Allem Ruhm zu trinken*'.

etw. trinkt etw. anderes sth. drinks or soaks sth. up, absorbs sth.; figur. with objects seen as 'drinking'; since Early NHG, e.g. Luther Bible transl. Hebrews 6,7: '*die erde, die den regen trincket*', Haller, 42: '*das . . . Thal . . . trinkt ein beständig Thau*'; often with *Ohr* as the subject, since the 18th c., e.g. F.Schlegel, *Luc.* 62: '. . .

Accente, die das Ohr nicht zu hören, sondern wirklich zu trinken scheint'.

sich Bettschwere ~ (coll.) to drink enough to make one thoroughly sleepy; this began as *sich ein Bett* ~,e.g. (T.) Friderich, *Sauffteuffel* 41 [1552], only in modern period with *Bettschwere*.

mit den Gänsen ~ (coll.) to drink nothing but water; since the 18th c., e.g. Wieland 1,132.

← See also under *Gans* (for *sauf Gänswein*).

~ *wie.* . . . to drink, booze like . . .; in many coll. comparisons, some of which have already been listed under *saufen* on p. 2065. To these can be added: ~ *wie ein Frosch*, f.r.b. Henisch [1616] (much earlier than stated on p. 2065), *wie ein Kapuziner* (recorded by Wander), *wie ein Loch*, e.g. Geibel, *Ein lustiger Musikante* and *wie ein Mühlrad* (recorded by Wander).

für (or *um*) *ein Trinkgeld* (coll.) for a mere pittance; *Trinkgeld* = 'tip' started as 'money paid for what one has drunk' (14th c.) and in the same c. developed into 'money given to sb. to buy himself a drink', also to 'reward for small services rendered' (sometimes called *Trinkpfennig*, recorded since 1562);since the 17th c. also for gifts which did not consist of money; lastly, since the 18th c. contemptuously for a small sum, inappropriate reward, e.g. Gleim, *Briefw.* [edit. K.] 1,173, cf. also *trinkgeldhungrig* = 'eagerly expecting a tip', modern, e.g. (Dwb) Bartels, *Dichterleben* 88 [1890]: '*trinkgeldhungrig wie nur ein Lakai*'.

schlaftrunken drowsy, drugged with sleep; since Early NHG, f.r.b. Maaler [1561], e.g. H.Sachs 2,88a [1591]: '*und war noch wol halber schlaftrunken*'. Later extended to the state of mind, e.g. Herder, *Z.Rel.u.Theol.* 7,93: '*noch weniger dürfen wir ihm* (i.e. the spirit of the period) *entsagen und . . . mit einem schlaftrunkenen Auge zurückblicken*'. The noun *Schlaftrunkenheit* only since the 18th c. (often in Herder, sometimes in the sense of 'dumb inertia').

← See also under *austrinken*, *Bart* (for *durch den Bart trinken*), *betrinken*, *bitter* (for *das Bittere getrunken haben*), *Blut* (for *Tapferkeit trinken*), *Bruder* (for *Bruderschaft trinken* and *Trinkbruder*), *durchtränken*, *ertränken*, *ertrinken*, *Fisch* (for *Fischtrank* and *Fischtrunk*), *Freude* (for *freudetrunken*), *Glas* (for *es ertrinken mehr im Glas dann in allen Wassern* and *ein Glas zuviel* or *über den Durst trinken*), *Hand* (for *sich auf seine Hand betrinken*), *Igel* (for *trinken wie ein Igel*), *Kelch* (for *den Kelch trinken*), *lahm* (for *bei Säufern lernt man trinken*), *Pfütze* (for *aus allen Pfützen trinken*), *Rebe* (for *Klagen ertränken*), *saufen* (for *jem. unter den Tisch saufen/trinken* and *Gesundheittrinken*), *sprechen* (for *trink, was klar ist*), *steif* (for *sich steif trinken*) and *Trunk*.

Trio: trio

das ~ trio (of people); originally (early in the 18th c.) only a mus. term; since the 18th c. also for 'three persons playing music' and 'three persons' (without ref. to music); e.l. (DWb) Henrici, *Ernst*

. . . *Ged*. 2,394 [1727].

Tritt: step, kick

der ~ (lit.) step, move made by sb.; since MHG, e.g. Seuse [edit. B.] 236; in this figur. sense the same as *Schritt*; often in *der erste* ~ *in etw.* = 'the start (in an office, profession, etc.)'.

jem.m or *einer Sache einen* ~ (or *Tritte*) *geben* to kick sb. or sth., put sth. aside (in anger or with contempt), also sometimes with the intention of inflicting pain; since the 18th c., e.g. Klopstock, *Gelehrtenrep.* 153 [1774] or Goethe 5,124 (W.): '. . . *wirst den vier Winden noch Tritte geben*'.

~ *fassen* to fall in step; derived from the mil. sense with ref. to marching 'in step'; then transferred to 'regular behaviour' (after some disturbance or aberration), 'acceptable conduct' (after having been 'out of step'); modern.

der Rücktritt resignation, retirement, withdrawal; late in the 18th c. derived from *von etw. zurücktreten*, e.g. Herder [edit. Müller] 11,76, Grillparzer 3,191: '*hast du gewählt, dann ist kein Rücktritt mehr*', f.r.b. Campe [1810].

der Trittbrettfahrer (coll.) undeserving beneficiary; literally 'traveller on the running-board of a moving vehicle'; pejor. term since the 2nd half of the 20th c. for sb. who benefits by the exertions of others, although he only joined them for selfish motives, became a 'hanger-on' and contributed little or nothing to the success of the enterprise.

← See also under *abtreten* (for *Abtritt*), *antreten* (for *Antritt*), *auftreten* (for *Auftritt*), *beitreten* (for *Beitritt*), *fehl-* (for *Fehltritt*), *Mißtritt* and *Schritt* (for *auf Schritt und Tritt* and *jem.m auf Schritt und Tritt folgen*).

trocken: dry

trocken (1) dry; with ref. to utterances and ways of speaking; derived from mediaeval doctrines about differing temperaments depending on juices in the body, in which melancholy persons were said to be 'dry'; since MHG, f.r.b. Maaler [1561]: '*trockenlich reden, das ist wenig und kaum oder ungern*', e.g. Goethe, *Faust I*, 2009: '*ich bin des trocknen Tons nun satt*', Huch, *Pitt u. Fox* 246: '*dieses halb trocken herausgesprochene Wort*' or ibid. 87: '*ihre Stimme hatte einen belegten, trockenen Klang*'; often in association with *dürr* (see p. 537) or contrasted with *feucht* (see p. 775); usually with a tinge of pejoration, but not pejor. in *trockener Humor*, which arose in modern times under Engl. influence.

trocken (2) dull, uninteresting, jejune; since the 18th c., when Lessing 8,426 still put it in inverted commas: '. . . *mit der "trocknesten" Aufschrift eines alten Denkmals*', e.g. Goethe, *Faust I*,521: '*der trockne Schleicher*', Schiller, *Räuber* 1,1: '*der trockne Alltagsmensch*'; hence *Trockenheit*, also since the 18th c., mainly with ref. to style, e.g. (Sp.) Zschokke, *Lebensgesch.Umr.* 42: '. . . *gedrängt ohne Trockenheit*'.

trocken (3) cold, unfriendly, plain; used as an

adj. and as an adv. since Early NHG, e.g. Luther, *S.Werke* 61,105: *'wir sagens dem Papst trucken heraus'*, Goethe, *Dicht.u.Wahrh.* 1,3: *'trockene Galanterie'*, Immermann, *Münchh.* 1,358: '. . . *nahm kurz und trocken seinen Urlaub'*; Adelung recorded: *'ein trockener Empfang'*.

trocken (4) dry, plain; with ref. to the absence of a beverage or some other addition; since Early NHG, e.g. Luther Bible transl. Prov. 17,1: *'ein trockener bissen'*, often with ref. to bread, e.g. *von trockenem Brot leben müssen*, but also extended. *Trockenes Fleisch* can mean 'meat without some relish or a gravy', *trockener Kaffee* is coffee without cake or biscuits. This began in Early NHG, e.g. Mathesius, *Luther* 68a [1576]: *'trucken tisch'* for 'meal without a beverage' (still today as *trockenes Gedeck*), f.r.b. Kramer, *N.Dict.* [1678]: *'trocken essen id est ohne trinken'*. A mediaeval example is *trockene Messe* (translating *missa sicca*) for 'Mass without a priest and wine'.

trocken (5) dried-out, emaciated, shrunk; since Early NHG, f.r.b. Maaler [1561], e.g. Goethe 45,231 (W): *'ein großer Mann, trocken und mager, eingeschrumpften Unterleibs'*.

trocken (6) (coll. or regional) on its own, without anything else being taken into consideration; mainly in adverbial locutions, e.g. (Sanders) *das ist ~ ein Verdienst von 100 Taler* or *'die Reise kommt an 100 Thaler, schon das Postgeld kostet trocken 30'*. This usage comes close to ~ = 'plain, downright', as in *trockene Lüge*, f.r.b. Stieler [1691]. One might even link ~ in sport contexts, e.g. *'mit einer trockenen Rechten schlug er ihn k.o.'* with this sense.

trocken (7) dry, restricted as to alcohol consumption; modern, e.g. *ein trockenes Land*; cf. ~ *sein* (coll.) = 'to remain abstinent', e.g. *er ist jetzt ~ und hat versprochen, es zu bleiben*.

trocken (8) dry; with ref. to fermented beverages as in *trockener Wein* or *Sekt*; recorded since Early NHG.

im Trocknen sein (coll.) to be in safety, out of the wood; originally = 'under cover, out of the rain'; figur. since the 18th c., e.g. Lessing 12,252: *'wenn ich nur erst wider auf dem Trocknen, d.i. aus meinen Schulden sein werde'*, also Schiller, *Räuber* 1,2 (with *kommen*) and *ibid.* 2,3 (with *sein*). Apparently not much used now, since recent dictionaries do not list it.

auf dem trocknen sitzen (coll.) to be stranded, on the rocks, in low water; it can refer to all kinds of difficulties, not only financial ones; in this form it arose in the 19th c. (not yet listed by Campe), but before then there was *jem. auf Trockne setzen* (coll.) = 'to put sb. into difficulties' (a nautical image), since the 18th c., e.g. Voß, *Theokrit* 1,51 [1808]; cf. Lessing 5,2: *'eine sehr leichte Antwort, mit welcher man nie auf dem Trocknen bleibt'*. ~ In joc. coll. *auf dem Trocknen sitzen* can also mean 'to have nothing to drink, sit before an empty glass'.

sein Schäfchen ins Trockene bringen (coll.) to make sure of safeguarding one's interests, see oneself all right; also sometimes with the notion of feathering one's own nest; usually in the diminutive, though *Schaf* or *Lämmer* also can be used; recorded since the 16th c., e.g. Goethe 12,121 (W.): *'schon so sicher, daß dein Schäfchen im Trocknen ist?'*. The argument that *Schiffchen* in its LG form *Schepken* led to *Schäfchen* has continued but not been decided.

sein Schiff ins Trockne bringen (coll.) to attain one's object, salvage sth.; an old nautical image, but younger than the previous entry; e.g. Leibniz, *Dt.Schr.* [edit. G.] 1,253: *'die teutschgesinnte Allianz . . . einzugehen und unser Schiff ins Trockne zu bringen'*.

jem. ~ scheren (coll.) to cheat, over-charge or fleece sb.; since the 13th c., e.g. *Buch der Rügen* (in *ZfdA.* 2,78) about knights: *'ir hiezt schersere vil baz. ir schert trucken unde naz'*, also H.Sachs [edit. K.-G.] 11,215: '. . . *hab im trucken ausgeschorn'*; later often = *anführen*, *verulken*.

← See also under *balbieren* (for *jem. trocken balbieren*) and *rasieren* (for *jem. trocken rasieren*).

ein trockener Wechsel (econ.) promissory note; translates Ital. *cambio secco*; in German since the 18th c.; Schiebe, *Kaufmänn.Handwb.* 136 [1833] recorded: *'trockene Wechsel sind von und auf sich selbst ausgestellte Wechsel'*.

der Trockenwohner (obs.) poor person allowed to live in a new building without paying rent until the house has dried out; coined in 1863 in Berlin; f.r.b. Ladendorf, *Hist.Schlagwb.* [1906], e.g. Raabe, *Werke* 2,6,416 (*Prinz.F.*): '. . . *habe keine Lust, den Trockenwohner für des Städtles Zukunftsbevölkerung zu spielen'*; now obs.

← See also under *April* (for *trockner April . . .*), *aufhängen* (for *jem. zum Lufttrocknen aufhängen*), *auftrocknen*, *Auge* (for *mit einem trocknen und einem nassen Auge* and *da blieb kein Auge trocken*), *austrocknen*, *dürr* (for *trockene Wahrheit*), *Faden* (for *es bleibt kein trockner Faden an einem*), *Faser* (for *keine trockene Faser mehr am Leib haben*), *Fisch* (for *wie ein Fisch auf trocknem Sand*), *Ohr* (for *noch nicht trocken hinter den Ohren sein*), *Oskar* (for *trockner Oskar*), *Pulver* (for *sein Pulver trocken halten*), *Staub* (for *staubtrocken*), *Stroh* (for *trocken wie Stroh* and *strohtrocken*), *Stunde* (for *die trockene Stunde*), *Sumpf* (for *einen Sumpf trockenlegen*) and *Träne* (for *jem.s Tränen trocknen*).

Trödel: lumber, rubbish; trade with cheap things

der ~ (1) (pejor.) rubbish; figur. with ref. to abstracts; since the 18th c., although pejoration began in polemic religious writings in Early NHG, e.g. Luther 34,1,212 and 26,234 (Weimar); e.g. (DWb) Lose, *Schattenrisse* 2,46 [1783]: '. . . *die Ettikette, diesen anständigen Trödel'*, Immermann, *Werke* [edit. B.] 2,168: *'der müffigste mystische Trödel'*, Heine 6,243: *'Minne und Glaube und wie der mittelalterliche Trödel sonst heißt'* (where the notions of 'antiquated' and 'worthless' are combined); hence also pejor. *Trödelkram*, as in Schiller, *Räuber* 2,3, *Trödelei* (rare) = 'occupation with old things or ideas', as in Mommsen 1,144: '*die spätere, der . . . Alterthumströdelei ergebene römische Bildung*' and *Getrödel* = pejor. ~, as in Tieck, *Novellenkranz* 2,240 (1831).

der ~ (2) (obs. or regional coll.) fun, entertainment; in some regions also = 'gay party, merry goings-on' and elsewhere = 'row, quarrel'; first in stud.sl., e.g. Immermann, *Cardenio* 3 [1820]: '*es macht mir keinen Trödel*' = 'I don't enjoy it'.

den ~ *satt haben* (coll.) to be tired of the whole wretched business; ~ treated as sth. tedious or annoying like *Kram*, *Zeug* and similar nouns; recorded since the 19th c., e.g. by Wander [1876].

trödeln (lit., rare) to deal (with some subject); from *trödeln* = 'to buy and sell, barter, trade'; pejor. since Early NHG, e.g. Luther 31,1,31 (Weimar): '*wie schendtlich sie mit der messen gehandelt und getreudelt haben*', Merck, *Ausgew.Schr.* [edit. Stahr] 186: '. . . *als derjenige, der mit spekulativer Weisheit getrödelt hat*'. Note that, according to a majority of scholars, *trödeln* = 'to move slowly, be dilatory, make little progress' does not belong to ~, but to regional coll. *trudeln* (in some regions *trotteln* or *drudeln*); this has many compounds such as *herumtrodeln*, *hin- und hertrödeln*, is much used in *die Zeit vertrödeln*; f.r.b. Schwan [1782]; hence also *trödelhaft* = 'sluggish(ly)', as in Herder (edit. M.) 13,188 and *Trödler* = 'dawdler, slow-coach', as in Lessing 12,400: '*er war der unglaublichste Verzögerer und Trödler*' (in modern coll. as *Trödelfritze*, femin. *Trödelliese*, *Trödelsuse*). A minority opinion believes in derivation from *trödeln* = 'to barter', which could include the notion of slowness and could have led to the sense of 'being dilatory'.

die Trödlerin, also *Trödlerschnecke* (zool.) carrier shell; a slug which Oken 5,446 recorded under its old classification as *Trochus conchyliophorus*; it received its German name from the fact that much 'rubbish', such as little stones, bits of shell, etc. cling to its back.

Trog: trough
der ~ (lit., rare) deep hollow (esp. one filled with water); perhaps influenced by Engl. mar. 'trough'; since the 19th c., e.g. *Gartenlaube* 10,436a about a ship: '. . . *fiel etwas ab, fuhr tief in den Trog der See*', where in the standard language one might use *Wellental*.

wie das Vieh am Troge (coll.) greedily, trying to grab what one can get; beginnings in Early NHG, e.g. in prov. as recorded by Franck [1541]; still in recent times, e.g. (T.) Stratz, *D.dt. Wunder* 53 [1916]: '*sie sind wie das Vieh am Troge, wenn sie sich bereichern! Jeder nimmt! Alles stiehlt!*'; cf. also figur. *Futtertrog*, as in Tim Kröger, *Nov.* 6,217 [1904]: '. . . *den Kampf um den Futtertrog der Ehe, der ehelichen Versorgung*'. See also under *Futter* for similar idioms.

← See also under *Ferkel* (for *wenn das Ferkel satt ist, stößt es den Trog um*), *Sau* (for *hinlaufen wie die Sau zum Trog* and *davonlaufen wie die Sau vom Trog*) and *Schwein* (for *wenn die Schweine satt sind, werfen sie den Trog um*).

Troglodyt: troglodyte
der ~ (lit.) primitive creature, savage; as a term of contempt since the 18th c., e.g. Haller, *Tagebuch* 2,326 [1787] on atheists: '. . . *alle Handlung wird unter diesen neuen Troglodyten nicht anders als baar gegen baar*', also Herder [edit. S.] 1,246.

Troika: troika
die (lit., polit.) troika, group or team of three people; often in polit. contexts with ref. to a ruling group of three, where it means the same as 'triumvirate'; 20th c.

Troja: Troy
ein Trojanisches Pferd (lit.) a Trojan horse, person or object offered or played into sb.'s hands with the aim of bringing about his downfall, wooden horse of Troy; from Virgil's account of the destruction of Troy; known since mediaeval times. The figur. meaning must have been obvious from the beginning to every reader of the story. See also under *Pferd* (p. 1858) for *das hölzerne Pferd*.

Trommel: drum
die ~ drum-shaped container; frequent in compounds, e.g. *Blechtrommel*, *Botanisiertrommel*, *Pflanzentrommel*, all only recorded since the 19th c., e.g. *Lotterietrommel* from which lots are drawn, as in Rahel, *Buch d.And.* 2,485 [1834]; cf. also L.Büchner, *Leb.* 21 [1861]: '*das silberne Trommelchen mit ausgesuchtem Backwerk*'. Numerous appliances used in various trades in which material is cleaned, polished or mixed, are also called ~; earliest recordings appeared in the 18th c., e.g. Nicolai, *Reise d.Deutschl.* 1,91 [1783].

die ~ *im Ohr*, *Ohrtrommel* eardrum, tympanum; called ~ until the 18th c., then usually *Ohrtrommel*; recorded by Kramer [1702] as *Ohrtrummel*.

die ~ or *Sticktrommel* embroidery-frame; since the 18th c., e.g. Wieland, *Liebe um Liebe* 1,49: '. . . *an der Trommel, stickte ein Blümchen in ihrer Stickerei*'; now usually called *Stickrahmen*, but in Dillmont, *Encycl.d.w.Handarbeiten* [1893] still referred to as ~.

das Getrommel, *die Trommelei* drumming; in wider sense = 'insistent noise'; figur. since the 18th c., e.g. Kl.Schmidt, *Kom.D.* 261 [1802]: '*dein Name widertönt mir lieblicher im Herzen als alle Trommelei der späten Folgewelt*' or Auerbach, *Tageb. aus Wien 98 [1849]*: '. . . *daß derartiges Wortgetrommel . . . Eindruck macht*'.

der ~ *folgen* to join the army; beginnings in Early NHG, e.g. H.Sachs, *Fab.* 2,113: '*pald ein solch man die trumel hort, so wil er spies und harnisch kaufen*'; later with *folgen*, e.g. Spangenberg, *Ausgew. Dicht.* 319 or Gellert 1,275; cf. synonymous *dem Kalbsfell folgen*, for which see p. 1426.

KEY TO PRINCIPAL ABBREVIATIONS

jem.m	jemandem (dat.)
Kluge	F. Kluge, *Etymologisches Wörterbuch der deutschen Sprache*, 11th ed., Berlin und Leipzig 1934.
Lehman	C. Lehman, *Florilegium Politicum*, etc., Frankfurt 1640.
Lexer	M. Lexer, *Mittelhochdeutsches Handwörterbuch*, Leipzig 1872—8.
LG	Low German
Lipperheide	F. Freih. v. Lipperheide, *Spruchwörterbuch*, 2nd ed., München 1909.
MHG	Middle High German
mil.	military
M. Latin	medieval Latin
N.	Northern Germany
NED	*Oxford English Dictionary, A New English Dictionary on Historical Principles*, Edited by Sir James Murray, Henry Bradley, W. A. Craigie and C. T. Onions. Oxford 1884—1928.
NHG	New High German
NW	North-Western Germany
obs.	obsolete
OE	Old English
offic.	in civil service language
OHG	Old High German
ON	Old Norse
OS	Old Saxon
Oxf.	*The Oxford Dictionary of English Proverbs*, compiled by W. G. Smith, Oxford, 1935.
p.	page
poet.	used mainly in poetic language
pop.	popular
pop. etym.	popular etymology
prov.	proverb, proverbial
sb.	somebody
Schmeller	J. A. Schmeller, *Bayerisches Wörterbuch*, Stuttgart 1827—37.
Schulz-Basler	G. Schulz und O. Basler, *Deutsches Fremdwörterbuch*, Strassburg und Berlin 1913ff.
s.e.	self-explanatory
sl.	slang
S. Singer	S. Singer, *Sprichwörter des Mittelalters*, Bern 1944—7.
sth.	something
SW.	South-Western Germany
Trübner	*Trübners Deutsches Wörterbuch*, herausg. v. A. Götze, Berlin 1939ff.
v.	verse, verses
vulg.	in vulgar use (obscene terms are included under this heading, but specially marked as such)
Waag	A. Waag, *Die Bedeutungsentwicklung unseres Wortschatzes*, 5th ed., Lahr 1926.
Wb.	Wörterbuch
Weigand	F. L. K. Weigand, *Deutsches Wörterbuch*, 5th ed., Gießen 1909—10.
Weist.	Weistümer; usually the collection by J. Grimm, Göttingen 1840—69 is referred to; Österr, is appended to the Austrian collections.
Westph.	Westphalia, Westphalian
zool.	zoological term.

Where later editions than those cited above have been quoted (especially in the cases of Büchmann, Dornseiff and Kluge), details of the editions used are given in the text.

The abbreviations for journals mostly follow the accepted practice (*MLR for Modern Language Review, MLN for Modern Language Notes, IF for Indogermanische Forschungen*, etc.), only some long titles have been still further abbreviated though still left recognizable (e.g. *Z.f.d.W.* for *Zeitschrift für deutsche Wortforschung, Z.f.d.U.* for *Zeitschrift für den deutschen Unterricht, Z.f.r.P.* for *Zeitschrift für romanische Philologie*, etc.). Other works, referred to or quoted have been mentioned in abbreviated but recognizable form. It is intended to give a comprehensive list of them when the dictionary is completed. From Fasc. 9 Goethe (W.) = Weimar edition, Schiller (S.) = Säkularausgabe.

ISBN 0 631 188223

An Historical Dictionary of German Figurative Usage

By KEITH SPALDING

PROFESSOR EMERITUS OF GERMAN, UNIVERSITY COLLEGE OF NORTH WALES, BANGOR

WITH ASSISTANCE FROM
GERHARD MÜLLER-SCHWEFE

PROFESSOR EMERITUS OF ENGLISH,
UNIVERSITY OF TÜBINGEN

Fascicle 53

Trompete – unterlegen

KEY TO PRINCIPAL ABBREVIATIONS

a.	archaic
Adolphi	O. Adolphi, *Das große Buch der Fliegenden Worte, etc.*, Berlin n.d.
Abd. Gl.	*Die Althochdeutschen Glossen*, ges. und bearb. von E. Steinmeyer u. Eduard Sievers, Berlin 1879—98.
Bav.	Bavaria, Bavarian
bot.	botanical term
Büchmann	G. Büchmann, *Geflügelte Worte*, 27th ed., ergänzt von A. Langen, Berlin 1915.
c.	century
Car.	Carinthia, Carinthian
cf.	compare
cl.	cliché
Cod.	codex
coll.	in colloquial use
comm.	used in language of commerce
dial.	dialect expression
Dornseiff	F. Dornseiff, *Der deutsche Wortschatz nach Sachgruppen*, Berlin und Leipzig 1934.
dt.	deutsch
DWb	*Deutsches Wörterbuch von Jacob Grimm und Wilhelm Grimm*, Leipzig 1854ff.
e.l.	earliest locus or earliest loci
etw.	etwas
Fast. Sp.	Fastnachtspiele, usually quoted after *Fastnachtspiele aus dem 15. Jahrbundert*, herausgeg. v. Keller, Stuttgart 1853.
Fick	F. C. A. Fick, *Vergleichendes Wörterbuch der indogermanischen Sprachen*, 3rd ed. Göttingen 1874.
f.r.b.	first recorded by
gen.	general
Götze	A. Götze, *Frühneuhochdeutsches Glossar*, 2nd ed., Bonn 1920.
Graff	E. G. Graff, *Althochdeutscher Sprachschatz*, Berlin 1834—42.
Hirt, *Etym.*	H. Hirt, *Etymologie der neuhochdeutschen Sprache*, 2nd ed.; München 1925.
Hirt, *Gesch.*	H. Hirt, *Geschichte der deutschen Sprache*, 2nd ed., München 1925.
hunt.	word or expression used by huntsmen
jem.	jemand (nom. or acc.)

© *Basil Blackwell Ltd., 1993 ISBN 0 631 188231*
Typeset by Hope Services, Abingdon
Printed and bound by Whitstable Litho Ltd., Whitstable, Kent.

vor der ~ *heiraten* (hist.) to get married whilst on active service; a drum took the place of an altar when the marriage was solemnized when the man was under arms; now only in hist. accounts, e.g. C.F. Meyer, *Nov.* 1,222: '*mit siebzehn hat er eine Fünfzehnjährige vor der Trommel geheiratet*'.

jem. m ein Loch in der ~ *machen* (coll., obs.?) to queer sb.'s pitch, spoil sb.'s pleasure, harm sb. deliberately; recorded since the 17th c., e.g. Lehman, *Floril.pol.* 2,795 [1662]: '*mäußdreck unter pfeffer mischen, der trummel ein loch machen*'; still in Thümmel, *Reise* 2,177 [1811] and Brentano, *Ges. Schr.* 7,312 [1852]; now obs.?

die Werbetrommel (also *Reklametrommel*) *für etw. rühren* (or *schlagen*) to make propaganda for sth. (or sb.); cf. Engl. 'to drum up custom'; *die* ~ *rühren* could mean 'to prepare for war', e.g. Opitz, *Poem.*, 1,52 [1629]: '*wenn Mars die trummel rührt*' or 'to recruit men for the army', e.g. H. Sachs [edit. K.] 9,485: '*wo sich die drummel rüret laut, so lauffen tzu die lantzknecht gleich*', but this is obs. and modern usage (since the 19th c.) refers to calling attention to sth.

das Trommelfell (med.) eardrum, tympanic membrane; since Early NHG, first as *Trummenfell* or *Trummelfell* for the hide of the drum, for part of the ear since the 18th c., in Schiller, *Räuber* 4,5 as *Trommelhaut*, in Adelung as *Trommelhäutchen*.

trommeln to drum with one's fingers, beat the devil's tattoo; it can express impatience or displeasure; current since the 18th c., e.g. Voß, *Sämtl.Ged.* 3,129 [1825]: '*fälscht ein Rebenhasser den Feuerwasser, frisch, trommelt auf den Tisch*'.

an or *gegen etw. trommeln* to beat or tap on or against sth.; e.g. *der Regen trommelte ans Fenster* or Raabe, *Hungerpastor* 3,10: '. . . *der Regen machtlos über seinem Kopfe auf dem Dache trommelt*'. Similarly, *jem. aus dem Bett trommeln* = 'to knock sb. up'; cf. Raabe, *Hung.* 3,106: '*Grips, welcher mit der Faust an seiner Tür trommelte*'; cf. also Goethe 8,170 on parsons: '. . . *wenn unsre auf der Kanzel herum trommeln*'. This usage began in the 18th c. (before then *trumpeln* was used in such contexts).

der Hase trommelt the hare taps or drums; describes the boxing movements made by hares (and rabbits); recorded by Oken, *Allg.Nat.Gesch.* 7,818 [1833ff]. Jean Paul used it neatly: '*der Hase trommelte auf Hinterfüßen den Abend aus mit Vorderfüßen*'.

nicht auf sich herumtrommeln lassen (coll.) to refuse to be ordered about or treated like dirt; since the 18th c., e.g. Schiller, *Wallensteins Lager* 11.

auf jem. lostrommeln (coll.) to thrash sb.; recorded since the 19th c.; Heine, *Verm.* 1,236 also used *auf etw. lostrommeln*; cf. also *jem. trommeln* (coll.) = 'to pummel (or pommel) sb.'.

Leute zusammentrommeln (coll.) to round up people, drum up support, take measures to win people (as supporters, customers, etc.); since the 18th c., e.g. Jean Paul [edit. H.] 1,152; also used with ref. to collecting or scraping together of things, as in Zelter (to Goethe 1,398): '. . . *um so viel Geld zusammenzutrommeln*'.

das Trommelfeuer drumfire, heavy barrage; in mil. contexts since 1915; soon also figur., e.g. O. Spengler, *Unterg.d.Abendl.* 2,577 [1922]: '*unter dem betäubenden Trommelfeuer von Sätzen, Schlagworten, Standpunkten, Szenen, Gefühlen . . .*', (Sp.) Werfel, *Abituriententag* 39 [1928]: '. . . *in Gottes besonderer Gunst stehen, um im Trommelfeuer der Erniedrigungen freundlich grinsen zu können*'.

die Maultrommel mouth-organ; one of the many terms for the instrument; since Early NHG, e.g. Fischart, *Garg.* 82b; Kramer recorded it in 1702 giving *Brummeisen* as an alternative. For other terms see under *Maul* (p. 1673).

Gott sei's getrommelt und gepfiffen! (coll.) thank goodness! expression of relief; modern coll.

was durch die Flöte gewonnen wird, geht durch die ~ *wieder fort* (prov.expr.) what has been attained in peacetime is lost again in war; the use of ~ for 'war' is old (cf. also Lenz, *Ged.* [edit. W.] 21: '*ach, ihr seid es, Bothen des Krieges, Herolde des Todes, ihr lautkrachenden Trommeln*'), but the phrase under discussion has only been recorded in this form since the 18th c., when Goethe IV,12,356 (W.) used it; still in (DWb) J.Grosse, *Ausgew.Werke* 3,333 [1909]; now obs.

← See also under *auftrommeln, austrommeln, Hase* (for *er bleibt bei seinen Worten wie der Hase bei der Trommel*) and *Sau* (for *sich zu etw. schicken wie die Sau zur Maultrommel*).

Trompete: trumpet

die ~ (lit.) the proclaimer of war; comparable in this sense to *Trommel* (see previous entry), e.g. Geibel, 108: '*der Hahn des Kriegs, die schmetternde Trompete*'; also with ref. to recruiting for the army, e.g. Uhland, 144: '*die Trompeten werben*', Goethe, *Herm.u.Dor.* 4: '*dich ruft nicht die Trommel, nicht die Trompete*' (cf. also *Faust I,* 891).

die Eustachsche ~ or *Ohrtrompete* (med.) the Eustachian tube; f.r.b. Bock, *Anat.* 690 [1838].

die ~ (zool.) needlefish, pipefish (*Syngnathus acus*); f.r.b. Oken, 6.96 [1839]; Oken also recorded ~ for 'moorish idol' (*Zanglus cornutus*), usually called *Abgottfisch*.

der Trompeter or *Trompeterfisch* (zool.) trumpetfish, tubenose (*Fistularia chinensis*); recorded by Oken.

die Trompetenschnecke (zool.) great triton (*Tritonium tritonis*); recorded since the 19th c., e.g. by Oken. *Trompetentierchen* for stentor (*Stentor*) has also been listed since the 19th c., as has been *Trompeterschwan* = 'trumpeter swan' (*Cygnus buccinator*).

der Trompeter or *Trompetervogel* (zool.) trumpeter (*Psophia crepitans*); recorded by Campe.

der Moraltrompeter von Säkkingen Schiller; abusive term coined by Nietzsche, *Werke* 8,117 [1888] with allusion to Scheffel's *Der Trompeter von Säckingen* [1854].

etw. trompeten to proclaim sth. loudly, shout it from the roof-tops; frequent since the 18th c., e.g. Zachariä 1,213: '*von Famen wird sein Lob trompetet aller Enden*', also Klopstock, *Od.* 2,19. Approaching the coll. when it is used for 'shouting', e.g. Arnim, *Isab.* 61 [1812] or Anzengruber, *Werke* (edit. H.) 8,12 [1886]: '*. . . hat nicht schlecht zum Trompeten ang'hoben*' (also Hauptmann, *Weber* 3).

trompeten to trumpet; with ref. to sounds made by animals, esp. elephants and cocks; since the 18th c., in comic exaggeration in Klopstock, *Gelehrtenrep.* 280 [1774]: '*. . . schwärmte die Mücke um die Nachtigall und trompetete Glossen*'. Noisy blowing of the nose and farting is also called *trompeten*, recorded since the 19th c., e.g. Cl. Brentano, *Ges. Schr.* 5,419: '*wenn sie sich schneuzen, trompeten sie ungemein mit der Nase*'.

sie trompetet alles aus (coll.) she blabs out everything, cannot keep things to herself; recorded since the 19th c., e.g. by Klix, 108 [1863].

das Trompetenpferd (coll., obs.) sb. who is not easily frightened; recorded since the 19th c., e.g. by Wander [1876] who refers to French *c'est un bon cheval de trompette* (Lendroy, 252).

← See also under *austrompeten, Mutter* (for *Muttertrompete*) and *Pauke* (for *mit Pauken und Trompeten*).

Tropen: see *Koller*.

Tropf: see *Tropfen*.

Tropfen: drop

der ~ (lit.) drop; in many poet. contexts, usually in compounds, e.g. Herder, *R.* 7,104: '*Liebe, du Thautropfe des Himmels*', Goethe, *Egmont* 2: '*ich habe nun zu der spanischen Lebensart nicht einen Blutstropfen in meinen Adern*', also *Schmerzenstropfen* for 'tears', as in Tieck, *Makb.* 1,4 (cf. also Heine, *Lied.* 160: '*die Perlenthränentröpfchen*').

nur ein ~ only a small amount; also *kein ~* = 'nothing at all'; since MHG, e.g. Walther v.d.V. 20,36: '*es regent bêdenthalben mîn, das mir des alles niht enwirt ein tropfe*' (cf. also French *ne voir goutte*), Schiller, *Jungfr.v.O.* 3,4: '*ein Tropfe Haß*', Heinse, *Ardingh.* 1,268: '*jeden Tropfen Lust mit Ach und Weh erkaufen*', in poetry even with ref. to light, e.g. Lenau, 43: '*. . . floß in kargen Tropfen durchs Laubgewölb das Licht*'; occasionally in *(nur) ein ~ im Ozean*, as in Gentz, *Rev.* 116 [1794]; cf. also Haller, *Vers.schw.Ged.* 210: '*mach . . . einen Tropfen Zeit . . . nicht zur Ewigkeit*', Hungari (edit.), *Dicht.-Fr.* 2,82 [1854]: '*nach Eimern zählt das Unglück, nach Tropfen zählt das*

Glück'. It is from this meaning of 'smallness' or 'nothingness' that *Tropf* = 'simpleton, dunce' is derived, current since Late MHG, first as *Tropfe* and closely connected with *Tropf* = 'paralysis, apoplexy' (also since Late MHG and still rcorded as current by Kramer [1702]), since it was believed that a drop of blood falling from the brain onto the heart caused apoplexy (f.r.b. Dasypodius [1536]).

ein ~ a drop; with ref. to a beverage, esp. wine in the idiom *ein guter ~* ; frequent in diminutive forms, since the 17th c., e.g. Kramer [1702]: '*ein Tröpflein Wein trincken*', e.g. Schiller, *Fiesco* 3,5: '*der Tropfe Wein*', Maler Müller 1,163: '*was ists doch eine edle Sach um ein gut Tröpfchen!*'.

etw. (or *jem.*) *tropft etw. auf jem.* (lit.) sth. (or sb.) send drops of sth. on sb.; beginnings in lit. contexts in the 16th c., where the general notion is 'to inject', e.g. (DWb) Barth, *Weiberspiegel* 3b [1566], then in poetry since the 18th c., e.g. Goethe 4,98 (W.): '*. . . tropftest Mäßigung dem heißen Blute*', Kl.Groth, *Quickborn* 14: '*die Sterne . . . tropfen in dunkle Herzen die Ruhe wie Perlenthau*', Stefan George, *Jahr d. Seele* 15: '*wir fühlen dankbar wie . . . Strahlenspuren auf uns tropfen*' (in an intrans. construction).

ein ~ auf den heißen Stein (prov.expr.) a mere drop in the bucket, of no more effect than a pebble dropped into the sea; in lit. only since the 19th c., e.g. Fr.L.Jahn, *Werke* [edit. E.] 2,605, Holtei, *Erz.Schr.* 25,24. B.Brecht wrote a *Ballade vom Tropfen auf den heißen Stein* (*Ged.* 3,170).

steter ~ höhlt den Stein (prov.) constant dropping wears the stone; in German (and in Engl.) from two sources, Ovid, *Epist. ex ponte* 4,10: '*gutta cavat lapidem*' and biblical '*Wasser wäscht Steine weg*' in Job 14,19; since MHG, e.g. Thomasin v.Zirkl., *W.Gast* 1921 or Hartmann v.Aue, *Erstes Büchl.* 1620, recorded as prov. by Franck [1541]: '*ein weycher tropff hölet auch die stein auß*'; also in verbal phrases, e.g. Matthisson, *A.* 9,65: '*den Stein tropft Regen hohl*'.

← See also under *Advokat* (for *Advokatentinte ist sehr teuer, denn sie wird aus Maurerschweiß gemacht, und der kostet einen Dukaten für jeden Tropfen*), *beträpfeln, Blut* (for *kein fremder Tropfen in meinem Blut*), *einträpfeln, Öl* (for *mit einem Tropfen demokratischen Öls gesalbt*), and *Regen* (for *regnet's nicht, so tröpfelts doch*).

Trost: consolation

mein ~ my solace, comfort; personification of 'sth. that provides consolation'; with ref. to one's children current since OHG, still today in *~ des Alters*; also applied to husband or wife, e.g. Goethe 39,109 (W.), in wider sense for 'protector' (or 'protection'), also frequently for 'friend', e.g. Luther Apocr. transl. Ecclesiasticus 6,16: '*ein treuer Freund ist ein Trost des Lebens*', J.E.Schlegel, *Werke* 1,10: '*Orestes war mein Trost*', also Goethe 7,210 (W.) or Fontane, *Ges.Werke*

1,4,29. From this extended to things which bring one consolation, often with ref. to alcohol, e.g. Lichtenberg, *Hog.Kupfer*, 1,47 [1794]: '. . . *im Begriff, einer Mamsell d'Eon . . . einen Schluck Trost zu reichen*'. *Tröster* can also be used, e.g. Hagedorn 3,77: '*du Tröster in Beschwerden, mein goldner Schlaf*', also *Trösterin* for 'the beloved', since MHG, e.g. Gottfried v.Neifen (in *Minnes.*, edit v.d.Hagen 1,51b): '*sorgen troesterinne, dir ist mîn jâmer kunt*', also *meins hertzn trösterin*, as in H.Sachs [edit. K.-G.] 20,133, and with ref. to abstracts, also since MHG, e.g. Goethe II,60,78 (W.): '*die edle Treiberin, Trösterin Hoffnung*', Wieland (Akad.Edit.) 1,13,163: '*die Zeit, die große Trösterin, den wahren Balsam hat*'. There are scores of compounds with *Trost, Tröster, Trösterin* and *Tröstung*, e.g. *Augentrost* for 'beloved', e.g. Weckherlin, 821 or Goethe, *Wahlverw.* 1,6: '*dadurch ward sie den Männern . . . ein wahrer Augentrost*' (here = 'balm to the eyes'). See also below.

der ~ (relig.) Jesus Christ; also used for 'God' and 'the Holy Spirit', seen as spiritual comfort, e.g. Psalm 52,9: '*siehe, das ist der Mann, der Gott nicht für seinen Trost hielt*' or Lamentations 4,20: '*der Gesalbte des Herrn, der unser Trost war, ist gefangen worden*' (where the A.V. has 'the breath of our nostrils, the anointed of the Lord'), also in ~ *der Welt*, e.g. Novalis, *Schr.* [edit. M.] 1,81: '*wo bleibst du, Trost der ganzen Welt?*' *Tröster* can also be used.

er ist nicht bei ~ (or *Troste*) (coll.) he is out of his mind; originally this described sb. who is inconsolable, unwilling to be helped by comforting words; since ca. 1700 in several forms: *nicht (wohl) bei* ~ *sein*, also with *recht*, e.g. Lichtenberg, *Verm.Schr.* 2,356, Wieland, *Att.* 2,2,130, J.G.Müller, *Lind.* 4,198 [1790]; also in question form: *bist du bei* ~ ?, as in Müllner, *Dram.W.* 5,225 [1828]; cf. *nicht bei Sinnen* (or *Verstand*) *sein* or coll. *er ist wohl nicht bei Groschen* (for which see p. 1149).

die Trostpille (coll.) consoling remark, act or payment; 20th c. coll., similarly *das Trostpflästerchen* (coll.), esp. with ref. to payments in compensation, since early in the 20th c., e.g. *Trostpflaster* in (DWb) *Tägl.Rundschau*, Nr. 481 [1904]; *Trostpille* arrived a little later.

← See also under *Gewehr* (for *Trostgewehr*), *Graus* (for *weltlicher Trost*), *Jungfer* (for *Jungferntrost*) and *Spital* (for *Spitaltröster*).

Troß: baggage; attendants

der ~ (1) followers, attendants, suite (of a prince, etc.); derived from ~ = 'baggage attendants', general since the 18th c., e.g. Klinger, *Giaf.* 122: '*der Troß von Höflingen*', often in compounds, e.g. *Dienertroß, Sklaventroß.* Heine, *Lied.* 30 also used *Getroß*: '*der Graf besoldete viel Dienergetroß*'.

der ~ (2) crowd, crew, bunch (of people);

more or less contemptuous; since Early NHG, e.g. Murner, *Luth.Narr* 2095: '. . . *wölt den lügentroß umb fieren*'; frequent since the 18th c., e.g. Günter, *Ged.* 382 [1735]: '*des Pöbels Troß*', Goethe, *Gespr.* 3,96: '. . . *bei dem Troß der ordinären Autoren und Autorinnen*'; also sometimes with ref. to abstracts, e.g. Herder [edit. S.] 24,96: '*über einen großen Troß von Einwürfen . . . hat uns Deutschen eine schöne Muse weggeholfen*', where ~ = 'mass of troublesome things, irksome rubbish'.

der ~ (3) (regional coll.) boor, uncivilized creature; for several dialects recorded since the 19th c., occasionally in lit., e.g. Immermann, *Werke* [edit. B.] 16,433: '*ein Ehrenmann beleidigt Damen nicht . . . hausbackner Troß!*'.

← See also under *Gewehr* (for *der gelehrte Troß*).

Trott: trot

der ~ (mus., obs.) rhythm, rhythmic movement; since the 18th c., derived from the sound effect of a trotting horse, e.g. Herder [edit. S.] 20,231; cf. also ~ *des Metrums* in Zelter (to Goethe) 2,427.

der (alte) ~ (coll.) routine, habitual way of doing things; since late in the 18th c., e.g. Pestalozzi, *L. und G.* 2,293, Mörike, *Ges.Schr.* 2,73: '*er machte seinen Trott so fort*'; often with *alt.*

im Hundetrott (coll.) at a brisk pace in short steps; since late in the 18th c., e.g. Seume, *Ged.* 288; Heine, 1,288 and 12,25 used *Hundetrab.*

der Trottel (or *Troddel*) (coll.) idiot, moron, nincompoop; probably derived from *trotten* = 'to plod, trudge, walk in an aimless fashion'; f.r.b. K.J.Weber, *Deutschland* 2,622 [1827]; first in use in Austria (cf. Schmeller-Fr., *Bayer.Wb.* 681 [1878]), then adopted by other areas, displacing *Kretin*; hence *troddelhaft* (since early in the 20th c.) and *vertrottelt*, also *Trottelei* = 'sluggish thinking, laziness in taking action', since early in the 20th c., e.g. O.Spengler, *Unterg.d.Ab.* 2,122 [1922]. There is also *trottelig* = 'brainless', but also = 'absent-minded' and 'forgetful'.

← See also under *Ochs* (for *Ochsentrott*).

Trotz: defiance, spite

der ~ defiance, resistance; figur. when treated as an object in such cases as *den* ~ *vertreiben, vergehen machen* (both recorded by Kramer [1702], *jem.s* ~ *brechen*, e.g. Keller, *Sinngedicht* 184, *jem.s* ~ *austreiben.*

jem.m. or *einer Sache* ~ *bieten* to defy sb. or sth.; since Early NHG, e.g. Luther 8,91a (Jena): '*wir . . . bieten ihrer heiligen weisheit trotz*', Lessing 10,54: '*ich biete aller Welt Trotz, mir ein einziges solches Exemplar zu zeigen*', Schiller, *D.Carl.* 2,12: '*Trotz sei geboten allen Königinnen*'. Also with ref. to things as the subject, e.g. *die Festung bot jedem Angriffe* ~ (as in Schiller). The entry on p. 313 requires correction.

~ *jem.m* (obs.) in competition with sb. at sth.,

undertaking to do sth. better than the other; this belongs to the old meaning of *trotzen* = 'to challenge, enter into a struggle with sb. for supremacy', current since MHG, e.g. Heinr. v. Freiberg, *Tristan* 4468; it can still be found in the 18th c., e.g. Hagedorn, *Epigr.* 95: '*trotz einer Elster schwatzt Ursin*'; also as *zu* ~ , as in Günther, *Ged.* 1043: '*wir liebten uns zu Trotz und scherzten um die Wette*'. In most cases it appears to have meant the same as *um die Wette*. Now obs.

trotz der or *des . . .* in spite of . . ., notwithstanding; this arose through ellipsis of *zu*; it required the genitive, insisted upon by 18th c. grammarians and used by Goethe, e.g. *Ben.Cell.* 1,2, but came to be used also with the dative, e.g. Lessing, *Em.Gal.* 5,5, Hölderlin, *Hyp.* 2,116: '*weil . . . trotz euch schön das Schöne bleibt*'. Older forms with *Tratz* and *Trutz* are obs., except in the combination of *Schutz und Trutz*, for which see p. 2197.

← See also under *bieten* (for *Trotz bieten*), *Kopf* (for *Trotzkopf*) and *Rüssel* (for *wer trotzt an der Schüssel, schadet sich am Rüssel*).

trübe: dull, dim, turbid

trübe (1) dull, dark, dismal; also 'melancholy'; removed from the phys. world to abstracts since OHG, first with ref. to *Mut, Herz, Gemüt, Sinn*, e.g. Notker, *Ps.* 30,11: '*die sint truoben muotes*'. Kramer [1702] recorded *trübes Gemüt*. Since the 17th c. also with ref. to gestures, looks, etc. which reveal a worried or sad mental condition, e.g. Goethe 16,125 (W.): '*warum ist deine Stirn so trüb?*', hence ~ *aussehen*, recorded by Kramer; with ref. to fears, thoughts, worrying intimations since the 18th c., e.g. Klopstock, *Od.* 1,3.

trübe (2) depressing, sad, regrettable; since the 17th c. with ref. to bereavement, illness or misfortune, e.g. Herder [edit. S.] 16,271: '*in trüber Einsamkeit*'.

trübe (3) dark, confused, inexplicable; only since late in the 18th c., often in *trübe Sache*, also used by Goethe IV,29,72 (W.).

trübe (4) dull (of sound); transfer to the acoustic sphere; since the 17th c., e.g. Gryphius, *Trauersp.* [edit. P.] 162: '*der trüben Hörner Klang*', Droste-Hülshoff, *Ges.Schr.* 2,244: '*. . . und lauter wird die Tropfmusik und trüber*'.

aus trüben Quellen schöpfen (lit.) to derive one's knowledge from a tainted source; with *Quelle* since the 18th c., e.g. Herder [edit. S.] 3,314, with *Lachen* or *Pfützen* since the 17th c.

trübes Wasser (coll.) bad feelings, dissent, enmity; since Early NHG, e.g. Luther 6,507a (Jena); still in the 19th c., but with the meanings of 'unpleasantry' or 'disreputable thing', e.g. Kotzebue, *Dram.W.* 1,212; possibly now only in some regions for 'bad state of affairs'.

das Wasser trüben to muddy the water; in phys. sense at least since Early NHG, when Luther,

Werke [edit. Clemen] 4,233 wrote: '*warum trübstu mir das wasser, das ich nicht trincken kan?*', then since the 18th c. in extended sense, e.g. Hippel, *Lebensläufe* 1,336 [1778]: '*die Sachwalter machens wie die Fischer, sie trüben das Wasser eh sie angeln*' (cf. similar remark by Goethe IV,20,222 (W.) on Görres and friends).

er sieht aus, als könnte er kein Wässerchen (or *Wässerlein*) *trüben* (coll.) he looks as if butter would not melt in his mouth, looks all innocent; current since the 16th c., e.g. Raabe, *Werke* 3,5,356: '*. . . macht fromme Augen, also ob er noch niemals ein Wässerlein getrübt hätte*'.

sein Urteil ist getrübt his judgment is clouded; refers to lack of objectivity; *getrübt* for 'clouded, falsified, deformed'; has been current since the 18th c., e.g. Goethe 7,155 (W.); hence also *ein Bild trüben* = 'to impart sth. false, negative, deprecatory to an image', as in Mommsen, *Röm.Gesch.* 1,545 [1856] on Hannibal: '*wenn auch Zorn, Neid und Gemeinheit seine Geschichte geschrieben haben, sie haben das reine und große Bild nicht zu trüben vermocht*'.

trübselig sad, melancholy (of persons), dreary, bleak (of conditions); first with ref. to events and conditions, e.g. Kirchhof, *Wendunm.* 1,472; since the 18th c. also applied to persons (cf. modern sl. *er ist eine trübe Tasse* = 'he is a bore'). From then onward it could also refer to bad or uninspiring works of art, e.g. Goethe, *Gespr.* [edit. B.] 4,296: '*so viele schwache und trübselige Gedichte*'. The noun *Trübseligkeit* was derived from the adj. in the 15th c.

der Trübsinn melancholy, low spirits, gloom; since the 18th c. recorded by Adelung, who also listed *trübsinnig*, which in fact appeared on the scene before the noun (middle of 18th c.); cf. also Goethe, *Iphig.* 1,2: '*wer hat des Königs trüben Sinn erheitert?*'. Occasionally *Trübheit* can be used for 'melancholy'.

ungetrübt (lit.) unclouded, unalloyed, perfect; since the 18th c., not listed by Adelung, but Campe [1811] recorded it with a quotation from *Deutscher Merkur* (no details): '*nur der Seele ungetrübter Frieden führt zu des Olympos Göttermahl*'; frequent now in *in ungetrübten Genuß von etw. gelangen* – 'to come into unalloyed enjoyment of sth.'.

die Trübung der diplomatischen Beziehungen (cl.) disturbing, dampening or clouding of diplomatic relations; modern, partly euphem.

← See also under *Auge* (for *trübe Augen haben*), *betrüben* (also for *Betrübnis*), *blasen* (for *Trübsal blasen*), *eigen* (for *Eigenliebe macht die Augen trübe*), *Fisch* (for *im Trüben fischen*), *Molch* (for *ein trüber Molch*) and *mürbe* (for *im Sand des Trübsals*).

Trubel: see *Jubel*.

Trug: deceit; fraud; lie; delusion

der ~ (lit.) deceit; personified; since the 17th

c., e.g. J.Böhme, *Sämtl.W.* [edit. Sch.] 3,179: '*wir sind . . . kinder des trugs*', Goethe 5,5 (W.): '*es schleicht . . . die List in deinen Schatten; sie suchet ihren Gatten, den Trug*' (also *Tasso* 4,1 and *Gespr.* [edit. B.] 2,89).

das ist Lug und ~ that is falsehood and deceit; as a fixed formula since Early NHG, f.r.b. Maaler [1561].

das Trugbild (lit.) phantom; introduced, or rather re-introduced by Herder after an absence of several centuries, e.g. in *Werke* [edit. S.] 19,125; f.r.b. Kinderling [1795].

der Trugschluß sophism, fallacy; coined early in the 18th c. and at first rejected by many purists, but by the end of the c. Wieland used it in pref. to *Agathon* [1767] and then it occurred frequently in Kant's writings. In music it can mean 'deceptive cadence'.

trügen to deceive; figur. with abstracts since OHG, e.g. Lehman 1,207 [1662]: '*Erfahrung treugt nicht*', Herder [edit. S.] 27,60: '*gefärbte Weisheit trügt*', Goethe, *Iphig.* 4,2: '*dir scheint es möglich, weil der Wunsch dich trügt*' (also Schiller, *Spaz.* 168).

sich trügen (a.) to be mistaken; since the 18th c., frequent in Herder's writings; now obs., displaced by *sich irren*.

der Schein trügt (prov.) appearances are deceptive; prov. in many versions, in Schottel [1663] as '*der Schein betrügt, die Wahrheit siegt*', in Lehman [1642] as '*was scheint, oft treugt*'; others have '*der Schein betrügt, der Spiegel lügt*'. The shortest form is modern, f.r.b. Simrock [1846].

← See also under *betrügen* (also for *Betrug*) and *Strick* (for *Truggestrick*).

Truhe: chest, trunk

die ~ (lit., a.) coffin; in occasional use in the 19th c. lit., e.g. Grillparzer 3,126: '*in der Truhe finde Ruhe, die dein Leben nicht genoß*'. also Freiligrath, *Sämtl.W.* 6,264; sometimes as *schwarze* ~ , as in Chamisso 3,360.

Trumm: large chunk; end of a thread

in einem ~ (regional coll.) in one go, without stopping; a ref. to spinning, meaning 'without a break in the thread'; hence regional *vom* ~ *kommen* = 'to lose one's thread' (in speech), *ihm ging das* ~ *aus* = 'he came to an end, he was at the end of his tether'. ~ = 'piece of sth.' can also be extended to abstracts, even in the diminutive, e.g. (T.) S.Keller, *D.e.Leben* 169 [1937]: '*an aller Freud hängt wie eine Zecke ein Trümmerlein Gefahr*'.

ein ~ *von einem Mann* (coll.) a hulk of a man; intensified as *Mordstrumm*; simple transfer from 'large object' as in *Klotz*, *Stück*, etc.; recorded since the 19th c., e.g. Spindler, *Vogelhändler* 1,268 [1841], recorded by Schmeller for Austro-Bav. areas. It can also be used with ref. to abstracts, e.g. *er hatte einen* ~ *von einem Rausch* = 'he was dead drunk'.

die Trümmer von etw. (lit.) the debris, wreckage of sth.; with ref. to abstracts since the 18th c., e.g. Wieland, *Danischm.* 44: '*was wir aus den Trümmern unsers Wohlstands geretten haben*', Schiller, *Räuber* 4,1: '*da liegen die Trümmer deiner Entwürfe*'.

zu Trümmern gehen to perish; since the 18th c., e.g. Schiller, *Fiesco,* 2,5: '*daß Genuas Freiheit zu Trümmern geht*' (but with ref. to persons as early as in Luther Bible transl. Hos. 10,14: '*da die mutter uber den kindern zu drümmern gieng*', now obs.).

etw. in Trümmer legen (or *schlagen*) to destroy sth.; figur. when the object is an abstract; since the 18th c.

Trümmer-. . . . . . of destruction and rubble; in compounds with ref. to the years immediately after 1945 when many German cities lay in ruins, e.g. *Trümmerjahre, Trümmerfilme*, etc.; since the fifties of the 20th c. Shortly after 1945 the term *Trümmerfrauen* was coined for the women who cleared away debris in cities destroyed by airraids, and this compound is still in use.

trümmerhaft fragmentary, in pieces; since late in the 18th c., e.g. Goethe, *Taghefte* [1818], Freytag, *Verl.Handschr.* 1,72: '*. . . ist . . . nur sehr trümmerhaft erhalten*'.

trümmern (obs.) to fall to pieces; still used by Schiller and Hölderlin; now obs. (see *zertrümmern* (2) below).

etw. zertrümmern (1) (trans.) to smash sth. to pieces; since Early NHG, e.g. H.Sachs [edit. K.] 7,204 (with *Gemüt*); Hölderlin in *Werke* [edit. J.-D.] 1,251 used *niedertrümmern*: '*Gesetze niedertrümmern*'.

zertrümmern (2) (trans.) to go to pieces; since the 16th c., e.g. Wickram, *Werke* [edit. B.] 4,180 or Arndt, *Ged.* 239 [1840]: '*zertrümmert liegt der Freiheit Haus*'.

← See also under *Meer* (for *Trümmermeer*) and *Mord* (for *Mordstrumm*).

Trumpf: trump

etw. ist ~ sth. is unbeatable, is all the rage; since the 18th c., e.g. Heine, *Tr.* XI: '*Gesinnung war Trumpf*'.

← See also under *Herz* (for *Herz ist Trumpf*).

jem.m einen ~ *aufsetzen* to outbid sb.; in the context of debate = 'to beat sb. in an argument, refute sb. effectively'; at least since the 19th c., e.g. Gutzkow, *R.v.G.* 3,297.

der letzte ~ the last trump, an important argument or proof which has been kept to the last; since the 19th c., e.g. (Sa.) Rank, *Gesch.arm.Leute* 102 [1853] but cf. the same notion in Goethe 26,255 (W.): '*. . . mit einem bedeutenden Trumpf zu schließen*'.

jem.m zeigen, was ~ *ist* (coll.) to show sb. how things really stand, what is being played; at least since the 19th c., frequent in Gotthelf's writings.

der ~ (regional) pointed remark, taunt, gibe; mainly in SW areas, e.g. in Gotthelf's writings; in the standard language *Stichelei* would now be used. This meaning must have been derived from ~ = 'coarse remark, insult', as in Lessing [edit. M.] 11,273 or Schopenhauer [edit. Gr.] 3,526; no longer listed in recent dictionaries.

Trümpfe ausspielen to use one's most effective arguments, play one's trump cards; at least since the 18th c., e.g. Goethe (to Schiller 1,259): '. . . *kann ich niemand übel nehmen . . . wenn er Trümpfe in die Hand kriegt, daß er sie auch ausspielt*'; similarly, *alle Trümpfe in der Hand haben* = 'to hold all the trump cards, be able to cope with all the difficulties that may arise'; sometimes *Trumpfkarte* is used.

jem. übertrumpfen to overtrump sb., go one better than sb.; since the 18th c., e.g. Goethe, *Gespr.* [edit. B.] 2,128: '. . . *einen . . . Teufel auftreten zu lassen, der die Andern übertrumpft*'.

etw. übertrumpfen to outdo or surpass sth.; since the 19th c., e.g. Riemer, *Mitt.üb.Goethe* 1,266: '. . . *daß seine Argumente durch Paradoxien übertrumpft wurden*'.

← See also under *abtrumpfen* and *ausspielen* (for *seinen letzten Trumpf ausspielen*).

Trunk: drink

der ~ (1) drink; figur. with abstracts since the 17th c., e.g. Olearius, *Pers.Baumg.* 39a [1696]: '*sie trinken den trunk der verachtung stets mit stillschweigen*'; frequent in figur. compounds, e.g. Rückert 1,116: '*der Feuertrunk geschöpft aus Traubenblut*', also in *Gifttrunk* (Schiller), *Schlaftrunk* (Goethe).

der ~ (2), also *Trunksucht* (addiction to) drink, drunkenness, intemperance; general since the 16th c., e.g. *dem* ~ *ergeben sein*, f.r.b. Kramer [1702], *Neigung zum* ~ , as in Goethe IV,26,294 (W.), also *dem* ~ *frönen* or *in* ~ *versunken sein* (both modern).

trunken vor (or *von*) *etw.* intoxicated with or drunk with sth.; since Early NHG, e.g. Luther Bible transl. Psalm 36,9: '*sie werden trunken von den reichen gütern deines hauses*', where the A.V. has 'they shall be abundantly satisfied with the fatness of thy house' (also Jerem. 46,10, Isaiah 49,26), Gellert, *Zärtl.Schw.* 1,2: '*ich bin vor Vergnügen ganz trunken*', Lessing, *Minna* 2,3: '*Sie sind trunken, trunken von Fröhlichkeit*'; cf. also *trunkne Augen* in Goethe, *Iphig.* 1,3 and *trunknes Ohr*, as in Schiller, *M.Stuart* 2,2. Hence *Trunkenheit*, as in Wieland, *Arist.* 3,6: '*Trunkenheit einer heftigen Leidenschaft*', Palleske, Schiller 1,329 [1858]: '. . . *zwischen Iffland'scher Nüchternheit und Schiller'scher Trunkenheit zu wählen*'. There are many lit. compounds, e.g. *Freudentrunkenheit*, as in Wieland, *Ob.* 5,12, also Wieland, *Werke* 17,408: '*Schwärmerei, diese schöne Seelentrunkenheit*', also *Mondscheintrunkenheit* in Heine, *Verm.* 1,7.

← See also under *betrinken* (for *wie betrunken*), *Elend* (for *das trunkene Elend*), *Fisch* (for *Fischtrunk*), *Freude* (for *freudetrunken*), *Schwede* (for *Schwedentrunk*), also entries under *angeheitert*, *austrinken*, *durchtränken*, *eintränken*, *ertränken*, *Hand*, *Trank*, *tränken* and *trunken* (also for *schlaftrunken*).

Truppe: troop

der Trupp or *die* ~ group of people; transfer from mil. usage (17th c.) to groups of civilian people = *Haufen, Schar*, e.g. Schiller, *Fiesco* 2,15: '*ein Trupp Pilgrimme*', Goethe 50,236 (W.): '*da überfiel den Hof ein Trupp verlaufnen Gesindels*'; also used as a collective term for animals = 'herd flock, etc.' since the 18th c., e.g. *ein Trupp Rinder*, and since the middle of the 18th c. with ref to professional groups, e.g. S.v.Laroche, Fr.Sternh. 1,330 [1771]: '*eine Truppe spanischer Musikanten*', hence such compounds as *Musikanten-, Schauspieler-, Wandertruppe*. The diminutive appeared in the 19th c., e.g. Keller, *Werke* 6,319: '*hierauf schwenkte das Trüppchen der Sieben ab*', in coll. *er hat ein Trüppchen Kinder* = 'he has quite a bunch of children', recorded by Heyne [1895]; *truppweise* (adv.) = 'in groups' was f.r.b. Stieler [1691].

← See also under *belegen* (for *mit Truppen belegen*), *einsetzen* (for *Truppen zum Einsatz bringen*), *heizen* (for *Truppen verheizen*), and *stoßen* (for *Stoßtrupp*).

Trutz: see *Trotz*.

Tube: tube

auf die ~ *drücken* (1) (coll.) to produce sentimental feelings, to do or produce sth. that is calculated to evoke sadness; ~ is a late 19th c. word imported from Eng., first as *Tübe*, then also as ~ ; in theatr. coll. the phrase can also be used for 'to over-act, lay it on thick', a ref. to the tubes of make-up material; both meanings arose in the 1st quarter of the 20th c.

auf die ~ *drücken* (2) (sl.) to accelerate, step on it; from sl. of motorists; since the twenties extended to 'to make strong efforts', also to 'to live to the full, burn the candle at both ends'.

Tuch: cloth

es ist wie ein rotes ~ *für ihn* (coll.)it acts like a red rag to a bull, it makes him mad or very angry; a ref. to bullfighting; only since the 20th c., e.g. Th.Mann, *Faustus* 396. See also under *rot* for idioms associating red with anger.

buntes ~ *kam vorbei* (coll., obs.) soldiers passed by; *zweierlei* ~ is also used; recorded since the 19th c., Raabe in *Hungerpastor* 2,84 used *bunt*, Stinde in *Buchholzens in Ital.* *zweierlei*; *zweierlei* ~ *lieben* is recorded by Hügel für Vienna for 'to run after soldiers'. Now a. or obs.

er ist leichtes ~ (regional coll.) he is a careless, thoughtless, superficial kind of person; recorded for many Alem. and Austro-Bav. areas since the 19th c. (though some phrases with ~ with ref. to the 'stuff that sb. is made of' are older); the adj. can vary, e.g. Hügel recorded the phrase for Vienna with *liederlich*.

in Tuchfühlung in close touch or contact; first in mil. contexts with ref. to soldiers in closed ranks; early in the 20th c. extended, e.g. *mit jem.m Tuchfühlung behalten* = 'to remain in close touch or direct contact with sb.', e.g. I.Seidel, *Lennacker* 226 [1938], also in *Tuchfühlung stehen mit jem.m* = 'to rub shoulders with sb.', *auf Tuchfühlung gehen* = 'to huddle together'.—Note that *betucht* = 'well-to-do' is not derived from ~ , but is of Hebrew origin.

← See also under *Brust* (for *gut unterm Brusttuch sein*), *doppelt* (for *das doppelte Tuch*), *Elle* (for *die Tuchhändler und die übrigen Ellenritter*), *Handtuch* (for several idioms), *Hunger* (for *am Hungertuch nagen*), *kauen* (for *am Hungertuch kauen*), *Leiche* (for *wie ein Leichentuch*), *Leintuch*, *schneiden* (for *das Tischtuch zerschneiden/entzweischneiden*), *Schnitt* (for *es ist gut, den Schnitt an fremdem Tuche zu lernen*) and *Tafel* (for *Tafeltuch*).

tüchtig: useful, usable
tüchtig (adv.) very much; extended from its original sense until it means no more than *sehr* (as in the cases of *ansehnlich, bedeutend, beträchtlich, erheblich, gehörig, gewaltig, mächtig, riesig*); since the 18th c., not yet mentioned in Kramer [1702], e.g. Schiller, *Räuber* 5,1: '*spotte mich tüchtig aus*'; in use both for degree and quantity as adj. and adv., e.g. Wieland, *Luc.* 6,55: '*eine tüchtige Portion Tollheit*'; cf. also coll. '*was Tüchtiges* = 'very much, properly', as in Merck, *Br.* 2,140: '*ich bombardiere dich diesmal 'was Tüchtiges*'.

← See also under *einpacken* (for *tüchtig einpacken*), and *einsacken* (for *tüchtig einsacken*).

Tücke: malice, guile, spite
die ~ (lit.) (example of) malice; in lit. sometimes seen as an object, e.g. Schiller, *Wall.Tod* 5,3: '*ihm spinnt das Schicksal keine Tücke mehr*'. ~ can also be personified, best known through Vischer, who in *Auch Einer* coined *die* ~ *des Objekts*, e.g. '*das Objekt lauert . . . solange irgendein Mensch um den Weg ist, denkt das Objekt auf Unarten, auf Tücke . . . so lauert alles Objekt . . . auf den Augenblick, wo man nicht achtgibt*'.

mit List und Tücke (coll.) with much trouble (and some cunning); the phrase began in Early NHG in its original sense 'with cunning and malice', e.g Luther 8,531 (Weimar) on the devil: '. . . *aller seyner tück und list gebraucht*', also in the now preferred order in *Tischr.* 1,480 (Weimar): '*mit listen und tücken*'. Only since the 20th c. in coll. use for 'with much trouble (and some cunning)'.

etw. hat seine Tücken (coll.) sth. is dangerous, cannot be trusted; off-shoot from ~ (lit.), see above; since the 18th c., e.g. Klopstock, *Spr.u.Dichtk.* 1,296 [1779].

tückisch insidious, treacherous; originally (like *heimtückisch*, which see below) only in descriptions of human behaviour, but in the 17th c. extended to abstracts, e.g. (DWb) Treuer, *Dädalus* 1,672 [1675]: '*das tückische glück*', Hebbel, *Werke* [edit. W.] 8,307: '*tückische Seuche*', frequent in *tückische Krankheit, tückisches Wetter*; cf. also Klabund, *Bracke* 106: '*ein Strohdach, das tückisch zu knistern begann*'.

tückisch (regional coll.) obstreperous, spiteful, rebellious; with ref. to 'difficult' people, recorded since the 20th c., e.g. for Berlin; in some areas it also occurs for 'disgruntled, grumpy'.

auf jem. tückisch sein (coll., a.) to be cross with sb.; recorded by Adelung, now regional or a., but in sl. *einen Tück auf jem. haben* (of 20th c. origin) still exists.

heimtückisch malicious, insidious; as an adj. since Early NHG, recorded by Stieler [1691], e.g. Fischart, *Garg.* 63a (as *heimdückisch*); derived either from *heimlich tückisch* or *hämisch tückisch* (Franck, *Weltb.* 130b [1534] has '*ein heimisch tückisch volk*' but H.Sachs has '*haimliche, hemische dück*'). The noun *Heimtücke* is now rare, the adj. also extended now to abstracts, events, even things, e.g. *ein heimtückischer Wind*.

tüfteln: fiddle, work on sth. delicate or tedious
tüfteln (also *difteln*) (coll.) to quibble, split hairs; also sometimes 'to ponder lengthily'; modern, e.g. R.Huch, *Dreißig.Kr.* 2,14: '*ich liebe das Tüfteln und Haarspalten nicht*'; hence *tüftelig* (coll.) = 'punctilious, fussy'; Fontane in *Br.* [edit. G.] 75 called it *tiftlig*, Storm used *düftlig*, also *Tüftelei* (coll.) = 'hair-splitting, sophistry', (since the middle of the 19th c. for 'work on sth. intricate or delicate'), in pejor. sense since the 2nd half of the 19th c.

Tugend: power, strength; virtue
die ~ (1) (a.) power, strength; this very old meaning of ~ was still alive in the 19th c. with ref. to the efficacy of medicines = *Heilkraft*, e.g. Goethe, *Cell.* 1,7 [1796]: '*durch die Tugend des Wermuths erlangte ich . . . wieder . . . Kräfte*', also Stifter, *S.Werke* 2,285, or to supernatural power = *Wunderkraft*, e.g. Wirnt v. Grafenberg, *Wigalois* 1484 and still in Wieland, *S.Werke* 22,109: '*ihr glaubt nicht, was der Ring für Tugenden besitzt*' (also *Geron* 376); now a., though occasionally used for 'good point, quality', for which the DWb. [1952] quoted an advertisement as an example: '*alle Tugenden eines guten Tabaks sind in der Zigarette . . . vereinigt*'.

die ~ (2) (personified) Virtue; personified since the Middle Ages when it was sometimes called *frou tugent* (e.g. in *Passional* [edit. H.] 329); often in prov.; Franck [1541] listed '*die tugend het hend vnd auge, die tugend ist schnöd, dann sie beut sich iedermann selbst an, die tugend kan sich selbs nit sehen*' (also as ~ *kennt sich selber nicht* in 17th c. collections); Sutor [1740] recorded: '*die Tugend ist eine Tochter Gottes, eine Schwester der Heiligen, eine Mutter aller Glückseligkeit*'; cf. also Schiller, *Shakespeares Schatten* 46 [1796]: '*wenn sich das Laster erbricht, setzt sich die Tugend zu Tisch*'. Modern examples of personification, esp. in prov. sayings, are too numerous to list (scores of them can be found in Wander IV,1378–73 [1876]).

die ~ (3) (a.) virtue (in the narrower sense of chastity); e.g. *sie bewahrte ihre* ~ ; general still in the 18th c., when Adelung recorded '*die Tugend einer Person in Verdacht ziehen*', e.g. Wieland 6,71: '*daß die Dame sich jederzeit durch eine sehr spröde Tugend unterschieden*' or 10,95: '*wie wohl die Frau die Tugend selber war*'.

der Tugendbold paragon of virtue; only since the 19th c. (following the group *Trunkenbold, Witzbold*, etc.) and usually ironic or sarcastic; e.g. (Kl.-St.) Viebig, *Erde* 257: '*der scheinheilige Tugendbold, der Doktor Hirsekorn*'.

← See also under *Adel* (for *Adel der Tugend haben*), *andrechseln* (for *angedrechselte Tugend*), *anschminken* (for *angeschminkte Tugend*), *Fron* (for *einer Untugend frönen*), *gesund* (for *Tugend ist die Gesundheit der Seele*), *Gewicht* (for *nach dem Gewicht der Tugend abwägen*), *Gold* (for *tombackene Tugenden* and *der Keuschheit güldne Tugend*), *Grenze* (for *wo jede Tugend mit dem Laster zusammenfließt* and *Licht, in dem die Grenzen der Tugend und Untugend schwimmen*), *Held* (for *Tugendheld*), *Jugend* (for *Jugend hat keine Tugend*), *Krone* (for *eine der vornehmsten Tugenden gekrönten Häupter*), *Liebe* (for *Liebe, Mutter der Tugenden* and *Gottesfurcht, die Mutter aller Tugenden*), *Muster* (for *Muster aller Tugend*), *Not* (for *aus der Not eine Tugend machen*), *Pfad* (for *von dem Pfad der Tugend ausirren*), *Plan* (for *sich üben auf dem Plan der Tugenden*), *Ritter* (for *Ritter der cynischen Tugend*) and *Spiegel* (for *Hausfrauentugend*).

Tulpe: tulip

die ~ (1) (lit., rare) lady; mainly with ref. to their pride, e.g. Herder [edit S.] 25,520: '*spröde Tulpen, die nicht duften, aber prangen und stolzieren*', Goethe 16,139 (W.): '*eitler Tulpen Pracht*', Heine [edit. E.] 3,157: '*die geschminkten Tulpen grüßten mich bettelstolz herablassend*'; dislike is also strong in Goethe 37,62 (W.): '*man muß ein Holländer seyn, um mit einer Tulpe zu sympathisiren*'.

die ~ (2) (coll., obs.) helmet of a Prussian soldier; since 2nd half of the 19th c., e.g. Hoffmann v. Fallersleben in *Wagners Archiv* 1,280 [1874]; now obs.

← See also under *Gewitter* (for *Gewittertulpe*).

die ~ (3) (coll.) tulip-shaped beer glass; recorded for many areas since the 19th c., at first mainly in the N.

die ~ (4) (zool.) blood clam, ark shell; f.r.b. Zedler [1745]; in Nemnich [1796] as *Lepas*

tintinnabulum; also the name of a snail, recorded by Campe [1810] as *Murex tulipa*.

die ~ (5) (sl.) odd creature, queer fellow; 20th c. sl., e.g. *du bist mir vielleicht eine* ~ = 'you are an odd creature, I must say'.

← See also under *Pokal* (for *Pokal einer Tulpe*).

tummeln: set going, exercise; hurry

der Tummelplatz playground, arena, scene; in phys. sense for 'place where one exercises sth.' recorded by Stieler [1691]; figur. since the 18th c., e.g. Schiller, *Fiesco* 2,3: '*nicht der Tummelplatz des Lebens—sein Gehalt bestimmt seinen Wert*' or Laukhard, *Leben u. Sch.* 162 [1792]: '*. . . sogar die Kanzel zum Tummelplatz seiner skandalösen Auftritte machte*'; with ref. to vices it can mean 'hotbed'.

← See also under *Getümmel* and *Pferd* (for *Jugendpferde, auf denen ich mich herumgetummelt hatte*).

tun: do

etw . . . ~ (1) to put, lay sth. somewhere; this goes back to the oldest meaning 'put, set, lay'; now rare and displaced by *geben, richten, stellen*, but still alive in *wohin hast du es getan?* = 'where did you put it?', *tu Geld in deinen Beutel* = 'put money in thy purse', as in Tieck's transl. of Shakespeare, *Othello* 1,3; mainly preserved in compounds such as *etw. abtun, etw. dazutun, sich hervortun* or *Dinge zusammentun*; cf. also Goethe 8,175 (W.): '*ich kann nichts davon noch dazu thun*'.

etw. ~ (2) to do, perform sth.; since OHG and still current, e.g. *er kann* ~ *und lassen, was er will*; it occurs in idioms with many nouns (though fewer than in MHG and Early NHG), e.g. in *Abbitte* ~ , *ein Gelübde* ~ , *Buße* ~ , *Erwähnung* ~ , *seine Pflicht* ~ , *jem.m Genüge* or *Schaden* or *unrecht* ~ . Also much used in coll. idioms such as *das tut's* – 'that does the trick, serves its purpose, suffices', *es gibt viel zu* ~ = 'there is a lot to be done', *ich habe nichts zu* ~ = 'I have nothing to do, am unemployed', *was hat er getan?* – 'what has he been up to? what is he accused of?'.

← See also under *Arbeit* (for *nach getaner Arbeit*), *Bescheid* (for *jem.m Bescheid tun*), *dienen* (for *getanen solt* and *eim etwas ze dienst thun*), *Flucht* (for *etw. auf der Flucht tun*), *Griff* (for *einen guten Griff tun*), *gut* (for *gut tun, gut daran tun, nicht gut tun, kein gut tun, sich etw. zugute tun* and *des Guten zuviel tun*), *lang* (for *etw. für die lange Weile tun*), *lassen* (for *dies sollte man tun und jenes nicht lassen*), *recht* (for *recht tun*), *Reise* (for *eine Reise tun*), *sagen* (for *gesagt, getan*), *Scheu* (for *tue recht und scheue niemand*), *Schritt* (for *der erste Schritt ist getan*), *Streich* (for *keinen Streich tun*), *Strich* (for *keinen Strich tun*) and *suchen* (for *ein Ansuchen tun*).

tun (3) + adj. or adv. to affect or display a certain attitude; since Early NHG, e.g. Luther Bible transl. Matth. 5,47: '*so jr euch nur zu ewern brüdern freundlich thut*', Gotthelf, *Schuld.* 395: '*thue nur nicht unterthänig*', and *fromm* ~ in Heine, *Verm.* 1,105.

← See also under *dick* (for *dick tun*), *dumm* (for *dumm tun*), *dünn* (for *dünnetun*), *fremd* (for *fremd tun*), *groß* (for *groß tun*), *gut* (for *gelehrt tun wollen*), *schön* (for *jem.m schön tun*) and *schwer* (for *sich schwer tun*).

tun (4) (intrans.) to act, be active; at least since the 17th c., e.g. Fleming, *Poemata* 75 [1651]: '*wäre wollen thun, ich ließe . . .*', Wieland 3,240: '*wenn ihr nicht thätet, würde bald die Welt ins Chaos zurückfallen*'; Adelung [1775] recorded: '*Tun lehrt tun*'.

jem.m etw. ~ (1) (obs.) to put a spell on sb.; still in the 18th c., e.g. (T.) Weiße, *Kom.Op.* 3,16 [1772]: '*wie kannst du dem Kerl so gut sein? Ich glaube, er hat dir's getan*'; now obs., displaced by *antun* (see p. 65).

jem.m etw. ~ (2) to harm sb.; in essence the same as the previous entry, but here with the special sense of inflicting some injury, e.g. Goethe, *Lehrj.* 1,3: '*was hat man dir, du armes Kind, gethan?*', near-coll., whereas *antun* takes its place in the standard language. A forerunner is *jem.m* ~ (obs.) = 'to behave towards sb', as in Luther 6,356b (Jena): '*wie sol ich ihm thun?*'.

mit jem.m zu ~ *haben* to (have to) deal with sb., be in contact, negotiations, etc. with sb.; since Early NHG, e.g. (DWb) Ayrer, 488: '*vor dir soll allen weibern grauen, daß sie mit dir nichts hetten zu thun*'. Sometimes (in modern period) used in the context of war or quarrels, e.g. Mommsen, *Röm.Gesch.* 1,583 [1856] and frequently with the notion of 'trouble', e.g. *wenn du damit nicht aufhörst, hast* (or *bekommst* or coll. *kriegst*) *du es mit ihm zu tun* = 'if you do not stop doing that, you will get into trouble with him'. Much older is *nichts mit jem.m zu* ~ *haben wollen* = 'to refuse to be associated with sb.'.

mit etw. zu ~ *haben* (1) to be busy or occupied with sth.; since Early NHG, also in the negative *damit will ich nichts zu* ~ *haben* = 'I will have nothing to do with that, I wash my hands of it', e.g. Luther Apocr. transl. Wisd. of Sol. 6,25: '*denn ich wil mit dem giftigen neid nicht zu thun haben*'.

mit etw. zu ~ *haben* (2) to be afflicted with sth., be troubled by sth.; a coll. off-shoot from the previous entry, used with ref. to illness; modern, not even mentioned in *DWb.* [1891]; e.g. *er hat (es) mit der Lunge zu* ~ = 'he has lung trouble'.

mit sich selbst zu ~ *haben* to be fully occupied with one's own problems; modern but cf. Goethe, *Faust* 4848: '*ein jeder hat für sich zu thun*'. Raabe used it in *Werke* 3,5,277 (*Akten d.V.*): '*man hatte damals so viel mit sich selbst zu thun*'.

so ~ *als ob . . .* to behave as though . . ., since

Early NHG, e.g. Wickram, *Rollwag.* 186 [1555]: '. . . *thet dergleichen, als wenn er nirgends da gewesen war*'; later with *so*, and in the regions by ellipsis *so* ~ = 'to pretend', e.g. *man so dun*, as recorded for Berlin coll.

es (mit jem.m) ~ (vulg.) to have sexual intercourse (with sb.); euphem. in origin, but vulg. in use; since Early NHG, e.g. (DWb) Manuel, *Elsli* 465: '*dann ich's sunst mit keim andern tät*'; also without *mit*, e.g. Grimmelshausen, *Simpliz.* 3,367: '. . . *daß ihr mirs noch einmal thun solt*'.

jem. . . . ~ to put, send, settle, instal sb. somewhere; belongs to the oldest meaning discussed above under *etw.* ~ (1); beginnings in OHG, general since Early NHG, e.g. *jem. in den Bann* ~ , as used by Luther, *An den Adel* (repr.) 34, Goethe, *Wahlverw.* 1,1: '*meine einzige Tochter that ich in Pension*'; Maaler [1561] recorded: '*ein knaben zu einem leermeister thun*'; cf. also Luther, *An den Adel* (repr.) 72: '*da rad ich niemand, das er sein kind hin thue*'.

das Seine ~ to do what one can, what one ought to do to the best of one's ability; since Early NHG, e.g. Luther, *An den Adel* (repr.) 76: '*ich thue das meine*', Schiller, *D.Carlos* 5,11: '*Kardinal, ich habe das meinige gethan, thun Sie das ihre*'.

(das) tut nichts (coll.) no matter, never mind; at least since the 18th c., e.g. Lessing, *Nathan* 4,2: '*thut nichts, der Jude wird verbrannt*'; cf. also *was tut's* (coll.) = 'what does it matter?'. since the 18th c., e.g. Klinger, *Theater* 2,100.

für jem. etw. ~ to help or serve sb.; at least since the 17th c., since Kramer [1702] recorded *viel für jem.* ~ , e.g. Schiller, *Picc.* 5,1: '*er thut so viel für uns und so ists Pflicht, daß wir jetzt auch für ihn was thun*'; before then *jem.m* ~ = 'to do a lot for sb., help sb. a great deal', recorded by Kramer, now obs.

tu was du nicht lassen kannst go ahead, if you feel that you must; suggests disapproval of sb.'s intentions and at the same time unwillingness to get into an argument over it; modern.

es ist um etw. zu ~ it is a matter or question of sth.; since Early NHG; Kramer [1702] recorded *es ist mir (nicht) darum zu* ~ , e.g. Schiller, *Räuber* 1,1; cf. also Schiller, *Picc.* 3,1: '*es scheint als wär es ihm um nichts zu thun, als nur am Platz zu bleiben*'.

mit etw. (or damit) ist es nicht getan that is not enough; belongs to *es tut es nicht* = 'it does not suffice', recorded by Kramer [1702], now only in coll. use; e.g. Schiller, *Fiesco* 4,6: '*izt ist es nicht mehr mit Murren und Verwünschen gethan*'.

um etw. (or jem.) ist es getan that (or he) is lost, at its end, must perish; since Early NHG, e.g. Goethe, *Faust I*, 1693: '*so sei es gleich um mich gethan*'.

du wirst gut daran ~ (or *du tätest gut daran*), *wenn . . .* (or *zu* + infinitive) you would be well advised, if you . . .; since the 17th c., e.g. (DWb) Logau [edit E.] 543: 'der den schöpffer weiß zu schaffen, thäte wol so gut daran, wann er eine welt auch schaffte, die ein solches glauben kann'.

sein (ganzes) Tun und Lassen his (entire) behaviour or conduct; since MHG, e.g. Wolfr.v.Esch., Parz. 405,14: 'mîn tuon odr mîn lâzen'; cf. also the entry under tu was du nicht lassen kannst (above) and du kannst tun und lassen, was du willst = 'I am not telling you what to do, you are a free agent'.

sein Tun und Treiben his activities; modern, e.g. Ranke, Werke 1,178 in reverse order: 'alles menschliche Treiben und Thun', which is now not the preferred order.

das ist nicht seines Tuns (obs.) that is not his usual way of behaving; still in the 18th c., e.g. in Wieland, Acharner 2: 'mit Gaukelkünsten zu täuschen ist seines Thuns nicht'; now obs.

es tut sich was (or etwas) (coll.) sth. is going on; modern; frequent in many contexts, e.g. in situations where one notices sth. which was to have been kept secret or when sth. happens at last for which one has been waiting.

tunlich (1) practical, manageable; first as tulich, and still in this form in Goethe, Dicht.u.Wahrh. 6: '. . . Sache, die ich mir im Stillen so thulich ausgebildet hatte'; in Lessing and Schiller as thunlich; also now as an adverb in the superlative, tunlichst bald = 'as soon as possible'. hence Tunlichkeit = 'practicability', f.r.b. Stieler [1691] as Thulichkeit.

tunlich (2) advisable; off-shoot from the previous entry; modern.

betulich obliging, concerned (and friendly), clumsily officious; in this sense in Goethe, Pater Brey: 'sobald die Kerls wie Wilde leben und nicht bethulich und freundlich sind'; now also containing the notion of being embarrassingly concerned, too eager to help (and therefore to interfere). Other meanings such as 'slowly and persistently' are rare or obs.

der Tunichtgut (sometimes Tunichtsgut) (coll.) good-for-nothing; since the 19th c., e.g. Alexis, Hosen d.H.v.B. 1,1,273.

'was tun, spricht Zeus' what is to be done? quotation from Schiller, Die Teilung der Erde 29, which has become a standing phrase, now often used in joc. coll.

sich umtun (1) (coll.) to get busy, bestir oneself; since Early NHG, e.g. Hätzlerin, Liederbuch 308 [1471]: 'tu dich umb, du bist noch jungk'; the phrase in etw. umgetan sein = 'to be well versed in sth., familiar with sth.', still current in the 18th c., is obs., displaced by erfahren, bewandert sein.

sich umtun (2) (coll.) to make enquiries, search for information; e.g. Goethe 50,238 (W.): 'lasset uns also zuerst bey guten Leuten uns umthun . . .'.

etw. umtun (coll., rare or obs.) to change, recast sth.; e.g. Goethe IV,35,192 (W.): 'wie die Natur uns täglich umarbeitet, so können wir's auch nicht lassen, das Gethane umzuthun'.

etw. vertun (1) (obs.) to achieve or manage sth.; since Early NHG, e.g. Fischart, S.Dom.Leb. 342 and still in the 18th c., e.g. Lessing, Dramat. 79: 'ein Dichter kann viel gethan und doch noch nichts damit verthan haben'; now obs., with verbs such as erreichen taking its place.

etw. vertun (2) (a.) to wear sth. out, use sth. up, consume or exhaust sth.; since MHG, e.g. Wolfr.v.Esch., Parz. 302,20; still current in the 19th c., e.g. (DWb) Eichendorff, Werke 3,436: '. . . Feuer, das nichts thut also verthun und verzehren'; now verbrauchen is preferred.

etw. vertun (3) to waste sth., with ref. to time since MHG, e.g. Gottfr.v.Str., Tristan 2094, f.r.b. Frisius [1556].

vertun (intrans., a.) to end, die, come to grief; e.g. Goethe, Faust II, 4759: 'der Alte fiel—der hat verthan'; with ref. to failure in R.Wagner, Meistersinger: 'der hat verthan und versungen ganz'.

sich vertun (coll.) to make a mistake, slip up; in many different contexts, e.g. with ref. to dealing cards wrongly, mixing things up, etc., modern (not yet recorded by Adelung, even in 2nd edit. of 1801).

da gibt es kein Vertun (regional coll.) that is an incontrovertible fact; modern and only current in some regions.

sich zusammentun (coll.) to get together, unite, combine; since Early NHG, e.g. (DWb) Buch d.Beisp. (Lit. Verein repr. 88), Goethe IV,11,329 (W.): 'so könnten wir uns wohl in den vorderen Zimmern zusammenthun'; in the standard language sich vereinen or (less stilted) sich zusammensetzen would be used.

Übermut tut selten gut (prov.) pride goes before a fall; sometimes also in the modern interpretation of Übermut in the sense of 'high spirits can have unpleasant consequences'; prov. since MHG; it occurs in Boner, where, however, the wording is uebermuot wirt niemer guot; recorded in modern form by Petri [1605].

← See also under abbrechen (for Abbruch tun), abtun, auftun, Auge (for kein Auge zutun), beitun, blicken (for jem.m einen Blick auftun), Bock (for einen Bocksprung tun), breit (for die Politiker thaten breit), Dampf (for jem.m Dampf antun), dartun, gerade (for etw. gerade tun), Gewalt (for einer Sache Gewalt antun), Hand (for die Hände voll zu tun haben and seine milde Hand auftun), Handlanger (for Handlangerdienste tun), hervortun, hintun, leiden (for sich ein Leid antun), Sache (for es tut nichts zur Sache, where I should have added that this was current as early as in the 17th c., recorded by Kramer in 1702), Schuld (for seine Schuldigkeit tun) and Sohn (for was der Vater erspart vertut der Sohn).

Tünche: whitewash

das ist nur ~ that is a mere veneer; pejor. since Early NHG (as Tünch) in H.Sachs 19,92 and in

Luther Apocr. transl. Ecclesiasticus 22,20. As a term implying deliberate deception since the 18th c. in the now current form *Tünche*.

etw. übertünchen to whitewash or gloss over sth.; since Early NHG; in the past participle *übertüncht* often = 'pretended, false, insincere', e.g. *übertünchte Höflichkeit*.

einer Sache etw. auftünchen (a.) to embellish sth. with sth.; since the 18th c., e.g. Goethe, *Von dt.Baukunst* 3: '*so hast du deinen Bedürfnissen einen Schein von Wahrheit und Schönheit aufgetüncht*'; now a.

← See also under *betünchen* and *Grab* (for *übertünchte Gräber*).

tunken: dip

etw. in etw. ~ (rare) to dip sth. into sth. else; figur. since the 18th c., e.g. Winckelmann, *S.Werke* [edit. E.] 1,56: '*der Pinsel, den der Künstler führet, soll in Verstand getunket sein*'; Börne, *Ges.Schr.* 358 [1840]: '*freie Schauspielbühnen . . . damit das arme Volk eine geistige Freude habe, worin es seine trockne Kruste tunke*'; more coll. in compounds, as in v.Horn, *Rh.D.* 2,271: '*Margareth hatte die Geschichte auszutunken*'; cf. also Kürnberger, *Novellen* 1,288 [1861]: '*fremde Schüsseln tunk' ich nicht aus*' (= 'I do not interfere in other people's affairs').

← See also *Pfütze* (for *Pfützentunker*).

jem. ~ (sl.) to degrade sb.; literally 'to hold or keep sb. down'; modern sl.

in der Tunke sitzen (coll.) to be in a mess, in trouble, in the soup; modern coll.

sein Brot in jem.s Suppe ~ (coll.) to live at other people's expense; e.g. (DWb) Forster, *Sämtl.Schr.* 9,77 [1843]; a. or obs.?

er tunkt sein Brot in jeder Brühe (coll.) he is up to any tricks, there are no flies on him; recorded since the 18th c., e.g. (DWb) J.G.Müller, *Siegfr. v.Lind* 1,211; now a. or obs.?

Polsterzipfel ~ (regional coll.) to sleep; in S. areas, e.g. Rosegger, *Schr.* 1,11,36 [1903].

Tunnel: tunnel

der ~ (coll.) basement cafe or restaurant; coined when the tunnel under the Thames was built (1829), as reported by Bucher in *Nat.Ztg.* 14,579: '*der Besitzer eines um dieselbe Zeit in Berlin erbauten . . . Vergnügslokals kam auf den Einfall, das . . . Kellergeschoß den Tunnel zu nennen und seitdem ist das Wort für ähnliche Anlagen zum Appellativum geworden*', e.g. Hoffmann v. Fallersleben, *Ges.Schr.* 7,303: '*morgen mir zu Ehren ein Frühstück im Tunnel des Hotel de Pologne*'. In 1827 the lit. society *~ über der Spree* (also inspired by the Thames tunnel) was formed.

← See also under *Neger* (for *Neger im Tunnel*).

Tüpfel: dot

kein ~ (or *Tupfen* or *Tüpfelchen*) (coll.) not one jot, iota, little bit; since Early NHG, recorded by Kramer [1702]; cf. *das Tüpfelchen auf dem i* (see

p. 1400) and its old synonyms *tittle* and *houbit* and the entry under *Jota*.

etw. aufs Tüpfelchen beachten or *einhalten* to observe sth. strictly in every detail; modern, e.g. Th.Mann, *Faustus* 359 (with *Versprechen halten*).

tupfen: tip, touch

tupfen (regional coll.) to make insinuations, gibes, make offensive allusions; for many regions recorded since the 18th c. with a variety of meanings (apart from the above-mentioned), such as 'to insult, annoy, reprimand, expose to ridicule, cheat, send packing'. The standard dictionaries do not list any of them.

Tür: door

die ~ (1) (lit.) door; in rare lit. use, above all in the Bible: John 10,7: '*ich bin die thür*'.

die ~ (2) (lit.) opening, gate; in relig. contexts since OHG, often in *~ des Himmels* or *der Hölle*, later also *des Todes ~*, as in Leibnitz 1,437: '. . . *daß wir . . . durch des todes thür zu dem leben folgen dir*'; also in secular lit. since MHG, e.g. *Iwein* 437: '*ûzerhalb des mundes tür*' or *Minnes.* 1,93a addressing *Minne*: '*tuo mir ûf der saelden tür*'; cf. also Schiller, *D.Carlos* 2,14: '*das Ohr der Neugier liegt nun an den Thüren des Glückes und der Leidenschaft*'.

die ~ (3) beginning; in poet. contexts since the 17th c., e.g. Logau 2,10,31 on January: '*unser thür ins erste jahr*'.

von ~ zu ~ from one person to the next; first in literal sense 'from door to door', since Early NHG when Maaler [1561] recorded: '*von einer thür zur anderen*', then extended, e.g. Geibel, *Ged.* 245: '*von Thür zu Thür wallet der Traum, ein lieber Gast*'; cf. *vor den Türen* (or *von ~ zu ~*) *sein Brot suchen* = 'to beg', recorded since the 18th c. See also under *Klinke* (for *Klinken/Türklinken putzen*).

jem.m die ~ zeigen (or *weisen*) to throw sb. out; since Early NHG, e.g. Fischart, *Bienenk.* 50b [1580]; also as *jem. vor die ~ setzen*, as in Goethe, *Aufger.* 42, or Goethe, *Faust* I,2801: '*zur Thür hinaus, wer sich entzweit*'; cf. also Luther 6,479a (Jena): '*du weisest mir eine thür, da kein weg ist*' = 'you send me off in the wrong direction (or to where I cannot find help)'.

an der unrechten ~ anklopfen to look for help, advice, etc. in the wrong quarter; also in wider sense = 'to choose the wrong route', e.g. Egenolff [1560]: '*die rechte thür verfehlen*', Eyering 1,799 [1601]: '*er hat gefehlt der rechten thür und ist darneben gangen für*', Lehman, 406 [1662]: '*wer nicht an der rechten thür anklopfft, den lest man nicht ein*'. Recordings for the positive version are older, e.g. *zur rechten ~ eingehen*, f.r.b. Agricola [1528].

ihm stehen alle Türen offen he is welcome everywhere; though recordings in this wording are late, the idiom must be old because of such phrases as *ein offenes Haus haben* (see p. 1256) or

Luther Bible transl. Rev. 3,8: '*ich habe fur dir gegeben eine offene thur*' (see p. 1805). The opposite is recorded by Eiselein [1838]: '*es sind ihm alle Thüren verriegelt*'. Cf. also *die ~ nicht zuschlagen* = 'to be prepared to continue negotiations'.

bei verschlossenen Türen with exclusion of the public; the phrase in its phys. sense is as old as OHG, e.g. Otfrid 5,11,3: '*bispartên durôn*', but is modern in the extended sense, as in *Verhandlung bei* (or *hinter*) *verschlossenen Türen*; see also *geschlossene Sitzung* under *schließen* (p. 2140).

die Politik der offenen ~ open-door policy; coined by Secretary of State John Hay on 6.9.1899 in a circular letter to all American ambassadors with ref. to trade with China. The phrase in Rev. 3,8 quoted above may have been of influence.

Tag der offenen ~ open day (in an institution, factory, etc. which is not ordinarily open to the public); 20th c.

sich eine ~ offenhalten to leave oneself an escape route; since the 19th c.

anders geht die ~ nicht zu (coll.) any other method is useless, this is the only practical way; 20th c. coll.; note, however, that the exclamation *ach, du kriegst die ~ nicht zu* (sl.) refers to open-mouthed stupefaction; 20th c. sl.

er ist hinter Türen ohne Klinke (sl.) he is in prison; 20th c. sl.

einer gibt dem andern die Türklinke in die Hand (coll.) there is a constant stream of callers (visitors, applicants, etc.); since early in the 20th c. in coll. use.

die Falltür (lit.) trap; at least since the 18th c., e.g. Musäus, *Ph.* 4,182: '*durch die Falltür der List . . . einzupraktizieren*'.

der Letzte macht die Türe zu (prov.) the surviving husband receives the entire inheritance; old legal prov., which excludes the relatives of the deceased woman from any share in the inheritance; listed in 19th c. prov. collections as 'old', but no early instances of its use are quoted.

← See also under *Angel* (for *etw. zwischen Tür und Angel erledigen, zwischen Tür und Angel* and *man muß den Finger nicht zwischen Tür und Angel stecken*), *auffliegen* (for *die Tür fliegt auf*), *aufrennen* (for *offene Türen aufrennen/einrennen*), *Auge* (for *Hosentürlaugen haben*), *eindonnern* (for *eine Tür eindonnern*), *einlaufen* (for *jem.m die Tür einlaufen*), *einrennen* (for *die Tür mit jem.m einrennen* and *offene Türen einrennen*), *fallen* (for *mit der Tür ins Haus fallen*), *Flügel* (for *Flügeltür*), *hinter* (for *hinter der Tür Abschied nehmen*), *Hintertür, hüten* (for *der Türhüter*), *kehren* (for *kehre vor deiner eignen Tür*), *klopfen* (for *an die/der Tür klopfen*), *Nase* (for *jem.m die Tür vor der Nase zuschlagen*), *offen* (for *ich habe dir gegeben eine offne Tür*), *pochen* (for *etw. pocht an die Tür*), *Riegel* (for *Riegel und Tür setzen* and *der Wahrheit Tür und Tor verriegeln*), *Sack* (for *habt ihr Säcke vor den Türen?*), *Schlag* (for *jem. mit der Tür schlagen*), *schließen* (for *jem.m die Tür schließen* and *jem.m ist weder Tür noch Tor verschlossen*), *Schritt* (for *der größte Schritt ist der aus der Tür*), *spät* (for *wer spät kommt, sitzt hinter der Tür*), *stehen* (for *etw. steht vor der Tür*), *Stuhl* (for *jem.m den Stuhl vor die Tür setzen*) and *Tor* (for *einer Sache Tor und Tür öffnen*).

Türke: Turk

ein ~ (coll., offensive) a boor, savage, cruel beast; used as a term of strong abuse and contempt, originally also of genuine fear, since the Middle Ages. Turks, the main followers of Islam with which the West came in contact, seen as the deadly enemies of the Christian world, are blackened in sayings and curses as cruel, savage, reckless, immoral, etc.; frequent examples in Luther's writings and in the regions still alive in *wild wie ein ~* , *dreinhauen wie ein ~* , *wüten wie ein ~* . A relic of such usage is the exclamation *Kruzitürken*, which combines the two antagonists, the Christian Church and Islam; still current in some regions (mainly in the S.).

einen Türken bauen or *stellen* (coll.) to put up a façade, fake sth.; also sometimes = 'to invent sth. on the spur of the moment and present it as though it were a proven fact or arrived at after long consideration'; current since the last quarter of the 19th c., though with *bauen* only since the 20th c. Arguments about its origin have continued. There are two facts which enter into the discussion and it is likely that both contributed. A mil. manuoeuvre concerned with assumed attacks or sham defensive actions was called *~* , f.r.b. Imme [1917], e.g. Ompteda, *Sylvester v. G.* 2,31 [1900] either because the chief ones were carried out on a parade ground on the *Tempelhofer Feldmark* which bordered on an old Turkish cemetery or because of an incident in 1895 when the German Emperor opened the Kiel Canal. Ships of many nations attended and as each approached the Emperor's flagship its national anthem was played. For Turkey the military band had no music and the conductor with great presence of mind made the band play *Guter Mond, du gehst so stille* as the Turkish national anthem. If one takes the two items together, they throw some light on the meanings 'staged event', as in *einen Türken stellen*, and 'invention on the spur of the moment' (for details see Krüger-Lorenzen, *Das geht auf keine Kuhhaut* 264ff). Others have rejected these mil. and naval explanations and have pointed to an apparatus invented by Wolfgang von Kempelen in 1768 in which a puppet dressed as a Turk played chess against all comers and won. This robot was directed by a small but brilliant chessplayer sitting in the table-like structure under the chessboard, pulling strings, who was invisible because the whole apparatus was confusingly fitted with mirrors. Although the use of *einen Türken stellen* may be less used now in the Army and in the theatre, it has grown in importance in the media, esp. in television programmes where, when a real event of interest has passed, people are paid to reproduce that event and it is shown on the small screen as a truthful picture of what happened. Similarly, the term is applied when an important interview is scheduled and a 'look-alike' is hired when the invited personality does not appear. In some cases *einen Türken bauen* can amount to criminal deception. There is now also a verb *türken* (coll.) = 'to fake sth., set up sth. which creates the illusion of truthful presentation', usually in the form *das ist getürkt*.

im Türkensitz sitzen to sit cross-legged; modern; see also under *Schneider* (for *Schneidersitz*).

der Türkenkoffer (sl.) plastic shopping bag; sl. of ca. 1975, attacked as offensive by believers in 'political correctness'.

das Türkenhütchen (zool.) European limpet (*Patella vulgata*); only in modern recordings.

← See also under *Kümmel* (for *Kümmeltürke*).

Turm: tower

der ~ (1) (poet., rare) tower of strength, fortress; occasionally in poetry, e.g. Geibel, *Ges.Werke* 1,186 [1883] on the beloved: '. . . *ist ihm sichrer Hort und Thurm*'. Beginnings in biblical language, e.g. Psalm 61,4; also with abstracts, e.g. (DWb) Logau 2,2,34: '*die ehr ist wie ein thurm*'.

der ~ (2) (chess) castle; for centuries the figure was called *Roche*, then called *~* under French and Italian influence; Adelung recorded it, but Campe and the *DWb.* ignored it totally.

im ~ (obs.) in prison; since Early NHG, e.g. Luther Bible transl. Psalm 66,11, still used in the 18th c. by Goethe and Schiller, e.g. *Räuber* 1,2 and *Hungerturm* as well as *Schuldturm* = 'debtors' prison' occurred in hist. writings even in the 19th c.; cf also Geibel, *Ges.Werke* 7,701 [1883]: '. . . *ein Jahr im Thurmverließ*'.

ein babylonscher ~ (or *Turmbau*) (lit.) a tower of Babel, grandiose or over-ambitious undertaking doomed to failure; allusion to the biblical story in Genesis 11. Heine 13,164 still used '*babylonischer Thurmbau*', but phrases with *Babel* are now preferred; see *Babelgedanke*, *babelhaft* and *Babeltum* on p. 176.

turmhoch as high as a steeple, very tall; as an adverb often = 'vastly'; since the 18th c., used by Goethe, e.g. Bismarck, *Reden* 7,200: '*unsere Beziehungen . . . stehen fest und turmhoch über der Tragweite von dergleichen kleinen Versuchen*'; frequently in *turmhoch überlegen sein* = 'to be vastly superior'; cf. Heine 6,114 on A.W. Schlegel: '*im Studium des Altdeutschen steht thurmhoch über ihn erhaben Herr Jakob Grimm . . .*'.

etw. auf etw. türmen (lit.) to pile sth. on sth. else; since the 17th c., e.g. (DWb) *Schles. Helikon*

52, Haller, *Vers.schw.Ged.* 203: '. . . *der falschen Größe gram, die auf der Bürger Grab des Herrschers theure Säulen thürmet*'; also in hyperbolic descriptions, e.g. G.Keller, *Werke* 6,294: '*eine gethürmte Schüssel voll*'. The pres. part. *türmend* can describe 'rising, soaring, stretching upward', as in Klopstock, *Mess.* 2,697: '*der thürmenden Felsen*' or it can stress the enormous size of sth., as in Schiller, *Wall. Tod* 1,4: '*eine Mauer . . . die mir die Umkehr thürmend hemmt*'; cf. *einer Sache etw. entgegentürmen*, as in Wieland 18,32. In reflex. use since the 18th c., as has been *sich emportürmen* (lit.). Note that *türmen* (coll.) = 'to run away, decamp' does not belong to *~* , but is a cant term probably derived from Hebrew *tharam* = 'to remove oneself'.

jem. eintürmen (regional) to imprison sb.; in some S. regions, e.g. G.Keller, *L.v.Seldw.* 1,186.

hochgetürmt (1) (lit.) towering, very high; since the 18th c., e.g. Mendelssohn, *Ph.* 1,62: '*eine hochgethürmte Welle*'.

hochgetürmt (2) (coll., obs.) proud, conceited, arrogant, stuck-up; current in the 18th and 19th c., e.g. Tieck, *Acc.*: '*diese hochgethürmte weise Hoffahrtsdame*',. Schubart 2,274: '*jeder aufgethürmte Trotzer*' expresses the same notion.

← See also under *auftürmen* and *Elfenbein* (for *Elfenbeinturm*).

turnen: do gymnastics

turnen (coll.) to move, clamber, scramble around; the verb was invented by F.L.Jahn in 1811, in coll. use since the middle of the 19th c., rare in lit., but G.Hauptmann used it in *Ratten* IV; frequent in compounds, e.g. Fontane, *Familienbriefe* 2,161 [1888]: '*sie turnt viel umher und ist in diesem Augenblick auf dem Wege nach Rostock*', Heine, *Börne* 270 [1840]: '*Menzel war der Erste, der in die alten Ideenkreise zurückturnte*'; *Turnerei*, current since the last quarter of the 19th c., is usually pejor. describing unnecessary activity (involving much moving about).

Turteltaube: see *Taube*.

tuschen: paint with water-colour or Indian ink

etw. ~ (lit.) to paint or colour sth.; figur. in lit. since the 18th c., mainly in descriptions of sb.'s beauty, e.g. (DWb) Dusch, *Verm.W.* 162 [1754]: '*die lichte . . . Haut war mit röthlichem Glanze getüschet*', Bürger, *Sämtl.W.* [edit. B.] 37b: '*wer tuschte so mit Kunst und Fleiß der Holden Wange roth und weiß?*'. Very occasionally in lit. compounds *antuschen*, *betuschen* or *übertuschen*, more often in *etw. hintuschen* (coll.) = 'to throw sth. on paper (in haste or carelessly)'.

etw. vertuschen to hush up, cover up, suppress sth.; though many scholars declare this to be unconnected with *~* , most of them admit that the painters' term must have influenced the development of *vertuschen*. The verb appeared in MHG as *verduschen*, could mean 'to extinguish', then 'to suppress', also with abstracts, as in *ein*

Gerede vertuschen, recorded by Frisius [1556], where the present-day meaning is clearly discernible.

tuschieren: touch

jem. ~ (obs.) to insult sb.; ultimately derived from French *toucher*, but more directly from stud.sl. *Tusch* = 'insult (requiring satisfaction by a duel)', current since the 18th c.; *jem. ~* was still used by Bürger, now obs.

Tusculum

das ~ (lit.) country seat or quiet place of retreat; based on the name of Cicero's estate near Rome and used mainly by Classical scholars and poets familiar with the Classics, e.g. *sich sein ~ erwählen* (as used by Herder), e.g. Droste-Hülshoff, *Briefe* [edit. S.-K.] 2,240 [of 1843]: '*die Aussicht auf mein künftiges kleines Tuskulum machte mir alles leicht*'.

Tüte: horn; paper-bag

die ~ (regional coll. and sl.) person, creature; in many pejor. descriptions of persons, first in some regions, e.g. *Trantute* = 'sleepy, lethargic person', recorded for Saxony by Müller-Fraureuth, now (since ca. 1950) among juveniles, e.g. *lahme* or *müde ~* = 'slow-coach, unenterprising chap', *traurige ~* = 'weakling'.

etw. in der ~ haben für jem. (coll.) to have sth. (disagreeable) to say to sb. or in store for sb., to have a bone to pick with sb.; modern (20th c.).

das kommt nicht in die ~ (coll.) nothing doing, out of the question; derived from a salesman wanting to put sth. damaged or rotten into one's bag; modern (? late 19th c.).

er hat keine Ahnung vom Tuten und Blasen (coll.) he does not know the first thing about it; current since the 16th c., f.r.b. Eyering, *Prov.* [1601]: '*er kan weder thütten noch blasen*', but much later with *Ahnung*.

der Tütendreher (coll., a.) shop-keeper; contemptuous, current mainly in 2nd half of the 19th c., used by Holtei and Alexis; now probably obs.

← See also under *flüstern* (for *Flüstertüte*) and *kleben* (for *er klebt Tüten*).

Tüttel: nipple

kein ~ (or *Tüttelchen*) (coll.) not the least bit or one iota; *~* = 'nipple' acquired the extended meaning 'dot, point', currently since the 15th c. and Luther used it in his Bible transl., e.g. Luke 16,17: '*. . . denn das ein tütel am gesetz falle*'; there was unavoidable interference from *Titel* = 'dot, small stroke in a letter' (recorded by Adelung), e.g. Bürger, *Kaiser u. Abt* 40: '*es soll auch kein Titelchen Wahres daran sein*'; cf. Storm, *Werke* 2,221: '*da beißt dir keine Maus auch nur ein Tittelchen ab*'.

Twen: person in his or her twenties

ein Doppeltwen (joc.coll.) a person in his or her forties who feels young (or wants to appear so); current since ca. 1960.

Typ: type

ein ~ (coll.) a type of person, individual, specimen; since early in the 20th c. in usually uncomplimentary refs., e.g. (T.) Dwinger, *Armee* 201 [1929]: '*beim Spaziergehen zeigte mir O. . . . einen "Typ". Mit diesem Namen bezeichnen wir die Sonderlinge unseres Lagers*'; often qualified by an adj., e.g. *ein komischer Typ* = 'an odd chap, queer specimen'. Not pejor. or coll. when describing a person as belonging into a certain class, e.g. *Hausfrautyp, Kämpfertyp, Unternehmertyp*, etc.

das ist mein ~ (coll.) that's the kind of person I like; 20th c. coll., also in compounds, e.g. *jem.s Traumtyp* (coll.) = 'sb.'s ideal'.

typisch! (coll.) that's typical of him or her, just what you would expect; 20th c. coll. ellipsis.

Tyrann: tyrant

ein ~ a tyrant (in wider sense of bullying or selfishly dominating person); general since the 18th c., also with ref. to abstracts, e.g. (S.-B.) Schlettwein, *Untersuch.* 8 [1764]: '*. . . den moralischen Egoismus, diesen Tyrannen der menschlichen Gesellschaft*', Fontane, *Sommer* 2,4,63 [1854]: '*die großen Tyrannen sind ausgestorben; nur in England lebt noch einer—der Sonntag*'; often in compounds such as *Haustyrann, Küchentyrann*, e.g. Meisl, *Quodlibet* 2,103 [1820]: '*wer hätte das von unserem sauberen Ehtyrann geglaubt*'; hence also *tyrannisieren* in wider sense 'to domineer, bully, tyrannise' since the 18th c., e.g. (T.) Schummel, *Revol.* 108 [1794]: '*. . . ihren Mann zu quälen und Kinder und Gesinde zu tyrannisieren*', also with abstracts, e.g. Iselin, *Gesch.d.Menschh.* 1,73 [1770]: '*so tyrannisieren die Einflüsse der äußerlichen Gegenstände den thierischen und den sinnlichen Menschen*' and *Tyrannei*, figur. in Schiller, *Philipp* 2,3,190: '*. . . eine solche Tyrannei des Gewissens—die schlimmste aller Regierungsformen*'.

← See also under *Mode* (for *die Mode ist die größte Tyrannin*).

tz

etw. bis aufs tz kennen (coll.) to know sth. in every detail; the same as *von A bis Z*, since in some old word lists and dictionaries *tz* was appended as the last letter after *Z*; recordings of the phrase are late, listed e.g. in Wander [1876]; e.g. (Sp.) Sternheim, *Bürger Schippel* 1,2 [1912]; there is also *bis ins tz* = 'to the utmost', e.g. Meyer, *D.richt. Berliner* 121 [1904]: '*bis in't tz*'.

U

jem.m ein X für ein U vormachen (coll.) to (try to) deceive sb.; this goes back to the period when no distinction was made in writing between U and V, and since numbers were given in Roman characters, X = 10 could be written by swindlers in such a way as to look like a V = 5; in print since the 16th c., e.l. of 1597 in *Germania* 13,270: '*er macht ein x wol für ein v, damit kam er der rechnung zu*'; cf. Wieland, *Wasserkufe* 561: '*wiewohl so einem schwachen verblüfften Kopf aus x ein u zu machen, kein großes Kunststück ist'*; Simrock [1846] recorded as prov.: *'laß dir kein x für ein u machen'*.

übel: ill, sick, evil, wicked

mir wird (or *ist*) ~ I am feeling sick; in phys. sense since the 17th c., but by the end of the c. also in extended sense of feeling disgust rather than phys. sickness, f.r.b. Kramer [1719]. Note, however, that *jem.m* ~ *zumute sein* and *jem.m* ~ *bekommen* date back to Early NHG.

~ *daran sein* to be badly off, be in a bad way or in a bad situation; beginnings in Early NHG in such idioms as ~ *ankommen* or *anlaufen* or *daran sein*, e.g. Arigo, *Decam.* 21. Later in *in übler Lage sein*. The phrase *es steht* ~ has been listed on pp. 2343 and 2345. Petri [1605] recorded several provs. beginning with *es stehet* ~ , *wenn . . .* = 'things are in a bad way, when . . .' and also listed: *'es gehet wol offt einem vbel, aber es weret nicht ewig'*.

nicht ~ not at all bad, quite acceptable; since the 17th c., e.g. Leibnitz, *Unvorgr.Ged.* 64: *'. . . daß sie das französische tendre, wenn es vom Gemüthe verstanden wird, durch innig . . . nicht übel gegeben'*; also sometimes as *so* ~ *nicht*.

kein übler . . . not a bad . . ., quite a good . . .; in essence the same as the previous entry, also since the 17th c., e.g. Ziegler, *As.Banise* 188 [1689], Schubart, *Leb.u.Ges.* 2,9: *'so wär' ich . . . kein übler Zeitungsschreiber worden'*, Schiller, *Wall.Lager* 5: *'das Mädchen ist kein übler Bissen'*.

~ *an etw. tun* (a.) to act wrongly in a certain matter, handle sth. badly; beginnings in Early NHG, f.r.b. *voc.theut.* [1482]; later with *an etw.* or *daran*, still in Goethe 21,78 (W.): *'daran thun Sie sehr übel'*; now a. or at least stilted.

zu etw. nicht ~ *Lust haben* to be inclined or more than ready to . . .; always in negative form; since the 18th c., e.g. Goethe IV,9,157 (W.).

wohl oder ~ willy-nilly, whether one likes it or not, *nolens volens*; since the 18th c., e.g. Hebel 2,235, sometimes as *gut oder* ~ , as in Droste-Hülshoff, *Werke*, 3,92.

etw. übelnehmen to resent sth., take sth. badly or in bad part; first as *für übel nehmen* or *halten*, also *in übel haben* or *halten* (Gellert still used *in* ~ *halten* in *Zärtl.Schw.* 1,6), later as ~ *nehmen*, f.r.b. Nieremberger [1753], since the 19th c. in one word. Hence *übelnehmerisch* = 'easily offended, touchy, resentful', since the 19th c., e.g. Anzengruber, *D.led.Hof.* 1,7 [1877]: *'besonders die Creszenz ist ein übelnehmerisches Ding'*, *Übelnehmer* and *Übelnehmerei*.

sich nichts übelnehmen (coll.) to have no qualms about what people think of one's behaviour, loose morals, etc., do as one pleases; Hetzel [1896] recorded it; cf. Ranke 3,76: *'. . . jener Kampf mit dem Islam . . . man nahm sich keine Gewaltsamkeit dabei übel'*.

. . .-übel (coll.) very sick; intensified in some coll. compounds such as *speiübel* and *sterbensübel*, both since the 20th c.

← See also under *Hund* (for *hundsübel*) and *kotzen* (for *mir wird kotzübel davon*).

zu allem Übel on top of everything else, in addition to all the other trouble; *Übel* here in the sense of 'misfortune, bad luck', current since Early NHG, but since the 19th c. in this phrase in wider sense when it can mean no more than 'bother, inconvenience'.

das kleinere Übel the lesser evil; taken from Cicero, *De officiis*; in German since Early NHG; sometimes in the superlative *kleinste* or *geringste*, though the comparative is in most cases the more appropriate form.

ein notwendiges Übel a necessary evil; Luther 10,2,293 (Weimar) used *'nöttigs ubel'*, but *notwendig* has been the preferred adjective since the 17th c.

etw. verübeln to resent sth., take sth. amiss; since the 18th c., recorded by Adelung, e.g. Alxinger, *Doolin* 269 [1797].

← See also under *abstellen* (for *ein Übel abstellen*), *alt* (for *ein altes Übel*), *aufnehmen* (for *etw. übel aufnehmen*), *fertig* (for *übelfertig*, also for *übelwollend* and *übelgesinnt*), *Gast* (for *übel zu Gast bei jem.m sein*), *heben* (for *ein Übel heben*, also *beheben* and *aufheben*), *Hirt* (for *viel Hirten, übel gehütet*), *Hund* (for *übel gebissen von etw.*), *Kunde* (for *übler Kunde*), *mitspielen* (for *jem.m übel mitspielen*), *rufen* (for *in üblem Ruf stehen*), *Schuld* (for *der Übel Größtes aber ist die Schuld*) and *stehen* (for *übel stehen*).

üben: exercise, practise

etw. ~ to exercise or perform sth., bring sth. to bear on sth. else; with abstracts since OHG in scores of cases such as *Barmherzigkeit, Gerechtigkeit, Gnade, Kritik, Milde, Rache, Verrat* ~ ; worth mentioning is only the lit. usage when an abstract exercises sth. abstract, since the 19th c., e.g. Schiller, *Wall.Tod* 1,4: *'das Jahr übt eine heiligende Kraft'*.

Übung macht den Meister (prov.) practise makes perfect; international; in German recorded since the 17th c.; older is *Übung bringt Kunst*, f.r.b. Franck [1541]: *'Vbung bringt künst'*.

← See also under *früh* (for *früh übt sich, was ein Meister werden will*).

über: over, above, beyond

jem.m ~ *sein* (coll.) to be superior to sb., be stronger than sb.; modern, presumably shortened from *überlegen sein*, e.g. (DWb) Timm Kröger, *Stille Welt* 276: *'er ist uns Beiden über'*.

mir ist (or *wird es*) ~ (coll.) I am sick and tired of it; modern coll.

etw. ~ *haben* (coll.) to have sth. left; same as *übrig haben*; modern coll.

~ *sein* (coll.) to have passed, to be a thing of the past; probably a shortened form of *vorüber sein*; current since the 16th c., now a. except in some regions.

~ *und* ~ (coll., obs.) in disarray, in confusion; since the 17th c., still used in the 18th c., e.g. Möser, *Ph.* 1,330, displaced by *drunter und drüber*; Luther 33,652 used '*über und drüber*', M.Claudius 1,12 has '*es geht Alles über und drunter*'.

~ *und* ~ all over, everywhere; since the 18th c., sometimes the same as 'completely', at others = 'more than enough', e.g. Bürger, 498b, Goethe used it with *rot werden* (others with *erröten*); Heinse, *Ardingh.* 1,142 has '. . . *küßte mich über und über*'; cf. also *er steckt* ~ *und* ~ *in Schulden* = 'he is up to his ears in debt'.

darüber (or *drüber*) (coll.) through it, on account of it, as a consequence of it; this should have been listed under *darüber* (p. 453); it has been current at least since the 18th c., e.g. Lessing, *Nathan* 5,5: '. . . *mir zu folgen, wenn sie drüber eines Muselmanns Frau auch werden mußte*'.

das Herüber und Hinüber (coll.) process of interchange, situation in which two things mingle or influence each other; since the 19th c., e.g. v. Raumer, *Gesch.d.Päd.* 3,2,116 [1847]: '*so entsteht ein Herüber und Hinüber zwischen Volksmundart und Schriftdeutsch*'.

kopfüber headlong; e.g. *sich kopfüber in etw.* (e.g. *Arbeit, Aufgabe*, etc.) *stürzen* = 'to plunge or fling oneself head first into sth.'. This is still in use, but *es geht mit jem.m kopfüber* = 'sb. is crashing into defeat, is coming to grief', as in Gutzkow, *R.v.G.* 5,333: '*da war's mit uns Kopfüber*' is no longer in use, nor is the verb *kopfübern* = 'to tumble head first', as in Gutzkow, *R.v.G.* 8,14; cf. also the notion of 'topsy-turvy' in Goltz, *Jugendleben* 1,278 [1852]: '*im Spektakel und Kopfüber der Welt und des Marktes*.

etw. ~ *sich nehmen* (a.) to undertake sth., be ready to deal with or shoulder sth.; still current in the 19th c., e.g. Ranke, *Werke* 1,115. Schiller used it in *D.Carl.* 2,10, but in later version changed it to '*auf sich*', which is now the standard form.

← See also under *darüber, darunter* (for *drüber und drunter*), *gegenüber* (also for *gegenüberstehen* and *gegenüberstellen*), *herübernehmen, hinüber, hinüberblicken, hinübergehen, hinübergreifen, hinüberreichen, hinüberreißen, hinüberrufen, hinüberschlafen, hinübersetzen, hinübertragen* and *hinüberwechseln*.

For idioms with *über* see also under *Achsel* (for *jem. über die Achsel ansehen*), *Bach* (for *überm Bach wohnen auch Leute*), *balbieren* (for *über den Berg schwatzen* and *über alle Berge sein*), *Bohne* (for *das geht übers Bohnenlied*), *bringen* (for *etw. über jem. bringen*), *Ecke* (for *über Eck*), *ergehen* (for *über sich ergehen lassen*), *Graben* (for *über den Graben kommen*), *Gras* (for *über etw. Gras wachsen lassen*), *grün* (for *jem. über den grünen Klee loben*), *Hals* (for *Hals über Kopf*), *Hand* (for *jem.m über die Hand wachsen, die Hand über jem.m halten*,

seine Hand über etw. haben and *die Hände überm Kopf zusammenschlagen*), *hauen* (for *jem. übers Ohr hauen, über die Schnur hauen* and *über die Stränge hauen*), *hermachen* (for *sich über jem. hermachen*), *hinauswollen* (for *über etw. hinauswollen*), *hinweg* (for *über etw. hinweg sein*), *hinweggehen, -heben, -huschen, -kommen, -können, -sehen, -setzen, Hund* (for *kommt man über den Hund, so kommt man auch über den Schwanz*), *Jahr* (for *übers Jahr*), *Kamm* (for *jem. übern Kamm scheren* and *alles über einen Kamm scheren*), *Knie* (for *jem. übers Knie legen* and *etw. übers Knie brechen*), *kommen* (for *über jem. kommen, etw. kommt über jem.* and *jem.m über etw. kommen*), *Kopf* (for *über Kopf* and *jem.m das Haus überm Kopf anzünden*), *Kreuz* (for *übers Kreuz stehen*), *kurz* (for *über kurz oder lang*), *Laus* (for *ihm ist eine Laus über die Leber gelaufen*), *Leisten* (for *alles über einen Leisten schlagen*, *Lippe* (for *das soll nicht über meine Lippen kommen*), *Maß* (for *über die Maße*), *Nacht* (for *über Tag und Nacht*), *Schatten* (for *über seinen Schatten springen*), *schütteln* (for *den Kopf über etw. schütteln*), *Schwelle* (for *über jem.s Schwelle kommen*), *Stab* (for *den Stab über jem.m brechen*), *Stein* (for *über Stock und Stein*), *Stock* (for *über Stock und Block*), *stürzen* (for *sich über etw. herstürzen*) and *Tisch* (for *jem. über den Tisch ziehen* and *es geht über Tisch und Bänke*).

überall: everywhere

überall (obs.) entirely, in any case; since OHG and still current in the 18th c., e.g. Schiller, *Picc.* 3,3: '*nur unter der Bedingung kann ich mich überall damit befassen*' or Kleist, *Prinz v.H.* 4,5: '*wenn's überall dein Wille ist*'.

er ist ein Überall und Nirgends (prov.expr.) he is everywhere and nowhere; describes a restless person as regards temperament, also sb. who cannot settle down anywhere; recorded since the 19th c. (Körte, Eiselein), e.g. Holtei, *Erz.Schr.* 20,190 describing himself as '*heimatlos—ein Überall und Nirgends*'. *Der Überall* on its own has been current since the 17th c., e.g. (DWb) Christstein, *Weltmann* 60 [1675].

~ *rufen* (mar.) to call all men on deck; recorded since the 19th c.

← See also under *Finger* (for *überall seine Finger haben*).

überarbeiten

etw. ~ to revise, retouch, rework sth.; since the 18th c., e.g. Winckelmann 5,27; in Tieck, *D.B.* 2,189 treated as a separable verb, which is now no longer permitted.

sich ~ to overwork, exhaust oneself through too much work; since the 18th c., recorded by Adelung, e.g. Heinse [edit. Schüd.] 7,29. Adelung also recorded *jem.* ~ = 'to produce work which surpasses sb. else's', but added the note '*ist ungewöhnlich*'.

überaus

überaus extremely; derived from *über aus* =

'everywhere', as used e.g. by H.Sachs [edit. K.] 1,269, but already in Luther 8,529 (Weimar) extended to 'very much': '. . . das diß den papisten überauß mißfallen wird'; f.r.b. Alberus [1540].

überbekommen

etw. ~ (coll.) to get sick and tired of sth.; since late in the 19th c., recorded in *DWb.* [1913].

überblicken: look over, survey.

etw. ~ to get a clear view or idea of sth., assess sth.; since the 18th c., e.g. (DWb) Meißner, *Alcib.* 3,263 [1781]; not recorded by Adelung, but Campe listed it with quotations from Sonnenberg.

der Überblick general view, clear perspective; coined in the 18th c. and criticised by Adelung who considered *Übersicht* as appropriate enough (a view which Campe obviously did not share).

← See also under *blicken* (for *Überblick* and *einen Überblick gewinnen*).

überbrücken: see *Brücke*.

überbürden: see *Bürde*.

überdecken: cover

etw. ~ (lit.) to cover sth. up, conceal, veil sth,; sometimes also = 'to mask'; since the 17th c., e.g. (DWb) Böhme, *Schr.* 3,267 [1620] or Gervinus, *Sh.* 1,59: '*dieser reinere Gedanke . . . ist durch den Reiz der Darstellung . . . überdeckt*'.

überdüstern: see *düster.*

übereilen: see *eilen.*

überein

überein-. . . in agreement or harmony; in several compounds, esp. *übereinkommen* = 'to come to an agreement', since MHG (see p. 1517) and *übereinstimmen*, since Early NHG, f.r.b. Kramer [1678], e.g. Luther Bible transl. Mark 14,56: '*jr zeugnis stimmete nicht uber ein*', also *überein werden*, since Early NHG, e.g. Pauli, *Sch. u.Ernst* [edit. B.] 6,6 [1522]: '*die schiffleut wurden überein*; (now generally *übereins werden*). Rare are *übereindenken* = 'to have the same ideas', as in Goethe 11,242 (W.), *übereinklingen* = 'to harmonise', as in Heine 7,296 and *übereintreffen* = 'to agree', since Early NHG, e.g. Luther 30,2,268 (Weimar). The nouns are *Übereinkunft*, f.r.b. Kramer [1678] and *Übereinstimmung*, f.r.b. Calepinus [1598], with ref. to music f.r.b. Stieler [1691].

überessen: see *essen.*

überfahren: drive over

etw. ~ (a.) to pass (quickly) over sth,; since Early NHG, f.r.b. Frisius [1556]; also = 'to deal with sth. quickly or superficially', f.r.b. Maaler [1561] who explained it as '*mit kurtzen worten darthun*' or = 'to touch lightly on sth.', current since MHG, still in Droste-Hülshoff, *Briefe* [edit. Sch.] 260: '. . . *Entschuldigung, daß ich Ihre lieben Geschenke . . . so leichthin überfahren muß*', or = 'to run (or read) quickly through sth.', as in Jean Paul, *Palingen.* 6,16, or = 'to revise sth. in places, make corrections here and there', f.r.b. Kramer

[1678], used by Jean Paul, *Briefwechsel* [edit. N.] 105. All these meanings are now a., displaced by *flüchtig behandeln, leicht berühren, überfliegen, schnell überarbeiten*, etc.

etw. überfährt jem. sth. comes over sb.; with such abstracts as *Schrecken, Furcht*, etc. since Early NHG and still now, e.g. Storm, 3,339: '*ein leiser Schauer überfuhr mich*'.

jem. ~ (coll.) to obtain sth from sb. by catching him unprepared; in wider sense sometimes = 'to walk over sb.'; modern, not yet mentioned in *DWb.* [1918].

← See also under *fahren* (for *über etw. hin fahren* or *dahinfahren*).

überfallen: fall over

etw. überfällt jem. sth. comes over sb.; in essence the same as *etw. überfährt jem.* (see above); since Early NHG, e.g. Luther Bible transl. Gen. 15,12: '*schrecken und große finsternis überfiel in*'.

jem. ~ (1) to attack sb. (unexpectedly); since MHG, e.g. *Wolfdietrich* D 9.37: '*wir werden übervallen . . . in der naht*'; now also used with ref. to illness which 'befalls' one. Hence *der Überfall* = 'surprise attack', general since Early NHG.

jem. ~ (2) to pay sb. an unexpected visit; since Early NHG, e.g. Pauli, *Sch. u.Ernst* [edit. B.] 6,6; hence *der Überfall* = 'unexpected visit', e.g. Schiller, *Kab.u.L.* 5,2: '*was führt Sie her? Was soll dieser Überfall?*'.

überfällig overdue; with ref. to a ship, plane, train,. etc. which has not arrived at the stipulated time, also in econ.. contexts with ref. to overdue payments; both are modern. A much older meaning 'superfluous' is obs.

← See also under *fallen* (for *herüberfallen, über jem. fallen* and *über etw. herfallen*).

überfliegen: fly over

etw. ~ to run one's eyes over or scan sth.; since the 18th c. (for earlier verbs see under *überfahren*), e.g. Herder 15,331.

etw. überfliegt etw. (or *jem.*) (lit.) sth. passes over or flits across sth. (or sb.); with such abstracts as *Röte, Unbehagen, Zorn*, since the 18th c., e.g. Holtei, *Erz.Schr.* 12,181: '*sein Anblick überfliegt ihr Antlitz mit einem Purpurschein der Freude*'.

← See also under *fliegen* (for *jem. überfliegen*).

überfließen: flow over

von etw. ~ (lit.) to overflow with sth.; with abstracts since Early NHG, e.g. Mentel's Bible 4,249 (Joshua): '. . . *hat vberflossen in boßheyt*', Wieland, *Klelia* 3,73: '. . .*überfließt von Dank*'.

← See also under *fließen* and *Überfluß.*

überfloren: see *Flor.*

überflügeln: see *Flügel.*

Überfluß: abundance

~ *bringt Überdruß* (prov.) abundance brings satiety or weariness; international; the nearest in Engl. (though not quite the same) would be 'plenty makes dainty', cf. French *l'abondance engendre la satiété.* For German recorded in many variant forms all mentioning some consequence of having too much of the good things in life, e.g. Lehman [1662]: *'von der vberflüssigkeit entspringt muthwillen'.*

überflüssig superfluous; in this sense since Early NHG, f.r.b. Frisius, e.g. Luther 32,361 (Weimar). The older meaning 'abundant' is now obs.

← See also under *Kommentar* (for *Kommentar überflüssig*).

überfluten: see *Flut.*

überfragen

überfragt sein to be asked too much, to be asked sth. for which one has no answer; since early in the 19th c., at first mainly in S., now general.

überfremden

überfremdet swamped, inundated or adversely influenced by outsiders, foreigners (in econ. contexts also by foreign capital); 20th. c. (not yet listed in *DWb.* [1918]).

überführen: lead over, transfer

jem. einer Sache ~ to find sb. guilty of sth.; derived from the meaning 'to convince'; since Early NHG.

Übergabe: see *übergeben.*

Übergang: see *übergehen.*

übergeben: hand over

sich ~ (1) to surrender; since Early NHG, derived from 'handing oneself over' to some superior power, esp. in *sich Gott* or *dem Teufel* ~ (e.g. Goethe, *Faust I,* 2866: *'und hätt' er sich auch nicht dem Teufel übergeben, er müßte doch zugrunde gehn'*), in the case of towns and fortresses from the 'handing over' of the keys. Later also with ref. to marriage, still in Lessing, *Minna v.B.* 4,6: *'... mich Ihnen zu übergeben'.* Because one wants to avoid confusion with *sich* ~ (2), *sich ergeben* (for which see p. 670) has gradually displaced *sich* ~ (1). The noun *die Übergabe* has remained in use, e.g. Schiller, *Jungfr.v.O.* (prol. 3): *'nichts von Verträgen! Nichts von Übergabe!'.*

sich ~ (2) to vomit; since the 16th c., e.g. Fischart, *Bienenk.* 270b [1588], derived from the MHG meaning 'to give sth. up, abandon sth.'; it was a transit .verb in Early NHG and became reflex. in the 17th c., probably under the influence of *sich erbrechen* (see p. 666).

übergehen: go over

etw. ~ (1) to go other sth. (revising or correcting); the same as *überarbeiten* (which see above); current since the 18th c., now becoming a.

etw. ~ (2) to pass over, omit, neglect sth.; since Early NHG, f.r.b. Maaler [1561], e.g. Luther 30,3,180 (Weimar): *'... all stillschweygend ubergangen';* also *jem.* ~ with ref. to 'passing sb. over', e.g. with ref. to omitted promotion, f.r.b. Nieremberger [1753].

etw. ~ (3) to have no longer any need for sth. which one has omitted to do; e.g. *ich habe den*

Schlaf (das Essen) übergangen = 'I do not feel sleepy (hungry) any more'; since the 19th c., belongs to the meaning 'to overcome' (e.g. an illness), current since Early NHG.

in etw. anderes ~ to merge with or fade into sth. else; since the 18th c., often with ref. to colours (cf. *Übergang* in Goethe, *Farbenlehre* 1,88, quoted on p. 1356), but also in descriptions of transitions from one state to another, e.g. Goethe 21,110 (W.): *'seine Ruhe ging in Verlangen über';* hence *der Übergang* = 'transition(al stage)', since the 18th c., frequent now in compounds, e.g. *Übergangsperiode, -stadium, -zeit.*

zu jem.m ~ to join sb.; with ref. to changing sides (in war or politics); since the 17th c., f.r.b. Kramer [1678]; also with ref. to changing one's religious persuasion, e.g. Goethe III,4,301 (W.); hence *Übergang,* since the 17th c., but *Übertritt* is now preferred.

zu etw. anderem ~ to pass on to sth. else; with ref. with a change in subject-matter in speech or writing, but also to emotions, e.g. Schiller, *M.Stuart* 1,6: *'ich kann so schnell nicht aus der Tiefe meines Elends zur Hoffnung übergehen',* also Goethe 22,137 (W.). Hence *Übergang* = 'change to sth. else', since the 18th c.

etw. übergeht jem. (regional) sth. comes over sb.; since MHG, recorded by Adelung as *'oberdeutsch',* still in use in some regions, e.g. (T.) A.Schott, *Im Hochriß* 180 [1922]: *'... wenn mich der Ärger einmal übergeht';* in the standard language *überkommen* is used.

← See also under *Auge* (for *die Augen gehen jem.m über*), *Fleisch* (for *es ist ihm in Fleisch und Blut übergegangen*), *glatt* (for *der Übergang sei eben und glatt*), *Grund* (for *Übergang von Schmerz zu Abscheu*) and *Ordnung* (for *zur Tagesordnung übergehen*); cf. also under *gehen* (for *Brücke, die über das Wasser ging, über etw. gehen* and *etw. über sich gehen lassen*) and *ergehen* (for *etw. über sich ergehen lassen*).

Übergewicht: see *Gewicht.*

übergießen: pour over

etw. übergießt etw. (lit.) sth. covers or spreads over, suffuses sth.; with nouns such as *Sonne* or *Mond* since the 17th c., also with abstracts such as *Glanz, Licht, Scham,* e.g. Lohenstein, *Armin.* 2,473b: *'... mit einem gantzen strome von schamröthe übergossen'.*

← See also under *Purpur* (for *sich gießet Purpur über Marmer bleich*).

jem. mit Spott, Vorwürfen, etc. ~ (lit.) to heap ridicule, reproaches, etc. upon sb.; since the 17th c., e.g. G.Keller, *Ges.Werke* 2,246: *'ich übergoß ihn mit einer Flut von Vorwürfen'.*

überglänzen: see *Glanz.*

übergolden: gild

etw. ~ (lit.) to embellish sth., make sth. distasteful acceptable; since Early NHG, when *Messing* ~ was in use for 'to make sth. cheap look valuable', later also with ref. to *Pillen, Medikamente*, when it means the same as *verzuckern* (cf. Engl. 'to sugar the pill'); hence *übergoldet* for 'made to look more attractive than it is', as in Wieland, *Luc.* 5,126: '*übergüldetes Joch*' or Gutzkow, *Ges.Werke* 1,144: '*dies . . . Publikum der Großstädte . . . mit seinem hohlen, übergoldeten Elend*'; cf. *das glänzende Elend* (on p. 625) for which some 18th c. writers used *übergüldetes Elend*.

übergreifen: reach over or across

etw. (or *jem.*) *greift über* sth. (or sb.) encroaches (on sth. or sb.); also used for 'to reach or extend beyond . . .', in wider sense 'to affect or impinge on sth.'; beginnings in MHG in legal contexts (cf. '*Rechte greifen, die nicht ihre sind*', quoted on p. 1129), general since the 18th c.; cf. also Goethe, *Dicht.u.Wahrh.* 5: '*die Krone . . . stand wie ein übergreifendes Dach vom Kopf ab*'; hence *der Übergriff* = 'encroachment, infringement, inroad', since the 14th c., first for 'illegal action, infringement of rules', in wider non-legal contexts since the 18th c.

überhaben

etw. ~ (1) (coll.) to have sth. over; mainly with ref. to money; variant of *übrig haben* (see under *übrig*), reduced form of *erübrigt haben*; since the 18th c.

etw. ~ (2) (coll.) to be fed up with sth.; ellipsis of *bekommen* or similar verbs; since the 19th c.

für etw. nichts ~ (coll.) to have no time for or interest in sth.; modern coll., identical in meaning with *übrig haben*, which see under *übrig*.

überhandnehmen

etw. nimmt überhand sth. spreads, increases, becomes prevalent; beginnings in MHG, with various verbs since Early NHG, e.g. Luther Bible transl. Psalm 9,20: '*. . . das menschen nicht überhand kriegen*' (where the A.V. uses 'prevail' and later German Bibles use *Oberhand haben*); with *nehmen* since the 15th c., e.g. Tauler, *Sermones* 75a [1508]: '*. . . gott . . . in dem menschen überhant näme . . .*'; later mainly pejor.; cf. also Schiller, *Tell* 4,1: '*der Sturm nimmt überhand*'. The entry under *nehmen* (p. 1775) is not detailed enough. See also the entry on *Oberhand* on p. 1801.

Überhang

der ~ (econ.) surplus; in accounting = 'carryover, residue'. Modern, not yet listed in *DWb* [1918].

das Überhangmandat (polit.) extra mandate; tech. term under modern proportional representation for a seat gained in addition to those won by a direct majority.

überhauchen: se *Hauch*.
überhäufen: see *Haufen*.
überheben: see *heben*.
überhirnt: see *Hirn*.
überhitzen: overheat

eine überhitzte Phantasie an overheated or too lively imagination; since the 18th c., e.g. Gutzkow, *R.v.G.* 6,340: '*Sie sind überhitzt, trunken*'; hence *die Überhitzung*, e.g. Bürger, 73: '*jene flammende Überhitzung, die damals die besten Köpfe oft mehr versengte als erleuchtete*'.

überholen: overtake

jem. ~ to surpass sb.; in phys. sense of 'overtaking' since Early NHG, figur. since the 18th c., wrongly dismissed by Adelung as '*oberdeutsch*'. The meaning 'to censure sb.', still used in the 18th c., e.g. by Bürger, is obs.

von den Ereignissen überholt overtaken by events; often in wider sense 'superseded, outdated, antiquated'; since the 19th c.

überhören: overhear

etw. ~ (1) to hear sth. and take no notice of it; since MHG, e.g. *Minnes.Frühl.* 163: '*des überhoere ich vil und thuon als ich des nicht verstê*', Luther Bible transl. Prov. 19,11: '*wer geduldig ist, der ist ein kluger Mensch, und ist ihm eine Ehre, daß er Untugend überhören kann*'.

etw. ~ (2) to fail to hear (unintentionally); at least since the 18th c., e.g. Schiller, *Fiesco* 2,17: '*ich könnte hier stehen . . . und ein Erdbeben überhören*'.

das möchte ich überhört haben (coll.) I'll pretent I did not hear that; in essence a reproof; modern coll.

überhüpfen: hop over

etw. ~ to skip sth.; since Early NHG, e.g. Luther 3,462b (Jena): '*. . . der heubtsachen müssig gehen und uberhüpfen*', as *überhupfen* f.r.b. Frisius [1556].

überirdisch: superterrestrial

überirdisch (1) supernatural; both in relig. and secular contexts for 'not of this world' since the 17th c., f.r.b. Schottel [1663]; frequent in Goethe's writings.

überirdisch (2) (lit.) divine; as a term of high praise since the 17th c. as an adj. (e.g. *überirdische Schönheit*) and as an adv. (e.g. *überirdisch schön*).

überjagen: see *jagen*.

überjähren

überjährt antiquated, outmoded; ~ started as 'to grow very old', and in this sense Luther used it in his transl. of Hebrews 8,13: '*was aber alt und uberjahrt ist . . .*'; since the 18th c. the past participle has been used pejor. for 'superannuated, too old'; *überjährig* can be used in the same sense.

überkalkt

überkalkt (a.) doting, senile, decrepit; since the 18th c., e.g. Wieland [edit. Hempel] 12,132: '*überkalchte Hand*'; now *verkalkt* would be used.

überkippen: tip over, overbalance

überkippen to crack, break; with ref. to a voice which becomes shrill or harsh; only since the 20th c.

überkochen: see *kochen*.

überkommen: see *kommen*.

überkreuzen: cross over

etw. ~ to cover sth. or move over sth. in a criss-cross fashion; from phys. *etw.* ~ = 'to cross' (e.g. a road); current since ca. 1800, e.g. Goethe 25,187 (W.): '*Geschäftsmänner, welche die* . . . *Welt mit unsichtbaren Fäden überkreuzen*'; also reflex. for 'to meet, come into contact', e.g. Goethe II,3,222 (W.): '*was für* . . . *Idiosynkrasien überkreuzen sich nicht!*'.

überkriechen: creep over

etw. überkriecht jem. (lit.) sth. creeps or comes stealthily over sb.; figur. since the 19th c., e.g. Heine [edit. E.] 3,286: '*melancholisch überkriecht uns der Gedanke, daß* . . .'.

überkriegen

etw. ~ (coll.) to get fed up with sth.; modern coll., the same as *etw. überbekommen*, which see.

überladen: overload

jem. (or *etw.*) ~ to put too heavy a burden on sb. (or sth.); with abstracts since MHG, see also the dictionary recording on p. 1575.

etw. ~ to overfill sth.; since the 18th c., e.g. Goethe 33,10 (W.)

überlassen: leave

jem.m etw. ~ to let sb. have sth.; since Early NHG, usually with ref. to objects, but also with such abstracts as *Amt, Regierung, Verwaltung*, e.g. *der König überließ seinem Sohn die Regierung*; cf. also *jem.m das Feld* ~ = 'to yield to some superior power, confess oneself beaten' (see also the entry on *das Feld lassen* or *räumen* on p. 756), also for 'to leave sth. to sb.' in such cases as ~ *Sie das mir* = 'leave that to me, let that be my worry'; sometimes with ref. to inheritance, f.r.b. Stieler [1691], where *hinterlassen* (for which see p. 1586) is now preferred, occasionally since the 18th c. as *an jem. etw.* ~ , now rare.

etw. der Vorsehung (dem Zufall) ~ to leave sth. to providence (chance); with such abstracts (also with *Gott*) since the 18th c., e.g. Gellert, *Werke* 10,146 (with *Vorsehung*).

jem. jem.m ~ to leave sb. in sb.'s care, entrust sb. to sb.; since the 18th c., e.g. Tieck, *Schr.* 4,40: '*Kinder dem Gesinde überlassen*'.

jem. seinem Kummer ~ to leave sb. to cope with his grief (on his own); general since the 18th c., e.g. Goethe 5,75 (W.): '*dann überlaßt ihn ihn der Pein*'. Often in *jem. seinen Gedanken* (or *seinem Schicksal*) ~ .

sich einer Leidenschaft ~ to abandon oneself to some passion; since the 18th c.; also with ref. to persons *sich jem.m* ~ , since the 18th c., e.g. Goethe 22,243 (W.).

jem. sich selbst ~ to leave sb. on his or her own; this can refer to abandonment or to the granting of absolute freedom; since the 18th c.; sometimes with ref. to abstracts, when in the past participle it means 'independent, free', as in Lessing

13,416, also used by Schiller.

← See also under *Pferd* (for *überlaß das Denken den Pferden*).

überlaufen: run over

überlaufen (intrans.) to defect, desert (to the enemy); f.r.b. Hulsius [1618], also sometimes as *hinüberlaufen*; hence *der Überläufer* = 'defector', current since the 15th c.

etw. ~ to run (with one's eyes) over sth., read sth. quickly; since MHG (also used by Luther), e.g. Goethe 25,101 (W.).

etw. überläuft jem. sth. comes over sb.; with ref. to unpleasant sensations, as in Adelung's recording: '*es überläuft mich ein Schauer, ein Angstschweiß*' (he also recorded *etw. überschauert jem.*); earlier Frisch [1741] had listed: '*es läuft mir ein Schauer über die Haut*'; current since Early NHG, e.g. Fischart, *Gesangb.* [edit. Kurz] 189: '*die angst mich überlaufen thut*'; *Schauder* can also be used, e.g. Goethe, *D.Epim.Erw.* 1,5: '*ein Schauder überläuft die Erde*'.

überlaufen (past participle) overrun, overcrowded, visited or besieged by too many people; cf. Adelung's examples: '*man wird an den Landstraßen immer von Bettlern überlaufen* . . . *der Arzt wird von Patienten überlaufen*' and his quotation from Hagedorn (no details): '*unzählig ist der Schmeichler Haufen, die jeden Großen überlaufen*'; now also with ref. to exceeded capacity or means, e.g. *der Kurs ist* ~ = 'there are more applicants than places for this course'.

der Überläufer (hunt.) wild boar in its second year; derived from ~ (hunt.) = 'to survive the first year'; recorded since the 18th c.

überlegen (1)

jem.m ~ *sein* to be superior to sb., surpass sb.; derived from *überliegen* = 'to lie on top' (e.g. in wrestling); since Early NHG, e.g. Luther [edit Bindseil] pref. to Dan. 7,364: '. . . *ein königreich dem andern uberlegen war*'; hence also as adj. or adv., e.g. Goethe 45,200 (W.): '. . . *sich mit dem weit überlegenen Voltaire vergleichen*', and the noun *die Überlegenheit* = 'superiority', only since the 18th c.

überlegen (2)

etw. ~ to consider, ponder sth.; derived from the sense 'to turn round' (cf. Engl. 'to turn sth. over in one's mind'); recorded since the 17th c., e.g. by Kramer [1678]; also used without the accusative, e.g. Goethe 4,295 (W.): '. . . *stets denkt und thut und niemals überlegt*', or as a noun, e.g. Goethe 9,18 (W.): '. . . *nicht zum Denken und Überlegen geboren* . . .'; noun *die Überlegung* = 'consideration', since late in the 17th c., recorded by Frisch [1741].

überlesen: read over

etw. ~ (1) to look sth. over hurriedly; derived from to read sth. (f.r.b. *voc.theut.* [1482]) in the 16th c., f.r.b. Alberus [1540].

etw. ~ (2) to miss sth. when reading, overlook

sth.; since the 19th c., e.g. (DWb) Gervinus, *Gesch.d.dt.D.* 3,373 (still missing in Sanders [1863]).

überliefern: hand on

jem. ~ to hand sb. over; since the 16th c., still in *jem. dem Gericht* ~ , but otherwise largely displaced by *ausliefern* or *überhändigen*.

überliefert werden to be handed down; with ref. to transmission by tradition; general since the 18th c., e.g. Kant, *Werke* [Acad. edit.] 3,9, often contrasted with 'handed down in writing', e.g. Lessing 3,92: *'denn gründen alle sich nicht auf Geschichte? Geschrieben oder überliefert!'*. Hence *die Überlieferung* = 'tradition, story handed down by tradition', since the 18th c.

übermachen

jem.m etw. ~ (lit.) to transmit sth. to sb.; in phys. sense of 'to transfer, hand over' since the 17th c., figur. with abstracts since the 18th c., e.g. (DWb) J.E.Schlegel 5,147: '. . . *hat mir auch ein Ungenannter einige Gedanken übermacht'*. Today *übermitteln* would be preferred, a modern word, even missing in *DWb*. [1921].

übermannen

jem. ~ (lit.) to overwhelm sb.; with abstracts as the subject since the Baroque, e.g. Hoffmannswaldau, *U.a.d.G.* 5,5: *'was übermannt mich denn hier die Eifersucht?'*.

übermäßig: see *Maß*.

Übermensch: see *Mensch*.

übermenschlich: see *Phänomen*.

übermitteln: see *übermachen*.

übermögen

jem. ~ (a.) to overpower, defeat sb.; since MHG, but now becoming obs. Modern dictionaries do not pay much attention to it, Duden [1989] does not list it at all, but some authors have used in it in this, e.g. (Sp.) Boree, *Dor u.d.Sept.* 9 [1940]: *'die Sonne hatte die Bürokratie übermocht'*. Now *übermannen, überwältigen* or *besiegen* would be used.

Übermut: see *tun*.

übernacht: see *Nacht*.

übernachten: see *Hotel*.

Übernahme: see *übernehmen*.

Übername

der ~ (1) surname, family name; since MHG, also called *Zuname* (which is now the usual term); f.r.b. Frisius [1556], who also listed *'zunamm'*.

der ~ (2) nickname; since Early NHG, e.g. (DWb) F.Platter, *Tageb.* 220; one of many terms, such as *Aftername, Ekelname, Schimpfname, Schmachname* and *Spitzname*. *Spitzname* is now the preferred term. For a list with dates see under *spitz* (p. 2308).

übernehmen: take over

etw. ~ to take over or accept sth.; with ref. to abstracts since the 17th c., f.r.b. Kramer [1702], e.g. Lohenstein, *Armin.* 1,28b [1689]: '. . . *die*

aufgetragene Würde willig zu übernehmen'; frequent in *die Verantwortung* = 'to take on the responsibility'; hence *die Übernahme*, since the 17th c., e.g. Harsdörffer, *Secret.* [1656].

jem. ~ (1) (obs. or regional coll.) to overcharge or cheat sb.; since MHG, now only in some regions.

jem. ~ (2) (a.) to demand too much of sb., put too much strain on sb.; a. in this sense, which was still current in the 19th c., but the reflex. *sich* ~ = 'to overexert oneself', also 'to overindulge', current since Early NHG, is still in use.

überpflastern: see *Pflaster*.

überpfropfen: see *Propfen*.

überpinseln: see *Pinsel*.

überquellen: see *Quelle*.

überquer: see *quer*.

überragen: see *ragen*.

überranken: see *Ranke*.

überraschen: surprise

etw. überrascht jem. sth. comes suddenly over sb.; figur. with ref. to such abstracts as *Gefühl, Schmerz, Liebe* since the 16th c.; similarly, *jem. überrascht jem.* = 'sb. pays sb. a surprise visit'; since the 16th c.

jem. mit etw. ~ to surprise and astonish sb. with sth.; the addition of the notion of 'causing astonishment' becomes more evident in 18th c. instances, though one must assume that astonishment must have been experienced in some cases before then; e.g. Goethe IV,42,261 (W.).

überraschend unexpected(ly); since the 18th c., e.g. Klinger, *Werke* 6,147: *'es ist überraschend tief und schön gedacht'*; *Überraschung* only became general in the 18th c., first for the sudden experiencing of sth., as in Lessing 17,65: *'die plötzliche Überraschung des Mitleides'*, then extended to surprise, unexpected or astonishing event as well as astonishment.

überrechnen: see *reichen*.

überreden: persuade

überredend (obs.) convincing(ly); since the 17th c., but by the 19th c. only rarely used, e.g. Schleiermacher, *Platon* 2,187: *'so überredend nun dieses klingt, so ist doch . . .'*; displaced by *überzeugend*.

überreichen: see *reichen*.

überreif: see *Pflaume* and *pflücken*.

überrennen: see *rennen*.

Überrest: see *Rest*.

überrieseln: see *rieseln*.

überrollen: roll over

jem. ~ to defeat, crush sb.; in phys. mil. sense since the 17th c., f.r.b. Kramer [1702]; now also with ref. to defeat by arguments, votes or other abstract powers, e.g. (Kl.-St.) H.Kant, *Aula* 213: '. . . *haben sich nie von dem sogenannten Zug der Zeit überrollen lassen'*.

übersäen: see *säen*.

übersättigen: see *satt*.

überschatten: see *Schatten.*
überschauen: see *schauen.*
überschauern: see *Schauer.*
überschäumen: see *Schaum.*
überscheinen: see *Schein.*
überschießen: see *schießen.*
überschlafen: see *schlafen.*
überschlagen: see *Schlag.*
überschleichen: see *schleichen.*
überschleiern: see *Schleier.*
überschmieren: see *schmieren.*
überschminken: see *schminken.*
überschnappen: see *schnappen.*
überschneiden: see *schneiden.*
überschnellen: see *schnell.*
überschreiben: see *schreiben.*
überschreiten: see *schreiten.*

Überschuß
der ~ surplus, excess; beginnings in Early
NHG, both for 'sth. extra, bonus', as in
Mathesius, *Sarepta* [1571], and for 'profit', as in
Wickram, *Werke* [edit. B.] 3,171, then *überschüs-
sig*, since the 17th c., f.r.b. Dentzler [1716];
occasionally as an adverb used for 'exceedingly'
(modern).

überschütten: see *schütten.*
überschwappen: see *schwappen.*
überschwellen: see *schwellen.*
überschwemmen: see *schwemmen.*
überschwingen: see *schwingen.*
übersehen: see *sehen.*
übersetzen: see *setzen.*
Übersicht: see *sehen* and *Sicht.*
übersiedeln: see *siedeln.*
übersilbern: coat with silver
etw. ~ (lit.) to disguise, fill or embellish with
silver; with ref. to deceitful covering of a base
metal with a silver coating since the 16th c.; cf.
also the criminal intent in Schiller, *Räuber* 2, 3:
'. . . *einen Schurken . . . der das Auge der
Gerechtigkeit übersilbert*', but also since Early
NHG used for 'to make attractive, embellish',
e.g. *eine bittere Pille* ~ ; lastly, with ref. to colour,
as in Zesen, *Verm.Hel.* 62 [1656]: '*der Mond übersilbert die Erde*'.

übersinnig
übersinnig (rare) eccentric, fantastic; also sometimes = 'abnormal', even 'crazy'; since the
Baroque, still occasionally in modern period, e.g.
Börne, *Ges.Schr.* 1,194: '*übersinnig ist der
Vicekönig, er hört das Gras wachsen*', where 'having extraordinary senses' is implied, whereas in
other modern examples the notion of 'madness'
is more prominent.

übersinnlich
übersinnlich transcendent, metaphysical; since
the 17th c. in philos. writings, e.g. Kant
[Acad.edit.] 5,106: '*Erkenntnisse von einer
übersinnlichen Ordnung*', Goethe, *Dicht.u.Wahrh.*
20: ' . . . *sich . . . dem Übersinnlichen zu nähern*',

but also now in general use for 'suprasensuous,
psychic'. See also under *Nacht* (p. 1741) for '*der
mit dicker Nacht erfüllte Raum des Übersinnlichen*';
the noun *Übersinnlichkeit* only since the 19th c.

übersonnen: see *Sonne.*
überspannen: see *spannen.*
überspielen: *etw. spielt in etw. anderes über* sth.
changes subtly into (or merges with) sth. else;
hinüberspielen also occurs; often with ref. to
colours (see the entry on *spielen* on p. 2298), but
also with other kinds of transition where sth.
gently merges with (or begins to take on the
appearance of) sth. else; since the 19th c.

überspitzt: see *spitz.*
überspringen: see *Funke* and *springen.*
übersprudeln: see *sprudeln.*

übersprühen
übersprühen (lit.) to scintillate, bubble over;
with abstracts since the 19th c., e.g. *übersprühen-
der Humor*; cf. Benedix, *Weste* 1,2: '*Dialog . . . der
übersprudelte von Witz*', where *übersprühen* could
also have been used.

überspülen: see *spülen.*
überstehen: see *stehen.*
übersteigen: see *steigen.*
übersteigern: see *steigern.*

überstimmen
jem. ~ to outvote sb.; since Early NHG, f.r.b.
Schönsleder, *Prompt.* [1647]. Figur. use of ~ in
musical contexts = 'to increase the volume or
pitch of a sound too much', still used by Herder
16,342, is a. or obs.

überstolpern: see *stolpern.*
überstrahlen: see *strahlen.*
überstreichen: see *streichen.*

überstreifen
in etw. ~ (or *hinüberstreifen*) (lit.) to wander,
range, roam into sth. (e.g. an area, subject); with
abstracts since the 19th c., synonymous with *in
etw. schweifen.*

überstreuen: strew over, besprinkle
etw. überstreut etw. or *jem.* (lit.) sth. strews or
scatters sth. over sth. or sb.; since the 18th c.,
e.g. Haller, *Tageb.* 1,206 (with '*mit Schwermuth*'),
G.Keller, *Werke* 5,337: '*die Sonne überstreute . . .
das Kind mit spielenden Lichtern*'.

überstricken
jem. ~ (obs.) to outwit, dupe sb., take sb. in;
in occasional use in 19th c., displaced by
übertölpeln or *übervorteilen.*

überströmen: see *Strom.*
überstülpen: see *stülpen.*
überstürzen: see *stürzen.*

übertäuben
etw. ~ to deaden or dull sth.; with abstracts
since the 18th c., e.g. Goethe 25,1,53 (W.): '*die
Stimme der Pflicht übertäuben*' (cf. also Schiller's
'*den Donner des erwachten Gewissens übertäuben*').
jem. ~ (obs.) to overpower or overwhelm sb.;
since Early NHG, still current in the 19th c., e.g.

Tieck, *Schriften* 16,318: '*die Fülle meines Glücks übertäubte mich*'; now obs.

überteuern
jem. ~ to overcharge sb.; since Early NHG, e.g. Luther 6,270 (Weimar) (where it is used as a noun), still in Seume, *Spaz.* 101, now obs., and only *etw.* ~ is used with ref. to goods for which too much is charged.

übertischt: see *Tisch*.

übertölpeln: see *Tölpel*.

übertönen: see *Ton*.

übertragen: see *tragen*.

übertreffen
jem. ~ to surpass sb.; assumed to be derived from 'throwing (a spear, stone) farther than sb. else', but not recorded in this phys. sense; figur. for 'to excel' since OHG, also in Luther Bible transl. Ecclesiastes 2,13: '*das die weisheit die thorheit übertraf*'. MHG *übertreffenlich* died out in the 18th c., displaced by *übertrefflich* (in occasional use since the 16th c.). Modern are *unübertreffbar*, *unübertrefflich* and *unübertroffen*.

übertrumpfen: see *Trumpf*.

übertünchen: see *Grab* and *Tünche*.

übertuschen: see *tuschen*.

überwachen: see *wachen*.

überwachsen: see *wachsen*.

überwallen: see *wallen*.

überwältigen
etw. überwältigt jem. (or *etw.*) sth. overwhelms sb. (or sth.); figur. when an abstract is the subject; since Early NHG; an abstract can also be seen as overwhelming another abstract, since Early NHG, e.g. Luther Apocr. transl. Wisd.of Sol. 7,30: '*die bosheit überweldiget die weisheit nimmermehr*'.

überwältigend overwhelming; since the 19th c. loosely used for 'grand, strong, impressive', e.g. *ein überwältigender Eindruck*, as in Freytag, *Bilder* 1,49.

überwälzen: see *wälzen*.

überwandern: see *wandern*.

Überwasser
~ *bekommen* or *kriegen* (rare) to gain the upper hand; the origin of this phrase is explained under *Oberwasser* (p. 1801); ~ is less used, but can occur, e.g. in Holtei, *Erz.Schr.* 13,224: '*Die Canaillen kriegen wieder Überwasser*'.

Überweib
das ~ (lit.) superwoman; this compound made two appearances in the language, first in the Baroque, when it was derived from *überweiblich* = 'exceeding womanly strength or characteristics', used since the 17th c.; O. Ludwig, *Werke* 4,29 referred to Maria Stuart as '*ein Überweib voll Entschlossenheit und Geist*'. When through Nietzsche *Übermensch* established itself, ~ came to be used by analogy, since early in the 20th c.

überweisen
jem. (eines Verbrechens) ~ (regional) to find sb.

guilty (of a crime); since Early NHG, used by Luther, e.g. Wieland, *Agathon* 10,6: '*nachdem er durch die Aussage überwiesen worden war*'; hence still in the 19th c. *ein überwiesener Verbrecher*. ~ is now confined to some regions, particularly to Austria, elsewhere displaced by *überführen*.

überwerfen
sich mit jem.m ~ to fall out with sb.; recorded by Stieler [1691], e.g. Goethe, *Dicht.u.Wahrh.* 2: '*man stritt, man überwarf sich*'.

etw. wirft jem.m etw. über (lit., rare) sth. covers, afflicts, burdens sb. with sth.; occasionally in lit., e.g. Goethe, *Tasso* 2,1: '*Schleier . . . den uns Alter oder Krankheit überwirft*'.

überwiegen
etw. überwiegt (intrans.) sth. predominates, prevails over, outweighs; since MHG, e.g. Klopstock 1,49: '*wäre sie, der bessern Thaten Schale so schwer, daß sie überwöge!*'; hence *überwiegend* = 'vast(ly), overwhelming', as in *mit überwiegender Mehrheit* = 'with or by a decisive majority'.

überwinden: overcome, conquer
jem. (or *etw.*) ~ to overcome, conquer, vanquish sb. (or sth.); figur. with abstracts since OHG, at first in relig. contexts; since the 18th c. with such abstracts as *Gefahr*, *Gewohnheit*, *Furcht*, *Mißtrauen*, but as early as OHG with ref. to *Krankheit*, *Schmerz*, etc.

sich ~ to bring oneself to doing sth. against one's inclinations or desires; since Early NHG, see the example from Franck under *Sieg* on p. 2259; hence *Überwindung*, e.g. *es hat ihn große Überwindung gekostet* = 'it required a great effort of will from him'.

überwogen: see *Woge*.

überwölken: see *Wolke*.

überwuchern: see *wuchern*.

überzählen: count
sich ~ (obs.) to miscount; still in the 18th c., e.g. Wieland, *Oberon* 11,43, recorded by Aler [1727], displaced by *sich verrechnen*.

überzeichnen
jem. ~ (lit.) to overdraw sb.; with ref. to a character in a work of fiction that is presented in an unbelievable or exaggerated way; modern, not yet listed in *DWb.* [1932].

überzeugen
jem. von etw. ~ to convince sb. of sth., persuade sb. to believe in sth.; tentative beginnings in the 16th c., established by the 18th c., f.r.b. Steinbach [1734]; hence also *sich* ~ , since the 18th c., e.g. Wieland, *Danischm.* 47: '*. . . wie er sich mit eignen Augen . . . überzeugen könnte*', and *Überzeugung* = 'conviction' in the extended sense since the 18th c.

← See also under *Brust* (for *mit dem Brustton der Überzeugung*) and *sein* (for *der Überzeugung sein*).

überziehen: draw over
etw. überzieht etw. anderes (lit.) sth. passes

across or suffuses sth. else; since the 17th c., e.g. *Röte überzog ihr Gesicht*.

etw. ~ to extend sth. beyond the set limit; loan translation of Engl. 'to overdraw' with ref. to accounts, then extended, e.g. *seinen Urlaub* ~ = 'to extend one's leave unduly, take too much time off', 20th c.

← See also under *Konto* (for *er hat sein Konto überzogen*).

jem. ~ (coll., separable) to tease sb.; also 'to take sb. to task; derived from phys. *übers Knie* ~ (for a beating); since Early NHG, e.g. Goethe 38,134 (W.): *'ich hab ihn gestern ein bisgen* (in later editions *ein bißchen) übergezogen*'; cf. the notes on *aufziehen* on p. 111.

ein Land mit Krieg ~ (a., inseparable) to make war on (or invade) a country; since MHG, still in 19th c. literature, but now a.

überzuckern: see *Zucker*.

überzwerch

etw. geht ~ sth. goes wrong, fails, misfires; derived from the sense 'oblique, slanting, from the side or the wrong direction'; since Early NHG, e.g. Keisersberg, *G.Spinn.* C6d [1510]: *'es ist alles überzwerch'*; cf. also adjectival use for 'wrong-headed, unreasonable', as in Grimmelshausen, *Simpliz.* 3,300: *'diese überzwerge thorheit'*.

übrig

für jem. or *etw. nichts* ~ *haben* (coll.) to have no time for sb. or sth.; since the 19th c., but not yet in Campe [1810]; also used positively: *dafür habe ich viel* ~ = 'that interests me a great deal, I am very keen on that'.

übrigbleiben to survive; since the 16th c., f.r.b. Alberus [1540]: *'ich bleib übrig, leb'*.

es bleibt einem nichts anderes ~ one is left with no choice, there is nothing else that one can do; since the 18th c.

ein übriges tun to do more than is required or was expected; since Early NHG, e.g. Luther 20,491 (Weimar): *'aber ich wil ein übrigs thun'*.

etw. erübrigen to save, spare, lay by sth.; since the 17th c., f.r.b. Stieler [1691].

das erübrigt sich that is superfluous or unnecessary; modern, e.g. *das dürfte sich erübrigen* = 'that will hardly be necessary', *jedes weitere Wort erübrigt sich* = 'there is no more to be said'; modern.

← See also under *kommen* (for *wer nicht kommt zur rechten Zeit, der muß essen, was übrig bleibt*) and *wünschen* (for *es läßt viel zu wünschen übrig*).

Übung: see *üben*.

Ufer: shore, bank

das ~ (lit.) the shore; figur. in many contexts since Early NHG, e.g. *jenes* ~ = 'the beyond', *das* ~ *des irdischen Lebens* = 'the shore of this world', *das sichere* ~ = 'the safe shore' (mainly in the sense of 'haven'), used sometimes poet. for

'married life', but also for 'the grave', as in Herder [edit. S.] 27,28: *'endlich landest du dort sicher am Ufer, in deinem Hafen: er heißt das Grab'*; occasionally used for 'edge, brink', as in *am* ~ *des Grabes*.

einer vom andern ~ (coll.) a homosexual; 20th c. jocular euphemism

uferlos limitless, unbounded; since the 18th c.; often also in *das geht ins Uferlose* = 'that is never ending', since the 19th c.

ausufern to get out of hand; mainly in the sense of 'to become irrational, nonsensical' e.g. with ref. to speculations; derived from the image of a river which overflows its banks; a very recent word, not even listed yet in Klappenbach-Steinitz [1964].

umufert (lit.,a) bounded, limited; since the 18th c., e.g. Zschokke 1,229: *'das Reich des nirgends umuferten Alls'*.

'zu neuen Ufern lockt ein neuer Tag' a new day invites us to explore a new shore, to experience a different kind of life; quotation from Goethe, *Faust I*, 701, now quasi-prov., often quoted when encouraging sb. to face the future with eagerness, also abbreviated as *zu neuen Ufern!* = 'start or attempt sth. new!'.

← See also under *Steuer* (2) (for *die besten Steuerleute stehen am Ufer*).

Uhr: clock, watch

wissen, was die ~ *geschlagen hat* to know the real state of affairs, understand the situation; since Early NHG, e.g. Murner, *Narrenbeschw.* 53 or repr. 53,60 [1512]: *'er soll versehen eine stat und weißt nit, was geschlagen hat'*; with mention of ~ later, since *Glocke* is the preferred noun.

← See also under *Glocke* (for *wissen, was die Glocke geschlagen hat*).

ein Mensch nach der ~ a person with very regular habits; since the 18th c., e.g. Platen, *Ges. Werke* 7,300: *'hier im Hause geht alles nach Uhr und Schnur'*. Hippel entitled one of his comedies *Der Mann nach der Uhr, oder der ordentliche Mann* [1765]

rund um die ~ (coll.) round the clock, for twelve hours; in wider sense = 'all day long'; modern, recorded since the 19th c.

nach ihm (or *nach seinen Gewohnheiten) kann man seine* ~ *stellen* you can set your watch by his regular behaviour; since the 19th c. (perhaps earlier, since people in Königsberg are reported as having set their time-pieces by Kant's regular walks); cf. also Lehman, *Flor.pol.* 2,693 [1662]: *'ein fürst ist des landes uhr, jeder richt sich nach demselben in wercken als wie nach der uhr in geschäften'*.

seine ~ *ist (noch nicht) ausgelaufen* (a.) his life has (not yet) reached its end; still in Goethe 19,151 (W.): *'meine Uhr ist noch nicht ausgelaufen, ich fühle es!'*, but then displaced by *abgelaufen*.

regelmäßig wie ein Uhrwerk as regular as a clock; beginnings of such refs. to regularity and orderliness can be found in the 17th c., e.g. Dannhauer, *Catechism.* 1,13 [1657]: *'eine wolgefaste ordnung, uhr und richtschnur'*, Zelter (to Goethe 5,136): *'das geht wie ein Uhrwerk'*, Goethe 21,183 (W.): *'unaufhaltsam wie ein Uhrwerk lief sie ihren Weg'*; cf. also *Uhrwerksmensch* (pejor.) = 'pedant', since the 19th c., and *nach der ~* = 'punctually'.

das menschliche Uhrwerk (lit.) the human organism; since the 17th c., e.g. Thomasius, *Vernunftlehre* 98 [1691]: *'das Uhrwerk des Leibes der Menschen'*, Ramler, *Einleit.i.d.sch.Wiss.* 2,7 [1758]: *'das Uhrwerk der Organe'*, also Raabe, *Werke* 2,5 and 2,2, where *'das Uhrwerk des Lebens'* occurs; cf. also comparisons such as *'der tod ist eine glokk, ein uhr so stündlich schlägt'* in Rist, *Parnassos* 109 or *'das Gewissen ist die einzige Uhr auf der Welt . . . die immer recht geht'* in Hebbel, *Briefe* [edit. W.] 6,243.

im Uhrzeigersinn moving from left to right; since the 19th c. *Uhrzeigerbewegung* and *-lauf*, less used now, were also recorded in the 19th c., e.g. by Karmarsch.

← See also under *ablaufen* (for *deine Uhr ist abgelaufen*), *ansagen* (for *die Uhr sagt an*), *Gevatter* (for *meine Uhr steht Gevatter*), *Mond* (for *die Uhr geht nach dem Mond*), *Pfand* (for *die Uhr geht nach dem Pfandhaus*), *Puls* (for *die Pulse der Taschenuhr*), *rund* (for *die Uhr rund*) and *Schmied* (for *Totenuhr*).

Uhu: eagle-owl *hausen wie ein ~* (lit.) to lead a (solitary, withdrawn) hermit's life; modern, e.g. H. Sudermann, *Katzensteg* 15 [1889]. See also under *klagen* for *Klagevogel* and *Klagefrau*.

Ukas: ukase *der ~* order, regulation; originally in Russian = 'tsarist order', in German since ca. middle of the 18th c., recorded by Adelung. Since the 19th c. often used in contemptuous remarks about unwelcome orders or restrictions esp. those which one considers as arbitrary, e.g. Tucholsky, *Gestern und morgen* 64: '. . . zerreißt alle ihre Ukasse in kleine Stücke', also in compounds and derivatives, e.g. Platen, *Ges. Werke* 6,17 [1843]: *'Ukasenton der Zärtlichkeit'*, or ibid. 5,168: '. . . *einen Tyrannen nach unsern ukasischen Begriffen'*, Heine, *Werke* [edit. of 1861] 4,27: *'die Berliner Ukasuisten und Knutologen'*.

Ulm

nach ~ appellieren (coll. obs.) to vomit; one of a group of idioms, in which a town is mentioned (others are Speier and Worms); f.r.b. Eiselein [1838]. See also under *appellieren*.

Ulme: elm *sich* (or *etw.*) *umschlingen wie die Rebe um die ~* (lit.) to cling to sb. (or sth.) like ivy; posts cut from elms are used in vinyards to support vines and this has given rise to many lit. comparisons and allusions, e.g. (DWb) Rachel, *Sat. Ged.* (repr.) 21: *'gleichwie die edle Reben sich*

nach der Ulmen tuhn . . .', Tiedge, *Werke* 3,81: *'umarmend wie den Ulm des Weines Ranke'*.

← See also under *Ranke* (p.1940) and *Rebe* (p.1955) for instances with *Ulm* and *Ulmenbaum*.

Ulmesbruder: see *Bruder*.

Ulrich: see *appellieren* and *Hans*.

um

um (1) for; with ref. to exchanges, sales or purchases; since OHG, e.g. Notker, *Ps.* 25,10: *'sie nobent unrecht umbe gold'*, Schiller, *Fiesco* 1,7: '. . . *daß ich keinen Heller um meine Unsterblichkeit gebe'*; often also in *um . . . willen* = 'for the sake of . . .', e.g. Schiller, *Räuber* 2,3: *'er mordet nicht um des Raubes willen'*.

← See also under *Auge* (for *Auge um Auge*), *Finger* (for *einen Finger der rechten Hand um etw. geben*), *ganz* (for *es geht ums Ganze*), *geben* (for *etw. um etw. geben*), *Gold* (for *Kupfer um Gold geben*), *Gott* (for *um Gottes willen*), *Himmel* (for *um Himmels willen*), *Katze* (for *jetzt gehts der Katze um den Schwanz*), *leben* (for *ums Leben*), *Lohn* (for *um einen Gotteslohn*), *Los* (for *das Los wird um etw. geworfen*), *Million* (for *nicht um eine Million*), *nichts* (for *viel Lärm um nichts*), *Nuß* (for *hier spielt man nicht um Nüsse*), *Preis* (for *um jeden Preis*), *Ritter* (for *um den Ritter schießen*) and *spröde* (for *um eines spröden Mädchens willen*).

um (2) for; with ref. to requests, demands, attempts to obtain sth.; often in such cases as *um etw. bitten*; since OHG, e.g. Goethe 2,31 (W.): *'und man fleht um euern Segen'*, *um Nachsicht bitten* = 'to ask for indulgence or forbearance', since early in the 18th c., *sich um etw. bemühen* = 'to try to obtain sth. or secure sth. for oneself or for others', only since the 18th c. with *um* (before then with genitive or with *mit*).

← See also under *angehen* (for *jem. um etw. angehen*), *anhalten* (for *bei jem.m um etw. anhalten*), *anhauen* (for *jem. um etw. anhauen*), *belangen* (for *jem. um etw. belangen*), *beten* (for *ums tägliche Brot beten*), *fechten* (for *um etw. fechten*), *kämpfen* (for *um etw. kämpfen*), *Maul* (for *jem.m ums Maul gehen*), *Nase* (for *jem.m etw. um die Nase streichen*), *reißen* (for *sich um etw. reißen*), *ringen* (for *um etw. ringen*), *rufen* (for *um Gnade rufen*), *schön* (for *um schön Wetter bitten*), *streiten* (for *sich um etw. streiten*) and *suchen* (for *jem. um etw. ersuchen*).

um (3) around, about; with ref. to surrounding, enclosing or circular movement; since OHG, e.g. Goethe 2,109 (W.): *'wenn alles still und finster um uns ist'*, Ranke, *Sämtl. Werke* 14,7: '. . . *Menge, die sich um sie sammelte'*, Droste-Hülshoff 2, 213: *'um den . . . Mund zieht sich ein weiches dämmerndes Verlangen'*.

← See also under *Brei* (for *um den heißen Brei herumgehen*), *drehen* (for *es dreht sich um . . .*), *Ecke* (for *etw. um die Ecke nehmen, jem. um die Ecke bringen* and *jem.m nicht um die Ecke trauen*), *Fichte* (for *jem. um die Fichte führen*), *Finger* (for *jem. um den Finger wickeln können*), *greifen* (for *um sich greifen*), *Hals* (for *jem.m um den Hals fliegen/fallen*), *herumgehen* (for *um etw. herumgehen*), *herumkommen* (for *um etw. nicht herumkommen können*), *Herz* (for *ist's . . . ums Herz*) *Kirche* (for *mit der Kirche ums Dorf gehen* and *die Kirche ums Dorf tragen*), *Kreis* (for *um etw. kreisen*), *Maul* (for *noch glatt ums Maul*), *Nase* (for *sich den Wind um die Nase wehen lassen*), *Ohr* (for *sich die Welt um die Ohren schlagen*), *Pappe* (for *jem.m Pappe ums Maul schmieren*), *Reif* (for *umb alle wîte ein ganzer reif*), *Reihe* (for *Reihe um* and *sich um jem. reihen*), *Ring* (for *einen Ring um jem. schließen* and *ringsum*), *ruhig* (for *es ist ruhig um diese Sache geworden*), *schauen* (for *um sich schauen*), *Schlange* (for *Luft, die um das schlängelnde Wasser spielt*), *schließen* (for *um etw. schließt sich etw. anderes*), *schlingen (1)* (for *etw. schlingt sich um etw.*), *schweben* (for *etw. schwebt um etw.*), *schwingen* (for *etw. um etw. anderes schwingen*), *schwirren* (for *etw. schwirrt um jem.*), *Sonne* (for *es sonnt rings um dich*), *sprossen* (for *der erste Flaum sproßt ums Kinn*), *still* (for *um den Mann ist es still geworden*) and *Uhr* (for *rund um die Uhr*).

um (4) by; with ref. to distances, weights, measures and values; since Early NHG, e.g. Mathesius, *Sar.* 168a [1571]: '. . . *umb die helfte leichter*', Geibel, *Werke* 5,7: '*der wie Saul das Volck weit überragt um eines Hauptes Länge*'.

← See also under *Daumen* (for *nicht um einen Daumen*), *Haar* (for *um ein Haar*), *Nase* (for *jem.m um eine Nase/Nasenlänge/Pferdelänge voraus sein*) and *Sonne* (for *um Sonnenferne*).

um (5) by; with ref. to time; since OHG, e.g. Tatian 207,2: '*umbi thia niuntun zit*', Goethe IV,40,4 (W.): '*um zwanzig Jahre verjüngt*'.

← See also under *Pfanne* (for *mehr zu tun haben als die Pfanne um Fastnacht*).

um (6) of; with ref. to losses or deprivations; often with *bringen* or *kommen*, sometimes shortened as in Schiller, *D.Carlos* 3,1: '*ich bin um meinen Schlummer*' (with ellipsis of *gekommen*); frequent also in modern coll. *jem. um etw. bemogeln, beschummeln, beschwindeln*.

← See also under *bringen* (for *jem. ums Leben bringen*), *gehen* (for *es geht ums Leben*), *Hals* (for *jem. um den Hals bringen*), *kommen* (for *ums Leben kommen*), *Kreuzer* (for *jem. um den letzten Kreuzer bringen*) and *kurz* (for *jem. um etw. kürzen*).

um (7) about, for; with ref. to concern, sympathy and other feelings concerning sb.; at least since MHG, e.g. *Angst um jem. haben* or *sich um jem. ängstigen* = 'to be worried or anxious about sb.', *sich um jem. kümmern* = 'to take care of or look after sb.', since the 17th c. (before then *sich bekumbern* was used). Also in book titles, e.g. A.Zweig, *Novellen um Claudia* [1912].

← See also under *geschehen* (for *es ist um ihn geschehen*) *Geschrei* (for *viel Geschrei um etw. machen*), *Leid* (for *um jem. Leid tragen*), *Schaden*

(for *es ist schade um etw.*), *scheren* (for *sich um etw. scheren* and *sich einen Dreck um etw. scheren*), *Sorge* (for *um jem. Sorge tragen*), *stehen* (for *es steht schlimm um ihn*), *trauern* (for *um etw. trauern*), *tun* (for *es ist um etw. zu tun* and *um etw. or jem. ist es getan*) and *wissen* (for *um etw. wissen*).

← *um* (8) by, for; describing sequences; since Early NHG, often with time, e.g. *Jahr um Jahr, Stunde um Stunde*, J.Paul, *Qu. Fixl.* 33: '*ein Jahrhundert um das andere*', but also with other nouns, e.g. Goethe 1,181 (W.): '*und so zog ich Kreis um Kreise*' or 4,93 (W.): '. . . *ein Küßchen um ein Küßchen gibst*'; cf. also *einen um den andern Tag* = 'every other or second day'.

um und um (1) everywhere, all around; since MHG, e.g. Luther 18,63 (Weimar): '*denn gottlosen umb und umb sind, wo die losen leute aufkomen*', Schiller, *Fiesco* 5,4: '*Feinde um und um*'; in some regions *um und an* can also be used in this sense, e.g. in Wieland's and Hebel's writings.

um und um (2) over and over; also sometimes = 'totally, thoroughly'; since MHG, with some verbs still in modern period, e.g. Storm, *Werke* 7,61: '*sie gruben allmählich alles um und um*'.

um sein to be over, to be past, to have run out; since Early NHG, e.g. Luther 19,243 (Weimar): '*bis die vierzig tage umbgewesen sind*', Schiller, *Turandot* 2,4: '*deine Frist ist um*', Goethe IV,8,281 (W.): '*im Fall . . . unsere Miethe um sei, wünschte ich die Prolongation derselben*'. For the entirely different *es ist mir um* see under *sein* (p. 2237).

der Weg ist um (coll.) that way is not the shortest one could take, means a detour; beginnings in Early NHG, recorded by Adelung and still current in many regions, e.g. O.Ludwig, *Ges.Schr.* 2,136: '*den Weg an der Herrnmühl vorbei, den geht sie nicht, der wär ihr zu viel um*'; cf. *Umweg* = 'detour'.

← See also under *nichts* (for *um nichts*) and *Note* (for *um eine Note zu hoch singen*).

umackern: plough over

etw. ~ (lit.) to rework, redraft or revise sth.; since the 18th c., sometimes pejor. in the sense of 'up-setting or destroying established things', e.g. in Jean Paul's writings. The general sense of 're-casting' puts this verb into a large group to which *umarbeiten* (since the 18th c.), *umbilden* (18th c.), *umfertigen* (17th c.), *umformen* (17th c.), *ummodeln* (18th c.), *umpflügen* (18th c.), *umprägen* (17th c.) and *umschmelzen* (17th c.) also belong. All describe a transforming process in which sth. existing is reshaped.

← See also under *Modell* (for *ummodeln*), *Pflug* (for *umpflügen*) and *prägen* (for *umprägen*).

umarbeiten: see *umackern*.

umarmen: embrace

jem. ~ to embrace sb.; figur. as a formula in letters since the 18th c., sometimes with the addition of '*in Gedanken*', also with abstracts, e.g. Schiller, *M.Stuart* 3,6: '*den Tod beherzt umarmen*'; hence figur. *Umarmung* (in letters).

sich ~ (lit.) to embrace, unite, meet in love; with abstracts since the 17th c., e.g. Lohenstein, *Armin.* (pref. lb3): '*künste und waffen sich umarmen*'; hence *Umarmung* = 'embrace', also since the Baroque.

umbacken *jem.* (or *etw.*) *zu etw. ~* (rare) to transform sb. (or sth.) into sth. else; since the 19th c., e.g. (DWb) Kruse, *Heinr. VII*, 10 [1898]: '*wie wardst du denn zum Prinzen umgebacken?*'. Sometimes *umbauen* can be used similarly, e.g. *die ganze Struktur umbauen*, since the 19th c.

umbauen: see *umbacken*.

umbiegen: bend over

etw. ~ to bend sth. into a different shape; figur. with ref. to abstracts since the 19th c., also reflex., e.g. (DWb) Hebbel, *Br.* [edit. W.] 2,298: '*der Punkt ist da, wo das Verhältniß sich umbiegt*'.

umbranden

etw. umbrandet jem. (lit.) sth. surges around sb.; in images of wild seas or storms since the 19th c., e.g. S.Zweig, *Balzac* 215: '. . . *von den Stürmen, die seine Existenz umbranden*'; also with ref. to loud applause. In the same contexts *umbrausen* (also since the 19th c.) can be used.

umbrausen: see *umbranden*.

umbringen

jem. ~ to kill sb.; f.r.b. Frisius [1556], but used in official documents as early as in the 15th c.; the reflex. *sich ~* = 'to commit suicide' was also recorded by Frisius. In religious contexts *etw. ~* = 'to defeat, overcome sth.' with ref. to abstracts has been used since the 16th c., e.g. (DWb) Gretter, *Erkl.d.Ep.S.Pauli* 348 [1566]: '. . . *die sünde und den todt überwinden und umbbringen*'.

etw. bringt jem. um sth. kills sb., leads to sb.'s death; since Early NHG, e.g. Luther Apocr. transl. Ecclesiasticus 31,30: '*denn der wein bringet viel leut umb*' or Bible transl. Prov. 1,32: '*der ruchlosen glück bringt sie umb*'; cf. coll. *das bringt mich noch um* = 'that will be the death of me', since the 18th c., e.g. Nestroy, *Ges.Werke* 1,11, also coll. *das bringt mich nicht um* = 'that does not harm me', recorded for many regions since the 19th c., *bring dich nur nicht um* (coll.) = 'don't kill yourself with so much effort', also the threat *ich bring dich um* = 'I'll kill you!'.

← See also under *glatt* (for *ich hätte ihn glatt umbringen können*).

das ist nicht umzubringen (coll.) that is indestructible; since the 19th c. recorded e.g. by Heyne [1895]; *unverwüstlich* is the standard term.

Umbruch

der ~ radical change; originally only a tech. term in mining and agriculture; only since the 20th c. figur. for 'change', also *im ~ sein* = 'to be

in a state of flux'. In the jargon of printers *~* describes 'page-proofs', derived from 'making-up', i.e. 'dividing the typed matter into pages and columns'.

umbuchen

etw. ~ to alter existing arrangements; 20th c., marginally figur., since the change is not always entered in a book; not yet listed in *DWb.* [1933].

umdrehen: turn round

sich ~ to change (completely); figur. since the 18th c., e.g. Schiller, *Räuber* 1,3: '*so hat die Welt sich umgedreht*'.

jem.m den Hals, das Genick, die Gurgel, den Kragen ~ to kill sb. (by twisting his neck); at first phys. and used with ref. to the slaughtering of birds, since Early NHG, but also applied to human beings, e.g. H.Sachs [edit. G.] 22,421: '*der dot im pald sein hals umbdret*'; also used in threats, in lit. since the 17th c., e.g. *dem dreh ich das Genick um*.

jem.m das Wort im Mund ~ to twist sb.'s words; since the 18th c., e.g. Lessing [edit. L.-M.] 18,236 (letter of 1777): '*einem Kinde . . . drehet man das Wort im Munde um*'; cf. somewhat different context in Nietzsche 1,2,8: '*kann man nicht alle Worte umdrehen? Und ist gut vielleicht böse?*'.

er wurde umgedreht (coll.) he was induced to change his mind, opinions, political allegiance (by force, threats, brain-washing); with ref. to spies: 'he was turned'; 20th c. coll.

er ist wie umgedreht (coll.) he has become a different person, you would not recognize him any more; since the 19th c., e.g. (T.) Ganghofer, *Dorfapostel* 268 [1900]; in the standard language *wie ausgewechselt* or *nicht wiederzuerkennen* would be used.

← See also under *Grab* (for *sich im Grab umdrehen*), *Hand* (for *im Handumdrehen*), *Magen* (for *es dreht mir den Magen um*), *Pfennig* (for *er dreht jeden Pfennig dreimal um*) and *Spieß* (for *den Spieß umdrehen*).

umfächeln

etw. umfächelt jem. (lit.) sth. wafts or sweeps smoothly around sb.; in the 18th c. still with a phys. basis, as in Goethe 12,191 (W.), fully figur. by the 19th c., e.g. G.Keller 1,234: '. . . *Abend, . . ., dessen Stille uns umfächelt*'.

umfallen: fall over

umfallen (coll.) to give up one's principles, give in to pressure, cave in, defect; since the 16th c., f.r.b. Rädlein [1711] apparently first in standard use, now coll. and pejor.

← See also under *Fliege* (for *umfallen wie die Fliegen*) and *Sack* (for *umfallen wie ein nasser Sack*).

Umfang

der ~ scope, extent; in phys. sense since MHG (*umbevanc*); figur. since the 18th c., e.g. *das Problem in seinem ganzen ~ untersuchen*, Goethe's mother to Lavater (30.12.1799): '*Ihr wollt den ganzen Umfang von der Krankheit und dem Tode unserer Fräulein Klettenberg wissen?*'.

umfangen: surround

etw. umfängt jem. (lit.) sth. surrounds sb., envelops sb.; figur. since Early NHG, e.g. Luther Bible transl. 2 Sam. 22,5: '*es hatten mich umbfangen die schmerzen des todes*', Schiller, *M. Stuart* 1,6: '. . . *des Kolosseums Herrlichkeit den Staunenden umfing*'; sometimes close to 'to contain', e.g. (Sp.) Zschokke, *Alamont.* 2,8: '. . . *was die Welt für mich Theures umfing*'.

umfassen: surround, embrace

etw. ~ (lit.)(1) to grasp sth., comprehend sth. in its totality; since the 18th c.; not much used now, but very frequent in *umfassend* = 'extensive, comprehensive' with ref. to *Kenntnisse, Maßnahmen*, also statements, e.g. *ein umfassendes Geständnis ablegen*.

etw. ~ (2) to include, take in, cover, include; with such abstracts as events and periods.

Umfeld

das ~ surrounding area, neighbourhood; in sociology and psychology used for 'milieu, surroundings'; a new word, not yet recorded in dictionaries of the 1st half of the 20th c.

umfloren: see *Flor* (1).

Umgang: walk round

der ~ (1) social intercourse, communication; since the 17th c., sometimes as *persönlicher, geselliger* or *gesellschaftlicher* ~, used both for the activity and for the persons concerned, e.g. Goethe 23,263 (W.): '*ein alter Freund . . . blieb sein einziger Umgang*'; in wider use possibly through Knigge's book *Über den Umgang mit Menschen* [1788]; since the 18th c. also euphem. for 'sexual intercourse'. The most frequently used compound is *Umgangssprache* = 'colloquial language', in the 18th c. usually as *Sprache des Umgangs*, e.g. Gottsched, *Crit. Dichtk.* 652 [1751]: '. . . *der Sprache des täglichen Umganges*', also sometimes as *Sprache des gemeinen Umgangs*. It could, however, also be used for 'language of communication' (without ref. to speech levels), as in Goethe, *Gespräche* 5,123 on French: '. . . *ist die Sprache des Umgangs und ganz besonders auf Reisen unentbehrlich*'; the compound established itself in the 19th c.

der ~ (2) occupation (with sth.); since the 18th c., e.g. Hagedorn, *Od.* 5,8: '*edlen Umgang mit den Münzen*', F. Schlegel (in *Athen.* 2,6): '. . . *in etwas näherem Umgange mit Wissenschaften und Künsten*'.

umgänglich sociable, affable, friendly; since the 18th c. (Adelung recorded '*umgängliches Betragen*'); hence *Umgänglichkeit*, also since the 18th c., e.g. Fontane 1,418: '. . . *die Tugend der Umgänglichkeit als eine spezifisch wienerische zu preisen*'.

unumgänglich necessary, unavoidable; literally 'sth. which one cannot avoid by going round it', therefore at first usually for 'unavoidable' (16th c.), later (18th c.) increasingly for 'necessary', but also used in emphasis as an adverb, as in Kant [Akad. edit.] 3,101: '*unumgänglich nothwendig*', where it means 'absolutely'; the noun *Unumgänglichkeit* = 'necessity' since the 17th c.

umgarnen: see *Garn*.

umgaukeln: flutter about

etw. umgaukelt jem. (lit.) sth. flutters or dances around sb.; with abstracts such as *Traum, Idee, Hoffnung* as the subject since the 18th c.

umgeben: surround

von etw. ~ *sein* (1) (obs.) to be afflicted by sth.; e.g. Luther Bible transl. Psalm 40,13: '*es hat mich umbgeben leiden on zal*', where the A.V. has in verse 12: 'for innumerable evils have compassed me about'; this sense of hostile 'surrounding' is now obs.

von etw. ~ *sein* (2) to be surrounded, sheltered, looked after by sth.; with such abstracts as *Liebe, Wärme, Pflege* since the 18th c., e.g. Goethe 22,62 (W.) or *Tasso* 2,1: '*die Schicklichkeit umgibt mit einer Mauer das zarte . . . Geschlecht*'.

← See also under *Loch* (for *umgeben sein*).

jem.s Umgebung sb.'s surroundings, associates, people around sb.; transfer from phys. 'environs, surroundings' to people; since the 18th c., e.g. Goethe IV,32,242 (W.) or Fichte, *Reden a.d.dt.N.* 463. *Umgegend* can be similarly transferred, e.g. *die ganze Umgegend redet davon*, modern.

umgehen: go round

etw. ~ (inseparable) to avoid, disobey or fail to observe sth.; since MHG for 'to avoid', since Early NHG for 'to disobey, contravene' with ref. to laws, as in Schiller, *M. Stuart* 1,7: '*Landesrecht umgehen*'.

← See also under *herumgehen* (for *um etw. herumgehen*).

etw. nicht ~ *können* to be unable to refrain from mentioning sth.; specialization of the previous entry; since the 17th c., e.g. Grimmelshausen, *Simpliz.* 4,263; cf. *etw. mit Stillschweigen* ~, since Early NHG, now with *übergehen*.

etw. geht um (1) sth. circulates; with ref. to abstracts such as *Nachricht, Gerücht*; since Early NHG, e.g. Fischart, *Werke* [edit. H.] 3,224: '*die tägeliche sprüchwörter, so unter den leuten umb gehen*'.

etw. (or *es*) *geht um* (2) some ghost is present, there are spooks about; since the 16th c., e.g. Schiller, *M. Stuart*: '*ich gehe nachts um wie ein gequälter Geist*'.

etw. geht mit einem um (coll.) sth. turns around in one's head or before one's eyes (making one dizzy); mainly with *Kopf*, e.g. Lessing [edit. L.-M.] 1,72: '*in meinem Keller selbst geht's um*', Schiller, *Räuber* 2,3; Adelung recorded '*das ganze Zimmer geht mit mir um*'.

← See also under *herumgehen* (for *etw. geht jem.m im Kopf herum* and *es geht mir wie ein Mühlrad im Kopf herum*).

mit jem.m ~ (1) (separable) to keep company with or have communication with sb.; since MHG, e.g. Goethe 42,2,168: '*sag mir, mit wem du umgehst, so sage ich dir, wer du bist*'.

mit jem.m ~ (2) (separable) to treat sb. (in a certain way); since MHG, e.g. Luther Bible transl. 1 Chr. 11,4: '*schendlich mit mir umbgehen*'; also with ref. to things, e.g. Lohenstein, *Armin.* 2,298a [1689]: '. . . *ist dieser wein wohl werth, daß man mit ihm sparsam . . . umbgehe*'.

mit etw. ~ (1) to deal or occupy oneself with sth.; since Early NHG, e.g. Luther Bible transl. Gen. 46,32: '*leute, die mit vieh umbgehen*'; cf. *Umgang* (2).

mit etw. ~ (2) to have sth. in mind, plan sth.; since MHG, not always with *mit*, e.g. Lessing in a letter to E.König [1772] has the phrase with *auf*; cf. also similar *etw. geht mit jem.m um*, as in Schiller, *Räuber* 1,2: '. . . *was ins Ohr sagen . . . das schon lang mit mir umgeht*'.

umgehend (1) (adj. and adv.) at once, immediate(ly); derived from the postal service: *mit umgehender Post*; since the 18th c.

umgehend (2). circulating, making the rounds; since the 18th c. with abstracts, e.g. Campe [1810] recorded it with *Krankheit*.

← See also under *Rad* (for *es geht noch manches um, eh das geschieht*).

umgießen: see *gießen*.

umglänzen
etw. umglänzt jem. (lit.) sth. bathes sb. in light or splendour; since the 18th c., e.g. Ebner-Eschenbach 3,51: '. . . *junges Haupt, das schon von der Morgenröte des Ruhms umglänzt wurde*'; *umglühen* can be used in similar contexts, but is rare.

umgreifen: grasp
umgreifend (a.) comprehensive, extensive; from ~ = 'to comprize' since the 18th c., displaced by *umfassend*.

umgrenzen: limit
etw. ~ (lit.) to circumscribe or limit sth. (e.g. a subject); figur. since the 18th c. mostly in the sense of 'surrounding', then usually for 'circumscribing'.

umgucken: look around
er wird sich noch ~ (coll.) he will have some (nasty) surprise coming to him, he is in for a shock; since the 19th c..

umgürten: gird
mit etw. umgürtet sein (lit.) to be girded (or girt) with sth.; with abstracts since MHG, now becoming a.

umhangen: see *hängen*.

umhängen: put around
einer Sache etw. ~ (lit.) to veil or clothe sth. with sth.; with abstracts since the 18th c.

← See also under *Mantel* (for *einer Sache ein Mäntelchen umhängen*).

umhauen: knock over
das haut mich um (sl.) that bowls me over, leaves me speechless; since early in the 20th c.

← See also under *hauen* (for *das haut mich vom Stuhl*) and *Neger* (for *das haut den stärksten Neger um*).

schon ein Glas haut ihn um (sl.) he gets drunk even on one glass; modern sl.

umhegen: surround with trees
jem. ~ (lit.) to cosset or shelter sb.; since the 17th c.

umherschweifen: see *schweifen*.
umhersprühen: see *sprühen*.
umhertreiben: see *treiben*.
umhin
nicht ~ *können* to have no choice but to . . .; since the 18th c., recorded by Adelung.

umhüllen: shroud
etw. umhüllt etw. sth. shrouds, covers, surrounds sth.; with abstracts since MHG, e.g. Schiller, *M.Stuart* 4,3: '*noch umhüllt Geheimnis seine Thäter*'.

umkehren: turn round
umkehren to change one's way of life, turn over a new leaf; since MHG, e.g. Böhme, *Schr.* 4,96 [1620]: '*sobald der mensch umbkeret und sich zu Gott wendet*'.

etw. ~ to turn sth. round, reverse sth.; with abstracts since MHG, e.g. (DWb) Alsfelder *Pass.Sp.* 149: '*do wart das wort Eva umbgekart, ave sprach der engel zart*'; also reflex. since MHG, e.g. Goethe 18,54 (W.): '. . . *daß sich unser Herz im Busen umkehret, wenn . . .*'.

← See also under *Blatt* (for *das Spiel wird sich umkehren*), *Hand* (for *im Handumkehren*), *Pflug* (for *nun hat der Fall sich umgekehrt*), *Schuh* (for *umgekehrt wird ein Schuh draus*), *Spieß* (for *den Spieß umkehren*), *Stein* (for *jeden Stein umkehren*) and *Stiel* (for *den Stiel umkehren*).

alles (or *das ganze Haus*) ~ to turn everything upside down, search everywhere for sth.; at least since the 18th c., e.g. Goethe IV,10,258 (W.) on a lost document: '*ich habe meine Garderobe und mein Zimmer umgekehrt und kann sie nicht finden*'.

← See also under *kehren* (for *das Oberste zuunterst kehren*).

auf halbem Wege ~ to stop halfway; since Early NHG, recorded in a prov. by Petri 2,1,6a [1605]: '*auff halbem wege ist gut umbkehren, wenn man irre geht*'.

← See also under *Grab* (for *sich im Grab umkehren*), *Magen* (for *es kehrt mir den Magen um*) and *Sack* (for *er ist wie ein umgekehrter Sack*).

umkippen: topple over
umkippen (regional and coll.) to keel over (of persons in a faint), to turn into the opposite, crack (with ref. to the voice), go off (with ref. to food and drink); recorded since the 19th c. for

many regions, coll. since the middle of the 19th c. for 'to give up one's former convictions or allegiances', synonymous with *umfallen* (which see); *umklappen* and *umknicken* (both coll.) have also been used in this sense (20th c.)

umklammern: clasp
den Feind ~ (mil.) to encircle or envelop the enemy; since the 19th c., e.g. Häusser, *Dt.Gesch.* 4,269: '. . . *die Stellung des Feindes . . . zu um-klammern*'.

umklappen: see *umkippen*.

umkleiden: clothe
etw. mit etw. ~ (lit.) to clothe sth. in sth. since MHG, e.g. Goethe IV,25,78 (W.): '. . . *wenn ich es auch mit noch so viel glatten Worten umkleiden wollte*'.

umknicken: see *umkippen*.

umkommen
umkommen to perish; with ref. to death of persons and animals (in war or by natural causes), go bad (with ref. to food and drink); f.r.b. Alberus [1540].
← See also under *Gefahr* (for *wer sich in Gefahr begibt, kommt darin um*).

umkränzen
umkränzt (lit.) encircled; since the 18th c., mostly in landscape descriptions, e.g. Nicolai, *Reise d.D.* 3,118 [1783]: '*rundherum mit Bergen umkränzt*'.

umkreisen: circle
etw. umkreist etw. (lit.) sth. moves or revolves around sth.; with such abstracts as *Geist, Gedanke, Hoffnung* since the 18th c.; not listed by Adelung, but recorded by Campe [1810], who also mentions use of ~ for 'to confine, limit, circumscribe', as to found in Herder (now obs.).
← See also under *Kreis* (for *Umkreis*).

umkrempeln
jem. ~ (coll.) to change sb. completely; since early in the 20th c., not even listed in *DWb.* [1936]; in recent sl. *umpolen* has appeared in this sense, using the image of reversing the electric polarity; sometimes used with ref. to a person's sexuality.

umlagern: besiege
etw. ~ to crowd around sth.; derived from the mil. sense in the 18th c.

umlauern
etw. umlauert jem. (lit.) sth. lies in wait for sb. with hostile intentions; since the 19th c. with abstracts, e.g. (DWb) Nestroy, *Ces.W.* 4,137: '*boshafte Verleumdung und Verrat umlauern meine Schritte*'.

umlaufen: see *herumlaufen*.

umlegen: lay down, fold or topple over
etw. auf verschiedene Personen ~ to divide, allocate or distribute (a charge, sum, tax, etc.) in equal or appropriate amounts among various people; since the 18th c., f.r.b. Aler [1727].
jem. ~ (sl.) to kill sb., do sb. in; modern sl.

umlenken: veer, turn aside
in etw. ~ to switch into sth., change course; since the 16th c. with ref. to persons who change their behaviour or adopt a different way of life, e.g. Schiller, *Picc.* 2,6: '. . . *umlenken in die alte breitgetretene Fahrstraße der gemeinen Pflicht*'.

umleuchten: see *leuchten*.

ummauern: see *Mauer*.

ummodeln: see *umackern*.

umnachten
umnachten (lit.) cover with darkness, plunge into darkness; since the 18th c., frequent in Klopstock's writings, e.g. *Mess.* 18,391; in *geistig umnachtet* used euphem. for 'mentally deranged'; cf. Schiller, *Turandot* 3,3: '*welch schwarze Ahnung mir den Sinn umnachtet*'.

umnebeln: see *Nebel* and *Rausch*.

umpanzern: cover with armour
umpanzert (lit.) covered with armour; modern, e.g. Heyse, *Par.* 3,233: '*das Eis, mit dem die Brust des . . . Trotzkopfs umpanzert war*'; see also *gepanzert* and *verpanzert* on p. 1827.

umpflügen: see *Pflug*.

umpolen: see *umkrempeln*.

umprägen: see *prägen*.

umpusten: see *pusten*.

umrahmen: see *Rahmen*.

umranken: see *Ranke*.

umräuchern: see *beräuchern*.

umrauschen: see *Rausch*.

umreihen: see *Reihe*.

umreißen: see *reißen*.

umringeln: see *Schlange*.

umringen: see *Ring*.

Umriß: see *reißen*.

umrühren: see *rühren*.

umsatteln: see *Sattel*.

Umsatz: see *setzen*.

umsäumen: see *Saum*.

umschaffen
etw. ~ (a.) to revise or rework sth.; esp. with ref. to writings, as in Lessing [edit. L.-M.] 9,185: '*eine . . . Erzehlung in ein rührendes Drama umzuschaffen*'; now a., displaced by *umarbeiten, umformen* and others listed under *umackern*.

umschalten: switch over
auf etw. anderes ~ to change or switch over to sth. else; very recent, derived from electrical switching, radio and television; ~ itself is not even listed in *DWb.* [1936].

umschatten: see *Schatten*.

umschauen: see *schauen*.

umschimmern: see *Schimmer*.

umschlagen: see *Schlag*.

umschlängeln: see *Schlange*.

umschleichen: see *schleichen*.

umschleiern: see *Schleier*.

umschließen: see *schließen*.

umschlingen: see *schlingen(1)*.

umschmelzen: see *schmelzen*.

umschmieden

etw. ~ to change, reshape sth.; since the 18th c., recorded by Adelung, now rare.

umschnallen: see *schmachten.*

umschnüffeln: see *schnüffeln.*

umschnüren: see *Schnur.*

umschreiben: see *schreiben* (also under *leuchten*).

umschulen

jem. (zu etw.) ~ to retrain sb. (for sth.); 20th c. coinage, not even listed in *DWb.* [1936].

umschwärmen: swarm around

jem. ~ to admire or idolize sb.; first for phys. 'flocking around', then, since middle of the 19th c. with ref. to the passionate feelings of the person who follows sb. around, e.g. Freytag, *Ges.W.* 3,16: '. . . umschwärmt von einem Heer Anbeter'; cf. *jem. anschwärmen* and *von jem.m schwärmen,* listed on p. 2204.

umschweben: float or hover around

etw. umschwebt etw. (or *jem.*) (lit.) sth. hovers around sth. (or sb.); since the 18th c., e.g. Goethe 11,292 (W.): '. . . Gesang, der wie ein Geisterlied das Ohr umschwebt'.

Umschweif: see *Schweif.*

umschweifen: see *Schweif.*

umschwellen: see *schwellen.*

umschwenken: see *schwenken.*

umschwirren: see *schwirren.*

Umschwung: see *Schwung.*

umsehen: see *sehen* (also under *leiten*).

umsetzen: see *setzen.*

Umsicht: see *sehen.*

umsonnen: see *Sonne.*

umsonst: see *bezahlen* and *heute.*

umspielen: see *Spiel.*

umspinnen: see *Spinne.*

umspringen: see *springen.*

Umstand

der ~ (1), *die Umständlichkeit* long-windedness, ponderousness, pedantry; at first with ref. to long-winded speech, recorded as *umbstend* by Riederer [1493]; since the 18th c. extended to ponderousness, fussy going into unnecessary detail, pedantry. Hence *der Umstandskrämer* (coll.) = 'fuss-pot', since the 18th c., recorded both for Swabia and Saxony. *Umstände machen* also referred at first to speech (16th c.), but now = 'to cause trouble or inconvenience' (with ref. to events, things or persons) and 'to go to much trouble, put oneself out', both since the 17th c.

der ~ (2) circumstance; influenced by Lat. *circumstantia;* current since Early NHG, e.g. Luther 12,492 (Weimar); often in *unter allen Umständen* = 'at all events, in any case'.

← See also under *Spiel* (for *durch Umständlichkeit . . . Kleinigkeitskrämerey*) and *Stand* (for *in anderen Umständen*).

umstehen: see *stehen.*

umsteigen: see *steigen.*

umstellen: see *stellen.*

umstimmen

jem. to cause sb. to change his mind, win sb. round; since the 17th c.

umstoßen: see *stoßen* (also under *Fliege*).

umstrahlen: see *Glorie.*

umstricken: see *Strick.*

umströmen: see *Strom.*

umstülpen: see *stülpen* (also under *Pfanne*).

umstürzen: see *stürzen.*

umtanzen: see *Tanz.*

umtaufen: see *taufen.*

umtoben

etw. umtobt jem. (lit.) sth. rages around sb.; since the 19th c. with ref. to abstracts, e.g. (DWb) Treitschke, *Dt. Gesch.* 5,242: '*in dem Wirrwarr . . . der den Minister umtobte*'.

umtönen: see *Ton.*

umtragen: carry around

sich mit etw. ~ (obs.) to have sth. in mind, plan sth.; still current in the 19th c. alongside *sich mit etw. tragen* which is much older and still in use (see p. 2470); now obs.

umtreiben: move around

jem. ~ to make sb. restless, worry or disturb sb.; with abstracts or persons as the subject; since Early NHG, e.g. Luther Bible transl. Hebrews 13,9: '*lasset euch nicht mit . . . frembden leren umbtreiben*'. - The reflex. *sich* ~ has made way for *sich herumtreiben* (for an example see under *Ring*) and *umhertreiben* (see p. 2479).

Umtrieb: see *Trieb.*

umtun: see *tun.*

umufern: see *Ufer.*

umwälzen: roll over

etw. ~ (lit.) to consider or ponder sth.; since the 19th c. with abstracts, e.g. (DWb) Immermann [edit. B.] 16,314: '*ich wälze wichtige Entschlüsse um*'.

die Umwälzung revolution; in phys. sense for 'rotation' since the 16th c.; figur. since the 18th c. for 'radical change', also in polit. contexts for 'revolution', e.g. by Goethe IV,14,40 (W.). Adelung objected: '. . . *Umwälzung, welches von einigen Neuern auf eine sehr ungeschickte Art für Revolution gebraucht wird, von welchem es ohne dieß nur eine buchstäbliche Übersetzung ist. Besser wäre Umwandlung*'.

umwandeln: walk around

jem. umwandelt etw. (lit., obs.) sb. goes over sth. (with a view to exploring it); mainly in the 18th c., now obs.

sich ~ (lit.) to change; figur. with abstracts since the 18th c.; similarly *umgewandelt werden* = 'to undergo a change', as in Goethe 42,2,10 (W.), also *sich wie umgewandelt fühlen,* since the 19th c. In legal contexts ~ can be used for 'to commute' (a sentence), not mentioned in *DWb.* (1936).

← See also under *umwälzen* (for *Umwandlung*).

umweben: weave around

umwebt or *umwoben* (lit.) gently surrounded or covered; since the 18th c., e.g. *von Wohlgeruch umwebt*; now very rare, if not obs., but *umwehen* in the same contexts, current since the 18th c. (Klopstock), is still in use.

Umweg: detour

etw. auf Umwegen tun to do sth. in a round-about way, surreptitiously or not quite legally; since Early NHG, often as *Umwege machen*, as in Goethe IV,3,85 (W.).

umwehen: see *umweben*.

umwenden: turn round

etw. wendet sich um sth. turns around, changes radically; with abstracts or in figur. locutions since Early NHG, in many cases used as an alternative to *sich umdrehen* or *sich umkehren* (which see).

← See also under *Napoleon* (for *umgewendeter Napoleon*).

umwerfen: throw over, topple

etw. wirft jem. or *etw. um* (coll.) sth. discon-certs or upsets sb. or sth.; with abstracts or such concrete nouns as *Alkohol* as the subject; since Early NHG, e.g. Luther 10,1,1,131 (Weimar); also sometimes in the sense of 'to destroy, over-turn, abolish'.

jem. ~ (lit.) to stir sb. deeply, shake sb. to the core; modern, e.g. (Kl.-St.) Feuchtwanger, *Oppermann* 232: '. . . *ein Mensch, der einen umwirft, zu neuen Gedanken zwingt*'. The chief notion is 'to change', which was also present in the reflex. *sich* ~ , current in the 18th c., now obs.

das ist umwerfend (coll.) that is smashing, a scream; in coll. of the 2nd half of the 20th c.; also in adverbial use, e.g. *umwerfend komisch* (coll.) = 'hilariously funny'.

umwickeln: wrap round

jem. mit etw. ~ (lit.,a) to fetter or ensnare sb. with sth.; expresses the notion 'to deprive sb. of free movement or the ability to defend himself', current since the 18th c., e.g. Wieland 34,304: '*während unser Gegner . . . uns mit runden Perioden umwickelt*'; *umwinden* can also be used, current since the 18th c., e.g. Wieland 3,78 or 15,7; cf. *unumwunden* = 'frankly, bluntly, without reserve', general since the end of the 18th c. (taking the place of *unbewunden*), as can be *umstricken* (for which see under *Strick*).

umwinden: see *umwickeln*.

umwittern

etw. umwittert jem. or *etw.* (lit.) sth. surrounds sb. or sth. (threateningly, in a sinister or uncanny way), besets sb.; since the 18th c., e.g. Goethe, *Faust* , 8: '. . . *vom Zauberhauch, der euren Zug umwittert*' or I,496: '*bist du es, der, von meinem Hauch umwittert, in allen Lebenstiefen zit-tert . . .?*'; not yet listed in Adelung.

umwogen

jem. or *etw.* ~ (lit.) to surround sb. or sth. in waves or crowds; figur. with abstracts only since the 19th c.

umwölken: cover with clouds

etw. umwölkt jem. or *etw.* (lit.) sth. darkens or shrouds sb. or sth.; since the 17th c., often in *jem.s Gemüt, Sinn, Augen* ~ , also in *umwölkte Stirn* (but *bewölkt* is also used); *unumwölkt* (lit.) = 'clear, unclouded' arose in figur. contexts in the 18th c.

umwühlen

etw. ~ to churn up sth., rummage around in sth.; since the 18th c., e.g. Goethe 2, 17 (W.): '. . . *sein Innerstes von Grund aus umzuwühlen*'.

umzäunen: fence in

etw. ~ (lit.) to limit, restrict, confine sth.; in general use with abstracts since the 17th c., but since Early NHG in purely religious contexts, e.g. Luther 26,335 (Weimar).

umziehen: see *halb, Reif* and *Traum*.

umzingeln: surround

etw. umzingelt jem. (lit., obs.) sth. surrounds sb. oppressively; with abstracts in the 18th and 19th c., but now obs.

umzirkt: see *sausen*.

umzüngeln

etw. umzüngelt etw. sth. licks around sth.; mainly with ref. to (phys. or figur.) snakes or fire since the 19th c.

unabänderlich

unabänderlich unalterable; positive *abänderlich* has not been in use for a long time (even in 1854 J.Grimm in *DWb.* only mentioned the negative in his entry on *änderlich* and Sanders [1860] stated '*ungewöhnlich außer in Zusammen-setzungen*', but Goethe used it in his *Farbenlehre*); the negative established itself in the 18th c. (Schiller, Fichte). Kramer [1702] recorded *unveränderlich*.

unabdingbar

unabdingbar (a.) absolutely necessary; derived from *abdingen* = 'to obtain sth. from sb. by bar-gaining', used by Schiller and Wieland. Locutions such as *er läßt sich nichts davon abdin-gen*, as recorded by Kramer [1702] made *abding-bar* possible (which *DWb.* [1854] and Sanders [1860] did not record). The negative was recorded in the 19th c., but is now dropping out of use (*DWb.* [1936] does not list it).

unabgeschliffen

unabgeschliffen (lit.) rough, coarse, unpolished; in occasional use since the 19th c.; see also under *schleifen* for *abschleifen, abgeschliffen, ungeschliffen* and *Ungeschliffenheit.*

unabgeschwächt

unabgeschwächt (lit.) undiminished; with such abstracts as *Interesse*; modern, not yet listed in Adelung or Campe.

unabhängig

unabhängig independent; antonym to *abhängig* (see p. 8), current since the 18th c., often in philos. contexts, the negative since late in the 18th c.; hence *Unabhängigkeit* which arose at the same time.

unabkömmlich

unabkömmlich (1) (mil.) reserved, employed in a reserved occupation; since the 19th c., when the mil. meaning was recorded in *DWb*. [1854].

unabkömmlich (2) indispensable; antonym to *abkömmlich* (see p. 9); since the 19th c., but apparently younger than ~ in its mil. sense.

unabkömmlich (3) engaged, unable to get away; *abkommen* for 'to get away, be spared' was recorded by Kramer (1702), but ~ = 'unable to get away, unavailable' apparently only arose in the 20th c.

unablässig

unablässig constant(ly), unremitting(ly); since Early NHG, e.g. Luther 32,319 (Weimar): '*unablessiger vleis*'; derived from *ablassen* = 'to discontinue', recorded by Steinbach [1734] and Frisch [1741]. Luther also used *unabläßlich* (also still to be found in Goethe's writings), but this is obs.

unablösbar

unablösbar, also *unablöslich* irredeemable; derived from *ablösen* = 'to redeem, repay'; since the 19th c. with ref. to debts, loans, etc., e.g. Keller, *Werke* 2,102: '*unablösliche Schuldverpflichtungen*'.

unabsehbar

unabsehbar unforeseeable, unpredictable f.r.b. Dusch [1754]; Klopstock in *Mess.* 4,282 still used '*nicht absehbar*'. See also *es ist nicht abzusehen* on p. 16.

unabsetzbar

unabsetzbar irremovable; only since the 19th c., still missing in Campe [1811]; mainly used with ref. to judges and officials; in econ. contexts for 'non-deductible' only since the 20th c.

unabsichtlich

unabsichtlich unintentional; since the 18th c., f.r.b. Campe [1811]; cf. *absichtlich* on p. 16. Goethe used *Absichtlichkeit*, but not *Unabsichtlichkeit* (which Campe recorded).

unabtretbar

unabtretbar (jur., econ.) unassignable, intransferable; displaced *unabtretlich*; f.r.b. Campe [1811].

unabweisbar

unabweisbar, *unabweislich* irrefutable, irrebuttable; only since the 19th c., e.g. Treitschke, *Dt.Gesch.* 5,52. It appears to be older than the antonym *abweisbar* (not yet listed in *DWb*. [1854]; *unabweislich* was used by Ranke, *Päpste* 1,168, f.r.b. Campe [1811].

unabwendbar

unabwendbar unavoidable; from *abwenden* (see p. 20); since the 18th c., f.r.b. Campe [1811].

unachtsam

unachtsam inattentive, careless; since MHG,

e.g. Zinkgräf, *Apophth.* 1,210 [1653]; hence also *Unachtsamkeit*, also since MHG, e.g. Tauler, *Pred.* 497b.

unanfechtbar

unanfechtbar incontestable, unimpeachable; from *anfechten* (see p. 39): in legal contexts = 'non-appealable'; since the 18th c.; Luther 1,395a (Jena) used *unanfechtlich* (now obs.). There is also *unangefochten* for 'uncontested'; modern.

unangebracht

unangebracht inappropriate, unsuitable; modern in this sense (for *angebracht* = 'suitable' and *übel angebracht* see p. 35); only recorded since ca. 1870, e.g. in the supplement to Sanders. 18th c.; Luther 1,395a (Jena) used *unanfechtlich* (now obs.). There is also *unangefochten* for 'uncontested'; modern.

unangemessen

unangemessen inappropriate; for *angemessen* see p. 53; the negative since the 18th c., f.r.b. Campe [1811].

unangenehm

unangenehm unpleasant; for *angenehm* see p. 53; since the 15th c., e.g. Schiller, *Fiesco* 3,10: '*eine unangenehme Geschichte*'; the litotes *nicht ~* = 'quite pleasant, not bad at all' was listed (and praised) by Kramer [1719].

unangetastet

unangetastet untouched, unaffected; since the 18th c., often with ref. to *Ruf*, *Ehre* and similar abstracts, frequent in Goethe, e.g. 49,1,237 or 27,183 (W.); see also below for *unantastbar*.

unangreifbar

unangreifbar unassailable; f.r.b. Campe [1811]; displaced *unangreiflich*.

unannehmbar

unannehmbar unacceptable; since late in the 18th c., possibly a loan from English.

unannehmlich

unannehmlich since the 16th c., in late 20th c. dictionaries no longer listed, but *Unannehmlichkeit* = 'trouble, unpleasantness, troublesome business', current since the middle of the 18th c., is still recorded.

unansehnlich: see ansehen.

unanständig: see anstehen.

unanstößig

unanstößig decent, proper, seemly; Luther used *unanstossig*, Kramer [1719] recorded *unanstößlich* (now obs.); see p. 63 for the change which *anstößig* underwent, which applies also to ~, recorded in its modern sense since Stieler.

unantastbar

unantastbar untouchable; from *antasten* (see p. 64); *antastbar* is not in use (possibly never was); the negative since the 18th c., recorded by Campe [1811].

unappetitlich

unappetitlich unappetizing; since the 18th c.

f.r.b. Rädlein [1711]; used not only with ref. to food and drink, but also figur. to persons, even to language, as in a letter by Zelter to Goethe in *Briefw.* 59.

Unart

die ~ bad habit, naughtiness, incivility; since MHG, but at first in more severe condemnation, e.g. *Passional* 188: '. . . *suntliche unart*', later in milder sense; cf. also Goethe, *Unterh.dt.Ausgew.*: '*es fehlte nicht an Arten und Unarten in seinem Hause*'. The adj. *unartig*, current since MHG, could refer to soil = 'unsuitable', minerals = 'yielding no ore of value', medicines = 'ineffective', children = 'illegitimate', appearance = 'ugly'; with ref. to morality since Early NHG, e.g. Luther Bible transl. 2 Thess. 3,2, later describing bad behaviour, e.g. Schiller, *Fiesco* 1,1.

← See also under *hoch* (for *die Unart ihres Betragens*).

der ~ (a.) naughty boy, unruly child; since MHG, recorded since the 18th c., e.g. Schwan [1784], now dropping out of use.

unaufgelöst: see *lösen.*

unaufgeschlossen

unaufgeschlossen hide-bound, unreceptive; for *aufgeschlossen* see p. 100; the negative only since the beginning of the 19th c., not yet recorded by Campe [1811].

unaufhaltsam

unaufhaltsam, also *unaufhaltbar* inexorable, unstoppable; from *aufhalten* = 'hold back, detain', as in Luther Bible transl. Gen. 24,56; *unaufhaltsam* in use since the 18th c. (frequent in Goethe), *unaufhaltbar* is about a c. older, but less used now.

unaufhörlich

unaufhörlich incessant(ly); *aufhörlich*, in use in Early NHG, is now obs.; the negative arose in the 16th c., f.r.b. Maaler [1561].

unaufrichtig

unaufrichtig insincere; for *aufrichtig* see p. 97; the negative recorded since the 17th c., e.g. by Kramer [1678].

unaufschiebbar

unaufschiebbar non-deferable, non-postponable; in use since the 19th c.; for *aufschieben* see p. 98.

unausführbar

unausführbar impracticable, unworkable; modern; surprisingly unrecorded in *DWb.* [1936], whereas *unausgeführt* is listed.

unausgeglichen

unausgeglichen (1) unstable; figur. with ref. to persons since the 19th c.

unausgeglichen (2) (econ.) unsettled; with ref. to accounts; since the 19th c. (*nicht beglichen* is preferred).

unauslöschlich: see *auslöschen.*

unaussprechlich

unaussprechlich inexpressible; since MHG, later (since the 17th c.) also used as an intensifying adverb = 'very much'.

unausstehlich: see *ausstehen.*

Unband, unbändig: see *Band.*

unbedachtsam: see *Tand.*

unbedeutend: see *bedeuten.*

unbedingt: see *bedingen.*

unbefangen: see *befangen.*

unbefleckt: see *beflecken.*

unbefriedigend

unbefriedigend unsatisfactory; only since the 19th c., f.r.b. Campe (1811), who also appears to have been the first to record *unbefriedigt* = 'dissatisfied'.

unbegreiflich: see *begreifen.*

unbegrenzt: see *begrenzen.*

unbegründet

unbegründet unfounded, groundless; since MHG (*unbegrunt*), later little recorded, but listed again in Campe [1811]. Kramer [1702] recorded *ungegründet* in this sense. The noun *Unbegründetheit* apparently only since the 19th c.

unbehauen: see *behauen.*

unbehaust: homeless

der unbehauste Mensch (lit.) man without a (spiritual or intellectual) home, homeless or uprooted man; ~ in phys. sense arose in MHG, the figur. meaning came into use (presumably) through Goethe, *Faust I*,3348: '*bin ich der Flüchtling nicht? der Unbehauste? Der Unmensch ohne Zweck und Ruh*' . . .'; given new significance by studies on modern rootlessness (since ca. 1950).

unbeherrscht

unbeherrscht intemperate, lacking self-control from *sich beherrschen* (see p. 222), not yet in Adelung, but recorded by Campe [1811].

unbeholfen: see *helfen.*

unbekannt: unknown

der große Unbekannte the Great Unknown; in Engl. before it became current in German, allusion to Job 36,26: '*siehe, Gott ist groß und unbekannt*'; in German apparently only since the 18th c. After the publication of the *Waverley Novels* [1814] the locution was applied to their anonymous author, then frequently as a nickname for Walter Scott, e.g. Pückler, *Br. eines Verstorb.* 3,14 [1826]: '. . . *kamen wir auf Walter Scott. Goethe war aber nicht sehr enthusiastisch für den großen Unbekannten eingenommen*', Gutzkow, *Ges.W.* 1,223: '*der "große Unbekannte", der Verfasser des "Waverley"*', but also used in more general contexts, e.g. Lenau, *Werke* 1,304 [1838]: '*als noch der Raucher drein gehaucht, der große Unbekannte*', Heinke 2,433: '. . . *des neuen Gotts, des großen Unbekannten*', perhaps an allusion to Acts 17,23. For details see Ladendorf, *Hist.Schlagwb.* 110 [1906].

die große Unbekannte the unknown or uncertain factor or information (relevant for a decision or a plan); the image is taken from mathematics and refers to 'the unknown' in an equation; modern.

unbelebt: see *beleben*.

unbeleckt

unbeleckt untouched, unaffected; for *beleckt* see p. 246; ~ is a 20th c. word, not yet listed in *DWb*. [1936]; e.g. *von irgendwelcher Zivilisation* ~ , when describing primitive people, iron. *von jeder Kenntnis* ~ = 'totally ignorant'.

unbemäntelt: see *bemänteln*.

unbemerkt

unbemerkt unnoticed; f.r.b. Stieler [1691]; Kramer [1702] recorded: '*ungemerckt = inobservatus, unaufmercksam = inattentus, non attentus, unmercklich = inobservabilis, unmercksam = negligens*', but not *unbemerkt*; *unbemerkenswert* appeared in the 18th c., *unbemerkbar* in the 19th.

unberaten: see *beraten*.

unberechenbar: see *berechnen*.

unberechtigt

unberechtigt unauthorized; since the 18th c., e.g. Wieland, *Oberon* 5,31.

unberufen: see *berufen*.

unberührt

unberührt untouched, unspoilt, unmoved; since OHG (*unbiruorit*), in Luther 10,2,241 (Weimar) as *unberürtt*.

← See also under *berühren* (for *unberührt* and *Unberührtheit*).

unbeschadet: see *Schaden*.

unbescheiden

unbescheiden presumptuous; since MHG, f.r.b. (DWb) *gemma* 3ba [1508]; the noun *Unbescheidenheit* (in modern sense) since the 18th c.

unbeschreiblich

unbeschreiblich indescribable; since MHG; mainly for 'so wonderful or terrible that one cannot describe it', but sometimes also for 'very mysterious, extraordinary', as in Goethe, *Faust* 12108: '*das Unbeschreibliche, hier ist's gethan*'.

unbeschrieben: see *beschreiben*.

unbeschrien: see *beschreien*.

unbeschwert: see *beschweren*.

unbeschworen: see *Schlange*.

unbesehen: see *besehen*.

Unbestand: see *König* and *niederbeugen*.

unbeständig: see *Grund*.

Unbeständigkeit: see *Marke*.

unbestechlich

unbestechlich unerring; the main meaning 'incorruptable' from *bestechen* (see p. 282) requires no comment. An extension to abstracts such as *Urteil* arose in the 18th c., e.g. Goethe IV,10,203 (W.): '*sein reiner unbestechlicher Blick*'.

unbestritten: see *bestreiten*.

unbesungen: see *besingen*.

unbetreten: see *betreten*.

unbeugsam

unbeugsam inflexible, unyielding; with abstracts since the 18th c., especially with *Wille*.

unbewacht: see *bewachen*.

unbewältigt

die unbewältigte Vergangenheit the past with which one has not yet come to terms; from *bewältigen* (see p. 302); ~ is a new word, coined after the end of the Third Reich. *Büchmann* (edition of 1967) states that the phrase *unbewältigte Vergangenheit* was first used in Summer 1955. For details see A.D. Nunn, *Polit. Schlagwörter in Deutschland* 191/2 [1974].

unbewandert

unbewandert inexperienced, unversed, unskilled, unfamiliar; for *bewandert* see p. 303; the negative in present-day sense only since the 19th c.

Unbeweglichkeit: see *steif*.

unbewunden: see *bewinden*.

unbrauchbar: see *Tand*.

Undank: see *Lohn* and *Stank*.

undankbar: ungrateful

undankbar thankless, unrewarding; with ref. to work which does not repay one's efforts; since the 18th c., e.g. Lessing 18,252: '*eine . . . undankbare . . . Arbeit*'.

undefinierbar

undefinierbar (pejor.) not really as it should be; to the neutral sense a (slightly) pejor. note has been added in the 20th c. suggesting that there is sth. odd about sth.

undeutlich: indistinct

undeutlich vague, faint; to the old phys. sense with ref. to writing or sound, current since the 17th c., an extension to abstracts was added in the 18th c., also in the litotes *nicht* ~ = 'quite clearly discernible', as in Lessing 9,83.

undicht

eine undichte Stelle a leak; for *dicht* with ref. to keeping one's mouth shut see p. 469; ~ is of recent date and usually refers to officials or employees who divulge confidential information (since 2nd half of 20th c.).

Unding: see *Quelle*.

undurchdringlich: see *geben*.

undurchschaubar

undurchschaubar obscure, enigmatic, mysterious; for *durchschauen* see p. 528. ~ had a forerunner in the 17th c. in *undurchschaulich*, still used by Schiller and recorded by Campe; ~ arose late in the 18th c., listed by Campe [1811].

uneben: see *eben*.

unecht

unecht inauthentic, spurious; with abstracts in many contexts since the 18th c., e.g. Goethe 24,296 (W.).

uneingeschränkt

uneingeschränkt unconfined, unrestricted; since the 18th c. in constitutional and religious contexts for 'unlimited'.

Uneinigkeit: see *setzen*.

Unempfindlichkeit: see *Frost*.

unerbittlich: see *Stunde*.

unerfindlich

unerfindlich inexplicable; ~ has had many meanings over the centuries, but only the legal meaning, current since MHG, explains the present sense; still called regional by Adelung and rejected by Campe, but in general use since the 19th c., esp. with the dative *es ist mir* ~.

unergründbar, unergründet: see *Grund*.

unerheblich

unerheblich insignificant, of no importance; from legal language influenced by Lat. *irrelevans*, current since the 16th c., f.r.b. Schöpfer [1550].

unerhört: see *erhören* (also under *enthülsen*).

unerkenntlich

sich ~ *zeigen* to be unappreciative; from *erkenntlich* = 'grateful' (see p. 677); first as *unerkanntlich*, f.r.b. Maaler [1561], then frequently as *unerkänntlich*, but since the 18th c. increasingly in modern spelling.

unerläßlich: see *Reue*.

unermeßlich: see *senken*.

unerrötend: see *erröten*.

unersättlich: see *Kehle*.

unerschlossen: unopened

unerschlossen unexplored; see entry on *erschlossen* on p. 685; the negative since the 18th c.; Goethe used it in *Faust* 6490.

unerschöpflich: see *schöpfen*.

unerschütterlich: see *erschüttern*.

unerschwinglich: see *erschwingen*.

Unersprießlichkeit: see *durchdringen*.

unerträglich: see *ertragen*.

unfaßlich, Unfaßlichkeit, Unfaßbarkeit: see *fassen*.

unfehlbar

unfehlbar (1) infallible, unfailing, unerring; since the 16th c., e.g. Fichte, *Nic.* 9: '. . . *daß sein Urtheil untrüglich und unfehlbar*'; in the 17th c. *unfehlbarlich* and *ohnfehlbar* were also current, both now obs. The noun is *Unfehlbarkeit*, e.g. Wieland 29,147: '. . . *den Ton der Unfehlbarkeit*'.

← See also under *steif* (for *Glauben an die Unfehlbarkeit*).

unfehlbar (2) (adv.) definitely; general since the 18th c., e.g. Lessing 12,460: '. . . *daß ich morgen unfehlbar von hier abreise*'.

unfein

unfein unmannerly, indelicate; cf. entry on *nicht fein* on p.p. 754/5; ~ since MHG, recorded since the 17th c., e.g. by Stieler [1691].

unfertig: see *fertig*.

unflätig: dirty

unflätig dirty, filthy; figur. when applied to a person's character or behaviour; since Early NHG, e.g. Luther Bible transl. Zeph.3,1 (where the A.V. uses 'filthy and polluted'). *Unflätigkeit* now applies not only to a person's behaviour or

character but also to an instance of indecency, e.g. *ein Buch voll von Unflätigkeiten*.

unfolgsam

unfolgsam disobedient; from *folgen* = 'to obey' (see p. 834). Current since Early NHG, e.g. Fischart, *Garg.* (repr.) 436; in modern lit. also used with ref. to things which do not behave as they should, e.g. (Sa.) Burmeister, *Geol.Bilder* 2,131 [1855]: '. . . *das unfolgsame, störrische Haar ihres Kopfes in die gewünschte Form zu zwängen*'.

Unfreiheit: see *Puppe*.

Unfriede: see *Friede*.

unfruchtbar: see *Frucht*.

Unfug: see *müde*.

unganz: see *ganz*.

ungeahnt: see *schnell*.

ungebacken: unbaked

das ist ungebackenes Brot (coll.) that is still a long way off; recorded by Campe [1811]; ~ for 'rude, uncouth', as in Early NHG lit., is obs., except perhaps in some regions for which it was still recorded in the 19th c.

ungebahnt

ungebahnt uncleared, not yet allowing free passage; belongs to figur. *einen Weg bahnen* (see p. 181); figur. ~ since the 17th c.

ungebändigt

ungebändigt uncontrolled, unrestrained; cf. figur. *bändigen* on p. 185; ~ since the 18th c., e.g. Goethe, *Faust I*, 194; cf. similar *ungezähmt*, *ungezügelt*.

ungebeten: see *bitten*, *Gast* and *gern*.

ungebeugt: see *beugen*.

ungebildet

ungebildet uncultured; for history of *gebildet* see pp. 315/6; the negative since the 2nd half of 18th c., e.g. Herder 16,25.

ungeboren: see *gebären*.

ungebrochen: see *brechen*.

ungebunden, Ungebundenheit: see *binden* (also under *Trieb*).

ungedeckt

ungedeckt (econ.) uncovered, unsecured; modern.

← See also under *Scheune* (for *ungedeckte Scheune*).

ungeduldig

ungeduldig impatient; for figur. *geduldig* see p. 937; ~ has had many meanings, some of them going back to OHG; it could mean 'unbearable' (same as *unerträglich*), still used by Lessing 6,219: '*ich fühle eine ungeduldige Last*', or 'disgruntled, bad-tempered', as in Goethe II,4,294 (W.), also 'intolerant, domineering', as still in Goethe 20,3 (W.). All are obs. now with the exception of 'impatient', current since Early NHG, in general with ref. to persons, but in lit. since the 18th c. also for things which are 'not willing to wait', e.g. Herder 29,81: '*die ungeduldig frühe Blume*'.

← See also under *platzen* (for *vor Ungeduld platzen*).

ungefähr

von ~ happening by chance, fortuitous; in the course of a long history MHG *ân gevaer* = 'without evil intention' coalesced to *ohngefähr* and ~ in the 15th c. The original sense made way for 'un-intentional(ly), by chance', esp. in *von* ~ = 'by accident, without being planned', often in *das kommt nicht von* ~ = 'that is not a case of pure chance', f.r.b. Klix [1863], generally used accusingly for 'sb. engineered that'. The noun *das Ungefähr* = 'fate, chance' is now dropping out of use.

ungefähr (adv.) approximately, around; the legal formula *âne vâre* which described an assurance given in good faith but which might not be exactly true could lead to ~ = 'approximately' (since the 16th c.); used with measurement, prices, etc., but also in wider contexts, e.g. Adelung: *'etwas nur ungefähr wissen'*.
← See also under *Haut* (for *ungefähr segeln*).

ungefärbt: see *Farbe*.

ungefestigt

ungefestigt weak, unstable; for *gefestigt* (figur.) see p. 772; ~, omitted in *DWb.*, is a modern term, mainly used with ref. to *Charakter*.

ungefüge: see *Haus*.

ungegliedert

ungegliedert disjointed, unstructured; first mentioned in 1651, according to *DWb.*; now used in many contexts, esp. in botany and architecture, but also with ref. to writings. Herder 22,209 used it in wider sense of 'vague, nebulous'.

ungegoren: unfermented

ungegoren (rare) immature, not fully developed occasionally in lit. with ref. to persons in the sense of *unausgegoren*, for which see under *ausgären*.

ungehalten

ungehalten displeased, annoyed; *gehalten* in the sense of 'reticent, reserved', as used by Goethe in *Wilh.Meister* 5,3: *'je gehaltener und gemessener sein ganzes Wesen ist . . .'.* must be taken as the root from which ~ grew in Early NHG, e.g. Luther, *Tischr.* 316: *'die jugent ist zaumloß, ungehalten und wilde'*; this sense weakened to 'angry, irritated', only since the 2nd half 18th c.; the nouns derived from it have dropped out of use.

ungehemmt

ungehemmt uninhibited, unrestrained, unchecked; not quite as strong as *hemmungslos* for which see p. 1289; ~ arose in the 17th c., e.g. Hagedorn 1,51: *'ein ungehemmter Geist'*; *Ungehemmtheit* appeared in the 19th c., but is not much used; Schiller once described sb. as *der Niegehemmte*.
← See also under *Strom* (for *ungehemmter Strom*).

ungeheuer

ungeheuer tremendous(ly); in MHG ~ meant 'hostile, dangerous, wild', an extension of the older sense of 'fearsome, uncanny'; then it became a term for magnitude and as early as in MHG used as an intensifier.

das Ungeheuer monster; derived from the adj. and current since OHG; ghosts or creatures one is afraid of, mainly first for wild beasts; extended to things or abstracts in the 18th c., e.g. Goethe, *W.-ö. Divan 1* (*Geständnis*): *'die Flamme, das Ungeheuer'*; also with ref. to persons, e.g. Moritz, *Anton Reiser* 233 [1786]: *'Reiser hielt sich wirklich damals für ein Ungeheuer an Bosheit und Undankbarkeit'*.

das vielköpfige Ungeheuer (lit.) the mob, (uncontrollable) crowd of people; translation of *belua multorum capitum* in Horace, *Sat.* 2,1,76; in German lit. since the 18th c., but not always for 'mob', e.g. Schopenhauer 1,145: *'die Philosophie als ein Unheuer mit vielen Köpfen'*.
← See also under *gären* (for *ungeheuerstes Unrecht*).

ungehindert: see *gehören*.

ungehobelt: see *Hobel*.

ungehörig

ungehörig improper, impertinent; for *gehörig* see under *gehören* (p. 956); ~ since the 17th c. in its present-day sense, e.g. Schottel, *Hauptspr.* [1663]. Older meanings which express *nicht zu etw. gehörend*, also 'incompetent' are obs.

Ungehorsam: see *Gewand*.

ungeklärt

ungeklärt not cleared up, unclarified; for figur. *geklärt* = 'clarified' see p. 1476; ~ is modern, not even listed in *DWb.* [1936]; often used with ref. to crime (*ein ungeklärter Fall*) and mysterious circumstances (*ungeklärte Verhältnisse*).

ungekränkt: see *Gewand*.

ungekrönt: see *König*.

ungeläufig

ungeläufig (1) (a.) unfamiliar; current since the 18th c., mainly in *etw. ist jem.m* ~ = 'sb. is not familiar with sth.', e.g. Lessing 13,422: '. . . *der ihm noch ungeläufigen Wahrheit*'; now a. or obs.

ungeläufig (2) uncommon, not in current use; with ref. to language, e.g. Mommsen, *Röm.Gesch.* 5,91: *'die ungeläufige Reichssprache'*; often in *ein ungeläufiger Ausdruck*, but strangely missing in many 20th c. dictionaries.

ungelegen

ungelegen inconvenient, awkward; since MHG, e.g. Luther Bible transl. Acts 27,12: *'vnd da die anfurt vngelegen war zu wintern . . .'.* Often now in *zu ungelegener Zeit* = 'at an inconvenient time', since the 17th c., e.g. Schoch, *Com.v.Stud.* 60 [1658], and ~ *kommen*, since the 18th c. The noun *Ungelegenheit*, current since MHG, has made way for *Unannehmlichkeit*.

ungelegt: see *Ei*.

ungelenke: see *Gelenk* (also under *Rad*).

ungelogen

ungelogen (coll.) truly, upon my word; ~ = 'truthful' is old, used by Luther 33,153 (Weimar) and even then added in emphatic statements; still current, but considered coll. - There is also regional coll. *das will ich ~ sein lassen* = 'I do not want to say, claim, maintain that', recorded since the 2nd half of the 19th c., e.g. in *D.richt. Berliner* and traced back by Büchmann, *Geflüg.W.* to Siegmund Haber who coined the phrase in the humorous journal *Ulk* [1873].

ungelöst: see *lösen* (also for *unaufgelöst*).

ungemein

ungemein uncommon; since Early NHG, e.g. Luther 7,382 (Weimar). Towards the end of the 18th c. also used adverbially for 'extraordinarily', e.g. Herder 9,475 and then as an intensifying adverb, e.g. *ganz ungemein amüsant*.

ungemessen

ungemessen (rare) enormous; figur. with abstracts since the 17th c., e.g. B. Frank, *Trenck* 13: '*eine ungemessene Ruhmsucht*'; now rare, displaced by *unermeßlich*.

ungemütlich

ungemütlich unpleasant; the negation of a group of meanings listed under *gemütlich* on p. 979; current since the 18th c., e.g. Goethe 7,158 (W.); hence ~ *werden* = 'to turn unfriendly, nasty'; since the 19th c., now also used coll. when threatening unpleasantness, e.g. Walser, *Halbzeit* 488: '. . . *sonst werd ich ungemütlich* . . .'.

ungenießbar: unpalatable

ungenießbar (1) unbearable; 18th c. transfer from food or drink to abstracts, esp. literature, e.g. Ranke, *Päpste* 1,486; hence *Ungenießbarkeit*, since the 19th c., e.g. Börne 1,60: '*die Ungenießbarkeit seiner Reden*'.

ungenießbar (2) insufferable, impossible (to get on with); since the 18th c. with ref. to people, e.g. *mein Chef war heute ganz ~*.

ungepflückt: see *pflücken*.

ungerade: see *gerade*.

ungerecht: see *Pfennig*.

ungereimt: see *Reim* (also under *führen*).

ungern: see *sehen*.

ungerochen: see *Mord*.

ungerupft: see *rupfen*.

ungesalzen: see *gesalzen* and *Salz*.

ungesättigt: see *satt*.

ungeschafft: see *schaffen*.

ungescheut

ungescheut without fear, candidly; in this sense since Early NHG, e.g. Luther 32, 466 (Weimar): '*das er ungeschewet die warheit sage*'; other meanings are obs.

Ungeschick: see *Gruß*.

ungeschlacht: see *Schlacht*.

ungeschlagen: see *Schlag*.

ungeschliffen: see *schleifen*.

ungeschmackt: see *Geschmack*.

ungeschmälert

ungeschmälert undiminished, unimpaired; from *etw. schmälern* (see p. 2149); not in Adelung, but listed in Campe [1811], omitted in *DWb*. [1936]. Now more often used for 'fully appreciated or acknowledged'; modern.

ungeschminkt: see *schminken*.

ungeschmückt: see *schmücken*.

ungeschoren: see *scheren* (I).

ungeschrieben

ein ungeschriebenes Gesetz an unwritten law; with *Gesetz* as early as in MHG for sth. that must be observed although there is no written authority for it.

ungesellig: see *Geselle*.

ungesiebt: see *Sieb*.

ungespitzt

den schlage ich ~ in den Boden (coll.) I'll smash him to pulp; threat of extreme violence; since the 19th c., e.g. Keller 6,330 (with *Erdboden*).

Ungestüm: see *gesotten* and *reißen*.

ungestraft: see *Palme*.

ungesund

allzuviel ist ~ (prov.) excess is always bad (or wrong); f.r.b. Agricola [1534].

← See also under *gesund*.

ungetauft: unchristened

ungetauft (coll.) undiluted; esp. with ref. to wine; cf. *getauft* on p. 2440; e.l. (DWb) Rist, *Parn.* 564.

ungeteilt: undivided

Sie haben meine ungeteilte Aufmerksamkeit you have my undivided attention; as a formula used since the 18th c., e.g. Goethe 47,150 (W.); sometimes joc. ironic = 'I am all ears for what you have to say'.

ungetrübt

~ *von jeglicher Sachkenntnis* (ironic) completely ignorant of the whole business; 20th c. coll.

← See also under *trübe* (for *ungetrübt*).

Ungetüm: spectre, demon

das ~ (1) dangerous beast, frightful creature; since the 18th c., often = *Untier*, e.g. Goethe, *Wanderj.* 3,5; also extended to persons = 'horrid individual', sometimes joc., as in Goethe IV,23,125 (W.), but also to things which are considered as dangerous as a wild beast, e.g. Goethe 31,30 (W.) applying the term to Mount Vesuvius.

das ~ (2) huge thing, monstre of a thing; since the 18th c., applied e.g. to a large tome or piece of furniture, also to big vehicles (Raabe, *Sämtl. W.* 1,4,18 used the term for a locomotive). Sometimes extended to abstracts, describing 'an enormous amount', as in (T.) Hertz, *Br. Rausch* 51 [1882]: '*ein Ungetüm von Zeit und Kraft*'.

das ~ (3) tumult, confusion; since the 18th c., e.g. Goethe 35,256 (W.) rejected by Adelung as regional coll. and no longer listed in recent dictionaries.

ungewaschen: unwashed

ungewaschen dirty, indecent, immoral, unfit, unauthorized; all these meanings go back to the condemnation of people who do not observe the (originally religious or ritual) laws concerning washing. The range of meanings is extensive and includes 'insolent' (with *Maul*), 'dishonest, thievish' (with *Hände*), 'ignorant' (with *Füße*), as in Luther 14,335 (Weimar): '*szo thuen alle, die mit ungewaszchenen fusszen, mit stiffeln in die bibel fahren*', 'indecent', as in Keisersberg, *Sünden d.M.* 61a: '*ungewaschne und unsaubere oder unzüchtige wort*'; now the whole range except with *Maul* has become a.

← See also under *Hals*, where the phrase *nun steh ich da mit meinem gewaschenen Hals* is listed. I should have added that *ungewaschen* can also be used in this idiom with the sense of disappointment that sth. expected did not happen.

ungewiß

ungewiß uncertain; used both with ref. to a person's uncertainty about sth. and to things and abstracts which are 'in doubt'; both since Early NHG.

← See also under *Ei* (for *ungelegte Eier geben ungewisse Küchlein*), *gären* (for *es ist ungewiß*), *reißen* (for *jem. aus seiner Ungewißheit reißen*) and *Sprung* (for *ein Sprung ins Ungewisse*).

Ungewitter: see *Gewitter*.

ungezähmt: untamed

ungezähmt unbridled, unrestrained, uncurbed; mainly now with ref. to *Leidenschaft*, but in wider use in earlier periods, where it could be = *unmäßig, maßlos* and could occur adverbially, e.g. Bodmer, *Noah* 3,179: '*ungezähmt lüstern*'; cf. also Goethe, *Tasso* 3,4: '*ungezähmter wirkt die Leidenschaft*'.

Ungeziefer: vermin

das ~ vermin; used as a term for anything that one considers as obnoxious since Early NHG, esp. people whom one despises, e.g. Schiller, *Kab.u.L.* 4,3 with ref. to the *Hofmarschall*; Börne, *Schr.* 1,172 called critics '*literarisches Ungeziefer*'; it can also be used with ref. to undesirable things, e.g. printer's errors, as in Heinse 9,324.

ungezogen

ungezogen impertinent, saucy; derived from 'not properly educated or disciplined' since Early NHG, e.g. Mentel's Bible Deuter. 21,20: '*vnser sun der ist widerspenig vnd vngezogen*' (where Luther used *ungehorsam* and the A.V. 'rebellious') it could also be used for 'indecent', e.g. Goethe 38, 382 (W.): '*die ungezogensten Zweydeutigkeiten*' (also Herder 23,214).

der ungezogene Liebling der Grazien the naughty darling of the Graces, Aristophanes; coined by Goethe in his epilogue to *Die Vögel* [1787]; in the 19th c. sometimes used as a description for H.Heine.

ungezügelt: see *Zügel*.

ungezwungen: unforced

ungezwungen informal, free and easy, natural; first with ref. to forms of speech in rhetoric (16th c.), since the 18th c. with ref. to behaviour.

ungläubig: see *Thomas*.

unglaublich

unglaublich unbelievable; as *ungleublich* in Luther Bible transl. Acts 28,8, later ~ , as in Schiller, *Räuber* 1,2; now also used for emphasis, e.g. *eine unglaubliche Menge* = 'a tremendous amount', as in Moltke 5,58.

ungleich: uneven

ungleich (obs.) bad(ly); with ref. to morals since Early NHG, e.g. Luther Bible transl. Levit. 19,35, where modern Bibles use *unrecht* (and the A.V. has 'unrighteousness'); still in use in the 18th c., e.g. Schiller, *Wall.Tod* 4,9: '. . . daß der fremde Mann nicht ungleich von mir denke*', but now obs.

← See also under *Schale* (for *in ungleichen Schalen wiegen*).

Unglück: misfortune

das ~ (personified) misfortune, bad luck; often personified, especially in prov., e.g. *das ~ kommt ungebeten*, f.r.b. Henisch [1616], . . . *lauert in jedem Winkel* (with which cf. Schiller, *Br.v.Mess.* 2271 on: '. . . lauernd umschleicht es die Häuser der Menschen*'), . . . *sitzt nicht immer vor armer Leute Tür*, recorded by Simrock [1846] or . . . *sitzt nicht immer vor einer Tür*, as in French *le malheur n'est pas toujours à la même porte*, . . . *hat breite Füße*, f.r.b. Schottel [1663], . . . *wächst über Nacht*, f.r.b. Petri II,70 [1605], *ein ~ kommt selten allein*, international, in German since MHG, recorded by Franck [1541] as '*keyn vnglück alleyn*', used by Luther (cf. *Sprichw.*, edit. H. 425), also as *ein ~ bringt das andere auf dem Rücken*, f.r.b. Petri, *~ schläft nicht* (Petri) or *~ feiert nicht*, also in Petri.

das ist kein ~ (coll.) that is no tragedy; in many contexts, esp. when calming sb's distress and surely old in such cases, but also sometimes in serious distinctions, as in Goethe 26,321 (W.): '*hierdurch entstand nun zwar kein Unglück, aber ein lächerliches Unheil*'; cf. Fontane, *Ges.Rom. u.Nov.* 7,63: '*Unglück, nicht Unsegen*'.

der Unglückstag unlucky day; very old superstitions (cf. Lat. *dies ater*) have made certain days *Unglückstage*, esp. the day of St. Magdalene, of St. George and of St. John, when one should not marry, travel, climb mountains or go to sea. In some cases particular reasons are adduced, such as for April 1, when Judas was supposed to have been born, August 1, when Lucifer was expelled from Heaven and December 1, when Sodom and Gomorrha were destroyed. Now only loosely used for 'day on which one has bad luck'.

eine unglückliche Figur abgeben (coll.) to look awkward, helpless, out of place; cf. Engl. 'to look like the picture of ill luck', recorded since 1678; this belongs to *unglücklich* with ref. to appearance or condition (not describing actual misfortune suffered, as in the case of Lat. *miser* or Engl. 'miserable, wretched') appeared in the 17th c. and spread in the 18th c. with a wide range such as 'unpleasant, ill-fitting, unsuitable, wretched, pitiable, contemptible'. Since the 15th c. *unglückselig* has also been used in the same contexts.

eine unglückliche Hand haben to be unlucky in everything one touches; *unglücklich* here in the sense of 'disastrous, bringing or causing misfortune', f.r.b. Frisius (1556). For this use of *Hand* see *milde Hand, offene Hand*, etc. on p. 1222. Since the 15th c. *unglückselig* has also been in use in contexts of this kind.

du machst mich noch unglücklich (coll.) you drive me to distraction; since the 18th c. *unglücklich* has been in use for 'raving, mad, demented', e.g. Goethe 23,28 or 11,121 (W.); in the coll. phrase it is used as hyperbole. Hence also *sich unglücklich machen* = 'to do sth. that one will come to regret (either because it will lead to misery or bring one in conflict with the law)', often in *mach dich nicht unglücklich!* = 'for heaven's sake don't do it!'.

er hat sich unglücklich gemacht (euphem.) he has committed suicide; recorded for some regions since the 19th c. (for origin see previous entry).

es ist selten ein ~ ohne Glück (prov.) no great loss but some small profit; also = 'it is an ill wind that blows nobody profit'; f.r.b. Sutor [1740], but there are many versions, some going back to MHG (cf. Spervogel quotation in Zingerle 156); Henisch [1616] has '*kein vnglück ist ohn glück*'.

Glück (or *glücklich*) *in der Liebe, ~* (or *unglücklich*) *im Spiel* (prov.) lucky in love, unlucky in games; modern prov., recorded since the 19th c., e.g. Eiselein [1838], Simrock [1846].

← See also under *ablösen* (for *ein Unglück löst das andere ab*), *abwenden* (for *ein Unglück abwenden*), *bringen* (for *Unglück bringen*), *fähig* (for *unglückliche Liebe*), *fallen* (for *es ist ein Unglück*), *Garn* (for *Garn des Unglückes*), *Geduld* (for *Geduld ist die beste Arznei im Unglück*), *Glück* (for *Glück im Unglück, bei allem Unglück doch ein Glück, Unglücksäpfel* and *Unglückspflanze*), *Hand* (for *des Unglücks rauhe Hand*), *hocken* (for *hocken wie ein Häufchen Unglück*), *Kind* (for *Unglückskind*), *Nacht* (for *Nacht des Unglücks*), *Rabe* (for *Unglücksrabe*), *Regen* (for *Unglück regnet herab*), *rennen* (for *ins Unglück rennen*), *Samen* (for *Unglückssamen*), *Schlitten* (for *in sein Unglück schlittern*), *schreiten* (for *das Unglück schreitet schnell*), *Schule* (for *das Unglück eine strenge Schule*), *Schwein* (for *Schweine und alte Weiber bedeuten Unglück*), *Stern* (for *Unglücksstern*),

stoßen (for *ein Unglück stößt jem.m zu*), *Stück* (for *du Stück Unglück*), *Stunde* (for *in einer unglücklichen Stunde geboren*), *stürzen* (for *jem. ins Unglück stürzen*) and *Tropfen* (for *nach Eimern zählt das Unglück*).

Ungnade
ungnädig (1) ungracious, unkind; since Early NHG, e.g. Franck [1534]: '*ungnedigen himmel haben*', Werfel (in *Öster.Erzähler* 1,549): '*das ungnädige Schicksal*'.

ungnädig (2) disgruntled, irritated, ill-tempered; since Early NHG.

← See also under *fallen* (for *in Ungnade fallen*) and *Gnade* (for *sich auf Gnade oder Ungnade ergeben*).

ungreiflich: see *greifen*.

ungründlich
ungründlich imprecise, careless, lacking in thoroughness; since Early NHG; the noun *Ungrund* = 'groundlessness, unfounded assertion', since Early NHG, is now obs. See also on p. 1165 for *unergründet, unbegründet* and *unergründlich*.

Ungunst: see *Gunst*.

ungut
ungut (1) (a.) bad, not acceptable; in meaning not as strong as *schlecht* or *übel*; still recorded by Campe [1811], now a.

ungut (2) (regional) unfriendly, annoyed; since MHG, still sometimes in *jem.m nicht ungut sein*, as in Nietzsche, *Zarath.* 246, or *ein ungutes Gesicht machen*, as in Heyse 4,374.

ungut (3) unpleasant, disagreeable; since Early NHG and still used in some regions.

ein ungutes Gefühl bei etw. haben to have misgivings or feel uncomfortable about sth.; since the 19th c.

← See also under *gut* and under *Herz* (both for *nichts für ungut*).

unhaltbar
unhaltbar (1) untenable; with ref. to things which one cannot keep (cf. *ein Versprechen nicht halten können*); f.r.b. Stieler [1691].

unhaltbar (2) untenable; with ref. to sth. which cannot be successfully maintained; since the 18th c.; Goethe in *Farbenlehre* used both *haltbar*, e.g. '*haltbare Theorie*' and *~* . It is assumed that *~* in this sense is a loan-translation of French *insoutenable*.

unhaltbar (3) untenable; from the mil. sense, e.g. *die Festung nicht halten können*; since the 17th c., perhaps a translation of French *intenable*.

Unheil: harm, mischief
das ~ (personified) Mischief; personified and seen as a demon since mediaeval times (cf. Grimm, *Mythol.* 2,731), e.g. Goethe, *Nat.Tochter* 911: '*Unheil ergreift mich*', Schelling 2,2,594: '*noch tausend andere Unheile wandern umher unter den Menschen*', also applied to persons, e.g. *er*

war das ~ *seiner Familie* (rare), where it can mean 'black sheep'. Hence *unheilvoll*, recorded by Campe [1811], which can mean *voll von* ~ = 'disastrous', but also *unheilbringend* = 'ominous' (cf. also *unheildrohend*), all current since the 18th c.; cf. also Schiller, *M.Stuart* 1,2: '*unheilspinnend*'.

← See also under *Brut* (for *Unheil brüten*), *Garn* (for *unheil ist al ze breit*), *Hals* (for *Unheilstifter*), *Rabe* (for *Unheilsrabe*), *stiften* (for *Unheil stiften*) and *Unglück* (for *lächerliches Unheil*).

unheilbar: incurable

unheilbar (1) incorrigible; in original sense for 'incurable' since Early NHG, loosely for 'incorrigible' since the 18th c.

unheilbar (2) irreparable; since the 18th c. with ref. to *Schaden* and similar abstracts, e.g. Goethe IV, 25,204 (W.) with *Mißstand*.

unheimlich

unheimlich uncanny, sinister, weird; for *heimlich* see under *Heim* (p. 1277); ~ since Early NHG, with change from 'foreign, unfamiliar' to 'fear-provoking', e.g. Heyse 10,13: '*dennoch war er mir unheimlich*'. Also in modern period used as an intensifying adverb, e.g. *es hat* ~ *viel Geld gekostet* (coll.), since 1st half of 19th c.

unhold

unhold (1) unfriendly; since OHG, first with ref. to persons, then with other nouns, e.g. Schiller, *M. Stuart* 5,6: '*feindliches, unholdes Land*', also adverbially, as in Lessing, *Nathan* 1,3: '*er gab so unhold, wenn er gab*'.

unhold (2) (a.) disinclined, averse; listed by Adelung as Upper German; now being displaced by *abhold* (which is itself becoming rare).

der Unhold monstre, fiend; current since OHG (*unholda*); e.g. Schiller, *Fiesco* 1,12 or Wieland, *Ob.* 6,92. Now sometimes used for 'rapist', 'molester of women or children'.

Uniform: uniform

die ~ *anziehen* to join the army; similarly, *die* ~ *ausziehen* = 'to leave the army'; both since the 18th c.

die ~ (rare) person in uniform; mainly with ref. to soldiers and policemen; since the 18th c., e.g. Schiller, *Brief.* 5,407: '*die Ankunft von zwei preußischen Uniformen*'; rare.

Unikum: unique thing

ein ~ *von* . . . an extraordinary example of . . ., a singular or striking specimen of . . .; modern word, not even mentioned in the chief *Fremdwörterbücher* of the 19th c., also not listed in *DWb.* [1936]; often with joc. or pejor. flavour, e.g. *sie trug ein* ~ *von einem Hut.*.

das ~ (coll.) queer creature, odd person, original; modern; usually in critical remarks though sometimes used in a tone of admiration; now also occasionally as a term of praise for 'joker, wit, wag', when it comes close to the praise *er ist einmalig* (coll.).

Unke: toad

die ~ (coll.) pessimist, prophet of doom, Jeremiah; since late in the 18th c.; hence *der Unkenruf* (coll.) = 'prophecy of doom', since the 19th c. and the verb *unken* (coll.) = 'to make pessimistic remarks, throw cold water over proposals, foretell disaster', since the 20th c.

wie eine ~ *leben* to live a hermit's life; since the 19th c., recorded e.g. by Wander [1876].

saufen wie eine ~ (coll.) to be a thorough drunkard; 19th c. coll.

Unkeuschheit: see *Pfütze* and *Strick*.

unklar: impure, dark

unklar (1) uncertain; with ref. to texts or meanings, as in Luther 26,405 (Weimar) or to situations and similar abstracts, e.g. *der Ursprung ist* ~ (= *ungeklärt*); often in *jem. im unklaren lassen* = 'to leave sb. guessing or in the dark'; sometimes also = 'incomprehensible'. The noun *Unklarheit* was f.r.b. Stieler [1691].

unklar (2) vague, not clearly defined; since the 17th c., mostly with ref. to sights or sounds; also sometimes = 'obscure'.

unklar (3) (mar.) not clear or ready (for sailing or naval engagement); since the 17th c., e.g. (Kluge, See.) Aldenburg, *West-Ind. Reiße* kla [1627].

Unkosten: costs

die Unkosten (coll.) trouble, effort; ~ began in the singular as *onkost* in MLG, in MHG since the 15th c. as *unkost*, in plural for 'expenditure, costs'; since the 17th c. in connexion with non-monetary 'expenditure', when it is now usually labelled 'coll.', e.g. *er hat sich sehr in* ~ *gestürzt* = 'he is gone to a lot of trouble'. See p. 2414.

Unkraut: weed

~ *vergeht* or *verdirbt nicht* (prov.) all weeds grow apace; international; in German recorded with many variants since 16th c., with *verderben* by Franck [1541], with *vergehen* by Tappius [1545]. See also under *Kraut* (p. 1544).

jem.m ~ *säen* to cause sb. harm; since Early NHG, of biblical origin (see the entry under *säen* for ~ *unter den Weizen säen*), e.g. G.Keller, *Salander* 197: '*wenn ihm schlechte Teufel* . . . *Unkraut in seine Geschäfte gesät haben*'; cf. also Gellert 7,72: '*sollte diese Leidenschaft nicht ein Unkraut sein, das* . . . *auf unser Herz gesäet worden?*'.

das ~ *wuchern lassen* to allow abuses to remain and multiply; e.g. (Sp.) Zschokke, *Alamontade* 2,31; similar phrases have been in existence since Early NHG; the opposite also occurs: *das* ~ *ausreißen, ausrotten, im Keime ersticken, vertilgen*, etc.; since Early NHG.

unlauter: impure, dirty

unlauter shady, unfair, reprehensible; in phys. sense mainly with ref. to water; with abstracts such as *Absicht, Benehmen*, etc. since the 18th c., often in *unlautere Geschäfte*.

unleidlich

unleidlich insufferable; ~ meant at first 'unwilling to submit', also 'intolerant', since Early NHG and still in Lessing, *Miss S.S.* 5,7, now obs. The pejor. meaning 'insufferable' also goes back to Early NHG, e.g. Luther 30,3,292 (Weimar); the meaning 'impatient', recorded by Kramer [1700] is no longer in use.

unlenksam

unlenksam unmanageable, intractable; since the 18th c., mainly with ref. to children, but also for adults sometimes, as in Goethe 8,55 (W.): '. . . *zu thätig, um ein Gelehrter, zu unlenksam ein Weltmann zu sein*'.

unlieblich: see *Gunst*.

unlösbar

unlösbar insoluble, unsolvable; figur. with ref. to problems only since late in the 18th c., f.r.b. Campe [1811].

unlöslich

unlöslich indissoluble; figur. with ref. to connexions, ties, etc. since the 18th c., e.g. Herder 29,679: '*unlösliche Bande*'.

unlustig: see *Frost*.

Unmasse

eine ~ vast amount; first in some regions, only since the 19th c. in the standard language; belongs to the small group of nouns in which *un-* does not produce a negation, but reinforces the simplex.

unmaßgebend and unmaßgeblich: see *Maß*.
unmäßig: see *Maß*.

Unmenge

eine ~ a great number, a large amount; the same use of *un-* for emphasis as in *Unmasse* (see above); since the 19th c., e.g. G.Keller, *Nachlaß* 219.

Unmensch

der ~ monster, beast, fiend; in earliest period used for sth. that lacks human attributes, then often in religious contexts for 'unbeliever, heathen', but since MHG also for sb. who is inhuman as regards morals or behaviour, e.g. Luther, *Hans Worst* (repr.) 62, Schiller, *Wall.Tod* 3,18. Hence *unmenschlich* = 'barbaric, cruel, beastly', since MHG, e.g. Nic.v.Jeroschin, *Kronike* [ca. 1350]: '*unmenschliche tât*', since Early NHG also used as an intensifier, e.g. Galmy, *History* 10a [1540]: '*unmenschliche freude*', Adelung: '*unmenschlich viel*'.

← See also under *Mensch* (for *Unmensch* and *unmenschlich*).

unmerklich: see *Kerbe* and *Knall*.

unmeßbar

unmeßbar immeasurable; figur. with abstracts since the Baroque, e.g. Lohenstein, *Armin.* 1,661b; adverbially it can be a hyperbole.

unmöglich: impossible

~ *werden* (coll.) to become impossible, socially disgraced, insufferable or a nuisance; modern; there is also *sich* ~ *machen*, e.g. G.Keller, *Seldw.* 2,254 '. . . *als Offizier unmöglich zu werden*'. ~ is sometimes also applied to things, meaning 'ludicrous, ridiculously inappropriate', e.g. *er trug einen unmöglichen Hut*.

← See also under *glatt* (for *glatterdings unmöglich* and *eine glatte Unmöglichkeit*).

unmündig: see *Mund*.

Unmut

der ~ ill-humour, displeasure; ~ occurred at first in a variety of meanings (not connected with *Mut* = 'courage'), such as 'terror', 'sadness', 'discord', but from MHG onwards increasingly in the present-day sense of *Mißmut*, e.g. Luther Apocr. transl. 1 Macc. 6,4 or Waldis, *Esop* 1,241 [1557]; hence *unmutig*, in the now current sense since Early NHG. See also the entry under *ungemütlich*.

unnachahmlich

unnachahmlich inimitable; in phys. and figur. senses since the 18th c., but *unnachahmbar* also occurs (used by Klopstock) and Lessing 1,39 has *unnachzuahmend*.

unnachgiebig

unnachgiebig unyielding, rigid, inflexible; for *nachgiebig* see under *nachgeben* (p. 1736); ~ since the 18th c., e.g. Goethe 18,321 (W.). Herder 28,501 used *unnachgebend*.

unnachsichtlich

unnachsichtlich (a.), *unnachsichtig* severe, strict, merciless; for *nachsichtig* and *nachsichtsvoll* see under *nachsehen* (p. 1739); in the 18th c. Kant still used *unnachsichtlich*, but *unnachsichtig* became the preferred form in the 19th c.

unnahbar

unnahbar inaccessible, unapproachable, standoffish; Campe [1811] listed it as a new word; Engl. influence is assumed by some.

unnatürlich

unnatürlich affected, forced, artificial; with ref. to manners, way of speaking, etc. since the 18th c.

ein unnatürlicher Tod death from unnatural causes, unnatural death; since Early NHG, sometimes euphem. for 'murder' or 'suicide', even used with ref. to 'execution'.

← See also under *raffinieren* (for *unnatürliches Raffinieren*).

unnennbar

unnennbar unspeakable; beginnings in MHG (*unnennelich*); the chief meanings are 'not having a name' (Wieland), 'extensive, vast' (Herder) and 'unutterable', all still in use, although the first of the three is rare; used as an intensifier since the 18th c. (comparable to *unaussprechlich, unbeschreiblich, unsagbar* and *unsäglich*).

unnötig: see *Porzellan* and *Schlinge*.

unnütz

unnütz (1) useless; since OHG (*unnuzzi, unnuzlich*); later with ref. to persons, e.g. Luther

Bible transl. Matth.25,30: *'den unnützen knecht'*; now *nutzlos* is preferred.

unnütz (2) unnecessary; general since Early NHG, e.g. Luther 30,243 (Weimar): *'du solt den namen deines Gottes nicht unnützlich füren'*; now rare.

unnütz (3) bad, wicked, wrong; since MHG; now usually *nichtsnutzig* (see p. 1798). For a discussion of the connexions between the three meanings see the helpful remarks in *Trübner*.

← See also under *nützen* (for *sich unnütz machen*) and *treiben* (for *unnützes Zeug treiben*).

unordentlich

ein unordentlicher Lebenswandel a disorderly (feckless, immoral, reprehensible) way of life; since the MHG period ~ has been applied not only to sth. which runs counter to the proper order of things but also to behaviour which conflicts with the moral order.

← See also under *Tor* (for *der Unordnung Tür und Tor öffnen*).

unpaß

unpaß, also *unpäßlich* indisposed, unwell; derived from *nicht zu paß sein*; recorded by Rädlein [1711], still used by Grillparzer, *Werke* 5,62; now mainly in regional *etw. kommt jem.m unpaß* = *ungelegen*, meaning that it is inconvenient.

unpoliert: see *polieren*.

unqualifiziert

unqualifiziert inappropriate (and weak or stupid), botched; pejor. development from 'unqualified' to the result of action by unqualified persons; since the 20th c.

unrasiert: unshaved

~ *und fern der Heimat* (joc. coll.) not looked-after by one's loved ones and therefore in poor condition; joc. self-pitying remark, 20th c. coll. ~ is not even listed in *DWb.* [1936]. It is generally assumed that the phrase, which became current in the 1st World War among soldiers is a parody of Platen's line in *Das Grab im Busento* [1820]: *'allzufrüh und fern der Heimat'*.

Unrast: see *Rast*.

Unrat

~ *wittern* to scent trouble, smell a rat; ~ has undergone several changes in its long history from 'lack of what is needed' to 'rubbish' (still current in phys. sense) to 'trouble', which is only preserved in the locution under discussion, current at least since the 18th c., e.g. Weiße, *Kom.Op.* 2,169 [1768], where ~ *merken* occurs; cf. also Goethe, *Faust* II,10315: *'Kriegsunrat hab' ich längst gespürt'*.

unrecht: wrong

so ~ *ist er nicht* he is actually quite acceptable; litotes, frequent since the 17th c. (Lehman, Zinkgräf); similarly, *so* ~ *hat er nicht* = 'there is some truth in (or justification for) what he says', used by Schiller in *Räuber*: *'so unrecht hat der*

Spiegelberg eben nicht'.

etw. ist jem.m ~ (coll.) sth. displeases sb.; general since the 19th c., e.g. Bettine, *Dies Buch* 2,410; cf. the polite (now oldfashioned) formula *wenn es Ihnen nicht* ~ *wäre* = 'if you will allow me to say so', as in O.Ludwig, *Werke* 2,83, also *bei jem.m* ~ *kommen* (coll.) = 'to be unwelcome, *persona non grata*', as in Lenz [edit. Tieck] 1,66.

jem.m ist ~ (regional coll.) sb. is not feeling well; since Early NHG and still in some regions (instead of standard *unwohl*).

← See also under *fallen* (for *in unrechte Hände fallen*), *falsch* (for *etw. in die falsche/unrechte Kehle bekommen*), *gären* (for *ungeheuerstes Unrecht*), *gedeihen* (for *unrecht Gut gedeiht nicht*), *recht* (for *an den Unrechten kommen*), *säen* (for *Unrecht säen*), *schreien* (for *schreiendes Unrecht*) and *Tür* (for *an der unrechten Tür anklopfen*).

unreif: see *reif* (also under *gären*).

unrein: see *rein*.

unreinlich: see *sudeln*.

unrettbar: see *retten*.

Unrichtigkeit: see *sauber*.

Unruhe: restlessness

die ~ (tech.) balance spring (e.g. on clocks and watches); since Early NHG and already in that period in comparisons, e.g. Fischart, *Podagr.* 16,6: *'. . . daß gemüt im leib wie die unru in der uren'* or Lohenstein, *Armin.* 2,962b: *'August alleine war die unruh in der uhr des gemeinen Wesens'*.

← See also under *Loch* (for *Unruhe ausstehen*).

unruhig: see *ruhen*.

unsagbar: see *sagen*.

unsäglich: see *bestürzen, sagen* and *schöpfen*.

unsanft: see *sanft*.

unsauber: see *sauber*.

unschädlich: harmless

jem. ~ *machen* to put sb. out of action; originally only used with ref. to things, then to persons, esp. with ref. to arresting of criminals; when extreme measures are resorted to, it means 'to eliminate sb. (through murder)'; 20th c. (not yet listed in *DWb.* [1936]).

unschätzbar

unschätzbar inestimable, incalculable, immense; since Early NHG, recorded by Stieler [1691], e.g. Schiller, *D.Carl.* 2,8 (with *Brief*). See also under *Schatz*.

unscheinbar: see *Schein*.

unschicklich: see *schicken*.

unschlüssig

unschlüssig undecided, irresolute; since Early NHG, recorded by Spanutius and Stieler; very frequent since the 18th c.; Goethe 8,194 (W.) used *halbunschlüssig*. Synonymous *unentschlossen* (see *entschlossen* on p. 657) arose in the 17th c., when Stieler recorded *Unentschlossenheit* (but not *unentschlossen*); Lessing 4,267 used *unentschlüssig*, which is now obs.

unschlagbar

das ist ~ (coll.) that can't be beaten; a new word (not recorded in *DWb.* [1936]), which arose in sport.

unschmelzlich: see *schmelzen.*

unschön: see *schön.*

Unschuld: innocence

seine Hände in ~ *waschen* to wash one's hands in innocence; biblical, from Psalm 26,6 and 73,13.

← See also under *Bein* (for *Verleumdung wirft die Unschuld übers Bein*), *gebären* (for *unschuldig wie ein ungeborenes/neugeborenes Kind*), *Gift* (for *nun hast du den Gifft an meiner Unschuld außgelassen*), *Kind* (for *unschuldig wie ein Kind*), *Land* (for *die Unschuld vom Lande*), *Lilie* (for *unschuldig wie eine Lilie*), *Paradies* (for *paradiesische Unschuld*), *reißen* (for *der unschuldige Socrates*), *Schlinge* (for *jem.s Unschuld Schlingen legen*), *spielen* (for *die gekränkte Unschuld spielen*), *Taube* (for *unschuldig wie eine Taube*) and *tauchen* (for *die Hände ins Blut der Unschuld tauchen*).

Unsegen

ein ~ *liegt* (or *ruht*) *auf etw.* (or *jem.m*) there is a curse upon sth. (or sb.); since the 18th c.; cf. also its use in passive contexts, as in ~ *leiden*, also since the 18th c.

unselig

unselig (1) hard, harsh, terrible, calamitous; figur. with abstracts since Early NHG, e.g. Luther Bible transl. Ecclesiastes 1,13, Goethe, *Iphig.* 1,3: '*viel unseliges Geschick der Männer*'.

unselig (2) accursed, bad, disastrous, wretched; with ref. to personal weaknesses, habits, etc. which are regrettable; since Early NHG, e.g. Luther Apocr. transl. Wisd. of Sol. 3,11.

unselig (3) (adv., coll. and regional) terribly; since Early NHG, e.g. S. Franck, *Chron.G.* 144b [1538]: '*unselig lang zeit*'; still used in some regions.

unseligen Angedenkens (or *Andenkens*) of cursed memory with ref. to events or persons one is loath to remember; used first positively with *selig*, taken from the language of chanceries (see the entry on pp. 35/6); with ~ since the 18th c.; Campe [1811] recorded it with a *locus* from Benzel-Sternau.

unser: see *Leute.*

unseriös

unseriös dubious, shady, questionable; used with ref. to persons or to business of a doubtful nature; modern (*DWb.* [1936] does not list the word at all); it can also be used for 'not to be taken seriously', as in Brecht, *Dreigroschenroman* 290: '*von ihm selber stand nur in den unseriösen Blättern etwas*'.

unsicher

einen Ort ~ *machen* to enjoy oneself in a place and stir things up there; when used jocularly, the notion of causing trouble through one's attendance disappears. In its original sense of 'making a place unsafe' since the 16th c., recorded by Frisius [1556]; loosely used since the 18th c.

← See also under *Kantonist* (for *unsicherer Kantonist*).

unsichtbar: see *Sicht* (also *stützen* and *überkreuzen*).

unsichtig: see *fassen.*

Unsinn

Unsinn (lit.) nonsense, wrongness; sometimes personified in lit., e.g. Schiller, *Jungfr.v.O.* 3,6: '*Unsinn, du siegst, und ich muß untergehn*'; also sometimes applied to persons, as in Schiller, *Demetr.* 1,475: '*Mehrheit ist der Unsinn*'.

~ *reden* to talk rubbish; recorded by Adelung, but presumably older; sometimes when contradicting shortened to *Unsinn!*; ~ *treiben* = 'to do sth. foolish, fool around' goes back to Early NHG, e.g. Steinhöwel, *Spiegel* 84b [1479]: '*söllich spil . . . treiben ist ein unsinn*'.

← See also under *bestehen* (for *durch diesen unsin bestan*), *blöde* (for *klassischer Unsinn*), *glatt* (for *hohler Unsinn*) and *rein* (for *Unsinn in Reinkultur*).

unsinnig

wie ~ like mad or possessed; in comparisons since the 18th c.

unsinnig (adv., coll.) unreasonably, exorbitantly, extremely (high); mainly with ref. to exaggerated demands, prices, etc., since the 18th c., but also with ref. to any other kind of excess, e.g. Goethe 22,229 (W.): '*unsinnig verliebt*'; in coll. use for 'very much', e.g. *er hat sich* ~ *gefreut*.

← See also under *Tag* (for *der unsinnige Pfinztag*) and *taub* (for *taub und unsinnig sein*).

unsolide: unstable

unsolide loose, dissipated, fickle, weak; figur. with ref. to persons; not yet recorded (even in its phys. sense) by Sanders [1865] or Heyne [1895], but used in lit. during the 2nd half of the 19th c., e.g. by Raabe.

unsportlich: see *Sport.*

unsterblich: see *sterben* (also *Burg* and *Tracht*).

Unsterblichkeit: see *Maikäfer, Trank* and *um.*

Unstern: see *Stern.*

unstet: see *Furz* and *schwarz.*

unstudiert: see *studieren.*

Unsumme

eine ~ a vast amount; use of *un-* to indicate 'large quantity', as in *Unmasse* and *Unmenge* (which see); since the 18th c., but in the 17th c. *Ohnsumm* occurred.

Untat

die ~ (1) misdeed, evil deed; since OHG.

die ~ (2) (obs.) miracle, astounding deed; still used by Herder [edit. S.] 9,440, now obs.

das ist kein Untätchen (regional coll.) that is no crime, no great fault, no serious drawback;

always in diminutive form, since MHG. Luther 5,491a (Jena) used *'unthetlin'*, others have *Untätele* or *Untätchen*; still in use is also *an ihm ist kein Untätchen* (regional coll.) = 'he is blameless, there is nothing wrong with him'.

unten

~ *bleiben* to remain in one's humble position; since Early NHG and still current for refusal or inability to climb up the social ladder; hence also *die* ~ = 'the lower classes'; cf. Goethe 1,355 (W.): *'der gute Wille von unten'*, meaning 'from the common people'.

untendurch sein (coll.) to cease to count, to have made oneself unpopular, to have lost; since the 19th c.

von ~ *auf dienen* to work one's way up from the bottom; since the 18th c., e.g. Wieland 3, 38, recorded by Adelung; cf. Goethe 24,26 (W.): *'ich wollte wenigstens von unten auf anfangen, ihm zu gleichen'*; Sometimes also as *von* ~ *hinauf* or *von* ~ *herauf*, since the 18th c.

← See also under *fix* (for *oben fix, unten nix*), *gischen* (for *oben gischt, unten nischt*), *hui* (for *oben hui, unten pfui*), *oben* (for *er weiß nicht, was oben und unten ist* and *jem. von oben bis unten mustern*), *Radfahrer* (for *nach oben bücken, nach unten treten*), *Radieschen* (for *sich die Radieschen von unten ansehen*) and *Rasen* (for *den Rasen von unten besehen*).

unter: under

See under *Auge* (for *unter Augen, unter vier Augen, jem.m unter die Augen kommen* and *jem.m etw. unter die Augen sagen*), *ausmessen* (for *ausgemessen sein unter . . .*), *Bank* (for *unter der Bank liegen* and *unter die Bank setzen/stellen*), *Bein* (for *die Beine unter den Arm nehmen*), *Berg* (for *unter dem Berg ausgucken*), *bleiben* (for *das bleibt unter uns*), *blind* (for *unter den Blinden ist der Einäugige König*, also listed *under König*), *Blut* (for *das Blut schießt jem.m. unter Augen*), *brennen* (for *der Boden brennt jem.m unter den Füßen*), *Bruder* (for *unter Brüdern, Brust* (for *gut unterm Brusttuch sein*), *Bürste* (for *jem.m. unter die Bürste kommen*), *Dach* (for *etw. unter Dach und Fach bringen*), *darunter* (for *drunter durch*), *Daumen* (for *unter jem.s Daumen sein*), *Decke* (for *unter der Decke sein* and *mit jem.m. unter einer Decke stecken*), *doppelt* (for *unter dem Doppeladler*), *drucken* (for *jem. unter Druck setzen*), *Eis* (for *unter das Eis gehen*), *Erde* (for *jem. unter die Erde bringen*), *Eule* (for *wie eine Eule unter Krähen*), *Fahne* (for *unter jem.s Fahne kämpfen*), *fallen* (for *unter eine Regel fallen, unter den Tisch fallen* and *unter die Mörder fallen*), *falsch* (for *unter falscher Flagge segeln*), *Feder* (for *etw. unter der Feder haben*), *Finger* (for *jem.m unter die Finger kommen*), *Fittich* (for *jem. unter seine Fittiche nehmen* and *unter den Fittichen der Nacht*), *Flagge* (for *unter fremder Flagge fahren*), *Flügel* (for *jem. unter seine Flügel nehmen*), *Fron* (for *unter Fröhnen*), *Fuchtel* (for *jem. unter seine Fuchtel*

bekommen), *Funke* (for *unter der Asche verborgen*), *Fuß* (for *jem.m den Boden unter den Füßen wegziehen, etw. unter die Füße treten, jem. unterm Fuß haben* and *die Füße unter jem.s Tisch haben*), *Gans* (for *wie eine Gans unter Schwänen*), *gehören* (for *unter jem. gehören*), *geraten* (for *unter etw. geraten*), *Gesicht* (for *jem.m unters Gesicht kommen*), *Gespan* (for *unter den andern Gespanen hervorragen*), *Gewehr* (for *unter dem gelehrten Troß*), *Glas* (for *unter Glas und Rahmen*), *glimmen* (for *das Feuer glimmt unter der Asche*), *Gras* (for *er läßt kein Gras unter seinen Füßen wachsen*), *greifen* (for *jem.m unter die Arme greifen*), *Gürtel* (for *ein Kind unter dem Gürtel tragen*), *Hand* (for *unter der Hand* and *etw. unter den Händen haben*), *Handikap* (for *unter einem Handikap leiden*), *Haube* (for *jem. unter die Haube bringen*), *Hemd* (for *jem.m. unters Hemd gucken*), *Hund* (for *es ist unter allem Hund*), *Hut* (for *Verschiedenes unter einen Hut bringen*), *Joch* (for *jem. unters Joch biegen*), *Jubel* (for *jem.m etw. unter die Weste jubeln*), *Jungfer* (for *wir sind ja unter uns Jungfern*), *Kaninchen* (for *unter dem Karnickel sein*), *Kanon* (for *unter aller Kanone*), *kehren* (for *das Oberste zuunterst kehren*, also listed under *oberst*), *König* (see *blind*), *Konstellation* (for *unter einer bösen Konstellation geboren sein*), *Krummstab* (for *unterm Krummstab ist gut leben*), *Laden* (for *unterm Ladentisch gekauft*), *leiden* (for *unter etw. leiden*), *Leute* (for *etw. kommt unter die Leute*), *Licht* (for *sein Licht unter den Scheffel stellen*), *Loch* (for *unterm fünften Knopfloch*), *Lupe* (for *etw. unter die Lupe nehmen*), *Maikäfer* (for *ein paar Maikäfer unter der Nase*), *Maske* (for *unter der Maske von . . .*), *Messer* (for *unters Messer müssen*), *Mikroskop* (for *etw. unters Mikroskop nehmen*), *mischen* (for *sich unter die Leute mischen*), *Mond* (for *unterm Mond*), *Mops* (for *das ist unterm Mops*), *Mütze* (for *nicht richtig unter der Mütze sein*), *Nagel* (for *sich etw. unter den Nagel reißen*), *Name* (for *unter dem Namen von . . .*), *Nase* (for *jem.m etw. unter die Nase reiben, er steckt gern etw. unter die Nase, unter der Nase gut zu Fuß sein* and *schnell unter der Nase sein*), *neu* (for *es gibt nichts Neues unter der Sonne*), *Niveau* (for *unter dem Niveau*), *null* (for *unter den Nullpunkt sinken*), *Ohr* (for *der Boden brennt unter jem.s Sohlen*), *Pantoffel* (for *unter dem Pantoffel stehen*), *Pelz* (for *unter dem Pelz gebacken*), *Pfahl* (for *das ist ein Pfahl unter Wasser*), *Planet* (for *unter einem glücklichen Planeten geboren sein*), *Prophet* (for *wie kommt Saul unter die Propheten?*), *Prügel* (for *mit Prügeln unter die Sperlinge werfen*), *Rad* (for *unter die Räder kommen*), *Rasen* (for *unter dem Rasen*), *rauben* (for *unter die Räuber gehen*), *Rose* (for *eine Rose unter Dornen*), *Roß* (for *das Roß unterm Schwanz zäumen*), *Rute* (for *unter jem.s Zuchtrute stehen*), *saufen* (for *jem. unter den Tisch saufen*), *schaffen* (for *unter andern*), *Schimmel* (for *ihm wird kein Schimmel unter den Füßen wachsen*), *Schlitten* (for *unter den Schlitten kommen*), *Schloß* (for *etw. unter sieben Schlössern haben*), *Schluß* (for *einen Schlußpunkt unter etw. setzen*), *schmachten* (for *unter einem Druck schmachten*), *schminken* (for *unter der Schminke der Einfalt*), *Schnitt* (for *jem. unter kurzem Schnitt halten*), *Schuh* (for *er hat auch schon fremde Schuhe unterm Bett gefunden*), *Schutz* (for *unter dem Schutz von . . .*), *seufzen* (for *unter Kriegslast seufzen*), *Sonne* (for *unter der Sonne*), *Spatz* (for *hast du Spatzen unterm Hut?*), *Spreu* (for *wie Spreu unter dem Korn*), *Staub* (for *unter den Talaren der Staub von tausend Jahren*), *stecken* (for *jem. unter etw. stecken*), *stehen* (for *unter etw. stehen*), *Stern* (for *unter fremden Sternen leben*), *stöhnen* (for *unter etw. stöhnen*), *Strich* (for *unterm Strich sein* and *einen Strich unter etw. ziehen*), *Stunde* (for *unter Stunden*), *Tag* (for *unter Tag*), *tappen* (for *unter die Menge tappen*), *Teppich* (for *etw. unter den Teppich kehren*), *Theke* (for *unter der Theke*), *Tisch* (for *köstlicher Tisch unter den Fremden*), *Titel* (for *unter dem Titel des Verdienstes*) and *treten* (for *unter die Waffen* or *unters Gewehr treten*).

unterbauen

etw. ~ (lit.) to underpin sth., provide a substructure or support for sth.; since Early NHG, at first with allusion to building activities, then extended. Hence *der Unterbau* = 'foundation, basis', figur. since ca. 1800.

unterbesetzt

unterbesetzt understaffed; only since the 20th c. and not yet listed in *DWb.* [1936]; belongs to *eine Stelle besetzen*, for which see p. 277.

unterbieten

das läßt sich nicht ~ that is rock-bottom, it would be difficult to find anything lower or worse; only since the 19th c. in contexts not connected with the auction room.

unterbinden

etw. ~ to prevent, stop, cut off or obviate sth.; in phys. sense mostly in med. contexts with ref. to 'ligature', from there extended in images as early as in Jean Paul, *Werke* [edit. H.] 7–10, 270: '*wem der sympathische Nerv des Lebens, die Liebe, unterbunden oder durchschnitten ist, der darf schon einmal seufzen*', general only since the middle of the 19th c.

unterbleiben

etw. unterbleibt sth. does not take place, ceases, stops; since Early NHG, e.g. Luther 34,1,28 (Weimar); for origin see the remarks under *bleiben* (p. 339).

unterbrechen

etw. ~ to interrupt sth.; probably began as a translation of Lat. *interrumpere*; figur. with ref. to speech as early as in MHG, e.g. (T.) Seifrid Helbling 3,190 (2nd half 13th c.): '*miniu wort niht underbrich*'. The noun *Unterbrechung* arose in Early NHG. The participle in the negative *ununterbrochen* has become a much-use adj. = 'contin-

uous', general since the 19th c.

unterbreiten

etw. jem.m ~ to submit sth. to sb.; derived from 'to put sth. before sb. (i.e. under the eyes of sb.) for signature', used first in Austrian civil service, then general; only since 1st half of 19th c.

unterbreitet werden (a.) to be made the foundation of sth.; also used for 'to be subjected to sth.', both only in the 19th c. in lit. language, now rare.

unterbringen

etw. ~ to house, lodge, place sth.; derived from 'to bring sth. under a (protecting) roof'; extended to abstracts since the 16th c.; in econ. contexts for 'to dispose of sth., invest sth.' since the 18th c.

jem. (or *etw.*) ~ (1) (obs.) to defeat sb., overcome sth.; since Late MHG, also in Luther Bible transl. 1 Chron. 23,18; still used by Goethe, *Rein.Fuchs* 12,365, now obs.

jem. ~ (2) to find a place, job, occupation for sb.; since the 17th c., e.g. Harsdörfer, *Teutsch.Sec.* 1,155 [1656].

jem. ~ (3) to place sb. (in one's mind or memory); since early in the 20th c., e.g. (Sp.) Werfel, *Abituriententag* 17: '*Doktor Sebastian tauchte in die reiche Maskengarderobe seiner . . . Richtererfahrung, um den Mann unterzubringen*'.

sich ~ (obs.) to manage to exist (or earn a living); since the 17th c., recorded by Kramer [1700] and still listed in 19th c. dictionaries but now obs., displaced by *sich durchbringen* for which see p. 517.

unterbuttern

jem. ~ (coll.) to get the better of sb., oppress sb.; since the 19th c., also in the negative locution now: '*ich laß mich nicht* ~ = 'I won't let them get me down', where *unterkriegen* is preferred in some areas.

etw. mit ~ (coll.) to spend sth. in addition to what one has already laid out; since the 20th, similar to coll. *etw. auch noch* (or *zusätzlich*) *hineinstecken*.

unterdrücken

etw. ~ to suppress, repress, quell, stifle sth.; renders Lat. *comprimere, reprimere, supprimere* and *deprimere*; since MHG, when *jem.* ~ = 'to oppress sb.' also arose.

← See also under *Leib* (for *einem Unterdrücker zu Leibe gehen*) and *stümmeln* (for *die teutsche sprache . . . verstimmelt und unterdruckt wurde*).

Untere

der ~ (1) the inferior or lower-placed person; since MHG, e.g. *Erec* 9332: '*swenne sich der ober man müeste sich dem unteren ergeben*'.

der ~ (2) knave, jack (in the German pack of cards); probably much older than the dictionaries indicate; Adelung listed it as *der Untere*, now *der Unter* is preferred.

unterernährt: undernourished

unterernährt (lit.) starved, deprived; figur. only since the 20th c., e.g. (DWb) Löns, *Dahinten in der Haide* 25: '*ein unterernährtes Herz*'.

unterfangen

sich einer Sache ~ (lit.) to undertake or venture on sth.; since Early NHG, often with the notions of 'daring' or 'presuming' implying courage or impudence; still in modern lit., e.g. Schiller, *M.Stuart* 4,4: '*was unterfangt Ihr Euch . . .*', considered as a. by Heynatz [1796] but still alive though seen as rather stilted and displaced by *sich etw. anmaßen* (for which see p. 52). The same applies to the noun *das Unterfangen*, current since the 17th c., still in occasional lit. use, e.g. G.Keller, *Nachlaß* 214: '*welch ein schulwidriges Unterfangen*'.

unterfüttern: line

unterfüttert (lit.) padded, swollen, enlarged; in occasional 20th c. lit. usage.

← See also under *stief-* . . . (for *die Stiefmutter ist des Teufels Unterfutter*).

Untergang

gegen ~ (lit.) towards the West; since Early NHG, often with addition of *der Sonne*, as in Megenberg, *Sphära* 11,30 or Luther Bible transl. Joshua 23,4; in modern period still in lit. language, e.g. Stifter, *Werke* 5,1,288: '*auf den Bergen gegen Untergang war es lichter*'; cf. the image in Brentano 3,85: '*mahnend zieht die Nacht den Mantel vor des Unterganges Thore*'.

der ~ death, destruction; recorded since the 16th c., e.g. by Decimator; with ref. to human death in Luther 18,480 (Weimar), who also used it with ref. to books, as in 6,616 (Weimar): '*aller meiner bücher untergang*'; with abstracts also since the 16th c., e.g. (DWb) Kirchhof, *Mil.disc.* 16 [1602]: '*der guten sitten untergang*', also in the prov. recorded by Franck [1541]: '*müssiggang der tugend undergang*'. Frequent in a number of locutions, e.g. *am Rande des Untergangs stehen, zum* ~ *reif sein, einer Sache droht der* ~ (also used by Goethe, e.g. 3,107 (W.)), *einer Sache den* ~ *schwören* or *etw. dem* ~ *weihen*.

← See also under *Rand* (for *an den Rand des Untergangs führen*).

untergeben

~ *sein* to be subject (to sth. or sb.); since Early NHG, when it occurred as in reflex. constructions, e.g. H.Sachs [edit. G.] 18,29: '*Christi joch sich untergeben*', also in Luther 10,1,1,505 (Weimar). In many cases used in contexts where *ergeben* (for which see on p. 670) would now be expected. See also the remarks under *geben* concerning *sich in etw. geben* and *sich dahingeben*.

der Untergebene subordinate or subject; since the 16th c., recorded by Stieler [1691]. It can be used with ref. to dependents, employees and subjects (e.g. of a king), but is now often avoided since considered objectionable.

untergehen: go down or under

untergehen to go under, come to an end, be lost or drowned, wane; since MHG with ref. to persons and abstracts; often with allusion to the setting sun, e.g. Keisersberg, *Kind. Israhel* M2d [1510]: '*das die sonn der vernunfft nit undergang*' or Goethe, *Tasso* 2231: '*es geht die Sonne mir der schönsten Gunst auf einmal unter*'. Sometimes with ref. to the end of the world, e.g. Luther Bible transl. Psalm 46,3: '*wenn gleich die welt untergienge*', with which cf. modern coll. *davon geht die Welt nicht unter* = 'that is not the end of the world, is not a really serious matter'; hence *in etw.* ~ = 'to be drowned or overwhelmed by sth.' e.g. *seine Rede ging im Lärm der Proteste unter*.

← See also under *Äon* (for *es kann die Spur von meinen Erdetagen nicht in Äonen untergehn*) and *Sonne* (for *laß die Sonne nicht über deinem Zorn untergehen*).

Untergestell: see *Gestell*.

untergraben

etw. ~ to undermine sth.; figur. since OHG, e.g. *Passional* [edit. H.] 205: '*die ere undergraben*'; since MHG also for various kinds of opposition, prevention, frustrating of sb.'s plans, e.g. G. Hauptmann, *Weber* II.

Untergrund

der ~ (1) basis, foundation; since the 18th c., but in essence an unnecessary coinage since *Grund* and *Grundlage* cover that area sufficiently.

der ~ (2) background; since the 18th c. (used by Goethe), but usually the same as *Hintergrund*.

der ~ (3) underground; in polit. and mil. sense taken over from Engl. in the 20th c. when 'underground movement' established itself. The adj. *untergründig* = 'hidden' with ref. to movement, connexion, meaning also arose in the 20th c.

Unterhalt

der ~ maintenance, upkeep, subsistence; in wider sense 'help, assistance'; since Early NHG, recorded by Stieler [1691]. For ~ (obs.) = 'entertainment' see under *unterhalten*.

unterhalten

etw. ~ to maintain, keep up sth.; since the 17th c., at first mainly for 'to provide a livelihood for sb. or ensure the continued existence of sth.', but extended in the 18th c. in numerous locutions, such as *Beziehungen mit jem.m* ~, *einen Briefwechsel* ~ , *ein Feuer* (also in mil. sense) ~ . It can also come close to *pflegen* = 'to foster' e.g. the arts, also since the 18th c.

jem. ~ to entertain sb.; beginnings in the 17th c., when it meant 'to refresh, provide pleasure', as recorded by Stieler [1691], then under the influence of French *entretenir* in the modern sense, e.g. Schiller, *Fiesco* 2,2: '*unterhalten Sie mich*'; also in reflex. use, both for *sich mit jem.m* ~ = 'to converse with sb.' and *sich* ~ = 'to entertain or amuse oneself (with sth.).'

sich von jem.m ~ lassen (a.) to allow oneself to be kept by sb.; at least since the 18th c., e.g. Goethe, *Lehrj.* 1,15; now the usual verb is *aushalten*, for which see p. 135.

die Unterhaltung entertainment; in the 18th c. *Unterhalt* could still be used for this, e.g. Gellert, *Fab.* 1,11 or Goethe, *Tasso* 3,2. *Unterhaltung* in the older sense occurs in Luther Bible transl. Jerem. 52,34 for 'maintenance, upkeep'; for 'entertainment' only since the 18th c.

← See also under *bewegen* (for *die Unterhaltung bewegte sich . . .*), *mischen* (for *die Unterhaltung wurde gemischt*), *plätschern* (for *die Unterhaltung plätscherte dahin*) and *Schnabel* (for *die Unterhaltung stand still*).

unterhandeln

mit jem.m ~ to negotiate with sb.; in the beginning (16th c.) the general notion was that of 'going between people' in various senses such as interpreting, mediating, acting as broker, so that *Unterhändler* could stand for 'actor' (on the stage) or 'broker' (in financial transactions) recorded by Maaler [1561]. The verb then concerned itself mainly with 'negotiating' between parties at war or in business contexts; *die Unterhandlung* = 'negotiation' also appeared in the 16th c.

unterhöhlen: see *Höhle.*

unterirdisch: subterranean

unterirdisch secret, covert, going on under the surface; with such abstracts as *Feindschaft* (also as an adv., e.g. *~ schwelend*), also *Bewegung* with ref. to activities secretly directed against forces in power; since the 18th c. for 'secret', as in Goethe IV,8,40 (W.), in polit. sense since the 19th c., e.g. Treitschke, *Dt.Gesch.* 3,141: '*überall . . . trieben die Geheimbünde ihre unterirdische Arbeit*'.

unterjochen: see *Joch.*

unterkommen

unterkommen to find accommodation, a situation, job; first in phys. sense of 'getting a roof over one's head' (17th c.), but also since 17th c. for 'finding a means of livelihood', also 'being provided for through marriage', f.r.b. Hulsius-Ravellus [1616]; the noun *das Unterkommen* has been current since the 17th c., as e.g. *ein Unterkommen finden*, e.g. Goethe II,9,140 (W.), though *Unterkunft*, current only since the 19th c., is now preferred for 'accommodation' and *Auskommen* for 'livelihood'.

etw. kommt jem.m unter sth. happens or occurs to sb.; since the 18th c., then displaced by *unterlaufen* or, in some contexts, *vorkommen*, but still alive in S. regions (e.g. in the writings of Nestroy, Anzengruber, Rosegger).

mit etw. ~ (coll.) to find acceptance or be applauded for sth. (which one has said or proposed); 20th c. coll., not yet listed in *DWb.* [1936].

unterkriegen: see *kriegen.*

Unterkunft: see *unterkommen.*

Unterlage

die ~ basis, foundation; from the numerous tech. meanings for 'sth. laid under sth. for support or cushioning' extended figur. to 'sth. firm on which to base sth.'; surprisingly, not listed in *DWb.* [1936], although Campe (1811) recorded it as figur. and quoted: '*man muß den Witz nie anders als auf der Unterlage echter Bescheidenheit, Sanftmuth und Gutherzigkeit spielen lassen*'. Hence in the plural also for 'relevant documents, papers' with ref. to (written) proofs of some event, evidence usable when making a statement; only since the 20th c.

eine ~ brauchen (coll.) to need sth. solid in one's stomach; used with ref. to drinking; therefore also in some regions (recorded since the 19th c.) *erst etw. unterlegen müssen.*

unterlassen

etw. ~ to stop or refrain from doing sth.; beginnings in OHG, rendering Lat. *intermittere*; general since the 16th c., recorded by Frisius [1556]; cf. also the remarks on *laß das* on p. 1585. Hence *Unterlassung*, recorded since the 16th c.

← See also under *Sünde* (for *Unterlassungssünde* and *Unterlassungsschuld*).

jem.m etw. ~ (regional) to leave sth. to sb. (in one's will); since Early NHG, still current in Austria, e.g. Raimund, *Diam.d.Geist.* 1,12; in the standard language *hinterlassen* is used.

ohne Unterlaß unceasingly; since Early NHG, e.g. Megenberg, *Buch d.Nat.* 217 [1650].

unterlaufen

etw. unterläuft sth. slips or creeps in; derived from 'running in (= occurring) unobserved'; since Early NHG, e.g. Luther 17,1,352 (Weimar): '*da mit ist untergeloffen vil gaucklei*' or Goethe 16,278 (W.); mainly with ref. to mistakes, accidental slips, confusion, etc.; often with *mit*, esp. in *etw. mit ~ lassen* = 'to include sth.', as in Lessing, *Abhandl. ü.d.Fabel:* '*. . . zwei Zeilen . . ., ob sie schon Phädrus als eine solche* [i.e. *Fabel*] *unter seinen Fabeln mit unterlaufen ließ*'. Cf. also Gutzkow, *Uriel Acosta* 1,1: '*. . . wie er . . . alles, was ihn umgibt, sich künstlich zu vergolden – Statt Gold läuft manchmal wohl auch Kupfer unter*'.

unterlegen: lay under

jem.m etw.~ (1) to impute sth. to sb.; refers to deceitful placing of sth. under sb. (with ref. to exchange of babies since Early NHG); in accusations since the 18th c., e.g. Lessing [edit. M.] 13,396: '*andern Leuten . . . Absichten . . . unterlegt, an die sie nie gedacht haben*'; now *unterstellen*, for which see p. 2360, is the preferred verb.

← See also under *Rücksicht* (for *jem.m. politische Rücksichten unterlegen*).

jem.m. etw. ~ (2) to put sth. (figur.) under sb.; mainly for support or relief; since Early NHG, e.g. Luther 28,711 (Weimar): '*. . . einen solchen gott haben, der seine hende wird dir unterlegen*'.

jem.m	jemandem (dat.)
Kluge	F. Kluge, *Etymologisches Wörterbuch der deutschen Sprache*, 11th ed., Berlin und Leipzig 1934.
Lehman	C. Lehman, *Florilegium Politicum*, etc., Frankfurt 1640.
Lexer	M. Lexer, *Mittelhochdeutsches Handwörterbuch*, Leipzig 1872—8.
LG	Low German
Lipperheide	F. Freih. v. Lipperheide, *Spruchwörterbuch*, 2nd ed., München 1909.
MHG	Middle High German
mil.	military
M. Latin	medieval Latin
N.	Northern Germany
NED	*Oxford English Dictionary, A New English Dictionary on Historical Principles*, Edited by Sir James Murray, Henry Bradley, W. A. Craigie and C. T. Onions. Oxford 1884—1928.
NHG	New High German
NW	North-Western Germany
obs.	obsolete
OE	Old English
offic.	in civil service language
OHG	Old High German
ON	Old Norse
OS	Old Saxon
Oxf.	*The Oxford Dictionary of English Proverbs*, compiled by W. G. Smith, Oxford, 1935.
p.	page
poet.	used mainly in poetic language
pop.	popular
pop. etym.	popular etymology
prov.	proverb, proverbial
sb.	somebody
Schmeller	J. A. Schmeller, *Bayerisches Wörterbuch*, Stuttgart 1827—37.
Schulz-Basler	G. Schulz und O. Basler, *Deutsches Fremdwörterbuch*, Strassburg und Berlin 1913ff.
s.e.	self-explanatory
sl.	slang
S. Singer	S. Singer, *Sprichwörter des Mittelalters*, Bern 1944—7.
sth.	something
SW.	South-Western Germany
Trübner	*Trübners Deutsches Wörterbuch*, herausg. v. A. Götze, Berlin 1939ff.
v.	verse, verses
vulg.	in vulgar use (obscene terms are included under this heading, but specially marked as such)
Waag	A. Waag, *Die Bedeutungsentwicklung unseres Wortschatzes*, 5th ed., Lahr 1926.
Wb.	Wörterbuch
Weigand	F. L. K. Weigand, *Deutsches Wörterbuch*, 5th ed., Gießen 1909—10.
Weist.	Weistümer; usually the collection by J. Grimm, Göttingen 1840—69 is referred to; Österr, is appended to the Austrian collections.
Westph.	Westphalia, Westphalian
zool.	zoological term.

Where later editions than those cited above have been quoted (especially in the cases of Büchmann, Dornseiff and Kluge), details of the editions used are given in the text.

The abbreviations for journals mostly follow the accepted practice (*MLR for Modern Language Review, MLN for Modern Language Notes, IF for Indogermanische Forschungen*, etc.), only some long titles have been still further abbreviated though still left recognizable (e.g. *Z.f.d.W.* for *Zeitschrift für deutsche Wortforschung, Z.f.d.U.* for *Zeitschrift für den deutschen Unterricht, Z.f.r.P.* for *Zeitschrift für romanische Philologie*, etc.). Other works, referred to or quoted have been mentioned in abbreviated but recognizable form. It is intended to give a comprehensive list of them when the dictionary is completed. From Fasc. 9 Goethe (W.) = Weimar edition, Schiller (S.) = Säkularausgabe.

ISBN 0 631 188231

An Historical Dictionary of German Figurative Usage

By KEITH SPALDING

PROFESSOR EMERITUS OF GERMAN, UNIVERSITY COLLEGE OF NORTH WALES, BANGOR

WITH ASSISTANCE FROM
GERHARD MÜLLER-SCHWEFE

PROFESSOR EMERITUS OF ENGLISH,
UNIVERSITY OF TÜBINGEN

Fascicle 54

untermalen – verwirren

KEY TO PRINCIPAL ABBREVIATIONS

a.	archaic
Adolphi	O. Adolphi, *Das große Buch der Fliegenden Worte, etc.*, Berlin n.d.
Ahd. Gl.	*Die Althochdeutschen Glossen*, ges. und bearb. von E. Steinmeyer u. Eduard Sievers, Berlin 1879—98.
Bav.	Bavaria, Bavarian
bot.	botanical term
Büchmann	G. Büchmann, *Geflügelte Worte*, 27th ed., ergänzt von A. Langen, Berlin 1915.
c.	century
Car.	Carinthia, Carinthian
cf.	compare
cl.	cliché
Cod.	codex
coll.	in colloquial use
comm.	used in language of commerce
dial.	dialect expression
Dornseiff	F. Dornseiff, *Der deutsche Wortschatz nach Sachgruppen*, Berlin und Leipzig 1934.
dt.	deutsch
DWb	*Deutsches Wörterbuch von Jacob Grimm und Wilhelm Grimm*, Leipzig 1854ff.
e.l.	earliest locus or earliest loci
etw.	etwas
Fast. Sp.	Fastnachtspiele, usually quoted after *Fastnachtspiele aus dem 15. Jahrbundert*, herausgeg. v. Keller, Stuttgart 1853.
Fick	F. C. A. Fick, *Vergleichendes Wörterbuch der indogermanischen Sprachen*, 3rd ed. Göttingen 1874.
f.r.b.	first recorded by
gen.	general
Götze	A. Götze, *Frühneuhochdeutsches Glossar*, 2nd ed., Bonn 1920.
Graff	E. G. Graff, *Althochdeutscher Sprachschatz*, Berlin 1834—42.
Hirt, *Etym*.	H. Hirt, *Etymologie der neuhochdeutschen Sprache*, 2nd ed.; München 1925.
Hirt, *Gesch*.	H. Hirt, *Geschichte der deutschen Sprache*, 2nd ed., München 1925.
hunt.	word or expression used by huntsmen
jem.	jemand (nom. or acc.)

© *Basil Blackwell Ltd., 1994 ISBN 0 631 194495*
Typeset by Hope Services, Abingdon
Printed and bound by Whitstable Litho Ltd., Whitstable, Kent.

← See also under *Kissen* (for *wir wollen ihm kein Kissen unterlegen*).

etw. ~ (a.) to submit sth.; since MHG rendering Lat. *supponere*; still used by Schiller, *Brief.* 3,317, where *schriftlich niederlegen*, sometimes also *vorlegen* would now be used.

einer Komposition einen Text ~ to base a composition on a text, set a text to music; since the 18th c., e.g. Goethe 20,151 (W.); also used in other contexts where sth. is used as the basis for sth. else, e.g. Goethe 42,2,239 (W.): '. . . *kein großer Unterschied, ob ich eine correkte Stelle falsch verstehe, oder ob ich einer corrupten irgend einen Sinn unterlege*'.

← See also under *Holz* (for *Holz unterlegen*) and *unterliegen* (for *unterlegen sein*).

unterliegen: lie under

unterliegen to be overcome, be defeated, succumb; with ref. to persons since MHG, e.g. *Passional* 254, Luther Bible transl. Psalm 116,6: '*wenn ich unterlige, so hilft er mir*'; first mainly separable, since late in the 18th c. always inseparable; in modern period also with ref. to death, e.g. *einer Krankheit* ~ = 'to succumb to an illness'. Hence also *jem.m unterlegen sein* = 'to be defeated by sb.', since the 17th c., then extended to 'to be inferior to sb.'. The noun *Unterlegenheit* was proposed by Campe [1813] as a substitute for *Inferiorität*, but it was generally accepted only in the 20th c.

einer Sache (abstract) ~ to be subject to sth.; since MHG in legal contexts translating Lat. *subjectum esse* with such abstracts as *Gesetz, Zoll, Bestimmung*, often with *Zweifel* in *es unterliegt keinem Zweifel* = 'there is no doubt about it', f.r.b. Heynatz [1797].

auf dem, der unterliegt, soll man nicht sitzen (prov.) don't let your superiority lead you to humiliating your opponent; modern prov., recorded only since the 19th c.

untermalen: see *malen*.
untermauern: see *Mauer*.
Untermensch: see *Mensch*.
unterminieren: see *Mine*.
unternehmen
etw. ~ to undertake sth.; until the 18th c. still reflex.; the range is extensive and includes the notions of 'daring, venturing, trying, executing sth.' in very many contexts.

← See also under *Mark* (for *Unternehmungen voll Mark und Nachdruck*), *Motor* (for *der Motor des Unternehmens*), *Razzia* (for *eine Razzia unternehmen*), *Schachtel* (for *Schachtelunternehmen*) and *toll* (for *etw. Tolles unternehmen*).

unterordnen: see *ordnen*.
Unterpfand: see *Pfand*.
untersagen: see *sagen*.
unterscheiden: see *Symptom* and *Tugend*.
unterschieben: see *schieben*.
Unterschied: see *einebnen*.

unterschlagen: see *Schlag*.
Unterschleif: see *schleifen*.
unterschreiben: see *schreiben*.
unterschwellig: see *Schwelle*.
untersetzt: see *setzen*.
untersinken: see *sinken*.
unterst
der Unterste the lowest or weakest (in a group or class); in cases where it need not be taken in the phys. or local sense at least since the 18th c., e.g. Goethe, *Herm.u.Dor.* 2: '*wenn in der Schule . . . du immer der Unterste saßest*'.

← See also under *kehren* and *oberst* (for *das Oberste zu unterst kehren*).

Unterstand
der ~ shelter, accommodation; ~ began in MHG with the senses of 'support', 'difference' and 'prevention', all obs. Equally obs. is the Early NHG meaning 'lower order or status', as in Luther 6,70 (Weimar), displaced by *unterer Stand*. Since the 16th c. in the present-day meaning of 'shelter, accommodation for the night', surprisingly unrecorded by Stieler, Frisch, Adelung and even Campe [1811].

unterstehen: see *Gesicht* and *stehen*.
unterstellen: see *stellen*.
unterstreichen: see *streichen*.
unterstützen: see *stützen*.
untersuchen: see *suchen*.
Untertan: see *beschränken, Fahne* and *raufen*.
untertänig: see *tun*.
untertauchen: see *tauchen*.
Unterton: see *Ton*.
untertreiben: see *treiben*.
unterwandern
unterwandert werden to become infiltrated (and weakened from within); a 20th c. word, not yet recorded in *DWb.* [1936], used in polit. contexts, e.g. *der linke Flügel der Sozialdemokraten war von Kommunisten unterwandert*.

unterwegs: see *treffen*.
Unterweisung: see *nehmen*.
Unterwelt
die ~ (1) (poet.) the grave; since the 18th c., e.g. Schiller, *Braut v. Mess.* 1507.

die ~ (2) Hell, Hades; since Early NHG; hence also *der Fürst der* ~ = 'the devil', as in Goethe, *Mitschuldigen* 429.

die ~ (3) the underworld, lowest classes of society; taken over from Engl. 'underworld'; only since late in the 19th c., e.g. Nietzsche, *Werke* 8,239. *DWb.* [1936] marked it '*unüblich*', but this is no longer correct, since it is now frequently applied to the criminal classes.

unterwerfen
jem. ~ to subjugate, conquer or overcome sb.; since Early NHG, though *unter sich werfen* also occurred, e.g. Luther 32,421 (Weimar): '*er kan straffen, die bösen unter sich werffen*'; with abstracts *etw.* ~ has been current for 'to subordinate sth.',

e.g. with ref. to one's will. Later mainly used in the sense of 'to submit', reflex. in *sich einem Befehl* or *Urteil* ~, e.g. Luther 7,852 (Weimar): '*sich williglich . . . solcher visitation unterwerfen*'.

unterwürfig subservient, servile, submissive; current since the 15th c. (before then *unterwürflich*); usually pejor., but sometimes non-pejor. when it means 'willing to serve under sb.', as in Schiller, *Picc.* 1,2: '*. . . das Vertrauen, das uns dem Friedland unterwürfig macht*'.

unterwinden
sich einer Sache ~ (obs.) to undertake to do, tackle sth.; from Early NHG, e.g. Luther Bible transl. Luke 1,1 to the 19th c., now obs.

unterwürfig: see *unterwerfen*.

unterzeichnen: draw under, sign
etw. ~ to agree with or approve sth.; since the 17th c., recorded by Stieler [1691]; sometimes = 'to continue to maintain sth., stand by sth.', as in Bismarck, *Br. a.s.Braut* 21: '*in der Hauptsache unterzeichne ich meine damaligen Ansichten*'.
auf etw. ~ (econ.) to subscribe to sth.; since the 18th c., e.g. Goethe 42,1,119 (W.): '*wer bei uns direct auf neun Exemplare unterzeichnet, erhält das Zehnte unentgeltlich*'; extended in a metaphor in Kotzebue, *Werke* 5,68: '*ein Kind an der Mutter Brust ist ein Freygast durch die Welt, von der Natur unterzeichnet*'.

unterziehen: draw under
sich einer Sache (abstract) ~ to undertake sth.; since Early NHG; although close to *sich unterwerfen* (see above), there are differences, as defined by Eberhard, *Syn.* 6,222: '*man unterwirft sich, indem man etwas leidet, man unterzieht sich, indem man etwas thut*' or (in the 1904 edit.): '*man unterzieht sich einer angenehmen Beschäftigung, unterwirft sich einer unangenehmen*'.
etw. einer Sache (abstract) ~ to subject sth. to sth.; translates Lat. *subducere*; current since Early NHG, now still frequently in *etw. einer Prüfung* ~.

untief: see *tief*.
Untier: see *Tier*.
untragbar
untragbar unbearable; only since the 19th c. and not yet in figur. contexts in Campe [1811]. Before then *unträglich* was used, e.g. Luther Bible transl. Matth. 23,4: '*vntregliche bürden*'.

untreu: see *treu* (also *Symbol, trauen* and *trennen*)
Untreue: see *Fuchs, Herr* and *Strick*.
Untugend: see *Fron, Grenze* and *überhören*.
unüberbietbar
unüberbietbar unsurpassable, matchless; from *überbieten* = 'to outbid', much used in the auction-room; figur. only since the 19th c.

unüberbrückbar: see *Brücke*.
unüberhörbar
unüberhörbar unmistakable; from *überhören* = 'to fail to hear' (see s.v.); since the 19th c.

unüberlegt

unüberlegt thoughtless, inconsiderate, unwise; also used for 'rash'; derived from *überlegen* (2), which see; since early in the 18th c.; *Unüberlegtheit* also appeared in the 18th c. (Lavater, Forster, Lichtenberg).

unüberschaubar: see *schauen*.
unübersehbar
unübersehbar (1) incalculable, vast; for *übersehen* see p. 2233; the negative adjective since the 18th c., both in phys. and figur. sense.
unübersehbar (2) obvious, clear; esp. with ref. to mistakes: *ein unübersehbarer Fehler*; only since the 19th c.

unübersetzbar
eine unübersetzbare Wendung an untranslatable phrase; für *übersetzen* = 'to translate' see p. 2250; ~ since the 2nd half of the 18th c. (Herder, Goethe), followed by *Unübersetzbarkeit*.

unübersichtlich
unübersichtlich badly arranged, unmethodical, involved; since the 19th c., but not yet listed by Campe [1811]; for *etw. übersichtlich machen* see p. 2255.

unübertragbar
unübertragbar not transferable; in econ. contexts = 'non-negotiable'; general since the 19th c.; for *übertragen* in this sense see p. 2472. Note that Goethe used *nicht übertragbar* (not *unübertragbar*) for 'not translatable'.

unübertrefflich
unübertrefflich unsurpassable, superb; since the 2nd half of the 18th c., probably influenced by Engl. 'insuperable'; though not listed by Campe [1811], used by him earlier in the same volume of his dictionary. See also under *übertreffen* for *übertreffbar, unübertreffbar* and *unübertroffen*.

unüberwindlich
unüberwindlich insuperable; since Early NHG, e.g. Luther 5,511b (Jena); sometimes also used for 'irrefutable', as e.g. adverbially in Forster, *It.* 2,46: '*unüberwindlich dargethan*' (now unusual); ~ occurs frequently in Goethe's writings and he also used *Unüberwindlichkeit*; cf. also *unüberwundene Abneigung*, as used by Goethe.

unumgänglich: see *Umgang*.
unumgehbar
unumgehbar (obs.) inevitable; since the 18th c.; older *unumgehlich* is also obs.

unumschränkt
unumschränkt unlimited; since the 18th c.; considered in *DWb.* [1936] as '*etwas gewählter als unbeschränkt*'; for *beschränken* in figur. sense see p. 271, for *schrankenlos* see p. 2178.

unumstößlich: see *stoßen*.
unumwölkt: see *umwölken*.
unumwunden: see *umwickeln*.
ununterbrochen: see *unterbrechen*.
ununterdrückbar
ununterdrückbar irrepressable, insuppressible; since the 17th c., now rare, if not obs.

ununterrichtet

ununterrichtet (euphem.) uneducated; since the 18th c., at least partly euphem.; used by Herder and Goethe.

ununterscheidbar

ununterscheidbar indistinguishable; since late in the 18th c.; Goethe used it in *Maximen u. Reflex.* 244.

ununterwürfig

ununterwürfig unwilling to submit, rebellious; with persons and abstracts since the 18th c.

unväterlich: see *Vater*.

unveränderlich: see *unabänderlich*.

unverantwortlich: see *verantworten*.

unverbesserlich

unverbesserlich (1) not amenable to improvement, unsurpassable; with ref. to things and abstracts since the 17th c., recorded by Kramer [1700].

unverbesserlich (2) incorrigible; with ref. to persons; since the 18th c., e.g. Wieland, *Agathon* 2,249.

unverblümt: see *Blume*.
unverdaut: see *verdauen*.
unverdient: see *treffen*.
unverdrüßlich: see *Philosoph*.
unverfälscht: see *Siegel*.
unverfroren: see *frieren*.
unvergleichbar: see *vergleichen*.
unverhofft: see *hoffen*.
unverhohlen: see *verhehlen*.
unverhüllt: see *Hülle*.
unverkennbar: see *verkennen*.
unverlangt: see *verlangen*.
unverletzlich: see *verletzen*.
unverloren: see *Glanz*.
unvermeidlich: see *vermeiden*.
unvermerkt: see *rücken*.
unvermögend: see *finden*.
unvermutet: see *Knall* and *vermuten*.
unvernehmlich: see *vernehmen*.
unvernünftig: see *Tier*.
unverrückbar: see *rücken* (also for *unverrückt*).
unverschämt: see *Scham*.
unversehens: see *sehen* (also *Schicksal*).
unversehentlich: see *Haut*.
unversiegbar: see *versiegen*.
unversöhnlich: see *Skorpion*.
unverständig and **unverständlich:** see *verstehen*.
unversucht: see *versuchen*.
unvertilgbar: see *vertilgen*.
unverträglich: see *vertragen*.
unverwehrt: see *verwehren*.
unverwelklich: see *Lorbeer*.
unverwelkt: see *verwelken*.
unverwüstlich: see *verwüsten*.
unverzüglich: see *verziehen*.

unverzwickt

nicht ~ (coll.) quite simple; modern litotes, only since 2nd half of the 20th c., but ~ has been current since the 16th c.

unvordenklich

unvordenklich (a.) long-past; now only in *seit unvordenklichen Zeiten* = 'since time immemorial' and *vor unvordenklichen Zeiten* = 'in time out of mind', but both are also becoming a.

unvoreingenommen

unvoreingenommen unprejudiced, impartial; since the 19th c.; Campe [1811] listed *voreingenommen*, but not the negative (Adelung recorded neither).

unvorgesehen: see *sehen*.
unvorsichtig: see *Vorsicht*.
unvorstellbar: see *vorstellen*.
unwägbar: see *wägen*.
unwahr: see *wahr*.
Unwahrheit: see *Fuchs*.
unwandelbar: see *nähen*.
Unweg: see *Weg*.

Unwesen

sein ~ *treiben* to cause trouble or terror, be up to mischief; ~ for 'bad or criminal behaviour' appeared in the 15th c., with *machen* since the 17th c., with *treiben* general since the 18th c.

Unwetter: see *Wetter*.
unwiderlegbar: see *widerlegen*.
unwiderruflich: see *rufen*.
unwidersprechlich: see *widersprechen*.
unwiderstehlich: see *widerstehen*.
unwiederbringlich: see *wiederbringen*.
Unwille: see *fassen, gären* and *Seite*.

unwillentlich

unwillentlich unintentional; since the 18th c.; also used adverbially, e.g. (Kl.-St.) Feuchtwanger (in *Dt. Erzähler* 2,139): '*die Arglose könnte unwillentlich etwas verraten*'.

unwillig

unwillig (1) unwilling, disinclined; since Late MHG, often the same as *unwillfährig*, current since the 17th c.

unwillig (2) angry; since Early NHG.

unwillkommen: see *willkommen*.

unwillkürlich

unwillkürlich involuntary, unintentional; with many abstracts since the 18th c., recorded by Heynatz and Campe.

unwirrsch

unwirrsch unfriendly, ill-natured; current since Early NHG, first for 'ugly, despised, unimportant', then neglected until the 19th c., when it returned for 'cross, testy, angry', also transferred from persons to things, mostly to the weather, since the 19th c.

unwirtlich: see *Wirt*.
Unwissenheit: see *glatt, Strom* and *Tod*.
unwürdig: see *Würde*.
Unzahl: see *Zahl*.
unzählig: see *überlaufen*.
Unze: ounce

keine ~ not an ounce, not the smallest bit; transfer from amount of weight since Early NHG, e.g. H. Sachs [edit. K.] 3,556: '*wusch auch darvon nye kein üntz*'; cf. Schiller, *Kab. u.L.* 4,3: '*ewig schade für die Unze Gehirn, die . . . in diesem undankbaren Schädel wuchert*'.

Unzeit
die ~ (1) wrong time; since MHG; now in such phrases as *zur* ~ *kommen* = 'to arrive at an inconvenient time', current since the 18th c.

die ~ (2) disastrous, catastrophic time; the notion of 'badness' is old in this compound (used as early as in OHG for 'night'); now (at least regionally) still in *es war eine* ~ *für* . . . = 'it was a hard, cruel period for . . .'.

unzerbrechlich : see *zerbrechen*.

unzerreißbar: see *zerreißen*.

unzerstörbar: see *zerstören*.

unzertrennlich: see *trennen*.

unzertrennt: see *trennen*.

Unzucht: see *treiben*.

unzugänglich: see *zugehen*.

unzukömmlich
unzukömmlich (1) unwarranted, uncalled-for; first used for 'unpleasant, undesirable' since the 17th c. with ref. to locations, towns, areas; only since the 19th c. with ref. to human behaviour, usually describing sth. which a person has no right to say or do, e.g. Th. Mann, *Werke* 9,962 (*Die Betrogene*): '*erlaube dir keine unzukömmlichen Wahrnehmungen*'.

unzukömmlich (2) (regional) insufficient; recorded since the 19th c., probably derived from the language of the civil service, mainly used in Austria.

die Unzukömmlichkeit (regional) trouble, unpleasantness, awkwardness; since the 19th c., mainly used in Austria and Switzerland.

unzulänglich
unzulänglich inadequate, deficient; much more used than the positive *zulänglich*; current since the 17th c., recorded by Kramer [1700], often used by Goethe and Wieland.

unzulässig: see *zulassen*.

unzumutbar: see *zumuten*.

unzurechnungsfähig
unzurechnungsfähig of unsound mind; mainly used in legal contexts, general since the 19th c., e.g. Gutzkow, *R.v.G.* 8,330; now also in wider sense for 'irrresponsible'.

unzuständig: see *Zustand*.

unzuträglich
unzuträglich unwholesome, prejudicial; since the 17th c., recorded by Stieler [1691]; sometimes also used for 'unacceptable' (e.g. in moral respects) with ref. to indecency, when it is synonymous with *ungehörig*, cf. Danzel, *Lessing* 151 [1850]: '*das plautinische Stück enthält noch einige Unzuträglichkeiten*'; this usage is now a.

unzutreffend: see *zutreffen*.

unzuverlässig: see *verlassen*.

unzweideutig: see *zwei*.

üppig
üppig sumptuous, rich, luxuriant; the original sense was 'exceeding the usual or required measure'; this could lead to a variety of meanings such as 'unnecessary, superfluous, abundant, rich', with ref. to behaviour also (since OHG) to 'vain, haughty, presumptuous'; the extension to plant growth and the human body occurred in the 18th c.

← See also under *Kurve* (for *kurvenüppig*) and *Mähne* (for *er hat eine üppige Mähne*).

uranfänglich: see *Königin*.

Urban: Urban
Urbans- . . . (regional) . . . of wine; since ~ is the Saint of vintners, or rather the chief one among several, mentioned as such in literature since the 16th c., compounds with ~ refer to wine, e.g. *Urbansbier* = 'wine', as in Fischart, *Garg.* (repr.) 128, who also used *Urbansjünger* for 'lover of wine'; the whole group is now obs., although relics still exist in some localities.

urban
urban urban, characteristic of life in a city; originally a loan from Lat. *urbanus* in its extended sense = 'civilized, refined, witty' (18th c.); only in the 20th c. extended to refer to life in a city (as opposed to 'rural'); hence also *urbanisieren* (late 19th c.) = 'to urbanize, incorporate in a city' and *Urbanität* = *großstädtischer Charakter* (20th c.).

urbar
etw. ~ *machen* to convert sth. to fertile ground; originally ~ related to financial matters and not to fertility since it referred to a condition of land in which it produced a fee payable to the landlord (since the 17th c.). In the 18th c. it came to mean 'cultivated, made fertile', e.g. Ramler, *Fab.* 1,249 [1783]: '*macht urbar, was versäumt gelegen*', and this could be extended to abstracts, e.g. (T.) A.W.v.Schlegel, *Athen.* 2,282 [1799] or Laroche, *Frl.v. Sternheim* 1,179.

Urbild
das ~ archetype, prototype; since the beginning of the 18th c. (cf. Singer in *ZfdW.* 4,131), first in philos. contexts, then in art with ref. to models or typical forms, then general for 'model'; since the 20th c. also a term in psychology; *urbildlich* was used by Kant and f.r.b. Campe [1811].

Urbursch: see *Moos*.

Urding: see *Quelle*.

ureigentümlich: see *Original*.

Urenkel: grandchild
die Urenkel (lit.) future generations; extension to persons not truly related and to abstracts; since the 18th c., e.g. Klopstock, *Oden* 1,11, Goethe 5,90 (W.), also 4,255 and 8,111 (W.)

Urfehde
~ *schwören* to swear an oath of truce; in wider

sense 'to promise to keep the peace'. ~ is 'vow to keep the peace', where *ur-* describes sth. negative (absence or abandonment of sth.), only current in OHG, MHG and Early NHG; cf. *urlog* = 'war', i.e. 'absence of agreement'. ~ *schwören* (or *geloben, geben, tun*) has been current since Early NHG; the old orthography *Urphede* still occurs in Goethe 39,125 (W.): '*die Urphede abschwören*'. The extended sense 'to promise' occurs e.g. in Schiller, *Tell* 5,1: '*Urphede schwur er, nie zurückzukehren*'. Luther 32,384 (Weimar) and others in the 16th c. used *Urfriede* for 'cessation of hostilities' where *Friede der Fehde* was turned into a new compound with total elimination of *Fehde*. For *Fehde* see p. 749.

Urfriede: see *Urfehde*.

urgieren: see *niederschlagen*.

Urheber

der ~ originator, creator, author; influenced by Lat. *auctor*; since the 15th c. (at first usually as *Urhaber*); in the beginning used for 'creator', e.g. Wieland, *Agathon* 3,2 on the Gods: '. . . sind entweder die Natur selbst oder die Urheber der Natur'; since the 16th c. also for 'author' (of books), f.r.b. Frisius [1556]; since the 18th c. extended to abstracts, e.g. Schiller, *Philipp II*: '*Elisabeth war die Urheberin ihrer Freiheit*'; *Urheberschaft* general only since the 19th c.

Urheimat

die ~ place of origin; only since the 19th c. for 'original home(land)' and figur. for 'place of origin (of things or abstracts)'.

Urian

Meister ~ (a.) the Devil; much has been written about this obscure word which probably began as an invented personal name, may perhaps belong to the *Jan-* group (like *Dummrian*, for which see p. 1411) or to another group patterned on Lat. words ending in *-ianus* (e.g. *Grobian*) but no agreement exists on that and its meanings are so diverse that guessing becomes idle. It has been current in literature since the 17th c., can mean 'devil', 'death', also (as in the case of *Johannes*) 'penis', or it can stand for any person whose real name one has forgotten, like *Dingsda* (for which see p. 479); lastly it can denote any person whom one finds unattractive. In 18th and 19th c. lit. the meaning 'devil' occurs more frequently than the others, now the term is dropping out of use.

← See also under *Meister* (for *Herr Urian*).

Urias: Uriah

der Uriasbrief letter of Uriah, fatal or treacherous letter; biblical, a ref. to 2 Sam.11,14 where the bringer of the letter is intended to be killed; in this sense used by Goethe 22,159 (W.), but since the 18th c. the word has been given the more general meanings of 'bad news', 'letter with unpleasant contents' and 'treacherous communication'. There were many compounds such as

uriasartig, Uriasempfehlung, but only *Uriasbrief* is still in use.

Urin: urine

das hab ich im ~ *gespürt* (vulg.) I have seen this coming, I had a gut feeling about that; modern low coll.

Urknall

der ~ the big bang; translates the Engl. term and describes the sudden explosion of concentrated matter which led to the creation of the universe; 20th c.

Urlaub: leave

See *hinter* (for *hinter der Tür Urlaub nehmen*), *Leiche* (for *wie eine Leiche auf Urlaub aussehen*) and *trocken* (for *seinen Urlaub nehmen*), also under *beurlauben*.

Urmutter

die ~ (lit.) first mother, ancestress; since the 18th c. used for 'nature' (cf. Engl. 'mother nature'), e.g. by Goethe IV, 35,26 (W.), for 'Eve' (also for equivalents in Classical mythology such as Neitha in Herder [edit. S.] 6,351), for 'earth' (cf. Engl. 'mother earth'); since the 19th c. also for 'first example or specimen of sth.'; the plural could stand for 'ancestors', e.g. Herder [edit. S.] 13,326. Gotthelf, *Werke* 1,322 used *Urmütterchen* for 'Eve'.

Urnacht

die ~ (lit.) chaos, darkness before light was created; since the 2nd half of the 18th c., e.g. Herder [edit. S.] 27,394.

Urne: urn

zur ~ *gehen* to (cast one's) vote, take part in an election; since the 18th c. the association between 'fate' and the 'urn' in which our personal 'lots' are kept has been used in lit., e.g. (S.-B.) Ramler, *Einl.i.d.Wiss.* 3,57 [1758]: '*unser aller Loos wird in einer Urne geschüttelt*'. From there it was but a short step to the meaning 'ballot-box' and phrases with ~ referring to elections; general since the 19th c.; hence also *der Urnengang* = 'walk to the polling-station' (cf. also Swiss coll. *Urnentanz* with ref. to the walk around the tables on which receptacles are placed into which the voters drop their voting-slips).

die ~ (lit.) container of the ashes; in lit. since ca. 1800, e.g. (S.-B.) Brentano, *Godwi* 1,62 [1801]: '*in der Urne meiner begrabenen Jugend*', Heine, *Werke* 1,134: '*dies Büchlein ist die Urne mit der Asche meiner Liebe*'.

Urquelle: see *Siegel*.

Ursache: cause

keine ~ (coll.) don't mention it, you're welcome; for many regions recorded since the 19th c.

← See also under *Lumpen* (for *Lumpenursache*).

kleine Ursachen, große Wirkungen (prov.) big oaks from little acorns grow; ~ has been coupled with *Wirkung* in many phrases since the 17th c., e.g. *gleiche Ursachen, gleiche Wirkungen, die inneren Ursachen der äußeren Wirkungen, Gesetz von ~ und Wirkung*, but the prov. is modern, not yet listed in Simrock [1846], recorded by Wander [1876].

Urschel: see *Ursula*.

Urschlamm

vom ~ (or *Urschleim*) *her* (coll.) since the earliest beginnings; a ref. to the 'primeval mud' from which life emerged; the phrase is recent, but both *Urschlamm* and *Urschleim* have been in use since ca. 1800, e.g. (DWb) Fr.Schlegel 15,59: '*aus dem Urschlamm hervorgekrochene Menschenstämme*'.

Urschleim: see *Urschlamm*.

Ursprung: see *Sprung*.

Urstand: see *Mensch*.

Ursula

die Urschel (coll.) slovenly wench, stupid woman, girl of loose morals; ~ became *Urschel* in many dialects and acquired various meanings all expressing contempt or disapproval; beginnings in the 16th c., e.g. Mathesy, 137a [1554]: '*sie ist eine tolle Vrsel*'; cf. also Goethe, *Hanswursts Hochzeit* 86–89, where the *Ursel* in question is obviously a girl of easy virtue.

Urteil: judgment

See under *abfallen* (for *das Urteil fällt ab*), *abschätzen* (for *abschätziges Urteil*), *absprechen* (for *absprechendes Urteil*), *anheften* (for *dem Urteil die Vollstreckung anheften*), *fällen* (for *ein Urteil fällen*), *link* (for *ein linkes Urteil*), *Salomon* (for *salomonisches Urteil*), *schief* (for *schief urteilen*), *schneiden* (for *schneidend urteilen*), *schnell* (for *Schnellurteil*), *schräg* (for *schräges Urteil*), *seicht* (for *seicht urteilen*), *Teil* (for *sich ein Urteil bilden, Urteil des Paris, Willkürlichkeit im Urteil zeigen, urteilsfähig, sich kein Urteil erlauben, sich selbst sein Urteil sprechen, von etw. urteilen wie ein Blinder von Farben, verurteilen, Vorurteil, vorurteilen* and *vorurteilsfrei*), *träufeln* (for *Urteilsspruch*), *treffen* (for *treffendes Urteil*) and *unfehlbar* (for *unfehlbares Urteil*).

Urvater: see *Vater*.

Urvieh

ein ~ (also *Urviech*) (coll.) a real character, odd creature, perfect scream; recorded for many dialects since the 19th c., sometimes as a term of praise = *Mordskerl*, also pejor. for '*komischer Kerl*', also '*grober Kerl*'; in lit. since the 19th c.

Urwald: primeval forest

ein ganzer ~ an impenetrable jungle; since early in the 19th c. ~ has been used figur. either to indicate lush growth (not kept in check) or large quantity of sth. impenetrable, e.g. Heine, *Börne* 200 [1840]: '*ganze Urwälder von Unwissenheit*'. There are many compounds expressing the same two notions, e.g. *urwaldartig, Urwalddickicht, -einsamkeit, -frieden, -labyrinth, Urwaldsdichte, -dickicht, -nacht*, all only since the 19th c. ~ can sometimes in joc. coll. refer to an untidy beard, even to pubic hair.

ein Benehmen wie im ~ (coll.) disgusting behaviour, shockingly bad manners; 20th c. coll.

Urwelt: see *Welt*.

Urwesen: see *Grund*.

urwüchsig: see *wachsen*.

uzen

jem. ~ (coll.) to tease sb., pull sb.'s leg; from *Uz*, the coll. form of the Christian name *Ulrich*; just as *Hans* led to *hänseln*, *Uz* allowed *uzen* (i.e. *jem. Uz nennen* = 'to make a fool of sb.') to arise; in many areas current since the 18th c., always coll., but in the *Sturm und Drang* period also to be found in lit.; hence *Uzer* and *Uzerei*, both coll.; the compound *Uzname* ,= 'nickname' also exists (not listed in *DWb*. [1936]).

← See also under *appellieren* (for *dem Utzen rufen*).

Vabanquespiel: see *Spiel*.

vagabundieren

vagabundieren to move around without a settled place (often also without a fixed income); this displaced *vagieren* (current since the 16th c.); Adelung listed '*im Lande herum vagieren*' without mentioning *vagabundieren*, but Campe recorded the verb. It began as 'to live as a vagabond', then figur. since ca. 1800.

vagabundierendes Geld (coll., econ.) capital which is frequently shifted from one currency into another for quick profit; since ca. 1930.

vagabundierender Strom (tech.) leakage current; 20th c., also called *Irrstrom, Kriechstrom* and *Streustrom*.

die Zeit vervagabunden to pass one's time wastefully; since the 19th c., e.g. (S.-B.) Goethe (in Diezmann, *Weimar* 19): '*der Abend gestern ward mit Würfeln und Karten vervagabundet*'.

Vakuum: vacuum

das ~ (lit.) vacuum, empty space, emptiness; since the 17th c., e.g. (S.-B.) *Gepflückte Fincken* 21 [ca. 1670]: '*hungerige Kragen, bellende Magen können das Vacuum gar nicht vertragen*', then transferred to abstracts, e.g. Becker, *Quantität* 15 [1962]: '*Talleyrand, der . . . Europa vor dem politischen Vakuum bei Napoleons Sturz bewahrte*'.

Valet: farewell

einer Sache (abstract) ~ *sagen* (a.) to abandon sth., give sth. up; cf. similar phrases in Engl. with 'saying goodbye'; Luther used ~ for 'end, final part'; Stieler (1691) recorded it with an abstract ('*studiren*') in the modern sense; Adelung listed *Valetrede* for 'farewell speech'.

Vampir: vampire

der ~ vampire, bloodsucker; figur. since late in the 18th c., e.g. (S.-B.) Laukhard, *Annalen* 1,51 [1798]: '*Zuchtspiegel für die politischen Vampyre*', Friedell, *Kulturgesch.* 3,455 (1931) on Strindberg: '*in mehreren Dramen kommen Personen vor, die die Rolle des Vampirs spielen; sie nähren sich vom Geist und Blut ihrer Mitmenschen*'; also in econ. contexts for 'extortioner, blackmailer, money-lender'; cf. also Grillparzer, *Ahnfrau* 2,5:

'*die Angst mit ihrem Vampyrrüssel saugt das Blut aus meinen Adern*'.

Vandale: Vandal

hausen wie ein ~, *vandalisch hausen* to behave (or destroy) like a Vandal; the name of this tribe established itself in German lit. late in the 18th c., in descriptions of senseless destruction or barbaric behaviour since the 2nd half of the 18th c., with *hausen* since the 1st quarter of the 19th c., e.g. (S.-B.) Wachenhusen, *Leben* 2,313 [1890]: '. . . *wo die abziehende Besatzung wie die Vandalen gehaust*'; hence also *vandalisch* and *vandalenmäßig* since the 18th c., but *Vandalentum* only since the 19th c.; *Vandalismus* (from French *vandalisme*) arose late in the 18th c. (Schiller still used the hybrid form *Vandalism*); in recent times *Wandale* has become the preferred spelling. For figur. use of *hausen* see p. 1259.

Vasall: vassal

der ~ (lit.) vassal, (dependent) follower; extended from legal feudal contexts to abstracts since late in the 18th c., with ref. to persons since ca. 1800; since that time also in many derivatives such as *Vasall(en)-schaft*, sometimes *Vasallität*, but *Vasallentum* only since the 20th c. Since the 1st half of the 19th c. in many compounds, chiefly in *Vasallenstaat*.

Vater: father

der ~ (1) (relig.) God; since earliest times (and also in this sense in the Classical world), e.g. OHG *truhtîn fater*; variant forms are *Gottvater*, *Himmelsvater*, *himmlischer ~*, since Early NHG, very frequent in the language of Pietists, also used by Lessing, occasionally *ewiger ~*.

← See also under *all* (for *Allvater*).

der ~ (2) (relig.) Father; at first with ref. to patriarchs, apostles, early teachers, hermits, then extended as a title for bishops, abbots (cf. *Abt*, derived from Aramaic *abba* = 'father'), then for 'priest' in general; hence also *Kirchenvater*, *geistlicher ~* and *der heilige ~* = 'pope', since MHG, e.g. Walther v.d.Vog. 33,13: '*der bâbest unser vater*'. In MHG the 'godfather' was also called *geistlicher ~* (now obs.).

der ~ (3) father, progenitor, originator; since OHG, when Lucifer was called '*des nîdis vatir*'; cf. Luther Bible transl. John 8,44 on the Devil and lies: '*ein lügner und ein vater derselbigen*', Apocr. transl. Wisdom of Sol. 10,1 on God: '*vater der welt*'; cf. also *der Krieg ist der Vater aller Dinge*. Sometimes *Urvater* is used (see below). Following Lat. usage historic personalities are called *~*, e.g. Herodotos, called *pater historiae* became *~ der Geschichte*, Opitz 1,53 referred to Prometheus as '*der vater der vernunfft und kunst und vieler werke*'. Cf. also Heine, *Werke* 6,269: '*Herr Uhland ist nicht der Vater einer Schule, wie Göthe oder Schiller*'. The phrase *der Wunsch war ~ des Gedankens* was coined by Shakespeare in *Henry IV,2*: 'thy wish was father, Harry, to that thought'.

der ~ (4) (geogr.) Father . . .' with ref. to mighty rivers, e.g. *~ Rhein*, since Early NHG, e.g. Fischart [edit. K.] 2,181 on the Limmat: '. . . *zu irem vater laufft inn Rhein*', as *~ Rhein* in Opitz 1,101, also Hölty: '*ein Leben wie im Paradies gewährt uns Vater Rhein*'. *~ Nil* and *~ Mississippi* also occur and are in essence translations.

der ~ (5) (theatr.) father-figure (in drama); since the 18th c., e.g. Lessing 12,472, but mainly in compounds such as *Heldenvater* or in *komischer ~*.

der ~ (6) custodian, manager, person responsible for sth.; in many compounds, e.g. *Bienenvater* = 'bee-keeper', since the 18th c., *Findelvater* = 'foster-father, person looking after an orphan', recorded since the 19th c., *Herbergsvater* = 'hostel manager', 19th c., *Nährvater* = 'fatherly protector', since the 17th c., when Abr. a S. Clara, *Etw.f.Al.* 1,189 applied the term to Christ, similarly *Pflegevater*, as in Lessing, *Nathan* 5,7.

der ~ (7) (mining) place of discovery (where ore was found first); f.r.b. Veith, *Dt.Bergwb.* 518 [1870]; the standard term is *(ursprünglicher) Fundort*.

~ Staat (coll.) the State; since late in the 19th c. (not yet listed in *DWb.* [1919]).

der Dichtervater (lit.) Homer; applied to Homer since the 18th c., e.g. Gotter 3,70: '*selbst Pope war dem kühnen Schwung zu schwach und streifte nur des Dichtervaters Sphäre*'.

der Landesvater (lit.) the sovereign; since the 18th c., f.r.b. Frisch [1741], e.g. Schiller, *30-jähr.Kr.* 2,3. For *Landesmutter* see p. 1730.

die Stadtväter the city fathers, magistrates; since the 19th c., often in half-joc. contexts; cf. Heine, *Werke* [edit. E.] 2,207: '*wir, Bürgermeister und Senat, wir haben folgendes Mandat stadtväterlichst an alle Klassen der treuen Bürgerschaft erlassen*'.

der Urvater (1) (obs.) great-grandfather; since the 15th c., still used by Goethe 26,222 (W.), now obs.

der Urvater (2) (lit.) God; since the 18th c., used e.g. by Herder [edit. S.] 6,331.

der Urvater (3) (rare) Adam; since the 16th c. and still in occasional lit. use.

der Urvater (4) father, progenitor; when used with ref. to things = 'first example' or to persons = 'creator or first master of sth.', e.g. Goethe 24,154 (W.) or R. Schumann, *Ges.Schr.* 2,214: '*S.Bach, der Urvater der Harmonie*'.

die Urväter the ancestors; frequent since the 18th c. (Herder, Goethe).

väterlich (1) (lit.) familiar since one's childhood; e.g. *die väterlichen Berge*, as in Schiller, *Tell* 2,1; cf. also Kerner, *Wohlauf noch getrunken*: '*ade nun, ihr Berge, du väterlich Haus*'.

väterlich (2) fatherly, in the manner of a father; hence often = 'caring, protective'; cf. *jem. bevatern* = 'to look after sb. like a father', since the 19th c.; cf. *bemuttern* (p. 251) and *bevettern* (p. 301), also Uhland, 48: '*ein Freund, ein vatergleicher*'.

väterlich (3) traditional, long-established; since Early NHG, e.g. Luther Bible transl. Acts 28,17: *'väterliche sitte'* or 1 Peter 1,18: *'väterliche weise'*.

der Vatermörder (coll.) choker; in the standard language *der Stehkragen*; since the 19th c., but still missing in Campe [1811], even in Meißner [1856], e.g. Gutzkow, *Serap.* 3,261 [1877].

die Vaterschaft paternity; modern, figur. in such cases where creation of sth. or authorship is referred to, e.g. Bismarck, *Reden* 16,39: *'. . . ich lehne die Verantwortlichkeit für die Gesetze . . . nicht ab, aber die Vaterschaft stammt durchaus nicht von mir'*.

zu seinen Vätern versammelt werden (bibl.) to die; based on Luther Bible transl. 2 Kings 22,20 and 2 Chron. 34,28, e.g. Rabner, *Werke* 1,117 [1777]: *'. . . daß der Arzt an Nichts weiter gedachte, als sie nach gehöriger Ordnung zu ihren Vätern zu versammeln'*.

Vaterfreuden entgegensehen to look forward to becoming a father; since the 19th c.; for figur. *entgegensehen* see p. 648, for the phrase with *Mutterfreude* see p. 1731.

Vaterstelle bei jem.m vertreten to take the place of a father to sb.; since the 18th c., e.g. Weise, *Kom. Op.* 3,256; see under *Stelle* for *an jem.s Stelle treten* and under *treten* for *jem. vertreten*.

ach, du dicker ~ ! (sl.) dear me! good heavens! usually expressing surprise; in sl. since ca. 1900, also as *ach, du heiliger* (or *himmlischer*) *~ !*, all examples of the avoidance of the word *Gott*.

'~ werden ist nicht schwer, ~ sein dagegen sehr' to become a father is not difficult, to be one, however, is; quotation from Wilhelm Busch, *Julchen*.

der will seinen ~ lehren Kinder machen (prov.expr.) he wants to teach his grandmother how to suck eggs, Jack Sprat would teach his grandame, teach your father to get children, teach your grandame to grope ducks (or to sup sour milk); in this wording recorded since the 19th c. (Eiselein, Simrock), but in Moscherosch, *Tech.All.* 511 [1656] as *'lehre du deinen Vater kinder zeugen'* with the French equivalent *'veux tu apprendre a fils de pescheur a manger poisson?'*.

aus! Dein treuer ~. (coll.) that's the end, there is no more to be said or done; jocular fictitious letter ending; 20th c. coll.

← See also under *dumm* (for *Vater stehen zu etw.*), *Erbe* (for *Vätertugend*), *Fleisch* (for *sein Vater war Fleischer*), *Folter* (for *das Vaterherz foltern*), *Freude* (for *ein weiser Sohn ist seines Vaters Freude*), *ganz* (for *ganz der Vater* or *der ganze Vater*), *Gefilde* (for *Vatergefilde*), *gerade* (for *Vater Adam*), *Glas* (for *dein Vater war kein Glaser*), *Grab* (for *der alte Vater würde sich im Grab umwenden*), *greifen* (for *greife nicht an das Vaterherz*), *Grube* (for *sie wird dem Vater nicht die Grube graben*), *heißen* (for *die Verwesung heiß ich meinen Vater*), *hervorbringen* (for *Gottes Vatergüte*), *Mutter* (for *jem.m Vater und Mutter sein*), *Nuß* (for *der Vater ist auf dem*

Nußbaum ersoffen), *offen* (for *Vaterherz*), *Rabe* (for *Rabenvater*), *Sohn* (for *seines Vaters Sohn, wie der Vater, so der Sohn* and *was der Vater erspart, vertut der Sohn*), *Stamm* (for *Stammvater*), *Stief-* (for *kein Stiefvater gegen sich sein*), *Sünde* (for *Sündenvater*), and *wachen* (for *das Vaterauge wacht*).

← See also below for separate entries on *Vaterland, Vaterstadt* and *Vaterunser*.

Vaterland: fatherland

das ewige (or *himmlische*) *~* (relig.) heaven; e.g. Wackernagel, *Kirchenl.* 3,139a, also Büchner, *Handkonkordanz* (for bibl. refs.) and A. Langen, *Der Wortschatz d.dt. Pietismus* 139 [1954].

er hat mehr Angst als Vaterlandsliebe (coll.) he is a coward; since ca. 1900 (not yet recorded in *DWb.* (1886).

wo es mir wohl geht, da ist mein ~ (prov.) my country is there where I am well off; cf. Lat. *ubi bene, ibi patria*; a modern prov., recorded since the 19th c., e.g. by Simrock [1846].

← See also under *Altar* (for *auf dem Altar des Vaterlandes opfern*), *anschließen* (for *ans Vaterland, ans teure, schließ dich an*), *beflügeln* (for *beflügle sein Herz mit Liebe zum Vaterland*), *Blume* (for *ihr Blumen des Vaterlands*), *Blut* (for *sein Blut lassen für das Vaterland*), *Boden* (for *des Vaterlandes vielgeliebter Boden*), *daheim* (for *der prophet nit hat ere in seim vatterlant*), *einpflanzen* (for *Einpflanzung der Vaterlandsliebe*), *führen* (for *undankbares Vaterland*), *gehören* (for *ins Vaterland des himmlischen Paradieses*), *Muse* (for *der Musen Vaterland*) and *rufen* (for *es ruft der Tod für das Vaterland*).

Vaterstadt: see *aneignen*.

Vaterunser: Lord's prayer

nicht ein ~ lang (coll.) for a very short time; since the 18th c., e.g. Thümmel 3,41; cf. also O. Ludwig, *Himm.* 163: *'ein halb Vaterunser lang hörte man nichts'*.

bet dein letztes ~ ! prepare yourself for death; at least since the 18th c. (sometimes no more than a threat), e.g. Hebel 3,163.

es ist wie das katholische ~ (coll.) it lacks strength and splendour; allusion to the fact that the Roman-Catholic form of the Lord's prayer lacks the line *'denn Dein ist das Reich und die Kraft und die Herrlichkeit'*; since the beginning of the 19th c.

← See also under *Backe* (for *man kann ihm ein Vaterunser durch die Backen blasen*) and under *Paternoster* for similar idioms.

vegetieren

(nur) ~ to lead a joyless life, merely vegetate; *~* meant originally 'to refresh, strengthen' (18th c.), then developed to mean 'to live like a plant (without being directed by the intellect)', hence pejor. = 'to live mechanically without intellectual or spiritual interests, have a wretched existence', since last quarter of the 18th c., e.g. *am Rande des Elends ~* = 'to eke out a miserable existence'.

Vehikel

das ~ (lit.) medium, means (of conveying sth.), vehicle; first in the language of medicine and pharmacology (18th c.), then transferred to abstracts, e.g. *etw. zum* ~ *machen* = 'to use sth. as a vehicle (also as a pretext)', *als* ~ *dienen* = 'to serve as a vehicle, means, method or way (to get what one wants)'; since the 2nd half of the 18th c.

Veilchen: violet

bescheiden wie ein ~ as undemanding, reticent or unselfish as a violet; cf. Engl. 'shrinking violet'; since MHG, when *demütig* appears to have been the preferred adjective; cf. the poems by Goethe entitled *Das Veilchen* and *Blümlein wunderschön* (in the latter *bescheiden* occurs).

veilchenblau violet-blue; since the 17th c., e.g. Grimmelshausen, *Simpliz.* [edit. K.] 1,373, but *veilchenfarbig* in the form *violvâr* = 'violet-coloured' as early as in MHG, e.g. *Minnes.* [edit. v.d.Hagen] 2,30b; cf. also Heine 2,95: '*die Mutter . . . hatte . . . blaue Augen, wie Veilchen in Milch gekocht*'.

ein prächtiges ~ *!* (sl.) a magnificent black eye! 20th c. sl.

← See also under *blau* (for *blau wie ein Veilchen*).

Veit: Vitus

der Veitstanz St. Vitus's dance, chorea minor; as an illness now also called Sydenham's chorea; describes jerky involuntary movements of parts of the body; the term has been current since Early NHG (also used by Luther) esp. in curses. St. Vitus, the Sicilian Saint, was credited with having cured the son of Diocletian in the 2nd half of the 4th c. He then became the patron Saint of people who suffered from chorea minor. In a strange process the names of Saints who cured illnesses became the names for the particular illness they were alleged to cure. By an equally strange development they became terms for the Devil (see also below on *Velten*).

ein ~ (coll.,obs.) a stupid person; in lit. from 17th c. onward, e.g. Abr. a S. Clara, *Judas, d.E.* 3,4 (1692): '*der ist wohl ein rechter Veitl, der nicht sicht, dass alles eytl*'; now obs., except in some dialects (cf. Frommann 3,315); Schmeller recorded *Veitl* for Bav. with the meaning of 'timid person'.

Velten: Valentin

Sankt ~ (obs.) the Devil; *Velten* is an old form of *Valentin*; in lit. since the 16th c., but probably older, as in the case of *Sankt Veit* (see above); full details on his numerous associations with wild dances, religious ecstasy, illnesses such as epilepsy and curses can be found in Trübner, *Dt. Wb.* 7,371 [1956].

Venedig: Venice

so spielt man in ~ (coll.) all tricks are mine and you have lost; triumphant phrase used by card-players when defeating an opponent by taking all tricks; assumed to be a ref. to the cruel legal system in Venice where even an innocent person could fall foul of the law and suffer punishment; modern (19th c.?).

Ventil: valve

das ~ outlet, vent, safety-valve; sometimes as a compound *Sicherheitsventil*; figur. occasionally as early as in the 16th c., but in general figur. use only since the 19th c., e.g. (S.-B.) *Hausblätter* 1,209 [1862]: '. . . *seinem feurigen Temperament durch das Sicherheitsventil einiger Flüche Luft zu machen*'; cf. also *etw. hat eine Ventilfunktion* = 'sth. serves as a safety-valve'.

etw. ventilieren (lit.) to consider sth. (carefully), examine or discuss sth.; since early in the 17th c., but after a considerable gap in the 20th c. a much-used verb, e.g. *eine oft ventilierte Frage* = 'a much-discussed question'.

Venus: Venus

(Frau) ~ Venus, Love (personified); since MHG, not only for 'love', but also for 'she-devil'.

eine ~ (lit.) a beautiful woman; since Early NHG, e.g. Heine 13,110: '*sie ist eine Venus*'.

die ~ (astron.) the planet Venus; the OHG name *uhto-sterno* and the MHG *morgensterne* were displaced by the Greek and Lat. term in Early NHG, e.g. Fischart, *Großm.* (repr.) 7.

die ~ *de Kilo* (sl.) very fat woman; rude pun on ~ *de* Milo; 20th c. sl.

(der) ~ *opfern* (or *räuchern*) (lit., a.) to pay one's tribute to Venus, make love; same as *Eros Tribut zollen* and similar locutions with *Amor* or *Liebesgott*: now a. or considered stilted.

im Venusberg weilen (lit.) to spend one's time in the pursuit of love; legends place the *Venusberg* in the Hörselberg, the mountain of love. In its caves ~ was alleged to hold court. Human visitors to it risked eternal damnation and *Eckart* (see p. 543) stood before the mountain warning humans against entering. Wagner's use of the *Tannhäuser* legend in his opera of that name gave the word wider currency, but *Venusberg* has been current since MHG. Sometimes *Garten der* ~ occurs in connexion with love (cf. *DWb.* IV, 1,1399 [1878]) which ties up with Lat. *hortulus cupidinis* and similar sexual images in German.

der Venusberg or *Venushügel* (med.) mons Veneris; translation of the med. Lat. term; recorded since the 18th c., e.g. Nemnich 3,597. – In chiromancy one of the raised areas in the palm is also called *Venusberg*.

Venusblümchen (coll., a.) freckles; f.r.b. Rädlein [1711], now a. or obs.; for the popular connexion between 'marks, spots' and 'flower' see the prov. on p. 358.

die Schuppenvenus (zool.) a scaly conch (*Venus squamosa*); recorded by Campe [1811].

Frau ~ *und das Geld regieren alle Welt* (prov.)

love and money rule all mankind; f.r.b. Tappius [1539] and still listed in modern prov. collections.

veraasen: see *Aas*.

verachten: despise

nicht zu ~ not at all bad, not to be sneezed at; ~ began as 'to overlook' (Early NHG) and became 'to despise'; *nicht zu* ~ with the notion of 'appreciating' appeared in lit. in the 1st half of the 19th c., e.g. Zschokke, *Selbstschau* 1,183 [1842].

jem. mit Verachtung strafen to treat sb. with contempt; since the 18th c., e.g. Herder [edit. S.] 22,223: '*kalte Verachtung . . . womit sie den Unwissenden zu strafen hätte*'.

mit Todesverachtung bravely; often in hyperbolic use, as in *mit Todesverachtung etw. essen* ,= 'to force oneself to eat sth. repugnant'; since the 19th c., e.g. Freytag, *Ges. W.* 17,173.

← See also under *aussetzen* (for *etw. der Verachtung aussetzen*), *Bein* (for *Verachtung gehet durch Marck und Bein*), *blühen* (for *eine nicht zu verachtende Nachblüte*) and *Kost* (for *er ist kein Kostverächter*).

veralten

veraltet out-moded, antiquated; since the 16th c. with abstracts (Luther used *voralden*); recorded by Adelung, e.g. Iffland, *Jäger* 2,9: '*veraltetes Vorurtheil*'.

← See also under *bestauben* (for *veraltete Sitte*).

verändern

etw. ~ to change sth.; with abstracts since Early NHG, e.g. Luther Bible transl. Job 14,20 (with *Wesen*) or Esra 6,11 (with *Worte*), Schiller, *Fiesco* 4,12: '*den Ton in Kälte verändert*'.

sich ~ to change; the original meaning 'to move or shift to another place' could in the reflex. verb lead to 'to move to sth. else, change one's job' and also 'to get married' (since this entails leaving the parental home); since MHG and still in some regions, e.g. *Buch d. Liebe* 354d: '. . . *daß sich mein mutter nicht hette verandert*'.

← See also under *April* (for *Herrengunst und Aprillenwetter sind veränderlich*), *einschneiden* (for *einschneidende Veränderungen*) and *Luft* (for *die Luft verändern* and *Luftveränderung*).

verankern: see *Anker*.

veranlagen: see *anliegen*.

Veranstaltung: see *abblasen*.

verantworten: see *antworten* (also for *verantwortlich* and *Verantwortung*).

veräppeln: see *Apfel*.

verarbeiten: see *bewältigen*.

verärgern

etw. ~ (obs.) to make sth. worse; since MHG (*verergern*); now obs., displaced by *verschlimmern* or *schlimmer machen*; the same applies to the reflex., used esp. with ref. to illness, displaced by *sich verschlimmern* or *schlimmer werden*.

jem. ~ to irritate, annoy, enrage sb.; since Early NHG when it meant 'to harm, inflict pain', but now describing 'irritating, causing annoyance'.

verarmen

verarmen to become impoverished; figur. with abstracts since the 18th c., e.g. Lichtenberg 5,279 [1800]: '*die reichste Sprache verarmt hierbei*'.

verarschen

jem. ~ (vulgar) to take the piss out of sb.; 20th c. vulgar sl.

verarten

etw. verartet (a.) sth. degenerates; figur. with abstracts since the 18th c., e.g. Mascou 2,132 [1726]: '*wie leicht die Freiheit . . . in ein wildes Wesen verartet*'; for similar locutions see *entarten, ausarten* (p. 120), also *aus der Art schlagen* (p. 75).

verarzten

jem. ~ to take care of sb., look after sb.; extension from medical treatment to non-medical contexts; in this sense since the 19th c.

← See also under *Arzt* (for *sein Geld verarzten* and the rough and threatening *jem. verarzten*).

verästeln: see *Ast*.

verausgaben

sich ~ to exhaust oneself, spend too much energy; mainly in sport with ref. to over-exertion; modern.

verbafelt: see *Bafel*.

verballhornen: see *Ballhorn*.

verbannen

etw. ~ (lit.) to banish sth.; derived from the sense 'to forbid' (16th c.) with many abstracts since the 18th c., e.g. Lessing, *Miss S.S.* 1,7: '*die Zweifel aus meiner Brust zu verbannen*'; cf. also Lessing, *Dram.* 18: '*seitdem die Neuberinn . . . den Harlekin . . . von ihrem Theater verbannte*'.

verbarrikadieren: see *Barrikade*.

verbasilisken: see *Basilisk*.

verbauen

etw. ~ go block sth.; since MHG first in phys. contexts, then with abstracts such as *Aussicht*, also reflex. *sich die Zukunft* ~.

verbauern

etw. ~ to give to sth. a rural appearance, significance or atmosphere, countrify sth.; since the 18th c., e.g. Goethe, review of Hebel, *All. Ged.*: '. . . *verwandelt der Verfasser diese Naturgegenstände zu Landleuten, und verbauert . . . das Universum*'.

← See also under *Bauer* (for *verbauern*).

verbeißen

etw. ~ to suppress sth.; also reflex. *sich etw.* ~ (e.g. *das Lachen*); since the 18th c., e.g. Schiller, *Kab.u.L.* 1,7.

← See also under *beißen* (for *sich auf die Lippen beißen* and *etw. in sich beißen*).

sich in etw. ~ to stick doggedly to or persist determinedly with sth.; derived from the inability of dogs to let go when their teeth are deeply embedded in the flesh of their enemy; transferred since the 18th c., e.g. Schiller to Goethe (letter of 17.12.179).

verbissen determined, fanatical, dogged; see

previous entry; only since the 19th c., since Steinbach [1734] only recorded it for 'biting, cutting, waspish' and Adelung also did not list the present-day meaning; also in adverbial use, e.g. *verbissen geführte Debatte*; noun *die Verbissenheit* = 'doggedness, (irrational) persistence' (19th c.).

verbergen

jem.m etw. ~ (lit.) to hide sth. from sb.; with abstracts since the 18th c., e.g. Bodmer, *Char.d.T.Ged.* [1734] on Hofmannswaldau: '*er . . . verbirgt uns die Natur*'.

sich einer Sache ~ (lit., obs.) to hide or stay away from sth.; since the 18th c., e.g. Herder, *R.* 7,16: '*sie, die wie ein Veilchen sich dem Lobe verbirgt*'; now still possible with *vor*, but not in the construction with the dative.

etw. (abstract) *verbirgt sich* (lit.) sth. hides or lies hidden; since Early NHG, e.g. Luther Apocr. transl. Wisd. of Sol. 17,3: '*jre sünde solten verborgen . . . sein*', Goethe, *Werther* (18.8.): '*. . . Kraft, die in dem All der Natur verborgen liegt*'.

sich ~ (lit., obs.) to dissemble; extension from 'to hide what is real', still in Schiller, *Tell* 2,1: '*verbirg dich wie du willst*'; displaced by *sich verstellen*.

etw. (abstract) *verbirgt sich schwer* sth. is difficult to conceal; e.g. Herder, *Cid* 48: '*der Freude Botschaft, sie verbirgt sich schwer*', where *sich* ~ *lassen* would now be preferred; cf. P. van der Aelst, *Lieder u. Rheymen* 80 [1602]: '*Lieb lest sich nicht verbergen, ist ein sprichwort, welchs war*'.

sich etw. nicht ~ to be aware or conscious of sth.; since the 18th c., e.g. Ranke, *Werke* 1,270: '*Luther verbarg sich jedoch nicht, daß das Urtheil in Rom leicht gegen ihn ausfallen könne*'.

← See also under *Brücke* (for *eine verborgene Brücke*) and *Hintertür* (for *ein verborgen hinderthürlein*).

verbessern

der Weltverbesserer idealistic reformer, utopian; since the 18th c., soon mainly pejor. (Schiller, Klinger), recorded by Campe [1811], e.g. Fallmerayer, *Fragm.* 2,29 [1845]: '*unberufene Weltverbesserer*'.

verbiegen

ein verbogener Charakter a twisted or warped character; since the 19th c., cf. (DWb) Spielhagen 18,46: '*wie das Schicksal auf ihm herumgehämmert haben mag, bis ein solcher . . . verbogener Nagel aus ihm wurde*'.

verbiestern

jem. ~ to confuse sb.; from LG where intrans. ~ at first meant 'to go wrong, lose one's way' (since 15th c.); since the 19th c. = 'to confuse'; there is also *jem.m etw.* ~ = 'to spoil sth. for sb.', which led to *verbiestert* (coll.) = 'grumpy'.

sich in etw. ~ to become immersed in sth., be totally absorbed by sth.; since the 19th c., often in *in eine Arbeit verbiestert sein*, as in Fontane, *Briefe* 2,1 (dated 1.7.1851).

verbieten

etw. (abstract) *verbietet etw.* sth. forbids sth.; since the 17th c., e.g. Goethe, review of de Salvandy, *Don Alonzo* [1824]: '*hierüber uns dießmal herauszulassen, verbeut uns Tag und Platz*'. Cf. S. Dach [edit. Öst.] 637: '*dein ernst verbeut es mir*'; cf. also *das verbietet sich von selbst* = 'that is out of the question'.

jem.m den Mund (or *das Maul*) ~ to forbid sb. to speak, ask sb. to shut up; sometimes used with *Rede* or *Wort*; one of the polite expressions which ask people to be quiet; others which are less polite can be found under *binden, Gosche, Maul (Maulkorb), Schnauze, schweigen* and *stopfen*; recordings with ~ are late (19th c.).

jem.m das Haus ~ to forbid sb. to enter one's house; since the 17th c., e.g. Grimmelshausen, *Simpliz.* [edit. K.] 4,337.

verboten (coll.) shocking, disgraceful; mainly in *verboten aussehen* = 'to look a disgrace'; possibly derived from *gehört verboten* = 'ought to be forbidden'; since ca. 1900.

was verboten ist, tut man am liebsten (prov.) forbid a thing, and that we will do; international saying, e.g. Ovid, *Am.* 3,4,17: '*nitimus in vetitum semper, cupimusque negata*', Chaucer, *Wife of B.* 'forbede us thing, and that desyren we'; in German since MHG (cf. Zingerle, 158), e.g. Renner: '*waz man uns wert, das wolle wir haben*', Luther, *Tischr.* 140b: '*was verboten ist, dawider thut man gern*', also in rhymed versions, e.g. *was man verbeut, das tun die Leut* (recorded since the 17th c., e.g. by Lehman).

← See also under *Feder* (for *der Feder verbieten*) and *Frucht* (for *verbotene Frucht*).

verbilden

etw. ~ (lit.) to corrupt, disfigure, spoil sth.; since Late MHG (e.g. used by the Mystics), e.g. Schottel, 5 [1663]: '*. . . daß sie zu unreinen Bastardworten werden verbildet*'.

jem. (lit.) to miseducate, spoil sb., shape sb.'s development in the wrong way; since the 18th c., e.g. Werder, *Kreuz a.d.O.* 1,9 [1823]: '*doch wird sie endlich tagen die Bildung in verbildet rohen Herzen*'; then in the noun *Verbildung*, e.g. Tschudi, *Thierleben* 5 [1856]: '*unsre so oft in kleinlicher Verbildung ruhende Weltanschauung*'.

verbimsen: see *Bims*.

verbinden

jem.s Wunden ~ (lit.) to bandage sb.'s wounds, alleviate sb.'s suffering; since the 17th c., e.g. Schottel, 756: '*. . . Samaritanus, welcher die Wunden meines Herzens verbindete*'.

sich mit jem.m ~ to associate oneself with sb., form an alliance with sb.; since Early NHG, e.g. Luther Bible transl. 2 Chron. 7,18 (where *verbünden* would now be used), also 1 Sam. 22,8: '*das jr euch alle verbunden habt wider mich*'; first with the dative, then with *mit*; hence also *verbunden sein mit jem.m* = 'to be married with sb.', e.g.

Wieland, *Winterm.* 2,221: '. . . *das schönste Weib mir zu verbinden*', and *die Verbindung* = 'union, alliance, association, marriage', since Early NHG, f.r.b. Dasypodius, 149c 9[1539], e.g. Schiller, *Kab.u.L.* 1,5 (with *eingehen*).

seinen Verbindlichkeiten nachkommen to discharge one's liabilities or commitments; *Verbindlichkeit*, derived from very much older *verbindlich* = 'obligatory, binding', since the 18th c.; for figur. *nachkommen* see p. 1737. An offshoot from this is *verbindlich* = 'friendly', from 'feeling obliged to sb.', since the 18th c.; still frequent in *verbindlich(st)en Dank* = 'much obliged, many thanks', modern.

← See also under *aktiv* (for *er ist bei der X Verbindung aktiv*), *angenehm* (for *das Angenehme mit dem Nützlichen verbinden*), *dreschen* (for *dem Ochsen . . . nicht das Maul verbinden*), *eng* (for *in enger Verbindung stehen*) and *Spiel* (for *er ließ seine guten Verbindungen spielen*).

verbissen: see *verbeißen*.

verbitten

etw. ~ to forbid sth.; since the 18th c., f.r.b. Steinbach [1734]; often in *sich etw.* ~ = 'to refuse to allow sth.' with such abstracts as *Ton* = 'manner of speaking': *ich verbitte mir diesen Ton*; cf. Goethe, *Faust* I,2505: '*den Namen, Weib, verbitt ich mir*'.

verbittern

jem.m etw. ~ to spoil sth. for sb., cause sb. misery or pain over sth.: since Early NHG, e.g. Fischart, *Garg.* 84 or Brant, *Narrensch.* 56 [1494].

etw. ~ to sour, embitter sth.; since Early NHG, e.g. Luther Bible transl. Jerem. 50,21: '. . . *das land, das alles verbittert hat*' or *Werke* 5,306b (Jena): '. . . *das schärfen, spitzen und verbittern sie aufs allerärgste*'.

verbittern (intrans.), *verbittert werden* to become bitter or angry; since Late MHG, e.g. Laßberg, *Liedersaal* 190: '*vür des honges süezikeit füer ich gar verbitert leit*', Cronegk, *Einsamk.* 23 [1751]: '*von Schwermuth verbitterte Tage*', also with abstracts in the reflex., e.g. Treitschke 3,69: '. . . *hatte sich die Stimmung . . . noch mehr verbittert*'.

verblasen: see *blasen*.

verblassen: see *blaß*.

verbleichen: see *bleich*.

verblenden

verblendet sein to be blinded, dazzled; since MHG, e.g. *Mystiker* [edit. Pf.] 1,33 or Luther Bible transl. Matth. 23,24; in erotic contexts also used for 'to be infatuated'. Transit. *jem.* ~ since Early NHG, e.g. H.Sachs [edit. K.] 1,238. Hence *die Verblendung*, general since the 18th c., sometimes as *Augenverblendung*.

verbleuen

jem. ~ (coll.) to thrash sb.; wrongly assumed by some to be connected with *blau* (as in *jem. blau schlagen*), but derived from *bleuen* = 'to beat', for which see p. 341; figur. only when the

'beating' refers to defeating in an argument or a game, but this would be unusual.

verblüffen: see *elf*.

verblühen: see *blühen*.

verblümen: see *Blume*.

verbluten: see *Blut*.

verbocken: see *Bock*.

verbohrt: see *bohren*.

verborgen: see *verbergen*.

verbösern: see *Essig*.

verbost: see *böse*.

verboten: see *verbieten*.

verbrämen

etw. ~ to veil sth., give a better appearance to sth. (e.g. by using a euphemism); derived from *brämen* (or *bremen*) = 'to adorn sth. with a brim, decorate or embellish sth.'; figur. with abstracts since the 16th c., *Verbrämung* only since the modern period. See also under *Nibelungen* (for *mit Nibelungentreue verbrämt*).

verbrauchen

verbraucht aussehen to look worn-out, exhausted; with ref. to language since the 18th c. for 'hackneyed', with ref. to persons since the 19th c.

verbrausen: see *brausen*.

verbrechen

etw. ~ (obs.) to destroy sth.; with abstracts since MHG, e.g. *Passional* [edit. H.] 301 and 383; with ref. to words = 'to corrupt, mutilate' still in the 17th c., now obs.

er hat etw. verbrochen (1) he has committed a crime; first in purely legal contexts, generalised since the 17th c., e.g. Klopstock, *Mess.* 8,316 referring to Jesus: '*aber dieser hat nichts verbrochen*'.

er hat etw. verbrochen (2) (coll.) he has perpetrated sth. bad, tasteless, laughable; half-joc. coll. version of the previous entry, e.g. *wer hat dieses schreckliche Gedicht verbrochen?*

← See also under *abfassen* (for *einen Verbrecher abfassen*), *anlegen* (for *ein Verbrechen anlegen*), *begehen* (for *ein Verbrechen begehen*), *beistecken* (for *einen Verbrecher beistecken*), *Schuld* (for *mit Verbrechen belastet . . .*) and *schwarz* (for *schwarzes Verbrechen*).

verbreiten

etw. ~ to spread sth.; with abstracts such as *Neuigkeiten, Nachrichten* etc. since the 18th c.; with ref. to people also used for 'to disperse'.

sich ~ to spread, diffuse, propagate itself; since the 18th c., when *Verbreitung* (figur.) also arose; hence also *sich über ein Thema* ~ = 'to go into much detail about some subject', modern.

verbrennen

sich das Maul (den Mund, die Schnauze) ~ to say too much; since the 17th c., first with *Maul*, f.r.b. Steinbach [1734], e.g. Weise, *Erzn.* 47 [1673].

← See also under *Finger* (for *sich die Finger*

verbrennen), *Hirn* (for *hirnverbrannt*), *Politik* (for *Politik der verbrannten Erde*) and *tun* (for *tut nichts, der Jude wird verbrannt*).

verbriefen: see *Brief.*

verbringen

etw. ~ to waste, get through sth.; mainly with ref. to *Geld, Vermögen*, etc., since MHG (cf. Diefenbach, *Gloss.* 187a); now only in some regions, elsewhere displaced by *durchbringen, vergeuden* or *verschwenden.*

nichts ~ (a.) to achieve nothing; Adelung recorded '*mit aller Mühe nichts verbringen*', where *erreichen* or *vollbringen* would now be used; see also *es zu nichts bringen* on p. 399.

etw. nicht ~ *können* (regional) to be unable or unwilling to bear or endure sth.; e.g. Rosegger, *Waldh.* 2,287: '. . . *einer, der das Gutsein nicht verbringen kann*'; little recorded, not mentioned in *DWb.* [1886].

verbröckeln: see *Brocken.*

verbrodeln: see *brodeln.*

verbrüdern: see *Bruder.*

verbrüten: see *Brut.*

verbummeln: see *bummeln* (also under *Genie*).

verbürgen: see *Bürge.*

verbuttern

sein Geld ~ (coll.) to spend one's money (wastefully or injudiciously); since the 20th c. (not yet mentioned in *DWb.* [1886]); cf. similar compounds listed under *Butter.*

Verdacht

See under *aufsteigen* (for *es steigt einem der Verdacht auf*), *beschleichen* (for *ein Verdacht beschleicht mich*) and *ertränken* (for *der Wein ertränke den Verdacht*).

verdächtig: see *Gevatter.*

verdammen

etw. (abstract) *verdammt ihn* sth. condemns him; with abstracts since the 18th c., e.g. Gotter 1,455 on posterity: '*vergessen bleibt, wen die verdammt*', Schiller, *M.Stuart* 1,7: '*Mord würde . . . keineswegs mich verdammen*'; the part.pass. *verdammt* became an adj. in curses for 'accursed, damned' in the 18th c., e.g. Goethe, *Faust I,* 2464: '*verdammtes Thier!*', later used adverbially as an intensifier, e.g. *es ist verdammt kalt* (coll.).

← See also under *Herz* (for *so uns unser Herz verdammet*) and *Pflicht* (for *verdammte Pflicht*).

verdampfen

etw. ~ (rare) to let sth. evaporate or abate; in lit. since the 19th c., e.g. Gutzkow, *Nov.u.Sk.* 5: '. . . *den Ärger wieder verdampfen*'; *verdämpfen* is also possible.

← See also under *Dampf* (for intransitive *verdampfen*).

verdanken: see *Dank* and *entsumpfen.*

verdauen

das kann er nicht ~ (regional coll.) he cannot get over that; with ref. to losses, disappoint-

ments, etc. in some regions; recorded since the 19th c.

← See also under *Bissen* (for *harte Bissen verdauen müssen*), *heiß* (for *Haus und Hof verdauen*), *Magen* (for *unverdaut im Magen liegen*) and *Stein* (for *du verdeust auch steinen heuser*).

verdecken

etw. (abstract) *verdeckt etw.*- sth. hides sth.; figur. since the 18th c., e.g. (DWb) Wieland 37,50; also *jem.m etw.* ~ = 'to hide sth. from sb.' (used by Goethe) and *etw.* ~ = 'to hide sth. (abstract)' since the 17th c., e.g. Schuppius, 694: '*viel verdeckten . . . ihr unglückseligkeit*'. *verdeckt* obscured, masked, disguised, concealed; since Early NHG, e.g. Luther 1,378b (Jena) and *Tischr.* 1,77 (where in both cases *verdackt* is used), as *verdeckt* since the 17th c. For 'obscure, cryptic, hidden' Luther used *verdeckt* in Apocr. transl. Wisd. of Sol. 8,8 and in Bible transl. 2 Cor. 4,3 (where the A.V. used 'hid').

verdenken

ich kann es ihm nicht ~ I cannot blame him for that, I cannot hold it against him (that he . . .); derived from *jem.* ~ = 'to think badly of sb.', since OHG (*firdenkjan*), with accusative still in Early NHG, since the 18th c. with the dative, e.g. Lessing [edit. L.] 3,43: '*so kann ich es ihm freilich nicht verdenken, daß . . .*'.

← See also under *Hals* (for *man könnte mir die Recension verdenken*).

verderben

See under *Appetit* (for *jem.m den Appetit zu* or *an etw. verderben*), *ausstreuen* (for *Dummheit und Verderb ausstreuen*), *Beispiel* (for *böse Beispiele verderben gute Sitten*), *Brei* (for *den Brei verderben*), *durchführen* (for *verdorben sein etw. durchzuführen*), *Ehre* (for *besser ehrlich gestorben als schändlich verdorben*), *Ei* (for *ein faules Ei verdirbt den ganzen Brei*), *einbrechen* (for *das Verderben bricht ein*), *gedeihen* (for *auf Gedeih und Verderb*), *Grund* (for *aus dem Grund verdorben* and *grundverdorben*), *rennen* (for *in sein Verderben rennen*), *Spiel* (for *jem.m das Spiel verderben*) and *Unkraut* (for *Unkraut verdirbt nicht*).

verdeutschen: see *deutsch.*

verdichten: see *dicht.*

verdienen

einen Namen ~ to deserve or be entitled to be given a (certain) name or title; since the 18th c., e.g. Lessing 7,142, often in the negative, e.g. Lessing 6,436: '*alles andre . . . verdienet diesen Namen nicht*' (also Herder 2,3).

seine ersten Brötchen ~ (coll.) to be in one's first job, start to earn one's living; 20th c. coll.

← See also under *ausputzen* (for *Unmacht zu einem Verdienst ausputzen*), *behandeln* (for *jem. nach seinem Verdienst behandeln*), *Brot* (for *bei jem.m sein Brot verdienen*), *einfassen* (for *er verdient in Gold eingefaßt zu werden*), *Galgen* (for *er verdient den Galgen*), *Kette* (for *wie sich Verdienst und*

Glück verketten), *Krone* (for *dem Verdienste seine Kronen*), *kuppeln* (for *sich einen Kuppelpelz verdienen*), *Salz* (for *er verdient nicht das Salz in der Suppe*) and *Sporn* (for *sich seine Sporen verdienen*).

Verdikt
das ~ verdict; loan from Engl. (early 19th c.); at first only in legal contexts, then generalised for '(negative) judgment, considered opinion', since middle of the 19th c., often in *ein* ~ *fällen* = 'to pronounce judgment, state one's considered opinion'.

verdoktern: see *Doktor*.

verdolmetschen: see *Dolmetsch*.

verdonnern: see *Donner*.

verdoppeln
da müßte ich mich ~ (coll.) there would have to be two of me (to cope with all this work); modern, e.g. Bismarck, *Red.* 7,21 with ref. to a load of work: '. . . *kann er sich nicht nur verdoppeln, sondern verzehnfachen*'; cf. Platen 4,278: '*jedes Hindernis erscheint verdoppelt*'.

verdorren
etw. verdorrt sth. withers or fades away; since the 18th c., e.g. Schiller, *Fiesco* 4,14: '. . . *verdorret das zarte Pflänzchen der Liebe*', Chamisso 4,147: '*das Herz ist allem Menschlichen verdorrt*'.

← See also under *ausschlagen* (for *aus der entlaubten, verdorrten Seele wird ein neuer Leib ausschlagen*).

verdrängen
jem. ~ to push sb. aside, oust or displace sb.; at least since the 18th c., e.g. Lessing, *Dram.* 34. See also under *drängen* for similar *jem. an die Wand*, or *beiseite, beiseits, seitwärts* or *zur Seite drängen*.

etw. ~ (psych.) to repress sth.; since the 20th c. with ref. to mental processes; hence also *Verdrängung* = 'repression'.

verdrehen
jem.m das Wort im Mund ~ to twist sb.'s words; since Early NHG with *verkehren* or *umkehren*, then with *umdrehen* and only in modern period recorded with ~, but this is deceptive, since *Wortverdreher* has been current since the 17th c. and *Wortverdrehung* since the 18th c.

jem.m den Kopf ~ to steal sb.'s heart, cause sb. to become infatuated, bowl sb. over; since the 19th c., e.g. Keller, *Werke* 6,278: '. . . *verdreht ihr den Kopf*'.

verdreht twisted, warped, crazy; since the 18th c., e.g. *ein verdrehter Kerl* = 'a crazy individual', as in Wildenbruch, *Quitzows* 1,8.

der Rechtsverdreher (1) shyster, sb. who twists the law; since ca. 1800, e.g. (DWb) Arnim, *Schaub.* 2,335 [1840]. Cf. also Schiller, *Kab.u.L.* 2,3: '*kann der Herzog Gesetze der Menschheit verdrehen?*'.

der Rechtsverdreher (2) (joc. coll.) lawyer; from the above in joc. coll. since the beginning of the 20th c.

← See also under *drechseln* (for *den Sinn verdrehen*) and *Gehirn* (for *sein Gehirn ist verdreht*).

verdreschen: see *dreschen*.

verdringen
jem. ~ (obs.) to displace sb.; still general in the 18th c., e.g. Lessing 3,423: '*dessen Zuname . . . durch einen andern verdrungen ward*', also Schiller, *D.Carlos* 2,9; obs., displaced by *verdrängen* (see above).

verdrücken
etw. ~ (coll.) to consume sth., put sth. away (with gusto or quickly); with ref. to food, e.g. *er hat's schnell verdrückt* = 'he gobbled it up'; modern coll., but ultimately derived from ~ = 'to put down, keep or hold down, defeat, hold in subjection', current from Early NHG until the 19th c.

← See also under *drücken* (for *sich verdrücken*).

verduckt: see *ducken*.

verdudeln
die Zeit ~ (regional coll.) to waste one's time, pass one's time in idleness; Wülcker in *DWb.* [1886] reported to have heard it in the Wetterau, I know it as current in Darmstadt; derived from *dudeln* = 'to make (bad) music, tootle, sing tunelessly'.

verduften
etw. verduftet sth. evaporates; figur. since the 18th c., e.g. Schiller, *Wall.Lager* 11. Also used reflex., as in Wieland 10,22 (as *verdüften*).

(sich) ~ (coll.) to make oneself scarce, slink away, disappear; since the 19th c., e.g. (DWb) Gutzkow, *Nov.u.Sk.* 141; it can be used both intransitively and as a reflex. verb.

verdummen: see *dumm*.

Verdumpfung: see *bezähmen* (for history also under *dumpf*).

verdunkeln
etw. ~ (1) (lit.) to darken sth., put sth. in the shade, obscure or cloud sth.; since Early NHG, f.r.b. Maaler [1561]: '*eim sein lob und eer verdüncklen*', Möser, *Osnab.* 1,256 [1780]: '*handelnde . . . Leute mußten geschwind die Landbesitzer verdunkeln*', Voß, *Odyssee* 16,212 [1806]: '*einen sterblichen Menschen zu verherrlichen – und zu verdunkeln*'; also in intrans. constructions = 'to become dark, cease to shine', e.g. Luther Bible transl. 1 Sam. 3,3: '*ehe die lampe Gottes verdunkelt*', also reflex., figur. since the 18th c., often with ref. to facial expressions but also such abstracts as *Zunkunft; sich verdüstern* can also be used.

etw. ~ (2) (legal) to obscure sth.; since Early NHG, e.g. Luther 5,288 (Jena); often now with ref. to criminal activities, also in the noun *Verdunklung*.

verdünnen
etw. verdünnt etw. sth. dilutes, waters down sth. else; since the 18th c., frequent with abstracts esp. in Jean Paul's writings; also used reflex. since late in the 18th c.

verdünnisieren: see *dünn*.

verdunsten

etw. verdunstet or *verdünstet* sth. evaporates; since the 18th c., e.g. by Wieland who also used it as a transitive verb for 'to let sth. evaporate, disperse sth.'

verdursten

etw. verdurstet (or *verdürstet*) (lit.) sth. dries up, becomes parched, withers; since ca. 1800 with abstracts, e.g. Rückert, *Ges. Ged.* 2,353: '*meine arme Liebe muß verdürsten*'.

verdüstern: see *düster* (also above under *verdunkeln*).

verebben: see *Ebbe*.

verebenen

etw. ~ (regional) to straighten sth. out, settle sth.; in some regions, esp. with such nouns as *Streit*, *Zwist*, also *eine Rechnung*; recorded since the 19th c., e.g. by Schmeller for Bav.

Verein: see *Meier*.

vereinen: see *Eisen* and *Herd*.

verekeln: see *Ekel*.

verengen: see *Kreis*.

vererden: see *Erde*.

verfädelt: see *Faden*.

verfahren

Todes ~ (obs.) to die; from Early NHG to the 19th c., still used by Jean Paul and Kotzebue; now obs.

mit etw. ~ to deal with sth.; since Early NHG.

mit jem.m (+ adverb) *~* to deal with sb. in a certain way; since Early NHG; in the early periods the simplex sufficed (see under *fahren*, p. 711).

den Karren ~ (coll.) to get things in a mess, make a botch of things; *~* for 'to go wrong' goes back to Early NHG, to be found e.g. in Keisersberg; the phrase with *Karren* established itself in the 19th c., e.g. Lenau, *S. Werke* [edit. B.] 428.

das Verfahren the procedure, in legal contexts proceedings; recorded since the beginning of the 18th c., e.g. Lessing 1,555.

← See also under *Cour* (for *behutsam verfahren*), *Deckel* (for *betrügerisches Verfahren*), *einleiten* (for *ein Verfahren gegen jem. einleiten*) and *Happen* (for *zu happig mit jem.m verfahren*).

verfallen

auf etw. ~ to conceive the (strange, wrong) idea of . . . ; since the 18th c., f.r.b. Steinbach [1734], e.g. Klopstock, *Werke* 12,159: '*wie konnten sie darauf verfallen, daß . . .*', where *ver-* supplies the notion of wrongness or inappropriateness.

← See also under *blühen* (for *durch die Zeit verfallen*), *gut* (for *der Herrschaft verfallen sein*), *Hals* (for *jem.s Hals ist verfallen*) and *herunterkommen* (for *in Verfall der Kräfte kommen*), also under *fallen* (p. 716) for the older form *vorvallen*.

verfangen: see *geben*, *Hase* and *schaffen*.

verfänglich

verfänglich tricky, awkward, embarrassing (or possibly) incriminating; in this sense only since the 17th c., f.r.b. Stieler [1691].

verfassen

etw. ~ to create, write, compose sth. derived from *etw. in Gestalt*, *in Worte*, *in ein Bild fassen* (see p. 734). Early examples with *~* are rare, but Luther used it in his Bible transl. Daniel 7,1, although in its modern sense it was not recorded before Frisch [1741].

verfaulwitzt: see *Hahn*.

verfechten

etw. ~ to fight or stand up for sth., defend sth.; since Early NHG, e.g. Franck, *Sprichw.* 107 [1541].

verfemen: see *Feme*.

verfesseln: see *Fessel*.

verfilzt: see *Filz*.

verfinstern: see *Bruder* and *finster* (also for *Verfinsterung*).

verflachen

verflachen to become shallow; with abstracts since the 18th c., e.g. Börne 1,48: '. . . *den verflachten Worten und Thaten*'; hence *die Verflachung*, e.g. Devrient, *Schausp.* 3,239: '*von Kotzebue datiert der Krebs der Verflachung . . . in der Schauspielkunst*'; see also p. 802 for *in Flachheit ausarten*.

verflackern

verflackern (intrans.) to die away; with ref. to the slow extinction of abstracts or persons since the 19th c., e.g. Beck, *Lieder v.a.M.* 257 [1846]: '. . . *daß der Theure rasch verflackert und verdirbt*'.

verflattern: see *flattern* and *flimmern*.

verflechten

verflochten (1) (lit.) bound together, intimately connected, entwined; since the 17th c., e.g. Herder, *Cid* 12: '*so verflochten ist ihr Herz*'; also used reflex. since the 17th c.

verflochten (2) (lit.) entangled, in confusion; frequent in Goethe's writings; cf. *das verworren Geflecht* on p. 810.

← See also under *Knäuel* (for *das Gefühl ist der verflochtene Knäuel*).

verfliegen: see *fest* and *Mücke*.

verfließen

etw. verfließt (lit.) sth. passes (away), goes by, vanishes; since the 17th c., often with ref. to *Zeit* and frequent in the past participle *verflossen*, e.g. Grimmelshausen, *Simpliz.* [edit. K.] 2,182: '*nach verflossenem küßmonat*'.

Dinge ~ things become indistinct; with ref. to things which become blurred, spread, diffused or lose firm definition as in the case of colours which 'run', or things can merge as in *ineinander ~*, often with *Grenze*; Campe [1811] recorded it in its figur. sense. He also listed *verflößen = verfließen machen*, which was still current in the 19th c., but is now obs.

seine verflossene Freundin (coll.) his ex-girl-friend; 20th c. coll. Also used as a noun: *seine Verflossene* (coll.).

verflittern: see *Flitter*.

verflößen: see *verfließen*.

verflucht: see *nähen*.

verflüchtigen: see *Flucht*.

verfluten: see *Flut*.

verfolgen

etw. ~ (1) to follow or observe sth.; with ref. to events which one 'follows' with one's eyes or 'goes after'; since the 18th c., e.g. Lessing 11,457: '*so wird er . . . auf mancherlei Spuren gerathen, aber keine verfolgen*'.

etw. ~ (2) to pursue sth.; mainly with ref. to studies; since the 18th c., e.g. Goethe, *Gesch.m.bot.Stud.*: '*die ganze Botanik, deren Studium wir so emsig verfolgten*'.

etw. ~ (3) (legal) to proceed with a charge in some matter; since the 18th c., f.r.b. Frisch [1741]. Hence *jem.* ~ = 'to prosecute sb.'.

jem. ~ to persecute sb.; since MHG, e.g. Luther Bible transl. Matth. 5,44 and Deuter. 28,45 (Mentel's Bible transl. still used '*jagen und leidigen*'). Abstracts can be the subject, e.g. Luther Bible transl. Prov. 13,21: '*unglück verfolgt die sünder*' (cf. Schiller, *Räuber* 3,2: '*das Unglück verfolgte mich*'), but an abstract can also be the object, since Early NHG, e.g. Luther, *Adel d.Nat.* (repr.) 80: '*die warheit verfolgen*'; cf. also *hinausverfolgen*, used by Lessing, and the numerous compounds with *Verfolgung*, e.g. *Christenverfolgung, Judenverfolgung*.

etw. verfolgt mich sth. haunts me; at least since the 18th c., e.g. Auerbach, *Ab.* 187: '*mitten in die ernstesten Studien hinein verfolgte ihn diese trübe Ahnung*'; often with *der Gedanke* as the subject.

der Verfolgungswahn (psych.) persecution mania; since the 19th c., when *DWb.* [1886] recorded it as *Verfolgungswahnsinn*.

← See also under *Kurs* (for *einen Kurs verfolgen*) and *Spur* (for *eine Spur verfolgen*).

verfrachten

jem. ~ (coll.) to bundle sb. off, get rid of sb.; 20th c. coll.

verfranzen: see *Franz*.

verfremden

verfremden (theatr.) to alienate or distance; in this sense only since the 20th c., much used in connexion with Brecht's theories on the mission of drama; hence also *Verfremdungseffekt* = 'alienation or distancing effect'.

verfroren

~ *sein* to be sensitive to cold; since the 18th c., recorded by Adelung; cf. the note on 'absence of embarrassment' in *unverfroren* (p. 856).

verführen

jem. ~ to seduce sb.; both in sexual contexts as well as in cases where 'leading astray' is meant; since Early NHG, e.g. Luther, *Adel d.Nat.* (repr.)

11; cf. note on *führen* in this sense (p. 873); hence also *sich* ~ *lassen*, since Early NHG. It can also be used for gentle 'seduction' to do sth. which he/she had not previously intended, e.g. *darf ich Sie zu einem Spaziergang* ~ ? f.r.b. Adelung [1780].

← See also under *Gewissen* (for *wenn man verführt oder angeführt wurde*) and *Labyrinth* (for *jem. in ein Labyrinth verführen*).

verführerisch: see *glatt*.

verfuhrwerken

sich ~ (coll.) to slip up, say the wrong thing; also 'to make a mess of things (esp. in business matters, when it can mean the same as *sich verkalkulieren*); since the 19th c., recorded by Wander [1876]; see for similar verbs under *Fuhrwerk* (p. 877).

vergaffen

sich in etw. ~ to become infatuated by sth.; originally 'to lose one's control through the sight of sth.'; since the 18th c. (Goethe, Wieland).

← See also under *gaffen* (for *sich in jem. vergaffen*) and *heute* (for *er ist so vergafft in sie*).

vergällen: see *Galle*.

vergaloppieren: see *Galopp*.

Vergangenheit

eine Frau mit ~ a woman with a (questionable) past; euphemistic omission of an adjective; 20th c.

← See also under *einholen* (for *die Vergangenheit einholen*), *Gespenst* (for *holdes Gespenst der Vergangenheit*), *Gold* (for *das Mattgold der Vergangenheit*), *Gras* (for *manches Stück Vergangenheit*), *Mehl* (for *Wurmmehl und Spinneweb der Vergangenheit*) and *unbewältigt* (for *die unbewältigte Vergangenheit*).

vergänglich: see *Dampf*.

Vergasung

bis zur ~ (coll.) ad nauseam; 20th c. coll.; not connected originally with the holocaust, but a chem. term to describe heating a material, such as coal, to the point when it becomes gasified. This was extended to mean 'to the highest pitch', then 'until it becomes unbearable' (1st quarter of the 20th c.). The association with processes of extermination practised in the Third Reich now inclines careful and sensitive speakers to avoid the phrase.

vergattern

die Wache ~ (mil., obs.) to instruct the guard; derived from ~ = 'to call together', still recorded in this sense by Adelung [1780], which belongs to *gattern* = 'to collect' (cf. Engl. 'to gather'). Now obs.

jem. zu etw. ~ (coll.) to ask or order sb. to do sth.; mainly with ref. to allotting sb. a disagreeable task, sometimes intended as a punishment; modern coll.

vergeben

(*das ist*) ~ *und vergessen* that is forgiven and forgotten, all over and done with; from *jem.m* ~

= 'to forgive sb.', since MHG; coupled with *vergessen* since Early NHG, e.g. Luther 7,33.

jem. mit Gift ~ (obs.) to poison sb.; since MHG, still used in the 18th c., e.g. Lessing 1,308 and 7,133, now obs.

sich ~ to deal (cards) wrongly; *ver-* here indicating a faulty action; f.r.b. Adelung.

sich nichts ~ not lose face, to suffer no loss of respect; from the original sense of ~ = 'to give away, lose'; since the 18th c., e.g. Freytag, *Verl.Hand.* 2,356; '*die Sorge . . . ist die, daß wir uns nichts vergeben*'; cf. also the adj. ~ = 'wasted, thrown-away, useless', beginnings in MHG.

← See also under *Beichte* (for *wie man beichtet, so wird einem vergeben*), *Hand* (for *meine Hand ist vergeben*), *Karte* (for *die Karten sind noch nicht ganz vergeben*), *Mal* (for *einmal stehet zu vergeben*) and *Sünde* (for *diese Sünde vergibt dir der Küster*).

vergebens
See under *dumm* (for *mit der Dummheit kämpfen Götter selbst vergebens*), *glatt* (for *vergebens brauchst du deine glatten Worte*), *Leber* (for *vergebens ist uns nicht die Leber einverleibet*), *Maul* (for *jem.m vergebens um das Maul gehen*) and *Mond* (for *nicht vergebens*).

vergehen
alles vergeht (or *ist vergänglich*) everything perishes or passes away; s.e. and international, to be found in Classical writers and in the Bible; cf. also such proverbs as *wenn alles vergeht, Tugend besteht* (recorded by Wander).

da vergeht einem der Spaß that ruins one's pleasure; nouns such as *Zeit, Lust, Zorn, Schmerz* or *Spaß* have been used with ~ = 'to pass away, disappear' since Early NHG.

sich ~ to go astray; since Early NHG, at first mainly with ref. to errors, later chiefly to immoral or criminal behaviour; hence *das Vergehen* = 'misdemeanour, crime, offence', only since the 18th c., e.g. Lessing (edit. L.) 2,2.

← See also under *anklingen* (for *der Anklang vergangener Zeiten*), *halten* (for *bis der Zorn vergeht*), *Herbst* (for *dem groß alle fräud und mut vergehet*), *hören* (for *dabei vergeht einem Hören und Sehen*), *Löwe* (for *die Lust vergeht*), *Rauch* (for *vergehen wie Rauch*), *Rede* (for *die Rede vergeht ihm*) and *Traum* (for *vergehen wie im Traum*).

vergeigen
er hat seine Prüfung vergeigt (sl.) he has failed his examination or test; also in sport. sl. for 'to lose the game'; recent sl.

Vergeltung: see *Rache*.

vergessen: forget
sich ~ to behave improperly; since MHG, e.g. *Marienlegenden* 129: '*swenne ir ûch vergezzet und daz obez ezzet*'. Cf. *sich selbst* ~ = 'to be unselfish, set one's own interests aside', which expresses an entirely different notion.

sich selbst nicht ~ to look after one's own interests, after number one; this is modern but

belongs to *sich nicht* ~ *mit etw.* = 'to provide oneself with sth.', since Early NHG, e.g. Fischart, *Garg.* (repr.) 81.

Vergißmeinnichtaugen (lit.) light-blue eyes; used by Schiller in *Kab.u.L.* 2,4.

← See also under *ändern* (for *glücklich ist, wer vergißt, was nicht mehr zu ändern ist*), *Atem* (for *zu atmen vergessen*), *bescheren* (for *vergiß das Zuknöpfen nicht*), *blitzen* (for *das unbegreifliche Vergessen*), *Graben* (for *den kommenden Tag vergessen*), *Traum* (for *vergessen wie ein Traum*) and *vergeben* (for *vergessen und vergeben*).

Vergessenheit
See under *fallen* (for *in Vergessenheit fallen*), *geraten* (for *in Vergessenheit geraten*) and *greis* (for *die flügelschnelle Zeit wird Vergessenheit*).

vergewaltigen
etw. ~ (lit.) to do violence to sth., murder sth.; with abstracts since the 17th c.

vergießen
Blut ~ to shed or spill blood; since Early NHG, frequent in Luther's writings, also in his Bible and Apocr. transl. (although he also used *Blut stürzen*, for which see p. 358); hence also the noun *das Blutvergießen*. See also under *Blut* (for *verbluten*).

← See also under *Träne* (for *Tränen vergießen*.

vergiften: see *Gesicht* and *Gift*.

verglast: see *ausbrennen*.

Vergleich
mit einem ~ *enden* (or *beigelegt werden*) to end in agreement, settlement or compromise; mostly at first in legal language; since the 17th c., f.r.b. Stieler [1691]; earlier in *sich mit jem.m vergleichen* = 'to come to an agreement with sb.', since the 16th c.

kein Vergleich (coll.) no comparison, nothing like it; younger than *ohne Vergleich*, f.r.b. Heinsius (1818), and *über allen Vergleich*, which is now obs. Cf. *unvergleichbar* = 'incomparable', since the 18th c. (Goethe, Herder).

← See also under *abfallen* (for *abfallen im Vergleich zu etw.*), *aufdunsen* (for *aufgedunsene Vergleichungen*), *heranziehen* (for *etw. zum Vergleich heranziehen*), *hinken* (for *vergleichendes Urteil*, where *der Vergleich hinkt* should have been listed), *Johannes* (for *Euch, ihr Johannistriebe, vergleich ich meine Liebe*), *mager* (for *ein magerer Vergleich ist besser als ein fetter Prozeß*) and *Natur* (for *in Vergleichung mit etw.*).

verglimmen: see *glimmen* and *glühen*.

verglühen
etw. verglüht sth. fades, burns out; with abstracts since the 18th c. Adelung quoted from Weiße (no details): '*glaubst du, die Raserey wird je in ihr verglühn?*'. Campe [1811] added Goethe's unusual '*du verglühst in dir selbst*' = 'you destroy yourself through the heat of your passion' (though Campe misquoted this and printed *an* instead of *in*).

vergnügt: see *Bein*.

Vergnügungsport: see *einlaufen*.

vergolden

See under *Feuer* (for *nicht im Feuer vergoldet*), *Finger* (for *du kannst dir deine Finger vergolden lassen*, further discussed under *Gold* on p. 1098) and *Gold* (for *ein Vergolder mit ästhetischem Mattgold*).

vergöttern: see *Gott*.

vergötzen: see *Götze* and *Opfer*.

vergraben

sich in seine Bücher ~ to immerse oneself in one's studies, bury oneself in one's library; since the 18th c.; Lessing 3,18 used *immer unter Büchern* ~ *sein*.

← See also under *graben* (for several idioms), *Nabob* (for *den Mammon ängstlich vergraben*) and *Pfund* (for *sein Pfund vergraben*).

vergreifen

sich an jem.m ~ to lay hands on, attack, assault, violate sb.; since Early NHG, frequent in Luther Bible transl., e.g. Gen. 37,27.

sich an etw. ~ to misappropriate sth.; with ref. to money = 'to steal or embezzle'; since Early NHG in many contexts describing 'harming, damaging, treating badly or irreverently'.

sich in etw. ~ to choose or use the wrong thing or method; since Early NHG, e.g. Megenberg, *Buch d.N.* [edit. P.] 91 with ref. to selecting the wrong medicine; now often with ref. to such abstracts as *Ausdruck* or *Ton*, e.g. Lessing, *Em. Gal.* 5,7: '*die Natur . . . vergriff sich im Thone*'.

vergriffen sold out, out of print; from comm. jargon meaning originally that too many customers have 'grabbed' sth.; recorded since Adelung [1780]. – Note that *vergriffen* can also occur for *abgegriffen* = 'well-thumbed, showing traces of frequent use' (Goethe used it in this sense).

← See also under *greifen* (for *vergriffene Sprachmünze*) and *Ton* (for *sich im Ton vergreifen*).

vergreisen: see *Greis*.

vergrimmt

vergrimmt (rare) angry, furious; recorded since the 16th c., now displaced by *ergrimmt*; *vergrollt* can also be used, e.g. with *Gemüt* (Bürger used *vergröllt* in this sense).

vergröbern

etw. ~ to coarsen sth.; with abstracts since the 17th c., used by Lessing and Goethe, recorded by Kramer in his *Hoch-Nider-Teutsch. Wb.* [1719].

vergrollt: see *vergrimmt*.

vergrößern

etw. ~ to increase, enlarge, widen or extend sth.; with abstracts since the 17th c., recorded by Stieler [1691].

← See also under *Glas* (for *Vergrößerungsglas*).

sich ~ (coll.) to extend one's premises, move to a bigger house; modern. Similarly, *sich verkleinern* for the opposite, also modern coll.

vergründet: see *Grund*.

vergrünen

vergrünen (lit., rare) to wither, perish; since MHG, but with abstracts only since the 17th c., recorded by Stieler [1691]: '*die schönheit vergrünt bald*'; *verblühen* and *verwelken* have displaced it.

vergurgeln: see *Gurgel*.

verhacken

jem.m den Weg ~ (rare) to block sb.'s path; since the 18th c.; F.H.Jacobi used it with *Paß*. See under *Paß* for alternatives such as *den Paß verhauen*, *verlegen* and *verschneiden*.

verhackstücken

etw. or *jem.* ~ (coll.) to make mincemeat of sth. or sb.; with ref. to severe criticism, thorough condemnation and cruel exposure of weaknesses; 20th c. coll. (mainly in N.).

jem.m etw. ~ (coll.) to spell sth. out to sb. (in great detail); 20th c. coll. (mainly in N.).

verhaften

mit (or *in*) *etw. verhaftet sein* to be rooted in or tied to sth.; belongs to ~ = 'to hold or tie together', since MHG, though then and still in Early NHG (e.g. in Luther) as *verheften*; now often with *Herkommen*, *Tradition*, *Gewohnheit* or *Zeit*; *jem.* ~ = 'to arrest sb.' is an off-shoot from this, f.r.b. Stieler [1691].

jem.m verhaftet sein (obs.) to be committed or under an obligation to sb.; from *sich* ~, frequent in *seine Hand* ~, as in Luther Bible transl. e.g. Prov. 6,1 and 22,26 (where the A.V. has 'be surety'); recorded by Adelung and still quite usual in the 18th c., e.g. Herder, *Br. z. Bef. d. Hum.* 3,28: '. . . *von Freunden . . . Gefälligkeiten annehmen . . . daß man ihnen verhaftet werde*'; now *verpflichtet* would be used.

verhageln

See under *Gesicht*, *gucken* and *Hagel* (for examples of *jem.m ist die Petersilie verhagelt*).

verhallen

etw. verhallt (lit.) sth. fades away, vanishes; in phys. contexts with *Stimme*, *Donner* and other natural phenomena; figur. only since the 18th c., e.g. in Herder or in Schiller, *Glocke* 424: '. . . *daß alles Irdische verhallt*'.

verhalten

jem. ~ (a.) to hide sb.; from ~ = 'to keep locked, hold back', since Early NHG, f.r.b. Maaler [1561], still used in the 19th c., e.g. Freytag, *Bilder* 1,178: '. . . *verhielt ihn heimlich*'. Hence also the adjective ~ = 'held back, suppressed' with ref. to feelings, tears, etc.

sich ~ to behave, conduct oneself (in a certain way); first with a noun in the genitive (since Early NHG), later with an adverb, f.r.b. Steinbach [1734], e.g. *sich still, neutral* ~.

so verhält sich's that's how things stand; since

the 18th c., e.g. Schiller, *Wall. Tod* 4,2: '*verhält sich's, wie Ihr sprecht . . .*'.

← See also under *abwarten* (for *sich abwartend verhalten*), *Atem* (for *mit verhaltenem Atem*), *brennen* (for *die verhaltene Abendglut*), *einholen* (for *Verhaltungsbefehle einholen*) and *halten* (for *sich recht verhalten*).

Verhältnis

das ~ relationship; frequent only since Herder, Goethe, Wieland and Kant who used it in many different contexts, but see next entry.

sein (ihr) ~ his (her) lover, girl (man); this is modern, but in Early NHG there are rare instances where ~ means 'person with whom one has a (helpful) relationship', e.g. (DWb) Melissus, *Ps.* N2b: '*du bist mein verhaltnis, du wirst mich . . . behüten*'.

die Verhältnisse conditions, circumstances, situation, means; only since the 18th c., f.r.b. Adelung [1780]; often with *leben*, e.g. *in beschränkten Verhältnissen leben* = 'to live in modest circumstances', *über seine Verhältnisse leben* = 'to live beyond one's means'.

← See also under *breit* (for *in einem breiteren Verhältnis stehen*), *Chaos* (for *chaotische Verhältnisse*), *drei* (for *das dreieckige Verhältnis*), *Mauer* (for *die Mauer der Verhältnisse*) and *Opfer* (for *ein Opfer der Verhältnisse*).

Verhandlung: see *anbahnen*.

verhängen

jem. verhängt etw. sb. imposes sth.; since Early NHG, e.g. Luther 2,183: '*. . . das Gott diese verfolgung . . . von wegen der sünde der menschen verhengt*'; mainly in legal contexts, e.g. *eine Strafe* ~.

← See also under *Boykott* (for *einen Boykott verhängen*).

verharren

See under *Mauer* (for *monarchisch verharren*) and *Mensch* (for *im Irrtum verharren*).

verhärten

See *hart* (and under *nachsetzen*).

verhaspeln

sich ~ to get muddled or tangled up, stumble over a word; since Early NHG, e.g. Keisersberg, *Post.* 185 [1522]: '*du bist verhasplet . . . mit zeitlichen sorgen*' (where *verstrickt in etw.* is the sense); reflex. much later, but mainly in coll. use.

verhaßt

See under *malen* (for *verhaßter Brief*) and *müssen* (for *das verhaßte Müssen*).

verhauchen

den Geist ~ (lit.) to give up the ghost, expire; euphem., since the 18th c.; *aushauchen*, for which see p. 135, is older and still preferred.

etw. verhaucht (intrans.) sth. fades away, vanishes; since the 18th c.

etw. verhaucht etw. sth. exudes sth.; since the 18th c.

← See also under *hauchen* (for *verhaucht werden*).

verhauen

etw. ~ to make a mess of sth., muck sth. up; in phys. sense used by miners, also by sculptors, then coll. in modern period for faulty activities, also reflex. *sich* ~ = 'to slip up'.

← See also under *Bahn* (for *jem.m die Bahn verhauen*), *Dimension* (for *jem. nach allen Dimensionen verhauen*), *Kunst* (for *jem. nach allen Regeln der Kunst verhauen*) and *Paß* (for *jem.m den Paß verhauen*).

verheben

jem.m etw. ~ (obs.) to forbid sb. sth.; since Early NHG and still in the 19th c., e.g. Rückert 6,350: '*niemand hat's ihm verhoben*', where *verboten* or *verwehrt* would now be used.

verheddern

sich ~ (coll.) to become entangled (in what one wants to say), get stuck; belongs to *Hede* = 'oakum' (and therefore a term from the areas of spinning or weaving like *verhaspelt, verwirrt*); since the 2nd half of the 18th c., sometimes as *verhäddern*, as in Zelter to Goethe (in *Briefw.* 3,364); hence *Verhädderung* (obs.) = 'quarrel, disagreement' (18th c.).

verheeren

etw. ~ (lit.) to destroy sth.; with abstracts only since the 19th c., e.g. (DWb) Platen, 321.

verheerend devastating, terrible; since late in the 19th c. (not yet recorded in *DWb.* [1891]), attacked by some as semantically inappropriate and also criticised when used positively for 'magnificent, marvellous' (e.g. by Th. Mann, *Zauberberg* 1,502).

← See also under *Heer* (for *verheeren* and *verheerend*) and *mähen* (for *der Zeit verheerende Sichel*).

verhehlen

etw. ~ to hide sth.; since Early NHG, e.g. Luther Bible transl. Psalm 40,11 and 2 Sam. 18,13; hence *verhohlen* = 'hidden, secret, surreptitious' and *unverhohlen* = 'frank(ly), open(ly)', since OHG (*unfirholan*).

verheiraten

ich bin mit dir doch nicht verheiratet (coll.) why should I feel obliged to do what you ask? modern coll. expression of refusal, but Goethe used it similarly for 'to be inextricably tied to sth.' with an abstract: '*sind wir nicht auch mit dem Gewissen verheirathet, das wir oft gerne los sein möchten*'.

verheißen

jem. ~ (regional) to scold, upbraid sb., give sb. a telling-off; recorded for some regions since early in the 20th c. (e.g. by Fischer, *Schwäb.Wb.* [1908]), but *jem. kurz und lang heißen*, for which see p. 1282, is older.

verheizen: see *heizen*.

verhetzen: see *hetzen*.

verhext: see *Hexe*.

verhimmeln: see *Himmel*.

verhockt: see *hocken*.

verhoffen: see *Brocken*.

verhöhnen

etw. ~ (lit.) to mock, deride, disparage sth.; in modern sense since Early NHG, f.r.b. Maaler [1561], e.g. Schiller, *M.Stuart* 3,4: '*der Völker Recht in mir verhöhnend*' (cf. the entries on *höhnen* and *hohnsprechen* on p. 1361).

← See also under *nachgeben* (for *ich hab des Herren Bund verhöhnt*).

verhökern

sich ~ (coll.) to sell oneself (or one's services) to the highest bidder; from *etw.* ~ = 'to sell in small quantities, retail', since Early NHG. The reflex. construction is modern coll.

verholzen

See under *Holz*, also under *hart* (for *Verholzung und Verhärtung der Laune*).

Verhör

jem. ins ~ *nehmen* to grill or quiz sb.; the older meanings = 'examination' and 'audience' are now obs., the legal sense = 'interrogation' is now the main one but has been extended to 'grilling' or 'quizzing', since the 18th c.

verhüllen

See under *Blatt* (for *mit Feigenblättern verhüllt*), *Buchstabe* (for *ein Blatt verhüllter Innigkeit*), *Hülle* (for *sein Haupt verhüllen, etw. verhüllen, sich in etw. verhüllen* and *verhüllt*) and *Nebel* (for *sein Bewußtsein verhüllen*).

verhungern

etw. ~ *lassen* (lit.) to starve sth., deprive sth. (abstract) of nourishment; since the 18th c., e.g. Jean Paul, *Lit Nachlaß* 4,133: '. . . *daß er seine Seele verhungern läßt*'.

wir sind schon am Verhungern (coll.) we are starving; modern coll.

jem. am steifen (or *ausgestreckten*) *Arm* ~ *lassen* (coll.) to exert pressure on sb., put the squeeze on sb.; 20th c. coll. threat (mixed with contempt) implying that one has sb. in one's power.

verhungert (lit.) wretched, miserable; since the 18th c., e.g. Lessing [edit. L.] 3,50. – There is also *verhungert aussehen* = 'to look half-starved', modern.

verhunzen

etw. ~ (coll.) to mess sth. up, botch or ruin sth.; only since the 18th c., since before then *verhundasen* expressed the same idea; f.r.b. Steinbach [1734], e.g. Lessing [edit. L.] 6,8. – See also under *aushunzen* for debate on origin.

verhuscht

verhuscht (coll.) shy, timid, self-effacing; belongs to *huschen* = 'to steal, slide or slip away'; used with ref. to persons (esp. children) who have little self-confidence; 20th c. coll.

verhüten

das Verhüterli (joc. coll.) condom; belongs to a group of nouns humorously formed with a Swiss ending such as *Peutêtreli* = 'cigarette-lighter'. 20th c. coll.

← See also under *Himmel* (for *das verhüte der Himmel*).

verhutzelt

verhutzelt (coll.) wizened; derived from *Hutzel* = 'dried or shrivelled (piece of) pear', for which see p. 1392; in lit. since the 19th c., but probably older in some regions.

verirren

ein verirrter Geschmack an out-of-the-way or stray taste, a taste revealing a degree of aberration; with abstracts since the 18th c., with *Geschmack* since the 19th, e.g. (Sp.) Keller, *Salander* 228: '. . . *Blechkränzen, mit denen der verirrte Geschmack die Denkmäler der Verstorbenen behing*'; cf. also Brod, *Leben m.e.Göttin* 105 [1923]: '. . . *ein verirrtes Gefühl, aber ich begreife es ganz gut*'. Sometimes *verirrt* can refer to 'mental derangement', as in Herder, *Lit.u.Kunst* 12,135: '*sanft Verirrte phantasieren gewöhnlich Idyllen*'.

← See also under *Gott* (for *Verirrung*), *irre* (for *verirrt machen*), *krank* (for *krankhafte Verirrungen*), *passen* (for *es kommt zu paß wie ein verirrtes Huhn dem Fuchs*) and *Schaf* (for *wie ein verirrtes Schaf*).

verjagen

See under *Grille* (for *Grillen verjagen*), *jagen* (for several idioms) and *Pinsel* (for *durch einen Pinselstrich verjagen der Flecken Überfluß*).

verjähren

verjährt outmoded, antiquated, oldfashioned; ~ developed from 'to become a year old' (Early NHG) to 'to become old, last a long time' (17th c.) and then to 'to become no longer useful or valid' (19th c.). This could easily turn into 'to be outmoded, oldfashioned'; as a past participle general since the 18th c.

etw. ~ (obs.) to obtain sth. as one's property through the passage of time; in legal language current in the 18th c., now obs.

verjubeln: see *Jubel*.

verjudassen: see *Judas*.

verjüden: see *Jude*.

verjüngen

sich ~ (1) (lit.) to be rejuvenated; with abstracts since the 18th c., e.g. Schiller, *Räuber* 4,4: '*als ob die Natur sich verjünge*'; there is also transit. *etw. verjüngt etw.*, with abstracts since the 18th c.

sich ~ (2) to taper, get thinner gradually; with ref. to columns, pillars, etc.; since the 18th c., e.g. Lessing 8,33: '*seine Figuren verjüngen sich von unten bis oben*'.

etw. ~ to reduce sth. in scale; since Early NHG, usually with *Maßstab*, e.g. *in verjüngtem Maßstab* = 'in reduced scale'.

← See also under *Ostern* (for *ein Ostern der Verjüngung*).

verkalkt: see *Kalk*.

verkalkulieren: see *kalkulieren*.

verkappt

See under *Kappe*, also under *Maske* (for *verkapptes Wesen*).

verkapseln

sich ~ to seclude oneself, live a solitary life; 20th c. (~ not recorded in *DWb.* [1885]).

verkarrt

die Sache ist ~ (coll.) the thing is ruined, messed up, has gone all wrong; belongs to *den Karrren verkehrt fahren* or *aus dem Gleis bringen*; recorded since the 19th c., e.g. by Wander [1876].

verkatert: see *Kater*.

verkaufen

etw. für ein Linsengericht ~ to sell sth. for a mess of potage, part with sth. for very low payment; an allusion to Genesis 25,34. See also under *Linse*, p. 1624.

etw. ~ (coll.) to present sth. as acceptable or worth having; e.g. *den Wählern das neue Programm der Partei* ~; this had its beginnings in Early NHG, e.g. Luther 7,67b (Jena): '*denn der teufel kan seine lügen nicht anders verkeuffen, denn unter dem lieben namen*'; Lessing, too, used the phrase frequently, e.g. *Werke* 4,54: '. . . Betriegers, welcher einem unwissenden Pöbel das Seltene für das Göttliche, und das Künstliche für das Wunderbare verkauft*'.

sich für etw. ~ to present oneself (falsely) as sth.; at least since the 17th c., e.g. Grimmelshausen, *Simpliz.* [edit. K.] 2,182: '. . . dem sie . . . sich vor ein jungffer verkauffte*', where *sich ausgeben* (*als* or *für etw.*) would now be used.

sich gut ~ (coll.) to make a good impression, impress people favourably; an off-shoot from the previous entry, current since the middle of the 20th c.

nichts mehr zu ~ *haben* (coll.) to have no more to say or to contribute; since the 19th c., recorded by *DWb.* [1885]; used esp. with ref. to people who keep quiet in company (mainly in critical remarks).

jem. ~ (1) (sl.) to cheat sb.; in essence an ellipsis of *jem. für dumm* ~; since the 19th c.

jem. ~ (2) (sl.) to denounce sb. (to the authorities); possibly an echo of the thirty pieces of silver received by Judas.

ich lasse mir Mäusedreck nicht für Pfeffer ~ (a.) I will not be cheated or swindled; since the 18th c., e.g. Wieland 20,59. For origin see under *Maus* (on *Mäusedreck unter den Pfeffer mischen*).

← See also under *aufstreichen* (for *im Aufstrich verkaufen*), *Bär* (for *die Bärenhaut verkaufen*), *Brille* (for *jem.m Brillen verkaufen*), *dumm* (for *jem. für dumm verkaufen*), *Ei* (for *das Ei unterm Huhn verkaufen*), *Elle* (for *nach der Elle verkaufen*), *Fleisch* (for *der Fleischverkäufer*), *Garten* (for *wer seinen Garten verkauft, kann nicht mehr darin krauten*), *Halm* (for *die Frucht auf dem Halm verkaufen*), *Hand* (for *etw. nach der Hand verkaufen*), *Handel* (for *ich bin der Creatur verkauft*), *Haut* (for *seine Haut verkaufen*), *Katze* (for *jem.m eine Katze im Sack verkaufen*), *nah* (for *etw. näher verkaufen*), *Petersilie* (for *sie verkauft Petersilie*), *rühren* (for *Kochlöffel zu verkaufen*), *Ruß* (for *er färbt den Ruß und verkauft ihn für Weizenmehl*), *teuer* (for *sein Leben so teuer wie möglich verkaufen*) and *verraten* (for *verraten und verkauft sein*).

Verkehlung: see *Kehle*.

Verkehr

jem. aus dem ~ *ziehen* (coll.) to lock sb. up, put sb. in prison; ~ here = 'circulation' (as in the case of money that is taken out of circulation); 20th c. coll.

← See also under *lösen* (for *ein Lösen des engeren Verkehrs*).

verkehren

mit jem.m ~ (euphem.) to have (sexual) intercourse with sb.; refers to *Verkehr* = '(sexual) intercourse'; the phrase *mit jem.m* ~ has only been current since the 18th c., f.r.b. Adelung, when it meant 'to have social intercourse with sb.', with a sexual meaning only since the 19th c.

da ist er an den Verkehrten gekommen (or *geraten*) (coll.) this time he has suffered a rebuff, come to the wrong address; usually indicating unwillingness to agree with (or help) sb.; modern coll.

garnicht so verkehrt (coll.) not at all bad or inappropriate; modern litotes; 19th c.

Kaffee verkehrt (coll.) coffee with a large addition of milk (or cream); since early in the 20th c., in Austria also called *ein Verkehrter*.

← See also under *beibringen* (for *es ist verkehrt, wenn . . .*), *Dampf* (for *sich in Dampf und Dunst verkehren*), *Geselle* (for *falsche Scham, die Gesellin eines verkehrten Verstandes*), *Grund* (for *grundverkehrte Bestimmung*), *Hemd* (for *in Hemdsärmeln miteinander verkehren*), *Kalb* (for *die Augen verkehren*), *Mund* (for *Feind des verkehrten Mundes*), *Mütze* (for *er hat seine Mütze verkehrt auf*), *Nacht* (for *die Nacht in Tag verkehren*) and *richten* (for *in jeder Richtung verkehrt*).

verkeilen

jem. ~ (coll.) to thrash, beat sb.; 19th c. coll.

sich ~ (coll., obs.) to fall in love; from stud.sl. since ca. 1800, e.g. Niebergall, *Bursch.Heimk.* 3,12 [1837].

er hat sich den Kopf verkeilt (coll.) he cannot be induced to change his mind, is deaf to all pleas; the notion is that of a *Keil* 'wedge' having been inserted to prevent all movement; modern (not yet mentioned in *DWb.* [1885]).

etw. ~ (coll.) to sell sth.; first in stud.sl., f.r.b. *Bemerk. eines Akad.* [1795], used by Goethe; other stud.sl. verbs in this category are *verkloppen*, *verkröschen*, *verkümmeln* and *vermöbeln*, all recorded in *Der flotte Bursch* [1831]; of these *verkloppen*, *verkümmeln* and *vermöbeln* have entered general coll.

verkennen

etw. ~ (1) to fail to recognize sth.; since the 18th c., e.g. Klopstock, *Mess.* 4,1325: '*dich verkennt die Welt, gerechter Vater, ich kenne dich*'.

etw. (or *jem.*) ~ (2) to misunderstand or misjudge sth. (or sb.); also sometimes used for 'to undervalue'; first recorded in past participle *verkannt* by Steinbach [1734] and general since the 18th c. (Klopstock, Lessing, Goethe). Hence *unverkennbar*, f.r.b. Campe [1811], used by Herder and Goethe.

← See also under *einschiffen* (for *taumelnd mich und die Welt verkennen*).

verkerben: see *Kerbe*.

verketten: see *Kette* (also under *Mond* for *Verkettung*).

verketzern: see *Ketzer*.

verkitscht: see *Schalmei*.

verkitten

Menschen (or *Abstrakte*) ~ (rare) to unite people, bind people (or things) together; since the 18th c., e.g. Goethe, *Wahlverw.* 1,9: '*wenn das Gesetz sie verkittet*'; now unusual, if not obs.

verklagen

etw. ~ to bewail sth., complain about sth.; since the 19th c., e.g. Fontane, *Frau J. Treibel*, chapt. 8: '. . . *abwechselnd die Menschen und die Verhältnisse verklagend*', where *sich beklagen* (or *beschweren* or the simplex *klagen*) *über etw.* is now preferred.

← See also under *Graf* (for *verklag mich beim Graf Teufel*) and *Pilatus* (for *einen bei Pontius und Pilatus verklagen*).

verklären

jem. ~ to transfigure sb.; at first mainly in relig. contexts (from Luther Bible transl. Matth. 17,2, where '*verkleret*' occurs), then secular contexts, where it describes a 'blissfully transfigured' appearance, e.g. Schiller, *M. Stuart* 3,6: '*wie dich der Zorn umglänzte, deine Reize mir verklärte*' (see also *verklärte Welt* on p. 2208), hence also *ganz verklärt aussehen* = 'to look ecstatic'. Sometimes ~ can be rendered with 'ennoble'.

verklärt blessed; with ref. to the dead; recorded by Kramer [1702], sometimes as *verklärte Seele*, as in Schiller, *M. Stuart* 5,7. Goethe used it frequently for *verstorben*.

← See also under *klar* (for *verklären* in secular and religious contexts), *Not* (for *Verklärungen der Poesie*) and *schwimmen* (for *wie Verklärung schwamm's*).

verklatschen: see *klatschen*.

Verklauselierung: see *Schale*.

verkleben: see *kleben*.

verkleiden

etw. ~ to disguise sth. (with the intention of deceiving); with abstracts since Early NHG, e.g. Fischart, *Garg.* 16 or Hagedorn 1,29: '. . . *verkleidet er, den Pöbel zu verblenden, den . . . Geiz in . . . Verschwenden*'; hence *sich in etw.* ~ since the 18th c.

verkleinern

jem. ~ to belittle sb.; since the 17th c., e.g. Zesen, *Ros.* 41; also *etw.* ~ = 'to belittle, diminish, derogate, detract from sth.', f.r.b. Kramer [1702]. In MHG *verkleinen* was used.

ein Wort ~ (ling.) to turn a word into a diminutive; f.r.b. Schottel [1663].

← See also under *Glas* (for *Verkleinerungsglas*) and under *vergrößern*.

verkleistern

etw. ~ (coll.) to patch sth. up or cover sth. over; mainly with ref. to quarrels or differences, f.r.b. Kramer [1702], e.g. Lessing [edit. L.] 5,42: '. . . *die Zweifel nicht bloß zu verkleistern, sondern . . . zu heben sucht*'; *bekleistern* can also be used; since the 18th c., e.g. Fr. Müller 3,148: '*seine Phantasie bekleistert ihm nicht die Augen*'.

jem. m die Augen ~ (obs.) to bribe sb.; recorded by Adelung [1780], now obs.

verklimpern

die Zeit ~ (coll., pejor.) to spend or waste one's time making (bad or worthless) music; Goethe used it in this sense, which is also present in regional *sein Geld* ~ = 'to waste one's money', where ~ derived from 'to remove with much noise', recorded since the 19th c.

etw. ~ (rare) to overcome or remove sth. by making music; e.g. Schiller, *Fiesco* 3,8: '*hast du deinen Zorn bald verklimpert?*'.

verklingen

etw. verklingt (lit.) sth. dies or fades away; at first only with ref. to sounds (as in Goethe, *Zueignung* in *Faust I*), then transferred in the 18th c., e.g. Goethe, *Ital. Reise* 1: '. . . *halb verklungene Sagen der Vorzeit*', Heine, *Reis.* 3,207: '. . . *einer längst verklungenen Zeit angehört*'.

verklopfen

jem. ~ or *verkloppen* (coll.) to beat, thrash sb.; recorded for several regions since the 19th c.

etw. ~ or *verkloppen* (coll.) to sell sth.; first in stud. sl., f.r.b. *Der flotte Bursch* [1831]; for guesses about origin see under *klopfen* (p. 1493).

sein Geld ~ (regional coll.) to waste one's money, spend recklessly; recorded since the 19th c., e.g. for Vienna by Hügel [1873], Gotthelf used it often, e.g. in *Schuldenbauer* 263 and 390 [1852]; for possible origin see previous entry.

← See also under *klopfen* and *Pfeife* (for *sich die Pfeife verkloppen*).

verkloppen: see *verklopfen*.

verknacken

jem. ~ (sl.) to put sb. inside, lock sb. up; 20th c. sl., not yet mentioned in *DWb.* [1885].

verknallen

jem. ~ (regional coll.) to sentence sb.; since the 2nd half of the 19th c. (recorded for the Frankfurt region).

sich in jem. ~ (coll.) to fall for sb.; also in *jem. verknallt sein* = 'to have fallen desperately in love with sb.'; 20th c. coll.

verknechten: see *Knecht*.

verkneifen: see *kneifen*.

verkniffen

verkniffen strained, pinched; since the 19th c., e.g. Treitschke, *Dt. Gesch.* 4,619: '. . . *die verkniffenen Züge des Fanatismus*'. Also used for 'suppressed, held back', from *etw. verkneifen* (see p. 1502), as in *verkniffener Grimm*, used by Raabe.

verknöchert: see *Knochen*.

verknoten

verknotet (lit.) knotted; figur. since the 18th c., e.g. Voß, *Antisymb.* 1,281: '. . . *diesen gordisch verknoteten Strick aufzulösen*'; for *gordisch* see p. 1108.

verknüpfen

See under *Knoten* (for *Knoten des wild verknüpften Sinnes*) and *Schlange* (for *länderverknüpfende Straßen*).

verknusen

etw. ~ (a.) to understand, comprehend sth.; LG ~ began as 'to squash, compress, crush' and became 'to digest'; in the course of the 19th c. it entered other parts of Germany, recorded for Berlin by Trachsel [1873], but is now a. if not obs.

ich kann ihn nicht ; (coll.) I cannot bear or stand him; since the 19th c., recorded by Wander [1876].

verkochen

etw. verkocht (lit.) sth. boils away, passes; at first with ref. to actual boiling, with the notion of disappearing in the course of long boiling since the 18th c., then with abstracts (see under *kochen* first item), but now only in such cases as *sein Zorn ist schon verkocht*, since the 19th c., recorded by Heyne [1895].

verkohlen: see *Kohl*.

verkommen

verkommen (1) to decay, go to wreck and ruin; since the 18th c., e.g. Bürger, 46b, Heine, *Verm.* 1,313: '. . . *wäre er in darbendem Elend verkommen*', Bismarck, *Reden* 16,41: '. . . *muß das Reich verkrüppeln und verkommen*'.

verkommen (2) (obs.) to make progress, get on; still recorded by Campe [1811], now obs. except in some regions, e.g. ich *werde schon* ~ = 'I'll get through, manage somehow', as in Swabian (cf. Fischer [1908]); *durchkommen* or *vorankommen* would now be used.

verkommen (3) (regional, Swiss) to agree; now only in Swiss regions, e.g. *mit jem.m* ~ = 'to come to an agreement with sb.', where in standard German *übereinkommen* would be used. It is an off-shoot from *mit jem.m* ~ = 'to get on with sb.', recorded by Adelung [1780], for which *auskommen* is now the usual compound.

es ist mir ~ (regional) I have lost it; current in some regions, e.g. Bav., where it can also be used for 'forgetting', e.g. *es ist mir* ~ = 'I have forgotten it' (where *entfallen* is the standard term).

~ *werden* (obs.) to become confused, get muddled; still used in the 19th c., e.g. Benedix, *Dram.Werke* 10,27 [1846].

verkorksen: see *Kork*.

verkörpern: see *Körper*, also under *dicht* and *durchfühlen*.

verkosten: see *kosten*.

verkrachen: see *Krach*.

verkraften

etw. nicht ~ *können* to be unable to handle, manage or bear sth.; only since the 20th c.

verkrallen: see *Kralle*.

verkrampfen

verkrampft tense, strained, inhibited; used with ref. to feelings or expressions showing tenseness; only since the 20th c. (*DWb.* [1885] does not even list ~).

verkriechen

See under *kriechen*, also under *Maus* (for *ich hätte mich am liebsten in ein Mauseloch verkrochen*) and *Molch* (for *gleich einem Molch verkrochen*).

verkröpft

verkröpft (lit.) disfigured; since the 19th c., e.g. Freytag, *Bild.* 1,5: '*ein unsicheres, langsames, verkröpftes Recht*'.

verkrümeln: see *krümeln*.

verkrüppeln: see *Krüppel*, also under *verkommen*.

verkühlen: see *kühl*.

verkümmeln: see *Kümmel*.

verkümmern

verkümmern to waste away, atrophy, decline, become stunted; since the 16th c., frequent since the 18th c. (Lessing, Goethe, Wieland), but *verkümmert* = 'afflicted by worries, withered, faded, in a state of decline' only since the 18th c. The transitive *etw.* ~, still recorded by Adelung for 'to reduce sth.' (e.g. sb.'s pay) is obs.

← See also under *Natur* (for *das Naturwesen war um seine Einfalt verkümmert*) and *Patsch* (for *mein Leben im nichtigen Patsch verkümmert*).

verkünden: see *gleiten* and *Schalk*.

verkündigen: see *schmettern* and *Schwabe*.

verkünstelt: see *schwemmen*.

verkuppeln: see *kuppeln*.

verkürzen: see *kurz*.

verlachen

etw. ~ to ridicule sth., treat sth. with contempt; current since the 15th c. and often without implying actual 'laughing'; f.r.b. Maaler [1561].

verlagern

sich ~ to shift; figur. with ref. to abstracts only since late in the 19th c., often with *Schwerpunkt*, *Gewicht* or *Interesse*. Campe[1811] did not record ~, even in its phys. meaning.

verlangen

etw. verlangt etw. sth. demands or requires sth.; figur. with an abstract as the subject since the 18th c., e.g. Wieland, *Oberon* 2,48: '*sein Groll verlangt dein Blut*', Goethe, *Ital. Reise* (6.10.1786):

'. . . *betrug . . . sich . . . toll, wie es leider die Rolle verlangt*'; hence *unverlangt* = 'not required, not asked for', since the 18th c., e.g. Lessing [edit. M.] 7,28; it can also mean 'uninvited', as in Goethe, *Jahrm.z.P.* 489.

jem. ~ to ask to see (or speak to) sb.; ellipsis, with *zu sehen* or *sprechen* omitted; since the 18th c., e.g. Schiller, *D.Carl.* 2,12: '*die Königin verlangt mich*'.

nach etw. or *jem.m* ~ to long for sth. or sb.; general since the 17th c., but in Early NHG there are instances of *mich verlangt zu . . .*, which can be taken as expressing 'longing', e.g. Luther Bible transl. Rom. 1,11: '*denn mich verlanget, euch zu sehen*'.

← See also under *baden* (for *brennendes Verlangen*), *brennen* (for *brennen mit Verlangen*), *dunkel* (for *unerkanntes Verlangen*), *Farbe* (for *unsere Zeit verlangt Farbe*), *faul* (for *Verlangen abspeisen*), *Fuß* (for *ein Lied verlangen*), *Gewicht* (for *man verlangt das heut zu Tage von einer Zeitung*), *leben* (for *in dem Menschenfreunde lebt ein gütiges Verlangen*), *recht* (for *verlang ich auch das Maul recht voll*), *Scheide* (for *zwischen Lieben und Verlangen ist die Scheidewand gefallen*), *Stachel*, *Strudel* and *verleben* (for *mich verlangte . . .*).

verlängern: see *Rücken*, also under *Stand* (for *Verlängerung*).

verläppern

etw. ~ (regional coll.) to spend or get through sth. bit by bit; derived from *Lappen*, i.e. *etw. in kleine Lappen zerschneiden* or *in Lappen zerfallen lassen*; recorded for many regions since the 19th c., e.g. *ein Vermögen* ~ = 'to get through a fortune gradually (and carelessly)'.

verlassen

See under *Bahn* (for *die rechte Bahn verlassen*), *Bezirk* (for *das Bezirk verlassen*), *Bock* (for *sich auf etw. verlassen wie der Bock auf die Hörner*), *Boden* (for *den festen Boden verlassen*), *Fuß* (for *den ordentlichen Weg verlassen*), *Geist* (for *von allen Geistern verlassen* and *verlassner Sünder*), *Gott* (for *gottverlassen* and *der Gottverlaßmichnicht*), *Mann* (for *verlaß sich nur niemandts auf einen andern*), *Posten* (for *verlaßt den Posten der Tugend nicht*), *Ratte* (for *die Ratten verlassen das sinkende Schiff*), *schneiden* (for *die Weinverlasser*), *spröde* and *Steg*.

Verlassenschaft: see *rund*.

Verlauf: see *link*.

verlaufen

verlaufen to happen, take its course, pass; since Early NHG, f.r.b. Schottel [1663]; now usually with adverbs, e.g. *es ist gut, schlecht, glücklich* ~.

sich ~ (1) to disperse; since the 17th c., e.g. *die Menge Menschen hat sich nun* ~.

sich ~ (2) to stray, go wrong; occasionally figur. with abstracts since the 18th c., e.g. (DWb) Kant 2,436 on reason: '. . . *daß sie . . . sich in transcendente Erklärungsgründe verlaufe*', where *sich verirren* would be preferred today.

← See also under *Markt* (for *wenn der Markt verlaufen ist*), *Parallele* (for *Entwicklungen verlaufen parallel*), *reiben* (for *reibungslos verlaufen*) and *Sand* (for *im Sand verlaufen*).

verlautbaren: see *laut*.

verlauten: see *laut*.

verleben

verleben to pass, spend; with ref. to time, since the 18th c., e.g. Schiller, *Wall.Tod* 3,4: '*mich verlangte, eine heitre Stunde im lieben Kreis der Meinen zu verleben*'; in the 18th c. frequent in past participle *verlebt* = 'past, spent', e.g. Herder, *Ph.* 13,120: '*dein Traum . . . ist verlebt*' or 10,130: '*das ganze verlebte Jahrhundert*', even *verlebte Sprachen* = 'dead languages', but this is now obs., as is *der verlebte Herr X* = 'the late Mr. X'.

sein Vermögen ~ (coll.) to spend all one has on one's everyday needs; modern coll.

verlebt aussehen to look dissipated; *verlebt* meant 'aged, senile, decrepit' from Early NHG to the 19th c., where *altersschwach* would now be used. Now *verlebt* is used pejor. to describe looks ravaged by loose living; not yet listed in *DWb.* [1885], but certainly current since early in the 20th c.

verledern

jem. ~ (coll.) to beat, belt sb.; modern coll.; cf. *jem.m das Leder gerben* (p. 1598).

verlegen (1)

etw. ~ (1) to move sth. (to another place); since the 17th c., occasionally with abstracts, e.g. (T.) Zahn, *Der Weg hinauf* 158: '. . . *so verlegte sie ihre Pflichten ins Freie*', f.r.b. Adelung with ref. to institutions, now also with ref. to time, e.g. appointments, e.g. *diese Verpflichtung kann ich nicht* ~, recorded by Sanders [1863]: '*den Termin verlegen*'. Reflexive use is also possible, e.g. Mörike, *Nolten* 488: '. . . *sich aus meinem Logis zu verlegen*' (now a.).

etw. ~ (2) to place sth. in a certain location or period; since the 18th c., e.g. Adelung [1780]: '*die Handlung eines Schauspiels nach Rußland verlegen*'.

etw. ~ (3) to mislay or misplace sth.; since Early NHG, e.g. Lessing, *Minna* 1,6.

etw. ; (4) (obs.) to provide, furnish sth.; still in the 18th c., recorded by Adelung: '*ein Land mit Waaren verlegen*'; now obs.

ein Buch ~ to publish a book; since the 16th c.; belongs to obs. *etw.* ~ = 'to defray the costs of sth.'; cf. Schirmer, *Kaufmannspr.* 202 [1911]; hence *Verleger* = 'publisher' and *Verlag*.

jem.m etw. ~ to block sb.'s access to sth.; since MHG, often with *Weg*, e.g. Luther Bible transl. 1 Sam. 15, 2, Lessing [edit. L.] 10,314; cf. also *eine Hündin* ~ = 'to lock up a bitch in heat'.

jem.m die Rede ~ (regional) to take sb.'s breath away, leave sb. speechless; recorded for some areas, e.g. Bav. since the 19th c.; cf. also *das verlegt einem den Appetit* = 'that takes one's appetite away'.

sich auf etw. ~ to turn to sth. (as a means of achieving one's ends); e.g. *sich aufs Bitten* ~ = 'to resort to entreaties', not yet in Adelung, but recorded by Campe [1811].

verlegen (2)

verlegen embarrassed; belongs to *verliegen* and meant originally '(to be) damaged', current since OHG and in some regions still current for 'exhausted, tired out'; in modern sense since the 18th c., f.r.b. Frisch [1741], e.g. Goethe, *Faust I*, 2060.

die Geldverlegenheit financial embarrassment or straits; since the 19th c., sometimes euphem. abbreviated to *Verlegenheit* (recorded in *DWb.* [1887]).

die Verlegenheitspause awkward silence; since the 20th c. (not yet mentioned in *DWb.* [1885]).

← See also under *fallen* (for *in Verlegenheit fallen*), *gucken* (for *mächtiglich verlegen*), *muffig* (for *Schimmel alter verlegener Worte*), *schlau* (for *jem. in einer Verlegenheit im Stich lassen*), *setzen* (for *jem. in Verlegenheit setzen*), *sparen* (for *jem.m die Verlegenheit ersparen*) and *stehen* (for *in Verlegenheit stehen*).

verleiden

etw. verleidet (obs.) sth. becomes hateful or disagreeable; current from the 17th to the 19th c., recorded by Kramer [1702], still used by Goethe, e.g. in *Dicht. u. Wahrh.* 6, now obs.

jem.m etw. ~ to spoil sth. for sb., take sb.'s pleasure in sth. away; since the 16th c., recorded by Stieler [1691], e.g. Schiller, *Kab.u.L.* 3,2; cf. also Luther Apocr. transl. Ecclesiasticus 33,21: *'ein weiser leßt jm gottes wort nicht verleiden'*.

verleihen

See *leihen*, also under *Matthäus* (for *Mätzchen den Anstrich der Karrikatur verleihen*), *Nacht* (for *Gott, der Jubel verleiht in der Nacht des Unglücks*), *polieren* (for *der Erziehung die letzte Politur verleihen*), *Preis* (for *jem.m den Preis verleihen*) and *sparen* (for *sparsame Reize verleih mir*).

verleimen

etw. ~ (rare) to glue sth. up, block sth.; e.g. Goethe, *Ital. Reise* (14.9.1786), but *verstopfen* is now preferred.

verleiten

jem. ~ to seduce or tempt sb.; since OHG usually with ref. to reprehensible actions, but in modern times also in contexts where it can mean 'to induce sb.' towards sth. positive, e.g. *man wird zum Nachdenken verleitet* (used by Goethe).

← See also under *Komödie* (for *in den Schulen verleitet*), *Messer* (for *den unwissenden Deutschen verleiten*) and *Schneider* (for *sich zu lustigen Geldschneidereien verleiten lassen*).

verlernen

etw. ~ to forget sth.; in this sense since the 17th c., sometimes in lit. also used for 'to give up', as in Klopstock, *Mess.* 7,405 or 'to abandon,

depart from', e.g. Treitschke, *Dt. Gesch.* 5,41: *'obwohl er die christlichen Tugenden . . . mehr und mehr verlernte'*; hence also *etw. noch nicht verlernt haben* = 'to be still able to . . .'. Unusual is Schiller, *D.Carl.* 1,2: *'o Roderich, wenn ich den Vater je in ihm verlernte'*, where *'zu sehen'* is omitted but to be understood.

← See also under *Geist* (for *der stolze Geist verlernte sich zu beugen*) and *rot* (for *er hat das Rotwerden verlernt*).

verlesen

etw. ~ (1) to read sth. out (in public, officially, solemnly); since the 15th c.

etw. ~ (2) to misread sth., make a mistake in reading sth.; modern, also used reflex. e.g. *ich habe mich* ~.

verletzen

etw. verletzt or *ist verletzend* sth. is hurtful, offensive, causes injury or harm; figur. when the subject is an abstract; since the 17th c., but marginally earlier, e.g. Luther Bible transl. Job 5,18: *'gott . . . verletzt und verbindet'*.

etw. (or *jem.*) ~ to hurt, damage, injure sth. (or sb.); figur. when the object is an abstract, since Early NHG, e.g. Luther 2,356 (Jena) with *Seele*, or Fischart, *Dicht.* [edit. Kurz] 3,346: *'wann man dein freyheit hat verletzt'*. Stieler [1691] recorded: *'am guten namen verletzet werden'*; hence *verletzlich*, translating Lat. *violabilis*, f.r.b. Dasypodius [1535], *verletzbar* (since the 18th c.), *unverletzlich* from Lat. *inviolabilis* since the 16th c., but *unverletzbar* only since the 18th c. (still missing in Adelung).

← See also under *einschneiden* (for *verletzte Gemüter*), *Luft* (for *Verletzer des Gastrechts*), *Melodie* (for *das Ohr verletzen*), *Seele* (for *jem. in tiefster Seele verletzen*) and *Spiel* (for *das verletzt die Spielregeln*).

verleugnen

jem. ~ to deny, disown, disavow sb.; since OHG (*farlougnen*), in general use through its appearance in the Bible, e.g. Mark 14,30.

etw. ~ to renounce, disclaim sth.; since MHG (*verlougenen*); also used several times in Luther Bible transl., e.g. Job 6,10. Often used for 'to deny the existence, importance of sth.', where *leugnen* can express the same notion; hence modern *es läßt sich nicht* ~ = 'it cannot be denied'.

sich ~ *lassen* to have oneself denied; mainly used for 'to have oneself reported as being not at home'; since the 18th c.

eine Farbe ~ to revoke, renege; in card games since the 19th c. for *nicht bekennen* = 'to fail to follow suit'.

er kann seinen Vater nicht ~ he looks very much like his father; modern.

sich selbst ~ to deny oneself, free oneself from one's desires or instincts; beginnings in Early NHG, e.g. Luther Bible transl. Matth. 16,24.

← See also under *Blut* (for *das Blut verleugnet*

← See also under *Blut* (for *das Blut verleugnet sich nicht*), *Natur* (for *seine Natur nicht verleugnen können*), *schicken* (for *weil er da war, konnte man ihn schicklich nicht verleugnen*) and *selbst* (for *Selbstverleugnung*).

verleumden

jem. ~ to defame, slander, libel sb.; current since MHG, at first in the inoffensive meaning 'to make public', f.r.b. Maaler [1561], used in Luther Bible transl. Psalm 101,5, also in the Apocr. Ecclesiasticus 5,16, also early in images, e.g. Logau (in Lessing 5,165): '*wer Verleumdung hört, ist ein Feuereisen, wer Verleumdung bringt, ist ein Feuerstein*'; cf. also *Verleumder*, e.g. Ecclesiasticus 5,17.

← See also under *Bein* (for *Verleumdung wirft die Unschuld übers Bein*), *bewerfen* (for *mit dem Staub der Verleumdung bewerfen*), *Natter* (for *die Nattern der Verleumdung zischen* and *Verleumdung nagt an meinem besten Mark*), *Panzer* (for *Stachel der Verleumdung*), *schwarz* (for *Verleumdung schwärzt nicht seinen Morgen*), *Spinne* (for *verleumdungsvolle Spinnen*) and *Stachel* (for *Giftstachel der Verleumdung*).

verlieben

verliebt in love, enamoured, love-sick; since the 17th c., with ref. to things general since the 18th c.; hence *Verliebtheit*, 18th c., e.g. Kant 10,294, *Verliebtsein*, 18th c., e.g. Zinzendorf, *Kinderreden* 327 [1758]. *Verliebnis* is unusual, *Verliebung* is a. if not obs. Frequently ~ is strictly separated from *lieben*, as in Lessing 1,78: '*du kannst lieben, doch verliebe dich nur nicht*'.

zum Verlieben schön (coll.) so attractive as to make one fall in love with it; modern.

die Köchin ist verliebt (coll.) the cook has been too generous with the salt – she must be in love; modern coll. See also under *Suppe*.

← See also under *elf* (for *in elftausend Jungfrauen verliebt*), *Käfer* (for *verliebt wie ein Käfer*), *Kater* (for *ein verliebter Kater*), *Narr* (for *närrisch verliebt*), *Nase* (for *verliebte Nasenlöcher machen*), *Ohr* (for *bis über die Ohren verliebt*), *Perle* (for *ein verliebter West*), *puffen* (for *verliebter Tor*), *Ratte* (for *verliebt wie eine tote Ratte*), *rauben* (for *die verliebten Räubereien*), *Stachel* (for *verliebtes Jugendbedürfnis*) and *sterben* (for *sich sterblich verlieben* and *sterblich/unsterblich verliebt*).

verlieblichen

etw. ~ (rare) to make sth. look, read, sound attractive or likeable; since the 18th c., e.g. Kosegarten, *Poesien* 1,8 [1798]: '*die du ... jegliche Pflicht verlieblichst*', Heine, *Lut.* 2,4: '*... haben ... Künstler die ... Schrecknisse der Passion mit ... Blumen ... verlieblicht*'.

verliederlichen

etw. ~ (a.) to dissipate sth. through wastefulness or carelessness; since Early NHG, f.r.b. Maaler [1561], still in the 19th c. with *Besitz, Gut, Vermögen*, now a.

verliegen

verliegen (obs.) to deteriorate, rot, suffer damage through not being used; since OHG and still in the 19th c., esp. in *verlegene Ware*, used e.g. by Goethe (in *Briefw. mit Schiller* 230) for 'sth. that has had its day'; now obs.

← See also under *verlegen (2)* and the example under *muffig*, listed among the cross-references at the end of *verlegen (2)*.

verlieren

der verlorene Sohn the prodigal son; biblical from Luke 15,11–32.

die Geduld ~ to lose (one's) patience; f.r.b. Rädlein (1711).

Worte ~ to waste words; general since the 18th c., e.g. Schiller, *Braut v. M.* 2269; '*meine Worte habe ich umsonst verloren*'; frequent in *darüber ist kein Wort mehr zu ~* = 'there is no need to say any more'.

er kann einfach nicht ~ (coll.) he is a bad loser; modern coll.

← See also under *Auge* (for *jem. aus den Augen verlieren*), *Bein* (for *verlier die Beine nicht*), *Daube* (for *Dauben und Reifen verlieren*), *Deckel* (for *verlorener Ruf*), *Ehre* (for *sie hat ihre Ehre verloren*), *eigen* (for *nichts Eigenes zu verlieren haben*), *Eisen* (for *sie hat ein Eisen verloren*), *Faden* (for *den Faden verlieren*), *Farbe* (for *Perspektive verlieren*), *Fasson* (for *die Fasson verlieren*), *Fledermaus* (for *sich in ihre Schlupfwinkel verlieren*), *Fuß* (for *festen Stand verlieren*), *Galopp* (for *den hat der Teufel im Galopp verloren*), *geben* (for *etw. verloren geben*), *Gedanke* (for *in Gedanken verloren sein*), *gelb* (for *das gelb hinter den ohren verlohren*), *Geschick* (for *das Geschick verlieren*), *Gesicht* (for *etw. aus dem Gesicht verlieren* and *Gesicht verlieren*), *Gewalt* (for *weil du mit aller Gewalt verlieren willst*), *Gewicht* (for *das sittliche Gleichgewicht verlieren*), *Gott* (for *gottverloren*), *Groschen* (for *der verlorene Groschen*), *halten* (for *verlorenes Spiel* and *seine Seele verlieren*), *Haufen* (for *der verlorene Haufen*), *Hopfen* (for *an ihm ist Hopfen und Malz verloren*), *Jungfer* (for *die Jungfernschaft verlieren*), *Kolonie* (for *ein verlorener Landstrich*), *Kranz* (for *den Kranz/das Kränzlein verlieren*), *Kurs* (for *sein Kurs hat seine Höhe verloren*), *lachen* (for *ein Lächeln, das sich ins Sardonische verliert*), *Latein* (for *sein Latein verlieren*), *Made* (for *den Madensack verlieren*), *Minute* (for *keine Minute zu verlieren*), *Mutter* (for *verlorenes Schaf*, listed also under *Schaf*), *nachholen* (for *verlorene Nächte nachholen*), *Nebel* (for *sich in Nebeln und Schwebeln verlieren*), *Nerv* (for *leicht die Nerven verlieren*), *Paroli* (for *sein Paroli verlieren*), *Pfahl* (for *den Mut verlieren*), *Polen* (for *noch ist Polen nicht verloren*), *Posten* (for *auf verlorenem Posten kämpfen*), *rechnen* (for *für verloren rechnen*), *Saft* (for *Saft und Kraft verlieren*), *Salbe* (for *diese Sprache ist an mir verloren*), *Salz* (for *Salz und Schmalz verlieren*), *Sand* (for *sich im Sand verlieren*), *Schaden* (for *swer verliuret, der muoz den spot zum schaden hân*), *Schanze* (for *die schanze verlieren*), *schenken* (for *der Spender hat den Arm verloren*), *Schlacht* (for *die Schlacht verlieren*), *Schlamm* (for *im Schlamme der Theorien verloren*), *schwimmen* (for *der verliurt grôzer arbeit vil*), *Traum* (for *traumverloren*) and *Verstand* (for *den Verstand verlieren*).

← See also under *verloren*.

verloben

sich ~ to become engaged; ~ began as 'to promise' (= *geloben*, for which see p. 975), f.r.b. Maaler [1561]; specialized for 'to promise marriage' since Early NHG; *der Verlobte* = 'fiancé' only since the 18th c., recorded by Campe [1811], still not mentioned in Adelung.

es verlobt sich mancher, der nicht Hochzeit macht (prov.) not every engagement leads to marriage; also in wider sense for 'a first step does not always lead to the decisive one'; recorded since the 19th c., e.g. by Wander [1876].

verlocken

jem. ~ to entice, tempt, seduce sb.; since MHG (*verlücken*), e.g. Luther Bible transl. Hos. 7,11: '*wie eine verlockte taube*' (where the A.V. has 'like a silly dove without heart'). See also under *locken* for phrases in which ~ can also be used.

verlodern: see *lodern* (also under *Feuer*).

verlogen

verlogen mendacious, (given to) lying; since OHG (cf. Graff 2,131); belongs to an obs. *verlügen*, which meant both 'to slander, libel' and 'to deny'; mainly used with ref. to persons, but since the 17th c. also with abstracts and things, e.g. Schupp, *Schr.* 310 [1663]: '*in diesen verlogenen zeiten*'.

← See also under *Mund* (for *falscher verlogener Mund*).

verlohnen: see *groß*.

verloren

an ihm ist ein Dichter verlorengegangen (coll.) he would have made (or could well have become) a poet; modern coll., not to be confused with *mit ihm haben wir einen Dichter* ~ with ref. to loss through death, which is older and not coll.

verlorene Liebesmüh wasted effort; modern, but Luther 5,79b (Jena) used '*mit verlorner mühe*'.

der verlorene Sohn the prodigal son; biblical from Luke 15,11–24.

daran ist nichts ~ (coll.) that is no great loss; since ca. 1900.

hier nichts ~ *haben* (coll.) to have no business to be here; meaning 'only if he had lost sth. he would have some justification to be here': similar to *hier nichts zu suchen haben*, but of different origin (see p. 2417).

← See also under *Kaiser* (for *wo nichts ist, hat der Kaiser sein Recht verloren*), *Sohn* (for *der Sohn hat's verloren*) and *Spiel* (for *das Spiel ist verloren* and *den verlorenen Sohn spielen*), also under *verlieren* for numerous locutions.

verlöschen

See under *Linie* (for *verlöschtes Dasein*), *naß* (for *einsam verlöschen*) and *Pfropfen* (for *verloschne Freundschaft*).

verlöten

einen ~ (sl.) to have a drink, take a snifter; since late in the 19th c., first in mil.sl. – For a vulg. sl. meaning relating to intercourse see Küpper, *Pons-Wb.* 881 [1987].

verlotsen: see *Lotse*.

verlottern

jem. verlottert sb. goes to the bad; since Early NHG; hence *verlottert* = 'dissolute', e.g. Wickram, *Nachb.* 78a [1556]: '*zwen verlotterte böse buben*'.

etw. verlottert sth. goes to wreck and ruin; Luther 1,367b (Jena) used for 'to corrupt': '*...viel schrift zuloddert und zumartert haben*', but this transit. use is obs. Intransitive since the 17th c., with such abstracts as *Leben* since the 19th c., e.g. *ein verlottertes Leben führen*. The past participle used with ref. to things means 'neglected, ruined, decayed'.

verludern: see *Aas*.

verlumpen: see *Lumpen*.

Verlust

der ~ loss; since OHG (*farlust*); even in the earliest periods used for 'death', with abstracts frequent since Early NHG, in Luther's writings as ~ *der Seele* or *der Seligkeit*, also in his Bible transl. Rom. 11,15. Hence also *einer Sache verlustig gehen* for 'to lose or be deprived of sth.', since the 17th c., now avoided as officialese.

← See also under *beikommen* (for *seinem Verlust beikommen*) and *Seite* (for *gleichseitiger Verlust*).

vermachen

jem.m etw. ~ to leave sth. to sb. (as a present or in a will); since Early NHG in present-day sense, f.r.b. Maaler [1561]; in modern coll. = 'to let sb. have sth.' (esp. if one is not interested in keeping it); noun *das Vermächtnis* = 'bequest, legacy', f.r.b. Stieler [1691]; figur. with abstracts since the 18th c. for 'legacy'.

← See also under *niederlegen* (for *im Herzen meiner Königin leg ich mein letztes kostbares Vermächtnis nieder*).

vermählen

sich ~ to marry; figur. for 'to unite, get together' since Early NHG, also used transitively, e.g. Gotter 2,250: '*mit diesem Ring vermähl ich dich der Tugend*', Schiller, *M.Stuart* 1,7: '*die Kronen Schottland und England friedlich zu vermählen*', also figur. *vermählt sein mit etw.* = 'to be wedded to sth.', cf. Keisersberg, *Granat.* a3b [1511]: '*vermahelt bist du got dem herren*'; hence *Vermählung*, f.r.b. Maaler (1561), figur. since the 18th c., e.g. (DWb) Klinger 11,86: '*die schönste Vermählung unserer Geisteskräfte ist die der hohen dichterischen Einbildungskraft mit der Vernunft des Mannes von Geschäften*'.

vermahnen: admonish

wer dich vermahnt, der liebt dich (prov.) when sb. admonishes you it means that he/she is fond of you; recorded since the 17th c., e.g. by Lehman [1640].

vermaledeit

See under *nirgends* (for *ein vermaledeiter Überall und Nirgends*) and *poltern* (for *vermaledeite Polterkammer*).

vermänteln: see *bemänteln*.

vermasseln: see *Tour*.

vermauern: see *Mauer*.

vermehren

See under *Kaninchen* (for *sich vermehren wie die Kaninchen/Karnickel*), *Knäuel* (for *sich selbst vermehrend wachsen*) and *Schuld* (for *wer seine Schulden bezahlt, vermehrt sein Vermögen*).

vermeiden

etw. ~ to avoid sth.; since OHG (*farmîdan*); *etw. läßt sich nicht* ~ = 'sth. is unavoidable' is modern, but *unvermeidlich* has been in use since MHG (*unvermîdelich*). The form *unvermeidentlich* is obs.

← See also under *bemänteln* (for *Bemäntelung vermeyden*), *naiv* (for *härtere Ausdrücke vermeiden*), *räudig* (for *den Thoren vermeide*), *Schein* (for *den Schein des Bösen vermeiden*) and *streiten* (for *bloß keinen Streit (nicht) vermeiden*).

vermeinen

See under *Bürde* (for *vermeint verletzte Ehre*) and *Präludium* (for *jren vermeinten jüngstentag*).

vermeintlich: see *steigen*.

vermelden

See under *neben* (for *neben dem allen ist zu vermelden*) and *Respekt* (for *mit Respekt zu vermelden*).

vermengen

sich mit etw. ~ (obs.) to concern oneself with sth.; general in the 18th c., e.g. Lessing 2,457: '*ich vermenge mich mit dem Unmöglichen nicht*', also Rabener, *Satiren* 3,253 [1768]; now obs. (*sich mit etw. befassen* or *auf etw. eingehen* are now used).

← See also under *mengen* (for several entries) and *Schwarm* (for *Vermengung*).

vermenschlichen: see *Mensch*.

vermerken

etw. (jem.m) übel ~ to take sth. amiss, resent sth.; since the 18th c.; Goethe, *Lehrj.* 4,19 used the milder '*nicht wohl vermerken*', and '*in ungutten nicht vermerken*' occurs as early as in Butschky, *Kanzl.* 341.

vermessen

See under *messen* and under *Schnecke* (for *vermessener Hase*), *steigen* (for *vermessene Entwürfe*) and *Straße* (for *Straßen vermessen*). *Vermessenheit*, current since Late MHG occurs in Luther Bible transl. Deuter. 18,22.

vermieten: see *Kammer*.

vermischen

See under *Fleisch* (for *sich fleischlich vermischen*) and *mischen* (for several entries).

vermissen

jem. ~ (1) to miss sb. (in the sense of being aware of the absence of sb.), ultimately derived from phys. 'missing' in the sense of 'failing to hit', since MHG, e.g. Luther Bible transl. 1 Sam. 20,18.

jem. (schmerzlich) ~ (2) to regret or feel deprived by sb.'s absence; since the 19th c., also negatively *ihn vermißt niemand* = 'his absence is not felt by anybody' (sometimes containing the notion of relief).

etw. ~ to be aware of the absence of sth.; sometimes in wider sense 'to fail to find sth.'; since the 17th c. also with abstracts, e.g. (DWb) Logau 3,79; hence also *etw.* ~ *lassen* = 'to be lacking in sth.'.

vermißt missing, lost (in battle or in a catastrophe); only since the 19th c.

vermitteln

vermitteln (intrans.) to mediate, reconcile; since the 17th c.; hence *Vermittler* = 'mediator', by the 18th c. also used with abstracts, e.g. by Goethe who called a certain *Unglück* '*eine milde Vermittlerin*' and *Kunst* '*eine erwünschte Vermittlerin*'; *Vermittlung* has been recorded since the 17th c.

etw. ~ to supply, provide, convey sth.; with abstracts since the 17th c., e.g. Grimmelshausen, *Simpliz.* [edit. K.] 1,331: '... *Gunst und ... Zutritt vermittelte*'; hence *vermittels(t)* = 'by means of, through the agency of'; since the 16th c., e.g. Luther, 1,115a (Jena).

vermöbeln: see *Möbel*.

vermodern

vermodern to decay, rot, distintegrate; figur. since the 18th c., e.g. Bürger 1,73 or C.F. Meyer, *Nov.* 1,153: '... *wäre die Welt längst vermodert wie ein wurmstichiger Apfel*'; now also in *geistig vermodert* (coll.) = 'mentally decrepit', since 2nd half of the 20th c.

vermögen

See under *herantragen* (for *etw. an die Herzen heranzutragen vermögen*), *Morgen* (for *warum bis morgen sparen, was wir heut vermögen*), *Parallele* (for *vermöge welcher ...*), *Sprache* (for *zu erwiedern vermögen*) and *trüb* (for *das Bild nicht zu trüben vermocht*).

Vermögen

See under *Kehle* (for *sein Vermögen durch die Kehle jagen*), *reichen* (for *reiche dem Armen nach deinem Vermögen*), *reiten* (for *baares Vermögen*), *Schlund* (for *das Vermögen verschlingen*), *schwimmen* (for *das Vermögen schwamm*), *sehen* (for *aufs Vermögen sehen*), *sparen* (for *das Vermögen sparen*) and *tragen* (for *sich über sein Vermögen tragen*).

vermoost: see *Moos*.

vermorscht: see *morsch*.

vermottet

vermottet (coll.) antiquated, out-of-date; since the 1st half of the 20th c. Cf. *mottenfräßig, mottenzerfressen* etc. listed under *Motte*.

vermotzt

vermotzt (sl.) disgruntled, dissatisfied with everything; since 2nd half of the 20th c.

vermüdet: see *müde*.

vermummen

vermummen to hide, mask, obscure, disguise; figur. since the 17th c., e.g. Bürger, *Entführung*: '*als nun die Nacht Gebirg und Thal vermummt in Rabenschatten*'. In recent coll. *seelisch vermummt* is used for 'unapproachable, brusquely rejecting friendly entreaties'.

vermürben: see *mürbe*.

vermuten

etw. ~ to suspect or believe sth. to be possible (or possibly true); at first and until the 18th c. in reflex. constructions (still recorded thus by Adelung and used by Schiller), then in ordinary transitive use, e.g. Schiller, *Räuber* 1,2: '*ich vermuthe so etwas*'; hence *vermutlich* = 'probable, likely', since the 17th c. and *unvermutet* = 'unexpected', since the 17th c., e.g. Schottel [1663]: '*seiner gemahlin . . . unvermuhtetes ableben*'; cf. also *wider alles Vermuten* = 'contrary to expectation', since the 17th c., e.g. Grimmelshausen, *Simpliz.* [edit. K.] 2,187 (Goethe and Schiller used *gegen mein Vermuten*); *über mein Vermuten* is obs.; *die Vermutung* has been current since Early NHG for 'supposition, suspicion'.

etw. ~ *lassen* to lead one to (or let one) expect or suppose'; since the 18th c., e.g. Schiller, *Kab.* 4,7: '*mehr Schelmerei als diese offene Bildung vermuthen läßt*'.

← See also under *aufspringen* (for *plötzlich aufspringende Vermutung*), *Gewicht* (for *würden vermutlich das Gleichgewicht gehalten haben*), *sein* (for *es sei denn, daß man solches vermuten wollte*) and *Tag* (for *das hätte ich mein Tag nicht vermutet*).

vernachlässigen: see *Ruck*.

vernagelt: see *Nagel* (also under *Brett* and *glatt*).

vernarben: see *Narbe*.

vernarren: see *Narr*.

vernascht

See under *Kloster* (for *vernascht wie eine Klosterkatze*) and under *schmecken* (for *ein Mädchen vernaschen*).

vernebeln: see *Nebel* (also under *benebeln*).

vernehmen

etw. ~ to hear, notice, learn sth.; since OHG (*farniman*), when even then it could be used in its present sense; the meaning 'to perceive, see' is now becoming rare. Hence *vernehmbar* = 'audible, noticeable', since the 18th c. and *vernehmlich*, since MHG, when it could mean 'understandable' and 'reasonable'; Goethe in *Dicht.u.Wahrh.* 3,12 still used it for 'comprehensible', now mainly = 'audible'. The negative *unvernehmlich*, since Early NHG, at first mainly for 'incomprehensible', as in Luther 30,3,626 (Weimar), then mainly for 'inaudible', e.g.

Lohenstein, *Armin*. 2,157a [1689], but *unvernehmbar* only since the 18th c. (Goethe used both, e.g. in IV,25,305 (W.)).

jem. ~ to examine, interrogate sb.; since the 17th c., hence *Vernehmung* = 'interrogation', since the 18th. c.

das Vernehmen (1) (a.) agreement:, since the 18th c., e.g. Schiller, *Kab.u.L.* 2,3: '. . . *in verrätrischem Vernehmen mit Frankreich*' (now *Einvernehmen* is preferred), less used now, but *in gutem Vernehmen mit jem.m* = 'on friendly terms with sb.' is still current.

das Vernehmen (2) report; mainly in *dem Vernehmen nach* = 'according to rumours, based on what one hears' and *nach sicherem Vernehmen* = 'according to reliable reports'.

← See also under *Kapitel* (for *ein gut capitel he vernahm*), *Markt* (for *durch der Märkte Rausch vernehmen ihrer Stimme Laut*), *stumm* (for *ich vernahm sein stummes Flehn*) and *tief* (for *Volk von tiefer Sprache, die man nicht vernemen kan*).

verneinen: see *herunterziehen*.

vernetzt: see *Netz*.

vernichten

See under *Nachdruck* (for *Nachdruck etlicher Wörter vernichtet*) and *stehen* (for *ganz vernichtet zu werden*).

Vernichtung: see *Splitter*.

Vernunft

~ *annehmen* to see reason, come to one's senses; general since the 18th c., e.g. (DWb) Jean Paul 2,130 or 2,185 but previously expressed by a variety of other verbs, e.g. *die ~ gewinnen*, as in Brockes 6,687, *die ~ wirken lassen*, as in Weise, *Die drei kl.L.* 151, *zur ~ kommen*, as in Luther Bible transl. Dan. 4,31.

← See also under *abgetakelt* (for *er takelt seine Vernunft ab*), *bändigen* (for *Vernunft wird durch Vernunft gebändigt*), *benebeln* (for *die Vernunft benebeln*), *bringen* (for *jem. zur Vernunft bringen*), *Damm* (for *Dämm' und Schanzen der Vernunft*), *entlehnen* (for *von der Vernunft Geduld und Trost entlehnen*), *Fackel* (for *vackel der vernunft*), *fortkommen* (for *der Vernunft alles Fortkommen absprechen*), *gängeln* (for *die Vernunft muß sich nicht gängeln lassen*), *Geschwister* (for *Andacht und Vernunft meist Stiefgeschwister*), *Gewehr* (for *das Gewehr der Vernunft strecken müssen*), *graben* (for *grab mit sinnes grabestickel in die vernunft*), *Griff* (for *Handgriff der Vernunft*), *klar* (for *dem klaer ez die vernunft*), *Kost* (for *die kalte Vernunft zu einem Götzen erheben*), *Platz* (for *der Vernunft Platz machen*), *Rat* (for *die Vernunft zu rat nehmen*), *sauber* (for *blinde vernunfft*), *schauen* (for *die prahlende Vernunft zur Schau zu führen*), *schieben* (for *die Vernunft herumschieben*), *schließen* (for *die Vernunft zuschließen*), *Schluß* (for *Vernunftschluß*), *Schnur* (for *die Vernunft zur Schnur brauchen*), *Schritt* (for *wo die Vernunft mit der Schrift nicht Schritt halten kann*), *senken* (for *Bleysenkel unserer*

Vernunfft), *sinken* (for *alle vernunft in die füße zusammengesuncken*), *stecken* (for *förmliche Vernunftschlüsse*), *stehen* (for *die Vernunft steht still*), *Stelze* (for *die Stelzen unserer Vernunft*), *sträuben* (for *dawider sträubt sich die Vernunft*), *suchen* (for *versuchte Vernunft*), *Tag* (for *eh die Vernunft in diesen Köpfen tagt*), *Thron* (for *die Vernunft von ihrem Throne stoßen*), *Trieb* (for *die Vernunft und alle Triebe wollten*), *untergehen* (for *die Sonne der Vernunft*), *Vater* (for *vater der vernunfft*) and *vermählen* (for *Vermählung der dichterischen Einbildungskraft mit der Vernunft*).

vernünfteln: see *hin*.

vernünftig

See under *Jahr* (for *zu seinen vernünftigen Jahren kommen*), *Mund* (for *ein vernünftiger mund ist ein edel kleinot*), *nehmen* (for *sich vernünftiger nehmen*) and *Stelle* (for *stellenweise ein vernünftiger Mensch sein*).

vernußbäumen: see *Nuß*.

veröden: see *öde* (also under *Lohn*).

veröffentlichen: see *Arbeit*.

verpacken

etw. ~ to wrap or parcel sth. up; in the 19th c. still only recorded in its phys. sense; since the 20th c. figur. for 'to present or prepare sth. in a certain way, dress sth. up'; hence *Verpackung*, e.g. *er legte seine Ideen in anziehender Verpackung vor*.

verpallisadieren: see *Pallisade*.

verpanzern: see *Panzer*.

verpäppeln: see *Pappe*.

verpassen

etw. ~ (1) (obs.) to spend (time) in waiting; since the 18th c. and still in the 19th c., e.g. Goethe, *Schäfers Klagelied*: 'Regen, Sturm und Gewitter *verpaß ich unter dem Baum*'; now obs.

etw. ~ (2) to miss sth.; since the 17th c., f.r.b. Stieler [1691], e.g. (Sa.) Wieland 12,171: '*den Anlaß zu verpassen*'; often in *eine Gelegenheit* ~ = 'to miss an opportunity'. Similarly, *jem.* ~ = 'to fail to meet sb.'

den Anschluß ~ (coll.) to miss the bus; taken from the language of railways, where it means 'to miss one's connexion'; 20th c. coll.

verpassen (intrans.) to pass (in card games); recorded since the 18th c., e.g. by Adelung, but the simplex *passen* is now preferred.

jem.m eins ~ (coll.) to paste sb. one, give sb. a box on the ear (or other kind of blow); not yet listed in 19th c. dictionaries, first mainly in mil. sl. of 1st World War, then general coll. – Vulg.sl. is *einer Frau ein Kind* ~ = 'to make a woman pregnant', since 1st quarter of the 20th c.

sich etw. ~ (sl.) to help oneself to sth.; this can refer to 'stealing', also to 'eating, drinking' or general 'helping oneself to sth.'; since the last quarter of the 19th c.

sich etw. ~ *lassen* (coll.) to accept sth. without contradiction, submit to sth.; since early in the 20th c., sometimes = *sich etw. aufschwätzen lassen*, also often = *etw. kritiklos hinnehmen*.

verpatzen

etw. ~ (coll.) to make a mess of sth., botch a job; 20th c. coll. (mainly in the S.), e.g. Klabund, *Borgia* 165; still missing in *DWb*. [1895].

verpauken

jem. ~ (coll.) to give sb. a beating; modern coll. (not recorded in *DWb*.).

verpennen

verpennen (sl.) to oversleep; modern sl.

etw. ~ (sl.) to forget sth.; modern sl.

den halben Tag ~ (sl.) to spend half the day in bed (or lazing about); modern sl.

verpesten: see *Pest* (also under *auswerfen*).

verpetzen: see *petzen*.

verpfänden: see *Pfand* (also under *einlösen*).

verpfeifen: see *Pfeife*.

verpflanzen: see *Pflanze*.

verpflichten

seine Verpflichtung gegen etw. abtragen to discharge one's obligation to sth.; figur. when the debt is owed to an abstract; at least since the 19th c., e.g. Raabe, *S.Werke* 3,1,262 on debts which one ones to one's country: '. . . *könnte ich alle meine Verpflichtungen gegen dich abtragen* . . .'. In the 18th c. with dative instead of *gegen*, as in Schiller, *Merkw.Beisp. e.weibl. Rache*: '*was hab ich euch für Verpflichtungen?*'.

← See also under *Adel* (for *Adel verpflichtet*) and *unablösbar* (for *Schuldverpflichtung*).

verpfuschen: see *pfuschen* (also under *stumpf*).

verpicht: see *pichen*.

verpissen

sich ~ (vulg.) to disappear, make oneself scarce; also in imperative *verpiß dich* = 'piss off!'. Derived from 'to go away in order to urinate'; recent sl.

verplanen

verplant messed up through faulty planning; 20th c.

verplant sein to be committed through fixed arrangements; e.g. *meine ganze Woche ist verplant* = 'my engagement-list for the entire week is full'; 20th c.

verplappern

sich ~ (coll.) to let the cat out of the bag, reveal sth. that was meant to be kept secret; beginnings in the 17th c., when Gryphius used '*verplappertes Maul*'. See also under *verplaudern*.

verplätten

jem. ~ (regional) to give sb. a beating; only since the 20th c.; similarly, *jem.m eins* ~ (coll.) = 'to hit sb., land a blow on sb.'

verplatzen

sich ~ (obs.) to let out sth. (in the course of conversation), reveal sth. (unintentionally, carelessly); current in the 18th c., e.g. (DWb) Klinger, *Theater* 2,173, now obs.

verplaudern

die Zeit ~ (or *verplappern*) to spend one's time chatting; since the 18th c., e.g. Goethe, *Mitschuld.* 1,4: '. . . *in stiller Nacht ein Stündchen zu verplaudern*'.

etw. ~ to reveal what should have been kept secret; since the 18th c., e.g. Goethe, *Die Aufger.* 1.1. Goethe also used *verplappern* in this sense. Unusual is ~ = 'to forget through talking too much', as in Schiller, *Fiesco* 2,15.

verplempern

etw. ~ (coll.) to waste sth.; belongs to *plempern* = 'to move to and fro', which could in the compound ~ lead to 'to spill', hence also 'to waste'; recorded since the 16th c. (cf. *Schweiz. Idiotikon* 5,101); often used with *Zeit* or *Geld* (Raabe has it with *Munition*).

sich ~ (coll.) to waste one's abilities, fritter away one's opportunities; reflex. extension of the previous entry; in earlier periods it could also refer to personal relationships so that it could be used for 'to fall (or be) in love' (17th c.), also in *sein Herz* ~ for 'to give one' love to sb.', containing the notion of unwise or careless behaviour, and *verplempert sein* = 'to be engaged', recorded by Adelung; this appears to have dropped out of use.

verpöbeln: see *Pöbel.*

verprassen

etw. ~ to squander sth., dissipate sth. in a life of luxury; since Early NHG (Luther used it as *verbrassen*), usually with ref. to *Geld, Vermögen, Haus und Hof* or *Erbschaft*; the use with *Zeit* for 'to waste one's time' is obs.

verprellen

jem. ~ (coll.) to annoy or harass sb.; mainly with ref. to overbearing, bossy behaviour; 20th c. coll. ~ can also be used for 'to intimidate'; this may be derived from hunt. jargon where ~ = 'to scare (away)'.

verprügeln: see *Strich.*

verpudeln: see *Pudel* (also under *Haar*).

verpuffen: see *Puff.*

verpulvern: see *Pulver.*

verpuppen: see *Puppe.*

verpusten: see *pusten.*

verputzen

etw. ~ (1) (coll.) to waste sth.; it had been suggested, e.g. in *DWb.*, that this was derived from *Putz* = 'finery' and therefore meant originally 'to spend frivolously on finery' which was extended to 'to waste', but this is no longer accepted and the phrase is taken to be derived from *putzen* or *ausputzen* = 'to clean'; since the 18th c.

etw. ~ (2) (regional coll.) to put sth. away, gobble sth. up; same as *verdrücken* (for which see p. 2550).

ich kann ihn nicht ~ (coll.) I cannot stand him; 20th c. coll. (perhaps only regional coll., since hardly recorded).

verquer: see *quer.*

verquicken: see *quick.*

verquisten

Farben ~ (N.) to splash or wastefully use colours; in pejor. contexts since the 18th c., e.g. Lessing [edit. L.] 7,448, also Heyse, *Par.* 3,219; mainly in Northern areas.

verrammeln: see *rammeln.*

verrasen: see *rasen.*

verraten

etw. (abstract) *verrät jem. sth.* betrays sb. or reveals sth. in or about him/her; with abstracts since Early NHG, e.g. Luther Bible transl. Matth. 26,75: '*deine sprache verrhet dich*'; sometimes also with abstracts as subject and object, as in Kant, *Anthr.* 127: '. . . *daß die Sprichwörter . . . menschenfeindliche Grundsätze verrathen*'; also reflex. *sich* ~ (1) = 'to become evident', e.g. Börne 1,3: '. . . *wie unglückliche Liebe leicht errathen wird, als sie sich leicht verräth*' or Hebel 8,68 '*die größte Weisheit verrathet sich in der einfachsten . . . Einrichtung der Dinge*'.

sich ~ (2) to betray oneself, give oneself away; since Early NHG, e.g. Luther 2,11b (Jena).

sich ~ (3) to guess wrongly; since the 18th c., but not much used because one wants to avoid confusion with the other meanings of *sich* ~.

~ *und verkauft sein* to be well and truly sunk, utterly lost; an older form ~ *und betrogen* was f.r.b. Maaler [1561], with *verkauft* also since Early NHG, e.g. *Buch d. Liebe* 372a [1587].

← See also under *Geist* (for *so wird er sich bald verrathen*), *gelb* (for *du verreter, wie bist du gelb*), *hinter* (for *Verrätherei lauscht hinter diesem Schwur*), *Karte* (for *jem.m die Karten verraten*), *meinen* (for *es verräthrisch meinen*), *Nase* (for *wir sind verrathen*) and *streicheln* (for *verräterisches Streicheln*).

verratzt

~ *sein* (coll.) to be lost, in dire straits; belongs to *Ratte/Ratz* and can be interpreted as associated semantically with *Ratte* (3) and such phrases as *verrecken wie eine Ratte, das ist für die Ratte* and *die Ratte in der Falle haben,* for which see pp. 1946/7; 20th c. coll. (still missing in *DWb.* [1895]).

verrauchen: see *Rauch* (also under *Geist*).

verrauschen: see *Rausch* (also under *stellen*).

verrechnen

sich ~ to miscalculate; since the 17th c., e.g. Weise, *Erzn.* 139 [1672], Schiller, *Kab.u.L.* 5,1: '*gib acht, ob du dich da nicht verrechnest, mein Kind*'.

← See also under *Gewalt* (for *hatte mich gewaltig verrechnet*) and *rollen* (for *hast du dich in mir verrechnet*).

verrecken

verrecken (vulg.) to die wretchedly, peg out, snuff it; originally with ref. to animals, since the 17th c. in vulg. use for human beings, e.g. Grimmelshausen, *Simpliz.* [edit. K.] 1,442 or Schiller, *Räuber* 5,1: '*wie eine Katze verreckt*'.

← See also under *Ratte* (for *daß wir zuletzt wie Ratten verrecken*).

er tut's ums Verrecken nicht (vulg.) he'd sooner die than do that, he is absolutely determined not to do it; modern (not listed in *DWb.*).

verreckt (1) (coll.) damned; as an expletive (synonymous with *verdammt, verflucht*) since the 19th c., e.g. C.F. Meyer, *Nov.* 1,139: '*es ist der verreckte Schwarze, der . . .*'; not mentioned in *DWb.* [1895].

verreckt (2) (hunt.) possessing fully developed antlers; with ref. to stags; f.r.b. Weber, *Univ.Wb.* [1734].

verreiben: see *reiben*.

verreisen: see *Onkel*.

verreißen: see *reißen*.

verrenken

sich den Hals nach jem.m (or *etw.*) ~ (coll.) to strain to see sb. (or sth.), watch sb. (or sth.) eagerly; with ref. to expectation or curiosity; modern coll.

sich den Steiß ~ (coll.) to bow and scrape; with ref. to obsequious or fawning behaviour; modern coll.

der Hirsch verrenkt (hunt.) the stag is growing new antlers; f.r.b. Weber, *Univ.Wb.* [1734].

lieber den Magen verrenkt als dem Wirt etwas geschenkt (prov.expr.) much rather get a stomachache than leave unconsumed what you have paid for; since the 19th c.

← See also under *Fuge* (for *sei unser Staat verrenkt und aus den Fugen*).

verrennen: see *rennen*.

verrichten

See under *Andacht* (for *seine Andacht verrichten*), *Geld* (for *guete wort und alt gelt das verricht alles*), *sausen* (for *Geschäfte verrichten*, also under *Schlag*) and *spannen* (for *Vorspanndienste verrichten*).

verriechen: see *riechen*.

verriegeln: see *Riegel* (also under *Tür*).

verringern

etw. (or *jem.*) ~ to diminish or reduce sth., belittle sb.; with abstracts since the 17th c.

verrinnen: see *rinnen* (also under *Sand*).

verrollen: see *rollen*.

verrosten

See under *Pickelhering* (for *das Geld verrostet in der Kisten ausgedorrter Pickelhäringe*), *Rost* (for several items) and *Teufel* (for *verrosten, das sie kein teufel im fegfeur erpanzerfegen könte*).

verrucht: see *herumdrücken*.

verrücken

nach (or *auf*) *etw. verrückt sein* to be crazy about sth., have an (unreasonable) desire for sth.; since the 18th c., also with ref. to persons, occasionally with *in*, as in Hippel, *Lebensl.* 2,230: '*ich bin nicht in sie verliebt, ich bin in sie verrückt*'; cf. also Kotzebue, *Versch. wider Willen* 6: '*alle hübsche Frauen verrücken mir den Kopf*'.

bist du verrückt? (coll.) are you mad? rhetorical question, since the 18th c., e.g. Hebel 3,242.

ich werd' verrückt (coll.) this makes me mad, drives me round the bend; since early in the 20th c. as hyperbole, but much earlier as a statement that one's *Sinn, Kopf, Gehirn* has become *verrückt*, e.g. Goethe, *Faust I*, 3383 or Schiller, *Turandot* 2,11; beginnings in Early NHG, when Maaler [1561] listed: '*der sinn oder verstand ist jm verruckt*', whereas Stieler [1691] only recorded '*verrückung des verstandes*' and not *verrückt*.

es ist zum Verrücktwerden (coll.) it is enough to make you mad, to drive you up the wall; since the 19th c.; cf. also (DWb) Heyse, *Kinder d. Welt* 1,206: '*eine . . . ganz zum Verrücktmachen geschaffene, junge Schlange*'.

wie verrückt (coll.) like mad, as if demented; since the 19th c., since early in the 20th c. also in *wie ein Verrückter* (coll.).

verrückt und drei sind neun (coll.) what nonsense! you must be raving; this maintains that sb. has an additional 'sense', i.e. *Unsinn, Wahnsinn* oder *Blödsinn*; since ca. 1850. It was followed by *verrückt und fünf sind neun* and *verrückt und drei sind sieben*, maintaining that sb. lacks one sense.

← See also under *Geist* (for *in dem Geiste eines gewissen verrückten Grafen*), *Hirn* (for *hirnverrückt*), *Hund* (for *das macht ja den Hund in der Pfanne verrückt*), *Kompaß* (for *jem.m den Kompaß verrücken*), *Konzept* (for *jem.m das Konzept verrücken*) and *rücken* (also for *verrückbar, unverrückbar* and *unverrückt*).

verrufen

See under *rufen* (for *etw. verrufen* (1) and (2) and *etw. in Verruf erklären*).

verrupfen: see *rupfen*.

Vers

der Versler (obs.) bad poet; current since 2nd half of the 18th c., from obs. *verseln* = 'to produce bad poetry'; still used by Immermann, *Werke* [edit. Boxberger] 20,164, but rare even then and now obs.

das Versmaß metre; Kramer [1702] recorded '*mas in versen*', but the compound did not appear until much later, still missing in Adelung, but listed by Campe [1811].

sich auf etw. keinen ~ *machen können* to fail to comprehend sth. fully; f.r.b. Klix, 114 [1863]: '*da mache sich einer einen Vers daraus*', e.g. (Sa.) Ernst, *Bilder a.d. Beamtenwelt* 414 [1858] and *er hat sich einen* ~ *daraus gemacht* = 'he has understood the meaning of it', as in Lewald, *Das Mädchen von Hela* 1,275 [1860]; cf. also *er macht sich aus allem einen* ~ = 'he cottons on to things quickly, is quick in the uptake' recorded by Zoozmann, *Zitatenschatz* 1330 [1919]. It has been suggested that these phrases may have arisen in days before the existence of newspapers when street ballad singers visited towns and villages with pictures of exciting or gruesome events which they showed accompanying them with self-made verses. If a picture failed to provide them with ideas for suitable verses, the phrase could have been used. The late appearance of the idiom – not recorded before the 2nd half of the 19th c. – casts doubt on this theory.

← See also under *Bann* (for *hab ich es verwiesen aus meiner Verse Bann*), *flicken* (for *ohne gewöhnliche Flickreime fließen die Verse*), *Fuß* (for *Füße eines Fußes*), *hinken* (for *hinkende Verse*), *holpern* (for *holprichster Vers*), *humpeln* (for *der Vers humpelt*), *Keule* (for *der Keulenvers*), *Schmied* (for *Verseschmied*), *Schweiß* (for *Verse schweißen*), *schwer* (for *einen Vers schwerfällig machen*) and *strecken* (for *Streckvers*).

versacken: sink

versacken (coll.) to go to the dogs; same as *versumpfen* (for which see p. 2420), but younger; only since the beginning of the 20th c., recorded with a locus of 1908 in *Frankfurter Wörterbuch* 3389; often used for 'to spend much time in public houses'.

jem.m versackt werden (coll., obs.) to become repugnant or hateful to sb.; rarely recorded, but Sanders quoted from *Charlotte v. Schiller u. ihre Freunde* 1,287 [1860]: '. . . *so wird er Einem recht versackt*'; obs.

versagen

versagen (intrans.) to fail to work or function properly; modern examples have been given on p. 2047, but the remark about its first appearance must be corrected, since the locution began in Early NHG with ref. to *Büchse*.

sich ~ lassen (obs.) to send one's excuses for not appearing; still in the 19th c., e.g. (Sa.) Baggesen, *Poet. Werke* 4,139 [1836]; now obs., displaced by *sich entschuldigen lassen*.

besser freundlich ~ als unwillig gewähren (prov.) it is better to refuse (sth. to sb.) than to grant it unwillingly; since the 17th c., e.g. Petri [1605]: '*freundlich versagen ist besser denn mit unwillen geben*'.

← See also under *blau* (for *etw., das ihr die Kinderfrau versagte*), *Hand* (for *seine Hand versagen*), *Molch* (for *der alte Molch versagte ihr gar die Hand*), *Ritt* (for *keinem einen ritt versagen*) and *sagen* (for *jem.m etw. versagen* (1) and (2), *sich jem.m versagen*, intrans. *versagen*, *Versager* (1) and (2)).

versalzen

See under *decken* (for *das Befehlen wird ihnen noch versalzen werden*), *kochen* (for *viele Köche versalzen den Brei*), *Pfeffer* (for *jem.m den Pfeffer versalzen*) and *Salz* (for *jem.m etw. versalzen*).

versammeln

See under *Feder* (for *zu seinen Federn versammeln*), *Pater* (for *ad patres versammelt werden*), *Punkt* (for *Ansichten auf einen Punkt versammeln*) and *sammeln* (for *etw. versammeln*).

versanden: see *Sand*.

Versatz

das Versatzstück (lit.) cliché, hackneyed phrase; now mainly used for 'word or phrase which can be given any meaning that suits one in a particular context'; originally it meant 'set piece on the stage, movable piece of stage decoration'; figur. only since the 20th c., e.g. (Sp.) D. Brüggemann, *Vom Herzen direkt in die Feder* 61 [1968]: '. . . *konnte "Liebe" nicht als Identifikation, sondern nur als rein ideologisches Versatzstück existieren*'.

~ *verjährt nicht* (legal prov.) goods left as surety cannot become the property of the lender however long repayment of the loan may be delayed; recorded as prov. since the 18th c., e.g. by Pistorius [1716] and Estor [1757] and still in 19th c. collections, e.g. in Graf [1864].

versauen: see *Sau*.

versauern: see *sauer* (also under *Essig*).

versaufen: see *saufen* (also under *Fell*).

versäumen

See under *nachholen* (for *das Versäumte einbringen*), *säumen* (for *ich habe nichts zu versäumen* and *versäumt ist nicht geschenkt*), *Schaf* (for *manche rasche Schäferstunde . . . haben wir versäumt*), *stecken* (for *das Fest versäumen*) and *urbar* (for *macht urbar, was versäumt gelegen*).

verschachern

etw. ~ to sell sth.; usually pejor. describing a treacherous or mean disposal of sth.; in lit. since the 18th c., e.g. Schiller, *Fiesco* 1,7 or Heine 17,25: '. . . *tödten uns sogar um zu verschachern unsre Haut und unsern Leichnam*'.

verschachtelt: see *Schachtel*.

verschaffen

jem. zu etw. ~ (obs.) to turn sb. into sth. else; with abstracts since the 18th c., e.g. Bürger, *Untreue über Alles*: '*zum häßlichsten Zwerge verschafft dich mein Wort*'; now obs. displaced by *verwandeln*.

sich etw. ~ to obtain sth., see to it that one gets sth.; figur. with abstracts since the 18h c., e.g. *sich Gehör ~* = 'to make people listen to one, make oneself heard', f.r.b. Steinbach [1734]; similarly, *sich Respekt or Gewißheit ~*; also in locutions where sb. obtains or procures sth. abstract for sb., e.g. *jem.m die Möglichkeit* or *die Gelegenheit* ;. In earlier periods *bringen* or *machen* were used.

was verschafft mir die Ehre? what can I do for you? used when addressing an unknown caller, also iron. for 'why come to me?'; similarly, *was verschafft mir das Vergnügen Ihres Besuchs?*; both now considered rather stilted.

verschafft aussehen (regional) to look worn out (through too much work); little recorded, but I know it as in frequent use in Hesse and Württemberg; another regional use is *jem.m etw. ~* = 'to leave sth. to sb. in one's will'.

← See also under *Paß* (for *verschafft ihm sichern paß*).

verschallen: see *Schall* (also under *tot* for *verschollen*).

verschämt: see *Tag* (also under *Scham* for *unverschämt*).

verschanzen

sich hinter etw. ~ to take cover or hide behind sth.; with abstracts since the 18th c., e.g. Schiller, *Kab.u.L.* 3,6: 'sie sind verschanzt vor der Wahrheit hinter ihre eigene Laster'; cf. Wander [1876]: 'er weiß sich gut zu verschanzen'. See also under *Schanze* (1).

verschärfen (1): see *scharf.*

verschärfen (2)

etw. ~ (cant) to sell sth. stolen; because of its origin this ought to be *verscherfen*, since it is derived from *Scherf* = 'small coin', still used by Klopstock in *Mess.* 16,281: 'den kupfernen Scherf' and in Rückert, *Ges.poet.W.* 11,376 (see also the entry on *Scherflein* on p. 2098); recorded since the 19th c., later also used in sl. for 'to flog sth.'.

verscharren

etw. ~ (lit.) to hide sth. away, bury sth.; figur. since the 18th c., e.g. Schiller, *D.Carlos* 2,8.

← See also under *Flug* (for *Winde, die so manches Dasein mit leichtem Flugsand verscharren*).

verschatten: see *Schatten* (also under *Nuance*).

verschauen: see *schauen.*

verschaukeln

jem. ~ (sl.) to diddle sb., get the better of sb., lead sb. up the garden-path; 20th c. sl.; cf. *jem. schaukeln* and *jem. einschaukeln* listed on p. 2087; ~ is presumably an offshoot from the latter.

verscheiden

verschieden (1) different; since the 17th c., f.r.b. Stieler [1691]; cf. also Kramer [1719]: 'verschiedene verschiedene, unterschiedliche Leute'; hence also *verschiedentlich* (1) = 'on different occasions', since the 18th c.; Frisch II,170 [1741] recorded 'unverscheidenlich', but also the form with the intrusive *t*.

verschieden (2) various, diverse; semantically the same development as in Lat. *diversus* and *varius*; since the 18th c.

verschieden (3) several, a few; derived from *verschieden* (2) in the 18th c.; hence also *verschiedenemal*, since the 18th c., used by Goethe, and *verschiedentlich* (2) = 'several times, sometimes, on various occasions'.

← See also under *Grund* (for *grundverschieden*), *scheiden* (for *verscheiden*), *schmelzen* (for *Schmelztiegel der verschiedenen Stile*), *Schuh* (for *das sind zwei verschiedene Schuhe*), *schwarz* (for *so verschieden wie schwarz und weiß*) and *schweben* (for *so Verschiedenes schwebet nicht gleich*).

verscheinen: see *Schein.*

verschenken

etw. ~ (lit.) to grant or bestow sth.; with abstracts since the 18th c., e.g. *seine Gunst* or *Hand* ~, as in Schiller, *M.Stuart* 2,9; cf. also Schiller's 'Liebe verschenkt, Egoismus leiht'; usually

the simplex is preferred (see p. 2096).

← See also under *Spur* (for *mit Großspurigkeit verschenken*) and *stechen* (for *er verschenkt die Wurst, ehe die Sau gestochen ist*).

verscheißern

jem. ~ (vulgar) to have sb. on, diddle sb.; cf. Engl. sl. 'to do the dirty on sb.'; 20th c. sl.

verscherzen: see *Scherz.*

verscheuchen: see *scheuchen.*

verschieben

See under *schieben* (also under *heute*).

verschieden: see *verscheiden.*

verschießen

See under *Bolzen* (for *Bolzen für jem. verschießen*), *Patrone* (for *er hat seine letzte Patrone verschossen*), *Pfeil* (for *er hat alle seine Pfeile verschossen*), *Pulver* (for *sein Pulver verschossen haben* and *sein Pulver nach Sperlingen verschießen*) and *schießen* (for *das Ehrenkleid, eh' es verschossen ist* and *sich in jem. verschießen*).

verschimmeln: see *Schimmel.*

verschimpfen: see *schimpfen* (also under *Scham*).

verschimpfiert

verschimpfiert (a.) disgraced; *verschimpfieren* has been current since MHG for *beschimpfen*; Schiller in *Kab.u.L.* 1,1 still used the best participle: 'das Mädel ist verschimpfiert auf ihr lebenlang'; now a.

verschissen

verschissen (vulg.) damned, blasted; mainly in curses and insults; in lit. since the 17th c., e.g. Grimmelshausen, *Simpliz.* [edit. K.] 4,65. Stieler [1691] recorded 'die gelegenheit ist verschissen' for 'the opportunity has been missed'.

bei mir hat er ~ (vulg.) I am through (or I have finished) with him; modern sl.; cf. *in Verschiß geraten* and *jem. in Verschiß tun* listed under *Scheiße.*

Verschiß: see *scheißen.*

verschlafen: see *schlafen* (also under *braten*).

verschlagen

See under *beziehen* (for *eine verschlagene Dame*), *buhlen* (for *wenn die buhlerische Luft sie verschläget an die Kluft*), *Luft* (for *etw. verschlägt jem.m die Luft* or *den Atem*), *naß* (for *der naß, verschlagen, diebisch knecht*), *Rank* (for *die bösen sind verschlagen*), *Rede* (for *etw. verschlägt jem.m die Rede*), *Schlag* (for several locutions) and *Schlitten* (for *er hat ihr den Schlitten verschlagen*).

verschlammt: see *Schlamm.*

verschlappen: see *schlapp.*

verschlechtern

sich ~ to grow worse; not recorded before Adelung late in the 18th c.; with abstracts since ca. 1800 (Goethe used it); hence *die Verschlechterung*, since the 19th c.

verschleiern: see *Schleier* (also under *frisieren*).

verschleifen: see *schleifen.*

verschleißen: see *schleißen.*

verschlendern: see *schlendern.*

verschleppen: see *schleppen* (also under *Taktik* for *Verschleppungstaktik*).

verschleudern: see *schleudern*.

verschließen

See under *Brust* (for *etw. in der Brust verschließen*), *pochen* (for *seine Herzensthür verschloß er vor dem Anpocher*), *ringen* (for *Tränen verschließen*), *schließen* (for *etw. verschließen* and *sich verschließen*) and *Tür* (for *bei verschlossenen Türen*).

verschlimmbessern

etw. ~ to make sth. worse when trying to improve it; coined by Lichtenberg, rejected by Campe who suggested *zerbessern* instead, but Lichtenberg's verb has found acceptance and it came to be used even in its reflex. form, e.g. by Raabe, *Sämtl. Werke* 1,3,192 (*Der heilige Born*). *Verschlimmbesserung* was then formed, used e.g. by Schopenhauer, *Parerga* 446.

verschlimmern

etw. ~ to make sth. worse; f.r.b. Stieler [1691]; general since the 18th c. (considered better than *verschlechtern* by Adelung), e.g. Schiller, *D.Carlos* 2,8 (with *Schicksal*); *Verschlimmerung*, also recorded by Stieler, followed suit in the 18th c.

verschlinden (1): see *Scherbe*.

verschlinden (2): see *Löwe*.

verschlingen (1)

See under *Auge* (for *etw. or jem. mit den Augen verschlingen*), *Mast* (for *wie die See so manchen Mast verschlinget*), *Mund* (for *schon verschlungen hat ihn der schwarze Mund*), *nichts* (for *der weite Schooß des Nichts verschlingt dein Meer von Glück*), *Schlund* (for *Schlund, welcher das Vermögen unerfahrner Jünglinge verschlingt*) and *Stein* (for *ein schwer zu verschlingender Brocken*).

verschlingen (2)

See under *Pfad* (for *die verschlungenen Pfade des Menschen*), *Ring* (for *knüpften reizende Ring mit verschlungener Hand*) and *schlingen* (for *sich verschlingen* and *verschlungen*).

verschlucken

See under *Kapuziner* (for *er hat einen Kapuziner verschluckt*), *laden* (1) (for *er hat einen Ladestock verschluckt*), *Lineal* (for *steif, als hätte er ein Lineal verschluckt*), *Mücke* (for *Mücken seihen und ein Kamel verschlucken*), *Pille* (for *eine unangenehme Pille verschlucken*), *schlingen* (2) (for *ein Wort, eine Silbe verschlucken*), *schlucken* (for *verschwinden wie vom Boden verschluckt*) and *Stachel* (for *jem.m Stachelbeeren zu verschlucken geben*).

verschlungen: see *verschlingen*.

verschlüsseln: see *Schlüssel*.

Verschlossenheit: see *Schimmel* (also under *schließen* for *Insichverschlossenheit*).

verschmachten: see *schmachten* (also under *niederfließen*).

verschmähen: see *Mist* and *Mörtel*.

verschmecken: see *Handwerk*.

verschmeißen: see *schmeißen*.

verschmelzen

verschmelzen (lit.) to melt or fade away; with abstracts in lit. since the 18th c., e.g. Goethe, *Divan* 2,11: '*wie leicht Gewölk verschmilzt ihr Gruß*'.

wie Wachs ~ to melt like wax; current since Early NHG, e.g. Luther Bible transl. Micha 1,4.

← See also under *Naht* (for *nahtlos verschmolz er das Fremde mit dem eigenen*) and *schmelzen* (for several entries).

verschmerzen: see *Schmerz* (also under *entwöhnen*).

verschminken: see *schminken*.

verschmitzt

verschmitzt roguish, impish; derived from *Schmicke* = 'rod, whip' which led to MHG *smitzen* = 'to thrash, whip', then – like *verschlagen* – extended in the past participle to mean 'roguish, impish' since the 16th c.; explained by Frisch [1741] with '*weil theils Kinder durch Schmitze der Ruthe klug werden*'; some scholars prefer Heyne's explanation in his *Dt.Wb.* of 1895 that it first described a punished cheat or counterfeiter and that the term was then extended and generalised; *Verschmitztheit* has been current since ca. 1800.

← See also under *Fuhrmann* (for *verschmitzt wie eine Fuhrmannspeitsche*).

verschmockt

verschmockt (coll.) written for effect or for causing a sensation; 20th c. coll.; describes cheap journalistic practices, unprincipled or unsubstantiated publicity-seeking writing; derived from *Schmock*, a journalist in Freytag's *Die Journalisten* [1853] whose name came to stand for 'hack writer, unprincipled journalist'; Freytag did not invent the name, but took it over from his friend J. Kaufmann's *Bilder aus Österreich* 15 [1851]; for further details see Kluge, *Etym.Wb.*, Ladendorf, *Schlagwb.* and Büchmann, *Gefl. Wörter*.

verschnappen: see *schnappen* (also under *herausplatzen* and *laufen*).

verschnarchen: see *schnarchen*.

verschnaufen

verschnaufen to take a breather, get one's breath back; since Early NHG, f.r.b. Frisch [1741], e.g. Bürger, 500b: '*lassen Sie mich nur ein wenig verschnaufen von Allem, was mich jetzt bestürmt*'; also used reflex., e.g. Heine, *Rom.* 170.

verschneiden

See under *Hammel* (for *ainen verschnitenen knecht*), *Natur* (for *Anstand hat den Naturmensch verschnitten*), *Paß* (for *jem.m wird aller Paß verschnitten*) and *schneiden* (for *etw. verschneiden, jem. verschneiden, Wein verschneiden* and *nichts verschneiden*).

Verschnitt: see *schneiden*.

verschnupfen: see *Schnupfen* (also under *Teufel*).

verschnüren: see *Schnur*.

verschollen: see *verschallen*.

verschonen

jem. ~ to spare sb., leave sb. unharmed or unpunished; beginnings in MHG, f.r.b. Maaler [1561], e.g. Luther Bible transl. Rom. 8,32 (with genitive), in Maaler with dative, since the 18th c. with the accusative, e.g. Schiller, *Kab.* 2,1; cf. also Schiller, *Jungfr.v.O.* 1,2: '*ich hab dein Ohr verschont*'.

jem. ins Buch der Verschonung schreiben (prov. expr.) to want to hear no more about sb., avoid future contact with sb.; since the 17th c. (cf. Wander 4, 1582 [1876]), now obs.?

← See also under *Brot* (for *der Jude wird mich nicht verschonen*), *König* (for *Verschonen das steht königlich*) and *Titel* (for *mit der Madame verschonen Sie mich*).

verschönen

See under *raffinieren* (for *Verschönen ist nichts als Überfeinerung und unnatürliches Raffinieren*) and *schminken* (for *die natürliche Schönheit der Geschichte mit der Schminke der Dichtkunst verschönen*).

verschönern: see *schön*.

verschossen: see *verschießen*.

verschränken

jem. or etw. ~ (a.) to restrict sb. or sth., limit or confine sth.; with abstracts since MHG and still in the 19th c., e.g. Bismarck, *Reden* 14,37: '*ich werde fortfahren, mir die Freiheit des Worts in keiner Weise verschränken zu lassen*'. Now *beschränken* and *einschränken* are used.

in etw. verschränkt sein (a.) to be wrapped up in sth., labour under sth.; since the 18th c., e.g. Goethe, *Nat.Tochter* 3,2: '*verschränkt in Trübsinn, Krankheit, Menschenhaß*'; a. or obs., displaced by *befangen sein*.

verschränkt (1) (obs.) confused; used pejor. in the 18th c., e.g. by Goethe.

verschränkt (2) involved; in linguistic contexts, e.g. Goethe, *Dicht.u.Wahrh.* 3,12: '*verschränkte Wortstellung*', where it comes close to *verschränkt* (1).

verschränkt (3) embracing; with ref. to rhymes, modern.

die Verschränkung (lit.) interlocking; since the 18th c., e.g. Goethe, *Wanderj.* -3,1: '*Zweigesang, der, bei Wiederholung und Verschränkung immer fortschreitend, den Hörenden mit fortriß*'.

← See also under *Knäuel* (for *die vielen verschränkten Fäden aus einem Knäuel zu winden*) and *Schranke* (for *verschränkt* in several senses, *mit verschränkten Armen zusehen* and *sich verschränken*).

verschrauben

See under *quer* (for *ein wenig quer und verschroben*), *rauben* (for *die verschrobenen Ideen*) and *Schraube* (for *verschraubte Ausdrücke, etw.* or *jem. verschrauben, verschroben* and *Verschrobenheit*).

verschreiben: see *schreiben*.

verschreien: see *schreien*.

verschroben: see *verschrauben*.

verschrumpelt: see *Gesicht*.

verschrumpfen: see *schrumpfen*.

verschüchtern

jem. ~ to intimidate sb.; from LG, in HG since the 17th c., recorded by Stieler [1691]; since the 18th c. frequent in past participle, e.g. Goethe, *Faust* II,2: '*verschüchtert fliehn*' and II,5: '*verschüchtert stehen*'.

verschulden

etw. ~ to be to blame for sth.; has been current since OHG, frequent since MHG in the general sense of 'to sin, commit sth. sinful', as recorded by Dasypodius [1535]: '*ich verschuld böses, ich sündige*', e.g. Luther Bible transl. Job 34, 6: '*ob ich wol nichts verschuldet habe*', Goethe, *Dicht.u.Wahrh.* 1,5: '*ich will auch gegen die nichts verschulden, die . . .*'; also in reflex. locutions since MHG, f.r.b. Maaler [1561]; *verschuldet sein* = 'to be guilty of sth.', as still used in the 18th c., is now obs., since it could be confused with *verschuldet sein* = 'to be in debt', general since the 18th c.

ohne mein Verschulden through no fault of my own; f.r.b. Steinbach [1734], e.g. Goethe, *Lehrj.* 4,20: '*wenn sie ein Gut ohne ihr Verschulden verloren haben*'.

← See also under *Grund* (for *daz hat der grundböswicht wol verschuldet*).

verschulen

etw. ~ to turn sth. (e.g. an institution) into a kind of school, give a school-like structure to sth.; since the 20th c. (not yet listed in *DWb.* [1905]).

verschult sein to be corrupted by education; modern, e.g. (DWb) Rosegger, *Sünderglöckel* 334 [1904]: '*ein Mensch, der nicht verschult und nicht verbildet ist*'. Sanders [1865] glossed ~ with '*durch Schulzwang verderben*' with a *locus* from Jahn, *Merke z.dt. Volksthum* 80 [1833].

verschustern: see *Schuster*.

verschütten

See under *Brei* (for *den Brei verschütten*), *Rachen* (for *etw. in jem.s Rachen verschütten*) and *schütten* (for several entries, also for *es bei jem.m verschütten*).

verschüttgehen

etw. geht verschütt (sl.) sth. is lost, has disappeared; derived from cant, where *verschütt* could mean 'in prison', 'arrested', 'lost', 'unhappy' and 'impoverished', recorded from 1840 onwards. The original source must have been LG *schutten* or *schütten* = 'to impede, block, enclose' (cf. HG *schützen*), but S.A. Wolf in his *Wb.d.Rotwelschen* [1956] has suggested that for the compound *verschütten* one must also consider Czech *chudy* = 'poor, worthless' as of influence if one wants to explain the meanings 'unhappy' and 'impoverished'. This seems unnecessary when one bears in mind some figur. locutions, as in Freytag, *Wald.* 5 (in *Dram. Werke* [1881]): '*der Inhalt meines Lebens ist verschüttet*'.

jem. geht verschütt (1) (sl.) sb. perishes, comes to grief, has gone for a burton; for origin see above; also used to describe disappearance without trace.

jem. geht verschütt (2) (sl.) sb. goes to the dogs, becomes depraved; 20th c. sl.

verschwammt
verschwammt (rare) flabby, bloated, spongelike; f.r.b. Sanders [1865]; *schwammig*, for which see p. 2200, is preferred.

verschwärmen
den Tag ~ to spend the day in revelry; cf. *schwärmen* (p. 2204); f.r.b. Campe [1811], e.g. Goethe, *Die Mitschuld.* 1,1.

verschwärzen
jem. ~ to make sb. appear in a bad light, blacken sb.'s name; cf. *schwärzen* (p. 2207) and the cross-references at the end of *schwarz*, also *anschwärzen* (p. 59); since Late MHG, recorded since 1482, e.g. Goethe, *Götz v.Berl.* 1.

verschweigen
See under *darbieten* (for *den treu verschwiegnen Busen darbieten*), *Grab* (for *verschwiegen wie das Grab*), *Grund* (for *einen Namen verschweigen*) *Hülle* (for *die Hülle der verschwiegnen Nacht*), *Mord* (for *es bleibt kein Mord verschwiegen*), *Sang* (for *das verschweigt des Sängers Höflichkeit*), *Siegel* (for *unter dem Siegel der Verschwiegenheit*) and *Stein* (for *verschwiegen wie ein Stein*).

verschwelgen: see *schwelgen*.

verschwellen: see *schwellen*.

verschwemmen: see *schwemmen*.

verschwenden
See under *auffallen* (for *unbesonnene Verschwendung*), *aufhalten* (for *sich über jem.s Verschwendung aufhalten*), *schlingen* (2) (for *Verschwendung von Hab und Gut*) and *verkleiden* (for *verkleidet den Geiz in Verschwenden*).

verschwenderisch
verschwenderisch wasteful, lavish, profuse; figur. when an abstract or thing is said to be wasteful; since the 18th c., e.g. Schiller, *M.Stuart* 1,6: '... *der Gestalten Fülle verschwenderisch aus Wand und Decke quoll*', Goethe, *Faust II*,3: '... *gebar ... verschwendrisch eignen Bluts*' (with unusual genitive); cf. also Herder, *Zur Phil. u.Gesch.* 4,275: '*die vielsamige Natur ... wie sie verschwendet!*'.

← See also under *treiben* (for *Ideal, das verschwenderisch Blüten treibt*).

verschwestern: see *Bruder*.

verschwiegen: see *verschweigen*.

verschwimmen: see *schwimmen*.

verschwinden
um die Ecke ~ (coll.) to make off in a hurry, make oneself scarce, disappear; beginnings in OHG, modern with *Ecke* (cf. synonymous *sich um die Ecke drücken*, for which see p. 543, also p.

506); cf. also *ich muß einmal ~* (coll., euphem.) = 'I have to go somewhere (to wash my hands)'; modern.

~ wie eine Eidechse to disappear rapidly, vanish in a trice; e.g. Eichendorff, *Taugenichts* 8; cf. *~ wie vom Erdboden verschluckt.* Other comparisons noted by Wander [1876] are *~ wie Pferdedreck im Mondschein* and *~ wie Quecksilber* (used by Grimmelshausen in *Springinsfeld*). For others see below under the cross-references.

etw. ~ lassen (coll.) to steal sth.; in earlier periods often = 'to spirit sth. away' as in the case of conjurors, e.g. Schade, *Sat.* (repr.) 3,174 [1525]: '*wie die gaukler thund "verschwind als der wind, das keiner wider find"*' (cf. the formula used: '*hokuspokus, verschwindikus!*'), but then also in partly euphem. use for 'stealing'.

etw. verschwindet neben etw. anderem sth. pales (or sinks) into insignificance compared to (or by the side of) sth. else; since the 18th c., e.g. Goethe, *Groß-Cophta* 2,2; cf. also *verschwindend wenig* (or *klein*) = 'insignificant little (or small)', also since the 18th c.

← See also under *Dunst* (for *der Trug verschwand*), *Hülle* (for *wie bald verschwand Sache und Bedeutung*), *Komet* (for *verschwand wie ein Komet*), *Kulisse* (for *hinter den Kulissen verschwinden*), *Meteor* (for *Götterlust, die wie ein Meteor verschwindet*), *Nacht* (for *die Nacht verschwand* and *Halbnacht, in der die Erde verschwand*), *schauen* (for *vom Schauplatz verschwinden*), *Schirm* (for *soll der Menschenwürde starker Schirm verschwinden*), *schlucken* (for *er verschwand wie vom Boden geschluckt*), *senken* (for *in der Versenkung verschwinden*), *sinken* (for *wie ein Echo an den Felsen verschwinden*), *Sorge* (for *die Sorge verschwindet*) and *Spur* (for *er ist spurlose verschwunden*).

verschwirren: see *schwirren*.

verschwistern
etw. mit etw. anderem ~ (lit.) to connect or combine sth. with sth. else; since the 18th c., e.g. E.v.Kleist, *Sämtl.Werke* 1,22 [1766]: '*den Schertz mit Küssen zu verschwistern*'.

etw. verschwistert sich mit etw. anderem (lit.) sth. connects itself closely with sth. else, enters into an alliance with sth. else; since the 18th c., e.g. (T.) Lindau, *Nur Erinn.* 2,148 [1917]: '*mit diesem Frohlocken verschwistert sich ganz eigenartig eine gewisse Wehmut*'; cf. also *sich verschwistert fühlen*, as in Wieland, *Idris* 5,79 or *sich verschwistert finden*, as in Brockes, *Ird.Vergn.* 1,129 [1739].

← See also under *rumoren* (for *mit Gespenstern sind die Diebe nah verschwistert*).

verschwitzen: see *schwitzen*.

verschwommen: see *schwimmen*.

verschwören
sich ~ mit etw. (lit.) to enter into a conspiracy with sth.; figur. in lit., when abstracts are seen as entering into a conspiracy; since the 18th c., e.g.

Schiller, *Räuber* 2,3: '*ich bin kein Dieb, der sich mit Schlaf und Mitternacht verschwört*'; cf. also Schiller, *M.Stuart* 3,6: '*verschwört sich Haß und Liebe mich zu schrecken?*'

sich hoch und heilig ~ *zu* ... to promise or assert solemnly to ...; contains a ref. to the oath; still in the 19th c., e.g. Fontane, *Ellernklipp* 132, now a., but *sich einer Sache* ~ = 'to dedicate oneself to sth.' is still in use.

etw. ~ to renounce sth.; derived from 'to swear that one will give up sth.'; since MHG, e.g. Goethe, *Dicht.u.Wahrh.* 2,9: '... *daß ich dergleichen Possen auf ewig verschwor*'; often also followed by a negative (which semantically could be considered redundant), as in Fischart, *Garg.* 347: '*er verschwor oft nicht zu trinken*', also Lessing, *Fab.* 4.14 or Goethe, *Lehrj.* 2,7: '*ich habe verschworen, nicht mehr an sie zu denken*', where *geschworen* would now be required.

jem.m etw. ~ (obs.) to promise or vow sth. to sb.; 'on oath' is implied but omitted; in 18th c. lit., e.g. Wieland, *Kl el.* 7,193: '... *daß er ... ihr tropfenweise sein Blut verschworen hätte*'; now obs.

alles hat sich heute gegen (or *wider*) *mich verschworen* everything has conspired against me today; same figur. usage as in Engl.; f.r.b. Adelung [1801] (with *wider*), e.g. Wieland, *Gold. Spiegel* 2,10, Schiller, *Räuber* 5,1.

die Verschwörung (1) (obs.) curse; still in the 18th c., e.g. Wieland, *M.u.Gly.* 2,26; now obs., displaced by *Fluch* or *Verwünschung*.

die Verschwörung (2) conspiracy; the shorter form of older *Zusammenverschwörung*; since the 18th c., e.g. Schiller, *Die Verschwörung des Fiesko zu Genua.*

← See also under *anspinnen* (for *eine Verschwörung anspinnen*) and *Sonne* (for *sonnenscheue Verschwörung*).

versehen

sich einer Sache ~ to expect sth. to happen; apart from expectation it can describe a guess or a vague feeling or intimation, in earlier periods even hope (Hulsius [1616] glossed it with *hoffen*); since MHG, general since Early NHG often in *des versehens* = 'according to expectation', as in Luther 2,81b (Jena). It is this meaning which led to *unversehens* = 'unexpectedly, suddenly' (in Luther's writings also as *unvorsehens*), in Stieler (in his *Nachschuß*) as *unversehener weise*, as *unversehens* recorded by Steinbach [1734]. The other meaning of *unversehens* = 'unintentionally' is rare, if not obs., displaced by *unabsichtlich*.

einen Sterbenden ~ to administer the last rites to a dying person; ellipsis of *mit den Sakramenten*, derived from ~ = 'to provide (sb. with sth.)', current since MHG, with ref. to last rites since Early NHG.

etw. ~ (*an jem.m*) to omit to do sth. for sb. (which needed attending to); belongs to ~ = 'to miss' (see examples below under the cross-refer-

ences, esp. under *Spiel* p. 2299 for prov. *versehen ist auch verspielt*), e.g. Luther 1,421b (Jena): '*wie er* [the Pope] *es versehen hat, das er ein mal was guts leret*'; Luther still used it with the person in the dative, Adelung recorded it with *bei*, but *an* is now preferred.

← See also under *hingehen* (for *es ist versehen ... aber einmal geht ja hin*), *Marke* (for *etw. mit einer Marke versehen*), *Nacken* (for *eh' man sich's versieht*), *Nu* (for *in einem Nu geschieht, das man im Jahr nicht versieht*), *Schanze* (2) (for *die Schanze schlecht versehen*), *schwer* (for *ein schweres Versehen*), *sehen* (for *etw. versehen, mit etw. versehen, sich an etw. versehen* and *das Versehen*), *Spiel* (for *versehen ist auch verspielt*) and *Uhr* (for *er soll versehen eine stat und weißt nit, was geschlagen hat*).

versehren

etw. ~ (lit.) to wound sth. (abstract); since MHG, used figur. either with an abstract as the subject, as in (DWb) Weichmann, *Poesie der Niedersachsen* 1,8 [1725]: '... *die Not, die uns versehret*', or where some abstract is seen as harmed or wounded, as in Rückert, *Hamasa* 2,94 [1846]: '*aufgebraucht ist unser Lieben, das die Zeit versehrte*'.

← See also under *Mark* (1) (for *das ist das Feur, das uns versehrt das Mark in allen Beinen*).

verseichten: see *seicht.*

versenden: see *senden.*

versengen: see *sengen* (also under *brennen*).

versenken

sich in etw. ~ (lit.) to immerse oneself in sth., become engrossed (or absorbed) in sth.; for the beginning of the image see under *einsenken*; as ~ since the 18th c., e.g. (Sa.) J.J. Engel, *Schriften* 8,37: '*in ein tiefes Nachdenken versenkt*', Herder [edit. J. Müller] 16,96: '*versenke dich in ihm, Gedanke!*'; hence *die Versenktheit*, e.g. (DWb) Vischer, *Ästh.* 2,247: '*eine Versenktheit in die Natur*'. Much older is transitive figur. use, e.g. *jem. in etw.* ~, as in Luther Bible transl. 1 Tim. 6,9: '*lüste, welche versenken die menschen ins verderben und verdamnis*' (also Psalm 56,2), Schiller, *Jungfr.v.O.* 3,2: '*versenkt in Lethe sei auf ewig das Vergangene*'.

etw. in etw. anderem ~ (lit.) to bury or drown sth. in sth. else; since the 18th c., e.g. Lessing [edit. L.] 11,25: '*das Wesentliche wurde in einer Sündfluth von willkürlichen Sätzen versenkt*'.

← See also under *Nadel* (for *Buch, zwischen dessen Blätter man eine Nadel versenkt*), *Schwester* (for *laß das Auge sich ins Schwesteraug versenken*) and *senken* (also for *Versenkung*). See also under *verschwinden* for *Versenkung.*

versessen: see *Mauer.*

versetzen

versetzen to retort; since the 17th c., derived from the old meaning 'to parry, ward off' (aggression by sb.); the view that it arose from *jem.m einen Hieb, Schlag*, etc. ~ and was turned into an intransitive verb has not found general acceptance.

sich mit etw. anderem ~ to mix or combine with sth. else; modern with abstracts, e.g. Freytag, *Bild.* 1,521: '... *wo altrömisches Volksleben sich mit germanischem Wesen versetzt hatte*'.

sich ~ (tech.) to change its course; used with ref. to rivers; recorded since the 18th c., e.g. by Jacobsson.

jem.m etw. ~ (obs.) to prevent sth. from reaching sb., block access of sth. to sb.; still in the 18th c., e.g. Goethe, *Faust I*,3809/10: '... *als ob die Orgel mir den Athem versetzte*'; now obs. (displaced by *benehmen*).

← See also under *Berg* (for *Berge versetzen wollen*), *Hieb* (for *hinterrücks versetzt er ihm einen Hieb*), *Kreis* (for *euch auf einen höhern Schauplatz zu versetzen* and *daß der Kunstrichter sich in den Gedankenkreis seines Schriftstellers versetze*), *Lage* (for *sich in die Lage von . . . versetzen*), *Mensch* (for *ihr seid noch Mensch genug, euch zu Euripides Admeten zu versetzen*), *Pfand* (for *versetzen ihren Hals zum Pfande*), *ruhen* (for *jem. in den Ruhestand versetzen*) and *setzen* (for *etw. versetzt jem.m etw.*, *jem.m etw. versetzen*, *etw. versetzen* (1) and (2), *jem. in einen Zustand versetzen* and *jem. versetzen* (1) and (2)).

verseucht: see *Seuche*.

versichern

See under *flexibel* (for *sonst versichere, daß ich ein flexibel Gemüthe bey ihm gefunden*), *Schanze* (1) (for *vor Gewalt versichert und beschanzt*), *sicher* (for *jem.m etw. versichern, versichert sein, Versicherung, sich einer Sache* or *Person versichern*, also *jem. verunsichern*), *Statt* (for *etw. an Eidesstatt versichern*) and *strafen* (for *seine Versicherungen Lügen strafen*).

versickern: see *sickern*.

versieben: see *Sieb*.

versiegeln

etw. ~ (lit.) to put a seal on sth., confirm sth.; since the 18th c., e.g. Schiller, *Kab.u.L.* 5,1: '*mit einem Eid gedachte er seinen Betrug zu versiegeln*', (H.) '*seine Treue mit seinem Tod versiegeln*'; *besiegeln* (which see on p. 277) is preferred.

← See also under *Grab* (for *versigelt mit Bapstlichen decreten*) and *Siegel* (for *Eingang zur versiegelten Urquelle der Natur, ihm blieb das Buch versiegelt* and *jem.s Lippen sind versiegelt*).

versiegen

versiegen to dry up; since MHG (*versîhen*), in comparisons since Early NHG, e.g. Luther Apocr. transl. Ecclesiasticus 40,13: '*der gottlosen güter versiegen wie ein bach*'; later often with *Quelle*, e.g. Goethe 36,41 (W.) or Herder, *Krit.Wälder* 1,4: '*Quelle des Gefühls, . . . die jetzt . . . beinahe versiegen ist*'; cf. also Zschokke, *Selbstschau* 1,139 [1842]: '*gänzliches Versiegen der Hilfsquellen*'. Note that *versiegbar* is not in use, but the negative *unversiegbar* has been current

with abstracts since the 18th c., e.g. Lessing [edit. M.] 10,27 or Goethe IV,37,294 (W.): '*jene unversiegbare Springquelle*'.

← See also under *Quelle* (for *wenn der mütterliche Milchquell versiegt ist, nie versiegt der Brunnquell ihrer Freude* and *die Quellen sind versiegt, wo ihre Freuden quollen*) and *Sand* (for *in dürrem Sand versiegen*).

Versifex: see *schäbig*.

versilbern

etw. ~ to convert sth. to cash; has been current since MHG for 'to cover with a layer of silver', for 'to sell' since Late MHG, only in modern period in near-coll. sense for 'to make money out of sth.'.

← See also under *hinunterbringen* (for *brachte das bittere Landleben nicht ohne die Versilberung des Stadtlebens hinunter*), *Pille* (for *die Bühne muß mir zur Versilberung der Pille dienen*) and *Silber* (for *etw. versilbern* (1) and (2) and *jem.m die Hände versilbern*).

versimpeln

versimpeln to become stupid or dull; since the 18th c., now also in non-pejor. sense for 'to content oneself with a life of simplicity and moderate demands'.

etw. ~ (1) (coll.) to lose, miss or ruin sth. through thoughtlessness or absentmindedness; since the 19th c., first recorded for Saxony in Albrecht, *Leipz. Mundart* [1881], now also in other areas.

etw. ~ (2) to simplify sth. or present it as negligible; often = *verharmlosen* or *zu sehr vereinfachen*; since 1st half of the 20th c., but *DWb.* [1895] quotes a passage from Moscherosch [1652] in which the word comes close to the modern meaning.

versingen

die Zeit ~ (rare) to while away the time with singing; in occasional use since the 18th c., e.g. Wieland, *Abderiten* 1,10: '*nachdem sie . . . den Abend vertanzt, versungen und verscherzt haben*'.

etw. ~ (obs.) to dispel sth. by singing; since the 17th c., e.g. Opitz 1,115: '... *ihr Winterleyd versingen*'; cf. also Herder [edit. S.] 8,500: '*das Lied . . . versingt ihr die Zeit der Einsamkeit*'.

← See also under *Leier* (for *ein versungen liedlin*).

versinken

die Versunkenheit in etw. (pejor.) fall into corruption, sin, depravity, etc.; since the 18th c., derived from ~ = 'to become depraved' (rarely used, since the simplex is sufficient), f.r.b. Campe [1811], e.g. Varnhagen van Ense, *Denkwürdigkeiten* 6,349 [1837]: '*die traurige Versunkenheit . . . jener Zustände*'.

← See also under *Blume* (for *in lauter Lust und Wonne fast versunken*), *Boden* (for *das wir versinken oder zu grund fallen werden*), *Sarg* (for *sei wie ein Sarg in deine Brust versunken*), *sinken* (for *vor Schmerzen versinken, du wirst nicht versinken, vor sich selbst versinken, in Laster* or *Trauer versinken* and *in etw.* or *jem. versunken sein*), *stumpf* (for *in Stumpfheit versinken*), *Traum* (for *traumversunken*) and *Trank* (for *in Trank versunken sein*).

versippt

versippt closely related; originally with ref. to family relationship, derived from *Sippe* = 'family, clan, relations'; extended to things and abstracts only in recent times, not yet mentioned in extended sense in *DWb.* [1895] and in Adelung and Campe not listed in any sense; e.g. *diese Banken sind* ~.

← See also under *Sippschaft*.

versitzen

See under *Mauer* (for *euch zu Sklaven versessen*) and *sitzen* (for *etw. versitzt* (1) and (2), *etw. versitzen, sich versitzen* and *auf etw. versessen sein*).

versklaven: see *Sklave*.

versohlen

See under *Bürste* (for *einen versohlen*) and *Sohle* (for *jem. versohlen* and *jem.m die Haut, das Fell, den Buckel versohlen*).

versöhnen

etw. ~ to reconcile, appease, placate sth.; belongs to *sühnen* (*versünen* still used by Luther); since the 17th c. in the form *versöhnen*, f.r.b. Schottel [1663]; with abstracts since the 18th c., e.g. Schiller, *Räuber* 5,2 or *Kab.u.L.* 4,5, Goethe, *Pandora* 817 [1810]: '*der Träume Gabe, sie versöhnt den grimmen Schmerz*', Freytag, *Soll u.H.* 1,28: '*. . . entbehren und fasten, um den Neid des Schicksals zu versöhnen*'.

sich mit etw. ~ to become reconciled to sth.; with abstracts only since the 19th c.

← See also under *glühen* (for *solang ein Busen noch der Versöhnung glüht*), *Groll* (for *wenn sich die grollenden Elemente versöhnen*) and *Pfand* (for *zum Pfand und Siegel redlicher Versöhnung*).

Versöhner

der ~ (relig.) Jesus Christ; in its general sense ~ (in MHG *versüener*) means 'conciliator'; applied to Christ since the 18th c., to any extent first by Klopstock, e.g. *Mess.* 9,28 and the Pietists, f.r.b. Adelung; cf. also its use with ref. to abstracts, since the 18th c., e.g. Hölderlin [edit. Litzmann] 2,30: '*o Vergessenheit! Versöhnerin!*' (but note that *Versöhnerin* has been current since MHG).

versonnen

versonnen dreamy, pensive, lost in thought; belongs to *Sinn* and has been current since MHG (*versunnen*), but in the sense of 'pensive, dreamy' only since the modern period, not yet mentioned in Campe [1811] or Meißner [1856].

versorgen

See under *Kragen* (for *den Kragen versorgen*), *Kuh* (for *Wissenschaft eine tüchtige Kuh, die ihn mit Butter versorgt*), *Maul* (for *zwanzig Mäuler zu versorgen haben*) and *Trog* (for *Kampf um den Futtertrog der ehelichen Versorgung*).

versparen: see *sparen*.

verspeien: see *speien*.

verspeisen: see *speisen*.

verspekulieren: see *spekulieren*.

versperren

See under *Fach* (for *etw. in einem Fach versperren*), *Paß* (for *der Paß vom Herzen nach der Zunge war versperrt*), *sperren* (for *etw. versperren* and *sich einer Sache versperren*) and *Tor* (for *mir ist verspart der saelden tor*).

verspielen

es ist noch nichts verspielt (prov.expr.) all is not lost yet; in this negative locution at least since the 18th c., e.g. Wieland, *D.Sylv.* 3,8, but earlier in positive statements such as *alles ist verspielt* = 'all is lost', e.g. (DWb) Lohenstein, *Sophon.* 1,505 [1689]; cf. Goethe 3,346 (W.): '*wenn all ihr Würdiges ist verspielt*'.

← See also under *Sack* (for *Sack und Seele verspielen*) and *Spiel* (for *etw. verspielen* (1) and (2) and *verspielt*).

verspießt: see *Spieß*.

verspinnen: see *spinnen*.

verspitzen

See under *Nase* (for *sich auf etw. verspitzen*) and *spitz* (for *sich auf jem. verspitzen*).

versplittern: see *Splitter*.

versprechen

See under *Berg* (for *jem.m goldne Berge versprechen*), *binden* (for *durch ein Versprechen gebunden sein*), *Edelmann* (for *Versprechen ist edelmännisch, Halten ist bäurisch*), *einlösen* (for *sein Versprechen einlösen*), *Geist* (for *die liebe Meyern hat versprochen . . .*), *halten* (for *ein Versprechen halten* and *versprechen, reinen Mund zu halten*), *Hand* (for *jem.m etw. in die Hand versprechen*), *heilig* (for *heiliges Versprechen*), *hoch* (for *etw. hoch und heilig versprechen*) *leer* (for *leere Versprechungen*), *Morgen* (for *Versprechen und Halten ist zweierlei*), *Parole* (for *bei bidermanns trew versprochen*), *Reihe* (for *das Höchste versprechen*), *Ring* (for *wer sich von dem goldnen Ringe goldne Tage nur verspricht*), *Rücken* (for *hinder dem Rücken mich manches verspricht*), *Sau* (for *ich hab's schon einer andern Sau versprochen*), *selig* (for *etw. bei seiner Seligkeit versprechen*), *Spanien* (for *ich versprach dir einmal spanisch zu kommen*), *sprechen* (for *etw. verspricht etw., sich viel von jem.m versprechen* and *jem.m einen Rosengarten versprechen*), *stopfen* (for *ich werde mit Versprechungen gestopft*) and *treu* (for *sie versprachen bei glauben und treuen*).

verspritzen: see *Tinte*.

Verstand

der ~ (personified) reason; seen as a person in many locutions, frequent since the 2nd half of the 18th c. with such verbs as *fassen, gebieten, regieren, richten, den Dienst versagen*, e.g. Goethe 23,270 (W.): '*der ungebundene freie Verstand sprach ihn los'*, often with verbs in the present participle, e.g. *der anschauende, der forschende, der zerlegende* ~, also sometimes in past participle, e.g. *der (un)geschulte* ~; for other examples see the list of cross-references below.

der ~ (obs.) meaning; since Early NHG, f.r.b. Maaler [1561], still in the 18th c., e.g. Klopstock 2,79: *'noch fassest du nicht des Gesetzes ganzen Verstand'*; now obs., displaced by *Bedeutung*.

es hat keinen Sinn und ~ it does not make sense; since Early NHG, e.g. Luther 34,1,383 (Weimar); cf. Goethe, *Faust I*, 550: *'es trägt Verstand und rechter Sinn mit wenig Kunst sich selber vor'*.

guten ~ *mit jem.m haben* (regional) to get on well with sb.; current since Early NHG, f.r.b. Maaler [1561], but now only in some S. regions, e.g. Bav.

des geht über meinen ~ that is not intelligible to me, I do not comprehend this; f.r.b. Dasypodius [1537] as *'es ist uber unsern verstandt'*.

den ~ *verlieren* to go out of one's mind, take leave of one's senses; in pathological contexts also = 'to go mad'; at least since the 17th c., since Kramer recorded it in 1702, but other synonymous locutions are older (MHG or Early NHG), such as *es hat ihm den* ~ *benommen, ihn des Verstands beraubt* or *den* ~ *verrückt* (or *verwirrt*). Lessing used it in *Em.Gal.* 4,7 and 5,5.

das mußt du mit ~ *essen* (*trinken*, etc.) you must savour that thoroughly (because it is sth. special); ~ here = 'discrimination, due consideration'; in use at least since the 18th c., e.g. Goethe, *Groß-Cophta* 3,9: *'die übrigen gruppiren sich mit Verstand'* or IV,21,238 (W.) with ref. to two bottles of wine: *'die eine hat uns schon besonders gut geschmeckt, die andere wollen wir mit destomehr Verstand trinken'*.

'~ ist stets bei wen'gen nur gewesen' real understanding has always been confined to a few people; quotation from Schiller, *Demetrius 1* in a passage which begins *'Was ist die Mehrheit? Mehrheit ist der Unsinn'*, continues with the near-prov. *'man soll die Stimmen wägen und nicht zählen'* and ends *'der Staat muß untergehn, früh oder spät, wo Mehrheit siegt und Unverstand entscheidet'*.

unverständig lacking in understanding, insensate, ignorant, stupid; since Late MHG (*unverstendic*); since the 18th c. occasionally with ref. to abstracts, e.g. (DWb) Reimarus, *Wahrh.d.n.Rel.* 600 [1766]: *'eine blinde unverständige Kraft'*. Much older is *unverständlich* = 'incomprehensible', current since OHG (*unfarstantlicho*). For *Unverstand* see the example in the Schiller quotation above.

← See also under *abgeschmackt* (for *dem gemeinen Verstand offenbar*), *Amt* (for *wem Gott gibt ein Amt, dem gibt Er auch Verstand*), *aufheitern* (for *tiefsinnigen Verstand mit Witz aufheitern*), *aus-*

polieren (for *Auspolierung des Verstandes*), *benagen* (for *der Verstand, der alles so gern benagt*), *benebeln* (for *den verstandt vernebeln*), *beschränken* (for *beschränkter Untertanenverstand*), *bringen* (for *jem. um seinen Verstand bringen*), *daheim* (for *sein Verstand ist nicht daheim*), *durchschneiden* (for *Durchschnittsverstand*), *Dutzend* (for *Verstand für ein Dutzend haben*), *gehen* (for *das geht über meinen Verstand*), *gesund* (for *nichts als gesunden Verstand*), *Glück* (for *er hat mehr Glück als Verstand*), *Haar* (for *lange Haare, kurzer Verstand*), *hüten* (for *die thürhüterin, das ist, der verstandt*), *Kasten* (for *der Verstandskasten*), *kommen* (for *zu Verstand kommen*), *löschen* (for *aus Unverstand*), *Lot* (for *du hast kein Lot Verstand*), *Magd* (for *die Elemente selbst sind Mägde des Verstandes*), *Messer* (for *messerscharfer Verstand*), *nah* (for *wir wollen dem Verstand nicht zu nahe treten*), *Nase* (for *einen durchdringenden Verstand haben*), *Oase* (for *Verstandeswelt*), *Pfau* (for *pfawen in der hoffart, gänß im verstandt*), *Pferd* (for *Pferdeverstand haben*), *Qual* (for *dem Verstand abgequälte Bilder*), *Reich* (for *Verstandesreich*), *saufen* (for *man säuft sich von Verstand*), *Schanze (1)* (for *sich im Unverstand verschanzen*), *Schlamm* (for *sein Verstand ist ganz verschlammt*), *schleifen* (for *ein Verstand, den Fleiß und Übung schliff*), *schließen* (for *Hertzen, deren Bund Verstand und Liebe schließt*), *schmecken* (for *all jhr dichten, kunst und ehr schmecket nach verstand und lehr*), *schneiden* (for *seinen schneidenden lebendigen Verstand*), *schreiben* (for *in den Verstand geschrieben*), *schwach* (for *schwach von Verstand*), *Schwanz* (for *der Verstand ist im Arsche*), *sechs* (for *du hast nicht für einen Sechser Verstand*), *seicht* (for *wie seicht sein Verstand war*), *Sinn* (for *Mangel am Verstande*), *spitz* (for *den Verstand spitzen*), *spucken* (for *. . . braucht nicht soviel Verstand*), *stark* (for *starker Verstand*), *stecken* (for *wenn der Verstand uns stecken lassen will*), *Steuer (2)* (for *weil sie den steuerman han vergessen, das ist verstand*), *still* (for *da steht einem der Verstand still*), *stutzen* (for *hier stutzt und stocket mein Verstand*), *Thermometer* (for *Magen ist oft der Thermometer des Verstandes*), *Tribunal* (for *das Tribunal des Verstandes*) and *tunken* (for *der Pinsel soll in Verstand getunket sein*).

verständig

See under *Sache* (for *sachverständig* and *der Sachverständige*), *Seele* (for *ein verstendiger mensch ist eine theure seele*) and *Verstand* (for *unverständig*).

verständlich

See under *schwer* (for *schwer verständlich*), *selbst* (for *selbstverständlich* and *Selbstverständlichkeit*) and *Verstand* (for *unverständlich*).

Verständnis

See under *lösen* (for *des Traums Verständnis löste mir ein Mönch*), *nah* (for *zum näheren Verständnis*), *scharf* (for *sin verstantnüsse etwz für baz gescherpfet würde*) and *Tick* (for *dessen Verständnis durch Zufall gekommen*).

verstärken: see *stark*.

verstatten

etw. ~ (obs.) to permit sth.; since the 16th c. and still used in the 18th c., e.g. Schiller, *M.Stuart* 4,5, now obs., displaced by *gestatten*.

← See also under *nehmen* (for *der Tochter nicht verstatten . . .*) and *Raum* (for *Spielraum, den sie verstattet*).

verstauben: see *Staub* (also under *Molch*).
verstauchen: see *stauchen* (also under *Pupille*).
verstauen: see *stauen*.

verstecken

See under *rennen* (for *Versteckens spielt*), *riechen* (for *es ist kein Pfennich so versteckt, den er nicht reucht*) and *stecken* (for *etw. verstecken, sich verstecken, versteckt, versteckt sein* and *etw./jem. muß sich vor jem.m verstecken*).

verstehen

zu ~ *geben* to give sb. to understand; since MHG, e.g. Luther Bible transl. Hebrews 11,14; since Early NHG also in the sense of 'to make sb. aware of sth., let sb. know sth.' (usually in a tactful or indirect way), and in this sense recorded by Adelung.

sich auf etw. ~ to be competent or versed, experienced in sth.; since MHG (but at first with genitive), e.g. *Erec* 3078, Luther Bible transl. Acts 25,20; later also with ref. to persons, e.g. *sich auf Leute* ~, as in Schiller, *D.Carlos* 2,11 or 2,15.

sich zu etw. ~ (a.) to agree (not very willingly) to do sth.; still general in the 18th c. and recorded by Adelung, but now becoming a.

wir ~ *uns* we understand each other, see eye to eye, are in agreement on that; since the 17th c., f.r.b. Kramer [1702], e.g. Klinger, *Werke* 4,103: '*wir verstehen uns über diesen Punkt so wenig, wie über viele andre*'.

das versteht sich (von selbst) that is understood, that goes without saying; f.r.b. Stieler [1691], e.g. Schiller, *Kab.u.L.* 1,5; with *von selbst* f.r.b. Adelung [1780].

wir wollen uns als neutral verstanden wissen we want to be considered as neutral; the locution is patterned on Lat. *intellectum velle aliquid*; in German since Late MHG, e.g. Lessing 11,299: '*ich will hierunter sowohl das Werk des Plaundes als das Kephalas verstanden wissen*'.

du redest wie du's verstehst what you say reflects your incomplete (or biassed) understanding of the matter; this belongs to a group led by *wie man es versteht* = 'according to one's lights'; Schiller used it in *Picc.* 2,6: '*du redst, wie du's verstehst*'.

ich verstehe nur Bahnhof (sl.) it's all double Dutch to me; also sometimes = 'I do not want to hear anything about that'. This arose at the end of 1918 when soldiers intent on getting their discharge or reaching home were only interested in finding a railway station and unwilling to talk about (or listen to) anything else.

er versteht's so wenig wie der Esel den Psalter (prov.) it is beyond his comprehension; e.g. Luther 26,341 (Weimar); there are many similar comparisons in the regions (for a list of them see Wander 4,1607 [1876]).

← See also under *Barometer* (for *sich schlecht auf den Barometer der Seele verstehen*), *Bauer* (for *was versteht der Bauer vom Saffran*), *blau* (for *ich verstehe den blauen Teufel*), *jagen* (for *der versteht das Jägerlatein*), *kaufen* (for *den Kauf der Zeit verstehen*), *Kind* (for *das kann ein Kind verstehen*), *Krähe* (for *soviel von etw. verstehen wie die Krähe vom Sonntag*), *Kuh* (for *die die geschrift verstênt also wênig als ein kuo*), *Mist* (for *jem.m etw. mit der Mistgabel zu verstehen geben*), *Pfeife* (for *er versteht den Pfiff*), *pflücken* (for *weil die Blumen eines großen Daseins abszupflücken verstand*), *Rand* (for *das versteht sich am Rande*), *Salz* (for *dies ist mit einem Körnchen Salz zu verstehen*), *Sau* (for *metavorice zu verstehn*), *schneiden* (for *die Weinverlasser verstehen den Wein zu schneiden*), *Schnitt* (for *sich auf den Schnitt verstehen*), *Sitte* (for *davon verstehst du nichts*), *Spaß* (for *er versteht keinen Spaß/Scherz*), *Spott* (for *um ein spott, verstehe wohlfeil*), *Sprache* (for *daß sie unsere Augensprache verstanden*), *Stimme* (for *ihr stumme Stim verstehn*), *trennen* (for *verstehen sie, vom Sein den Schein zu trennen*) and *unterlegen* (for *ob ich eine correkte Stelle falsch verstehe*).

versteifen

sich ~ (econ.) to rise, become dearer; with ref. to the market value of shares on the stock exchange, e.g. *der Markt in X hat sich versteift* = 'shares in X have risen in price'; 20th c.

← See also under *steif* (for *sich auf etw. versteifen* and *versteift*).

versteigen: see *steigen*.
versteinern: see *Stein* (also under *Mandel* and *stehen*).
versteint: see *Stein* (also under *Gesicht*).

verstellen

See under *einhüllen* (for *der Khalife hüllte sich in Verstellung ein*), *einwiegen* (for *mit Verstellung mich erst einzuwiegen*), *lauern* (for *hinter scheinbarer Offenheit lauerte die tiefste Verstellung*), *Schein* (for *wer spät im Leben sich verstellen lernt*), *Schranke* (for *da brach . . . die Schranke der Verstellung*) and *stellen* (for *etw. verstellen, jem.m etw. verstellen* and *sich verstellen*).

versteuern: see *Steuer* (2).

verstieben

etw. verstiebt (lit.) sth. is scattered like dust, is dispersed in wider sense also = 'vanishes'; figur. with abstracts since the 18th c., e.g. Goethe 9,274 (W.): '*des weisen Mannes Rath verstiebt zu nichts*', Ranke 15,209: '*die Gedanken Buckinghams verstoben als seien sie nicht gewesen*'; cf. also Klopstock, *Werke* 7,182: '*wenn ich, wie ein Staub, verstiebe, wird mit mir mein Gott vereint*'; now *zerstieben* is preferred.

verstiegen: see *steigen*.

verstimmen: see *Stimme* (also under *Absicht* and *munter*).

verstocken

See under *ergreifen* (for *Verzweiflung ergreift nur Verstockte*), *Hirn* (for *das Hirn der Zeit ist ehern, es ist verstockt, vertaubt*), *steif* (for *wollen wir allein uns eigensinnig steifen und verstocken*) and *Stock* (for *verstockt, Verstocktheit* and *sich verstocken*).

verstohlen

See under *blond* (for *meine tiefste und verstohlenste Liebe*), *decken* (for *Glut verstohlner Lüste*), *stehlen* (for *verstohlen* (1) and (2)) and *streuen* (for *keine kleinen verstohlnen Metaphern*).

verstolpern: see *stolpern*.

verstopfen

See under *Ohr* (for *der Begierden Ohren mit Tugend-Wax verstopft* and *seine Ohren verstopfen*), *Schlauch* (for *wer kan die wasserschleuche am himel verstopffen*), *schlüpfen* (for *wie er alle Schlupflöcher verstopft hat*) and *stopfen* (for *etw. verstopfen* (1) and (2) and *sich verstopfen*).

verstören

See under *davontragen* (for *meine verstörten Nerven*), *Schlaf* (for *verstöre seine Ruhe nicht*) and *stören* (for *verstört* and *Verstörung/Verstörtheit*).

verstoßen

See under *fressen* (for *bald verstoß ich sie*), *nachkommen* (for *ein solcher Verstoß*), *Öl* (for *alles Öl der Hoffnung war verstoßen*), *Spiel* (for *das verstößt gegen die Spielregeln*) and *stoßen* (for *jem. verstoßen, etw. verstoßen, der Verstoß* and *in Verstoß geraten*).

verstreichen

die Zeit verstreicht (the) time passes; ~ has been used figur. with abstracts since MHG (also in reflex. locutions); with ref. to *Zeit* f.r.b. Stieler [1691]; often with *lassen* since the 17th c., e.g. Goethe 23,18 (W.): *'wie thöricht der Mensch seine Zeit verstreichen läßt!'*.

die Tiere ~ (hunt.) the animals disperse, move away from their previous habitat; since the 18th c., also used reflexively.

← See also under *streichen* (for *etw. verstreichen*).

verstreiten

sein Vermögen ~ (a. or regional) to spend one's fortune with litigation; f.r.b. Stieler [1691], still used in the 18th c., but then confined to some regions, esp. Bav. – ~ could also be used with ref. to time: *die Zeit* ~ = 'to spend one's time arguing'; this, too, is now only recorded for Austro-Bav. areas.

verstreuen: see *streuen*.

verstricken: see *Strick*.

verstrubbeln: see *frisieren*.

verstümmeln: see *stümmeln* (also under *hinüberreißen*).

verstummen: see *stumm* (also under *tief*).

Versuch

der ~ (lit.) essay; introduced by Montaigne [1580] for 'essay', taken over in German in the 18th c., e.g. Schiller's dissertation *'Versuch über den Zusammenhang der thierischen Natur des Menschen mit seiner geistigen'* [1780], hence also *poetische Versuche*, as in Seidel, *Ges. Werke* 1,272.

das Versucherle (regional coll.) sample (esp. of food); same as standard German *Kostprobe*; mainly in SW areas, recorded for Swabia in Fischer 2,1371 [1908].

einen Versuchsballon steigen lassen to fly a kite; from French *ballon d'essay*; used with ref. to unconfirmed reports or tentative statements made to elicit a reaction by sb. or the general public; 20th c.

← See also under *Kaninchen* (for *Versuchskaninchen*), *schüchtern* (for *ein schüchterner Versuch*), *schwimmen* (for *Versuche der Formulierung*) and *Turm* (for *Tragweite von den gleichen kleinen Versuchen*).

versuchen

sich ~ to put oneself to the test; in wider sense = 'to examine oneself'; at first mainly in relig. contexts, e.g. Luther Bible transl. 2 Cor. 13,5: *'versuchet euch selbs, ob jr im glauben seid'*; now *untersuchen* is preferred.

sich in etw. ~ to try one's hand at sth.; derived from ~ = '(to try to) experience'; since the 17th c.

nichts unversucht lassen to try everything, leave no stone unturned; since the 19th c.

Versuchen (or *ein Versuch*) *kann nichts schaden* (prov.) there can be no harm in trying; this restates Ovid's *quid tentare nocebit*; recorded by Wander [1876]; Simrock [1846] recorded as prov. *'versuchs und häng die Angel ein; was gilt's, es werden Fische dein'*.

unversucht schmeckt nicht (prov.) what you have not tasted has no taste; in wider sense = 'what has not been tried is valueless'; f.r.b. Pistorius [1715].

← See also under *Angel* (for *jem. zu angeln versuchen*), *Heil* (for *sein Heil versuchen*), *Masche* (for *es mit einer andern Masche versuchen*), *Meister* (for *sie versuchten Gott immer wieder*), *Quadrat* (for *die Quadratur des Kreises versuchen*), *sehen* (for *versuochtiu swert*), *Sisyphus* (for *versuchte die Sisiphusarbeit*), *sprengen* (for *vergeblich versucht man, die überkommenen Formen zu sprengen*) and *suchen* (for *etw. versuchen* (1) and (2), *jem. versuchen* (1) and (2), *sich versuchen an etw., versucht sein* and *in Versuchung geraten*).

Versucher

der ~ tempter, seducer; since MHG in various contexts, but later often used as a term for the devil through Luther's use of it in his Bible transl., e.g. Matth. 4,1.

Versuchung: see *Strick* (also under *suchen*).

versumpfen: see *Sumpf*.

versündigen: see *Sünde*.

versüßen

etw. ~ to sweeten sth., make sth. more acceptable or agreeable; figur. since the Baroque, e.g.
Zesen, *Ros.* 226 (with *Zeit*), Gellert, *Fab.* 2,34
(with *Mühe*), Schiller, *Räuber* 2,1: '*dein Zorn
versüßt ihm seinen Triumph nur*'; frequent with
Pille.

← See also under *Essig* (for . . . *ist der Essig
meines Bluts versüßt*), *Kelch* (for *den sauren Kelch
des Ehstands zu versüßen*) and *Pille* (for *die Pille
versüßen*).

vertagen

etw. ~ to postpone sth.; the original meaning
'to fix a date for sth. (mainly a court appearance)' contains the notion of 'postponing', which
began to come to the fore in the 16th c. (cf.
Teuerdank 77,62 [1517]). It could mean, when
used with a personal object, 'to order sb. to
appear on a certain day' (since the 13th c.), but
this is obs., and its use by Goethe in *Götz* 1 only
indicates a deliberate retention of the language of
his ENHG source and does not mean that this
sense was still current in the 18th c. – Equally
obs. are two meanings recorded by Campe
[1811]: 'to miss a date' and 'to omit an item on
the agenda'.

sich ~ to adjourn; with ref. to formal meetings
(cf. *tagen* = 'to hold a conference' and *Tagung*
discussed under *Tag*), which are to be resumed
at some future date; since the 19th c., but not yet
recorded by Campe [1811].

vertändeln: see *Tand* (also under *Schlüssel*).

vertappen: see *Tappe.*

vertaubt: see *Hirn.*

vertauschen

See under *Busen* (for *den Busen zu vertauschen*),
König (for . . . *nicht mit dem König von England
vertauschen*), *Mond* (for *nicht mit dem Kaiser im
Mond sein neues Glück vertauscht hätte*), *Rolle* (for
die Rollen vertauschen) and *tauschen* (for *etw. vertauschen* (1), (2) and (3)).

verteidigen

etw. ~ to defend sth.; with abstracts since
Early NHG, e.g. Luther Apocr. transl.
Ecclesiasticus 4,33: '*verteidige die warheit bis in
den tod*'; Luther also used it in cases where the
chief sense is 'to protect', as in Isaiah 38,6.

← See also under *doppelt* (for *sünd vertheidigen
heißt doppelt sündigen*), *Herd* (for *den eignen Herd
verteidigen*) and *Rede* (for *Verteidigungswaffe*).

verteilen

See under *Jugend* (for *diu verteilte jugend*), *kurz*
(for *bei der Verteilung zu kurz gekommen*) and *Teil*
(for *etw. verteilen* and *sich verteilen* (1) and (2)).

verteufeln: see *Teufel.*

vertiefen

See under *Samt* (for *das schwarze Geäst vertiefte
noch das Sammetdunkel*), *studieren* (for *ins Studium
vertieft sein*) and *tief* (for *etw. vertiefen, jem. vertiefen, Vertiefung* and *sich vertiefen*).

vertieren

etw. vertiert jem. sth. brutalizes sb.; since the
19th c., frequent in *vertiert sein* = 'to be inhuman'
in political invectives; hence also *Vertiertheit* and
Vertierung recorded by Campe [1811].

vertilgen

etw. ~ to destroy, eradicate sth.; with abstracts
since MHG, f.r.b. Frisius; often also used for 'to
abolish, cancel', e.g. Schiller, *Br.v.Mess.* 423: '*die
Rechnung gegenseitig zu vertilgen*'; hence *vertilgbar*
and *unvertilgbar*, since the 18th c.

← See also under *Nebel* (for *ich vertilge deine
sünde wie ein nebel*), *schlingen* (1) (for *bis dieses
böse Schlingkraut vertilgt*), *Spur* (for *eine Spur vertilgen*) and *Unkraut* (for *das Unkraut vertilgen*).

Vertrag

ein leoninischer ~ (jur.) a contract or agreement
under which one party obtains the entire profit
or an undue advantage; this alludes to the
Esopian fable 260 dealing with the lion's share.
See under *Löwe*, p. 1635 for *Löwenanteil.*

in diesem Haus ist kein ~ (regional coll.) in this
house they are always at each other's throats;
recorded since the last quarter of the 19th c.; cf.
sich mit jem.m vertragen (below).

← See also under *abschließen* (for *einen Vertrag
abschließen*), *Anker* (for *einen Vertrag verankern*),
auflösen (for *einen Vertrag auflösen*), *aufnehmen*
(for *mit jem.m einen Vertrag aufnehmen*), *aufsetzen*
(for *einen Vertrag aufsetzen*), *binden* (for *durch
einen Vertrag gebunden sein*), *brechen* (for *den
Vertrag brechen*), *eingehen* (for *Eingehen eines
Vertrags*), *mager* (for *besser einen mageren Vertrag
als einen fetten Sentenz zu erwarten*) and *übergeben*
(for *nichts von Verträgen!*).

vertragen

sich mit jem.m ~ to get on well with sb.; since
Early NHG, f.r.b. Frisius, e.g. Luther 34,1,60
(Weimar); derived from *jem.* ~ = 'to bear with
sb., be tolerant towards sb.', since MHG, e.g.
Luther Bible transl. 2 Cor. 11,19: '*jr vertraget
gerne die narren, dieweil jr klug seid*' (cf. also obs.
jem.m etw. ~ = 'to forgive sb. sth., tolerantly
allow sth. to sb.', since MHG, e.g. *Iwein* 870:
'*daz ich im sîniu wort vertrage*', f.r.b. Maaler
[1561]). Also extended to things, f.r.b. Kramer
[1702], e.g. *diese zwei Farben* ~ *sich* = 'these two
colours go well together, harmonize', and to
abstracts, e.g. *sein Benehmen verträgt sich nicht mit
seiner Stellung* = 'his behaviour is not appropriate
to (or does not befit) a man in his position'; since
the 18th c., e.g. Lessing, *Miss S.S.* 4,4. – Cf. also
the prov. *vertrag, leid und meid*, recorded by
Henisch [1616].

die Sache verträgt keinen Aufschub the matter
brooks no delay (or postponement); since the
17th c., e.g. Lohenstein, *Armin.* 2.44a: '*ihre
reichsgeschäffte vertrügen kein langes abseyn aus
Thracien*'; cf. *es leidet keinen Aufschub* listed on
p. 98.

~ *werden* (obs.) to become worn out; in wider sense = 'to perish'; since MHG, mainly with ref. to the effect of time, hence still in the 19th c. in *von der Zeit ~ werden* = 'to be or become worn out, become obsolete or useless', but now obs., except in phys. contexts with ref. to clothes.

ich könnte eine heiße Suppe ~ (coll.) some hot soup would not come amiss (or would do me good); often as a polite request. This extends the usual meaning of *etw. ~ können* = 'to be able to stand, bear, consume without suffering harm'; cf. similar Engl. coll. 'I would not mind some hot soup'; modern coll.

jem.m das Geld ~ (obs. or regional) to take one's money to sb. else, buy elsewhere; since the 17th c., f.r.b. Kramer [1702]; now only in some regions.

verträglich sein to be good-natured, peaceable, easy to get on with; since Early NHG, hence also *unverträglich*, since Early NHG (*unverdregelich*), e.g. Goethe 47,138 (W.). Another meaning of *unverträglich* used by Goethe 29,63 (W.) = 'unbearable' is obs., displaced by *unerträglich* or *unausstehlich*.

etw. ist verträglich mit etw. anderem sth. is compatible with sth. else; with abstracts since the 17th c., e.g. Goethe 25,6 (W.); hence *unverträglich* = 'incompatible', since the 17th c., e.g. Lohenstein, *Armin.* 2,1147a, Goethe 41,2,131 (W.).

← See also under *Jude* (for *das verträgt er wie der Judenmagen den Schweinespeck*), *packen* (for *Pack schlägt sich, Pack verträgt sich*), *Pfaffe* (for *Pfaffenmagen kann alles vertragen*), *Rauch* (for *wer das Feuer genießen will, muß auch den Rauch vertragen können*), *schwirren* (for *diesen Schwirr vertrage ich kaum*), *Stiefel* (for *einen Stiefel vertragen können*) and *Stoff* (for *eine stoffärmere . . . verträgt dagegen Witzarabesken*).

vertrauen
zu große Vertraulichkeit erzeugt Verachtung (prov.) familiarity breeds contempt; from Classical sources (e.g. Pub. Syrus 102 '*parit contemptum nimia familiaritas*') and international, e.g. French *trop de familiarité engendre mépris*, but in this wording late in German (19th c., e.g. Wander [1876]).

sich mit etw. (abstract) *vertraut machen* to familiarize oneself with sth.; hence also *mit etw. vertraut werden* for 'to get used to sth.'; since the 18th c. with abstracts, e.g. Lessing, *Miss S.S.* 1,7: '*ich war mit dem Laster zu vertraut geworden*'; since the 19th c. often with *Gedanke* and *machen*, but also in lit. with ellipsis of *machen*, as in O.Ludwig, *Scudery* 4,14: '*. . . bittet er . . . daß Ihr mit dem Gedanken Euch vertraut*'.

← See also under *blind* (for *blindlings zu vertrauen*), *Fuß* (for *auf vertrautem Fuß* and *Fuß der Vertraulichkeit*), *Heim* (for *so vertraulich*), *Maul* (for *den ich zum Vertrauten gemacht hatte*), *Natter*

(for *vertrau du schönen Geistern dich*), *Pauke* (for *die Vertrauenspauke anschlagen*), *Rückhalt* (for *ich darf unser Schicksal nicht ihr vertrau'n*), *Sache* (for *Sache des Vertrauens*), *Sakrileg* (for *das vertraute Gut eines Verstorbenen*), *schauen* (for *wird man ihm viel vertrauen*), *schenken* (for *jem.m sein Vertrauen schenken*), *schleichen* (for *sich in jem.s Vertrauen schleichen*), *sein* (for *in der vertraulichen Sprechart* and *gesetzt, daß Doris auch es dem Damöt vertraut*), *setzen* (for *sein Vertrauen auf etw./jem. setzen*), *Sorge* (for *laß dies dein mir vertrautes Gut nur einzig meine Sorge sein*), *stecken* (for *jem.m etw. im Vertrauen stecken*) and *stehlen* (for *sich in jem.s Vertrauen stehlen*).

vertreiben
Farben ~ to apply colours in such a way that they blend or gently merge; at least since the 18th c., when it was figur. extended to literature, as in Lessing, *Dram.* 20: '*einige . . . Pinselstriche zu lindern und mit den übrigen in eine sanftere Haltung zu vertreiben*').

← See also under *Gilde* (for *vertriebene Fürsten*), *Grille* (for *Grillen vertreiben*), *mästen* (for *die sich vom Raube der vertriebnen Bürger mästen*), *muffig* (for *dein muffig Wesen vertreiben*), *Opium* (for *Zeitvertreib*), *Paradies* (for *Erinnerung . . . Paradies, aus welchem wir nicht vertrieben werden können*), *Platz* (for *jem. von seinem Platze vertreiben*), *Raupe* (for *es vertreibt die Motten*), *Reh* (for *ihm lange Weil vertreibe*), *Schwert* (for *was uns aus dem Paradies vertreibt*), *Sorge* (for *eim die sorg abnemen und vertreyben*), *treiben* (for *Zeitvertreib* and derivatives) and *Trotz* (for *den Trotz vertreiben*).

vertreten
See under *eingreifen* (for *daß jeder sein Ort, Beruff und Ampt vertretten . . . soll*), *Gewicht* (for *die herangewachsene Generation in der Familie zu vertreten*), *Kuh* (for *die Kuh hat vier Beine und vertritt sich doch*), *link* (for *steht er gegen den Vertretungsstaat*), *praktizieren* (for *wir haben das praktische Christentum zu vertreten*), *Schuh* (for *etw. längst an den Schuhen vertreten haben*), *Stelle* (for *ich selbst vertrete Mutterstelle*), *Tenor* (for *vertritt der Hauptredacteur . . . die Stelle des ersten Tenors*), *treten* (for *jem. vertreten* (1) and (2), *etw. vertreten*, *Vertreter*, *vertretbar*, *jem.m den Weg vertreten* and *sich die Füße vertreten*) and *Vater* (for *Vaterstelle bei jem.m vertreten*).

Vertreter
ein übler ~ (regional coll.) a nasty specimen; first recorded for Berlin in 1904 by H. Meyer in *D.richt.Berliner*.

vertrinken: see *Lumpen*.

vertrocknen
See under *Mumie* (for *mumienhafter, vertrockneter Styl*) and *Saft* (for *wie Saft vertrocknet*).

vertrödeln
etw. ~ (coll.) to forget to do sth.; also used for 'to postpone sth. again and again'; since the 18th

c., e.g. Goethe in a letter to Fr.v.Stein of 12.12.1781 on *Egmont*: '*dieses lang vertrödelte Stück*'.

← See also under *Trödel* (for *die Zeit vertrödeln*).

vertrottelt: see *Trott*.

vertrunken: see *vertrinken*.

vertun

See under *Sohn* (for *was der Vater erspart, vertut der Sohn*) and *tun* (for *vertun, etw. vertun* (1), (2) and (3), *sich vertun* and *da gibt es kein Vertun*).

vertuschen: see *tuschen*.

verübeln: see *übel*.

verüben

etw. (abstract) *verübt etw.* (rare) sth. (abstract) dispenses, transacts, performs sth.; ~, recorded since the 17th c., is now used with ref. to reprehensible actions, but could still be used in the 18th c. without expressing disapproval, occasionally with abstracts as the subject, e.g. Goethe 15,1,343 (W.): '*Gnade, die liebende, Schonung verübende*'.

← See also under *Stelle* (for *Orte nämlich, wo ein Frevel verübt worden ist*).

verunglimpfen

etw. verunglimpft jem. (or *sth.*) sth. (abstract) denigrates sb., blackens sb.'s character; ~ has been recorded since the 15th c. but not with the present-day meaning, which became current in the 16th c., f.r.b. Frisius with ref. to sb. slandering sb., e.g. Luther 26,264 (Weimar); figur. with abstracts as the subject since the 18th c., e.g. with *Betragen*, as in Iffland, *Spieler* 5,6: '. . . *das verunglimpft den Monarchen und den Dienst*', where one of the objects is also an abstract.

verunglücken: see *Säule*.

verunreinen: see *verunreinigen*.

verunreinigen

etw. ~ to soil sth., sully, besmear or besmirch sth.; since the 16th c., e.g. Luther 15, 256 (Weimar): '. . . *das keyn befleckung . . . unsern heyligen glauben verunreyne*'; also reflex. with abstracts since Early NHG (as ~ usually since the 18th c.), e.g. Goethe 38,270 (W.): '. . . *sich den Mund . . . mit . . . Lästerungen verunreinigen*'.

verunsichern: see *sicher*.

verunstalten

etw. ~ to disfigure, corrupt sth.; first as *verungestalten* (Early NHG), since the 18th c. as ~, sometimes with ref. to abstracts such as *Sprache*; hence also *Verunstaltung*, general since the 19th c.

veruntreuen: see *treu*.

verunzieren

etw. ~ to spoil the appearance of sth.; recorded since the 17th c., e.g. by Schottel [1663]; figur. with ref. to abstracts since the 18th c., occasionally also used for 'to disparage sth., give sth. a bad name'.

verurteilen

See under *scharf* (for *jem. scharf verurteilen*), *scheitern* (for *zum Scheitern verurteilt*), *schmachten* (for *zu schmachten verurteilt*) and *Teil* (for *etw. verurteilen* and *Verurteilung*).

vervagabunden: see *vagabundieren*.

vervielfachen

etw. ~ to redouble sth.; f.r.b. Campe [1811]; with abstracts such as *Anstrengungen, Bemühungen* since the 18th c.; synonymous *vervielfältigen* has been current since the 17th c., with abstracts also since the 18th c.

vervielfältigen: see *vervielfachen* (also under *Anfang*).

vervögeln: see *Vogel*.

vervorteilen

jem. ~ (obs.) to overcharge, defraud or get the best of sb.; since Early NHG, e.g. H. Sachs, *Fab.* 2,78, still used by Schiller in *Räuber* 4,2; now obs., displaced by *übervorteilen*.

verwachsen

verwachsen (past participle) (1) overgrown; figur. since Early NHG, e.g. Luther 10,1,1,35 (Weimar) on justice: '*aber dieser weg ist gantz vorwachsen*'.

verwachsen (past participle) (2) distorted, misshapen, deformed; in phys. (mainly med.) contexts since the 17th c., figur. since the 18th c., e.g. Klopstock, *Gel.Rep.* 87: '*eine verwachsene Seele*'.

etw. ~ to grow out of sth.; since the 18th c. mainly with ref. to clothes, but also in figur. contexts since the 18th c., as in (DWb) Lichtenberg, *Aphor.* 1,76: '*er hatte seine Bibliothek verwachsen, so wie man eine Weste verwächst*'.

die Wunde ist ~ the wound has healed; in phys. contexts since Early NHG, f.r.b. Maaler [1561]; much later sometimes with ref. to figur. 'wounds', although *vernarben* and *heilen* are preferred; in consoling coll. use, however, *das verwächst sich* is still alive.

mit etw. ~ *sein* to be deeply rooted in sth., feel at one with sth.; derived from the notion of organic growing together or fusing; since the 18th c., e.g. Goethe IV,35,118 (W.) or Treitschke, *Dt. Gesch.* 5,44: '*ein patriotischer Adel . . . fest verwachsen mit seinem Staate*'; sometimes also in reflex. locutions; the noun *Verwachsenheit* only since the 19th c.

verwägen: see *verwegen*.

verwahren

sich gegen etw. ~ to object to sth., protest; at first mainly in legal contexts (with the noun used since the 15th c.); derived from the older meaning 'to protect, keep safe'; general since the 18th c.; cf. *bewahren* on p. 302.

← See also under *einlegen* (for *Verwahrung einlegen*), *Engel* (for *ein Ding verwahren wie vorm Dieb*), *entstürzen* (for *rasch entstürzt das Gefühl sich der Verwahrung*), *reißen* (for *verwar in . . . auf das er sich von dir nicht reiße*) and *Schloß* (for *das Schloß ist übel zu verwahren, dazu jedermann einen Schlüssel hat*).

verwahrlosen: see *auswerfen*.

verwaist: see *Waise*.

verwalten: see *Portefeuille*.

verwandeln

See under *Mühle* (for *ihre Einbildung verwandelt Windmühlen in Riesen*) and *Posse* (for *etw. in eine Posse verwandeln*).

verwandt

verwandt related; apparently figur. when used for relationship not based on blood, but actually returning to the old wider meaning expressing some kind of 'connexion'; at first (since Early NHG) for 'closely connected, attached, emotionally near', as in Goethe IV,21,85 (W.): '*im Grunde bin ich von Jugend her der Rechtsgelahrtheit näher verwandt als der Farbenlehre*', sometimes expressing the notion of common origin, as in Schubart, *Ged*. 3,36: '*geselle dich immer zur Erde, mein Staub, bist ja mit ihm verwandt*', often used with ref. to languages (*verwandte Sprachen*). Since the 17th c. with abstracts, e.g. Abr. a Santa Clara, *Judas* 1,4: '*Schlemmerey und Ohnsauberkeit, dann dise beede gemainiglich verwandt seind*'; hence *verwandte Ansichten, Gefühle, Empfindungen*, etc. See also the cross-references below.

← See also under *aufsteigen* (for *ein Verwandter der aufsteigenden Linie*), *Ecke* (for *um tausend Ecken verwandt*), *entfernen* (for *entfernter Verwandter*), *Grenze* (for *Grenze . . . wo jede Tugend mit dem verwandten Laster zusammenfließt*), *Haufen* (for *Überhäufung verwandter Gegenstände*), *laufen* (for *verwandte Bilder*), *Pelz* (for *verwandt bis auf den Pelzkragen*), *Saite* (for *eine verwandte Saite*), *schieben* (for *verwandte Schmerzen*) and *Seele* (for *seelenverwandt, Blutverwandte, Geistes- und Seelenverwandte*).

verwanzen: see *Wanze*.

verwarnen: see *Ton*.

verwaschen: see *waschen*.

verwässern: see *Wasser*.

verweben

etw. in etw. anderes ~ (lit.) to weave sth. into or fuse sth. with) sth. else; since the 18th c., e.g. Goethe, *Werther* I: '*Züge . . . die ich . . . in meine Lebensart verweben kann*'; also reflex., e.g. Goethe, *Wahlverw.* 1,12: '*so verwebten . . . sich Abwesendes und Gegenwärtiges . . . durcheinander*'.

← See also under *Leib* (for *was im Klärchen leibt und lebet ist durch und durch mit ihm verwebet*).

verwechseln

jem.m zum Verwechseln ähnlich sein (or *gleich sehen*) to be the spitting image of sb., look confusingly similar; since the 18th c.; for similar locutions see under *ähnlich* (p. 26).

← See also under *Kammer* (for *verwechselt das Bäumchen*).

verwegen

sich ~ (or *verwägen*) (obs.) to dare, venture (courageously or in a foolhardy spirit); since MHG, still current in 1st half of the 19th c., e.g. Wieland, *Ob.* 10,6: '*der ist des Todes . . . der je des Frevels sich verwäget*', now obs.; cf. *verwegen* = 'daring, audacious' and *etw. wagen*.

← See also under *Nagel* (for *die verwegnen Finger des Jünglings*), *nah* (for *redet verwegen meiner Ehre zu nah*), *Pfund* (for *ein Gran Verwegenheit*), *Schritt* (for *zurück, Verwegner!*), *Seil* (for *seiltänzerische Verwegenheit*) and *stecken* (for *steckest aus Verwegenheit dein Ziel oft über allen Sternen*).

verwehen

See under *haschen* (for *hasch die Freuden, eh sie der Sturm verweht*) and *Rauch* (for *wie ein Rauch vom Winde verweht*).

verwehren

unverwehrt permitted, unimpeded; current since MHG even with abstracts, e.g. Seuse, *Dt.Schr.* 106,8 or Goethe 42,2,459 (W.).

← See also under *Ausweg* (for *jem.m ist der Ausweg verwehrt*) and *Ding* (for *das Reden verwehren*).

verweichlichen: see *weich*.

verweigern

sich einer Sache ~ (obs.) to reject sth.; in the 17th c. the genitive was used in this locution, but by the 18th c. the dative came to be preferred, e.g. Lessing [edit. M.] 9,265: '*er verweigert sich dem großmütigen Anerbieten*'. This is now obs. (displaced by *ablehnen* or *zurückweisen*). Equally obs. is *einer Sache verweigert sein* = 'to be denied sth.', which Lessing still used.

← See also under *Tribut* (for *Achtung ist ein Tribut, den wir dem Verdienst nicht verweigern können*).

verweilen

mit etw. ~ (obs.) to delay with (or postpone) sth.; f.r.b. Steinbach [1734]: '*mit der Strafe verweilen*'; now obs.

die Zeit ~ (obs.) to pass the time (staying somewhere); often close to *sich aufhalten, bleiben* and still used in the 19th c., but displaced by *verbringen*.

jem. ~ (obs.) to detain sb. for some time, cause sb. to stay for a while; as *etw. ~* since the 17th c., f.r.b. Stieler [1691], with persons often in the 18th c., used by Herder and Schiller; now obs.

etw. (abstract) *verweilt an (auf, bei) etw.* sth. dwells, rests, lingers on sth. (or sb.); since the 18th c., often with *Blick* (or *Auge*) as the subject, e.g. C.F. Meyer, *Nov.* 2,46: '*sein Blick verweilte . . . auf dem . . . Krieger*'.

verweisen

See under *Bann* (for *hab ich es verwiesen aus meiner Verse Bann*), *einstecken* (for *steckte die Verweise ein*), *Hieb* (for *ein empfindlicher Verweis*), *Strich* (for *verweise ich die ganze Notiz unter den*

Strich) and *Topf* (for *der Topf verweist es dem Kessel, daß er schwarz ist*).

verwelken

etw. verwelkt sth. withers; in phys. sense since MHG, with abstracts since Early NHG, when Luther used it in his transl. of Psalm 1,3: often still in comparisons with plants, e.g. Luther 8,214 (Weimar): '*wie das grune kraut werden sie verwelcken*'.

unverwelkt, unverwelklich imperishable; in both forms with abstracts since Early NHG; less used is *unverwelkbar*, but it occurs in Heine [edit. E.] 7,514: '*unverwelkbare Herrlichkeiten meines Bewußtseins*'.

← See also under *Kelch* (for *verwelkter Kelch*), *riechen* (for *verwelkter Strauß der Vergangenheit*) and *Ruhm* (for *mein herrliches Rühmchen wird in der Blüthe verwelken*).

verwenden

jem.m den Kopf ~ (obs.) to turn sb.'s head, confuse sb.; ~ here in the old sense of 'to turn', 'twist', still used by Goethe in *Pater Brey* 10: '*da kam ein Teufelspfäfflein ins Land, der hat mir Kopf und Sinn verwandt*'; now obs., displaced by *verdrehen*.

← See also under *prüfen* (for *nicht eine Stunde auff die Prüfung ihres Gewissens verwandt haben*) and *selig* (for *auf eine armselige Pflanze seine Kunst verwenden*).

verwerfen

etw. ~ to reject or condemn sth.; with abstracts since MHG; now in a variety of contexts for 'to condemn as false', 'reject as useless or inappropriate', 'abandon as wrong', also 'disown, quash or overrule' in legal contexts.

verwerflich reprehensible, objectionable, bad; current since the 16th c., often at first with ref. to persons for 'sinful, immoral', then also with abstracts, e.g. *ein verwerflicher Gedanke*; hence *unverwerflich* = 'trustworthy, reliable', with ref. to persons, esp. in legal contexts and 'irrefutable' with ref. to statements, proofs, etc., since Early NHG, f.r.b. Stieler [1691], e.g. Luther 18,504 (Weimar).

sich an jem. ~ (regional) to throw onself away on sb., degrade oneself (through marrying sb. who is unworthy); still in S. areas in this c.; in the standard language *sich wegwerfen* is used.

ein verworfener Tag (regional) a day of bad luck; since MHG; Wednesday and Friday were classed as *verworfen* and considered unsuitable for doing the weekly wash, baking bread or taking cattle out of their winter quarters into the fields; April 2 and 3 also fell into this category (cf. Fischer, *Schwäb.Wb.* 2,1411, also the entry on *Unglückstag* on p. 2527); *verworfen* = 'accursed', as used in Early NHG, e.g. by H. Sachs, is obs.

← See also under *Geselle* (for *verworfene Sitten*), *nisten* (for *wie viel Verworfenheit nistet in unserem Gemüt*) and *Schlamm* (for *verworfene Pöbelseele*).

verwesen

etw. verwest sth. perishes, disintegrates; figur. since Early NHG, e.g. Luther Bible transl. Prov. 10,7: '*der gottlosen name wird verwesen*'; hence *Verwesung* = 'decay', e.g. Mommsen, *Röm.Gesch.* 3,512 (1857): '*Verwesung der Nation*'.

← See also under *säen* (for *es wird geseet verweslich*) and *trauern* (for *die Blumen trauerten ihrer Verwesung entgegen*).

verwettert

See under *niederträchtig* (for *ein verwettertes niederträchtiges Asthma*) and *Teufel* (for *daß meine Frau einen verwetterten Hochmuthsteufel im Kopfe hat*).

verwichen: see *darstellen*.

verwichsen: see *Wichse*.

verwickeln

etw. (or *jem.*) *in etw.* ~ to involve sth. (or sb.) in sth., get sth. mixed up in sth. else; since the 18th c., e.g. Wieland, *Agathon* 3,4 [1766]: '*er verwickelte die Republik in ungerechte und unglückliche Kriege*'; hence *in etw. verwickelt sein* = 'to be embroiled in sth.' (18th c.) and reflex. *sich in etw.* ~; the noun *Verwicklung* can mean 'entanglement', 'confusion', but also 'complexity' (see next entry).

verwickelt complicated, involved, intricate; general since the 19th c.

← See also under *Bollwerk* (for *Bollwerk von verwickelten metaphysischen Unterscheidungen*), *Hand* (for *sich verwickeln lassen*), *Knoten* (for *Knoten, welche auch die Verwickelung genannt werden*) and *Rätsel* (for *er verwickelt den räthselhaften Besuch in räthselhafte Erklärungen*).

verwilden: see *verwildern*.

verwildern

verwildern to run wild, degenerate; since MHG, also as *verwilden*, still used by Schiller, *Räuber* 1,2: '*verwilde zum Tyger, sanftmüthiges Lamm*', e.g. (Sp.) Brod, *Leben m.e.Göttin* 137: '*die erste Grobheit in unserem Briefwechsel, der bisher nie verwildert, nie ausgeartet war*'; also reflex., as in Goethe, *Erwin* 2,6: '*verwildre dich, Natur!*'.

verwilligen: see *nachlassen*.

verwinden

etw. nicht ~ *können* to be unable to get over (or recover from the effects of) sth.; since MHG, e.g. (T) Graf Rudolf Kb 27; in most cases = *nicht über etw. hinwegkommen können* (see p. 1345), sometimes = *überwinden*.

← See also under *Henker* (for *den Nachgeschmack verwinden*).

verwirren

See under *anrichten* (for *Verwirrung anrichten*), *Babel* (for *babylonische Verwirrung*), *entwirren* (for *die verworrensten Geschäfte*), *Fittich* (for *Taten des verworrnen Sinnes*), *fitzen* (for *Wahrheit aus seiner verworrenen Schreibart heraus zu fitzen*), *flechten* (for *das verworrene Geflecht der Umstände*), *Garn*

KEY TO PRINCIPAL ABBREVIATIONS

jem.m	jemandem (dat.)
Kluge	F. Kluge, *Etymologisches Wörterbuch der deutschen Sprache*, 11th ed., Berlin und Leipzig 1934.
Lehman	C. Lehman, *Florilegium Politicum*, etc., Frankfurt 1640.
Lexer	M. Lexer, *Mittelhochdeutsches Handwörterbuch*, Leipzig 1872—8.
LG	Low German
Lipperheide	F. Freih. v. Lipperheide, *Spruchwörterbuch*, 2nd ed., München 1909.
MHG	Middle High German
mil.	military
M. Latin	medieval Latin
N.	Northern Germany
NED	*Oxford English Dictionary, A New English Dictionary on Historical Principles*, Edited by Sir James Murray, Henry Bradley, W. A. Craigie and C. T. Onions. Oxford 1884—1928.
NHG	New High German
NW	North-Western Germany
obs.	obsolete
OE	Old English
offic.	in civil service language
OHG	Old High German
ON	Old Norse
OS	Old Saxon
Oxf.	*The Oxford Dictionary of English Proverbs*, compiled by W. G. Smith, Oxford, 1935.
p.	page
poet.	used mainly in poetic language
pop.	popular
pop. etym.	popular etymology
prov.	proverb, proverbial
sb.	somebody
Schmeller	J. A. Schmeller, *Bayerisches Wörterbuch*, Stuttgart 1827—37.
Schulz-Basler	G. Schulz und O. Basler, *Deutsches Fremdwörterbuch*, Strassburg und Berlin 1913ff.
s.e.	self-explanatory
sl.	slang
S. Singer	S. Singer, *Sprichwörter des Mittelalters*, Bern 1944—7.
sth.	something
SW.	South-Western Germany
Trübner	*Trübners Deutsches Wörterbuch*, herausg. v. A. Götze, Berlin 1939ff.
v.	verse, verses
vulg.	in vulgar use (obscene terms are included under this heading, but specially marked as such)
Waag	A. Waag, *Die Bedeutungsentwicklung unseres Wortschatzes*, 5th ed., Lahr 1926.
Wb.	Wörterbuch
Weigand	F. L. K. Weigand, *Deutsches Wörterbuch*, 5th ed., Gießen 1909—10.
Weist.	Weistümer; usually the collection by J. Grimm, Göttingen 1840—69 is referred to; Österr, is appended to the Austrian collections.
Westph.	Westphalia, Westphalian
zool.	zoological term.

Where later editions than those cited above have been quoted (especially in the cases of Büchmann, Dornseiff and Kluge), details of the editions used are given in the text.

The abbreviations for journals mostly follow the accepted practice (*MLR for Modern Language Review, MLN for Modern Language Notes, IF for Indogermanische Forschungen*, etc.), only some long titles have been still further abbreviated though still left recognizable (e.g. *Z.f.d.W.* for *Zeitschrift für deutsche Wortforschung, Z.f.d.U.* for *Zeitschrift für den deutschen Unterricht, Z.f.r.P.* for *Zeitschrift für romanische Philologie*, etc.). Other works, referred to or quoted have been mentioned in abbreviated but recognizable form. It is intended to give a comprehensive list of them when the dictionary is completed. From Fasc. 9 Goethe (W.) = Weimar edition, Schiller (S.) = Säkularausgabe.

ISBN 0 631 194495

An Historical Dictionary of German Figurative Usage

By KEITH SPALDING

PROFESSOR EMERITUS OF GERMAN, UNIVERSITY COLLEGE OF NORTH WALES, BANGOR

WITH ASSISTANCE FROM
GERHARD MÜLLER-SCHWEFE

PROFESSOR EMERITUS OF ENGLISH,

UNIVERSITY OF TÜBINGEN

Fascicle 55

verwirtschaften – wegsein

KEY TO PRINCIPAL ABBREVIATIONS

a.	archaic
Adolphi	O. Adolphi, *Das große Buch der Fliegenden Worte, etc.*, Berlin n.d.
Ahd. Gl.	*Die Althochdeutschen Glossen*, ges. und bearb. von E. Steinmeyer u. Eduard Sievers, Berlin 1879—98.
Bav.	Bavaria, Bavarian
bot.	botanical term
Büchmann	G. Büchmann, *Geflügelte Worte*, 27th ed., ergänzt von A. Langen, Berlin 1915.
c.	century
Car.	Carinthia, Carinthian
cf.	compare
cl.	cliché
Cod.	codex
coll.	in colloquial use
comm.	used in language of commerce
dial.	dialect expression
Dornseiff	F. Dornseiff, *Der deutsche Wortschatz nach Sachgruppen*, Berlin und Leipzig 1934.
dt.	deutsch
DWb	*Deutsches Wörterbuch von Jacob Grimm und Wilhelm Grimm*, Leipzig 1854ff.
e.l.	earliest locus or earliest loci
etw.	etwas
Fast. Sp.	Fastnachtspiele, usually quoted after *Fastnachtspiele aus dem 15. Jahrbundert*, herausgeg. v. Keller, Stuttgart 1853.
Fick	F. C. A. Fick, *Vergleichendes Wörterbuch der indogermanischen Sprachen*, 3rd ed. Göttingen 1874.
f.r.b.	first recorded by
gen.	general
Götze	A. Götze, *Frühneuhochdeutsches Glossar*, 2nd ed., Bonn 1920.
Graff	E. G. Graff, *Althochdeutscher Sprachschatz*, Berlin 1834—42.
Hirt, *Etym.*	H. Hirt, *Etymologie der neuhochdeutschen Sprache*, 2nd ed., München 1925.
Hirt, *Gesch.*	H. Hirt, *Geschichte der deutschen Sprache*, 2nd ed., München 1925.
hunt.	word or expression used by huntsmen
jem.	jemand (nom. or acc.)

© *Blackwell Publishers Ltd., 1995 ISBN 0 631 198067*
Typeset by Hope Services, Abingdon
Printed and bound by Whitstable Litho Ltd., Whitstable, Kent.

(for *jem.m das Garn verwirren*), *Grund* (for *Grundstein einer verworrenen Geschichte*), *hereinbrechen* (for *Unheil und Verwirrung*), *Knäuel* (for *einen alten verworrenen Zustand zu entwickeln*), *Knoten* (for *die verworrenen Knoten des wild verknüpften Sinnes*), *plaudern* (for *ein naher Bach plauderte verwirrend in seine Gedanken hinein*), *Rätsel* (for *Knoten seiner verworrenen Lebensrätsel*), *scheckig* (for *verworren, schäckig, wild umdrängt uns hier ein fratzenhaft Gebild*), *Schlinge* (for *er warf Schlingen verwirrend um mich her*), *Sprache* (for *Sprachenverwirrung*), *sprechen* (for *Verwirrung, welche die Gesellschaft zu sprengen drohte*), *Strick* (for *durchs verwirrte Truggestrick*), *treiben* (for *das verworrene Streben*) and *Trieb* (for *das verworrene Getriebe der Zeit*).

verwirtschaften: see *Wirtschaft.*

verwischen

etw. verwischt etw. anderes sth. blurs, obscures, wipes out sth. else; figur. since MHG, e.g. *Martina* (edit. Keller) 174: '*der sünden spor verwuschen*', Arnim, *Isabella* 51 (1812): '*die Vergangenheit hat ein verwischtes Gesicht, wie eine Alabasterstatue, die lange unter der Traufe gestanden*', (Sp.) Huch, *Pitt u. Fox* 195: '*das Bild ihrer Großmutter . . . verwischte sich mehr und mehr*'; hence *unverwischt* (MHG *unverwischet*), e.g. Keller, *Gr.Heinr.* 2,185: '*unverwischte lebendige Jugendlichkeit*'.

← See also under *reiben* (for *durch Verwischung und Verreibung abgestumpft*).

verwittern: see *Wetter.*

verwogen

verwogen (regional and coll.) courageous, audacious; secondary form of *verwegen*, current since Late MHG; Schiller still used it in *Alpenjäger*: '*hinter ihr verwogen folgt er mit dem Todesbogen*'.

~ *wie ein Leierkastenmann* (coll.) as cheeky as can be; recorded by Klix [1863]; Frischbier [1865] recorded for Prussia: '*verwogen wie ein Stint*'.

verwöhnen

vom Glück nicht verwöhnt sein to have been not kindly treated by fate; recorded since the 19th c., e.g. by Heyne [1895]. Positive versions are older, e.g. Goethe 9,49 (W.): '*das Glück verwöhnt uns gar leicht durch seine Gaben*'.

← See also under *Kloster* (for *verwöhnt wie eine Klosterkatze*).

verworfen: see *verwerfen.*

verworren: see *verwirren.*

verwunden

etw. wird verwundet sth. is injured, wounded; with abstracts since MHG, e.g. Konr.v. Würzburg, *Troj.* 21703: '*daz iuwer herze sî verwunt*'.

eine verwundbare Stelle a sensitive spot, a place where one is vulnerable; with *Stelle* frequent since the 19th c., e.g. (DWb) Pückler, *Briefw.*

1,385 [1873]: '*das ist die Stelle, wo ich verwundbar bin*', with *Seite* already in the 18th c., e.g. Goethe IV,29,160 (W.): '*wer befehden will, muß nicht so viele schlechte verwundbare Seiten blos geben*'; often the same as *wunder Punkt* (which see under *wund*), sometimes with allusion to Achilles' heel or to the vulnerable spot on Siegfried's shoulder.

ein verwundetes Feld (mining) area which has been explored or mined previously; recorded since the 17th c.

← See also under *Geist* (for *wann man nach einem geist schlegt, so verwundt man sich selber*), *Stachel* (for *nimm jeden Stachel, der verwunden könnte*) and *treffen* (for *hast mich verwunt mit der minne*).

verwundern

das verwundert mich an ihm (obs.) I admire that in him; still recorded by Adelung [1780] along with '*eines Verstand verwundern*', but Campe [1811] classed it as '*verwerflich*'; it became obs., and *bewundern* has taken its place.

← See also under *fechten* (for *es ist zum Verwundern*), *Geist* (for *mit solchem geist, das sichs jederman verwundert*), *Grund* (for *nit zu verwundern, daß . . .*), *malen* (for *Verwunderung malt sich in jem.s Gesicht*), *mitschwingen* (for *schmerzliche Verwunderung*), *stier* (for *stiere Verwunderung*), *strecken* (for *Schornsteine streckten noch verwundert die langen weißen Hälse aus der Einsamkeit*) and *Tod* (for *sich des Todes verwundern*).

verwünschen

verwünscht (1) damned, wretched; weaker than *verflucht*, often expressing disappointment, e.g. Schiller, *Kab.u.L.* 3,1; also used on its own as an exclamation = 'blast!, dash it!'.

verwünscht (2) bewitched, enchanted; since the 18th c., e.g. Goethe 22,261 (W.): '*in diesem artigen Tiere stak ein verwünschter Prinz*' (also Schiller, *Fiesco* 1,1; a variant form is *verwunschen*, e.g. Eichendorff, *Taugenichts* 76: '*ein verwunschener Prinz*'.

verwunschene Tage (regional) days of bad luck; same as *verworfene Tage* (which see under *verwerfen*); Fischer recorded it for Swabia.

← See also under *Olymp* (for *so verwünschte ich den gesammten Olymp*), *Spiegel* (for *Neid, Furcht, Verwünschung sind die traurigen Spiegel*) and *tun* (for *izt ist es nicht mehr mit Murren und Verwünschen getan*).

verwursteln: see *Wurst.*

verwurzeln: see *Wurzel.*

verwürzen: see *Würze.*

verwüsten

etw. (abstract) *verwüstet etw.* sth. (abstract) devastates or ravages sth.; since Early NHG, e.g. Luther Apocr. transl. Wisd. of Sol. 6,1; '*vngerechtigkeit verwüstet alle land*'; cf. also *ein verwüstetes Gesicht* = 'ravaged face', where corruption or misfortune are taken as having caused disfigurement or ugliness; since Early NHG, f.r.b. Frisius [1556]: *'verwüste vnd vngestaltne angsicht'*.

unverwüstlich indestructible; occasionally in Early NHG, general only since the 18th c. (but not yet recorded by Adelung [1780]), e.g. Goethe II, 6, 216 (W.) with *Trieb*; with ref. to persons frequent since the 19th c. for 'inveterate', also for 'irrepressible'.

← See also under *Saat* (for *verwustet mîner frouden sât*).

verzagen

etw. verzagt (lit., rare) sth. loses its strength, fades; rare anthropomorphism, occasionally in modern lit., e.g. Eichendorff, *Sämtl. Werke* 1,314: *'wenn die Bäume all verzagen . . .'*.

← See also under *bellen* (for *verzagter Hund bellt am meisten*) and *Knie* (for *das ir hertz mus verzagen*).

verzählen: see *Reise*.

verzahnen

verzahnt (1) interlinked, dovetailed; since late in the 18th c., first listed by Adelung [1780] with ref. to metal parts forged in such a way that they interlock.

verzahnt (2) indented, forming deep recesses; mainly in geogr. contexts with ref. to coast-lines; since the 19th c.

sich ~ to interlock; since the 19th c., e.g. G. Keller, *Werke* 6,258: *'so eng verzahnen sich die Übergänge der Kultur ineinander'*.

verzanken

etw. ~ to spend or waste sth. through quarrels or litigation; since Early NHG, e.g. *Zimmersche Chron.* [edit. Bar.] 2,595; also with *Zeit*: *die Zeit ~* = 'to waste time with (unnecessary) quarrels'.

verzapfen

Unsinn ~ (coll.) to talk rubbish, concoct sth. senseless; derived from *~* = 'to draw from a cask' (by turning the *Zapfen* = 'tap'); since the 19th c. Heyne [1895] called it stud.sl. (and this is repeated by Küpper), but Kluge, *Dt.Student.* [1895] does not list it. It is of regional coll. origin.

Dinge ~ (rare) to link or combine things; belongs to *Zapfen* = 'tenon' as used in building; figur. since the 19th c., e.g. (DWb) O. Ludwig, *Ges. Schr.* 5,37 on philosophizing: *'. . . kann verbinden, was die Kunst . . . nur mechanisch zu verzapfen vermag'*.

verzärteln

jem. ~ to coddle, spoil sb. through too much indulgence; f.r.b. Stieler [1691]; in lit. occasionally figur., e.g. Schiller, *Fiesco* 2,3: *'es ist ein schwaches, verzärteltes Ding, mein Herz'*.

← See also under *Gewächs* (for *daß er weder verzärtelt noch eitel gemacht werde*), *Mädchen* (for *verzärtelte, mädchenhafte Weichlinge*), *Möbel* (for *in einer so verzärtelten Haußhaltung*) and *schön* (for *das bedeutende Rauhe nicht verzärteln*).

verzaubern

verzaubert enchanted; originally = 'bewitched'

(in the sense of 'affected or changed by witchcraft'); in the 17th c. extended in comparisons such as *wie* or *gleichsam verzaubert*, then, as in Engl., further extended to 'delighted, carried away with enjoyment', since the 18th c., e.g. Goethe 28,5 (W.): *'sah ich meine Hörerinnen . . . von meiner seltsamen Darstellung aufs äußerste verzaubert'*; hence *die Verzauberung*, since late in the 18th c., e.g. Forster, *It.* 1,199: *'mit welchem Taumel, welcher Verzauberung das alle meine Sinne ergreift'*.

verzechen

etw. ~ to spend sth. on convivial drinking; since the 16th c., e.g. *sein Vermögen ~* = 'to spend all one possesses on drink', also with ref. to time spent in drinking, e.g. Zschokke 8,304: *'P. verzechte den Abend bei den Fuhrleuten'*.

verzehnfachen: see *verdoppeln*.

verzehren

sich in etw. ~ (lit.) to be consumed by sth., pine away with sth.; derived from the original sense 'to destroy, consume'; figur. often with allusion to heat, fire, flames; frequent in lit. since the 18th c., e.g. Goethe 10,195 or 21,106 (W.); often in present participle with abstracts, e.g. *verzehrender Haß, Eifer, verzehrende Leidenschaft, Liebe*; since early in the 18th c.

← See also under *Friede* (for *Friede ernährt, Unfriede verzehrt*), *Heu* (for *menschen kinder, die als hew verzeret werden*), *Motte* (for *von Motten und Würmern verzehrt werden*), *Parasit* (for *der Parasit Paris, der die Säfte des Landes verzehrt*), *Pfennig* (for *der ungerechte Pfennig verzehrt den gerechten Taler*), *Scheffel* (for *eh du den Scheffel Salz mit dem neuen Bekannten verzehret . . .*), *schlafen* (for *Wachen nach Reichtum verzehrt den Leib*) and *Stroh* (for *wie des fewrs flamme stroh verzehret*).

verzeichnen

etw. ~ (1) to register, record, secure, score sth.; figur. with ref. to *Erfolg, Gewinn* and other achievements; only since the 19th c., not yet recorded by Sanders, even in his *Ergänzungswb.* of 1885, nor by Heyne [1895], e.g. *die Mannschaft konnte letztes Jahr mehrere Siege ~*; similar to *etw. aufweisen können*, which is older (see p. 109).

etw. ~ (2) to misrepresent or distort sth.; first in phys. sense of 'drawing wrongly', then (mainly in lit. context) = 'to present a wrong picture of sth.', since the 18th c., e.g. *in dem Buch ist der Charakter von X verzeichnet*; hence *Verzeichnung*, since the 19th c., e.g. Treitschke, *Dt.Gesch.* 5,397: *'grobe Verzeichnungen'*.

Verzeichnis: see *Sünde*.

verzeihen

etw. ~ (1), *sich einer Sache ~* (obs.) to renounce sth.; from Late MHG to the 18th c., still in Wieland, *Ob.* 8,68: *'so mag sie ihrer nun auf ewig sich verzeihen'*; now obs., displaced by *auf etw. verzichten*.

etw. ~ (2) to forgive sth.; current since Early NHG, e.g. Luther Bible transl. Psalm 19,13: '*verzeiht mir die verborgen feile*'. As a standing phrase also in *Gott verzeih dir's* = 'may God forgive you', e.g. Schiller, *Räuber* 4,3: '*Gott der Herr verzeihs euch*' or *Kab.u.L.* 1,2: '*Gott verzeih' mir's*'.

alles verstehen heißt alles ~ (prov. expr.) to understand is to forgive; translates French *tout comprendre c'est tout pardonner*; modern, but cf. older sayings which recommend forgiveness such as Franck, *Prov.* 1,158 [1541]: '*verzeihe dir nichts vnd andern vil*', also Petri [1605]: '*Verzeihen ist die beste Rache*'.

← See also under *schwach* (for *wie könnt ihr dieser die Schwachheit für so ein Scheusal verzeihen*).

verzerren

etw. ~ to distort sth.; in phys. sense since MHG; for 'distort' since the 17th c., figur. since the 18th c., often with *Bild*, e.g. Goethe, *Gespr.* [edit. Bied.] 2,90, also with *Sprache*; sometimes = 'to caricature, falsify, pervert', e.g. Klinger, *Werke* 3,260: '*ein Philosoph wie Voltaire . . . der . . . alles Gute verzerrte, wo er es fand*'; hence *Verzerrung*, figur. since the 18th c.

← See also under *Gebelle* (for *Verzerrung galt für Witz, Klopffechten und Gebelle für Leidenschaft*).

verzetteln

etw. ~ to fritter or throw sth. away; derived from *zetten* (obs.) = 'to spread, disperse, distribute' (and not connected with the language of weavers, discussed under *anzetteln*); with abstracts f.r.b. Stieler [1691]: '*das Mägdlein hat ihre Ehre verzettelt . . . die Gunst verzetteln*' (he also recorded '*Ehrenverzetlung*') and '*verzetlichter Mensch = negligens, incuriosus*', which is obs.). Keller, *Salander* 48 used '*die Zeit verzettelte sich*'. Now often reflex. for 'to dissipate one's energies or occupy oneself with too many things and unimportant matters', e.g. (H.) Treitschke, *Dt. Gesch.* 5,371: '. . . *hatten sich aus dem verzettelnden Eintagsschaffen hinausgesehnt*'.

verziehen

(sich) ~ to linger, delay, hesitate, be tardy; the basic idea is negative expressing 'not moving forward' and therefore capable of being used in a variety of senses, sometimes transitively, at others reflexively, such as *(ver)zögern, zurückhalten, aufschieben, säumen, verweilen*; since MHG, frequent in Luther Bible transl. e.g. Exodus 22,29, Jerem. 15,15, Luke 18,7, Apocr. transl. Ecclesiasticus 4,3, general in the 18th c., e.g. Goethe 23,35 (W.) and regionally and in poetry even in the 20th c., but now considered a. The meaning is still preserved in *Verzug* (which see) and in *unverzüglich* = 'at once, without delay' (in Early NHG *unverzogen* and *unverzogenlich*).

etw. ~ (a.) to distort sth.; contains the notion of phys. 'pulling sth. into a wrong shape, disar-

ranging sth.'; in MHG also used for 'to dilute' (drinks), then in (still phys.) 'screwing up' (face, lips), recorded by Kramer [1702]; since the 18th c. with abstracts, e.g. Herder, *R.*9,209: '*es wird ein verzogen, elend Werk*', Raabe, *Sämtl. Werke* 2,1,200 (*Abu T.*): '*sein Vortrag war . . . eine Fata Morgana, welche manches verzog und auf den Kopf stellte*'. Hence *Verziehung*, as in Lessing, *Em.Gal.* 1,4: '*die Verziehung muß nicht bis zur Grimasse gehen*'.

jem. ~ to educate sb. wrongly or badly; = *falsch erziehen*; current since the 16th c., e.g. Goethe, *Wahlverw.* 1,2: '*das einzige verzogene Kind reicher Eltern*' or *Dicht.u.Wahrh.* 2,10: '*der verzogene Jüngste*'; abstracts can be the subject, e.g. *das Glück* or *zuviel Schonung verzog ihn* (since the 18th c.); hence *die Verziehung* = 'faulty education', f.r.b. Ludwig [1716].

sich ~ to move away, melt away, fade, disappear; since Early NHG in phys. contexts, figur. since the 18th c. often with allusion to the weather, as in Schiller's '*das Kriegsgewitter verzog sich*'; now also in coll. use for 'to go away, make oneself scarce', also in the order *verzieh dich!* = 'scram, buzz off'.

er verzog keine Miene he did not bat an eyelid, showed no emotion; current since the 19th c., e.g. (Sa.) Kriegk, *Weltgesch.* 1,284 [1844]: '*wenn sie dabei auch nur eine Miene verzogen*', Stifter, *Sämtl. Werke* 1,273.

← See also under *Kasten* (for *auf dem Kasten muß der Fräulein verzogener Name stehn*), *nachkriechen* (for *das der tod nit verzeucht*) and *Schoß* (for *die verzogenen Schoßkinder der Regierung*).

verzieren

brich dir keine Verzierung ab (coll.) don't put on airs, get off your high horse; also sometimes = 'don't make so much fuss'; it is assumed by some that the phrase refers to the points on a nobleman's crown, the number of which denotes his rank. Others have suggested that *Verzierung* stands for 'nose' pulled up high by a conceited or haughty person (cf. the entry on *hochnäsig* on p. 1763); it originated in Berlin around the middle of the 19th c. Later, off-shoots are *sich sämtliche Verzierungen abbrechen* (coll.) = 'to be most anxious to please sb. or to obtain sth. by hook or by crook', since early in the 20th c., and *bei ihr ist die Verzierung abgebrochen* (coll.) = 'she is no longer attractive', since the twenties of the 20th c.

das wird dir (or *dabei wirst du dir*) *keine Verzierung abbrechen* (coll.) that would not harm your image or damage your reputation; synonymous with *dadurch wirst du dir nichts vergeben* (which see under *vergeben*); 20th c. coll. The *DWb.* entry, compiled in 1955, does not record phrases with *abbrechen*.

← See also under *Name* (for *diese Grillen*

verziert ihr mit dem Namen der Tugend), *Phrase*
(for *Verzierungsphrase*) and *Schnörkel* (for *führt er
in seine Sitten Schnörkel und Verzierungen ein*).

verzinken

jem. ~ (cant) to grass on sb.; since the 19th c.
in the language of criminals. There is also *eine
Frau* ~ (obscene) = 'to have intercourse with a
woman'; since early in the 20th c., derived from
Zinken (obscene) = 'penis'.

verzogen: see *verziehen.*

verzögern

See under *Taktik* (for *Verzögerungstaktik*) and
Trödel (for *der unglaublichste Verzögerer*).

verzopft: see *Zopf.*

verzuckern

Unangenehmes ~ to sugar the pill; less used
than the locution with *versüßen* (which see); ~ in
its phys. sense has been recorded since the 16th
c.; for 'to make sth. (abstract) pleasant or acceptable since the 17th c., f.r.b. Stieler [1691]; often
with *Pille.*

verzückt: see *Region.*

Verzug

Gefahr ist im ~ there is danger ahead or immi-
nent; this phrase has changed its meaning completely. It meant originally 'to hesitate or to delay
would be dangerous', based on *periculum in mora*,
used by Livy, bk. 38,25, in German since the
17th c., e.g. (DWb) Chemnitz, *Schwed.Kr.* 2,36
[1653]: '*es were dan, das periculum in mora vnd die
sache keinen verzug leiden wolte*'. This sense
remained established for a long time, e.g. Möser,
Sämtl.Werke [edit. Ab.] 2,286: '*wo Gefahr auf
dem Verzuge haftet*', even Ganghofer in *Jäger v. F.*
357 still used it: '*jeder Verzug ist Gefahr für sein
Leben*'. Through misunderstanding of *Verzug* and
interpreting *im Verzug sein* as *im Anzug sein* the
new meaning arose in the middle of the 19th c.
and is now dominant.

der ~ (a.) badly or wrongly educated person;
derived from *jem. verziehen* (which see), first for
the abstract = *Verziehung*, since the 18th c., e.g.
Haller, *Vers. schweiz.Ged.* 29 [1753], later for the
person affected = 'badly educated child', e.g.
Raabe, *Sämtl. Werke* 1,1,55 (*Chron.d.Sperl.*); now
a.

← See also under *verziehen* (for *unverzüglich*).

verzupfen

etw. ~ to pull sth. to pieces; figur. with ref. to
criticizing or destructive handling of sth.; since
the 19th c., e.g. (Sa.) *Dt.Museum* 1,2,408
[1851]: '*Jene verzupften das Wichtige, Diese
bauschten das Unbedeutende auf*'; *zerzupfen* can
also be used in this sense.

verzweifeln

verzweifelt (adv.) terribly, abominably; derived
from the sense 'desperately, hopelessly' and
meaning at first 'leading one or driving one to
despair', e.g. Luther Bible transl. Jerem. 30,12:
'*dein schade ist verzweivelt böse*', but since the 18th

c. often for 'confounded', e.g. Gellert, *Loos* 2,2:
'*die verzweifelten Mücken*', Lessing, *Minna*: '*der
verzweifelte Nachbar*', later as an intensifying
adverb, e.g. G. Hauptmann, *Vor Sonnenaufg.* 1:
'*eine Gesellschaft, die trockenen Gaumens beisam-
men hockt, ist und bleibt eine verzweifelt öde und
langweilige*'.

← See also under *Brust* (for *an der Hoffnung
Liebesbrust erwarmet starrende Verzweifelung*),
fassen (for *Verzweiflung faßt jem.*), *Grab* (for *dieß
Grab der Verzweiflung*), *Lage* (for *die Sachen haben
eine verzweifelte Lage bekommen*), *leihen* (for *die
Verzweiflung soll mir Kräfte leihen*), *morsch* (for
Verzweiflung reißt ihn fort), *Nase* (for *die
Goldbarren stechen mir verzweifelt in die Nase*),
Quinte (for *wer hütet sich für solche verzweifelte
Quinten*), *Rede* (for *die Verzweiflung redet aus ihm*),
reißen (for *in Verzweiflung hinabgerissen werden*),
Sack (for *verzweifelter balg und lügensack*),
schlucken (for *Verzweiflung in sich schlucken*),
Schnecke (for *der Witz der Verzweiflung*), *schwingen*
(for *Verzweiflung schwingt in jem.s Worten*), *setzen*
(for *nur ein verzweifelter Spieler setzt alles auf einen
einzigen Wurf*), *sprechen* (for *Lieb und Verzweiflung
spricht aus beyden*) and *trinken* (for *in der Traube
goldnem Blut trinken Sanftmuth Kannibalen, die
Verzweiflung Heldenmuth*).

verzweigen

verzweigt branched, ramified; transferred from
the world of plants since the 18th c., often with
ref. to family, as in Goethe 46,53 (W.) or
abstracts as in Rückert, *Ges.poet.W.* 8,601: '*ein
Baum der Weltvernunft, verzweigt in seine Ranken*'.

sich ~ to become entwined; since the 19th c.,
e.g. (DWb) Fouqué, *Ausgew.W.* 8,86: '*da schon
verzweigte sich unser Geschick und wir wollen es
fürder so innig verzweigen . . .*'; sometimes expressing the notions of intermingling, even of absorption; cf. joc. coll. *sich um jem.* ~ = 'to embrace
sb.'. 20th c. coll.

verzwergen: see *Zwerg.*

verzwickt

verzwickt (1) complicated, involved; the verb
verzwicken arose in MHG for 'to fasten with
tacks or pegs', figur. for 'to tie together, entangle', but also for 'to restrict'; from the notion of
entanglement there was but a short step to 'com-
plication, involvement' leading in Early NHG to
the adjective ~, e.g. Schiller, *Räuber* 1,1:
'*verzwickte Consequenz*'.

verzwickt (2) (rare) strange, inexplicable; since
the 19th c., e.g. (T.) Immermann, *Münchh.*
1,1,17: '*sie schießt zuweilen so verzwickte Blicke auf
mich*'.

verzwickt (3) uncomfortable, uneasy; since the
19th c., e.g. G. Keller, *Sinnged.* 100: '*sie durch
. . . Scherzworte aus der verzwickten Stimmung her-
auszubringen*'.

verzwickt (4) (adverb. coll.) terribly, awfully;'
modern, used like *verflixt*, e.g. *ein* ~ *schlechtes*

Geschäft = 'a damn bad bargain', mainly in the S.; *verzwackt* also occurs in some regions.

← See also under *unverzwickt*.

Vesper
Sizilianische ~ spielen (obs.) to wipe out all one's opponents; a ref. to the Sicilian Vespers (March 30, 1292), when the citizens of Palermo murdered every French person in the city; still recorded in the 19th c., e.g. by Wander [1876], but hardly understood now except by historians; cf. Goethe 7,163 (W.): '*. . . wird eine umgekehrte sicilianische Vesper unternommen: der Fremde ermordet den Einheimischen*'.

Vestalin
die ~ (lit.) virgin; Vestals had to remain spotless virgins until they were thirty years old; cf. Campe's entry: '*bei den Römern eine Priesterin der Vesta; uneigentlich eine unbefleckte Jungfrau*'; in 18th c. literature the term could even be applied to a man; hence also *vestalisch* = 'chaste', e.g. Wieland, *Agathon* 1,222: '*Danae (von der man ohnehin keine vestalische Tugend forderte) . . .*'.

Veteran
der ~ veteran; originally described a soldier who had finished his service, then a person who had spent a long time in an occupation (for which Campe unsuccessfully suggested *Ältermann* as a substitute), then in wider sense an elderly person (18th c.); only in the 20th c. extended to things of considerable age, such as motorcars; not yet mentioned in *DWb.* [1913], older in Engl.

Vettel
die ~ (pejor.) wench, loose (or ugly) woman; recorded for 'old woman' by Maaler [1561], then used pejor. for 'harlot' since the 17th c., occasionally in lit. as a term of abuse, e.g. Platen, *Verm. Ged.* 2,3: '*meine Muse, jene Vettel*', with ref. to Fortuna used by G. Keller, *Werke* 6,95 (*Züricher Nov.*), often with the addition of *alt* even where age is irrelevant; cf. Luther Bible transl. Timothy 4,7: '*der vngeistlichen aber vnnd altvettelschen Fabeln* (= old-wives tales) *entschlahe dich*'; Steinbach [1734] recorded '*altvettelische Mährlein*'; in the 17th c. *vettelisch* and *vettelhaft* arose, recorded by Stieler [1691].

← See also under *anvettermicheln* (for *anvetteln*).

Vetter
ein . . . . ~ (regional) a . . . fellow, chap, type; *~* could be used so loosely, e.g. addressing peasants or a person whose name one did not know that the extension to 'chap, fellow' is easily understandable; hence *ein toller ~* = 'an unpredictable or irresponsible fellow', *ein netter ~* (ironic) = 'a nice (meaning "unpleasant") type'; recorded in 19th c. regional dictionaries but probably older; cf. entries on similar use of *Michel* (p. 1691).

beim ~ sein (regional coll., obs.?) to be lodged

in a pawnshop; cf. Engl. coll. 'uncle' used in the same way; f.r.b. Albrecht [1881] for Leipzig.

die Vetternwirtschaft nepotism; there are many terms for this, esp. *Vetterleswirtschaft, Vetterles machen* (Swabian), *Vetterschaftswesen, Vetterschaftlichkeit*, all recorded since the 19th c., widespread in Alemannic dialect areas.

die Vetternstraße ziehen (coll.) to move from one relative to the next and enjoy their hospitality; current in the 19th c., now obs.

← See also under *anvettermicheln, bevettern, heben* (for *zweitens hob er keine Vettern in den Sattel*), *link* (for *Vettern von links/rechts*), *Michel* (for *sich anvettermicheln*) and *Schwabe* (for *ein schwäbischer Vetter*).

vexieren
vexier dich! (coll. obs.) leave me (or them) alone, go to the devil; still used in the 18th c. when telling sb. who has been offensive to stop and take himself off, e.g. Goethe, *Egmont* 1: '*vexier Er sich!*', now obs.

die Vexiergasse (lit., rare) cul-de-sac; occasionally with ref. to abstracts, e.g. G. Keller, *Seldw.* 1,223: '*Gefühl . . . welches sich in eine Vexiergasse verrannt hat*'.

Vieh
das ~ beast, brute, uncouth or dumb person; cf. Lat. *pecus* used frequently by Cicero as a term of contempt; in German since the Middle Ages, but at first mainly in comparisons, the adjective *vihelich* and the abstract *vihelicheit* = 'brutality'; Luther 10,2,426 (Weimar) used the noun as a term of abuse: '*die Creter sind yhe lügener gewesen, böße viech unnd faule beuche*', also Lessing, *Minna* 3,2 on Just: '*aber mit dem Vieh ist nichts anzufangen*'. Frequent in comparisons: *dumm* or *roh wie ein (Stück) ~*; cf. also *ein ~ von einem Menschen* (Adelung recorded: '*solche Viehe von Menschen*'). Use in affectionate coll. speech is also possible, mainly in the diminutive *Viecherl*. It can also occur half-pityingly for a stupid but good-natured person, as in Wieland 12,7: '*Pervonte war . . . im Übrigen ein gutes Vieh, den nie der Kitzel stach, nach Wann, Warum und Wie . . . zu fragen*'.

ein berühmtes (or *großes*) *~* (coll.) a famous (or outstanding) personality; less used than *ein großes Tier* (for which see p. 2455), but used occasionally, e.g. by H. Hesse on Schiller in *Klingsor* 369 [1931]: '*und doch ist jetzt das aus ihm geworden, daß er ein berühmtes Vieh ist*'; cf. Heine, *Werke* [edit. E.] 3,232: '*. . . . daß er kein Jesuit war, sondern ein ganz gewöhnliches Vieh Gottes*'.

saufen wie das liebe ~ (coll.) to drink without knowing when to stop; perhaps best known through the rhymed advice: *sauft Wasser wie das liebe ~ und denkt, es wär Krambambuli* (a strong spirit distilled in Danzig); sometimes associated with solitary drinking, as in Fischart, *Garg.* 96a: '*allein sauffen ist viehisch*'; cf. also Wieland, *Horaz Br.* 1,114: '*schifsvolk das . . . zum Vieh sich säuft*';

das liebe ~ has been a standing expression since the 17th c., e.g. Rabener, *Werke* 5,22: '*ihr Deutschen lebt hier so ordentlich und gesund, wie das liebe Vieh . . .*'. In this case lack of good sense and discernment is being attacked, but today *wie das liebe* ~ criticizes bad manners, also indecent behaviour.

viehisch brutal, coarse, crude, animal-like; since MHG, e.g. Luther Bible transl. Daniel 4,13: '*ein viehisch herz*', Schiller, *Räuber* 1,1: '*Stillung viehischer Begierden*'. The noun is *Viecherei* (coll.) and has three meanings: it can mean the same as *Viehsarbeit* = 'unpleasant job, work that requires brute strength', or *viehische Gemeinheit* = 'vile or despicable act' or *viehische Einstellung* = 'beastly attitude'; recorded for some regions since the 19th c., but inadequately treated in *DWb.* [1913]: '*auch Viecherei = unverantwortliches verhalten, wüstes treiben, gemeinheit u.ä. hört man gelegentlich*' with no dates or locations mentioned.

viehmäßig (adverb) brutally, indecently, shamefully, in a beastly manner; since the 18th c. with ref. to objectionable behaviour.

viehs-. . . or *viechs-*. . . (coll.) terribly, extraordinarily, very . . .; in many compounds (often synonymous with compounds formed with *sau-*. . ., for which see p. 2061), mainly in derogatory descriptions, e.g. *viechsdumm*, *viechsblöd*, but occasionally also in positive contexts, e.g. *viechsgescheit*, also in nouns, e.g. *er ist ein Viechskerl, er hat eine Viehnatur*, when it can refer to strength, but also with ref. to stupidity, as in *Viehdummheit*, used by Herder and Jean Paul.

ein Hundevieh or *Hundsviech* (coll.) a beastly creature; in print since the 19th c., recorded by Sanders [1860], still missing in *DWb.*, e.g. Holtei, *Mensch* 2,141: '*Hundeviecher*'.

ein Mordsvieh (coll.) a big brute; this can be applied to animals when it describes size and strength and to human beings when it is abusive; missing both in *DWb.* and Sanders.

Stimmvieh voters in whom one is only interested as long as one gets their support; abusive term coined in the USA, particularly with ref. to Irish voters who could be easily swayed and were called 'voting cattle'; German travellers reporting on this translated the term with *Stimmvieh* from ca. 1860 onwards; Nietzsche was apparently the first writer of consequence to use the term. In political debates at the close of the 19th c. working-class people who voted for the Social Democrats were contemptuously referred to by this term; details in Ladendorf, *Histor. Schlagwörterbuch* 303 [1906].

Kleinvieh macht auch Mist (prov.) many a mickle makes a muckle, many drops make a shower, every little helps (as the old woman said when she pissed in the sea); recorded since the 19th c., e.g. by Simrock (1846).

← See also under *best* (for *das beste Vieh*), *Eisen* (for *eisernes Vieh*), *Feder* (for *Federvieh*), *herabsetzen* (for *setzen wir alsdann den Menschen unter das Vieh herab*), *Horn* (for *ja wohl ein Vieh, von dem gehörnten Vieh!* and *Hornvieh*), *leer* (for *leeres Vieh*), *Rind* (for *Rindvieh*), *Stand* (for *Viehstand*) and *Trog* (for *wie das Vieh am Troge*).

viel

~ *haben von jem.m* to be very much like sb.; e.g. *er hat viel von seinem Vater* = 'he takes very much after his father'; see also under *haben* (p. 1191).

er weiß ~, *was das bedeutet* (regional coll.) he has no idea of what this means; ironic in essence; current since the 18th c., when Adelung recorded it: '*ich bekümmere mich viel darum = wahrlich nicht*'.

er redet ~ , *wenn der Tag lang ist* (prov. expr.) he talks a lot, but not much of it is worth taking seriously; modern coll.

die Vielzuvielen (lit.) the common herd; coined by Nietzsche in *Werke* 6,63.70.

wer ~ *verlangt, bekommt garnichts* (prov.) all covet, all lose; recorded since the 16th c., e.g. Franck [1541]: '*wer zu vil wil han, dem wirt zu wenig*'.

← See also under *aufheben* (for *viel Aufhebens machen*), *auskommen* (for *mit vielem hält man Haus*), *Bach* (for *viele Bäche machen einen Strom*), *bedenken* (for *wer gar zu viel bedenkt, wird wenig leisten*), *bedeuten* (for *viel zu bedeuten haben*), *berufen* (for *viele sind berufen, aber wenige sind auserwählt*), *bringen* (for *wer vieles bringt, wird manchem etwas bringen*), *Bruder* (for *viele Brüder machen schmale Güter*), *Eiche* (for *viele Streiche fällen die Eiche*), *Feder* (for *nicht viel Federlesen(s) machen*), *fehlen* (for *es fehlte nicht viel*), *fragen* (for *was frag ich viel nach Geld und Gut*), *Freund* (for *viel Geld, viel Freunde*), *geben* (for *viel auf etw. geben*), *gehören* (for *es gehört nicht viel dazu*), *gut* (for *vil armuot, so viel er sich . . . zu Gute thut, des Guten zuviel tun*), *haben* (for *damit hat es viel auf sich*), *halten* (for *viel von etw. halten*), *Hand* (for *viele Hände machen leichte Bürde*), *heißen* (for *im Krieg disputiert man nicht viel*), *Herz* (for *sie zeigt viel Herz* and *viel Herz*), *Hirt* (for *bei viel Hirten wird übel gehütet*), *Holz* (for *das ist viel Holz*), *Hund* (for *viele Hunde sind des Hasen Tod*), *irre* (for *wer viel fragt, geht viel irr*), *Koch* (for *viele Köche verderben den Brei*), *Kopf* (for *so viel Köpfe, so viel Sinne*), *nichts* (for *viel Lärm um nichts*), *Sack* (for *zu viel zerreißt den Sack*), *sagen* (for *es sagt nicht viel, weiß nicht viel zu sagen* and *hat nicht viel zu sagen*), *schwimmen* (for *der verliurt grozer arbeit vil*), *sein* (for *so viel an mir ist*), *sprechen* (for *sich viel von jem.m versprechen*), *Teufel* (for *im Grunde fragt kein Teufel Viel nach meinem Siechthum*), *tun* (for *viel zu tun haben, viel mit sich selbst zu tun haben* and *viel für jem. tun*) and *ungesund* (for *allzuviel ist ungesund*).

vielbeinigt: see *Tier*.

vielfältig: see *gut*.

Vielfraß

der ~ (1) glutton, greedy person; as a term of abuse since the 16th c., e.g. Eyering [1601]: '*er ist ein rechter vielfrass*', Goethe 45,154 (W.): '*weil Ihr ein Nichtswürdiger, ein Vielfraß . . . seid*'. Jean Paul called the public '*Viel-und-alles-Fraß*'.

der ~ (2) (zool.) wolverine, glutton; f.r.b. Gesner, *Thierbuch* [1583]; also sometimes (and wrongly) applied to 'hyena' from Late MHG until the 18th c. Other voracious animals called ~ are 'pelican' (recorded by Frisch [1741]), also some beetles and some snails but these are local terms not listed in scientific systems of classification, although Campe [1811] mentions them as names for *Speckkäfer* (*Dermestes lardarius*) and *Warzenkäfer* (*Cantharis fusca*).

vielköpfig: see *Ungeheuer*.

vielleicht

vielleicht (coll.) very much; ~ was originally a fusion of two words *vil lîhte = sehr leicht* (cf. similar combinations Engl. 'perhaps'. Lat. *forsitan*, French *peut-être*); in coll. use since late in the 18th c. for emphasis, contrary to its original meaning, e.g. *da hat er sich* ~ *geirrt* = 'in that case he is very much mistaken', also in envy or admiration, e.g. *der hat* ~ *Geld!* = 'he is rolling in it!'.

Vielliebchen

~ *mit jem.m essen* to share a double-kerneled almond or hazelnut with sb.; not connected with *lieb*, but developed from French *philippine*, which in German became *Filipchen* and then ~ ; since the 19th c. (not yet recorded by Campe [1811]), e.g. Fontane, *Werke* 3,335 (*Frau J.Tr.*): '*. . . bot Corinna . . . ein Vielliebchen an*'. Many customs, including bets, fines, exchanged kisses, presents, addressing each other with *du* henceforth, are associated with ~ (for some of them see *DWb.* 12,2,241, also Brewer, *Dict. of Phrase and Fable* (under *Philopena*)).

vielsagend

vielsagend meaningful; since the 18th c.; see the entries under *sagen* on *es sagt nicht viel* and *es hat nicht viel zu sagen*.

vielschichtig see *Schicht*.

vielseitig: see *Seite*.

vielversprechend

vielversprechend promising; in the sense of 'leading one to expect much' since the 18th c., e.g. Wieland, *Lucian* 4,604 [1788]; cf. the entry under *sprechen* on *sich viel von jem.m versprechen*.

Vielwisser

ein ~ (pejor.) a Mr. know-all; in approving or praising sense since the 17th c. as *Viel-wissender*; pejor., but again only as *Vielwissender*, since the 18th c. The form ~ is modern, not even mentioned in *DWb.* [1919]; cf. similar pejor. *Vielredner(ei)* and *Vielschreiber(ei)*, all modern.

vier

die Viere the four elements (fire, water, air, earth); not frequent in this shortened form, but used occasionally, e.g. Goethe, *Faust I*, 1272: '*. . . brauch ich den Spruch der Viere*' and 1292: '*keines der Viere steckt in dem Tiere*', König, *Ged.* 77 [1745]: '*in jeden Säugling pflegt von ihr vertheilt zu werden ein unterschiednes Vier: Lufft, Wasser, Feuer, Erden*'.

auf allen Vieren on all fours; since MHG, mainly with *kriechen*; f.r.b. Stieler [1691], e.g. Luther 24,96 (Weimar): *so man solt mit allen vieren zu yhm kriechen*'.

an (or *auf*) *allen Vieren* (coll.) in every respect; since the 17th c. in negative locutions, e.g. (DWb) Wickram, *Werke* 5,135: '*das ich ein narr sey an allen vieren*'; Fischer recorded for Swabia: '*der ist auf allen Vieren nix*'; since the 18th c. often with *beschlagen* (see entry on *beschlagen* on p. 268.

nicht bis ~ *zählen können* (coll.) to be stupid; since Early NHG, e.g. Luther 6,516b (Jena): '*geringe und einfeltige leute, die nicht viere können zelen*'.

~ *Hosen aus einem Tuch* (regional coll.) two persons who are very much alike; recorded since the 16th c., now only in some regions (recorded for the Tyrol by Schoepf).

das Buch der ~ *Könige* (joc. coll.) pack of cards; in allusion to the Books of Kings in the Old Testament; recorded since the 19th c.

← See also under *Auge* (for *vier Augen sehen mehr als zwei* and *unter vier Augen*), *Buchstabe* (for *setz dich auf deine vier Buchstaben*), *Ecke* (for *eine Stadt an allen vier Ecken/Enden anzünden*), *Stand* (for *der vierte Stand*), *Straße* (for *alle vier Straßen der Welt*), *strecken* (for *alle Viere von sich strecken*), *Wand* (for *in seinen vier Wänden*) and *Wind* (for *in alle vier Winde*).

viereckig

viereckig (1) coarse, clumsy, lacking polish; with ref. to persons since the 18th c., recorded by Adelung who defined it as '*grob, plump*', e.g. F.Th. Vischer, *Werke* 2,45: '*das Volk fand sie etwas viereckig und derb*'; cf. *ein eckiger Mensch* (for which see p. 544) and *anecken* = 'to give offence', based on the same notion.

viereckig (2) (regional) unpleasant, awkward, nasty; with ref. to abstracts, e.g. (T.) A. Schott, *Im Hochriß* 8 [1922]: '*heut ist schon so ein viereckiger Tag*'.

← See also under *Sonne* (for *die Sonne viereckig sehen*).

Viergespann

das ~ (lit.) group of four people; extension of the original meaning 'team of four (horses or oxen)'; since the 19th c., e.g. (H.) Treitschke, *Dt. Gesch.* 5,214 quoting Bunsen: '*welch ein Viergespann . . . Schinkel, Cornelius, Rauch, Mendelssohn!*'; also used for 'four children (in one family)', as in Arndt, *Sämtl. Werke* 1,10: '*wir haben ein Viergespann von Buben*'.

vierkantig: see *Kante*.

Vierkleeblatt

das ~ (lit.) group of four (closely connected) people; in occasional use since the 19th c., e.g. (DWb) Raabe in *Westermanns Monatsh.* 49,25: '*dummes Zeug! sprach das gesammte Vierkleeblatt*'.

Vierräuberessig

der ~ (obs.) *acetum aromaticum*; Campe [1811] offers a (legendary) explanation: '*eine Art Essiges, durch welchen vier Räuber zur Zeit einer Pest sich vor der Ansteckung gesichert haben sollen (Vinaigre à quatre voleurs)*' and quotes an example from Jean Paul (no details).

vierschildig

vierschildig (hist.) having four (noble ancestors both on the father's and on the mother's side; recorded by Campe (not by Adelung); probably only used by historians and members of the nobility; for *Schild* in the sense of 'escutcheon' see p. 2110.

vierschrötig: see *Schrot*.

vierspännig

~ *fahren* (coll.) to be well-off; meaning 'rich enough to keep a coach and four horses'; in this sense a., but in this c. there is *mit jem.m* ~ *fahren* (coll.) = 'to have made a good (also lucrative) choice in one's partner'.

Viper

die ~ (lit.) viper; figur. as a term of abuse, as in Schlegel's transl. of Shakespeare, *Richard II*, 3,2: '*o Schelme, Vipern, rettungslos verdammt*'. Immermann, *Werke* [edit. B.] 14,281: '*du kleine Viper du!*'; cf. also Ebner-Eschenbach, *Sämtl. W.* 4,263: '*Pfeile ... ins Viperngift der Verleumdung getaucht*'; for comparable terms see under *Natter* (p. 1768), *Otter* (p. 1821) and *Schlange* (p. 2127).

virulent

virulent (lit.) virulent; originally a med. term describing the effects of health-threatening bacteria, germs, etc., in modern period transferred to denote what is dangerous and liable to spread, esp. with ref. to emotions such as *Fanatismus*, *Haß*, etc.

vis-à-vis

da stehst du machtlos ~ (coll.) there's nothing that you can do about that; since early in the 20th c., first among juveniles, now general in mock-resignation.

Visier (1): visor

mit offenem ~ openly, frankly; a ref. to the visor of one's armour; since the 18th c. in the extended sense, e.g. Herder [edit. S.] 8,131.

das ~ *herunterlassen* to put up one's guard; signifying that one expects an attack; the opposite is *das* ~ *lüften* = 'to raise the visor-part of one's armour' (fearing no attack), e.g. Börne, *Ges.Schr.* 10,71 or Immermann [edit. B.] 12,77 (with *aufschlagen*).

Visier (2): backsight

jem. ins ~ *nehmen* to keep an eye on sb., watch sb. intently; ~ here = 'backsight of a rifle'; modern.

visieren

etw. ~ (lit.) to contemplate or consider sth.; modern, e.g. Th.Mann, *Werke* 11,611: '*das Himmlische, von Menschenvernunft aus visiert*'.

Visitation: see *unterwerfen*.

Visite: see *Stipp*.

Visitenkarte

seine ~ *abgeben* (coll.) to call, pay a visit; figur. when no card was actually left but sth. can be seen which indicates that sb. (or sth.) called, e.g. with ref. to signs of destruction: *da hat der Sturm seine* ~ *abgegeben*.

eine gute ~ *für diese Gegend* (coll.) a good recommendation (or advertisement) for this area; used also in other contexts for sth. which shows off the quality of sth.; 20th c. coll.

Vitamin

~ *B* (sl.) good connections; *B* stands for *Beziehungen*; in such contexts as *wenn man diese Stellung haben will, braucht man* ~ *B*; 20th c. sl.

Vitriol

voll ~ full of venom; with ref. to caustic remarks, reviews, etc.; since the 18th c., when Adelung recorded *vitriolisch* in an extended sense.

Vogel

ein ~ (coll.) a person; when used on its own, the meaning depends on the context, e.g. Goethe 8,84 (W.): '*ich hab ihn losgelassen, den Vogel* [i.e. Weislingen]', Fontane, *Werke* 1,2,164: '*wir dürfen diesen Vogel nicht wieder aus den Händen lassen*', but usually, since Early NHG, with an adjective, e.g. Luther 20,579 (Weimar): '*ein seltzamer vogel ein christ*', C.F. Weiße, *Lustspiele* 1,54: '*ich denke, Sie sind mir ein schlauer Vogel*', Goethe 5,1,171 (W.) on the Brothers Schlegel: '*auch wär es billig, diesen frechen Vögeln auch tüchtig was am bunten Zeug zu flicken*', Schiller, *Fiesco* 1,1: '*hätt ichs je gedacht, daß der finstere Verrina ... noch ein so lustiger Vogel würde*', or in compounds for which see entries below and among the cross-references.

ein ... -vogel (a. or regional) (zool.) a ... creature; in earlier periods anything which could fly was called ~, e.g. Megenberg [1350] included the bat among the birds, Luther in his Apocr. transl. Ecclesiasticus 11,3 has '*die biene ist ein kleins vögelin*' and in *Werke* 16,152 (Weimar) he applied the term to *Heuschrecke*; hence *Buttervogel* for 'butterfly', also called *Sommervogel* and *Honigvogel* for 'bee', usually in the diminutive *Honigvögelein*, still used in the 18th c., e.g. by Bürger, *Ged.* 101b [1778]. In some regions these terms are still alive.

er hat einen ~ (coll.) he is not quite right in the head; recorded for many areas since the 19th c.;

cf. Engl. coll. 'he has a bee in his bonnet'; allusions to that bird which has built its nest in sb.'s head are frequent, cf. such phrases as *dich pickt's wohl* (see p. 1874) or *er hat einen Piepmatz im Kopf* (see p. 1875).

der Dämmerungsvogel (lit., obs.) spy, undercover agent; e.g. Musäus, *Volksmärchen* 2,139 [1826]; for figur. *Dämmerung* see p. 447.

die Tage der Eisvögel (lit., obs.) the halcyon days; *Eisvogel* (obs.) occurs in Fischart, *Garg.* 211b and 230a as a term of abuse for a cunning person; with ref. to *Halcyonen* since the 17th c., e.g. (S.-B.) Herrenschmid, *Coronologie* 11 [1622]: '*Gott gebe seinem betrübten evangelischen kirchlein die erwünschte Halcyonia oder eyssvögelins tag*'; still in the 18th c., e.g. Wieland 21,338: '*Halcyonische Tage ... sind die während der Brütezeit der Halcyonen (Eisvögel)*'. The phrase is obs., but *Eisvogel* as a zool. term for 'kingfisher' (which was originally *Eisenvogel*), is still alive.

ein Glücksvogel (1) (coll.) a fortunate person, lucky dog; since Early NHG; for the opposite see under *Fink* and *Pech* for *Pechvogel*.

ein Glücksvogel (2) a bird which (or the sight of which) brings luck; since the 17th c., f.r.b. Henisch [1616], e.g. Rosegger, *Schriften* 3,3,131 referring to the swallow: '*das ist kein gutes Zeichen, wenn dieser Glücksvogel ausbleibt*'.

der Goldvogel golden bird; a term used in many contexts with several meanings; it was first used for birds which had some yellow in their plumage (still recorded by Oken [1837] for *galbula*), then for rich persons, esp. in the diminutive for girls of marriageable age with a rich father (in lit. since the 19th c.); in coll. use it denoted 'gold coin', also called *gelber* ~ (cf. Engl. sl. 'yellow bird'). Lastly, it can occur as a term of endearment, e.g. H. Hesse, *Narz.u.G.* 11 [1948], also as *Goldvöglein*, since the 19th c.

der Lockvogel lure, decoy; used both for a bird-shaped lure and figur. for a person used to entice sb. to do what one wants; since Early NHG in comparisons or figur., e.g. Luther Apocr. transl. Ecclesiasticus 11,31, Fischart, *Garg.* 145b, Schiller, *Fiesco* 2,15, Goethe, *Götz* 2 (Bamberg).

der Pfingstvogel (regional, zool.) oriole; so called because it arrives in Germany around Whitsun; also called *Kirschvogel* in some areas; the standard term is *Pirol*. As *Pfingstvogel* (*Oriolus galbula*) f.r.b. Nemnich.

der Piepvogel (joc. coll., obs.) Order of the Eagle; f.r.b. Albrecht [1881] for Leipzig. There are also other regional meanings, esp. 'girl' in joc. coll. of NE regions, recorded by Dähnert [1781] and 'weakling' in some N regions, recorded by Danneil [1859].

der Schreivogel (coll.) loudmouth, noisy person; since Early NHG, e.g. (DWb) Thurneißer, *Magna Alchym.* 1,82 [1583]; still used in modern period, e.g. by Alexis in *Hosen d.H.v.B.* 2,3,14,

although *Schreihals* (for which see p. 1206) is preferred.

der Spaßvogel joker; general since the 18th c., f.r.b. Adelung, e.g. Lessing 10,175, Wieland 5,246, also used by Goethe.

der Spottvogel mocker; since Early NHG, e.g. Keisersberg, *S.d.Munds* 53a, f.r.b. Rädlein [1712]; also called *Spottdrossel*.

der Wandervogel rambler, hiker; original sense 'bird-of-passage', extended to persons in 1st half of the 19th c.; since early in the 20th c. a term for a member of a group devoted to exploring the countryside and enjoying life in the open air; cf. *DWb.* [1922]: '*wandervogel kommt jetzt als name von vereinen, die die wanderung pflegen, vor*'; the designation was invented by Wolf Meyen at a meeting of nature enthusiasts in Steglitz on November 4,1901 (details in *Trübner* 8,43 [1957]).

der ~ (1) (obscene) the penis; rarely in print, but current at least since the 19th c., sometimes used as an euphem. when talking to little boys, usually in the diminutive form *Vögelchen*.

der ~ (2) (sl.) bailiff's mark on impounded buildings or goods; so called because of the eagle on the seal; also called *blauer* ~ since early in the 20th c.; another term for it is *Kuckuck* (see p. 1561).

der ~ (3) (mil. sl.) uniform button which has the picture of an eagle; since the 19th c. and still in the 2nd World War.

der ~ (4) (sl.) aircraft; since the 1st decade of the 20th c.; cf. later *müder* ~ (mil. sl.) = 'slow aircraft' (2nd World War).

ein ~ *federlos* (old riddle) snow; the full text of the riddle is: *ein* ~ *federlos kam und flog auf einen Baum blattlos, da kam eine Frau mundlos* [i.e. the Sun] *und aß den* ~ *federlos*; recorded since the 19th c., e.g. *DWb.* [1862] and Wander [1876].

vögeln (obscene) to screw; in transit. and intrans. use first for the mating of birds; since ca. 1300 transferred to human intercourse; in early periods not often in print, but Stieler [1691] recorded it, also the noun *Vögelung* = 'coitus' and a large number of verb compounds.

die Vögel, die zu früh singen, holt die Katze (prov.) if you sing before breakfast, you'll cry before night; recorded for many areas since the 19th c., e.g. Simrock [1846]; see also under *früh* (p. 864).

besser ein ~ *im Bauer als Tausende in der Luft* (prov.) one bird in the hand is worth two in the bush; variants are *besser ein* ~ *im Netz als hundert im Fluge, ... in der Hand als zehn über Land, besser eine Feder in der Hand als einen* ~ *in der Luft* (or *am Strand*); some versions were recorded as early as in the 17th c., others by Simrock [1846] and Wander [1876].

es ist ein böser ~ , *der sein eignes Nest beschmutzt* (prov.) it is an ill bird that fouls its own nest;

international, in Engl. since the 13th c., in German recorded since the 16th c., e.g. Franck [1541].

er läuft wie ein blinder ~ (prov.) he moves very slowly; used by W. Grimm in *Kinder- u. Hausmärchen* (cf. H. Röllecke (ed.), *Das Sprichtwort in den Kinder- u. Hausmärchen der Brüder Grimm* 17 [1988]).

Vögel von einer Feder (or *Farbe*) *fliegen gern zusammen* (prov.) birds of a feather flock together; in German (and in Engl.) recorded since the 16th c., e.g. by Tappius [1539] and Franck [1541]; in Franck as *vögel von einn federn fliegen gern zusamen*; cf. also *das sind Vögel von einer Feder* = 'there is nothing to choose between them', as recorded by Lehman [1640].

← See also under *abschießen* (for *er hat den Vogel abgeschossen*), *anfallen* (for *die Vögel fallen hier an*), *Busch* (for *der eine klopft auf den Busch, der andre fängt den Vogel*), *Butter* (for *Buttervogel* in two meanings), *Canaille* (for *Canaillenvogel*), *Chor* (for *der Vögel frühes Chor*), *Feder* (for *den Vogel kennt man bei den Federn*), *Finger* (for *ihm erzählt es ein Vögelchen oder sein Finger*), *Fink* (for *Pechvogel*), *Flügel* (for *beschirmen wie die vögel thun mit flügeln* and *vogelschnell*), *fressen* (for *friß Vogel oder stirb*), *früh* (for *die Vögel, die zu früh singen*), *Gabel* (for *die Gabel des Vogels*), *Garn* (for *Zauberfädchen, die auch die erfahrenen Vögel gern umgarnen*), *Gesang* (for *am Gesang erkennt man den Vogel* and *süßer Gesang hat manchen Vogel betrogen*), *Hanf* (for *vergnügt* etc. *wie der Vogel im Hanfsamen*), *los* (for *ein loser Vogel*), *Luft* (for *frei wie der Vogel in der Luft*), *Nacht* (for *Nachtvogel*), *Nest* (for *ein großer Vogel will ein groß Nest haben*), *Paradies* (for *Paradiesvogel*), *Pech* (for *Pechvogel*), *piepen* (for *Piepvogel*), *rar* (for *ein rarer Vogel*), *rauben* (for *Raubvogel*), *rupfen* (for *einen Vogel rupfen*), *Salz* (for *dem Vogel Salz auf den Schwanz streuen*), *sauber* (for *du bist ein sauberer Vogel*), *schräg* (for *ein schräger Vogel*), *Strauß* (for *Vogel-Strauß-Politik treiben*) and *Tasche* (for *er hat einen toten Vogel in der Tasche*).

Vogelbauer

das (also *der*) ~ or *Vogelkäfig* (coll.) small enclosed space; originally = 'birdcage', occasionally extended as in Goethe 26,12 (W.)

Vogelflug

im ~ (rare) in a hurry; used by Goethe IV,4,88 (W.); *im Fluge* is the usual phrase (for which see p. 828).

vogelfrei

vogelfrei (1) outlawed, without legal protection; f.r.b. Frischlin [1588], e.g. Franck [1528]: '. . . *vogelfrey geachtet werde*', Goethe 14,111 (W.): '*stoßt zu! der Kerl ist vogelfrei*'; the original sense is 'handed over to the birds which can eat him', as explained by Dentzler [1716] '*der dem Vogel im Luft erlaubt*'; often in *jem. für* ~ *erklären*, f.r.b. Adelung.

vogelfrei (2) free as a bird, unencumbered; since the 15th c., usually = 'free from feudal service, imposts, tithes, etc.', but then also in wider sense for 'free, unfettered', as in Luther 33,647 (Weimar).

Vogelkäfig: see *Vogelbauer.*

vogelleicht

vogelleicht (1) in effortless motion, agile like a bird; f.r.b. Campe [1811], e.g. P. Heyse, *Ges.Werke* 3,159 [1873]: '*bald trägt sie ein Nachen vogelleicht dahin*'.

vogelleicht (2) (lit.) light-hearted, easy-going; modern, e.g. (Sp.) Boree, *Dor u.d.Sept.* 139: '*eine vogelleichte Freiheit erfüllte mein Herz*'.

Vogelleim

zäh wie ~ as tough as birdlime, holding on like strong glue; since the 18th c., e.g. H.v.Kleist, *Hermannsschlacht* 5,1; cf. also v. Arnim, *D.Buch gehört* . . . 2,371.

Vogelnest

das ~ (coll.) bun (i.e. hair arranged in the shape of a bird's best); recorded for SW areas since the 19th c.; see also under *Nest* (p. 1780).

Vogelschau

die ~ or *Vogelperspektive* bird's-eye view; first as *Vogelperspektive*, since the 18th c., e.g. Goethe 30,65 (W.); in an effort to replace this with a German word *Vogelschau* was introduced in the 19th c., but is still not used in tech. contexts where the older word predominates.

Vogelscheuche: see *scheuchen.*

Vogelwat: see *Feder.*

Vöglein: see *sorgen.*

Voland

Junker ~ (obs.) the Devil; the term ~ is old and could describe monsters, spectres or evil spirits; it occurred in MHG as *volant*, as *falant* recorded by Stieler [1691]; with ref. to the devil in *Fast.Sp.* 2,926 as '*böser volant*'; Goethe still used it in *Werke* 14,203 (W.): '*Platz! Junker Voland kommt*'; now obs.

Volk

das ~ (1) (pejor.) the common people, the lower orders; in OHG ~ was used with ref. to an armed group, troop, and it can still be used when an army is meant, as in *unter das* ~ *gehen* = 'to join the army', extended to naval contexts in *Schiffsvolk*; pejor. since Early NHG, as in Luther Bible transl. Levit. 4,27, where '*gemeines volk*' occurs; hence *ein Mann aus dem Volke* = 'a man of humble origin'; contemptuous in Schiller, *Kab.u.L.* 2,1: '*soll ich mein Zimmer mit diesem Volk tapezieren?*'.

das ~ (2) (obs. or regional) the servants; since MHG for 'attendants, servants', e.g. *Nibelungenl.* 708; still used in some SW regions in the 19th c., e.g. Gotthelf, *Schuldenb.* 310: '*als das Volk vom Tische aufbrach, war der Bauer der letzte*'; Adelung remarked about this sense: '*nur noch im gemeinen Leben*'.

das ~ (3) (crowd of) people; since Early NHG, e.g. Luther Bible transl. Judges 7,2: *'des volks ist zu viel, das mit dir ist'*, Matth. 8,1: *'folgete jm viel volks nach'*; cf. *bevölkern*, listed on p. 301. In some cases of compounds ~ = 'inhabitants', e.g. *Landvolk*, which began in MHG for 'inhabitants of a country', but since the 15th c. has come to be used for 'countryfolk, village people' in contrast to *Stadtvolk*; f.r.b. *voc.inc.theut.* mlb [1482], e.g. Hagedorn 3,55: *'uraltes Landvolk, eure Hütten verschont der Städter Stolz und Neid'*.

das ~ (4) (zool.) group, family, genus, lot, colony of animals; since Early NHG, e.g. Luther Bible transl. Prov. 30,26: *'caninichen ein schwach folk'*, Freytag, *Soll u.H.* 1,12: *'auf der Weide saß ein Volk Sperlinge'*.

Volks-. . . (1) folk-. . . , originating among the (common) people, part of a national tradition; in many compounds, several of them coined by Herder or by Romantics inspired by the *Sturm und Drang*, such as *Volksart* = 'traditional feature, national characteristic' (Herder), *Volksausdruck* = 'common expression' (Herder), also *Volkskunst, --märchen, -sage, -tanz, -tracht*. In the 19th c. Förstemann coined *Volksetymologie* = 'popular etymology' and *Volkskunde* arose for 'folklore'. *Volkslied* became a hotly contested term around 1770 when Herder and people around him collected 'folksongs', whereas Rationalists of the Enlightenment used the term in the sense of *Lieder für das* ~ (first collection by Nicolai [1776]). Herder confused the issue further by including poems by Sappho, even by Goethe and Matthias Claudius in his collection, whereas others were to be taken as 'songs created by the nation' and not attributable to a known author.

Volks-. . . concerning itself with the (common) people, produced for the people, enjoying popularity; some of the compounds in this category arose in the 18th c., e.g. *Volksaufwiegler* = 'demagogue', *Volksblatt* = 'cheap newspaper for mass consumption', *Volksbuch* = 'chap book', but later the term for 'book that has acquired or is intended to attract a mass readership'. Many established themselves in the 19th c., such as *Volksbelustigung,- bücherei, -bühne, -musik*. In some cases ambiguity exists, e.g. *Volksredner* can be 'speaker of humble origin' or 'mob orator', *Volksdichter* can be 'popular author' or 'national poet' (used by Herder), *Volkssprache* can mean 'the vulgar tongue' but also 'the vernacular (language)'.

das Jungvolk young people; used as a general description for children and adolescents, only since early in the 20th c. (still missing in *DWb.*, Sanders and Heyne), but in the Third Reich it also became the designation for children aged between 10 and 14 years organised in the *Hitlerjugend*.

Volkstum national characteristics, nationhood, nationality; coined by Jahn in *Deutsches Volkstum*

[1810] and quickly accepted (although J. Grimm considered *Volktum* as more appropriate); the adjective *volkstümlich* was coined by Herder for 'popular', but due to Jahn the meaning 'characteristic of the people, bearing the national imprint' also came into use. Goethe used *Volkheit* (e.g. Werke 42,2,194 (W.)), formed by analogy with *Christenheit*, but this has dropped out of general use.

← See also under *aufgären* (for *das Volk begann aufzugären*), *aufwühlen* (for *das Volk aufwühlen*), *auserwählen* (for *das auserwählte Volk*), *bevölkern*, *Bürde* (for *der Völker Fluch auf mich gebürdet*), *Gasse* (for *Gassenvolk*), *Haufen* (for *ein Haufen Volk*), *Hottentotte* (for *Hottentottenvolk*), *Kaviar* (for *Kaviar für das Volk*), *Märchen* (for *in der Erinnerung des Volkes*), *Markt* (for *von des volkes wuofte*), *Stoff* (for *das rauhe Volk gefällt mir*), *Strom* (for *laufft zu das volck gleich wie ein strom*), *Teufel* (for *Teufelsvolk*), *Tücke* (for *einheimisch tückisch volk*), *um* (for *der wie Saul das volck weit überragt um eines hauptes länge*) and *Wirtschaft* (for *Volkswirtschaft*).

Volksbegehren
das ~ (polit.) petition for a referendum; 20th c. coinage, as is *Volksentscheid* for 'referendum'.
Volksmeer see *Meer*.
Volksmund: see *Mund*.
Volksredewut: see *Diarrhöe*.
Volksstimme: see *Stimme*.
Volkstümlichkeit: see *stellen*.

voll
voll (1) complete, not lacking in anything; figur. with ref. to persons or abstracts since MHG, e.g. Reinmar v. Zweter 164: *'ein voller mensch vünf sinne hât'*, Iwein 2428: *'volle tugend'*.

voll (2) full; with ref. to abstracts since MHG, e.g. with ref. to times and numbers general since Early NHG, e.g. Luther Bible transl. Romans 11,12: *'wenn jre zal vol würde'* (cf. also Schiller, *Tell* 2,2: *'er hatte seine Jahre voll'*). With other abstracts since MHG, e.g. *'nîdes was er voller'* (in *Fundgruben* 2,25,33), Luther Bible transl. Psalm 44,16: *'mein antlitz ist voller schande'*, Schiller, *Fiesco* 2,4: *'ein Cavalier . . . voll Talenten und Kopf'*, *Räuber* 5,2: *'ein Leben voll Abscheulichkeit und Schande'*. Since the 17th c. in many adjectival compounds. Kramer [1702] recorded *'dünckelvoll, einbildungvoll, eifervoll, freudenvoll, gnadenvoll, lebensvoll, schmertzenvoll, traurenvoll* and *trostvoll'* (adding *'e simili'*). Gottsched took exception to *sinnvoll, trostvoll*, etc. wanting to see them replaced by *sinnreich, trostreich*, etc., but many compounds in this group have established themselves firmly, esp. *anspruchsvoll*, used by Wieland, though Goethe used *anspruchsreich, ehrfurchtsvoll, einsichtsvoll, erwartungsvoll, geheimnisvoll* and *hoffnungsvoll*, all since the 18th c., but *geheimnisvoll* probably since the 17th c., because Rädlein [1712] recorded it.

voll (3) full of sth., much moved or carried away by sth.; with ref. to personal feelings and emotional reactions. Kramer [1702] recorded *voll* (or *voller*) *Angst, Betrübnis, Schrecken, Freude, Verwunderung, Mut* and *Scham*, e.g. Goethe, *Kenner u. Enth.*: 'mein Busen war so voll und bang'; often in ~ *von etw. sein*, sometimes used when sth. is the topic of conversation by many, as in *die ganze Stadt ist* ~ *davon*, e.g. Schiller, *Verbr.a.v.Ehre*: 'die ganze Gegend ist voll von dir', also *alle Mäuler sind* ~ *davon*.

voll (4) (coll.) drunk, plastered; derived from ~ *von* = 'full of, replete with' which can be used with ref. to food and drink, but acquired its special sense 'drunk' in MHG, e.g. *vol sîn* in *Dt.Myst.* 1,78, *vol werden* in Konr.v.Megenberg, *Buch d.Nat.* 230,24; often in comparisons ~ *wie . . .*, e.g. Löns, *Hausbur* 134 [1910]: '. . . nach einer Stunde voll wie ein Entendarm'; for others see among the cross-references below.

jem. nicht für ~ *nehmen* (or *rechnen*) to refuse to take sb. seriously, consider sb. as not quite sound (in mind); probably belongs to ~ (1); see also under *rechnen* (p. 1956) for *jem. für etw. rechnen, ansehen, betrachten* or *halten*; such phrases must have been current in some form at least since the 17th c., because Kramer in 1702 recorded 'einen für voll ansehen'. Some scholars have suggested that the phrase originally referred to coins having or not having their 'full' weight.

~ *des süßen Weines* (bibl.) intoxicated; bibl. from Acts 2,13; as a standing phrase (often in joc. coll. or euphem. contexts) at least since the 17th c., when Kramer recorded it as such.

voll und ganz fully, entirely; similar to *ganz und gar*, but only current since the 19th c., frequently attacked as jargon when in the 2nd half of the 19th c. it became a fashionable phrase in polit. speeches; some authors, e.g. Storm used *ganz und* ~.

die Handvoll handful; first used for 'as much as a hand can hold', f.r.b. Maaler [1561] and in this sense used by Luther in his Bible transl. 1 Kings 20,10; now also used for 'a few', even for 'five' with ref. to the number of fingers.

← See also under *Arm* (for *Armvoll*), *Bauch* (for *ein voller Bauch studiert nicht gern*), *Brust* (for *aus voller Brust* and *die Knospe spaltet die volle Brust*), *Ei* (for *voll wie ein Ei*), *einlaufen* (for *mit vollen Segeln*), *Foh* (for *einen Korb/Sack voll Flöhe hüten*), *Fuder* (for *ganze Fuder voll*), *Galopp* (for *in vollem Galopp*), *Geige* (for *jem.m hängt der Himmel voller Geigen*), *Gott* (for *gottvoll*), *gut* (for *zween gut löffel voll*), *Hagel* (for *blitzhagelvoll*), *Hals* (for *aus vollem Hals*), *Hand* (for *alle Hände voll zu tun haben* and *mit voller Hand*), *Hose* (for *die Hosen voll haben*), *Huck* (for *sich die Hucke voll lachen*), *Kanal* (for *den Kanal voll haben*), *Kanone* (for *kanonenvoll*), *Kehle* (for *aus voller Kehle*), *Kelch* (for *sie hat den vollen Kelch der Freuden aus-*

getrunken), *Kiste* (for *Kisten und Kasten voll haben*), *Maß* (for *das Maß ist voll*), *Mond* (for *leuchtet er wie der volle Mond* and *er ist voll wie der Mond*), *Mund* (for *ein Mundvoll* and *wes das Herz voll ist, des geht der Mund über*), *Nase* (for *die Nase voll haben*), *Pfropfen* (for *vollgepfropft* and *gepfropft voll*), *Rand* (for *bis zum Rande voll von Bitterkeit*), *rappeln* (for *gerappelt voll*), *recht* (for *verlang ich auch das Maul recht voll*), *Sack* (for *ein Sack voll* and *Sackvoll*), *Saft* (for *saftvoll*), *saufen* (for *sich toll und voll saufen*), *Schmalz* (for *das Lied ist voll Schmalz*), *schöpfen* (for *aus dem Vollen schöpfen*), *Schüssel* (for *er hat immer aus vollen Schüsseln gegessen*), *schweppern* (for *geschweppert* or *geschwadert voll*), *Segel* (for *mit vollen Segeln gehen*), *sitzen* (for *etw. sitzt voll(er) . . .*), *sprengen* (for *volle Brust*), *spritzen* (for *voll wie eine Spritze*), *sprudeln* (for *Herzlichkeit sprudelte voll und natürlich*), *Stand* (for *anstandsvoll*), *stecken* (for *etw. steckt voll von . . .*), *stehen* (for *stund vol disteln, weils voll schämbart steht, voller Leute, voll Steine, die Augen stehen voll Wasser/Tränen* and *die Segel stehen voll*), *Stern* (for *sternvoll* and variants), *Strand* (for *voll wie eine Strandhaubitze*), *Strom* (for *in vollen Strömen*), *Stube* (for *eine Stube voll Kinder haben*), *tausend* (for *voll wie tausend Mann*), *Temperament* (for *voll Temperament*), *Tisch* (for *tisch vol arme leut speiset*), *toll* (for *sich toll und voll saufen*), *Ton* (for *das Volle, Langtönende unsrer Sprache*) and *Tour* (for *auf vollen Touren laufen*).

vollauf: see *Stoff*.

Vollblut

das ~ person of pure descent; at first with ref. to animals of pure race, thoroughbreds, a loan from Engl., in German texts only since the 2nd half of the 18th c. mainly with ref. to horses (when the term *Vollblütler* is also used); in the 19th c. applied to persons of 'pure' descent, often mockingly to members of the nobility, but also seriously for 'showing the proper characteristics of the type', e.g. *Vollblutfranzose* = 'typical Frenchman' or 'Frenchman to the core', also in praise (cf. the adjective below).

vollblütig full-blooded, vigorous, energetic; since the 17th c. in phys. med. sense 'plethoric', f.r.b. Stieler [1691], figur. only since the 19th c. The antonym is *blutarm* = 'anaemic', used figur. for 'weak' (apart from 'very poor', where *blut-* is used as an intensifying prefix).

Vollblut-. . . (coll.) complete . . . , thorough . . . ; in compounds, mainly of the pejor, kind, e.g. *Vollblutphilister*, e.g. (DWb) Bog.Goltz, *Jugendleben* 2,288, *Vollblutschuft*, e.g. Bernoulli, *Overbeck u. Nietzsche* 2,104, often in *Vollblutidiot*, since early in the 20th c. (there is also synom. *Vollidiot*).

vollbringen

etw. ~ to achieve, accomplish, perform sth.; cf. entries on *es zu etw. bringen* (p. 399) and *etw. vor sich bringen* (p. 400); frequent since MHG, as has been the noun *Vollbringung*, with ref. to time sometimes used like *verbringen*, e.g. Körner, *Männer u. Buben*: '. . . Regennacht . . . wachend vollbracht'.

← See also under *dienen* (for *nach vollbrachtem Dienste*) and *Ritter* (for *eine Sache ritterlich vollbringen*).

Volldampf: see *Dampf.*

vollenden

etw. ~ to complete sth.' since MHG, when often used synon. with *vollbringen; vollendigen*, since MHG, still used in the 19th c., has become obs.

er hat vollendet (lit.) he has passed way; since the 15th c., e.g. Mentel's Bible transl. [1466], where Luke 13,32 is translated: '*an dem dritten tag vollend ich*' (Luther put: '*werde ich ein ende nemen*').

vollendet perfect, immaculate; past participle used as an adjective since the 18th c., e.g. Goethe 25,1,182 (W.).

vollends completely; first (in Early NHG) as *vollend*, since the 17th c. with final *s*, f.r.b. Kramer [1702]; rare now in cases, where it means *nun gar* = 'even', as in Schiller, *Don Carlos* 2,2: '*vollends Thränen? Unwürdger Anblick*', or 'especially', as in Lessing, *Nathan* 2,5: '*vollends Ihr, Ihr seid mir gar nichts schuldig*'.

← See also under *Meißel* (for *der vollendet sprang aus dem Meißel der . . . Künstlerin*), *Saft* (for *der edelste Saft sich in künftigen Jahren vollende*) and *Trank* (for *ich muß den Gifttrank dieser Seligkeit vollends ausschlürfen*).

vollfressen: see *Ranzen.*

vollführen

etw. ~ to perform, execute sth.; at first (in MHG) ~ = *vollbringen* or *vollenden* with the main notion of bringing sth. to its conclusion; this was still alive in the 18th c., but then the range of meanings contracted and only the sense 'to perform, execute' is in current use, e.g. Goethe, *Was wir bringen* (Forts. 3): '*unfrei vollführ ich nur ein strenges Muß*', where *ausführen* (1) (see p. 130) could also be used (or *machen, tun*).

Vollgas

mit ~ (sl.) vigorously, with energy (and speed); from motoring contexts where it means 'at full throttle' and ~ *geben* = 'to step on it'; since the 1st half of the 20th c.

vollhauen: see *Jacke* and *Kasten.*

völlig: see *Seele.*

volljährig

volljährig (lit.) mature; the ordinary meaning is 'of age, having attained majority', current since the 18th c., f.r.b. Adelung (MHG had *gejâret*); in figur. sense since the 19th c., e.g. Laube, *Ges. Werke* 16,102.

vollkacken: see *Kacke.*

vollkommen

vollkommen (1) (a.) complete, entire; from

MHG to the 18th c. when it was still used with ref. to appearance, e.g. Adelung 4,1235 [1801]: '*im Gesichte vollkommen seyn*' = 'to have a full (well-rounded, fleshy) face'; in some regions still used for 'wide, broad'.

vollkommen (2) perfect; from 'having reached its full extent, value, shape, degree' since MHG (even in abstracts), used by Luther in his Bible transl. Matth. 5,48; hence *die Vollkommenheit*, since MHG, when *unvollkommen* also appeared.

vollkommen (3) (adv.) completely, totally, thoroughly; since the 18th c. without containing the notion of perfection, becoming synon. with *völlig*, e.g. Goethe 35,303 (W.): '*die vollkommen poetische Gewitterwolke*'.

aus eigner Machtvollkommenheit on one's own authority, making use of one's unlimited authority; beginnings in MHG, but without *eigen*; as a set phrase with *eigen* it is modern.

← See also under *rund* (for *gut rund vnnd vollkommen ding reden*), *schön* (for *in vollkommener Übereinstimmung*), *Siegel* (for *das Siegel der Vollkommenheit*), *steigen* (for *ynn eynen vollkommeneren stand gestiegen*) and *treffen* (for *das trifft vollkommen*).

vollkriegen: see *Laden.*

vollmachen

um die Sache, Angelegenheit, das Unglück, etc. *vollzumachen* (coll.) to crown it all; modern (not yet mentioned in *DWb.* [1931]).

Vollmacht

die ~ (legal) proxy; translates Lat. legal *plenipotentia* = 'full power', in German recorded since 1372; often in *jem.m* ~ *erteilen* = 'to empower sb.', also *jem. bevollmächtigen* (recorded in *DWb.* [1854]). ~ is also used for the document in question, since the 18th c., recorded by Adelung.

Vollmond

das Vollmondsgesicht (coll.) face like a full moon; since the 17th c., f.r.b. Kramer [1702]. See also under *Mond* for *Mondgesicht.*

er hat einen ~ (sl.) he is as bald as a coot; first in mil. sl., recorded by Imme, *Soldatenspr.* 69, but *Mondschein* is older (see p. 1708).

← See also under *Mond* (for *glänzen/leuchten wie ein Vollmond*).

vollmundig

vollmundig full-bodied; mainly with ref. to alcoholic drinks; recorded for several regions since the 19th c., now in general use.

~ *daherreden* (coll.) to brag, talk in a swanky way; 20th c. coll.

vollnehmen

See under *Backe* (for *die Backen vollnehmen*) and under *nehmen* (for *das Maul vollnehmen*).

vollnudeln: see *Nudel.*

vollpinseln: see *Ohr.*

vollplärren: see *plärren.*

vollquaken: see *quaken.*

vollquatschen: see *Ohr*.

vollreden: see *Ohr*.

vollreif: see *reif* (also for *Vollreife* and *vollreifen*).

vollrichten: see *Muster*.

vollrosig: see *Rose*.

vollsacken: see *Sack*.

vollschlagen

See under *Hucke* (for *jem.m die Hucke vollschlagen*), *Jacke* (for *jem.m die Jacke vollschlagen* and *sich die Jacke vollschlagen*), *Ohr* (for *lass dir weder die ohren volschlagen . . .*) and *Ranzen* (for *sich den Ranzen vollschlagen* and *jem.m den Ranzen vollschlagen*).

vollschlank

vollschlank (euphem., coll.) plump, a little over-weight; 20th c. coll. which avoids such terms as *fett* or *dick*, e.g. (T.) Lerch, *Glück auf Sperlingslust* 172 [1934]: '*du sollst nicht Dickchen sagen, ich bin höchstens vollschlank*'.

vollschlauchen: see *Schlauch*.

vollschreiben: see *Rand*.

vollständig

vollständig complete, thorough, total; ~ only arose in the 16th c., used like *vollkommen*, since the 17th c. extended to use with abstracts and persons, e.g. Keller, *Ges.Werke* 4,48 (*Leute v.Seldw.*): '*nie trifft . . . ein vollständiger Narr auf einen unbedingt klugen Fröhlichen*'; as an adverb since the 17th c., usually = *völlig* or *ganz*.

← See also under *Ende* (for *ein vollständiges Bild*) and *Sack* (for *einen Sack vollständig ausschütten*).

vollstecken: see *Säckel*.

vollstimmig: see *Grund*.

vollstopfen: see *Ranzen* and *stopfen*.

vollstrecken

etw. ~ to perform, execute sth.; originally = 'to extend, prolong' (phys. and figur.), f.r.b. Frisius [1556], then = 'to perform, do' (also in Frisius), but also in the narrower sense of 'to perform or execute sth. that has been ordered by somebody else', e.g. (DWb) Boltz, *Terenz* 76a [1539]: '*mein geheiß hettest wöllen volstrecken*'.

Vollwaise

Vollwaise orphan; recorded since the 19th c.; when only one parent has died, *Halbwaise* is used.

vollziehen

etw. ~ (1) to perform sth.; current since OHG, often = *vollstrecken* (including the notion that sb.'s command is being obeyed), but usually = *vollbringen*.

etw. ~ (2) (legal) to make sth. valid; with ref. to treaties, judgments, etc., since the 17th c., recorded by Kramer [1702]. Often merely = 'to sign', and used by Goethe III, 7,130 (W.) in this sense.

etw. vollzieht sich sth. takes place, happens, occurs; only since the 2nd half of the 19th c.

Vollzugsorgan: see *Organ*.

von

von or *vom* (1) from, away from; with ref. to persons, things or abstracts with many verbs in their figur. sense or in phrases.

← See under *abbringen* (for *jem. von etw. abbringen*), *abfallen* (for *von jem.m abfallen*), *abkommen* (for *von etw. abkommen*), *abrücken* (for *von jem.m abrücken*), *abschieben* (for *eine Schuld von sich abschieben*), *abschneiden* (for *abgeschnitten von etw.*), *abschütteln* (for *Vorwürfe von sich abschütteln*), *absehen* (for *absehen von etw.*), *absondern* (for *sich von der Welt absondern*), *abspringen* (for *von einem Thema abspringen*), *abstehen* (for *von etw. abstehen*), *abtreten* (for *von etw. abtreten*), *abwälzen* (for *das wält mir einen Stein vom Herzen ab*), *abweichen* (for *von etw. abweichen*), *abziehen* (for *seine Hand von jem.m abziehen*), *Apfel* (for *der Apfel fällt nicht weit vom Stamm*), *Auge* (for *die Augen von jem.m abwenden* and *es fallen jem.m die Schuppen von den Augen*), *ausgehen* (for *ausgehen von etw.*), *Bock* (for *die Böcke von den Schafen sondern* and the same idiom under *scheiden*), *Butter* (for *mir fällt die Butter vom Brot* and *Finger von der Butter*), *Decke* (for *die Decke von etw. wegziehen*), *entbinden* (for *von etw. entbunden werden*), *entfernen* (for *entfernt sein von etw.*), *entkleiden* (for *sich von etw. entkleiden*), *entlasten* (for *von etw. entlastet werden*), *entwöhnen* (for *jem. von etw. entwöhnen*), *erwecken* (for *von den Toten erwecken*), *Esel* (for *vom Gaul auf den Esel kommen*), *fallen* (for *vom Fleisch fallen* and *mir fällt ein Stein vom Herzen*), *Faust* (for *rasch von der Faust gehen* and *von der Faust weg*), *Feder* (for *von den Federn aufs Stroh kommen*), *fern* (for *das sei ferne von mir*), *Ferse* (for *von der Ferse bis zum Scheitel*), *Fessel* (for *etw. entfesselt jem. von etw.*), *Finger* (for *die Finger von etw. lassen*), *Fleck* (for *nicht vom Fleck kommen*), *frei* (for *frei von . . .*), *Fuchs* (for *der Fuchs schleicht vom Taubenschlag*, also the similar idiom under *Katze*), *Fuß* (for *etw. mit Füßen von sich stoßen*), *geben* (for *etw. von sich geben*), *gelb* (for *das Gelbe vom Schnabel wischen*), *glatt* (for *glatt vonstatten gehen*), *Grund* (for *von Grund auf*), *Haar* (for *jem. m die Haare vom Kopf fressen*), *Hals* (for *jem.m vom Hals bleiben*), *halten* (for *jem. von etw. abhalten, sich von etw. nicht abhalten lassen* and *sich von etw. enthalten*), *Hand* (for *von der Hand in den Mund leben* and *etw. geht jem.m leicht von der Hand*), *hauen* (for *das haut mich von Stuhl*), *Herodes* (for *von Herodes zu Pilatus geschickt werden*), *Herz* (for *es kommt vom Herzen*), *Holz* (for *vom Hölzchen aufs Stöckchen kommen*), *Hund* (for *damit kann man keinen Hund vom Ofen locken*), *hundert* (for *vom Hundertsten ins Tausendste gehen*), *Kirche* (for *weiter von Gott*), *kommen* (for *von jem.m kommen, von etw. kommen* and *von einem ins andere kommen*), *Kopf* (for *von Kopf bis Fuß*), *lachen* (for *vom Erhabenen zum Lächerlichen ist nur ein Schritt*), *Leber* (for *frisch von der Leber weg*), *Leder* (for *vom Leder ziehen*), *Leib* (for *vom Leibe bleiben* and *sich etw. vom Leibe schaffen*), *link* (for *die Linke kommt von Herzen*), *los* (for *los von etw. sein*), *Mund* (for *sich etw. vom Mund absparen, jem.m geht alles glatt vom Munde ab* and *vom Munde aus gen Himmel fahren*), *nachlassen* (for *von etw. nachlassen*), *Nacken* (for *vom Nacken bis zu den Hacken*), *Nagel* (for *etw. von einem Nagel auf einen andern hängen* and *die Nägel von etw. lassen*), *nehmen* (for *er nimmts von den Lebendigen*), *Nuß* (for *die Nuß vom Baum schwätzen*, where *von* should read *vom*), *Pelle* (for *jem.m nicht von der Pelle rücken*, where *jem.* should read *jem.m*), *Piedestal* (for *jem. von seinem Piedestal reißen*), *Pike* (for *von der Pike auf dienen*), *Pilatus* (for *jem. von Pontius zu Pilatus schicken*), *Postament* (for *jem. von seinem Postament herunterholen*), *Pritsche* (for *von der Pritsche fallen*), *Regen* (for *vom Regen in die Traufe kommen*), *reißen* (for *das reißt einen vom Stuhl*), *rollen* (for *etw. rollt vom Band*), *scheiden* (for *von etw. scheiden*), *Scheitel* (for *vom Scheitel bis zur Sohle*), *Schippe* (for *dem Tod von der Schippe springen*), *Staub* (for *den Staub von den Füßen schütteln*), *Seele* (for *sich etw. von der Seele reden/schreiben*), *Seite* (for *jem.m nicht von der Seite kommen*), *Socke* (for *von den Socken sein*), *Sperling* (for *es fällt kein Sperling vom Himmel*), *sprechen* (for *sich etw. von der Seele heruntersprechen*), *Stapel* (for *etw. vom Stapel laufen lassen*), *Statt* (for *von statten gehen*), *Stelle* (for *von der Stelle kommen*), *Stengel* (for *vom Stengel fallen*), *strecken* (for *alle Viere von sich strecken*), *Teufel* (for *dem Teufel vom Karren gefallen*), *Thron* (for *jem. vom Thron stoßen*), *Tisch* (for *etw. vom Tisch bringen*), *trennen* (for *etw. von etw. trennen* and *jem. von jem.m trennen*).

von or *vom* (2) from, of; with ref. to origin or descent; with verbs used figur. and in set expressions.

See under *ableiten* (for *ein Wort von einem anderen ableiten*), *alt* (for *von alters her*), *Art* (for *Art läßt nicht von Art*), *bauen* (for *Männer vom Bau*), *Eltern* (for *nicht von schlechten Eltern*), *Gott* (for *Gottes Wort vom Lande*), *Haus* (for *von Hause aus*), *herkommen* (for *von etw. herkommen*), *herleiten* (for *etw. von etw. anderem herleiten*), *hernehmen* (for *etw. nimmt etw. von einer Sache her*), *herschreiben* (for *sich von etw. herschreiben*), *hier* (for *du bist wohl nicht von hier*), *Land* (for *die Unschuld vom Lande*), *Leder* (for *Bergmann vom Leder* and *Bergmann von der Feder*), *Linie* (for *von jem.m abstammen*), *nehmen* (for *vom Stamme Nimm*), *Rang* (for *vom ersten Rang*), *Robe* (for *ein Herr von der Robe*), *Sattel* (for *vom Sattel leben*), *Seite* (for *von seiten der Mutter*), *stammen* (for *stammen von . . .* and *herstammen von . . .*), *Stange* (for *von der Stange kaufen*) and *Straße* (for *der Mann von der Straße*).

von or *vom* (3) from; with ref. to place or movement in a certain direction:

See under *Abend* (for *von Abend her*), *arg* (for *das Ärgernis kommt von oben*), *Blatt* (for *vom Blatt*), *draußen* (for *von draußen zumachen*), *hinten* (for *von hinten her, von hinten bis vorn* and *jem. am liebsten von hinten sehen*), *Kanzel* (for *von der Kanzel fallen*), *Mai* (for *Tränen, die den Mai von seinen Wangen ätzen*), *Mund* (for *von Mund aus*), *niesen* (for *von hinten niesen*), *oben* (for *jem. von oben bis unten mustern*), *Ohr* (for *von einem Ohr zum andern*), *Olymp* (for *vom Olymp*), *Pfad* (for *von dem Pfad der Tugend ausirren*), *Radieschen* (for *sich die Radieschen von unten ansehen*), *riechen* (for *etw. von weitem riechen*), *Seite* (for *von allen Seiten*), *Tanz* (for *vom Tanz zum Rosenkranz gehen*), *trennen* (for *Trennung von Tisch und Bett*), *Tür* (for *von Tür zu Tür*) and *umgeben* (for *von etw. umgeben sein*).

von or *vom* (4) from, since; with ref. to time.

See under *datieren* (for *nicht von heute*), *gestern* (for *er ist nicht von gestern*), *Hand* (for *von langer Hand*), *heute* (for *nicht von heute*), *Hose* (for *von den ersten Hosen an*), *Jahr* (for *von Jahr zu Jahr*), *Mal* (for *von Mal zu Mal*) and *Schnee* (for *Schnee von gestern*).

von or *vom* (5) of, made of, consisting of; with ref. to the possession of certain characteristics or in classifications where sb. or sth. is compared to sb. or sth. or is allotted a place in some category.

See under *besessen* (for *vom Teufel besessen*), *Blech* (for *nicht von Blech*), *Eisen* (for *er ist von Eisen*), *Fleisch* (for *von Fleisch und Blut sein* and *er ist von Schelmenfleisch gemacht*), *fließen* (for *sein Auge fließt von Tränen*), *Format* (for *ein Mann von Format*), *Geruch* (for *im Geruch von etw. stehen*), *glühen* (for *die Brust glüht jem.m von Tränen*), *Gold* (for *die Minuten sind von Gold*), *Hund* (for *übel gebissen von etw. sein*), *klar* (for *ein klarer Fall von . . .*), *Koloß* (for *ein Koloß von . . .*), *Kranz* (for *ein Kranz von Menschen*), *Meer* (for *ein Meer von . . .*), *Metall* (for *von feinstem Metall*), *Muster* (for *von einem schlimmen Wercke ein Muster nehmen*), *nichts* (for *von nichts kommt nichts*), *Pappe* (for *nicht von Pappe*), *Pflug* (for *von vogelwat ist mein pflug*), *Porzellan* (for *wie von Porzellan*), *Rasse* (for *ein Mensch von Rasse*), *rufen* (for *ein Mann von Ruf*), *schwarz* (for *schwarz von Menschen sein*), *Seele* (for *eine Seele von einem Menschen sein*), *sein* (for *von etw. sein*), *Sibylle* (for *vom Teufel selbst bestellt sein*), *Soldat* (for *er ist vom tollen Soldaten gebissen*), *Sorte* (for *von der Sorte*), *Spiel* (for *vom Spielteufel besessen sein*), *Stand* (for *ein Mann von Stand*), *starr* (for *von etw. starren*), *Stroh* (for *das ist nicht von Stroh* and *ich bin nicht von Stroh*), *Strom* (for *die Augen strömten von Tränen*), *Teufel* (for *vom Teufel besessen* and *dem Teufel vom Karren gefallen*), *Traum* (for *ein Stück von einem Träumer*), *Trumm* (for *ein Trumm von einem Mann*), *Unikum* (for *ein Unikum von . . .*), *verwöhnen* (for *vom Glück nicht verwöhnt sein*) and *Welt* (for *ein Mann von Welt*).

von or *vom* (6) about, concerning; with ref. to a subject with which one deals in some way or other.

See under *blind* (for *wie der Blinde von der Farbe urteilen*), *Galgen* (for *im Hause des Gehängten spricht man nicht vom Strick*), *Glück* (for *er kann von Glück reden*), *Kuh* (for *von der Poesie sprechen wie eine Kuh von der Muskatnuß*), *Lied* (for *ein Lied von etw. singen können*), *sprechen* (for *sprich gut von deinen Freunden*), *tausend* (for *der Glaube vom tausendjährigen Reich*), *Teufel* (for *es träumt ihm vom Teufel*), *tot* (for *von den Toten soll man nur Gutes reden*) and *Tüte* (for *keine Ahnung vom Tuten und Blasen*).

von selbst (1) on one's own initiative, voluntarily; general since the 17th c.; Kramer [1702] recorded '*etwas von sich selber tun*', also '*von sich selbst*'; the shorter form *von selbst* was recorded by Frisch [1741]. Cf. also *aus sich selbst* and *aus sich heraus* (p. 120).

See also under *Teufel* (for *dem Teufel darf man nicht rufen, er kommt von selbst*) and *verstehen* (for *das versteht sich von selbst*).

von selbst (2) by itself, automatically; in essence the same as the previous entry, but used with ref. to things; Kramer refers to *aus sich selbst* in this connexion.

von mir aus (coll.) as far as I am concerned; presumably an ellipsis with a past participle such as *gesehen* omitted; since the 19th c., e.g. (DWb) Nestroy, *Werke* 2,33: '*von mir aus kann der ganze Wald in Flammen stehn*'.

er könnte sich 'von' schreiben, wenn . . . (coll.) he would be quite somebody, if . . . one would take him for an aristocrat if . . . ; 20th c. coll., also used for 'he could call himself fortunate if . . .'. Some lexicographers have placed the beginning of the phrase in the middle of the 20th c., but I have heard my parents use it (ca. 1920).

← See also under *abheben* (for *etw. hebt sich vom Hintergrund ab*), *abstechen* (for *von etw. abstechen*), *bringen* and *Not* (for *vonnöten*) and *Otto* (for *von wegen Otto*).

vor

vor (1) before, in front of; with ref. to place.

See under *Anker* (for *vor Anker liegen*), *Auge* (for *Gnade vor jem.s Augen finden, es wird einem grün und gelb vor Augen, sich etw. vor Augen halten, etw. schwebt jem.m vor Augen and den Tod vor Augen haben*), *Blatt* (for *kein Blatt vor den Mund nehmen*), *blau* (for *es wird einem blau vor den Augen* – see also the similar phrases listed under *bunt*, *Nacht* and *schwarz*), *Brett* (for *er hat ein Brett vorm Kopf*), *durchwühlen* (for *stellte sich das hell vor seine Seele*), *entrollen* (for *Möglichkeiten vor ihrem Blick entrollt*), *Fackel* (for *der die Fackel voran vor unserm Lessing trug*), *Flinte* (for *mitnehmen was einem vor die Flinte kommt*), *führen* (for *jem.m etw. vor Augen führen*), *gehen* (for *vor etw. gehen*), *Gesicht* (for *etw. kommt jem.m vors Gesicht*), *Hand* (for *man sieht die Hand vor den Augen nicht*), *Hannibal* (for *Hannibal ist vor den Toren*), *Herr* (for *ein großer Jäger vor dem Herrn*), *Holz* (for *Holz vor der Hütte*), *Hund* (for *etw. vor die Hunde werfen* and *vor die Hunde gehen*), *Hut* (for *vor jem.m den Hut ziehen*, also under *Mütze* (for *vor jem.m die Mütze abnehmen*), *Klafter* (for *daß ihr Klaftern tief vor mir versinken woltet*), *Klinge* (for *jem. vor die Klinge fordern*), *Knie* (for *das Knie beugen vor jem.m*), *kommen* (for *vor jem. kommen*), *kriechen* (for *sich vor jem.m verkriechen*), *Loch* (for *jem. vors Loch schieben*), *Nase* (for *vor der Nase, etw. vor die Nase halten, die Tür vor der Nase zuschlagen* and *jem. jem.m vor die Nase setzen*), *nichts* (for *vor dem Nichts stehen*), *Perle* (for *Perlen vor die Säue werfen*), *Pfanne* (for *einen/eins vor die Pfanne kriegen*), *reißen* (for *vor den Riß stehen*), *Sack* (for *habt ihr Säcke vor den Türen?*), *Sau* (for *vor die Säue gehen*), *Scheit* (for *vor einem Scheiterhaufen stehen*), *schießen* (for *ein Schuß vor den Bug*), *Schlag* (for *vor den Kopf geschlagen sein*), *schließen* (for *die Augen vor etw. schließen*), *Schloß* (for *er hat ein/kein Schloß vorm Mund*), *Schritt* (for *den Schritt vor die Tür machen*), *schwimmen* (for *etw. schwimmt jem.m vor den Augen*), *Sonne* (for *jem. steht jem.m vor der Sonne*), *stehen* (for *etw. steht vor der Tür, vor etw./jem.m stehen* and *ich sehe es vor mir stehen*), *stellen* (for *jem. vor etw. stellen*), *stoßen* (for *etw. vor sich her stoßen* and *jem. vor den Kopf stoßen*), *stramm* (for *er muß vor seiner Frau strammstehen*), *Stuhl* (for *jem.m den Stuhl vor die Tür setzen*), *treten* (for *etw. tritt jem.m vor Augen*), *Tribunal* (for *jem. vor das Tribunal ziehen*) and *Unglück* (for *das Unglück sitzt nicht immer vor einer* or *armer Leute Tür*).

vor (2) before; with ref. to time.

See under *Abend* (for *man soll den Tag nicht vor dem Abend loben*), *Ding* (for *vor allen Dingen*), *essen* (for *vor Essens wird kein Tanz*, see also under *Sichel* for the similar *vor Sichelhenke ist kein Tanz*), *fünf* (for *fünf Minuten vor zwölf* or *Torschluß*), *Gerste* (for *den Hafer vor der Gerste schneiden* and under *Hafer* the similar *den Hafer vor dem Korn schneiden*), *Hand* (for *vor der Hand*), *Hochmut* (for *Hochmut kommt vor dem Fall*), *Opfer* (for *vor der Messe zum Opfer gehen*), *Regen* (for *er kommt immer drei Tage vor dem Regenwetter heim*), *ruhen* (for *die Ruhe vor dem Sturm*), *Schlag* (for *nicht vor dem ersten Schlaganfall*), *schreien* (for *schreien vor dem Schlag wie ein Hund*), *Sorge* (for *Sorge macht alt vor der Zeit*), *Tau* (for *vor Tau und Tag*), *taufen* (for *er hat vor der Taufe geniest*) and *Tor* (for *kurz vor Torschluß kommen*).

vor (3) with, out of, on account of; with ref. to actions or conditions which are an emotional response to sth. or lead to a visible result.

See under *abbeißen* (for *sich die Zunge abbeißen vor Lachen*), *auffahren* (for *auffahren vor Schrecken*), *aufzehren* (for *sich aufzehren vor*

Ärger), *ausschütten* (for *sich ausschütten vor Lachen*), *brennen* (for *brennen vor Eifer*, etc.), *drehen* (for *es dreht sich alles vor meinen Augen*), *dunkel* (for *es wird einem dunkel vor den Augen*), *fressen* (for *jem. vor Liebe fressen mögen*), *glühen* (for *vor etw. glühen*), *Hose* (for *vor Lachen in die Hosen machen*), *hüpfen* (for *hüpfen vor Freude*), *kleben* (for *vor Dreck kleben*), *können* (for *können vor Lachen*), *krank* (for *die Kränke vor Ärger kriegen*), *Kugel* (for *sich kugeln vor Lachen*), *platzen* (for *vor Ungeduld platzen*), *rauchen* (for *er raucht vor Zorn*), *Schaum* (for *schäumen vor Wut*), *Schein* (for *scheinen vor etw.*), *Schlag* (for *sich überschlagen vor...*), *schnauben* (for *vor etw. schnauben*), *staunen* (for *starr/stumm vor Staunen*), *stehen* (for *etw. steht vor Dreck*), *wteif* (for *steif vor Schrecken*), *stinken* (for *vor Faulheit stinken*), *strotzen* (for *vor etw. strotzen*), *stumm* (for *stumm vor etw. sein*) and *toll* (for *toll vor etw. sein*).

vor (4) from; with ref. to attitudes, conditions or events which elicit a reaction in or from sb.

See under *alt* (for *Alter schützt vor Torheit nicht*), *behandeln* (for *wer ist vor Schlägen sicher*), *entsetzen* (for *vor den sich junge und alte entsetzen*), *fliehen* (for *fleuch fur der sünde wie fur einer schlange*), *Furcht* (for *Furcht vor etw.*), *Kreis* (for *sicher vor euch und der Hölle*), *Nagel* (for *der Nagel an der Wand ist vor ihm nicht sicher*), *scheu* (for *vor etw. zurückscheuen*) and *Teufel* (for *er fürchtet sich davor wie der Teufel vorm Weihwasser*).

vor (5) before; with ref. to precedence or preference; e.g. Schiller, *Wall.Tod* 3,15; '*Ihr scheint mir's wert vor andern*'.

← See also under *Gewalt* (for *Gewalt geht vor Recht*), *Gnade* (for *Gnade vor Recht ergehen lassen*) and *Macht* (for *Macht geht vor Recht*).

vor (6) (regional coll., adv.) from, of; in such locutions as *da muß er sich vor hüten* or *wo hast du Angst vor?*, where in the standard language *davor* and *wovor* are used.

← See also under *Gott* (for *da sei Gott vor!*).

vor (7) (a. or regional) before, previously; still used in the 18th c., e.g.Schiller, *Fiesco* 3,7: '*bleibt alles wie vor*'; in the standard language *zuvor* or *vorher* have displaced this.

vor (8) (obs.) for; in such locutions as *vors erste*, as in Lessing, *Minna* 2,8, where *für* must now be used.

← See also under *krank* (for *ein Mittel vor einen krancken Staat*).

← See also under *gehen* (for *vor sich gehen*) and *hin* (for *vor sich hin*).

vorab

vorab (1) (obs.) in advance; since MHG; Adelung described it as a. and used in civil service jargon; now obs.

vorab (2) above all; since Early NHG, also used for 'first of all' and, arising from that for 'especially'; in modern period also in compounds such as *etw. vorabsagen* = 'to say sth. by way of

introduction' or *etw. vorabaufnehmen* = 'to prerecord sth.'.

Vorabend

am ~ on the eve (of); at first only used with ref. to the eve of Church festivals (17th c.), but since the 18th c. for the eve of any day, e.g. Goethe 26,298 (W.).

← See also under *Abend* (for *am Vorabend großer Ereignisse*).

vorahnen

etw. ~ (lit.) to anticipate sth., have a presentiment or foreboding about sth.; Stieler [1691] recorded it as *vorahnden*, Adelung omitted it, but it was current in the 18th c., even with abstracts, as in Goethe 17,39 (W.): '*künftige Kraft [wird] ihm in der jungen Faust vorahnend zucken*'. The noun *die Vorahnung* was f.r.b. Stieler and has remained in use, whereas *vorahnen* is now much less used than *vorausahnen*.

voran: see *langsam*.

voranbringen

etw. ~ to advance or further sth.; in phys. sense 'to bring forward', but now often figur. with ref. to abstracts, e.g. *das Geschäft* or *die gute Sache tüchtig* ~.

voraneilen

einer Sache ~ to rush ahead of or make faster progress than sth.; with abstracts since the 18th c.

vorangehen

etw. geht voran sth. makes progress; modern; surprisingly missing in *DWb.* [1931]; cf. similar (now obs.) *emporgehen* listed under *gehen* and *vorankommen* (see below).

wie im Vorangehenden erwähnt as stated above; referring to an earlier passage in a text; since the 19th c.

← See also under *Beispiel* (for *mit gutem Beispiel vorangehen*).

vorankommen

vorankommen to advance, make progress, get ahead; since the 19th c.; cf. similar *fortkommen*, discussed on p. 837 and *vorwärtskommen* (see below).

voranmachen

mit etw. ~ (coll.) to make progress with sth.; at least since the 18th c., recorded by Campe [1811] who called it '*niedriges aber deswegen noch nicht verwerfliches Wort*'.

mach voran! (coll.) hurry up, get on with it, get a move on! since the 19th c.

voranschicken

etw. ~ (a.) to say (or write) sth. by way of introduction; general in the 18th c., still used in the 19th c., but then displaced by *vorausschicken* (which see under *schicken*).

Voranschlag: see *anschlagen*.

vorantreiben: see *treiben*.

Vorausbestimmung: see *bestimmen*.

vorausdenken: see *Sprung*.

vorauseilen: see *eilen*.

vorausflattern: see *flattern*.

vorausgehen

etw. geht jem.m voraus sth. precedes sb.; since the 18th c. with such abstracts as *Ruf*, as in *ihm geht der Ruf voraus, daß er . . .* = 'he has the reputation that he . . .', e.g. (DWb) Sturz, *Schriften* 1,115 [1779]: '*als Hume in Paris erwartet wurde, ging ihm sein Name voraus*'.

etw. geht einer Sache voraus sth. precedes sth. else; since the 18th c. with ref. to prefacing sth., as in Goethe 41,2,345 (W.) or with events which precede sth. (18th c.), also with ref. to sth. already mentioned earlier in a text (same as *vorangehen*, which see above). No figur. extension of any kind was listed by Adelung or Campe.

← See also under *Teufel* (for *das Alter geht voraus*).

voraushaben

etw. vor jem.m ~ to be superior to (or excel) sb. in sth., have an advantage in sth. over sb.; figur. since the 18th c., recorded by Campe [1811]; also possible with abstracts, e.g. Herder (edit. S.) 20,352: '*so viel die Ode vor der Elegie an Schwunge voraus hat*'.

← See also under *Flug* (for *was haben denn diese zween Bürger voraus?*) and *Schein* (for *wer spät im Leben sich verstellen lernt, der hat den Schein der Ehrlichkeit voraus*).

vorauskosten: see *kosten*.

vorausnehmen

etw. ~ to anticipate sth.; with abstracts since the 18th c., e.g. Herder [edit. S.] 16,379: '*ein thörichtes Vorausnehmen der Zukunft*'; *vorwegnehmen* is now preferred.

voraussagen

etw. ~ to predict, forecast, prophesy sth.; since the 17th c., f.r.b. Kramer [1702], e.g. *das hätte ich dir ~ können* = 'I could have told you that this would happen', as in Knigge, *Reise nach B.* 86 [1792].

Voraussagung: see *Spiel*.

vorausschicken: see *schicken*.

voraussehen

See under *Geist* (for *im Geiste etw. voraussehen*) and *Rose* (for *eine rosenrote Zukunft voraussehen*).

voraussein

er ist seinem Alter voraus he is forward for his age, more advanced or mature than his age would suggest; modern; *voransein* can also be used in this context.

← See also under *Nase* (for *jem.m um eine Nasenlänge voraus sein*), *Pferd* (for *sie ist ihm um eine Pferdelänge voraus*) and *Schnecke* (for *die Weiber alle sind voraus*).

voraussenden: see *schicken*.

voraussetzen

See under *setzen* (for various examples and for *Voraussetzung*), also under *Grund* (for *jene Einfachheit wird nicht vorausgesetzt*).

Voraussicht: see *Sicht*.

voraussichtlich: see *Sicht*.

vorauswerfen: see *Schatten*.

vorauswittern: see *Faust*.

Vorbau

sie hat einen mächtigen ~ (joc. coll.) she carries all before her, has a well-developed bust; recorded for some regions since early in the 20th c., e.g. by Müller-Fraureuth.

vorbauen

einer Sache~ to take measures to prevent or avoid sth.; it is assumed that this related originally to the forward extension of fortifications; current since the 16th c., e.g. Fischart (edit. H.) 3,12, f.r.b. Stieler [1691], but the noun *vorbawung* as early as in Orsäus, *Nomenclator* [1623], explained by Adelung with '*Veranstaltungen treffen, daß es nicht geschehe*'.

vorgebaut ist besser als hinterhergeschaut (prov.) making provision for what might happen is better than having to regret a missed opportunity; recorded since the 19th c., e.g. by Wander [1876].

← See also under *Butter* (for *hätte fernerem Unglücke vorbauen können*) and *klug* (for *der kluge Mann baut vor*).

vorbedeutend

See under *bedeuten* (also for *vorbedeutungsvoll*) and under *gehen* (for *das geht vorbedeutend durch sein ganzes Leben*).

Vorbedingtheit: see *Klammer*.

vorbehalten: see *Schritt*.

vorbeiflattern: see *flattern*.

vorbeibenehmen

sich ~ (coll.) to misbehave; modern coll., not yet listed in *DWb*. [1934].

vorbeigehen

See under *Nase* (for *mit der Nase in der Luft vorbeigehen*), *neben* (for *neben etw. vorbeigehen*), *Rose* (for *sie ist einmal an einer Rose vorbeigegangen*), *sagen* (for *gehen Sie ja aber keinen . . . vorbei*) and *Schaden* (for *schade um jeden Schlag, der vorbeigeht*).

vorbeikommen: see *Tuch*.

vorbeirauschen: see *Rausch*.

vorbeireden

aneinander ~ to talk at cross-purposes; 20th c.; *DWb*. [1934] calls it '*neuere . . . Bildung*'.

an einer Sache ~ to fail to speak to the point; modern, not yet mentioned in *DWb*. [1934].

vorbeirennen: see *Schwein*.

vorbeischießen: see *schießen*.

vorbeischleichen: see *schleichen*.

vorbeischlendern: see *schlendern*.

vorbeischmiegen: see *schmiegen*.

vorbeisein

etw. ist vorbei sth. is past, over, finished; extension from movement in a phys. sense to time; since the 17th c.; Steinbach [1734] recorded it and Adelung listed it with the remark that *vorüber* was the better term. Goethe used it frequently, e.g. *Faust I*, 1706; *es ist vorbei mit jem.m* has many meanings and Adelung listed three of them: '*er ist verschieden, oder auch er ist unglücklich, in gleichen es ist nichts mit ihm zu machen*'. To this can be added that it also means 'he is past it, no longer at the height of his strength, ability, creativity, etc.', which became current in the 19th c.

← See also under *auslachen* (for *ist die Gefahr vorbei, wird der Heilige ausgelacht*) and *schnappen* (for *es war schnapps vorbei*).

vorbeistreifen: see *hart*.

vorbelastet

vorbelastet handicapped (by heredity, political past, previous convictions, etc.); a 20th c. compound, not yet recorded in *DWb*. [1934]. See also under *belasten* (for *erblich belastet*).

vorbereiten: see *Hand*.

Vorbereitungsschule: see *Schule*.

vorbestraft: see *Stigma*.

vorbeten

jem.m etw. ~ to tell sb. sth. over and over again, impress sth. on sb.; since the 18th c., e.g. (DWb) Gottsched, *Schaub.* 4,450. See also under *predigen* for the much older synonymous *vorpredigen*.

vorbeugen

einer Sache ~ to prevent, preclude, obviate sth.; similar to *vorbauen* (which see above) but probably not connected with fortifications but derived from phys. ~ = *entgegentreten, den Weg versperren*; current since the 16th c.

Vorbewußt

der ~ (obs.) prior knowledge; since the 16th c., when it occurred as *fürbewust*; still used in the 18th c., recorded by Adelung and Campe, e.g. Lessing, *Minna* 2,2: '*mit und ohne Vorbewußt des Herrn*', then displaced by *vorheriges Wissen* or *Vorauswissen*; O. Ludwig, *Schriften* 5,169 still used *Vorbewußtsein* which has also become a. or obs.

Vorbild

das ~ (1) (rare) prefiguration, image which precedes sth.; ~ has been current since OHG, Luther used it in the form *furbilde*; cf. Goethe 8,281 (W.): '*der Kerker ists, des Grabes Vorbild*', see also Goethe 3,85 (W.): '*ein beginnendes Vorbild lag unter die Hülle gebeugt*'.

das ~ (2) model, example, paragon; since the 16th c., recorded by Maaler [1561]; used esp. in *sich jem. zum* ~ *nehmen* = 'to model oneself on sb.', *jem. ist jem.s* ~, e.g. Silesius, *Seelenlust* (repr.) 21: '*Jhesus Christus soll allein meiner seelen vorbild sein*'; cf. Goethe, *Lehrj.* 8,3: '*Vorbilder, nicht zum Nachahmen, sondern zum Nachstreben*'.

etw. jem.m vorbilden (lit.) to present, offer, suggest sth. to sb.; since the 18th c., e.g. Goethe, *Claud.* 2: '*wes weiß es, was die Furcht den guten Kindern vorgebildet*'.

etw. bildet etw. vor (lit.) sth. represents, symbolises, stands for sth.; recorded by Adelung: '*die eherne Schlange bildete Christum vor*', where *vorstellen* would now be preferred.

etw. ist schon vorgebildet sth. has already been formed or envisaged; with abstracts since the 19th c., e.g. Freytag, *Bild.* 1,518 with ref. to change: '*. . . weil diese im Volk längst vorgebildet war*', where sth. like *in der Vorstellung bereits existierte* would now be used.

sich etw. vorbilden (obs.) to imagine sth.; since the 17th c., f.r.b. Kramer [1700]: '*sich eine Sache schwer oder leicht vorbilden*', still used by Goethe, e.g. *Werke* IV, 8,52 (W.): '*ich habe . . . mir die Arbeit leichter vorgebildet*'; *vorstellen* has taken its place.

das ist vorbildlich that is exemplary, would serve as a perfect example; first (in Early NHG) in theol. contexts, then also in secular writings, but in the modern sense only general since the 19th c.

← See also under *Salz* (for *als Vorbild diente*).

vorbohren

vorbohren (intrans.) (coll.) to make a preliminary effort of sounding sb. about sth. that one wants; belongs to *bohren* = 'to get to work on sb.' (see p. 370); 20th c. coll., recorded in *DWb*. [1934].

Vorbote: see *Bote*.

vorbrechen

etw. bricht vor (lit.) sth. appears, bursts, shines forth; mainly with ref. to light, sun or moon, with *Flammen* in Gryphius, *Trauersp.* [edit. P.] 96 (Gryphius also used ~ with ref. to *Thränen*); in most cases *ausbrechen* (see p. 123) or *hervorbrechen* (see p. 1309) are now preferred in the standard language.

vorbringen

etw. ~ to bring or put sth. forward, produce sth.; with abstracts since the 16th c., often with ref. to speech, e.g. Kramer [1700]: '*er konte für weinen kein deutliches wort vorbringen*', where *hervorbringen* (which see on p. 1309) is now preferred, but with ref. to ideas, arguments, complaints, excuses ~ is the correct verb; f.r.b. Stieler [1691]: '*alles was er vorbrachte, waren lappalien*'.

vorder: see *hinter* (also under *alt*).

Vordergrund: see *rücken*.

Vordermann

etw. (or *jem.*) *auf* ~ *bringen* (coll.) to make sth. conform, make sb. get into (or toe the) line, follow instructions or agreed policy' from mil. jargon; since 2nd half of the 20th c., also extended to mean 'to put sth. in order, arrange sth. to one's own satisfaction'.

vordrängen: see *drängen*.

vordringen

in etw. ~ to penetrate into or make good progress in sth.; with ref. to abstracts such as

Wissensgebiet, Thema, Problem since the 18th c., also in pres. part. *vordringend* with abstracts, e.g. Goethe II,4,4 (W.): '*sein vordringendes leidenschaftliches Gemüth*'.

etw. dringt vor sth. advances, progresses, spreads, gains in influence; since Early NHG, e.g. Leibniz, *Dt. Schriften* 1,345: '. . . *das verlangen zu dem frieden bei den meisten vorgedrungen*'.

← See also under *Schwester* (for *eilt, seinen Schwestern vorzudringen*).

voreinnehmen: see *einnehmen* (for *voreingenommen*).

vorerzählen

jem.m etw. ~ to tell or report sth. to sb.; in neutral contexts since the 18th c., e.g. Lessing (edit. M.) 5,234 or Goethe 19,254 (W.), but also pejor. in modern coll. use where the truth of the story is doubted, as in *du kannst mir doch nichts* ~ = 'you can't make me believe that story'.

vorführen

jem. or *etw.* ~ (coll.) to ridicule or expose sb. or sth.; derived from phys. ~ = 'to demonstrate' in last quarter of the 20th c., mainly in political contexts.

← See also under *Stirn* (for *eh man ihn mir, Stirne gegen Stirne, vorgeführt*).

Vorfuß: see *Fuß*.

Vorgabe: see *vorgeben*.

Vorgang

der ~ (1) proceedings, course of events; since Early NHG, f.r.b. Stieler [1691], e.g. Goethe 23,283 (W.), Schiller, *Kab.u.L.* 3,1, influenced by Lat. *processus*. Adelung made a distinction between *Vorfall* and ~: '*Vorgang unterscheidet sich dadurch von Vorfall, daß dieses eigentlich von plötzlich sich ereignenden Umständen, Vorgang aber ohne diesen Nebenbegriff . . . gebraucht wird*'; this still applies. The numerous other meanings of ~ which were much used from MHG to the 18th c., such as 'way of approach' (used by Luther), 'progress', 'advance' (also in mil. contexts), 'precedence' (displaced by *Vortritt* or *Vorrang*), 'earlier appearance' (from which was derived 'example set by sb.') had all practically disappeared by the end of the 18th c.

der ~ (2) file, dossier, documents about a legal case or commercial transaction; extension of ~ (1) to papers relating to a particular course of events; general only since the 20th c. (not even mentioned in *DWb.* [1935]).

Vorgänger

See under *Nadel* (for . . . *Vorgängern des Piranese*) and *Schimmer* (for *der Stil seines großen Vorgängers*).

Vorgarten

Glatze mit ~ (sl.) bald, tonsure-like patch; since 1st quarter of the 20th c.; if the bald patch is in front, *Glatze mit Hintergarten* is used (since ca. 1950).

der Vorgartenzwerg (sl.) unpleasant or unattrac-

tive person; comparison with a garden gnome; since the 1st half of the 20th c. (ca. 1930, according to Küpper).

vorgaukeln: see *Schatten*.

vorgeben

etw. ~ (1) (obs.) to utter, say sth.; since Early NHG, e.g. Luther Bible transl. Job 6,31; Adelung called it '*veraltet*', displaced by *vorbringen* or *(aus)sagen*.

etw. ~ (2) to pretend sth.; since Early NHG with ref. to sth. which is untrue, e.g. Schiller, *Kab.u.L.* 5,2: '. . . *die Sie zu lieben vorgeben*'; hence also *unter dem Vorgeben* = 'under the pretence or pretext', as in Raabe, *Sämtl.W.* 2,5,224 (Fontane used *Vorgabe* for 'pretext', e.g. in *Frau J.Treibel*, chapt. 6).

vorgeblich (a.) alleged(ly); general since the 18th c. with ref. to false statements, recorded by Campe, used by Lessing, Kant and Wieland, still by some 19th c. writers, but then displaced by *angeblich*, which see on p. 41.

vorgehen

jem.m ~ (a.) to lead the way for sb. to follow; since Late MHG, but *vorangehen* or *vorausgehen* are now used.

was geht da vor? what is happening there? since Early NHG, f.r.b. Stieler [1691]; used like *vor sich gehen, sich abspielen* or *stattfinden*, also *vorfallen* or *vorkommen* in some contexts, e.g. Schiller, *M.Stuart* 1,8.

das (or *der*) *geht vor* that (or he) is more important than anything (or anybody) else; since the 16th c., e.g. Luther Bible transl. 2 Sam. 24,4: '*des königes wort gieng vor*'; hence also *jem.m* or *einer Sache* ~ = 'to be superior to sb. or sth. else', since Early NHG, e.g. Fischart, *Praktik* (repr.) 24: '*das silber würd dem bley vorgehen*', Herder [edit. S.] 23,242: '*dies macht sein Verdienst, worinn er sogar dem Britten vorgeht*' (where *übertreffen* is now used). The dictionary recordings show the spread: Maaler [1561]: '*alters halber vorgen = elter seyn*', Steinbach [1734]: '*er gehet allen vor = maximus omnium est*', Frisch [1741]: '*vorgehen = den Vorzug haben, vornehmer sein*'.

mit einer Sache ~ to procede with sth.; since the 18th c.

gegen jem. ~ to proceed against sb.; from phys. ~ = 'to advance, attack', mainly mil.; since the 18th c.

vorgängig (a.) previous, past; since Early NHG, still used in the 18th c. (Goethe, Schiller) and sometimes in the 19th c. (Fontane), but now a.

← See also under *diplomatisch* (for *man muß diplomatisch vorgehen*), *drastisch* (for *ein drastisches Vorgehen*) and *Schaf* (for *wo ein Schaf vorgeht, folgen die anderen nach*).

Vorgeschmack

der ~ foretaste; figur. since Late MHG, e.g. Tauler, *Sermones* 39a [1508]: '*wann es ist ain warer vorgeschmack des ewigen lebens*'.

Vorgesetzte: see *vorsetzen* (also under *nehmen*).

vorgreifen

etw. ~ to anticipate, forestall sth.; since MHG, e.g. *Passional* [edit. K.] 375, Goethe 41,2,222 (W.).

vorgreifen to jump ahead; mainly with ref. to a narrative when sb. deals with sth. before anything else, as. in Goethe, *Dicht.u.Wahrh.* 1: '...muß ich hier mit der Schilderung meines Geburtsortes vorgreifen'.

jem.m in etw. ~ to encroach on sb. (e.g. his rights or his decision-making); since the 18th c., e.g. Kotzebue, *Kleinst.* 1,15: 'man muß dem lieben Gott nicht vorgreifen'; cf. p. 1129: 'Rechte greifen, die nicht ihre sind'.

einer Sache ~ to deal with sth. prematurely (or earlier than other people); sometimes referring to prescience (since the 18th c.), but predominantly in contexts where such anticipation is not approved of, when it can mean 'to prejudge a matter' (suggesting either haste or prejudice).

auf etw. ~ to take or draw on sth. in advance (of the due date); modern, e.g. *ich habe schon auf mein nächstes Monatsgehalt vorgegriffen* = 'I have drawn on my next month's salary'.

vorhaben

jem. ~ (coll.) to see sb. for the purpose of instructing, blaming or reprimanding him; natural extension of 'having sth. before one so as to deal with it' (since MHG). The extension occurred in the 18th c., recorded by Adelung, e.g. Goethe 21,280 (W.).

etw. ~ to intend to do sth., plan sth.; the phys. meaning *etw. vor sich haben* in the sense of being occupied with it could easily be extended to planning to do sth. with sth.; since Early NHG, e.g. Schiller, *Fiesco* 4,3: 'Fiesco hat einen Spaß vor'; often in *was hast du mit ihm* (or *damit*) *vor?* = 'what are you intending to do with him (or it)?, *Böses* ~ 'to plot mischief', *er hat es gut mit dir vor* = 'he means well by you, wants to do what is best for you'; sometimes it can also be used with ref. to sth. with which one is occupied at the time; hence *vorhabend* (a.) = 'intended', since Early NHG, still used in the 18th c., e.g. Lessing [edit.M.] 10,157, also *das Vorhaben* = 'plan, project', since Early NHG, e.g. Mathesius, *Sar.* 39a [1571].

vorhalten

jem.m etw. ~ to reproach sb. for sth.; 'to hold sth. before sb.' as an example to be followed could lead first to 'to admonish sb.', in use since the 17th c., then in the 18th c. the stage was reached when 'admonition' turned to 'reproach'; f.r.b. Steinbach [1734].

vorhalten to last (for a certain period); first with ref. to objects such as provisions, also *Geld*, as in Goethe 25,165 (W.); only since the 19th c. with abstracts, e.g. *seine gute Laune wird nicht*

lange ~. Cf. similar *anhalten* and idioms under *halten* which also express the notion of lasting.

← See also under *Spiegel* (for *jem.m einen Spiegel vorhalten*).

Vorhand: see *ausspielen*.

vorhanden

See under *Grund* (for *so muß ein Grund vorhanden seyn*), *Mittel* (for *es ist nur ein Heilmittel vorhanden*) and *Schatten* (for *auch nicht der Schatten einer Gefahr vorhanden*).

Vorhang

der ~ *ist gefallen* the matter is over and done with; transfer from the theatre; current since the 18th c., e.g. Haller, *Ged.* 151, Gotter 1,171 [1787].

← See also under *Eisen* (for *der eiserne Vorhang*).

Vorherbestimmung: see *bestimmen*.

vorhergehen

vorhergehen to precede; figur. since the 17th c., usually synonymous with *vorangehen* or *vorausgehen*, sometimes with *vorgehen* (see above); hence also *Vorhergang* = 'preceding event' (18th c.), 'example or pattern set by sb. or sth. previously', as in *nach dem Vorhergang* = 'following the previous procedure' (19th c.) and *vorhergängig* = 'previous, preceding', used by Goethe and some 19th c. authors, but displaced by *vorherig*, current since the 18th c., also used by Goethe, but considered inferior to *vorig* by Adelung and classified as 'niedrig, aber deshalb noch nicht verwerflich' by Campe.

← See also under *Schritt* (for *jeder folgende Zustand ist von dem vorhergehenden getrennt*).

vorherig: see *vorhergehen*.

vorherrschen: see *herrschen* (also for *vorherrschend* and *Vorherrschaft*).

vorhersagen

etw. ~ to predict, prophesy sth.; since the 17th c., f.r.b. Kramer [1700]. It can also be used for 'foretell' where it is a question of feeling sure that sth. will happen; since the 18th c.; in most contexts synonymous with *voraussagen*.

vorhersehen: see *sehen*.

Vorhersehung: see *Sicht*.

vorhexen: see *Hexe*.

Vorhochzeit

die ~ (coll., euphem.) intercourse before marriage; recorded since the 19th c., e.g. by Wander [1876].

Vorhof: see *Hof*.

Vorhölle

die ~ (1) (relig.) limbo; destination of unbaptized children and souls of people who died before Christ brought salvation; since MHG (*vorhelle*).

die ~ (2) (lit.) antechamber to hell (or a place as terrible as hell); sometimes used like purgatory; since the 18th c., e.g. Goethe 17,33 (W.), Hebbel [edit. W.] 1,5,61 on harlots: '... um sie *durch die Vorhölle des Ehestandes bußfertig zu machen'.*

Vorhut

die ~ vanguard; loan translation of French *avantgarde*; in mil. sense since Early NHG, but in figur. use also since Early NHG, e.g. (DWb) Zwingli, *Dt. Schriften* 1,322; cf. *auf der ~ stehen* = 'to stand in the vanguard', e.g. Eichendorff, *Incogn.* 64: '*wir steh'n ja hier auf der Vorhut der Kultur'.*

vorig: see *Rumpf* (also under *vorhergehen*).

vorkämpfen

vorkämpfen to lead the struggle for sth., act as pioneer in sth.; since the 18th c., little used now, but the noun *Vorkämpfer* (for which see under *kämpfen*) is in frequent use.

sich ~ to struggle to get ahead, fight one's way forward; modern (not mentioned in *DWb.* [1936]), but in frequent use with ref. to intellectual or political struggles.

vorkauen

jem.m etw. ~ to spoonfeed sth. to sb., prepare sth. for sb. so that he/she can understand or make use of it; since Early NHG, e.g. Fischart, *Bien.* 39a: '*es hätte denn die . . . kirch . . . uns also die päpp und brei . . . vorgekauet'*, f.r.b. Stieler [1691].

vorkehren

vorkehren (a.) to take measures with the object of dealing with sth., avoiding sth., protecting sth., etc.; since Early NHG, but now rare, since *Vorkehrungen treffen*, current since the 18th c., is preferred.

etw. ~ (1) to prepare sth.; still usual in the 18th c., e.g. Bürger, 302b: '*ich . . . kehr' ein grimmig Unheil vor'*; now little used, displaced by *vorbereiten* or *ins Werk setzen*.

etw. ~ (2) to show or reveal sth.; mainly with ref to revealing one's feelings or attitudes, e.g. *heute hat er seine böse Seite vorgekehrt* = 'today he revealed his nasty nature'; see also under *rauh* (for *die rauhe Seite herauskehren*); Steinbach [1734] recorded '*Fleiß vorkehren'*.

Vorkette: see *ausstrahlen*.

vorknöpfen

sich jem. ~ (coll.) to take sb. to task, give sb. a serious warning or reprimand; since late in the 19th c., not yet mentioned in Sanders (even in his *Ergänzungswb.* of 1885); *DWb.* [1936] recorded it with the gloss '*in moderner Umgangssprache*'; cf. Engl. 'to buttonhole sb.'.

sich etw. ~ (coll.) to take sth. in hand for close examination or study; since the middle of the 1st half of the 20th c., e.g. *die alten Akten muß ich mir ~, ehe ich den Bericht abfassen kann*; not yet recorded in *DWb.* [1936].

vorkommen

einer Sache ~ (obs.) to try to avoid or obviate sth.; in transitive locutions since Early NHG, e.g. Luther Apocr. transl. Ecclesiasticus 30,30: '*der kann viel böses vorkommen'*, where it means 'to prevent', then intrans. with the dative, still in Lessing, *Dram.* 77; now obs., displaced by *vorbeugen* or *zuvorkommen*.

etw. kommt vor sth. occurs, happens; derived from phys. 'to come forward, appear' (cf. phrases with *Auge, Gesicht, Ohr*), e.g. Luther Bible transl. 1 Cor. 1,11; also in locutions with a person in the dative, as already in Luther Bible transl. 1 Kings 20,20: '*er schlug, was ihm vorkam'*. Later in wider sense for 'to occur' in many contexts, e.g. *dieses Wort kommt bei Goethe vor, so etwas ist noch nicht vorgekommen*, apologetic *es soll nicht wieder ~* = 'it shall not happen again'; also in the modern coll. off-shoot *wie kommen Sie mir vor?* = 'who do you think you are? how dare you? you are being offensive', since early in the 20th c.

← See also under *Blei* (for *die mir wie schweres Blei vorkamen*), *bunt* (for *was nur immer in einem . . . Leben vorkommen mag*), *Familie* (for *das kommt in den besten Familien vor*), *fremd* (for *jem.m fremd vorkommen*), *öde* (for *daß mir alles so öde vorkommt*), *piepen* (for *sie kommt mir wie eine Henne . . . vor*) and *Spanien* (for *das kommt mir spanisch vor*).

vorkramen: see *Kram*.

Vorlage: see *durchpeitschen* and *vorlegen*.

vorlängst: see *eilen*.

vorlaufen

jem. läuft jem.m vor (obs.) sb. surpasses sb. else; since MHG and still used by Jean Paul and by Goethe, but now obs., displaced by *übertreffen*.

jem. läuft jem.m (or *einer Sache*) *vor* sb. precedes sb. (or sth.); since Early NHG, e.g. Luther 20,220 (Weimar); sometimes = 'to be ahead of or earlier than sb. or sth.', e.g. Goethe II,3,163 (W.): '*das Schicksal hat er mit allen denen gemein, die ihrer Zeit vorlaufen'*; hence *der Vorläufer* = 'precursor, forerunner', in relig. contexts often with ref. to St. John the Baptist as precursor of Christ, as in Luther 10,1,225 (Weimar): '*von dem komen heyst auch s. Johannes seyn vorleuffer'*; since the modern period frequent in secular contexts.

etw. läuft vor sth. extends forward; figur. with abstracts or non-moving objects since the 18th c., e.g. Campe quoting Voß (no details): '*eine harmonische Bucht erstreckt . . . zwei vorlaufende Arm'*.

← See also under *laufen* (for *wenn man Andern gleich- oder gar vorläuft*).

vorläufig

vorläufig (adj. and adv.) provisional, temporary; since the 17th c., but not recorded before the 18th c. (e.g. by Adelung). See also on p. 2137 under *schleppen*, where unfortunately the heading '*schleppen*' has been omitted.

vorlaut

vorlaut pert, forward, cocky; used not only for speaking before one is asked but also in wider sense, e.g. for 'taking action before having obtained permission', as in Schiller, *Räuber* 4,5; also with abstracts or objects without a voice, esp. with *Wesen*, as in Goethe 42,2,193 (W.), e.g. Schiller, *Fiesco* 3,4 (with *Sonnenstrahl*) or Keller, W*erke*, 6,7 (with *Buch*).

vorlegen

etw. ~ to submit or present sth.; since Early NHG, e.g. Luther Bible transl. Deuter, 30,15; hence *die Vorlage* = 'submission, presentation', in political contexts = 'bill', both only since the 19th c., but older *Vorlage* = 'model, pattern' occurs only on the phys. level.

jem.m Geld ~ to advance money to sb.; since early in the 20th c., recorded by Schirmer, *Kaufmannsspr.* 206 [1911].

Tempo ~ (sl.) to increase speed; first in the language of car drivers, then extended; 20th c. sl.

← See also under *durchpeitschen* (for *eine Vorlage durchpeitschen*) and *schwach* (for *dir die schwache Seite vorzulegen*).

vorleiern

See under *Leier* (for *welcher nichts als elende Hochzeitslieder der Welt vorleiert*) and *Lied* (for *da alle meine Widersacher fast immer einerlei Liedlein mir vorgeleiert haben*).

vorlesen

vorlesen or *eine Vorlesung geben* or *halten* to deliver a lecture; in extended sense also used when the lecture is given extempore; since Early NHG, f.r.b. Maaler [1561], the noun *Vorlesung* since the 16th c.

← See also under *Jungfer* (for *Jungfernvorlesung*) and *Register* (for *der Richter ließ ihm sein langes Sündenregister vorlesen*).

vorleuchten: see *leuchten*.

vorliebnehmen: see *nehmen*.

vorliegen

etw. liegt vor sth. exists, has come into existence or has become available, has been submitted; figur. only since the 19th c. with such abstracts as *Absicht, Grund, Irrtum, Plan* or *Verwechslung*, usually the same as *etw. besteht* or *ist vorhanden*.

vormachen

jem.m etw. ~ (coll.) to fool, kid, humbug, hoodwink sb.; originally = 'to demonstrate sth. to sb., show sb. how to do sth.', since Early NHG, f.r.b. Maaler [1561], then probably due to performances by entertainers, magicians, the notion of 'deception' entered the phrase; since the 17th c., e.g. *er läßt sich nichts* ~, = 'he is nobody's fool', *in seinem Beruf macht ihm keiner etw. vor* = 'he is not surpassed by anybody in his profession', *bald wirst du mir etw.* ~ *können* = 'soon you will be able to teach me a thing or two'.

sich etw. ~ (coll.) to delude, kid, fool oneself; since early in the 19th c.; cf. also coll. *wir brauchen uns doch nichts vorzumachen* = 'we might as well be frank'.

← See also under *blau* (for *jem.m blauen Dunst*

vormachen) and *U* (for *jem.m ein X für ein U vormachen*).

Vormacht

die ~ *haben* to enjoy predominance or supremacy; only since the 19th c. (still missing in Meißner [1856]); frequent since the 20th c. in *eine Vormachtstellung innehaben* or *besitzen*.

vormalen: see *malen*.

vormals: see *satt*.

Vormarsch

im ~ *sein* to advance, gain influence, adherents, etc.; derived from its mil. connotation in the 20th c. See also under *Marsch* (p. 1660) for *auf dem Marsch sein*.

vormärzlich: see *März*.

Vormauer: see *Mauer*.

vormessen

jem.m etw. ~ (obs.) to allot, mete out sth. to sb.; mainly with ref. to sth. that is destined for sb. (by fate); f.r.b. Stieler [1691]; sometimes also = 'to prescribe'; still in occasional use in the 19th c., now obs., displaced by *(zu)erteilen* or *bestimmen*.

Vormund

jem.s ~ *sein* to restrain, control sb., keep sb. in check; ~ is in its ordinary current meaning a 'guardian'. It is derived not from *Mund* = 'mouth', but from OHG *munt* = 'hand' and 'protection', current as *foramunto* since the 10th c. in many meanings such as 'protector, trustee, advocate, syndic, magistrate'; figur. with ref. to abstracts since the 16th c., e.g. (DWb) Rachel, *Sat.Ged.* (repr.) 36: '*die höchste Weißheit muß der Thorheit Vormund sein*'.

dir sollte man einen ~ *setzen* (or *dir gehört ein* ~ *gesetzt*) (coll.) you need sb. to keep you in check; in its ordinary sense at least since the 18th c., e.g. Goethe 11,92 (W.), but modern in its coll. extension where it is used as a reprimand to an irresponsible person. A similar phrase with *Kuratel* (*er sollte unter Kuratel stehen*) is now dropping out of use.

← See also under *bevormunden* and *dumm* (for *Gott ist der Dummen Vormund*).

Vornahme: see *vornehmen*.

Vornäsigkeit: see *denken*.

vorne

See under *Auge* (for *er hat Augen hinten und vorne*), *hinten* (for *hinten und vorne, von hinten bis vorn, es fehlt hinten und vorne, jem. hinten und vorn betrügen, nicht wissen, wo vorne und hinten ist* and several other idioms), *liegen* (for *in diesem Wettkampf lag er immer vorne*), *Nase* (for *die Nase vorn haben*) and *Tanz* (for *so geht der Tanz wieder von vornen an*).

vornehm

See under *Ast* (for *der vornehmste Ast der Familie*), *Phrase* (for *er wird vom hohen Pferd herab gräflich vornehm über mich herabphrasen*), *schief* (for *schief ist vornehm*), *schön* (for *die vornehmen und artigen Leute*), *Spiel* (for *als man mich schon so vornehm hielt mich zu mißbrauchen*), *stellen* (for *wenn sich jemand sehr vornehm beträgt*), *Tier* (for *ein groß und vornehm Thier zu werden*) and *Tour* (for *nun machen Sie bloß nicht auf 'vornehme Tour'*).

vornehmen

etw. ~ (1) to examine sth., take a close look at sth., take sth. in hand; derived from *etw. vor sich nehmen* (as e.g. in Goethe 49,205 (W.)), since the 17th c. still in partly phys. sense, figur. f.r.b. Kramer [1702]: '*man hat eure Sachen vorgenommen*', e.g. Gellert, *Betschw.* 1,7; cf. the entry on p. 1225 on *etw. in, vor* or *an die Hand nehmen*.

etw. ~ (2) to carry out, make, undertake, perform sth.; close to (1), f.r.b. Kramer, but examples in literature are much older, e.g. H.Sachs [edit. K.] 9,293: '*man redt oder hielt silentium, was man nur im kloster fürnum*'. The past participle *vorgenommen* = 'undertaken', since the 17th c., e.g. Grimmelshausen, *Simpliz.* [edit. Kurz] 4,237, can verge on 'decided upon', for which see *sich etw.* ~ below; still frequent in *vorgenommene Änderung, Auswahl* or *Trennung*, but in earlier times with ref. to many more abstracts such as *Krieg, Mord, Weg*.

sich etw. ~ to resolve, decide on sth.; since the 17th c., e.g. Lehman 2,833 [1662], f.r.b. Kramer [1702]; cf. synonymous now obs. *etw. vor sich nehmen*.

jem. ~ to give sb. a talking-to; first in the wider sense of 'to admit to one's presence, deal with sb. (by way of examination, treatment, etc.)'; now also quite usual with the notion of reprimanding; beginnings in the 17th c., e.g. Opitz 1,176: '. . . *mich sehr scharpff hier vorgenommen*', Goethe 41,2,172 (W.). Also used in threats of phys. assault: '*den werde ich mir vornehmen*' = 'I shall deal with him'.

eine Maske ~ to disguise oneself, dissemble; e.g. Wedekind, *Frühl.Erw.* 3,7; for older *eine Maske anlegen* or *(an)nehmen* see p. 1664.

die Vornahme undertaking, the putting into effect of sth.; still missing in Adelung, but recorded by Campe [1811], now mainly in civil service jargon.

← See also under *dick* (for *das dicke Ende wieder vornehmen*), *herumgehen* (for *habe ich den Wallenstein vorgenommen*) and *holen* (for *den Kerl werde ich mir mal vornehmen*).

vornehmlich: see *sehen*.
vororgeln: see *Orgel*.
vorpauken: see *Pauke*.
vorpinseln: see *Pinsel*.
vorpirschen
sich ~ to make one's way forward cautiously or with difficulty; from *pirschen* in hunt. jargon for 'to stalk'; modern, recorded by *DWb.* [1937].
vorposaunen: see *Posaune*.
Vorposten: see *Posten*.

vorpredigen: see *predigen*.
vorpreschen
vorpreschen to rush ahead, storm forward, rush things; from *preschen* in the language of riders; f.r.b. Campe [1811], e.g. (DWb) Liliencron 8,207 [1896].
vorquatschen
jem.m etw. ~ (coll.) to talk rubbish to sb.; for related locutions see *quatschen* (p. 1925); recorded only since the 20th c., e.g. in *DWb.* [1937].
vorquellen
etw. quillt vor sth. gushes out; in wider sense 'sth. comes to the fore, appears'; cf. *quellen*, also *hervorquellen* on p. 1926; figur. with abstracts since the 17th c., e.g. (DWb) Thomasius, *Von der Artznei* 286 [1696]: '. . . *aus Besitz der Tugend vorquellenden Wahrheiten*'.
vorragen: see *ragen*.
Vorrang: see *Rang*.
Vorrat
der ~ supply, store, stock; figur. with abstracts since Early NHG, e.g. Luther 30,2,639 (Weimar): '*wer dolmetzschen wil, mus großen vorrath von worten haben*', Schiller, *Kab.u.L.* 2,6.

die Vorratskammer store-cupboard; occasionally figur., as in Schiller, *Philos.Briefe* (in Goedeke 4,55): '*Millionen Gewächse trinken von den vier Elementen. Eine Vorrathskammer steht offen für alle*'.
vorrechnen: see *Finger*.
Vorrecht
das ~ (1) prior right or claim; since the 16th c., at first mainly in legal contexts.

das ~ (2) privilege; since the 17th c., often in pejor. contexts, e.g. (DWb) Tiedge 4,189 [1823]: '*den Vorzug giebt Natur, das Vorrecht Tyrannei*', v. Ebner-Eschenbach 1,41: '*der größte Feind des Rechtes ist das Vorrecht*'.

das ~ (3) advantage; natural extension of ~ (2); since the 19th c., e.g. (T.) v. Polenz, *Grabenhäger* 2,199 [1897]: '*Malte hatte nun mal das Vorrecht, grob zu sein*'.
Vorrede
die ~ preface; at first only with ref. to speech, f.r.b. Maaler [1561], but since the 16th c. also with ref. to printed matter, e.g. Luther Apocr. transl. 2 Macc 2,33: '*das nicht die vorrede größer werde denn die ganze historie*'.

jem.m etw. vorreden to tell sb. sth. which is not true; originally the locution described general verbal communication, but since the 17th c. increasingly with the imputation of untruth; f.r.b. Stieler [1691]; coll. in *ich lasse mir doch von Ihnen nichts* ~ = 'you cannot humbug me with that tale'.
vorreiten: see *reiten* (also for *Vorreiter*).
Vorritt: see *Ritt*.
vorrücken
vorrücken (intrans.) to advance; cf. the entries

under *rücken* on *vorwärtsrücken* and related compounds; in phys. sense with ref. to troops since Early NHG, then with abstracts mainly with ref. to time, e.g. Goethe, *Wanderj.* 1,5: '*ein schöner Morgen war im Vorrücken*', *im vorgerückten Alter* = 'at an advanced age', *in vorgerückter Stunde* = 'at a late hour'.

jem.m etw. ~ (obs. or regional) to draw sb.s attention to sth.; mainly by way of reproach; since the 17th c., but now only in some S. regions, e.g. C.F. Meyer, *Nov.* 1,147: '*du hast mir nichts vorzurücken*'; *vorhalten* or *vorwerfen* are used in the standard language.

vorrupfen

jem.m etw. (regional, S.) to reproach sb. with sth.; recorded for many regions since Early NHG, frequent in Abr. a Sancta Clara, e.g. *Etwas für Alle* 1,219, still in some S. areas in the 19th c. alongside synonymous *aufrupfen*, used by Gotthelf, *Uli d.P.* 151 (which also has been current since Early NHG).

← See also under *rupfen*.

Vorsatz

der ~ (1) intention; translates Lat. *propositio*; since OHG, e.g. Luther 2,59 (Weimar), Lessing, *Nathan* 3,3: '*Entschluß ist Vorsatz, That*', Schiller, *Wall. Tod* 4,6: '*ermorden wollt Ihr ihn? Das ist mein Vorsatz*'; hence *mit* (also *aus*) ~ = 'intentionally', since the 17th c., and *vorsätzlich*, f.r.b. Kramer [1702].

der ~ (2) (ling., obs.) prefix; since the 17th c., recorded by Adelung, still occasionally used in the 19th c., now obs., displaced by *Vorsilbe*.

← See also under *geben* (for *doch bleib ich dem Vorsatz getreu*), *heilig* (for *ein heiliger Vorsatz*), *Hölle* (for *der Weg zur Hölle ist mit guten Vorsätzen gepflastert*), *springen* (for *meine Seele springt von Vorsatz zu Vorsatz*) and *steif* (for *ein steifer Vorsatz*).

Vorschau

die ~ preview, forecast; since the 17th c., in figur. contexts since the 19th c. with ref. to printed announcements about future events, then in the 20th c. in film and television parlance for 'trailer'.

Vorschein: see under *Nessel* and *Schein* (for *zum Vorschein kommen*).

vorscheinen: see *Schein*.

vorschieben: see *schieben*.

vorschießen: see *schießen*.

vorschimmern: see *Schimmer*.

vorschlafen: see *Naht*.

Vorschlag

See under *fallen* (for *der Vorschlag ist gefallen*), *herantreten* (for *sind mit dem Vorschlag herangetreten*), *Schlag* (for *ein Vorschlag zur Güte*) and *Seite* (for *dieser Vorschlag gefiel mir*).

vorschlagen: see *Schlag*.

Vorschmack: see *blühen*.

vorschmecken *etw.* ~ (obs.) to experience

(the sensation of) sth. before it actually happens; since MHG, but recordings appear to be late (Campe), used by Herder e.g. in edit. S. 24,372 and Goethe IV,3,170 (W.), but now obs. Obs. is also the meaning 'to experience (the sensation of) sth., before others have experienced it', for which *DWb.* quotes one *locus* from Riehl, *Nat.gesch.d.dt. Volkes* 1,271 (1851).

etw. schmeckt vor sth. predominates, comes to the fore more clearly; with ref. to taste since the 18th c., recorded by Adelung; figur. with ref. to abstracts since late in the 18th c., e.g. (DWb) Hebbel [edit. W.] 1,12,326: '*wenn auch in der Polemik . . . die schwäbische Empfindlichkeit ein wenig vorschmeckt*'.

vorschmeißen

jem.m etw. ~ (coll.) to reproach sb. with sth.; recorded for many regions since the 19th c., listed by Campe [1811] with a quotation from Bürger. For synonymous verbs used in other areas see *vorrücken* and *vorrupfen* above; the standard term is *vorwerfen*.

vorschneiden

jem.m etw. ~ to apportion (or grant) sth. to sb.; the range of the compound is wide and can (or could?) refer to grudging, willing or affectionate 'granting'; Kramer [1702] recorded this only with ref. to *Arbeit* ('*den Gesellen die Arbeit vorschneiden*'); more truly figur. with abstracts since the 18th c., e.g. Schiller, *Fiesco* 2,2: '. . . schneidet ihm ihre Karessen wirthschaftlich wie einem Kostgänger vor*', (DWb) Gaudy 8,161 [1844]: '. . . seine Traumportion von Morpheus sich vorschneiden zu lassen*'.

vorschnell

vorschnell rash, hasty, precipitate; since MHG; at first usually with ref. to persons, with abstracts since the 17th c. (with *Wort, Urteil, Versprechen*), frequent as an adverb, e.g. Goethe 24,103 (W.), Schiller, *M.Stuart* 5,15; cf. synonymous *voreilig* (p. 558).

← See also under *schnell*.

vorschreiben

etw. (abstract) *schreibt etw. vor* (lit.) sth. prescribes, demands or requires sth.; with an abstract as the subject since the 18th c., e.g. Goethe 21,208 (W.): '. . . die Musik die Bewegungen des Körpers leitet . . . und ihnen zugleich das Maß vorschreibt*'.

← See also under *Regime* and *schreiben*.

vorschreiten: see *stehen*.

Vorschrift: see *schreiben*.

Vorschub: see *schieben*.

Vorschubleistung

die ~ (legal) aiding and abetting; specifically in legal contexts for 'dealing in stolen goods' or 'acting as a receiver of stolen goods'; the general sense since the 19th c., e.g. (DWb) Anzengruber 1,279 [1890], the legal special sense since the 20th c.

Vorschuß

der ~ advance payment; since the 17th c., recorded by Kramer [1702]; derived from *vorschießen* (see p. 2107); hence also *auf* ~ = 'in expectation of money or a refund', as in (DWb) Gökingk, *Ged.* 3,235 [1780]: '*er starb, und ward mit großer Pracht, wie wohl auf Vorschuß nur, begraben*'; sometimes with abstracts where 'sth. granted beforehand' is the general sense, e.g. O. Ludwig 5,329 [1891]: '. . . *wird der Dichter meist einen Vorschuß von Glauben sich ausbitten müssen*'.

← See also under *Lorbeer* (for *Vorschußlorbeern bekommen*).

vorschützen: see *Schutz* (also under *auffallen*).

vorschweben

See under *Blut* (for *daß ihr die verkehrten Urtheile der Leute vorgeschwebt hätten*), *Hintergrund* (for *dem diese Sorgen unablässig vorschwebten*) and *schweben* (for detailed treatment).

vorschwindeln: see *Schwindel*.

vorsehen

See under *Postillion* (for *der Großvater hat sich schlecht vorgesehen*) and *sehen* (for detailed treatment).

Vorsehung

See under *Hand* (for *Hand der Vorsehung*), *niederbeugen* (for *die Vorsehung hat tausend Mittel . . .*), *ruhen* (for *Religion ruht auf der Überzeugung einer allgemeinen Vorsehung*), *Speiche* (for *wenn man der göttlichen Vorsehung Speichen andichtet*), *Sperling* (for *die Vorsehung ist dabei, wenn Sperlinge fallen*), *Spiel* (for *Vorsehung spielen*), *Spur* (for *die Spuren der Vorsehung entdecken*) and *überlassen* (for *etwas der Vorsehung überlassen*).

vorsetzen

See under *Fuß* (for *den besten Fuß vorsetzen*) and *setzen* (for detailed treatment, also for *Vorgesetzter*).

vorsichbringen

etw. ~ (coll.) to achieve sth. (positive); sometimes in financial contexts = 'to make a profit'; Eiselein 623 [1840] recorded '*wir wollen was vor uns bringen*'.

vorsichgehen

etw. geht vor sich (coll.) sth. progresses or prospers; first in MHG as *für sich gehen*, with *vor* since Early NHG, in prov. sayings often used in an ironic negative to describe failure to progress, e.g. *er geht vor sich wie die Hühner scharren, er geht vor sich wie die Krebse kriechen* (both recorded by Lehman [1630]), to which Wander added the more recent '*es geht vor sich, wie mit einer Schnecke auf einem Theerfaß*'. See also under *gehen* (9) on p. 946 and the entry on *vor sich gehen* on p. 950.

Vorsicht

~ *ist besser als Nachsicht* (prov.) cautious proceeding is better than later regrets; there is no comparable Engl. saying, but French has *il faut mieux voir avant qu'après*; German recordings are late (Mayer, *Baiersche Sprichw.* [1812], Müller, *Jugendfreund* [1816]), but Schottel [1663] has '*Vorsichtigkeit viel Unfall meidt*'; for related phrases see under *nachsehen* (p. 1739), also one under *bedenken* (p. 107).

← See also under *Sicht* (for detailed treatment) and under *Himmel* (for *ließ die Vorsicht walten*), *Mutter* (for *Vorsicht ist die Mutter der Porzellankiste*), *Platz* (for *hier ist Vorsicht am Platz*), *Polizei* (for *die große Polizei der Vorsicht*), *Rücksicht* (for *Vorsicht und Rücksicht*), *schlüpfen* (for *meine Vorsicht verdoppeln*) and *Schlüssel* (for *warf die Schlüssel weiser Vorsicht weg*).

vorsichtig

See under *Sicht* (for detailed treatment), also under *Eltern* (for *er ist in der Wahl seiner Eltern vorsichtig gewesen*) and *Scherbe* (for *Zeus den Ring der Welt vorsichtig aufgehangen*).

vorsintflutlich: see *Sintflut*.

Vorsitz *den* ~ *haben* to be in the chair, be chairman; derived from the verb *vorsitzen* and f.r.b. Corvinus [1646]; hence also *der Vorsitzer*, still used by Kleist, *Käthchen v.H.* 1,1 which has made way for *Vorsitzender*. See also under sitzen (p. 2268).

vorsitzen: see *sitzen*.

Vorsitzender: see *machen*.

Vorsorge

~ *treffen* to take precautions, make provisions; the chief sense is 'to provide for sth. in the future'. In earlier periods ~ and *Fürsorge* were used without distinction, but since the 18th c. the two nouns have become differentiated with ~ relating to measures to provide for eventualities and *Fürsorge* denoting the care of or provision for people (as already stated by Adelung [1787]).

← See also under *Grund* (for *daß die göttliche Vorsorge ein bloßer Traum wäre*).

Vorspann

der ~ (1) help, helper; derived from ~ = 'team of horses or oxen' provided for transport (since mediaeval times, when it constituted one of the feudal obligations to supply ~), then extended in the 18th c. to 'to provide help', esp. in ~ *geben* = 'to lend a helping hand'.

der ~ (2) (lit., film) introduction; used first for writings before the main body of a work, e.g. a prologue; since the 19th c.; in the 20th c. extended to films where it describes a 'trailer' giving titles, names of actors, etc.

einen ~ *nehmen* (regional coll.) to take some food or drink before coping with a strenuous task; recorded for S. areas, e.g. *Schweiz. Idiotikon* 10,241.

← See also under *spannen* (for further details).

vorspannen

See under *Schimmel* (for *wenn die Schimmel nicht ziehen, muß man Füchse vorspannen*) and *spannen* (for *jem. vorspannen*).

vorsparen: see *sparen*.
vorspiegeln: see *Spiegel*
Vorspiel: see *Spiel*.
vorspielen
See under *Spiel* (for *jem.m etw. vorspielen*) and *Theater* (for *jem.m ein Theater vorspielen*).
vorsprechen
See under *einsprechen* and *sprechen* (for *bei jem.m vorsprechen* and *etw. spricht vor*).
vorspringen
jem.m ~ (1) (a.) to jump ahead of sb.; figur. with ref. to 'being earlier', e.g. through anticipation; Goethe used it in *Wahlverw.* 1,4. Now a. or obs.
jem.m ~ (2) (a.) to advance (e.g. in rank) before sb. else; since the 18th c., recorded by Adelung [1801] who equated it with '*schnell über jem. befördert werden*'. This is a. - Quite unusual is Goethe's use of ~ in '*vorspringende Gegenwart*', as in *Tagebuch* (4.10.1786), where it comes close to *in die Augen* (or *in den Sinn*) *springen*. Trübner defined it as '*Ausdruck besonders lebhafter Anschaulichkeit*'.
← See also under *springen* (for *vorspringen* (1) and (2)).
Vorsprung
der ~ lead, advantage (over sb. or sth.), achievement which is superior to sb. else's; with ref. to distance since MHG, to time since Early NHG, since the 18th c. also with ref. to abstracts, with ref. to superiority, e.g. (DWb) Jung Stilling 4,529: '. . . *daß die Philosophie bei weitem den Vorsprung hat*'.
~ *haben vor jem.m* to be older than sb. else; e.g. Goethe, *Gespr.* [edit. B.] 10,212: '. . . *so viele Jahre als seine Mutter Vorsprung habe*'.
← See also under *gewinnen* (for *jem.m einen Vorsprung abgewinnen*).
Vorstand
einen ~ *haben* (legal, a.) to (have to) appear before a court; still recorded by Adelung, now obs., though in some areas ~ has continued to be used for 'surety given by sb. to enable bail to be granted', synonymous with *Bürgschaft*.
der ~ principal, chairman, manager; derived from MHG ~ *haben* = 'to occupy the principal place'; in the modern period used for the person (or group of persons) in charge; general since the 19th c.
vorstechen
etw. sticht vor (a.) sth. stands out, predominates among things; since the 17th c., recorded by Adelung who also mentions its figur. use with abstracts; *hervorstechen* is now preferred; see under *stechen* (p. 2339).
vorstecken: see *Pflock*.
vorstehen
vorstehen (intrans., legal) to appear before a court; f.r.b. Hulsius-Ravellus [1616]; still recorded as current by Sanders [1865], now only in some regions.

etw. steht vor sth. precedes, has been mentioned above; first in civil service jargon, since the 18th c. general with ref. to texts, mainly in the present participle *vorstehend*, e.g. Herder [edit. S.] 15,200, Goethe 25,82 (W.).
einer Sache ~ to preside over or direct sth.; beginnings in MHG, general since Early NHG, e.g. Luther Bible transl. 1 Tim. 3,5, Genesis 24,2; still used with ref. to *Amt, Geschäft, Haushalt*, etc. (cf. the entry under *Vorstand* above); sometimes close to 'to supervise', as in Goethe, *Wanderj.* 1,2.
jem.m ~ (obs.) to surpass or be superior to sb.; since the 16th c., e.g. Franck, *Zeytbuch* 243a [1531], still occasionally used in the 19th c., e.g. Immermann [edit. B.] 5,100.
etw. steht jem.m vor (1) sth. appears before or is present in sb.'s mind; usually *etw. steht vor jem.m* or *steht* or *schwebt jem.m vor Augen* (see p. 118) and similar to *vorschweben*; current since Early NHG; Adelung recorded it and glossed it with *ahnen*; still used by Goethe, e.g. III,1,182 (W.) and in the 19th c., now unusual or a.
etw. steht jem.m vor (2) (obs.) sth. is going to happen to sb., will have to be faced by sb.; f.r.b. Frisius [1556], still used in the 18th c., e.g. Lessing, *Nathan* 3,4, Goethe, *Briefe a.d.Schweiz* (13.11.1779); displaced by *bevorstehen*
vorstellen
See under *stellen* (for detailed treatment), also under *Hölle* (for *die Hölle als heiß vorstellen*), *machen* (for *du kannst mich der Dame vorstellen*) and *Nacht* (for *sich den Tag als Tag der Abrechnung vorstellen*).
vorstellig: see *stellen*.
Vorstellung
See under *brennen* (for *in welchen alle seine Vorstellungen sich sammeln*), *entbinden* (for *entbindet in uns die Vorstellung von Zeiten*), *hinausgehen* (for *das geht über meine Vorstellungen hinaus*), *mitschwingen* (for *in deren Begriff Vorstellungen mitschwingen*), *schmeißen* (for *eine Vorstellung schmeißen*) and *schräg* (for *schräge Vorstellung*).
vorstoßen: see *stoßen* (also for *Vorstoß*).
vorstrecken
jem.m Geld ~ to advance money to sb.; since the 16th c., e.g. Grimmelshausen, *Simpliz.* (repr.) 323. The older meaning 'to give as a present, donate sth.' is obs. - See also under *fühlen* (p. 872).
Vorstufe
die ~ preliminary stage; f.r.b. Campe [1811], in literature apparently only since the 1st half of the 19th c.
vortasten
vortasten (lit.) to make cautious or tentative enquiries, approach sth. with care, put out feelers; modern, e.g. Th. Mann, *Werke* 6,219 (*Faustus*): '*das erste vortastende Gespräch*'; it can also be used in mil. contexts for 'probing, exploring the terrain before one's own position'.

vortäuschen: see *täuschen*.

Vorteil

See under *Teil* (for detailed treatment), also under *anbiegen* (for *der angebogene Vorteil*), *ersehen* (for *seinen Vorteil ersehen*), *Feier* (for *der vortheil hat bald feierabend*), *Schaf* (for *kein Vortheil für die Heerde, wenn der Schäfer ein Schaf ist*), *sehen* (for *er sieht nur seinen Vorteil*) and *Spiel* (for *es liegt das Spiel nicht ganz zu meinem Vortheil*).

vorteilhaft

vorteilhaft advantageous, favourable; originally = 'yielding a profit', since the 17th c., f.r.b. Stieler [1691], with abstracts since the 18th c., e.g. Lessing [edit. M.] 9,110; now also by transfer from the seller's point of view to the buyer's describing sth. that is a bargain; since the 19th c.

← See also under *stechen* (for *vorteilhaft abstechen*).

vortraben: see *traben*.

Vortrag

See under *tragen* (for detailed treatment), also under *Glück* (for *allein der Vortrag macht des Redners Glück*) and *Schlaf* (for *schläfriger Vortrag*).

vortragen

See under *tragen* (for detailed treatment), also under *Blatt* (for *eine Erzählung mit Fertigkeit vorzutragen*), *Schaum* (for *seine Meinung ohne ein Schäumchen vorzutragen*) and *Schnabel* (for *nur diejenige Prosa vorzutragen . . .*).

vorträglich: see *tragen*.

vortrefflich

See under *treffen* (for detailed treatment), also under *bieten* (for *deine Sprache eine vortrefliche Sprache ist*) and *schicken* (for *diese Umstände sich vortrefflich zusammenschickten*).

Vortrefflichkeit

See under *gern* (for *sittliche Vortrefflichkeit*) and *Speer* (for *Vortrefflichkeit* as a title).

vortreiben

etw. ~ to advance sth., make progress with sth.; figur. only since the 19th c. See, however, under *treiben* for *vor sich treiben* and *etw. vorantreiben*.

vortreten

etw. tritt vor sth. stands out; since the 18th c.; *hervortreten* (for which see p. 1310) is preferred, but ~ was still used in the 19th c., though 20th c. dictionaries list it only in phys. contexts, where it can mean the same as *vorstehen*; its 19th c. use in the sense of *vorkommen* is no longer current.

Vortritt

den ~ *haben* to have or enjoy precedence; f.r.b. Kramer [1702], e.g. Schiller, *Fiesco* 5,16, also with abstracts as the subject, as in Schiller, *D.Carlos* 2,2: '*den Vortritt hat das Königreich*'.

Vortrupp

der ~ vanguard; from the mil. sphere; figur. apparently only since the 2nd half of the 18th c. (Jean Paul), then in frequent use for people forming the vanguard in the fight for sth.

vortun: see *hervortun*.

vorüber

aus (or *vorbei*) *und* ~ (coll.) finished, all over and done with, a thing of the past; modern; cf. also ~ *ist* ~, as in Lenau [edit. Barthel] 502.

← See also under *Aranjuez* (for *die schönen Tage von Aranjuez sind nun vorüber*).

vorübergehen

etw. geht vorüber sth. passes, blows over; with ref. to time; since the 16th c., e.g. Klopstock, *Od.* 2,91: '*ganze lange Jahrhunderte sind vorübergegangen*', Hebbel [edit. W.] 12,253: '*Jean Pauls . . . Geburtstag ist ohne Sang und Klang in Deutschland vorübergegangen*'; cf. entries under *vergehen*, *vorbeigehen*, also *vorbeisein*.

an etw. ~ to ignore sth., pass sth. over (in silence); since the 17th c., e.g. Lehman 2,724 [1662]: '*man muß hören und vorüber gehen*'; Kramer [1700] recorded '*ein Ding mit Stilschweigen vorbeygehen*' also '*gehe für über und sprich kein Wort*'.

im Vorübergehen in passing, *en passant*; since the 17th c.; Kramer [1700] recorded it as '*im Vorbeygehen/im Fürübergehen = passando*'; Goethe used *im Vorbeigehen*.

etw. ist an jem.m vorübergegangen sth. has passed sb. by; figur. general since the 18th c. Matth. 26,39: '*so gehe dieser Kelch von mir*', which led to the more frequent '*so gehe dieser Kelch an mir vorüber*'; cf. Droste-Hülshoff 3,211: '*Herr, ist es möglich, so laß diese Stunde an mir vorübergehn*'; also frequently in the negative, e.g. *die Krankheit ist nicht spurlos an ihm vorübergegangen* = 'his illness has told (or left its mark) on him'.

vorübergehend temporary, passing, brief(ly); since the 17th c.; Kramer [1700] recorded it as '*vorbeygehend/fürübergehend*'. In the 18th c. *vorbeieilend* appears to have been just as frequently used, e.g. Goethe 42,1,52 (W.), Lenz [edit. Tieck] 3,160.

← See also under *heben* (for *laß diesen Kelch an mir vorübergehn*) and *Strom* (for *bis die Strömung vorübergegangen ist*).

vorübergleiten

etw. ~ *lassen* to let sth. pass without reacting to it; since the 18th c., e.g. Immermann [edit. B.] 4,14; cf. Goethe 2,69 (W.) with *Blick* as the subject.

← See also under *gleiten* (for *die Bewegungen des Lebens gleiten vor seinem innern Sinn vorüber*).

vorüberlassen

etw. ~ (coll.) to allow sth. to pass; usually with ref. to time; essentially an ellipsis with *gehen* omitted; f.r.b. Steinbach [1734], e.g. C.F. Meyer 1,25 (*Jenatsch*); Goethe used it frequently.

vorüberrinnen: see *gleiten*.

vorüberschießen

vorüberschießen to pass quickly before one's eyes (or sth.); since the 18th c. (Jean Paul, Schiller). ~ can also be used like *vorbeischießen* (for which see under *schießen*).

vorüberschleichen: see *schleichen*.

vorübertreiben: see *treiben*

vorüberwandeln

vorüberwandeln (poet.) to pass; in lit. since the 18th c., e.g. Klopstock, *Mess.* 16,213: 'hundert Monde sind vorübergewandelt'.

vorüberziehen

vorüberziehen to pass; frequent with ref. to clouds or storms since the 16th c., e.g. Goethe 43,225 (W.), Herder [edit. S.] 12,313. It occurs also with ref. to figur. storms.

Vorurteil

See under *auffallen* (for *Streich, der seinen Vorurteilen auffallen wird*), *bekämpfen* (for *ein Vorurteil bekämpfen*), *hegen* (for *Vorurteile hegen*), *fassen* (for *ein Vorurteil fassen*), *Glück* (for *Vorurtheile pflegen eben kein Glück zu machen*), *heften* (for *wo Vorurteil den Ruhm an helle Laster heftet*), *Mauer* (for *er umgab sich mit einer Mauer von Vorurteilen*), *Nebel* (for *durchdringt den Nebel grauer Vorurteile*), *scheu* (for *mit weniger Vorurteilen oder Scheuklappen*), *schnell* (for *leben Kinder in Schnellurtheilen, um nicht zu sagen in Vorurtheilen*), *springen* (for *über ein Vorurtheil wegspringen*), *steigen* (for *Mauern angebohrner Vorurtheile*), *Teil* (for *Vorurteil*, also *vorurteilen* and *vorurteilsfrei*) and *veralten* (for *veraltetes Vorurtheil*).

Vorwacht

~ *halten* (lit., a.) to be on outpost duty, serve as outpost; derived from mil. contexts; since the 17th c., occasionally still used in the 19th c., e.g. Raabe, *Schüdd.* 112 [1870].

vorwalten

etw. waltet vor (1) (a.) sth. predominates; from civil service jargon; f.r.b. Adelung [1780]; often used by Goethe, now a.

etw. waltet vor (2) (a.) sth. exists; the compound has the same meaning as older *obwalten*; f.r.b. Adelung: 'es waltet kein Zweifel vor'; often in 18th and 19th c. in *unter vorwaltenden Umständen* = 'under existing or prevailing conditions', used by Wieland and Goethe, now a.

← See also under *Surrogat* (for *der Humor ist eins der Elemente des Genies, aber sobald er vorwaltet, nur ein Surrogat desselben*).

Vorwand

der ~ pretext; of legal origin; in this sense since the 17th c., f.r.b. Reyher, *Thesaur.* [1686], e.g. Schiller, *M.Stuart* 1,8; often in the phrase *unter dem* ~ = 'under the pretext', since the 17th c., f.r.b. Kramer [1702], used by Kant (Akad.Ausg.) 3,247.

← See also under *haschen* (for *wozu Spanien von jeher nur gern den Vorwand gehascht het*) and *schmücken* (for *schmückst mit heil'gem Vorwand deine That*).

vorwärts

Marschall Vorwärts Blücher von Wahlstatt (1742–1819); title given to the Prussian military commander (incidently first by the Russians) because of his aggressiveness in the War of

Liberation (chiefly in 1814); in literature first in Brentano 2,47, f.r.b. Hübner, *Zeitungslex.* [1824].

etw. ~ *und rückwärts aufsagen können* (coll.) to know sth. by heart or inside out, be able to quote chapter and verse (without having to look it up); modern coll.

← See also under *Rücken* (for *vorwärts eilt die Zeit*).

vorwärtsdringen

vorwärtsdringen to advance, make progress; since the 18th c., also with abstracts as the subject, e.g. Goethe, *Faust I*, 1093 or (DWb) Ranke 3,406: 'die vorwärtsdringenden Tendenzen'.

vorwärtsgehen

vorwärtsgehen to advance, make progress; in figur. contexts since the 19th c., e.g. Goethe IV,19,175 (W.).

← See also under *Sache* (for *die Sache geht vorwärts wie eine Laus auf einer Teerbüchse*).

vorwärtskommen

vorwärtskommen to get ahead, make headway; since the 18th c., e.g. Goethe 7,158 (W.), frequent in *so kommen wir nicht vorwärts* = 'by this method we do not get any further'.

vorwärtstreiben: see *Krampf*.

vorwegkosten: see *kosten*.

vorwegnehmen

etw. ~ to anticipate sth.; figur. with ref. to doing or inventing sth. before sb. else; general since the 19th c., e.g. Keller, *Sämtl.W.* 2,200 (*Fähnlein*): '. . . nimmt dir aber ein Anderer diesen Gedanken vorweg'.

vorweisen

etw. ~ *können* to be able to show sth. to one's credit (such as knowledge, experience); from phys. ~ = 'to show', current since Early NHG; with ref. to achievements since the 18th c. – Goethe in *Dicht.u.Wahrh.* 8 used *vorzeigen* in a similar sense: '. . . mir Genesung und gesunde Thätigkeit in der nächsten Zeit vorzuzeigen'.

vorwerfen

jem.m etw. ~ to reproach sb. with sth.; since Early NHG, e.g. Luther Apocr. transl. Tob.2,23, where *fürwerfen* is used: '. . . warf sie jm sein elend für', Lessing, *Minna* 5,1: 'damit ich mir nichts vorzuwerfen habe'; hence *vorwerfend* = 'reproachful', as in Schiller, *M.Stuart* 2,9: 'vorwerfend wär mir ihres Mangels Anblick', and *vorwurfsfrei*, as in (Sp.) Trenck, *Lebensgesch.* I,231.

← See also under *Brot* (for *täglich vorgeworfen, er esse Gnadenbrot*) and *Tonne* (for *dem Walfisch eine Tonne vorwerfen*).

vorwiegen

etw. wiegt vor sth. predominates; from *mehr wiegen als etw. anderes*; in Early NHG as *für wiegen*, later as ~ , f.r.b. Hederich [1777]. Frequent as an adverb in the present participle *vorwiegend* = 'mainly', seen by some as a combination of *vorherrschend* and *überwiegen*, current only since the 19th c.

Vorwissen: see *setzen*.

Vorwitz: see *durchwühlen*.

Vorwort

das ~ (1) (obs.) plea in favour of sb.; still used by Goethe, *Rein. Fuchs* 7: '. . . *der Königin Vorwort leicht zu gewinnen*'. In earlier times *Fürwort* was used, both now obs.

das ~ (2) (ling., a.) preposition; f.r.b. Schottel, *Sprachkunst* [1641], but abandoned in course of time, because *Präposition* and *Verhältniswort* proved more acceptable, though some 20th c. grammarians still used it sometimes, as do Austrians.

das ~ (3) preface, prologue; translates Lat. *praepositio*; f.r.b. Schottel [1663].

← See also under *bevorworten*.

Vorwurf

der ~ (1) reproach; f.r.b. Stieler (1691), e.g. Schiller, *Kab.u.L.* 3,1: '*die Vorwürfe Ihres Gewissens*'. For further examples see the numerous cross-references below.

der ~ (2) (lit.) subject, theme; Adelung called it a recently coined word for Lat. *objectum*; mainly in such phrases as *etw. zum ~ für eine Arbeit wählen*. *Thema* is the generally preferred term, *Gegenstand* can also be used.

← See also under *abschütteln* (for *Vorwürfe von sich abschütteln*), *ausgießen* (for *seinen Unwillen in bitterste Vorwürfe ausgegossen*), *aussprudeln* (for *was da für Vorwürfe aussprudeln*), *Dusche* (for *die Dusche von Vorwürfen auszuhalten*), *eintragen* (for *jem.m Vorwürfe eintragen*), *fassen* (for *falsche Vorwürfe treffen flach*), *gelb* (for *er trieb die Vorwürfe so weit* . . .), *Keule* (for *deine Vorwürfe lasten wie Keulschläge*), *Köcher* (for *soll ich des Vorwurfs Köcher vor Euch leeren*), *Magazin* (for *ein Magazin unendtlicher Vorwürffen*), *Natter* (for *die Natter des Vorwurfs*), *Pfeil* (for *Pfeile des Vorwurfs*), *prasseln* (for *Vorwürfe prasselten auf ihn nieder*), *setzen* (for *dein Vorwurf setzet mir ein Messer an die Kehle*), *Splitter* (for *der Splitter des Vorwurfs eiterte*), *Stachel* (for *des Vorwurfs Stachel*), *Staffel* (for *der Vorwurf weitergereicht*) and *übergießen* (for *jem. mit Vorwürfen übergießen*), also under *vorwerfen* (for *vorwurfsfrei*).

vorzählen: see *zählen*.

vorzaubern: see *zaubern*.

Vorzeichen

das ~ (1) omen; since MHG, f.r.b. *voc.theut.* [1482].

das ~ (2) early indication of sth. that is likely to happen; since the 18th c.

das Gleiche mit umgekehrten ~ (coll.) the same thing but (to be taken) the other way round; 20th c. coll.; sometimes *mit negativen* ~ occurs in the same sense, e.g. Th. Mann, *Faustus* 384 [1948].

vorzeigen: see *vorweisen*.

Vorzeit

die ~ antiquity, prehistory; since the 18th c.,

much used by the Romantics (often with *grau*); hence *vorzeitlich* = 'prehistoric', since the 19th c., but *vorzeitig* = 'premature', current since the 18th c.

← See also under *einleben* (for *die Dichtkunst der hellenischen Vorzeit*) and *Zeit* (also for *vorzeiten*), also under *sehen* (for Luther's use of *vorzeiten*).

vorziehen

etw. ~ (1) to prefer sth.; beginnings in OHG (cf. Notker (edit. Piper) 2,280), but in general use only since MHG, f.r.b. Stieler (1691).

etw. ~ (2) to move sth. to an earlier date; with ref. to projects, items in a program, etc., often with *zeitlich*; since the 20th c.

etw. zieht sich vor sth. extends; in local contexts, e.g. *das Gebirge zieht sich weit nach Norden vor*; since the 19th c., but not yet listed by Campe [1811].

← See also under *bleich* (for *ein tugendbleiches Kind mir vorgezogen*) and *Schlag* (for *einen Schlagbaum vorziehen*).

Vorzug

See under *Grund* (for *verlangte auf Grund dieses Vorzugs* and *wir fangen an in Deutschland, auf den Vorzug der Gründlichkeit stolz su werden*) and *streichen* (for *strich alle Vorzüge heraus*).

vorzüglich: see *hinübergehen*.

vorzugsweise: see *sympathetisch*.

vulgär

vulgär (1) vulgar, coarse, offensive; since the middle of the 18th c. in the pejor. sense; taken over from French *vulgaire*.

vulgär (2) trivial, unscientific, superficial, intended for mass consumption; since the middle of the 19th c., hence *etw. vulgarisieren* = 'to present sth. in a simplified or unscientific form'; since the 1st half of the 19th c., f.r.b. Oertel, *Gramm. Wb.d.dt.Spr.* [1831].

Vulkan

der ~ (lit.) volcano; figur. in wider sense for sth. or sb. that can or is likely to erupt with explosive force; since the 18th c., e.g. (S.-B.) Forster, *Br. über Ital.* 1,129 [1789]: '*der Vulkan ihrer Einbildungskraft ist erloschen*', Schlözer, *Jugendbr.* 80 [1845]: '*Paris ist der Vulkan Europas*'; hence *vulkanisch*, as in Goethe, *Br.* V,24 [1780]: '*vulkanische Wuth*'.

etw. vulkanisieren (1) (lit., rare) to put sth. in a state of unrest or agitation; since the 2nd half of the 18th c.

etw. vulkanisieren (2) (tech.) to vulcanize sth.; loan from Engl.; since the middle of the 19th c.

der Vulkanist (hist.) believer in the theory that the major features of the earth's surface can be explained as the consequences of volcanic activity; also called *Plutonist*; since late in the 18th c., e.g. Goethe, *Br.* III, 272 [1823].

← See also under *Tanz* (for *ein Tanz auf dem Vulkan*).

wach

wach awake, alert, lively; since the 16th c., at first mostly with *Auge* or *Herz* (as in Goethe, *Morgenklagen*: '. . . *war mein Herz beständig wach geblieben*'), then in phrases with abstracts, e.g. Bürger, 42b: '*noch ist mein Gewissen wach*', Schiller, *M.Stuart* 2,8: '*da wird in mir die Hoffnung wach*'; by a further extension ~ *werden* can in lit. mean 'to come into existence, become visible or audible', since the 18th c., e.g. Hagedorn 2,125: '*eh er stirbt wird seine Stimme wach*', Schiller, *Braut v.M.* 1,7: '*das Echo des Berges wird wach*'. Hence *die Wachheit* in wider sense, only since the 20th c. (not yet mentioned in *DWb.* [1901]), e.g. *die Wachheit des politischen Bewußtseins*.

wach- . . . awake; in verbal compounds, mostly of a phys. nature, but some such as *wachrufen* and *wachrütteln* can occur with abstracts, e.g. Heyse, *Par.* 2,349: '*Vatergefühle wachzurufen*' or the example quoted under *rütteln* (p. 2035).

Wache

die ~ *für etw.* (lit.) watchful care (or concern) for sth.; since the 18th c., e.g. Berens in Herder [edit. S.] 17,411: '*Belohnung der Wachen für den Wohlstand . . . seiner Mitbürger*', derived from ~ = 'watchfulness, care', as used by Luther 3,324 (Jena); frequent in earlier periods in *Hut und* ~ *halten* = 'to be watchful', e.g. P. Gerhardt [edit. G.] 118,27.

~ *halten* to be on guard; with abstracts as the subject since the 18th c., e.g. Lessing [edit. L.] 1,21: '*unter diesem Dache . . . hält Armuth treue Wache*'; in lit. things can also be seen as 'standing guard', as in C.F.Meyer, *Huttens l.T.* 6: '*die Wache hält ein Eichbaum*'. ~ *stehen* can be used in the same way.

← See also under *ablösen* (for *eine Wache ablösen*), *Donner* (for *auf die Donnerwache stehen*), *nackt* (for *einen Nackten auf die Wache stellen*), *Schild* (for *Schildwache*) and *Stall* (for *Stallwache haben*).

wachen

wachen to be or stay awake; figur. at first with ref. to *Auge* or *Herz*, then with abstracts such as *Gewissen* or *Rache* (for examples see pp. 1038 and 1931).

← See also under *aufwachen*, *bewachen* and *erwachen*.

wachhalten

etw. ~ to keep sth. awake (or alive); since the 18th c., at first mainly as *wach erhalten*, but then compounded with *halten*; in phys. sense in Goethe, *Lehrj.* 4,16; since the 19th c. figur. with abstracts, such as *Erinnerung*, e.g. Grillparzer, *Werke* 9,14.

Wachs

weich wie ~ *sein* to be (too) readily yielding or tolerant, too quickly influenced; since MHG; hence also ~ *in jem.s Händen sein*, e.g. Schiller,

Jungfr.v.O. 3,4, *wachsweich sein*, since the 17th c., e.g. Grimmelshausen, *Simpliz.* [edit. K.] 1,34 and *Wachsfigur* (sl., pejor.) = 'easily influenced person', since ca. 1900. Pejoration has also strengthened in *wachsweich sein*, in which lack of determination is now criticized.

wächsern waxen, pale, lifeless; a modern term in its figur. sense, though Steinbach [1734] recorded *wachsfarben*; e.g. (H.) Taylor, *Antinous* 232 [1881]: '. . . *Leiche, die kalt und wächsern vor ihm lag*', Wildenbruch, *Nov.* 105: '*regungslos wie ein wächsernes Bild*'; *wachsbleich* also occurs (modern).

← See also under *gelb* (for *vor bosheit gelb ward als ein wax*), *Nase* (for *jem.m eine wächserne Nase drehen*), *Ohr* (for *der Begierden Ohren mit Tugend-Wax verstopft*) and *verschmelzen* (for *wie Wachs verschmelzen*).

wachsam: see *betrügen* and *richten*.
Wachsamkeit: see *betrügen*.

wachsen

See under *Auge* (for *jem.m aus den Augen wachsen*), *Bart* (for *laß dir keinen Bart darüber wachsen*), *Blatt* (for *das unsre kirche teglich wechst*), *einziehen* (for *unter den henden größer gewachsen*), *Feder* (for *ihm wachsen die Federn*), *Fleisch* (for *ihr ist kein Nonnenfleisch gewachsen*), *Garten* (for *das ist nicht in seinem Garten gewachsen*), *grau* (for *sich keine grauen Haare wachsen lassen*), *Hand* (for *jem.m über die Hand wachsen*), *Kraut* (for *gegen den Tod ist kein Kraut gewachsen*), *Mist* (for *das ist nicht auf seinem Mist gewachsen*), *Pfeffer* (for *ich wollte, du wärst, wo der Pfeffer wächst*), *Pilz* (for *du wechst und nimmest zu wie die morchel im meyen* and . . . *daß die Großen wie Pilze aus der Erde wachsen*), *Schnabel* (for *reden, wie einem der Schnabel gewachsen ist*) and *Schnee* (for *etw. wächst wie ein rollender Schneeball*).

← See also under *anwachsen*, *auswachsen*, *durchwachsen*, *einwachsen* and *erwachsen*.

Wachtel: see *Spinat*.

Wächter

der ~ guardian; sometimes used for 'spiritual guardian, keeper, protector', e.g. *heiliger* ~ , as in Luther Bible transl. Dan. 4,10, and Schiller, *Räuber* 5,2: '*im Rath der himmlischen Wächter*'.

← See also under *Nacht* (for *Nachtwächter* (1) and (2) and *Nachtwächterstaat*).

Wachtturm

der ~ (lit.) watch-tower; figur. since the 18th c., e.g. Herder [edit. S.] 17,304: '*Universitäten sind Wacht- und Leuchtthürme der Wissenschaft*'.

wackeln

wackeln to wobble, shake, be in a shaky or insecure state; in religious contexts since MHG, e.g. Luther 8,139b (Jena) on faith: '. . . *der nicht wancket, wackelt, bebet, zappelt* . . .', or Schiller, *Räuber* 2,3: '*die Ehrlichkeit wackelt wie ein hohler Zahn*'.

etw. ins Wackeln bringen to cause sth. to totter;

this is modern, e.g. Bismarck, *Reden* 14,22: '. . . *die Verfassung . . . ins Wackeln zu bringen*', but earlier there was *etw. wackelnd machen*, as recorded by Kramer [1702].

← See also under *Gehirn* (for *so wackelt der Staat*).

wacker

wacker (adj. and adv.) active, energetic, proper(ly); belongs to *wachen* and therefore expressed initially the notion of 'lively', as in Fischart, *Trostb.* '*wacker wie der hase auf dem acker*'; referred in Early NHG mainly to human behaviour (e.g. Luther Bible transl. Luke 21,36, Prov. 20,137), increasingly used as a term of praise in the sense of 'efficient, competent', sometimes extended to things, as in Luther Bible transl. Jer. 1,11: '*einen wackern stab*', lastly, employed as an intensifying adverb = *tüchtig, ordentlich*, since the 18th c., e.g. Kotzebue, *Pagenstr.* 5,2: '*diesen Befehl wacker einzuschärfen*'.

← See also under *gehören* (for *das man hie jmerdar wacker lebe*) and *Gelage* (for *borgen frei wacker in das Gelack*).

Wade: calf

bei mir eiskalte ~ (mil.sl.,obs.?) without me, leave me out of it; mil.sl. of 2nd World War, same as *ohne mich!*

Waden-. . . (joc.coll.) calf-. . ., leg-. . .; mainly in Berlin sl., e.g. *Wadenkneifer* = 'tight trousers' and *Wadenoper* = 'opera containing ballet' (cf. Engl. coll. 'leg-show'), both recorded in 9th edit. of *D.richt. Berliner* [1925]. There is also *Wadenbeißer* (sl.) = 'sb. who is in the habit of passing critical remarks'.

Wadel: see *Esel*.

Waffe: tool; weapon

die ~ (1) weapon; transfer to the non-phys. sphere; since MHG, e.g. A.v.Eyb, *Eheb.* 27,8: '*die zunge des menschen . . . ist ein woffen zu liegen und zu triegen*', also in Luther Bible and Apocr. transl. e.g. 2 Cor. 6,7 and 10,4, Rom. 6,13 and 13,12, Lessing, *Nathan* 3,4: '. . . *mit Waffen, die ich nicht gelernt zu führen*', Goethe, *Iphig.* 1,3: '*unedel sind die Waffen eines Weibes*'; it occurs in several set phrases, e.g. *jem. mit seiner eignen* ~ *schlagen* (which Ludwig (1716) recorded with *erlegen*), *mit gleichen Waffen kämpfen* (since the 17th c.), *jem.s* ~ *gegen ihn selbst kehren* (modern). Kramer [1702] recorded *Geisteswaffe*.

die ~ (2) arm or branch of the armed forces; the same as *Waffengattung*; modern, as is *Waffengattung*, not yet recorded by Campe [1811]. The plural can be used for 'the armed forces', since Early NHG; cf. also *Waffen führen* = 'to make war', *in Waffen stehen* = 'to be at war', since the 17th c. - Ludwig [1716] recorded *die feindlichen Waffen* for 'the enemy troops'.

sich waffnen (now usually *wappnen*) to arm oneself; in phys. and figur. sense since MHG,

e.g. Konr. v. Würzburg, *Troj.* 4181, Schlegel in transl. of Shakespeare, *Hamlet* 3,1: '*sich waffnend gegen eine See von Plagen*'.

der Waffenstillstand armistice; patterned on French *armistice*; recorded since 1669 (cf. Kluge s.v.); in modern period also figur. for 'cessation of (non-phys.) hostilities', e.g. *einen Waffenstillstand schließen* = 'to cease quarrelling'.

← See also under *bewaffnen, entwaffnen, führen* (for *keine hinlängliche Waffe für den, der sie führt*), *Gewehr* (for *ein gute wehr und waffen, nur wie Waffen in einer Gewehrkammer* and *all under gewehr und waffen*), *greifen* (for *zuo iren waffen griffen*), *ruhen* (for *die Waffen ruhn*), *Schild* (for *Schild und Waffe*) and *strecken* (for *die Waffen strecken*).

wägbar

nicht ~ imponderable; phys. ~ has been current since the 18th c., recorded by Campe [1811], *nicht* ~ , not referring to actual 'weighing' since later in the 19th c.

Wage (1): scales, balance

die ~ (1) (now usually spelt *Waage*) Libra, sign of the zodiac, of Classical origin, denoting the time between September 24 to October 23; f.r.b. Stieler [1691], e.g. H.Sachs [edit. K.] 4,255: '*die sonn war in der wag*'; hence also *er or sie ist eine* ~ (coll.) = 'he or she is Libra or a Libran', modern (not yet recorded in *DWb.* [1903]).

die ~ (2) (lit.) the scales; figur. with abstracts in such phrases as *die* ~ *der Gerechtigkeit*, e.g. Lessing, *Em. Gal.* 5,5 or *die* ~ *der Weisheit*, e.g. Wieland, *Agathon* 8,4.

etw. fällt in die ~ (a.) sth. must be taken account of, has to be considered as relevant; general in the 18th c., e.g. Schiller, *D.Carlos* 2,10, Kleist, *Prinz v.H.* 4,2, but now *etw. fällt ins Gewicht* is preferred (which see under *Gewicht*).

die ~ *halten* to (have the power to) determine the outcome; mainly with ref. to the gods or some power 'holding the scales' in their hands, e.g. Goethe, *Ital. Reise*: '*über meine sicilianische Reise halten die Götter noch die Wage in Händen*'.

jem.m die ~ *halten* to equal sb., be able to hold one's own against sb.; since the 17th c.

sich die ~ *halten* to balance out; in early periods phrases with *gleich* were used to express this notion (since MHG), with *halten* only since the 17th c.

← See also under *Gewicht* (for *niht werk ze wage ligt, wo Gott nicht in der woge ist* and *auf der Wage der Gerechtigkeit*), *Gold* (for *seine Worte auf die Goldwage legen*), *stehen* (for *ûf der wage stên*) and *Zunge* (for *das Zünglein an der Wage*).

Wage (2): venture

die ~ (obs.) venture, hazardous enterprise; old word, resurrected by Wieland, *Ob.* 5,72, but it did not establish itself, displaced by *Wagnis*.

Wagehals

See under *Glück* (for *der Teutsche ist ein*

Wagehalß) and *Hals* (for *noch schwimpt er wie ein verwegner wagenhals*, also for *waghalsen* and *waghalsig*).

wagen
gewagt dangerous; transfer from 'hazarded' to 'hazardous', the former still used by Goethe in *Briefe* 2,52 (letter to Kestner [1771]); since Early NHG, f.r.b. Maaler [1561]. In the 19th c. *gewagt* was further extended to mean 'risqué, not quite decent', e.g. Freytag, *Bild.* 1,519.

← See also under *frisch* (for *frisch gewagt ist halb gewonnen*), *gehen* (for *mit ihnen einige Gänge zu wagen*), *gewinnen* (for *es muß gewagt sein, wagen gewint*), *Hals* (for *den Hals wagen*), *Kopf* (for *Kopf und Bart daran wagen*) and *Schinken* (for *einen Schinken zu erjagen, muß man eine Bratwurst wagen*).

Wagen: cart, vehicle
der ~ am Himmel (bibl.) the Great Bear; e.g. Luther Bible transl. Job 9,9: '*der wagen am himmel*' (where Mentel's Bible also has *wagen*, whereas the A.V. has 'Arcturus').

der ~ (lit.) the carriage; in literature sometimes with abstracts, e.g. *wer auf dem ~ der Hoffnung fährt, hat die Armut zum Gefährten* or *wer auf dem ~ des Reichtums fährt, der hat den Neid zum Kutscher und Langeweile zur Begleiterin*, both recorded by Wander [1876] without details about sources.

jem.m an den ~ fahren (regional coll.) to offend or hurt sb.; recorded for Silesia [1865], as quoted by Wander, and for Leipzig by Albrecht [1881]; also used as a warning: *laß dir nicht gegen den ~ fahren* = 'be on your guard, don't let people take advantage of you'.

laßt uns (abwarten und) sehen, wie der Wagen läuft (coll.) let us (wait and) see how things will turn out; modern in this form and not recorded in *DWb.*; see under *laufen* (p. 1590) for similar *wie die Sache läuft*.

← See also under *fünf* (for *er ist das fünfte Rad am Wagen*), *gelten* (for *der Geltungstriebwagen*), *grün* (for *der grüne Wagen*), *Ochs* (for *er seezt den wagen für die rinder*), *Pferd* (for *die Pferde hinter den Wagen spannen*), *reiten* (for *auf einem Wurstwagen reiten*), *Schimmel* (for *er hat den Schimmel vor den unrechten Wagen gespannt*), *Schlaf* (for *er steht da wie ein entgleister Schlafwagen*) and *Sonne* (for *der Sonnen-wagen*).

wägen: weigh
erst ~ , dann wagen (prov.) look before you leap; recorded since the 18th c., e.g. by Pistorius [1714–16]. An older form occurs in H.v.Schweinichen's diary (completed in 1602): '*bewiegs, ehe du wägst*'; cf. also *wagen ist besser als wägen* (prov.), recorded by Simrock [1846].

← See also under *abwägen, auswägen, darwägen, gewogen* and *wiegen* (also for *erwägen*).

Wagnis: see *reißen*.

Wagschale
See under *fallen* (for *in die Wagschale fallen*), *Gewicht* (for *auf der Wagschale einer kalten Überlegung* and *die Wagschale der guten Werke*) and *Schale* (for several examples).

Wahl: choice, election
See under *abstimmen* (for *in einer Wahl abstimmen*), *eng* (for *engere Wahl*, also *freie Wahl*), *frei* (for *vrie wal*), *Qual* (for *wer die Wahl hat, hat die Qual*) and *treffen* (for *eine Wahl treffen*).

wählen
gewählt elegant, choice, refined; meaning that a careful choice has been made (cf. Kant's remarks on *wählen* with ref. to aesthetics in *Anthrop.* §63); since Early NHG, e.g. H.Sachs, *Fabeln* [edit. K.-D.] 3,40.

← See also under *auserwählen* and *auswählen*.

wählerisch
wählerisch choosy, particular; f.r.b. Stieler [1691], but still as *wählig* in the 18th c., e.g. Lessing, *Dram.*18 (even in the 19th c. in Grillparzer). Adelung criticized the term and wanted it replaced by *wählisch*, but ~ proved stronger.

Wahlgang: see *gehen*.
Wahlpuff: see *Puff*.
Wahlverwandtschaft
die ~ elective affinity; originally a term in chemistry, first used in Latin form by Bergman (1775), translated as ~ by Weigel [1779] and by Tabor [1782]; transferred to human relationships by Goethe in his novel *Die Wahlverwandtschaften* [1809].

Wahn: see under *Blut* (for *argen wahn machen*), *Fieber* (for *Fieberwahn*), *Nebel* (for *Nebel des Wahnes*) and *Schleier*.

Wahnbild: see *Gegenbild*.
wähnen: see *halb*.
Wahnsinn
See under *Beute* (for *des Wahnsinns Beute*), *brennen* (for *in seinem Gehirn brannte der Wahnsinn*) and *hell* (for *heller Wahnsinn*), also under *Cäsar* (for *Cäsarenwahnsinn*) and *rufen* (for *Wahnsinn ruft man dem Calchas*).

wahnsinnig
das ist ~ that is mad or crazy; in modern period often in coll. hyperbolic phrases such as *du machst mich noch ~* = 'you are driving me mad or round the bend', *wie ~* 'like mad' in such comparisons as *er fährt wie ~* = 'he drives like a madman', in such exclamations as *~ !* = 'that is fantastic, quite unbelievable!', since the 19th c. also used as an adverbial intensifier, e.g. *~ verliebt, es hat ~ viel Geld gekostet*.

wahr: true
wahr right, suitable, appropriate; since the 18th c., e.g. Goethe, *Lehrj.* 4,2: '. . . *die wahre Tracht eines Fußgängers*'; hence also *das ist nicht ganz das Wahre* = 'that is not quite the right thing'; often = 'sensible', as in *das ist das einzig Wahre* = 'that is the only sensible thing to do'.

das ist schon nicht mehr ~ (coll.) that happened ages ago; modern coll.

← See also under *bleiben* (for *wahr bleibt wahr*), *Daniel* (for *ein wahrer Daniel*), *Drache* (for *sie ist ein wahrer Drache*), *helfen* (for *so wahr mir Gott helfe*), *Jakob* (for *der wahre Jakob* and *ein wahrer Jakob*), *schön* (for *zu schön um wahr zu sein*), *sprechen* (for *sprich was wahr ist*) and *stehen* (for *so wahr ich hier stehe*).

wahren: see *Gesicht* (also under *bewahren* and *verwahren*).

währen

See under *Ehre* (for *ehrlich währt am längsten*), *lang* (for *was lange währt, wird endlich gut*) and *schön* (for *Schönheit wehret nicht lange*).

wahrhaft: see *Nase*.

wahrhaftig: see *steif*.

Wahrheit

See under *begraben* (for *zum Begräbnis der Wahrheit gehören viele Schaufeln*), *betäuben* (for *Verleumdung, deren Mund die Wahrheit selbst betäubet*), *biegen* (for *wie wird der die warheit biegen*), *Binse* (for *Binsenwahrheit*), *brennen* (for *brennender Durst nach Wahrheit*), *Ehre* (for *um der Wahrheit die Ehre zu geben*), *einschlafen* (for *auch Wahrheiten schlafen ein*), *fallen* (for *wobei die Wahrheit zu kurz fiel*), *Fiedel* (for *wer die Wahrheit geigt . . .*), *Gefäß* (for *schrecklich . . . deiner Wahrheit sterbliches Gefäß zu sein*), *Geige* (for *jem.m die Wahrheit geigen*), *Gewicht* (for *die Mittellinie der Wahrheit*), *Gold* (for *den goldnen Strich der Wahrheit erkennen*), *Herberge* (for *Herberge der Warheit*), *Korn* (for *es steckt ein Körnchen Wahrheit darin*), *Mann* (for *die Wahrheit unter allerlei Larven*), *nackt* (for *die nackte Stärke der Wahrheit*), *Narr* (for *Narren, Kinder und trunkene Leut sagen die Wahrheit*), *pirschen* (for *ze birsen ûf die wârheit*), *ruhen* (for *nur auf der Wahrheit ruht die Wahrsagung*), *schweben* (for *zwischen Trug und Wahrheit schwebet*), *Schweif* (for *ewig aus der Wahrheit Schranken schweift des Mannes wilde Kraft*), *stehen* (for *wo man das Placebo singt, muß die Wahrheit zurückstehen*) and *Tochter* (for *die Wahrheit ist der Zeit Tochter*).

wahrnehmen: see *blenden*.

wahrsagen

wahrsagen to prophesy; in use since the 14th c., also in Luther Bible transl., e.g. Micha 3,11: '*ire prophete warsagen umb geld*' or Hesek. 21,21; with pejor. flavour even as early as in Early NHG (contrasted with positive *weissagen*).

Wahrsager: see *selten*.

Wahrsagung: see *ruhen*.

Wahrscheinlichkeitsrechnung: see *Lot*.

Waise

die ~ (metrics) rhymeless line in a rhymed poem; beginnings at the time of the *Meistersinger*, when ~ was used for a line in a stanza which had no clear (formal) connexion with other parts of the stanza.

eine ~ sein (lit. rare) to be bereft, bare or not possessed of sth.; since MHG, e.g. Walther v.d.V. 20,22: '*dâ stên ich als ein weise vor*' (also Wolfram v.E., *Parz.* 169).

er ist das reinste Waisenkind in dieser Sache (coll.) he has no knowledge about or experience in this, is a mere novice, totally incompetent; for origin see the previous entry; in this form since the 19th c.; cf. also Heine [edit. E.] 3,164: '*diese Waisenkinder des Ruhmes*'.

gegen x ist y ein Waisenknabe (coll.) y cannot be compared to x; usually indicating that x is sth. objectionable whereas y is almost angelic by comparison; beginnings in MHG, e.g. H.v.Freiberg, *Tristan* 1350: '*her Tristan . . ., der valscheit ein weise*'; *unschuldig wie ein Waisenknabe* also occurs, but the phrase under discussion has not been recorded before the last quarter of the 19th c. (cf. *DWb.* 13,1058).

Wald: wood, forest

ein ~ von . . . a mass or multitude of . . .; since MHG, e.g. W.v.Eschenbach, *Parz.* 66,24: '. . . hât der küneg . . . von speren einen ganzen walt*', Schiller, *Ring d.Pol.*: '*der Schiffe mastenreicher Wald*', also *~ von Lanzen* in *Tell* 3,3; *ein ~ von Haaren* occurs for 'big mop of hair' (also sometimes with ref. to bushy eye-brows). With abstracts since the 18th c., e.g. Herder, *Ph.* 13,318: '*in dem Walde von Begriffen*'.

Wälder (lit., obs.) collection of poems or small lit. items; since the 17th c., first in Opitz, *Dt.Poet.*158 [1624], in imitation of Lat. *silvae*, the term used by Quintilian for poems based on sudden inspiration; still used by the Brothers Grimm in *Altdeutsche Wälder* [1813], now obs.

in die Wälder zurückkehren (obs.) to abandon cultured society and civilized life; this reflects the old concept of ~ as a fearsome place only inhabited by wild creatures or outlaws; cf. Günther, *Ged.* 275: '*in den Wäldern will ich irren, vor den Menschen will ich fliehn*'.

der ~ ist heller (a.) things are looking up; still used by Schiller, *Räuber* 1,1.

in den ~ rufen (or *reden*) (a.) to waste one's effort; since MHG, e.g. Neidhart (in Zingerle, 163); still recorded by Wander [1876]: '*das war in den Wald geredet*' = 'that did not lead to any result'.

Wald und Wiesen-. . . (coll.) common and garden, everyday; in compounds since the 19th c. for things which are too common to be noteworthy.

der Waldargus (zool.) the butterfly *Pararge aegaria*; f.r.b. Nemnich; *Argus* refers to the eye-like markings on the wings.

← See also under *Baum* (for *er sieht den Wald vor lauter Bäumen nicht*), *Bett* (for *Waldweiber*), *Bruder* (for *Waldbruder*), *entkleiden* (for *der walt hat sich enkleidet gar*), *Furcht* (for *die Furcht hütet den Wald*), *hineinschallen* (for *wie es in den Wald hineinschallt, so schallt es heraus* - see also the variant under *rufen*), *Hinterwäldler, Krone* (for *Waldkrone, Waldeskrone* and *waldgekrönte Berge*), *schnarchen* (for *schnarchen wie ein Waldesel*), *Seele* (for *wie ein Waldvöglein*), *Teufel* (for three different meanings of *Waldteufel*) and *Urwald*.

Walfisch: whale

der ~ (astron.) Cetus; large constellation in the Southern sky; f.r.b. Ch. Wolff, *Mathem.Lex.* [1716].

← See also under *Tonne* (for *dem Walfisch eine Tonne vorwerfen*).

walken: full, mill

jem. ~ (coll.) to thrash sb.; at least since the 18th c., e.g. H.v.Kleist, *Amphitryon* 2,2; mainly now in coll. compounds, such as *verwalken*.

← See also under *durchwalken* and *Geist* (for *walkte seine Frau*).

Walküre: Valkyrie

eine ~ (coll.) a veritable Juno, imposing, majestic-looking woman; since the 19th c., after Richard Wagner had made the word familiar through his opera *Die Walküre* [1876].

Wall: earth work, rampart

ein ganzer ~ (lit.) a huge pile; since the 18th c., mainly in mil. contexts, e.g. *ein ~ von Leichen*.

der ~ (lit.) protective rampart or obstacle; since Early NHG, e.g. Goethe, *Egmont* 1 (with ref. to Egmont forming an obstacle), Rückert, *Ges. Ged.* 3,418 on Mainz: '. . . *Stadt . . . einst Deutschlands Schutz und Wall*', also extended to abstracts, e.g. *er verschanzt sich hinter einem ~ von Argumenten*.

wallen (1): flow, move

etw. wallt jem.m entgegen (lit.) sth. surges or stretches out towards sb.; in poet. contexts since the 18th c., e.g. Klopstock 8,135: '. . . *wallt mein Herz dem nahen Siege mit Ungestüm entgegen*', Gotter 3,454: '*werd ich hier ein Herz entdecken, das mir entgegenwallt?*'. Abstracts can also be the subject, as in Gotter 1,438: '. . . *wallen . . . das Elend und der Unbestand in tausend Bildern ihm entgegen*'.

← See also under *aufwallen, Blut* (for *sein Blut wallt*), *durchwallen* and *Feuer* (for *Feuer, die elektrisch mich durchwallen*).

wallen (2): travel *wallen* (lit.)

to move solemnly or with deliberation, walk in a stately fashion; began as 'to travel' in OHG, then also for 'to move from place to place without a permanent home', as in Luther Bible transl. 1 Peter 1,17, also for 'to go on a pilgrimage' (now obs.); for 'procede solemnly' since the 18th c.

← See also under *Wallfahrt* (for *nachwallen*).

Wallfahrt: pilgrimage

eine ~ machen or *unternehmen* to go on a pilgrimage; first only in relig. contexts when it could also occur figur. for 'journey through life', as in Luther Bible transl. Genesis 47,8, then secularized, e.g. *jährlich macht dieser Wagner-Verehrer*

eine ~ nach Bayreuth; this began as early as in Early NHG, e.g. Götz v. Berlichingen (reprint of his diary, 31): cf. also Klinger, *Zw.* 31: '*Grimaldi wallt dir eine düstre Wallfahrt nach*'. Hence also *wallfahrten*, since the 16th c., for which *wallen* (2) could also be used.

Wallung: see *Peitsche*.

wälsch: see *welsch*.

Wälschheit: see *impfen*.

Walstatt: battle-field

auf der ~ bleiben to perish or be defeated in battle; originally with ref. to war, but since the 18th c. also in non-mil. contexts with ref. to other kinds of struggle such as debates or elections.

walten: see under *Gott*

(for *Gott walts's*), *Himmel* (for *ich ließ den Himmel und die Vorsicht walten*), *Natur* (for *ewig waltende Natur*), *Surrogat* (for *vorwalten*) and *vorwalten*.

Walze: see *Dampf*.

wälzen: roll, heave

etw. auf jem. ~ to shift sth. onto sb. else; with such abstracts as *Last* or *Schuld*, since the 17th c., e.g. (DWb) Thomasius, *Kl.Schrifften* 69 [1707], Goethe, *Nat.Tochter* 1,7 (very frequent in Schiller's writings).

Gedanken ~ (lit.) to turn thoughts over in one's mind; since Early NHG, influenced by Lat. *volvere*. – Marginally figur. is *Bücher ~* (coll.) = 'to pore over books, search among many books'; modern.

sich in etw. ~ to wallow in sth.; only with ref. to vices (*Laster, Unzucht, Wollust*) since Early NHG, e.g. Grimmelshausen, *Simpliz.* [edit. K.] 3,10.

etw. überwälzen to pass sth. on, shift responsibility for sth. to sb. else; with such abstracts as *Kosten* or *Verantwortung*, mainly with ref. to shedding responsibility and passing it to sb. else, e.g. *vom Bund auf die Länder*; modern (in Campe [1811] not yet recorded in figur. sense).

← See also under *abwälzen, aufwälzen, Faß* (for *sein Faß wälzen*), *Getriebe* (for *Körperweltgewühle wälzet eines Rades Schwung zum Ziele*) and *herumwälzen*.

Walzer: waltz

der Walzerkönig (coll.) Johann Strauß; since the 2nd half of the 19th c.

Wälzer

der ~ (coll.) heavy tome; since the 18th c., recorded by Adelung.

Wamme, Wampe: belly, womb

die ~ (regional coll.) pot-bellied person; transfer from 'belly' to the entire person; in many regions in different forms such as *Wamper, Wamperling* and in compounds such as *Freßwampe, Wampenkessel, Wampenschieber* (frequent in various forms in Abr.a Sancta Clara, *Etwas für Alle*).

die Mutterwamme (obs.) the womb; occasionally figur. in poetry, e.g. Rückert, *Mak.* 2,226:

'*die Trägheit . . . ist . . . der Hilfsbedürftigkeit Mutterwamme*'.

etw. wamsen (regional coll.) to eat sth. greedily, stuff oneself with a lot of sth.; in many regions, also as *wambsen*.

wampig fat, bloated; extension from 'belly' to other parts of the body, e.g. Heine [edit. E.] 3,42: '*ein glänzend wampiges, dummkluges Gesicht*'.

Wams: doublet, jacket

jem.m das ~ ausklopfen (coll.) to thrash sb.; cf. Engl. coll. 'to dust sb.'s jacket'; f.r.b. Kramer [1719], e.g. Grimmelshausen, *Simpliz.* [edit. K.] 1,289; hence also *jem. wamsen*, since the 18th c., recorded by Adelung; only occasionally in lit., e.g. Jean Paul, *Flegelj.* 1,59. there are also the compounds *durchwamsen* and *verwamsen*.

jem.m Hosen und ~ ausziehen (obs.) to take away sb.'s entire possessions; *Hosen und ~* described originally sb.'s entire clothing, then extended to all his possessions; recorded by Adelung, now obs.

Wand: wall

Wände von . . . (lit.) walls of . . .; seen as a 'large mass forming a barrier or an obstacle'; beginnings in poetry in MHG, e.g. W.v.Eschenbach, *Parz.* 69,19, but in general lit. use only since the 18th c., e.g. Goethe 24,59; cf. also such instances as Freytag, *Soll u.H.* 3,8: '*heute steht die Vergangenheit als eine dunkle Wand zwischen ihm und mir*'.

in seinen (eigenen) vier Wänden in one's own home; *vier Wände* for 'house, home' has been current since MHG, but the phrase only appeared in the 18th c., f.r.b. Nieremberger [1753].

alles, was an die ~ pissen kann (vulg.) every male; biblical in origin, from 1 Sam. 25,34 (in A.V. as 'any that pisseth against the wall' and the same in Luther, but modern Bibles print: '*einer, der männlich ist*'); still used in the original wording in the 19th c., even in lit.

gegen eine ~ reden to speak without making any impression; cf. French *parler à un mur*; with some verbs such as *predigen* since Early NHG, f.r.b. Dentzler; with *reden* recorded by Eiselein [1838], who quotes as a Lat. parallel *per parietem loqui*.

es ist um die Wände hochzugehen (coll.) it is enough to drive you up a wall or round the bend; current with various verbs since the 16th c., e.g. Goethe, *Faust I*, 3939: '*um's Haar sich auszuraufen und an den Wänden hinauf zu laufen*'.

jem. an die ~ spielen (coll.) to put sb. in the shade, place sb. in an inferior position; now with many verbs, but first with *spielen* since it arose in theatr. jargon, since early in the 20th c., from ca. 1920 onwards with other verbs, e.g. *jem. an die ~ reden, singen, quatschen, schlagen*, all meaning 'to demonstrate one's superiority'.

er gehört an die ~ gestellt (coll.) he ought to be shot; a ref. to executions; modern as a coll. phrase;

weiß (or *blaß* or *bleich*) *wie eine ~* as white as chalk; e.g. Wieland, *Gandalin* 8,413: '*wie die Wand so weiß*'; cf. also Heyse, *Nov.* 2,3: '*vor der Thür stand der Nebel jetzt schon wie eine weiße Wand*'.

hier wackelt die ~ (coll.) sth. exciting or important is going on here; often with the punning addition *hier muß 'was los sein*; assumed to have originated as the cry of showmen in a fair promising that the public will laugh so much that the walls will be shaking; first in Berlin since the 1st quarter of the 19th c.; cf. Klix [1863]: '*da muß ja gleich eine alte Wand wackeln*'.

scheiß die ~ an! (vulgar) damn it! mainly as an exclamation of great disappointment, frustration or irritation; 20th c. sl., first in mil.sl.

wie an die ~ gepißt (vulg.) terribly bad and worthless (with ref. to inferior paintings); coined by the painter Max Liebermann (1st quarter of 20th c.).

← See also under *drängen* (for *jem. an die Wand drängen*), *drücken* (for *jem. an die Wand drücken*), *einrennen* (for *so dumm, daß man mit ihm Wände einrennen könnte*), *Fliege* (for *ihn ärgert die Fliege an der Wand*), *kahl* (for *kahle Wände*), *Kalk* (for *er wird wie der Kalk an der Wand*), *kleben* (for *an der Wand kleben*), *Kopf* (for *mit dem Kopf durch die Wand fahren wollen*), *malen* (for *den Teufel an die Wand malen*), *nackt* (for *die nackte Wand*), *Nagel* (for *der Nagel an der Wand ist vor ihm nicht sicher*), *Ohr* (for *die Wände haben Ohren*), *Rede* (for *wenn die Wände reden könnten*), *Rücken* (for *mit dem Rücken zur Wand stehen*), *Schande* (for *der Horcher an der Wand hört seine eigne Schand*), *Schatten* (for *er gleicht dem Schatten an der Wand*), *Scheide* (for *die Scheidewand*), *Spanien* (for *die spanische Wand*) and *trennen* (for *eine Trennwand errichten*).

Wandel: change; conduct

See under *führen* (for *einen Wandel führen*) and *Handel* (for *Handel und Wandel*).

wandelbar: see *geschmeidig*.

wandeln: change; stroll

See under *anwandeln, durchwandeln, finster* (for *Volk, das im Finstern wandelt*), *Konversation* (for *er ist ein wandelndes Konversationslexikon*), *Leichnam* (for *ein wandelnder Leichnam*), *Lexikon* (for *ein wandelndes Lexikon*), *Natur* (for *die wandelnde Natur*), *Schornstein* (for *er ist ein wandelnder Schornstein*), *Spur* (for *in or auf jem.s Spuren wandeln*), *umwandeln* and *verwandeln*.

Wandelstern: planet

ein ~ (lit., obs.) a comet-like person; *~* was recorded for 'planet' by Adelung who considered it '*unschicklich*' except for poetry, partly because it could also mean 'comet'. Campe [1811] added that it can occur figur.: '*uneigentlich, ein Ding,* *welches sich um ein anders als das hauptsächliche bewegt, sich nach demselben richtet und davon abhängt'*. He did not yet note that the main 19th c. meaning, which was 'comet', could occur figur. with ref. to 'illustrious personality', as in Goethe 28,283 (W.) referring to Lavater and Basedow: *'man behandelte mich nicht . . . bloß als den Dunstschweif jener beiden großen Wandelsterne'*, or to a 'restlessly striving personality', as in Fürst Pückler, *Briefw.u.Tageb.* 1,293: *'. . . sind sie ein Komet, ein Wandelstern, der rastlos durch die unendlichen Räume strebt'*. These and other figur. extensions quoted in *DWb.* 13,1643 [1911] are all obs.

Wanderfreude: see *Strom*.

Wanderlust: see *einsitzen*.

wandern: wander, walk

wandern (1) to pursue a path, go on one's way; since MHG, e.g. Ottokar, *Reimchronik* [edit. S.] 74958, also in Luther Bible transl. Psalm 23,4: *'ob ich schon wandert im finstern tal'*, Goethe, *Diwan (Tefkir Nameh)*: *'drum laßt uns rasch und brav und kühn die Lebenswege wandern'*, cf. also *den Weg alles Fleisches ~ =* 'to die' and Steinbach's [1734] recording *'er wandert in den Himmel'*; since the 18th c. increasingly with other abstracts, e.g. Burmeister, *Geol.Bilder* 2,238 [1855]: *'. . . Weg, den die Kultur bisher gewandert hat'*.

wandern (2) (cant) to escape; f.r.b. Ostwald, *Rinnsteinsprache* 165.

etw. wandert (1) (lit.) sth. moves around, travels, spreads; since MHG (first with *maer*), then with such abstracts as *Gerücht, Kunde, Sitte, System*, etc.

etw. wandert (2) sth. moves or lands somewhere (through having been conveyed there); passive use in essence; general since the 18th c., e.g. H.v.Kleist, *Käth. v.H.* 2,8: *'in eure Kerker klaglos würd ich wandern'*, Goethe 36,55 (W.): *'man sah das letzte Blatt mit Vergnügen in die Druckerey wandern'*; frequent now in *so ein Schund wandert in den Papierkorb =* 'such rubbish lands in the wastepaper basket'.

etw. wandert (3) sth. roams; since Early NHG, e.g. (DWb) Spreng, *Ilias* 201b [1610]: *'eins mannes sinn und mut . . . wanderet . . . an frembde ort . . . mit sein gedancken'*, recorded by Ludwig [1716]: *'er wandert mit seinen Gedancken weit umher =* he has rambling thoughts, or a wandering mind'; often with *Auge, Geist* or *Gedanke* as the subject, Wieland 10,7 has it with *Blick*.

etw. wandert über (lit.) sth. moves to a different territory, migrates; since the 18th c., e.g. W.v.Humboldt, *Ges.Werke* 3,261: *'die Wörter sind es vorzüglich, die von Nation zu Nation überwandern'*.

← See also under *auswandern, bewandert, durchwandeln* (for *durchwandern*) and *einwandern*.

Wanderstab: see *greifen*.

Wanderung: walk, journey

die Gratwanderung perilous journey or undertaking, balancing act; literally 'walk along mountain ridges'; in phys. sense since the 19th c., e.g. Barth, *Kalkalpen* 480 [1874], figur. since the 20th c.

die Seelenwanderung transmigration of souls; in its religious sense established since the 18th c., recorded by Adelung who also mentions its Greek form *Metempsychosis*; used by Herder, e.g. *Werke* [edit. S.] 15,243. Jean Paul used it frequently for 'journey undertaken by the soul', e.g. *Flegelj.* 2,57 or *Titan* 2,90.

Wandervogel: see *Vogel*.

Wandler: walker

See under *Nacht* (for *nachtwandlerisch*) and *Schlaf* (for *schlafwandlerisch*).

Wandschmied: see *Schmied*.

Wange: cheek

See under *gelb* (for *die Wangen gelb und grün*), *Purpur* (for *Wangen, die mit Milch und Purpur prangen*), *Salz* (for *Salz und Brot macht Wangen rot*) and *Strom* (for *siegswerthe Röthen überströmten flammend die Wang*).

Wankelmut: see *Gewicht*.

wanken: totter, waver

wanke nicht stand fast, do not waver; biblical, Luther Bible transl. Prov. 4,27: *'wanke nicht weder zur Rechten noch zur Linken'* (where the A.V. has 'turn not to the right hand nor to the left'). Luther also used it in the Psalms, e.g. 38,17; 69,24 and 107,27. In *Werke* 8,139b (Jena) Luther used it with ref. to *Glaube*; cf. also Wieland 2,49: *'daß Don Sylvio, wo nicht völlig wankte, doch ziemlich erschüttert wurde'*. Frequent in compounds such as *daher-, dahin-, einher-wanken*, or *entgegenwanken*, as figur. in Heine, *Lut.* 2,58: *'das Ministerium wankte seinem Untergang entgegen'*.

unwankbar unshakable, steady, firm; *wankbar* is hardly ever used, but *unwankbar* occurs fairly often in lit., current since the 17th c., e.g. Kuhlmann, *Kühlpsalter* 1,185 [1684], Wieland 11,275, Heinse, *Ardingh.* 1,96 [1794]: *'. . . Entschluß . . . stahlfest und unwankbar'*. In Rückert, *Mak.* 2,65 *Unwankbarkeit* occurs; synonymous *unwankelbar* is older and occurs in H.Sachs [edit. K.] 12,45 as *ohnwankelbar*, as *unwankelbar* in Luther 2,137 (Weimar), now obs.

← See also under *Knie* (for *jem.m wanken die Knie*)

Wanst: see *Ranzen*.

Wanze: bug

die ~ (1) (coll.) disagreeable person, vermin; since Early NHG in many contexts, e.g. Luther, *Tischr.* 293a: *'wer Erasmum zudrückt, der würget eine wantzke'*, used for 'parasite', 'intrusive person', since the 19th c. also for 'troublesome investigative reporter' since the 20th c. also for 'kibitzer', hence *wanzen* (coll.) = 'to kibitz'.

die ~ (2) (regional) drawing-pin; cf. French *punaise*; the usual term for standard *Reißzwecke* in Hesse, f.r.b. Pfister, 329.

die ~ (3) (joc.coll.) small car, mini; since the fifties of the 20th c., perhaps under influence of Engl. 'beetle'.

die ~ (4) (coll.) bug, device for overhearing people's conversation; from Engl. 'bug' since ca. 1930; the standard term is *Abhörgerät*.

unbeholfen wie eine schwangere ~ (sl.) clumsy; first in mil.sl. of 1st World War, then general sl.

frech wie eine ~ (coll.) very cheeky; since ca. 1900.

wenn das nicht gut für die Wanzen ist (,so weiß ich nicht, was besser ist) (prov.expr.) that should do the trick, ought to be strong enough to do the job; joc. expression used when extreme measures have been taken to deal with sth. unimportant; since the 1st half of the 19th c., f.r.b. (Wander) *Klosterspiegel* 92 [1841]: *'wenn das nit gut für die Wanzen ist, so wess ich nit, was gut wär', sagte der Berliner, als er hörte, daß die Spanier die Klöster sammt Mönche und Nonnen verbrennen'*, Simrock [1846]: *'wenn das nicht gut für die Wanzen ist'*. Various anecdotes reporting that this saying was coined by a bystander who saw a brothel burn and the prostitutes jump out of the windows and Wander's example [1876]: *'wenn das nicht gut für die Wanzen ist, sagte der Bauer, als sein Haus brannte'*, can be treated as later embroideries made up in the regions. In my youth I still heard it used by my parents' generation, but recent dictionaries do not record it.

verwanzt (coll.) filthy; originally = 'infested with bugs', then widened to refer to dirty conditions in general; since the 19th c.

Wappen: coat-of-arms
See under *führen* (for *ein Wappen führen* and *etw. im Wappen führen*) and *Rede* (for *das redende Wappen*).

wappnen: arm
sich mit etw. ~ to forearm oneself with sth.; figur. with abstracts since Early NHG, e.g. in Luther's writings (in 18,440 with *wappen*, in 10,2,474 with *wapnen*). In wider sense *gewappnet sein* = 'to be prepared', since the 19th c. – The phrase *mit bewappnetem Auge* = 'with the help of spectacles' has been displaced by *mit bewaffnetem Auge*, for which see p. 302.

Ware: goods, commodities
Ware (sl.) drugs; euphemism used by addicts and dealers since ca. 1960.

angreifische ~ sth. that tempts people to touch it; sometimes with ref. to an attractive woman (inviting a phys. approach), as in Immermann, *Münchh.* 1,137: *'ein Frauenzimmer, was die Mannsleute angreifen, pflegt von Hause aus angreifische Waare zu zein'*. Goethe used it with ref. to 'theft-inviting' objects, for which see p. 43.

heiße ~ (coll.) illegal, smuggled or stolen goods; since the 1st quarter of the 20th c. (also used for 'drugs'); cf. entry under *heiß* (p. 1279).

gute ~ *hält sich* (prov.expr.) quality goods last; usually quoted with ref. to one's state of health, as much as to say 'I am not bad for my age'; modern.

leichte ~ (coll.) things (or persons) of little value or importance; since the 17th c. in many contexts including abstracts; sometimes used for 'girls of easy virtue'; cf. similar *leichtes Tuch* (p. 2454).

← See also under *absetzen* (for *Waren absetzen*), *bücken* (for *Bückware*), *flüstern* (for *Flüsterware*), *halten* (for *ein Frauenzimmer, welche mit ihrer Waare nicht feste hielt*), *Hering* (for *Heringsware*), *Rauch* (for *Rauchwaren empfangen*) and *schwarz* (for *schwarze Ware*).

warm: warm
warm (1) enthusiastic, full of fervour or ardour; beginnings in MHG where it could mean 'desirous for sth.'; Luther's use, e.g. in 10,162 (Weimar) is nearer to 'full of fervour', by the 18th c. = 'enthusiastic', e.g. Wieland 5,181.

warm (2) excited, agitated; since the 17th c., f.r.b. Stieler [1691]; it is this which led to ~ = 'furious' in the 18th c., e.g. Schiller, *Fiesco* 4,14. Cf. the entry under *Kopf*.

warm (3) lively, fresh, youthful, hearty, loving, lovable; the group only established itself in the 18th c.; often with *Leben*, e.g. Schiller, *Kab.u.L.* 3,4 or *Blut*, e.g. Goethe 1,13, or 1,45 or 6,24 (W.). The range includes 'passionate', e.g. Herder [edit. S.] 22,181, Wieland, *Agathon* 4,1, Goethe, *Faust I*, 1799, also 'enamoured', as in Lessing, *Em.Gal.* 1,4, 'temperamental', as in Lessing, *Nathan* 5,8. 'warm' emotions from 'tender-hearted' to 'sensuous' are represented, also with abstracts, e.g. Wieland 5,149: *'warme Einbildungskraft'*.

warm (4) devoted, affectionate; since the 18th c., often with *Freund*, but also with *Eifer, Gefühl, Herz, Seele* or *Teilnahme*, e.g. Goethe 17,122 (W.). Often close to 'enthusiastic' (see above); cf. also the entries under *erwärmen* (p. 692).

warm (5) comfortable, pleasant, agreeable; beginnings in Early NHG, e.g. Luther's use of *'umb einen rock wermer'* in 16,31 (Weimar) for 'getting or feeling better'; since the 18th c. often in *in etw.* or *mit jem.m* ~ *werden* = 'to warm to sth. or sb.', recorded by Kramer [1702], e.g. Lessing 12,245: *'von Wolfenbüttel aus wieder eine Reise, ehe ich noch da warm geworden'*.

warm (6) warm; an off-shoot from *warm* (3), used with ref. to colours, sounds or tunes since the 18th c., e.g. Wieland, *Ob.* 7,51 or Goethe 25,1,234 (W.); frequent in *warme Worte*.

warm (7) (adv.) warmly; mostly with *danken* or *empfehlen*, also as *wärmstens*; since the 18th c. (Goethe used it with *danken*).

etw. ist noch ~ sth. is still fresh, of (quite) recent date; since Early NHG; sometimes with allusion to milk straight from the cow or sth. still hot from the pot, with *Braten* in Schiller, *Fiesco* 1,9: hence also *warme Fährte* = 'recent or fresh track' in hunt. jargon (since the 18th c.), but also transferred and used with ref. to the pursuit of criminals; cf. *brühwarm* listed in the cross-references.

es wird einem ~ *ums Herz* one experiences a heart-warming emotion; this can refer to affection or love, but also to feelings of being safe or protected; since the 18th c., e.g. (DWb) Wieland 21,63, Goethe, *Faust I*, 3492; recorded by Adelung.

etw. ~ *halten* to look after, preserve or nurture sth.; since the 17th c., recorded by Kramer [1702], since the 18th c. also with ref. to abstracts.

jem.m ~ *machen* to excite, disturb or worry sb.; since the 17th c., e.g. Logau 1,8,35, Wieland, *Musarion* 1: '*macht dir mein Antrag warm?*'; cf. *es wird einem* ~ *bei der Sache*, recorded by Stieler [1691]. - Note the dative, since when the accusative is used, *jem.* ~ *machen* describes 'pleasing sb. or making sb. enthusiastic about sth.', as in Herder [edit. S.] 15,262: '*sie machen mich nicht warm, sondern böse, wenn sie . . .*'.

(sich) jem. ~ *halten* to make sure that sb. remains well-disposed (towards oneself); since the 18th c., recorded by Frisch [1741].

dort geht es ~ *zu* (coll.) there is much going on there; this can refer to 'heated' discussions, 'hot' battles or 'lively' goings-on; Adelung recorded it, mentioning its various contexts; still current, at least in some regions.

mit jem.m ~ *werden* (coll.) to begin to take to sb., arrive at a friendly relationship with sb.; since the 19th c.

sich ~ *anziehen müssen* (coll.) to have to reckon with sth. difficult or unpleasant, be prepared for the worst; coll. of the 2nd half of the 20th c. but Müller-Fraureuth in 1911 recorded: '*da muß mer warm angezogen sein = viel Geld einstecken haben*' for areas of Saxony. This may be connected, but could also simply refer to 'being well-padded, rich'., since other areas have *ein Warmer* for 'rich man'.

ein warmer Bruder (coll.) a homosexual; since late in the 18th c., e.g. Döblin, *Berlin Al.* 404.

warme Zeichen (astrol.) the signs of Aries, Leo and Sagittarius; translates *signa calida*; f.r.b. Ch. Wolff, *Mathem. Lex.* 1269 [1716].

lieber warmer Mief als kalter Ozon (sl.) rather have warm air, even if it is stuffy than fresh air which is too cold; 20th c. sl., in essence another version of the joc. saying: *es ist schon mancher erfroren, aber noch keiner erstunken*

← See also under *blasen* (for *kalt und warm blasen*), *Blut* (for *warmes Blut* and *mit warmem*

Blut), *Brühe* (for *etw. brühwarm erzählen*), *Eisen* (for *man muß das Eisen schmieden, solange es warm ist*), *kalt* (for *daß du kalt oder warm wärest*), *Kopf* (for *jem.m den Kopf warm machen*), *Nest* (for *sich ins warme Nest setzen*), *Niere* (for *seine Nieren liegen warm*), *Regen* (for *warmen Regen abbekommen*), *Semmel* (for *es geht weg wie warme Semmeln*) and *sitzen* (for *warm sitzen* and *warmgesessen*).

Wärme: warmth
die ~ warmth; figur. use following the adj. *warm* (3); since the 18th c. (not yet recorded by Kramer [1702]).

← See also under *binden* (for *gebundene Wärme*), *Nest* (for *Nestwärme*) and *schinden* (for *Wärme schinden*).

wärmen: warm
etw. wärmt jem.s Herz sth. warms sb.'s heart ;beginnings in OHG, where (e.g. in Notker's Psalms) the Holy Spirit is described as 'warming' a person, but general and in secular contexts only since the 18th c., when *warm* and *Wärme* were extended to the emotional sphere.

← See also under *aufwärmen*, *Droschke* (for *sich durchwärmen wie ein Droschkenkutscher*), *durchwärmen*, *erwärmen* (also for *herzerwärmend*), *Glanz* (for *sie glänzen nicht, diese Tugenden, aber sie wärmen*) and *Hand* (for *sich Hände wärmen*).

Wärmflasche: hot-water bottle
die ~ (joc. coll.) partner in bed; modern coll.

die ~ (sport.sl.) stone in curling; so called because in shape it resembles an old-fashioned tin hot-water bottle; only since the 2nd half of the 20th c.

warmgesessen: see *sitzen*.

warnen: warn
etw. warnt (lit.) sth. warns; figur. with abstracts as the subject since Early NHG, e.g. Luther 34,2,80 (Weimar), recorded by Franck [1541]; frequent since the 18th c., e.g. Goethe 1,16 (W.) or *Iphig.* 4,1: '*die Sorge . . ., die mich warnt*'.

Warnung: see *Tag*.

Warschau: see *Ordnung*.

Warte: watch-tower
auf hoher ~ (lit.) on a high vantage-point; figur. since Early NHG, e.g. Freiligrath, *Werke* [edit. Z.] 1,264: '*der Dichter steht auf einer höhern Warte als auf den Zinnen der Partei*'.

Warteinweilchen: see *nichts*.

warten: wait
etw. wartet auf jem. sth. awaits sb.; figur. with abstracts as the subject since Early NHG, e.g. Luther Bible transl. Acts 20,23: '*bande und trübsal warten mein daselbs*' (cf. also Psalm 145,15); also in non-lit. use now, e.g. *in meinem Amtszimmer wartet viel Arbeit auf mich*.

darauf habe ich gerade gewartet (ironic) that is all I wanted (i.e. the last thing I wanted to have or see); modern.

auf etw. ~ to wait for sth.; with abstracts since MHG, at first with the genitive; frequent in the

Bible, e.g. Job 30,26, Psalm 48,10, later with *auf*, e.g. Schiller, *Picc.* 2,6: '*du wirst auf die Sternenstunde warten, bis dir die irdische entflieht*'.

warte nur! (coll.) just wait, give me time; implying a threat that punitive action will soon be taken; since the 18th c., used in this sense by Goethe, Schiller and Kleist, e.g. Müllner, *Dram.Werke* 5,315: '*wartet nur! Euch heiz' ich wohl noch ein*' Immermann, *Münchh.* 1,283: '*nun warte! Dafür sollst Du heute Deine Strafe kriegen.*'.

← See also under *abwarten, aufwarten, fein* (for *fein lange auf sich warten läßt*), *Schlag* (for *einen Schlag warten*) and *schwarz* (for *er kann warten, bis er schwarz wird*).

warum: why
das ~ the reason; first used by the Mystics, e.g. Eckhardt (in *Myst.* 2,131), Wieland, *N.Amadis* 79: '. . . *und vom Warum das Warum erklärt*' er an *den Fingern Euch her*', Goethe even used *die Warums* in 11,188 and 37,201 (W.); Stieler [1691] recorded '*es ist ein köstliches warüm vorhanden*'.

~ nicht gar! (coll.) why should I? denotes refusal, but sometimes also astonishment; first in N. coll. in the 18th c., then also elsewhere; much older is *~ nicht?* = ' (and) why not?', since the 15th c. denoting a concession, willingness to yield to sb.'s argument or proposal, sometimes as *~ denn nicht*.

jedes Warum hat sein Darum (prov.) there is a reason for everything; recorded by Simrock [1846] as '*kein Warum ohne Darum*'.

Warze: see *bereden*.

Wäsche
dumm aus der ~ gucken (coll.) to look dumbfounded, flummoxed; modern coll.

jem.m an die ~ gehen (coll.) to assault sb.; modern coll.

← See also under *Katze* (for *Katzenwäsche*).

waschecht: see *echt*.

waschen: wash
sich ~ (bibl., lit.) to make oneself clean, purify oneself; non-reflex. since MHG in relig. contexts, then reflex. as in Luther Bible transl. Isaiah 1,16 (where the A.V. has 'wash you, make you clean'), also Schiller, *Phaedra* 4,2: '*du giebst dich schuldig, um dich rein zu waschen*'.

jem.m den Kopf ~ (coll.) to give sb. a reprimand, tell sb. off; general since the 17th c.; from older *jem. ~* = 'to punish, beat sb.' (still alive in some regions).

eine Antwort, Ohrfeige, etc., die sich gewaschen hat (coll.) a most effective, sound answer, box on the ear, etc.; since the 17th c., f.r.b. Ludwig [1716], e.g. Weiße, *Kom.Opern* 3,9.

Geld aus verbotenen Einkünften ~ (coll.) to launder money from illegal sources; loan from Engl., since the last quarter of the 20th c.

er hat ein ungewaschenes Maul (coll.) his speech is full of obscenities; details on p. 2527.

verwaschen unclear, indistinct; cf. Engl. 'wishy-washy'; derived from phys. 'faded through frequent washing or pale through too much thinning with water'; modern in figur. sense with abstracts.

← See also under *abwaschen, aufwaschen, auswaschen, Gesicht* (for *er hat viel Gesicht zu waschen*), *Gurgel* (for *die Gurgel waschen*), *Hals* (for *da steh' ich da mit meinem gewaschenen Hals*), *Hand* (for *seine Hände in Unschuld waschen* - also listed under *Unschuld* - and *eine Hand wäscht die andere*), *Lauge* (for *jem. mit scharfer Lauge waschen*), *Mohr* (for *einen Mohren weiß waschen wollen*), *Pelz* (for *den Pelz waschen und nicht naß machen*), *rein* (for *ich wasch ihn rein von aller Schuld*), *sauber* (for *etw. sauber waschen*), *Schimmel* (for *des verjährten Grolles Schimmel wascht ihn ab*), *Schmutz* (for *seine schmutzige Wäsche in der Öffentlichkeit waschen*) and *ungewaschen*.

waschhaft
waschhaft (a.) talkative; since Early NHG, e.g. Luther Apocr. transl. Ecclesiasticus 25,26: '*weschaftig weib*': *Waschhaftigkeit* has been in use since the 18th c., e.g. Wieland, *Sylv.* 7,3. Adjective and noun are no longer listed in recent dictionaries.

Waschlappen: see *Lappen* (also for *waschlappig*).

Waschung: see *Kehle*.

Waschweib: washerwoman *er ist ein ~* (coll.) he is a thoughtless gabbler, incurable gossip; applied to men since the 18th c. (Schiller used '*kaudern wie ein Waschweib*'), recordings only since the 19th c. in the pejor. sense.

Wasser: water
das ~ des Lebens (bibl.) God's word and revelations; since MHG, based on Revelations 22,17.

zu ~ werden to dissolve into nothing, fade away, become worthless; since Early NHG, e.g. Luther 26,383 (Weimar): '. . . *wird sein tropus zu wasser*', Goethe 46,279 (W.); hence also *etw. zu ~ machen* = 'to reduce sth. to nothing', since the 16th c., still in Lessing, *Minna* 5,3; now obs.

. . . wie ~ in great amounts, in masses; since MHG, e.g. Luther Bible transl. Psalm 73,10: '. . . *lauffen inen zu mit hauffen, wie wasser*' (cf. also Psalm 79,3).

etw. läuft jem.m vom Munde wie ~ sb. speaks sth. fluently; with ref. to rapid speech or to knowledge of a foreign language; since MHG, e.g. *Passional* [edit. K.] 415.

etw. läuft an jem.m ab wie ~ it is like water off (or on) a duck's back; since the 18th c., with a different noun in Goethe, *Briefe* 8,118 (W.): '*es fliest wie Wasser an einem Wachstuch ab*'.

ein Stein (or *eine Perle*) *von reinstem ~* a gem (or a pearl) of the purest water; f.r.b. Frisius [1556], e.g. Goethe 17,145 (W.), Schiller, *Kab.u.L.* 1,4 (with *klar*).

ein Schlag ins ~ a fruitless undertaking; in this form only since the 19th c., but *ins* ~ *schlagen* = 'to achieve nothing' goes back to MHG, e.g. Th.v.Zirclaria, *Wälsche Gast* 14644 and Eyering [1601] recorded '*es ist nichts denn ein wasserschlagen*'; cf. also *das ist ins Wasser geschrieben* = 'that does not last, will disappear as soon as it is done', since the 18th c., used by Goethe.

jem.m nicht das ~ *reichen können* to be far inferior to sb.; derived from the mediaeval custom of appointing a servant (or a page at court) to hold out a bowl with water to guests after a meal; as a phrase current since Early NHG, even with abstracts, as in Luther 4,155a (Jena): '. . . *von diesen historien . . . das inen alle andere das wasser nicht reichen*' (cf. also his transl. of 2 Kings 3,11); f.r.b. Stieler [1691]; in later periods sometimes with *bieten* instead of *reichen*.

das ~ *tritt (schießt, läuft) jem.m in die Augen* sb. breaks into tears; ~ with ref. to tears has been in use since MHG; with *treten* recorded by Steinbach [1734], with *schießen* the phrase occurs in Wieland, *Lucian* 1,287.

mit allen Wassern gewaschen experienced, clever, familiar with all the tricks; modern with *allen*, but in similar phrases current since the 17th c. (cf. *DWb*. 13,2239).

durch ~ *und Feuer für jem. gehen* to face all kinds of dangers or difficult times for (the love of) sb.' figur. since the 18th c.

ins ~ *gehen* (coll.) to drown oneself; presumably old, but in lit. apparently only since the 18th c.; cf. Goethe 21,163 (W.), where *springen* is used.

jem. über ~ *halten* (coll.) to keep sb. safe, rescue sb.; often with ref. to rescues of sb. in financial difficulties; literally 'to keep sb. afloat'; at least since the 18th c., e.g. (DWb) Bode, *Montaigne* 5,11; Goethe in *Briefe* 29,156 (W.) used it in a reflex. construction for 'to stay unperturbed and happy'.

das ~ *läuft einem im Mund zusammen* (coll.) it makes one's mouth water; at least since the 17th c., e.g. Grimmelshausen, *Simpliz.* [edit. K.] 1,99: '. . . *daß mir das maul gantz voll wasser ward*'; with *zusammenlaufen* in H.v.Kleist, *Amph.* 3,8.

über dem ~ *wohnen auch Leute* there are people on the other side of the ocean, too; also in wider sense 'you are not the only person in the world'; since the 17th c., e.g. Moscherosch, *Phil.* 2162 [1642]; cf. *das große* ~ = 'the ocean', often with ref. to the Atlantic and emigration to America (only since the 19th c.).

jem.m ~ *in die Schuhe schütten* (coll.) to offend sb.; also used for 'to play sb. a trick', e.g. Kirchhof, *Wendunm.* 1,366; earlier used for 'to put the blame for sth. on sb.', recorded by Petri [1605]: '*es wolte jederman gern sein unrein wasser in eines andern schuh schütten*'; see also under *Schuh* for *jem.m in die Schuhe brunzen.*

sie hat nahe ans ~ *gebaut* (coll.) she weeps very easily, sheds tears over every little mishap; recorded since the 19th c., e.g. by Albrecht for Leipzig [1881], e.g. Holtei, *Lammf.* 1,35.

das ~ *ist das Auge der Landschaft* water is the eye of the landscape; German lexicographers attribute this saying to Lenne, landscape gardener in Potsdam; he may have coined it, but he could have heard it in its Engl. form from sb., since Lean in his *Collectanea* 4,175 [1902–4] recorded it as prov. in Engl.

bei ~ *und Brot sitzen* to be in prison; the phrase is old with ref. to living in reduced circumstances (cf. also Eiselein's recording [1838]: '*Einen auf Wasser und Brot setzen*'), but later used particularly with ref. to prison.

← See also under *Aal* (for *wer einen Aal fangen will, macht erst das Wasser trüb*), *abgraben* (for *jem.m das Wasser abgraben)* *abschlagen* (for *sein Wasser abschlagen*), *abschrecken* (for *Wasser abschrecken*), *Bach* (for *Wasser in den Bach tragen*), *Balken* (for *Wasser hat keine Balken*), *begießen* (for *jem. mit kaltem Wasser begießen*), *Bims* (for *Bims bringt selten Wasser*), *Blut* (for *Blut ist dicker als Wasser*), *brechen* (for *der Krug geht solange zum Wasser, bis er bricht*), *Brot* (for *sein Brot aufs Wasser werfen*), *dienen* (for *Feuer und Wasser sind zwei gute Diener*), *entlaufen* (for *dem Regen entlaufen und ins Wasser fallen*), *ertränken* (for *Wein im Wasser ertränken*), *ertrinken* (for *es ertrinken mehr im Glas als im Wasser*), *fahren* (for *das alte Fahrwasser*), *fallen* (for *die Wasser fielen* and *ins Wasser fallen*), *faul* (for *vom faulsten Wasser*), *Feuer* (for *Feuer und Wasser mischen wollen*), *Fisch* (for *gesund wie ein Fisch im Wasser, ich han in grozen wazzern vil gevischet* and in *trübem Wasser ist gut fischen*), *fließen* (for *meine Augen fließen mit Wasser*), *gießen* (for *Wasser in jem.s Wein gießen* and *Wasser in ein Sieb gießen*), *Gurgel* (for *Gurgelwasser*), *Hals* (for *das Wasser geht ihm an den Hals*), *hinabfließen* (for *bis dahin fließt noch viel Wasser den Rhein hinab*), *Kapuziner* (for *Kapuzinerwasser*), *Kiel* (for *in jem.s Kielwasser folgen*), *Knie* (for *aller knie werden so vngewis stehen wie wasser*), *kochen* (for *dort wird auch nur mit Wasser gekocht*), *Mühle* (for *das ist Wasser auf seine Mühle*)), *Müller* (for *es fehlt dem Müller an Wasser* and *jeder Müller leitet das Wasser auf seine Mühle*), *Rotz* (for *Rotz und Wasser weinen*), *saufen* (for *mensch, der unrecht seufft wie wasser, Blut saufst du wie Wasser* and *sauffe Wasser wie ein Ochs*), *Schaukel* (for *Schaukelwasser*), *Schaum* (for *falsch wie Schaum auf dem Wasser*); *Scheide* (for *das Scheidewasser*), *schöpfen* (for *Wasser mit dem Sieb schöpfen wollen*), *schwimmen* (for *auf dem Wasser schwimmen, er hat in allen Wassern geschwommen* and in *jem.s Kielwasser schwimmen*), *Seele* (for *jem.m geht das Wasser an die Seele*), *Spree* (for *er ist mit Spreewasser getauft*), *spülen* (for *die Suppe schmeckt wie Spülwasser*), *Stange* (for *eine Stange Wasser in die Ecke stellen*), *stehlen* (for *gestohlen Wasser ist Wein*), *still* (for *er ist ein stilles Wasser* and *stille Wasser sind tief*), *Strumpf* (for *deine Strümpfe ziehen Wasser*), *Teufel* (for *er fürchtet sich davor wie der Teufel vorm Weihwasser*), *trübe* (for *trübes Wasser, das Wasser trüben* and *er sieht aus als könnte er kein Wässerchen trüben*), *Überwasser* (for *Überwasser bekommen*), *Vieh* (for *sauft Wasser wie das liebe Vieh*) and *wild* (for *wildes Wasser*).

Wasserapostel
der ~ sb. who recommends water as a panacea; slightly derogatory; since the 19th c.

wasserarm
wasserarm suffering from a shortage of water; it can refer to areas with a scarcity of rivers, to 'arid' soil and also to rivers with a deficient flow of water, as in Klopstock, *Messias* 20,701; hence *Wasserarmut*, since the 19th c.

Wasserast
der Wasserast (regional) wild shoot; since the 18th c.; Adelung recorded it adding '*welche auch Wasserschüsse heißen, zum Unterschiede von Holz- und Fruchtästen*'; Campe [1811] stated that *Wasserschoß* was the better term.

Wasserberg: see *Berg*.
Wasserblase: see *Blase*.
Wasserblühen: see *blühen*.

Wasserdichter
der ~ (rare) inferior poet, producer of insipid literature; since the 18th c., e.g. Heine [edit. E.] 5,326.

Wasserfall
reden wie ein ~ (coll.) to talk incessantly (and very rapidly); since the 19th c., e.g. Heine [edit. E.] 5,109. Similarly, *er hat die Wassersucht* (coll.), recorded by Wander [1876].

Wassergeträufel: see *flüstern*.
Wasserglas: see *Sturm*.
Wassergrab: see *Grab*.
Wasserhose: see *Hose*.
Wasserjungfer: see *Jungfer*.

Wasserkopf
der ~ (coll.) stupid fellow; term of abuse since early in the 19th c.

ein ~ (sl.) overstaffed authority; since the first half of the 20th c.

wässern
See under *bewässern*, *durchwässern* and *Heu* (for *der eine wässert die Wiese, der andre fährt das Heu ein*).

Wasserpfarrer
der ~ (coll.) Sebastian Kneipp; the parson Kneipp (1821–97) became famous through his treatment of many ailments by the application of water; since early in the 20th c.

Wasserrate: see *Ratte*.
wasserscheu: see *scheu*.
Wasserschlagen: see *Wasser*.
Wasserspiegel: see *Spiegel*.

Wasserstiefler: see *Strumpf*.

wasserstoffblond
wasserstoffblondes Haar (coll.) hydrogen peroxide blond hair; a ref. to chemically bleached hair; since early in the 20th c.

Wasserstrahl
jem.m einen kalten ~ *senden* (coll.) to calm sb. or urge sb. to calm agitation; coined by Bismarck early in 1874, when he called his request to French authorities to put an end to the agitations of French bishops in Alsace-Lorraine '*einen kalten Wasserstrahl*' The phrase ultimately goes back to one listed under *begießen*.

Wassersucht: see *Wasserfall*.

waten: wade
in etw. ~ (1) (lit.) to wade in sth.; since MHG, used especially with ref. to *Blut* or *Sünde*; e.g. Schiller, *Räuber* 4,2 (with *Totsünde*).

in etw. ~ (2) (coll.) to have more than enough of sth.; hyperbole as in the case of *schwimmen*; since the 19th c., e.g. G.Hauptmann, *Weber* 38.

watscheln
See under *Ente* (for *watscheln wie eine Ente*) and *Gans* (for *watscheln wie eine Gans*)

Watte: cotton wool
jem. in ~ *packen* (or *wickeln*) (coll.) to treat (or shelter) sb. with great care; since the 19th c., e.g. (H.) Wildenbruch, *Nov.* 14 on a spoilt daughter: '. . . *daß er sie in Watte packte*'.

hast du ~ *in den Ohren?* (col.) can't you hear? recorded since the 19th c., e.g. *D.richt.Berliner* 110 [1882].

wattieren: pad
mit etw. wattiert (coll.) stuffed, crammed full of sth. (other than cotton wool); since the 19th c., used e.g. with ref. to a well-padded wallet; e.g. Gutzkow, *R.v.G.* 4,252.

Webe: weaving, woven material
das Gewebe (1) (lit.) tissue, veil, atmosphere; here *weben* = 'to weave' and *weben* = 'to move about' (cf. the entry under *webern* below) are combined, and Herder used *Gewebe* frequently in this sense, e.g. '*ein schwebendes Gewebe*', '*Gewebe der Luft*'; Goethe used it in *Nat.Tochter* 1,1: '*laß dieser Lüfte liebliches Geweb uns leis umstricken*'; cf. Mörike, *Ges.Schr.* 1,52: '*wie ein Gewebe zuckt die Luft manchmal*'.

das Gewebe (2) tissue; here 'movement' plays no part, but figur. usage refers to the structure or combination of parts in sth. woven (by loom or nature); since early in the 18th c., e.g. Lessing, *Die Religion* 1: '*das thörichte Geweb aus Laster, Fehl und Tugend*' (cf. Engl. 'a tissue of lies'); frequently used by Herder, e.g. '*im Gewebe meiner Natur*', '*das Gewebe seines Buchs*', '*das Gewebe sichtbar machen, was menschliche Natur heißt*'; then also used by Wieland, Goethe and Klinger.

das beste ~ *wird zu Haus gesponnen* (prov.) home-made things are best; a rare survival of ~, recorded by Wander (1876).

← See also under *Duft* (for *nicht mit so duftiger Web umspannt die Balken Arachne*), *Netz* (for *das Gewebe seiner Talente*), *Spinne* (for *Spinnewebe, Spinnwebe* and *Spinnengewebe*) and *weben* (for *Gewebe des Schicksals*).

weben: weave

etw. ~ (lit.) to contrive or produce sth.; with many abstracts, e.g. *jem.s Schicksal* since the 17th c., frequent with *Kette, Netz, Verbindung* since the 18th c., e.g. Schiller, *Glocke* on *Ordnung*: '. . . . *die das theuerste der Bande wob, den Trieb zum Vaterlande*'; there is also *Ränke ~* = 'to hatch plots, intrigue, plot and scheme', modern with *~* (earlier with *schmieden, spinnen* or *ersinnen*). It can also occur in reflex. locutions, e.g. Wieland, *Oberon* 7,90: '*ein neues zartres Band webt zwischen ihnen sich*'. There is also *an etw. ~* e.g. Wieland 17,179: '*spinnen und weben wir Alle an dem unendlichen Gewebe des Schicksals*'.

← See also under *Duft* (for *es webt um meine Wipfel noch der Erinnrung Duft*) *durchweben, einweben, Faden* (for *jetzt mußte gewoben werden* and *aus grobem Faden gewebt*), *leben* (for *leben und weben*), *Netz* (for *er webte fein mit falschem Mund das Netz*), *Spinne* (for *er hört die Spinnen weben*), *spinnen* (for *Metaphysicus webt ein durchsichtiges Gespinste*), *Teppich* (for *er webt emsig seines Liedes Riesenteppich*) and *verweben*.

Weberknecht

der ~ (zool.) daddy-long-legs; this crane-fly of the Order *Opiliones* has many names in German, one of them, *Müller*, listed on p. 1718. Other terms recorded for it since the 18th c., are *Geißhirt, Habergeiß, Müllermaler, Schuster* and *Zimmermann* (details in *DWb.* 13,2663).

webern: move to and fro

webern (a.) to move to and fro; an old word, now obs.; Luther used it in his Bible transl. Psalm 65, 9, where modern editions put '*weben*' and the A.V. has 'makest the outgoings of the morning and evening to rejoice'; Droste-Hülshoff still used *~* when writing of a phantom: '*es webert auf und nieder*'.

Webfehler

er hat einen (coll.) he is nuts; modern coll.

Webstuhl: loom.

der ~ (lit.) loom; figur. only since the 18th c. with such abstracts as *Traum, Geist, Natur*; best known perhaps through *~ der Zeit* in Goethe, *Faust I*, 508 (also used by Stolberg, Heine, Geibel); cf. also *etw. in den ~ spannen* = 'to commence work on sth.', as in H.Hesse, *P.Camenzind* 242.

← See also under *Rose* (for *die ganze Erde war ein Webstuhl rosenroter Träume*).

Wechsel: change; bill of exchange

See under *Keller* (for *Kellerwechsel*), *reiten* (for *Wechselreiter*), *Szene* (for *Szenenwechsel*) and *trocken* (for *trockener Wechsel*).

Wechselbalg: see *Balg*.

Wechselfall

der ~ (mainly in pl) unpleasant change(s), vicissitudes; can include a wide range from mishap to catastrophe, certainly in most cases a 'change for the worse'; since early in the 18th c., f.r.b. Ludwig [1716], e.g. Goethe, *Briefe* 40,209 (W.): '. . . *was für Wechselfälle . . . mich beunruhigt haben*'.

wechseln: change

See under *abwechseln, austauschen* (for *auswechseln*), *Bruder* (for *die reimarten wechseln*), *Farbe* (for *die Farbe wechseln*), *Karte* (for *sie wechselten die Karten*), *Kugel* (for *Schicksal, das immer wechselnd seine Kugel dreht* and *Kugeln wechseln mit jem.m*), *Ring* (for *den Ring mit jem.m wechseln*), *Spiel* (for *der Farben wechseln Spiel*), *steigern* (for *wir wechseln, wir steigern das Spiel*), *Tapete* (for *die Tapeten wechseln*) and *verwechseln*.

Wechselneigung: see *deuten*.

wechselseits: see *erwärmen*.

wechselweise: see *tragen*.

wecken: wake

etw. ~ to rouse, wake, awaken or arouse sth.; figur. with abstracts (or things taken in their extended sense) since Early NHG, e.g. Luther Bible transl. Isaiah 50,4: '*er wecket mir das ohr*', Schiller, *M.Stuart* 3,1: '*warum aus meinem süßen Wahn mich wecken?*', *Glocke* 381: '*gefährlich ist's den Leu zu wecken*'; often in *Erinnerungen, Gefühle, Gedanken ~* , but with *Mut* already in MHG.

jem. zu etw. ~ (lit.) to stimulate, encourage, incite sb. to some activity; without *zu etw.* as early as in MHG (though locutions with *uf* occur); with *zu* (or *für*) *etw.* general since the 18th c., e.g. Klopstock, *Oden* [edit. M.] 2,158: '*der Künste Blumen können zur Heiterkeit auch wieder wecken*', Novalis [edit. Minor] 1,18: '*noch weckst du, muntres Licht, den Müden zur Arbeit*'.

← See also under *aufwecken* and *erwecken*.

wedeln: see *Schwanz* (also for *Schwanzwedeln*).

weder

weder . . . noch . . . neither . . . nor; since MHG, e.g. *Nibelungenl.* 2185: '*weder schilt noch wâffen*'; later also *weder . . . weder . . .*, as in Goethe, *Iphig.* 3,1: '*weder Hoffnung, weder Furcht*', *Faust I*,2607: '*bin weder Fräulein, weder schön*'. For *entweder . . . oder* see p. 661.

← See also under *aus* (for *weder aus noch ein wissen*), *ein* (for *weder eins noch keins*), *Fisch* (for *weder Fisch noch Fleisch*), *hauen* (for *weder gehauen noch gestochen*), *leiden* (for *weder zu Liebe noch zu Leide*), *Stiefel* (for *es hat weder Stiefel noch Sporn*) and *Strich* (for *weder Strich noch Stich halten*).

Weg: way

der ~ (1) (bibl. and lit.) way of life, path (followed or to be followed), behaviour, conduct; taken over from Hebrew and from the Greek of the New Testament and frequent in the Bible, e.g. Psalms 1,1; 1,6; 37,5 and 119,9, Jerem. 32,19. Latin *vitae via* led from MHG onwards to *lebens weg*, e.g. Goethe, *Tasso* 4,2 and *Herm.u.Dor.* 5,204; frequent in *der rechte ~* , recorded since the 12th c. (for other locutions with adjectives see the list of cross-references below). *Gottes Wege* (cf. Psalm 103,7, Jerem. 55,8, Romans 11,33) has been current since Early NHG; later also in *die Wege der göttlichen Vorsehung* and secularized in *die Wege des Schicksals* or *des Zufalls* (cf. also Schiller, *Fiesco* 3,4: '*himmlische Vorsicht . . . deine Wege sind sonderbar*').

der ~ (2) the (right) approach, the (proper) course to adopt, the (suitable) method; with such verbs as *finden, kennen, suchen, weisen, wissen* or *zeigen* frequent since Early NHG, e.g. Luther 16,265 (Weimar) with *finden*, with *zeigen* f.r.b. Frisius [1556], e.g. *den rechten ~ zum himmel weisen*, as in Ringwald, *Christl. Warn.* Dla. – Note that *jem.m den ~ zeigen* can also be used for 'to show sb. the door, send sb. packing', f.r.b. Stieler [1691], e.g. Kotzebue, *Dram.Spiele* 2,266: '*zeig ihm den Weg zur Pforte*'.

der ~ (3) (personified) the way; personified in the nominative with such verbs as *gehen, führen, tragen* or *hintragen*, all since MHG; since the 18th c. also with *sich winden* or *schlängeln, steigen, fallen, sich ziehen, laufen, gleiten* or *sich teilen*; for details and examples see under the cross-references.

des Weges or *seines/ihres Weges gehen, fahren, laufen*, etc. to go on one's way, follow one's course; in phys. sense since Early NHG, figur. only since the 18th c., e.g. Herder [edit. S.] 17,232, when ~ had come to be used in the sense discussed under ~ (1).

seinen ~ machen to make progress, advance, succeed, prosper; in phys. sense for 'to go on one's way'; figur. for 'to advance, make one's way successfully' only since the 18th c., e.g. Schiller, *Picc.* 1,1, but since the 19th c. also with abstracts for 'to gain support, spread'.

etw. ist auf dem Wege zu etw. sth. is in the process of . . ., is about to . . ., has begun to . . .; figur. since the 18th c., e.g. Schiller, *Räuber* 2,3: '*wenn Deutschland so fortmacht, wie es bereits auf dem Wege ist . . .*'; with a person as the subject in Schiller, *Kab.u.L.* 3,6; frequent in *er ist auf dem Wege zur Besserung*.

etw. fällt auf den ~ (a.) sth. makes no impression, fails to have any positive result, does not bear fruit; also with *an* instead of *auf*; a ref. to the seeds not growing roots because they have not been put in fertile soil from Matth.13,4; still current in the 19th c., e.g. Gutzkow, *Zaub.v.Rom* 5,270; now a., if not obs.

etw. ist auf guten Wegen (a.) sth. is progressing well, developing satisfactorily; since Early NHG, f.r.b. Maaler [1561], still used by Lessing, *Misog.*

1,4 and Goethe 22,232 (W.); now a., but there is still *etw. hat gute Wege* = 'sth. is taking its proper course, is happening as it should (or as one hoped)'; since the 18th c., e.g. Lessing, *Nathan* 4,7, F.H. Jacobi 5,163: '*und so hatte Alles gute Wege*'.

damit hat es gute Wege (coll.) that is not a pressing matter, need not trouble us yet; ironic in essence; at least since the 19th c.

etw. liegt auf dem (or *im*) *Wege* sth. fits into one's plans, thoughts or activities; the ref. is to some place which one passes on a journey and which one includes in one's itinerary; therefore sometimes = 'it offers itself conveniently'; since the 18th c. in lit. (used by Schiller), now rare, perhaps obs.; the negative also occurred, e.g. (DWb) F.v.Schlegel 6,149: '*das würde eine eigne Abhandlung erfordern, die jetzt nicht auf unserm Wege liegt*'. Cf. obs. *es ist aus dem Wege* = 'it is inappropriate', used from MHG period until the 18th c.

jem.m (or *einer Sache*) *aus dem Wege gehen* to avoid sb. (or sth.); since Early NHG, e.g. Luther 19,418 (Weimar); with abstracts only since the 18th c.

etw. aus dem ~ räumen (or *schaffen*) to remove sth., push sth. aside; since Early NHG, also occasionally with ref. to abstracts and persons; later (at least since the 18th c.) also for 'to abolish or destroy sth.' and with ref. to persons 'to kill sb.', when it became synonymous with *aus der Welt schaffen*, for which see p. 2073.

aus dem ~ geraten to lose one's way (also one's thread); figur. when straying from one's subject, having become side-tracked; since the 18th c., e.g. Lessing, *Laok.* 2.

im Wege sein (or *stehen*) to be in the way, constitute a hindrance; since Early NHG, f.r.b. Maaler [1561]; see also *im ~ stehen* (p. 2347).

jem.m etw. in den ~ legen to cause sb. trouble with sth., obstruct sb. with sth.; since Early NHG (also with *setzen* and *stellen*); also in reflex. locutions as in Luther 32,424 (Weimar): '. . . *das sich der teufel . . . ynn wege legt*', Goethe 21,278 (W.): '*ein unerwartetes Hinderniß legte sich in den Weg*'; recorded by Ludwig [1716].

etw. in die Wege leiten to prepare (the ground for) sth.; first in civil service language, initially with *bringen*, since the 18th c. with *leiten*, e.g. Goethe, *Briefe* 12,23 (W.).

in alle Wege (coll.) in every way, totally; Luther 3,94a (Jena) used *in allweg*, also *allewege* in Psalms transl. 119,44 for 'always'; Lessing and Wieland used *in alle Wege*. Some modern writers still use it for 'always' in the form *allerwegen*, whereas Goethe in *Nachspiel z.d. Hagestolzen, 2.Gruppe* used it for 'everywhere': '*Getreide, mannshoch, allerwegen*'. His use of *allerwegs* in *Faust I*,3014 is ambiguous and could mean 'always' or 'everywhere'.

jem.m nicht über den ~ trauen to trust sb. as far as one can see him; since the 18th c., e.g. (DWb) Gotter 3,131, Herder [edit. S.] 24,71. In earlier periods *jem.m nicht weiter trauen als die Augen sehen* was used (since Early NHG).

den ~ unter die Füße nehmen (regional coll.) to start on one's way, get going; beginnings in MHG, when *den ~ vor sich nehmen* was used; with *Füße* since Early NHG, f.r.b. Frisius [1556], now mainly in Alemannic regions. There is a variant with *unter die Beine nehmen* and sometimes *zwischen* can be used, e.g. Heine [edit. E.] 3,25: '*jetzt will ich den Weg zwischen die Beine nehmen*'.

etw. zuwege bringen to achieve, manage sth.; since Early NHG, e.g. Luther Bible transl. Ezek, 28,4 and Acts 22,28.

jem.m auf halbem Wege entgegenkommen to meet sb. halfway; figur. with ref. to compromises since the 18th c., e.g. Goethe 3,29 (W.) or *Iphig.* 1,2.

auf halbem Wge stehenbleiben to fail to pursue sth. to the end; since the 18th c., e.g. (DWb) Gerstenberg, *Recensionen* (repr.) 78.

bei Wege (regional, N.) by the way, in passing; recorded since the 18th c. for N. areas, occasionally in lit.; in some regions *nicht bei Wege* means 'not at all', rare in lit., though it occurs in Immermann, *Münchh.* 1,106.

eineweg (regional coll.) at any rate; in some regions used for *jedenfalls* or *immerhin*, e.g. (Sa.) Scherr, *Graziella* 1,273 [1852]: '*jedennoch thut mirs eineweg leid ums Kätherle*'.

eines Weges (regional coll.) rather, to some extent; in some contexts close to the previous entry, e.g. (Sa.) v.Horn, *Rh.D.* 2,18: '*daß die Liebe blind sei, ist doch eines Wegs dumm*'.

auf keine Wege (obs.) in no way, not at all; still general in the 18th c. and used by Goethe; others used *in keine Wege*, e.g. Müllner, *Dram. W.* 4,199; it followed on *in keinen ~*, as in Luther 5,327a (Jena), also as *in keinem ~*, as in Schweinichen *Leben* [edit. v.Büsching] 2,133; now *keineswegs* has displaced the longer forms, since the 18th c., also used by Goethe.

der Unweg (obs.) wrong way, impassable road (or method), cul-de-sac; since MHG, figur. since Early NHG, e.g. Luther Bible transl. Job 12,24, Lehman 1,141 [1662]: '*irrwisch . . . führen die leut immer auf unweg*'. Adelung skill recorded it as current for 'wrong road', now obs. except in some dialects where it can also mean 'detour'; the adj. *unwegsam*, current since OHG, is still in use.

von Worten zu Werken ist ein weiter ~ (prov.) from words to deeds is a great space; at least since the 17th c., when Lehman 1,153 [1662] recorded it; the Engl. version recorded since the 16th c.

wo ein Wille ist, ist auch ein ~ (prov.) where there's a will, there's a way; late in German (still missing in the standard prov. dictionaries of the 19th c.), and in Engl., too, in current form only since the 19th c.

← See also under *abbringen* (for *vom rechten Weg abbringen*), *abschneiden* (for *jem.m den Weg abschneiden*), *Abweg* (also for *abwegig*), *Ausweg*, *Bahn* (for *einen Weg bahnen*), *bauen* (for *wer am Wege baut, hat viele Meister*), *betreten* (for *das Betreten eines Weges, Fahrweg der Gedanken, Betreten des Rechtswegs, Betretung des Gnadenwegs* and *den betretenen Weg verlassen*), *dehnen* (for *der Weg dehnt sich*), *eben* (for *jem.m die Wege ebnen*), *ein* (for *eine viertel Stunde in Einem Weg*), *einschlagen* (for *einen Weg einschlagen*), *entführen* (for *sie werden edle Gemüther dem geraden Wege der Pflicht entführen*), *erleichtern* (for *gut Gespräch erleichtert den Weg*), *Fahrweg*, *Finger* (for *ihm sind die Finger bei der Arbeit im Wege*), *Fleisch* (for *den Weg alles Fleisches gehen*), *führen* (for *der weg der do furt zu dem leben* and *es führte mich der Weg*), *Fuß* (for *den ordentlichen Weg verlassen*), *gehen* (for *so geht der Weg bald herauf, bald herab* and *hier geht kein Weg*), *gerade* (for *der gerade Weg, geradezu ist der nächste Weg, geraden Wegs* and *geradenwegs*), *geraten* (for *daß du nicht geratest auf den Weg der Bösen*), *glatt* (for *der weg stat offen nacht und tag*), *glitschen* (for *du hast einen langen weg für dich genummen*), *Grind* (for *nur halbe Wege säubern*), *halb* (for *halbweg*), *Herkules* (for *Herkules am Scheideweg*), *Hölle* (for *der Weg zur Hölle ist mit guten Vorsätzen gepflastert*), *irre* (for *Irrweg*), *kalt* (for *auf kaltem Wege*), *Kreuz* (for *am Kreuzweg stehen*), *krumm* (for *krumme Wege gehen*), *laufen* (for *ein Weg läuft, seinen Weg laufen* and *etw. läuft jem.m in den Weg*), *Mittel* (for *Mittel und Wege finden* and *Mittelweg*), *neben* (for *nebenhin geht auch ein Weg*), *Rom* (for *alle Wege führen nach Rom*), *Scheide* (for *am Scheideweg*), *Schlag* (for *jem.m den Weg verschlagen*), *schleichen* (for *Schleichweg*), *sperren* (for *jem.m den Weg/Rückweg sperren*), *Steg* (for *Wege und Stege*), *stehen* (for *jem.m im Wege stehen*), *Stein* (for *jem.m Steine in den Weg legen*), *trennen* (for *unsere Wege trennen sich hier*), *um* (for *der Weg ist um*), *umkehren* (for *auf halbem Wege umkehren*), *Umweg*, *verlegen* (for *jem.m den Weg verlegen*) and *wandern* (for *die Lebenswege wandern* and *Weg, den die Kultur bisher gewandert hat*).

weg: away

See under *abschneiden* (for *es ist weg wie abgeschnitten*), *Ende* (for *da ist das Ende von weg*), *Faden* (for *an einem Faden weg*), *Faust* (for *von der Faust weg*), *Fleck* (for *vom Fleck weg*), *gerade* (for *geradeweg*), *heben* (for *hebe dich weg von mir*), *Leber* (for *frisch von der Leber weg*), *sein* (for *er ist weg*) and *weit* (for *weit weg*).

wegangeln

jem.m etw. ~ (coll.) to snatch sth. from sb., deprive sb. skilfully of sth.; since the 18th c., e.g. Wieland, *Agathon* 8,3; the same in essence as *wegfischen* (see p. 800); cf. also *weggabeln* (p. 897), *wegkapern* (p. 1436), *wegmolchen* (p. 1705) and *wegschnappen* (p. 2159).

wegarbeiten

jem. ~ (obs.) to surpass sb. at work; f.r.b. Kramer [1702], still in occasional use in the 19th c., now obs.

wegbannen

etw. ~ (lit.) to banish sth.; with abstracts since the 18th c., e.g. Goethe 13,1,345 (W.), Herder [edit. S.] 12,180, but *verbannen* (see p. 2546) is the preferred compound; see also the notes on *bannen* (p. 186).

wegbeißen

jem. ~ (coll.) to get rid of sb. by making life unpleasant to him; same as *fortbeißen* (see p. 235), but older, used by Luther 32,42 (Weimar).

wegbeizen

etw. ~ (rare) to remove sth. by harsh methods; figur. with abstracts since the 18th c., now rare.

wegblasen

See under *blasen* (for *blas mir den Staub weg, jem. wegblasen* and *wie weggeblasen*), *Luft* (for *als Spreu wegblasen*) and *Rauch* (for *Rauch des Lebens wegblasen*); cf. also *fortblasen* (p. 836).

wegbleiben: see *Luft*.

wegblicken

von etw. ~ to overlook sth. deliberately; figur. when no actual 'looking' is involved, since the 18th c., recorded by Campe [1811], but not yet by Adelung.

wegblühen: see *blühen*.

wegbrennen

wegbrennen (intrans.) (lit.) to burn away; figur. with ref. to 'consuming itself in heat' since the 18th c., e.g. Herder [edit. S.] 9,376; also possible in transitive locutions for 'to destroy sth. by fire, heat, passion', unusual with ref. to health, as in Goethe, *Briefe* 1,217 (W.); cf. also *etw. aus etw. brennen* in the quotation from Goethe, *Tasso* 1,3 on p. 393.

wegbringen

jem. von etw. ~ to deprive sb. of sth., make sb. give up sth., wean sb. from sth.; with abstracts since the 18th c., e.g. Goethe 8,277 (W.).

etw. ~ (1) (obs.) to be finally left with sth., keep sth. as a residue; with abstracts since Early NHG, still current in the 18th c., e.g. Lessing 12,116: '*der einzige Vortheil, den ich davon wegbringen werde . . .*'; now obs.

etw. ~ (2) to remove sth.; with abstracts only since the 19th c. (not yet listed in Adelung or Campe).

wegbügeln

etw. ~ (coll.) to iron or smooth out sth. (differences, difficulties, etc.); modern (Campe [1811] only mentions the phys. meaning); cf. *ausbügeln* (p. 124) and *geradebügeln* (p. 421).

wegbugsieren: see *bugsieren*.

wegdrängen

wegdrängen (intrans.) to wish to distance one-self from sb. or sth.; belongs to intrans. *drängen*, as in *es drängt mich* = 'I feel an urge . . .' (see p. 492); modern in this sense, which is not even listed in *DWb.* [1922]. Older in transit. *jem.* or *etw.* ~ , figur. with abstracts since the 18th c., e.g. Herder [edit. S.] 15,520.

wegdrücken

sich ~ to slip away; current since the 18th c., e.g. Goethe, *Egmont* 5, but coll. *sich verdrücken* (see p. 506) is preferred.

wegen

von ~ (coll.) no, not to be thought of, out of the question; expressing opposition or refusal; since ca. 1800.

~ *mir* (coll.) as far as I am concerned . . . I don't mind (if . . .); in locutions where one wants to express indifference about sb.'s actions or plans, e.g. ~ *mir kann er wählen, wen er will.* It occurs in the same kind of contexts as *von mir aus* (which see on p. 2600).

← See also under *Otto* (for *von wegen Otto*).

wegfallen: see *fallen* (also for *in Wegfall kommen*).

wegfangen: see *fangen*.

wegfegen: see *fegen*.

wegfischen: see *Fisch*.

wegflattern: see *flattern*.

wegfliehen: see *Glück*.

wegfluten: see *Flut*.

wegfressen: see *fressen*.

weggabeln: see *Gabel*.

weggehen

weggehen (1) to pass (away); with ref. to time since Early NHG, but now less frequently used than *vergehen* (see p. 2553); cf. also *hingehen* (2) on p. 1333.

weggehen (2) to go away, disappear; since Early NHG, e.g. Schottel, *Hauptspr.* 1118 [1663]: '*die Krankheiten kommen zu Pferde, . . . gehen aber zu Fuß . . . wieder weg*'.

weggehen (3) (euphem.) to die; since the 18th c., e.g. Herder [edit. S.] 26,14: '*genieße dein Leben, als müssest morgen du weggehn*'; cf. *hingehen* (3) on p. 1333.

← See also under *Semmel* (for *es geht weg wie frische/warme Semmeln*).

Weggenosse

der ~ (lit.) companion on a journey, fellow-traveller (but not in the polit. sense); modern term, patterned on *Zeitgenosse*; not listed in *DWb.*

weggleiten

über etw. ~ (lit.) to pass lightly over sth. (as though it were of no importance); since the 18th c., e.g. (DWb) Kant 5,74.

weggucken

über etw. ~ (coll.) to overlook sth. deliberately; occasionally in lit., e.g. Schiller, *Kabale u.L.* 1,1;

cf. *hinwegsehen* (p. 1345), also *wegblicken* and *wegsehen*.

weghaben

etw. ~ (1) (coll.) to have (obtained, acquired) sth.; f.r.b. Stieler [1691]; in modern period usually with ref. to an unpleasant acquisition such as an illness, e.g. (DWb) Prutz, *Holberg* 248: '*wenn die Republik einmal einen Knacks weg hat . . .*', Bismarck, *Ged.u.Erinn.* 2,85: '*. . . wir hätten die französische Ohrfeige weg*'; also with ref. to death, as in Bürger's *Macbeth* transl. 5,3: '*. . . die Königinn - hat's weg*'.

etw. ~ (2) (coll.) to have grasped, got the hang of sth.; since the 18th c., f.r.b. Ludwig [1716], e.g. Lessing, *Miss S.S.* 4,8.

jem. ~ (1) (coll.) to be rid of sb.; since Early NHG, e.g. Luther 29,105 (Weimar); Campe [1811] recorded '*ich habe den Überlästigen glücklich weg*'.

jem. ~ (2) (coll.) to have sb.'s number, see through sb., realize what sb. is up to; since the 18th c., e.g. Lessing, *D.j.Gel.* 1,6.

einen ~ (coll.) to be drunk; ellipsis of the 19th c. for several regions; in some areas it is also used for 'he is not quite right in the head', with ellipsis of *Hieb* or some similar term indicating brain damage.

er hat es bei mir weg (coll.) I am through with him; at least since the 18th c., e.g. Lessing, *Misogyn* 3,6, recorded by Adelung; mainly in E. areas.

wegheben: see *heben*.

weghelfen: see *Troß*.

wegholen

sich etw. ~ (coll.) to bring away or catch sth.; figur. with abstracts, esp. unwanted ones, e.g. *er hat sich eine Ansteckung weggeholt*, where *geholt* would suffice - see *holen*.

wegkapern: see *kapern*.

wegkommen

etw. ist weggekommen sth. has been lost (or stolen), has gone astray; since Early NHG, e.g. Luther Bible transl. Ecclesiastes 12,6 (where the A.V. has 'be loosed').

aus (or *bei*) *etw. gut (schlecht, übel)* ~ to come off well (badly); since ca. 1700 e.g. Lessing 7,354, Goethe 8,25 (W.), Schiller, *Kab.u.L.* 2,1; cf. *rupfen* (for *ungerupft entkommen*, where *ungerupft wegkommen*, used by Goethe in a letter to Schiller (5,161) could have been added), *Auge* (for *mit einem blauen Auge davonkommen*) and entries under *davonkommen* (p. 457).

über etw. ~ to get over sth.; general since the 18th c. in two contexts, either for 'to overcome (e.g. difficulties)' = *überwinden*, as in Goethe 49,32 (W.), or for 'to get over (disappointment, set-back)' = *sich hinwegsetzen*, as in E.Th.A.Hoffmann 4,82: '*was den Ärger betrifft, über den wird er wegkommen*'; cf. entry on *hinwegkommen* (p. 1345).

wegkriegen: see *Mund*.

weglassen: see *Loch*.

weglaufen

weglaufen to run away, desert; since Early NHG both for desertion by a marriage partner and in mil. contexts, lastly also with ref. to servants who have absconded.

etw. läuft nicht weg (coll.) sth. is not going to run away, will still be there later; since the 19th c.

← See also under *Hahn* (for *über alles läuft er doch weg, wie der Hahn über die Kohlen*).

wegmachen

sich ~ (coll.) to make oneself scarce, steal away; since Early NHG, e.g. Luther Bible transl. Psalm 55,8 (where the A.V. has 'I would hasten my escape'); Steinbach [1734] recorded '*er machte sich über Hals über Kopf weg*'; in coll. usage also = 'to die', recorded since the 18th c., e.g. (DWb) v. Canitz, *Ged.* 223.

etw. (coll.) to achieve, accomplish sth.; since the 17th c., e.g. Goethe, *Br.* 10,247 (W.): '*ich bin fleißig und mache meine Sachen weg*'; hence admiringly: *der macht was weg!* (coll.) = 'he gets through an amazing lot, is a quick worker'; modern.

sie hat das Kind weggemacht (coll.) she has had an abortion; 20th c. coll. (not yet recorded in *DWb*. [1922]).

wegmolchen: see *Molch*.

Wegnarr: see *Narr*.

wegnehmen

See under *Bissen* (for *jem.m den Bissen vorm Mund wegnehmen*) and *nehmen* (for *sie nehmen es Gott vom Altar weg* and other entries under *nehmen* (1), where *wegnehmen* could also be used).

wegpacken

pack dich weg! (coll.) buzz off! scram!; *sich* ~ = *sich wegmachen* has been current since the 17th c.; see under *packen* for synonymous *davonpacken, fortpacken* and *hinwegpacken* (p. 1823).

wegpflücken: see *pflücken*.

wegputzen: see *putzen*.

wegraffen: see *raffen* (also for *hinwegraffen*).

wegrasieren

etw. ~ to remove sth. completely, wipe sth. out; figur. only since the 20th c., recorded by *DWb*. (1922).

wegräubern: see *rauben*.

wegräumen: see *forträumen*.

wegrauschen: see *Rausch*.

wegreden

jem.m etw. ~ to relieve sb. of sth. by talking about it; since the 18th c., when Jean Paul used it, e.g. (Sa.) Spielhagen, *Pr.* 8,191: '*du kannst mir diese fürchterliche Last . . . nicht wegreden*.

wegreißen: see *reißen*.

wegrinnen

wegrinnen (lit., rare) to flow or trickle away; in occasional figur. use since the 18th c., e.g.

Goethe 16, 328 (W.): '*das Kleinliche ist alles weggeronnen*'; cf. similar compounds listed on p. 1999.

wegrücken

von jem.m (or *etw.*) ~ to distance oneself from sb. (or sth.); since the 19th c. (not yet in Campe in figur. sense), e.g. Immermann, *Münchh.* 4,30; cf. *ferner* or *weit weg rücken* on p. 2016.

wegrufen

etw. ruft jem. weg (lit.) sth. calls sb. away, bids sb. to go away; figur. since the 18th c. with abstracts as the subject, e.g. Goethe 9,427 (W.): '*mich rufen andre Sorgen weg von hier*'.

wegrutschen

etw. rutscht weg (coll.) sth. slips away; occasionally figur., as in Goethe, *Briefe* 23,242 (W.): '*die Zeit rutscht weg, man weiß nicht, wo sie hinkömmt*'; cf. *fortrutschen* (p. 2034).

wegsacken

wegsacken (coll.) to fall down, collapse, faint; modern, not listed in *DWb.* [1922]; cf. *umfallen wie ein Sack* (p. 2040).

wegsäubern: see *sauber*.

wegsaugen

etw. ~ (lit.) to suck sth. away; since late in the 18th c. (but in Campe [1811] only recorded in its phys. meaning), e.g. (Sa.) Waldau, *Nach der Natur* 3,235 [1850]: '*der Zudringliche hatte ihr alle Luft weggesaugt*'.

wegschaffen

etw. ~ to remove, eliminate sth.; with ref. to abstracts since Early NHG; it can also refer to persons = 'to drive away, dismiss'; cf. also *beiseite* (for *beiseite schaffen*), *Hals* (for *sich etw. vom Halse schaffen*) and *Leib* (for *sich etw. vom Leibe schaffen*).

sich ~ to commit suicide; modern, not listed in *DWb.* [1922].

Wegscheide

an einer ~ *stehen* (lit.) to stand at a crossroads; ~ has been in use for 'crossroads, fork in the road' since Early NHG; figur. for 'point where a choice between alternatives has to be made (or was made)' only since the 19th c. (in Campe '*Wegescheide*' is listed only in its phys. sense), e.g. *an einer historischen* ~ *stehen*.

Wegscheißer

der ~ (regional coll.) sty (in the eye); recorded for many regions since the 19th c., though probably much older; a sty was traditionally considered to be punishment for sb. who had defecated on the road (or in some areas, in a cemetery, against a lime tree or even when facing the moon). The standard term is *Gerstenkorn* (for which see p. 993).

wegscheren: see *scheren (2)*.

wegscheuchen: see *scheuchen* (also under *Hof*).

wegschieben

etw. (von sich) ~ to push sth. away, decline

acceptance of sth.; with abstracts such as *Sorge* or *Verantwortung* since the 18th c. (not recorded by Kramer [1702] who only listed synonymous *etw. von sich schieben*).

wegschlagen

etw. von der Hand ~ (obs.) to manage or deal with sth. without any trouble or great effort; e.g. Lessing 12,517; now obs.

wegschleichen: see *schleichen*

wegschleudern

etw. ~ (lit.) to throw sth. away; since the 18th c., e.g. Schiller, *M.Stuart* 5,10: '*welch Glück des Himmels hab' ich weggeschleudert!*'; often the same as *verschleudern* = 'to waste' (see *schleudern*).

wegschlüpfen: see *schlüpfen*.

wegschmeißen

etw. ~ (coll.) to discard or eliminate sth.; rare with abstracts, but often in figur. contexts where no 'throwing' is involved, e.g. Goethe 32,79 (W.). It can also be used for 'to waste' (since the 18th c.)

sich ~ (coll.) to throw oneself away, make oneself cheap; since the 19th c., often with ref. to a marriage to a partner who is socially inferior; cf. *sich wegwerfen*.

wegschmelzen

etw. schmilzt weg sth. melts away; with abstracts since the 18th c., e.g. Lichtenberg 4,263: '*so schmolzen jene Werke der Kindheit weg*'.

wegschnappen: see *schnappen*.

wegschnarchen: see *schnarchen*.

wegschneiden: see *schneiden*.

wegschwemmen: see *schwemmen*.

wegschwinden

etw. schwindet weg (lit.) sth. fades away, disappears; figur. since the 18th c., e.g. Goethe, *Götz v.B.* 1.

wegsehen

etw. ~ to remove sth. by looking at it; marginally figur., like *wegdenken*; since Early NHG, e.g. Luther 46, 361 (Jena): '*du wirst die schlangen nicht wegsehen*'.

von etw. ~ to turn (one's eyes) away from sth.; figur. when not referring to actual 'seeing' since the 18th c., e.g. Herder [edit. S.] 5,81. Sometimes, also since the 18th c., used for deliberately ignoring sth. (cf. *hinwegsehen* on p. 1345).

wegsein

er war ganz weg (coll.) he was astonished, beside himself (with surprise); since the 18th c.; cf. similar *außer sich sein* (p. 173), *aus der Fassung bringen* (p. 735), *aus dem Häuschen sein* (p. 1257).

wegsein (coll.) to be unconscious, to have fainted; also used for 'to be drunk' (18th c.), 'to have fallen asleep' (19th c.), 'to be not quite right in the head' (19th c.) and 'to be dead' (20th c.).

über etw. ~ (coll.) to have overcome (or got over) sth.; recorded since the 19th c.; cf. *hinaussein* (p. 1330).

KEY TO PRINCIPAL ABBREVIATIONS

jem.m	jemandem (dat.)
Kluge	F. Kluge, *Etymologisches Wörterbuch der deutschen Sprache*, 11th ed., Berlin und Leipzig 1934.
Lehman	C. Lehman, *Florilegium Politicum*, etc., Frankfurt 1640.
Lexer	M. Lexer, *Mittelhochdeutsches Handwörterbuch*, Leipzig 1872—8.
LG	Low German
Lipperheide	F. Freih. v. Lipperheide, *Spruchwörterbuch*, 2nd ed., München 1909.
MHG	Middle High German
mil.	military
M. Latin	medieval Latin
N.	Northern Germany
NED	*Oxford English Dictionary, A New English Dictionary on Historical Principles*, Edited by Sir James Murray, Henry Bradley, W. A. Craigie and C. T. Onions. Oxford 1884—1928.
NHG	New High German
NW	North-Western Germany
obs.	obsolete
OE	Old English
offic.	in civil service language
OHG	Old High German
ON	Old Norse
OS	Old Saxon
Oxf.	*The Oxford Dictionary of English Proverbs*, compiled by W. G. Smith, Oxford, 1935.
p.	page
poet.	used mainly in poetic language
pop.	popular
pop. etym.	popular etymology
prov.	proverb, proverbial
sb.	somebody
Schmeller	J. A. Schmeller, *Bayerisches Wörterbuch*, Stuttgart 1827—37.
Schulz-Basler	G. Schulz und O. Basler, *Deutsches Fremdwörterbuch*, Strassburg und Berlin 1913ff.
s.e.	self-explanatory
sl.	slang
S. Singer	S. Singer, *Sprichwörter des Mittelalters*, Bern 1944—7.
sth.	something
SW.	South-Western Germany
Trübner	*Trübners Deutsches Wörterbuch*, herausg. v. A. Götze, Berlin 1939ff.
v.	verse, verses
vulg.	in vulgar use (obscene terms are included under this heading, but specially marked as such)
Waag	A. Waag, *Die Bedeutungsentwicklung unseres Wortschatzes*, 5th ed., Lahr 1926.
Wb.	Wörterbuch
Weigand	F. L. K. Weigand, *Deutsches Wörterbuch*, 5th ed., Gießen 1909—10.
Weist.	Weistümer; usually the collection by J. Grimm, Göttingen 1840—69 is referred to; Österr, is appended to the Austrian collections.
Westph.	Westphalia, Westphalian
zool.	zoological term.

Where later editions than those cited above have been quoted (especially in the cases of Büchmann, Dornseiff and Kluge), details of the editions used are given in the text.

The abbreviations for journals mostly follow the accepted practice (*MLR* for *Modern Language Review*, *MLN* for *Modern Language Notes*, *IF* for *Indogermanische Forschungen*, etc.), only some long titles have been still further abbreviated though still left recognizable (e.g. *Z.f.d.W.* for *Zeitschrift für deutsche Wortforschung*, *Z.f.d.U.* for *Zeitschrift für den deutschen Unterricht*, *Z.f.r.P.* for *Zeitschrift für romanische Philologie*, etc.). Other works, referred to or quoted have been mentioned in abbreviated but recognizable form. It is intended to give a comprehensive list of them when the dictionary is completed. From Fasc. 9 Goethe (W.) = Weimar edition, Schiller (S.) = Säkularausgabe.

ISBN 0-631-19806-7

An Historical Dictionary of German Figurative Usage

By KEITH SPALDING

PROFESSOR EMERITUS OF GERMAN, UNIVERSITY COLLEGE OF NORTH WALES, BANGOR

WITH ASSISTANCE FROM
GERHARD MÜLLER-SCHWEFE

PROFESSOR EMERITUS OF ENGLISH, UNIVERSITY OF TÜBINGEN

Fascicle 56

wegsetzen – wohlig

KEY TO PRINCIPAL ABBREVIATIONS

a.	archaic
Adolphi	O. Adolphi, *Das große Buch der Fliegenden Worte, etc.*, Berlin n.d.
Ahd. Gl.	*Die Althochdeutschen Glossen*, ges. und bearb. von E. Steinmeyer u. Eduard Sievers, Berlin 1879—98.
Bav.	Bavaria, Bavarian
bot.	botanical term
Büchmann	G. Büchmann, *Geflügelte Worte*, 27th ed., ergänzt von A. Langen, Berlin 1915.
c.	century
Car.	Carinthia, Carinthian
cf.	compare
cl.	cliché
Cod.	codex
coll.	in colloquial use
comm.	used in language of commerce
dial.	dialect expression
Dornseiff	F. Dornseiff, *Der deutsche Wortschatz nach Sachgruppen*, Berlin und Leipzig 1934.
dt.	deutsch
DWb	*Deutsches Wörterbuch von Jacob Grimm und Wilhelm Grimm*, Leipzig 1854ff.
e.l.	earliest locus or earliest loci
etw.	etwas
Fast. Sp.	Fastnachtspiele, usually quoted after *Fastnachtspiele aus dem 15. Jahrbundert*, herausgeg. v. Keller, Stuttgart 1853.
Fick	F. C. A. Fick, *Vergleichendes Wörterbuch der indogermanischen Sprachen*, 3rd ed. Göttingen 1874.
f.r.b.	first recorded by
gen.	general
Götze	A. Götze, *Frühneuhochdeutsches Glossar*, 2nd ed., Bonn 1920.
Graff	E. G. Graff, *Althochdeutscher Sprachschatz*, Berlin 1834—42.
Hirt, *Etym.*	H. Hirt, *Etymologie der neuhochdeutschen Sprache*, 2nd ed.; München 1925.
Hirt, *Gesch.*	H. Hirt, *Geschichte der deutschen Sprache*, 2nd ed., München 1925.
hunt.	word or expression used by huntsmen
jem.	jemand (nom. or acc.)

© *Blackwell Publishers Ltd., 1996 ISBN 0 631 201858*
Typeset by Hope Services, Abingdon
Printed and bound by Whitstable Litho Ltd., Whitstable, Kent.

von etw. ~ (coll.) to be carried away by sth.; with ref. to enthusiasms or to having fallen in love; since the 18th c.; cf. *ganz hin sein* (p. 1328).

← See also under *sein* (for *er ist weg*).

wegsetzen
sich über etw. ~ to make light of or disregard sth., refuse to take sth. to heart; since the 18th c., e.g. Klopstock 12,72, but *sich hinwegsetzen* (which see on p. 1345) is preferred; cf. also *hinwegkommen*.

wegspringen: see *springen*.

wegspülen
etw. ~ (lit.) to wash or flush sth. away; since the 18th c.; also used for 'to drown sth. (by drinking alcohol)', for which see under *hinunterspülen* (p. 1344).

wegstecken
er kann das nicht ~ (coll.) he cannot cope with that; used in two contexts: a.) 'he fails to manage or achieve it', b.) 'he cannot get over (or manage to forget) it'; both are 20th c. coll. (not yet recorded in *DWb.* [1922]).

wegstehlen: see *stehlen*.

Wegsteuer
die ~ *nicht mehr haben* (regional coll.) to be unsteady on one's feet; usually referring to intoxication; recorded by Eiselein, 630 [1838] and still by Wander [1876]; strangely missing in *DWb.* [1922], also not listed in recent *Duden* editions, but in my youth I heard it used frequently.

wegtauchen
wegtauchen (coll.) to slip away unobtrusively, make oneself scarce; 20th c. coll.; cf. *untertauchen* (p. 2439).

wegtreten
weggetreten sein (coll.) to be absentminded, a little distracted; 20th c. coll.

wegwaschen: see *Spur*.

Wegweiser
der ~ guide; since Early NHG used for persons (also for stars), by Adelung recorded for persons but not yet for publications, whereas Campe listed it for both; Eiselein [1838] recorded ~ *und Leithammel* and referred to Latin *dux caperque* as a parallel.

wegwerfen
etw. ~ to throw sth. away, dispose of sth.; with abstracts since Early NHG; for 'to waste' since the 18th c. (cf. *Geld zum Fenster hinauswerfen* on p. 761); cf. also the entry on *fortwerfen* (p. 840). Of recent origin are *Wegwerfgesellschaft* and *Wegwerfware*.

sich ~ to throw oneself away, make oneself cheap, waste oneself; often with ref. to a marriage to a socially or intellectually inferior partner; not yet listed by Adelung, but recorded by Campe [1811].

wegwerfend dismissive; with ref. to words, remarks or gestures; since the 19th c., but not yet recorded by Campe.

← See also under *ausdrücken* (for *etw. wegwerfen wie eine ausgedrückte Zitrone*), *Spiel* (for *etw. wegwerfen wie ein altes Spielzeug*) and *Sturm* (for *ist der Sturm vorbei, wirft man's Gebetbuch weg*).

wegwischen
etw. ~ (lit.) to wipe sth. away; with ref. to abstracts since the 18th c., e.g. Wieland [Acad. Edit.] 1,2,3 or Herder [edit. S.] 20,112.

wegzaubern
etw. ~ to remove sth. (as if) by magic; mainly in such comparisons as *verschwinden wie weggezaubert*, since the 18th c., e.g. (DWb) Kleist, *Briefe* [edit. B.] 88.

Wegzehrung
die ~ (relig.) viaticum; at least since the 17th c., often also as *heilige* or *letzte* ~.

wegziehen
See under *Fuß* (for *jem.m den Boden unter den Füßen wegziehen*), *Geiß* (for *nur so viel wie eine Geiß wegziehen kann*) and *Riegel* (for *die Ereignisse haben seiner Denkart manche Hemmriegel weggezogen*).

Weh: pain, sorrow
das Wohl und ~ the weal and woe; old formula, current since Early NHG, first with ref. to an individual's condition, e.g. H.Sachs [edit. K.-G.] 17,53: '. . . *haben gelitten wol und weh mit einander*'; since the 18th c. also with ref. to communities, the State, etc., e.g. Herder [edit. S.] 27,207.

die Geburtswehen birth pangs, labour pains; figur., at first mainly with ref. to lit. productions since the 18th c., but the extension to non-phys. labour pains goes back to Greek (Socrates).

die Nachwehen painful consequences, aftermath; figur. since Early NHG, when Keisersberg used the term, even then in the plural, in the forms *die nachweegen* and *nachwewen*, recorded by Aler, *Dict.* [1727]: '*die Nachwehe wird kommen = sera poenitentia te subibit*'.

← See also under *ach* (for *ach und weh schreien*), *falsch* (for *falsche Wehen*), *Heimweh* and *Saal* (for *ich winsle voll von Weh in diesem Thränen-Saal*).

wehen: blow
See under *anwehen*, *Saite* (for *im wunderbaren Wehn der Abendglocken*), *verwehen* and *Wind*.

Wehmut: wistfulness, nostalgia
See under *einlullen* (for *Gefühl der Wehmut*), *ergreifen* (for *Wehmut ergreift mich*), *Mond* (for *der Mond schaut mit Wehmuth darauf hinab*) and *schleichen* (for *Wehmut schleicht mir ins Herz hinein*).

wehmütig: see *trauern*.

Wehmutter
die ~ (obs. or regional coll.) midwife; since Early NHG, e.g. Luther Bible transl. Gen. 3517, also 38,25 and Exod. 1,15; still in use in some areas, in some regions as *Wehfrau*, but in the standard language displaced by *Hebamme*; cf.

also Gildemeister's transl. of Shakespeare, *Richard II*, 2,2: '*du Green, bist meines Wehs Hebamme worden*'.

wehren: resist, defend oneself

See under *Abwehr, Brust* (for *Brustwehr*), *fertig* (for *die handfertige, wehrhafte Frau*), *Hand* (for *sich mit Händen und Füßen wehren*), *Haut* (for *werte sich mit ernstheit ze hiute und ze hâre*), *Nagel* (for *sich mit stumpfen Nägeln wehren*), *verbieten* (for *waz man uns wert, das wolle wir haben*) and *verwehren* (for *unverwehrt*).

wehtun: hurt

See under *Finger* (for *ihm tut kein Finger mehr weh*), *Fliege* (for *nicht so viel wie einer Fliege im Auge weh tät*) and *Name* (for *daß es dir namhaft weh tut*).

Weib: woman, wife

See under *alt* (for *altes Weib, Altweib*), *betrügen* (for *ein schön Weib ist ein stummer Betrug*), *binden* (for *wie eng gebunden ist des Weibes Glück*), *Blücher* (for *geblüchert, was Weiber, Wein und Würfel angeht*), *ein* (for *man und wîp mir ist all ein*), *Fisch* (for *reden wie ein Fischweib*), *Floh* (for *weiber hüten: einer wannen vol flöh hüten*), *Hyäne* (for *da werden Weiber zu Hyänen*), *Kind* (for *Weib, Kind und Kegel*), *Kreuz* (for *ach gott, ein creuz und weib hast geben mir*), *Krone* (for *ein tugendsam weib ist eine krone ihres mannes*), *Kröte* (for *ein wîp ich heime lie, diu ist ein toerschiu krot*), *Not* (for *Not lehrt ein alt Weib tanzen*), *Nuß* (for *Nußbäume, Esel und Weiber wollen geschlagen sein*), *Rasse* (for *ein Weib von Rasse*), *schwach* (for *Schwachheit, dein Nam' ist Weib*), *Teufel* (for *Teufelsweib*), *Überweib* and *Waschweib*.

Weiberblume

die ~ (obs. or regional) menstruation; in print since the 16th c. (also as *Weiberfluß*); see also under *Blume* (pp. 355 and 356).

Weiberfeind

der ~ misogynist; loan-translation from Greek; in German since the 16th c., f.r.b. Stieler [1691]. When Lessing called his play *Der Misogyn* [1748], some critics objected maintaining that ~ would have been a more appropriate title. *Weiberfeindschaft* followed in the 18th c., recorded by Campe [1811], but not yet by Adelung, *weiberfeindlich* a little later (not yet listed by Campe).

Weiberfleisch: see *Fleisch*.

Weiberfluß: see *Weiberblume*.

Weibergeschichte

er hat Weibergeschichten he has affairs; *Geschichte* here used in the pejor. or erotic sense discussed on p. 1001; current since the 18th c.

weiberhaft

weiberhaft womanish, effeminate; f.r.b. Stieler [1691]; not as strong when used in criticism of men as is *weibisch* (which see below).

Weiberhand

in ~ (lit.) when done or pursued by women;

usually in negative judgements, as in Schiller's *Wallenstein*: '*die beste Sach in Weiberhand verdirbt*'; cf. similar instances of figur. use of *Hand* on p. 1218.

Weiberheld

der ~ lady-killer; in use since the 18th c.; cf. *Held in Liebessachen* and *Schlafzimmerheld* on p. 1283.

Weiberherrschaft: see *Regiment*.

Weiberherz

ein ~ *haben* to be a coward; was f.r.b. Stieler [1691]; with ref. to weakness or cowardice in use since the 17th c. (cf. entries on *weiberhaft* and *weibisch*).

Weiberklätscherei: see *klatschen*.

Weiberknecht: see *Knecht*.

Weibermär

die ~ (or *das Weibermärchen*) old wives' tale, unbelievable story; the oldest form appears to have been *alter weiber märlin*, as in Nigrinus, *Papist.Inqu.* [1582]; Maaler [1561] recorded '*alt weyber fablen*', and for the 17th c. *Weibermährlein* has been recorded; Lessing 1,176 used *Weibermährchen*; recordings for ~ are late (Campe [1811]. See also under *Märchen* (p. 1654) for *Altweibermärchen*, where it should be added that Budaeus, *Gedanken v.e.Hystorie* 28 [1732] used '*von alten Weibermährgen*'.

Weibermühle

Weibermühle, also *Altweibermühle* fountain of youth; the idea of regaining youth by magic is, of course, older than the German language and examples in many parts of the world are too numerous to be listed here (for literature on the German form of it see the list in Röhrich, *Lex.d.spr.Redensarten* 1132 [1973]). *Jungbrunnen* appears to be the oldest term describing magical regaining of one's youth (see under *Born*, p. 374). *Weibermühle* has been recorded for many areas since the 19th c., but dictionaries have neglected it (no trace in Kramer, Adelung or Campe), yet even now the term is used in joc. remarks such as *die müßte man in die* ~ *schicken* and on floats in carnival processions *Weibermühlen* are a popular feature.

Weibernarr: see *Narr*.

Weiberrat: see *Frucht*.

Weiberregiment: see *Regiment*.

Weiberrock

er läuft jedem ~ *nach* (coll.) he chases every petticoat; modern coll., not mentioned in *DWb.* [1915]; phrases with *Schürze* (see p. 2194) are in more general use.

Weiberträtscherei: see *Gevatter*.

Weibertreue: see *Kitt*.

weibisch

weibisch womanish, effeminate; now always pejor., but neutral in MHG and Early NHG, e.g. Luther Bible transl. 1 Peter 3,7; it could indicate weakness, timidity or cowardice from the 16th c.

onwards and was recorded in the derogatory sense by Frisius [1556]. In the 16th c. also the second pejor. meaning 'effeminate, effete, epicene, luxury-loving' entered literature. By the 18th c. the negative meanings began to predominate, e.g. Kant 10,282: '*Lachen ist männlich, Weinen dagegen weiblich (beim Manne weibisch)*'.

weiblich

weiblich (1) feminine; since OHG for 'characteristic of (or appropriate to) a woman' and soon also applied to a man showing feminine traits; with abstracts since MHG, e.g. Wolfram v.E., *Parz.* 24,8: '*sî hete wîplîchen sin*' or 252,16: '*wîplîcher kiusche ein bluome*', Walther v.d.V. 109,27: '*ir wîplîch güete*'; frequent since Early NHG with such abstracts as *Zartheit (zerte), Treue, Scham, Scheu, Anmut, Sorgsamkeit*, etc., but also pejor. with *Furcht, Eigensinn, Schwachheit*, etc. Often in statements which contrast (alleged or generalizing) feminine with male properties, e.g. (DWb) Grillparzer, *Werke* 9,6: '*von einem mehr weiblichen, taktartigen, als männlichen, denkenden Verstande*', Novalis [edit. Minor] 2,204: '*die Eigenschaft ist das weibliche Prinzip, das Subjekt; der Reiz ist das männliche Prinzip, das Objekt*', Schopenhauer [edit. Gr.] 1,91: '*die Vernunft ist weiblicher Natur: sie kann nur geben, nachdem sie empfangen hat*'.

weiblich (2) (bot.) female; with ref. to plants; loan from Latin, e.g. *femineus flos* = *weibliche Blüte*; recorded since Early NHG, e.g. Alberus, *Dict.* Ggiija, Herder, *Zur Relig.* 7,12 on palms: '*man verhüllet die männliche Blüthensprosse in die kleinen Zweige der weiblichen Blume*'.

weiblich (3) (grammar) feminine; from Lat. *femininus*, e.g. *genus femininum*; in German since the middle of the 15th c.; see under *Geschlecht* (p. 1004) for a quotation from Schottel [1663].

weiblich (4) (metr.) feminine; with ref. to rhymes; from French, e.g. *vers féminin*; in German since Opitz, *D.Poeterey* (repr.) 42 on the alexandrin: '*der weibliche Verß hat dreizehen, der männlich zwölff sylben*'; endings are called ~ when they consist of two syllables of which the latter is unstressed (also called *fallend*, for which see p. 715).

weiblich (5) (lit.) mild, gentle, tender; with ref. to natural phenomena, since the 18th c., e.g. Wieland, *Werke* 1,3,30: '*dieses milde weibliche Mondlicht*'.

weiblich (6) (tech.) female; used for parts of instruments, tools or mechanical devices which fit into or are enveloped by a corresponding 'male' part; current since the 19th c.; Sanders recorded from Payne, *Panorama d.Wissen.* 298a: '*... Anwendung eines weiblichen Zahnrads, welches in den inneliegenden Drehling greift*'. See also under *Mönch* (p. 1706) for a similar description of parts which fit into one another (with ref. to 'concave' and 'convex'), also the corresponding entries

under *Nonne* (6) and (8) (p.1790), also the similar terms such as *Muttergewinde* and *Mutterschraube* under *Mutter* (p.1732). Surprisingly, *weiblich* (6) was not listed in *DWb.* [1915], nor does it appear in *Duden. Dt. Univ.Wb.* [1989].

ein weibliches Wesen (joc.) a woman; joc. or with affected disinterestedness; modern, but cf. such 18th c. examples as in Wieland 11,190: '*wenn was Weibliches sich am Fenster zeigt*'. There is, of course, also *sie hat ein weibliches Wesen*, which refers to the possession of femininity to a pronounced degree.

ein weiblicher Saphir a light-blue sapphire; recorded since the 19th c., e.g. by Sanders [1871], but probably older in the jewelry trade.

← See also under *Geschlecht* (for *weibliches Geschlecht*), *Mann* (for *die ganze weibliche Gesellschaft*) and *Rätsel* (for *das große Räthsel des weiblichen Herzens*).

Weiblichkeit

eine ~ (coll.) a woman; as an abstract describes 'femininity, feminine features or traits', e.g. S.v.Laroche, *Frl.v. Sternheim* 2,187: '*hierauf beschrieb er meine eigenen Weiblichkeiten, wie er sie nannte*', Kant 10,340: '*die Weiblichkeiten heißen Schwächen*'. The transfer of this abstract making it a person in the phys. sense is modern, not even mentioned in *DWb.* [1915]; it occurs in Th.Mann 2,819 (*Zauberb.*): '*er zeigte sich verliebt in all und jede erreichbare Weiblichkeit*'.

die ~ (rare) the women, the women-folk; the abstract here taken as a collective noun; since the 18th c., e.g. Jean Paul, *Lev.* 678: '*das Fehlbetragen der Weiblichkeit im Hause einer Gebärerin*'.

die holde ~ (joc.,cl.) the fair sex; since the 19th c. with *hold* used iron. or with mock respect; cf. Hoffmann v. Fallersleben, *Werke* 1,288: '*du holdes Bild der Weiblichkeit zogst auch mit ihm von hier*'.

Weibsbild: see *Bild*.

Weibsmensch: see *Weibsstück*.

Weibsstück

das ~ wench, bitch, immoral (or slovenly, dirty, fickle) woman; since the 16th c., always derogatory, neglected in early dictionaries, recorded by Ludwig [1716], e.g. Th.Mann 7,563 (*Lotte*): '*... sein Umgang mit Frauen, die man nur als Weibsstücke bezeichnen kann*'. Adelung recorded ~ , adding that some areas use *Weibsmensch* in the same pejor. sense. See also under *Fleisch* (for *ein Stück Weiberfleisch*) and *Stück* (for *ein Stück Weibs*).

weibstoll

weibstoll woman-mad, obsessed with women; modern, not even listed in *DWb.* [1915], but earlier there was synonymous *weibsüchtig*, which Campe [1811] recorded.

weich: soft

weich gentle, soft, tender, kind; with many abstracts, e.g. *weiche Seele, Stimmung, weiches Herz, Gefühl*. Goethe used *unentschiedener weicher Zustand, weiche Heiterkeit, weiche Trauer*. The range has been wide since the MHG period and stretches from positive 'lenient, receptive, sensitive, tolerant' to negative 'weak, negligent, lacking energy, yielding too easily', e.g. *zu ~ sein*, as in Luther Apocr. transl. Ecclesiasticus 30,7, *~ werden*, as in his Bible transl. 1 Thess. 3,3.

einen weichen Keks haben (sl.) to be off one's rocker; 20th c. sl., when *Keks* came to be used in sl. for 'head' (as in *etw. geht jem.m auf den Keks* (sl.) = 'sth. annoys sb., gets on sb.'s nerves').

eine weiche Währung (econ.) a soft currency; loan from Engl.; 20th c.

weiche Überblendung (tech.) (gentle) dissolve; fading-out of a picture and gently replacing it by another in films and television; 20th c.

jem. verweichlichen to make sb. soft or effeminate, mollycoddle sb.; only since late in the 18th c., not yet listed by Adelung, e.g. Goethe, *Gespr.* [edit. B.] 5,141: '. . . *Schwestern, die . . . ihn verweichlichten*'.

etw. verweichlichen (lit.) to soften sth., tone down the harshness of sth.; since the 18th c., e.g. Herder [edit. S.] 24,267.

verweichlichen (intrans.) to grow soft; since ca. 1800. often in past part. in pejor. contexts; hence also *Verweichlichung* = 'softness'.

← See also under *Birne* (for *er hat eine weiche Birne*), *Brei* (for *weich wie Brei* and *breiweich*), *Butter* (for *weich wie Butter* and *butterweich*), *Daune* (for *daunenweich*), *Gewissen* (for *er hat ein weiches Kissen: ein noch unentweiht Gewissen*), *Holz* (for *weiches Holz zu spalten haben*), *Kissen* (for *auf dem weichen Kissen unsrer Siege*), *Knie* (for *weich in den Knien werden*), *Pflaume* (for *pflaumenweich*), *rauh* (for *ein weicher Kern in rauher Schale*), *Seide* (for *der Wimper weiche Seide* and *seidenweich*), *Seite* (for *jem.m die weiche Seite geben*), *sitzen* (for *im ganzen Kanton saß Keiner so warm und weich wie er*) and *Wachs* (for *weich wie Wachs* and *wachsweich*).

Weichbild

das geistige ~ (lit.) the intellectual or spiritual area, field or ambience; *~*, current since MHG for 'area of a town and its immediate surroundings and its juridical system', acquired, in the 16th c., the same extended meaning as *Bannkreis* (for which see p. 186). Since the last quarter of the 20th c. *das Ambiente* has come to be preferred to figur. *Weichbild* and *Bannkreis*.

Weiche: points, switch

die Weichen stellen to set the course, determine which direction developments will take; from the language of railways (*Weichen* were invented by Charles Fox in 1832), but much later than figur. extensions of some railway terms (such as *totes Gleis* on p. 1073); even Wildhagen-Héraucourt in 1967 did not record figur. use; hence also *Weichen dazwischenschalten* = 'to interfere with developments', e.g. by creating diversions, only since the last quarter of the 20th c.

weichen (1): yield, get out of the way

von etw. ~ to desist, move away or abstain from sth.; in the Middle Ages this occurred as *etw. ~* with the accusative, e.g. *Teuerdank* [edit. G.] 27: '*ich hab allezeit gewichen falscheit*', soon after that with *von*, e.g. Luther Bible transl. Prov. 3,7: '*fürchte den herrn und weiche vom bösen*', but with ref. to persons already in MHG, e.g. *Passional* [edit. K.] 171,73: '. . . *mit den gedanken er . . . von vatere und von mutere weich*'.

nicht wanken und ~ to stand firm, persevere; originally used with ref. to buildings, f.r.b. Frischlin; later extended to human 'firmness, determination', predominantly in the negative, first as *nicht ~ und wanken*, e.g. Bürger, *Len.u.Bland.*: '*wollte nicht weichen noch wanken von dar*', also in Schiller, Tieck and Novalis, but in reverse order in Goethe 22,23 (W.).

einer Sache or *jem.m an etw. ~* (obs.) to be inferior to sth. or sb. in some respect; recorded by Adelung and still used by Goethe, e.g. in *Ital. Reise* 1: '. . . *große . . . Canal weicht keiner Straße in der Welt*', where *nachstehen* would now be used.

etw. (abstract) *weicht* sth. departs, passes away, ceases; since Early NHG, e.g. (DWb) Luther Bible transl. (1st version) 1 Sam. 15,32: '*also weicht des tods bitterkeyt*' (later changed to '*also muß man des Todes Bitterkeit vertreiben*'), or Luther, *Werke* 18, 508 (Weimar): '*meyne tage sind gewichen wie eyn schatten*'.

einer Sache (abstract) *~* (lit.) to yield or give way to sth.; since the 18th c., e.g. Lessing 2,323 or Schiller, *Kab.u.L.* 4,5: '*meine Grundsätze weichen deiner Liebe*'.

← See also under *abweichen* (also for *Abweichung von der Regel*), *ausweichen, Schritt* (for *nicht einen Schritt weichen*) and *Seite* (for *jem.m nicht von der Seite weichen*).

weichen (2): soak

etw. weicht (obs.) sth. grows soft; recorded since the 16th c., but rarely with abstracts; in the 19th c. some writers revived it with *Herz*, e.g. Scheffel, *Ekkehard* 293: '*da weichte Etzels Herze*', but the much older compound *erweichen* prevented figur. use of the simplex.

etw. ~ (lit., rare) to soften sth., since MHG, later mainly with *Herz* (cf. previous entry), as in Schiller's *Aeneid* transl. 1,53: '*er ist Meister der Herzen und weicht sie mit Worten der Liebe*'; only *erweichen* is now used.

← See also under *einweichen, erweichen* and *Stein* (for *ich bin kein Stein, ich lasse mich alsdenn erweichen*).

Weichheit: see *flach*.

Weichherzigkeit: see *einreiben*.

weichlich: see *pimpeln*.

Weichlichkeit: see *einlullen* and *flach*.

Weichling: see *Mädchen*.

weichmütig

weichmütig tender-hearted, deeply (or easily) touched or moved; since the 18th c., e.g. Bode, *Yoricks e.R.* transl. 3,66 [1768]: '*ob ich gleich immer weichmüthig werde, wenn ich daran denke*', Th. Mann 7,53 (*Kön. Hoh.*): '*er selbst war weichmütig und zu Tränen geneigt*'; *Weichmütigkeit* followed in the 19th c., e.g. (Sa.) König, *Kön.Jer.* 1,95 [1855].

weichwollig: see *Flaum*.

Weide: food; pasture

etw. ist ~ für jem. (lit.,obs.) sth. delights sb.; since MHG, e.g. Heinr.v.Neustadt, *Apollonius* 2021: '*mînes herzen weide*'; still current in the 18th c., when Adelung recorded '*das ist Weide für sein Herz*' and Schiller used it in *Turandot* 5,2: '*dieser Schmerz . . . ist eurem Auge süße Weide*'; now obs.

← See also under *Auge* (for *Augenweide*).

weiden: feed

jem. ~ (relig.) to feed, nurture, sustain sb.; now only in Luther Bible transl. Psalm 23,2: '*er weidet mich auf einer grünen Aue*' with ref. to God as the good shepherd.

die Augen ~ (lit.,obs.) to feast one's eyes on sth.; since MHG, e.g. Ulrich v.Tür., *Willehalm* 216b: '*sîniu ougen er sô weidet . . .*'; f.r.b. Maaler [1561]: '*die augen weiden = lumina pascere*'; later poetically extended in the wider sense (and in intrans. usage), e.g. Goethe, *Werke* 2,60 (W.): '. . *die andern armen Geschlechter . . . wandeln und weiden in dunkelm Genuß*' and *Gesang d.Geister ü.d.Wasser*: '. . . *in dem glatten See weiden ihr Antlitz alle Gestirne*', where ~ = 'to exist, live' and ~ = 'to enjoy' have coalesced.

sich an etw. ~ to revel in (or enjoy the sight of) sth.; since Early NHG, e.g. Luther 20,522 (Weimar): '*du solt dich ym glauben weyden, das du ein solchen herren hast*'; also used for reprehensible 'gloating', e.g. (DWb) Zimmermann, *Einsamk.* 1,99: '*er weidete sich an allem Bösen, wie ein Esel am Feigenbaum*'.

weidlich: see *Fisch*.

weigern: see *bitten* (also under *Tribut* for *verweigern* and under *verweigern*).

Weihe: consecration

die ~ (lit.) solemnity; derived from the relig. sense 'consecration, ordination, initiation', and even when the context is secular, the notion of sth. bordering on the sacred, awe-inspiring, also inspirational is present to some extent; since the 18th c., e.g. Goethe 46,85 (W.): '. . . *Seelen, die eine höhere Weihe mit in's Leben bringen*', Platen, *Gaselen* 123: '*was giebt dem Freund, was giebt dem Dichter seine Weihe?*'. Often it can be taken as sth. with a solemn or sacred aura or poignancy, as in Heine [edit. E.] 3,395: '*das Mitleid ist die letzte Weihe der Liebe*', Klinger, *Damokl.*1,1:'. . . *um die spartanischen Sitten durch der Musen Weihe sanft zu färben*', Fontane, *Werke* 1,1,110: '*auch dem Profanen gab er eine Weihe durch die Art, wie er es behandelte*'; exercizing it or imparting it as a gift is usually expressed by *verleihen* (for which see p. 1609).

weihen: dedicate, consecrate

etw. (or jem.) ~ (lit.) to dedicate or consecrate sth. (or sb.); secularized (often in mockery) since MHG, but seriously in lit. since the 18th c., e.g. Klopstock, *Oden* [edit. M.-P.] 1,7: '*sehr wenig Könige weihen ihr erhabenes Amt durch ein gottnachahmendes Wohlthun*', Schiller, *D.Carlos* 4,21: '*mein Herz, nur einem Einzigen geweiht*'; in wider sense *jem.s Andenken Tränen ~* (for *Tränen ~* see Herder [edit. S.] 27,51). The opposite *etw. entweihen* = 'to profane or desecrate sth.' retains its association with sacredness; cf. *unentweiht* with ref. to *Gewissen* (p. 1040).

← See also under *einweihen* and *Untergang* (for *etw. dem Untergang weihen*).

Weihkessel: see *Teufel*.

Weihnachten: Christmas

sich auf etw. freuen wie ein Kind auf ~ (coll.) to look forward to sth. very eagerly; since the 19th c.; cf. Voß, *S.Ged.* 2,14 [1802]: '*und süß ängstete mich, wie zu Weihnacht, kindliche Sehnsucht*'.

ein Gefühl wie ~ (coll.) a feeling of happy contentment, peace, comfort; it can also suggest joyful anticipation of pleasant events; since early in the 20th c., but cf. Storm, *Br.i.d.H.* 68: '*mir wird schon ganz weihnachtlich*'.

das ~ (coll.) Christmas present; the concrete sense was first used (since Early NHG) for various things associated with Christmas, e.g. a painting of the Bethlehem stable, also for the Christmas tree or a crib, but since the 18th c. mainly for 'Christmas present', e.g. (DWb) Rahel v. Varnhagen, *Buch d.And.* 1,306 [1806]: '*ich schicke Ihnen ein kleines Weihnachten*', Goethe IV,6,229 (W.): '*ein gutes Weihnachten*', even used by him in the plural, e.g. III,13,16 (W.).

← See also under *Gesicht* (for *Weihnachtsgesicht*).

Weihkessel: see *Teufel*.

Weihrauch: incense

jem.m ~ streuen (lit.) to praise sb. (highly); this can be extended to 'flattering'; current since the 2nd half of the 18th c.; Bismarck, *Reden* 14,422 used *verbreiten*.

der Weihrauchvogel (zool.) oriole (*Oriolus oriolus*); not connected with ~; it was originally called *wîrûk* (cf. Suolahti, *Dt. Vogelnamen* 171 [1909] and changed by pop.etym. to *Weihrauchsvogel*.

← See also under *beweihrauchen* (also for *beweihräuchern, Beweihräucherer* and *Beweihräucherung*), *einsaugen* (for *sog den Weihrauch ein, den ihm Österreich und Spanien streuten*) and *streuen*.

Weihwasser: see *Teufel*.

weiland: formerly, long ago

sein ~ Vater (obs.) his late father; still current in the 19th c., e.g. C.F. Meyer, *Ang.Borg.* 230; now obs.

Weile: time, period

die ~ (1) (lit.) tedium, boredom; since the 17th c., still frequent in the 18th c., e.g. Bürger, 66a: '*. . . Euch plagt viel Weile*', Schiller, *M.Stuart* 1,1: '*. . . des Kerkers traurge Weile zu verkürzen*'; now *Langeweile* or *Langweile*, current as a compound since the 18th c. (Goethe once called it '*Mutter der Musen*') is preferred. – Note that the opposite *Kurzweil* for 'pastime, entertainment' has been current since MHG and could even be used for 'love(r)', as in *Buch d. Liebe* 276.

die ~ (2) (rare) expectation; modern, e.g. Kürnberger, *N.* 2,243: '*. . . blieb sie eine Beute der grausamen Weile*'; cf. Wieland 12,187: '*mit Witz, Geduld und Weile*' (interpreted by some as 'patient waiting').

mit der ~ soon but not yet, in time to come; still in occasional use, e.g. Wieland 2,61.

gut Ding will ~ haben (prov.) a proper job takes time; since Late MHG, e.g. *Liederb.d. Hätzlerin* 162; recorded in the principal prov. collections since Franck [1541].

← See also under *eilen* (for *Eile mit Weile*), *lang* (for *etw. für die lange Weile tun*) and *Tod* (for *tödlich langweilig*).

Weilchen: short time

See under *fein* (for *ich blieb ein feines Weilchen stehn*) and *nichts* (for *Warteinweilchen*).

weilen

weilen (lit.) to stay, remain; re-introduced into the lit. language by Klopstock who used it for 'to stay (with sb.)', transitively for 'to make sb. stay' and (in *Mess.* 9,448) for 'to hesitate'. Now only used for 'to stay, remain', in wider sense 'live', as in *er wird nicht mehr lange unter uns ~* (euphem.) = 'he will not live much longer' (cf. Luther Bible transl. John 13,33: '*ich bin noch eine kleine weile bey euch*'), and for 'to last', as in Th.Mann, *Dr. Faustus* 207 [1947]: '*diese . . . Minuten weilten mir zu lange*'.

Wein: wine

der ~ (personified) wine; in many sayings, some of them recorded since Early NHG, e.g. Franck [1541]: '*der wein nimpt keyn blat fürs maul*', '*der wein sagt war*', '*es nimpt der wein mehr hin, dann das schwerdt*', Petri [1605]: '*der wein macht bös leut*', '*. . . schleicht leicht ein*', '*schweigt nicht*' (also *lest nichts verschwiegen*), '*vertreibt die grillen*', Lehman [1630 and 1641]: '*der wein schemt sich nicht*', '*sperrt alle fenster auff im kopff*'; cf. also '*der Wein erfindet nichts, er schwatzts nur aus*' (Schiller, *Piccol.*).

der ~ ist . . . . wine is . . . ; in many lit. images, such as *der Dichter Postpferd* (cf. Lehman's '*ist der Poeten Heiliger Geist*'), *der Spiegel der Seele*, where

Engl. has 'wine is the mirror of the mind', for which Erasmus quoted a parallel in Aeschylus (cf. Oxf.714), *Satans sübes Gift, die Waage der Menschen, ein listiger Kämpfer, ein Roß ohne Zügel, ein Schleifstein* (used by Abraham a Sancta Clara), *ein Schlüssel zum Herzen* (also used by A.a.Sta.Clara), *ein Spotter* (recorded by Petri [1605]), *ein Wahrsager* (recorded by Franck [1541]), *der Alten Milch*, recorded by Petri, cf. French *le vin est le lait des vieillards*, Engl. 'wine is old men's milk', recorded since the 16th c., whereas Lehman has '*wein ist der alten pferd*'.

neuen ~ in alte Schläuche füllen to pour new wine into old bottles; derived from the Bible (Matth. 9,17). The general sense is 'to put sth. forward as new which in reality is merely a slight variant of sth. old'; it can also be used in criticism of sb.'s preoccupation with a subject, as in the example quoted under *Schlauch*.

der ~ erfreut des Menschen Herz (bibl.) wine makes glad the heart of man; quotation from the Bible, Psalm 103,15, frequently used in lit., also by Goethe, e.g. *Götz* 1; Tunnicius, 542 [1515] listed it in LG as '*de wyn vrouwet de lude*'.

guter ~ braucht keinen Kranz (or *Reif, Busch*) (prov.) good wine needs no bush; recorded since Early NHG, e.g. Franck [1541] '*gutter wein darff keins aussgesteckten reyffs*'. In Engl. recorded since the 15th c.; cf. Lehman [1630]: '*guter wein rufft sich selbst auss*'.

im ~ist Wahrheit (prov.) in wine there is truth; from Classical sources such as Lat. *in vino veritas*; international, e.g. French *dans le vin on dit la vérité*; Engl. 'in wine there is truth' has been recorded since the 16th c., but Engl. also has 'wine in, truth out', recorded since the 16th c. and quoted by Dickens; cf. also 'what soberness conceals, drunkenness reveals'.

← See also under *baden* (for *den Wein baden*), *Blücher* (for *tüchtig geblüchert, was Weiber, Wein und Würfel angeht*), *blühen* (for *wenn der junge Wein blüht* and *rühret sich der Wein im Fasse*), *decken* (for *Wein decken*), *drei* (for *Dreimännerwein*), *einschenken* (for *jem.m den Wein des Zorns einschenken* and *jem.m reinen Wein einschenken*), *einschmeicheln* (for *mehr des einschmeichelnden Weins genossen als billig war*), *ertränken* (for *etw. im Wein ertränken* and *Wein ertränken*), *Essig* (for *aus dem besten Wein wird der sauerste Essig*), *Feuer* (for *des Weines Feuerkräfte*), *Fisch* (for *der Fisch will dreimal schwimmen: im Wasser, im Schmalz und im Wein*), *Flasche* (for *Wein auf Flaschen ziehen*), *Gans* (for *Gänsewein*), *Geist* (for *der Geist des Weines*), *glühen* (for *glühender Wein* and *Glühwein*), *Hefe* (for *des Lebens Wein ist abgezogen*), *leicht* (for *leichter Wein*), *lieben* (for *mit dem Wein in der Flasche liebäugeln*), *Perle* (for *jenen Perlenschaum des Weins* and *wohl perlet im Glase der purpurne Wein*), *rot* (for *Sponwein*), *saufen* (for *daß ich's in jedem Glas Wein zu saufen kriege* and

*sauffe Wasser wie ein Ochs, Wein wie ein König),
Schlauch* (for *Börne, der allen Wein des Lebens in
die Schläuche der Politik füllte), schneiden* (for *den
Wein schneiden), schwer* (for *schwerer Wein), spinnen* (for *der Wein spinnt), steigen* (for *der Wein stieg
mir in den Kopf), taufen* (for *den Wein taufen*) and
Träne (for *ein Tränlein Wein*).

Weinberg: vineyard

ein Arbeiter im ~ des Herrn (bibl.) a labourer in
God's vineyard; alludes to Matth. 20,1–16; in lit.
since the 16th c., e.g. Fischart, *Bilderged.* [1571];
at least since the 18th c. secularized so that one's
~ was taken as 'one's field of activity', e.g.
Goethe 37,190 (W.), in modern vulg. usage used
for the activity of begetting children, recorded in
DWb. [1925]

Weinbuben: see *Hefe.*

weinen: weep

weinen (lit.) to weep; in personifications, at first
(since MHG) with *Auge* or *Herz* as the subject,
as in Freiligrath, *Sämtl.W.* 5,347: '*mein Herze
weint*', but then also with abstracts and objects,
e.g. Spee (in Wackernagel, *Dt.Lesebuch* 2,247):
'*die Wolken weinen sehr*', Ramler, *Lyr. Ged.* 345
[1772]: '*bald weint aus euch der Schmerz*',
Fr.Th.Vischer, *Asthet.* 3,648: '*ein tiefes Weinen der
Natur*'; in poetry brooks, springs and willows can
'weep', frequent since Klopstock.

es ist besser, das Kind weine als der Vater (prov.)
better children weep than old men; used with ref.
to loss through death, in German recorded since
Franck [1541], in Engl. since the 14th c.

← See also under *Auge* (for *sich die Augen
ausweinen), ausweinen, beweinen, bitter* (for *bitter-
lich weinen), Blut* (for *Blut or blutige Tränen
weinen), Gier* (for *Gierde lauert, Unschuld weint),
Kind* (for *weinen wie ein Kind), Krokodil* (for *wie
der krokodil thränen weint* and *der zum mord
waint), lachen* (for *mit einem lachenden und einem
weinenden Auge*), *nah* (for *mir war das Weinen
näher als das Lachen), Rotz* (for *Rotz und Wasser
weinen), Sack* (for *Lachen und Weinen in einem
Sack haben), Tod* (for *zu Tode weinen*) and *Träne*
(for *einer Sache keine Träne nachweinen*).

weinerlich: see *sprechen.*

Weinfaß: see *Faß.*

Weinflasche: see *Flasche.*

Weingärung: see *gären.*

Weingeist: see *Geist.*

Weinlaune

etw. in ~ versprechen to promise sth. while in
one's cups; ~ appeared in the sixties of the 18th
c. and was used by Goethe 9,102 (W.) and Jean
Paul soon after that but not recorded before
Sanders [1863]; the phrase with *versprechen*
became current in the 19th c.

weinrot: see *rot.*

weinselig: see *selig.*

weise: wise, prudent

die ~ Frau (a.) midwife; the term was originally

associated with the occult and described a soothsayer or sorceress, but recorded since Early
NHG for 'midwife' (*weise Mutter* or *weise Muhme*
also occurred); displaced by *Hebamme.*

der Weise (lit., rare) the wise (but unworldly or
inexperienced) man; since the 18th c. occasionally in contexts where a thinker is looked upon
with pity, amusement or (slight) contempt for his
ignorance about real life and its enjoyments. The
adjectives vary: Zachariae, *Poet. Schr.* 1,49
[1763] used "*dunkle Weisen*', W. Müller, *Ged.*
2,20: '*tiefe Weise*', Schiller pities '*den armen
Weisen*' and Goethe IV,1,91 (W.) has '*von kalten
Weisen rings umgeben, sing ich, was heiße Liebe sey*'.

~ wie Salomon as wise as Solomon; for details
see under *Salomon* (p. 2051).

die Weisen aus dem Morgenland the wise men
from the East, the Magi; from Matth. 2,1.

der Königsberger Weise Kant; Goethe 41,1,136
(W.) used the expression which has entered lit.
language.

← See also under *Daniel* (for *so weise wie
Daniel), durchlöchern* (for *der Verstand eines Weisen
ist wie ein voller Beutel), Geschenk* (for *Geschenke
machen den Weisen blind), gesund* (for *alles, was
dem Weisen hier auf der Erde kann gesunden), Narr*
(for *ein Narr kann mehr fragen als zehn Weise
beantworten können), Nase* (for *naseweis* and derivatives), *Sache* (for *in seiner eignen Sache ist niemand weise genug), schweigen* (for *schweigen wie ein
Weiser* and *. . . der swîge und sî ein wîser man*),
sieben (for *die sieben weysen mayster), Stein* (for *der
Stein der Weisen*) and *Tor* (for *ein weiser Tor*).

Weise: manner, method; melody

die ~ (rare) instruction, precept, demand; off-
shoot from the usual meanings, current since
Early NHG, e.g. Luther Bible transl. Gen. 26,5,
also Deuter. 11,12, where it renders Lat. *prae-
cepta; Anweisung* or *Weisung* might often be preferred, but ~ in this sense still occurs, e.g. Seidel,
Lennacker 448 [1938].

das ist keine Art und ~ that is not the proper
way to behave; *Art und ~* has been recorded
since Maaler [1561]; in this phrase which
expresses criticism of sb.'s behaviour it is modern.

jedem gefällt seine ~ (prov.) everybody is
pleased with his own conduct; recorded since the
16th c., e.g. Franck [1541]: '*eim jedem gefelt seine
weise wol, drumb ists landt der narrn voll*'.

← See also under *gackern* (for *viel von Weise
eines Liedes zu gacken), Spiel* (for *ein schlechter
Spielmann, der nur eine Weise kann), Stelle* (for
stellenweise) and *Vater* (for *väterliche weise*).

weisen: show, direct

etw. weist auf etw. sth. indicates sth.; with
abstracts since Early NHG, e.g. Fischart, *Binenk.*
154 [1588] dealing with the meaning of a symbol, Herder [edit. S.] 23,88: '*seine Fehler selbst
weisen auf eine höhere Stufe des menschlichen Geistes*';

cf. similar *auf etw. hinweisen*. A 20th c. newcomer is *vorwärtsweisend* = 'trend-setting'.

mit Fingern auf jem. ~ to point the finger of scorn at sb., treat sb. with contempt or derision; since Early NHG, e.g. Luther 18,93 (Weimar), recorded by Kramer [1702]; see also under *Finger* for similar idioms.

etw. von sich ~ to turn sth. away, refuse to have anything to do with sth.; since the 18th c., e.g. Schiller, *Wall.Tod* 1,4: '. . . nicht die Versuchung von mir wies'.

etw. von der Hand ~ to reject sth.; variant of the previous entry, also current since the 18th c., in the 19th c. often in polit. contexts.

← See also under *anweisen, aufweisen, beweisen, brennen* (for *zurückweisen*), *Ehre* (for *Ehre erweisen*), *Finger* (for *Nachweisung einer Sache in wenig Worten*), *führen* (for *Beweis führen* and *Gegenbeweis*), *Loch* (for *das Loch weisen, welches der Zimmermann im Hause offen gelassen hat*), *nehmen* (for *Unterweisung*), *Schranke* (for *jem. in die Schranken zurückweisen*), *Spiel* (for *Platz anweisen*), *überweisen, Tür* (for *jem.m die Tür weisen*), *unabweisbar* (also for *abweisbar* and *unabweislich*), *verweisen, vorweisen, Weg* (for *den rechten Weg zum Himmel weisen*) and *Wegweiser*.

Weisheit: wisdom *du kannst deine* ~ *für dich behalten* nobody wants your pearls of wisdom; ironic ~ has been current since MHG, often in mockery of the authorities, e.g. *die* ~ *des Senats* (*Parlaments, der Behörden*), ~ *des grünen Tisches,* ~ *der Bierbank*.

die ~ *ist aller Dinge Anfang* (prov.) wisdom is at the beginning of all things; derived from Psalm 111,10: '*die Furcht des Herrn ist der Weisheit Anfang*', and Prov. 4,7 '*denn der Weisheit Anfang ist . . .*' must also be considered as a partial source.

~ *ist des Lebens Auge* (prov.) wisdom is the eye of life; there appears to be no corresponding prov. in Engl.; in German since Franck [1541] who quoted it with its Lat. parallel *oculus vitae sapientia*.

'*der* ~ *letzter Schluß*' wisdom's ultimate conclusion, the answer to everything; quotation from Goethe, *Faust II*, 11574.

← See also under *anfangen* (for *die Furcht des Herrn ist der Weisheit Anfang*), *arm* (for *es verdirbt vil wisheit in eines armen mannes buch*), *Dame* (for *die Dame Weisheit*), *Danaide* (for *was schöpft ihr Weisheit aus dem Gefäße der Danaiden?*), *durchgehen* (for *Staatsweisheit*), *Ende* (for *sie sind mit ihrer Weisheit am Ende*), *fressen* (for *er denkt, er hat die Weisheit mit Löffeln gefressen*), *Gasse* (for *die Weisheit auf der Gasse*), *Glück* (for *ein Quentchen Glück ist besser als ein Pfund Weisheit*), *klug* (for *die Weisheit soll die Klugheit zu ihrer Dienerin haben*), *Kram* (for *Allerweltsweisheitskrämer*), *leuchten* (for *er wird mit Weisheit euch umleuchten*), *Mittag* (for *im Mittagspunkte von seiner Weisheit*), *Mutter* (for

Mutter der Weisheit), *Perle* (for *die Perlen der Weisheit*), *Rocken* (for *Rockenweisheit*), *rufen* (for *ruft nicht die Weisheit, und die Klugheit läßt sich hören?*), *Schnecke* (for *Schneckengang der ruhigen Weisheit*), *schöpfen* (for *die ihre Weisheit aus den reinsten Quellen schöpften*), *Schule* (for *Schulweisheit*), *steil* (for *steile Höhen besucht die ernste forschende Weisheit*), *Strahl* (for *Strahlen der göttlichen Weisheit*), *Trödel* (for *der mit spekulativer Weisheit getrödelt hat*), *übertreffen* (for *das die weisheit die thorheit übertraf*), *überwältigen* (for *die bosheit überweldiget die weisheit nimmermehr*), *verraten* (for *die größte Weisheit verrathet sich in der einfachsten Einrichtung der Dinge*), *Vormund* (for *die höchste Weißheit muß der Thorheit Vormund sein*) and *Wage* (for *die Wage der Weisheit*).

Weisheitszahn: wisdom-tooth
die Weisheitszähne kommen spät und fallen bald wieder aus (prov.) wisdom-teeth come late in life and drop out soon; modern prov., recorded by Eiselein [1838] and Simrock [1846]; cf. also regional *dem sind die Weisheitszähne noch nicht gekommen*, recorded by Wander [1880] and Holtei, *Erz.Schr.* 25,85: '*möchte dir doch der Weisheitszahn wieder wachsen, den du . . . dir . . . selbst ausgerissen zu haben scheinst*'.

weislich: see *einhüllen*.

weismachen
jem.m etw. ~ (also formerly and incorrectly *weißmachen*) to tell sb. a yarn, fool or hoodwink sb.; beginnings in OHG '*einen eines wîsî tuan*' (Otfrid) and in MHG, still without the notion of 'deceit' as '*einen eines dinges wîs tuon*' = 'to instruct sb. in, enlighten sb. about sth.'; with ref. to deceitful information since the 17th c., e.g. Goethe 8,67 (W.): '*macht das Kindern weiß, die den Rübezahl glauben*'. Frequent in such phrases as *er läßt sich* (or *ihm kann man*) *nichts* ~ = 'he is nobody's fool', *mach das einem andern weis* (coll.) = 'tell that to the marines', *laß dir nichts* ~ = 'don't be fooled'.

sich etw. ~ to make oneself believe, pretend (to oneself), persuade oneself (that . . .); since the 18th c., e.g. Goethe 19,112 (W.): '. . . habe ich mir weiß gemacht, daß ich die Bergwerke . . . besuchen wollte; ist aber im Grunde nichts dran . . .'.

← See also under *Eichhorn* (for *jem.m weismachen, der Teufel wär' ein Eichhörnchen*).

weissagen
etw. weissagt etw. sth. prophesies sth., foretells sth., close to *wahrsagen*; with abstracts since MHG, e.g. Hartm.v. Aue, *Iwein* 3097: '*im wîssagte sîn muot . . .*', J.M. Miller, *Ged.* 271 [1783]: '. . . das düstre Morgenroth . . . weissagt meinen Tod'; cf. v. Haller *Usong* 137 [1771]: '*eines Weisen Mutmaßungen werden Weissagungen*'.

der Weissager (lit.) prophet, (in wider sense) sth. that announces coming events (= *Verhersager*); since the 18th c., e.g. (DWb) Breitinger, *Crit.Dichtk.* 1,338: '. . . von den

Cometen als Weissagern allgemeiner Landplagen', also with the notion of 'promising', e.g. Klopstock, *Oden* [edit. M.-P.] 1,165: *'o Gefühl, Weissager inniger ewiger Ruh'*.

← See also under *rumoren* (for *Geist der Weissagung, der in seinem Innern rumorte*).

weiswerden

etw. ~ (regional coll.) to get to know or understand sth., hear of sth. which one did not previously know; beginnings are early, e.g. *Heliand* 273, current in MHG, but recordings are late and even Kramer [1702] only recorded it for 'to become wise, acquire wisdom'; in modern sense recorded by Ludwig [1716]; still frequent in many regions, but rare in lit., where *gewahr werden*, *erfahren* and *merken* are used instead.

weiß: white

See under *blühen* (for *blütenweiß* and *blühweiß*), *brennen* (for *sich weiß brennen*), *Fleck* (for *Flecken auf der weißen Weste*), *Fledermaus* (for *weiße Fledermäuse*), *grün* (for *grüne Weihnachten bringen gern schneeweiße Ostern*), *Kalk* (for *weiß wie Kalk*), *Kohle* (for *weiße Kohle*), *Kreide* (for *kreideweiß*), *Lilie* (for *weiß wie eine Lilie*, *lilienweiß*), *Marmor* (for *weiß wie Marmor* and *Marmorweiße*), *Maus* (for *weiße Mäuse sehen*), *Milch* (for *weiß wie Milch* and *milchweiß*), *Nase* (for *eine weiße Nase haben*), *Rabe* (for *ein weißer Rabe*), *Salbe* (for *es ist wie weiße Salbe*), *Schnee* (for *weiß wie Schnee* and *schneeweiß*), *Schwan* (for *weiß wie ein Schwan* and *schwanenweiß*), *schwarz* (for *jem.m schwarz für weiß geben, so verschieden wie schwarz und weiß, aus schwarz weiß machen, nicht wissen, was schwarz und weiß ist, sagt er schwarz, so sagt sie weiß, etw. schwarz auf weiß haben* and *er ist nicht schwarz und nicht weiß*), *Semmel* (for *weiß wie Semmel*), *Sperling* (for *ein weißer Sperling*), *Stab* (for *an den weißen Stab kommen*) and *Wand* (for *weiß wie eine Wand*).

Weißbluten

die Bevölkerung wurde bis zum ~ *ausgepreßt* the population was bled white; since the 1st quarter of the 20th c.; there is also *sich weißbluten* = 'to exhaust oneself financially', which is even more recent.

Weiße: whiteness

Weiße hat diese Nacht Grünern erschlagen (regional coll., obs.?) the first snow fell last night; recorded by Klix [1863] and Wander [1880].

← See also under *Auge* (for *jem.m nicht das Weiße im Auge gönnen*).

Weißbuch

das ~ (polit.) White Paper (issued by the Government); loan-translation from Engl., so called because of its binding; current since the 2nd half of the 19th c.

Weißfisch

der ~ (coll., obs.) good-for-nothing; refers to the comparative inferiority of ~ ; since the 18th c., e.g. Goethe 8,86 (W.) (*Götz*); still in Storm,

Werke 6,37; now obs.

Weißgerber: tanner

er ist unter den Weißgerbern gewesen (coll., obs.?) he looks exhausted (run-down, tired); recorded since the 19th c., e.g. by Wander [1880]; obs.?

Weißglut

jem. bis zur ~ *bringen* (or *reizen*) to bring sb. into a great rage; since the beginning of the 20th c.; cf. the entry under *Glut* (p. 1094).

Weißkopf

ein ~ an old man; since the 19th c. (much younger than *Graukopf*, for which see p. 1127), e.g. (DWb) Fontane, *Ges. W.* II,3,44: *'Weißköpfe, alte Troupiers'*.

weißwaschen: see *Mohr*.

weit: wide, far

weit (1) far; used figur. in a great number of locutions, principally in *etw. geht zu* ~ = 'sth. goes too far, exceeds what is permitted', since Early NHG, e.g. Lessing [edit. M.] 2,334, hence also *so* ~ *es geht* = 'as far as is possible (or permissible)', e.g. Goethe 22,101 (W.) and *wie* ~ *etw. geht* = 'how far sth. extends or lasts'; close to it is *etw. führt zu* ~ = 'sth. leads one too far (away from the point)', but also sometimes synon. with *etw. geht zu* ~ ; the phrase with *führen* is not recorded by Kramer [1702] who lists many related expressions belonging here: ~ *entlegen*, *einen weiten Umschweif nehmen* (now obs.), ~ *sehen*, ~ *langen*, ~ *fehlen*, ~ *suchen* (which Goethe 21,59 (W.) used), *(nicht)* ~ *kommen, wenn es* ~ *kommt* (where *hoch* is now preferred), *nicht* ~ *her sein, etw.* ~ *wegwerfen, zu* ~ *gehen, sich zu* ~ *in eine Sache vertiefen, zu* ~ *kommen, so weit ists kommen, in so* ~ *er mein Bruder ist, liebe ich ihn* (which has dropped out of use), *es einem* ~/*bey weiten bevorthun* (now obs.), *er ist* ~/*bey weiten größer als* . . . (where *bei weitem* is now used) and *von weiter her seyn* (now: *von* ~ *her sein*). He does not list *etw.* ~ *holen müssen*, current since Early NHG and used by Luther 26,445 (Weimar), nor ~ *vom Schuß* = 'safe from danger, out of harm's way', current since Early NHG, e.g. Fischart, *Podagr.Tr.* B2a; cf. ~ *davon ist gut vorm Schuß* (prov.), recorded since the 16th c., e.g. by Franck. ~ *weg* = 'far away' has been in use with abstracts since the 18th c., e.g. Chr. Weiße, *Polit. Red.* 261: '. . . *Gott wolle . . . Kranckheit . . . weit . . . weg verbannen'*.

weit (2) distant; as in *ein weiter Freund, weiter Verwandter, seine weitere Bekanntschaft*; at least since the 17th c., as borne out by Kramer's [1702] recordings *'von weiten verwandt'* and *'einem von weiten verwandt seyn'*.

weit (3) wide, elastic; the notion is that of extension without strict limitations, e.g. Schiller, *D.Carlos* 3,3: *'ein weites Wort'*; it can border on 'tolerant' or 'generous', as in *ein weites Herz*.

weit (4) comprehensive, broad; with such abstracts as *Auslegung, Bedeutung, Begriff, Sinn*, formerly also with *Verstand*, as in Kramer [1702]: '*etwas in weitem Verstande nehmen*'. Goethe used '*im allerweitesten Sinn, weite Frage, weite Ideen, Glaube weit, eng der Gedanke*'.

weit (5) extensive, large, big, wide; with such abstracts as *Gebiet* or *Unterschied*, e.g. Heine, *Lut.* 2,60: '*das weiteste Wissen*'.

~ *und breit* far and wide, for miles around; general since the 17th c., e.g. Logau (in Lessing 5,264): '*der beste Redner weit und breit und um und um*'; cf. similar *in der weiten Welt* = 'in the (big) wide world'. Kramer recorded '*in die weite Welt gehen*'. He also listed '*ein weites und breites von etw. machen*' and '*weit und breit berühmt seyn*'.

so ~ *wie* . . . as far as . . . ; old in comparisons, e.g. Luther Bible transl. Psalm 36,6: '*so weit der Himmel ist* . . . *so weit die Wolken gehen*'.

weit (adv.) far, considerably; expressing degree of extent; general since Early NHG, f.r.b. Frisius [1556], e.g. ~ *größer*, as in Luther 10,1,1,549 (Weimar), ~ *besser* or ~ *lieber*, as in Goethe 1,138. Hence also ~ *anders* = 'totally different', ~ *nicht so gut wie* . . . = 'not as good as . . . by far', ~ *nicht genug* = 'far from (being) sufficient'.

so ~ *sein, daß* . . . to have reached the point (or moment) where (or when) . . . ; ellipsis with *gekommen* omitted; with *gekommen* since the 16th c. (also *so* ~ *ist es gegangen*, since the 16th c.), without it but with *sein* general since the 18th c., e.g. Herder [edit. S.] 5,19 or Goethe 25,241 (W.); cf. also *so* ~ *zurück sein*, as in Goethe 46,86 (W.): '*so weit war damals noch die Pädagogik zurück*'.

es ist nicht ~ *her* (coll.) it is of little value or importance; reflects admiration of sth. which come from far away (often attacked as a German weakness); also contemptuously (but less frequently) used with ref. to persons, e.g. Grimmelshausen, *Teutscher Michel* 21 [1673]: '*du bist nit weit her*'.

was einem zu eng ist, ist dreien zu ~ (prov.) what is felt to be too narrowly circumscribed by one person is considered to be too broad (or loosely circumscribed) by three others; recorded in modern period by Fischer for Swabia, but there is an older and more extensive form in Franck, *Sprichw. Klugreden* 170b [1548]: '*was zweyen gerecht ist, ist eim zu eng, dreien zu weit*'.

← See also under *allein* (for *allein auf weiter Flur*), *Apfel* (for *der Apfel fällt nicht weit vom Stamm*), *Beil* (for *das Beil zu weit werfen*), *bringen* (for *etw. so weit bringen, daß* . . .), *Büchse* (for *ein Büchsenschuß weit entfernt*), *Elle* (for *ellenweit*), *eng* (for *enges recht ist weit unrecht*, . . . *gerne hât wîten friund und engen rât* and *das weiteste Wissen verdammt uns zur engsten Passivität*), *fehlen* (for *weit gefehlt* and *es feilet nicht weit*), *Feld* (for *das steht noch im weiten Feld*), *fern* (for *das steht noch in weiter Ferne*), *gerade* (for *lenkte er von weitem dahin*), *Gewissen* (for *es haben so viele so weite Gewissen*), *greifen* (for *so weit in die Unendlichkeit hinaus greift unser Geist*), *herrlich* (for *wie wir's dann zuletzt so herrlich weit gebracht*), *Himmel* (for *himmelweiter Unterschied* and *weit gefehlt*), *hinaus* (for *er ist weit über diese Kleinigkeit hinaus*), *hinausgreifen* (for *weit in etw. hinausgreifen*), *hinausjagen* (for *auf dem weiten Erdenrunde*), *hinausreichen* (for *das reichet über jene Zeit weit hinaus*), *hinausschieben* (for *die Zeit weit hinausschieben*), *holen* (for *weit hergeholt*), *Horizont* (for *einen weiten Horizont haben*), *Kreis* (for *etw. zieht weite Kreise*), *langen* (for *wie weit wir damit langen*), *Meile* (for *meilenweit*), *Pforte* (for *die weite Pforte*), *Pilger* (for *durchpilgern den weiten Raum*), *reichen* (for *großer Herren Arm reicht weit, soweit das Auge reicht, soweit das Zepter meines Vaters reicht* and *überrechnete, wie weit ich damit reichen würde*), *riechen* (for *etw. or jem. von weitem riechen*), *Saphir* (for *des weiten Himmel-Raumes saphirene Gewänder*), *schicken* (for *einen weit in verre land schicken*), *schießen* (for *weit vom Ziel schießen*), *Schritt* (for *ein sehr weiter Schritt*), *Schuh* (for *in weiten Schuhen gehen*), *Seele* (for *seine Seele ist weit fort*), *springen* (for *nicht weit springen können*), *Sprung* (for *weite Sprünge machen*), *stecken* (for *ein weit entferntes Ziel erreicht*), *Tor* (2) (for *das Tor der Poesie weit geöffnet*), *treiben* (for *treibe trawrigkeit weit von dir*) and *Weg* (for *von Worten zu Werken ist ein weiter Weg*).

weitaus

weitaus (adv.) far, by far; only since late in the 18th c., not even listed by Campe [1811]; *DWb.* quotes from Lavater, *Handbibl.f.Fr.* 5,34.

weitbauschig: see *Bausch*.

Weitblick

~ *haben* to be far-sighted; figur. only since the 19th c.; the same applies to *weitblickend* = 'far-sighted'.

Weite: width

die ~ (1) far distance; in phys. sense since the 16th c., e.g. Fischart, *Bien.* 186a; then in wider sense, sometimes = 'the wide world', sometimes = *Ferne*, as in Goethe 2,114 (W.) or Chamisso 4,29: '*jene räthselhafte blaue Weiten*'.

die ~ (2) (lit.) broadness, wideness, scope; with ref. to sb.'s mentality (cf. *weit*(4)); first with *Herz*, as in Mentel's Bible 3 Kings 4,29: '*der herr gab weysheit salomon vnd gar uil witzigkeit vnd di weite des hertzen*', where Luther (1 Kings 4,29) rendered it with '*reichen Geist*'; it can refer to 'broad-mindedness, tolerance of outlook, generosity of mind', but is now rare (recent dictionaries do not list it).

← See also under *Kragen* (for *Kragenweite*), *Spiel* (for *etw. ins Weite spielen*), *suchen* (for *das Weite suchen*) and *tragen* (for *Tragweite*).

weiten: widen

etw. ~ (a.) to widen, expand, extend sth.; since the 18th c. figur. with *Auge* or *Herz*; with *Gemüt* in Herder [edit. S.] 22,244. Now *erweitern* is preferred, for which see p. 693.

sich ~ (lit.) to swell, expand; first as an intransit. verb in Early NHG, when Maaler [1561] recorded it; reflex. figur. use belongs to the modern period with such abstracts as *Verständnis, Horizont* or *Interesse*.

← See also under *ausweiten*.

weiter: further

~ *nichts* nothing else or further; at least since the 17th c., since Kramer recorded it in 1702. Adelung [1780] also listed: *'es ist nichts weiter in der Sache geschehen . . . was wollt ihr weiter . . . was weiter daraus werden wird . . . ohne weitere Umstände, keine weitere Erklärung . . . bis auf weiteren Befehl'*. It is interesting that *ohne weiter(e)s* = 'without further ado, easily, readily' and *bis auf weiteres* = 'for the present, pending further developments' are still missing in his list.

← See also under *ausholen* (for *weiter ausholen*), *bringen* (for *es nie weiter bringen können als . . .*), *greifen* (for *daß wir weiter um uns greifen müssen* and *daß Napoleon in Italien weiter um sich griffe*), *Grenze* (for *dehnen sich die Grenzen weiter aus*), *herauskommen* (for *wenn auch weiter nichts dabei herauskäme*), *herbringen* (for *Althergebrachtes weiter führen*), *herumdrehen* (for *weiter ausbreiten*), *hinaufklettern* (for *um weitere zehntausend Mark*), *hinter* (for *Liebelei, die weiter nichts hinter sich hat*), *lassen* (for *um weiter vorzugehen*), *Nase* (for *nicht weiter als seine Nasenspitze*), *Schlag* (for *immer weiter vom Ziel*), *springen* (for *es springt weiter mit . . .*), *Stab* (for *den Stab weiter setzen*) and *Text* (for *weiter im Text*).

weitererzählen

weitererzählen (1) to go on with one's narrative; modern; see the example under *gehen* (p. 947).

weitererzählen (2) to pass on what one has heard; modern with ref. to gossip, talebearing, e.g. Schopenhauer, *Werke* [edit. Gr.] 2,78.

weiterfahren

weiterfahren to continue; since Early NHG, e.g. Luther 32,521 (Weimar): *'nu feret er weitter und wil sich verkleren . . .'*; it can mean 'to continue to speak', but *fortfahren* should be used. *DWb.* [1922] puts it strongly *'weiterfahren in der Bedeutung fortfahren ist fehlerhaft'*; Duden, *Univ.Wb.* [1989] classifies it as regional (S.German, Swiss).

weiterführen: see *herbringen*.

weitergeben

etw. ~ to pass sth. on; figur. only since the 19th c., e.g. *die Mehrkosten an den Kunden* ~ ; it can also mean 'to spread', e.g. with ref. to a rumour.

weitergehen: go on

etw. geht weiter sth. continues; figur. since the 18th c., e.g. Goethe 21,73 (W.); often in *so kann das nicht* ~ = 'things cannot go on like this'.

weiterhelfen: see *Himmel* (p. 1323).

weiterkommen

weiterkommen to get further, make progress; figur. only since the 19th c.

weiterlaufen

etw. läuft weiter (coll.) sth. goes on running, continues to function; since the 19th c. with such abstracts as *Geschäft, Unterricht*; cf. *laufen*(2) and (6).

weiterleiten

etw. ~ (lit.) to forward or further sth.; with abstracts since the 18th c., e.g. Herder [edit. S.] 15,507.

weitern

See under *eng* (for *die Gebirghöhe der Freiheit weitert die Seele*) and *erweitern* (also under *weiten*).

weiterspinnen: see *Faden*.

weiterstricken: see *Strick*.

weitertragen: see *tragen*.

weitertreiben: see *treiben*.

weiterwissen

nicht (mehr) ~ to be at one's wit's end, be stuck; occurs mainly in negative locutions; modern (not listed in *DWb.*).

weiterwursteln

weiterwursteln (coll.) to go on muddling; modern, e.g. Th. Mann 1,346 (*Buddenbr.*): *'. . . sich gehen zu lassen und so weiterzuwursteln'*.

weitgehend

weitgehend far-reaching, extensive, wide; in many contexts since late in the 18th c., e.g. Fontane, *Werke* I,1,535; *'die weitgehendsten Hoffnungen'*.

weitgreifend

weitgreifend comprehensive, extensive; since the 18th c. mainly with such abstracts as *Folgen* or *Problem*; cf. similar *weitreichend*, which is used with the same abstracts.

weitherzig

weitherzig warm-hearted, generous, tolerant; since late in the 18th c., e.g. Treitschke, *Dt. Gesch.* 5,367. Hence *Weitherzigkeit*, since the 19th c.

weitläufig

weitläufig (1) spacious, extensive; with ref. to territories; since early NHG, used by H. Sachs as *weitlauffig*.

weitläufig (2) detailed; with ref. to speech or texts (often slightly pejor. for 'too wordy, including too many inessentials'); since Early NHG, e.g. Luther 18,213 (Weimar), where *weytleufftig* occurs.

weitläufig (3) distant; with ref. to personal relationships (as in *entfernt* and *weit*); since the 17th c., recorded by Kramer [1702].

← See also under *eng* (for *von so weitläuftigem Kopfe*).

weitreichen: see *reichen* (also for *weitreichend*).

weitschauend

weitschauend far-sighted; same as *weitblickend* (see above); current since the 17th c.

weitschichtig: see *Schicht*.

weitschweifig

See under *schweifen* (also for *Weitschweifigkeit*)

and under *kraus* (for *ding von weitschweifigen sachen*).

Weitsicht

die ~ (lit.) far-sightedness; only since the 19th c. when it was derived by back formation from the adjective *weitsichtig*, which has been current since the 16th c.; cf. *Weitblick* above.

weittragend

weittragend far-reaching; recent in figur. sense; used mainly with *Folgen* or *Konsequenzen*.

weitverzweigt: see *Zweig*.

Weizen: wheat

See under *blühen* (for *sein Weizen blüht*) and *Spreu* (for *die Spreu vom Weizen sondern*).

welk: withered

welk faded, withered; in its current phys. sense relating to plants appeared in the 10th c.; much later transferred to the human body for 'weak, decrepit, shrunk', e.g. Goethe, *Faust I*, 458; Adelung [1780] recorded '*welke Brüste*'.

welken to wither, fade; frequent in lit. with ref. to abstracts since the 18th c., e.g. Schiller, *M.Stuart* 2,3: '. . . *Jugendkraft, welkt jene nicht mit jedem Schritt zum Grabe?*', Holtei, *Vagabunden* 48: '*kecke Wünsche, die unerfüllt welken*'. There are many compounds, e.g. *dahinwelken*, as in Wieland 10,131: '*sie welkt dain, des Lebens Blüthezeit*', *abwelken*, as in Heine 6,46: '*unsre Gefühle sind abgewelkt*' and in a comparison in Wieland 11,274: '*ihre Wangen sind wie ein abgewelkter Kranz*', *hinwelken*, as in Bürger, 484b; *hinwegwelken* and *seinem Ende entgegenwelken* also occur. The most frequently used compound is *verwelken*, since Early NHG, used by Luther in his Bible transl. He also used *unverwelklich* in 1 Peter 5,4, which also occurs in Goethe 4,183 (W.) and Heine [edit. E.] 7,514, *Unverwelklichkeit* in Goethe 4,183 (W.); he even used the rare *unverwelkend*.

← See also under *verwelken*.

Welle: wave

die ~ (1) (personified) the wave; personified since OHG, when Notker used it with *uberfarin*; then it occurred with many verbs of action in Luther 10,3,215 (Weimar) and was also used by him in his Bible transl. Isaiah 51,15 with *wüten*; it has also been frequent with *schlagen* since MHG (cf. Goethe 9.352 (W.): '*Wellen, die das Ufer schlagen*'); other verbs used are *spielen*, as in Goethe 2,73 (W.) and the unusual *hinanklettern* in Goethe 37,66 (W.); he also used *steigen* and *weichen*.

← See also under *rauben* (for *ein Raub der Wellen*).

die ~ (2) wave-like motion (or sth. of wave-like appearance); since the 18th c., e.g. E.v.Kleist 1,79: '*wie reizend fließt die Saat in grünen Wellen fort*', Brockes 9,366 on fields of corn: '*ein reges Meer voll trockner Wellen*', Wieland 11,162: '*des jungen Busens sanfte Wellen*' or Wieland 12,275:

'*daß sein Blut in sanftern Wellen fleußt*'. When used with ref. to emotional 'waves', it can mean the same as *Wallung* (to which it is etymologically related), e.g. Thümmel, *Sämtl.Werke* 4,185, where '*die innern Wellen*' occurs; cf. also W.v. Humboldt, *Ges.W.* 1,372: '*des Gefühles Welle*'.

die ~ (3) wave; with ref. to temporary occurrence constituting an increase of a condition or an influence, now mainly describing a trend or fashion which sweeps in like a wave; it is modern, not yet listed in Sanders [1865], but his *Erg.Wb.* [1885] recorded *Aufruhrwelle* = 'wave or series of revolts' and similar *Unruhwelle*. General only since the 20th c., e.g. St.Zweig, *Balzac* 55: '*von England ist eine neue Welle herübergekommen, nachdem die frühere sentimentale . . . in Europa abgebrandet ist*'. Frequent in compounds such as *Streikwelle* = 'series of strikes', *Modewelle*, *Protestwelle*; hence also *mit der ~ fortschwimmen* = 'to follow the trend'. Closely related is the use of *Welle* (3) with ref. to the weather describing a limited period of a certain type of weather, e.g. *Hitzewelle*, *Kältewelle*, *Frostwelle*, all still missing in 19th c. dictionaries.

die ~ (4) flood; used with ref. to a body of persons or of events advancing successively; since the 18th c., when Goethe used '*die Wellen reitender Männer*'; frequent in compounds, e.g. *Feuerwelle*, used by Goethe (but missing in *DWb.* [1862], or Droste-Hülshoff, *Ged.* 484 [1844]: '*das Morgenroth . . . spülte kleine Feuerwellchen her*', also *Menschenwelle*, as used by Schiller in *Kran.d.Ibykus* 79. Goethe also used *Wolkenwelle* (missing in *DWb.*).

die Wellen (lit.) the sea; since the 17th c., e.g. *sich auf den Wellen versuchen* = 'to become a sailor', as in Goethe IV,36,102 (W.), or *den Tod in den Wellen finden* = 'to be lost at sea'; cf. Adelung's [1780] entry: '*figürlich bedeuten die Wellen wohl auch das Meer, oder sonst ein großes Wasser*'.

Wellen schlagen to cause a stir; the phrase covers a wide range from 'to cause trouble or a sensation' to 'to have many consequences'; only since late in the 19th c., e.g. G.Keller, *Nachl.* 19: '*ein freundlicher Kreis . . . schlug . . . weitere Wellen und Wellchen*'; cf. Bismarck, *Red.* 16,189: '*wenn . . . aus dem Leben schieden, so hat das gewiß in weiten Kreisen einen Wellenschlag gemacht*'. It is this idiom which in the 20th c. produced a number of coll. or sl. phrases such as *die Wellen gehen hoch* = 'there is much excitement or commotion', its opposite *keine Wellen machen* = 'to cause no stir', *quatsch keine Wellen!* = 'don't boast (or exaggerate) so much!' and *eine dicke ~ angeben* (sl.) 'to boast atrociously'.

die grüne ~ (coll.) sequence of green traffic lights; coll. of the 2nd half of the 20th c., e.g. *wir kamen rasch vorwärts, denn wir hatten mehrere grüne Wellen*.

er hat eine ~ (regional coll.) he is drunk; only recorded since the 20th c.

← See also under *Glas* (for *zu Glas erstarrt des Wassersturzes Welle*), *Rausch* (for *umrauscht uns mächtig des Gefühles Welle*), *schlingen* (2) (for *die Wellen verschlingen jem.*), *schwanken* (for *ein ewiges Schwanken auf der Welle des Glücks*) and *stürzen* (for *Sturzwelle*).

wellenartig

wellenartig wave-like, undulating; recorded since the 2nd half of the 18th c.

Wellenberg

der ~ (lit.) mountainous wave; since the 18th c.; cf. *Wasserberg* on p. 257.

Wellenbrecher

der ~ break-water; modern, possibly influenced by the Engl. term (although *DWb.* doubted that); since the 20th c. also used figur. for sb. or sth. that calms an onslaught of some force.

wellenförmig

wellenförmig wave-shaped, undulating; f.r.b. Schwan [1784]. Used with ref. to art since the 18th c. when *wellenförmige Linie* (also called *die Schönheitslinie*) established itself under influence of Engl. 'waving line'; Goethe used it in geological contexts, e.g. III,9,98 (W.)

Wellengrab: see *Grab*.

wellenhaft

wellenhaft (lit.) wave-like, undulating; since the 18th c., e.g. Goethe 50,303 (W.). See also example on 822.

Wellenlinie

die ~ wavy line; since the 18th c., e.g. Lessing [edit. M.] 5,370; see also the entry under *wellenförmig*.

Wellenschlag: see *Welle*.

Wellensittich

der ~ (zool.) budgerigar (*Melopsittacus undulatus*); named after the wavy lines on its feathers; recorded only since the 19th c.

Wellental

das ~ (lit.) trough (of a wave); figur. to describe the low point in the ups and downs of one's life; only since the 20th c.

wellenweise

wellenweise (adv.) in the shape or resembling the behaviour of a wave; since the 17th c. and therefore earlier than *wellenartig, -förmig*, etc.; *wellig*, too, appeared in the 17th c., recorded as *wellicht* by Stieler [1691]; *wellichtig* was recorded in the 16th c.

wellig: see *wellenweise*.

Welsch: Celtic

welsch (also *wälsch*) (pejor.) treacherous, false,unreliable; the term began as 'Celtic' (cf. Volcae, Wales and Cornwall), but when nationals of Romance origin settled in Gaul, it changed to 'Romance'. It was spelt *welsch*, until Adelung postulated *wälsch* as the correct form; since the 19th c. again the old spelling (though the 13th

vol. of *DWb.* [1909] still preferred *wälsch*). It is often used for 'French', e.g. *die welsche Schweiz* or *Welschland* for 'French-speaking Switzerland' or 'Italian' (in 1741 Frisch wrote: '*Welsche heissen unter dem Pöbel nicht nur die Italiäner, sondern auch die Franzosen*'). Pejoration began in MHG (cf. Walther v.d. Vogelweide 34,11), was reinforced in the 16th c. through hostility to Rome, in the 17th c. through the publications of linguistic purists, and later through anti-French sentiments until it became partly-pejor. as 'foreign' and then totally pejor. For detailed treatment see L.Weisgerber, *walhisc, die geschichtliche Leistung des Wortes welsch* [1948].

das Kauderwelsch double Dutch, incomprehensible jargon, gibberish; since the 17th c. for 'abstruse, confused speech', frequent in Grimmelshausen, *Simpliz.* , also since the 17th c. with ref. to languages which one does not know (Goethe once referred to Hebrew as *kauderwelsches Idiom*); sometimes it can mean the same as Engl. 'gobbledegook'. There is also a verb *kauderwelschen* = 'to talk in a way nobody can understand', current since the 18th c. For the derivation of *kauder* from the Swiss city of Chur see Kluge, *Etym.Wb.*

das Rotwelsch cant, language of the criminal underworld; since MHG, e.g. *Passional* [edit. H.] 221: '*der kuniginnen rat walsch was in verborgen*', where it describes language incomprehensible to outsiders. Whilst *welsch* stands for 'incomprehensible', *rot* is still unsolved. It certainly has no obvious connexion with the colour, but attempts to connect it with *Rotte*, e.g. Frisch [1741]; '*es scheint Rott-Welsch des zusammengerotteten Gesindes Sprach zu seyn*', have met with considerable doubt.

welschen (a.) to speak indistinctly or in terms nobody can understand; also sometimes = 'to use foreign words unnecessarily'; now a. in all senses.

← See also under *Suppe* (for *jem.m ein welsch Süpplein geben*).

Welt: world

die ~ (1) (personified) the World; in lit. since MHG, e.g. *frou welt*, as in *Minnesinger* [edit. v.d.Hagen] 2,135b. It is assumed to have been imported from near-Eastern beliefs. In these the world was seen as false, cruel and untrustworthy, and this is still reflected in early German lit., until later in the Middle Ages it was regarded more positively as God's creation, though often it remained associated with wickedness, as in Luther, *Briefw.* 8,353 (Weimar): '*die welt ist nicht allein des teuffels, sondern der teuffel selber*'. *Kind dieser* ~ and *Weltkind* (see p. 1465) also contain the negative flavour (and an element of personification).

die ~ (2) mankind, humanity, (the population of) the world; general since MHG, e.g. *alle werlt*

= 'everybody', *deheine werlte* = 'nobody', *junge werlt* = 'young people', Luther Apocr. transl. Ecclesiasticus 10,7: '*den Hoffärtigen ist Gott und die Welt feind*', Schiller, *Räuber* 3,2: '*die ganze Welt eine Familie*', Goethe, *Dicht.u.Wahrh.* 18: '*Lavater wollte die ganze Welt zu Mitarbeitern*'. Frequent in compounds, e.g. *Mitwelt* = 'fellow human beings, the present generation', recorded as new by Campe [1809], used by Schiller, *Wall.* prol.44 and Goethe, *Elegien* 5: '*Vor- und Mitwelt spricht lauter und reizender mir*', *Nachwelt* = 'posterity', f.r.b. Stieler [1691], e.g. Lessing 1,3 on the poet: '*er, den Welt und Nachwelt liest*', Goethe, *Faust I* (*Vorsp.*): '*gesetzt, daß ich von Nachwelt reden wollte, wer machte denn der Mitwelt Spaß?*', *Umwelt* = 'environment', recorded as new by Campe [1811], taken up as a substitute for *Milieu*, used by Goethe in 30,27 (W.) of 1816 and IV,36,63 (W.) of 1821 (cf. *ZfdW.* 7,58), *Vorwelt* = 'former ages, the past, past generations', f.r.b. Kramer [1702]; cf. Goethe quotation above under *Mitwelt*. For others see separate entries below and the list of cross-references.

die ~ (3) (pejor.) sinful humanity (seen as disobedient to God's commandments); see remarks under *~* (1); general with many adjectives since Early NHG, e.g. *arge ~*, as in H.Sachs, *Fab.* 2,75, *böse ~*, as in Fischart, *Garg.* 94. Kramer [1702] listed: '*die arge, lose, blinde, falsche, eitele, verderbte, verrätherische, unreine etc. Welt*'; pejor. also in *verkehrte ~* = 'topsy-turvy world' and in exclamations such as *was ist das für eine ~ !*

die ~ (4) people of breeding or culture, good society, upper classes and their behaviour or standards; since the 17th c., sometimes with adjectives such as *feine, elegante, vornehme*, but also on its own (now a.), e.g. Schiller, *Fiesco* 2,2: '*der Graf hat Person, Welt, Geschmack*' or *Kab.u.L.* 4,7: '*wo sie Manieren und Welt lernen kann*'.

die ~ (5) (lit.) world, some entity comparable to a world; since Early NHG, e.g. Luther Bible transl. James 3,6: '*Vnd die Zunge ist auch ein Fewer, eine Welt vol vngerechtigkeit*', Goethe, *Kenner u.Enthus.* :'*Mein Busen war so voll und bang, von hundert Welten trächtig*'; cf. *eine ~ von Vorstellungen, ~ der Träume*.

die ~ (6) world (of some category, group, class or family); beginnings in the 16th c., e.g. *die ~ der Diplomatie, die christliche ~, die gelehrte ~, die ~ der Philosophen*, also in the natural sciences, e.g. *die ~ der Säugetiere, die gefiederte ~* for 'the feathered world' (not yet mentioned in *DWb.* [1878]).

die ~ (7) the world, confines or environment of sb.'s life or interests; since the 17th c. in such phrases as *Bücher sind seine ~, er baute sich eine eigene ~ auf*.

eine (sometimes *die*) *~* (coll.) anything in the world, a great deal; hyperbole of quantity; begin-

nings in Early MHG,frequent since Early NHG, e.g. Luther, *Tischr.* 1,417 (Weimar): '*ich geb ein welt vmb die legenden der patriarchen*', f.r.b. Serz [1797]: '*ich wollte die ganze Welt nicht nehmen*'; later often in *nicht um die ~* = 'not for anything (in the world)', e.g. H.v. Kleist, *Werke* 3,242 (*Kohlhaas*): '*nicht um die Welt!*'. Into this group fall also *es kann die ~ nicht kosten* = 'it cannot cost a lot, is probably affordable', recorded since the 19th c., and the boastful or over-confident *was kostet die ~ ?* (coll.) = 'I could manage anything now, no problem at all', which started in the 18th c. in stud.sl. The notion of 'great deal, vast amount' is also present in such phrases as *er sieht nicht aus, als ob er die ~ einreißen könnte* (coll.) = 'he is not likely to get far or to set the Thames on fire', current since the 18th c., e.g. (DWb) Kretschman, *Sämtl.Werke* 3,1 [1786]: '*ey nun – der wird die Welt nicht wegtragen!*'. Kramer [1702] recorded *eine ~ von Menschen* for 'lots of people', but this use of *~* for 'many people' has been current since OHG, e.g. Luther 28,526 (Weimar): '*eine grosse welt volcks*'.

meine ~ my love; term of endearment, comparable to *mein Alles*; though only recorded since the 19th c., surely much older in the language of lovers and poetry.

alle ~ ! my word! by Jove! current since MHG, used by Walther v.d.Vogelweide 28,31: '*al die werlt*', where it is a joyful exclamation. It is assumed by some that it is a shortened form of *alle ~ rufe ich zum Zeugen*, though I prefer to interpret it as *alle ~ soll es hören*. In modern usage it expresses admiration or amazement.

was in aller ~ . . . . what in heaven's name (made you do it?); similarly *was, warum, wie in aller ~*; in earlier periods with *um* instead of *in* and probably going back to *um aller ~ willen* (cf. *um Gottes willen*, for which see p. 1101); f.r.b. Serz [1797], and in lit. frequent since early in the 19th c.

um alles in der ~ ! (coll.) for heaven's sake! exclamation of irritation or impatience; since the 18th c. also frequent in the negative *um alles in der ~ nicht* = 'not at any price', as in Wieland 1,162, or *um die ~ nicht*, as in Stilling 1,64; cf. such similar negations as in Gellert, *Zärtl.Schw.* 1,4: '*mir wird nichts in der Welt zu schwer sein*'.

die alte ~ (1) the world of the Ancients, the Classical world; at least since the 17th c.; Kramer [1700] recorded '*die alte Welt* = *l'antica simplicità*', e.g. Goethe 46,66 (W.), where Rome is called '*Mittelpunkt der alten Welt*'. See also the entry under *alt* (p. 29).

die alte ~ (2) Europe; probably since the 17th c., although Kramer [1702] recorded only *neue ~* for 'America' and did not list *alte ~* for 'Europe'.

die alte ~ (3) (coll.) the elderly; modern, used with ref. to older people in a mixed gathering, also called *die alten Herrschaften*.

zur alten ~ gehören (or von der alten ~ sein) to follow oldfashioned ways; mostly in praise = 'to have strict long-established standards (and be averse to modern laxity)'; recorded since the 16th c., e.g. by Tappius [1545].

es ist jetzt eine andere ~ conditions are quite different now; since Early NHG, e.g. Luther 11,270 (Weimar): 'es ist itzt nicht mehr eyn welt wie vortzeytten'; Steinbach [1734] recorded: 'es ist itzt eine andere Welt'; the phrase belongs to ~ (6).

das ist nicht aus der ~ that is not very far (from here); since Early NHG, e.g. Fischart, S.Dicht. [edit. Kurz] 1,57: 'dann Vlm, das ist nicht auß der welt, noch Thübingen . . . ', Gökingk, Ged. 1,292: 'und sechs und dreißig Meilen ist ja nicht aus der Welt'. Goethe used 'nicht außerhalb der Welt'.

die bessere ~ the other world, the Beyond, Heaven, Paradise; one of several terms used for the world after death; earlier die andere ~ was also used; general since the 18th c., e.g. Schiller, Räuber 4, 4; cf. Schiller, Kab.u.L. 2,4: 'in dieser oder in jener Welt'; Kramer [1702] recorded in jener ~. Cf. also Usteri, Dicht. 1,5 [1831]: 'so wallt man leicht ins beßre Vaterland'.

nichts auf der ~ besitzen to be penniless (or without family); recorded by Kramer [1702].

eine Kind zur ~ bringen to bear a child; phrases with ~ and bringen have been current since MHG, relating to birth are numerous, first in MHG, e.g. Marienlieder [edit. W.Grimm] 95,16: 'ein kint zû der werlde bringen', followed by zur (or in die) ~ kommen, e.g. Fischart, Garg. 40 or Goethe 26,11 (W.) and ein Kind in die ~ setzen (see p.2249). These phrases could also be figur. extended to relate to abstracts such as a performance, works of literature or music, at least since the 17th c., e.g. Grimmelshausen, Simpliz. [edit Scholte] 160: '. . . sein Schelmenstück . . . auf die Welt zu bringen', Goethe IV,34,101 (W.): '. . . daß die zu spät zur Welt geborenen Hefte freundlich aufgenommen . . . werden', Beethoven, S.Briefe [edit. Kalischer] 5,273: 'ih hoffe noch einige große Werke zur Welt zu bringen'. See also under bringen.

er hat das mit auf die ~ gebracht he was born with that; with ref. to innate or inherited traits of character or features; modern (not yet recorded in DWb. [1885]), but cf. entry under mitbringen, which shows the beginning of this phrase.

die bucklige ~ (regional) very hilly region; used in general contexts, but also for specific regions, e.g. in Austria for the Mühlviertel in Upper Austria (recorded since the 19th c., e.g. by Wander [1880]).

die ~ ist ein Dorf (coll.) the world is but a little place after all; expression used when meeting an acquaintance far away from home; since ca. 1900, equivalent to 'fancy meeting you here of all places'; the Engl. version cited is also modern.

die dritte ~ the Third World; used for the developing countries; first in the press, since 1962 (details in A.D.Nunn, Polit. Schlagwörter 70 [1974]).

die erste ~ (a.) the world before the Flood; Kramer [1702] still recorded it as 'die Vorwelt vor der Sündflut', and it was still occasionally used in 19th c. lit., but is now rare or a.

in die ~ hinein leben to live without a care about tomorrow; since the 17th c., e.g. Merck, Briefe [Darmstadt 1835 edit.], but in den Tag hinein leben is now preferred for which see p. 2427. See also under Gelage (p. 969).

die ganze ~ liegt im Argen (bibl.) the whole world is full of sin; quotation from Luther Bible transl. 1 John 5,19 (where the A.V. has 'the whole world lieth in wickedness'), recorded as prov. by Petri 2,129 [1605].

die halbe ~ lots of people, practically everybody; hyperbole; cf. halb (2) on p. 1201 (for the entirely different Halbwelt see p. 1202).

solange die ~ besteht (or steht) since time immemorial; recorded by Steinbach [1734] with steht.

das (or sowas) hat die ~ noch nicht gesehen (coll.) this is unbelievable or unheard-of; modern coll.; cf. non-coll. examples such as Lessing 8,8; 'alles, was die Welt noch bis itzt von elenden Übersetzern gesehen hat', also Goethe IV,33,35 (W.)

deswegen (or darum, davon) geht die ~ nicht unter (coll.) that is not the end of the world, is not tragic; modern, since early in the 20th c. (cf. Küpper, Pons 916 [1987]).

es ist eine verkehrte ~ everything is wrong (or topsy-turvy) in the world; since the 17th c., f.r.b. Kramer [1700]). Cf. die ~ steht auf dem Kopf, used by Alexis in Hosen d.H.v.B. 293.

die ~ verlassen to die; euphem. in origin; often the phrase implies suicide; at least since the 17th c., recorded by Kramer [1702], frequent in Goethe's writings (e.g. in Werther). In earlier times der ~ Urlaub geben, aus der ~ scheiden and ab der ~ wandern occurred, later also die ~ quittieren or segnen. A different (transitive) die ~ verlassen = 'to abandon or forsake the world' is older and occurs in Luther 2,13b (Jena).

die vierte ~ the underdeveloped countries of the world; since the 2nd half of the 20th c. in econ. and press jargon.

vor der ~ (1) in public; since Early NHG, recorded since the 15th c.

vor der ~ (2) or in den Augen der ~ in the eyes of the world, in public opinion; since the 17th c., e.g. (DWb) Moscherosch, Gesichte 1,153 [1650], Lessing 2,295: 'genug, daß ich in den Augen der Welt für ein Frauenzimmer ohne Tadel galt'.

vor die ~ treten to appear in public, also to come out publicly with sth.; with ref. to appearance on the stage or publishing sth.; modern.

ein Wanderer zwischen zwei Welten (lit.) wanderer between two different worlds or modes of thought; since the 18th c., when Herder and after him Goethe used *zwischen zwei Welten wandeln*; in modern period given wider currency through *Der Wanderer zwischen beiden Welten* by W.Flex [1916]; cf. also Th.Mann 9,270 (*T. Kröger*): '*ich stehe zwischen zwei Welten, bin in keiner daheim*'.

die kleine ~ (lit.) man; also = 'microcosm'; since MHG, e.g. Frauenlob [edit. Ettmüller] 437: '*die minner werlt, daz ist der mensch*', Fischart, *Werke* (edit. Hauffen) 1,371: '*daher der mensch heißt die klein welt, weil er die groß welt in sich hält*', Thümmel 3,80: '*die kleine Welt, der Mensch*'; cf. also Wieland 2,52: '*innerhalb der kleinen Welt seines Hirnschädels*' and Heine, *Werke* [1861 edit.] 6,87 where *kleinweltlich* = 'forming a microcosm' occurs.

'*ich verstehe die* ~ *nicht mehr*' I do not understand the world any more; quotation from the end of Fr. Hebbel's *Maria Magdalena* [1844].

die ~ *will betrogen sein* (prov.) if the world will be gulled, let it be gulled; wrongly attributed by some (e.g. *Oxf.* 732) to Cardinal Caraffa, as he entered Paris in 1556, but Luther who died in 1546 used it (cf. *Luthers Sprichwörter* [edit. Heuseler] 392). The fuller form is *die* ~ *betrügt und will betrogen sein*, sometimes used in the Lat. version *mundus vult decipi, ergo decipiatur*.

← See also under *Abschied* (for *der Welt den Abschied geben*), *absondern* (for *sich von der Welt absondern*), *absterben* (for *der Welt absterben*), *all* (for *allerwelts* and *Alltagswelt*), *alt* (for *in der alten Welt*), *Angel* (for *die Welt aus den Angeln heben*), *aufschlagen* (for *die Welt liegt aufgeschlagen wie ein Gesangbuch da*), *befördern* (for *jem. in eine bessere Welt befördern*), *Beutel* (for *so geht es in der Welt*), *blasen* (for *etw. in die Welt hinausblasen*), *Brett* (for *dort ist die Welt mit Brettern vernagelt* and *Bretter, die die Welt bedeuten*), *bringen* (for *ein Kind zur Welt bringen*), *Dank* (for *der Welt Dank or Lohn*), *darlegen* (for *schließen die moralische Welt auf*), *durchschlagen* (for *dich durch die ganze Welt durchschlagen*), *düster* (for *der blinden und dustern Welt*), *eigen* (for *eine eigene Welt*), *Einklang* (for *in sein Herz die Welt zurücke schlingt*), *Ende* (for *in allen vier Enden der Welt* and *bis ans Ende der Welt*), *erblicken* (for *das Licht der Welt erblicken*), *Feuer* (for *in die wellt speyen*), *Folie* (for *er legt sich als Folie der ganzen Welt unter*), *fortkommen* (for *kan in der ganzen welt fortkommen*), *fragen* (for *mit Fragen kommt man durch die Welt*), *Freiheit* (for *die ganze Welt hätte wissen dürfen*), *Fürst* (for *der Fürst dieser Welt*), *Geist* (for *Geisterwelt*), *Geld* (for several proverbs), *Geschmack* (for *ungeschmacke welt*), *Gewicht* (for *sie treiben das lebende Uhrwerk der Welt, er selbst ist das Gewicht der Welt* and *du trägst wie Atlas seine Welt*), *Glück* (for *mit einer Glückshaube auf die Welt gekommen*), *Gold* (for *genem der gulden welt*), *Gott* (for *Gott und die Welt*), *Grind* (for *wunderbar Ding ums Regiment*

dieser Welt), *Grund* (for *sich eine schuldlos reine Welt zu gründen*), *gucken* (for *der Guckindiewelt*), *halb* (for *Halbwelt*), *herumschlagen* (for *Muth, mich die Welt zu wagen*), *Jammer* (for *doch ist diu werlde ein jâmertal*), *Kind* (for *Kindheit der Welt* and *Weltkind*), *Kranz* (for *dem Mimen flicht die Nachwelt keine Kränze*), *laufen* (for *die Welt läuft* and *Lauf der Welt*), *Lohn* (for *Undank ist der Welt Lohn*), *Markt* (for *wo vier Welten ihre Schätze tauschen ... auf dem Markt der Welt*), *Meer* (for *das Meer der Welt*), *Mut* (for *dem Mutigen gehört die Welt*), *Nabel* (for *der Nabel der Welt*), *Netz* (for *Annoncen in die Welt geschleudert*), *neu* (for *die neue Welt* (1) and (2)), *nobel* (for *nobel geht die Welt zu Grunde*), *Ohr* (for *sich die Welt um die Ohren schlagen*), *Papier* (for *papierne Welt*), *rauh* (for *in die rauhe Welt schicken*), *Rede* (for *die Welt von uns reden machen*), *Reihe* (for *alles in der Welt läßt sich ertragen*), *Runzel* (for *die Welt ist faltig, schrammig und runtzelheudig*), *schaffen* (for *etw. aus der Welt schaffen*), *scheiden* (for *aus der Welt scheiden*), *Schein* (for *die Welt des schönen Scheins*), *schicken* (for *einen in die Welt schicken*), *schmücken* (for *Schmuck der Welt*), *schön* (for *die schöne Welt*), *schwarz* (for *es liebt die Welt das Strahlende zu schwärzen*), *sehen* (for *sah sich wol umb in der welt*), *setzen* (for *ein Kind in die Welt setzen*), *Sinn* (for *gott helt auch die welt dafur ...*), *Spiel* (for *kaum hatt' ich mich in die Welt gespielt* and *die Welt ist ihm ein Spielplatz der Begierden*), *sterben* (for *abgestorben den Satzungen der Welt* and *gestorben für die Welt*), *Stück* (for *ein Stückchen Welt*), *studieren* (for *durchstudiert die groß' und kleine Welt*), *Sumpf* (for *ihre Geisteswelt versumpfte zu einem Aberglauben*), *taufen* (for *die getaufte Welt*), *Theater* (for *Theater der Welt*), *Tracht* (for *mein Busen war von hundert Welten trächtig*), *Traum* (for *Traumwelt*), *trennen* (for *uns trennen Welten voneinander*), *umfangen* (for *was die Welt für mich Theures umfing*), *untergehen* (for *wenn gleich die Welt untergienge*), *Unterwelt*, *Vater* (for *Vater der Welt*), *Venus* (for *Frau Venus und das Geld regiern alle Welt*) and *weit* (for *in der weiten Welt*).

weltabgewandt
er lebt ~ (lit.) he lives as a recluse, has turned his back on the world; modern, listed in *DWb.*, which also recorded *weltabgeschieden*, in use since the 19th c.

Weltall
das ~ the universe; since the 18th c., alongside *Weltenall*, used by Herder and Jean Paul.

Weltalter
das Weltalter period; in use since the 17th c. both for a period of time and for the people living in that particular period.

← See also under *alt* (for *Weltalter, Zeitalter*).

Weltampel: see *Ampel*.

Weltangst
die ~ (lit.) terror of feeling alone or deserted in a world conceived as hostile or indifferent; first in Spengler, *Unterg.d.Abendl.* 1,238 [1918].

Weltanschauung

die ~ (lit.) world-view, philosophy of life, ideology; also in Engl. used as ~; coined by Kant, *Werke* (Acad.Edit.) I,5,255 [1790], quickly taken up by many, also ridiculed by some in the 19th c. when the term had come to be used for sb.'s personal convictions, particularly in politics. See also under *anschauen* (p. 56).

← See also under *verbilden* (for *unsre so oft in kleinlicher Verbildung ruhende Weltanschauung*).

Weltapfel: see *Apfel*.

Weltaufkommen

das ~ (econ.) world production; 20th c. econ. jargon, not yet listed in *DWb*. [1955]

Weltauge

das ~ (1) (poet.) the Sun; as *Auge der Welt* already in OHG (Notker), as a compound since the 16th c.

das ~ (2) (mineral.) (variety of) opal; f.r.b. Hübner [1776]; Goethe used it in III,8,163 (W.); it is also called *Hydrophan*.

Weltball

der ~ the globe; f.r.b. Stieler [1691].

Weltbeglücker

der ~ (lit.) saviour of the world, deliverer of the world from misery; Herder [edit. S.] 19,113 used it for Christ; later often ironic for 'idealist who thinks that he can save mankind' (19th c.).

Weltbejahung

die ~ (lit.) positive attitude to life; since the 19th c., when the opposite *Weltverneinung* also arose.

weltbewegend

weltbewegend world-shaking; since the 19th c.; Heine [edit. E.] 7,79 called Goethe '*weltbewegender Dichter*'; hence also *das ist nicht* ~ (coll.) = 'that is nothing to make a song and dance about', 20th c. coll. – Synonymous *welterschütternd* is older but figur. use established itself only ca. 1800; Heine 6,330 used '*welterschütternde Bedeutung*'.

← See also under *gischen* (for *ein weltbewegender Mensch steht wie ein Gigant*).

Weltbild

jem.s ~ sb.'s conception of the world (or of life); the compound made its first appearance in OHG when Notker used it rendering Lat. *imago mundi*, but it only came into general use in the 19th c.; Goethe used it in 1818 in 49,1,153 (W.)

Weltbürger

ein ~ a citizen of the world, cosmopolitan; translated in the 18th c. from Greek *kosmopolites*, e.g. Wieland, *Nachl.d.Diog.* 31.

← See also under *Gilde* (for *auch wird der freie Weltbürger sich schwerlich in eine enge Gilde einzunften lassen*).

Weltenbummler: see *bummeln*.

Weltende

er wohnt am ~ (coll.) he lives at the back of beyond; 19th c. coll.; see also under *Ende* for *am Ende der Welt*. *Weltende* for terminal 'end of the world' arose in the 18th c., not yet recorded by Kramer [1702], used by Herder (cf. also the entry under *Ende* for *bis ans Ende der Welt* (p. 632)).

Weltenlenker: see *lenken*.

Weltenstürmer: see *Sturm*.

weltentrückt: see *entrücken*.

weltfern: see *fern* (also for *weltentrückt, weltflüchtig, weltfremd* and *weltverloren*).

Weltflucht

die ~ (lit.) flight (or withdrawal) from the world (or from life); derived from the adj. *weltflüchtig* (current since the 17th c.) in the 18th c. Hence *Weltflüchtling*, in use since the 19th c. but rare.

weltfremd

weltfremd (1) unknown to everybody; since Early NHG, e.g. (DWb) Mechtel, *Limb. Chron.*, used by Goethe 24,144 (W.).

weltfremd (2) ignorant of the (real) world, unwordly; also = 'incapable of coping with life's problems'; since the 19th c.

weltfremd (3) starry-eyed, idealistic; often with pejor. tinge; since late in the 19th c.

Weltfrömmigkeit: see *Haus* (p. 1259).

Weltgericht

das ~ (relig.) the day of judgment; since Early NHG, but Luther in his transl. of John 12,31 still has '*itzt gehet das gerihte uber die welt*'; Simon Dach used the compound which is still in use, although *das Jüngste Gericht* is more often used (see under *Gericht* on p. 989). The meaning 'judgment which will be passed on the world' in non-relig. contexts arose in the 18th c., e.g. Schiller, *Resignation* 85: '*die Weltgeschichte ist das Weltgericht*'.

weltgerieben: see *reiben*.

Weltgeschichte

das hört (sich) die ~ *auf* (coll.) that is the limit, the last straw; also = 'that is unbelievable'; modern coll.

in der ~ *herumreisen* (coll.) to gallivant all over the place; inappropriate addition of *Geschichte* where *Welt* alone is sufficient; current since the 19th c., recorded by Müller-Fraureuth for parts of Saxony, but also used elsewhere.

← See also under *Geschichte* (for *neues Blatt der Weltgeschichte*), *Gewand* (for *Weltgeschichte ... das Gewand der Gottesgeschichte*), *Gold* (for *in den goldenen Rollen der Weltgeschichte*) and *Treppe* (for *ein Treppenwitz der Weltgeschichte*); also under *Weltgericht* (above).

Weltgetümmel: see *Getümmel*.

weltgewandt

weltgewandt (lit.) versed in worldly affairs, urbane; since early in the 19th c., e.g. (DWb) Eichendorff, *Sämtl.W.* 3,342; from this derived *Weltgewandtheit*, current since the 19th c.

Weltgewissen

das ~ (lit.) the conscience of mankind; since the 1st quarter of the 20th c.; occasionally personified with *sprechen* oder *protestieren*, as in the case of *Gewissen*, for which see p. 1038. Cf. *ans* ~ *appellieren* = 'to appeal to the conscience of mankind'.

Weltherrschaft: see *groß*.

Weltkind: see *Kind*.

weltklug

weltklug experienced and wise in practical things; since Early NHG; sometimes = 'politically or tactically clever' as opposed to 'truly wise and considering eternal values', as in Luther 24,311 (Weimar); recorded by Stieler [1691]; hence *Weltklugheit*, recorded by Frisch [1741], used by Goethe, e.g. 11,63 (W.).

Weltkörper: see *Grund* (p. 1164).

Weltkreis: see *decken*.

Weltlauf

See under *einheimisch* (for *mit dem . . . Weltlauf einheimisch und innig bekannt gewesen*), *gern* (for *es geht nach der welt laufft*), also under *schicken* (for *sich in der wält lauff schicken*).

weltläufig

weltläufig (1) (lit.) experienced in wordly affairs, cultivated and sociable; since the 15th c., at first referring principally to experience gained by contact with many people or things (as in *bewandert* and *erfahren*); in modern times mainly with ref. to social graces, cultivated behaviour in society, as in Th.Mann, *Buddenbrooks* 1,135: '*ein wohlerzogener und weltläufiger Mann*'; hence *Weltläufigkeit*, since the 19th c., e.g. Böll, *Dienstfahrt* 68 (also used by Th.Mann in *Buddenbrooks*).

weltläufig (2) occurring frequently, usual; since Early NHG, but *landläufig* is now preferred (see under *Land*, p. 1581).

weltläufig (3) (regional, obs.) weak-minded; a regional term on which Goethe III,4,119 (W.) provides details.

Weltleute: see *Strom*.

weltlich

weltlich (1) worldly, mundane, secular, temporal, profane (as opposed to spiritual or religious); since OHG, e.g. H.Sachs, *Fab.* 2,85: '*in . . . geistlich und weltlich regimenten*'; cf. Luther's use alongside *zeitlich*, as in 18,321 (Weimar): '*alle von welltlichen zeytlichen sachen*'.

weltlich (2) worldly-minded; since MHG, e.g. Tauler, *Pred.* [edit. Vetter] 87: '*weltliche lute und sundige menschen*'.

← See also under *fassen* (for *der Imperator faßte die Religion in dem weltlichsten Bezuge*) and *Gericht* (for *Gebiet der weltlichen Gesetze*); also below under *Weltling*.

Weltling

der ~ worldling, child of this world; since Early NHG; Schottel [1663] recorded '*du Weltling*

magst haben nur weltliche Gaben'; cf. similar *Weltkind* (under *Kind*).

Weltmacht: see *Macht*.

Weltmann: see *unlenksam*.

weltmännisch

weltmännisch in the manner of (or as befits) a man of the world; since the 18th c., e.g. Goethe 28,335 (W.), f.r.b. Campe [1811].

Weltmeer

See under *schöpfen* (for *das große Weltmeer in eine Trinkschale zu schöpfen*), also under *Meer* (for *das Meer der Welt*).

Weltmeinung

die ~ public opinion; since the 17th c. (but not yet recorded by Kramer [1702]); see also under *offen* for *öffentliche Meinung*.

weltoffen

weltoffen (1) evident, available for all the world to see, public; the same as *weltoffenbar*, since the 19th c.

weltoffen (2) open-minded, out-going; describing a willingness to be sociable and ability to make contact with most people. At first (in the 19th c.) it referred to countries (and their inhabitants) for 'open to foreigners and tolerant towards them'; now principally with ref. to fellow human beings.

Weltordnung

die ~ world order; beginnings in Early NHG, but general only since the 18th c.; cf. *Ordnung* for *Ordnung regiert die Welt* and *Ordnung erhält die Welt* on p. 1816, also the quotation containing *Weltenordner* on p. 1815.

← See also under *Geschrei* (for *Angstgeschrei um die moralische Weltordnung*).

Weltplan

der ~ (lit.) the planned course of the world; since the 2nd half of the 18th c.; Schiller used it in *Resignation* 49: '. . . *des kranken Weltplans schlau erdachte Retter*'; *Weltenplan* also occurs, e.g. Gutzkow, *R.v.G.* 9,106 or in the humorous aria in Lortzing's opera *Zar und Zimmermann* (text by Römer and von Biedenfeld): '*beschlossen ist's im Weltenplan, ich werd ein hochberühmter Mann*'.

Weltrang: see *Rang*.

Welträtsel: see *Rätsel*.

Weltraummacht: see *geben* (p. 928).

Weltreich

das ~ empire; since the 16th c. as a political and geogr. concept, but earlier as antonym to *Himmelreich* in relig. contexts.

mein ~ (ironic) my surroundings, the world I call my own; since the 19th c., e.g. (DWb) Anzengruber, *Ges. Werke* 9,246: '*mein grünes Weltreich geht über sein Fassungsvermögen*'; cf. *meine Welt*, listed under *Welt* (7).

Weltruf

der ~ world reputation; only since the 19th c. and not yet in Campe (1811).

Weltrund

das ~ the earth, globe; recorded by Stieler [1691]; Schiller used *Rund der Welt* in *D.Carlos* (see under *rund*, p. 2030).

Weltschmerz: see *Schmerz.*

Weltschöpfer

der ~ (also *Weltenschöpfer*) creator of the world, God; since the 17th c., though not yet recorded by Stieler [1691] or Kramer [1702].

Weltseele: see *Thron.*

Weltteil: see *Teil.*

Welttheater: see *Theater.*

Weltton: see *Marionette.*

weltumfassend: see *Planet.*

Weltuntergang

der ~ the end of the world; as a compound only since later in the 18th c., used by Schiller, e.g. in *Die unüberwindliche Flotte*, f.r.b. Campe [1811], but not yet in Adelung, even missing in his 2nd edit.; cf. the near-coll. *in Weltuntergangsstimmung sein* = to be plunged into a feeling of black despair'.

Weltverbesserer: see *verbessern.*

weltvergessen

weltvergessen (lit.) oblivious of the world, sunk in meditation, immersed in one's thoughts; since the 18th c.; hence *Weltvergessenheit*, also since the 18th c.

Weltverhängnis: see *entgegenwerfen.*

weltverlassen: see *Gott.*

Weltverneinung

die ~ (lit.) rejection of the world; since the 19th c.; see also under *Weltbejahung* above.

Weltvernunft: see *verzweigen.*

weltweise

weltweise (1) (a.) wise, learned, capable of dealing with problems; since OHG *weralt-wîsi*, MHG *werlt-wîse*, but now a.

weltweise (2) (a.) clever, possessing worldly wisdom, experienced; since MHG, but now a.

der Weltweise thinker, scholar, philosopher, philosopher; since OHG *werlt-wîso*; Luther used it in his Bible transl. of 1 Cor. 1,20; still alive, but rare.

Weltweisheit

die ~ philosophy; since MHG *werltwîsheit*; in relig. contexts at first often as antonym to *Gottesweisheit*; used by Luther, e.g. *Tischr.* 2,8 (Weimar); since the 17th c. general for 'philosophy', also as a title for the university subject.

← See also under *Kram* (for *Allerweltsweisheitskrämer*).

weltweit

weltweit (1) comprising the entire world; since the 17th c., f.r.b. Stieler [1691].

weltweit (2) extending over the whole world; since the 19th c., mainly with ref. to communications and trade.

weltweit (3) immensely wide, very extensive; hyperbole; since the 18th c., e.g. *es ist ein weltweiter Unterschied, das ist weltweit entfernt von der Wahrheit.*

Weltwunder

die sieben ~ the seven wonders of the world; based on Lat. *mirabilia mundi*; in German since Early NHG, e.g. (DWb) Mathesius, *Ausgew. Werke* [edit. L.] 4,475: '. . . der siben grossen weltwunder eines'. The seven ancient wonders were: the pyramids, the hanging gardens of Babylon, the Mausoleum, the temple of Diana at Ephesus, the statue of Jupiter by Phidias, the Pharos of Alexandria and the Colossus of Rhodes. Later other lists of seven were made (see Brewer, *Dict. of Phrase and Fable* 1185 in the 14th edit. of 1989.). Sth. unusual or impressive can be called *ein achtes* ~, as in Storm 7,247 (*Schimmelreiter*).

das kleine ~ (ironic) the little marvel; ironic use of ~ for sth. that is a wonderful thing to sb., although it is in reality sth. fairly ordinary; sometimes with ref. to the admiration of parents for their babies, as in P.Heyse, *Mer.* 319: '*wenn Einer nach dem kleinen Weltwunder schielte*'.

Weltzirkel: see *treiben.*

weltzugewandt

weltzugewandt (lit.) worldly, appreciative of the pleasures of this world; recent term, often the same as *weltoffen* (2), which see above.

Wende: turning, turning-point

die ~ (1) change; figur. from its beginnings in OHG, where it could describe 'conversion'; then in a great number of contexts, often with ref. to time (*Zeitenwende*, ~ *des Jahrhunderts*) or to personal development, also to the peripateia in drama.

die ~ (2) (polit.) the collapse of the German Democratic Republic bringing about the reunification of Germany; since ca. 1990.

← See also under *Sonne* (for *Sonnenwende*).

Wendehals: wryneck

der ~ (polit.) turncoat, renegade; derived from the name of the bird wryneck (*Jinx torquilla*) and applied to people who after the *Wende* in October 1989 (see above) changed their political convictions overnight and feigned genuine belief in democracy.

Wendeltreppe: see *Treppe.*

Wendekreis

der ~ tropic; loan-translation of Lat. *tropicus circulus* and its Greek equivalent; since the 2nd half of the 17th c.; used figur. by Gutzkow in *Ges. Werke* 2,393, but this is rare.

wenden: turn

See under *abwenden*, *anwenden*, *aufwenden*, *Auge* (for *die Augen von jem.m abwenden*), *bewenden* (also for *dabei hat es sein Bewenden*), *Blatt* (for *das Blatt wird sich wenden*), *drehen* (for *sich drehen und wenden*), *einwenden* (also for *Einwendung* and *Einwand*), *Gott* (for *so wandte sie sich andern Göttern zu*), *kehren* (for *die Kehrseite hervorwenden* and *Kehrtwendung*), *Kittel* (for *den Kittel umwenden* or *wenden*), *Licht* (for *sich dem Licht zuwenden*), *Napoleon* (for *ein umgewendeter Napoleon*), *prüfen* (for *nicht eine Stunde auff die Prüfung ihres Gewissens verwandt haben*), *Rede* (for *redegewandt*), *Schoß* (for *all dieß war einem Schoßkind zugewendet*), *selig* (for *seine Kunst verwenden*), *umkehren* (for *sich zu Gott wenden*), *umwenden, unabwendbar, verwenden* and *weltzugewandt*).

Wendepunkt: see *schweben*.

wendig

wendig agile, nimble, versatile, adaptable; used since OHG period to render Lat. *mutabilis*, MHG *wendec*; Corvinus [1646] recorded it in a pejor. sense: '*versutus . . . wendig, tückisch, listig*', which can still be present today, but does not predominate; Heyne was surprisingly wrong when he stated in his *Dt.Wb.* [1895] that ~ only occurred now in compounds; it was current in his time and is still used today.

← See also under *abwenden* (for *jem. abwendig machen*), *auswendig, dringen* (for *notwendige besserung*) and *inwendig* (for *etw. in und auswendig kennen*).

Wendung: turn

eine ~ zum Besseren (Schlechteren) nehmen to take a turn for the better (worse); beginnings in the 17th c., since Kramer [1702] recorded *Gemütswendung* and *Glückswendung*; frequent in *eine glückliche ~ nehmen*.

die Redewendung figure of speech, expression, phrase; f.r.b. Stieler [1691], e.g. Goethe in *Serbische Lieder* (on the German language): '*sie weiß sich in Worte, Wortbildungen, Wortfügungen, Redewendungen . . . so wohl zu finden . . .*'; he also used ~ in this sense, e.g. in a review of *Volkslieder der Serben*: '*. . . Fremdartiges aufzunehmen, sowohl in Wort als Bildung und Wendung*'; cf. also his poem *Christgeschenk*: '*Dir möcht ich dann mit süßem Redewenden poetisch Zuckerbrot zum Fest bereiten*'.

← See also under *kehren* (for *Kehrtwendung*) und *unübersetzbar* (for *eine unübersetzbare Wendung*).

wenig: little

meine wenige Person (a.) my humble self, yours truly; self-belittling formula, still recorded by Adelung, now a., but *meine Wenigkeit* with the same meaning is still alive, though treated jocularly.

mehr oder weniger more or less; since Early NHG, e.g. Luther, *Adel* (repr.) 41.

nichtsdestoweniger nevertheless, yet; since the 17th c., e.g. Grimmelshausen, *Simpliz.* [edit. S.] 122, still in three words; earlier *nichts des weniger* or *nichts des zu weniger* were used (16th c.); now written in one word.

nicht ~ quite a lot; litotes, current since the 17th c., e.g. (H.) Zesen, *Rosen.* 2: '*. . . belustigte sich nicht wenig*'.

weniger denn (or *als*) *nichts* less than nothing; since Early NHG, e.g. Luther Bible transl. Psalms 62,10.

er hat einen zu ~ (coll.) he is not quite right in the head; *einen* refers to one of the five senses; since the 18th c.

und weniger (sl.) let's deduct a little from what you are saying; interjection to a boastful or exaggerating person; since the middle of the 20th c.

viele Wenig machen ein Viel (prov.) little and often fills the purse; phrasing varies, e.g. *~ zu ~ macht zuletzt viel* or *~ und oft macht zuletzt viel*, recorded by Simrock [1846], but as early as in 1541 Franck recorded: '*wenig zu wenig gethan macht zuletzt viel*'.

← See also under *auskommen* (for *mit vielem hält man haus, mit wenigem kommt man aus*), *bedenken* (for *wer gar zu viel bedenkt, wird wenig leisten*), *Beil* (for *die das Beil am wenigsten tragen, reden am meisten von Feiertagen*), *berufen* (for *viele sind berufen, aber wenige sind auserwählt*), *Blut* (for *blutwenig*), *fehlen* (for *so wenig sonst*), *fragen* (for *frag ich wenig darnach*), *geben* (for *wenig auf etw. geben*), *gehören* (for *dazu gehört sehr wenig*), *Geschrei* (for *viel Geschrei und wenig Wolle*), *gewinnen* (for *wenig raum gewinnen*), *glatt* (for *abgeschliffen, wenigstens geglättet*), *haben* (for *er hat wenig von seinem Vater*), *halten* (for *uns andere für ein wenig mondsüchtig halten*), *Kopf* (for *wenig aber hat er Sinnen*), *Mond* (for *er kümmert mich so wenig wie der Mann im Mond*), *spät* (for *ein wenig zu spät ist viel zu spät*), *sterben* (for *zum Leben zu wenig und zum Sterben zuviel*), *Stern* (for *hatte ich abermal wenig Stern*), *Stil* (for *wenig klare, aber bezeichnende Schlagwörter*), and *viel* (for *wer zu vil wil han, dem wirt zu wenig*).

wenn: when, if

das Wenn the (great, unpleasant, awkward) if; since the 18th c., e.g. Henrici, *Ged.* 4,261 [1737]: '*ach! wäre doch das Wörtlein wenn nicht auf der Welt gebohren*'; frequent in phrases beginning with *wenn's wenn nicht wär* followed by *wär mancher Bauer ein Edelmann* or *so wär mein Vater ein Ratsherr* (or more recent: *wär mein Vater Millionär*); cf. Engl. 'if wishes were horses, beggars would ride'. Often coupled with *aber*, e.g. *mancher söffe das ganze Meer, wenn nur nicht das ~ und Aber wär*, recorded by Simrock [1846], Lewald, *Prinz L.Ferd.* 4,186 [1849]: '*die Feldherren von Wenn und Aber*'; cf. French prov. *n'était le si et le mais, nous serions tout parfaits*.

~ auch even if (or though); since Late MHG, e.g. Luther 28,24 (Weimar): '*wenn es auch ein engel vom hymel were*'.

als (or *wie*) *~* as if; this followed on *als ob* and began in the 16th c.; Goethe used it, e.g. 2,77 (W.), even in the extended version *wie als wenn* (not mentioned in *DWb.* [1958]).

~ schon, denn schon (coll.) if it is to be done, then let it be done properly; modern.

na ~ schon (coll.) does that matter? modern; in many cases the same as Engl. coll. 'so what?'.

~ anders (a.) provided that; Adelung still recorded it, but now it is ignored by most lexicographers; displaced by falls or vorausgesetzt daß.

wennen (coll.) to bring forward objections or raise difficulties; since the 19th c., e.g. da gibt's nichts zu wennen = 'that is going to happen, no ifs and buts'; cf. der Wennich und der Hättich sind zwei arme Brüder, recorded by Wander [1880].

wer das Wenn erstiegen, sieht das Aber liegen (prov.) you have hardly overcome one obstacle, when you are faced with new problems; f.r.b. Simrock [1846].

← See also under aber (for der Mann, der das Wenn und das Aber erdacht, hat sicher aus Häckerling Gold schon gemacht), Affe (for wenn ein Affe in den Spiegel hineinguckt, kann kein Apostel herausschauen), aufhören (for wenn's am schönsten ist, soll man aufhören), Auge (for wenn zwei Augen sich schließen and wenn dich dein Auge ärgert), Beichte (for selbst wenn der Teufel Beichte säße), bellen (for wenn ein alter Hund bellt, soll man hinausschauen), bitter (for wenn die Maus satt ist, schmeckt das Mehl bitter), Bock (for wenn die Böcke lammen), Himmel (for wenn der Himmel einfällt, sind alle Spatzen tot and variants), hoch (for wenn's hoch kommt), Horn (for wenn der Esel Hörner bekommt and das nützt soviel, wie wenn man einem Ochsen ins Horn petzt), Hund (for ja, wenn der Hund nicht . . .), Kalb (for wenn das glück wol will, so kälbert aim ein ochs and wenn's Kalb ersoffen ist, deckt der Bauer den Brunnen zu), Katze (for wenn die Katze aus dem Haus ist, tanzen die Mäuse auf dem Tisch), Meier (for ich will Meier heißen, wenn . . . .), Mond (for wenn er so groß wäre wie er dumm ist . . .), Not (for wenn die Not am größten ist Gott am nächsten), Ostern (for wenn Ostern auf den Charfreitag fällt and wenn Ostern und Pfingsten auf einen Tag fallen), Schnee (for und wenn der ganze Schnee verbrennt), schneien (for wenn es Rosen schneit), sein (for wenn das so wäre, wenn ich dich/du wäre and als wenn mir was fehlte), stellen (for auch/selbst wenn er sich auf den Kopf stellt), Stelze (for und wenn der Teufel auf Stelzen ginge) and Strang (for wenn alle Stricke reißen).

Wenzel

der ~ (regional coll.) jack (in card games); is a hypocoristic form for the name Wenzeslaus; in lit. since the 18th, in coll. use probably older.

der . . . wenzel (1) (coll.) . . . fellow, . . . chap; in compounds mainly in E. regions, e.g. Badewenzel = 'bath attendant'; also sometimes used as a term of abuse, e.g. Lausewenzel = Dreckskerl, as in F. Müller, Fausts Leben 100 [1778].

der . . . (2) (zool.) bird of the Sylvia or Motacilla family; in the regions as Brust-, Bunt-, Hecken-, Kloster- or Rotwenzel, mainly for Rotkehlchen = 'robin'.

← See also under Scharwenzel.

wer

es hat ~ angerufen (coll.) sb. has rung up; Stieler [1691] only recorded irgend wer for 'somebody', as shortened ~ in lit. since the 17th c., e.g. Logau, Sinnged. (repr.) 127 and 544, Goethe 15,1,12 (W.): 'verbiete wer, was alle wollten, der hat ins Wespennest gestört'; cf. also ~ sonst and ~ anders = 'who else', both general since the 19th c. Note, however, that more clearly defined locutions have been used since Early NHG, e.g. S.Dach [edit. Ö.] 735: 'ist wer unter uns'.

~ weiß ~ (coll.) somebody (unknown to me); at least since the 17th c., when ~ weiß wo, wann, wie were recorded.

er ist ~ (coll.) he is somebody (of importance), not to be overlooked or left out of account; e.g. er wollte ~ sein (coll.) = 'he wanted to be (or become) sth. special, wanted to be taken notice of', also possible in the plural: wir sind auch ~.

← See also under A (for wer A sagt, muß auch B sagen), Aal (for wer einen Aal fangen will, macht erst das Wasser trüb), Adam (for wer was do ein Edelman), beizen (for wer drohet, der beizt mit einem toten Falken), bejahen (for wer schweigt, bejaht), bekommen (for wer from ist, der bekompt trost vom herrn), bringen (for wer vieles bringt, wird manchem etwas bringen), Decke (for wer sich nicht nach der Decke streckt, dem bleiben die Füße unbedeckt), essen (for wer nicht kommt, hat gegessen), gewinnen (for wer nicht wagt, der nicht gewinnt), Gewalt (for wer Gewalt hat, der hat Recht), Glas (for wer im Glashaus sitzt, soll nicht mit Steinen werfen), glauben (for wer's glaubt wird selig and wer's nicht glaubt, zahlt einen Taler), Grube (for wer andern eine Grube gräbt, fällt selbst hinein), haben (for wer nicht will, der hat), hängen (for wer hangt, der langt and wer's lang hat, läßt's lang hängen), hoch (for wer hoch steigt, wird tief fallen), Honig (for wer erst Essig gekostet hat, dem schmeckt der Honig desto süßer), hören (for wer nicht hören will muß fühlen), Kalb (for wer Glück hat, dem kalbt der Ochs), kommen (for wer selten kommt, kommt wohl and wer nicht kommt . . . and variants), lachen (for zuletzt lacht, lacht am besten), Mühle (for wer auf meine Mühle kommt, ist mein Freund, wer zuerst zu der Mühle kommt, mahlt zuerst and wer nicht staubig werden will, bleib aus der Mühle), Pfennig (for wer den Pfennig nicht ehrt, ist den Taler nicht wert), sagen (for wer sagt, was er will, muß hören, was er nicht will), Schaden (for wer den Schaden hat, braucht für den Spott nicht zu sorgen), Schaf (for wer das Schaf hat, dem gehört auch die Wolle) and wenn (for wer das Wenn erstiegen, sieht das Aber liegen).

werben: seek to acquire

etw. wirbt (lit.) sth. tries to obtain, enrol, win over sth.; figur. when the subject is a thing or an abstract, as in Goethe, *Faust I*,891: '*die Trompete lassen wir werben*', Geibel,*Tod d.Tib.*: '*ein Fragen, das nur scheu um Antwort wirbt*'. Much older (since Late OHG) is *jem. wirbt um etw.*

← See also under *bewerben* (for *Bewerbchen*), *Handwerk* (for *Rache ist mein Gewerbe*), *nachgehen* (for *jeder seinem Gewerbe nachgeht*), *Quelle* (for *Erwerbsquelle*), *Trommel* (for *Werbetrommel*) and *Zweig* (for *Ge-* or *Erwerbszweig*).

werden

werden (1) to arise, be born, occur; since OHG with ref. to persons or things, e.g. Schiller, *Phoen.*370: '*und dann wardst du*', Goethe 2,129 (W.); sometimes in lit. as *wachsen und* ~; hence *etw. ist im Werden*, as in Goethe, *Faust I* (*Vorsp.* 185): '*da ich noch selbst im Werden war*'; also in pres. part. *werdend* in poetry since the 18th c., e.g. Klopstock, *Mess.* 14,743 or 17,217; cf. Goethe, *Faust I* (*Vorsp.* 183): '*ein Werdender wird immer dankbar sein*', and *werdende Mutter* = 'pregnant woman'.

werden (2) to become or turn into sth.; since OHG, e.g. Luther Bible transl. Gen. 1,5: '*das ward aus abend und morgen der erste tag*' or 3,22: '*Adam ist worden als unser einer*' (also 9,20), Schiller, *Kab.u.L.* 1,7: '*Sie werden mir zum Räzel*'. By the 17th c. in many phrases, e.g. Kramer [1702] recorded '*etwas werden, was willst du werden, er wird noch was werden, was ich noch nicht bin, das kan ich noch werden . . . etwas aus etwas werden, was wird aus dem Kinde werden, ich weiß nicht, was draus werden wird, aus Kindern werden Leute . . . nichts aus etwas werden*' and many more. See also the cross-references below.

es ist ihm worden (obs.) it has been given to him, has become his property; since MHG, e.g. Walther v.d.Vog. [edit. Kr.] 20,26, Herder, *Stimmen d.V.* 1,13; still used in the 19th c, now obs. except in poetry, displaced by *ist sein Eigentum geworden*, *ihm zugefallen*, *zuteil geworden*.

wird's bald? (coll.) hurry up! get a move on! since the 18th c., e.g. Lessing [edit. L.-M.] 2,4; it can also be an enquiry = 'will it come right soon?' with ellipsis of *fertig*, *in Ordnung kommen* or *werden*.

er wird wieder (coll.) he is getting better; ellipsis of *gesund*; cf. Adelung's recording '*es wird besser mit ihm*'.

wo werd' ich denn! (coll.) I wouldn't dream of it, out of the question; refusal; modern.

← See also under *Abend* (for *o Herr, laß Abend werden*), *anders* (for *mir wird ganz anders*), *Angst* (for *angst und bange werden*), *Asche* (for *zu Asche werden*), *bilden* (for *das hergebracht Werdende*), *bunt* (for *das wird mir zu bunt* and *es wird einem bunt vor den Augen*), *Bürge* (for *Bürge werden*), *fertig* (for *mit jem.m fertig werden*), *Fleisch* (for *ein Fleisch werden*), *gelb* (for *vor bosheit gelb ward als ein wax*), *gut* (for *das kann ja gut werden*), *Herr*

(for *einer Sache Herr werden*), *irre* (for *irre werden an dir*), *jung* (for *jung werden* and *wieder jung werden*), *Kalk* (for *er wird wie der Kalk an der Wand*), *kalt* (for *diu werdent drumbe kalt*), *Kind* (for *zum Kinde werden* and *kindisch werden*), *klug* (for *aus etwas nicht klug werden*), *lang* (for *das Essen wird mir lang im Hals* and *was lange währt, wird endlich gut*), *müde* (for *etw. müde werden*), *nichts* (for *viele Nichts sind zu etw. geworden* and *aus nichts wird nichts*), *Rat* (for *wer sich an Gott leßt, des ende wird gut radt*), *rauben* (for *etw. wird ein Raub von etw.*), *rot* (for *rot werden*), *satt* (for *etw.* or *einer Sache satt werden*), *sauer* (for *etw. wird jem.m sauer*), *schlecht* (for *schlecht werden*), *Schuh* (for *umgekehrt wird ein Schuh draus*), *schwer* (for *etw. wird jem.m schwer*), *sein* (for *was nicht ist, kann noch werden*), *sterben* (for *dieses stirb und werde*), *still* (for *er ist ein stiller Mann geworden* and *um den Mann ist es still geworden*), *Tag* (for *es wird Tag*), *übel* (for *mir wird übel*), *über* (for *mir wird es über*), *Vater* (for *Vater werden*), *verrückt* (for *ich werd' verrückt* and *es ist zum Verrücktwerden*), *wach* (for *wach werden*), *warm* (for *mit jem.m* or *in etw. warm werden*), *Wasser* (for *zu Wasser werden*) and *weich* (for *weich werden*).

Werdegang

der ~ career, development; only since late in the 19th c.; in earlier periods *Gang* alone sufficed (cf. pp. 971–2).

werfen: throw

Anker ~ to settle down (in a place); figur. only since the 19th c. (but not yet listed by Campe [1811]).

Junge ~ to produce off-spring or young; at least since the 18th c., when Steinbach [1734] recorded: '*der Hund wirfft = canis parit catulos*'; mainly used with ref. to cats, dogs and horses.

jem. ins Gefängnis (*in den Kerker*) ~ to imprison sb., throw sb. into jail; since Early NHG, recorded by Maaler (1561).

jem.m etw. an den Kopf ~ to hurl sth. (e.g. insults, accusations) at sb.; since the 18th c., e.g. Lessing 2,339.

sich auf etw. ~ to turn (or devote oneself) to sth. (as an occupation or field of study); since the 18th c., e.g. F.Schlegel, *Lucinde* 122 [1799]: '. . . *Studien, auf die sich oft sein jugendlicher Enthusiasmus mit gefräßiger Wißbegierde warf*'.

sich jem.m zu Füßen ~ to submit humbly; figur. extension of 'to throw oneself down at sb.'s feet'; since the 18th c., e.g. Schiller, *D.Carlos* 4,16.

etw. auf die Leinwand ~ to project on the screen; since the 20th c. with ref. to films.

jem. niederwerfen to subdue, overcome sb.; first in mil. contexts, e.g. Aventin, *Chron.* 5,19,8 [1566]: '*die Römer wurden nidergeworfen*'; also with such abstracts as *Aufstand*, *Putsch*, etc.

sich vor jem.m niederwerfen (lit.) to submit to sb.; the same as the entry with *zu Füßen* (see above); since the 18th c.

die Krankheit hat ihn niedergeworfen the illness has confined him to a sickbed; since the 18th c., e.g. Hagedorn 2,97. Sometimes used like *niederschlagen*, e.g. *von der schlimmen Nachricht niedergeworfen*.

← See also under *abwerfen, anwerfen, aufwerfen, Auge* (for *ein Auge auf jem. werfen*), *auswerfen, Bach* (for *das Pfund in den Bach werfen*), *Beil* (for *das Beil zu weit werfen*), *Bein* (for *du wirst noch mit meinen Beinen Äpfel abwerfen*), *Beutel* (for *Beutel werfen*), *bewerfen, blind* (for *wie man aufwarf den blinden Graben* and *eilte die Hündin nicht, so würfe sie nicht blinde Junge*), *Bord* (for *etw. über Bord werfen*), *Brühe* (for *alles in eine Brühe werfen*), *Brust* (for *sich in die Brust werfen*), *Bündel* (for *jem.m das Bündel vor die Tür werfen*), *Daus* (for *wenn man wirfft der meysten augen*), *Decke* (for *wie warf ich ... Blick auf Blick*), *einwerfen, Eisen* (for *etw. zum alten Eisen werfen*), *entgegenwerfen, falsch* (for *ein falsches Licht darauf werfen*), *Fenster* (for *Geld zum Fenster hinauswerfen*), *Flinte* (for *die Flinte ins Korn werfen*), *fortwerfen, Garten* (for *jem.m einen Stein in den Garten werfen*), *Gaul* (for *das wirft den stärksten Gaul um*), *Geld* (for *ins Wasser geworfenes Geld*), *Gewehr* (for *das Gewehr ins Korn werfen*), *Gewicht* (for *ihn aus dem Gleichgewicht werfen konnten*), *Gift* (for *an die man seine Liebe nicht wegwerfen darf*), *Glanz* (for *sich in Glanz werfen*), *Glas* (for *wer im Glashaus sitzt, soll nicht mit Steinen werfen*), *Glück* (for *seine Wünschelrute auszuwerfen*), *Hals* (for *sich jem.m an den Hals werfen*), *Handtuch* (for *das Handtuch werfen*), *Haufen* (for *etw. über den Haufen werfen*), *hinzukommen* (for *Licht werfen auf etw.*), *Holz* (for *jem.m das Hölzel werfen*), *Horn* (for *jem.m das Seil über die Hörner werfen*), *hundert* (for *das hundert ins tausend werfen*), *Jacke* (for *jem.m etw. in die Jacke werfen*), *Jungfer* (for *Jungfern werfen*), *Knie* (for *sich auf die Knie werfen*), *Knüppel* (for *jem.m Knüppel zwischen die Beine werfen*), *Licht* (for *Licht auf etw. werfen*), *Los* (for *das Los wird um jem. geworfen*), *Löwe* (for *wenn sie sich darauf werfen, Lionnes zu werden*), *Mittel* (for *ins Mittel werfen*), *Nacken* (for *den Kopf in den Nacken werfen*), *neun* (for *alle Neun werfen*), *Perle* (for *Perlen vor die Säue werfen*), *Prügel* (for *mit Prügeln unter die Sperlinge werfen*), *Schale* (for *sich in Schale werfen*), *Schatten* (for *etw. wirft seinen Schatten voraus*), *Schein* (for *Scheinwerfer*), *Schinken* (for *mit der Wurst nach dem Schinken werfen*), *Schlag* (for *Schlaglichter werfen*), *schmücken* (for *mit Schmuckwörtern um sich werfen*), *Schoß* (for *sich einer Sache in den Schoß werfen*), *Schwert* (for *sein Schwert in die Wagschale werfen*), *Seil* (for *jem.m ein Seil um den Hals werfen*), *Seite* (for *mit der Wurst nach der Speckseite werfen*), *Spatz* (for *Spatzen werfen*), *Spiel* (for *zurückgeworfene Lichtstrahlen*), *Staat* (for *sich in Staat werfen*), *Staub* (for *jem. in den Staub werfen*), *Stein* (for *den ersten Stein auf jem. werfen* and *jem. mit Steinen*

bewerfen), *Straße* (for *hinauß werff ich dich auf die straßen*), *Tiegel* (for *zwei Dinge in einen Tiegel werfen*), *Tölpel* (for *jem. über den Tölpel werfen*), *Topf* (for *alles in einen Topf werfen*), *überwerfen, umwerfen, unterwerfen, verwerfen, vorwerfen* and *weit* (for *etw. weit wegwerfen*).

Werg: see *Rocken*.

Werk: work, activity; product *das ~* (1) work; with ref. to writings, compositions and other works of art; translates Lat. *opus* in this sense; since OHG; f.r.b. Frischlin [1594] with ref. to books, Hulsius [1618] with ref. to sculpture and other works of art, only since the 18th c. with ref. to compositions.

das ~ (2) (lit.) effect; figur. when a thing or an abstract is seen as 'going to work and effecting sth.', e.g. Wieland (Acad.Edit.) 1,13,46: '*des Ringes Werk ist dieß, so lang ihn der beschützt, kann ihm am Leben nichts geschehn*'; hence also *das ~ der Flammen* = 'what the fire brought about'; modern; often the same as *Wirkung*; cf. also *es war das ~ eines Augenblicks* = 'it happened in the shortest possible time'; since the 18th c.

gute Werke tun to perform good deeds; in the religious sense with ref. to works agreeable to God since OHG; cf. Petri's [1605] recording: '*gute werck machen nicht Christen, sondern Christen machen vnd thun gute werck*'; later also in non-relig. contexts with ref. to charitable work.

viel Werks von etw. machen (obs. or regional coll.) to make a great to-do about sth.; since the 17th c., recorded by Kramer [1702]; now obs. except in dialects (Fischer records it for Swabia); *Aufhebens* is now used.

etw. ist im Werke sth. is being done, is in progress; in many contexts for 'etw. is being performed, produced, written, published, plotted, perpetrated, etc.'; since the 17th c., e.g. H.v. Kleist, *Zerbr.Krug* 28: '*ein Schabernack ist wider mich im Werk*'. In most cases '*ist im Gang*' (for which see p. 951) would now be preferred.

Kotzebues Werke studieren (or *lesen*) (sl.) to vomit; punning combination of *kotzen* with the name of the writer August von Kotzebue (1761–1819); as early as one year after his assassination by Sand the phrase became current.

das Laufwerk (coll.) the legs; first in mil.sl. of 2nd World War (derived from the track of mil. vehicles), then in general sl. esp. among teenagers.

das Machwerk product, creation; since the 18th c., f.r.b. Adelung; first in neutral sense, e.g. Kant 1,227: '*die Geschäftsmänner, die ihr Machwerk (savoir faire) verstehen*', but also (and now usually) pejor. since the 18th c., e.g. Goethe, *Tag- und Jahreshefte* [1805] on speeches alleged to have been written by Cicero: '*später untergeschobenes Machwerk*'.

← See also under *Bergwerk, blenden* (for *Blendwerk*), *Bollwerk, danieder* (for *das*

Gaukelwerk der schwarzen Kunst), *drucken* (for *Druckwerk* and *Saugwerk*), *Ende* (for *das Ende krönt das Werk*), *Fach* (for *Fachwerk*), *flicken* (for *das ist Flickwerk*), *fordern* (for *jetzt fodert mich ein dringend Werk von hier*), *frei* (for *freie Werke*), *frisch* (for *nur frisch ans Werk*), *führen* (for *etw. ins Werk führen*), *Fuhrwerk* (also for *hinausfuhrwerken*), *gehen* (for *aufs genauste zu Werke gehen*), *Geschmeiß* (for *verderben wir das werck*), *Gewicht* (for *das lebende Uhrwerk der Welt*), *Hand* (for . . . *Hand zu Werke lege*), *Handwerk* (also for *Handwerksneid*), *laufen* (for *Spielwerk schöner Farben*), *Markt* (for *die Werke großer Männer*), *Meister* (for *Meisterwerk* and *das Werk lobt den Meister*), *Mund* (for *Mundwerk* and *Maulwerk*), *Orgel* (for *Orgelwerk*), *Paternoster* (for *Paternosterwerk*), *Rad* (for *Räderwerk*), *schreiten* (for *zum Werk schreiten*), *sehen* (for *mit Umsicht zu Werke ging*), *setzen* (for *etw. ins Werk setzen*), *Stück* (for *Stückwerk* and *das ganze Werk ist von einer Natur und aus einem Stücke*), *stumpf* (for . . . *sein Werk nur auf die Hälfte bringt*), *suchen* (for *Todeswerk*), *Tag* (for *Tagbergwerk* and *jch mus wircken die werck . . . so lange es tag ist*), *Uhr* (for *Uhrwerk* and *Uhrwerksmensch*) and *Weg* (for *von Worten zu Werken ist ein weiter Weg*).

werkeln
werkeln (regional coll.) to work away, keep on being busy, make oneself useful, potter about; in essence the same as *arbeiten*; in lit. since the 17th c., e.g. Lehman 3,85 [1662], not recorded by Kramer, Adelung or Campe. Since in Austria a hurdy-gurdy is called *Werkel*, ~ can also occur regionally for 'to turn the handle of a hurdy-gurdy'.

Werkeltagsgedanken: See *Flitter*.

werkgetreu
werkgetreu faithful to (the spirit of) the original; a new word, not yet recorded in *DWb*. [1959].

Werkmeister: foreman
der ~ (1) (relig.) the Creator, God; since MHG, f.r.b. Frisius [1556], now rare but still used in relig. contexts, e.g. Stifter, *Sämtl.W.* 1,58: '*was hat denn der unergründliche Werkmeister vor . . .*'.

der ~ (2) (lit.) originator, producer; since the 17th c. for 'sb. (or sth.) who (or which) causes sth. to happen', e.g. (DWb) Harsdörffer, *Poet. Trichter* 3,354 [1653]: '*der Mund . . . ist der Werkmeister der Worte*', Herder (edit. S.) 5,378 where a lexicographer is called '*Werkmeister eines Wörterbuchs*'.

Werkstatt: workshop
die ~ workshop; in phys. sense since Late MHG, figur. since Early NHG, e.g. Luther 7,575 (Weimar) on Maria: '*ich byn nur die werckstat, darynnen ehr (= God) wirckt*', Goethe 4,259 (W.): '*wenn wir dich, o Vater, sehen in der Werkstatt der Natur*'. Petri [1605] recorded '*trübsal ist die rechte werckstat der hoffnung*'. – *Werkstätte* can also

be used in this extended sense (since the 16th c.). – The entry under *Statt* (p. 2336) lacks details and dates.

werkstellig: See *stellen* (p. 2361).

Werkstudent
der ~ student who works during the university vacations in order to finance further studies; in print since 1922 after a meeting of students at Erlangen in July 1921.

Werkzeug: tool
das ~ tool; figur. use influenced by Lat. *instrumentum* in its extended sense; in German since the 16th c., at first with ref. to things, e.g. Luther 49,406 (Weimar) (with *Hand*), Lessing (edit. L.-M.) 2,295: '*Gift und Dolch sind zu barmherzige Werkzeuge*', then to abstracts, esp. *Wort* or *Sprache*, e.g. Börne's '*Worte sind meine Werkzeuge*'.

Wermut: wormwood
bitter wie ~ bitter as wormwood; in lit. since Early NHG, used both in Mentel's and in Luther's Bible transl. Prov. 5,4, where the A.V. has 'bitter as wormwood'.

der Stern ~ (obs.) the star Absinthium (or Wormwood); taken over from the Lat. name used in Revel. 8,11; the A.V. puts 'the star Wormwood', Luther translated '*vnd der name des Sterns heisst Wermut*'; very rarely used now, but Raabe, *Sämtl.Werke* (edit. Klemm) II,1,86 has '. . . *um nicht bitterer zu sein als jener Stern Wermut, der alle Brunnen und Wasser der Erde untrinkbar machte*'.

ein Tropfen ~ *im Becher der Freude* (lit.) a bitter drop in the cup of joy; in wider sense = 'a bitter experience or disappointment'; beginning as *mit* ~ *tränken* after the Bible (Lamentations 3,15, where the A.V. has 'he hath made me drunken with wormwood'); since the 17th c. as *jem.m* ~ *einschenken* and since the 18th c. in locutions with *Becher*. *Wermutstropfen* became current in this phrase in the 2nd half of the 18th c., e.g. Herder (edit. S.) 32,328.

← See also under *bitter* (for *dann bitterst du dein Leid mit Wermut*).

Wermutbruder
der ~ (or *Wermutpenner*) (coll.) tramp, vagrant addicted to alcohol; in wider pejor. sense = 'drunkard'; 20th c. coll.; cf. similar Amer.sl. 'wino'.

wert: worth, esteemed, dear
einer Sache ~ *sein* to deserve sth.; since MHG, e.g. Luther Bible transl. Luke 10,7: '*eyn erbeytter ist seyns lohns werdt*', Goethe 21,83 (W.): '. . . *daß er eines solchen Glückes nicht werth sei*', Schiller, *Kab.u.L.* 4,5: '*diese Millerin . . . ist es werth meine Tochter zu sein*'; frequent in *es ist (nicht) der Mühe* ~ = 'it is (not) worth the trouble', since the 18th c.

etw. ist jem.m lieb und ~ sth. is dear to sb., is very much appreciated; in various forms since

MHG, e.g. *Lancelot* (edit. Kluge) 1,286: '*ich han uch sere lieb und sere wert*'; Luther 51,115 (Weimar) used '*hoch und werd halten*', H.Sachs in *Fab.* 1,393 has '*wirdig und wert*', Goethe, *Dicht.u.Wahrh.* 10: '*Dinge . . . die mir lieb und werth sind*'.

der Allerwerteste (euphem. coll.) the behind, bottom; since early in the 19th c.; hence *einen blauen Allerwertesten haben* (sl.) = 'to have been given a beating', since early in the 20th c.

eine Summe ~ sein (econ.) to be worth, possess or have an annual income of a certain sum; a loan from Engl., at least since the 18th c., e.g. Wieland, *Sylv.* 2,3: '*ein kleiner Edelmann, der jährlich kaum hundert Pistolen werth ist*'.

← See also under *ausreden* (for *eine gute Ausred' ist drei/ein Batzen wert*), *Batzen, drei, Groschen, Kreuzer, Pfennig* (for *keinen Batzen, Dreier, Groschen, Kreuzer, Pfennig wert*), *Dach* (for *mehr wert als . . .*,) *Ehre* (for *eine Ehre ist die andere wert*), *Feld* (for *im Felde, da ist der Mann noch was wert*), *Galgen* (for *den Galgen nicht wert sein*), *Geld* (for *das ist Geld wert* or *geldeswert*), *Gold* (for *Mädchen, du bist viel Geld werth* and *Gold(es) wert sein*), *halten* (for *jem. wert halten*), *Herd* (for *eigner Herd ist Goldes wert*), *klein* (for *wer das Kleine nicht ehrt, ist das Große nicht wert*), *Nuß* (for *nicht eine taube Nuß wert* and *keine Nußschale wert*), *Pfennig* (for *wer den Heller nicht ehrt, ist des Talers nicht wert*), *Prophet* (for *nummant wert geholden vor einen prophet in synem lande*), *Pulver* (for *keinen Schuß Pulver wert sein*), *Rede* (for *etw. ist (nicht) der Rede wert*), *Schuh* (for *nicht wert sein, jem.m die Schuhriemen zu lösen*), *Schweiß* (for *des Schweißes der Edlen werth*), *Sünde* (for *eine Sünde wert sein*) and *treiben* (for *wer mag wohl, werthes Kind, dein Zeitvertreiber seyn*).

Wert: value

der ~ value, significance, importance; the noun was derived from the adjective; transfer from monetary value to abstracts began as early as in OHG when *werd* meant not only 'price or value of sth.' and 'precious object', but also 'excellence, splendour'. *Das hat keinen ~* extended its meaning in modern times from 'that is of no value' to 'that is futile, useless, leads to no positive result'.

Wert-. . . (econ.) (relating to) value; in many compounds since the 19th c., when economists, esp. Carey, Ricardo and Karl Marx established *Wertlehren* and G.Simmel wrote his *Philosophie des Geldes* [1900]; the chief figur. ones are *Wertabstufung, -begriff, -beständigkeit, -erhöhung, -erschließung, -erzeugend* and *-zuwachs*. In the 2nd half of the 20th c., evidently due to Marxist ideas, compounds with ~ increased in the German Democratic Republic. Of non-econ. (often philos. or legal) origin are *Wertschätzung* = 'esteem' (since the 17th c.), *Wertsein* (since the 18th c., used by Herder), *Wertunterschied* and *Werturteil*, both since the 19th c.

← See also under *auslegen* (for *man muß nicht seinen Wert auslegen*), *beilegen* (for *ich lege der Sache keinen Wert bei*), *Geld* (for *Geldeswert*), *legen* (for *Wert auf etw. legen*) and *Stelle* (for *Stellenwert*).

werten

etw. or *jem. ~* (1) to appreciate, think highly of sth. or sb.; beginnings in OHG, but much less used than *wertschätzen* or *für wert halten*, but in lit. more frequently used in the 20th c. than in earlier periods.

etw. or *jem. ~* (2) to assign a certain value to sth. or sb.; only since the 19th c., mostly in such locutions as *als etw. gewertet werden*, where it competes with *bewerten*, a relatively new word not yet recorded in *DWb.* or by Sanders [1865].

wertfrei

wertfrei (lit.) objective, unprejudiced, unbiassed; a 20th c. term; other adjectives expressing the same notion are *wertfremd* and *wertindifferent*, all coined early in the 20th c.

Wesen: existence, being, nature, essence

das fünfte ~ (lit., a.) quintessence; since Early NHG, translates Lat. *quinta essentia* (borrowed from the Greek term in Phythagoras), e.g. Lohenstein, *Ros.* 84 [1733]: '*ich bin die Liebe selbst, ihr Kern, ihr fünftes Wesen*'; cf. Wieland 25,382: '*das Element der Himmelskörper aber ist der . . . Äther . . . , ist ein fünftes Element, die quinta essentia . . . woher . . . Quintessenz stammt, womit wir das Allerfeinste bezeichnen*'.

sein Sein und ~ (lit.) his entire being, his personality in all its aspects; at least since the 18th c., used e.g. by Wieland 14,20.

viel (also *groß*) *~ um* (or *aus, über, von*) *etw. machen* to make much fuss about sth., attach undue importance to sth.; since Early NHG. In some areas *Wesens* is preferred, other use *groß Gewese*, which occurs e.g. in L.Feuchtwanger, *Die häßliche Herzogin* [1923].

'*Und es mag am deutschen ~ einmal noch die Welt genesen*' the German way of life may yet heal mankind; quotation from a poem by Geibel (1815–84) entitled *Deutschlands Beruf* [1861]. Geibel referred to the good features in the German character and expressed no jingoistic sentiments. Later nationalists interpreted it differently and Emperor Wilhem II in particular used it in a way that was offensive to other countries, especially when *mag* was replaced by *soll*.

das böse ~ (euphem., obs.) epilepsy; one of the old euphem. terms for illnesses which one did not want to mention by name (taboo avoidance); now probably no longer used; a variant form was *Bösding*.

← See also under *Anker* (for *Anker meines Wesens*), *Anwesen, blähen* (for *das geblähte und aufgedunsene Wesen*), *einnehmen* (for *ein einnehmendes Wesen*), *Fabel* (for *Fabelwesen*), *führen* (for *ein Wesen führen*), *Gicht* (for *eine Gicht, ein spielendes Wesen*), *groß* (for *was großes Wesen ist ein Kuß*), *Grund* (for *jenes gründerhafte Wesen*), *Schatten* (for *weidet uns mit Schatten, da wir das Wesen selbst haben könnten*), *Schein* (for *Schein eines gottseligen Wesens*), *Schmiß* (for *meinem Wesen etwas Keckes zu geben*), *Schwamm* (for *man kann nichts machen aus dem schwammigen Wesen*), *Stück* (for *Zerstückelung meines Wesens*), *Unruhe* (for *die unruh in der uhr des gemeinen wesens*), *ungehalten* (for *je gemessener sein ganzes Wesen ist*), *Unwesen* and *verarten* (for *die Freiheit in ein wildes Wesen verartet*).

Wesenkette: se *Glied.*

wesentlich

See under *beigesellen* (for *nicht zum Wesentlichen (principale), sondern zum Beigesellten (accessorium) gehören*) and *versenken* (for *das Wesentliche wurde in einer Sündfluth von willkürlichen Sätzen versenkt*).

Wespe: wasp

die ~ (1) (lit.) aggressive or dangerous person; since Early NHG, e.g. S. Franck, *M.Encomion* 56b [1534] in an attack on monks.

die ~ (2) irritable person; since Early NHG; hence modern (regional) *er hat Wespen im Kopf* = 'he is in an irritable mood'; in some areas *wefzig* occurs for 'irritable' (recorded for Swabia by Fischer).

die ~ (3) (lit., rare) statement which is bound or likely to cause irritation or discomfort; Goethe IV,11,213 (W.) used the term, but it is rare. There is, however, regional coll. *jem.m Wespen ins Ohr setzen* = 'to cause sb. trouble, make sb. worried', recorded by Wander with a *locus* of 1864. See also under *Nest* for *Wespennest* = 'group of ill-intentioned people' (p. 1780). Lichtenberg, *Verm.Schr.* 4,368 [1800] has '*ein füchsisch, wespisch, wölfisch, teuflisches Verfahren*'.

sieben Wespen stechen ein Roß tot (prov.) seven wasps can kill a horse; recorded by Zoozmann, *Zitatenschatz* (3rd edit.); general meaning: 'a great many small troubles combined can overcome even a strong character'; used by Scheffel, *Ekkehard* 3,5. Wander [1875] has referred to Lat. *cave multos, si singulos non times*'. There is a variant of the phrase with *Reiter* instead of *Roß*.

← See also under *Frucht* (for *die schlechtsten Früchte sind es nicht, woran die Wespen nagen*, where it should have been stated that this occurs in *Trost* by Bürger).

Wespennest: see *Nest.*

Wespenschlank

wespenschlank (also *wespenhaft*) wasp-like; used with ref. to a woman's figur, esp. the slim waist, e.g. Gaudy, *Erz.* 77: '*eine so wespenschlanke Taille*'; Sanders [1865] recorded *wespenhaft.*

Wespenschwarm *der ~* multitude of disagreeable things (thoughts or people); since the 19th c., e.g. *einen ~ aufrühren* = 'to stir up a hornets' nest'.

Wespentaille *mit ~* wasp-waisted; international, e.g. Ital. *vitina di vespa*; in German lit. since the 19th c., e.g. Gutzkow, *R.v.G.* 4,445 [1852]: '. . . *eine vollkommen runde Taille, eine richtige Wespentaille*'.

wespisch: see *Wespe.*

West: west wind

See under *Hauch* (for *nur noch der Hauch verliebter Weste belebt das schwanke Laub der Äste*), *Perle* (for *Kräuter, die ein verliebter West mit frühen Perlen tränkt*) and *Regen* (for *vollen Blütenregen schüttelt schon der laue West*).

Weste: waistcoat *eine reine (saubere) ~ haben* (coll.) to be without a stain on one's reputation; since the 2nd half of the 19th c., according to Büchmann used by Bismarck as early as in 1864 but in printonly in his *Ged.u.Erinn.* 2,60 [1911].

← See also under *Fleck* (for *keinen Fleck auf der (weißen) Weste haben*) and *Jubel* (for *jem.m etw. unter die Weste jubeln*).

Westen: West

der wilde ~ the Wild West; at first (ca. 1890) as *der Ferne ~*, since it lies beyond the original 13 States of the U.S.A.; then as *Wilder ~*, popularized through the adventure stories, particularly those by Karl May. – *Ein wilder West*, used by Goethe and others, refers, of course, to a 'fierce west wind'.

der goldene ~ the Golden West; originated shortly after 1848 when gold was discovered in California.

der ~ (polit.) the West; referred after 1945 to the German Federal Republic; in newspapers since the middle of the fifties of the 20th c. – Older, of course, in geogr. sense for 'Western countries', also in mil. contexts for 'Western front', as in Remarque's book *Im Westen nichts Neues* [1929].

Westentasche: waistcoat pocket

sich die Finger in der ~ brechen (coll.) to be unbelievably unlucky; since the 19th c., e.g. Gaudy, *Sämtl. Werke* 2,130 [1844], also used by Fontane in *Br.a.s.Familie* 1,216 [1905]. An older phrase with the same meaning is *er bricht seine Finger im Hirsebrei*, which see on p. 1347.

mit dem rechten (linken) Auge in die linke (rechte) ~ sehen or *gucken* (coll.) to squint; recorded for some areas (e.g. Schleswig-Holstein) since the 19th c.

das bezahlt er aus der ~ (coll.) that is no more than petty cash to him; 20th c. coll.

← See also under *Tasche* (for *etw. kennen wie seine eigne Westentasche* and *im Westentaschenformat*).

Westerhemd: see *Hemd.*

westlich: see *Pudel.*

wett: even, quits

etw. macht zwei Leute ~ sth. makes two people quits; since MHG, when it was *wette tuon*; with *machen* since the 17th c.; Kramer [1702] recorded 'etwas wieder wett machen', e.g. Grillparzer, Sämtl. W. 5,117: 'du hast mich nie geliebt, je, ich dich auch nicht! Das macht uns wett'; often in etw. mit etw. ~ machen = 'to make up or compensate for sth. with sth.' (e.g. repay a service with a similar service), as in Grillparzer 7,55: 'was sie für mich bezahlt, ist dann wohl wett durch manchen Dienst'; in lit. also with abstracts, e.g. Schiller, Fiesco 5,1: 'ich machte Größe mit Größe wett'.

← See also under bauen (for sich wett bauen).

Wettbewerb der ~ competition; coined in the 2nd half of the 19th c. as a substitute for the foreign term Konkurrenz, esp. in comm. contexts. For the history of Bewerb see under bewerben.

Wette: wager

um die ~ (mit jem.m) etw. tun to vie with sb. in doing sth.; with ref. to all kinds of competitions (but not implying a bet) since Early NHG, e.g. Luther Aprocr. transl. Wisdom of Sol. 15,9: 'das er umb die wette erbeite mit den goldschmiden' (where the A.V. has 'striveth to excell goldsmiths'); Maaler [1561] recorded: 'erstlich in wett weyß. Certatim. Wenn ye einer den anderen übertreffen will'.

ich gehe jede ~ ein, daß . . . (coll.) I'll bet you anything that . . .; since the 18th c., e.g. Gellert, Sylvia 2: 'dennoch wett ich viel, Ihr habt nichts vorzubringen'. There are, as in Engl., several phrases in which a bet is proposed but is not seriously contemplated.

← See also under Gans (for mit der wilden Gans um die Wette leben), Schlag (for die Wette biet ich and eine Wette? nun gut, so schlagt sie vor) and Trotz (for liebten uns zu Trotz und scherzten um die Wette).

Wetteifer: see glühen.

wetten: wager

mit jem.m ~ to enter into a wager with sb.; since Early NHG; Maaler [1561] recorded: 'wollen mit eim wetten = sponsione prouocare'; he also listed 'man wettet oder hat ein gewett'.

ich wette (or könnte ~), daß . . . I could take any bet that . . .; cf. the similar entry under Wette, where no actual wager is intended; since MHG, e.g. Luther 30,2,38 (Weimar): 'ich dürfft umb einen finger wetten . . .'; cf. modern darauf wette ich meinen Kopf.

so haben wir nicht gewettet (coll.) I won't go along with that, that goes against our agreement; rejection of a proposal which would benefit the other and leave oneself at a disadvantage; the phrase does not refer to an actual bet; modern coll.

Wetter: weather

das ~ (1) (personified) the weather; often personified, e.g. (DWb) Lehmann, Schaupl. 546 [1699]: 'das Wetter hatte einen grossen Bären ins Städtel gejagt', Kramer [1702] recorded it with gehen, stehen, daherkommen and unfreundlich;

often with drohen; cf. also such phrases as des Wetters Wut or grausames ~ .

das ~ (2) (lit.) misfortune, disastrous event; since Early NHG, often with ref. to war or turbulence in politics, as in Luther 18,62 (Weimar): 'da geht eyn new wetter her', Goethe 41,1,5: 'die Wetter des Krieges'; hence also die ~ des Schicksals and das ~ vorüberziehen lassen = 'to wait until things have calmed down', f.r.b. Faber, Thes. [1587]: 'bis dis wetter fürüber zeucht'.

das ~ (3) tribulation, trouble, affliction, suffering; closely connected with ~ (2) but more concerned with personal or domestic events; since Early NHG, e.g. seelisches ~ as in Raabe, Sämtl. W. 1,6,8: 'das Wetter in meiner Seele mag sich ändern'. When used with positive adjectives it describes a settled, contented or happy state of mind, as in Nietzsche, Werke 8,7: 'mit meinem guten Wetter ist es vorbei'; cf. modern coll. gut ~ machen = 'to make efforts to create a pleasant atmosphere, make sb. or people feel at ease'.

das ~ (4) thunderstorm, tumult, uproar, quarrel (including violent reprimand or punishment); when used figur., in essence the same as Gewitter in its many meanings for which see pp. 1040–42; since Early NHG, e.g. Luther 1,391 (Weimar), recorded by Kramer [1702].

wie ein ~ like a stormy blast, quickly and devastatingly; the comparison occurs in the Bible Prov. 1,27 (where the A.V. has 'as a whirlwind'), e.g. Goethe 8,140 (W.): 'wir hinauf wie Wetter und zum Fenster herunter mit dem Kerl'.

Wetter! (coll.) damn! as a curse since the 17th c., recorded by Kramer [1702], e.g. Wieland 34,240: 'mich soll der Donner und das Wetter, wenn . . .', Lenz 1,92: '. . . daß das Donnerhageltausend Wetter . . .', Lessing 1,72: 'fluche, Freund, nicht alle Wetter auf deinen eigensinngen Vetter'. Schiller used Hagel und ~ , Donner und ~ , Wieland ~ auch and zum ~ .

alle ~ ! (coll.) my word! exclamation of admiration or surprise; modern (in earlier period potz ~ could be similarly used).

gut ~ für . . . (coll.) the right kind of climate (or opportunity) for sth.; rare in lit., but Schiller used it in Kab. u. L. 4,9: 'gut Wetter für Kuppler'.

Wetter- . . . (coll.) amazing . . ., terrific . . .; in coll. compounds since the 18th c.; derived from ~ = 'curse, reprimand', extended to 'deserving a reprimand or curse', but then also containing a degree of admiration, e.g. Wetterjunge, Wetterkerl, Wettermädchen'; Weiße, Kom. Opern 3,79 [1770] used Wettermädchen; others became current in the 19th c. Campe [1811] recorded Wetterjunge and Wetterkerl, but only in condemning sense. Cf. similar compounds formed with Blitz, Donner or Mord.

← See also under brauen (for es braut sich ein Wetter zusammen), Donner (for Donnerwetter), drei (for ein Gesicht wie drei Tage Regenwetter), ducken (for *duck dich . . . das Wetter will sein Willen han*), *Ei* (for *ein Wetter zum Eierlegen*), *einschlagen* (for *da soll ja das Donnerwetter einschlagen* and *das wetter schlecht oft eine*), *Gewitter* (also for *Ungewitter* and many compounds), *Hund* (for *bei diesem Wetter jagt man keinen Hund hinaus* and *Hundewetter*), *Regen* (for *Regen und schönes Wetter machen* and *Regenwetter*), *Sau* (for *Sauwetter*), *Scheiße* (for *Scheißwetter*), *Schlag* (for *umschlagen wie Aprilwetter*), *schön* (for *um schön Wetter bitten*), *Tau* (for *Tauwetter*) and *Wind* (for *in Wind und Wetter*).

Wetterecke *die* ~ (coll.) bad-weather area; modern, also figur., e.g. (DWb) Freytag, *Briefe* [edit. Tempeltey] 370: '. . . *nicht ganz so arg werden, als es sich in der Wetterecke gegen das arme Deutschland zusammenzieht*'; similarly *Wetterwinkel*, modern, in phys. sense since the 19th c. (figur. examples have not come to my notice).

Wetterfahne: see *Fahne*.

Wetterfrosch: see *Thermometer*.

wettergegeißelt: see *Geißel*.

Wetterhahn See under *drehen* (for *Wetterhanen die sich mit jedem Wind drehen*) and *Hahn* (for *unbeständig wie ein Wetterhahn* – also for *wetterwendisch*).

Wetterkröte: see *Kröte*.

Wetterleuchten See under *aussehen* (for *aussehen wie die Gänse, wenn's wetterleuchtet*), *durchblitzen* (for *durchblitzt von dem Wetterleuchten seines Witzes*) and *Feuer* (for *wir wollen auf ihre Köpfe herabfeuern wie Wetterleuchten*).

Wetterloch: see *Loch*.

wettern: thunder *wettern* to rave, rage, curse, shout reprimands; cf. *Wetter* (4); since Early NHG, e.g. Luther 31,1,81 (Weimar), f.r.b. Steinbach [1734].

← See also under *anwettern* and the cross-references under *verwettert*.

wetterwendisch *wetterwendisch* unsteady, fickle, unreliable; first lit. appearance in Luther's writings who used it in his Bible transl. Matth. 13,21 and Mark 4,17 (where the Mentel Bible has '*unstet*' and the A.V. 'endure but for a time') and frequently elsewhere which brought about wider use of the word; f.r.b. Alberus, *Nov.Dict.* [1540]. See also under *Wetterhahn*.

Wetterwinkel: see *Wetterecke*.

Wettrennen: see *rennen*.

Wettstreit: see *Schiene*.

wetzen: sharpen

seinen Schnabel an jem.m ~ (coll.) to make critical or derogatory remarks about sb.; the phrase has a long history. It began as *seine Zunge* ~ in MHG and still occurs with *Zunge* today, as in (DWb) I.Seidel, *Lennacker* 169 [1938]: '*unsere Lutheraner . . . die sich die Zungen schon schartig an ihm gewetzt*'; *Maul* can also be used; cf. Goethe 41,1,181 (W.): '*ohne den kritischen Zahn zu wet-*

zen'. See also under *scharf* (pp. 2078–80) for similar phrases and under *Zunge* (for *scharf geschliffene Zunge*).

etw. ~ to sharpen sth.; since Early NHG with such abstracts as *Worte*, e.g. Luther 23,420 (Weimar): '*wie denn die gottlosen yhre wort wissen zu wetzen*', *Verstand*, *Vernunft* and *Sinne*, e.g. (DWb) Pegius, *Geburtsstundenbuch* pref. 3a [1570]: '*so werden jhre verständt dardurch gewetzet*'.

wetzen (coll.) to dash, run, rush, flit; derived from *die Sohlen* ~ = 'to grind down one's shoesoles by running'; since late in the 19th c.

jem.m eine ~ (sl.) to give sb. a box on the ear; derived from ~ = 'to do sth. violent' (since the 18th c.), then specialized for 'to hit out', modern, e.g. (DWb) Steguweit, *D.tör.Jungfr.* 9 [1937]: '*dafür wetzte sie dem Buben zwei hinter die Löffel*'.

Wetzstein: whetstone

etw. ist ein ~ *für etw. anderes*; sth. serves to sharpen sth. else; with abstracts since Late MHG, e.g. ~ *des Verstandes* or *Witzes*, e.g. Herder [edit. S.] 23,67: '*das Französische . . . ein Wetzstein des Urtheils*'; sometimes close in meaning to Engl. figur. 'catalyst'.

wibbelig

ein wibbeliger Mensch (regional coll.) a restless creature; belongs to *wiebeln* or *wibbeln* = 'to crawl' (with ref. to insects) and = 'to move around in a crowd', current since Early NHG; in some regions transferred to restlessness in human beings; recorded in some idiotica since the 19th c.

Wichs: polish

Wichs(e) bekommen (coll.) to get thrashed; since the 18th c., e.g. Hermes, *Soph. Reise* 2,406 [1769]; cf. *wichsen* (below).

in vollem or *voller* ~ (coll.) dolled up, in one's best clothes; first in stud. sl., f.r.b. Kindleben, *Stud.-Lex.* [1781], but general coll. since the 19th c., often in *sich in* ~ *werfen* (cf. similar phrases with *Glanz* (p. 1060) and *Staat* (p. 2324)).

~ *geben* (coll., obs.) to pay for sb.'s food or drink, stand a round; first in stud.sl. *wichsen* = 'to pay for sb.'s food or drink', f.r.b. Vollmann, *Bursch.Wb.* [1846]; with the noun since the 19th c., e.g. G. Keller, *Br.u. Tageb.* 2,56 [1841]; now obs.

die ~ (coll.) the matter, thing, business; usually in the phrase *das ist alles eine* ~ = 'that's the same thing, nothing to choose between them'; recorded for many areas from Berlin to the Alsace since the 19th c.

wichsen: polish

jem. ~ (coll.) to thrash sb.; originally = 'to treat with wax, polish'; verbs which describe vigorous hand movements are often extended to express 'to beat'; since the 18th c., e.g. Lessing, *Mätresse* 45, recorded by Adelung [1780].

jem. m etw. ~ (sl., obs.) to stand sb. a drink, pay for sb.'s drink (or food); first in stud. sl. (see *Wichs* above), in general coll. since the 19th c., now obs., but *aufwichsen* = 'to entertain one's guests' is still current in some regions (see under *aufwichsen*, p. 110).

wichsen (vulg.) to wank, toss off, masturbate; 19th c. sl., prudishly unrecorded in *DWb.* and *Trübner.*

gewichst (1) (coll.) cunning, crafty, sly; modern coll.

gewichst (2) (regional coll.) alert, handy, helpful; only recorded for the South-Western corner, e.g. by Martin-Lienhart [1907] for the Alsace.

← See also under *ab-, auf-, aus-* and *durchwichsen.*

Wicht: see *räudig* (also under *Gesicht*).

wichtig: weighty, important.

sich ~ *machen* to give oneself airs, assume an air of importance; in lit. since the last quarter of the 18th c.; hence also *ein wichtiges Gesicht machen, sich ein wichtiges Ansehen geben*, etc. and the prov. *wer sich* ~ *macht, wird ausgelacht*, recorded by Wander [1880], hence also *Wichtigtuer* (coll.) = 'pompous ass'.

← See also under *auswerfen* (for *von Wichtigkeit sein*), *belangen* (for *von wichtigem Belang*), *Blut* (for *alles Wichtige leicht behandelt*), *Gewicht* (for *gewichtig, Gewichtigkeit, halbgewichtig* and other compounds) and *Gold* (for *von Gold, so wichtig*).

Wicke: vetch

in die Wicken gehen (coll.) to get lost; the same as *in die Binsen gehen* (see p. 320); O. Weise (in *Zs. fdMundarten* 3,211 [1902] has suggested that hunters originated the phrase since a hare or partridge is safe if it manages to reach a vetch field, but this has been rejected by others who have pointed out that the vetch harvest is over when the hunting period begins. Recorded for many regions since the 19th c. and by Höfer in *Aus dem Volk* [1852].

Wickel: bunch, gathering

jem. am ~ *kriegen* (coll.) to get hold of sb. by the scruff of the neck; ~ began as 'wad or roll of wool or yarn' and developed to 'bandage', also 'nappy' (cf. *Wickelkind* = 'babe in arms'); in the 18th c. it came to be applied to the 'pigtail' and from there to 'bunch of hair'; the phrase arose in the 18th c.

wickeln: wrap

jem. aus etw. ~ (lit.) to free sb. from sth. (difficulty, entanglement); modern; Heyne [1895] recorded *'jem. aus einem ärgerlichen Handel wickeln'*: hence *herauswickeln*, also reflex. for 'to free oneself', since the 19th c., e.g. (H.) Häusser, *Dt. Gesch.* 4,315: '. . . *aus schwierigen Lagen . . . sich mit bedächtiger Klugheit herauszuwickeln'.*

in etw. gewickelt sein (lit.) to be enveloped in sth.; since the 18th c., e.g. Schiller, *Fiesco* 2,18: *'in den Windeln der Üppigkeit lag das erstaunliche*

Werk der Verschwörung gewickelt'.

jem. ~ (1) (sl.) to beat sb.; since the 19th c., either iron. or euphem. in origin (? from 'wrap up carefully').

jem. ~ (2) (sl.) to flatter sb., try to get into sb.'s good books; probably an off-shoot from *jem. einwickeln* (see p. 612); current since early in the 20th c.

sich zusammenwickeln (lit.) to become wrapped up in sth.; e.g. Eichendorff, *Taug.* 31: *'ich wickelte mich gleich einem Igel in die Stacheln meiner eigenen Gedanken zusammen'.*

← See also under *abwickeln, auswickeln, einwickeln, entwickeln* (also for *Entwicklung*), *Finger* (for *jem. um den (kleinen) Finger wickeln können*), *Garn* (for *sich aus diesem liebesgarne zu wüklen*), *Geschichte* (for *ihn so gut als möglich aus der Geschichte zu wickeln bemüht sei*), *schief* (for *er ist schief gewickelt*), *umwickeln, verwickeln* and *Watte* (for *jem. in Watte wickeln*).

Widder: ram

der ~ (1) (astron.) the Ram, Aries; according to Pliny 1,8 coined by Kleostratos of Tenedos [ca. 520 B.C.] under Egyptian influence (Greek *krios*, Lat. *aries*); in German since MHG period, e.g. Goethe IV,2,220 (W.): '. . . *bereit ich alles, um mit Eintritt der Sonne in den Widder eine neue Produktion zu beginnen'*; hence *der Widderpunkt* = 'Vernal Equinox', f.r.b. Campe [1811], and coll. *er ist ein* ~ = 'he is an Aries', modern.

der ~ (2) (tech.) battering ram; also called *Sturmwidder*; translates Lat. *aries* (in this tech. sense), recorded in OHG as *uuidar*; e.g. Goethe 49,1,261 (W.), Schiller, *Zerst.v.T.* 86: *'die Thüre liegt in Trümmern, vom Widder eingerannt'.*

der hydraulische ~ (tech.) hydraulic ram, Archimedes screw; probably translation of French *belier hydraulique*; in German recorded since 1853.

der doppeltgehörnte ~ (bibl.) the ram with two horns; interpreted as 'power of the ruler'; from the Book of Daniel 8. Persian rulers when going into battle wore a ram's head of gold, Zeus, too, was symbolically represented by a ram.

der goldene ~ (poet.) the Sun; in old myths of the Near East the ram is seen as a symbol of propagation and fecundity and this created such images as *der schwarze* ~ for 'rain' and *der weiße* ~ for 'Sun', also *der goldne* ~, as in Schiller, *Hero u. Leander*: *'als des goldnen Widders Flug Helle . . . über deine Tiefe trug'*; *'das goldwollige Fell des Widders'* in Goethe 49,97 (W.) refers to the Classical story about Jason and the golden fleece.

er ist ein alter ~ (coll.) he is an old lecher; recorded by Wander [1880]; cf. *geil wie ein Bock* (p. 363).

in das Zeichen des Widders kommen (coll., a.) to be cuckolded; since the 17th c., e.g. Abr. a Sa.Clara, *Judas* 1,316 [1687] and still in comedies (esp. in Vienna) in the 19th c., now a.

← See also under *treten* (for *die Sonne tritt aus dem Zeichen des Widders in das des Stiers*).

wider: against

~ *Erwarten* contrary to expectation; since the 18th c., e.g. Schiller, *Tur. 3,3*.

wer nicht ~ uns ist, der ist für uns (bibl.) he that is not with me is against me; bibl. from Luke 11,23, recorded as prov. by Henisch [1616].

← See also under *Abrede* (for *das ist wider die Abrede*), *belfern* (for *wider uns pelfern*), *Gift* (for *wider den gifftigen ketzer Martin Luther*), *Kopf* (for *ich kann nicht mit dem Kopf wider die Wand laufen*), *Mauer* (for *zur ehernen mauer wider die könige Judas*), *schwimmen* (for *wider den Strom schwimmen*), *streben* (for *weil sie strebt wider trew und ehr*), *Strich* (for *wider den Strich denken*), *Strom* (for *es geht mir alles wider den Strom*) and *Wurst* (for *Wurst wider Wurst*).

widerborstig: see *Borste*.

widerfahren *etw. widerfährt jem.m sth.* happens to sb., befalls sb.; ~ (until the end of the 18th c. often as *wiederfahren*) means 'to happen, occur', also in MHG 'to meet' which led to 'to meet with sth., experience sth.' thus producing the modern meaning, recorded since the 17th c. In the Mentel Bible of 1466 it occurs in Exod. 18,16: '. . . *so in widerfert etlicher krieg*'. Adelung [1796] recorded: '*es soll dir nicht die geringste Beleidigung widerfahren*'. Hence also *jem.m etw. ~ lassen* in positive sense = 'to grant or bestow sth. to sb.', as in Schiller, *Geisterseher*: '*Verehrung, die man seinem Geist widerfahren ließ*'.

widerhaarig *widerhaarig* (rare) obstreperous, contrary, rebellious; since ca. 1800 (but not yet recorded by Campe [1811]); in lit. first in Jean Paul 1,120: '*starres, widerhaariges Volk*', then quite frequent in the 19th c., but now rare; cf. French *à contre poil* and *widerborstig* (above).

Widerhaken: barb

der ~ (lit.) drawback, negative aspect of sth. seemingly positive; since MHG and often in contexts where the simplex *Haken* can express the same sense (see p. 1200); recorded since Frisius [1556] and since then used in the present-day sense, e.g. (DWb) Francisci, *All. Rache 26* [1668]: '*dann fand sich in seiner zusage immer ein widerhakke*', Leisewitz, *Jul.v.T. 2,5*: '*Widerhaken . . . im Herzen*', but also later for 'reservation', as in Storm, *Sämtl.W. 6,218*: '*Archimedes hatte noch ein Bedenken oder wenigstens einen Widerhaken im Gemüthe*'; not frequently used now in figur. sense. The same applies to *widerhakig*, used by some 19th c. authors.

Widerhall: echo

See under *ermüden* (for *Jubelschall . . . ermüdet den Widerhall*), *Hall* (for *Gegenbild oder Widerhall, der Widerhall seiner Thaten* and *Widerhall erwecken* or *finden*) and *schlafen* (for *in Bergesklüften schläft der Widerhall*).

widerhältig ~ *sein* (a.) to be resistant, able to

withstand a great deal; derived from *widerhalten* (obs.) = 'to offer resistance', with ref. to a strong constitution since the 18th c. The adj. appeared towards the end of the 18th c., f.r.b. Campe [1811], e.g. Grillparzer [edit. Sauer] 13,250: '*mein Körper ist sonst stark und widerhältig*'; now *widerstandsfähig* (current since the 19th c.) is preferred and ~ is not even listed in late 20th c. dictionaries.

widerlegen *etw.* ~ to refute sth.; in general use since the 16th c., e.g. Luther, *Tischr. 3,47* (Weimar). Hence *Widerlegung* (since 16th c.) and *widerlegbar* = 'refutable, rebuttable', since 18th c., joining *widerleglich*, current since the 16th c., still used by Goethe 22,294 and II,2,135 (W.), now rare; *Widerlegbarkeit* arose in the 19th c.

← See also under *einziehen* (for *die schriftklugen kundten nicht widerlegen*).

widerlich *widerlich* (1) repulsive, repugnant, revolting; with ref. to things, persons and abstracts since the 17th c.

widerlich (2) (lit.) showing displeasure or repugnance; mainly with ref. to facial expressions, e.g. Goethe 15,297 (W.) on Faust: '*er macht ein widerlich Gesicht*' (*angewidert* would express the same sense); in some regions ~ can also mean 'dissatisfied, disgruntled, ill-humoured', recorded since the 18th c. for Saxony.

widerlich (3) (adv.) unpleasantly, to a disagreeable degree; modern when negatively intensifying, as in ~ *süß*, but cf. also ~ *mißfallen*, used by Goethe 15,61 (W.).

← See also under *Dunst* (for *Dunstkreis ihrer so widerlich zusammengärenden Leidenschaften*).

Widerling *der* ~ (coll.) unpleasant person, revolting creature; since early in the 20th c.

widernatürlich *widernatürlich* (1) unnatural, perverse; since Late MHG, but with ref. to human behaviour which conflicts with the normal only since the 18th c.

widernatürlich (2) contradictory, expressing opposition or dissent; since Early NHG, used by Luther; now rare.

widernatürlich (3) supernatural; with ref. to things beyond human understanding, e.g. miracles; since Early NHG, f.r.b. Frisius [1556].

Widerpart *der* ~ (1) adversary, opponent; since MHG; e.g. Schiller, *Tell 2,2*: '*er ist mein Widerpart*'; *Widersacher* or *Feind* would now be preferred.

der ~ (2) opposite, sth. or sb. that constitutes a contrast; since the 19th c., e.g. Hauff 3,13: '. . . *Frau, die der Widerpart von ihm war*'. It could, however, also be used for *Gegenstück* = 'counterpart, mate, partner', as in Goethe 6,188 (W.), but this is now obs. See also under *Gegenstück* (p. 943).

jem.m ~ *halten* to oppose sb., adopt a hostile attitude towards sb.; in this locution since the 17th c.

← See also under *Borste* (for *helt jederman das Widerpart*).

Widerprall: see *prall*.

widerrechtlich *widerrechtlich* unlawful, illegal; though in existence since the 16th c., little used before the 18th c., f.r.b. Apinus, *Gloss.* [1728]; also in adverbial use, e.g. Beethoven, *S.Briefe* [edit. Kal.] 1,126: '*jene . . . widerrechtlich unternommene Ausgabe meiner Werke*'; now *rechtswidrig* (not yet recorded by Adelung and Campe) is preferred.

Widerrede *die* ~ contradiction, objection; since the 12th c.; *ohne* ~ = 'unquestionably', current since MHG, f.r.b. Stieler [1691] is still used, but ~ itself less than *Widerspruch*. ~ could also be used for 'written refutation or protest', as in Luther 26,268 (Weimar), but this would not be acceptable now.

← See also under *Geist* (for *der ohne Widerrede einer der schönsten Geister unter uns ist*).

Widerruf: see *rufen*.

widerrufen: see *rufen*.

widerruflich *widerruflich* revocable; recorded since the 15th c., predominantly in legal contexts, e.g. Kramer, *Teutsch-ital.* 2,382 [1702]: '*ein Testament ist allzeit widerrufflich*', *widerrufliche Anstellung* = 'appointment on probation', *widerrufliche Erlaubnis* = 'permission which can be withdrawn at will'. See also under *rufen* for this and *unwiderruflich*.

Widersacher *der* ~ adversary, opponent, enemy; current since the 14th c., at first mainly in legal contexts, since Early NHG also in mil. and in relig. contexts where *der* ~ can stand for 'Satan, Devil'; cf. Luther 10,3,356 (Weimar).

← See also under *halten* (for *aber unser widersacher halten nur so hart über den ehelosen stand*) and *Leute* (for *unsere widersacher lesens viel mehr, denn unsere leute*).

Widerschall *der* ~ (a.) echo; cf. synonymous *Widerhall*; current since the 12th c., now a. or rare, displaced by *Widerhall* (and *Echo*).

Widerschein *der* ~ (lit.) reflection, reflected light; since MHG (*widerschîn*); figur. first among mediaeval Mystics, but general only since the 18th c., partly phys. with ref. to (figur.) light thrown on sth., fully figur. with ref. to events, e.g. Heine [edit. Elster] 3,70: '*die Dame war fast erschrocken über den trüben Widerschein ihrer Bemerkung*', Rinser, *Lobel* 40: '*dieses Lächeln . . . trat wie ein Widerschein auf ihr eignes Gesicht*'.

widersetzen: see *setzen*.

widersetzlich: see *setzen*.

Widersinn *der* ~ (1) (obs.) distaste, repugnance; since the 17th c., still used by Goethe 27,187 (W.), now obs., displaced by *Widerwille* or *Abneigung*.

der ~ (2) absurdity, nonsense; since the 16th c., close to *Unsinn*.

widersinnig *widersinnig* absurd, nonsensical;

since the 16th c., e.g. Luther 8,546 (Weimar).

widerspenig: see *ungezogen*.

widerspenstig *widerspenstig* recalcitrant, obstreperous; derived from *Span* (2), for which see p. 2282; in MHG as *widerspaenec*, later *widerspenig* (see previous entry); Luther used it, e.g. in Bible transl. Psalm 5,11.

widerspiegeln: see *Spiegel*.

Widerspiel *das* ~ (1) (a.) the opposite; since the 14th c., e.g. the title page of Scheidt's edition of *Grobianus* [1551]: '*thun das widerspil*' = 'do the opposite'. Displaced by *Gegenteil*.

das ~ (2) counteraction; since Early NHG for all kinds of opposition (Luther used '*widderspil thun*'), now usually for the activity of opposing forces, *das* ~ *entgegengesetzter Kräfte*. Occasionally ~ is also used for 'opponent, adversary'.

← See also under *Spiel*.

widersprechen: contradict

See under *Atem* (for *er widerspricht sich zehnmal in einem Atem*), *Laie* (for *wenn ein laienhafter Schüler zu widersprechen wagt*) and *sprechen* (for obs. *etw. widersprechen*).

Widerspruch: protest; contradiction

See under *blank* (for *die blank und bloßen Widersprüche*), *dunkel* (for *Widersprüche heben*), *Geist* (for *regt sich der Geist des Widerspruchs*), *Seele* (for *Trotz ist, Widerspruch die Seele mir*) and *strotzen* (for *etw. strotzt von Widersprüchen*).

Widerspruchsgeist *der* ~ (1) spirit of contradiction; since the 2nd half of the 18th c. and used by Goethe II,8,124 (W.); see also under *Geist* for *Geist des Widerspruchs* in Goethe 25,1,121 (W.).

der ~ (2) (coll.) sb. who loves to oppose what is generally accepted or contradicts whatever one says; since the 2nd half of the 19th c.

Widerstand: opposition

See under *Schritt* (for *passiven Widerstand entgegensetzen*), *spannen* (for *spannt sich die Seele zu Widerstand*), and *treffen* (for *auf Widerstand treffen*), also under *stehen* (p. 2349).

widerstandsfähig: see *widerhältig*.

widerstehen: oppose, resist

See under *anfangen* (for *widersteh dem Anfang*), *Schlag* (for *kannst dem Schicksal widerstehen*), *stehen* (for *jem.m widerstehen*), *steif* (for *aller anfechtung widerston*) and *streiten* (for *Begierden widerstehen*).

widerstreben: resist

See under *streben* (also under *Satan*).

Widerstreit: conflict See under *heben* (for *in einem Widerstreit geraten*) and *streiten* (for *im Widerstreit liegen, sein* or *sich befinden*).

widerstreiten See under *durchstürmen* (for *die widerstreitendsten Gefühle*) and *streiten*.

Widerwärtigkeit: repulsiveness

See under *Flut* (for *Flut und See der Widerwertigkeit*) and *glatt* (for *daß die Tugend durch Widerwärtigkeit geglättet werde*).

Widerwille: aversion, disaste

See under *Haar* (for *mit Widerwillen erfüllt werden*) and *Natur* (for *dieser Widerwille ist gänzlich von der Natur des Eckels*).

widmen: dedicate

sich einer Sache ~ to devote oneself to sth., occupy oneself with sth. (with dedication); transfer from relig. and spiritual dedication to secular affairs; since the 18th c., e.g. (DWb) Schubart, *Tonkunst* 192 [1806]: '. . . *sich ganz dem Clavier zu widmen*'.

sich jem.m ~ (lit.) to engage oneself to serve sb. (as a friend); since the 18th c., e.g. Goethe 22,85 (W.): '. . . *daß er sich ihr zum Freund widme*'; *jem.m etw.* ~ = 'to dedicate sth. to sb.' led to *Widmung* in non-relig. contexts, since the 17th c., recorded by Stieler [1691], in the sense of 'written dedication' (e.g. in a book) since the 18th c.

widrig

widrig (1) hostile; since the 16th c., e.g. Luther, *Briefw.* 9,321 (Weimar): '. . . *von dem widderigen teil* [i.e. our enemies] *vns zugemessen*'.

widrig (2) unpleasant; beginnings in Late MHG, general only since the 18th c. (though with ref. to things since the 17th c.), e.g. Goethe 19,265 (W.): '*widriges schwarzes Ansehn*', Schiller, *Kab.u.L.* 1,2: '*widriger Kerl*'.

widrig (3) adverse (close to ~ (1)); first mainly with ref. to *Wind*, and with *Wind* often used figur., as in Goethe 21,247 (W.), then with many abstracts since the 18th c., e.g. Schiller, *Kab.u.L.* 1,4: '*die Stürme des widrigen Schicksals*'.

widrig (4) (rare) recalcitrant, obstreperous, disobedient; at first with ref. to persons, f.r.b. Frisius [1556], then to things occasionally since the 19th c.

← See also under *blasen* (for *daß zween widrige solten in ein Horn blasen*) and *unterfangen* (for *welch ein schulwidriges Unterfangen*), also under *widerrechtlich* (for *rechtswidrig*).

wie

wie (1) like, as; only since Early NHG, when it began to displace *als*, though *als wie* continued for a long time, e.g. Goethe 10,242 (W.): '*du bist so elend nicht, als wie du glaubst*', and *als* in comparisons is still alive in the regions and 19th c. grammarians argued about the proper uses of *wie* and *als*. Examples of ~ in comparisons are too numerous to be listed.

wie (2) how; since OHG in direct questions. For examples see the cross-references below.

~ *das?* (coll.) why? shortened forms of ~ *ist (es) denn das, daß* . . . (Late MHG) or ~ (*ist*) *dem* (Early NHG); f.r.b. Frisius [1556].

wie (3) how (very or much); indicating the high degree or amount of sth. with adjectives (less with verbs); since OHG, e.g. Luther Bible transl. 1 Thess. 2,10: '*wie heilig vnd gerecht vnd vnstrefflich wir bey euch . . . gewesen sind*'; frequent in exclamations, e.g. Hartm. v. Aue, *Arm.Heinr.*

286: '*wie schône er sîn genôz!*', Goethe 11,287 (W.): '*wie schön und wie herrlich, nun sicher einmal im Herzen des Liebsten regieren!*'.

wie (4) such as, for instance; in enumerations current since Early NHG, f.r.b. Calepinus [1598]; derived from ~ *da ist* (or *sind*) and ~ *zum Beispiel*, f.r.b. Rädlein [1711].

wie (5) (coll.) isn't that so? modern; question added after a statement inviting confirmation by the other person, e.g. Böll, *Billard* 196: '*du hast Erfahrung in solchen Dingen, wie?*'.

wie (6), also ~ *bitte?* I beg your pardon? what did you say? shortened question as in French *comment?* in some areas more politely ~ *beliebt?* derived from the fuller form ~ *sagt Ihr?*, f.r.b. Kramer [1702]: '*wie sagt Ihr? wie? = come dite?*'. Adelung [1786] commented: '*als ein höfliches Fragewort für das härtere was gebraucht*'.

aber (or *und*) ~ ! (coll.) not half! not how! very much so; modern coll. and widespread in the regions, e.g. Müller-Fraureuth, *Obersächs.* 2,664 [1914]: '*hast du ordentlich gegessen? Na und wie!*', Martin-Lienhart, *Elsäss.* 2,778: '*es regnet und wie!*'. Cf. French *et comment!*

nichts ~ *fort (weg, raus)!* (coll.) let's be off and quickly! recorded only since the 20th c., e.g. by Fischer for Swabia. See also under *nichts* (for *wie nichts* (1) and (2)).

das Wie the manner or method; since the 16th c., e.g. Luther, *Tischr.* 4,484 (Weimar), Lessing [edit. L.-M.] 8,24: '. . . *von Natur weit begieriger, das Wie als das Warum zu wissen*', Fontane, *Cecile* chapt. 22: '*das Wie seines Todes wurde vertuscht*'; it can also be used for 'reason' or 'excuse', as in Goethe, *Die wandelnde Glocke* 3–4: '*Sonntags fand es stets ein Wie, den Weg ins Feld zu nehmen*'.

~ *du mir, so ich dir* (prov.) tit for tat; international; in German in this form only recorded since the 19th c.

← See also under *Atem* (for *wie atmet rings Gefühl der Stille*), *gehen* (for *es gehet wie es kan, sage mir, wie gêt ez dir nû? ach geh, wie häßlich du bist, wie geht es mit . . . and wie er geht und steht*), *Glanz* (for *wie kommt mir solcher Glanz in meine Hütte?*), *Gott* (for *Gott weiß wie*), *Herz* (for *wie mir's ums Herz ist*), *Kind* (for *wie sage ich's meinem Kinde?*), *kommen* (for *wie ist das or ist es zu . . . gekommen, wie es gerade kommt, wie sind Sie gerade auf ihn gekommen, wie käm ich darhinder* and *wie man dann von einem in das ander kompt*), *nehmen* (for *man muss nehmen wies kompt* and *wie man das nimmt*), *nichts* (for *wie nichts* (1) and (2)), *rufen* (for *wie gerufen kommen*) and *sein* (for *wie kann das sein, abgelaufen wie es sollte* and *wie kannst du nur so sein*).

wiebeln: move in a mass

etw. wiebelt von . . . sth. is alive with . . ., is in movement in all directions; originally (since 16th c.) describing the movements of large numbers f insects, ants, etc.; transferred to swarming masses of people or frantic movement of a person since the 16th c., e.g. Grimmelshausen, *Simpliz.* 1,425: '*es wiebelte und kriebelte und krapelte und zappelte wie eine Mauß im Schmaltz-Kübel*', recorded by Adelung: '*es kriebelt und wiebelt alles von Menschen*'; now obs.

Wiedehopf: see *stinken*.

wieder: again

hin und ~ (1) (a.) here and there, scattered in all directions, everywhere; since MHG, e.g. Luther Apocr. transl. Wisd. of Sol. 18,10, still in Goethe 22,40 (W.): '*wo eine Menge kleiner Geräthschaften hin und wieder lagen*', and occasionally used in the 19th c., now a. and no longer listed in late 20th c. dictionaries.

hin und ~ (2) from time to time, occasionally; since Early NHG; the same as *dann und wann*.

~ und ~ again and again; successor to *~ und aber*, current since the 17th c., e.g. Goethe IV,8,63 (W.). Goethe also used *immer ~* (current since the 18th c.), e.g. IV,29,80 (W.).

aber dann ~ but then again; expressing doubts concerning a position one had previously adopted where *~* corresponds to 'on the other hand' (thus returning to its original meaning 'against'); since MHG, e.g. Wolfram v.E., Parz. 389,11: '*nû nach dem grâle wê unt doch wider nach ir minne*'; cf. *ich möchte es tun, und doch auch ~ nicht.*

nie ~ never again; since the 18th c. (MHG used *nie mêre*); Adelung [1777] recorded: '*es soll nie wieder geschehen*'.

← See also under *abblühen* (for *des Lebens Mai blüht einmal und nicht wieder*), *geben* (for *sie gab sich wieder gesprächig wie früher*), *gehen* (for *morgen geh ich wieder bunt*), *hin* (for *hin und wieder* (1) and (2)), *das Hin und Wieder jener Bewegungen*), *Lot* (for *es ist alles wieder im Loth*), *nichts* (for *für nichts und wieder nichts*), *nüchtern* (for *schnell wieder ernüchtert*) and *schöpfen* (for *wieder Luft schöpfen können*).

wiederabkühlen: see *auskühlen*.

wiederanfangen: see *ausholen*.

Wiederaufbau *der ~* rebuilding, reconstruction; since the 18th c., figur. with ref. to abstracts since the 19th c. For the verb *wiederaufbauen* there are examples of figur. use in the 17th c., e.g. Opitz, *Teutsche Poem.* (repr.) 9: '. . . *würde vnd lob wider auffzubawen*'.

← See also under *aufbauen* (for *seine Gesundheit wieder aufbauen*) and *Gold* (for *der Wiederaufbau und das Wirtschaftswunder*).

Wiederauferstehung *die ~* resurrection; in relig. sense since Early NHG, e.g. Luther 1,689 (Weimar), in secular contexts since the 18th c., e.g. Goethe 11,7,179 (W.), Heine [edit. E.] 6,506: '. . . *Zeit der Wiederauferstehung oder, besser gesagt, der Wiedergeburt der antiken Weltanschauung*'.

wiederaufleben *wiederaufleben* revive; since the 18th c., e.g. Goethe 47,289 (W.); in comm. contexts there is *etw. ~ lassen* = 'to reinstate sth.' (e.g. an insurance); modern. Hence *die Wiederauflebung*, since the 18th c.

Wiederaufnahme *die ~* (1) resumption of or return to former ideas, plans, etc.; since the 19th c., also in legal contexts for 'revision'.

die ~ (2) resumption of ties, friendships; since the 19th c.; also used in the theatre for 'revival', in med. contexts for 'readmission', in others for 'reversion'.

wiederaufnehmen: see *Faden*.

wiederaufrichten *etw. ~* to rebuild, reform, renew sth.; since Early NHG, now rare.

jem. ~ to give fresh heart or courage to sb., strengthen sb.'s back; since the 18th c.; also with abstracts, e.g. *jem.s Gemüt, Seele* or *Sinn ~* .

Wiederaufsteig *der ~* return to former heights, recovery; modern, often used in polit. contexts in the national-socialist period.

Wiederauftreten *das ~* (lit.) return or reappearance (of some phenomenon or event); also used for the reappearance of an actor on the stage; cf. *auftreten* (p. 107); since the 19th c.

Wiederausbruch *der ~* renewed outbreak; since early in the 19th c., mainly with ref. to illness or war (cf. *Ausbruch* on p. 124).

wiederbekommen: see *Birne*.

wiederbeleben: see *beleben*.

wiederbringen *etw. ~* to reproduce, repeat, restore or return sth.: in many contexts since OHG.

Wiedereinführung *die ~* reintroduction, reinstatement, reinstallment; this and the verb *wiedereinführen* current since the 16th c., f.r.b. Calepinus [1598].

Wiedereinsetzung: see *Glorie*.

Wiedererlangung: see *stehlen*.

Wiedererscheinung: see *Geißel*.

wiederfinden: see *Faden*.

wiedergeben See under *entschweben* (for *das kann ich nicht wiedergeben*), *greifen* (for *es zu greifen, wiederzugeben*), *lehren* (for *laß dir dein Lehrgeld wiedergeben*) and *Schule* (for *laß dir dein Schulgeld wiedergeben*).

wiedergeboren: see *gebären*.

Wiedergeburt: rebirth See under *baden* (for *das Bad der Wiedergeburt*), *Geburt* and *Wiederauferstehung*.

wiedergutmachen: see *gut* (p. 1176)

Wiederhall: see *Seele*.

Wiederherstellen: see *herstellen*.

wiederholen *etw. ~* to repeat sth.; first apparently in print in Luther's writings, e.g. *Tischr.* 4,310 (Weimar), f.r.b. Maaler [1561], but Luther also used '*holet es widder*' in 24,152 (Weimar); hence *die Wiederholung*, since late in the 16th c.

sich ~ to repeat oneself or itself; since the 18th c., e.g. Herder [edit. S.] 23,71, also in impersonal locutions *es wiederholt sich* = 'it happens again', e.g. Goethe 49,17 (W.) and with persons as the subject also since the 18th c., e.g. Fontane, *Ges.W.* 5,153 (*Stechlin*): '*man darf sich wiederholen*'; lastly with ref. to things which put in a further appearance, since the 19th c., e.g. Mügge, *Afraja* 151 [1854]: '. . . *mit roten und grünen Fäden . . ., die sich an seiner Mütze . . . wiederholten*'.

wiederholt repeated(ly); since the 17th c.; often as an adverb, also as *wiederholentlich* (mainly 18th and 19th c., now becoming rare).

im Wiederholungsfall in case of recurrence; since late in the 18th c., mainly in legal contexts.

der Wiederholungskurs (or *-lehrgang*) refresher course; since the 19th c.

wiederkäuen: see *kauen*.

Wiederkehr: see *bunt*.

wiederkommen *er kommt wieder wie der böse Pfennig* (or *Groschen*) or *wie falsch Geld* (prov.expr.) he always turns up again, there's no escaping from him; since the 17th c., a variant is *er kommt wieder wie eine Mücke*, f.r.b. Gruter [1610].

← See also under *Pfennig* (for *ein böser Pfennig kommt allzeit wieder*).

wiederschmecken: see *schmecken*.

wiedersehen: see again

das siehst du nicht wieder (coll.) you'll never get that back again, you can say good-bye to that; modern coll. with ref. to loans, where ~ = *wiederbekommen*.

Wiedersehn macht Freude (joc.coll.) I should be glad to see that back again (in my possession); joc. paraphrase when lending sb. sth. of the phrase *Wiedersehn macht Freude* = 'it is a great pleasure to meet again'.

← See also under *finden* (for *im Augenblick, da er uns wiedersieht*), *kehren* (for *seit ich diesen Menschenkehricht wiederseh*), *nimmer* (for *auf Nimmerwiedersehen*) and *Philipp* (for *bei Philippi sehen wir uns wieder*).

Wiedervereinigung: see *Glück* (p. 1086).

Wiege: cradle

See under *Bahre* (for *von der Wiege bis zur Bahre*), *Glück* (for *Anblick ihres schlummernden Glückes in der Wiege*), *Gold* (for *warum ist er nicht in die goldne Wiege geboren?*), *Grab* (for *von der Wiege bis zum Grab*), *Grazien* (for *die Grazien haben nicht an seiner Wiege gestanden*), *Kind* (for *das Kind aus der Wiege werfen*) and *singen* (for *es wurde mir nicht an der Wiege gesungen*).

wiegen (1): rock, sway, cradle

etw. or *jem.* ~ (lit.) to treat sb. gently, caress sth. or sb.; since the 18th c., e.g. Günther, *Sämtl.W.* [edit. Krämer] 5,48: '*der Himmel wiege dich mit seiner Seegenshand*'; cf. Goethe 1,68 (W.): '*der Abend wiegte schon die Erde*'.

sich in etw. ~ (lit.) to nurture or cherish sth.; since the 17th c.; now mainly with such abstracts

as *Hoffnung, Illusion, Sicherheit* or *Traum*, where often the notion of 'lulling oneself into a feeling' is present and in many cases the locution comes close to 'to delude oneself with sth.'. In the modern period transitive use has also become possible, e.g. *jem. in Sicherheit* ~ , as in E.Jünger, *Gord. Knoten* 147 [1953].

← See also under *einwiegen* and *Spiel* (for *wiegt Hännschen mich sanft auf seinem Schoß*).

wiegen (2): weigh See under *Daumen* (for *den Daumen zum Fleisch wiegen*), *Gewicht* (for *es will das theure Recht nicht blind gewogen seyn, er ist gewogen und übergewichtig befunden worden* and *abwiegen*), *Gold* (for *ich wäge dir in mit golde, aufwiegen* and *widerwegen*), *Schale* (for *mit ungleichen Schalen wiegen*), *spitz* (for *etw. spitz wiegen*), *Tonne* (for *das wiegt eine Tonne*), *überwiegen* and *vorwiegen* (also for *vorwiegend* and *überwiegend*).

Wiegendruck *der* ~ incunabulum, printed book published before the year 1501; first in Lat. form *uncunabulum*, based on Lat. *incunabula* = 'beginnings, early period'. Two registers (written in Lat.) of early printed books by Philippe Labe [1653] and Cornelius van Beughem [1688] called them *incunabula*. The German term only arose in the 1st half of the 19th c. and became general in the 2nd half after the terms *Erstlingsdruck* and *Druckerstling* (recommended by Campe [1813] for *Incunabel*) had dropped out of use.

Wiegenfest: see *herauskommen*.

Wiegenlied: see *einlullen*.

wiehern: neigh, whinny

wiehern (1) (obs.) to be full of lust, show signs of ardent desire; translates Lat. (figur.) *hinnire*; since MHG, e.g. Luther Bible transl. Jerem. 5,8 (where the A.V. has 'every one neighed after his neighbour's wife'); mainly describing sexual lust, but it could also occur for lusting after honour, glory, etc., as in Klopstock, *Oden* 1,115. Now obs.

wiehern (2) (coll.) to guffaw, laugh loudly; since the 18th c., e.g. E.Th.A. Hoffmann, *Sämtl.W.* 2,241: '*das wiehernde Gelächter der Menge*'.

← See also under *bewiehern*.

Wien: Vienna

ein Paar Wiener (coll.) a couple of Frankfurters (sausages); recent and only recorded since the 2nd half of the 20th c.

etw. wienern to polish sth.; from mil.sl., because *Wiener Kalk* (or *Putzlack*), a polishing powder, was used in the Army for cleaning the metal parts of equipment; later also current in civilian life; modern.

jem.m eine wienern (sl.) to slap sb.; *eine* stands for *eine Ohrfeige*; 20th c. sl.

← See also under *Umgang* (for *die Tugend der Umgänglichkeit als eine spezifisch wienerische zu preisen*).

Wiese: meadow *die* ~ (poet.) meadow; personified in poetry since MHG, e.g. Neidhart v. Reuenthal 18,16: '*seht wie sich vreut boum unde wise*', Mörike, *Sämtl. Schr.* [edit. Göschen] 1,109: '*noch träumen Wald und Wiesen*'.

das ist für.ihn eine gemähte ~ (prov.expr.) that is just what he wanted, just what the doctor ordered; same as *ein gefundenes Fressen* (see p. 851); f.r.b. Dentzler, *Clavis l.l.* [1716], used by Grimmelshausen, still current in some regions.

wo die Wies ist gemein, ist das Gras gerne klein (prov.) when sth. is held in common (ownership), everybody exploits it and nobody looks after it; since MHG, recorded by Freidank (cf. Zingerle, 175) and still listed in 19th c. collections, e.g. by Simrock [1846].

← See also under *Gicht* (for *Gichtwiese*), *Gras* (for *in* or *auf fremden Wiesen grasen*), *Heu* (for *der eine wässert die Wiese, der andre fährt das Heu ein*) and *Spiel* (for *Spielwiese*).

Wiesel: weasel *flink, behend, schnell wie ein* ~ as agile as a weasel; recorded since the 18th c.; *eifersüchtig, emsig, frisch, gesund* and *vergnügt wie ein* ~ also occur; the compound *wieselflink* appeared in the 20th c.; hence also *wieseln* = 'to run fast' and 'to be very active', since the 19th c.

wieviel: see *aussetzen*.

Wiking: Viking *die Wikingerfahrt* (lit.) adventurous expedition; since the 19th c., even in metaphors, as in (DWb) O.Spengler, *Unterg.d.Ab.* 1,390: '*den Menschen des Barock erfüllt die unersättliche Leidenschaft für die Wikingerfahrten der Seele*'.

wild: wild, untamed, uncultivated

wild (1) wild, tumultuous, ferocious, violent; derived from one of the original meanings 'untamed, uncontrolled'; sometimes applied to such phenomena as weather, e.g. Schiller, *Tell* 4,1: '*ihr wilden Elemente*', Goethe 20,249 (W.): '*je wilderes Wetter . . .*', also to battles, floods or conflagrations, but since the 18th c. increasingly with ref. to human emotions or behaviour, when it can mean 'wild, boisterous, unruly, passionate', e.g. Goethe, *Haidenröslein*: '*und der wilde Knabe brach . . .*', with ref. to girls = 'hoydenish', to entertainment = 'riotous, turbulent, uproarious', e.g. Lessing, Minna v.B. 4,6: '*Sie hätten die zweitausend Pistolen an einem wilden Abend verloren*', Schiller, *Kab.u.L.* 2,1: '*wilde Ergötzungen*'; hence also *es* ~ *treiben, es geht* ~ *zu,* ~ *auffahren*, as in Schiller, *Räuber* 3,1 and 5,1, *mach es nicht zu* ~ (coll.) = 'put a break on it, keep it within bounds'. See also some examples among the cross-references.

wild (2) distressed, gloomy, upsetting; with ref. to people's feelings, as in Luther 18,94 (Weimar): '*. . . den man wild und unrügig machten*', Goethe 2,146 (W.): '*düster wild an heitern Tagen*', or abstracts provoking such feelings, as in *wilde Träume*.

wild (3) (coll.) wild, mad, angry, furious; since MHG, esp. now in *jem.* ~ *machen,* ~ *werden, es ist zum Wildwerden, wie* ~ = 'madly, without consideration' and *sich wie ein Wilder benehmen*. – Note that *jem.* ~ *machen* could also mean 'to make sb. wicked, immoral', as recorded by Steinbach [1734]: '*die Gemüther durch Gewohnheit des Bösen wild machen*', but this is no longer current. See, however, ~ (4) which comes close to the notion of wickedness.

wild (4) wild, ferocious, cruel; since Early NHG, e.g. Luther Bible transl. Gen. 16,12: '*er wird ein wilder mensch sein*' (where the A.V. also has 'wild'), Lenz, *Ged.* [edit.W.] 79: '*am Herzen wild als Tiger*', also with ref. to abstracts, e.g. Schiller, *Tell* 1,2: '*wilde Zwietracht*', Bürger, 167: '*wilde Mordbegier*'.

wild (5) unauthorized, since the 17th c., e.g. with ref. to quacks, later also to people exercising a trade without having become a member of the guild. Now mainly in *wilder Streik* = 'wildcat strike', *wildes Parken* = 'illegal parking', *wilde Badestelle* = 'beach or river bank where bathing is not allowed'. See also below for *ein Wilder* (1) and (2).

wild (6) wild, confused, disorderly; since Early NHG; both Luther and Goethe used it with *Unordnung*; it often occurs with *Durcheinander*.

wild (7) dishevelled, unkempt, uncared-for; closely related to ~ (6); since the 18th c., e.g. Goethe 18,41 (W.): '*du siehst wild aus*'; also in Lessing 8,12 with ref. to an untidy beard; sometimes also with ref. to abstracts, e.g. *eine Vorstellung in wilder Form darbieten* where absence of strict direction is the principal criticism.

wild (8) wild, unreasonable, irrational, not based on sound evidence; since the 18th c., but not yet recorded by Adelung or Campe; often with *Vermutung* = 'wild guess', *Behauptung* = 'unfounded assertion', *Raterei* = 'sheer guesswork', ~ *drauflosreden* (coll.) = 'to talk without thinking'.

wild (9) rough, rude, uncouth; since MHG, then and still now often with *Sitten*; connected with the sense 'barbarian' and ultimately derived from 'uncultivated'.

wild (10) (adv.) atrociously, badly, irresponsibly; since the 17th c., e.g. Abr.a.Sta. Clara, *Judas* 1,37: '*. . . stinkt es gar wild*', Goethe III,1,224 (W.): '*ich sudle heut Abend wild, aber es ist besser etwas als nichts*'; as an intensifying adverb still current in several (mainly Southern) regions, where ~ *schön,* ~ *hübsch* and ~ *närrisch* have been recorded.

~ *sein auf jem.* (coll.) to be very angry with sb.; belongs to ~ (3); since the 18th c., e.g. Lessing 1,13: '*Alexander, hör' ich, ist auf mich gewaltig wild*'.

~ *sein auf etw.* (coll.) to be crazy (or wild) about sth.' derived from ~ = 'lascivious, full of lust', current since MHG; now coll. to express a strong liking (not necessarily of an erotic nature).

~ *wachsen* to grow wild; in phys. sense used with ref. to plants; in modern period transferred to human upbringing, mainly in the compound *aufwachsen*, e.g. Gutzkow, *R.v.G.* 1,45: '*Professor Bergs Schüler wachsen alle etwas wild auf*', meaning 'grow up without proper education or strict discipline'.

es ist nicht halb so ~ (coll.) things are not as bad as that (after all); in contexts where an excessively gloomy view is corrected; modern coll.

wildes Blut haben to be passionate, hotheaded, temperamental; since the 18th c., e.g. (DWb) Müllner 1,68; *heiß* is preferred.

wilde Ehe concubinage, cohabitation; since MHG, first in the verbal locution ~ *leben*, as in (L.) *Chron.d.dt.St.* 11,641: '*er hat wild mit seim weib gelebt*'; with *Ehe* since the 18th c., e.g. Hermes, *Soph. Reise* 3,34 [1771].

wildes Fleisch proud flesh, granulations; since MHG; it occurs also in Megenberg, *Buch d.Nat.* 383, f.r.b. Diefenbach, *Gloss.* 239b.

wilde Flucht headlong flight; modern; belongs to ~ (6).

wildes Gestein dead or barren rock (which does not yield ore in sufficient quantity to make its treatment worthwhile); since Early NHG; the same as *taubes Gestein*, for which see p. 2438.

wilder Trieb wild impulse; since the 18th c., e.g. Goethe 14,61 (W.): '*entschlafen sind nun wilde Triebe*'; in bot. *wilder Trieb* = 'sucker'.

wildes Wasser or *Wildwasser* wild mountain stream, unregulated water course; since Early NHG; cf. *Wildbach* = 'mountain stream which has created its bed by sweeping away the sandy soil or by tree-fellers sliding tree trunks down the mountain side'; since the 19th c.; sometimes figur. for 'torrent', as in (DWb) H.Kurz, *Sonnenwirth* 1,91: '. . . den Wildbach seines Schicksals in ein fortan friedliches Bette geleitet*'.

wildes Weh (lit.) fierce uncontrollable pain (or emotional stress); belongs to ~ (1); e.g. Heine, *Lorelei*: '*den Fischer . . . ergreift es mit wildem Weh*'.

wilde Wehen false labour; same as *falsche Wehen* (see p. 724); recorded since the 18th c., e.g. Amaranthes, *Frauenzimmer-Lex.* [1715].

er ist vom wilden Affen gebissen (sl.) he is mad, off his rocker; modern; see variants with *Narr* and *Watz* (p. 235).

es geht ~ *über Eck her* (coll.) things are in turmoil or in disorderly confusion; since the 19th c., e.g. Holtei, *Mensch.* 1,96; locutions with *bunt* (which see on p. 425) are preferred.

ein Wilder (1) (stud.sl.) a student who refuses to join a corporation; f.r.b. *D.Göttinger Student* [1813]; now obs.

ein Wilder (2) (polit.) independent member of parliament, diet or local council; derived from *Wilder* (1); since the middle of the 19th c., e.g.

(Ladendorf) Laube, *Das erste dt. Parl.* 3,41 [1849]: '*eine gewisse Anzahl sogenannter 'Strandläufer' oder 'Wilder' . . ., die zu keiner bestimmten Partei gehörten*'; later further extended to examinees who presented themselves without having attended an institution which prepared them for entry into the profession.

leben wie ein Wilder (coll.) to live in an uncivilized or primitive way; 20th c. coll.; cf. *wilde Leute* as recorded by Steinbach [1734] for *homines sylvestres*.

'*wir Wilden sind doch bessre Menschen*' we savages are better human beings after all; quotation from Seume's poem *Der Huron* (in *Ged.* [1801]).

toben wie zehn nackte Wilde im Schnee (sl.) to kick up a terrible shindy; 20th c. sl.

~ *in der Jugend bringt im Alter Tugend* (prov.) wild youngsters become virtuous old men; f.r.b. Petri [1605].

ins Wilde etw. tun to act unreasonably, do sth. without proper reflexion or consideration; belongs to ~ (8); since the 18th c., e.g. Möser, *Ph.* 2,31: '*Andere, welche ins Wilde gefordert hatten*'; cf. similar ~ *drauf los* = 'impetuously', recorded since the 19th c., e.g. Sanders (1865); cf. the entry on *ins Gelage hinein* on p. 969.

← See also under *Eber* (for *wild wie ein Eber*), *Feuer* (for *wildes Feuer*), *Fuchs* (for *fuchswild*), *Gans* (for *mit der wilden Gans um die Wette leben*), *Gast* (for *Sie sind ein wilder Gast*), *glühen* (for *von wilder Lust geglüht*), *Hafer* (for *wilden Hafer säen*), *Heer* (for *das wilde Heer*), *herb* (for *die wucherer füren wild gewärb*), *Hummel* (for *eine wilde Hummel*), *jagen* (for *die wilde Jagd*), *nackt* (for *raubt eine wilde Horde uns die Schätze*), *Natur* (for *Naturvölker, die wir Wilde nennen*), *Sau* (for *die wilde Sau spielen*), *Spiel* (for *den wilden Mann spielen*), *Stier* (for *wie ein wilder Stier*), *Strom* (for *wilder Strom*), *Ton* (for *die heil'ge Lippe tönt ein wildes Lied*), *treiben* (for *weg treibt der wilde Strom in grausamer Zerstörung*), *ungehalten* (for *die jugent ist zaumlos, ungehalten und wilde*), *verwildern* (also for *verwilden*) and *Westen* (for *der wilde Westen*).

Wild: game, wild animal

das ~ (lit.) prey, booty; since the 18th c., e.g. Schiller, *Tell* 4,3 referring to Geßler: '*ich laure auf ein edles Wild*', E.A.West, *Donna Diana* 3,2 with ref. to a desired woman" '*sie jagen Euch das Wild recht in den Schuß*'; cf. also Meißner, *Ged.* 163: '*Menschenwild, gehetzt von Menschenhunden*', Börne, *Menzel d.Fr.* 71: '*man ist Policeihund oder Policeiwild*'; much earlier in comparisons, as in Steinbach's [1734] quotation from Hofmannswaldau (no details): '*und wär ich Feindinn nicht allhier dein beßter Rath, so hätte dich das Garn als wie ein Wild gefangen*'.

← See also under *abfangen* (for *ein Stück Wild abfangen*), *ausspüren* (for *wie das Wild von Jagdhunden ausgespürt*) and *Flucht* (for *daz flühtege wilt*).

Wildbach: see *wild* (under *wildes Wasser*).

wildbewegt See under *bewegen* and *Rad* (for *in der Geschicke wildbewegtes Rad zu greifen*).

Wildbret: game, wild animal

Wildbret (1) (lit.) choice food; since Early NHG, e.g. Grimmelshausen, *Simpliz.* [edit. K.] 1,409: '*schimlich brod . . . mein bestes wildbret*' or 1,157 on a spider: '*. . . sich eines netzes gebrauchet, ihr wildpret zu belaustern*'.

Wildbret (2) (lit.) prey; same as figur. *Wild* (see above), e.g. Goethe 14,47 (W.) with ref. to a girl: '*geschwind! daß wir das Wildpret nicht verlieren*'; also with ref. to abstracts such as ideas which one 'chases', e.g. Luther 7,639 (Weimar) or Goethe 27,102 (W.).

← See also under *Bissen* (for *daß ein solch wildbret und niedlich bißlin in ihre netze kriegten*).

Wilde: wilderness

die ~ (1) (lit.,a.) wilderness; same as *Wildnis*; since Early NHG; occasionally in lit. in figur. use, e.g. Uhland, *Ged.* [1864 edit.] 130: '*aus dieses Erdenlebens rauher Wilde an deiner Wandrung frohes Ziel gekommen*'.

die ~ (2) (lit.,obs.) wildness; same as *Wildheit*; figur. since the 17th c., e.g. Abr. a Sta. Clara, *Etw.f.Alle* 1,11.

← See also under *wild* for locutions derived from the adjective.

Wildermann *Wildermann* (also *Wildemann*) (obs.) fierce man of huge size and great strength living in the forest; since OHG (cf. Grimm, *Sagen* 1,211); Goethe referred to the term in *Faust II* (15,54 (W.)): '*die wilden Männer sind's genannt*'. Since both words were also in use for 'miner, gold-digger', figures of miners appeared on some coins which were called *Wildemannstaler, -gulden* or *-dukaten*, only known now to collectors of coins of the 16th and 17th c.

wildern *wildern* to poach; recorded since the 18th c., e.g. by Adelung; earlier *wilddieben* was used.

etw. wildert (lit.) sth. grows in wild confusion; since the 18th c., e.g. Voß 5,259: '*noch wildert rings der Barbarei verjährter Wust*'.

jem. wildert sb. rampages or roams about (noisily or destructively); in this extended sense f.r.b. Steinbach [1734]; e.g. *Kinder ~ auf den Straßen*.

jem. ~ (lit.,rare) to make sb. wild (unruly, rebellious); since the 18th c.; Sanders [1865] quoted from Jean Paul (no details: '*wenn seine geistliche Lage . . . ihn mehr mildert als wildert*'.

etw. wildert (or *wildenzt*) sth. tastes or smells like game; with ref. to meat; *wildzen* and *wilderenzen* are also used, and some forms of this group have been recorded since the 16th c.

← See also under *verwildern*.

Wildernis: wilderness

die ~ (lit.,a.) wilderness; figur. since the 17th c., still in Goethe 15,71 (W.): '*. . . zur Einsamkeit, zur Wildernis entweichen*'; now displaced by *Wildnis*.

Wildfang: see *einbilden*.

wildfremd *wildfremd* totally unknown, quite unfamiliar; first with ref. to persons not belonging to the area and in this sense tautological since *fremd* and *wild* both contain the notion of 'alien'; since Early NHG; in the 18th c. extended to abstracts, e.g. *wildfremde Sprache*; Goethe used it with ref. to *Mordtaten* in 49,2,68 (W.): '*. . . gelesen und besprochen, aber wie etwas Wildfremdes, das uns nichts angeht*'.

Wildheit *die* ~ wildness, ferocity, barbarity; since the 18th c., e.g. Hagedorn 1,20: '*der . . . der Zwietracht Wildheit zähmt*', Wieland 31,440: '*Freiheit ohne . . . wächst gar bald in Barbarei und Wildheit aus*', Freiligrath 1,5: '*die Wildheit der Berserker*'. It can also be used with ref. to artistic performance for 'abandon, passion, ferocity', e.g. Th. Mann, *Budd.* 308: '*spielte die Geige . . . mit einer Wildheit, einer Leidenschaft . . .*'.

← See also under *Gitter* (for *die ganze Wildheit lag . . . und lauerte*).

Wildling *der* ~ uncivilized person, savage; since the 18th c., e.g. Voß 4,400, but also extended to 'rebel, sb. who deliberately ignores the rules', e.g. Gervinus, *Shakespeare* 1,47: '*in die Reihe dieser Wildlinge trat Shakespeare in seinen Jugendsitten sichtbar ein*'; cf. Jean Paul, *Fat.* 2,203: '*o du Wildling von Engel!*'

Wildnis: wilderness

die ~ (lit.) wilderness; figur. since the 18th c., e.g. Goethe, *Nat. Tochter* 5,7: '*o! hätt' ich nicht . . . mich zurück zu dieser Wildnis frechen Städtelebens . . . gewendet*'; also figur. with ref. to objects, e.g. Stifter 1,177: '*eine Wildnis dunkelbrauner Haare*', P.Heyse, *Mer.* 20: '*Hut, auf dem eine Wildnis von Hahnenfedern . . . wuchert*'.

Wildpret: see *Wildbret*.

Wildsau: see *Sau*.

Wildwasser: see *wild*.

Wilhelm: William

den dicken ~ *markieren* (or *spielen*) (coll.) to play the big dicken white chief; also 'to brag a lot'; first in mil.sl. of 1st World War; origin uncertain, perhaps it refers to *Kaiser Wilhelm* II who loved ostentation and made boastful speeches, perhaps to Dutchmen (= *Willem*) who were considered to be too well-fed and prone to give themselves airs.

ein falscher ~ (coll.,a.) a switch, tress of false hair; 19th c., now little used.

Wille(n): will

der ~ (personified) the will, volition; personified since Early NHG, often at first with *tun*, e.g. Eyering 1,602: '*der will ists und thuts alles*', Schottel, *Haubtspr.* 1127 [1662]: '*der will thut viel*', Schiller, *Wall. Tod* 4,8: '*den Menschen macht sein Wille groß und klein*', Goethe, *Iphig.* 1,1: '*. . . bewahrt mich . . . ein hoher Wille, dem ich mich ergebe*'; also with *sagen, diktieren* or *beherrschen*, as in Bismarck, *Ged.u.Erinn.* 2,22; cf. also C.F.Meyer, *Nov.* 2,12 on floating in a boat:

'. . . *dem Willen des Stromes sich überlassend*'.

der freie ~ (philos.) free will; since Early NHG, e.g. Luther 26,503 (Weimar): '. . . *verdamme ich . . . alle lehre, so unsern freien willen preisen*'. Although some dictionaries point to French *esprit libre* as of influence, this can be discounted in view of much earlier use in German.

der gute ~ good will; this covers a wide range from 'benevolence' and 'friendliness' to 'readiness to help' and 'charitable disposition'; since MHG. Goethe 2,10 (W.) also used '*freundlicher Wille*' for 'kind friendliness'. – Note that Engl. financial 'goodwill' is in German *der Goodwill*, not *der gute* ~ .

mit gutem Willen willingly, gladly; since MHG (cf. Engl. 'with a good will', as in Shakespeare, *Henry V*, 4,8); cf. Luther Bible transl. Phil. 1,16: '*etlich umb den guten willen*' (where the A.V. in 1,15 translates: 'some also of good will'). There is also the negative as in Wieland, *Lucian* 4,27: '. . . *daß es mit allem guten Willen nicht möglich war*'; hence also modern *beim besten Willen nicht*.

der letzte ~ last will (or testament); firmly established through Zesen's advocacy for Lat. *testamentum*, but current since Early NHG, e.g. Luther 8,521 (Weimar): '*ein testament ist nicht anders denn ein letzter wil*' (cf. also *ibid.* 26,547).

der ~ *zum Leben* the will to live; as a philos. concept coined by Schopenhauer, e.g. *Werke* 1,372. Nietzsche later coined *der* ~ *zur Macht* = 'the will to power'.

mit Willen (1) willingly; since OHG, e.g. Luther 10,1,1,451 (Weimar): '*was wir nit mit willen thun, das thun wir nit*'; now displaced by locutions with *willig* or *gewillt sein*. The opposite was *wider Willen*, since OHG, f.r.b. Alberus; now usually *widerwillig*.

mit Willen (2) intentionally, deliberately; since Early NHG, f.r.b. Alberus, Nov.Dict.; now usually *absichtlich*.

jem.m seinen ~ *lassen* to let sb. have his way; since MHG, e.g. Luther 10,1,1,653 (Weimar): '*wie ein kind, dem man seinen willen lest*'.

jem.m zu Willen sein (a.) to comply with sb.'s wishes, give in to sb.; since MHG; sometimes used for 'to oblige, obey, yield'; Luther used it in his Bible transl. Matth. 5,25; cf. also *sich jem. zu Willen machen* (a.) = 'to bend sb. to one's will, force sb. to yield', also used in sexual contexts; now a.

den guten ~ *für die Tat nehmen* (prov.expr.) to take the good intention (or will) for the deed; since MHG, e.g. *Minnes*. [edit. v.d.Hagen] 1,303b: '*dâ setze ich guoten willen für die tât*' or *Lohengrin* 7647: '*so nemet willen für die werc an*'. The entry on p. 2436 places the beginnings of this expression at too late a date.

← See also under *ausmachen* (for *den willen tun des himmlischen Vaters*), *blind* (for *blinder Wille*), *brechen* (for *jem.s Willen brechen*), *ducken* (for *das Wetter will sein Willen han*), *durchgehen* (for *der gute Wille geht mit der Überlegung durch*), *fassen* (for *nach unserm Willen* and *Unwillen fassen*), *gären* (for *solche Unwill bey dem gemeinen Man gejohren*), *geben* (for *den Willen dareingeben*), *gefallen* (for *Ausdruck einer mit Unwillen begleiteten Verwunderung*), *geschmeidig* (for *ihre Zöglinge . . . ganz in ihren Willen gelassen macht*), *Gewicht* (for *fremdem Willen gehorchen* and *rascher Wille*), *halb* (for *Ihr hattet sonst nie einen halben Willen*), *herrschen* (for *jem.m seinen Willen zuherrschen*), *hervorbringen* (for *wider unsern Willen hervorbringen*), *Himmel* (for *des Menschen Wille ist sein Himmelreich*), *lassen* (for *mein Bruder wird ihn nicht mit Willen lassen*), *Marionette* (for *wider ihren Willen deine Marionetten sind*), *sein* (for *daß der Will' auff ihrer Seite sey*), *Seite* (for *Seitenblicke sowohl des Unwillens und Ekels*) and *Weg* (for *wo ein Wille ist, ist auch ein Weg*).

For *um . . . willen* see under *Frieden, Gans, geben, Glück, Gott, Himmel* and *Mammon*.

Willenlosigkeit: see *geschmeidig*.

willens: see *entbinden* and *sein* (p. 2239).

willensstark: see *stark* (also for *willenstark*).

willfährig: see *Hand*.

willig: willing

See under *ausliefern* (for *die erregte und willige Sinnlichkeit*), *ducken* (for *sich willig unters Joch ducken*), *Esel* (for *dem willigen Esel wird alles aufgepackt*), *geben* (for *so geb ich mich auch willig drein* and *freiwillig*), *Geist* (for *der Geist ist willig*), *Pferd* (for *ein willig Pferd soll man nicht zuviel reiten*), *übernehmen* (for *die Würde willig übernehmen*) and *unwillig*.

willigen: see *erklären* (also under *eingehen* for *verwilligen*).

willkommen: welcome

See under *groß* (for *grôze willekomen sîn*) and *Jude* (for *willkommen wie eine Sau im Judenhaus*), also under *bewillkommnen*.

Willkür: arbitrariness

See under *Haken* (for *durch die Willkür in einander gehäkelt*) and *stellen* (for *er stellte es nun in meine freie Willkür*).

willkürlich: see *versenken* (for *unwillkürlich* see p. 2539).

wimmeln: swarm, be teeming

jem. abwimmeln (coll.) to send sb. packing, get rid of sb.; modern; similarly *jem. hinauswimmeln* (coll.), which Heyne [1895] called '*burschikos*'; in compounds of this group the sense of ~ is 'to drive away'.

das Gewimmel throng, moving mass of sth.; in phys. sense since the 17th c., then extended in the 18th c. to abstracts, e.g. *das Gewimmel des Lebens* or *der Welt* (also *Weltengewimmel*), Herder, *Krit. Wälder* 2: '*das Gewimmel von Citationen*', Stifter, *Feldblumen* 15: '*die Töne . . . wurden ein Gewimmel*'.

← See also under *Ameise* (for *es wimmelt wie in*

einem Ameisenhaufen) and *treiben* (for *die wimmel-nde Menschenfluth der großen Stadt*).

wimmern: whimper

wimmern to whimper, whine, moan, groan; the original meaning was 'to make a plaintive noise', usually applied to people and birds, e.g. Schottel, *Haubtspr.* 749 [1662]: '*es kimmert und wimmert der Nachtigall Kind*'; then extended, e.g. Grillparzer, *Ahnfrau* 4: '*wimmernd heult der Sturm von außen*'; hence also *das Gewimmer*, at first meaning the same as *Gewimmel*, e.g. Wickram, *Pilger* 4,810: '. . . *von jägern ein gewimmer*', then in modern sense, also in Wickram, *Knabenspiegel* 1,9: '*was sie joch hand für ein gewimmer*'; cf. Fouqué, *Ged.* 1,108: '*es klingen Worte durch die Nacht als wie mit leisem Klaggewimmer*', Heine [edit. E.] 5,338: '*das ewige Wehmutgewimmer*'.

um etw. ~ to beg plaintively for sth.; since the 18th c., e.g. Gökingk, *Ged.* 2,215: '*um Liebe zu wimmern war nichts für ihn*', Schiller, *D.Carlos* 5,10: '*wenn Sie um Mitgefühle wimmern*'.

Wimmer- . . . (coll., pejor.) whining . . .; with ref. to instruments since the 19th c., e.g. *Wimmerholz* = 'violin or guitar', *Wimmerkasten* = 'piano' and *Wimmerschinken* = 'lute'.

Wimpel: see *Schiff*.

Wimper: eyelash

mit keiner ~ (or *nicht mit den Wimpern*) *zucken* not to bat an eyelid; in Schiller, *Tell* 3,3: '*ich will . . . nicht zucken mit den Wimpern*' the phys. sense still predominates; figur. since the 19th c., e.g. (Sp.) Huch, *Pitt u.Fox* 204: '*ohne mit den Wimpern zu zucken, kann ich zusehen . . .*'

die Wimpern der Morgenröte (bibl.) the dawning of the day; from Job 3,9 where the A.V. misses the poetic image in the original, but Luther caught it well with '*die wimpern der morgenröthe*' (after earlier *augenbrün*); Mentel's Bible transl. had '*aufgang des aufsteygenden morgenrötes*'.

was die ~ *hält* (poet.) as much as your eyes can take in; from Keller, *Abendlied*: '*trinkt, o Augen, was die Wimper hält, von dem goldnen Überfluß der Welt!*'.

← See also under *klimpern* (for *er läßt sich nicht an den Wimpern klimpern*) and *Seide* (for *der Wimper weiche Seide*).

Wind: wind

der ~ (personified) the wind; personified in many idioms with *brausen, singen, klagen, pfeifen, weinen, rütteln, peitschen, sich drehen*, e.g. Lessing, *Freigeist* 3,1: '*ein kleiner Wind . . . kann ihn wieder herabstürzen*', Goethe 21,111 (W.): '*die Winde der Nacht saugten begierig den Hauch auf*', 49,82 (W.): '*in die Flammen als wie in Segel stößt der Wind*', Platen, 124: '*es legt sich der Wind*'. For other examples see below under the cross-references.

nur ein ~ nothing of substance or importance; since MHG, e.g. Muskatblüt [edit. Grote] 16, N. 83: '*es ist doch alles gar ein wint*'; in many locutions, e.g. *etw. wird* (*zu*) ~, *löst sich in* ~ *auf*, etc.

für ~ *achten, eitel* ~, *leerer* ~; sometimes it can contain the notions of deceit or untruth; cf. also Luther Apocr. transl. Wisd. of Sol. 5,15: '*der Gottlosen Hoffnung ist . . . wie ein Rauch, vom Winde verweht*', Goethe 37,222 (W.): '*das hofften wir und griffen – in Wind*'.

geschwind, leicht, unbeständig wie der ~ light, fleeting, fast like the wind; there are many of these comparisons, frequent since Early NHG, e.g. *eilen wie der* ~, N. Manuel [edit. B.] *Todtentanz* 90: '*wie der wind alle ding unbestendig sind*', Goethe 5,126 (W.): '*da geht alles wie der Wind*', Wieland 12,88: '*dem Winde gleich lief Hann davon*', Heine 15,34 '*da hüpft aus dem Kreise, so leicht wie der Wind, ein mageres Wesen*'; Henisch [1616] recorded '*geschwind wie der wind*'. See also below under the cross-references.

der ~, *das himmlische Kind* the wind, heaven's child; Hildebrand in *DWb.* [1873] considered it as possibly pre-Christian in origin and referred to Grimm, *Mythol.* 598, also to *Kindermärchen* No. 15. Sütterlin in *DWb.* [1913] pointed out that some such phrase occurred as early as in an old Indian tale about Nala and Damayanti. The expression is still alive, recorded by Martin-Lienhart 2,831 [1907] for the Alsace, but I have also heard it in Hesse and elsewhere.

~ *bekommen von etw.* to hear or get to know of sth., become aware of sth.; since Early NHG from the language of hunting; the verbs vary, usually *bekommen* or *kriegen* (both Goethe in 11,107 (W.) and Schiller in *Räuber* 2,3 used *kriegen*), but *haben* also occurs, e.g. Lessing, *Em.Gal.* 3,2, frequent in Grimmelshausen's writings.

vom ~ *leben* to live on air, exist on nothing; since MHG, when *des windes leben* was current; Petri [1605] recorded: '*vom wind kann niemand leben*', e.g. Goethe IV,3,14 (W.): '*jetzt aber brauch ich Geld denn niemand lebt vom Winde*'; *von der Luft leben* is now the preferred phrase.

viel ~ *machen* (coll.) to spout nonsense, indulge in empty talk, say much that is irrelevant; it can also contain the notions of boasting or exaggerating; cf. Gellert, *Schr.* 1,216 [1769]: '*zu groß zu Pralerei und Wind*'; formerly also with *vormachen*, but *machen* is now the usual verb; hence also *um eine Sache viel* ~ *machen* (coll.) = 'to make a great deal of fuss about sth.'. Cf. related idioms such as *mit* ~ *schwanger gehen*, as in Günther, *Ged.* 416 [1735], '*Staatsleute voller Wind*' in Zachariae, *Schriften* 1,82 or '*Eitelkeit, gefüllt mit Wind*' in Arndt, *Werke* 5,194. Note that there is an entirely different *es macht einen* ~ (regional coll.) = 'it causes quite a stir', since the 18th c., still in Viennese coll., recorded by Hügel.

den ~ *hinter sich haben* to be favoured by circumstances; of nautical origin; often with the notion of 'being sheltered', e.g. (Sp.) Keller, *Salander* 142: '*wenn er ein ruhiges Plätzchen hinter*

dem Wind hat . . . daß er sich noch erholen kann';
cf. also *hinter dem ~ schifft der Kluge* (prov.),
recorded by Wander [1880] and regional coll.
hinter dem ~ sein = 'to be out of danger', recorded
for the Palatinate. There are similar phrases with
Rücken.

etw. in den ~ schlagen to disregard sth. (negligently, obstinately or frivolously); general since
Early NHG, f.r.b. Frisius, e.g. Herder 17,210:
'*Verstandesehre geht über alle Ehre . . . also nicht in
den Wind zu schlagen*'; cf. similar phrases with
befehlen, as in Luther 1,383 (Weimar): '*befelh dem
lieben wind . . . die ubrigen vorgeben wort*' or
streuen, as in Stifter, *Werke* 2,100: '*streue die
Erinnerung in die Winde*'.

etw. in den ~ schreiben to ignore sth., take no
notice of sth.; modern, in essence the same as the
previous entry, but also containing the notion of
'not expecting a positive result from sth.' perhaps
influenced by *er schreibt in das Wasser*, as in
Moscherosch, *Höllen-Kinder, Phil.* 1,450.

in alle vier Winde in all directions; since OHG
(*fona feor wintun*); e.g. Goethe IV,2,275 (W.):
'. . . *schweifen in alle vier Winde*', W.Müller 1,120:
'*so sing ich meinen Jubelgesang hinaus in alle vier
Winde*'; cf. Goethe, *Faust I*, 2980: '*wer weiß, wo
es nun die vier Winde haben*'. Hence also *in alle
(vier) Winde zerstieben*.

es weht ein frischer ~ there is a fresh breeze
blowing or another kind of wind is now blowing.
The phrase is ambiguous, since it can refer to the
temperature or speed of the wind, e.g.
Eichendorff 3,9: '*der frische Wind an seinem Hute
pfiff*', but in many cases *frisch* is = 'new, different', when it means *ein anderer ~* ; cf. Grimm,
Märchen 1,172 (1843): '. . . *merkte, daß kein guter
Wind wehte*', also *merken, woher der ~ bläst*, Keller,
Salander 143: '*draußen im Bunde wehte der näm-
liche Wind*' and *der ~ der Veränderung* = 'the wind
of change', e.g. R.Zundel in *Die Zeit*, 30.3.1962:
'. . . *der 'Wind der Veränderung', von dem
Macmillan einmal sprach*'; cf. also *der ~ der Welt
weht durch etw.* = 'events or influences of the
world have their effect on sth.'.

vom ~ zerstreut or *zerstoben* scattered by the
wind; since Early NHG, e.g. Lehman, *Flor.*
1,305 [1662]: '. . . *so vom wind zerstreuet wird*'; cf.
also *vom Winde verweht*, which was chosen as the
German title of Margaret Mitchell's *Gone with
the Wind* [1936]. See also under *Spreu* and
idioms with *fliegen*.

in ~ und Wetter in every kind of weather; since
Early NHG, e.g. Luther 18,351 (Weimar): '. . .
kein wind noch wetter sich schrecken lassen' and
figur. in 30,3,291: '. . . *in solchen seltzamen leuften
. . . keinem winde noch wetter zu trauen*'.
Sometimes the locution can refer to changes
brought about through the passage of time, as in
(Sp.) Keller, *Salander* 119: '*wenn die Menschen
sich in Wind und Wetter leise ändern*'.

durch etw. Aufwind bekommen to be given an
impetus or fillip; from the language of gliding;
20th c.

← See also under *auslaufen* (for *Wind, welcher
in einen Sturm auslief*), *Baum* (for *hoher Baum
fängt viel Wind*), *blasen* (for *viel boses windes unter
augen blasen* and *weggeblasen als der wind ein
bawmblat hinwegwehet*), *blühen* (for *Lebensblüte,
welche der Wind verweht*), *brausen* (for *er kam
gebruset als ein windesbrut*), *brunzen* (for *gegen den
Wind brunzen*), *buhlen* (for *wie so gelinde erwärmen
die westlichen Winde das Ufer*), *drehen* (for *wetterhanen die sich mit jedem wind trehen*), *durchwehen*
(for *der Wind der Anfechtung*), *Ecke* (for *bläst der
Wind aus dieser Ecke?*), *fangen* (for *der Wind fängt
sich an dieser Stelle*), *Fittich* (for *auf den Fittichen
des Windes*), *fliegen* (for *flieg ich des Windes Flug*),
Flug (for *gleich den Winden, die so manches Dasein
verscharren*), *Flügel* (for *auf den Flügeln des Windes*
and *Sturmwindsflügel*), *geben* (for *Gott gibt leisen
Wind, wenn die Schafe geschoren sind*), *Gefieder*
(for *keines Windes Gefieder*), *gehen* (for *das
Schifflein gehet für den Wind* and *es geht ein un-
freundlicher Wind*), *Geißel* (for *vom Wind
gegeißelt*), *Glück* (for *wer Glück hat, mahlt ohne
Wind und Wasser*), *gut* (for *die Seele nach dem Tode
in alle Winde*), *heulen* (for *der Wind heult*), *kehren*
(for *den Mantel nach dem Wind kehren*), *Kugel* (for
wie der Wind wechseln des Geschickes Loose), *legen*
(for *der wind leget sich*), *Loch* (for *bläst der Wind
aus diesem Loch*), *Mantel* (for *den mantel henken
gen den wind*), *Meile* (for *der Käse stinkt drei
Meilen gegen den Wind*), *Mund* (for *der Winde
Mund erzählts dem Meer*), *Mütze* (for *eine Mütze
voll Wind*), *Nase* (for *sich den Wind um die Nase
wehen lassen*), *Pflug* (for *die Winde pflügen*),
Posaune (for *als Heilige posaunt in alle Winde*),
Rauch (for *wie ein Rauch vom Winde verweht*),
reden (for *in den Wind reden*), *Rohr* (for *rohr im
ried, das ein jeder wind umtreibt*), *säen* (for *wer
wind seet, wird sturm erndten*), *sanft* (for *unsanfter
Wind*), *sausen* (for *der Sausewind*), *schnell* (for
schnell wie der Wind, windschnell and *Windes-
schnelle*), *Segel* (for *jem.m den Wind aus den Segeln
nehmen* and *das ist Wind in seine Segel*), *Spreu* (for
zerstreut werden wie Spreu vom Winde), *streichen*
(for *einen Wind streichen lassen*), *Sturm* (for *sit der
kreftige wint daz (haus) stürmet*), *Tritt* (for *wirst
den vier Winden noch Tritte geben*) and *verschwinden* (for *verschwind als der wind*).

Windbeutel: see *Beutel*.

winddürr: see *Flederwisch* (and *Hering*).

Windei: wind egg

das ~ dud; also in wider sense for 'sth. that has
no substance, worthless product'; in phys. sense
recorded since the 16th c., a transl. of Lat. *ovum
subventaneum*, based, according to Varro, on the
belief that the wind had fertilized it; figur. since
the 17th c. for 'sth. of no real substance', e.g.
Lessing 8,119: '*die Henne ward über ihr Ei so laut*

und es war noch dazu ein Windei', Chamisso 5,149: *'um Gottes willen kein Windei der Henne eures Ruhmes untergelegt'*.

Windel: nappy *noch in den Windeln sein (liegen, stecken)* to be still in its early stages, very young, immature, undeveloped; at least since the 17th c., e.g. Schiller, *Fiesco* 2,18: *'in den Windeln der Üppigkeit lag das erstaunliche Werk der Verschwörung gewickelt'*.

← See also under *austauschen* (for *in Windeln unsre Kinder ausgetauscht*).

windelweich ~ *werden* (coll.) to relent, become soft-hearted or too lenient; modern, e.g. Graf, *Mitmenschen* 181: *'Zurede macht mich windelweich'*.

jem. ~ *schlagen* (coll.). to thrash sb. mercilessly; since the 18th c., e.g. Kotzebue, *Pagenstr.* 3,4.

winden: wind *gewunden* tortuous, devious, roundabout; figur. with ref. to speech. since the 18th c., with *Phrase* in Goethe, *Faust II*,1, with *Sätze* in Treitschke 4,656. Cf. Schiller, *Br.v.Mess.* 120: *'des unverständlich krummgewund-nen Lebens'*.

← See also under *Aal, auswinden, bewinden* (also for *unbewunden* and *unumwunden*), *durchwinden, Faden* (for *den man nicht herauswinden kann*), *Gewand* (for *windet uns in Wolken ein*), *Gewinde* (for *ihr Schlangengewind windet die Mythologie*, also for *Krausgewinde, Fruchtgewinde, Blumengewinde* and *Irregewinde*), *Knäuel* (for *Fäden aus einem Knäuel zu winden, zu einem Knäuel aufwinden* and *immer auf- und abzuwinden*), *Kranz* (for *jede Blume windet er zum Kranz*), *Ranke* (for *durch die rohe Welt hindurchgewunden*), *Schlange* (for *sich winden wie eine Schlange*), *überwinden, umwickeln* (for *umwinden*), *unterwinden, unüberwindlich* and *verwinden*.

Windfang: draught-screen

der ~ (1) (obs.) irresponsible person, scamp; with ref. to children also = 'imp'; since the 17th c., e.g. Weise, *Dr.kl.Leute* 49: *'der kleine windfang wil groß pralens . . . treiben'*, Gottsched, *Schaub.* 6,108: *'lüderliche junge Windfänge seid ihr!'*; influenced by *Windbeutel* and *Wildfang*; now obs.

der ~ (2) (cant) cloak, overcoat; since Early NHG, e.g. Luther 26,640 (Weimar); still listed as current in the cant of criminals; cf. Kluge, *Rotwelsch* 1,55 and 485.

der ~ (3) (hunt.) the nose of deer; f.r.b. Tüngen, *Waidmannspract.* 315.

Windflüchter *der* ~ (isolated) tree deformed or crippled through standing in a place exposed to strong wind; modern, not listed in *DWb.* [1916].

Windfuß: see *Fuß*.

Windharfe *die* ~ wind harp, aeolian harp; modern; cf. the entries unde *Aeolus* (p. 67) and *Harfe* (p. 1240).

Windhauch: see *Gerippe*.

Windhose: see *Hose*.

Windhund: see *Hund*.

windig: windy

windig unreliable, uncertain, shaky, tricky; since the 18th c., e.g. Günther, 1034: *'das Ding sieht windigt aus'*, C.F.Meyer, *Nov.*, 1,161: *'es steht in diesem Punkte bei euch selbst sehr windig'*; also with ref. to a person's character, e.g. Hebel 2,232: *'windiger Gesell'*; with abstracts often = 'deceitful', as in Treitschke 5,384: *'windige Ränke'*, or = 'lame, thin' with ref. to excuses or explanations.

Windkopf: see *Kunkel*.

Windmühle: windmill See under *Mühle* (for *sich mit Windmühlen schlagen*), *Riese* (for *Windmühlen für Riesen ansehen*) and *Schlag* (for *er hat einen Schlag von der Windmühle*).

Windmüller: see *Müller*.

Windrose: see *Rose*.

Windsack: see *Sack*.

Windsbraut: see *Braut*.

windschief: crooked *windschief* crooked, distorted; by pop.etym. associated with *Wind* = 'wind', but really derived from *Wind* (obs.) = 'wound' (see p. 1105); transferred in the 17th c. to people's character or behaviour, also sometimes to their appearance, as in Keller, *Werke* 2,47: *'wie blühende . . . Männer ganz windschiefe und blasse Weibchen heiraten'*, and to abstracts, e.g. Lessing [edit. L.-M.] 13,116: *'windschiefe Frage'*, Musäus, *Volksmärchen* 1,iv [1804]: *'windschiefes Urtheil'*.

windschnell: see *schnell* (also for *Windschnelle*).

Windspiel: see *Spiel*.

windstill

windstill calm, unperturbed, quiet; figur. since the 16th c., e.g. (DWb) Hippel, *Lebensl.* 1,40 [1778]: *'Leute von dieser windstillen Art im Leben'*, Jean Paul [edit. H.] 7,90: *'die windstillen . . . Freuden'*.

Windstille *die* ~ calmness, undisturbed conditions; figur. since the 18th c., often with allusion to storms or heavy seas, e.g. Wieland, *Agathon* 2,178: *'. . . Ruhe gleich einer Windstille auf dem Meer'*, (Sp.) Huch, *Pitt u. Fox* 210: *'so war wieder eine Windstille um sein Herz herum'*, Keller, *Salander* 233: *'nachdem . . . eine friedliche Windstille eingetreten und die Zukunft heller geworden schien'*.

windvoll *windvoll* (lit., rare) brainless, empty; since the 18th c., e.g. Knigge, *Roman m.L.* 1,166: *'ein Haufen windvoller Köpfe'*.

Wink: wave, nod, sign

jem.m einen ~ *geben* to give sb. a hint, tip (in financial contexts); since the 18th c., e.g. Wieland, *Luc.* 3,6: *'wenn Zeus . . . einem einen gnädigen Wink verleiht . . .'*, ibid. 349: *'. . . kleine Umständchen geben uns über Sitten etc. Winke'*, 6,54: *'. . . daß er von seinem Vorhaben keinen Wink bekäme'*, 11,240: *'. . . daß ich den Wink nicht sah, den Warnungswink, der mich noch retten wollte'*.

in einem ~ in the twinkling of an eye; e.g. Wieland, *Ob.* 4,18: '*in einem Wink erhob sichs aus dem Rasen, in einem Wink ist alles weggeblasen*'; cf. Klopstock, *Mess.* 13,219: '*schnell wie ein Wink*' or Bürger, *Werke* [edit. B.] 469a: '*im Nu des Augenwinks*'.

nur ein ~ only a hint, trace, tiny bit; since the 18th c., e.g. Lavater, *Physiol.Fr.* 1,14 [1775]: '*um einen Wink verfehlt*', also used by Goethe.

← See also under *betäuben* (for *die Verhältnisse betäuben den Wink der Natur*), *gehen* (for *gehorche meinen Winken*), *halb* (for *wollen wir nach deinem Wink unabläßlich streben*) and *Laternenpfahl* (for *ein Wink mit dem Laternenpfahl/Zaunpfahl*), also under *Herr* (for *Herrenwinker*).

Winkel: angle

der ~ (1) hiding-place, secluded spot; frequent since Early NHG, e.g. Luther Bible transl. Acts 26,26: '*denn solchs ist nicht im winckel geschehen*' (where the A.V. has 'for this thing was not done in a corner'), or Apocr. transl. Ecclesiasticus 23,28; often in ~ *der Seele* or *des Herzens*, current since the mediaeval Mystics, e.g. Goethe 21,47 (W.): '*in den innersten Winkeln seiner Seele*' or Platen 2,64 on the poet's duty: '*erleuchten soll er klar der Seele tiefste Winkel*'; hence also *Herzenswinkel* (lit.), e.g. (Sa.) Rank, *Schön Minnele* 184 [1853].

der ~ (2) dump, place into which one throws rubbish; since Early NHG, e.g. Fischart, *Bienkorb* 2a, Lessing 8,508: '*der rechte Winkel, in welchen ich so Etwas . . . hinwerfen kann*', also Goethe 32,62 (W.); cf. Heine, *Verm.* 1,26: '*im Makulaturwinkel eines Buchladens*', J.G. Müller, *Lind.* 4,247: '*in einem Plunderwinkel seines Gehirns*'; cf. also Keller, *L.v.Seldw.* 183: '*man lichtete die alten Winkeleien in der Gesetzsammlung*'.

der ~ (3) backwater, place off the beaten track; since MHG usually slightly pejor., f.r.b. Maaler (1561); often in *im äußersten* ~ = 'at the back of beyond', since the 17th c.

auf meinem ~ (lit.) in my (small) sphere of activity; since the 18th c., e.g. Pestalozzi, *Sämtl.Schr.* 4,328: '*. . . gradsinnig thu ich auf meinem Winkel, was mir recht scheint*'.

im ~ *sitzen* to (wish to) remain unnoticed, keep out of the way; in various locutions since Early NHG, e.g. Sudermann, *Heimat* 164: '*wir sollen still in den Winkeln hocken und da hübsch sittsam warten, bis irgendein braver Freiersmann daherkommt*'.

in allen Winkeln der Welt (lit.) (even) in the remotest corners of the earth, everywhere; since the 16th c. and still in the modern period, e.g. Laube, *Ges.Schr.* 1,85: '*. . . sah ich mich vergeblich um in allen Winkeln der Welt*'.

der Blickwinkel point of view; even in its phys. sense not yet in *DWb.* [1860] and Sanders [1865]; figur. since late in the 19th c.

der Gesichtswinkel (lit.) point of view; in phys. sense recorded by Campe, figur. since the 19th c. in such locutions as *etw. unter einem anderen Gesichtswinkel betrachten*; recorded by *DWb.* [1897] where it is described as synon. with *Gesichtspunkt* (current since the 17th c., cf. Engl. 'point of view').

das Glück im ~ happiness in a secluded place away from the tumult of the world; chosen by H. Sudermann for the title of his play [1896] and now used as a prov. expression, sometimes slightly mockingly.

← See also under *durchwehen* (for *durchwäet alle winkel deiner seelen*), *Loch* (for *aus dem loch und winkel solche lere solt anfahen*), *scheuchen* (for *den geheimsten Winkel des Herzens*), *schlüpfen* (for *Schlupfwinkel*), *schmollen* (for *Schmollwinkel*), *tot* (for *der tote Winkel*) and *Unglück* (for *Unglück lauert in jedem Winkel*).

Winkeladvokat *der* ~ hedge-lawyer, shady or unqualified lawyer; since the 18th c., e.g. Fontane, *Ges.Werke* 1,6,9: '*Blätter, in denen . . . verlogene Winkeladvokaten ihre Weisheit zu Markte bringen*'.

← See also under *Advokat* (where e.l. Stinde (1885) should be changed to since the 18th c.) and *schüren* (for *Winkeladvokaten schüren*).

Winkelehe *die* ~ secret marriage; since MHG, f.r.b. Emelius, *Nomenclator* 177 [1592]; still used in the 18th c., now obs. The same applies to *Winkelheirat*, current since MHG.

Winkelei: see *Winkel.*

Winkelgeschäft *das* ~ (obs.) secret business, surreptitious trade or undertaking; since Early NHG, e.g. Luther 5,244b (Jena): '*die Ehe ist ein öffentlicher Stand . . . nicht ein Winkelgeschäft*'.

Winkelheirat: see *Winkelehe.*

Winkelhölzer: see *Winkelzug.*

Winkelsache *die* ~ (a.) trifling matter, unimportant thing; since the 18th c., e.g. Schleiermacher, *Zur Philos.* 1,652; now a. or obs.

Winkelschlange: see *Schlange.*

Winkelschreiber *der* ~ unauthorized clerk, writer who does not dare to acknowledge his authorship; in wider sense 'contemptible scribbler, hack'; since the 16th c., e.g. Luther 30,3,447 (Weimar), (Sp.) Trenck, *Lebensgesch.* 2,104: '*. . . von . . . bezahlten Winkelschreibern angefeindet*'.

Winkelstadt *die* ~ unimportant town; since the 19th c., e.g. Gutzkow, *Ges.W.* 4,367; cf. *Winkel* (3). Now obs., but *Winkelschule* (coll.) = 'backwoods school' still exists.

Winkelversammlung *die* ~ secret (or illegal) meeting; mainly used with ref. to gatherings of people intent on overthrowing existing institutions; since Early NHG, f.r.b. Heupold, *Dict.* 114 [1620].

Winkelzug *der* ~ dishonest act, trick, shift, dodge; describes 'deviation from the straight line, twist'; this was done phys. with *Winkelhölzer* which led to *Winkelhölzer suchen* = 'to resort to excuses, evasions, subterfuges', used by Luther, *Tischr.* 185a, f.r.b. Stieler [1691]. With such *Winkelhölzer* one made a ~ , current since Early NHG, often with *machen*, f.r.b. Schottel [1663].

winken: wave, beckon, wink

etw. winkt sth. beckons; figur. with objects or abstracts since the 18th c., e.g. Wieland, *Ob.* (1st version) 2,38: '*dort winken runde Waden*', Uhland, *Ged.* 27: '*des Lebens Früchte winken euch*', Keller, *Salander* 50: '*wenn er sich ein Ziel sichtbar winken sieht*'; cf. *in Aussicht stehen* or *stellen* (p. 155).

der Mädchenwinker (coll., a.) handkerchief in outer left breast pocket of a man's jacket; since ca. 1920, according to Küpper.

← See also under *abwinken*, *Nacht* (for *die einsame Nacht winkt mit dem bleyernen Zepter ihrem düsteren Zug*), *Pfahl* (for *jem.m mit dem Zaunpfahl winken*) and *Scheune* (for *mit dem Scheunentor winken*).

winseln: whine

winseln (lit.) to cringe, beg; transfer from animal sounds to human (despicable) imploring; since the 17th c., e.g. Uz 1,160: '*ich winsle nicht um Trost*'; unusual is Grabbe 1,43: '*laut rauscht das Laub – es winselt nach Vergänglichkeit*'. Hence *das Gewinsel*, since the 17th c., recorded by Kramer [1702], who also recorded '*sein Unglück bewinseln*', which is no longer in use.

← See also under *Saal* (for *ich winsle voll von Weh in diesem Thränen-Saal*).

Winter: winter

der ~ (lit.) winter (or last period) of life; since the 15th c., e.g. Gökingk, *L.zw.Lieb.* 58: on life: '*im Winter schleicht sie* (i.e. *Lust*) *den Gang der Schnecken*'. *Des Alters* ~ has been current since Early NHG.

das macht mir keinen Sommer und keinen ~ (coll.) it is all the same to me, does not cause me a moment's worry; modern coll.

der ~ *verzehrt, was der Sommer beschert* (or *gewährt*) (prov.) winter finds out what summer lays up; modern in this form (the Engl. version has been recorded since the 15th c.), but cf. Eyering, *Prov.* 3,94: '*wer im sommer nicht samlet ein, mus im winter ein bettler sein*' and phrases with ~ as '*strenger Herr*'.

grüner (or *milder*) ~ *macht den Kirchhof fett* (or *reich*) (prov.) green winter, fat churchyard; in Engl. recorded since the 17th c., apparently later in German.

Sommer wie ~ throughout the year; as a formula since MHG, e.g. Walther v.d.V. 35,16, Keller, *Ges.W.* 4,217: '*. . . behauptete seinen Platz . . . Winter und Sommer*'.

← See also under *anschleichen* (for *der Winter kommt angeschlichen*), *blühen* (for *da blüht der Winter schön*), *einfrieren* (for *um dich Winter, in dir Winter*), *Flucht* (for *Flucht des Winters*), *Gewalt*

(for *jetzt wird es aber mit Gewalt Winter*), *Gewand* (for *der Winter hat das Maigewand der armen Flur geraubt*), *Gras* (for *es wächst dem Winter zum Trotze das Gras*), *hereinbrechen* (for *während der Winter hereinbrach*) and *schneien* (for *Winter in meiner Seele*).

Winterfenster: see *Fenster*.

Wintergeselle: see *Geselle*.

Winterkleid *die Felder haben ihr* ~ *angelegt* (lit.) the fields are covered with snow; in various locutions since the 15th c., e.g. O. Ludwig, *Ges. Schr.* 1,48: '*dann schmilzt in Frühlingswonne das starre Winterkleid*'. In zool. ~ is also used for 'winter plumage' (since the 19th c.).

Winterkönig *der* ~ (hist.) king for one winter; refers to Frederick V of the Palatinate, King of Bohemia for one winter (1619–20).

winterlich: see *blühen*.

Winternacht: see *betrügen*.

Winterschlaf: hibernation

der ~ hibernation; in original sense with ref. to animals since the 16th c.; for (human) 'time of rest, lazy period' since the 18th c., e.g. Jean Paul [edit. H.] 7/10,346: '*im März, wo die höheren Stände wegen ihres sitzenden Winterschlafes mehr vollblütig als kaltblütig sind*', or Goethe IV,12,101 (W.): '*meine naturhistorischen Arbeiten sind . . . wieder aus ihrem Winterschlafe geweckt worden*'; cf. Walther v.d.V. 39,6: '*möhte ich verslâfen des winters zît!*'.

Winterseite *die* ~ North side; since the 19th c. in recordings, but probably in existence earlier since Kramer [1702] listed *Sommerseite* for 'South side'. Cf. *er ist auf die Winterseite gefallen* (regional coll.) = 'he has fallen on his behind', since the 19th c.

Winzling

der ~ tiny creature (or thing), insignificant person; derived from *winzig* in the 2nd half of the 20th c., not yet listed in *DWb.* [1937].

Wipfel: see *Duft*.

Wippchen

Wippchen (pl) dodges, tricks, pretence, lame excuses; derived from obs. *Wipf* = 'jump', associated with entertainers such as conjurers, jugglers, illusionists, etc.' this led to ~ *machen* = 'to show off one's tricks' and is still alive in ~ *vormachen*, mainly in *mach mir doch keine* ~ *vor*, f.r.b. Klix [1862], current in many regions, also as *Wippkens*, *Wuppken* or *Wüppken*. In my youth I heard the ditty *mach mir doch kei* ~ *vor, setz mir doch kei Floh ins Ohr*. Now ~ is dropping out of use.

Wirbel: whirlpool; vortex

der ~ (1) tumult, commotion, whirl, hurlyburly; since Early NHG with ref. to emotions in tumult, f.r.b. Frisius, and unsettling conditions which affect people, e.g. Goethe IV,2,33 (W.): '*die Wirbel der Gesellschaftlichkeit hatten ihn verschlungen*'.

der ~ (2) chaos, muddle, vortex; since the 17th c., e.g. Goethe 11,166 (W.) or Hebbel, *Briefe* [edit. W.] 2,164: '*in dem bisherigen Wirbel beständiger Aufregungen*'. The meaning 'chaotic notions, wrong ideas', as in Luther 23,234 (Weimar), is obs., but the related meaning 'dizziness, vertigo' is still alive; cf. Kramer's [1702] listing of *Wirbelgeist -hirn, -kopf* and *-sucht*.

vom ~ *bis zur Zehe* from top to toe, all over; ~ for 'head' has been current since MHG, used by Luther, but the locution is modern, e.g. Fontane, *Ges.W.* 1,2,27: '*er ist Pole vom Wirbel bis zur Zehe*'.

einen ~ *machen* (coll.) to make a great fuss, kick up a lot of noise; derived from ~ (1) + the acustic meaning of ~ = 'drum roll', modern, not yet listed in *DWb.* [1937].

← See also under *Geist* (for *nenne mir den Wirbel, der an Körper Körper mächtig reißt*) and *Strom* (for *ein Strudel, ein Wirbel, eine fortreißende Stromschnelle*).

wirbeln: whirl

wirbeln (lit.) to whirl, swirl, rush around; figur. since the 17th c., Kramer [1702] recorded: '*es wirbelt mir . . . der Kopf oder das Hirn*' and '*einem wirbelicht im Kopf seyn, einen Wirbel im Kopf haben*', e.g. Raabe, *Hungerpastor* 3,73: '*Gedanken wirbelten schneller im Kreis*'. Frequent in compounds such as *aufwirbeln* (see p. 110 for *es wirbelt viel Staub auf*), *durcheinanderwirbeln*, *emporwirbeln, umwirbeln*, all in lit. use, many of them since the 17th c. (Kramer listed several).

Wirbelwind: whirlwind

ein richtiger or *wahrhaftiger* ~ a real bundle of energy; figur. ~ has been current in comparisons since Early NHG; application to persons appeared in the 18th c., e.g. Herder [edit. S.] 31,385: '*jener Wirbelwind von einem Menschen . . .*'; cf. Goethe 39,137 (W.): '*das Volk ist unbändig wie ein Wirbelwind*'.

wirken: produce, weave

etw. verwirken to forfeit sth.; *verwirken*, current since OHG has had many meanings, e.g. in Luther Bible transl. it occurs for 'to commit' (e.g. a crime) and for 'to deserve, merit'. These meanings are obs., only the meaning (also current since OHG) which has what Adelung called '*die destruirende Bedeutung der Partikel ver*' is still in (lit.) use, e.g. *er hat sein Leben verwirkt*; Adelung also recorded '*jemandes Gnade . . . die gute Meinung seiner Freunde verwirken*'. It is a stronger term than (*sich etw.*) *verscherzen*. Hence *die Verwirkung*, current since the 16th c.

← See also under *auswirken, beschränken* (for *das Wirken der Menge beschränkt sich im Kreise des Augenblicks*), *Decke* (for *hinter der Decke verborgen zu wirken*), *durchwirken, einwirken, Gewalt* (for *wirkend auf und nieder wandeln*), *Gold* (for *Gotfrid, der guldin getihte worhte*), *Natur* (for *würkende Natur*), *Tag* (for *wirken so lange es Tag ist*) and

ungezähmt (for *ungezähmter wirkt die Leiden schaft*).

wirklich: real

etw. verwirklichen to realize sth.; late derivation from ~ , not yet recorded by Adelung, but in Campe [1811] listed with 18th c. *loci*, including Schiller's '*und trunken sah ich schon das Künftige verwirklicht*' (from *Macb.* 1,11); Herder [edit. S.] 12,277 used it and it occurs frequently in Goethe's writings. Goethe also used the noun *Verwirklichung*, e.g. in 24,341 (W.).

← See also under *Gift* and *leben*.

Wirklichkeit: reality

See under *finden* (for *alles fand sich in der Wirklichkeit ganz anders*) and *Hand* (for *die Wirklichkeit in die Hände bekommen*).

Wirklichkeitsentfremdung: see *Elfenbein*.

Wirkung: effect

See under *abklingen* (for *die Wirkung klingt ab*), *einschneiden* (for *von einschneidender Wirkung*), *Gericht* (for *eine gute Wirkung tun*) *Gewächs* (for *die Wirkung der Dichtkunst*), *sublimieren* (for *sublimierende Wirkung*) and *Ursache* (for *kleine Ursachen, große Wirkungen*).

Wirkungskreis See under *austreiben* (for *Mensch, der seinen Wirkungskreis aus sich geschaffen und ausgetrieben hat*), *eng* (for *ein enger Wirkungskreis*) and *Kreis* (for *von den naturkundigen sphaera activitatis . . . der würckungskreis benamset*).

wirren: see *beugen* and *verwirren*.

Wirrwarr: see *umtoben*.

Wirt: host *der* ~ (biol.) host (to a parasite); since the 2nd half of the 19th c., f.r.b. Sanders, *Erg.Wb.* [1871].

unwirtlich inhospitable; first as *unwirtbar* (17th c.), now obs., displaced by *unwirtlich* in the 18th c. (Klopstock in *Mess.* 2,245 used *unwirtbar* in the 1st edit., then substituted *unwirtlich*); f.r.b. Campe [1811]. When it is used with ref. to weather, it means 'inclement, rough'.

← See also under *duzen* (for *Geld im Säckel duzt den Wirt*), *Gast* (for *das Glück sei dir mehr Wirth als Gast*), *Glas* (for *Schloßwirt*), *Himmel* (for *beim Gastwirt zum blauen Himmel*), *Kreide* (for *Herr Wirth, leihet mir jetzt eure Kreide*), *rechnen* (for *die Rechnung ohne den Wirt machen*) and *verrenken* (for *lieber den Magen verrenkt als dem Wirt etw. geschenkt*). See also under *bewirten*.

Wirtin: see *Dromedar*.

Wirtschaft See under *Futter* (for *Futterkrippenwirtschaft*), *Latein* (for *lateinische einfältige Wirthschaft*), *Polen* (for *eine polnische Wirtschaft*), *Schatten* (for *Schattenwirtschaft*) and *Teufel* (for *dem hat der Teufel ein Ei in die Wirtschaft gelegt* and *Teufelswirtschaft*).

wirtschaften *etw. verwirtschaften* to ruin sth., squander sth. through mismanagement; since the 18th c., also occasionally reflex. e.g. Anzengruber, *Ges.W.* 9,239: '*dann hat ein Anderer sich hier verwirtschaftet*'.

← See also under *abhausen* (for *abwirtschaften*), *abwirtschaften* and *Beutel* (for *aus welchem Beutel ich gewirtschaftet hatte*).

wirtschaftlich: see *vorschneiden*.

Wirtschaftswunder: see *Gold*.

Wirtshaus See under *Kirche* (for *wo Gott eine Kirche baut, baut der Teufel ein Wirtshaus* and *neue Kirchen und neue Wirtshäuser stehen selten leer*) and *Reif* (for *ein gut Würtshauß bedarff keines Reyffs*).

Wirtshausmatador: see *Matador*.

Wisch: scrap of paper
See under *Flederwisch*, *Grütze* (for *erklärten den Wisch für die Geburt eines elenden Grützkopfs*) and *irren* (for *Irrwisch*).

wischen: wipe
ich konnte mir den Mund ~ (coll.) I had to leave empty-handed; a ref. to the end of the meal with nothing to one's advantage to follow; at least since the 17th c., when Lehman, *Flor.pol.* 1,129 [1662] recorded: '*die schwächere . . . müssen das maul wischen und davon gehen*'.

jem.m das Maul ~ (coll.) to send sb. packing, give sb. a refusal; since the 18th c., e.g. Goethe 16,14 (W.): '*sie wischt dem Doctor das Maul*'; also sometimes as *übers Maul*. – The locution *das Maul ~* = 'to protest one's innocence', also 'to make light of the wrong one has done', which is derived from the Bible (Prov. 30,20), in A.V. rendered with 'she eateth, and wipeth her mouth, and saith, I have done no wickedness'), also used by Luther (in *Sprichw.*, edit. Thiele 317), is obs.

← See also under *arm* (for *an armer Leute Hoffahrt wischt der Teufel den Arsch*), *auswischen*, *Bart* (for *sich den Bart wischen*), *durchwischen*, *entwischen*, *erwischen*, *Nase* (for *wer dem Kinde die Nase wischt, küßt der Mutter den Backen*), *reiben* (for *durch Verwischung abgestumpft*), *ruhen* (for *die hätte genug vor ihrer Tür zu wischen*), *Schuh* (for *jem.m die Schuhe wischen* and *die Schuhe an jem.m abwischen*) and *verwischen*.

Wischer *jem.m einen ~ geben* (coll.) to reprimand sb.; since the 18th c., e.g. Lessing 10,161: '*Wischer bekommen*', Heyse 1,305: '. . . *dem Postgehülfen . . . einen kräftigen Wischer gebend*'.

← See also under *auswischen* (for *Auswischer*).

Wischiwaschi *das ~* (or *der Wischwasch*) (coll.) twaddle, nonsense, empty talk, poor piece of writing; the origin is not quite clear; Murray on 'wish-wash' in *NED* suggested derivation from 'dishwater, slops', whereas in *DWb.* [1937] Insam and Beyschlag preferred to think of *waschen* (*Gewäsch*) in the sense of 'gossip, loose talk' (and this seems preferable); general since the 18th c., both as *Wischwasch* and as *~*, e.g. Lessing [edit. M.] 2,18, H.v.Kleist [edit. E.Schm.] 1,232.

wissen: know
um etw. ~ to be aware of sth.; describes vague uncertain knowledge; since MHG, e.g.

Wolfr.v.E., *Parz.* 805,12, Goethe 22,207 (W.). Sometimes *von etw. ~* can also be used to indicate partial knowledge. This too, began in MHG.

sich viel (or *nicht wenig*) *um* (or *auf*) *etw. ~* (a.) to be conceited about or proud of sth.; since the 17th c., frequent in 18th c., rare in the modern period (not always with ref. to actual 'knowledge'), e.g. Eichendorff, *Sämtl.Werke* 2,404: '. . . *der sich nicht wenig damit wußte, daß . . .*'; Fontane used *auf* in this locution.

allwissend all-knowing; old in relig. contexts, then secularized, e.g. Goethe, *Faust I*, 1582: '*allwissend bin ich nicht, doch viel ist mir bewußt*'; hence also *Allwissenheit*.

der Besserwisser Mr. know-all, smart aleck; in *DWb.* as '*dünkelhafter Besserwisser*'; modern; hence also *Besserwisserei*, as in Klinger, *Werke* 12,124 and *besserwisserisch*.

jem.m Dank ~ to be grateful to sb.; beginnings in OHG, f.r.b. Henisch [1616]; same as *jem.m für etw. dankbar sein*.

sich nicht zu lassen ~ to be beside oneself; modern, e.g. Keller, *Leute v. Seldw.* 1,19; cf. Goethe, *Ballade*: '*er kann sich vor Freude nicht lassen*'; now becoming obs.

von jem.m nichts ~ wollen to want to have nothing to do with sb.; probably since the 17th c., if one judges by recordings of *von etw. nichts ~ wollen* (e.g. in Kramer [1702]), though with ref. to persons the locution may have become current later.

die Eule weiß nichts vom Sonntag (prov. expr.) you cannot expect understanding from that quarter; in essence the same as such phrases as *was soll die Kuh mit der Muskatnuß* (see p. 1563) or *er schickt sich dazu wie der Esel zum Lautenschlagen* (see p. 696); f.r.b. Blum [1780] and still listed in Simrock [1846].

← See also under *anfangen* (for *ich weiß nichts damit anzufangen*), *aus* (for *weder aus noch ein wissen*), *auswendig* (for *etw. auswendig wissen*), *Barthel* (for *er weiß, wo Barthel den Most holt*), *behalten* (for *wer vom Winter Böses weiß, mag's für sich behalten*), *bevorworten* (for *welches er immer zu bevorworten weiß*), *bleiben* (for *mit einer Sache nicht zu bleiben wissen*), *blühen* (for *wer weiß, was mir noch blühen könnte*), *Bock* (for *was der Bock an sich selber weiß, traut er der Geiß*), *Bube* (for *er weiß nicht, ob er ein Bübchen oder Mädchen ist*), *drei* (for *was dreie wissen, erfahren bald dreißig*), *drücken* (for *wissen, wo der Schuh drückt*), *Ende* (for *am Ende weiß man, wieviel es geschlagen*), *finden* (for *man wird ihn zu finden wissen*), *Fuchs* (for *der Fuchs weiß mehr als ein Loch*) *gackern* (for *weder gicks noch gacks von etw. wissen*), *Gasse* (for *das weiß jederman und wohnt in allen Gassen*), *Gewicht* (for *denn wir christen müssen das wissen*), *Gott* (for *der von Gott und der Welt nichts weiß, weiß Gott* and *das wissen die Götter*), *Grütze* (for *die weltweisen aber wöllen alles wissen*), *Haar* (for *das weiß ich auf *ein Haar), Hase* (for *wissen wo der Hase läuft, wissen, wo der Hase im Pfeffer liegt* and *mein Name ist Hase, ich weiß von nichts), hauen* (for *so hette ich im wol über die schnauszen zu hawen gewust), heiß* (for *was ich nicht weiß, macht mich nicht heiß), herschreiben* (for *was weiß ich), Himmel* (for *das weiß der Himmel), hinaus* (for *ich weiß nicht wo hinaus), hinten* (for *nicht wissen, wo vorne und hinten ist), Kopf* (for *er weiß nicht, wo ihm der Kopf steht* – also under *stehen), link* (for *nicht mehr wissen, was links und rechts ist), Loch* (for *mehr Löcher als eines wissen), Mann* (for *an den Mann zu bringen wissen), Maus* (for *er weiß, wie man den Mäusen pfeift), Melodie* (for *er weiß die Melodie, aber nicht den Text), Mittel* (for *wenn man die Ursache weiß, so weiß man auch das Gegenmittel), recht* (for *bilde mir nicht ein, was Rechts zu wissen), sagen* (for *sag nicht alles, was du weißt), Satan* (for *das weiß der Satan), sein* (for *wir sind von gestern her und wissen nichts), Tat* (for *nach der Tat weiß jeder guten Rat), tausend* (for *das weiß der Tausendste nicht), Uhr* (for *wissen, was die Uhr geschlagen hat), ungefähr* (for *etw. nur ungefähr wissen), verstehen* (for *wir wollen uns als neutral verstanden wissen*) and *weiterwissen.*

← See also under *Esel* (for *Unwissende), Vielwisser* (p. 2591), also under *Gewissen* (pp. 1038–40), *gewiß* (p. 1040), *ungewiß* (p. 2527) and under *glatt, Strom* and *Tod* (for *Unwissenheit).*

Wissen: knowledge
See under *ausweiten* (for *das Wissen ausweiten), Dunst* (for *mit eurem Wissen ist es Dunst), eng* (for *das weiteste Wissen verdammt uns zur engsten Passivität), Gesicht* (for *ein praktisches Wissen), gut* (for *kramte viel Wissens aus), Macht* (for *Wissen ist Macht), Stück* (for *unser Wissen ist Stückwerk*) and *weit* (for *das weiteste Wissen).*

Wissenschaft: knowledge, science
~ *ist . . .* knowledge is . . .; in numerous sayings such as ~ *ist das Licht des Lebens, der beste Reichtum, ein guter Wanderstab* (cf. Engl. prov. 'knowledge is no burthen'), *eine gute Erbschaft, Macht* (cf. Bible, Prov. 24,5), all listed in Wander 5,318 [1880]. He also quoted from Aeneas Sylvius (Pope Pius II, 1405–64): '*Wissenschaften sind das Silber gemeiner Leute, das Gold des Adels, das Kleinod der Fürsten*'.

← See also under *blühen* (for *blüht kein Heil in unserer Wissenschaft* and *letzte Ausblüte an dem Baum der Wissenschaft), Blume* (for *Lehrer der schönen Wissenschaften), greifen* (for *den Wissenschaften unter die Arme greifen), gut* (for *alte Scheinwissenschaft), Kunst* (for *das ist keine Kunst, es ist nur eine Wissenschaft), leuchten* (for *eine Leuchte der Wissenschaft), Mutter* (for *Erfahrung ist die Mutter der Wissenschaft), Nuß* (for *ich gebe für deine ganze Wissenschaft keine hohle Nuß* and *meine Wissenschaft läßt sich in eine Nußschale packen), Strahl* (for *die Wissenschaften werfen einen Teil ihrer Strahlen . . .), stützen* (for *der eigentliche*

Stützpunkt der Wissenschaft) and *Umgang* (for *näherer Umgang mit Wissenschaften und Künsten).*

wissenschaftlich: see *Gewicht*
wissentlich: see *entgegengehen*
Wißbegier(de) See under *Gefräß* (for *gefräßge Wißbegier*, also under *werfen*) and *schnappen* (for *die Wißbegierde schnappt begierig*).

wittern: scent, sense
etw. ~ to sense or suspect sth., become aware of sth. in the wind; from the jargon of huntsmen; first as *anwitern* in Hademar v.Laber, *Jagd*, v.57 (14th c.) in phys. sense, then as ~ and in the 18th c. transferred to describe human awareness or intimation of sth., e.g. Keller, *Sinngedicht* 98: '*sie schien den Handel zu wittern, wurde mißtrauisch*', Werfel, *Abituriententag* 307: '*er hat in ihr eine Schlinge gewittert*'; recently also used for 'to expect to see or experience sth., await sth. (confidently)'; *erwittern* has now dropped out of use.

Witterung von etw. bekommen (or *aufnehmen*) to become aware, get wind of sth.; from the language of huntsmen since the 18th c.; further extended in *keine Witterung für etw. haben* = 'to have no instinct for (or ability to sense) sth.'; only since the 20th c.; cf. similar Engl. phrases with figur. 'nose'.

verwittert weather-beaten, worn-out, decayed; figur. with ref. to persons only since late in the 18th c. (Campe [1811] only listed it for objects which have disintegrated).

← See also under *auswittern, Gewitter* (for *auswittern, gewittern, loswittern* and *ungewittern), Morgen* (for *Morgenluft wittern), Stall* (for *das Pferd wittert den Stall), umwittern* and *Unrat* (for *Unrat wittern).*

Witwe: widow
die ~ (poet.) the widow; in poetic comparisons or in metaphors since the 17th c., e.g. Opitz, *Dt.Poem.* 2,44 [1629] on a town: '*. . . sieht einer witwen gleich, ist leer auf allen gassen*', Hölderlin [edit. L.] 1,155: '*Mutter Erde! rief ich, du bist zur Witwe geworden*', Stifter [edit. S.] 1,212: '*. . . dem Schlosse Krumau, dieser grauen Witwe der verblichenen Rosenberger*', v.Hippel, *Lebensl.* 1,253: '*. . . Blume, die der Sturm wie eine Wittwe beugt*'.

alle Witwen sind reich (prov.) widows are always rich; the Engl. version has been recorded since 1678 (cf. John Gay, *Beggar's Opera* 1,10: 'the comfortable estate of widowhood is the only hope that keeps up a wife's spirits'); cf. also the Russian prov. in Altmann VI,401: '*eine reiche Witwe ist keine Witwe*'. Kramer [1702] recorded '*junger und reicher Witwen Thränen trucknen bald*'.

← See also under *grün* (for *grüne Witwen), Öl* (for *das Ölkrüglein der Witwe), Sonntag* (for *Sonntagswitwe*) and *Stroh* (for *Strohwitwe).*

Witwer: see *Stroh*
Witz: wit, witticism, joke
etw. ist ein ~ (coll.) sth. is incongruous, farcical,

a ridiculous affair; esp. with ref. to clothing; 20th c. coll.

der ganze ~ (coll.) the whole affair, matter, business; weakening of the original sense, which began in the 18th c. in such cases as Lichtenberg's '*der ganze Witz ist's Wörtlein "Witz"* '; often in *das ist gerade der* ~ = 'that's the point that matters or that explains things'.

mach keine Witze! (coll.) you don't say! get away! modern coll.; similarly in such questions as *das soll wohl ein* ~ *sein?* = 'you must be joking'.

Kürze ist die Seele des Witzes brevity is the soul of wit; quotation from Shakespeare, *Hamlet* 2,2, in German since the 18th c., sometimes in rhymed form *Kürze ist des Witzes Würze*.

← See also under *aufheitern* (for *tiefsinnigen Verstand durch Witz aufheitern*), *Beutel* (for *daß er Witz genug hat, in seinen Beutel zu lügen*), *blind* (for *an rehten witzen blint*), *blitzen* (for *die Sprache blitzt mit Witzen*), *dick* (for *ei, wie ist dein Witz so dick*), *Dreck* (for *ein dreckiger Witz*), *einflößen* (for *doch thut der Wein durch eingeflößten Witz . . . Wunderwerke*), *entbrennen* (for *doch bloß gehörter Witz hat nie ein Herz entbrannt*), *faul* (for *ein fauler Witz*), *Garn* (for *der witze garn*), *Gegend* (for *daß diese Gegend des deutschen Wtzies noch am wenigsten angebaut sei*), *geschmeidig* (for *Hippias besaß einen behenden und geschmeidigen Witz*), *Geselle* (for *der Witz ist der Furcht Gesell*), *Gewalt* (for *gewalt den witzen angesiget*), *Gips* (for *Gipsabgüsse von Witz*), *Grenze* (for *der Witz ist hart an der Grenze*), *Grütze* (for *ohne Witz und Gritz*), *Hintertreppe* (for *Hintertreppenwitz*), *klug* (for *Klugwitz*), *Leder* (for *machest Witze so ledern wie dein Schinken*), *Mutter* (for *Mutterwitz*), *Nebel* (for *Unglück vernebelt Witz und Verstand*), *Quentchen* (for *ein Quentchen Witz zu einer Zentnerfracht erhöhen*), *schnappen* (for *an der Grenze unseres Witzes, wo euch Menschen der Sinn überschnappt*), *Schnecke* (for *der Witz der Verzweiflung überflügelt den Schneckengang der ruhigen Weisheit*), *Treppe* (for *ein Treppenwitz der Weltgeschichte*) and *übersprühen* (for *übersprudelte von Witz*).

Witzarabeske: see *Stoff*
Witzberger: see *Abdera*
witzig See under *Gewalt* (for *die mitt gwalt went witzig syn*) and *Sinn* (for *witzige Einfälle*).
Witzigkeit: see *Weite*
witzsprühend: see *Glanz*
wo: where

~ *brennt's denn?* (coll.) why are you in such a hurry? what's the fuss about? since the 19th c., recorded by Hetzel [1896].

~ *werd' ich denn!* (coll.) why should I do such a thing, I would not dream of it; rejection of an imputation or a suggested course of action; modern coll., sometimes shortened to *i* ~ .

← See also under *Beutel* (for *wo mein Beutel aufgeht, da raucht meine Küche*), *bleiben* (for *wo bleibt . . .?*), *brennen* (for *wo brennt's?*), *Fuchs* (for *wo Fuchs und Hase sich gute Nacht sagen*), *geben* (for *wo gibt's denn so was!*), *hinführen* (for *wo wird das hinführen?*), *Hund* (for *wo die Hunde mit dem Schwanz bellen*), *Pfeffer* (for *ich wollte, du wärst, wo der Pfeffer wächst*), *Schaf* (for *wo ein Schaf vorgeht, folgen die andern nach*), *singen* (for *wo man singt, da laß dich ruhig nieder*), *Taube* (for *wo Tauben sind, fliegen Tauben zu*), *Vaterland* (for *wo es mir wohl geht, da ist mein Vaterland*) and *Weg* (for *wo ein Wille ist, ist auch ein Weg*).

Woche: week

in die Wochen kommen (or *in den Wochen liegen*) (a.) to be brought to bed (through confinement); *die Wochen* were originally *die Sechswochen*, general in Early NHG, Luther still used it, also *die Sechswöcherin*; since the 18th c. without *Sechs*, e.g. Gellert, *Loos* 2,1: '*wenn seine Frau in die Wochen kam*'.

die angerissene ~ (coll.) the second part of the week; since the middle of the 19th c. (cf. *anreißen* on p. 55).

die stille ~ (coll.) the time of menstruation; since early in the 20th c.

tausend Wochen alt (joc.coll.) of marriageable age; first recorded in N. areas (ca. 1800); with ref. to teenage girls; hence also *ein Tausendwochenbaby* (sl.), 20th c.

er sieht in die andere ~ (coll.) he squints; since the 19th c.; also in Dutch *ziet naar de andere week*. It can also be used to describe a dreamy look.

die ~ *zwier, (der Weiber Gebühr), schadet weder mir noch dir, macht des Jahres hundertvier* (prov.) twice a week; old rule concerning frequency of intercourse; according to Wander used by Luther, still recorded in 19th c. dictionaries (Eiselein, Simrock, Körte); different and more demanding in French *il faut se reveiller deux fois la nuit pour rendre le bien de sa femme*.

← See also under *anfangen* (for *die Woche fängt gut an . . .*), *brach* (for *einige Wochen brach liegen*), *Butter* (for *Butterwoche*), *Flitter* (for *noch in den Flitterwochen*), *Geige* (for *in vierzig Wochen wird sich's zeigen, was man gespilt hat uf der Geigen*), *grün* (for *die grüne Woche*), *gucken* (for *in die nächste Woche gucken*), *Käse* (for *Käsewoche*), *Sonntag* (for *wenn zwei Sonntage in einer Woche kommen*), *still* (for *die Stille Woche*) and *verplanen* (for *meine ganze Woche ist verplant*).

wochenlang: see *glotzen*
Wochenrundschau *die* ~ (sl.) dish consisting of last week's leftovers; since the 2nd half of the 19th c.; also later called *Wochenschau* (suggested by the name of 'newsreel') and (*gedrängte Wochenübersicht*, often applied to minced steak or rissoles, first in Berlin sl., late in the 19th c.

der Wochentölpel (regional coll.) mumps, *parotitis epidemica*; so called because it lasts for about a week during which the patient has a disfigured appearance suggesting stupidity; since the 17th c. The usual terms are *Mumps* and *Ziegenpeter*.

Woge: big wave, surge

die ~ (1) (lit.) flood, wave; transfer from moving water to wind (as in Klopstock), clouds, fog, light or sand; since the middle of the 18th c.; hence *das Gewoge* = 'movement to and fro or in waves', figur since late in the 18th c., recorded by Campe.

die ~ (2) (lit.) wave, rush, surge, upsurge; since the 17th c., with abstracts in the field of acustic phenomena, in the first instances containing the notion of threatening 'flood', e.g. '*Wasserwogen der Anfechtung*' (Schupp), *Unglückswogen*, recorded by Stieler [1691]; since the 19th c. in such phrases as *~ der Begeisterung, Empörung, Sympathie*, also *von Beifall*, etc. In many cases the same as figur. *Welle, Flut* or *Strom*. Frequent in compounds, e.g. (Sp.) Huch, Pitt u. Fox 331: '. . . hatte er sich frisch in eine neue Lebenswoge gestürzt'.

← See also under *branden* (for *wenn jugendlich des Zornes Wogen branden*), *gießen* (for *Öl auf die Wogen gießen*), *glatt* (for *die Wogen von etw. glätten*) and *steigen* (for *Häufleins, das in den Wogen der Menschenfluth steigt und sinkt*).

wogen: move in waves

etw. überwogt etw. (or *jem.*) (lit.) sth. covers, swamps or overwhelms sth. (or sb.); since late in the 18th c., e.g. L.v.François, *Frau E.Z.* 269: '*ein Glutstrom überwogte sein Gesicht*'. In the 19th c. many other compounds became current, e.g. *anwogen, auf und ab wogen, durchwogen, emporwogen, fortwogen, hin und her wogen* (used figur. by Goethe), *heranwogen*, e.g. Scherr, *Bl.* 1,300: '*den Thron gegen die heranwogende Demokratie zu decken*, *hervorwogen*, e.g. Ense, *B.* 3,296: '*inmitten der hervorwogenden Stimmen der öffentlichen Meinung*', *verwogen*, used by Jean Paul for 'fade away' with ref. to sounds.

← See also under *Geschmeide* (for *im wogenden Geschmeide*), *Gift* (for *Giftschwaden meine Brust so oft umwogt*), *Gold* (for *all dies wogende Gold*), *schwellen* (for *wogend Lichtmeer*), *Strom* (for *durch einander wogende Empfindung*), *Strudel* (for *ich woge in einem Wonnestrudel*) and *umwogen*.

Wogengefilde: see *Gefilde*.

Wogengewitter: see *Gewitter*.

Wogengrab: see *Grab*.

woher: *ach, ~ denn ?* (coll.) nonsense! recorded for several regions since the 19th c.

wohl: well *~ tun* (1) to do good (deeds); since OHG, occurs in Mentel's Bible in Philipp. 4,14, also in Luther's transl., e.g. Jerem. 4,22 and Matth. 5,44; cf. also *du tätest ~ daran* = 'you had better . . . , you would be well advised to . . .', since the 17th c., recorded by Kramer [1702].

~ tun (2) to do (sb.) good, provide relief or satisfaction; since the 17th c., f.r.b. Corvinus

[1646]; cf. Kramer [1702]: '*das thut einem so wol als einem Säulein das man krauet*'.

gehab dich ~ good luck to you, best wishes; originally (15th c.) a phrase of encouragement = 'be cheerful, confident'; since the 18th c. used as a formula when taking leave and wishing sb. well; f.r.b. Dentzler [1716].

jem.m ist nicht ~ bei der Sache sth. makes sb. feel uneasy; since the 17th c., recorded by Kramer.

das kann man ~ sagen one can say that (without fear of contradiction); used as a formula of affirmation or confirmation; recorded by Kramer; cf. similar phrases with *schon, ruhig* or *getrost* (see p. 2045).

sehr ~ certainly; formula used by servants on receiving an order, now mainly ironic, e.g. *sehr ~* , *sagte Johann, als der Herr zu ihm sagte "du bist ein Schuft"*, recorded by Wander [1880].

wer ~ ist, der bleib daheim (prov.) he that would be well needs not go from his own house; both for Engl. and German recorded since the 17th c., e.g. Henisch [1616], shorter in Lehman [1662]: '*wem wohl ist, der bleibe*'; cf. French *mieux vaut tenir que courir*; cf. also Franck [1541]: '*wem wol ist, der schweig*' and '*wem zu wol sei, der neme ein weib*'.

← See also under *aussinnen* (for *wohl ausgesonnen*), *beichten* (for *wohl gebeichtet ist halb gebüßt*), *bekommen* (for *wol dem Menschen, der Verstand bekommt* and *ez ist in wol bekomen*), *betragen* (for *daß ich mich sein wohl betragen mocht*), *Ding* (for *so möhten wir der minne dinc nâch wunsche wol getríben*), *Ecke* (for *dir haben sie wohl eine Ecke abgefahren*), *Eis* (for *wenn's dem Esel zu wohl wird, geht er aufs Eis*, also under *Esel*), *fahren* (for *wohl fahren* and *niht wol gevarn*), *fühlen* (for *sich wohl fühlen in der eignen Haut*), *Füllen* (for *wohl sein Lebtag nicht*), *Fuß* (for *es lernet sich wol, wenn . . .*), *ganz* (for *möchte ich wohl wissen, wohl öfters* and *ich erinnere mich wohl*), *gefallen* (for *wer im selbem wol gevallet*), *gehen* (for *auf daß es dir wol gehe, laß dirs wol gehn* and *es gehet alles wol vor sich*), *gescheit* (for *Sie sind nicht wohl gescheidt*), *haben* (for *man hat sich wohl in seiner Gegenwart* and *es hat sich wohl*), *Keim* (for *wohl geziemen*), *leben* (for *leb wohl!*), *merken* (for *wohl gemerkt*), *Pudel* (for *pudelwohl*), *Rätsel* (for *ich bin dir wohl ein Rätsel*), *recht* (for *wol den ze hove, der heime rehte tuot*), *sagen* (for *hübsch ist sie wohl, doch . . .*), *sein* (for *du bist wohl nicht bei Trost*), *treu* (for *ich weiß wohl, daß . . .*), *trinken* (for *ich möchte wohl ein Spiegel sein*) and *übel* (for *wohl oder übel*).

Wohl: well-being, welfare.

etw. dient dem ~ (von, des, der) . . . sth. benefits sth. or sb.; phrases with the noun *~* appear only to have arisen in the 18th c., although *~ und Weh* goes back to Early NHG, was used by H. Sachs and Luther and Stieler [1691] recorded: '*das*

KEY TO PRINCIPAL ABBREVIATIONS

jem.m	jemandem (dat.)
Kluge	F. Kluge, *Etymologisches Wörterbuch der deutschen Sprache*, 11th ed., Berlin und Leipzig 1934.
Lehman	C. Lehman, *Florilegium Politicum*, etc., Frankfurt 1640.
Lexer	M. Lexer, *Mittelhochdeutsches Handwörterbuch*, Leipzig 1872—8.
LG	Low German
Lipperheide	F. Freih. v. Lipperheide, *Spruchwörterbuch*, 2nd ed., München 1909.
MHG	Middle High German
mil.	military
M. Latin	medieval Latin
N.	Northern Germany
NED	*Oxford English Dictionary, A New English Dictionary on Historical Principles*, Edited by Sir James Murray, Henry Bradley, W. A. Craigie and C. T. Onions. Oxford 1884—1928.
NHG	New High German
NW	North-Western Germany
obs.	obsolete
OE	Old English
offic.	in civil service language
OHG	Old High German
ON	Old Norse
OS	Old Saxon
Oxf.	*The Oxford Dictionary of English Proverbs*, compiled by W. G. Smith, Oxford, 1935.
p.	page
poet.	used mainly in poetic language
pop.	popular
pop. etym.	popular etymology
prov.	proverb, proverbial
sb.	somebody
Schmeller	J. A. Schmeller, *Bayerisches Wörterbuch*, Stuttgart 1827—37.
Schulz-Basler	G. Schulz und O. Basler, *Deutsches Fremdwörterbuch*, Strassburg und Berlin 1913ff.
s.e.	self-explanatory
sl.	slang
S. Singer	S. Singer, *Sprichwörter des Mittelalters*, Bern 1944—7.
sth.	something
SW.	South-Western Germany
Trübner	*Trübners Deutsches Wörterbuch*, herausg. v. A. Götze, Berlin 1939ff.
v.	verse, verses
vulg.	in vulgar use (obscene terms are included under this heading, but specially marked as such)
Waag	A. Waag, *Die Bedeutungsentwicklung unseres Wortschatzes*, 5th ed., Lahr 1926.
Wb.	Wörterbuch
Weigand	F. L. K. Weigand, *Deutsches Wörterbuch*, 5th ed., Gießen 1909—10.
Weist.	Weistümer; usually the collection by J. Grimm, Göttingen 1840—69 is referred to; Österr, is appended to the Austrian collections.
Westph.	Westphalia, Westphalian
zool.	zoological term.

Where later editions than those cited above have been quoted (especially in the cases of Büchmann, Dornseiff and Kluge), details of the editions used are given in the text.

The abbreviations for journals mostly follow the accepted practice (*MLR for Modern Language Review, MLN for Modern Language Notes, IF for Indogermanische Forschungen*, etc.), only some long titles have been still further abbreviated though still left recognizable (e.g. *Z.f.d.W.* for *Zeitschrift für deutsche Wortforschung, Z.f.d.U.* for *Zeitschrift für den deutschen Unterricht, Z.f.r.P.* for *Zeitschrift für romanische Philologie*, etc.). Other works, referred to or quoted have been mentioned in abbreviated but recognizable form. It is intended to give a comprehensive list of them when the dictionary is completed. From Fasc. 9 Goethe (W.) = Weimar edition, Schiller (S.) = Säkularausgabe.

ISBN 0-631-20185-8

90000>

9 780631 201854

An Historical Dictionary of German Figurative Usage

By KEITH SPALDING

PROFESSOR EMERITUS OF GERMAN, UNIVERSITY OF WALES, BANGOR

WITH ASSISTANCE FROM

GERHARD MÜLLER-SCHWEFE

PROFESSOR EMERITUS OF ENGLISH, UNIVERSITY OF TÜBINGEN

Fascicle 57

Wohlbefinden – ziehen

KEY TO PRINCIPAL ABBREVIATIONS

a.	archaic
Adolphi	O. Adolphi, *Das große Buch der Fliegenden Worte, etc.*, Berlin n.d.
Ahd. Gl.	*Die Althochdeutschen Glossen*, ges. und bearb. von E. Steinmeyer u. Eduard Sievers, Berlin 1879—98.
Bav.	Bavaria, Bavarian
bot.	botanical term
Büchmann	G. Büchmann, *Geflügelte Worte*, 27th ed., ergänzt von A. Langen, Berlin 1915.
c.	century
Car.	Carinthia, Carinthian
cf.	compare
cl.	cliché
Cod.	codex
coll.	in colloquial use
comm.	used in language of commerce
dial.	dialect expression
Dornseiff	F. Dornseiff, *Der deutsche Wortschatz nach Sachgruppen*, Berlin und Leipzig 1934.
dt.	deutsch
DWb	*Deutsches Wörterbuch von Jacob Grimm und Wilhelm Grimm*, Leipzig 1854ff.
e.l.	earliest locus or earliest loci
etw.	etwas
Fast. Sp.	Fastnachtspiele, usually quoted after *Fastnachtspiele aus dem 15. Jahrbundert*, herausgeg. v. Keller, Stuttgart 1853.
Fick	F. C. A. Fick, *Vergleichendes Wörterbuch der indogermanischen Sprachen*, 3rd ed. Göttingen 1874.
f.r.b.	first recorded by
gen.	general
Götze	A. Götze, *Frühneuhochdeutsches Glossar*, 2nd ed., Bonn 1920.
Graff	E. G. Graff, *Althochdeutscher Sprachschatz*, Berlin 1834—42.
Hirt, *Etym.*	H. Hirt, *Etymologie der neuhochdeutschen Sprache*, 2nd ed.; München 1925.
Hirt, *Gesch.*	H. Hirt, *Geschichte der deutschen Sprache*, 2nd ed., München 1925.
hunt.	word or expression used by huntsmen
jem.	jemand (nom. or acc.)

© *Blackwell Publishers Ltd., 1997 ISBN 0 631 204326*

Typeset by Hope Services, Abingdon
Printed and bound by Whitstable Litho Ltd., Whitstable, Kent

ewige, wahre, höchste wol'. Some dictionaries even in the 18th c. left it unrecorded or merely mentioned it without comment or examples.

zu ~ , **auf Ihr ~ !** your health! a toast or a good wish; only since the 18th c., with *trinken* apparently only since the 19th c., e.g. (DWb) Fontane, *Ges.W.* 1,5,26: '*so bitt ich denn, die Gläser zu füllen, um auf das Wohl Hermionens zu trinken*'.

← See also under *Finger* (for *das Wohl des Staates an seinen Fingern haben*), *geraten* (for *aufs Geratewohl*), *merken* (for *das Merkewohl*) and *Weh* (for *das Wohl und Weh*).

Wohlbefinden: see *Mittel*.

Wohlbehagen: see *tragen*.

wohlbehalten: see *behalten*.

wohlen: *etw. wohlt jem.m* (regional) sth. give sb. a warm or pleasant feeling; only in some areas of the SW, e.g. Gotthelf, *Schuldenbauer* 283 or Hesse, *Auch* 2,67. In Swabian *jem.m ~* can also mean 'to be fond of sb.' and 'to favour sb.'.

wohlerzogen: see *Blatt*.

wohlfeil: cheap.

See under *Besen* (for *die Besen kann man am wohlfeilsten geben, die man schon fertig stiehlt*), *Beutel* (for *er hab es noch so wohlfeil*), *geben* (for *es wohlfeil geben*), *kaufen* (for *so wohlfeil, mit einem so geringen Schaden*) and *Sohn* (for *wohlfeiler wird meiner Mutter Sohn sich nimmermehr ergeben*).

Wohlgefallen: See under *auflösen* (for *sich in Wohlgefallen auflösen*), *dienen* (for *eim etwas ze dienst und wolgefallen thun*), *Geschmack* (for *finde ich kein Wohlgefallen*), *Interesse* (for *Interesse wird das Wohlgefallen genannt, das wir mit der Vorstellung der Existenz eines Gegenstandes verbinden*) and *Sohn* (for *lieber Sohn, an welchem ich Wohlgefallen habe*). See also under *rauben* (for *was uns wohl gefällt*).

wohlgehen: See under *gehen* (for *auf das es dir wolgehe*), *gut* (for *es ist gut geduldig seyn, wann es eim wohlgeht*) and *Vaterland* (for *wo es mir wohlgeht, da ist mein Vaterland*).

wohlgeläutert: see *gediegen*.

Wohlgereimtheit: see *auslaufen*.

Wohlgeruch: See under *Meer* (for *Meer von Wohlgerüchen*) and *Strom* (for *strömte Wohlgeruch hinein*).

Wohlgestalt: see *trinken*.

wohlgewählt: see *Mittel*.

wohlhabend: *~ sein* to be well-to-do, well off, prosperous; since the 15th c. in present-day meaning, e.g. Goethe, *Wahlverw.* 2,1; Goethe also used *das Wohlhaben*, e.g. in 25,39 (W.), but *Wohlhabenheit* is preferred, f.r.b. Diefenbach, *Glossarium* 6a for *abundantia* (*locus* of ca. 1500); *Wohlstand* is used more frequently.

wohlig: comfortable, cosy.

wohlig comfortable, cosy; Heyne [1895] wrongly states '*erst des späteren 18. Jh.*', since the word has been in existence since the 17th c. and was recorded by Kramer [1702], e.g. Goethe,

Fischer: '*wie's Fischlein* [here in the dative] *ist so wohlig auf dem Grund*', Keller, *Nachlaß* 225: '*mitten in . . . wohliger Bewegung*'; *Wohligkeit* occurs in 20th c. lit., but is rare (not even recorded in *Duden Universalwb.* [1989]).

Wohlklang: see *Gelenk*.

wohlklingend: See under *hochtrabend* (for *hochtrabend und wolklingend were*) and *Kern* (for *eine kernichte wohlklingende Prosa*).

Wohllaut: See under *Gold* (for *Wohllaut schläft in der Saiten Gold*) and *Opfer* (for *die Vögel opfern Wohllaut ihrem Ohr*).

Wohlstand: See under *bestreuen* (for *seine geringste That war mit Wohlstand und Anmuth bestreuet*), *saugen* (for *dem Sog des Wohlstandes nicht widerstehn*) and *Wache* (for *Belohnung der Wachen für den Wohlstand seiner Mitbürger*).

wohlstehend *~ sein* (rare) to be well-to-do, well off; in occasional use as a back-formation from *Wohlstand* since the 19th c., e.g. Storm, *Sämtl. W.* 1,207: '*einem wohlstehenden Kaufmann*'.

wohlstimmig: see *Echo*.

Wohltat: See under *ausposaunen* (for *Mann, der seine Wohltaten ausposaunet*), *Finger* (for *jem.m seine Wohltaten an den Fingern vorrechnen*), *Garten* (for *jem. mit einer Wohlthat überraschen*) and *Geißel* (for *er lernte sie nie als eine Wohltat, nur als eine Geißel kennen*).

wohltun: See under *Opfer* (for *wohlzutun und mitzuteilen vergesset nicht*) and *weihen* (for *durch ein gottnachahmendes Wohlthun*).

Wohlwollen: See under *gehen* (for *mein allgemeines Wohlwollen trieb mich*) and *halten* (for *ein so edles Wohlwollen unverändert durchhalten zu sehen*).

wohnen: dwell *mit jem.m ~* (bibl.) to cohabit with sb.; e.g. Luther Bible transl. 1 Peter 3,7; *zusammenleben* would now be used. *etw. wohnt in etw.* (lit.) sth. dwells or has established itself in sth., resides in sth.; since the 18th c., e.g. Schiller, *M.Stuart* 1,7: '*ein tiefer Sinn wohnt in den alten Bräuchen*', *Glocke*: '*in den öden Fensterhöhlen wohnt das Grauen*', also his saying '*die Wahrheit wohnt in der Sonne*'.

einer Sache wohnt etw. inne sth. possesses sth., sth. is to be found or contained in sth.; mainly with ref. to certain attributes, qualities, etc.; only since the 19th c., e.g. Heine [edit. of 1861] 5,194: '*welche soziale Bedeutung jenem Hauptbuche innewohnt*'; *inwohnen* is also used, e.g. Börne [edit. of 1840]: '*weil jeder geheimen Verbindung aristokratische Verderbnis inwohnt*'.

← See also under *beiwohnen*, *besitzen* (for *sei im Besitze, und du wohnst im Recht*), *bewohnen*, *durchwohnen*, *einwohnen*, *gehen* (for *sie beide wohnen auf der Menschheit Höhen*), *Hölle* (for *der Groll der*

Hölle wohnt in ihrem Busen), Raum (for *leicht beieinander wohnen die Gedanken), Seele* (for *in einem schönen Leib wohnt eine schönre Seele* and *zwei Seelen wohnen, ach! in meiner Brust*) and *Wasser* (for *über dem Wasser wohnen auch Leute*).

wohnlich: see *Mensch.*

Wohnung: see *frei.*

wölben: see *Saphir.*

Wölbung: vault *eine ~ bilden* (lit.) to form a dome or vault; referring to its function as a protecting cover; modern, e.g. Bismarck, *Reden,* 14,180 on the union of the three Empires: '*diese Verbindung an sich bildet ein starkes Dach und eine starke Wölbung*'; see also figur. *Gewölbe* (p. 1043).

Wolf: wolf *wenn man den ~ nennt, kommt er gerennt* (prov. expr.) talk of the devil, *lupus in fabula*; there are many phrases of this type and the one with *Esel* has been listed under *Esel;* another is *wer vom ~ spricht, findet ihn an seiner Tür,* and to some extent related is *den Teufel an die Wand malen* (for which see under *malen*). Franck [1541] recorded the rhyming form with *nennt/gerennt,* Corvinus [1646] recorded *wenn man von dem wolff redet, so steckt er in der nechsten hecken,* but *der ~ in der Fabel* appeared only in the 18th c., *lupus in fabula* was recorded by Stieler [1691] with *der wolf kommet.*

er hat den ~ gesehen (prov. expr.) he has had a severe shock, he is (still) terribly afraid or shaken; since the 16th c. in two forms, e.g. Franck [1531]: '. . . *erstumpt gleich als hab ihn ein wolff gesehen*' and Tappius, *Adag.* [1545]: '*er hat einen wolff gesehen*'.

unter die Wölfe geraten to fall into the hands of or become involved with rapacious, cruel, rough or immoral people; *~* as a dangerous beast occurs in the Bible, e.g. Matth. 7,15 or 10,16 and transfer to people became current in MHG, e.g. Walther v.d.V. 33,30 attacking the Pope: '*sîn hirte ist zeinem wolve im* [i.e. Germany] *worden under sînen schâfen*'; frequent in Luther's writings, e.g. in 7,361 (Weimar), where he calls the Pope '*o du wolff der christenheit*'; he also used *wölfisch* with ref. to cruel or immoral persons or conditions.

er bessert sich wie ein junger ~ he grows worse all the time; f.r.b. Tunnicius, 585 [1514] in LG form, then in Stieler [1691] in HG.

ein ~ ändert sein Haar, aber nicht seine Art the wolf may lose his teeth, but never his nature; in Engl. recorded since 1616 (cf. Oxf. 723); in German since MHG in many versions, e.g. Franck [1541]: '*der wolf endert sein har und jar, aber nit sein art*', Stieler [1691]: '*der wolf wird zwar älter, aber nicht frömmer*'; the shortest form

is *~ bleibt ~*; a modern rhymed version is *der ~ verändert nur die Haar; wer bös ist, bleibt es immerdar,* f.r.b. Gerlach, also in Wander [1880].

sich den (or *einen*) *~ gehen, laufen* or *reiten* to get sore or chafed; refers to chafing which is in med. language *intertrigo* or *attritus:* since Early NHG, e.g. H. Sachs, *Dicht.* [edit.G.] 1,97: '. . . *get blasen und den wolf darzu*'; in early periods also called *arswolf,* e.g. Fischart, *Garg.* 125b.

sich einen ~ reden (coll.) to talk oneself hoarse (trying to convince sb.); modern coll., derived from the previous entry.

schlank wie ein gesättigter ~ very fat; ironic comparison; recorded by Hetzel [1896].

(wie) durch den ~ gedreht sein (coll.) to be or feel completely exhausted; *~* here refers to the *Fleischwolf* = 'mincer'; modern coll.

etw. in den ~ befördern to shred sth.; *~* here = *Reißwolf* = 'shredder, devil', in the textile trade also = *Lumpenwolf,* which tears wool or cotton into fibers. Recorded by Karmarsch, *Techn.Wb.* (edit. of 1854) 2,816; hence *wolfen* (tech.) = 'to tear up in a shredder or devil', also recorded by Karmarsch.

der ~ (zool.) name for many insects, birds or fishes which are considered to be particularly noxious, dangerous or aggressive; the group is too large to be considered here in its entirety (esp. if one wanted to include purely regional terms). The chief ones are *~* or *Bienenwolf, Immenwolf* (*Phaelona melonella*) = 'robber wasp', recorded by Stieler [1691], *~* or *Meerwolf, Meerteufel* = 'coot', recorded by Oken, *Allgem. Nat.Gesch.* [1833], see p. 2448, *~* or *schwarzer Kornwurm* (*Calandra canarea*) = 'corn weevil'. Eppendorf in *Plinius* 193 [1543] wrote: '*die kleynsten spinnen, so man die wölfe nennet*'. In Swabia the 'death's-head-moth' is called *~* , in Saxony, according to Stieler, *Uter maris* is called *~* , elsewhere it is a term for 'stickleback', usually called *Stichling,* recorded frequently since Campe [1811]. There is also *Bienenwolf* for 'woodpecker', so called because of its feeding on bees settled in tree trunks, a very old term, according to W. and J. Grimm in *DWb.* [1854], recorded by Adelung, but Kramer [1702] listed *Bienenwolf* only for the 'robber wasp' (see above).

der ~ (mus.) a certain dissonance, also called *Orgelwolf,* described by Hübner [1714] as '*eine gewisse Tertz mit einem Semitonio, welche schwer zu stimmen und immer etwas falsch heulet*', whereas Jacobssohn, *Tech. Wb.* 3,175a [1781–95] defined it as '*Stimmungsfehler der Orgelpfeifen, der sogenannte dritte falsche Ton*'. It was f.r.b. *Theatrum machinarum* 6,146 [1614].

der ~ (astron.) a Southern constellation; the name may be of Babylonian origin though this has been rejected by W.Gundel (see A. Scherer, *Gestirnnamen bei den indogerm. Völkern* 192 [1956]); recordings in German are late, e.g. (DWb) Chr. Wolff, *Mathem. Lex.* 1423 [1747]: '*Wolff, lupus ist ein südisches Gestirne nahe an dem Centauro unter dem Scorpion, so bey uns nicht aufgehet*'.

der ~ *frißt kein Ziel* (prov., a.?) nothing can change the time when repayment is due; cf. Lat. *lupi nullum terminum comedunt. Ziel* here = 'fixed date of repayment'; since the 16th c., f.r.b. Faber [1587]; cf. also Aler, *Dict.* 1,1045a [1727]: '*der Haußzins steht nie still, der Wolff frist keinen Haußzins*'. It can still be found in 19th c. lit., but may now no longer be in use, esp. since *Ziel* for 'date of repayment' is now rare. Wander [1880] printed the modern version *Wölfe fressen keine Schuld*.

ein Dieb kennt den andern und ein ~ *den andern* (prov.) a thief knows a thief as a wolf knows a wolf; in Engl. since 1539 (cf. Oxf. 649); also in German since the 16th c., e.g. (DWb) *Klugreden* 23a [1548]; the prov. which deals with their mutual protection occurs in Luther 18,493 (Weimar): '*eyn teuffel jagt den andern nicht . . . ein wolff beschreiet den andern nicht*'.

wer einen ~ *großzieht, wird zum Dank von ihm gefressen* (prov.) offer a wolf a home and he will eat you; versions of this warning have been current since MHG and Zingerle in *Die dt. Sprichw. im Mittelalter* [1864] listed: Spervogel: '*swer den wolf ze hûse ladet, der nimt sîn schaden*' and Morolf II,479: '*ledestu den wolf heim ze hûs, er enkommet nit ân schaden darûz*'.

wenn ein ~ *den andern frißt, ist Hungersnot* (prov.) it's a hard winter when wolf eats another; in Engl. since 1579; in German f.r.b. Tappius [1545]: '*es muß ein grosser hunger im büsche sein, wann ein wolff den anderen isset*'; Stieler recorded it in 1691.

er frißt wie ein ~ he eats voraciously; old comparison, recorded e.g. by Kramer [1702].

es geht klein her, sagte der ~ , *als er Schnaken fraß* (prov., Wellerism) sometimes one must be content with little; beginnings in Early NHG, e.g. (DWb) *Klugreden* 158b (1548): '*es ist besser etwas dann nicht, sprach ein wolff, verschland er ein schnacken*'; the modern form was recorded by Hetzel [1896].

der Mensch ist dem Menschen ein ~ (prov.) man is to man a wolf; from Plautus, *Asinaria* 2,4,88: '*lupus homo homini*'; for Engl. recorded since the 16th c., in German probably equally old in view

of the popularity of Plautus' works in educated circles, but early recordings and examples have eluded me.

← See also under *absehen* (for *der Wolff hat ein Absehen auffs Schaaff*), *beschreien* (for *bliebe der Wolf im Wald, so würd er nicht beschrien*), *Ding* (for *ir ding its hungerig als des wolfs magen*), *Eber* (for *die Wölfe jagen sich*), *Gevatter* (for *wer beim Wolfe Gevatter stehen will, muß einen Hund unter dem Mantel haben*), *heulen* (for *wer unter Wölfen ist, muß mit ihnen heulen*), *Hund* (for *zwischen Hund und Wolf*), *Lamm* (for *das Lamm den Wölfen befehlen*), *Ohr* (for *einen Wolf bei den Ohren halten* and *den Wolf beim Ohr fassen ist schwer*), *Rachen* (for *etw. aus dem Rachen des Wolfs erhalten*), *rauben* (for *vor euch raubisch diebischen welfen* and *der Räuber ist des Wolfes Bruder*) and *Schaf* (for *sî tragent ûzen schafgewant und innen wolves herz sî hant, der Wolf im Schafpelz* and *die gezählten Schafe frißt der Wolf auch*).

Wolfsauge: *das* ~ (lit.) blackish-yellow eye; f.r.b. Aler [1727], but also describing an eye which is full of lust (or cruelty), e.g. (DWb) Kürnberger, *Nov.* 3,109 [1862].

Wolfsblick: *der* ~ (lit.) hostile look; since the 19th c., used by Freytag and Treitschke.

Wolfsgebiß: *ein* ~ *haben* to have a set of sharp teeth; used by Goethe II,7,198 (W.); the noun also occurs in the comparison *scharf wie ein* ~; modern.

Wolfsgrube: *die* ~ (mil.) ditch between inner and outer wall of fortifications; original meaning 'wolf-trap' (same as *Wolfsfalle*) and still the only meaning given in Adelung, but in the 18th c. specialized in mil. context, f.r.b. Chr.Wolff, *Mathem. Lex.* [1747].

Wolfshunger: *einen* ~ *haben* to be extremely hungry; at least since the 17th c., since recorded by Kramer [1702] as '*fame lupina*', in Adelung as '*unnatürlicher heftiger Hunger*'. Cf. Plautus, *Stich.* 605: '*quasi esuriens lupus*'.

Wolfsmonat: *der* ~ (regional or obs.) December; recorded by Kramer [1702], in Adelung glossed as regional.

Wolfsrachen: *der* ~ (med.) cleft palate; modern (not yet listed by Adelung or Campe), recorded by Bock, *Lehrbuch d. Diagnostik* 116 [1853]. The scientific term is *cheilopalatognathoschisis*.

Wolfsschlucht: '*werft das Scheusal in die* ~' throw that monster where wolves have their lair; quotation from *Der Freischütz* by F.Kind. In modern lit. ~ is occasionally used for 'wilderness, hateful place full of obnoxious people'.

Wolke: cloud *die* ~ (1) cloud, plume; transfer

from clouds in the sky to phenomena on earth which resemble clouds, e.g. Wieland 16,191: '*Wolken von Weihrauch*'; frequent in *Wolken von Sand, Staub, Tabak, Mücken*, also in compounds; since the 18th c.

die ~ (2) cloudlike mass of textiles of tissue; since the 18th c., mainly with ref. to curtains, lace, fluffy or loosely flowing garments; recorded by Adelung, used by Goethe, e.g. Spielhagen, *Probl.Nat.* 6,214 [1861]: '*die Dame, die in einer Wolke von Musselin und Spitzen herabschwebte*'; cf. also Huch, *Pitt u. Fox* 142: '*er entfernte unauffällig eine kleine Haarwolke vom Waschtisch*'. Recently extended to acustic phenomena, e.g. *Klangwolke*.

die ~ (3) (a.) crowd, heap, mass; since Early NHG, first in the Bible where the Mentel Bible has in Hebr. 12, 1: '*wolcken der gezeug*', Luther had '*wolcken der zeugen*', which he changed in 1530 to '*haufen zeugen*'; still in the 18th c., e.g. Wieland, *Luc.* 1,129: '*eine ganze Wolke von Zeugen zu Gewährsmännern*', occasionally still in 19th c. lit.

die ~ (4) (lit.) cloud, sth. which casts a shadow on sth. or sb.; with abstracts since MHG, e.g. Herder, *Ph.* 4,190: '*die Wolke des Argwohns, des Kummers, der Mühe und Sorgen umnebelt ein Gesicht, das . . .*'; hence *Wolken stehen auf seinem Gesicht*, as in Hebbel, *Mar.Mag.* 1,4; cf. also Gutzkow, *Uriel Ac.* 1,1: '*doch muß die Wolke weichen zwischen ihr und meinem Glück*', Huch, *Pitt u.Fox* 104: '*er würde jede drohende Wolke verscheuchen*'. *Gewölk* can be used in the same way, e.g. Luther, *Der 117. Psalm* F3b: '*der gnadenhimmel ist mechtiger denn der sunden gewölcke*', Varnhagen v. Ense, *Denkw.* 2,46: '*die erlittenen Drangsale hatten ihm ein trübes Gewölk auf der Seele zurückgelassen*'; cf. Pyrker, *Sämtl.W.* 367 [1839]: '*des Nachtgrauns Trauergewölk*'.

etw. or *jem. bis an die Wolken erheben* (lit.) to praise sb. to the skies; since the 16th c., e.g. Wieland, *Agathon* 2,122 or Pfeffel, *Prosaische Vers.* 10,29 [1810]. See under *heben* (p. 1265) for the more frequently used *jem. in den Himmel heben*.

das ist 'ne ~ (sl.) that's great! 20th c. sl.

etw. steht auf Wolken (lit.) sth. has no solid basis, stands on a shaky foundation; modern, e.g. Varnhagen v. Ense, *Tageb.* 5,221 (1861): '*das ganze Ministerium . . . stehe auf Wolken*'.

kein Himmel ohne Wolken (prov.expr.) no sky is ever cloudless; in essence the same as *keine Rose ohne Dornen* (p. 2009); Abr. a Sta. Clara used it in *Judas d.E.* 1,161.

etw. umwölken (lit.) to cloud, overshadow sth.; since the 17th c., e.g. Klopstock, *Oden* (edit. M.-P.) 2,122: '*die Stunde, die uns traurig umwölkt*', Goethe IV,23,184 (W.): '*. . . Falschheiten, die sich mit Bombast umwölken*'; frequent in past part. *umwölkt*, esp. with *Stirn*, as in Lessing (L.-M.) 4,460, but also with *Auge, Antlitz* or *Sinn*. See also under *bewölken* for *bewölkte Stirn*; no longer in use is Klinger, *Werke* 4,82 (1809): '*es wölkte sich finster vor meiner Stirne*'.

← See also under *auftreiben* (for *das Leben trieb seine rabenschwarzen Wolken auf*), *Ball* (for *dem Gläubgen müssen selbst die Wolken sich zu Füßen ballen*), *durchstechen* (for *die Sonne spinnt sich in purpurne Wolken*), *entladen* (for *da entladet er sich wie eine schwere Gewitterwolke*), *fallen* (for *wie aus allen Wolken gefallen*), *fliegen* (for *fliegen wie die Wolken*), *Flocke* (for *Flockenwolken*), *Gebirge* (for *silberne Gebirge aus Wolken*), *Gewächs* (for *ihr Wolken hochgeboren*), *Gewand* (for *Badegewand von Wolken*), *Gewitter* (for *zwei gewittertragende Wolken*), *Glück* (for *sein Glücksgestirn verstecke nie in finstre Wolken seine Strahlen*), *Gott* (for *die Wolke verschwinden zu sehen*), *haften* (for *mit ihm spielen Wolken und Winde*), *Rachen* (for *der Wolken schwarzer Rachen*), *reichen* (for *seine Gebet reicht bis in die Wolken*), *rollen* (for *wenn der Vater aus rollenden Wolken segnende Blitze sät*), *Schoß* (for *der Wolken schwarzer Schoß*), *schweben* (for *in den Wolken schweben*), *Traum* (for *die Wolken sind die Träume des Himmels*), *weinen* (for *die Wolken weinen sehr*) and *weit* (for *so weit die Wolken gehen*).

Wolkenbruch: See under *aufklären* (for *es klärt sich auf – zu einem Wolkenbruch*) and *Hagel* (for *Wolkenbruch und Hagel!*).

Wolkenburg: see *Burg*.

Wolkenfeger: *der ~* (mar.) moonsail, moonraker; the same as *Mondsegel*; recorded since the 19th c.

Wolkenkratzer: *der ~* skyscraper; taken over from Amer.-Engl. in the last decade of the 19th c.

Wolkenkuckucksheim: *das ~* cloud-cuckoo land; see the entry on p. 1561 which, however, needs amplification: Wieland coined *Wolkengukguksburg* and Voß *Kukukswolkenheim* before ~ established itself.

wolkenlos: *wolkenlos* (lit.) untroubled; occasionally figur. in lit., e.g. Schiller, *Räuber* 4,1: '*so wolkenlos heiter*'.

Wolkenmeer: see *Meer*.

wolkennah: see *Gipfel*.

Wolkensaum: see *Scheitel*.

Wolkenschafe: see *Grund*.

Wolkenschieber: *der ~* (1) (coll.) big man, hefty chap; in some regions also = 'vagabond, vagrant', recorded since 2nd half 19th c.; in cant also used for 'peasant', f.r.b. Ostwald, *Rinnsteinspr.* 168.

der ~ (2) (coll.) big wide-brimmed hat; modern, e.g. Löns, *D.zw.Gesicht* 252.

der ~ (3) (mar.) moonsail, moonraker; same as *Wolkenfeger* (see above), modern.

der ~ (4) (coll.) dreamer, fantast; 20th c. coll.; refers to *Wolke* = 'sth. without substance or solidity'.

Wolkenschlacht: see *Schlacht.*

Wolkenwelle: see *Welle.*

Wolle: wool *ein in der* ~ *gefärbter Demokrat* a convinced (committed, steadfast) democrat; cf. Engl. 'dyed in the wool'; sometimes *in der* ~ *gefärbt* can also contain the notions of reliability and trustworthiness; since Early NHG, e.g. Keisersberg, *Brös.* 2,69b [1517].

in der ~ *sitzen* (coll.) to be comfortable, well-off; since the 18th c., e.g. Droysen, *Arist.* 278 [1835], Heine, *Reis.* 2,203, f.r.b. Lohrengel [1860]; hence also *in die* ~ *kommen* = 'to become well-off'.

jem.m in die ~ *fahren* (or *greifen*) (coll.) to attack sb. verbally or physically; since Early NHG, e.g. Luther 34,2,312 (Weimar), f.r.b. Lehman 2,582 [1662].

jem. in ~ *bringen* (coll.) to make sb. furious; this could be connected with the previous entry, but Dolmayr in *DWb.* maintains that it is derived from ~ = 'fibers, fluffy stuff (on budding plants)', f.r.b. Frisch [1741], although the idiom with *bringen* has not been recorded before the 19th c.

~ *lassen müssen* (coll.) to suffer a loss or defeat; modern in figur. contexts, e.g. Echtermeyer, *Ausw.dt.Ged.* 84 [1847].

Wolle (coll.) (human) hair; since the 18th c. the hair on the head of black men has been called ~ , e.g. Herder [edit. S.] 13,231, but it can also refer to fluffy beards, e.g. Goethe, *Philostr. Gem.* 39: '*feine Wolle sproßt um die Wange*'; cf. *wolliges Haar* as in Th.Mann, *Buddenbr.* 294.

sich in die ~ *reden* (coll.) to talk oneself into a rage; modern, belongs to *jem. in* ~ *bringen.*

mancher geht nach (or *auf*) ~ *aus und kommt geschoren zurück* (prov.) many go out for wool and come home shorn; in Engl. recorded since 1599, in German since the 17th c., e.g. (DWb) Bastel v.d.Sohle, *Harnisch* 82 [1648].

besser die ~ *verlieren als das Schaf* (prov.) better give the wool than the sheep; in Engl. recorded since 1573, in German also since the 16th c., e.g. Fischart, *V.S. Dom.* [edit. K.] 159.

Schaumwolle (lit.) bluff, untenable proposition, wild talk; cf. the entry on *Schaum* (p.2087). In

the 18th c. *Schaumwolle* was used in the phys. sense of 'vapour', then transferred in modern period.

← See also under *Geschrei* (for *viel Geschrei und wenig Wolle*), *Schaf* (for *wer das Schaf hat, dem gehört auch die Wolle*) and *Schlag* (for *Haare unter die Wolle schlagen*).

wollen: wish, desire, will

jem. will, etw. sei . . . (a.) sb. maintains or insinuates that sth. . . .; still in modern period, but becoming a.; in essence an ellipsis with *behaupten, meinen, sich* or *jem.m einbilden* left out; e.g. Schiller, *Räuber* 2,1: '*der Doktor will, ich sei im Umkehren*'.

das will überlegt sein that has to be considered, requires some thought; describing a requirement; since the 18th c., often indistinguishable from *müssen*, frequent in *das will erledigt* (*getan*, etc.) *werden*; also in the negative where objects are seen as having a will, e.g. *das Feuer will nicht brennen, die Tür will nicht aufgehen*; lastly in cases where an infinitive has been left out, e.g. *meine Füße wollen nicht mehr* = 'my feet have given up', where *mitmachen, arbeiten, funktionieren* has been omitted; cf. also *was willst du mir* (ellipsis of *antun*), since the 18th c., e.g. Kleist [edit. Schm.] 2,21: '*was wollen diese Amazonen uns?*'; also *was wollen mit . . .* (ellipsis of *erreichen, bezwecken,* etc.), as in Goethe, *Faust I,* 4924 or Schiller, *D.Carlos* 1,5.

hier ist nichts zu ~ (coll.) nothing doing, you (or we) will not get what you (or we) want; since the 19th c., recorded e.g. by Heyne [1895]. It means the same as the phrase with *holen,* for which see p.1361.

wer will, der kann (prov.) where there's a will, there's a way, to him that will ways are not wanting; international, e.g. French *qui veut peut et qui ose fait*; but German recordings in this wording are late (e.g. Eiselein [1838], Simrock [1846]); cf. Goethe's '*du kannst, so wolle nur*' in *Faust I.*

← See also under *Bruder* (for *willst du nicht mein Bruder sein . . .*), *einwollen* (for *es will mir nicht in Kopf hinein*), *essen* (for *wer nicht will, hat schon gehabt*), *Gott* (for *so Gott will* and *wills Gott*), *heißen* (for *das will nichts* or *etw. heißen*), *heraus* (for *herauswollen*), *hinaus* (for *hinaus wollen* and *hoch hinaus wollen*), *schwimmen* (for *der Fisch will schwimmen*) and *Wohlwollen.*

Wollust: See under *ausliefern* (for *Sinnlichkeit der Wollust ausliefern*), *ausschlürfen* (for *den Becher der reinen Wollust ausschlürfen*), *einschenken* (for *den Wein der Wollust einschenken*), *ermatten* (for *in Wollüsten ermattet seine Tugend*), *gebären* (for *die Wollust im Essen und Trinken*), *Gold* (for *der goldne*

Schein der Wollust) and Himmel (for Götterwollust).

Wollustflammen: see *entsprudeln*.

wollustgirrend: see *girren*.

wollüstig: See under *beschneiden* (for *wollüstige Auswüchse*) and *Getümmel* (for *wollüstiges Getümmel*).

wollustvoll: see *fassen*.

Wonne: See under *Blume* (for *in lauter Lust und Wonne*), *drehen* (for *schon dreht sich der Boden vor Wonne mit mir*), *entspringen* (for *da von mir ein wunne entspranc*), *Folie* (for *hat Ihre Wonne die Verzweiflung so nötig zur Folie?*), *Freude* (for *Gott, der meine Freude und Wonne ist*), *Himmel* (for *Himmelswonne*), *Maß* (for *seiner Wonne Maaß ist groß*), *schaffen* (for *ich wil Jerusalem schaffen zur wonne*), *schwimmen* (for *in wunno swimman*), *See* (for *See mehr denn gewünschter Wonne*) and *Strom* (for *Schauer der Wonn'*).

Wonnegefühl: See under *durchglühen* (for *durchglühte mich das Wonnegefühl*) and *rein* (for *ätherreines Wonnegefühl*).

wonneleer: see *leer*.

Wonnestrudel: see *Strudel*.

Wort: word *sein ~ hat Gewicht* what he says carries weight, is taken notice of; similarly *sein ~ hat Geltung*; *~* here used in wider sense of 'opinion, judgment'; since the 18th c., e.g. Goethe IV,31,10 (W.); it can also be used (in singular or plural) with ref. to the utterances or sayings of a writer (cf. Goethe 6,40 (W.): '*erst werd ich Sinn, sodann auch Worte finden*'), and several magazines (some of them religious) have appeared with the title *Das Wort*.

das ~ haben to be entitled to speak; at first (in Early NHG) in the sense of speaking in a dominating way, but since the 19th c. in the milder sense of speaking after having been granted permission to do so (e.g. in a formal meeting, political assembly, etc.).

etw. nicht ~ haben wollen to refuse to admit sth.; since Early NHG, e.g. Goethe 21,94 (W.). There is also *etw. nicht wahr haben wollen*, a younger phrase.

hast du da noch Worte? does that not leave you speechless? expression of surprise or indignation; modern.

das letzte ~ the final say, the definite decision, the last word; old in *das letzte ~ haben wollen* for 'to insist stubbornly that one is right' (cf. *rechthaberisch sein*), recorded by Kramer [1702], but for 'final say' only in modern period.

ein ~ mitreden to contribute to a discussion or decision about sth.; recorded by Kramer [1702], e.g. Stifter, *Sämtl.W.* 5,1,181.

das ~ nehmen to speak; same as *das ~ ergreifen* (which see under *ergreifen*); general since the 18th c., e.g. Lessing [edit. L.-M.] 3,13,244: '*Daja, nimm das Wort*'; cf. *zum ~ kommen*, also current since the 18th c., e.g. *er konnte* (or *man ließ ihn*) *kaum zum ~ kommen*, and *sich zu ~ melden* = 'to ask permission to speak, (in public meetings) ask for the floor'.

jem. beim ~ nehmen to take sb. at his word; since the 17th c., recorded by Kramer [1702].

etw. tritt ins ~ (lit.) sth. becomes public knowledge; in lit. at least since the 18th c., e.g. Goethe 25,1,241 (W.); in earlier periods *zu ~ werden* (obs.) was used.

Worte wechseln mit jem.m to exchange words or converse with sb.; since the 17th c., recorded by Kramer [1702]; hence *der Wortwechsel*, which can often be of an unfriendly sort, also since the 17th c.

auf ein ~ just for a few words (if you can spare the time); also for 'may I say something?' or in hostile contexts 'let me say just this . . .', even confidentially for 'a word in your ear'; at least since the 17th c., recorded by Kramer [1702].

auf mein ~ ! on my word of honour; assertion of the truthfulness of one's statement; at least since the 17th c., recorded by Kramer.

mit ~ und Tat in word and deed; first as *mit und Werk* (already in *Heliand* 2612), then with *Tat* since Early NHG, recorded by Kramer. Cf. also his entry: '*seine Wort mit den Thaten bekräftigen/wahr machen*'.

im wahrsten Sinne des Wortes in the true sense of the word; modern.

das berittene ~ Gottes (mil.sl.,obs.) chaplain to the Forces; only in mil.sl in 19th and early 20th c., now obs.

← See also under *abkaufen* (for *jem.m die Worte abkaufen müssen*), *ableiten* (for *ein Wort von einem andern ableiten*), *abschneiden* (for *jem.m das Wort im Munde abschneiden*), *abspeisen* (for *der Bauch läßt sich nicht mit Worten abspeisen*), *abwägen* (for *seine Worte abwägen*), *all* (for *Alltagsworte*), *anklammern* (for *sich an jedes Wort anklammern*), *aufschließen* (for *ein Wort aufschließen*), *aussprechen* (for *du sprichst ein großes Wort gelassen aus*), *bedingen* (for *jedem Wort klingt der Ursprung nach*), *Bein* (for *ein gutes Wort bricht einem kein Bein*), *beißen* (for *Worte beißen nicht*), *bekleiden* (for *etw. mit Worten bekleiden*), *beschwingen* (for *mit beschwingten Worten*), *best* (for *jem.m die besten Worte geben*), *beugen* (for *ein Wort beugen*), *biegen* (for *ein Wort biegen*), *binden* (for *sich an die wort nicht binden*), *Blume* (for *reden vil geblümter wort*), *Blut* (for *Worte des Friedens wechseln*), *brechen* (for *kläglich mit gebrochenen Worten*),

Brücke (for *wenn das Wort eine Brücke wäre . . .*), *dartun* (for *die warheit mit wenig worten darthun*), *Dreck* (for *treck der wüsten schamperen wort*), *dritt* (for *jedes dritte Wort*), *durchweben* (for *mit fremden Worten durchwebt*), *Ebbe* (for *wenn der Wind der Worte ihn wegweht*), *eigen* (for *man kann sein eignes Wort nicht hören*), *ein* (for *mit einem Wort*), *einbürgern* (for *ein Wort einbürgern*), *einlegen* (for *gute Worte für jem. einlegen*), *einwandern* (for *das Wort ist eingewandert*), *eng* (for *wie wol das wort zu enge ist*), *entfahren* (for *ein Wort entfährt ihm*), *entfallen* (for *eh ihm noch das Wort entfallen*), *entfliegen* (for *kein einigs wort sol uns entfliegen*), *entlehnen* (for *ein Wort entlehnen*), *ergreifen* (for *das Wort ergreifen*), *ersticken* (for *von Wut erstickt in mir das Wort*), *fallen* (for *jem. m ins Wort fallen* and *das kein wort des herrn ist auff die erden gefallen*), *fassen* (for *etw. in Worte fassen*), *fein* (for *in feine Worte gekleidet*), *finden* (for *nicht Worte finden können* and *ein gutes Wort findet eine gute Statt*), *Fleisch* (for *das eingefleischte Wort*), *fliegen* (for *es flog noch manches wilde Wort, auch flogen Worte hin und wieder, wort sint niht gewegen* and *mit hochfliegenden Worten rühmen*), *fließen* (for *ûz den die gâbe fliezent der worte*), *Flügel* (for *geflügelte Worte*), *Flut* (for *daß frei das Wort durch alle Lüfte möge fluten*), *führen* (for *das Wort führen*), *füllen* (for *Worte füllen den Bauch nicht* and *Füllwort*), *Fuß* (for *mit diesem Wort war das Gesetz unter meine Füße gerollt* and *Abschiedswort*), *geben* (for *ein Wort gab das andere*), *Gehege* (for *oh welch ein Wort entfloh dem Gehege deiner Zähne*), *gehen* (for *lass gottis wort seynen gang haben, man halte am reinen Gotteswort, das Wort geht nicht in den Vers* and *noch gängige Wörter*), *Geld* (for *nicht für Geld und gute Worte*), *Gewalt* (for *um sein Wort zu halten*), *Gewicht* (for *da wort, niht werk ze wage ligt*), *Glanz* (for *der Worte göldner Glantz*), *glatt* (for *jem. m glatte Worte geben*), *gleißen* (for *mit gleissenden worten*), *Gold* (for *jedes Wort war so schwer wie Gold, guldîniu wort, goldene Worte* and *seine Worte auf die Goldwage legen*), *Gott* (for *Gottes Wort vom Lande*), *Gras* (for *hat auch müssen manches Wort ins Gras beißen*), *groß* (for *im großen Sinne des Wortes* and *das wort sol mir mein hertz gross machen*), *gut* (for *laut Pakt und gutem Wort* and *jem. m gute Worte geben*), *haften* (for *weil ich nicht auff meinen Worten haffte*), *halten* (for *Wort halten* and *suchte in diesem Wort selbst einen Halt*), *Handlanger* (for *wolbestellter Handlanger des Wortes Gottes*), *herrschen* (for *gern führt sie das herrschende Wort*), *hoch* (for *ich kann nicht hohe Worte machen*), *hohl* (for *beides sind hohle Worte*), *Kehle* (for *das Wort bleibt einem in der Kehle stecken*), *knutschen* (for *Worte/Wörter knutschen*), *kurz* (for

mit kurzen Worten), *leer* (for *Leerheit der Worte*), *lehnen* (for *Lehnwort*), *Mann* (for *ein Mann ein Wort*), *Markt* (for *Markt der schönen Worte*), *Material* (for *Worte sind Fabrikate*), *Mord* (for *ez ist ein altgesprochen wort*), *muffig* (for *mit dem Schimmel alter verlegner Worte*), *nehmen* (for *jem. m das Wort aus dem Mund nehmen, Jawort* and *das Wort ist aus dem Lateinischen genommen*), *Ohr* (for *dein Wort in Gottes Ohr*), *Öl* (for *worte gelinder denn ole*), *prägen* (for *das Prägen von glitzenden Wörtern*), *pressen* (for *ein Wort pressen*), *reden* (for *jem. m das Wort reden*), *Saat* (for *diese Worte waren eine Saat*), *Sack* (for *große Worte machen den Sack nicht voll*), *schlafen* (for *Worte wie verschlafene Kinder*), *Schlag* (for *jem. m mit einem Wort das Mark aus den Gebeinen schlagen* and *Schlagwort*), *schleifen* (for *er kann Worte schleifen*), *schneiden* (for *schneidende Worte*), *schmücken* (for *Schmuckwort*), *schön* (for *mit schönen Worten erschüttern*), *Schranke* (for *verschränkte Worte*, *Schule* (for *Wörter, die nach der Schule schmecken*), *schwören* (for *auf des Meisters Worte schwören*), *Schwulst* (for *sie lauten von schwulstigen worten*), *spitz* (for *Spitzwort*), *springen* (for *ein Wort über die Zunge springen lassen*), *Stachel* (for *mit dem Stachel meiner Worte*), *stehen* (for *die wort stehen klar da fur augen*), *Stelle* (for *Wörter nicht nur ein Stellenwert . . .* and *ein gutes Wort findet eine gute Stelle*), *Stich* (for *Stichwort 1–5* and *Stichwörter*), *streiten* (for *mit Worten läßt sich trefflich streiten*), *Strich* (for *göttliches Wort* and *gottes wort*), *Strick* (for *der Lüge trüglich Wort*), *Strudel* (for *ihre Worte strudeln*), *täuschen* (for *uns Deutschen fehlt es an einem Wort für . . .* and *junges Wort*), *Trank* (for *meine wort ersetigend als ein gutes tranck*), *umdrehen* (for *jem. m das Wort im Mund umdrehen*, also *under verdrehen*), *umkleiden* (for *mit viel glatten Worten umkleiden*), *ungewaschen* (for *ungewaschne wort*), *verkleinern* (for *ein Wort verkleinern*), *verlieren* (for *Worte verlieren*), *verschaffen* (for *zum häßlichsten Zwerge verschafft dich mein Wort*), *verschränken* (for *die Freiheit des Worts verschränken*), *Vorrat* (for *vorrath von worten*), *Vorwort* (also for *Fürwort* and *Verhältniswort*), *warm* (for *warme Worte*) and *Weg* (for *von Worten zu Werken ist ein weiter Weg*).

wortarm: *eine wortarme Sprache* a language with a small vocabulary; since the 17th c., e.g. Schottel, *Haubtspr.* 13 [1663]. Hence *Wortarmut*, since the 19th c.

Wortaufwand: *großer ~* (lit.) excessive use of words; since the 18th c.

Wortbau: *der ~* (lit.) word formation, verbal structure; since the 18th c., both (and at first) for 'diction, style', as in Herder [edit. S.] 20,85 and with ref. to the formation of words, also in Herder, e.g. in [edit. S.] 27,278.

Wortbild: see *Bild*.

Wortbildung: *die* ~ word-formation; since the 2nd half of the 18th c., also = 'morphological aspect of a word'.

Wortbruch: *der* ~ breaking of one's word, breach of promise; f.r.b. Stieler [1691], though the appearance of *wortbrüchig* in Schottel's writings as early as 1648 indicates that the noun existed long before Stieler recorded it; Goethe IV,9,92 (W.) used *Wortbrüchigkeit*.

Wörtchen: *nur ein* ~ (or *Wörtlein*) just a short communication (reply, sign of life); since the 17th c.; Goethe used it as *Wörtgen* in IV,5,36 (W.); cf. emphatic *davon ist kein* ~ *wahr* = 'there is not one word (or iota) of truth in it'.

← See also under *Schlag* (for *kein Wörtchen zu überschlagen bitten*).

Wortchrist: *der* ~ (pejor.) Christian in words only, merely nominal Christian; since the 16th c.; cf. similar pejor. *Wortdienst*, as in (DWb) Harsdörffer, *Frauenzimmer-Gespr.* 8,63 [1649]: '*Wortdienst ohne Werke*'.

Wortdienst: see *Wortchrist*.

Wortdrechsler: *der* ~ manipulator or twister of words; mainly pejor. with the imputation that words are by him wrongly interpreted or their sense perverted; since the 19th c. *Wortverdreher*, current since the 17th c., is more frequently used.

Wörterbuch: *das* ~ dictionary; f.r.b. Comenius, *Sprachenthür*[1631]; *ein Buch von Wörtern* occurred a century earlier in Alberus [1540] as the German for '*dictionarium, vocabularium*'. For the history of the word see the prefaces to *DWb*. vols 1 and 5 by J.Grimm and R.Hildebrand, where, however, the use of ~ by Comenius was not yet mentioned and credit for first use was given to Gueintz in a letter to Fürst Ludwig von Amhalt (March 1,1640): '*so were es gut, daß ein Wörterbuch (lexicon) ans Tagelicht keme*'.

Wörterfabrik: *die* ~ , also *Wortfabrik* (lit.) word factory coined by Lessing in comments on Wieland's felicitous diction, where he praises Wieland's '*glückliche Wörterfabrik*'; cf. Lessing [edit. L.-M.] 16,81.

Wörtersturm: see *Sturm*.

Wortfamilie: *die* ~ , also *Wörterfamilie* family of words; since the 2nd half of the 18th c., used by Herder [edit. S.] 6,185.

Wortfeld: *das* ~ (ling.) word field; introduced by Jost Trier, *D.dt.Wortschatz . . .* 1 [1931].

Wortfetzen: *die* ~ (plural) disjointed (or bits of) words, scraps of conversation; modern, still missing in *DWb*. [1951]; cf. the quotation from Wieland on *Fetzen*, p.775.

Wortformel: see *Geist* (p.964).

Wortfügung: *die* ~ , also *Wörterfügung* (ling.) syntax; although attributed by some lexicographers to Schottel [1663], the term was used by Ratichius, *Allg.Sprachlehr* [1619] and Gueintz, *Sprach.* [1641].

Wortführer: *der* ~ spokesman (for a group), chairman (of a meeting); since the 17th c.; also, since the 18th c., sometimes for a person who interferes belligerently in conversations or negotiations (not allowing others to have their say), e.g. G.Keller, *Ges.W.* 1,139; cf. p.876 for *das Wort führen, das große Wort führen* and *das Wort alleine führen*.

Wortgebimmel: see *bimmeln*.

Wortgebrauch: *der* ~ word usage, use of words appropriate to their meaning; since the 17th c., e.g. Goethe II,6,195 (W.), Herder [edit. S.] 6,185.

Wortgefecht: see *fechten*.

Wortgeklimper: see *klimpern*.

Wortgeklingel: *das* ~ (pejor.) empty talk; since the 18th c., e.g. Herder [edit. S.] 17,174.

Wortgeläut(e): see *läuten*.

Wortgemengsel: see *Gemengsel*.

Wortgeplänkel: see *Geplänkel*.

Wortgeplätscher: *das* ~ sound of speech without understandable (or important) content; see the entry under *plätschern* (p.1853); the noun since the 19th c., e.g. (DWb) Raabe, *Sämtl.W.* 1,5,65.

Wortgepränge: *das* ~ verbal splendour or pomp, stilted or artificially contrived way of expressing oneself; since the 17th c., e.g. Lessing [edit. L.-M.] 8.294: '*mit mehrerem Wortgepränge will ich dieses Leben meines Dichters nicht einführen*'; Grimmelshausen on the title illustration of his *Teutscher Michel* used *Sprach-Gepreng*.

Wortgeprassel: see *prasseln*.

Wortgerippe: see *Gerippe*.

wortgetreu: *wortgetreu* faithful, exact; with ref. to translations = *wörtlich*, but also = 'repeating or rendering exactly the text (of some document, message)', since the 18th c., e.g. Oppenheim, *Jahrb.f.Pol.u.Lit.* 10,367, but not yet recorded by Campe [1811].

Wortgetrommel: see *Trommel*.

Wortgewand: see *Gewand*.

Wortgewebe: *das* ~ (lit.) tissue or web of words; since the 18th c., e.g. Wieland 14,142:

'*gleich einer ermüdeten Spinne saß er im Mittelpunkte seiner Gedanken- und Wortgewebe*'.

Worthülse: *die* ~ cliché, empty term; in pejor. use in polit. contexts; since the last quarter of the 20th c.; cf. Engl. figur. pejor. '(mere) shell'.

wortkarg: *wortkarg* taciturn, brief (or curt) in conversation; since late in the 18th c., f.r.b. Heynatz [1796], e.g. Goethe 30,207 (W.); sometimes also with ref. to a writer who expresses himself tersely or concisely, such as Tacitus, e.g. Fr.L.Jahn, *Briefe* [edit. Meyer] 203: '. . . *den wortkargen und gedankenschweren Tacitus*'.

Wortklauber: see *klauben* (also for *wortklauben* and *Wortklauberei*).

Wortkram: see *Kram* (also for *Wörterkram*).

Wortkrieg: see *Krieg*.

Wortkunst: *die* ~ (lit.) eloquence, mastery of style; since the 16th c., less used than *Redekunst* and *Stilkunst*; the meaning 'etymology', still recorded by Kramer [1702], is obs.

Wortlaut: *der* ~ wording, exact text of sth.; current since the 17th c., f.r.b. Stieler [1691], but now no longer connected with sound only but used with ref. to a text (printed or written), since the 17th c.

wortlos: see *halten* (p. 1214).

Wortmalerei: *die* ~ (lit.) word-painting, imagery; see the entry '*die Szene, welche die Worte malten*' on p.1648; as a noun since the 2nd half of the 18th c.

Wortmeldung: *die* ~ request for leave to speak; modern, mainly in polit. contexts.

wortreich: see *reich*.

Wortsalat: *der* ~ (coll.) jumble of words; modern; belongs to the group of compounds recorded on p.2050.

Wortschall: *leerer* ~ (lit.) empty phrase(s); in acustic sense since the 17th c., pejor. since the 18th c. for 'sound without substance', e.g. Herder [edit. S.] 17,230, Goethe 42,2,133 (W.); often with *leer* or *taub*.

Wortschatz: see *Schatz*.

Wortschmied: *der* ~ (lit.) inventor of artificial words; since Early NHG; also used in the more pejor. sense for 'idle talker, purveyor of nonsense', as in Schottel, *Ethica* 583 [1669]; for similar pejor. compounds see p.2154.

Wortschnüffler: see *schmuggeln*.

wortschön: see *schön*.

Wortschöpfer: *der* ~ coiner of new words; since the 18th c., e.g. Gottsched, *Beob.* 62 [1758]; see on p.2175 for *neue Wörter schöpfen*.

Wortschwall: see *Schwall*.

Wortsparer: see *sparen*.

Wortspiel: see *Spiel*.

Wortstreit: See under *Spiel* (for *habe man die Sache in einen Wortstreit gespielt*) and *Streit* (for *Wortstreit*).

Wrack: see *alt*.

Wucher: *der* ~ gain, profit; originally = 'outcome, progeny', then in financial contexts, at first neutral for 'gain, dividend', then since Early NHG increasingly in derogatory sense, though Luther used it also in its positive sense, negatively in his *Sermon gegen den Wucher*. Figur. only since the 18th c. with ref. to sth. that brings or constitutes 'gain'; Schiller [edit. G.] 5,132 on virtue wrote: '. . . *ist sie mehr als hoher Wucher mit der Liebe Freuden*' and in 5,1,113: '*woher auf einmal der karge Wucher mit der Zeit?*'.

Wucherer: See under *Gold* (for *ein Wuchrer nur, der sich das goldne Kalb zum Götzen ausersehn*), *groß* (for *apotecker sind die grösten wucherer*) and *herb* (for *die wucherer füren wild gewärb*).

Wuchergewächs: see *Gewächs*.

wuchern: *wuchern, um sich* ~ (lit.) to run riot, be rampant; since the 18th c., e.g. Görres, *Hlg.All.* 252 [1822]: '*jene immer mehr um sich wuchernde Verwilderung der Gemüther*', Schiller, *Resignation*: '*jenseits der Gräber wuchern deine Schmerzen*', in milder sense for 'to increase' in Platen 4,320: '*es wuchert Glück und Segen, wo du weilst*'. Frequent also in lit. compounds, e.g. *aufwuchern*, e.g. Platen 2,271: '*wo man . . . aufwuchern Talent an Talent sah*', Treitschke, *Dt.Gesch.* 5,265: '. . . *wuchern die Legenden der Parteien am üppigsten auf*', Spielhagen, *Pr.* 2,5: '*dieser giftige Samen wuchert auf und überwuchert der Liebe rothe Rosen*', *sich auswuchern* = 'to spread (alarmingly)' (19th c.), *durchwuchern* (19th c.), *emporwuchern*, as in Heine [edit. of 1861] 14,12: '*die Lügengerüchte, die so tödtlich frech emporwuchern*', also Duller, *Grabbes Leben* 59 [1838] (missing in *DWb.* [1862]), *fortwuchern*, as in Devrient, *Gesch.Schausp.* 2,55: '. . . *diese schäferliche Unwahrheit auf dser Bühne fortwuchern sehen*', *nachwuchern* (19th c.), *überwuchern* and *vorwuchern* (both modern).

mit etw. ~ to speculate with (or profit, gain by) sth.; at least since the 18th c. with abstracts, e.g. Wieland, *Luc.* 4,375: '*die Hetäre habe mit ihren Reizen so glücklich gewuchert*'.

jem. auswuchern to empoverish sb. by exorbitant demands; since Early NHG, e.g. Luther 8,93b (Jena): '*er wuchert fürsten, herrn, land und leute aus*'; no longer listed in recent dictionaries.

etw. einwuchern (lit.) to earn sth. or gain sth. in return; since the 18th c., e.g. Lessing 1,143: '*Undank statt Erkenntlichkeit einwuchern*', where (*ein*)*ernten* would now be preferred.

etw. erwuchern to acquire sth. through usury (or other gainful activity), since MHG, e.g. Muskatblüth [edit. v.Groote] 244; general with abstracts since Early NHG, e.g. Fischart, *Garg.* 74a: '. . . *gegenlieb erwuchern*'; cf. Jean Paul, *Holzschn.* 110: '*eine Schönheit erwuchern*'.

etw. verwuchern (a.) to lose sth. (through one's own fault); figur. in the 19th c., when Sanders [1865] recorded '*seinen guten Namen verwuchern*'; no longer listed in *DWb*. [1954].

verwuchert (rare) ruined, delapidated; still alive in phys. sense (though the *Duden* of 1989 surprisingly does not list it), but rare in figur. sense; it occurs in (DWb) Langgässer, *Siegel* 153 [1946].

← See also under *Pfad* (for *auf krummen Pfaden wuchert der Schaden*), *Pfund* (for *mit seinem Pfund wuchern*) and *Unkraut* (for *das Unkraut wuchern lassen*).

Wuchs: *der Nachwuchs* offspring, (in wider sense) new blood; first in botanical contexts, since the 18th c. with ref. to the next generation, e.g. Hebel 2,195: '*der liebe Gott bescheert mir Nachwuchs*'.

← See also under *auswachsen* (for *Auswuchs*).

Wucht: weight, impetus, pressure

die ~ (lit.) strength, energy, weight; with abstracts since the 18th c., f.r.b. Kindleben [1781], e.g. Lessing [edit. L.-M.] 1,251: '(*das*) *gibt seinen Worten Wucht*'; later also with the notion of 'pressure, burden', as in Geibel 2,147: '*des Kummers Wucht*'; cf. also G.Keller, *Nachlaß* 52: '*geistige Wucht*'.

eine ~ *von* . . . (sl.) a lot of . . .; in sl. since ca. middle of the 20th c. It can be used with the notion of appreciation, e.g. *das ist eine* ~ ! = 'that's marvellous!', also with ref. to punishment (= *Tracht Prügel*), e.g. *gleich bekommst du eine* ~ = 'I'll give you what for in a moment, you're in for a hiding'.

sich wuchten (stud.sl.,obs.) to disappear without paying one's bill; same as *zechprellen* (cf. similar sl. *sich verdrücken*, which see under *drücken*); recorded since 1802; hence *Wuchterei* = *Zechprellerei*, in stud.sl. since late in the 18th c., e.g. Laukhard, *Mein Leben* 5,113 [1796].

← See also under *brechen* (for *die Wucht brechen*).

wudeln: see *gedeihen*.

wühlen: grub, root, rummage.

in etw. ~ to rummage around or burrow in sth.; beginnings of figur. usage in MHG, e.g. *in sich* ~ , e.g. *Passional* [edit. K.] 61; with the notion of 'agitating, stirring or shaking vigorously', as in Uhland, *Ged.* 45: '*seit der Sturm in Blüthen wühlet*', or of 'searching', as in *in Büchern* ~ , e.g. Taylor, *Antinous* 357 [1886], or of 'hurtful digging into sth.', as in Schiller, *Kab.u.L.* 5,2: '*wollen Sie auch in der Wunde noch wühlen*'.

in Geld ~ (coll.) to be rolling in money; 20th c. coll.

etw. wühlt (*in jem.m*) sth. gnaws in sb.; with abstracts since the 17th c., e.g. Goethe, *Tasso* 1,4: '. . . *der Wahnsinn hin und her zu wühlen scheint*' (also 4,95 and 14,182 (W.)).

gegen jem. (or *etw.*) ~ to engage in subversion against sb. (or sth.); in mainly polit. contexts since the middle of the 19th c., e.g. Häusser, *Dt.Gesch.* 3,134; hence *Wühler* = 'agitator', used by Keller, *Nachl.* 110, also for 'demagogue', hence *Wühlhuber*, coined by the journal *Fliegende Blätter* ca. 1850 (cf. *Gschaftlhuber* on p.998).

das Gewühl turmoil, restless moving, burrowing, subversive agitation, throng (of people); since the 17th c. in various contexts derived from the verb. Kramer [1702] listed it. He also recorded figur. *sich in etw. hineinwühlen* '*wie die Roßkäfer*'.

← See also under *aufwühlen*, *durchwühlen* (also for *die Fluten wühlen*, *schmerzdurchwühlt* and *Durchwühlung*), *Gebein* (for *wie wühlet der Schmerz mir im Gebein*), *Geiz* (for *hier durchwühlt der Geiz seiner Koffer goldnes Eingeweide*) and *Maulwurf* (for *wühlen wie ein Maulwurf*).

Wühlhuberei: *die* ~ (polit.) systematic activity designed to undermine existing conditions; since the middle of the 19th c. (see the entry on *Wühlhuber* under *wühlen* above); G.Keller used the word in *Salander* 181.

Wühlmaus: vole *die* ~ (coll.) agitator; modern coll. (e.g. *Die Zeit*, March 30, 1962); same as *Wühlhuber* (see above).

wund: sore *ein wunder Punkt* a sore spot; modern and used also with *Fleck* and *Stelle*, e.g. Goethe IV,22,32 (W.). Hence also *die wunde Stelle berühren* or *an den wunden Punkt rühren*; since the 19th c.

← See also under *einbeizen* (for *sein wundes Herz*), *Ort* (for *der wunde Ort*) and *Schwert* (for *diu von der sünden swert ist wunt*).

Wundärztin: see *Magd*.

Wunde: wound *alte Wunden soll man nicht aufreißen* (prov.) do not open up old wounds; recorded since the 17th c., e.g. by Gruter [1610] and Lehman [1642].

die Wunden heilen übel, die man sich selber schlägt (prov.) self-inflicted wounds take a long time to heal; modern, recorded since the 19th c., e.g. by Eiselein and Simrock.

einer Sache Wunden zufügen to injure sth.; figur. since Early NHG when no phys. wounds are referred to, as in Luther. *Tischr.* 3,478 (Weimar), still in modern use where harm done to sth. can be called ~ , also in compounds, e.g. *Stadtwunde* for a disfigurement of some feature in a town.

← See also under *ausbluten* (for *die Wunde muß erst ausbluten*), *Blut* (for *blutet an Wunden des Herzens*), *Eiter* (for *eine eiternde Wunde*), *frisch* (for *frische Wunde*), *gaffen* (for *die gaffende Wunde*), *Gewicht* (for *daß mit dem Scherz es wie mit Wunden ist*), *Heil* (for *die Zeit heilt alle Wunden*), *Narbe* (for *ihr Tod schlug mir Wunden, wenn die Wunden alle vernarbt* and *welche Wunde vernarbte nicht der Mensch?*), *reißen* (for *alte Wunden aufreißen*), *Schwäre* (for *den Finger auf die schwärende Wunde legen*), *verbinden* (for *jem.s Wunden verbinden*), *verwachsen* (for *die Wunde ist verwachsen*), *verwunden* and *wühlen* (for *in der Wunde wühlen*).

Wunder: wonder '*das ~ ist des Glaubens liebstes Kind*' the miracle is faith's dearest child; quotation from Goethe, *Faust I*, 766; cf. also the occasionally quoted '*nun sag mir eins, man soll kein Wunder glauben*' from *Faust I*, 2336.

ein ~ währet nicht länger als neun Tage (prov.) a wonder lasts but nine days; international, but the number of days varies: in German and Engl. nine, in Italian and Greek three. In Engl. since the 14th c. (used by Chaucer), in German apparently later. Eiselein recorded it in 1838 and Wander lists no earlier recordings.

← See also under *Berg* (for *Berge und Wunder*), *besäen* (for *Milde mit Wundern besät*), *blau* (for *sein blaues Wunder erleben*. I should add the correction here that Nigrinus in *Inquisition* 406 [1583] has '*man sihet den blawen wunder*', a much earlier instance than I quoted under *blau*), *Geschöpf* (for *das Wunder ist des Augenblicks Geschöpf*), *Gesicht* (for *kein Wunder, wenn . . .*), *Gold* (for *Wirtschaftswunder*), *Hauch* (for *was Wunder, wenn . . .*) and *Loch* (for *es nehme ein Wunder*).

wunderbar: See under *blühen* (for *erblüht die Rede wunderbar*), *dämmern* (for *es dämmerte mir wunderbar*), *ergänzen* (for *ergänzten sich zu wunderbarer Einheit*), *gehen* (for *wunderbar und ahnungsvoll*), *Grind* (for *es ist ein wunderbar Ding*), *treten* (for *ist das so wunderbar, daß . . .*) and

verkaufen (for *das Künstliche für das Wunderbare verkauft*).

Wunderkind: *ein ~* a child prodigy; first in relig. contexts used for Jesus by Pietists in their hymns, also to be found in the writings of Goethe and Novalis. Then in the usual modern sense applied first to Christian H. Heinekjen of Lübeck, as mentioned in Jean Paul 27,167: '. . . *als das Lübecker Wunderkind, Christian Heineken getauft, das schon im ersten Jahre mehr von der Bibel auswendig konnte, als andere Leute im letzten übertreten oder vergessen haben*', but there is one earlier occurrence in poetry: Weckherlin, *Ged.* (edit. Fischer) 2,440: '. . . *bist du ein Wunderkind gewesen . . . dreyjährig kontest du schon lesen*'. – With allusion to *Wirtschaftwunder* Hugo Hartung called a novel about Germans in the 'fifties *Wir Wunderkinder* [1957].

Wunderkur: see *Herkules*.

wunderlich: See under *Christ* (for *ein wunderlicher Christ*), *drehen* (for *sein Glück dreht sich wunderlich*), *Gast* (for *wunderliche Gäste*), *gehen* (for *Appetit auf wunderliches Zeug*), *hergehen* (for *es geht wunderlich in der Welt her*), *Kopf* (for *ein wunderlicher Kopf*) and *Spiel* (for *das Glück spielt oft wunderlich*).

wundern: See under *Gebild* (for *zerrinnt vor dem wundernden Blick*), *Laie* (for *da staunt der Fachmann und der Laie wundert sich*) and *verwundern*.

wundersam: see *blühen* (p.353).

wunderscheu: see *Scheu*.

wunderschön: *~ ist Dreck* (or *nichts*) *dagegen* (regional coll.) not as wonderful as he/she thinks it is; as an ironic comment recorded for some regions since the 19th c.; cf. Wander 5,452 [1880]. For the phrase . . . *ist Dreck dagegen* see under *Dreck*.

Wunderstreich: see *einbilden*.

Wundertier: see *Tier*.

Wundertüte: *die ~* surprise packet; cf. Engl. 'bag of mysteries'; usually a cone-shaped paperbag given to a child; it contains sweets but also some (unexpected) toy or other small gift; 20th c.

Wundfieber: see *glühen*.

wundschreiben: see *Finger*.

Wunsch: wish *Wünsche offenlassen* to be incomplete or unsatisfactory; modern. Hence also *etw. läßt keine Wünsche offen* = 'sth. is completely satisfactory'.

dein ~ ist mir Befehl your wish is my command; modern, mostly jocular.

auf vielfachen ~ eines einzigen Herrn (joc.coll.)

at repeated requests of a single gentleman; pun
on the two meanings of *vielfach*; modern.

← See also under *anbrüten* (for *Wünsche
anbrüten*), *Auge* (for *jem.m jeden Wunsch an den
Augen absehen*), *beschränken* (for *deine Wünsche
beschränkt der Ernten ruhiger Kreislauf*), *beseelen*
(for *von dem Wunsche beseelt*), *Blut* (for *seinen
blutigen Wunsch zu widerrufen*), *fromm* (for *ein
frommer Wunsch*), *Frucht* (for *Wünsche und seine
Blüthen*), *gehen* (for *daz ging in wol nâch wunsche
vort*), *Geißel* (for *von neuen Wünschen gepeinigt*),
Grenze (for *des Landguts Hag war meiner Wünsche
Grenze*), *halten* (for *eines Wunsches Kraft enthält er
in sich*), *Herz* (for *Herzenswunsch*), *Spiel* (for *zu
jung, um ohne Wunsch zu sein*), *stehen* (for *sein
Wunsch nur nach dem Grabe*), *stehlen* (for *die
geheimen Wünsche aus seinen Augen stehlen*), *tragen*
(for *mit frechen thörichten Wünschen hat sich mein
Busen getragen*), *Trug* (for *dir scheint es möglich,
weil der Wunsch dich trügt*) and *Vater* (for *der
Wunsch war Vater des Gedankens*).

Wünschelrute: See under *anlegen* (for *die
Wünschelrute anlegen*), *Glück* (for *seine
Wünschelruthe nach einem neuen Glücksborn
auszuwerfen*) and *Rute* (for *Erfahrung bleibt die
beste Wünschelrute*).

wünschen: wish *es läßt viel (nichts) zu ~ übrig*
it leaves much (nothing) to be desired; since the
19th c., but not yet recorded by Campe [1811].

das möchte ich meinen ärgsten Feind nicht ~ I
would not like that to happen to my worst
enemy; since the 19th c.

etw. wünscht (nach etw.) (lit.,rare) sth. longs for
sth.; objects seen as expressing a wish; only in
lit., e.g. Gryphius, *Freuden- u. Trauersp.* 691
[1663]: '*das ausgedörrte Feld "wündscht" nach dem
Thau*'.

was man wünscht, das glaubt man gern (prov.)
what one would like to happen one is prone to
believe in; modern prov., only since the 19th c.,
recorded by Eiselein and Simrock.

← See also under *alt* (for *was man in der
Jugend wünscht hat man im Alter die Fülle*), *bitten*
(for *Bittens und Wünschens geht viel in einen Sack*),
gehen (for *ich wünschte, es ginge garnicht*), *Grille*
(for *ein Grill, der sich auch solche Thorheit wünscht*), *Herz* (for *er ist nach meinem Herzen, so wie
ich ihn wünsche* and *so verwünscht gescheidt*) and
verwünschen (also for *Verwünschung*).

Würde: worth, dignity, honour
in Amt und Würden in possession of an official
position and its prestige; since the 18th c., e.g.
Kotzebue, *Kleinst.* 1,4, Raabe, *Sämtl. Werke*
1,3,374; *in Rang und ~* can also occur; cf. Luther
Bible transl. Psalm 49,21: '*wenn ein mensch in der

würde ist', where it describes an important position. The change to 'dignity' with ref. to character occurred at the end of the 18th c. (partly
under Kant's influence), when Schiller in *Anmut
und Würde* [1783] defined ~ as '*Ausdruck einer
erhabenen Gesinnung*', also as '*Ruhe im Leiden*' (cf.
also his *Würde der Frauen* [1795]). The adj.
würdelos was f.r.b. Stieler [1691] for 'undigni-
fied', but *würdevoll* only appeared in the modern
period.

nach Würden (obs.) as it deserves, as its value
and worthiness call for; Luther used it in his
Apocr. transl. Ecclesiasticus 42,17, and it still
occurs in the 18th c., e.g. Wieland 11,200: '. . .
sonst hätt' ich Sie nach Würden ausgeschmäht'; now
obs.

es ist unter meiner ~ (lit.) it is beneath my dignity; since the 18th c., e.g. Goethe, *Groß-
Cophtha* 2,2 [1791]; hence *unter aller ~* = 'totally
unacceptable (without injury to one's dignity),
beneath contempt'.

Bürde bringt ~ (prov.) hard work earns distinction; also as *auf die Bürde folgt die ~* ; international, cf. Lat. *fructus honos oneris* or *fructus
honoris onus* and *labores pariunt honores*; Steinbach
[1734] recorded the version *Würden sind Bürden*,
which is in more general use.

← See also under *einfließen* (for *die Vorstellung
der Würde der Menschheit*) and *Wiederaufbau* (for
würde vnd lob wider auffzubawen).

Würdenträger: dignitary
der ~ dignitary; only coined in the 1st quarter
of the 19th c. (Campe [1811] did not record this
but listed synonymous *Würdner*, which is obs.).

würdig: worthy *würdig* worthy, dignified; first
in OHG as a transl. for Lat. *dignus*, then following the noun *Würde* in its changing meanings.
Frequent in compounds of which *ehrwürdig* =
'venerable' and *glaubwürdig* = 'credible' appear to
be the oldest, both recorded by Maaler [1561].
Stieler [1691] listed *denkwürdig* = 'memorable',
Kramer [1702] added several which are now a.
or obs., also *liebwürdig* = 'lovable', which was displaced by *liebenswürdig* in the 18th c. (f.r.b.
Steinbach [1734]) with the weaker meaning
'kind', *merkwürdig* = 'remarkable' and *strafwürdig*
= 'punishable, deserving punishment'. Steinbach
added *erbarmungswürdig* = 'pitiful'.

menschenwürdig humane, worthy of a human
being; now mainly for 'fit for human beings';
current since the 18th c., e.g. Goethe, *Wanderj.*
3,3: '*gewisse menschenwürdige Gesinnungen*'.

merkwürdig (1) (obs.) worth noting, memorable, remarkable; f.r.b. Steinbach [1734]; hence
Merkwürdigkeit, since the 18th c.

merkwürdig (2) strange, odd, peculiar; since the 19th c., e.g. Immermann, *Münchh.* 1,168; now much more frequently used than *merkwürdig* (1).

nichtswürdig (1) unworthy, worthless, not doing justice to the worth of sth.; displaced *nichtswertig*; f.r.b. Rädlein [1711]; it can be synonymous with *unwürdig*, and Lessing in *Vademecum* skilfully contrasted the two adjectives: '*Sie sind zum Exempel ein unwürdiger Übersetzer des Horaz, sind Sie deswegen ein nichtswürdiger?*', where he refers to *nichtswürdig* (2); cf. *menschenunwürdig* = 'not fit for human beings, degrading', a 20th c. word, not yet listed in *DWb.* [1885].

nichtswürdig (2) despicable, contemptible, base; f.r.b. Aler [1727], but older since Stieler [1691] recorded *Nichtswürdigkeit*, though he did not list *nichtswürdig*; e.l. Lessing, *Em.Gal.* 3,8.

unwürdig unworthy; since OHG, influenced by Lat. *indignus*; meanings cover a range from 'worthless' and 'lacking in dignity' (since Early NHG) to 'undeserving of honour', e.g. Goethe 21,92 (W.). The noun *Unwürdigkeit* has been current since MHG.

← See also under *blenden* (for *wird der Würdige zurückgesetzt*), *eindrücken* (for *daß symbolische Handlungen alles eindrücklich, ehrwürdig und feierlich machten*), *erbarmen* (for *den Weisen, der würdig sich regieret*) and *verspielen* (for *wenn all ihr Würdiges ist verspielt*).

würdigen: *etw.* or *jem.* ~ to appreciate sth. or sb.; since MHG (*wirdigen*); as early as in MHG extended to 'to acknowledge, recognize, dignify, honour, pay tribute to sth. or sb.', but all still reflecting the original meaning of 'taking account of the value of sth. or sb.', e.g. Schiller, *M.Stuart* 5,7: '*Gott würdigt mich, durch diesen unverdienten Tod die frühe schwere Blutschuld abzubüßen*' or Goethe 9,313 (W.). In lit. there is also *etw. würdigt jem.m etw.*, e.g. Wieland, *Ob.* 8,45: '*die Freud' veredelt, würdigt ihr des Tagwerks Niedrigkeit*'. The noun *Würdigung*, current since the 15th c., followed the verb in all its meanings. – Note that *würden*, still used by Herder and *würdern*, which still occurs in Goethe's writings, are obs. Luther 1,195b (Jena) used *wirden* and in his Bible transl. Levit. 27,25 *wirderung* occurs, where the A.V. has 'estimations'.

jem. keines Blickes (*keiner Antwort*) ~ to refuse to look at (answer) sb. (in the sense of not deigning or condescending); in such negative locutions since the 17th c. with *Antwort* and *Anblick*, e.g. Grimmelshausen [edit. Keller] 2,560, with *Blick* since the 18th c.

etw. or *jem. herabwürdigen* (lit.) to denigrate

sth. or sb.; since the 18th c., e.g. Lessing 10,11, Heinse, *Ardingh.* 1,349, frequent in Wieland's writings where *Herabwürdigung* also occurs often; *entwürdigen* (lit.) = 'to degrade, abase' also arose in the 18th c. and is still current, but *entwürden* is obs.

Wurf: throw *der* ~ (1) (zool.) litter, number of young produced at the same time; in lit. since the 16th c., e.g. Keisersberg, *Postill* 4,31 [1522], recorded by Stieler [1691]. Mainly used with ref. to dogs and pigs, although occasionally also to other animals, e.g. cats and sheep.

der ~ (2) (coll.) small amount of liqueur (which one tosses back); recorded since the 19th c., e.g. by Heyne [1895].

jem. in ~ *bringen* (regional) to propose sb. for an appointment or office, make sb. a candidate for a post; since the 18th c., now only current in some SW regions.

der erste ~ or *Hinwurf* the first draft or version, initial sketch; cf. *etw. aufs Papier werfen*; since the 18th c., e.g. Schiller, *Briefw. mit Goethe* 1,8: '*wegen der langen Zwischenzeit, die zwischen dem ersten Wurf und der letzten Hand verstrichen sein muß*'; Herder used both *erster* ~ and *Hinwurf*.

jem. kommt jem.m in den ~ sb. comes across sb.; often with ref. to unexpected meetings, where *Schuß* or *Weg* can also be used, e.g. Goethe 8,58 (W.), since the 16th c., but now only in some regions. There is also *etw. kommt jem.m in den* ~ = 'sth. occurs to sb., comes to sb.'s mind', both with ref. to things and ideas (where it is the same as *in den Sinn kommen*); since the 18th c., used by Herder and Kant and still by some 20th c. writers, although it has remained unrecorded in late 20th c. dictionaries.

ein glücklicher (or *großer*) ~ (1) a happy outcome, fortunate piece of success; since the 18th c., e.g. Schiller, *Lied a.d.Freude*: '*wem der große Wurf gelungen, eines Freundes Freund zu seyn*'; cf. Fichte, *Sämtl.Werke* 6,81 [1846]: '*nicht das Werk einer verständigen kalten Berechnung, sondern ein Wurf des Ohrgefähr*' or Ense, *Biogr.Denkm.* 4,387: '*mit einem glücklichen Wurf aus dem Stegreife*'. In many contexts ~ means the same as Engl. 'hit', since the 18th c. in *einen großen* ~ *tun* = 'to score a big hit', often at first with ref. to successful works of lit., then extended more recently to other successes in the world of entertainment.

ein glücklicher ~ (2) (a.) a neat formulation, apposite remark, clever way of putting sth., *bon mot*; Goethe used it in 6,168 (W.), but it has not been recorded in recent dictionaries.

der ~ *ist gefallen* (a.) the matter has been decided, the decision has been made, e.g.

Schiller, *D.Carlos*: '*jetzt ist der Wurf gefallen, Sie sind für mich verloren*'. The locution with *Würfel* is now much more frequently used.

← See also under *abwerfen* (for *Abwürfling*), *anwerfen* (for *Anwurf* and *Anwürfling*), *aufwerfen* (for *Aufwurf*), *einwerfen* (for *Einwurf*, also for *Gegenwurf*), *entwerfen* (for *Entwurf*), *Glück* (for *Glückswurf*), *setzen* (for *nur ein verzweifelter Spieler setzt alles auf einen einzigen Wurf*), *Stein* (for *einen Steinwurf weit*), *vorwerfen* (for *vorwurfsfrei*) and *Vorwurf*.

Würfel: der *der ~ ist gefallen* the die is cast; Classical, used by Caesar when he crossed the Rubicon (49 B.C.): '*iacta alea est*'. There are many locutions which refer to the fall of the dice in connexion with fate and decisions, e.g. (DWb) Kirchhof, *Mil.Disc.* 181 [1602]: '. . . in zweifel wie der würffel fallen werde', H.v. Kleist, *Werke* (edit. E.Schmidt) 2,391: '*der Ort, an dem die Würfel fallen sollen*', Goethe, *Faust II*, 10295: '*wer weiß wie noch die Würfel fallen*', D.Fr. Strauß, *Ges. Schr.* 8,203: '. . . damit war über Schubarts Leben . . . die Würfel geworfen'. Related to this is *die ~ liegen noch auf dem Tisch* = 'the decision has not yet been made, the outcome cannot yet be foreseen', since the 17th c., still in 19th c. lit. (Kleist, Grillparzer, Geibel), now a.

der ~ (math.,tech.) cube, hexahedron; transl. of Lat. *cubus*; in German lit. since the 16th c.; recommended by 19th c. purists as German alternative for *Kubik* or *dritte Potenz* = 'cube, power of three'.

er will mit drei Würfeln neunzehn (or *mehr als achtzehn*) *Augen werfen* (prov.expr., a.) he attempts more than can be achieved, overestimates his capabilities, has too high expectations; since the 17th c., recorded by Kramer [1702] with '*mehr denn 18*', used by Kleist, *Werke* [edit. E.Schm.] 2,445 with '*neunzehn*'.

← See also under *Auge* (for *die Augen eines Würfels*), *blind* (for *blinde Würfel*) and *Blücher* (for *geblüchert, was Weiber, Wein und Würfel angeht*).

würfeln: dice; throw dice

würfeln (lit.) to gamble, let chance decide, make an arbitrary decision; since the 18th c., e.g. Klopstock, *Oden* [edit. M.-P.] 2,133: '*das würfelnde kalte Scheusal . . . der Krieg*', Gutzkow, *Ges.W.* 9,27: '. . . würfelte er den Völkern ihre Schicksale*'; also *um etw. ~* , as in Bauernfeld, *Ges.Schr.* 7,11: '*der Congress ist eine Art Spieltisch – Europa würfelt um seine Staaten*'.

etw. ~ (1) to dice sth., make sth. cube-shaped; since the 16th c.; Adelung recorded '*die Semmel würfeln*'.

etw. ~ (2) to arrange sth. or lay sth. out in a checked pattern; since the 17th c. with ref. to textiles and floors; frequent in *gewürfelt* = 'checked'. – Note that *gewürfelt* = 'clever, cunning' does not belong to *~* , but to *worfeln* = 'to winnow'.

etw. ~ (3) to move (or throw) sth. about in a haphazard fashion; since the 16th c. and occasionally still (in lit.) in modern period, frequent in compounds, e.g. *durcheinanderwürfeln* = 'to mix up, throw together', and *zusammenwürfeln* = 'to put together without a set plan, lump together', both since the 18th c.

mit etw. ~ (obs.) to interpret sth. arbitrarily; since Early NHG, e.g. Luther 7,395 (Weimar) and elsewhere; Schiller used it as a transitive verb, with *mit* it still occurred in the 19th c., now obs.

← See also under *auswürfeln*.

Würfelnatter: die *~* (zool.) dice (or tesselated) snake (*Natrix tessellata*); modern (?), missing in Adelung, Campe and *DWb*.

Würgelbirne: *Würgelbirnen fressen* (*müssen*) (coll.,obs.) to be hanged; *Würgelbirnen* are pears of extreme hardness which are liable to choke one; hence transfer to the notion of 'being hanged'; still recorded by Ludwig, *Teutsch-Engl. Wb.* [1716]: '*er wird Worgelbirne or Hangelbirne fressen müssen* = he will be hanged'; now obs. See also the entry under *Birne* (p.321).

würgen: strangle; choke

jem. ~ (a.) to kill sb.; development from 'to choke, strangle' to 'to kill' (since the 16th c.), also with abstracts as the subject since Early NHG, e.g. H.Sachs [edit. *Lit.Verein*] 3,160: '. . . nöten, auff das sie uns würgen'; cf. Luther 33,211 (Weimar): '*das leben wurget den todt*'.

an etw. ~ to have difficulties with coping with (understanding, digesting) sth.; first with *über* (used by Luther), then with *an* (e.g. Petri, *Weißh.* [1605]), used by Goethe IV,19,187 (W.) with ref. to a book by Steffens, alive in many regions.

etw. in sich hineinwürgen (or *reinwürgen*) to stuff oneself with sth.; also 'to have trouble in getting sth. down'; modern.

das Gewürge (1) drudgery, strain, laborious procedure; modern, not yet in Campe.

das Gewürge (2) (a.) carnage, (wholesale) slaughter; recorded by Campe [1808]. Adelung did not record either meaning.

← See also under *Birne* (for *an einer hänfenen Holzbirn erworgen*), *erwürgen*, *hängen* (for *mit Hängen und Würgen*), *hinunterwürgen*, *Lamm* (for *was hat dieses Lamm getan, daß Sie es würgen?*) and *Wanze* (for *der würget eine wantzke*).

Würgengel: *der* ~ (1) (bibl.,lit.,a) destroyer; originally biblical as the name of the angel sent by God to kill man, Exod. 12,7ff; Luther gave the term wider currency through his writings (although he did not use the term in his transl. of Exodus 12, but used *Verderber*, where the A.V. has 'destroyer'). It was then extended to visitations by epidemics, mainly the plague, e.g. Hamann, *Schriften* 6,225: '*der Würgengel hat auch mein Haus verschont*', and the cholera (for details see J.Grimm, *Dt. Mythologie, Handwb. d.dt. Aberglaubens* and *DWb.* 14,2,2213 [1960].

der ~ (2) (lit.) murderer; applied to abstracts, first in relig. contexts such as *Sünde* or *Laster*, then to other things which destroy sth., since the 18th c., e.g. Heine, *Sämtl.Werke* [edit. E.] 7,561: '*verlangen Sie von mir keine Systematie; das ist der Würgengel aller Korrespondenz*'.

der ~ (3) (hist.) murderer; applied to persons since the 18th c., e.g. Gentz, *Schriften* 1,121: '*Gott und sein Würgengel Bonaparte*'.

der ~ (4) (zool.) species of falcon (*Lanius excubitor*); since the 17th c., but first applied to owls, by Adelung recorded for 'falcon'; details in Suolahti, *Dt. Vogelnamen* 148 [1909].

Würgszene: see *Pinsel*.

Wurm: worm *der* ~ (1) (lit.) man; with ref. to his pitiful nature, insignificance and helplessness; biblical in origin (cf. Job 25,6 and Psalm 22,7); frequent since MHG and still alive in lit., e.g. Klopstock, *Der Genügsame*: '*dem Wurm, der Mensch heißt, jähriget, blühet, verblüht und abfällt* ', Goethe, *Faust I*, 653: '*dem Wurme gleich ich, der den Staub durchwühlt*'. Hence in *armer* ~ , *armes Würmchen*, e.g. Goethe, *Faust I*, 3131: '. . . *das arme Würmchen selbst zu tränken*', G.Keller, *Salander* 76: '*die armen Würmer*' (referring to two girls); cf. also Luther Bible transl. Isaiah 41,14: '*du Würmlein Jakob*' (in A.V. 'thou worm Jacob'); also extended to the collective *Gewürm*, e.g. Lessing 1,160: '*wer ist die Welt . . . ein blind Gewürm!*'.

der ~ (2) man; seen as sth. despicable and sinful; cf. Schiller's choice of *Wurm* as a suitable name for the villain in *Kabale und Liebe*; since Early NHG, e.g. Luther 28,86 (Weimar), often with *böse, schändlich, giftig*, e.g. Goethe 14,255 (W.): '*wandle den Wurm* (meaning Mephistopheles) *wieder in seine Hundsgestalt*'.

der ~ (3) (lit.) affliction, gnawing pain; since OHG, referring to 'bites' inflicted (cf. *Gewissenswurm* below); sometimes called '*ein nagender Wurm*', as in Lehman 1,299 [1662], Haller, *Über d.Urspr. des Übels*, bk.2 [1734]: '*der Sorgen Wurm verzehrt den Balsam unsrer Säfte*'

and *Vers.Schw.Ged.* 90: '*nie untergräbt sein Herz bereuter Laster Wurm*', Hagedorn, *Poet.W.* 2,128: '*Wurm des Widerspruchs, der Haupt und Zunge nagt*', Klinger, *Werke* 3,234: '*wie Faust den Wurm, der an seinem Herzen zu nagen anfing . . . zu betäuben suchte*'. Tieck, *Don Quix.* 2,57: '*o Neid, du nagender Wurm der Tugenden*'.

der ~ (4) whim, mood, fancy, caprice; cf. Engl. 'maggot'; since the 17th c. (Grimmelshausen, Schupp), e.g. Lessing 10,297: '*woraus nimmst du diesen Wurm ihm ab?*'; often in *er hat einen* ~ (18th c.), e.g. Goethe 2,231 (W.): '*ein jeder Mann hat seinen Wurm, Copernicus den seinen*'; also as ~ *im Kopf*, as in Wieland 5,247, ~ *in der Hirnschale*, as in Freytag, *Verl.Handschr.* 3,87; sometimes *Tollwurm* is used, e.g. Bürger, 488a or Musäus, *M.* 4,39.

der böse (giftige, teuflische) ~ (bibl.,a.) the serpent; refers to the serpent in paradise; since MHG, frequent in Luther's writings, still in Schiller [edit. G.] 3,158: '*daß ich dich hasse – hasse wie den Wurm des Paradieses*'.

es sitzt ein ~ *drin* (coll.) there is sth. fishy about that, it is not as good as it looks; cf. Engl. coll. 'there is a bug in it'; refers to fruit containing a worm; modern.

er badet Würmer (joc.coll.) he has gone fishing; recent coll.

nackt wie ein ~ (coll.) completely naked; recorded by Wander (1880); hence also *wurmnackt* (rare).

jem.m einen ~ *unters Dach jubeln* (sl.) to put an exciting (but usually mad) idea into sb.'s head; belongs to ~ (4); in sl. since 2nd half of the 20th c.

ein Bandwurm (1) (coll.) sth. inordinately lengthy; since the beginning of the 20th c. used for long words, sentences, book titles also in compounds such as *Bandwurmwort, -satz*, etc.

ein Bandwurm (2) (lit.,rare) a troublesome thing; e.g. Jean Paul 1,36: '. . . *daß es keinen mehr zehrenden Bandwurm giebt als eine Hausfranzösin*'; Börne 2,80 used it in a pun with *Ordensband*.

jem.m einen Bandwurm abtreiben (coll.) to subject sb. to strict discipline; *abtreiben* here means 'to give sb. a strong medicine (which will dispose of his tapeworm)'. In some regions *es geht ihm ein Bandwurm ab* occurs for 'he gives sth. away most unwillingly', i.e. he is so mean that he does not even wish to part with his tapeworm.

das Gartenwürmchen (lit.,rare) snail; occasionally in lit. comparisons (where ordinarily one would expect *Schnecke*), e.g. Grillparzer, *Sappho* 2,6: '. . . *Innigkeit, die . . . gleich dem stillen Gartenwürmchen das Haus ist und Bewohnerin zugleich*'.

der Gewissenswurm worm of conscience; since Early NHG, e.g. S.Dach [edit. Öst.] 255: '*dein gewissenswurm stirbt nicht in ewigkeit*', an echo of Luther Bible transl. Isaiah 66,24: '*ir wurm wird nicht sterben*', Schiller, *D.Carlos* 1,2 (first version only). Anzengruber wrote a play *Der G'wissenswurm* [1874]. See also under *Biß* (for *Gewissensbiß*).

← See also under *Akt* (for *Aktenwurm*), *Buch* (for *Bücherwurm*), *drehen* (for *er hat den Drehwurm*), *Erde* (for *Erdenwurm*), *Holz* (for *Holzwurm*), *Johannes* (for *Johanneswürmchen*), *krumm* (for *auch ein Wurm krümmt sich*), *Maria* (for *Marienwürmchen*), *Nase* (for *jem.m die Würmer aus der Nase ziehen*), *öde* (for *öd und taub wie eine nuß, welch der wurm gestochen*) and *Ohr* (for *Ohrwurm* and *Ohrwürmchen*).

würmeln: *würmeln* (obs.) to be critical, make biting remarks; used by Heine in *Über Börne* 369 and *Troll* 76, but not traceable elsewhere.

wurmen: *etw. wurmt jem.* (coll.) sth. irritates, annoys, bothers sb.; refers to the constant gnawing of a woodworm (*Holzwurm*) according to some, or to a worm in one's stomach (*Bandwurm*) according to others; the latter view is supported by '*Wurmen im Leibe*', which occurs in Droysen, *Arist.* 3,135 [1835]; since the 2nd half of 18th c., when Goethe 11,412 (W.) used it with the dative: '*wie's ihnen wurmte*', in Werther first with *mich*, changed to *mir*. Adelung recorded its use with the dative, Campe with the accusative, now always with the accusative, e.g. Wassermann, *Moloch* 173. Hence also *es wurmt bei* (or *in*) *jem.m*, often in lit. with *im Herzen*. Sometimes used transitively, e.g. Lenau, *Neuere Ged.* 81: '*wenn Haß dich wurmt*'; regarding the image cf. French coll. *cela m'asticote* = 'that annoys me', which belongs to *asticot* = 'maggot'.

wurmen (a.) to ponder, cogitate; contains the notions of some anger or bad mood; e.g. Gutzkow, *Bl.* 1,323: '*in dieser Art wurmte Blasedow fort und überredete sich, daß . . .*'.

Wurmfortsatz: appendix
so überflüssig wie der ~ totally superfluous; since early in the 20th c.
der ~ (polit.sl.) small partner in a coalition; coined ca. 1969, according to Küpper, *Pons* 930 [1987].

Wurmgesindel: see *Gesinde*.

wurmisch: *wurmisch* (obs.) disgruntled; used by Lessing, *Nathan* 5,5; others used *wurmig* in this sense; *wurmig* can, however, also mean 'odd, moody' (= *einen Wurm haben*), the same as *wurmhaftig*, current since the 17th c., e.g. J.G. Müller, *Lind.* 1,107 [1781]. Adelung [1780]

recorded: '*wurmig = einen Wurm habend, d.i. seltsam, wunderlich. Ein wurmiger Mensch. Wurmig werden, ärgerlich, verdrießlich*'. Only *er hat einen Wurm* is still alive in coll. usage.

wurmisieren: *wurmisieren* (obs.) to ponder, cogitate; cf. *wurmen* (a.) above; since the 18th c., e.g. Tieck, *Nov.Kr.* 4,47 and G.Keller, *Leute v.Seld.* 368; now obs.

Wurmmehl: see *Mehl*.

wurmstichig: wormy *es ist* ~ it is rotten, unsound, corrupt; transfer from fruit to other things, since MHG, also used by Luther, with ref. to abstracts and persons, but ~ *im Hirn*, as recorded by Lehman (and with *Haupt* in Schottel) is no longer current.

← See also under *vermodern* (for *vermodert wie ein wurmstichiger Apfel*).

Wurst: sausage ~ *wider* ~ (prov.expr.) one good turn deserves another; also 'tit for tat'; derived from the old custom of sending a sausage to one's neighbour when a pig has been killed, which always led to the gift of a sausage in return (in phys. sense still alive in country areas); f.r.b. Alberus, *Nov.Dict.* [1520], e.g. Albertinus, *Landstörzer* 636 [1619]: '*wurst um wurst*'; hence also such sayings as *eine* ~ *über den Zaun und eine* ~ *herüber erhält die Freundschaft* and *man schickt Keinem* ~ , *man weiß denn, daß er auch ein Saw werde schlachten*, the former in Wander [1880], the latter recorded by Lehman [1662]. Later the phrase was also used with ref. to an unfriendly act repaid by another, when it became 'tit for tat' (= *wie du mir, so ich dir* and similar sayings).

das ist mir ~ (or *Wurscht*) (coll.) that is all the same to me; first in stud.sl., f.r.b. (Kluge, Stud.) *Das Leben auf Universitäten* [1822], then general, e.g. G.Keller, *Werke* 8,220; Bismarck (in a letter of 1853) wrote of '*Stimmung gänzlicher Wurschtigkeit*' (= 'complete indifference'). The origin of the locution is still unclear. Some scholars refer to the fact that a sausage has two identical ends so that it makes no difference where one begins to cut it up; others point to the relatively small value of a sausage (e.g. Luther, *Br.* 9,501 (Weimar) or Tieck, *Nov.Kr.* 4,141: '. . . *eine geräucherte Wurst . . . Nahrungsmittel des gemeinen Mannes, frugale Kost*'), so that it could be interpreted as 'it is of so little value that I do not care' (cf. *wurstige Sache* below).

es geht um die ~ (or *Wurscht*) (coll.) much is at stake, it is do or die now, now or never, now comes the crunch; late in lit. and in dictionaries (19th c.), but derived, as is generally assumed, from competitions in which a sausage formed the prize (as in the similar case of Engl. 'to bring home the bacon'). Albrecht recorded it for Leipzig [1881].

das ist eine wurstige Sache (sl.) that is a trifle, not worth talking about; first in stud.sl., f.r.b. *Der flotte Bursch* [1831].

die ~ (1) sth. that is sausage-shaped; applied to things of various kinds (many of them relating to gadgets or parts of machinery). The chief ones are 'excrement', used by Luther, *Tischr.* 1,137 (Weimar) and still alive today, also in baby-talk, where *Würstchen machen* occurs. Another meaning is 'penis' current since the 15th c., esp. in the *Fast.Sp.*, and still alive in vulg. speech. Articles of clothing which produce a bulge (= *Wulst*) were called ~ , esp. *Miederwurst* and *Brustwurst*, since the 17th c., recorded by Kramer [1702]. The meaning 'purse' occurs in Grimmelshausen, *Simpliz.* [edit. Scholte] 361, which in some regions led to *jem.m die* ~ *anschneiden* = 'to lighten sb.'s purse, take money off sb., esp. in gambling', whereas in other parts of the country the same locution means 'to take sb. to task' (e.g. Stinde, *Fam. Buchholz* 1,97 [1884] written in Berlin coll.). In cant ~ is used for 'knapsack' (= *Felleisen*) of journeymen.

die ~ (2) (obs.) kind of carriage in which the space between the axles was upholstered with a half-round bulge on which people could sit astride. The carriage derived its name from this particular seating arrangement; current since the 17th c., the noun and *auf der* ~ *herumfahren* recorded by Kramer [1702]. Adelung listed it, as well as *Wurstwagen* and *Wurstschlitten*, added the phrase '*auf der Wurst herumfahren . . . d.i. von einem Ort zum andern schmarotzen zu gehen; von der ehemahligen Gewohnheit des Landadels, auf solchen Wurstwagen zu ihres Gleichen herum zu fahren, und daselbst so lange zu schmausen, als noch etwas vorhanden war*'.

eine lange ~ (coll.) a long (but narrow) stretch or area; since the 19th c., e.g. Holtei, *Erz.Schr.* 20,88: '*es ist eine verzweifelt lange Wurst, diese Straße*'; also applied to a long valley between mountain ranges.

das ist eine andere ~ (*mit zwei Zipfeln*) (prov. expr. that is something quite different; cf. French *c'est une autre paire de manches*; modern.

wie der Mann ist, brät man ihm die ~ (prov.) one treats people according to their importance (merit, wealth, etc.); since the 17th c., sometimes shortened to *wie der Mann, so die* ~ , f.r.b. Schellhorn, *Sprichw.* 7 [1797].

← See also under *braten* (for *er will immer eine Extrawurst gebraten haben* and *mit einer Bratwurst*

versiegelt), *Division* (for *die Divisionswurst*), *Ende* (for *jedes Ding hat ein Ende, bloß die Wurst nicht, die hat zwei*), *Hans* (for *Hanswurst*), *Hund* (for *den Hund nach Bratwürsten aussenden, den Hund nach der Wurst schicken, einen Hund an eine Wurst binden* and *einem Hund die Würste spicken*), *Leber* (for *die gekränkte Leberwurst spielen*), *predigen* (for *kurze Predigten und lange Bratwürst haben die Leute/Bauern gern*), *Seite* (for *mit der Wurst nach der Speckseite werfen*) and *stechen* (for *er verschenkt die Wurst, ehe die Sau gestochen ist*).

Wurstblatt: *das* ~ *Wurschtblatt* (also *Käseblatt*) (coll.) inferior newspaper, rag; so called, because considered only fit for wrapping up sausage (or cheese); since early in the 2nd half of the 19th c., e.g. Hoffmann v. Fallersleben, *Ges. Werke* 8,98; Fritz Reuter, *Briefe* [edit. W.] 764 used *Wurstblättchen*, J.Grimm (in a letter to P. Wigand) used *Wurstzeitung*.

Würstchen: *ein armes* ~ (coll.) a poor helpless creature; usually expressing pity, but also used with contempt, meaning 'a nonentity, nobody'; since the 19th c., not yet in Campe [1811].

wurstegal: *das ist mir* ~ (coll.) I could not care less; 20th c. coll. tautology, missing in *DWb.* and *Duden*, but quite common; L.Röhrich listed it in his *Lex.d. sprichw. Redensarten*.

Wurstel: *der* ~ (coll.) fool, comic figure (in a play), entertainer; coll. shortened form of *Hanswurst*, but not only used in theatr. contexts. It can mean 'foolish or clumsy person', but also 'sb. who has the gift to make one laugh'; Goethe used it in 38,47 (W.); still current in the regions, esp. in the S. and in Austria (cf. *Wurstlprater*).

Würstel: *das ist auf einmal verschwunden wie das* ~ *vom Kraut* (coll.) that went in a trice; comparison with the quick disappearance of the most attractive part of a dish from sb.'s plate; recorded by Hetzel [1896].

wursteln: *wursteln* (also *wursten*) (coll.) to fiddle with things, work aimlessly or leisurely (or without much skill); since the 2nd half of the 19th c. (in Sanders [1865] still missing, but listed in his *Ergänz.Wb.* of 1871), probably earlier in some regions; alive as a simplex and in many compounds, e.g. *einwursteln* = 'to wrap up untidily', e.g. Freytag, *Markus König*, chapt.7 (missing in *DWb.* [1862]), *fortwursteln* = 'to muddle on, continue working in a leisurely or ineffectual way' (not yet in *DWb.* [1878]) also *weiterwursteln* (even missing in *DWb.* [1955]) and *verwursteln* = 'to get things in a muddle', for which the earliest recording appears to be Hügel's for Vienna [1873]. The nouns *Gewurstel* and *Wurstelei* appeared in the 19th c.

Wurstfinger: *er hat* ~ (coll.) he has fingers like sausages; in lit. since early in the 20th c., e.g. (Kl.-St.) E.Claudius, *Grüne Oliven* 150: '. . . *streicht sich mit den unförmigen Wurstfingern über den Leib*'; in pl also as *Würstefinger*.

Wurstkessel: see *auskennen*.

Wurstmarmor: *der* ~ (tech.) pudding marble; in appearance like sliced *Blutwurst* (black pudding); recorded since the 19th c.

Wurstmesser: *das* ~ (joc.coll.) sabre; 19th c. coll.

Wurstnickel: *der* ~ (regional coll.,a.) worthless fellow; used by Goethe 38,446 (W.); for *Nickel* for *Nikolaus* see p.1784.

Wurststil: *der* ~ (coll.) unattractive, messy, confused or disjointed style; since the 18th c., e.g. (DWb) Hamann (in Fr.H.Jacobi, *Werke* 4,3,133).

Wurstsuppe: *so klar wie* ~ (ironic coll.) totally incomprehensible; modern, in some areas, e.g. Switzerland, *Wurstbrühe* is also used. See also under *Brühe* (for *so klar wie Kloßbrühe*).

Würze: spice *etw. verleiht* (or *gibt*) *einer Sache* ~ sth. adds spice (or a special savour, flavour, spice, aroma) to sth.; since the 18th c. with abstracts, e.g. Lessing [edit. L.-M.] 9,299, Seume, *M.Sommer* 76: '*es gehört zur Würze . . . wenn sie über die kleinen Schattierungen verschieden denken*', J.J.Engel, *Herr L.Stark* 196 [1801]: '*das Vergnügen sei nur Würze und wolle nur als Würze genossen werden*'; sometimes in *die* ~ *des Daseins* (or *Lebens*, e.g. Gutzkow, *Ges.Werke* 6,255: '. . . *Freuden und Würzen des Lebens entbehren*', which allowed Tieck to use *Daseinswürze* in his transl. of Shakespeare, *Cymbeline* 1,7; often in ~ *des Gesprächs, der Unterhaltung, des Mahls*, since the 19th c.

in der Kürze liegt die ~ (or *Kürze hat* ~) (prov.) brevity imparts spice to a statement; cf. Shakespeare, *Hamlet* 2,2: 'brevity is the soul of wit'; modern, e.g. Tucholsky, *Panter* 298: '*die Kürze ist nicht nur die Würze des Witzes, sie ist die Würze jedes guten Stils*'.

← See also under *Kraut* (for *Langeweile ist ein böses Kraut, aber auch eine Würze, die viel verdaut*).

Wurzel: root *die* ~ (1) root; figur. since MHG, e.g. Trimberg, *Renner* 7325 or 7808, Wolfram v. Eschenbach, *Willehalm* 48,24: '*wurzel sîner tugent*', Luther, *Tischr.* 1,723 (Weimar): '. . . *eine mutter, ursprung und wurzel aller irrthume*', Börne [edition of 1829] 10,54: '*die Preßfreiheit . . . diese Wurzel und Blüthen aller Freiheit*', Schiller, *Tell* 2,1: '*hier sind die starken Wurzeln deiner Kraft*'. The statement in 1 Tim. 6,10: '*geitz ist eine*

wurtzel alles vbels' has been quoted (or paraphrased) in lit. since MHG. Sometimes ~ comes close to 'earliest stage of sth., beginning', since OHG, e.g. Otfrid 1,2,27 where it stands for 'ancestor, progenitor', later also for 'father, mother', until it became established for 'beginning'.

die ~ (2) (math.) root; originally an Arabic term, translated into Lat. as *radix*, taken over as a loan-translation into German as ~ in Late MHG, mainly at first for 'square root'; *die* ~ *ziehen* translates Lat. *radicem extrahere*.

die ~ (3) (ling.) root (of a word); since the 16th c., e.g. Mathesius, *Sarepta* 166b [1571], Schottel, *Haubtspr.* 61 [1663]: '*die ersten wurtzelen oder die stammwörter der teutschen sprache*'.

die ~ (4) (regional coll.) occurs in several regions in a variety of meanings; in Bav. for 'loose-living fellow' (perhaps a relic of ~ = 'wicked person', recorded by Corvinus [1646]), in Alsace for 'little chap', in Hesse for 'little busy energetic and strong fellow' (a term of appreciation), in Swabian for 'tough chap'. In stud.sl., recorded since 1841, it meant 'sanctimonious fellow' (for which *Mucker* is the usual term).

etw. mit allen Wurzeln ausgraben to eradicate sth. completely; in several locutions since the 18th c., e.g. Bode, *Yorick's e.R.* 1,117 [1768]: '*bis an die Wurzel abgesichelt*', Wieland, *H.B.* 1,62: '*das Übel an der Wurzel zu schneiden*', Iselin, *Tr.* 185: '*alles Übel der Gesellschaft aus der Wurzel zu heben*', Goethe used *die* ~ *aller Ungeduld ausreißen*; cf. also the image with *abgraben* in Auerbach, *D.* 4,290: '*einem Baum den Bach abgraben, der seine Wurzeln tränkt*' and the comparison in Fallmerayer, *Morea* 1,46 [1830]: '*Sparta welkte ab, wie ein Baum, dessen Herzwurzel das Beil zerschnitten hat*'.

. . .-wurzel (med.) root (of an organ of part of the body); in many compounds all listed in C.E.Bock, *Anat.* [1838], the chief of which are *Haarwurzel* = 'root of a hair', f.r.b. Stieler [1691], used by Goethe, *Nagelwurzel* = 'nail root, matrix', f.r.b. Stieler, *Nasenwurzel* = 'root of the nose', f.r.b. Zedler, *Univ.* 23,700 [1732–54], cf. Lessing 3,56: '*eine Nase mit Wurzel und Stiel wegbeißen*' and *Zahnwurzel* = 'dental root', e.l. (DWb) Paracelsus, *Chir.Schr.* 153 [1618] as *zanwurtzen*, in present form only since the 19th c.

etw. auf's Würzelein (or *aus dem Würzele*) *wissen* (regional coll.) to know sth. thoroughly; mainly in Swabian, e.g. (Fischer) D.Fr.Strauß, *Briefe an S.T.* 226: '*alles aus dem Würzele wissen*' (written by Strauß's mother in 1824).

← See also under *ausreißen* (for *jem. ausreißen, ehe er Wurzel faßt*), *Axt* (for *es ist schon die Axt den Bäumen an die Wurzel gelegt*), *erröten* (for *bis unter die Haarwurzeln erröten*), *fassen* (for *Wurzel fassen*), *greifen* (for *Wurzel greifen*) and *Grund* (for *so Grund als Wurzel fasse* and *ehrgeytzigkeit, die wurtzel aller grundboßheit*).

wurzellos: *wurzellos* rootless; figur. since Early NHG; used with ref. to persons who are 'homeless, unsettled, not firmly grounded' and to abstracts which are 'groundless, having no firm basis'.

Wurzelmann: *der* ~ mandrake; the original meaning is 'collector of or dealer in roots, herbs, etc.' and recorded in this sense only by Adelung [1780], but also the term used for little all-knowing spirits living in forests (cf. Grimm, *Mythol.*) and for 'mandrake' (= *Alraun*), in romantic lit. since ca. 1800.

Wurzelmännchen: *ein* ~ desiccated little (old) man; in lit. since the 19th c., e.g. Freytag, *Dram.W.* 9 [1858]: '*er blieb ein trocknes Wurzelmännchen*', Droste-Hülshoff, *Br.* [edit. S.-K.] 2,326: '*ein kleines grauköpfiges Wurzelmännchen*'. ~ can, however, also be used for 'mandrake'.

wurzeln: take root, be rooted

wurzeln to take root; with ref. to settling down in a place (with ref. to persons) as early as in OHG (where *Wurzel fassen* or *sich festsetzen* would now be used), later with abstracts, e.g. Herder [edit.S.] 12,29: '*alte Eindrücke . . . wurzelten . . . tief in diese . . . Lebensart*', Goethe, *Vier Jahreszeiten*: '*Neigung besiegen ist schwer; gesellet sich aber Gewohnheit, wurzelnd, allmählich zu ihr, unüberwindlich ist sie*'. Hence also *zum Wurzeln kommen* = 'to achieve a settled existence, settle down', *etw. wurzelt in jem.m* and *gewurzelt sein in etw.*, e.g. Gotthelf, *G.* 395: '*. . . daß ihre Kinder in Gott gewurzelt . . . sind*', also Hoffmannswaldau, *Begräbnisged.* 6: '*was seine hand geschrieben, das wurzelt noch in uns*'; hence transitive *jem. in etw. wurzeln* = 'to settle or establish sb. in sth.', since MHG and still in Herder [edit. S.] 5,478: '*. . . um die Menschheit in ersten Neigungen, Sitten . . . zu wurzeln*', which is now a., but passive *gewurzelt sein in etw.* is still alive, e.g. Abr. a Sta. Clara, *Reimb dich* 237: '*auß gewurtzleter schlimmer Gewonheit*', often with *tief*, e.g. Mommsen, *Röm.Gesch.* 3,422: '*eine so tief gewurzelte Herrschaft geht nicht unter . . .*'; hence also locutions with *fest*, as in Goethe's '*den Irrthum so bei sich festwurzeln zu lassen*'. Sometimes the notion of 'origin' comes to the fore, as in (DWb) Gilhusius, *Grammat.* 4,128 [1597]: '*in hoffart alle*

sünde wurtzln'.

etw. auf etw. or *jem.* ~ (lit.,obs.) to fix, hold or fasten sth. on sth. or sb.; mainly with *Auge* or *Blick*, since the 18th c., also used by Schiller, e.g. Tieck, *Schr.* 6,16: '*da wurzelte mein Auge in das Gras*', now obs., as is *jem. festwurzeln* (lit.) = 'to hold sth. fast' (so as to prevent his movement or speech), same as 'to make sth. get stuck' (when unable to answer), as in Musäus, *Ph.* 1,84. The relative *sich festwurzeln* also existed, e.g. Grabbe, *Nap.* 227.

an (or *in*) *den Boden gewurzelt sein* to be rooted to the spot; since the 18th c., e.g. Wieland 24,237: '*eine heilige Ehrfurcht hielt mich in den Boden gewurzelt*'.

verwurzeln to settle, become established; since the 18th c., e.g. *in seinem Glauben verwurzelt sein* = 'to be deeply rooted in one's faith'; *verwurzelt sein* can also refer to 'to be intimately connected'. Adelung did not record *verwurzeln* at all, but Campe [1811] listed it with a quotation from Goethe: '*mein Dasein ist mit dem Dasein meines Bruders so innig verbunden und verwurzelt, daß . . .*'.

← See also under *anwurzeln, auswurzeln, Berg* (for *in den Kämpfen des 16.Jh. wurzelt mit etw. hinter dem Berge halten*), *denken* (for *Zeit, um tief einzuwurzeln*), *einwurzeln, entwurzeln* and *Grund* (for the quotation from Herder mentioned above).

würzen: flavour

etw. ~ to give flavour to sth., spice sth.; figur. since the 16th c., e.g. Franck, *Sprichw.* 1,189a [1541]: '*hunger der gut koch würtzt jn alles*', Lenz, *Hofmeister* 3,4: '*das würzt das Gespräch wie Pfeffer den Gurkensalat*', Schiller, *Verschw. Bedemars*: '*er würzte die Schmeicheleien mit einer beträchtlichen Menge Spanischer Pistolen*', Wieland, *Amadis* 16,7: '*. . . den Scherz mit Sokratischen Lehren zu würzen* and *Werke* 15,201: '*was der Topf beschert, würzt Hunger zu Götterkost*', Börne 2,201: '*die Meinung ist die Küche, worin alle Wahrheiten . . . geschmort und gewürzt werden*'.

stark gewürzt highly spiced, strongly seasoned; figur. with ref. to abstracts such as *Rede, Redensart* or *Witz* (esp. such which border on the salacious) since the 19th c., e.g. (T.) Wolzogen, *Südd.Gesch.* 238 [1925]: '*. . . Hunger nach stark gewürzten Anekdoten und saftigen Witzen*'.

etw. verwürzen (1) to overspice sth.; since the 17th c., recorded by Kramer (1702) who equated it with *überwürzen*; figur. later for 'to spice sth. too highly', e.g. Rückert, *Mak.* 1,4. Surprisingly, *Duden* [1989] does not list *verwürzen* at all.

etw. verwürzen (2) (obs.) to deprive sth. of its

flavour, make sth. tasteless or insipid; at least since the 18th c., e.g. Bürger, 70a: '*das darf nicht Fürstengunst verwürzen*', recorded by Campe [1811] who defined it '*die Annehmlichkeit verderben, des Angenehmen berauben*'; also in the variant 'to remove the bitter taste of sth. by a sweeter flavour', as in Günther, 1041: '. . . *die dir so manches Leid durch ihren Kuß verwürzt*'. Both meanings are obs.

← See also under *durchwürzen, einspinnen* (for *ihre mit eingesponnenem Witz gewürzten Stücke*), *Gewürz* (for *du willst das Gewürze würzen, Gewürzgärtlein* and *Schmeichelgewürz*) and *Krämer* (for *Gewürzkrämer*).

Wust: jumble See under *durchwühlen* (for *der finstern Schriften Wust*), *Graus* (for *in des Nordens Wust und Graus*) and *wildern* (for *der Barbarei verjährter Wust*).

wüst: empty, deserted; chaotic

wüst (1) (pejor.) rude, coarse, terrible, foul, outrageous; first (in Late MHG) for 'dirty, ugly', which led, from the 18th c. onward to 'disgusting, unpleasant' and then to stronger pejor. meanings with ref. to persons and abstracts, e.g. *ein wüstes Benehmen, ein wüster Gauner, wüste Zustände, eine wüste Spekulation*; sometimes in lit. even used for 'monotonous, tedious' (19th c.).

wüst (2) (pejor.) awfully, terribly; intensifying adverb; modern, e.g. *er wurde ~ mißhandelt, sie haben dort ~ gehaust* or (more coll.) *es hat ~ gestürmt*.

← See also under *brennen* (for *er hat sich wüst gebrannt*), *Knäuel* (for *der Bürgerkriege wüsten Knäuel*) and *treiben* (for *sinnlos durchs wüste Leben*).

Wüste: desert *die ~* (lit.) desert, waste, empty uninhabited area; f.r.b. Maaler [1561]; in comparisons since Early NHG, e.g. Luther 18,510 (Weimar): '*darumb so ist sein leben gleich wie eine wüsten* . . .' (cf. Kant, [Acad.edit.] 1,8,234: '*Wüsten sind eigentlich Örter, die von der Natur dazu bestimmt . . . scheinen, daß die Menschen nicht darin wohnen können*'); hence *in die ~ gehen* = 'to retire to a solitary place, flee from society', since Early NHG, e.g. Goethe 24,236 and 2,77 (W.).

jem. in die ~ schicken to send sb. packing, dismiss or expel sb.; derived from the biblical image of the scapegoat (Levit. 16,10, where the A.V. uses 'wilderness'), general for dismissals, expulsions (mainly as a punishment) only since the 19th c.

es ist eine (wahre) ~ it is a veritable desert, sth. utterly barren; general since the 18th c., e.g. Grillparzer, *Sämtl. W.* [edit. S.] 9,206: '*die Wüste der neuesten deutschen Poesie*', also in poet. images,

as in 18th c. '*des Meeres öde Wüste*', in comparisons, as in Hebbel, *Br.* [edit.W.] 1,64: '*der Katalog ist wie eine Wüste, in welcher man sich nach Quellen umsieht*'. Earliest (since MHG) in relig. contexts for a spiritually empty place or thing; cf. *Ezzolied* where the compound *werltwuostunge* occurs. Frequent now also in compounds such as *Stadtwüste* or *Steinwüste*.

← See also under *Blume* (for *Schicksal, das uns zum Grabe durch Blumenflor und Wüste führt*), *Graus* (for *zu Graus und Wüste*), *Haus* (for *wo das Recht wird in der Wüste wohnen*), *heulen* (for *in der wüsten, da es heulet*), *predigen* (for *ein Prediger in der Wüste*), *rufen* (for *der Rufer in der Wüste*), *Schiff* (for *das Schiff der Wüste* and *Wüstenschiff*) and *schlafen* (for *itzo geh' ich in die Wüsten*).

wüsten: devastate

mit etw. ~ to squander sth.; derived from *~* = 'to devastate, ruin or damage', current since OHG, mainly with ref. to fields and buildings, displaced by *verwüsten*. The meaning 'to squander' began in MHG, but the locution *mit etw. ~* appeared only in the 18th c., recorded by Adelung, who remarked that *verwüsten* was '*gangbarer und edler*'.

← See also under *Saat* (for *verwustet mîner frouden sât*) and *verwüsten* (also for *unverwüstlich*).

Wüstheit: see *einnehmen*.

Wut: fury *wut- . . .* (lit.) furious; in compounds in which the second part is figur., e.g. *wutentbrannt, wuterfüllt, wutschnaubend*, all in lit. since the 18th c.

die Liebeswut (lit.,a.) nymphomania; since the 18th c., frequent in Goethe's writings, e.g. *Deutscher Parnaß*, Schiller used it in *Phädra* 3,5, Wieland in *Ob.* 9,20 (in *Werke* 3,170 he used *Nymphenwut*); now a.; cf. *Mannwut* (missing in DWb. 6 [1885]) and *Weiberwut*, since the 18th c., e.g. Zimmermann, *Einsamk.* 1,212 [1780].

← See also under *aufschäumen* (for *vor Wut aufschäumen*) *ausbeißen* (for *seine Wut an etw. ausbeißen*), *auslassen* (for *seine Wut an jem.m auslassen*), *Berserker* (for *Berserkerwut*), *borgen* (for *die Gerechtigkeit soll meiner Wuth ihre Arme borgen*), *brechen* (for *die Wut brechen*), *Dampf* (for *seine Wut dämpfen*), *einfeuern* (for *wo Wut die Herzhaftigkeit einfeuert*), *ergreifen* (for *Wut ergreift jem.*), *ersticken* (for *vor Wut ersticken*), *fressen* (for *da steh ich denn und fresse meine Wuth*), *Funke* (for *sein Auge funkelt Wuth*), *gebieten* (for *gebiete dieser Wuth*), *Geier* (for *an meinem Busen nagt die Wuth grausamer Seelengeier*), *Geißel* (for *geißle weit der Flamme Wuth umher*), *geraten* (for *in Wut geraten*), *gleich* (for *die entfesselte Wut der sozialen*

Gleichmacher), *Schaum* (for *schäumen vor Wut*), *stumm* (for *verstummt vor der Partheien Wuth*) and *toll* (for *toll und blind vor Wuth* and *Wuth tollkühner Reiterei*).

wüten: rage See under *Eingeweide* (for *gegen sein eigenes Eingeweide wüten*), *Schlange* (for *jr wüten ist gleich wie das wüten einer schlangen*) and *Teufel* (for *er wütet wie der Teufel*).

wütend: See under *erstürmen* (for *mit wütender Anstrengung*), *Feuer* (for *das Pferd feuerte wütend aus*), *Sand* (for *was ist Eduard als ein wüthend Meer*) and *See* (for *wüetunden se*).

Wüterei: see *belagern.*

Wutgesicht: see *Gesicht.*

wütig: see *brüllen.*

X: see *U.*

Xanthippe: *eine ~* a Xant(h)ippe, termagant, shrewish wife (or woman); a ref. to the ill-natured wife of Socrates; in German lit. general since Early NHG, e.g. Fischart, *Garg.* (repr.) 448. Heine [edit. E.] 2,219 altered it to *Xantuppe* for humorous effect and the sake of the rhyme. Cf. the verse *Xanthippe war ein böses Weib, der Zank war ihr ein Zeitvertreib*, quoted since the 19th c.; *xanthippisch* appeared in lit. in the 17th c.

X-Bein: *X-Beine haben* to be knock-kneed; 19th c.; cf. *Courths-Mahler* (for *Courths-Mahler-Beine*).

x-beliebig: *jeder x-beliebige Mensch* (coll.) any Tom, Dick and Harry; since the 19th c.

x-fach: *das X-fache bezahlen* (coll.) to pay umpteen times as much; also adverbially for 'umpteen times'; similarly *zum x-ten Mal* and *x-mal*, all since the 19th c.

X-Haken: *der ~* picture hook; 19th c.

Ypern: see *aussehen.*

Ysop: hyssop *jem. mit ~ besprengen* (bibl.,obs.) to purify sb.; from Psalm 51,7 (cf. also Numbers 19,18: '*und ein reiner Mann soll Ysop nehmen und ins Wasser tauchen und die Hütte besprengen und alle Geräte und alle Seelen, die darin sind*'); recorded as a standing phrase by Kramer [1702]: '*besprenge mich mit Ysop, so werde ich rein werden*'; still to be found in 19th c. lit., now obs.

von der Ceder bis zum ~ (bibl.,obs.) everything from A to Z; at first with ref. to Solomon's wisdom, quoted by Goethe 37,295 (W.), then used loosely to describe comprehensive knowledge, e.g Kotzebue, *Sämtl.Dram.W.* 1,314: '. . . *der alles weiß und kennt, von der Ceder bis zum Ysop*'; now obs.

zach: see *zäh.*

zack: *zack zack* (coll.) like greased lightning; indicates sth. that happens quickly (possibly connected with sth. as *zackig* as lightning); since the 18th c., e.g. Musäus, *Volksm.* 2,70: '*zak zak war er zum Thor hinaus*'; hence (*mach*) *zack zack* (sl.) = 'get a move on, get weaving' and the order *zack zack! -=* 'at the double!'.

er ist auf Zack (sl.) he is on the ball, there are no flies on him; also *etw. ist auf Zack* = 'sth. is in good order, works well' and *jem. or etw. auf Zack bringen* = 'to put sb. or sth. into shape, smarten sb. or sth. up'; all three locutions arose around 1940 and may have started in mil.sl.

Zacken: prong, point

das wird dir keinen ~ aus der Krone brechen (coll.) that won't impair your standing, hurt your dignity, lower your prestige; since the 19th c.; see the same phrase with *Perle* (p.1846).

er hat einen ~ (coll.) he is (a little) drunk, slightly tipsy; in lit. since the 2nd half of the 19th c., e.g. Stinde, *Fam. Buchholz* 1,160.

er hat einen (ganz gehörigen) ~ drauf (sl.) he is speeding like mad; 20th c. sl.

Zacken (regional) haermorrhoids; at least since the 18th c., when Adelung recorded it and glossed it with *Feigwarzen* (for which see p.753).

zackerieren: *mit jem.m ~* (regional coll.,N.) to argue, bicker, find fault with sb.; from French *sacré*; concerning the derivation cf. *zackerlot*, a regional variant of *sackerlot*, used by Lenz, *Werke* 2,2183 as an exclamation. See p.2049.

zackig: notched, indented

zackig alert, energetic, snappy, brisk; since late in the 18th c., in lit. first in Jean Paul, *Katzenb. Badereise*: '*ein wilder, zackiger Doktor*'.

zag: timid *zag* (lit.) timid; current since OHG, usual in MHG, then dormant, reintroduced in the 19th c. in lit. usage, as was the noun *der Zage* = 'coward', but *zaghaft*, as in Luther Bible transl. Isaiah 37,27 or Schiller, *Fiesco* 5,5 is preferred. In lit. *zagend* also occurs, as in Heine, *Sal.* 1,266: '*das Mädchen erwartet den Bräutigam zagenden Herzens*'. The noun is *Zaghaftigkeit*, and in critical comments *Zagerei* can be used, e.g. Bürger, 170a.

zagen: quail, flinch

zittern und ~ to tremble, show fear; in this alliterative combination since Early NHG, e.g. Luther Bible transl. Mark 14,33: '*fieng an zu zittern und zu zagen*' (where the A.V. has 'began to be sore amazed and to be very heavy'), f.r.b. Steinbach [1734].

← See also under *verzagen.*

zäh: tough *zäh* (1) miserly, close-fisted, tardy in paying; since MHG, f.r.b. Maaler [1561]; Adelung recorded: '*ein zäher Bezahler, das Geld gehet zähe von ihm*'.

zäh (2) tough, steadfast, determined; since Early NHG in praise or criticism for 'tenacious, dogged, grim', e.g. *seinen Standpunkt ~ behaupten* = 'to be unyielding in maintaining one's point-of-view', as in Huch, *Pitt u. Fox* 323. It can also be used for 'clinging to tradition, conservative', as in Schiller, *Kab.u.L.* 1,7 and in pejor. sense for 'reactionary'.

zach (1) (regional) tough, dogged, tenacious; the same as *zäh* (2); current in S. areas.

zach (2) (regional) stingy, close-fisted; the same as *zäh* (1); current in E. areas.

zach (3) (regional) timid, reticent; close to *zag* or *zaghaft*; mainly in N. areas.

← See also under *Harz* (for *Ideen ein zäheres Harz*), *Juchten* (for *zäh wie Juchten/Juchtenleder*), *Katze* (for *zäh wie eine Katze* and *Katzen und alte Jungfern haben das zäheste Leben*), *Leder* (for *zäh wie Leder* or *Handschuhleder*) and *Vogelleim* (for *zäh wie Vogelleim*).

zähflüssig: viscous
der Verkehr ist ~ traffic moves very slowly; 20th c. figur. extension which can also be applied to conversations or negotiations which make slow progress.

Zähheit: *die ~* (also *Zäheit*) toughness, unpolished (or crude) condition; figur. since the end of the 18th c., e.g. Fichte, *Nicolai* 43: '*seine Späße behielten eine gewisse dicke Zähheit, Plattheit*'. On the whole, *Zähigkeit*, which can also mean 'tenacity, enduring quality', is preferred.

← See also under *suchen* (for *an Zähheit sucht es seinesgleichen*).

Zahl: number *die ~* (ling.) number (in gramm. contexts); translation of Lat. *numerus*, current in German since the 17th c., used by Schottel. It is interesting to note that Kramer [1702] did not yet know *Einzahl* and *Mehrzahl* and listed instead '*eintzelne Zahl*' and '*mehrer Zahl*'.

etw. hat keine ~ (a.) sth. cannot be counted, is countless; there are several expressions describing the vastness of numbers. In MHG *âne zal* and *sunder zal* were used, e.g. *Nibelungenl.* 481,5, and Heine 1,233 still used *sonder Zahl*. In Luther Bible transl. one finds *es ist dessen keine zahl* (e.g. Song of Songs 6,7 and Job 9,10), in the Apocr. Ecclesiasticus 37,28 there is *es hat keine ~*, in the Psalms 40,13 and 104,25 *es ist ohne ~* occurs; cf. Arndt, *Ged.* 479 [1840]: '*Gott ist der Ohnezahl, vor dem die Zeit vergeht*'. Locutions with *unzählich* then appeared. Kramer [1702] recorded '*eine unzehlige Zahl*', but not yet *Unzahl*, which is also still missing in Adelung, although it has been current since the 17th c., was used by Logau; Campe [1811] recorded it with quotations from Goethe and Bürger.

er macht bloß die ~ voll he merely makes up the number; of Classical origin; Wieland in H.B. 1,68 translated *nos numerus sumus* with '*wir machen bloß die Zahl voll*'. In Early NHG locutions with *mehren* occur, e.g. Fischart, *Bien.* 42a: '. . . *zahln den haufen zu mehren gerechnet werden*'; Eyering II,323 [1601] recorded: '*er hilfft nur die zahl vermehren*'.

ungerade ~ ist eine heilige ~ (prov.) odd numbers are sacred; recorded as prov. only since the 19th c., e.g. by Eiselein and Simrock. Eiselein thought of a Classical source and quoted Vergil: '*numero Deus impari gaudit*'. *DWb.* [1877] did not record it and one wonders which odd number gave rise to the prov., if it is not of Classical origin. Was it *drei* (*aller guten Dinge sind drei*, a ref. to the Trinity?) or *sieben*? Wander [1876] recorded *sieben ist eine heilige Zahl* (as current in Ulm). One could think of the seven sacraments, the seven gifts of the Holy Spirit or the seven words of Christ uttered on the cross. One might also think of legal contexts, esp. the insistence on odd numbers of judges (cf. *Gerichtsverfassungsgesetz* of 1898: '*die Anzahl der Richter muß eine ungerade sein*') and the fact that it was an old Germanic practice that an oath by seven men had the strength of documentary evidence (cf. Grimm, *Weisth.* 3,146).

eine krumme ~ (comm.sl.) a deceptive figure showing an attractive-looking price; since ca. 1900 when shops began to price articles at 2,99 marks instead of three marks; not yet listed by Schirmer in his *Wb.d.dt. Kaufmannssprache* [1911].

← See also under *beweisen* (for *Zahlen beweisen*), *einschließen* (for *Titanen ohne Zahl*), *einschmelzen* (for *die Zahl ist eingeschmolzen*), *Galgen* (for *die Galgenzahl*), *gehen* (for *er geht mit der Jahreszahl*), *Gold* (for *die goldene Zahl*), *rechnen* (for *welche in der Zahl der Poeten wollen gerechnet werden*), *rot* (for *rote Zahlen schreiben*), *rund* (for *runde Zahlen*) and *Schnaps* (for *die Schnapszahl*).

zählebig: *zählebig* tenaciously clinging to life, so tough as to be able to survive; beginnings in Early NHG, when Maaler [1561] recorded: '*ein langwirig zäch leben, wenn etwas lang beharret ze stärben, lenta vivacitas*', but the adj. with ref. to humans is modern; Adelung and Campe did not record it.

Zahlemann: *jetzt geht's zu* (or *an*) *~ und Söhne* (joc.coll.) now you must pay, the time to settle has come; fictitious name of a firm which is assumed to have sent an invoice; current since the middle of the 'fifties of the 20th c.

zahlen: pay See under *Auge* (for *bezahlt*

instead of *gebüßt* in the quotation on p.120), *auszahlen, bezahlen, Geld* (for *Lehrgeld zahlen müssen*), *glauben* (for *wer's nicht glaubt, zahlt einen Taler*), *Ferse* (for *mit fersengelt zahlen*), *Heim* (for *jem.m etw. heimzahlen*), *Münze* (for *jem. mit gleicher Münze bezahlen*), *Natur* (for *die Schuld der Natur bezahlen*), *pressen* (for *bezahle, locke, presse bei*), *Schuld* (for *wer seine Schulden bezahlt, vermehrt sein Vermögen*), *Schule* (for *das Schulgeld mit ihrer armen Seele bezahlen*), and *Tribut* (for *den Tribut der Natur zahlen*).

zählen: count *zählen* (1) to number, comprise, contain; e.g. *die Stadt zählt eine halbe Million Einwohner*; since the 17th c., e.g. Abr. a Sancta Clara, *Etwas f.A.* 141 [1699]: '*gleichwie in der Catholischen Kirche viel schöne Ritterorden gezehlt werden*', Schiller, *M.Stuart* 2,3.

zählen (2) to be worth . . ., count as . . .; mainly in games, e.g. *jeder Spielgewinn zählt zwei Punkte*; modern and surprisingly not even listed in *DWb.* [1956].

zwanzig Jahre ~ to be twenty years old; at least since the 18th c., e.g. Schiller, *Picc.* 2,2 and *M.Stuart* 1,6; also with ref. to objects, e.g. Heine 2,189: '*das Röcklein . . . zählte schon sehr viele Lenze*'.

meine Tage sind gezählt my days are numbered, I have not much longer to live; since the 18th c., e.g. Schiller, *M.Stuart* 1,2, Heine 2,389: '*gezählt sind deine Lebenstage, Atta Troll*'.

etw. zählt (etw.) sth. counts, matters, is of significance; beginnings in Early NHG and even then more frequently in negative statements, e.g. Luther Bible transl. Ecclesiastes 1,15: '*krum kann nicht schlecht werden, noch der feil gezelet werden*' (in modern versions: '*krumm kann nicht schlicht werden noch, was fehlt, gezählt werden*', in A.V. 'that which is crooked cannot be made straight and that which is wanting cannot be numbered'); now mainly in *das zählt nicht* = 'that does not count or matter', also with ref. to persons, e.g. Goethe, *Nat. Tochter* 1,5: '*in solcher großen Menge zählt er nicht*'; cf. also *für nichts* ~ = 'to consider as (worth) nothing', as in H. Sachs (edit. Keller) 3,220: '*dich armut man für nichts zelet*' (where *halten* would now be used).

etw. (or *jem.*) *als* (formerly *für*) *etw.* ~ to consider or count sth. as sth.; with *für* since MHG, e.g. H.Sachs, *Fast.Sp.* 734,27: '. . . *den zelen di weisen fur ainen gauch*', then with *als*, e.g. Häusser, *Dt.Gesch.* 3,13: '*die Reservearmee . . . war kaum mehr als eine Stütze zu zählen*'.

etw. zählt nach . . . sth. can be counted or measured in . . . (or amount to . . .); modern, e.g. J.G.Seidel, *Ged.* 3 [1877]: '*nach Eimern zählt*

das Unglück, nach Tropfen zählt das Glück'.

auf jem. ~ *können* to be able to count or rely on sb.; since the 18th c., e.g. Schiller, *Fiesco* 3,4; cf. also *Tell* 1,3: '*ein jeder zählt nur sicher auf sich selbst*'.

auf etw. ~ to count or rely on sth.; with abstracts since the 18th c., e.g. Schiller, *Kab.u.L.* 3,2; hence also *ich zähle darauf, daß* . . ., as in Goethe IV,6,331 with the notion of firm expectation.

jem. zu (also *unter*) *etw.* ~ to count or consider sb. to belong to sth., include or rank sb. among . . . (e.g. a certain group); since MHG, e.g. *Liedersaal* [edit. Laßb.] 3,48,865: '*er ist zen wîsen nicht gezelt, der gallen für daz honig welt*', also in passive locutions such as *unter eine Gruppe, Klasse etc . gezählt werden*, as in Goethe, *Dicht.u.Wahrh.* 17; also as a reflex. *sich zu etw.* ~ , as in Luther Bible transl. 2 Cor. 10,12: '*wir thüren uns nicht unter die rechen oder zelen, so sich selbs loben*'.

die Häupter seine Lieben ~ (joc.) to check whether everybody is there; originally a quotation from Schiller, *Die Glocke*: '*er zählt die Häupter seiner Lieben*', turned into a joc. statement about a head count.

er zählt die Ziegeln auf den Dächern (prov.expr.) he loafs around, does nothing useful; f.r.b. Stieler [1691]; cf. also the prov. *man muß erst das eigne Dach decken, ehe man die faulen Schindeln auf des Nachbars Dach zählt*, recorded by Wander [1865].

← See also under *abzählen, aufzählen, auszählen, Bissen* (for *jem.m die Bissen in den Mund zählen*, where it should have been mentioned that *vorzählen* can also occur in locutions of this type and that *Happen* can be used instead of *Bissen*), *drei* (for *als ob er nicht bis drei zählen könnte, er kann wol fünf zehlen* and *ehe man bis drei zählt*), *erzählen, Finger* (for *das kann man an den fünf Fingern zählen* and *etw. an den Fingern herzählen können*), *Knopf* (for *sich etw. an den Knöpfen abzählen*), *mitzählen, Reise* (for *wenn einer eine Reise tut, so kann er was verzählen*), *Rippe* (for *bei ihm kann man die Rippen zählen*), *Schaf* (for *die gezählten Schafe frißt der Wolf auch*), *überzählen, Verstand* (for *man soll die Stimmen wägen und nicht zählen*) and *vier* (for *nicht bis vier zählen können*).

Zahlensinn: *er hat einen guten* ~ he has a good head for figures; f.r.b. Campe [1811]; approx. at the same time similar *Zahlentalent* arose.

Zahler: *die schlimmsten* ~ *sind die besten Mahner* (prov.) people who are tardy in paying are very quick in dunning their debtors; Adelung recorded '*ein scharfer Mahner ist gemeiniglich ein* *böser Zahler*', then in the wording of the prov. in Eiselein [1838] and Simrock [1846]. In Early NHG *gut Borger und bös Zahler* occurred, e.g. H.Sachs [edit. Keller-Götze] 21,322.

Zahlpfennig: *der* ~ counter, jetton; token used in games and not real money, therefore often pejor. for 'sth. of no value'; since Early NHG, e.g. Luther 16,405 (Weimar) and still in use, although *Spielgeld* and *Spielpfennig* are the more usual terms.

Zahltag: *es kommt einmal der* ~ the day of reckoning will come eventually; with ref. to judgment, retribution or revenge since the 19th c. Hence the modern saying *Wahltag ist Zahltag*.

Zahlung: *die* ~ (lit.) payment; figur. with ref. to having to pay for sins or crimes since Early NHG, e.g. Luther 10,1,182 (Weimar), Fischart, *Bien.* 158a.

← See also under *abschlagen* (for *Abschlagszahlung*).

zahlungsfähig: *zahlungsfähig* solvent; coined as a replacement for *solvent*, recorded by Campe [1811] who also listed *zahlungsunfähig* for 'insolvent'.

zahlungskräftig: *zahlungskräftig* (comm.coll.) affluent, well able to pay; 20th c. coll., not yet recorded in *DWb*. [1956].

zahm: tame *zahm* (1) tame, gentle; originally with ref. to animals which have been tamed, domesticated or broken in; since OHG extended to human beings, esp. in *jem.* ~ *machen* = 'to tame sb., bring sb. to heel, quieten sb.'; recorded by Maaler [1561], and ~ *werden* = 'to become tame, amenable', e.g. *Minnes.* [edit.v.d.H.] 2,96; even abstracts can be made 'tame' (as in Engl.) so that Schlegel could translate *Hamlet* 3,4: 'the hey-day in the blood is tame' with '*der Tumult im Herzen zahm*'. The meanings 'timid' and 'subdued', current in earlier periods, are obs.

zahm (2) mild, restrained, moderate; also pejor. for 'dull, insipid, unexciting'; with abstracts since the 18th c., e.g. *zahme Kritik*, hence Goethe's *Zahme Xenien* (as opposed to *Wilde*).

fingerzahm very tame; now with ref. to birds which are so tame that they sit on one's finger, but in earlier periods it meant 'to easily led that one finger suffices for sb.'s control'; perhaps first with ref. to horses, as suggested by Benecke in *B.M.Z.* 3,890b, but the early examples he adduced all refer to people. Eiselein [1838] recorded: '*er ist so zam worden, daß man ihn um einen Finger wickeln kann, er ist fingerzam*', introducing a derivation which is not generally accepted.

← See also under *Hand* (for *so zahm, daß er aus der Hand frißt*).

zähmen: tame *jem.* ~ to tame or quieten sb.; the same as *zahm machen* (see above), since MHG, e.g. Konr.v.Würzburg, *Troj.* 14215, Goethe 10,184 (W.): '*hier kommt der rauhe Freund, wir wollen sehn, ob wir ihn zähmen können*'. Also reflex. for 'to restrain or control oneself' since Early NHG, e.g. Goethe 27.81 (W.) on Günther: '*er wußte sich nicht zu zähmen*'.

etw. ~ to tame, subdue, restrain sth.; often with ref. to parts of the body such as *Mund*, *Maul*, *Zunge* or *Hand* since Early NHG (with *Herz* since MHG), then with abstracts, with *begirde* and *laster* recorded by Maaler [1561], with *wollust* and *bosheit* in Stieler [1691]; *bezähmen* is also used; the noun *Zähmung* became current in Early NHG, e.g. Luther 16,232 (Weimar): '*das fleisches zemung*'. Hence *ungezähmt* since the 18th c., e.g. with *Leidenschaft* in Goethe, *Tasso* 3,4.

← See also under *bezähmen* and *Schwung* (for *bezähmt der Rede wilden Schwung*).

Zahn: tooth *der* ~ (1) tooth; transfer to objects which can be compared to teeth; international; in German since MHG, for which Diefenbach, 173a recorded: '*der eisni zan oder seche in einem pflug*'; Maaler [1561] recorded it with ref. to comb and saw, Stieler [1691] listed the compounds *Kammzäne* and *Sägzäne*, Frisch [1741] recorded '*Sicheln mit Zähnen*'; anchors, harrows and forks have *Zähne*, and since the 18th c. the term has been extended to wheels; *Zahnrad* appeared in the 18th c. and was recorded by Adelung.

der ~ (2) (coll.) desire, idea (at the back of one's mind), illusion, (secret) hope; in several idioms such as *laß dir diesen* ~ *ausziehen* (coll.) = 'get rid of that idea (or hope)', since the 17th c., e.g. (DWb) Lohenstein, *Cleop.* 35: '*reiß dir nur selber diesen zahn der lüsternheiten aus*', and *sich keinen* ~ *wachsen lassen* (coll.) = 'to feel no desire or longing for sth.', listed in *DWb*. [1956]. See also the entries below on *jem.m lange Zähne machen*, *jem.m wässern die Zähne nach etw.* and *mit langen Zähnen essen*.

der ~ (3) (teenager sl.) girl; always with a qualifying adjective, e.g. *steiler* ~ ='very attractive girl', *leckerer* ~ ='pretty girl', *nasser* ~ = 'inexperienced girl', *toter* ~ = 'ugly girl', also in the compound *Goldzahn* = 'steady girlfriend'. All these arose ca. 1955, but merely revive a usage that has been current in the cant of the underworld, where Yiddish *sona* = 'harlot' led to *sen, sian, zan* = 'woman' and *sennele* = 'girl'; cf. Brecht, *Dreigroschenoper*: '*und der Haifisch, der hat Zähne, und die trägt er im Gesicht'*, where *Haifisch* stands for Yiddish *cheifez* = 'pimp, procurer' and *im Gesicht tragen* = 'to control', so that the song means 'the pimp has prostitutes and he controls them'.

bewaffnet bis auf die Zähne armed to the teeth; since MHG, e.g. Konr.v.Würzburg, *Troj.* 3495: *'Mars mit sînen scharn gewapent sêre biz ûf die zene'*.

die Zähne blecken to bare one's teeth (in anger or as a threat); derived from animal behaviour (horses, dogs); with ref. to human hostility since Early NHG, e.g. Luther Bible transl. Lamentations 2,16: *'deine feinde . . . blecken die zeene'* (where the A.V. has '. . . gnash the teeth'); *fletschen* can also be used, e.g. Lessing [edit. L.-M.] 10,233 and Goethe 14,226 (W.), where *entgegenfletschen* occurs.

die Zähne wetzen to sharpen one's teeth (with the object of preparing oneself for an attack); mainly with ref. to criticism, since the 17th c., e.g. (Sp.) Happel, *Acad. Roman* (repr.) 138 [1690]: *'wer weiß, wer seinen Zahn hingegen wieder wetzt'*; see also the entry under *wetzen*.

mit den Zähnen knirschen to gnash one's teeth; recorded by Stieler [1691]; with ref. to pain Luther 10,2,147 (Weimar) used *jem.m knirschen die Zähne*. There is also *die Zähne knirschen* (used transitively) for 'to feel or show anger, hostility or frustration', since Early NHG, e.g. Goethe IV,1,138 (W.): *'ich knirschte die Zähne und sah zu'* (also Schiller, *Kab.u.L.* 3,4). Luther in his Apocr. transl. Ecclesiasticus 30,10 also used *kirren*: *'deine zeene zu letzt kirren müssen'* (in the Engl. version 'lest thou gnash thy teeth in the end'); cf. also his use of *zusammenbeißen* in his transl. of Psalm 37,12: *'beißet seine zeene zusamen uber jn'* (in A.V. 'gnasheth upon him with his teeth').

auf die Zähne beißen to control or restrain oneself; since Early NHG; see also the previous entry.

jem.m lange Zähne machen to make sb. crave for sth., whet sb.'s appetite; this often refers to feeling lascivious and contains the notion discussed under ~ (2); since Early NHG, e.g. Fischart, *Garg.* (repr.) 1,30 and Grimmelshausen, *Vogelnest* 2,6. See also the quotation from Wieland on p.1582. Hence also *mit langen Zähnen essen* = 'to relish one's food or eat greedily', recorded by Adelung. Note the entirely different regional coll. *mit langen Zähnen essen* on p.1582.

jem.m werden die Zähne stumpf sb.'s teeth are set on edge; from Classical and bibl. sources, e.g. Bible Jerem. 31,30: *'welcher Mensch Herlinge ißt,*

dem sollen seine Zähne stumpf werden' (in A.V. 'every man that eateth the sour grape, his teeth shall be set on edge'). Hence *mit stumpfen Zähnen* = 'with aversion, without appetite', as in Herder 27,31: '. . . *kostet er alles mit stumpfem Zahne'*. Stieler [1691] recorded: *'stumpe zähne = dentes stupidi'* and Adelung wrote: *'die Zähne werden stumpf, wenn sie von einer Säure die Kraft zu beißen verliehren'*, repeated by Campe [1811], but since then the locution appears to have dropped out of use. Simrock [1846] still recorded as prov. *'wer den Andern Saures essen sieht, dem stumpfen die Zähne'*. One wonders whether the idioms with *stumpf* led to *mit langen Zähnen essen* = 'to eat without enjoyment or appetite' mentioned above and recorded on p.1582 through a simple change of *stumpf* (no longer understood?) to *lang*. This would also explain the 19th c. idiom *von etw. lange Zähne kriegen* = 'to get tired of or be bored with sth.'.

jem.m wässern die Zähne (nach etw.) sth. makes sb.'s mouth water; since the 17th c., used e.g. by Abraham a Sancta Clara, *Etw.f.A.* 2,142.

jem.m die Zähne weisen (or zeigen) to bare one's teeth, offer resistance, show determination to fight; since the 17th c., e.g. Moscherosch, *Phil.* 2,49 [1650], Gutzkow, *R.v.G.* 3,191: *'diesen Menschen muß man nur die Zähne weisen und sie werden zahm'*.

jem.m etw. aus den Zähnen ziehen (coll.) to drag sth. (e.g. information, confession) out of sb.; since late in the 19th c.

jem. zwischen den Zähnen haben (coll.) to chide, criticize or mock sb.; this is the same as *jem. durch die Hechel ziehen* and *jem. hecheln* (see p.1267) or *jem. durchhecheln* (p.524), since not human teeth but the teeth of a hackle or flax-comb are referred to; the phrase is younger than those with *Hechel* (general only since the 19th c.); hence also *den Leuten zwischen (or in) die Zähne kommen (or geraten)* (coll.) = 'to get talked about, give people cause for adverse comment, acquire a bad reputation'.

etw. zwischen den Zähnen murmeln to mumble or murmur sth., say sth. under one's breath; since the 18th c., e.g. Lessing 10,129, Goethe 40,134 (W.), Schiller, *Räuber* 4,2, Wieland 8,232: '. . . *murmelte er zwischen seinen zusammengebißnen Zähnen'*; also as *durch die Zähne murmeln*, as in Schiller, *Kab.u.L.* 5,7. similar locutions with *brummen, knurren* or *summen* also exist.

ihm tut kein ~ mehr weh he is dead; at least since the 17th c., when Stieler [1691] recorded: *'es thut ihm kein Zan mehr wehe'*.

auf jem. einen ~ haben (coll.) to dislike sb., be cross with sb.; also as *jem. auf dem ~ haben*; the idiom, current in the S. and W. since the 18th c., is probably a loan translation of French *avoir une dent contre quelqu'un*; Goethe used it in 8.64 (W.): '*die weltlichen Stände . . . haben alle einen Zahn auf mich*'. Some lexicographers have suggested that ~ in this case = 'foresight (on a rifle)', usually *Korn* (see p.1531) and that the phrase therefore means the same as *jem. aufs Korn nehmen* (for which see under *Korn*).

einen süßen ~ haben (coll.) to have a sweet tooth; since the 2nd half of the 19th c.

einen tollen ~ draufhaben (or *fahren*) (sl.) to drive at a mad speed; this has a phys. basis because the action of accelerating involved (at one time) a gearwheel with teeth; 20th c. sl.; hence also *ein paar Zähne wegnehmen* (sl.) = 'to reduce speed'.

der ~ der Zeit (1) (lit.) the ravages of time; a quotation from Shakespeare, *Measure for Measure* 5,1, but the image has Classical antecedents (see *Der Neue Büchmann* 322 [1994]).

der ~ der Zeit (2) (joc.coll.) false tooth (or teeth), denture; 20th c. joc.coll.

← See also under *Auge* (for *Augenzähne* and *Auge um Auge, Zahn um Zahn*), *ausbeißen* (for *sich die Zähne an etw. ausbeißen*), *Backe* (for *man kann seine Zähne durch seine Backen zählen*), *beißen* (for *die Zähne zusammenbeißen/zusammenschlagen/aufeinander pressen/aufeinanderbeißen/zusammenschließen*), *benagen* (for *vom Zahn der Zeit benagt*), *Drache* (for *trachenzän*), *fühlen* (for *jem.m auf den Zahn fühlen*), *Gehege* (for *das Gehege der Zähne*), *Geifer* (for *herauszugeifern, was ihm in die Zähne schießt*), *Gift* (for *Giftzahn*), *Haar* (for *Haare auf den Zähnen haben*), *hohl* (for *das ist für einen hohlen Zahn*), *Kalb* (for *Kälberzahn*), *knacken* (for *er satzte wacker ein, daß Zähn und Schwarte knackte*), *knirschen* (for *mit den Zähnen knirschen*), *lang* (for *lange Zähne kriegen* and *mit langen Zähnen essen*), *Maus* (for *Mausezahn* and *Mausezähnchen*), *Milch* (for *dem sind die Milchzähne längst ausgefallen*), *Neid* (for *des Neides Zahn*), *Perle* (for *Zähne wie Perlen*), *Stock* (for *auf dem Stockzahn lächeln* and *hinter den Stockzähnen lachen*), *wackeln* (for *die Ehrlichkeit wackelt wie ein hohler Zahn*), *Weisheitszahn* and *wetzen* (for *den kritischen Zahn zu wetzen*). See also under *Gebiß* (for *ein Gebiß wie Sterne*).

Zahnbrecher: *schreien wie ein ~* (coll.) to scream at the top of one's voice; ~ is now obs., but the phrase is still alive. It refers to the fact that itinerant quacks shouted at the top of their voices at fairs where they proclaimed their skill; f.r.b. Steinbach [1734].

← See also under *schreien*.

Zähneklappern: see *heulen*.

zahnen: *etw. ~* , *auszahnen, einzahnen* or *verzahnen* to fit an object with teeth-like notches, make sth. serrated; Adelung recorded *zahnen* with ref. to wheels and combs, Campe listed it as *zähnen*. On the whole, the compounds are preferred today, but philatelists speak of *gezähnte Briefmarken*.

Zahnfleisch: *auf dem ~ gehen* or *kriechen* (sl.) to be totally exhausted, absolutely knackered; 20th c. sl.

Zahnklempner: *der ~* (coll.) dentist; modern joc. coll.

← See also under *verzahnen*.

Zahnstocher: toothpick

der ~ (1) (coll.) midget, little creature; term of contempt for small or weak-looking persons; in lit. since the 18th c., e.g. Goethe 9,176 (W.).

der ~ (2) (mil.sl.) toothpick; contemptuous or joc. term for lances, bayonets, swords or daggers in mil.sl.; f.r.b. Horn, *Dt.Soldatenspr.* 70 [1905].

Zähre: tear *Zähren* (pl) (lit.,obs.) verses; this imitates Late Latin usage taken up by poets of the 17th c.; in occasional use still in the 18th c., e.g. (DWb) Kästner, *Verm.Schr.* 1,141 [1755]: '*kein Dichter mahlt mit kunsterfüllten Zähren, wie tief dein Tod in so viel Seelen dringt*'. Now obs. (Adelung and Campe no longer recorded it).

← See also under *Perle* (for *auf den jungen vollen Busen perlengleiche Zähren rollen*) and *saugen* (for *nun müssen Bach und Klee genug Verliebter Zähren saugen*).

Zampano: *er ist ein ~* (coll.) he is a Zampano-type; ref. to a film hero in Fellini's *La Strada* (1954), a boastful, loud, successful type of mountebank to whom everything seems possible. Ephemeral?

Zange: pincers, pliers

etw. klemmt (kneift, petzt) jem. wie eine ~ sth. torments sb., holds sb. in an iron grip; since MHG, e.g. *Minnes.* [edit. v.d.Hagen] 2,287a: '*minne klemmet rehte alsam ein zange*', C.Keller 6,92: '*von der Liebe wie mit Zangen gekneipt*'; see similar idioms under *beklemmen* and *klemmen*.

jem. zwischen (or *in*) *die ~ nehmen* (coll.) to put sb. under pressure, put the screws on sb.; since the 19th c., e.g. Sanders, *Erg.Wb.* [1871]. Hence also *jem. in der ~ haben* (coll.) = 'to have sb. just where one wants him'.

die ~ (coll.) termagant, battle-axe, xanthippe;' since the 17th c., at first mainly as *Beißzange*, e.g. in Abr. a Sa. Clara, *Judas* 1,29 [1686].

die Freßzange (zool.) masticating organ; used with ref. to the two front teeth of horses and, more widely, for the masticatory parts (*tenaculum*) of insects. Jean Paul used it jocularly for the human mouth in *Flegelj.* 1,110.

← See also under *angreifen* (for *man kann ihn nicht mit der Zange angreifen*), *beißen* (for *Beißzange*) and *Feuer* (for *Feuerzange*).

zangenförmig
zangenförmig (biol. and tech.) forcipate(d), cheliform; since the 18th c., f.r.b. Campe [1811].

Zangenangriff
der ~ (mil.) pincer attack; modern and not listed in *DWb.* [1956], although there other mil. terms are recorded, such as *Zangenring,-schanze, -system* and *Zangenwerk* (all relating to fortifications); the oldest appears to be *Zangenwerk*, f.r.b. Fäsch, *Kriegs-Lex.* 270 [1726].

Zangengeburt: forceps delivery
die reinste ~ (coll.) a very difficult process, tough job; since the 1st half of the 19th c.

Zangengriff
der ~ (sport) double grip; in wrestling; 20th c.

Zankapfel: see *Apfel.*

zanken: quarrel; scold
wenn Zwei ~ um ein Ei, steckts der Dritte bei (prov.) two dogs strive for a bone, and the third runs away with it; international, e.g. Lat. *inter duos litigantes tertius gaudet*; see also under *dritte* (for *der lachende Dritte*); quite different, but also prov., is the advice to keep out of a quarrel: '*wo zween zancken, da sey nicht der dritte*', recorded by Petri [1605].

← See also under *Haar* (for *der zankt mit eim der nit da ist*), *Schatten* (for *er zankt sich mit seinem eignen Schatten*) and *verzanken.*

Zanksucht
See under *Götze* (for *Uneinigkeit und Zancksucht*) and *Sucht* (for *Zanksucht*).

Zankteufel
jem. hat den ~ im Leibe (or *ist ein leibhaftiger ~*) sb. is a quarrelsome person by nature; *~* appeared in the 16th c., f.r.b. Stieler [1691]. The phrases with *im Leibe* or *leibhaftig* are modern, e.g. Gotthelf, *Ges.Schr.* 20,404.

Zapfen: tap, bung
ein voller ~ (coll., obs.) sb. who is the worse for drink; recorded by Adelung, now obs., but regionally *er hat einen ~* = 'he is (slightly) drunk' is still alive.

zapfen
See under *abzapfen*, *anzapfen* and *verzapfen.*

Zapfenstreich
den ~ blasen to sound the tattoo; *~* was introduced (or at least firmly established) by Wallenstein in an attempt to curb drinking by his men late into the night. All sutlers had to bung up their barrels, i.e. *den Zapfen streichen*, on a given signal (first by trumpet, later by drums) called *der ~* ; f.r.b. Stieler [1691]. Engl. 'tattoo' (from 'tap to') and Amer. 'taps' still show the connexion with *Zapfen* = 'tap'. *Über den Zapfen hauen* (mil.sl.) means 'to break curfew regulations', where *Zapfen* stands for *~.*

jetzt ist ~ (coll.) now it's time for bed; modern, also used in public houses for 'time, gentlemen, please'.

Zapfstelle
eine ~ für jem.s Ansprüche a source from which to satisfy sb.'s demands; a ref. to a petrol pump; 20th c.

Zappelbeinleutchen
Zappelbeinleutchen (lit.) people swinging from the gallows: coined by Heine in *Lied.* 21. Cf. similar *Galgenschwengel* on p. 900.

zappeln: wriggle, fidget
jem. ~ lassen (coll.) to keep sb. on tenterhooks or in suspense; since Early NHG; cf. also Weise, *Kom. Opern* 1,165: '*er mag ein Weilchen zappeln*'.

zappeln (coll.) to move in short but quick steps; since the 17th c., f.r.b. Stieler [1691], also recorded as *zäppeln* and *zeppeln*. Frequent in compounds such as *daherzappeln, hinaufzappeln*; Adelung recorded '*er ist fort gezappelt*' and Campe: '*da kömmt er gezappelt*'; hence also the noun *der Zappelgang*.

das Gezappel wriggling (to get out of some difficulty); also *Gezäppel* or *Gezeppel*; in figur. sense only since the 19th c. The older meaning 'disorder, unrest' is obs.

← See also under *Fisch* (for *zappeln wie ein Fisch*) and *Tod* (for *zu Tode zappeln*).

Zappelphilipp
der ~ (coll.) fidget, restless child; taken from one of the stories in *Struwwelpeter* [1845] by Heinrich Hoffmann.

zappen
zappen (coll.,tech.) to switch continually from one channel to another on a television set; this belongs to the same root as *zappeln* = 'to move to and fro'; since last quarter of the 20th c.; details in M.Jäckel, *Fernsehwanderungen. Eine empirische Untersuchung zum Zapping* (München, 1993).

zappenduster
es ist ~ (coll.) it is pitch-dark; probably belongs to *Zapfenstreich* which produces total darkness in the barracks when it has been sounded; since late in the 19th c.(?), not recorded in *DWb.* [1956]; I have known it since my youth.

damit ist es ~ (coll.) things are bad where that is concerned; also *für dich ist's* ~ = 'you are in for it'; from the previous entry; 20th c. coll.

zart

See under *Flaum* (for *flaumzart*), *Geschlecht* (for *das zarte Geschlecht*, also under *umgeben*) and *umkehren* (for *ave sprach der engel zart*).

zartbesaitet: see *besaiten*.

zärteln: see *verzärteln*.

zartfühlend: see *fühlen*.

Zartgefühl: see *fühlen*.

Zärtlichkeit

See under *girren* (for *girrte schmachtend Zärtlichkeiten*), *rauben* (for *wann die Zärtlichkeit die verliebten Räubereien recht spricht*), *temperieren* (for *außer der temperierten Zärtlichkeit*) and *Ukas* (for *Ukasenton der Zärtlichkeit*).

Zäsur: caesura

eine ~ *setzen* (lit.) to mark a turning point; also 'to constitute a halt in some development'; from metrical language transferred in the modern period, e.g. *das Jahr der ersten bedeutenden Zäsur in seinem Leben* or *die erzwungene Pause in der Zeit des Dritten Reichs setzte eine Zäsur in seiner Laufbahn*, therefore meaning sometimes *Einschnitt*, at others *Unterbrechung*.

Zauber: magic, witchcraft

der ~ (1) spell, charm; with ref. to the strong experience produced by a person or abstract in sb.; since the 18th c., e.g. S.v.Laroche, *Frl. von Sternberg* 2,37: '*Zauber der jungfräulichen Schamhaftigkeit*', O. Jahn, *Mozart* 4,407: '*der Zauber seiner Persönlichkeit*', Geibel, *Ges.W.* 2,62: '*o welche Zauber liegen in diesem kleinen Wort:daheim!*'.

der ~ (2) (coll.) business, affair, thing, caboodle, palawer; pejoration of ~ (1), modern and even unrecorded in *DWb*. [1956]; one can see tentative beginnings in such instances as Gutzkow, *Ges.W.* 9,46: '*. . . die tollsten Zauber . . . erzählen*', but fully established only in the 20th c.; frequent in *ich bin den ganzen* ~ *müde, was kostet der* ~ *? den* ~ *kenne ich schon lange*.

etw. ist ein ~ (now usually *zauberhaft*) sth. is sheer magic, a marvel, most enchanting; since the 18th c., closely related to ~ (1), but in essence a hyperbolic comparison, e.g. Platen 7,183 on Venice: '*bei Nacht ist die Stadt ein wahrer Zauber*' The adj. *zauberhaft* has increasingly displaced the locution with the noun and has at the same time become a coll. hyperbole.

das ist ein fauler ~ (coll.) that is humbug, eyewash, a sham, sth. bogus; *faul* here = 'unconvincing, ineffective (see p. 740); the idiom became current in the 19th c., e.g. Fontane, *Ged.* 76:

'*Wissenschaft ist fauler Zauber*'.

der Budenzauber (coll., a.) riotous party, rave-up; coined in the 19th c., but now displaced by a variety of teenager terms such as *Party, Show, echt Action*.

~ *machen* (sl.) to make a fuss, exaggerate; since the 2nd half of the 19th c., mainly in *mach keinen* ~ = 'don't make such a fuss'.

← See also under *binden* (for *deine Zauber binden wieder*), *brechen* (for *den Zauber brechen*), *Geist* (for *nenne mir den Zauber, der . . .*) and *Haken* (for *ein Zauber häkelt mich wieder*).

zauberhaft: see *Zauber*.

Zauberhauch: see *umwittern*.

Zauberin

die ~ (lit.) sorceress, bewitching woman; since the 18th c.; in Wieland, *Gold. Spiegel* 2,1 as *Zauberin*, in Goethe, *Götz* 2 as *Zauberin*.

zaubern

. . . -zaubern . . . by magic; in many compounds, all since the 18th c., e.g. *einzaubern*, as in Wieland 19,321: '*den eingezauberten Liebesteufel loszuwerden*', *entzaubern* = 'to remove the charm or magical power from sb. or sth.', frequent in Wieland, *heran-, her-* or *hinzaubern* = 'to produce sb. by magic' (Goethe used *heranzaubern*), *umzaubern* = 'to change by magic', esp. in *jem. m. etw. vorzaubern* = 'to produce sth. magical for sb.' and *weg-* or *hinwegzaubern* = 'to remove sth. by magic or as though by magic'.

icht kann nicht ~ (coll.) I'm no magician, I can't do the impossible; modern as a coll. phrase; the same as *ich kann nicht hexen* (see p. 1820).

← See also under *bezaubern* and *verzaubern*.

Zauberschlaf: See *Duft*.

Zauberschlag: see *Schlag*.

Zauberspruch: see *binden*.

Zauderer

der ~ (hist.) Leopold Joseph Graf von Daun (1705–1766), Austrian Fieldmarshall; called *der* ~ because of his delaying strategy after the Roman general Quintus Fabius Maximus who acquired the name *Cunctator* because of his hesitating strategy in the war against Hannibal.

← See also under *predigen* (for *was predigt er Zauderer?*).

zaudern: see *Tod*.

Zaum: bridle

der ~ (li.) curb, bridle; figur. with ref. to abstracts in lit. since the 18th c., e.g. Wieland 24,43: '*die Gerechtigkeit sei ein Zaum, den bloß die Nothwendigkeit den Menschen über den Hals geworfen*'. See also under *Zügel* for similar locutions.

jem. m or *einer Sache einen* ~ *anlegen* to curb sb. or sth., restrain or keep sb. or sth. in check; since

MHG, e.g. Konr. v. Würzburg, *Troj.* 15076, Tauler, *Sermones* 147 [1518]; sometimes with *ins Maul legen*, as in Luther 6,466 (Weimar) or *in die Lippen legen*, as in Gryphius, *Freud- u. Trauersp.* 17 [1663], also with *einlegen* as in Zinkgref, *Apoph.* 1,417 [1628]; with *anlegen* still in the 18th c., e.g. Herder, *Ph.* 10,267, but locutions with *halten* are more frequently used.

jem. or *etw. im ~ halten* to curb or check sb. or sth.; younger than the previous entry, but established by Early NHG, when Luther used it in his Bible transl. James 3,2 and Maaler [1561] recorded it; specifically with abstracts in Steinbach [1734]; '*er hällt die Begierden im Zaume*'; now even in coll. phrases such as *das Mundwerk im ~ halten*; frequent also in the reflex. *sich im ~ halten* = 'to restrain or control oneself'. The locution *etw. im ~ reiten* = 'to curb sth'., as in Mathesius, *Predigten* 94, where it is used with *Sünde*, is obs.

jem. m in den ~ greifen (a.) to halt sb.'s progress; in phys. sense since Early NHG, e.g. H. Sachs [edit. K.] 3,486: '. . . *griff ihn in zaum*', later figur., but phrases with *Arm*, *Rad* or *Speiche* (for which see on pp. 73,718 and 1933) are preferred.

den ~ schießen lassen (a.) to relax (or abandon entirely) one's control over sth. or sb; the notion is the same as in *jem. m den ~ lang lassen* = 'to allow sb. considerable freedom of action'. Locutions of this type have been current since the 17th c., e.g. with *schießen* in Olearius, *Pers. Baumg.* 99b [1696] or Grimmelshausen, *Simpliz.* bk. 5, chapt. 7; Eyering recorded in prov. collection [1601–4] *den ~ nicht zu lang lassen*, Maaler [1561] listed '*den Zaum lassen - dare fraena*', and Steinbach [1734] recorded it with an abstract: '*den Begierden den Zaum lassen*'.

den Kappzaum anlegen (obs.) to enforce control (over sth.), curb sth.; *Kappzaum* = 'cavesson', as used for wild young horses, was f.r.b. Stieler [1691]; frequently used figur. in the 17th and 18th c., e.g. *Kappzaum der Vernunft* in Lohenstein, *Ibr. S.* 5,16 [1679], Bodmer, *Gd.* 10: '*der geistlichen Gewalt den Kappzaum angelegt*', Möser, *Verm. Schr.* 1,127: '*die Religion sei . . . ein Kappzaum für den Pöbel*'.

← See also under *betreiben* (for *meine Geduld reißt den Zaum ab*), *hängen* (for *wissen, wo die Zäume hängen* and *einem Pferd den Zaum hängen*), *locker* (for *den Zaum locker hält*) and *Rappe* (for *den Rappen beim Zaum halten*).

zäumen

etw. verkehrt aufzäumen (coll.) to set about sth. (in) the wrong way; modern version of the phrase listed on p.210.

aufgezäumt (lit., rare) prepared and ready for anything; occasionally in lit. in the 19th c., but now rare if not obs.

← See also under *aufzäumen*, *bezäumen* (also for *Bezäumung* and *einzäumen*) and *Roß* (for *das Roß unterm Schwanz zäumen* and *das ross soll man nicht beym ars auffzäumen*).

zaumlos: see *ungehalten*.

Zaun: fence

der ~ (lit.) fence, hedge, shield, obstacle, shelter; in a variety of contexts which have in common that sth. guards or shelters sth.; since Early NHG, e.g. v. Haller, *Rest.* 4,43 on the Church: '*sie ist . . . der Zaun, der die Heerde der Gläubigen schützt*', Hippel, *Lebensl.* 3,2,184: '. . . *ohne Gesetze, ohne Zäune. . . herumwandeln*', Treuer, *Däd,* 1,139: '*Augenbrau ist der Augen Schutzwehr und Zaun*', an image that had occurred before in Megenberg, *B.d.Natur* [edit. Pf.] 10,24 [1350]: '*daz die augenpraw sein recht als die zeun umb einen garden*'; cf. *die Welt hinterm Bretterzaun* = 'the world beyond one's own mental horizon', e.g. v. Wolzogen, *Wie ich mich . . . .* 69 [1923]: '*hinter dem Bretterzaun meiner ererbten Vorstellungen*'. See also under *Brett* (p. 395) for *ihm ist die Welt mit Brettern vernagelt*.

einen Streit vom ~ brechen to provoke a quarrel; since Early NHG, e.g. H. Sachs [edit. G.] 17,370: '*brach offt ein hader von eim zaun*'. It is assumed that the phrase refers to getting hold of the nearest weapon to hand when starting a fight and therefore tearing out a stake or post from the nearest fence; used by Luther in *Werke* 5,287b (Jena).

etw. vom ~ brechen to produce (or say) sth. impromptu, off the cuff; derived from previous entry and used with ref. to some abstracts, e.g. *eine Ursache vom ~ brechen* (or *reißen*) - 'to invent a cause or reason' since Early NHG, or *man muß Gelegenheit von einem Zaune brechen*, since the 18th c. and still current in the 20th c., though *aus dem Stegreif etw. tun* (for which see p. 1975) is preferred.

er wird damit nicht hinterm ~ halten (coll.) he will not keep this (information, piece of scandal, etc.) to himself; modern coll. Older and more frequently used is *mit etw. (nicht) hinter dem Berge halten* (see p. 258).

etw. auf den ersten besten ~ hängen (coll.) to let all the world know sth. as quickly as possible, publish sth. without delay; modern coll., e.g. Droste-Hülshoff (in letter to Schücking, 154): '*wenn er was Nettes weiß, so hat die arme Seele keine Ruhe, bis er es auf den ersten besten Zaun gehängt hat*'.

jem.m etw. über den ~ *werfen* (coll.) to do sb. a favour, render sb. a service; modern coll. Much less used than *ich werf dir auch einmal einen Stein in den Garten* (see p. 916).

nicht hinterm ~ *geboren* (or *aufgewachsen, aufgelesen*) *sein* (coll.) to come from a good home (or respectable family); recorded since the 18th c., e.g. by Adelung; hence *hinter dem* ~ *geborenes Kind* = 'illegitimate child'; see also under *Straße* (for *er ist nicht auf der Straße gefunden*).

sein Gewissen an den ~ *hängen* (a.) to disregard the voice of one's conscience; still in the 18th c., e.g. M. Möller, *Erkl. d. Evang.* 528 [1729]: '*also hänget mancher sein Gewissen an den Zaun*'; the phrase with *Nagel* is preferred (see p. 1749).

wir leben ~ *an* ~ (coll.) we are next-door neighbours; modern, e.g. (T.) Binding, *Opfergang* 24 [1944]; cf. *ein Schwatz übern* ~ (coll.) = 'a talk with one's neighbour'.

beizeit auf die Zäun, so trocknen die Windeln (prov.) don't hesitate! get on with it! since Early NHG, f.r.b. Franck [1541]: '*beyzeit auff die zeun, so trucknen die windlen*'; Merck quoted it to Goethe, when the latter hesitated about publishing *Götz* and *Werther*.

wo der ~ *am niedrigsten ist, will jeder übersteigen* (prov.) everybody looks for the easiest way to achieve his object; since Early NHG, recorded by Tappius, 220b [1545], also used by Luther in *Tischr.* 226a.

← See also under *Gevatter* (for *Gevatter übern Zaun*).

Zaunbillet

ein ~ *nehmen* (coll.) to enjoy sth. (e.g. a concert) without paying (by staying outside the enclosed area); since the 19th., f.r.b. Trachsel, 67 [1873] (for Berlin).

zaundürr

zaundürr very thin, emaciated; with ref. to persons since the 18th c., used by Jean Paul, recorded by Campe [1811].

zäunen

See under *bezäunen, einzäunen* and *umzäunen*.

Zaungast

der ~ onlooker (esp. an uninvited or non-paying one); cf. *Zaunbillet* above; since the 19th c., f.r.b. Brendicke (for Berlin).

Zaunkönig: see *König*.

Zaunpfahl

See under *Pfahl* (for *jem.m mit dem Zaunpfahl winken*) and *stupfen* (for *ein Stupfer mit einem Zaunpfahl*).

Zebedäus: Zebedy

der ~ (coll.) the penis; biblical name from Matth. 4,21; the coll. meaning since the 17th c. (Küpper's

dating in *Pons* is wrong), e.l. (Müller-Fraureuth) Paullini, *Zeitkürz.Erb.-Lust* 2,97 [1695]: '*der neugewählte Papst müßte sich den zebedäum vorher fein betasten lassen*'; Teuchert in *DWb.* [1956] suggested stud. sl. origin, which receives some support from Fischer, *Schwäb. Wb.* where it is mentioend that the term occurs in the stud. sl. of Basel. Müller-Fraureuth 2,694 [1914] thought that the notion of *Zipfel* might have contributed to the creation of the term. Küpper in *Pons* 939 [1987] adds as a gloss: '*Zebedäus, Vater der Apostel Johannes und Jakobus, die als unzertrennlich geschildert werden. Hieraus ergab sich im Ital. die Bezeichnung zebedei – Hoden*'. *Frankfurter Wörterbuch* 18,3619 [1985], one of the many idiotica which list the term, adds: '*Ausdruck der älteren Generation*'.

Zebra: zebra

Zebra- . . . (zool.) striped . . .; in several animal names, such as *Zebrakatze - Felis maniculata domestica, Zebrasalm = Haplochiton zebra, Zebraschnecke = Achatina zebra, Zebrawolf = Thylacinus cynocephalus, Zebrazunge = Synaptura zebra*; all recorded in Brehm, *Thierleben*

das ~ (mil.sl.) quartermaster sergeant; since 1st World War, f.r.b. Bächtold-Stäubli [1922].

das ~ (stud.sl.) a lot (of drink); a pun based on the fact that a large helping of beer is called *Streifen*. Since a zebra has many stripes, a ~ is much more than one *Streifen*; since the 1st half of the 20th c.

Zechbruder: see *Bruder*.

Zeche

die ~ *bezahlen müssen* to have to pay the price, foot the bill; since Early NHG, e.g. Franck [1541]: '*er würt einmal zeche zahlen*' and '*ich muss die zech bezahlen*', Forster, *Br.* 2,234: '*wer wird die Zeche bezahlen? Wer wird das Opfer sein?*'; *ausbaden* can also be used; see p. 121.

← See also under *ankreiden* (for *hier kreiden sie die Zeche nicht anders an als gleich auf den Kopf*), *Bein* (for *er trinkt sich eine große Zeche ans Bein*) and *Kreide* (for *für jetzt ist ihm seine Zeche abgeschrieben*).

zechen: carouse

zechen to drink, booze, carouse; as a simplex now little used, but 17th c. *bezechen* = 'to make drunk' and *sich bezechen* are still alive, whereas the compounds *dickbezecht*, as in Ramler, *F.* 3,129 and *wohl bezecht*, as in Wieland, *Luc.* 5,156 are no longer in use. Still possible is *durchzechen*, as in *die Nacht durchzechen*, e.g. Wieland, *H.B.* 2,180, but Goethe used compounds which are now obs., e.g. in a review in *Frankf.Gel.Anz.* 86: '. . . *sein Glas Bier mit Heldenappetit auszechend*' or *Seefahrt*: '*mir Geduld und guten Muth erzechend*'.

← See also under *verzechen*.

Zechenbaron

ein ~ (coll.) rich mine owner; refers to the fact that around the end of the 19th c. many mine owners were ennobled; now in pejor. use. See under *Baron* for similar compounds.

Zecher: see *Klaue*.

Zechpreller: see *prellen*.

Zechprellerei: see *prellen*.

Zecke: tick

er hängt (or *beißt*) *sich fest wie eine* ~ (coll.) one cannot get rid of him, he sticks to one like a leech, clings like ivy; since Early NHG and still in use in some regions, but phrases with *Klette* (for which see p. 1488) are preferred.

voll (or *vollgefressen*) *wie eine* ~ (coll.) as fat or full as a tick; since Early NHG, e.g. Fischart, *Garg.* (repr.) 227; Kramer [1702] recorded: '*er ist so fett wie eine Zecke*'; cf. '*frißt sich, sauft sich an wie eine Zeck*', recorded by Fischer for Swabia.

← See also under *Trumm* (for *hängt wie eine Zecke*).

Zehe: toe

die ~ small piece of root; only applied to garlic, ginger and horseradish; recorded since the 15th c., in Kramer [1702] also in the diminutive: '*ein zehelein knoblauch*'.

unversehrt bis zur kleinen ~ totally unharmed; e.g. Goethe, *Götz* 1 (Jaxthausen): '*er ist ganz von der äußersten Haarspitze bis zum Nagel des kleinen Zehs*'. As early as in MHG phrases of this kind corresponding to Engl. 'from tip to toe' were current, e.g. *Minnes.* [edit. v.d.H.] 3.439a: '*von ir scheitel ûf ir zêhen*'.

jem.m auf die Zehen treten (coll.) to offend sb.; in early examples the meaning appears to have been 'to hurt sb.', as in Lohenstein, *Arm.* 2,251: '*der tod . . . tritt keinem behertzten auf die zehen*', but in the modern period 'to offend' is the general meaning, e.g. Schubart, *Leben* 2,16: '*wenn ich . . . von einem lutherischen Freunde auf die Zehen getretten werde*'.

sich auf die Zehen stellen müssen (coll.) to have to make an effort to comply, do what is expected; similar to, but not quite the same as Engl. 'to have to be on one's toes'; 20th c. coll.

er hat Schmerzen in der kleinen ~ (coll.) he imagines that he is ill; belittling sb.'s complaints; modern.

über die große ~ *gehen* (regional coll.) to walk pigeon-toed; in some regions, whereas in others *onkeln* is used, for which see p. 1813.

← See also under *aushöhlen* (for *aushöhlen bis auf die Zehen*), *Ferse* (for *von jem.m lieber die Fersen als die Zehen sehen*) and *Wirbel* (for *vom Wirbel bis zur Zehe*).

Zehenspitze

auf Zehenspitzen quietly, furtively, cautiously; modern, *auf den Zehen* is older, esp. with *schleichen* (used by Schiller). The older form was *Zehspitze*; cf. Herder [edit. S.] 22,294: '*nie stehen wir auf der Zehspitze eines peinlichen Strebens*'.

zehn: ten

alle Dreizehn treiben (regional coll.) to play all sorts of tricks, get up to all kinds of mischief; modern, e.g. Spindler, *Vogelhändler* 4,251 [1841], recorded for Bav. by Schmeller.

eine alte Mutter Fünfzehn (coll.,obs.) an old hag; e.g. O.G.Müller, *Lind.* 2,326 [1790], now obs.

← See also under *Finger* (for *alle zehn Finger nach etw. lecken*), *Freund* (for *Freunde in der Not gehn zehn auf ein Lot*), *fünf* (for *kurze Fünfzehn machen*), *Gaul* (for *zehn Gäule kriegen mich von hier nicht weg*) and *Narr* (for *ein Narr kann mehr fragen als zehn Weise beantworten können*).

Zehner

ein falscher Siebenzehner (regional coll.) a crook, swindler; the same as *ein falscher Fünfziger* (for which see under *falsch* and the additional note under *fünf*); e.g. Spindler, *Vogelhändler* 4,118 [1841]: '*bist du's nicht, falscher Siebenzehner!*'; a *Siebenzehner* was a coin worth 17 Kreuzer.

zehnt

der Zehnte weiß nicht . . . few people know . . ., not one in ten knows . . .; mainly in prov. sayings, recorded since the 19th c., e.g. by Simrock [1846]: '*der Zehnte weiß nicht, wo den Elften der Schuh drückt*' and '*der Zehnte weiß nicht, wovon der Elfte lebt*'; Klix, 124 [1862] recorded: '*das kann der Zehnte nicht vertragen*'.

zehren

etw. zehrt sth. consumes, makes sth. waste away (also lose weight); since MHG; this can be used with ref. to diseases which make sb. waste away, but since the 18th c. with other abstracts seen as 'gnawing' at one's substance, e.g. Goethe IV,22,300 (W.): '*der Augenblick zehrt schon wieder an unserm Marck*', *Iphig.* 16: '*ihm zehrt der Gram das nächste Glück vor seinen Lippen weg*', Fontane, *Ellernklipp* 480: '*sie hat eine Sehnsucht, und Sehnsucht zehrt, sagt das Sprichwort*'.

von etw. ~ to live, feed or continue to exist on sth.; transfer from phys. existing on food and drink to abstracts, at least since the 16th c., e.g. Henisch [1616]: '*zehr spärlich vom gewinn*' = 'be careful or slow in consuming or spending what you have gained', now mainly in *von dem Erbe, von Erinnerungen, vom alten Glück* ~, e.g. Huch, *Pitt u.Fox* 239: '*nun zehrte er sehr von der Vergangenheit*'.

zehren (cant) to beg; also = 'to extort money';
this usage in the language of criminals can be
seen as a return to the old notion of 'tearing
(away)' present in ~; f.r.b. Ostwald, *Rinnsteinspr.*
(Appendix).

← See also under *aufzehren, auszehren, Bär*
(for *Bären, die immer an eignen Pfoten zehren*),
Schnur (for *von der Schnur zehren*), *Schweiß* (for
hab ich von ewerm schweiß gezert) and *verzehren*.

Zehrgeld: see *Zehrpfennig.*

Zehrpfennig

der ~ travelling allowance; at first (MHG) the
actual money taken by or given to sb. to help him
along on his journey; in relig. contexts also used
for 'Communion', in modern period = 'travelling
allowance', figur. since 18th c., e.g. Goethe
IV,6,150 (W.): *'dein liebes Andencken . . . ist mir
. . . der beste Zehrpfennig, den ich auf die Reise mitnehmen kann'.*

Zehrung

die heilige (or *letzte*) ~ (relig.) extreme unction;
~ was 'provender' (esp. for a journey), in MHG
also used for 'meal', even 'banquet'; now a. if not
obs., but with *heilig* or *letzt* still current in
Catholic areas, e.g. Ganghofer, *Dorfapostel* 403.

die ~ (med.,obs.) consumption; still in
Kortum, *Jobs.* 3,153 [1784]; now obs., but
Auszehrung is still understood though it, too, is
becoming obs., displaced by *Schwindsucht.*

← See also under *auszehren* (for *Auszehrung*).

Zeichen: sign, mark

seines Zeichens (or *seinem* ~ *nach*) *ein* . . . by
trade or profession a . . .; first with ref. to trades-
men who marked their products with a sign (or
initials), but then transferred to professions, e.g.
Kügelgen, *Jugenderinn.* 228: *'ein Privatgelehrter,
seines Zeichens Mineralog'*; also in joc.coll., e.g.
seines Zeichens ein Esel, as in Freytag, *Verl.
Handschr.* 5,5.

das ~ (1) mark; with ref. to things not
intended to serve as a sign or mark, e.g. s scar, as
in Goethe, *Lehrj.* 5,10: '. . . *einen Teller an den
Kopf geworfen, davon sie noch das Zeichen trage'.*

das ~ (2) sign, indication; since MHG, e.g.
Nibelungenl. 928, Megenberg, *Buch d.N.* [edit.
P.] 38,17: *'diu zaichen davon man waiz, ob ain
fraw swanger sei worden'*, and therefore also =
'symptom' in med. contexts; cf. also ~ *von* (or
with genitive) = 'sign of . . .', as in Goethe
22,216 (W.): *'das Kind gab kein Zeichen von
Schmerz von sich'*, Körner, *Jos.H.*1: *'kein Zeichen
des Lebens'.* More figur. in *ein* ~ *der Zeit* = 'a sign
of the times', for sth. which is characteristic of or
symptomatic for the period; since Early NHG,
e.g. Luther Bible transl. Matth. 16,3: *'könnet jr*

denn nicht auch die zeichen dieser zeit vrteilen?' (in
A.V. 'can ye not discern the signs of the times?'),
and in cases where ~ means 'portent': *etw. für ein
gutes* ~ *halten*, as in Goethe 43,20 (W.), Schiller,
M.Stuart 2,1: *'ein Zeichen böser Vorbedeutung'*,
Lied v.d.Glocke 86/7: *'ob das Spröde mit dem
Weichen sich vereint zum guten Zeichen'.* In most
contexts *Anzeichen* can also be used, but this
only became current in the 18th c.

das ~ (3) sign, expression, token; since Early
NHG, e.g. Luther Bible transl. Numbers 21,9:
*'machte Moses eine eherne schlange und richtete sie
auff zum zeichen'*; now mainly in ~ *des Dankes,
der Teilnahme* or *Trauer.*

das ~ (4) symbol; since Early NHG, e.g.
Keisersberg, *Bilgers.* B3a: *'biet dinem nechsten die
hand, das zeichen des friedens'* (cf. Schiller's *'ein
Schwerdt! das Zeichen des Kriegs'*); cf. also Luther
26,164 (Weimar): *'zum zeichen dieses bundes hat er
die tauffe eingesetzt'.* It is from this meaning (or ~
(3)) that ~ came to be used in the sciences and
in music; cf. also *die Sprache ist ein System von* ~.

das ~ (5) proof; in this case a sign that sth. can
be taken as evidence; derived from ~ (2) in the
modern period, e.g. Alexis, *Hosen d.H.v.B.*
1,2,316: *'zum Zeichen, daß mein Herr unschuldig'*,
where *Beweis* would be the usual noun.

das ~ (6) constellation; also used for 'phase'
(of a planet considered to be of influence), as in
Schiller, *Wall.Tod* 5,5: *'die Zeichen stehen grauen-
haft . . . ein greulich Zeichen steht im Haus des
Lebens'.* In astrology used for 'sign of the zodiac,
e.g. *in einem guten (schlechten)* ~ *geboren*, where
Engl. uses 'star' or 'constellation'. There are
numerous phrases relating to signs of the zodiac,
e.g. *auch unter den zwölf himmlischen* ~ *gibt's einen
Skorpion* = 'even in distinguished groups of
people there can be a black sheep', used by Abr.
a Sta. Clara (quoted in Wander, *Parömiakon*
308), *er ist in das* ~ *des Widders gekommen* = 'his
wife has become unfaithful to him', recorded by
Wander [1880].

etw. steht unter dem ~ *der/des* . . . (lit.) sth. is
marked by sth. (abstract); derived from ~ (6);
only with abstracts, modern, e.g. (DWb)
Boltzmann, *Pop.Schr.* 403: *'der erste Theil meiner
Reise stand unter dem Zeichen der Eile'*; see under
stehen (p. 2345) for *etw. steht* (2).

~ *und Wunder* wonders and signs; originally
biblical, frequent in Acts 2,19, also 2,22 and 43;
given wider currency through Schiller, *Wall.
Lager* and now frequent in such phrases as *da
müßten* ~ *und Wunder geschehen* = 'that would
require a miracle', *es geschehen* ~ *und Wunder* =
'wonders will never cease' (when commenting on

an event one had not expected to occur) or *es geschehen jetzt keine ~ und Wunder mehr* = 'the age of miracles is past' (19th c.).

← See also under *ausrufen* (for *gut Wein darf kein Zeichen vorm Haus*), *befestigen* (for *Befestigungszeichen*), *bezeichnen* (for *sintemal alle zeichen geringer sind denn das ding, so sie bezeichnen*), *einwirken* (for *wie anders wirkt dies Zeichen auf mich ein*), *geben* (for *ein Lebenszeichen geben*), *Geist* (for *ein Zeichen, daß sie wenig Geistigkeit haben*), *halten* (for *ein Haltezeichen aufrichten*), *Kain* (for *Kainszeichen* and *Zeichen Kains*), *stehen* (for *die Sonne stand im Zeichen der Jungfrau*) and *Vorzeichen*.

zeichnen: draw, mark

etw. ~ (1) (lit.) to depict, describe, delineate, indicate sth.; with ref. to verbal communication; since the 17th c., recorded by Stieler [1691], e.g. Goethe 44,12 (W.: '*Herr Ludwig hatte mit Worten gezeichnet, daß . . .*', Gerstenberg, *Schl.Lit.* (repr.) 35: '*den Charakter eines Helden zeichnen*'; hence *fest gezeichnet* = 'firmly or clearly delineated' with ref. to abstracts. Sometimes no more than *zeigen* = 'to show', as in Lessing 6,368: '*der . . . Wege weiter bahnet und neue Pfade . . . zeichnet*'. Also in compounds, esp. in *vorzeichnen*, as in Wieland 16,163: '*Tanz . . . der . . . die feinsten Schattierungen der Leidenschaft den Augen vorzeichnete*'.

etw. ~ (2) to subscribe to sth., commit oneself to the purchase of sth. or contribution towards sth. (e.g. a charity); since the 18th c., e.g. Goethe 37,85 (W.): '*. . . zeichnete eine ansehnliche Summe Dukaten*'; general in business, esp. stock exchange contexts since the 19th c.

etw. ~ (3) to sign (as sender or as responsible) sth.; beginnings in Early NHG, but general only much later, since Kramer (1702) only records *unterzeichnen* for this sense and in the 18th c. it seems to have been used mainly for documents of importance, where it still survives whereas for ordinary letters *unterzeichnen* is used.

gezeichnet sein to be marked; both in biol. contexts with ref. to coats, feathers etc. of animals or plants and with ref. to people; since the 16th c., e.g. Keisersberg, *Bros.* 2,88: '*es ist ein sprichwort, hüt dich vor denen, die die natur gezeichnet hat*', Goethe 22,194 (W.): '*wohl ist sie recht an Augen und Stirne gezeichnet, daß man sich vor ihr hüten möge*'; cf. also Klopstock, *Mess.* 7,141 or Heinse (edit. Sch.) 4,71: '*vom Stempel der Liebe mächtig gezeichnet*'.

vorgezeichnet (lit.) traced out beforehand, predestined; since the 18th c., mainly with *Weg*, *Laufbahn* or *Entwicklung*, e.g. Wieland, *Luc.* 6,147, Goethe 26,204 (W.): '*auf jenen Weg wieder zurückkehren, den ihm die Natur einmal vorgezeichnet hat*'.

jem. ~ (regional coll.) to scold, reprimand, correct sb. sharply; this goes back to Early NHG *~* (also *zeichen*) = 'to hurt sb. (so as to leave a mark)', still used by Goethe 22,132 (W.): '*man muß euch Männer scharf zeichnen, wenn ihr merken sollt*'; now only in some regions (if not obs.).

← See also under *abzeichnen, auszeichnen, bezeichnen, überzeichnen, unterzeichnen* and *verzeichnen*.

Zeichnung: drawing

die ~ (1) depiction; with ref. to verbal 'drawing' or imaging (from *zeichnen* (1) above); since the 18th c., e.g. Breitinger, *Dichtk.* 1,494: '*Zeichnung der Charakter*', W. Hauff, *Sämtl.W.* 2,373: '*flüchtige Zeichnungen der Sitten*'.

die ~ (2) (act of) signing; from *zeichnen* (3) since the 18th c., e.g. Lessing [edit. M.] 2,239: '*Zeichnung des Friedens*' (where *Unterzeichnung* would now be used). Later in comm. contexts.

die ~ (3) marking; cf. *gezeichnet sein* (under *zeichnen*); since the 18th c., e.g. Goethe 4,320 (W.) about a snake: '*nach der Zeichnung deiner Ringe*'.

← See also under *geben* (for *die Zeichnung gibt eine ungefähre Vorstellung*) and *verzeichnen* (for *Verzeichnung*).

Zeidelbär: see *Bär*.

Zeigefinger

den ~ heben to raise a forefinger; as a sign of warning or admonition since the 18th c. (also with *aufrecken, aufstrecken* or *drohen*); now also as a verb *zeigefingern* (coll.) = 'warn or admonish', 20th c. (not yet listed in *DWb.* [1956]).

← See also under *Rheumatismus* (for *er hat Rheumatismus zwischen Daumen und Zeigefinger*).

zeigen: show

etw. ~ to show, exhibit, reveal sth.; with abstracts (as in Engl.) with *Mut, Lust, Reue*, etc., general since Early NHG, e.g. Luther Bible transl. James 2,18: '*zeige mir deinen glauben mit deinen wercken*', Lavater (in Wackernagel 4,573): '*sie machen die ewige Ordnung zur willkürlichsten Taschenspielerin, die immer etwas Anderes zeigt*', Goethe, *Egmont* 2: '*du zeigst einen guten Geschmack*', Raabe, *Leute a.d.W.* 121: '*die Frau . . . zeigte Charakter*', Th.Mann, *Faustus* 242: '*wir Künstler zeigen auch das Sein*'. Objects can form the subject of the phrase, e.g. *die Münzen zeigen die Daten seiner Regierungszeit* or abstracts can be the subject, e.g. *seine Antworten ~ seine Unwissenheit*. Cf. the prov.expr. *hier zeige, was du kannst* = 'now show what you are capable of, *hic Rhodus, hic salta*' (see p. 2433).

sich ~ (1) to step forward (or before the public), make a public appearance; general since the 18th c., e.g. Lessing 4,307; '*er hat sich der Welt als ein Kunstrichter gezeigt*', Goethe, *Herm.u.Dor.* (Kall. 308): '*sich unter Leuten zu zeigen*'; also with the notion of showing one's capabilities, prove oneself and pejor. in *das Kind will sich* ~ = 'the child wants to show off'; cf. also *mit ihm kann man sich* ~ = 'one need not be afraid or ashamed of being seen in his company'.

sich ~ (2) to behave or appear in a certain way, frame of mind or attitude, show oneself (angry, amused, friendly, etc.); general since the 17th c., e.g. Abr. a Sta. Clara, *Wien* 144: '*zeigen sich . . . feindlich*', Goethe 7,162 (W.): '*zeigt sich geneigt*'; often now in *sich erkenntlich* ~ = 'to show one's appreciation'.

sich ~ (3) to appear, become discernible; with *es* as the subject at least since the 18th c., recorded by Kramer [1702], but with abstracts as the subject only since the 18th c., e.g. (DWb) Klinger, *Werke* 1,22: '*wie sich die Leidenschaften bey meinen Kindern zeigen*', Goethe 46,26 (W.): '*hier zeigt sich ein merkwürdiger Unterschied*'; cf. the cliché with *Hoffnungsstrahl*.

dem werd' ich was ~ (coll.) I'll show him! used as a threat, but also sometimes as a boast; modern, e.g. J. Seidel, *Lennacker* 464: '*denen wer'n wir's schon zeigen*'.

es wird sich ~, *wer die längsten Beine hat* (prov.) we shall see who gets to the top first (or achieves most); recorded by Wander [1880].

← See also under *anzeigen*, *betreffen* (for *seine Betroffenheit in seinem Gesicht zu zeigen*), *bezeigen*, *Esel* (for *jem.m den Esel zeigen* and *jem.m zeigen*, *wo sein Pferd ein Esel ist*), *Feige* (for *jem.m die Feigen zeigen*), *Feld* (for *seine Talente zu zeigen*), *Ferse* (for *die Fersen zeigen*), *Finger* (for *mit den Fingern auf jem. zeigen*), *Geige* (for *in vierzig Wochen wird sich's zeigen*), *halten* (for *zeigte, daß . . .*), *Harke* (for *jem.m zeigen, was eine Harke ist*), *Herz* (for *sie zeigt viel Herz*), *Leder* (for *wir zeigen, wo uns das Herz sitzt*), *Licht* (for *jem./etw. in einem guten Licht zeigen*), *Loch* (for *jem.m zeigen, wo der Zimmermann ein Loch gelassen hat*), *Mameluck* (for *Mut zeiget auch der Mameluck*), *Rücken* (for *jem.m den Rücken zeigen*), *Schulter* (for *jem.m die kalte Schulter zeigen*), *Teufel* (for *jem.m den Teufel im Glas zeigen*), *Tür* (for *jem.m die Tür zeigen*), *vorweisen* (for *vorzeigen*), *Weg* (for *jem.m den Weg zeigen*) and *Zahn* (for *jem.m die Zähne zeigen*). See also under *Finger* (for *Fingerzeig*).

Zeiger

er ist wie ein ~ *an der Uhr* (prov.expr.) he lets other people direct him, he has no will of his own; used by Luther, recorded since the 17th c., e.g. by Lehman, still listed in Simrock [1846].

← See also under *Uhr* (for *Uhrzeigersinn*, *-bewegung* and *-lauf*).

zeihen

'*wer unter euch kann mich einer Sünde* ~ *?*' who among you can call me sinful? in A.V. John 8,46: 'which of you convinceth me of sin?'; although ~ is little used now, this quotation is still alive; *bezichtigen* is now the preferred verb; the synonymous compound *bezeihen*, still used by Lessing in *Nathan* 3,7, is obs.

← See also under *verzeihen*.

Zeile: line

ein paar Zeilen (*schreiben*) (to write) a short letter or note, just a few lines; general since the 18th c., e.g. Gellert, *Zärtl.Schw.* 1,1.

zwischen den Zeilen lesen to read between the lines; international, e.g. French *lire entre les lignes*, Ital. *leggere fra le righe*; in German surprisingly late, not yet listed in Kramer [1702], but general since the 19th c., e.g. Fontane, *Werke* I,2,162.

← See also under *binden* (for *die Zeilen in ein Joch zu binden*), *Glanz* (for *in jede Zeile ein . . . Wort einflechten*), *schinden* (for *Zeilen schinden*) and *Schlag* (for *Schlagzeilen machen*). See also under *Tag* (for *kein Tag ohne Linie*, where *Zeile* can also be used).

Zeisig: siskin

ein lockerer ~ (coll.) a gay spark, easygoing or lighthearted lad; sometimes pejor. when it means a 'fast liver'; since the 18th c., e.g. Körner, *Nachtw.* 4: '*ich war kein lockerer Zeisig*'; Goethe in *Dicht.u.Wahrh.* 9 used '*ein feiner Zeisig*'.

zeisiggrün (a.) green with a yellow tinge; since Early NHG, when some dictionaries defined it as *grüngelb* or *gelbgrün*; still current in the 19th c., used e.g. by E.Th.A. Hoffmann, *Sämtl. Werke* [edit. G.] 14,126.

← See also under *sauber* (for *ihr saubern Zeisige!*).

Zeit: time

die ~ (1) (personified) time; seen as an active agent in scores of phrases, e.g. Goethe, *Prometheus*: '*hat nicht mich zum Manne geschmiedet die allmächtige Zeit*', Schiller, *Sprüche des Konfuzius*: '*dreifach ist der Schritt der Zeit*', Schubart 2,65: '*die geile, hungrige Zeit, immer Kinder gebärend, immer Kinder verschlingend*', Wieland 12,308: '*Geduld! Die Zeit macht alles offenbar*', Heine, *Lut.* 2,198: '*von der Hand der Zeit, die die Stirne so häßlich fältelt*'. For others see among the cross-references below.

die ~ ist . . . time is . . .; there are numerous imaginative or colourful definitions, e.g. Herder, *Ph.* 10,348: '*die Zeit ist ein Gedankenbild nachfolgender in einander verketteter Umstände, sie ist ein Maß der Dinge nach der Folge unsrer Gedanken*', Falk, *Der Mensch u.d.H.* 97 [1798]: '*das erstgeborne Kind der Ewigkeit, die Zeit*', Rückert, *W.* 5,245: '*was ist die Zeit? Ein Fluß der Ding und der Gedanken*'.

die ~ (2) (ling.) time; loan transl. of Lat. *tempus*; in German since the 17th c.

jem.m die ~ bieten (a.) to give sb. the time of day, greet sb.; since MHG and still in the 19th c.; cf. Goethe, *Dicht.u.Wahrh.* 1,4: '*nachdem sie auf freundliche Weise guten Abend geboten*'.

seine ~ ist gekommen (1) (euphem.) his time has come, he is near death; first in relig. contexts and in use since OHG; *die letzte ~* (obs.) was used for 'death', 'time of death'; cf. *aus der ~ in die Ewigkeit abberufen werden* (relig.); *aus der ~* in this sense since Early NHG. On the other hand, *ihre ~ ist gekommen* (euphem.) can also mean 'her confinement is near'; current since Early NHG; cf. Eyering, *Prov.* 1,71: '*hab schon gerechnet auß mein zeit*', also the non-euphem. *locus* in J.Grob, *Dichter.Vers.* 65: '*weil deinem lieb ir bäuchlein wil geschwellen, so hast du hohe zeit, ein hochzeit anzustellen*'.

seine ~ ist gekommen (2) (lit.) now is the time that he achieves recognition, gets his chance, comes into his own; general since early in the 19th c.

er hat die längste ~ gedient (coll.) he was given up work; also 'he has been dismissed'; *die längste ~* (coll.) indicates the end of a certain period in varying contexts, e.g. *er ist dort die längste ~ gewesen* (coll.) = 'he is no longer there', 'he wants to be there no longer' and 'he must leave there'; recorded since the 19th c. In ordinary use it can, of course, also mean 'he was there longest'.

~ nehmen (sport) to be counted out (in boxing); 20th c. jargon; hence also *über die ~ kommen* = 'to go the distance'.

auf ~ spielen (sport) to play for time, delay the game so as to gain an advantage'; 20th c. jargon.

alles hat seine ~ (bibl.) to everything there is a season; both bibl. from Ecclesiastes 3,1: '*omnia tempus habent*' and from Classical sources, e.g. Virgil: '*omnia fert aetas*'; cf. Engl. prov. 'there is a time for all things', also 'timely blossom, timely ripe'; recorded as prov. in German by Agricola [1528]: '*ein ygklich ding hat sein zeyt*'.

alles zu seiner ~ (prov.expr.) all in good time; close to the previous entry; since Early NHG when Franck [1541] listed '*alles mit der zeit*'.

die alte ~ war immer besser (prov.) things were always better in the past; since Classical times, e.g. Diogenes: '*semper superioris anni proventus melior*', Horace: '*laudator temporis acti se puero*'; since MHG in lit., e.g. *Wigalois* 262: '*diu zît hât sich verwandelt gar: ie lange lenger boesent diu jâr*'; cf. the modern regretful exclamation *das war'n noch Zeiten* and the cliché *die gute alte ~*.

andere Zeiten, andere Weise (Gedanken, Sorgen, Lehre, Lieder, Sitten) (prov.) things change with the times; in many variant forms, some recorded since the 16th c., e.g. Franck [1541]: '*andere zeit, andere freud*', Lehman [1662]: '*ander zeit, ander Gott, ander Jahr, ander Glück*'; cf. Lat. *tempora mutantur, nos et mutamur in illis*; cf. also the contrasting hymn by Paul Gerhardt *alles Ding währt seine ~, Gottes Lieb in Ewigkeit*.

laß dir ~ (*und iß Brot dazu*) (prov.) don't rush things; modern prov. recorded since the 19th c. (Simrock, Körte).

man muß die ~ nehmen, wie sie kommt (prov.) take time, when time is, for time will away; international, e.g. Horace: '*tu quacumque deus tibi fortunaverit horam, grata sume manu, nec dulcia differ in annum*'; in German since MHG, e.g. *Freidank* 114: '*lât iu die zît gevallen wol, sît noch ein boeser komen sol*'. Sometimes *wahrnehmen* takes the place of *nehmen*.

mit der ~ gewöhnt man sich an alles (prov.) in time one gets used to everything; international, e.g. Cicero: '*nullus dolor est quem longinquitas temporis minuat atque molliat*'. Proverbs beginnings with *mit der ~* are very numerous (for a long list see Wander V,543/4); several have been recorded since the 17th c. (Petri, Lehman).

von ~ zu ~ ein Haar, so wird das Haupt kahl (prov.) little by little in course of time everything disappears; recorded since Tunnicius, 81 [1515] in LG wording.

~ gewonnen, alles gewonnen (prov.) he that gains time gains all things; in Engl. since the 17th c. (cf. Oxf. 231), in German only recorded as prov. since the 19th c., e.g. by Körte, used by Fontane, *Werke* 1,5,90.

~ bringt Rosen (prov.) in the course of time joy (or fulfilment) will come; cf. Engl. prov. 'in space comes grace'; since Early NHG, e.g. H.Sachs, *Meisterl.* [edit. G.] 24,208: '*zeit bringt rosen, spricht von Nürnberg Hans Sachs*'; usually with the notion that patience is required, e.g. Suhrmeister 35 [1869]: '*d'Zit bringt Rose, aber z'erst Knöpf*'.

~ und Stroh machen die Mispeln reif (prov.) time and straw make medlars ripe; in Engl. since the 16th c. (cf. Oxf. 658), in German recorded

since Lehman [1642]: '*mit der zeit auffm Stroh werden die Mespeln zeitig*'.

~ *ist Geld* (prov.) time is money; beginnings in Classical lit.; in its present Engl. form since the 18th c., e.g. B. Franklin, *Advice to Young Tradesman* [1793]; taken over by German in the 19th c.

← See also under *ändern* (for *die Zeiten ändern sich*), *anklingen* (for *der Anklang vergangener Zeiten*), *anmessen* (for *etw. der Zeit anmessen*), *Ärmel* (for *niemand hat die Zeit vnd Gelegenheit im Ermel*), *außer* (for *außer der Zeit*), *benagen* (for *vom Zahn der Zeit benagt*), *besetzen* (for *meine Zeit ist besetzt*), *betrügen* (for *die Zeit betrügen*), *blühen* (for *Blütezeit*), *brechen* (for *brechen durch die Zeit*), *bringen* (for *die älte der Zeit viel änderungen mit sich bringt*), *Dieb* (for *er stiehlt unserm Herrgott die Zeit weg*), *drängen* (for *dieser Zeiten drängender Moment* and *die Zeit drängt*), *einnehmen* (for *eine gewisse Zeit einnehmen*), *Eisenbahn* (for *es ist die höchste Zeit/Eisenbahn*), *Engel* (for *des Menschen Engel ist die Zeit*), *entbinden* (for *entbindet in uns die Vorstellung von Zeiten*), *entgegentreten* (for *einer Zeit entgegentreten*), *entrinnen* (for *die Zeit entrinnt*), *entstürmen* (for *die Zeit entstürmt*), *erfüllen* (for *als die Zeit erfüllet war*), *ernten* (for *Erntezeit*), *ersehen* (for *seine Zeit ersehen*), *Flaum* (for *flaumenleichte Zeit der dunkeln Frühe*), *Flügel* (for *die Zeit hat Flügel*), *fordern* (for *zu süßen Sorgen bleibt nun keine Zeit*), *frei* (for *Freizeitsgestalterin* and *-gestaltung*), *Frühling* (for *Frühlingszeit*), *Fuge* (for *die Zeit ist aus den Fugen*), *Furche* (for *die Furche der Zeit*), *Geburt* (for *Geburtshelfer der Zeit*), *gehen* (for *die Zeit, wenn ihre Waaren am besten gehen*), *Geist* (for *was ihr den Geist der Zeiten heißt* and *geistarme Gleichgültigkeit unsere Zeit bewältiget*), *Gelegenheit* (for *man muß der Zeit und Gelegenheit die Hand bieten*), *gerben* (for *mich haben die Zeiten gegerbt*), *gewinnen* (for *Zeit gewinnen*), *Gold* (for *die goldene Zeit*), *Granit* (for *tief in den grauen Granit der Zeit*), *Gras* (for *mit der Zeit findt sich alles* and *wenn die Zeit ihr Gras hätte wachsen lassen*), *grau* (for *lasset uns unsere graue Zeit verlassen*, *vor grauer undenkbarer Zeit* and *in grauender Zeit*), *Grund* (for *wolte sehen zallen ziten, was noch ruhte in der Zeiten Grund* and *Gründerzeit*), *Hals* (for *beizeiten*), *heben* (for *in der neueren Zeit*), *heilen* (for *die Zeit heilt alle Wunden/alles Leid*), *herumbringen* (for *die Zeit herumbringen*), *hoch* (for *hohe Zeit*), *Höhe* (for *auf der Höhe der Zeit*), *Kamm* (for *es kommen lausige Zeiten*), *kommen* (for *wer nicht kommt zur rechten Zeit* and *kommt Zeit, kommt Rat*), *Kreis* (for *ausgefüllt der Kreis der Zeit*), *kurz* (for *die Zeit lehrt mich kurz sein*, *Wartezeit* and *die Zeit kürzen*), *laufen* (for *die Zeit läuft*), *Leder* (for *wie war die Zeit so ledern*), *lehren* (for *die Zeit wird es lehren*), *lieben* (for *du liebe Zeit*), *mager* (for *magere Zeiten*), *mähen* (for *der Zeit verheerende Sichel*), *nehmen* (for *sich Zeit nehmen*), *Olim* (for *zu Olims Zeiten*), *Patina* (for *Zeit, die durch ihre Patina mitmalt*), *Pilger* (for *Tod den Arm bietet über den Graben der Zeit* and *Pilgerzeit*), *Rad* (for *das Rad der Zeit*), *Rat* (for *kommt Zeit, so kommt Rat* and *kommt Zeit und Stunde, so kommt auch Rath*), *rauben* (for *ein Raub der Zeit*, *die Zeit raubet alles*), *reif* (for *die Zeit ist reif*), *Rose* (for *Rosenzeit*), *Sand* (for *goldne Zeit*), *sausen* (for *am sausenden Webstuhl der Zeit*), *schicken* (for *sich in die Zeit schicken*, *schinden* (for *Zeit schinden*), *Sorge* (for *Sorge macht alt vor der Zeit*), *sparen* (for *spare in der Zeit*), *Spiel* (for *das Stück spielt in der Zeit, als . . .* and *die Zeit verspielen* in two senses), *stehen* (for *um diese Zeit sind die Frauen in ihren stehenden Jahren*), *Stein* (for *Steinzeit*), *Strom* (for *der Strom der Zeit* and *fortströmende Zeit*), *Stunde* (for *zu jeder Zeit*, *zur gleichen Zeit* and *es ist an der Zeit*), *Tag*(for *der Zeit dienen*), *Tochter* (for *die Wahrheit ist der Zeit Tochter*), *tot*(for *die Zeit totschlagen*), *Trödel* (for *die Zeit vertrödeln*), *Tropfen* (for *mach einen Tropfen Zeit nicht zur Ewigkeit*), *ungelegen* (for *zu ungelegener Zeit*), *Unzeit, vagabundieren* (for *die Zeit vervagabunden*), *verdudeln* (for *die Zeit verdudeln*), *vergehen* (for *die Zeit vergeht*), *verklingen* (for *längst verklungene Zeit* and *Vorzeit*), *versehren* (for *unser Lieben, das die Zeit versehrte*), *verstreichen* (for *die Zeit verstreicht*), *vorlaufen* (for *seiner Zeit vorlaufen*), *vorweisen* (for *in der nächsten Zeit*), *Vorzeit, Webstuhl* (for *Webstuhl der Zeit*), *Wucher* (for *der karge Wucher mit der Zeit*), *Zahl* (for *Ohnezahl, vor dem die Zeit vergeht*), *Zahn* (for *der Zahn der Zeit*) and *Zeichen* (for *Zeichen der Zeit*).

Zeitablauf
der ~ (lit.) lapse of time; only since late in the 19th c., also in legal contexts.

Zeitabschnitt
der ~ period, epoch; since the 2nd half of the 18th c. and at first rejected; for *Abschnitt* see p. 15.

Zeitalter
See under *alt* and *ehern* (for *das eherne Zeitalter*).

Zeitanschauung
die ~ (1) (philos.) concept of time; since the 18th c., used by Herder [edit. S.] 21,60; cf. *Zeitbegriff* below.

die ~ (2) view taken at a certain period; since the 19th c., e.g. *nach unserer* ~ *ist das grausam*; cf. *die Anschauung* (2) on p. 56.

Zeitanspielung

die ~ (lit.) allusion to contemporary conditions; since the 18th c., used by Herder [edit.S.] 18,133; for *Anspielung* see p. 60, where the date should be corrected to 'late 18th c.'.

Zeitaufwand

der ~ expenditure of time; since the 18th c., e.g. Wieland, *Luc.* 5,84. For *Aufwand* see p. 104 (under *aufwenden*).

zeitaufwendig

zeitaufwendig taking up or requiring much time; only since ca. middle of the 20th c., not yet recorded in *DWb.* [1956].

zeitbedingt

zeitbedingt (1) caused by circumstances at the time; since the 18th c., when Goethe used *Zeitbedingung*, though 18th c. examples of the adjective have eluded me.

zeitbedingt (2) seasonal; modern and not yet recorded in *DWb.* [1956].

Zeitbedrängnis

die ~ (1) pressure of time; since the 19th c.

die ~ (2)(lit.) depression suffered through the conditions of the period; more usual would be *Bedrücktheit durch die Zeit*; Heine [edit. E.] 2,487 used it.

Zeitbetrachtung

die ~ (lit) contemplation of time or of the times; f.r.b. Stieler [1691]; in philos. sense used by Schopenhauer [edit. G.] 2,548; he also used *Zeitbewußtsein* (in 5,78) equating it with '*die Zeitideen*'.

zeitbezogen

zeitbezogen (lit.) time-oriented; used both with ref. to past periods and (more often) to the present time, when it means 'topical'; *DWb.* does not list it, though 19th c. *Zeitbeziehung* is recorded. Duden, *Univ. Wb.* [1989] does not list either word.

Zeitbild: see *Bild*.

Zeitbombe

dort tickt eine ~ there a time-bomb is ticking away.

Zeitdruck

unter ~ *stehen* or *sein* to be pressed for time; modern, missing in *DWb.* [1956]; see p. 505 for *im Druck sitzen* or *sein* and *jem. unter Druck setzen*.

Zeitenräuber: see *rauben*.

Zeitenschoß: see *ruhen*.

Zeitempfinden

das ~ sense of time; modern; *Zeitgefühl* and *Zeitsinn* can also be used (see below). ~ is not listed in *DWb.* [1956].

Zeitfrage

die ~ (1) contemporary problem, question occupying people's minds at a particular time; since early in the 19th c.

die ~ (2) question of time; in the phrase *nur eine* ~ it is suggested that sth. is likely to happen eventually, perhaps soon; general since the 19th c.

die ~ (3) a matter (or question) of available time; e.g. *das ist eine* ~ *für mich* = 'I will do this if I can find the time (or fit it in)'; *DWb.* [1956] does not list this 20th c. usage.

Zeitfraß

das ist ein ~ (lit.) that is sth. which takes up a lot of time (devours much time); occasionally in 20th c. lit., e.g. (Sp.) Boree, *Dor u.d. Sept.* 8.

Zeitgeist

See under *link* (for *schroff gegen die linke Seite des Zeitgeistes*), also under *Geist*, p. 962 (for *Geist der Zeiten*).

Zeitgemälde

das ~ (lit.) picture (or depiction) of (a period of) time; the same as *Zeitbild*; only since the 19th c.

Zeitgenosse: see *Rat*.

zeitgenössisch   *zeitgenössisch*   (1)

belonging to the same period, contemporary; since the 19th c., e.g. Zschokke 1,257: '. . . *die Griechen nicht nur die zeitgenössischen Völker, selbst die spätern übertrafen*', S. Zweig, *Balzac* 124: '*zeitgenössische Memoiren*'.

zeitgenössisch (2) contemporary, present-day; 19th c.

Zeitgeschmack

der ~ taste (or fashion) of a period; since the 2nd half of the 18th c., e.g. Schütze, *Hamb. Theat. Gesch.* 709 [1794]: '. . . *von Zeit-, Mode- und Familiengeschmack beherrscht*'.

Zeitgrund

der ~ (lit.) historical background; used by Schiller (though *zeitlicher Hintergrund* would be clearer). He is more explicit in *D. Carlos* 4,9: '*o wer weiß, was in der Zeiten Hintergrunde schlummert*'; cf. Kind, *Ged.* 2,151 [1817]: '*und was noch ruhte in der Zeiten Grund*'.

aus Zeitgründen for reasons of time; 19th c.

zeitig

zeitige Birnen fallen zuletzt in Kot (prov.) ripe pears eventually fall into dirt; recorded since the 17th c. (Henisch [1616] and Lehman [1642]); Wander explains it as a ref. to immoral desires.

← See also under *früh* (for *was eine Nessel werden will, brennt zeitig* and *was früh zeitig wird, fault bald*), *Frühling* (for *ich habe zeitig ausgedient*) and *Zeit* (for *mit der Zeit auffm stroh werden die mespeln zeitig*).

zeitigen

zeitigen to ripen, bring to maturity; since MHG (*zîtigen*) and even then in figur. use, e.g. (DWb) Berhold v. Chiemsee 234: '*die sünd . . . zeytigt im freyen willen*', Goethe 13,1,174 (W.); since the 18th c. mainly in the wider sense 'to produce, bring about, yield', where, however, *hervorrufen* and *hervorbringen* are generally preferred.

Zeitigungsprobe: see *reif*.

zeitlich

See under *kleben* (for *kleben an dem was zeitlich ist*), *schlecken* (for *um eine zeitliche Freud schlecken wir die Finger*), *Segen* (for *das Zeitliche segnen*), *Stein* (for *steinzeitlich*) and *verhaspeln* (for *verhasplet mit zeitlichen sorgen*).

Zeitlupe

in ~ (film) in slow motion; its long history contains several metaphorical transfers, since *Lupe* belongs to Lat. *lupa* = 'she-wolf' and was transferred to describe a circular tumour under the skin. By a further transfer it came to apply in French to 'lense for enlargement'. French *loupe* came into German as *Lupe*, f.r.b. Campe [1801]. In the first half of the 20th c. ~ was coined in the film industry. Hence coll. *im Zeitlupentempo arbeiten* = 'to work at a very slow pace'.

Zeitpunkt: see *bezielen*.

Zeitrad: see *Rad*.

Zeitraffer

der ~ (film) quick motion technique; since the 1st half of the 20th c.; cf. *raffen* (2) on p. 1935.

zeitraubend

zeitraubend time-consuming; modern (not yet recorded by Sanders [1865]); see under *rauben* for *Raub der Zeit* and *Zeitenreuber*.

Zeitraum: see *Raum*.

Zeitschrift

die ~ journal, periodical; introduced to render French *journal* in the last quarter of the 18th c., in lit. since 1784, used by Herder [edit. S.] 16,431 and Goethe III,2,208 (W.), not yet listed by Adelung; hence *Zeitschriftsteller* since the end of the 18th c., listed by Campe, who, however, also recorded *Zeitschriftler* and *Zeitschrifter*, now both obs.

Zeitspanne: see *spannen*.

Zeitspiegel

der ~ (lit.) mirror of (the events or conditions) of time; since the 17th c., e.g. Grabbe [edit.B.] 4,235: '*die Bühne soll der Zeitspiegel sein*'; cf. O. Ludwig 5,53: '*Shakespeare ist der Spiegel, nicht das Spiegelbild seiner Zeit*'.

Zeitstrom

der ~ (lit.) the current of time; since the 17th c., e.g. Goethe 42,2,171 (W.): '*im Zeitstrom mit fortzuschwimmen*'; Luther used *Strom der Zeit* (see p. 2400).

Zeitströmung

der ~ (lit.) current, trend, tendency, development of a period; since the 19th c., e.g. D.Fr.Strauß, *Ges.Schr.* 3,117: '*gegen diese Zeitströmung schwimmen*', Werfel, *Bernadette* 178; cf. *die fortströmende Zeit* on p. 2401.

Zeitstück: see *Stück*.

Zeitung: news; newspaper

die ~ newspaper; first in LG as *tiding* = 'report about an event, (piece of) news'; cf. Luther 34,2,497 (Weimar): '*frölich zeitung sagen*'; as ~ since last quarter of 15th c. for 'newspaper' (first example in Augsburg [1482]), established as a regular publication since 1609 (Straßburg); *zur* ~ *gehen* (coll.) = 'to become a journalist' is a 20th c. phrase, as is *in die* ~ *kommen*, both for 'to have sth. of one's own printed in a newspaper' and 'to be reported on in a newspaper'.

eine lebendige ~ (coll.) a walking newspaper, sb. who always knows (and gossips about) everything that is going on; recorded since the 19th c. for several (mainly SW) areas, in some as *Dorfzittig*; older is *Zeitungsweib* 'gossip', in use since the 18th c.; cf. under *Chronik* (p. 439) for a similar phrase.

Zeitungs- . . . (pejor.) newspaper – . . .; pejor. in *Zeitungsdeutsch* = 'journalese' (19th c.), *Zeitungsfutter* = 'stuff on which newspapers feed (or thrive)', since the 19th c. e.g. Hebbel [edit. W.] 3,6,197, *Zeitungsgeschrei, -geschwätz, - geklatsch, - geträtsch, -gewäsch* = 'newspaper gossip' with ref. to sensationalized reporting, unfounded speculation, trivial chit-chat, etc., some since early in the 19th c., but *Zeitungsschmierer* has been current since the 18th c.

← See also under *betreten* (for *den allgemeinen Fahrweg der Gedanken betrete deine Zeitung nicht*) and *Glas* (for *Zeitungen, als Brenngläser der näheren Zeit*).

Zeitungsente: see *Ente*.

Zeitverbindung: see *geben* (p. 928).

Zeitvertreib

See under *greifen* (for *nach einem Zeitvertreib zu greifen*), *Haut* (for *über meinen bisherigen Zeitvertreib lachten sie . . .*), *Opium* (for *Zeitvertreib sollte der Name eines Opiats sein*), *treiben* and *Xanthippe* (for *Zank war ihr ein Zeitvertreib*).

Zeitvertreiber

See under *kurz* (for *wegkürtzer und zeitvertreiber*), *platt* (for *Scherze platter Zeitvertreiber*) and *treiben* (for *wer mag wohl dein Zeitvertreiber sein*).

Zeitwort

das ~ (ling.) verb; proposed for Lat. *verbum* by Schottel and Gueintz (both in 1641), rejected by Adelung [1786] as *unschicklich* (still condemned in his 2nd edit. of 1801), but accepted by Heynatz [1797] and given wider currency by Jean Paul.

Zeitzeuge

der ~ witness of (and reliable reporter on) a period; only since the 2nd half of the 20th c., not yet listed in *DWb.* [1956].

Zelle: cell

die ~ small community, cell; since MHG (from Lat. *cella*), first for 'small room, compartment, monastic or prison cell'; since the 19th c. used in biological contexts for 'smallest unit in living matter', though R. Hocke was the first to use the term in this sense in 1667, e.g. Auerbach, *Dt. Volkskalender* of 1861, 101: '*diese kleinen Gebilde hat man Zellen genannt*'. Only since the 20th c. applied to '(small group of) people', e.g. *in dieser Partei existiert auch eine anarchistische* ~.

die kleinen grauen Zellen (coll.) the little grey cells, the grey matter (=brain); even if (possibly) in existence before Agatha Christie introduced Hercule Poirot, certainly general in German only since her crime stories became popular in Germany (2nd half of the 20th c.).

die enge ~ (lit.) one's little home (contrasted with the outside world); e.g. Goethe, *Faust I*, 1194: '*ach wenn in unsrer engen Zelle die Lampe freundlich wieder brennt*'; cf. Schiller, *Spaziergang* 7/8: '*entflohn des Zimmers Gefängnis*'.

← See also under *Keim* (for *Keimzelle*).

Zelot

der ~ (lit.) fanatic; originally only used in relig. contexts (after *zelotes* in the *Vulgate*, where Luther used *Eiferer*); in secular contexts since the 16th c., e.g. Mathesius, *Sar.* 155 [1562]; Herder [edit. S.] 9,176 used *Zeloteneifer* and in 9,151 *Zelotengeist* for 'fanaticism'; *zelotisch* = 'intolerant' is still restricted to relig. contexts.

Zelt: tent

das ~ (lit.) canopy, vault; mainly with ref. to the sky from Job 36,29: '*die wolcken auszubreiten wie ein hoch gezelt*', almost literally taken over by Herder [edit. S.] 6,13; Goethe 4,31 (W.) used *blaues* ~ and in *Faust* 5434: '*Zelt des Tages*'; then in the compounds *Himmels-, Sternen-, Wolkenzelt*; cf. also Geibel 3,116: '*kein Lüftchen ging vom blauen Zelt*'.

das grüne ~ (poet.) the green canopy provided by large trees; since the 19th c. Hence also *Blätterzelt*.

sein ~ *aufschlagen* (cl.) to settle, take up one's residence (in a certain place); since the 17th c. in

figur. contexts.

← See also under *abbrechen* (for *die Zelte abbrechen*) and *spannen* (for *Himmel, spann dein blaues Zelt*).

Zement: cement

etw. dient als ~ sth. serves as a binding agent, cements sth. (also abstracts); since the 18th c., e.g. Lichtenberg (in Wackernagel 4,807) on servants: '. . . *sind ein Cäment in der Verbindung von Begebenheiten, das Alles zusammenhält, was sonst nicht halten will*', (S.-B.) Wezel, *Tob. Knaut* 4,243 [1776]: '*eine Flasche Wein, dieses bindende Cäment der Freundschaft*'.

zementieren

etw. ~ (lit.) to make sth. firm and lasting, cement sth.; only since the fifties of the 20th c., frequent now also in the compounds *einzementieren* and *festzementieren*.

Zenit: zenith

im ~ *stehen* (lit.) to be at the highest point (summit, peak) of sth.; 19th c. transfer from astron. language, e.g. *den* ~ (or *Zenitpunkt*) *erreichen*, often in *im* ~ *der Macht, des Glücks, des Lebens* or *Ruhms*, e.g. Heine, *Lut.* 2,117: '*in diesem Augenblick ist der Stern Rothschild im Zenith seines Glanzes*'; Scherr in *Blücher* 5,244 [1865] used *Zenithhöhentage*.

Zenithöhe: see *Höhe*.

Zensur: see *glatt*.

Zentner: hundredweight

der ~ heavy load; in imprecise statements or as hyperbole since the 18th c. in lit., e.g. Schiller, *Räuber* 3,1: '*dieser Zentner muß von meiner Seele*'; hence in compounds, e.g. *Zentnerlast* (in a letter by E. König to Lessing in 1772), *zentnerweise* = 'by or in huge amounts', Huch, *Pitt und Fox* 275: '*mit ihrem zentnerschweren Gewicht*'.

← See also *Quentchen* (for *ein Quentchen Witz zu einer Zentnerfracht erhöhen*).

zentrifugal: see *Gravitation*.

Zephir: see *rund*.

Zepter: sceptre

unter jem.s ~ under sb.'s sovereignty or power; ~ used in wider sense in various contexts since MHG (e.g. Wolfram v. Eschenbach, *Parz.* V,26), mainly for 'power', since Early NHG, e.g. Mentel's Bible transl. Gen. 49,10: '*das zepter wirt nit abgenomen von iuda*' (in the A.V. 'the sceptre shall not depart from Judah') Agricola, *Sprichw.* [1528]: '*das scepter soll augen haben*'; Steinbach [1734] quoted from Hoffmannswaldau: '*den zepter der liebe und des regiments zugleich in ihren händen zu führen*', Haller [edit. Hirzel] 138: '*der Zepter wird so oft . . . verflucht*', also for 'sovereignty', e.g. Schiller, *Tell* 5,1: '*wie verlautet, wird das Scepter gehn aus Habsburgs Haus zu einem andern Stamm*'; *jem.m das ~ entreißen* = 'to deprive sb of his (regal) power', *das ~ niederlegen* = 'to abdicate', even in modern joc. coll. *das ~ schwingen* = 'to show who is boss'. Bürger in his *Ilias* transl. 2,136 used '*die scepterführenden Regierer*' and in 1,392 '*Scepterführer*' for 'ruler'. *Zepterträger* can mean 'ruler' since MHG, but also 'official carrying the sceptre in ceremonies', recorded by Campe.

das Narrenzepter bauble, baton carried by jesters as an emblem of the court jester's licence; it used to be made of reeds; formerly (since MHG) also referred to as *Kolbe des Toren*; in carnival jollifications in Catholic areas *Prinz Karneval führt das Narrenzepter* = 'reigns supreme' occurs even today.

← See also under *führen* (for *den Zepter führen*).

zerarbeiten

jem. ~ (obs.) to criticize sb. severely; cf. Engl. coll. 'to work sb. over'. Lichtenberg still used it in *Briefe* [edit. L.} 1,316; cf. also related *jem. ~* (obs.) = 'to wear sb. down', as in Klinger, *Werke* 1,9: '*Melancholie . . . die mich zerarbeitet*'. A new development (only since the 19th c.) is *zerarbeitet* = 'worn or marked through too much work', e.g. *zerarbeitete Hände*.

sich ~ (rare) to be overworked, suffer through having worked too much; since the 18th c., e.g. Weiße, *Kom. Opern 1,10* [1777]; also with *Kopf*, as in Klinger, *Werke* 11,130; cf. *sich überarbeiten* (p. 2504), which is now the preferred verb.

zerbeißen

eine Antwort ~ to bite back, swallow, repress a reply; connected with *sich die Zunge ~* = 'to bite one's tongue (in an effort not to offend or to reveal sth.); modern, e.g. O. Ludwig, *Ges.Schr.* 2,36: '*. . . zerbiß die Worte zwischen den Zähnen*'.

vom Wetter zerbissen (lit.) weather-worn; modern, e.g. Raabe, *Hungerpastor* 3,196.

zerbersten

vor Lachen ~ (*wollen* or *mögen*) to burst with laughing; hyperbole, current since the 17th c., but the simplex is preferred (see p. 261).

Zerberus

ein wahrer ~ (coll.) a watchful keeper, vigilant watch-dog; a ref. to Cerberus of Classical mythology, the three-headed dog guarding the entrance to the underworld; modern, often jocular.

zerblasen: see *blasen* (also for *Zerblasenheit*).

zerblättern

etw. zerblättert (lit.) sth. disintegrates; figur. since the 19th c., e.g. (DWb) E.M.Arndt [edit. R.-M.] 3,83: '*der Kindheit lustige Blumenwelt zerblättert unter meinen Händen*'.

zerbrechen

etw. zerbricht (lit.) sth. breaks, shatters, disintegrates; with abstracts general since the 19th c., e.g. Hebel 3,334: '*als die Macht der Römer . . . anfing zu zerbrechen*'. The past participle *zerbrochen* can also be used with ref. to persons = 'frail, infirm, weak', e.g. Immermann, M. 3,248: '*ein armer, alter zerbrochener, abgebrauchter Mann*'.

← See also under *brechen* (for *sich den Kopf. das Gehirn zerbrechen*), *Fessel* (for *die Fesseln zerbrechen*), *Glas* (for *die berge zerbrechen alse daz glas* and *mit ihrer zerbrochenen Sopranstimme*) and *Scheibe* (for *es ist eine zerbrochene Scheibe in der Stube*).

zerbrechlich: see *Glas*.

zerbröckeln: see *Brocken* (also for *Zerbröckelung*).

zerdrücken

Tränen ~ to press back one's tears, avoid showing emotion; since the 19th c., e.g. Dahn, *Kampf u.R.* 1,236: '*. . . mit Mühe . . . zwei Thränen des Zornes zerdrückte*', but also in coll. = 'to shed tears' (with implied suggestion that they are false).

zerdrückt (lit.) depressed, cast down; since Early NHG; often = *bedrückt*, but also used for 'shattered', e.g. Droste-Hülshoff, *Ges.Schr.* [edit. Sch.] 1,418: '*verlassen, aber einsam nicht, erschüttert, aber nicht zerdrückt*'.

← See also under *Mus* (for *man wurde fast zu Mus zerdrückt/zerquetscht*).

zerfahren

etw. zerfährt sth. goes to pieces, becomes disordered; in phys. sense since OHG and then figur. in cases where *zerbrechen*, *zergehen*, *zerschellen*, etc. would now be used. In modern period with abstracts in the past participle *zerfahren*, esp. in the writings of *Jungdeutschland*, where it became a fashionable term used with ref. to persons for 'giddy, scatter-brained, distracted' and this was extended to abstracts, e.g. Raabe, *Sämtl.W.* 2,5,179: '*in diesem zerfahrenen Jammerleben*' or ibid. 2,1,39: '*in dieser . . . zerfahrenen, aus Rand und Band gekommenen . . . entgleisten . . . Existenz*', Rosegger, *Gottsucher* 206: '*. . . war so zerfahrenen Gemütes, daß er vergaß . . .*'. Hence *Zerfahrenheit* since the middle of the 19th c., e.g. Raabe, *op.cit.* 2,5,346: '*deine eigene Zerfahrenheit kennst du*'.

Zerfall

der ~ (1) decay, decline; derived from the verb in the 18th c., e.g. Schiller, *Räuber 2,3*.

der ~ (2) (obs.) discord, dissension, dispute; since the 19th c. and still in 19th c. lit. (although left unrecorded in Adelung and Campe), e.g.

Auerbach, *Schr.* 3,167; now obs., but *mit jem.m zerfallen sein* (see below) is still in use.

zerfallen

zerfallen to decay, fall into ruin, disintegrate; since Early NHG, e.g. Schiller, *Wall.Prologue* 70: '*zerfallen sehen wir die alte feste Form*'; also with the notion of death or annihilation in *in nichts ~*, used by Goethe.

etw. zerfällt in zwei Teile sth. is divided into two parts; figur. since the 18th c.

unter mehrere Personen ~ (a.) to be distributed among several persons, be shared by several people; sine Early NHG; Goethe still used in 22,253 (W.): '*wie meine Besitzungen . . . unter sie* [i.e. the children] *zerfallen würden*'; now a.

mit jem.m ~ (*sein*) to be at odds with sb.; since the 17th c.; later in *mit sich selbst und der Welt ~ sein* = 'to be at odds with oneself and the world, to be dissatisfied with life'; hence *Zerfallenheit*, since early in the 19th c.

zerfasern: see *zerfetzen*.

zerfetzen

etw. ~ (lit.) to tear sth. to pieces; figur. since the 18th c., e.g. (DWb) F.A.Wolf (letter to Heyne [1797]): '*zusammenhangendes Raisonnement zerfetzen und zerfasern*'; Herder [edit.S.] 16,250 used it with ref. to words. There is also *jem. ~* = 'to tear sb. (or his writings) to pieces', e.g. Börne 4,30 on a bad writer: '*man soll ihn hinrichten, aber nicht zerfetzen*'.

jem. 's Ohr (or *Nerven*) *~* (lit.) to lacerate sb.'s ears (or nerves); hyperbole; since the 19th c.

zerflattern: see *flattern*.

zerfleischen

sich ~ to tear each other apart; since Early NHG, e.g. Luther 18,330 (Weimar): '*euch selbs unter einander mussen zufleysschen wie die wütigen Bestien*', Treitschke, *Dt.Gesch.* 1,113: '*nach wie vor zerfleischte sich das unselige Volk*'.

zerfließen

zerfließen (lit.) to vanish, perish, dissolve; since Early NHG, e.g. Luther Bible transl. Isaiah 64,1: '*die berg zerfließen vor dem antlutz des herrn*' (where the A.V. has 'flow down'), Hoffmannswaldau, *Ged.* 1,193: '*. . . der krieg . . . läßt das deutsche reich in flammen fast zerfließen*', Keller, *Salander* 197: '*in der zerflossenen Traumwelt*'; also with ref. to the dispersal of people, e.g. Luther Bible transl. 1 Sam. 14,16, where Luther first put '*zurfloß*'', then '*zurann*'' and in his last version '*verlieff sich*' (in A.V. 'melted away').

in Tränen ~ to dissolve in tears; beginnings in the language of the Mystics with ref. to ecstasy, which led to such instances as '*die zevliezent . . .*

in andaht' in Megenberg, *Buch d.N.* 308; later among Pietists with *Wonne, Tränen*, etc.

zerflossen (lit.) over-sensitive, effeminate, vapid; since the 18th c., usually pejor., as in Goethe 47,304 (W.): '*zerflossenes, schlaffes Wesen*', still in lit. in the 20th c., e.g. (Sp.) Wassermann, *Moloch* 227: '*. . . daß er ganz und gar nicht zerflossen war*'.

← See also under *dämmern* (for *des Lebens Dämmerungen zerfließen ihm im Licht*).

zerflittern: see *Flitter*.

zerfressen

zerfressen eroded, corroded, eaten, ravaged; figur. *~* appeared in Early NHG, when Luther used it with ref. to leprosy, also reflexively in 32,491 (Weimar): '*das wir uns . . . zumartern und zufressen mit unsern eigen sorgen*'.

zerfurchen: see *Furche*.

zergehen

zergehen to perish, disappear, melt away; since OHG; Luther used *~* and *vergehen* almost indiscriminately, although in his Bible transl. *vergehen* predominates; it can include the notions of 'dissolving, melting away, disintegrating', but the meanings 'to come to nought, be abolished, die, die out' have become obs.

← See also under *Schnee* (for *zergehen wie Schnee vor der Sonne*).

zergliedern

etw. ~ to dissect sth., take things apart; figur. since the 17th c., chiefly in linguistic and philos. contexts for 'parsing' and 'analysing', but also extended to music and chemistry.

← See also under *schmieren* (for *ein zergliedertes Buch ist doch bildender als ein zusammengeschmiertes*).

zergreifen: see *Griff*.

zerhacken

zerhackt clipped, broken, chopped up, fragmentary; since the 18th c., e.g. *elektronisch zerhackte Music*, but *abgehackt* is preferred in most contexts.

zerkämpfen: see *kämpfen*.

zerkauen

ein Thema ~ to treat a subject in every detail, dissecting a subject; mostly pejor., sometimes = 'to flog sth. to death'; since the 18th c.; recorded by Campe [1811] with a quotation from Herder (no details).

← See also under *kauen*.

zerkeilen

jem. ~ (rare) to thrash sb.; since Early NHG, but *verkeilen* (for which see p. 1457) is now preferred.

zerketzern: see *Ketzer*.

zerklauben

sich den Kopf ~ to worry about sth., strain at understanding sth.; much less used than the idiom with *zerbrechen*; modern, e.g. G. Hauptmann, *Weber* 105 (cf. *klauben* (2) on p. 1478).

zerklemmen

sich zerklemmt fühlen (rare) to feel oppressed, heavy at heart; modern, used by Zelter in a letter to Goethe, but *beklemmt* (which see p. 240) is the usual term.

zerklopfen

jem. ~ (coll.) to beat sb.; since the 18th c., e.g. Tieck, *Octav.* 391.

zerklüften

Menschen ~ (lit.) to cause divisions among people; since the 19th c., e.g. Treitschke, *Dt.Gesch.* 1,56: '*Gegensätze, die das Reich zerklüfteten*', Gutzkow, *R.v. G.*5,73; cf. *eine große Kluft befestigen* on p. 1496.

zerknirschen: see *knirschen* (also for *Zerknirschtheit*).

zerknittern

zerknittert (coll.) crestfallen, remorseful; derived from ~ = 'to crumble, crease', in past participle = 'wrinkled' with ref. to the face; figur. when applied to feeling; 20th c. coll., close to standard *zerknirscht*.

zerlegen

etw. ~ to analyse, strip down, dissect sth.; phys. in many contexts, figur. when used in mathematics, physics and chemistry since the 18th c., Frisch [1741] recorded it for 'to analyse'.

← See also under *Verstand* (for *zerlegender Verstand*).

zerlösen

etw. zerlöst sich (lit.) sth. dissolves; modern, e.g. Huch, *Pitt u. Fox* 214: '*das Gefühl des Neides . . . zerlöste sich*'; *sich auflösen* is the preferred verb (see p. 93).

zermalmen

See under *Decke* (for *brich, Himmelsdecke, und zermalme mich*) and *Fessel* (for *zermalmten die eisernen Fessel der Regel*).

zermartern

See under *Hirn* (for *sich das Hirn zermartern*), *Marter* (for *sich zermartern*) and *zerfressen*.

zermürben: see *mürbe* (and under *reiben* for *Zermürbung*).

zernagen: see *nagen*.

zernichten

etw. ~ (lit.) to annihilate or utterly destroy sth.; figur. since the 18th c., e.g. Lessing, *Freigeist* 2,2, Treitschke, *Dt.Gesch.* 4,242, but *vernichten* is the preferred verb.

zerpflücken: see *pflücken*.

zerplatzen

See under *Neid* (for *vor Neid zerplatzen*) and *platzen* (for *vor Zorn zerplatzen, ungedult wil mir mein hertz im leibe zerplatzen, zerplatzen wie eine Seifenblase* and *zerplatzte Luftblasen*).

zerpressen: see *pressen*.

zerquetschen: see *Mus*.

zerreden

etw. ~ to destroy the attractiveness of sth. (a topic or a piece of writing) by over-elaborate analysis, flog sth. to death; only since the 20th c. and not yet recorded in *DWb.* [1956].

zerreiben: see *reiben*.

zerreißen

zerrissen sein (lit.) to be torn apart, deeply disturbed (mainly through conflicting emotions); since the 17th c. (at first mainly in relig. contexts), e.g. Goethe 11,164 (W.): '*bin ich's? die Zerschlagene, die Zerrissene, die in der bedeutenden Stunde so ruhig, so muthig ist?*', 20,119 (W.): '*Charlotte war innerlich zerrissen*'.

sich lieber ~ *lassen, als . . .* to be rather torn limb from limb than . . .; since Early NHG, recorded by Eyering, *Prov.* 3,77.

jem. am liebsten ~ *mögen* (coll.) to feel like wanting to tear sb. to pieces; modern coll.; sometimes *in der Luft* is inserted.

sich förmlich für jem. ~ to go to no end of trouble for sb.; modern.

sich die Mäuler (or *das Maul*) ~ (coll.) to wag one's tongue; with ref. to calumny, libel, defamation since the 17th c., e.g. Schupp, *Schr.* 406 [1663].

im Kopf zerrissen sein (regional coll.) to be mad; since the 17th c., rcorded by Kramer [1702], still current in Bav.

← See also under *Faden* (for *den Faden zerreißen, des Denkens Faden ist zerrissen* and *unzerrissen*), *Faser* (for *keine Faser seiner Verbindungen zerreißen*), *Herz* (for *herzzerreißend*), *Krause* (for *sich die Krause zerreißen*), *Nerv* (for *nervenzerreißend*), *Netz* (for *das Schuldennetz zerreißen*), *Paß* (for *er hat seinen Paß zerrissen*), *Pelz* (for *ist da der Pelz zerrissen*), *Rechnung* (for *die Rechnung ist zerrissen*), *Sack* (for *zuviel zerreißt den Sack*), *Schuh* (for *etw. schon lange an den Schuhen zerrissen haben*), *Seil* (for *zureißen jre bande*), *Strick* (for *man zerreißt den Strick, wo am dünnsten ist*), *Ukas* (for *zerreißt alle ihre Ukasse in kleine Stücke*) and *zerspleißen*.

Zerreißprobe: see *Probe*.

zerren

jem. ~ (obs.) to annoy, upset or tease sb.; Stieler [1691] recorded it with ref. to dogs, but it

has been current for (human) *reizen, necken* since
Early NHG, e.g. Knigge, *Rom.*, 2,35: '*zerre
keinen mit einer unwahren Nachricht*'; recorded for
many regions since the 19th c.; sometimes used
for 'to plague, pester', as still in Goethe, *W.
Meister* 7, 8. Now obs.

sich mit jem.m ~ (coll.) to quarrel with sb.; this
belongs to Early NHG ~ = 'to fight, resist' and
LG 'to quarrel'; listed for several dialects, in
Heyne [1895] given as generally current, but
omitted in the principal 20th c. dictionaries.

etw. ~ (rare) to contort sth.; since Early NHG,
used by Luther, and Goethe 37,16 (W.) has
'*gräslich zerrt er die Geberden*', where *verzerren*
would now be used.

etw. hin und her ~ to pull sth. about; with
abstracts since the 18th c., e.g. Goethe
IV,27,345 (W.).

an etw. ~ (1) to try to take sth. away; with
abstracts since the 18th c., e.g. Goethe, *Gespr.*
[edit. B.] 5,65: '*sie zerren an meinem Ruhm*'.

an etw. ~ (2) (lit.,rare) to move or pull sth.
fiercely; occasionally with an abstract as the
agent, as in Schiller, *Glocke* 365: '*da zerret an der
Glocken Stränge der Aufruhr*'.

← See also under *verzerren*.

zerrinnen
See under *Finger* (for *etw. zerrinnt jem.m unter
den Fingern*), *Gebild* (for *da zerrinnt . . . der Nebel
des Wahnes*) and *gewinnen* (for *wie gewonnen, so
zerronnen*).

zerrupfen: see *rupfen.*

zerrütten
See under *fallen* (for *Sinn, den Fälle nicht zerrüttet*), *klar* (for *die schönsten verhältnisse so zerrüttet werden*), *Rauch* (for *wenn ihn einer zerrüttet*)
and *rütteln* (for *wenn nicht zerrüttet, doch gewalt-
sam durcheinander gerüttelt*).

zersäbeln: see *Säbel.*

zersägen: see *Säge.*

zerscheitern: see *scheitern.*

zerschellen: see *Schelle.*

zerschlagen
See under *gießen* (for *die Form zu zerschlagen,
worin sie mich goß*), *Panzer* (for *den Panzer zerschlagen*), *Porzellan* (for *unnötig Porzellan zerschlagen*) and *Schlag* (for *etw. zerschlagen, sich
zerschlagen, wie zerschlagen sein*, also for
Zerschlagung).

zerschmelzen
See under *glatt* (for *zerschmeltzen glatterdings*),
Niere (for *mir selbst zerschmolzen die Nieren davon*)
and *schmelzen* (for *sein Hab und Gut ist zerschmolzen, mein hertz ist wie zerschmoltzen wachs*
and *in Tränen zerschmelzen*).

zerschmettern
See under *Sand* (for *zerschmettert ihn wohl gar
an den boden*), *Scheitel* (for *Gestirne, die zer-
schmetternd sich berühren*) and *schmettern* (for *jem.
or den Feind zerschmettern*).

zerschneiden: see *schneiden.*

zersetzen
See under *gären* (for *faule Gärung des sich zer-
setzenden Geistes*) and *setzen* (for *etw. zersetzen*
and *zersetzende Kräfte*).

Zersetzung
See under *greifen* (for *gegenseitige Zersetzung*)
and *setzen* (for *Zersetzung durch gegenwirkende
Mittel*).

zersiedeln
eine Landschaft ~ to spoil a landscape by filling
it with settlements of low density; 2nd half of
20th c. official jargon.

zerspalten: see *Spalt.*

zerspellen
etw. zerspellt das Herz (rare) sth. rends one's
heart; since the 18th c., e.g. Bürger, *Br.Graur.*:
'*vergebner Gram zerspellt das Herz*'; now rare.

zerspleißen
sich ~ (lit., rare) to tear oneself apart; since the
18th c., e.g. Bürger, *Kaiser u. Abt*: '*das Pfäfflein
zerriß und zerspliß sich mit Sinnen*'. Now rare.

zersplittern: see *Splitter.*

zerspringen
See under *Bogen* (for *allzu straff gespannt zerspringt der Bogen*), *Gift* (for *vor Gift zerspringen
mögen*), *Glas* (for *etw. zerspringt wie Glas*) and
springen (for *jem.m zerspringt der Kopf* and *vor
freuden zuspringen*).

zerstäuben: see *Staub.*

zerstieben: see *Wind.*

zerstören
See under *Grund* (for *auf den grundt zerstören*),
stören (for *zerstören* and *Zerstörung*) and *Strudel*
(for *in dem Strudel der Zerstörung*).

zerstoßen
See under *Glas* (for *mit meinem Herrn Vater ein
paar Gläser zu zerstoßen*) and *Kopf* (for *den Kopf
worüber zerstoßen*).

zerstreuen
See under *Fach* (for *die vielen zerstreuten
Erfahrungen*), *Flitter* (for *zerstreue nicht . . . deinen
Geist*), *Glied* (for *in ihren zerstreuten Gliedmaßen*),
herausgehen (for *sich zu zerstreuen wünschte*),
Professor (for *ein zerstreuter Professor*), *Rauch*
(for *die stille That zerstreut der Worte dicken
Rauch*), *sprengen* (for *sich zerstreut machen*),
streuen (for *Menschen zerstreuen, etw. zerstreuen,
jem./sich zerstreuen*) and *Wind* (for *vom Wind zerstreut*).

Zerstreuung

See under *Geist* (for *Gleichgültigkeit unsere Zeit bewältiget durch Zerstreuung*), *Kopf* (for *Zustand der Zerstreuung*), *streuen* and *Stück* (for *vielfache Zerstreuung*).

zerstückeln

See under *Buße* (for *mit einem Lückenbüßer das Zerstückelte scheinbar vereinigen*) and *Stück* (for *zerstückeln* and *Zerstückelung*).

zerstücken: see *Stück*.

zerteilen

See under *Gold* (for *diese Zerteilung nennt man wohl auch den goldenen Schnitt*) and *Teil* (for *ich kann mich nicht zerteilen*).

zertrennen

See under *Faden* (for *den Faden zertrennen*) and *trennen* (for *zertrennen, unzertrennt* and *unzertrennlich*).

zertreten: see *Ton*.

zertrümmern: see *Trumm*.

zerwerfen

etw. ~ (a.) to reject sth.; since the 19th c., e.g. Jean Paul, *Hesp.* and still in Freytag, *Verl.Handschr.* 1,5, but unusual, since *verwerfen* (see p. 2584) has been the preferred verb over a long period.

mit jem.m zerworfen sein to be at odds with sb.; since MHG, e.g. Walther v.d.Vogelweide 106,27: '*des zerwurfen sie sich gar*'.

in sich zerworfen sein (lit.) to be in an inner turmoil; since the 19th c., but Bürger, 35a: '*sie zerwarf sich im Schlummer und träumte, wie schwer!*' indicates a phys. basis for the phrase (see also the following). Hence *die Zerworfenheit*, since the 19th c.

zerworfen (lit.) dispersed, scattered; for 'scattered' as early as in OHG; in many modern cases = *zerstreut* or *auseinander getrieben*; now rare; equally rare, if not obs. is the meaning 'disordered, confused, untidy', as still used by Jean Paul [edit. H.] 6,8.

Zerwürfnis

das ~ (lit.) discord, dissension; f.r.b. Frisius (1556), not listed in Adelung or Campe, though in general use by the 19th c., e.g. Heine, *Lut.* 1,207 or Zschokke 1,269.

Zeter: cry for help, complaint, wailing

~ *schreien* or *rufen* to cry murder, raise a hue and cry; since MHG, at first mainly in legal contexts, but general at least since the 18th c., e.g. Lessing, *Anti-Goeze* 3: '*der du das laute Zeter über sie anstimmst*', Schiller, *Fiesco* 3,5. now often combined with *Mordio* (see p. 1711).

Zetergeschrei: see *Sprache*.

zetern

zetern to wail, lament, scold; in lit. only since the 18th c. (used by Schiller), e.g. Fontane, *Werke* I,1,67: '*er zetert nicht, er verdammt nicht*'; often in *wider* or *gegen etw.* ~, as in Treitschke, *Dt. Gesch.* 5,176: '*er zeterte wider den Kölnischen Kastengeist*'.

Zettel

See under *Beichte* (for *Beichtzettelnase*), *denken* (for *jem.m einen Denkzettel geben*) and *Gift* (for *Giftzettel*).

zetteln

gegen jem. or *mit jem.m* ~ (a.) to take (subversive, hostile) actions against sb.; belongs to MHG *zetten* = 'to distribute, spread'; still in lit. in the 19th c., e.g. C.F.Meyer, *Ang. Borgia* 29; now a. if not obs.

← See also under *anzetteln* and *verzetteln*.

Zeug: material, stuff

ins ~ *gehen* to take measures, put one's back into it; this goes back to mediaeval times when for combat one had to put on *Tournierzeug* or *Rüstzeug*; e.g. Keller, *Werke* 6,199; Goethe 24,168 (W.) used it with *fahren*; also as *sich ins* ~ *legen* (or *werfen*); old in the regions, general in lit. since the 19th c.; hence also *sich für jem. ins* ~ *legen* = ' to stand up for sb., support or defend sb.'.

dummes ~ (stuff and) nonsense; since the 18th c., often in *tolles* ~ (Goethe, Müllner, Tieck, Wieland, *Luc.* 6,407), *unnützes* ~ in Wieland, *Luc.* 5,31, letter to Merck (in *Briefw.* 1,329): '*alles dumme, schiefe und platte Zeug*', *Luc.* 6,198: '*mit diesem unverständlichen, langweiligen, kopfbrechenden Zeuge, das sie ihm vorschwatzt*', Goethe also used *wildes* ~ and *wunderliches* ~, and *das* ~ often for 'worthless piece of writing'; sometimes pejor. *Zeugs* is used, e.g. Klinger, *Leid.W.* 74: '*meinen Sie denn, ich wollte mir den Kopf vollpfropfen mit dem Zeugs?*', Fontane, *Jenny Tr.*: '*da wird immer von alten, einfachen Zeiten geredet; dummes Zeug!*'.

liederliches ~ worthless, dissolute, feckless people; since the 18th c., recorded by Adelung, e.g. Goethe, *Faust I*, 1369–70: '*und dem verdammten Zeug, der Thier- und Menschenbrut, dem ist nun gar Nichts anzuhaben*'.

jem.m etw. am ~ *flicken* to find fault with sb. or sb.'s work; since the 18th c., e.g. Goethe 5,171 (W.).

arbeiten, was das ~ *hält* to work hell for leather, for all that one is worth; originally 'what material or tools can stand (without breaking)'; general since the 19th c., e.g. Keller, *Leute v.Seldw.* 362.

im ~ sein (regional) to be energetic, efficient, competent; in lit. since the 19th c., e.g. Brentano, *Ges.Schr.* 8,261: '*beständig im Zeug und voll Begeisterung*'; hence also regional *wieder im ~ sein* = 'to be fit again' Wander recorded as prov. *er ist von dem rechten Zeuge gemacht* = 'he is made of the right stuff'.

das ~ zu (or *für*) *etw. haben* (coll.) to have the necessary ability, skill, talent for sth., to have got what it takes; since the 19th c., e.g. Keller, *Nachlaß* 136, Heyse 1,164: '*nicht in Eurem Schüler war Zeug zum Philologen*'.

das ~ (euphem.) the genitals; since OHG and still in use in coll.

← See also under *abdreschen* (for *abgedroschenes Zeug*), *falsch* (for *falsche Farben, welche den Zeug zerfressen*), *gehen* (for *Appetit auf wunderliches Zeug*), *Kopf* (for *Zeug schwatzen, das weder Kopf noch Schwanz hat*), *rüsten* (for *Rüstzeug*), *Sau* (for *Sauzeug*), *Spiel* (for *Spielzeug*), *Vierkleeblatt* (for *dummes Zeug*) and *Werkzeug*.

Zeuge: witness

See under *Bein* (for *Gebeine der Heiligen zu Zeugen anrufen*), *entlasten* (for *Entlastungszeuge*), *Gewissen* (for *das Gewissen wacht, dein Zeuge*), *rufen* (for *die thränen ruf ich zeugen an*), *stoßen* (for *Zeugen, die sich an meinem Lebenswandel stoßen*), *stumm* (for *ein stummer Zeuge*), *tot* (for *der tote Zeuge*) and *Wolke* (for *wolcken der zeugen*).

zeugen: beget, engender

etw. zeugt etw. (lit.) sth. engenders, produces, brings about sth.; since the 17th c., sometimes with allusion to the sense 'to beget', as in Kästner, *Verm.Schr.* 1,183: '*o Land, das mich gezeugt*', but more frequently with the extended sense 'to produce', e.g. (DWb) Raupach, *Dram. Werke e.G.* 5,273: '*denn das Bedürfnis zeuget die Gewohnheit und die Gewohnheit zeuget das Gesetz*', where *erzeugen* is now the usual verb (see p. 694).

← See also under *erzeugen* and *überzeugen*, also under *bezeigen* (for wrong use of *bezeugen*).

Zeugnis: statement, testimonial

etw. ist (ein) ~ für etw. anderes (lit.) sth. is a testimony to (or evidence of) sth. else; since Early NHG, e.g. Luther 32,60 (Weimar): '*das es sol sein ein gewisser zeugnis und urkund seiner auferstehung*', Möser, *Ph.* 1,167: '*so lange dieser Name ein redendes Zeugnis bleibt, daß . . .*', Ense, *Humb.* 318: '*ein schönes Zeugnis der dortigen wachsenden Gesittung*'; often meaning 'proof', since Early NHG, e.g. Luther Bible transl. Matth. 26,65: '*was dürffen wir weiter zeugnis?*'; frequently used verbs are *ablegen* (esp. in Goethe's writings) and *reden*, e.g. Lessing, *Nathan* 2,5.

← See also under *arm* (for *sich ein Armutszeugnis ausstellen*), *Haar* (for *Zeugnis geben*) and *klar* (for *klare zeugnuss der schrift*).

Zeus: see *tun*.

Zibebe: raisin

Zibeben- . . . (regional coll.) dealer in raisins; in contemptuous compounds for 'grocer', mainly in Austrian coll., e.g. *Zibebenhengst*, recorded by Schirmer, *Kaufmannsspr.* 214 {1911}; Nestroy, *Ges. Werke* 5,178 used *Zibebenjüngling* for 'grocer's assistant'.

Zicke: nanny goat

die ~ (1) (regional coll. and sl.) woman, girl; esp. as a term of abuse for an unpleasant woman; when applied to girls it can describe a silly girl, elsewhere a prim girl, in some areas a girl with red hair; recorded since the 19th c., e.g. for Alsace and Saxony. Now also used in teenager sl.

die ~ (2) (regional coll.) dishevelled wig; recorded for N. areas since the 19th c.

Zicken

~ machen (coll.) to act irresponsibly or foolishly; derived from *Zickzacksprünge, -wege* or similar compounds (though some scholars have suggested a connexion with the jumps of goats (*Zicken*)); in various contexts, mainly for 'foolish actions, improvident adventures, dangerous experiments', also for 'extramarital escapade' (same as *Seitensprung*, for which see p. 2242); since the 19th c., e.g. G. Hauptmann, *Rose Bernd* 24; predominantly in the plural, but *ne Zicke machen* = 'to make a mistake' has been recorded for Berlin by *D. richt. Berliner* [8th edit.] 195.

Zickenbart

der ~ (regional coll.) goatee; recorded since the 19th c. for Berlin and Brandenburg regions.

Zickzackkurs

der ~ (polit.) frequently changing policy; current since the last decade of the 19th c., when Wilhelm II dismissed Bismarck and changed his own course several times. Outside politics, *~* can, of course, also describe any erratic course followed by sb. or sth.

Ziege: goat

die ~ (vulg.) bitch, hag; contemptuous term for 'woman', esp. an old one, since MHG, e.g. Ottokar, *Öster.Reimchr.* 7382; in the 20th c. revived in teenager sl. (also as *Zicke*).

die Gewitterziege (coll.) shrew; see the previous entry, also *Gewitter* (4) on p. 1040; recorded in modern dictionaries of abusive terms, e.g. by Kapeller.

dürr or *mager wie eine ~* (coll.) as thin as a rake; recorded for several regions since the 19th c.

er meckert wie eine ~ (coll.) he bleats like a goat; recorded since the 18th c., but at first with *Bock*, e.g. Hederich, *Teutsch-lat. Lex.* [1736]; cf. Goethe's notes on *Frankfurter Theater* about Demmer:' '. . . *hat was Meckerndes in der Stimme*'.

die ~ (also *Zicke*) (coll.) the ten in card games; in print since the 19th c., recorded e.g. by Müller-Fraureuth 2,703 [1914].

er hat es in sich wie die ~ *das Fett* (prov. expr.) he is much more astute than he lets you think, there's more to him than one would think judging by appearances; a ref. to the fact that goats though appearing lean have a great deal of fatty substance inside them; recorded for many regions since the 19th c., also as general by Sanders [1865].

die Himmelsziege (coll., obs.) bicycle in bad state of repair; late 19th c. coll., e.g. (T.) J.Lauff, *Pittje P.* 48 [1903]. An entirely different meaning is mentioned by Oken 7,506 [1833–41]: '*die Heerschnepfe fliegt oft hoch in die Luft und meckert wie eine Ziege, heißt daher auch Himmelsziege*'.

die Sündenziege (joc.coll.) female scapegoat; playful variant of *Sündenbock*; current since the 19th c. (Börne); now obs.

die ~ *beim Schwanz haben* (regional coll.) to fail in one's undertaking, to have got nowhere; recorded since the 19th c.; for the quite different *die Ratte am Schwanz fassen* see p. 1948.

die ~ *ist die Kuh des armen* (or *kleinen*) *Mannes* (prov.) the goat is the poor man's cow; also in (or from?) French *la chèvre est la vache du pauvre*; recorded by Wander [1880].

er hat die ~ *in den Garten gelassen* (prov.expr.) he has done something very unwise; current in several (esp. E.) regions; cf. the much more general *den Bock zum Gärtner machen* (p. 364).

man darf nicht verlangen, daß das Böcklein im Hof herumspringe, ehe die ~ *geworfen* (prov.) don't count your chickens before they are hatched; at least since the 18th c., used by Wieland 24,227 in this wording, but there are several variants.

alte Ziegen fressen auch gern Salz (prov.) even old women are not free from lust; at least since the 17th c., recorded by Pistorius [1716].

← See also under *Bock* (for *ein grindiger Bock ist einer goldnen Ziege wert*), *fahl* (for *man hat ihn auf einer fahlen Ziege ertappt*), *grün* (for *wer sich grün macht, den fressen die Ziegen*) and *meckern* (for *Meckerziege*). See also under *Geiß* for related phrases (pp.966/7).

Ziegel: brick, tile

nicht einmal ein ~ (coll.) not even a tiny part (of a building); in several phrases since the 18th c., e.g. Gellert, *Schr.* 3,77 [1774]: '*sie hätte dir*

nicht einen Ziegel von ihrem Rittergut vermacht', Prutz, *Ob.* 2,26: '*von dem Gebäude gehörte ihm, wie man zu sagen pflegt, nicht mehr der Ziegel auf dem Dache*'.

jem.m ist ein ~ *auf den Kopf gefallen* (prov.expr.) sb. has met with unexpected trouble; recorded by Lehman [1662]; G.Keller in *Salander* 71 has it: '*ein Ziegel ist uns auf den Kopf gefallen*' (with ref. to the discovery of secret love affairs of their daughters).

den letzten ~ *auflegen* to complete a piece of work; recorded since the 19th c.

~ *weißwaschen wollen* (prov.expr.) to embark on some fruitless endeavour; since MHG, e.g. *Freidank* 88,15, recorded by Franck, *Spr.* 1,4a [1545] as '*ein ziegel waschen*'. Others have recorded ~ *und Mohren lassen sich schwer weißwaschen*.

rot wie ~, *ziegelrot*, *ziegelfarbig* brick-red; at least since the 18th c., e.g. Gotter 3,139: '. . . *und röthet mein Gesicht gleich einer neuen Ziegel*'.

Ziegel- . . . (comm.) brick-shaped . . .; in compounds used in trade, e.g. *Ziegeltee* for tea remainders pressed into cakes shaped like a brick, recorded by Brehm [edit. L.-P.] 1,533, e.g. (T.) Sven Hedin, *Transhimalaja* 1,160 [1922] and *Ziegelkäse*, recorded by Martiny, *Wb.d.Milchwirtschaft* 7

dort wächst Gras auf den Ziegeln (regional) nobody lives there any more; modern.

der Rotziegel (zool.) the snail *Chiton ruber*; recorded since the 19th c., e.g. by Sanders [1865], but not in *DWb.* [1893].

'*so viele Teufel dort wie* ~ *auf den Dächern*' as many devils there as tiles on the roofs; quotation from Luther 15,214 (Weimar): '*wenn ich gewust hette, das so vil teufel auf mich gezilet hetten, als zigel auf den dechern waren zu Worms, were ich dennoch eyngeritten*', which has become almost prov.

← See also under *Dach* (for *kein Dachhase auf den Ziegeln*) and *Kehle* (for *Kehlziegel*).

Ziegenbart

der ~ (coll.) goatee; since Early NHG, used by Wieland and Goethe, both for the beard and a man with such a beard, but its use for cantankerous, irritable, even wild or coarse persons has disappeared. See also under *Bock* for *Bocksbart* and *Zicke*.

Ziegenfuß: see *Fuß*.

Ziegenpeter: see *Peter*.

Ziegenspeck: see *Speck*.

Ziegenzunge

unter einer ~ *ist nicht viel zu verwahren* (prov., obs.) women cannot be relied upon to keep secrets; *Ziege* here = 'woman'; recorded by Wander [1880].

ziehen: pull, draw

jem. zieht etw. sb. draws or takes sth.; with many abstracts in various contexts, general since the 18th c., e.g. *jem. zieht etw. in Erwägung* = 'sb. takes sth. into consideration', recorded by Adelung. Similarly *Gewinn (aus etw.)* ~ = 'to get or receive a profit from sth.', *eine Lehre (aus etw.)* ~ = 'to learn sth. (from sth.)', used by Hagedorn; *Nutzen (aus etw.)* ~ = 'to derive benefit (from sth.)' is probably the oldest of these phrases; it was recorded by Maaler [1561]; *einen Vorteil (aus etw.)* ~ = 'to gain an advantage (from or through sth.)' was not yet recorded by Adelung, although Günther, *Ged.* 15 [1735] used it. There on p. 696 one also finds: '*so mancher wird noch Trost aus meinen Liedern ziehn!*'. For other phrases falling into this category see the list of cross-references.

jem. zieht jem. am Narrenseil sb. makes a fool of sb.; since the 17th c.; Steinbach [1734] recorded it with a quotation from Günther.

jem. zieht jem. an sich sb. draws sb. unto himself, causes an attachment (friendship, etc.) to arise; from bibl. sources, e.g. Luther Bible transl. John 6,44: '*es sey denn das jn ziehe der Vater, der mich gesand hat*' (cf. an earlier example in *Ezzo* 28,6); frequent in the language of the Mystics, still used in modern period, e.g. Novalis [edit. M.] 4,111. Also used in the wider sense of 'to attract, cause to come', as in Wieland, *Agathon* 2,161 with '*an seinen Hof*', Lessing [edit. M.] 7,4 with '*zu seiner Parthey*'; cf. also Wieland 23,405: '*der Zaubervogel, womit sie ihn an sich gezogen*'.

jem. zieht etw. auf sich sb. incurs sth., causes sth. to come upon him; with such abstracts as *Haß* or *Verachtung*; since the 18th c., used by Goethe.

jem. zieht etw. auf jem. (a.) sb. takes sth. to refer to sb. since Early NHG, used by Luther 11,435 (Weimar), still in Schiller, *Wall. Tod* 4,3: '*wir zogens auf den Türken*', for 'we assumed it to refer to the Turk'; also in *jem. zieht etw. auf sich* = 'sb. takes sth. as aimed at (or referring to) himself', used by Goethe. Now a., displaced by *beziehen*.

jem. (or etw.) zieht die Aufmerksamkeit auf jem. (or *etw.* or *sich*) sb. (or sth.) draws attention to sb. (or sth., himself, itself); modern.

jem. zieht jem. auf seine Seite sb. gains sb. as his supporter, draws sb. over to his side (in a struggle or argument); general since the 18th c., recorded by Adelung, who also listed: '*jem. an sich ziehen, auf seine Parthey ziehen*', but much

earlier Frisius [1556] recorded the related '*einen auf sein meinung ziehen*' for 'to induce sb. to share one's own views'; cf. Steinbach [1734]: '*mit Geschenken einen an sich ziehen*'.

jem. zieht die Konsequenz (earlier *die Folge*) *aus etw.* sb. draws the (necessary) conclusions from sth.; since the 18th c., e.g. Hagedorn, *Poet. W.* 2,28: '*soll ich daraus die Folge ziehn?*'; Goethe 41,1,341 (W.) used *Folgerungen*; with *Konsequenz* since the 19th c.; cf. also Raabe, *Hungerpastor* 3,24: '*. . . und das Facit zog, daß . . .*'.

jem. zieht etw. aus einer Quelle (*einem Buch, einer Rede*, etc.) sb. derives sth. from some source (by way of appropriating, excerpting, quoting, etc.); since LateMHG, e.g. Tauler, *Serm. registr.* 2d [1528]: '*die . . . predigen . . . sind gezogen auß sant Marcus ewangelio*'.

jem. zieht jem. aus einer Gefahr (*einer Not, einem Zweifel*) sb. pulls sb. out of danger, frees sb. from distress or doubt; since the 18th c. with many abstracts; not yet in Kramer [1702], although he listed similar phrases with *herausziehen*; now often coll. with *aus der Klemme* or *Patsche*.

jem. zieht jem. in etw. sb. drags sb. into sth., involves sb. in sth.; f.r.b. Steinbach [1734]: '*einen in eben das Unglück ziehen*'; now usually with *hineinziehen* (used by Schiller); cf. *jem. ins Vertrauen* ~ = 'to take sb. into one's confidence' (Adelung recorded this with *Geheimnis*: '*sie haben mich mit in ihr Geheimniß gezogen, haben es mir anvertrauet*').

jem. zieht etw. in etw. (anderes) sb. gives to sth. a turn, twist towards sth. else; since the 18th c. with abstracts, e.g. *eine Anschauung ins Lächerliche ziehen*; cf. Wieland 35,337: '*Begebenheiten, die so leicht in Mißbrauch gezogen werden konnten*'.

jem. zieht ein Kind (a.) sb. brings up a child; since OHG, frequent since MHG, e.g. Wolfram v.E., *Parz.* 141,13: '*dô zôch mich mîn muoter*', recorded by Alberus, *N.Dict. gen.* [1540]: '*du zeugst in nit, verzeugst in*'; Steinbach [1734] quoted: '*wie man die Kinder zieht, so hat man sie*'; later *aufziehen* and *erziehen* came to be preferred, but with ref. to animals (recorded e.g. by Kramer) ~ is still used.

jem. zieht jem. mit etw. in Verdacht sb. throws suspicion on sb. over sth.; since the 18th c., recorded by Adelung.

jem. zieht jem. vor Gericht sb. takes sb. to court, brings an action against sb.; first with *bringen* or *fodern*, since the 17th c. with ~, e.g. Rabener, *Sat.* 4,233 [1751], recorded by Kramer [1702].

jem. zieht Scham auf jem.s Wangen (lit.) sb. causes sb. to blush with shame; since the 18th c., e.g. Klinger, *Werke* 2,333: '*so würd ich die Schaam auf eure Wangen ziehen*'.

jem. zieht einen Flunsch (coll.) sb. looks disgruntled, angry; modern coll.

jem. zieht jem.m eine (coll.) sb. hits sb., boxes sb.'s ears; since the 18th c., but now only in some regions.

jem. läßt einen ~ (vulgar) sb. breaks wind; as wide-spread as synonymous phrases with *fahren* and *streichen*, probably older than the dictionaries suggest.

etw. zieht jem. sth. pulls, drags, attracts, moves sb.: frequent since MHG in phrases too numerous to list, esp. with prepositions, e.g. *etw. zieht jem. in etw.* or *zu etw.*; see also the list of cross-references.

etw. zieht sth. sells well, is popular, finds approval; since the 18th c., first in comm. contexts; e.g. Goethe, *Gespr.* [edit. B.] 5,165: '*eine gute Oper . . . soll man . . . so lange . . . geben, als sie irgend zieht und irgend das Haus füllt*'.

etw. zieht etw. (anderes) nach sich sth. leads to (or brings about) sth. else; since the 17th c., recorded by Kramer [1702], e.g. Gutzkow, *R.v.G.* 7,187: '*in Dingen, die eine so große Lebensänderung würden nach sich gezogen haben*'.

die Sonne zieht Wasser there will be rain; recorded by Tappius [1545]; also in joc. coll. as a remark about a child that is near to tears, since the 19th c., recorded by Hetzel [1896].

ihre Strümpfe ~ Wassser (coll.) her stockings have slipped down her calves; modern coll.

etw. zieht sich durch die ganze Geschichte sth. runs through the entire story (like a thread), sth. is present throughout (e.g. as an idea or a motif); modern; also used with *laufen* (for which see p. 1590).

etw. zieht ins Land sth. passes or elapses; with ref. to time, e.g. *manches Jahr ist seither ins Land gezogen* = 'many a year has passed since then'; first with *gehen* (see p. 1580), later with ~.

etw. zieht eine Wolke über etw. (lit.) sth. clouds sth., casts a gloom over sth.; in Early NHG *eine Wolke vor die Sonne ~* was used; later also without mentioning of *Sonne*, e.g. Goethe IV,10,281 (W.) on the darkening of a joyful hour: '*. . . hätte nur nicht . . . die Nachricht von Schillers Übel . . . eine Wolke davor gezogen*'.

etw. zieht jem. empor (lit.) sth. raises sb. (or sb.'s spirits), lifts sb. up; since the 18th c., e.g. Wieland 5,15: '*meine Seele schien davon wie aus ihrem Leibe emporgezogen*'.

etw. in sich ~ (lit.) to imbibe, inhale, absorb sth.; modern, e.g. Platen 4,256: '*ich . . . zog den Ton in mich in vollen Zügen*'; cf. also Wieland

11,163: '*mit jedem Blick sie ganz in sich hineinzuziehen*'.

etw. ins Enge, Kleine, Kurze ~ (a.) to reduce, abbreviate, condense sth.; since the 16th c., recorded by Steinbach [1734], still used by Goethe (with *Enge*) and by Bürger (with *Kurze*); in the past also used in ling. contexts. Now *zusammenziehen* and *(ver)kürzen* are used instead.

etw. zieht sich (in etw.) hinein sth. permeates or enters sth.; with abstracts such as *Geruch* or *Geschmack* since the 18th c.; *reinziehen* occurs in more coll. usage.

sich aus etw. ~ to extricate oneself from sth., withdraw from sth.; modern, often with *Affaire* or *Sache*.

die Börse ~ to pay, fork out money; since MHG, e.g. Osw.v. Wolkenstein [edit. Sch.] 60,23: '*nu ziecht die riem, gesellen*', in Early NHG with *Seckel* (Fischart), much later with *Beutel*, *Börse* or *Portemonnaie* (see e.g. under *Beutel*); Goethe 43,295 (W.) used it with *Börse*.

einen Ton ~ (mus.) to prolong a note; since Early NHG, Kramer [1702] recorded '*die Stimme im Singen ziehen*'; also used with the notion of raising or dropping the voice: *die Stimme über sich* or *unter sich ~*. Goethe 45,12 (W.) used '*der . . . seine Sylben zieht*'.

in die Stadt ~ to move into town; since the 18th c.; Kramer recorded it and *ausziehen* and *einziehen* (but not yet *umziehen*). Steinbach [1734] listed '*aus dem neuen Hause in das alte zurückeziehen*', but *er ist verzogen* = 'he lives no longer at this address' is modern.

mitziehen to join in a campaign, an expedition, trip, etc.; f.r.b. Stieler [1691], e.g. Voß, *Il.* 9,352: '*da ich im Danaervolke noch mitzog*' (as a warrior).

Dinge in einen Wettstreit ~ to make things compete with each other; since the 18th c., e.g. Lessing 6,501: '*nie sind Malerei und Poesie in einen gleichen Wettstreit gezogen worden*'.

ein Schmerz zieht jem. a pain hurts or troubles sb., is felt by sb.; since the 17th c.; Kramer [1702] recorded '*es zeucht mich der Krampf*', e.g. Goethe IV,5,42 (W.): '*gestern Abend kriegte ich noch Ziehen im Kopf*'.

der Tee (Kaffee) muß ~ the tea (coffee) must draw; derives from *etw. ausziehen, herausziehen* or *in sich hineinziehen* with ref. to the essence or aroma; modern.

← See also under *abziehen*, Adam (for *den alten Adam ausziehen*), *anziehen*, *aufziehen*, Auge (for *alle Augen auf sich ziehen*), *ausziehen*, Bank (for *sich in die Länge ziehen*), *betrachten* (for *in Betracht ziehen*), Beutel (for *er zieht nicht gern den*

jem.m	jemandem (dat.)
Kluge	F. Kluge, *Etymologisches Wörterbuch der deutschen Sprache*, 11th ed., Berlin und Leipzig 1934.
Lehman	C. Lehman, *Florilegium Politicum*, etc., Frankfurt 1640.
Lexer	M. Lexer, *Mittelhochdeutsches Handwörterbuch*, Leipzig 1872—8.
LG	Low German
Lipperheide	F. Freih. v. Lipperheide, *Spruchwörterbuch*, 2nd ed., München 1909.
MHG	Middle High German
mil.	military
M. Latin	medieval Latin
N.	Northern Germany
NED	*Oxford English Dictionary, A New English Dictionary on Historical Principles*, Edited by Sir James Murray, Henry Bradley, W. A. Craigie and C. T. Onions. Oxford 1884—1928.
NHG	New High German
NW	North-Western Germany
obs.	obsolete
OE	Old English
offic.	in civil service language
OHG	Old High German
ON	Old Norse
OS	Old Saxon
Oxf.	*The Oxford Dictionary of English Proverbs*, compiled by W. G. Smith, Oxford, 1935.
p.	page
poet.	used mainly in poetic language
pop.	popular
pop. etym.	popular etymology
prov.	proverb, proverbial
sb.	somebody
Schmeller	J. A. Schmeller, *Bayerisches Wörterbuch*, Stuttgart 1827—37.
Schulz-Basler	G. Schulz und O. Basler, *Deutsches Fremdwörterbuch*, Strassburg und Berlin 1913ff.
s.e.	self-explanatory
sl.	slang
S. Singer	S. Singer, *Sprichwörter des Mittelalters*, Bern 1944—7.
sth.	something
SW.	South-Western Germany
Trübner	*Trübners Deutsches Wörterbuch*, herausg. v. A. Götze, Berlin 1939ff.
v.	verse, verses
vulg.	in vulgar use (obscene terms are included under this heading, but specially marked as such)
Waag	A. Waag, *Die Bedeutungsentwicklung unseres Wortschatzes*, 5th ed., Lahr 1926.
Wb.	Wörterbuch
Weigand	F. L. K. Weigand, *Deutsches Wörterbuch*, 5th ed., Gießen 1909—10.
Weist.	Weistümer; usually the collection by J. Grimm, Göttingen 1840—69 is referred to; Österr, is appended to the Austrian collections.
Westph.	Westphalia, Westphalian
zool.	zoological term.

Where later editions than those cited above have been quoted (especially in the cases of Büchmann, Dornseiff and Kluge), details of the editions used are given in the text.

The abbreviations for journals mostly follow the accepted practice (*MLR for Modern Language Review, MLN for Modern Language Notes, IF for Indogermanische Forschungen*, etc.), only some long titles have been still further abbreviated though still left recognizable (e.g. *Z.f.d.W.* for *Zeitschrift für deutsche Wortforschung, Z.f.d.U.* for *Zeitschrift für den deutschen Unterricht, Z.f.r.P.* for *Zeitschrift für romanische Philologie*, etc.). Other works, referred to or quoted have been mentioned in abbreviated but recognizable form. It is intended to give a comprehensive list of them when the dictionary is completed. From Fasc. 9 Goethe (W.) = Weimar edition, Schiller (S.) = Säkularausgabe.

ISBN 0-631-20432-6

An Historical Dictionary of German Figurative Usage

By KEITH SPALDING

PROFESSOR EMERITUS OF GERMAN, UNIVERSITY OF WALES, BANGOR

WITH ASSISTANCE FROM
GERHARD MÜLLER-SCHWEFE

PROFESSOR EMERITUS OF ENGLISH, UNIVERSITY OF TÜBINGEN

Fascicle 58

Ziel – Zylinder

University of Memphis Libraries

KEY TO PRINCIPAL ABBREVIATIONS

a.	archaic
Adolphi	O. Adolphi, *Das große Buch der Fliegenden Worte, etc.*, Berlin n.d.
Ahd. Gl.	*Die Althochdeutschen Glossen*, ges. und bearb. von E. Steinmeyer u. Eduard Sievers, Berlin 1879–98.
Bav.	Bavaria, Bavarian
bot.	botanical term
Büchmann	G. Büchmann, *Geflügelte Worte*, 27th ed., ergänzt von A. Langen, Berlin 1915.
c.	century
Car.	Carinthia, Carinthian
cf.	compare
cl.	cliché
Cod.	codex
coll.	in colloquial use
comm.	used in language of commerce
dial.	dialect expression
Dornseiff	F. Dornseiff, *Der deutsche Wortschatz nach Sachgruppen*, Berlin und Leipzig 1934.
dt.	deutsch
DWb	*Deutsches Wörterbuch von Jacob Grimm und Wilhelm Grimm*, Leipzig 1854ff.
e.l.	earliest locus or earliest loci
etw.	etwas
Fast. Sp.	Fastnachtspiele, usually quoted after *Fastnachtspiele aus dem 15. Jahrbundert*, herausgeg. v. Keller, Stuttgart 1853.
Fick	F. C. A. Fick, *Vergleichendes Wörterbuch der indogermanischen Sprachen*, 3rd ed. Göttingen 1874.
f.r.b.	first recorded by
gen.	general
Götze	A. Götze, *Frühneuhochdeutsches Glossar*, 2nd ed., Bonn 1920.
Graff	E. G. Graff, *Althochdeutscher Sprachschatz*, Berlin 1834–42.
Hirt, *Etym.*	H. Hirt, *Etymologie der neuhochdeutschen Sprache*, 2nd ed., München 1925.
Hirt, *Gesch.*	H. Hirt, *Geschichte der deutschen Sprache*, 2nd ed., München 1925.
hunt.	word or expression used by huntsmen
jem.	jemand (nom. or acc.)

© *Blackwell Publishers Ltd., 1997 ISBN 0 631 207910*

Typeset by Hope Services, Abingdon
Printed and bound by Whitstable Litho Ltd., Whitstable, Kent

Beutel), *beziehen*, *Bilanz* (for *die Bilanz ziehen*), *blasen* (for *ihm ein federn ziehen lassen*), *Draht* (for *jem. am Draht ziehen*, also for *Drahtzieher* and *Drahtzieherei*), *dringen* (for *zusammenziehen*), *einlegen* (for *zog mir Erkältungen zu*), *einziehen*, *erziehen*, *Esel* (for *zieht ein Esel übern Rhein*), *Feld* (for *zu Feld ziehen*), *Fell* (for *jem.m das Fell über die Ohren ziehen*), *Flasche* (for *das darf man nicht auf Flaschen ziehen*), *fühlen* (for *seine Fühler einziehen*)

Fuß (for *jem.m den Boden unter den Füßen wegziehen*), *Gabel* (for *jem. in die Gabel ziehen*), *Gehäuse* (for *sich zurückziehen*), *gehen* (for *ein blinder Appetit auf . . . tumme Speisen zieht* and *stille Flöte! Deine Gänge ziehn die Herzen*), *Geist* (for *sie ziehen uns an*), *Geiß* (for *nur so viel wie eine Geiß wegziehen kann*), *Geschmeide* (for *Furchen ziehen*), *Gesicht* (for *ein Gesicht ziehen*), *Glas* (for *weil ich in krieg will ziehn*), *Glatze* (for *zieh ab, Glatzkopf!*), *Glück* (for *die Lotterielose für sie zu ziehen*), *Gummi* (for *etw. zieht sich in die Länge wie Gummi*), *Haar* (for *etw. zieht mich an den Haaren, jem. bei den Haaren zu etw. ziehen* and *etw. an den Haaren herbeiziehen*), *halb* (for *dreimal umgezogen ist halb abgebrannt*), *Halm* (for *jem.m den Halm durchs Maul ziehen* and *das Hälmchen ziehen*), *Hammel* (for *jem.m die Hammelbeine langziehen*), *Haut* (for *jem.m die Haut über die Ohren ziehen*), *Hechel* (for *jem. durch die Hechel ziehen*), *Hecht* (for *es zieht wie Hechtsuppe*), *Heim* (for *heimziehen*), *herabziehen*, *heranziehen*, *herbeiziehen*, *herunterziehen*, *hinterziehen*, *hinunterziehen*, *Hut* (for *vor jem.m den Hut ziehen*), *Joch* (for *wir ziehen im gleichen Joch*), *Kakao* (for *jem. durch den Kakao ziehen*), *Karren* (for *den Karren aus dem Dreck ziehen*), *Kasten* (for *verzogener Name*), *Konto* (for *er hat sein Konto überzogen*), *Korkenzieher* (for *Korkenzieherlocke*), *Kreis* (for *durch Deutschlands Kreise zogst, zieh deinen Kreis* and *etw. zieht weite Kreise*), *Kruste* (for *zieht eine Steinkruste über unser Herz*), *kurz* (for *den kürzern ziehen*), *lang* (for *mit langer Nase abziehen*), *Länge* (for *etw./sich in die Länge ziehen*), *Leder* (for *vom Leder ziehen*), *leer* (for *jem. leer abziehen lassen*), *Leine* (for *Leine ziehen* and *an einer Leine ziehen*), *Licht* (for *das Licht hochziehen*), *Linie* (for *eine klare Linie ziehen*), *los* (for *auf jem. losziehen*), *Magnet* (for *etw. zieht etw. an wie ein Magnet*), *matt* (for *mattwarm zog die Luft*), *Maul* (for *ein Maul ziehen*), *Mensch* (for *ich ließ sie ein menschlich Joch ziehen* and *zieh dich etw. menschlicher an*), *Mitternacht* (for *die Mitternacht zog näher schon*), *nachkriechen* (for *das der tod nit verzeucht*), *nachziehen* (also for *Nachzügler*), *Nase* (for *jem. an der Nase herumziehen, jem. an der Nase ziehen,*

jem.m die Würmer aus der Nase ziehen and *jem.m eine Feder durch die Nase ziehen*), *Natur* (for *zieht das Herz des Weltmanns zusammen*), *Niete* (for *eine Niete ziehen*), *privat* (for *sich ins Privatleben zurückziehen*), *Rat* (for *jem. zu Rate ziehen*), *Register* (for *alle Register ziehen*), *Reif* (for *bevor dieß Haupthaar der Reif umzieht*), *Riegel* (for *manche Hemmriegel weggezogen*), *Ring* (for *jem.m einen Ring durch die Nase ziehen*), *Scheide* (for *eine Scheidewand ziehen*), *Scheitel* (for *er kann sich den Scheitel mit dem Schwamm ziehen*), *Schleuse* (for *so zieht ihr eure Schleusen auf*), *Schlinge* (for *den Kopf aus der Schlinge ziehen*), *Schluß* (for *Schlüsse aus etw. ziehen*), *Schlüssel* (for *daß sie die Schlüssel ihres Herzens abgezogen*), *Schnute* (for *eine Schnute ziehen*), *Schoß* (for *die verzogenen Schoßkinder*), *Schulter* (for *die Schultern ziehen*), *Schwanz* (for *den Schwanz einziehen*), *Schwert* (for *ein Flammenschwert sieht sie den Todesengel ziehn*), *Spur* (for *etw. zieht seine Spur*), *Stiefel* (for *den Stiefel ziehe ich mir nicht an*), *Strang* (for *seinen Strang ziehen*), *Strich* (for *einen Strich unter etw. ziehen*), *Summe* (for *die Summe ziehen*), *Tau* (for *das Tauziehen*), *Tisch* (for *jem. über den Tisch ziehen*), *Traum* (for *ein süßer Traum umzieht sein Haupt*), *überziehen*, *um* (for *um den Mund zieht sich ein Verlangen* and *so zog ich Kreis um Kreise*), *ungezogen*, *Uniform* (for *die Uniform anziehen/ausziehen*), *Untergang* (for *mahnend zieht die Nacht den Mantel vor des Unterganges Thore*), *unterziehen*, *Verkehr* (for *jem. aus dem Verkehr ziehen*), *verziehen*, *Vetter* (for *die Vetternstraße ziehen*), *wegziehen*, *Weiblichkeit* (for *zogst auch mit ihm von hier*), *Wettereck* (for *es sich . . . zusammenzieht*), *Wurzel* (for *die Wurzel ziehen*), *Zahn* (for *laß dir diesen Zahn ausziehen* and *jem.m etw. aus den Zähnen ziehen*), and *zeitbezogen*.

Ziel: limit, aim, target

das ~ limit, boundary, border; since MHG, esp. in the phrase *jem.m ein* ~ *machen* (now obs.) = 'to fix or set a limit (which sb. must not overstep)', e.g. Rudolf v. Ems, *Weltchron.* 11,535; with *stecken* frequent since Early NHG, e.g. Franck, *Spr.* 1,74b [1545], f.r.b. Frisius [1556], still occasionally in recent times, e.g. (DWb) Weinheber, *Späte Krone* 29 [1936]: '*gesetzt ist hier dem Weg ein Ziel*'; f.r.b. Maaler [1561]: '*das zil und end eins jeden dings = terminus*'; hence the phrase *er kennt kein* ~ = 'he recognizes no limitations', as in Cronegk, *Schr.* 2,104 [1760]. Often ~ comes close to 'end, conclusion' and has been used in this sense since MHG.

jem. wird das ~ (*von Angriffen*) sb. becomes the target (of attacks); since Early NHG, when Luther 18,384 (Weimar) wrote about himself:

'der Luther ist das mal und zill des widersprechens'; cf. Stifter, *Sämtl. W.* 3,191: 'er war . . . das Ziel von manchen schönen Augen'. See also p. 2310 for *Zielscheibe des Spottes sein*.

ihr ~ ist gekommen (obs.) the time of her confinement has arrived; still used by Wieland in (Sa.) *Werke* 20,229, now obs.

sich zum Ziele legen (a.) to accommodate sb., make things easier for sb.; recorded by Körte, *Spr.* [1837], used by Bismarck, *Briefe* (letter to Gerlach) 174, now a.

← See also under *aufstecken* (for *ein Ziel aufstecken*), ausstecken (for *ein Ziel ausstecken*), blau (for *ob nicht ihr Ziel allzufern im Blauen liege*), Einöde (for *gesonderte Pfade gehn zum hohen Ziel*), erfliegen (for *erfleuch das Ziel der Ehre*), geben (for *ein Ziel will ich dir geben*), Grenze (for *zil und grentzen setzen*), Maß (for *Maß und Ziel gibt das beste Spiel* and *übermizzet niht sin zil*), schießen (for *schießen sie neben dem Ziel vorbey, weit vom Ziel* and *sie haben ihr Ziel überschossen*), Schiff (for *ein solches Ziel kann man als einen Stern ansehen*), Schlag (for *kommt immer weiter vom Ziele*), stecken (for *ein Ziel stecken* and *ein hochgestecktes Ziel erreicht*), and Wolf (for *der Wolf frißt kein Ziel*).

zielen

See under *abzielen, bezielen, blau* (for *mancher zielt ins Blaue und trifft ins Schwarze*) and *halten* (for *da die teufel alle augenblicke auf uns zielen*).

Zielgruppe

die ~ (econ.) target group; 20th c. term for 'category of people at whom one aims one's publicity or propaganda'.

Zielpunkt: see *stecken*.

Zielscheibe: see *Spott*.

Zielsprache

die ~ (ling.) target language; 20th c. term, not yet listed in *DWb.* [1956].

zielstrebig: see *streben*.

Zielwasser

ich brauche ~ (sl.) I need a strong drink (so as to become a better shot); first in mil.sl., recorded by Maußer, Imme and Delcourt; in my youth I heard it used by rifle club members.

ziemen

See under *herb* (for *es ziemt uns noch weniger*) and *Scherz* (for *Scherz, welche euch nicht ziemen*).

ziemlich

ziemlich (coll.) fair, sizeable; *~* began as 'right and proper, appropriate, suitable' with ref. to conduct, but from the 17th c. onward acquired a quantitative meaning = 'moderate, fair', e.g.*ein ziemliches Einkommen* = 'a fair income', also in adverbial use for 'rather', e.g. *~ gut* = 'quite good, not bad'.

← See also under *Fleck* (for *ein ziemlicher Fleck*), herausreden (for *ob er gleich sich so ziemlich herausgeredet hatte*) and Kopf (for *zimliche Kopf-Arbeit darzu gehöret*).

Zier: see *Flor* (1).

Zierbengel: see *Bengel*.

Zierde: See under *Arbeit* (for *Arbeit ist des Bürgers Zierde*), Blume (for *du Blume und Zierde aller Feenritter*), Gier (for *bist aller Jungfrawn zirde*) and glatt (for *verlor sich in Glätte und Zierde*).

zieren: See under *Blume* (for *mit redebluomen volzieren ein lop* and *mit vielen Blumen ausgeziert*), Esel (for *er ziert die Gesellschaft wie der Esel den Roßmarkt*), Glied (for *eine steife gezierte Person*), Grenze (for *darneben thet sie auch fein zieren . . . tugent*), Name (for *diese Grillen verziert ihr mit dem Namen der Tugend*), Phrase (for *Verzierungsphrase*), Schnörkel (for *Schnörkel und Verzierungen*) and verzieren.

zierlich: see *lecken*.

Zierat: see *schnell*.

Ziffer

die ~ (1) letter (of the alphabet); since Early NHG, e.g. Luther 33,432 (Weimar), Schottel, *Haubtspr.* 58 [1663]: '. . . durch die Zusammenfügung etzlicher Zieferen ein solches Wort . . . werde vorgestellt'.

die ~ (2) chiffre, secret sign (in a code); since the 17th c. under French influence, f.r.b. Duez [1664]; cf. Luther, *Tischr.* 416b: '. . . mit seltzamen, wunderbarlichen buchstaben und ziffern geschrieben, daß es niemand lesen kondte'.

die ~ (3) (legal) subparagraph; since the 19th c. in legal documents and laws. Also used for 'item' in treaties and agreements. Since the 19th c.

← See also under *entziffern*.

Zifferblatt: see *Blatt*.

Zigarette: see *schinden*.

Zigarettenlänge

nur eine ~ (coll.) only a short while; 20th c. coll., not yet listed in *DWb.* [1956], though current several decades before.

Zigarre

eine ~ (sl.) a reprimand; first in mil. sl. of 1st World War, f.r.b. Imme, *Soldatenspr.* 88, now general sl.

Zigarrenfritze: see *Friedrich*.

Zigeuner: gypsy

ein ~ a vagabond, bohemian; in lit. for a person with no fixed abode since Early NHG, when dictionaries often derived the name from *(herum)ziehen*, whereas Frisch [1741] connected it with Lat. *circulari*. Thieves, abductors of children were also compared to *~*, since gypsies have

have for centuries been accused of these crimes, but more frequently their reputation as soothsayers is mentioned in lit. and prov., e.g. H.Sachs [edit.K.] 5,11: *'ich main, dast ein zigeuner seist, weil all mein haimligkeyt du weist'*, Agricola, *Spr. Cla* [1534]: *'du gebest eynen bosen Zygeüner, du kanst nicht wahrsagen'*, also Aler [1727], mentioning further bad features: *'er gibt einen guten Zigeuner ab - raro a mendacio sibi temperat; homo vanus est et futilis'*. The accusation that gypsies are liars is old, e.g. Luther 23,166 (Weimar): *'wenn mir yemand solche bucher . . . brecht . . . so denke ich gewislich, es hette sie ein Zygeuner odder loser bube gemacht'* and this equation ~ = 'liar' is recorded for many dialects. Only since ca. 1800 a more Romantic view has been taken and actors, bohemians and people with a roving way of life have come to be called ~, e.g. Goethe 23,24 (W.). Pestalozzi, *Werke* 10,177 used *Zigeunergelüste* for 'desire to live a life free from legal constraints and the censorship of a settled community'.

← See also under *schwarz* (for *schwarz wie ein Zigeuner*) and *Topf* (for *der schwarze Topf heißt den schwarzen Kessel Zigeuner*).

zigeunerhaft
zigeunerhaft gypsy-like, nomadic, bohemian; since the 18th c., e.g. Goethe 24,355 (W.); it can refer to bohemian behaviour, but also to disorderly appearance of a person, house, etc. Stieler [1691] recorded the earlier *zigeunerisch* and glossed it with *'vagabundus, pannosus et vage'*.

Zigeunerleben
ein ~ führen to lead a gypsy-like, nomadic, bohemian, unconventional life; recorded since the 17th c. (Eyering [1601]), e.g. Dahlmann, *Gesch.franz.Rev.* 6 [1845]: *'das Volk führt kein menschliches Leben mehr, es ist ein Zigeunerleben'*. Hence also the verb *zigeunern*, recorded since the 16th c., e.g. H.Hesse, *P. Camenz.* 126 [1907]: *'wie ich in diesem verfluchten Nest (= Paris) zigeunerte, verbummelte'*.

Zimmer: room
das ~ (lit.) abode, dwelling; mainly in relig. and mythol. contexts; since the 16th c., e.g. Klaj, *Geburt J.Chr.* 53: *'da hat der sternen fürst sein zimmer aufgeschlagen'*, Gottsched, *Anm.Gel.* 833 [1757]: *'der Glanz des Ewigen füllt Zeus bestirntes Zimmer'*. - *Gezimmer*, used in many contexts for 'building' (made of wood) since OHG, is now obs.

← See also under *Engel* (for *es geht/fliegt) ein Engel durchs Zimmer*), *Gefängnis* (for *entflohen des Zimmers Gefängnis*) and *hüten* (for *das Zimmer hüten*).

Zimmermann
See under *Axt* (for *die Axt im Haus erspart den Zimmermann*), *Loch* (for *jem.m zeigen, wo der Zimmermann ein Loch gelassen hat*) and *Weberknecht*.

zimmern
jem. zimmert etw. sb. builds, erects, constructs sth.; originally meant 'to build sth. (of wood)', but since Early NHG extended to other things and abstracts, f.r.b. Stieler [1691], e.g. *Bücher ~*, as in Fischart, *S.Dicht.* [edit. K.] 1,45, (DWb) Wurstisen, *P.Ä. Hist.* 1,149 [1571]: *'es zimmeret . . . ein jeder nur seine innwendigen fürsätz'*, A.Seghers, *Die Toten b.j.* 591 [1950] *'Anneliese hatte sich . . . eine Art Glaubensbekenntnis gezimmert'*, also Goethe 5,1,107 (W.) and in his *Gespr.* [edit. B.] 6,269: *'schon zimmere Xenien genug . . . gegen sie '*; hence also *jem. zimmert an jem.m* or *etw.*, as in Luther 41,582 (Weimar) with ref. to God: *'denn er hat an uns angefangen . . . zu zimern und bawen'*. There are several compounds, e.g. *mitzimmern*, as in (Sp.) Keller, *Salander* 236: *'seit er so rüstig an dem öffentlichen Wohle mitgezimmert und gebastelt'*.

etw. zimmert etw. (lit.) sth. creates sth.; with abstracts since the 18th c., e.g. Bode, *Montaigne* 3,84 [1793]: *'die Bosheit zimmert und schmiedet für sich selbst die Peinbank'*.

← See also under *Schraube* (for *zimmert und schraubt sie durch künstliche Versuche zusammen'*).

Zimmerpflanze
eine ~ (coll.) sb. who prefers staying at home to outside pursuits; 20th c. coll.; sometimes containing the notion of 'delicate constitution' unable to stand the rigours of life outside his home.

Zimt (1): cinnamon
zimtbraun or *zimtfarben* cinnamon-coloured, yellow with a reddish tinge; recorded since the 1st half 19th c.

Zimt (2)
~ machen (sl.) to make a great fuss about sth.; probably from Yiddish *zimmes machen*, which entered some regions, esp. Berlin ca. 1880; origin still not certain and some lexicographers have suggested that it could be derived from ~ (1) = 'cinnamon', since this was sold in tiny paper bags; for details of the derivation from Yiddish see Wolf, *Jiddisches Wb.* 194 [1962] and his *Wb. des Rotwelschen* 349 [1956]. Some recent dictionaries, such as Klappenbach-Steinitz mark it as Yiddish, differing from the listing in *DWb.* [1956]; rare in lit., but Tucholsky, *Ganz anders* 14 has *'erst viel Geschrei und mächtiger Zimt'*.

der ~ (1) (sl.) rubbish, worthless stuff, nonsense; modern, from the previous entry, e.g. *wirf den* ~ *weg*.

der ~ (2) (cant) sign, hint, (secret) mark; from Yiddish *simon* = 'sign' and *simmenen* = 'to mark' (but influence of Fr. *signe* has also been suggested); by its very nature not in lit. and recordings began in the 20th c. (see the first entry above).

der ~ (3) (cant) money, (small) change; recorded for the language of the underworld by Ostwald, *Rinnsteinspr.* [1906]; hence *roter* ~ = 'jewelry, gold', f.r.b. E.Rabben [1906].

Zimtstengel: see *Stengel*.

zingeln: see *umzingeln*.

Zinke(n): point, peak, prong, tooth

der ~ (1) (vulg.) penis; current since early NHG.

der ~ (2) (coll.) (prominent) nose, conk; since Early NHG, e.g. H. Sachs [edit. K.-G]. 14,63 and 21,107, recorded by Frisch [1741] and later for many dialects, also for mil.sl. and stud.sl.

der ~ (3) (cant) sign; derived either from Lat. *signum* or French *signe* and used by the criminal underworld at least since the 18th c. It occurs in ~ *stecken* or *stechen* = 'to mark sth.', which goes back to phys. sticking branches in the ground so as to show a route or warn others and then in the wider sense for 'to give a warning sign or provide information', e.g. by signs on doorposts or marks on trees. ~ can also occur for the personal mark (or cryptic signature) of a felon, e.g. Kurz, *Sonn.* 305: '. . . *seinen Zinken, d.h. sein Wappen oder Wahrzeichen, dergleichen jeder von ihnen sein eigenes führt*'. This is also called *Gaunerzinken*. In Freytag, *Bild.* 2,240 it occurs as *Spitzbubenzinken* and Löns in *Wehrwolf* 50 used *Warnzinken*; cf. also *Ruttzinken* (cant) = 'agreed secret mark in or on letters', recorded since the middle of the 19th c.

der ~ (4) (sl.) (tobacco) pipe; 20th c. coll. or sl.

seine ~ *abrennen* (coll.,a.) to sow one's wild oats; the same as *die Hörner ablaufen* (see under *ablaufen* and *Horn*). ~ here refers to the tines on antlers; in lit. at least since the 18th c., e.g. Goethe 8,96 (W.): 'habt ihr ein paar Zinken abgerennt?'; now a. if not obs.

er hat einen ~ (regional coll.) he is drunk; recorded since the middle of the 19th c.

← See also under *fünf* (for *die fünfzinkige Gabel*).

zinken

zinken (1) (cant) to give a (warning) sign; see

Zinken (3) above; recorded by Ostwald, *Rinnsteinspr.* 137.

zinken (2) (cant) to mark cards with secret signs, rig; cf. *Zinken* (3), e.g. Langgässer, *D.u.Siegel* 307 [1946]. Hence *Zinker* (cant) = 'card sharper, broadsman', also used for 'forger'.

zinken (3) (cant) to inform (on sb.), grass; hence also *Zinker* (cant) = 'informer' and used for *Spitzel* = 'police informer', 'stool-pigeon'.

zinken (4) (vulg.) to have intercourse; cf. *Zinke(n)* (1) above.

← See also under *verzinken*.

Zinne: merlon

die Zinnen der Berge (lit.) the mountain pinnacles; ~ is a man-made 'merlon' (in pl. = 'battlements'); transferred in lit. since MHG, mainly with ref. to mountains, e.g. *hoher Felsen Zinnen*; poet. extended with personification in Chamisso, *Werke* 4,21: '*die starren Zinnen des Gebirges trauern*'. In poetry also used for 'height(s), highest points', as in *Zinnen des Verstandes* (quoted in *DWb.* from Neumark) or *Zinnen der Zeiten*, used by Rilke.

Zinnober: cinnabar

rot wie ~ , *zinnoberrot* vermilion; since MHG, e.g. Hartmann v. Aue, *Erec* 2295; often at first with ref. to toiletries, mainly facial make-up, as in *zinnoberrote Wangen*, later also in other contexts (flowers, berries, minerals).

das ist ~ (sl.) that is rubbish, twaddle, first in mil.sl., f.r.b. Imme, *Soldatenspr.* 13. Often used like *Zimt* (which see) and therefore also sometimes = 'fuss', e.g. *mach so keinen* ~ !

Zinsen

etw. mit Zins(en) und Zinseszinsen zurückzahlen (*bezahlen, heimzahlen*) (coll.) to repay sth. (by way of revenge) with interest; in this special sense in lit. since last quarter of the 19th c.; cf. Lessing, *Nathan*, 1,3: '*auch Zins vom Zins der Zinsen? – Freilich . . . bis mein Kapital zu lauter Zinsen wird*', also *etw. mit Zinsen* (not in financial sense) *vergelten, erstatten* or *bezahlen*, since the 18th c.

schwarze ~ (sl.) interest received but not declared to the tax authorities; since the middle of the 20th c.

← See also under *bringen* (for *es bringt Zinsen*) and *Geld* (for *das Geld brütet Junge, wenn es auf Zinsen geliehen wird*).

zinsen

etw. zinst (lit.,a.) sth. brings profit (or income); in financial sense since the 14th c., figur. with abstracts since the 18th c., e.g. Musäus, *Volksmärchen* 3,14: '*so zinste ihm doch der Schatz seiner geheimnisvollen Weisheit reichlich*'.

Zinshahn

See under *glühen* (for *glüheten wie die roten zinßhäne*) and *Hahn* (for *rot wie ein Zinshahn*).

Zinskneifer

der ~ (regional coll.) usurer, loan-shark; since the middle of the 19th c.

Zipfel: small tapering piece

ein ~ (coll.) a little bit; with abstracts since Early NHG, e.g. *FastSp.* 2,858: '*so hab ich oft ein zipfel reu*'; also as *ein Zipfelchen*, e.g. (Sa.) Prutz, *Ob.* 2,116: '*bis endlich das Schicksal ermüdete und ihm ein Zipfelchen Glück zuwarf*'; cf. *zipfelweis* = 'in small portions', as used by Wieland.

der ~ (1) (coll.) penis (esp. of a young boy); since at least the 17th c., since Kramer recorded it in 1702.

der ~ (2) (coll.) stupid fellow; since the 19th c. recorded for many areas, though the meanings, mostly pejor., vary. They include 'clumsy, coarse, immoral, greedy and mean', but 'stupid' predominates.

etw. beim rechten ~ fassen (or *anpacken*) (coll.) to deal properly with sth., go the right way about sth.; beginnings in Early NHG, e.g. Luther 10,1,1,118 (Weimar), general since the 17th c., e.g. Heine, *Sämtl. W.* (edit. E.) 1,432: '*fliegt dir das Glück vorbei einmal, faß es beim Zipfel*', with *recht* in Hippel, *Lebensl.* 3,2,376 [1778] and Raabe, *Sämtl. W.* 1,3,11. In phrases with *Gelegenheit, Chance*, etc. *Schopf* (which see p. 2175) is more frequently used and less coll. than ~.

er denkt, er hat es an allen vier Zipfeln (coll.) he thinks that he has made quite sure, is in full control; *an allen vier Zipfeln* has been in use since Early NHG (Roth, *Catech. Pred.* [1573], Faber, *Thes.* [1587]); the coll. phrase suggesting possible failure arose later.

dem seine Wurst hat drei ~ (regional coll.) he thinks he is sth. special, a cut above the rest; recorded e.g. for Swabia by Fischer-Pfleiderer.

← See also under *Bett* (for *nach dem Bettzipfel schnappen*), *Sack* (for *den fünften Zipfel am Sack suchen*), *saugen* (for *Saugenzipfel*) and *Wurst* (for *das ist eine andere Wurst mit zwei Zipfeln*).

Zipfelmütze: nightcap

eine ~ tragen to be an unadventurous, sleepy person, dull philistine; since the 19th c., e.g. Fontane, *Stechlin* chap. 15: '*gefahrlose Berufe, die sozusagen eine Zipfelmütze tragen, sind mir von jeher ein Greuel gewesen*'; cf. Bleibtreu, *Verrohung d. Lit.* 6 [1903]: '*der Philister zieht sich die so beliebte Zipfelmütze über und geht wieder schlafen im alten Schlendrian*'.

zipp

er kann nicht ~ sagen (coll.) he is shy or speechless (with fear); ~ imitates the cheep of birds (cf. the similar use of *piep*, discussed on p. 1875), in use since the 18th c.; since the 19th c. also in *nicht mehr ~ sagen können* = 'to be exhausted', e.g. Fontane, *Familienbriefe* 2,27.

Jungfer Zipp (coll., a.) affected girl; from regional coll. *zipp* = 'affected, prudish, haughty', since the 19th c. in some regions; cf. also *zippenglisch* = 'affected English', as used by Laube, *Ges. Schr.* 8,361 [1875].

Zippe

die alte ~ (coll.) the old hag; also in some areas 'that odious woman'; recorded since the 19th c.; origin has been much debated but is still not clearly established, since ~ has many meanings. It could mean 'puppy, bitch, ewe, goat' and could therefore have become a term of insult, but influence of *zipp* (see above) has also been considered with ref. to 'affected behaviour, prudishness, twittering way of speaking' and ~ = 'song thrush' in lit. since the 18th c., cannot be ignored. Müller-Fraureuth, *Wb. d. obersächs.* 703 and 708 [1914] considered the meaning 'goat' as the most likely source. – When used with ref. to men, *alte ~* means 'coward'.

die Zippschwester, also *Kaffeezippe* (regional coll.?) coffee addict; recorded by Amaranthes, *Frauenz.-Lex.* [1700]; now *Kaffeetante* (see p. 2431) and *Kaffeeschwester* (see p. 2218) are the usual coll. terms.

Zippelpelz: see *Pelz*.

Zipperlein: gout

das ~ haben to suffer from gout; ~ started as a term for sb. '*der zippert*', i.e. walks with unsteady short steps, current since the 15th c.; then transferred to the illness (alongside *Podagra*), recorded by Stieler [1691], considered regional coll., but then accepted as a standard term by Campe [1811] and used in lit., e.g. by Wieland in *Ob.* 12,67; cf. Jean Paul, *Herbstbl.* 2,140: '*zipperleinhaftige Geschäftsmänner*'.

da könnte man das ~ kriegen (regional coll.) that is enough to give one the jitters, drive one up the wall (with impatience); current in several regions, recorded since the 19th c., e.g. for Frankfurt (cf. *Frankfurter Wb.* 3642).

← See also under *piepen* (for *ein Zeus piept am Zipperlein*).

Zirkchen: see *Bezirk*.

Zirkel: circle

ein ~ von Personen a circle (or cohesive group) of people; since the 18th c. under influence of

French *cercle*; e.g. Göckingk 1,73: '*ein Zirkel drei geliebter Schwestern*', Platen 4,274: '*der Kalif . . . im Zirkel seiner Kronbeamten*'; Schiller used *Familienzirkel* (now usually *Familienkreis*); cf. also Eichendorff, *Gesch.Dram.* 198 [1834] where *Damentheezirkel* occurs. – Many idioms with ~ are outnumbered by those which use *Kreis*. See under *Kreis* for *Kreis der Familie, der Freunde*, etc., *häuslicher Kreis, den Kreis auslaufen, Kreis der Zeit, Bannkreis, Zauberkreis, Kreis der Welt, Teufelskreis, störe meine Kreise nicht*, in all of which ~ can take the place of *Kreis* in lit., but rarely in everyday usage.

der ~ (lit.) circular reasoning, vicious circle; at least since the 18th c., e.g. Lessing 6,240: '*der . . . Beweis ein offenbarer Zirkel*'; cf. *Teufelskreis*, which is also derived from Lat. *circulus vitiosus*

ein viereckiger (earlier *viereckter*) ~ a contradiction in terms; since the 18th c., e.g. Mendelssohn, *Ges. Schr.* 4,2,72; cf. also Lichtwer, *Schr.* [edit. Pott] 83 [1825]: '*so wollen Sie vielleicht des Zirkels Viereck finden*'.

die Quadratur des Zirkels squaring of the circle; cf. *Quadratur des Kreises* (p. 1924), where the date (20th c.) must be corrected, since the phrase, a translation of Lat. *quadratura circuli*, has been current in German since ca. 1700; cf. also Fontane, *Frau J.T.* chap. 19: '*etliche Zirkelquadratur- und Perpetuum-mobile-Sucher . . . die das Unmögliche zustande bringen wollen*'.

← See also under *böhmisch* (for *böhmische Zirkel machen*), *Kreis* (for *ich steige jetzt in diesen gebannten Zirkel*) and *saufen* (for *sich aus dem Zirkel saufen*).

zirkeln

zirkeln to circulate, go from one person or place to the next; with abstracts since the 18th c., e.g. Bürger, 10b: '*so zirkeln immer Lust und Genuß*', Wieland 24,333: '*die Freuden zirkeln von Land zu Land*'.

etw. ~ to produce sth. with great care; derived from 'to do sth. with a pair of compasses or other instruments'; since the 18th c., often in past participle *gezirkelt* for 'painstakingly executed (with great accuracy)'; sometimes ironic, when it can mean 'carefully cautious so as not to give offence', as in Storm, *Sämtl.W.* 4,237, or 'pedantic, contrived' (since the 18th c.).

← See also under *abgezirkelt*.

zirkulieren

zirkulieren to circulate, move around; since the 17th c., influenced by Lat. writings, also by French *circuler*; with ref. to blood recorded since Kramer [1702] (but as *zirkelieren*), e.g. Goethe, *Faust I*, 1372; '*und immer zirkuliert ein neues, frisches Blut*'; with ref. to writings passed around

among friends since the 18th c., then also in wider sense with abstracts.

Zirkus: circus

der ~ (coll.) uproar, disarray, rumpus, fuss; since very early in the 20th c. with a wide range of meanings, e.g. for sth. which is loud and lively, sth. which is faked (as in *einen* ~ *aufführen* for 'to appear furious or disgusted, etc.'), sth. which is felt to be a farce (esp. in mil.sl.); around the middle of the 20th c. 'presenting a (false) picture of being very busy' was added to the list of meanings.

Zirkus- . . . circus- . . .; in compounds where the second part is figur., mainly in *Zirkuskönig* or *-vater* for the director of a circus and *Zirkusmutter* for his wife.; since 1st quarter of the 20th c.

zischeln: whisper

über jem. ~ (pejor.) to make defamatory remarks about sb. behind his back; ~ for 'to speak in a low voice' and 'to tell sb. sth. in secret' (since the 18th c.) could easily acquire a pejor. extension, and this happened towards the end of the 18th c., e.g. Goethe 11,135 (W.): '*sogar zischelte man einander in die Ohren, sie seien niemals getraut gewesen*', Grass, *Blechtrommel* 138: '*die Kaffeetanten zischelten*'; hence also pejor. *Zischelei* and *Gezischel* (modern).

zischen: hiss

zischen (coll.) to rush, move quickly; derived from the sound made by quick movement, e.g. *gestern spät kam er ins Haus gezischt*; modern; hence also *Gezisch* (modern) in various contexts.

einen ~ (sl.) to have a quick one, a snifter; meaning a drink (of some alcohol); modern sl., recorded in *DWb.* [1956].

← See also under *gären* (for *es kocht mein Blut und zischt und gärt*), *glatt* (for *sie zischt mit glatter Zunge*), *Natter* (for *die Nattern der Verleumdung zischen*) and *Schlange* (for *Schlangengezisch*).

Zitadelle: citadel

die ~ (lit.) citadel, fortress, bulwark; figur. since Early NHG, first with ref. to the Virgin Mary and to God, later to houses, as in Goethe IV,49,265 (W.) or ships (used by Schiller with ref. to the Armada), but also to abstracts, as in Riehl, *Nat.Gesch.d.Volkes* (3,12 [1851]: '*das Haus ist die Citadelle der Sitte*'.

Zitat: quotation

das Götz-Zitat gebrauchen (euphem., coll.) to use the quotation from Götz; a ref. to Goethe's *Götz von Berlichingen* (39,110 (W.)); since the 19th c., cf. notes under *lecken* (p.1598) and *einladen* (for *eine Einladung, der man nicht nachzukommen braucht*).

← See also under *Gold* (for *mit allen meinen Citaten . . . sie sind echt wie 24 karätiges Gold*).

zitatenfest

~ *sein* to be skilled in quoting accurately; modern, e.g. Th.Mann, *Lotte i.W.* 13; cf. *bibelfest* and *kapitelfest* on p. 769.

Zitatenschatz

der ~ (lit.) treasury or lexicon of quotations; 20th c. compound, often used (even in the title) for Büchmann's *Geflügelte Worte*; for figur. *Schatz* in this sense see p. 2084.

zitieren

See under *Gespenst* (for *Gespenster zitieren*) and *Glanz* (for *zitierte zahlreiche Glanzstellen*).

Zitrone: lemon

gelb wie eine ~ lemon-yellow; Ruland, *Alchem. Lex.* [1612] recorded *citrinfarb* and *citronfarb*, Kramer [1702] *Zitronengelb* and *Zitronenfarb*.

← See also under *ausdrücken*, *ausquetschen* and *Handel* (for *mit Zitronen handeln*).

Zitronenvogel

der ~ (1) (zool.) dotterel (*Charadrius morinellus*); recorded by Brehm, *Thierleben* 6,68. The standard term is *Mornell*.

der ~ (2) (zool.) brimstone butterfly *Gonepterix rhamni*); also called *Zitronenfalter*; recorded by Brehm, *Thierleben* 9,376, used by Fontane in *Ges.Werke* 1,6,406.

der ~ (3) (regional coll., a.) postman; mainly in Saxony, where until 1866 postmen wore a yellow uniform; e.g. Wetzel, *Dresdner Parnaß* 35 [1841].

zittern: tremble

~ *vor*. . . . to tremble or shake with . . .; since MHG with *Furcht*; Grimmelshausen used it with *Zorn*, Goethe with *Verlangen*; it also occurs with *Freude*, *Ungeduld*, *Wut* and other emotions; *erzittern* can also be used, but only in lit.; hence also *das Gezitter* (modern).

← See also under *beben* (for *ein zitterndes flammendes Beben*), *durchzittern*, *Espe* (for *zittern wie Espenlaub*), *fühlen* (for *was du mit Zittern glaubst*), *Gallert* (for *zittern wie Gallert*), *Gewitter* (for *von Gottes Strafgewittern zittern*), *Götze* (for *zittre du vor deines Götzen Zorn*), *irre* (for *Menschen von zitternder Nerve*), *Laub* (for *zittern wie Laub*), *Schaft* (for *wenn das blutende Herz am eisernen Schaft der Notwendigkeit zittert*), *Staub* (for *ich trat dein zitterndes Alter in den Staub*) and *zagen* (for *zittern und zagen*).

Zitterpartie

die ~ (sport) cliff-hanger, game which is undecided until the very end; also called *Zitterspiel*; both since 2nd half of the 20th c.

Zitterprämie

die ~ (joc.coll.) danger-money; since 2nd half of 20th c.

zivil: civil

zivil (1) moderate, reasonable; modern, e.g. *zivile Preise* ~ 'moderate prices'.

zivil (2) decent, well educated; modern, but becoming a., though still used adverbially, e.g. *jem.* ~ *behandeln* = 'to deal in a civil way with sb.'.

Zivilcourage

die ~ courageous conduct of a citizen, determination to stand up for one's convictions; first used and probably coined by Bismarck [1864]; coined as the opposite of courage of a soldier on the battlefield; frequent since early in the 20th c., e.g. ~ *aufbringen*.

Zivilisation: see *unbeleckt*.

Zobelfang: hunt for sable.

der ~ (obs.) acquisition of sth. very valuable; still used in the 18th and early 19th c. (Hamann, Jean Paul), now obs.

jem. auf ~ *schicken* (obs.) to banish sb., send sb. into the wilderness; still used in the 19th c. (Hebel, Nestroy), now obs.

zocken

zocken (cant) to gamble; in cant, derived from Yiddish *zchokken*; only in general use since recent times. The compound *jem.m etw. abzocken* (sl.) = 'to win sth. from sb. by cheating' may belong here, but for LG *enem das sinige aftokken* has been recorded since the 18th c., which suggests a different origin.

Zofe

die ~ (lit.) lady's maid; figur. with abstracts since the 18th c., e.g. Günther, *Ged.* 1028 [1735]: '*das Glück ist eine Zofe, so sich nach ihrer Frau, der Unbeständigkeit, in allem richten muß*', Treitschke, *Hist. u.polt. Aufs.* 1,4: '*die Bühne nach Shakespeares Tode . . . ward eine Zofe der Stuarts*'.

← See also under *Stunde* (for *die Stunden, die ihre Zofen sind*).

zögern

zögern (lit.) to hesitate, procrastinate; figur. with abstracts. Often in participial phrases or in cases, where things are seen as 'hesitating', as though they had a will of their own, e.g. Kosegarten, *D.* 2,21: '*zu erwarten der Fremden zögernde Ankunft*', Thümmel 3,186: '*wieviele Menschenalter wird dieser Übergang noch zögern?*', Schiller, *Spruch des Confuzius*: '*zögernd kommt die Zukunft hergezogen*' (cf. also Schiller, *Kab.u.L.* 5,2: '*die Gewichte der zögernden Wanduhr*'). Unusual is *einer Sache* ~ = 'to fail to follow quickly upon sth.', as in Becker, *Weltgesch.* 13,449: '*diesem Entschlusse zögerte die Ausführung*', and still rarer is *etw. heranzögern*, as in Goethe 14,229 (W.); *'fort! Dein Zagen zögert den Tod heran'*.

← See also under *verzögern*.

Zögling: pupil

der ~ (lit.) pupil; with abstracts as the teacher since the 18th c.; frequent in Herder's writings, also in the phrase ~ *der Natur*, as in Seume, *Ged.* 190; often = *Jünger* = 'disciple' (see p. 1416), e.g. ~ *der Musen* or *der Grazien*, jocular in Heine 3,18: *'Eseltreiber mit ihren grauen Zöglingen'*.

← See also under *dressieren* (for *Therese dressirt ihre Zöglinge, Natalie bildet sie*) and *Geburt* (for *jeder Unmut ist eine Geburt, ein Zögling der Einsamkeit*).

Zoll (1): inch

keinen ~ *breit weichen (vorrücken)* to yield (advance) not by one inch; general since the 19th c.; Bismarck, *Ged.u.Erinn.* 2,105 used it with *zurückweichen*, it also occurs with such abstracts as *Zeit*, e.g. Eichendorff 2,175:' . . . *daß die Zeit auch nur um einen Zoll . . . weiter fortrückte'*.

~ *um* ~ by small steps, one bit after another; since the 19th c. sometimes with abstracts, e.g. Droste-Hülshoff 2,98: *'bevor uns Krankheit Zoll um Zoll verzehrt'*; hence also *zollbreit* (a.) = 'gradual(ly)', as in *zollbreite Abtragung einer Schuld* (where *in Raten* or *ratenweis* would now be used).

'jeder ~ *ein König'* every inch a king; quotation from Shakespeare, *King Lear* 4,6, which has become a prov. expression, general since the 19th c., not only with *König*, e.g. Vischer, *Auch Einer* 1,1: *'jeder Zoll ein Geschäftsreisender in Baumwolle'*; see also p. 1522.

Zoll (2): tax, fee, toll

der ~ (lit.) tribute, acknowledgement, reward; in lit. with abstracts since MHG (*zol nemen* or *geben*), frequent since the 17th c., e.g. Grob, *Poet. Spaz.*80 [1700]: *'so ist auch Reu und Spott des Grimmes Zoll'*, Lessing 1,362: *'jeder lächelnde Blick dünkt uns der Zoll unserer Verdienste'*, Chamisso 1,143: *'nimm entgegen meines Dankes Zoll'* (cf. Hebbel, *Genov.* 1,2: *'als Zoll des Danks für unsern schönen Bund'*); hence also for 'payment', as in *den* ~ *entrichten* = 'to render what one is obliged to grant or give', e.g. Günther, *Ged.* 109 [1735]: *'Seufzer sind der theure Zoll, welchen wir der Erde geben'*; Wieland 20,155 used it with ref. to *Ehstandspflicht*.

← See also under *bezahlen* (for *den Zoll der Menschlichkeit bezahlen*).

zollen

jem.m etw. ~ to pay, grant, render sth. to sb.; with such abstracts as *Dank, Ehrfurcht, Beifall, Tribut* since the 17th c., f.r.b. Stieler [1691], e.g.

Platen 1.79: *'Gehorsam wußte dir die Welt zu zollen'*. The sense of 'to endow sb. with sth.', as in Goethe's line *'da er* [i.e. God] *mir . . . Talent gezollt, hat er mir Viel vertraut'*, is now obs.

← See also under *Tribut* (for *jem.m Tribut zollen*).

zollfrei

Gedanken sind ~ (prov.) thoughts pay no (or are free from) toll; in Engl. f.r.b. Camden [1636], in German since Early NHG, e.g. E. Alberus, *Fabeln* (repr.) 104–7, 34 [1534/50]: *'gedancken aber, wie der windt, in allen landen zollfrey sind'*, Abr. a Santa Clara, *Judas* 1,8: *'Gedancken seynd zoll frey'*.

Zone: zone

See under *einfrieren* (for *eingefrorene Zone*), *Gegenfüßler* (for *Gegenfüßler der melodschen Zone*), *grau* (for *die graue Zone*) and *Schlag* (for *von Fremden Zonen bin ich her verschlagen*).

Zopf

der ~ (lit.) formality, antiquated tradition, pedantry; men of rank and soldiers (on the order of King Friedrich Wilhelm I of Prussia) wore pigtails in the 18th c., seen from the 1st half of the 19th c. onwards not merely as an outdated fashion but also as embodying antiquated thinking and despotic rule. The students and other Liberals attending the *Wartburgfest* [1817] burned it solemnly as a symbol of autocratic government; hence such refs. to ~ as in Hoffmann von Fallersleben, *Leben* 6,2: *'daneben war freilich viel Philisterei und Residenzlerei, und im Bürgerstande viel Zopf*. It could then describe 'pedantry', 'bureaucratic resistance to change' and 'adherence to outdated customs' (often as *alter* ~). Hence the rare *Zopftum*, as e.g. in Heine 2,435: *'der lange Schnurrbart ist eigentlich nur des Zopfthums neuere Phase'*. Hence *zopfig* = 'antiquated, old-fashioned', in this sense only since the 19th c.

jem.m einen ~ *andrehen* (obs.) to make fun of sb.; recorded since the 19th c., also for 'to find fault with sb.' and 'to reprimand sb.'; occasionally in lit., but now obs.

sich einen ~ *trinken* (col. 1,a.) to get drunk; sometimes *Haarbeutel* is used instead of ~ (see p. 1187); since the 19th c., mainly in stud.sl., e.g. Heine 1,310: *'mein Deutschland trank sich einen Zopf'*; now a.

ein ~ *Menschen* (regional) a long line of followers (e.g. behind a coffin at a funeral); rare in lit., but G. Hauptmann used it in *Weber* 49.

vom ~ *zur Zehe* (obs.) from top to toe; Goethe 1,36 (W.) used the phrase, but modern dictionaries no longer list it.

Zopfstil

der ~ (lit.) rococo style; since the 19th c., mainly with ref. to buildings, e.g. Stifter 14,257, Gutzkow, *Ges.W.* 6,18, but occasionally extended as in (DWb) Ebner-Eschenbach 1,67: '*es gibt Menschen im Zopfstil: viele hübsche Einzelheiten, das Ganze abgeschmackt*'. Hence *verzopft* can mean 'turned into sth. which reflects rococo style', but it can also be the same as *bezopft*, for which see p. 309.

Zopfzeit

die ~ (lit.) the 18th c.; with ref. to its taste, rococo style, fashions and outlook; usually pejor. (see above under *Zopf*); only since the 19th c., e.g. Stifter 14,248 (Gutzkow used it and also *Zopfperiode*); sometimes combined with *Perücke* in *die Zopf- und Perückenzeit* (see p. 1847).

Zorn: rage

den hat Gott im ~ *erschaffen* (coll.) God made him (when he was) in a rage; used with ref. to a person who is unsuited for his job; since early in the 19th c., e.g. Raabe, *Horacker* 92.

der ~ (personified*)* rage; personified in many prov. since MHG; one of the oldest is *der* ~ *ist blind*, less used as a prov. now than in the phrase *blinder* ~ ; e.g. Renner 13984: '*zorn ist gên allen witzen blint*' (cf. also '*der* ~ *wirft blinde Junge wie die Hündin*', recorded still in Simrock [1846]); another MHG example is '*zorn totit schire den unschuldigen wie den schuldigen*'. 17th c. collections contain from Petri [1605]: '*zorn ist ein böser ratgeber*', from Henisch [1616]: '*zorn und gelt verwirren die welt*', from Lehman [1663]: '*Zorn ist ein wackrer Haushund*' (also '*zorn ist wie ungelöschter Kalk*').

← See also under *anzünden* (for *ihr habt ein Feuer meines Zornes angezündet*), *Art* (for *je edler Art, je leichter Zorn*), *ausstreuen* (for *streue aus den Zorn deines Grimmes*), *bersten* (for *vor Zorn bersten*), *bewegen* (for *wie er in zorn bewegt ist gewesen*), *bitzeln* (for *es bitzelt alles in mir vor Zorn*), *branden* (for *wenn jugendlich des Zornes Wogen branden*), *Dampf* (for *seinen Zorn dämpfen*), *einfressen* (for *der alte eingefreßne Zorn*), *entbrechen* (for *Junos Brust entbrach der Zorn*), *führen* (for *si vuorte beide ein grôzer zorn*), *Gefäß* (for *gefeße des zorns*), *Geifer* (for *das nicht sein zorn vnd eiffer werde dorn vnd geiffer*), *Gewitter* (for *des Zorns Gewittergluth*), *Gift* (for *die Giftblüte ihres Zorns*), *glatt* (for *dies glättet meinen Zorn*), *Glied* (for *Stillingen fuhr der Zorn durch die Glieder*), *glimmen* (for *des zornes funke . . .*), *glühen* (for *ihre Augen glühen Zorn*), *Götze* (for *zittre du vor deines Götzen Zorn*), *greifen* (for *das uns nit griff der gottes zorn*), *halten* (for *biß dir der zorn vergat*), *Hefe* (for *wandte sich jetzt ihr Zorn*), *lodern* (for

warum ihr Zorn so heftig lodert), *Mord* (for *Mordszorn*), *Rauch* (for *dann wird zein Zorn und Eifer rauchen* and *der Zorn ist bey ihm verrauchet*), *Schale* (for *die schalen des zorns Gottes*), *Schaum* (for *vor Zorn scheumen*), *schießen* (for *daz im in daz hirne schoz ein zorn*), *schmelzen* (for *daß all sein Zorn davon verschmolz*), *schwanger* (for *wie mit Zorn ihr Blick sich schwängert*), *Sonne* (for *laß die Sonne nicht über deinem Zorn untergehen*), *vergehen* (for *da vergeht einem der Zorn*) and *verklären* (for *wie dich der Zorn umglänzte*).

zorndurchrüttelt: see *rütteln*.

zornig: See under *ausstoßen* (for *zornige Worte ausstoßen*), *bezahlen* (for *wenn zornige Hund einander zausen*) and *Puter* (for *zornig wie ein Puter*).

Zornkelch: see *Kelch*.

Zote: See under *reißen* (for *Zoten reißen*) and *schmieren* (for *grobe zotten, pasquillen*).

zubeißen: see *Span*.

zubinden: see *Sack*.

zublasen

jem.m etw. ~ (rare) to suggest sth. to sb.; with ref. to whispered, secret, often malicious communications, where *einblasen* (see p. 230) is the preferred compound; f.r.b. *voc.theut.* [1482]; now rare, if not obs.

zubringen

den Tag in Sorgen ~ to pass or spend one's day in worries; since Early NHG, e.g. Luther 29, 564 (Weimar): '. . . *dieses leben fein friedlich . . . zubracht werde*'; always used with details as to time or place or with adverbs; *verbringen* is now preferred in this context.

jem.m etw. ~ to convey or bring sb. sth.; since the 19th c. occasionally with abstracts, e.g. Mommsen, *Röm.Gesch.* 1,196: '*dies . . . Alphabet ist . . . den Italikern zugebracht worden*'; still in *jem.m eine Nachricht* ~ ; older is the phrase with ref. to children 'brought into' a marriage from a previous marriage, since Early NHG, e.g. Steinhöwel, *Äsop* 49 [1477], also its use with ref. to a dowry, f.r.b. Frisius [1556]; cf. also its special use with ref. to 'drinking to' sb., where phys. 'bringing a glass to sb.' led to *jem.m eins bringen*, discussed on p. 398, or ~, as in Goethe, *Faust I,*736: '*der letzte Trunk sei nun . . . dem Morgen zugebracht*'.

zubrocken: see *zubüßen*.

Zubrot

von ~ *leben* to exist on earnings made on the side, casual jobs; in gastron. sense ~ (f.r.b. Stieler [1691]) = 'entremets' (cf. Kindleben, *Stud.Lex.* 224: '*Zubrodt nennt der gemeine Mann Fleisch und Zugemüse*'), used figur. in Goltz, *Zur Physiog.* 48: '. . . *der Mutterwitz . . . ist gleichsam das Zubrod dem täglichen Brode, das Dessert zur Arbeit'*. Now it refers to extra income earned (by tips, overtime, second job, etc.); modern, not yet mentioned in *DWb*. [1954].

zubüßen

etw. ~ müssen to have to provide a further sum, spend additional money; from *Zubuße* = 'additional payment'. (used by Goethe), but also containing the notion of '(painful) loss', as in *einbüßen*. Adelung [1780] recorded '*sein Vermögen bey etw. zubüßen*' and referred to *zubrocken*, where he gave as an example '*ich habe dabey zehn Thaler zugebrockt, nach und nach aus meinem Vermögen dabey aufgewandt*'; Trübner quoted from P. Ernst, *Glück v. Lautenthal* 160 [1933]: '*seit zwei Jahren hat er kein Gehalt bekommen, und außerdem hat er auch von seinem Eignen zugebüßt*'.

zubuttern: see *Butter*.

Zucht: breeding, upbringing

die ~ (1) (obs.) progeny, offspring; meaning '*was man aufgezogen* or *erzogen hat*'; in the past this could be applied to humans, since Early NHG, e.g. Zwingli, *D.Schr.* 1,95 where Jesus is called '*die himmelisch zucht und geburt*'; still in Wieland, *Gold.Spiegel* 2,14: '*eine Zucht von Priestern aus seiner Schule hervor gehen zu sehen*'; now only used with ref. to animals.

die ~ (2) discipline; also used for 'disciplined behaviour'; since MHG, also in pl, as in *Nibelungenl.* 371: '*in ritterlichen zühten die herren tâten daz*', Luther Bible transl. Prov. 15,10, where Luther put ~, but modern Bibles *Züchtigung* (in A.V. 'correction'); hence *jem. in ~ halten* = 'to keep strict control over sb.', recorded by Kramer [1702], e.g. v. Kügelgen, *Jugenderinn.* 53 [1871]: '. . . *ein Hauslehrer, der . . . uns Kinder allesamt in Zucht halten sollte*'; cf. *in allen Züchten*, as in Keller, *Werke* 6,59: '*ob man dem Kinde nicht in allen Züchten und mit aller Vorsicht den . . . Knaben Johannes zum Gespielen geben könnte*'. The formula *in ~ und Ehren* has been current since Early NHG, e.g. H.Sachs, *Fab.* 2,106 (cf. obs. *mit züchten*, as in Fischart, *Garg.* 55). Sometimes in lit. things can be seen as imposing discipline, e.g. (Sp.) Brod. *Leben m.e.Göttin* 217: '. . . *daß sie in die strenge Zucht ihrer . . . Zimmer zurückgekehrt ist*'.

die ~ (3) (coll.) noisy or rowdy behaviour, wild goings-on; negative off-spring from ~ (2) in such comments as *das ist eine tolle* (or iron. *schöne*) *~* ; since the 19th c., recorded by Heyne [1895].

~ ist . . . disciplined behaviour is . . ., good manners are . . .; since MHG in many sayings and prov., esp. in *~ ist der beste Schmuck*, still used in modern period, e.g. Gutzkow, *Werke* 3,2,875: '*Zucht ist der Schule Schmuck*'. Others are: *~ ist das beste Heiratsgut* (or *der beste Brautschatz*), *. . . gesunde Arzenei, Vorrat aller Tugend* (listed in Wander [1880]).

die beste ~ sind gute Worte und harte Strafe (prov.) the best upbringing requires kind words and harsh punishment; recorded by Simrock [1846]; cf. Hardegger (in *Minnes.* II,134a): '*sô wizzet ouch ein dinc vür wâr, daz âne zuht nieman wart tugende rîche*', for other MHG prov. see Zingerle, *Die dt. Sprichwörter im Mittelalter* 183–5 [1864]; Franck [1541] listed '*wie die zucht also die frucht*', in more recent times changed to *Liebe ohne ~ trägt keine gute Frucht*.

← See also under *bloß* (for *sich der Zucht und Ehrbarkeit entblößen*), *Grenze* (for *zucht und scham war an der stiren*) and *Salz* (for *ohne die Übung heilsamer Zucht*), also under *Inzucht* and under *treiben* (for *Unzucht treiben*).

züchten: breed

eine Kategorie von Leuten ~ to produce a certain kind of people; *~* ordinarily refers to the breeding of animals, but in Early NHG it could mean 'to beget' with ref. to people. Quite different is its use since the 19th c. for 'to produce by education (training, discipline)', as in Bismarck, *Ged.u. Erinn.* 1,23: '*wir züchteten schon damals das Offiziersmaterial*'. Abstracts can be *gezüchtet* in modern lit., e.g. (Sp.) Huch, *Pitt u. Fox* 341: '*Autoritätsglauben, gezüchtet durch Gewohnheit und gedankenlose Nachbeterei*'.

sich etw. ~ to produce sth. (by one's efforts but sometimes to one's own detriment); modern in such phrases as *durch seinen Erfolg hat er sich Konkurrenz* (or *Konkurrenten*) *gezüchtet* = 'his successful activities have led to the emergence of competitors'.

etw. hochzüchten (coll.) to bring about top performance in or of sth.; *~* here in the wider sense of 'to produce'; in many contexts, in sport with ref. to special training, in motoring for 'to beef, soup or hot up' (an engine); 20th c. coll.

züchtigen: chastise

wen der Herr lieb hat, den züchtiget er (bibl.) whom the Lord loveth he chasteneth; from Hebr. 12,6.

← See also under *Gott* (for *den lieben Gott zu machen und zu züchtigen und zu plagen*), *kosten* (for *Worte, mit denen er meinen Verrat züchtigen sollte*) and *Skorpion* (for *jem. mit Skorpionen züchtigen*).

Zuchtrute: see *Rute*.

Zuck: see *Ruck*.

zucken: twitch, jerk

See under *Achsel* (for *achselzuckend*), *blitzen* (for *Geistesblitze zuckend durch die Gesellschaft fahren*), *Gicht* (for *Gichter zuckten durch alle Glieder*), *Schulter* (for *mit den Schultern zucken*), *Schwert* (for *zuckten nun auch die zweischneidigen Schwerter, Lästerzungen genannt*), *vorahnen* (for *künftige Kraft wird ihm in der Faust vorahnend zucken*) and *Wimper* (for *mit keiner Wimper zucken*).

Zucker: sugar

wie ~ like sugar; ~ seen as sth. very agreeable, pleasant and desirable in many comparisons and phrases since MHG, e.g. Stricker (in *Dt. Texte d. Mittelalters* 17,115): '*daz ir ietweders lip dem andern suzer muz sin danne zucker und zimin*'; Luther 34,1,63 (Weimar) used it for sth. pleasant, also in 17,1,335 Weimar): '*eytel zucker und honig ist in istis verbis*', in a more unusual sense in 33,546 concerning the relief of a tormented person: '*ein fürst oder richter ist demselbigen als ein vater und zucker*'; hence in the comparisons, *süß wie* ~ and *zuckersüß*, current since MHG; cf. also its use in modern sl., where *der reine* ~ could occur for sth. wonderful, fabulous, e.g. (T.) Wolzogen, *Südt. Gesch.* 201 [1925]: '*ein Kostüm . . . der reine Zucker*', an idiom which is still alive. In the Baroque period ~ became a fashionable word among poets seeing love as the sugar of life (as in Günther, *Ged.* 601). Many compounds were coined, e.g. '*Brüstlin wie zween Zucker – Ballen*' (in G.Greflinger, *Seladon* [1644]). Others were *Zuckerrosen*, *-lider*, *-mündchen*, *-kind*, *-wange* (details in M.Windfuhr, *Die barocke Bildlichkeit* 260 [1966]). Even oxymora occurred such as *zuckersüße Pein*.

etw. ist (ein) ~ (lit.) sth. is (or works) like sugar; since the 17th c., when abstracts could be compared to sugar, e.g. Lehman 1,233: '*frewd ist des lebens zucker*', Butschky, *Pathmos* 177: '*geduld . . . ist ein zukker aller beschwernüsse*'.

ich bin doch nicht von (or *aus*) ~ (coll.) I can put up with the rain, shan't melt away; 19th c. coll.

er bläst ihr ~ *in den Hintern* (or *Arsch*) (vulg.) he spoils her terribly, makes himself ridiculous (or cheap) with all this adoration, flattery or sycophancy; modern.

← See also under *Affe* (for *seinem Affen Zucker geben*), *Gift* (for *giftküchlin, das mit zucker uberzogen ist*), *Schaum* (for *der Zucker unsers Lebens ist nur ein Schaum*) and *streuen* (for *an statt des Zuckers, welcher auf die Rede gestreuet wird*).

Zuckerbäckerstil

der ~ (archit.) wedding-cake style; derogatory in criticism of a decorative style overloaded with elaborate adornments; a 20th c. term, often used with ref. to buildings in the Soviet Union erected after 2nd World War.

Zuckerbrot: see *Peitsche*.

Zuckerhut: see *Hut*.

Zuckerlecken

das ist kein ~ (coll.) that is definitely no pleasure, far from being sth. that one enjoys; phrases with ~ have been current at least since the 18th c., e.g. Lessing 3,205: '*sie denken wer weiß was für Zuckerlecken bey einem Manne ist*'; alive now only in *das ist kein* ~, always in the negative, recorded e.g. by Müller-Fraureuth [1914]. *Honiglecken* can be used as an alternative.

mit ~ *etw. tun* (coll., a.) to do sth. eagerly and most gladly; still in the 19th c., e.g. L.v. Francois, *Reckenburg.* 117 [1871]: '*sähe ihn deine Gnädige, sie bezahlte mit Zuckerlecken seine Schulden*'.

zuckern

etw. überzuckern to make sth. appear attractive; *überzuckern* can be used for phys. 'to sugar, sweeten' and 'to sweeten sth. to excess', both since at least the 17th c., recorded by Kramer [1702]. According to context the extended senses can refer to flattery or deception, mainly to make sth. appear more attractive than it really is.

← See also under *verzuckern*.

Zuckerpüppchen: see *Puppe*.

zudäppisch: see *lang*.

zudecken: cover

See under *Kalb* (for *wenn's Kalb ersoffen ist, deckt der Bauer den Brunnen zu*), *Mantel* (for *mit dem Mantel der christlichen Liebe zudecken*) and *Pflaster* (for *etw. mit einem Pflaster zudecken*).

zudrehen: see *Öl*.

zudringen: see *Schirm*.

zudringlich: see *drängen*.

Zudringlichkeit: see *Geschlecht*.

zudrücken: see *Auge*.

zuerkennen: see *Palme*.

zuerst

See under *erst* (for *wer zuerst kommt, mahlt zuerst*, also under *Mühle*), *Faß* (for *was zuerst ins Faß kommt, darnach schmeckt es*) and *link* (for *mit dem linken Bein zuerst aufgestanden*).

zuerteilen: see *Palme*.

Zufall

der ~ (1) (med., obs.) fit, attack; used in medicine over a long period, recorded by Stieler [1691], still alive in the 19th c., e.g.

E.Th.A.Hoffmann, *Sämtl.W.* 1,152, Schiller (in a letter to Goethe of 13.3.1798); Goethe IV,10,211 (W.) used '*körperliche Zufälle*'; now displaced by *Anfall*.

der ~ (2) (obs.) event, occurrence; recorded in *voc.theut.* [1482], still used by Raabe, *Sämtl.W.* 1,3,190: '. . . *die Ankömmlinge über die Zufälle und Beschwerden ihrer Reise zu befragen*' (where the predominant meaning 'unpleasant event' is clear); now obs.

der ~ (3) chance, accidental happening; derived from ~ (2) when used with such adjectives as *unerwartet, ohngefähr, plötzlich*, e.g. in the early instance in S.Franck, *Sprichw.* [1541]: '*in gehem zufal*'; in early dictionaries often equated with Lat. *fortuna* or *fors*, but established in modern sense only since the 17th c., e.g. Schiller, *Wall.Tod* 2,3: '*das war ein Zufall . . . Es giebt keinen Zufall, und was uns blindes Ohngefähr nur dünkt. . . .*'.

der ~ (4) (lit.) (personified) chance; as a person can be taken as *blind*, can have *Launen* and *Tücken*, can *fügen* and *lenken*, play with mankind (Goethe 2,147 (W.) used *Spiel des Zufalls*). It is also seen as having a will in *der* ~ *wollte, daß . . .*, as in E.Th.A.Hoffmann, *Werke* [edit. G.] 6,144. For other instances see under the cross-references.

← See also under *Gewächs* (for *Staaten als Gewächse des Zufalls*), *Glied* (for *der Zufall liegt mir noch in den Gliedern*), *Gott* (for *der Zufall ist der wahre Gott der politischen Welt*), *Grube* (for *Gruben, die der Zufall ihrer Eitelkeit in den Weg legt*), *lösen* (for *Gott sey Dank, daß mir der Zufall die Zunge lös't*). and *sammeln* (for *sehr leicht zerstreut der Zufall, was er sammelt*).

zufallen

etw. fällt jem.m zu sth. is awarded, granted, given, left to sb.; since Early NHG, e.g. Luther Bible transl. Matth. 6,33: '*trachtet . . . nach dem reich Gottes . . . so wird euch solches alles zufallen*', Goethe IV,8,156 (W.): '*wer Rom gesehen hat, dem muß alles andre zufallen*'; frequent with *Amt, Aufgabe, Erbe* and *Preis*. See also under *fallen* (p.720) for *an jem. fallen, ze lône fallen, zum erbteil fellet* and *dir fällt es*, where ~ would later be used.

zufällig See under *Geist* (for *die zufälligen Erscheinungen*), *Grund* (for *grundverkehrte Bestimmung des Zufälligen*) and *Schein* (for *unter den besonderen zufälligen Zügen*).

Zufälligkeit: see *Kette*.

zufliegen

etw. fliegt jem.m zu sth. comes without effort into sb.' mind or possession; with abstracts since the 18th c., e.g. Herder [edit.S.] 17,237 on Esop: '(*die Fabeln*) *flogen ihm gleichsam . . . zu*', Klinger, *Werke* 1,107: '*das Geld fliegt dir zu*'; cf. also the cl. *alle Herzen flogen ihm zu*. Older is *jem.m* ~ = 'to run to sb.', as in (DWb) *Der wohlgeplagte Priester* 155 [1695]: '*wenn man gehört, Johannes Chrysostomus werde predigen, so seynd die leute wie zugeflogen*'.

← See also under *Taube* (for *wo Tauben sind, fliegen Tauben zu*).

Zuflucht

See under *Hauch* (for *sie nahm ihre Zuflucht zum Clavier*, also under *nehmen*, p. 1775) and *Rest* (for *zu den Büchern ihre Zuflucht genommen*).

zufrieden

sich ~ *geben* to declare oneself content or satisfied; since Early NHG when it could still refer to *Friede* = 'peace', but then extended, general since the 18th c., e.g. Schiller, *D.Carlos* 3,7 where *mit etw.* ~ *sein* = 'to be satisfied with or approve of sth.' and *sich* ~ *geben* occur together: '. . . *will wissen, wie man in Madrid mit Euch zufrieden sei . . . gebt Euch zufrieden*'.

← See also under *darben* (for *die Weisheit darbet nie zufriedne Wonne*), *gehen* (for *ich war wohl zufrieden, mit ihnen einige Gänge zu wagen*), *Gold* (for *man muß die Gans zufrieden lassen, sie legt gute Eier*), *gut* (for *was frag ich viel nach Geld und Gut, wenn ich zufrieden bin*), *Stand* (for *mit seinem Stand zufrieden sein*) and *stellen* (for *jem. zufrieden stellen*).

Zufriedenheit

See under *durchströmen* (for *ihr Herz durchströmt Zufriedenheit*), *Friede* (for *die Zufriedenheit Gottes mit den Menschen*) and *Schoß* (2) (for *im Schooße der Zufriedenheit*).

Zufuhr: see *abschneiden*.

zuführen

etw. seiner Bestimmung ~ to direct sth. to its destined purpose; figur. locutions with abstracts began in the 18th c., e.g. (DWb) J.A.Cramer, *Nord. Aufs.* 1,74 [1758]: '*die Augen sind nur Canäle, die bestimmt sind, der Seele Vorstellungen zuzuführen*'; since the 19th c. with *Bestimmung, Ende* and *Lösung*.

Zug

der ~ (1) movement (and the people in it, also things or animals which move together), procession, expedition, crusade, march, parade; since late in MHG, general since Early NHG, f.r.b. Frisius [1556]; hence *Zugfreiheit* = 'freedom of movement'. Very frequent in compounds such as *Auszug* (see p. 174), *Beutezug* (see p. 300), *Einzug, Fackelzug, Feldzug* (see p. 756), *Festzug, Kreuzzug* (see p. 1549), *Kriegszug, Luftzug, Nachzug, Raubzug* (see p. 1949) *Siegeszug* (see p.

2259), *Streifzug* (see p. 2392), *Umzug, Verzug* (see p. 2588), *Viehzug* (cf. Goethe IV,12,334 (W.): '*die Straße . . . war mit Zügen sehr schönen Viehes belebt*') and *Windzug*. Since the 18th c. frequent with ref. to the movement of clouds, e.g. Goethe 15,245 (W.): '*nach Osten strebt die Masse mit geballtem Zug*'. The appearance of railways (from the forties of the 19th c. onward) contributed *Blitzzug* (see p. 349) and its opposite *Bummelzug* (see p. 423), *Eilzug, Postzug*, etc. For special figur. uses and phrases see below.

der ~ der Ereignisse, des Tages, der Zeit, etc. the course taken by events, the occurrences of the day, the developments of the period; in cases of this type ~ still indicates movement but within a named space; since early in the 19th c., e.g. Goethe, *Faust* 8971: '. . . *Geduld, des Vortrags langgedehnten Zug still anzuhören*', Stifter, *Werke* 3,160: '*Beide folgten dem sanften Zuge dieser Tage*'; cf. also *es liegt im ~ der Zeit* = 'it is part of the prevailing tendency or fashion'.

auf einen ~ at one go, at a stretch; since the 17th c., e.g. Schiller, *Turandot* 1,3: '*ich muß auf einen Zug die schönste Frau der Erde und ein Kaisertum mit ihr gewinnen*'. Similarly: *im Zuge sein* = 'to be going on, proceeding', *in ~ kommen* = 'to get going', e.g. Wieland, *Att.* 2,2,85: '*er kommt unvermerkt in den Zug und schwatzt mehr als er gefragt wird*', *etw. in ~ bringen* = 'to get sth. going, set sth. in motion', *alles ist auf einem guten ~* = 'it is all progressing satisfactorily', Kramer [1702] recorded '*einen guten Zug (Geldzug) thun*', *etw. bleibt im ~* = 'sth. continues to make (the intended) progress', *es ist kein ~ drin* = 'it is stagnant, lacks drive', *~ um ~* = 'without a break, in rapid succession', recorded by Kramer: '*Zug um Zug handeln*'.

der ~ (games) move; first in chess, since MHG, then also in other board games, e.g. *einen ~ zurücknehmen* and *der ~ ist an jem.m*, both of which occur in Lessing, *Nathan* 2,1 and 2,2: '*nimm diesen Zug zurück*' and '*nun ist der Zug an ihm*'; then extended to contexts not related to games, e.g. *er ist am ~* = 'it is his turn (to move, act, etc.)', 'the ball is in his court'; see also under *Schach* for *Schachzug*

der mathematische (englische, etc.) ~ der Schule the mathematical (English, etc.) side of the school; called ~ because a set course is followed over a certain period of time; 20th c.

sich zum Abzug rüsten to prepare to depart; extended from mil. contexts (e.g. *zum Abzug blasen*) to ordinary departure; since the 17th c., e.g. Weckherlin, *Ged.* 226 [1648]: '*die wilde thier nehmen ihren abzug*'; with *rüsten* it appeared later

(but *rüsten* has been used with *Fahrt* and *Reise* since Early NHG).

etw. ist im Anzug sth. is approaching, developing (in the direction of the speaker), brewing; since the 18th c., often with *Wetter, Gewitter, Sturm* taken in phys. sense but also figur. when used for 'trouble, outbreak of fury or violence', e.g. Schiller, *Fiesco* 3,5; occasionally used for 'approach' of sth. in wider sense, e.g. Wieland 34,104: '. . . *daß eine neue Arie im Anzug sei*', Klinger, *Werke* 9,168: '*einen Roman im Anzug sehen*'.

seinen Einzug halten (lit.) to appear, enter; in Kramer [1702] still only with ref. to mil. 'march into sth.', later with ordinary 'moves', e.g. into a house; still later for 'coming, arriving' with ref. to abstracts, e.g. *der Frühling hält seinen Einzug* = 'Spring has come'. Phrases with *einziehen* are preferred in ordinary usage (see p. 613).

der Gegenzug counter-move, opposing move; in phys. sense since the 17th c., but not yet recorded by Stieler [1691] or Kramer [1702]; in various contexts since the 18th c. with ref. to games, processions, draughts, in polit. contexts since the 19th c. when it also came to be used with ref. to railway trains.

der Mattzug final blow, move or action which brings about decisive defeat; transfer from chess in the 19th c.; Sanders quoted from Prokesch v.O. (in *Dt. Viertelj.* 1,1) on Napoleon's defeat: '. . . *sie zielten alle auf den Mattzug, der bei Leipzig gegeben wurde*'; cf. related *Meisterzug*, since MHG (*meisterzuc*), e.g. Görres, *Ath.* 138: '*nun zieht er den Meisterzug und spricht: Schach dem König!*'.

den Rückzug antreten to retreat; in wider sense 'to withdraw (statements, demands, etc.)'; first (in 17th c.) in phys., mainly mil. contexts, but since the 18th c. also figur. for 'to yield', used by Schiller; cf. Gutzkow, *R.v.G.* 5,69: '*ich will mir den Rückzug auf ein festbegründetes Leben nicht ganz abschneiden*'; for figur. *antreten* see p. 65.

einen Umzug halten (lit.) to move around (in a kind of procession); figur. since the 19th c., e.g. Heine, *Verm.* 1,150: '*Phantasien, die des Nachts im Hirn den bunten Umzug halten*'.

etw. in (or zum) Vollzug bringen (legal) to execute sth.; current since MHG (*volzuc*); with *bringen* since the 18th c., but *setzen* and *kommen* also occur; in wider sense = 'to establish sth., bring sth. about', e.g. Gutzkow, *Werke* 9,157: '*die Russen verlangten den Vollzug des Friedens von Bukarest*', Ayrenhoff, *Werke* 1,310: '. . . *Beyde setzen ihr Heil in den Vollzug so heiliger Pflichten*'.

der leichteste Windzug (or *Luftzug, Windstoß*) *wirft ihn um* (coll.) the slightest gust of wind knocks him over, he is a delicate creature; modern coll.

ein ~ durch die Gemeinde (coll.) a stroll, a leisurely walk (for some fresh air); 20th c. joc. coll. phrase, similar to *Verdauungsspaziergang* or *Ernüchterungsgang*.

im falschen ~ sitzen (coll.) to have made a wrong decision, put one's shirt on a loser; ~ here = '(railway) train'; 20th c. coll.

dieser ~ ist abgefahren (coll.) that opportunity has been missed, that chance has been lost; another ref. to railways; 20th c. coll.

der ~ (2) feature, trait; derived from ~ = 'stroke, line, mark' in writing, painting and sculpture, f.r.b. Faber [1537], e.g. Dürer, *Unterw.d.Messung* [1525], Goethe 5,87 (W.); hence *Namenszug* = 'signature'. This was extended to '(facial) feature, trait' (still missing in Stieler and Kramer), used by Zesen, *Rosen.* [1645], Wieland, 5,239: '. . . *ob ihm gleich kleine Züge entwischten*', and at the same time also for 'trait' with ref. to the character, outlook or behaviour of persons, but with ref. to abstracts only since the 18th c., e.g. Wieland, *Luc.* 4,52: '. . . *den skythischen Charakter, in welchem Naturwildheit, Verwegenheit . . . wesentliche Züge sind*'. Compounds are numerous, e.g. *Charakterzug*, as in Gervinus, *Lit.* 5,175: '. . . *Originals, in dem Karikaturzüge Charakterzüge der Menschheit sind*', *Familienzug*, used by Schiller, also Eichendorff, *Gesch.Dr.* 24, *Gemütszug*, modern, e.g. Meißner, *Sansara* 3,285 [1855]: '*ein abergläubiger Gemüthszug, der in mir steckt*', *Gesichtszug*, not yet recorded by Stieler and Kramer, used by Lessing, Goethe and Schiller, e.g. *D.Carlos* 4,13; cf. Kant's observation on married people: '*die Vertraulichkeit und Neigung . . . bringt . . . ähnliche Mienen hervor, die . . . in stehende Gesichtszüge übergehen*', also the punning sl. phrase *ich hau dich, daß dir die Gesichtszüge entgleisen*, recorded in *D.richt. Berliner* 85 [1924] in dialect form, *Grundzug*, used by Goethe, also Wieland 30,291, *Lokalzug*, since the 19th c., e.g. Gödeke, *Grundr.Gesch.Lit.* 795 [1862]: '. . . *daß das Schicksal eines Dichters unbeschadet der Lokalzüge . . . als Schicksal . . . überhaupt gefaßt wird*' (*Lokalzug* can also mean 'local train', belongong to ~ (1)), *Meisterzug*, since the 18th c., e.g. Goethe, *Lehrj.* 4,14 on Ophelia: '*nur mit wenig Meisterzügen ist ihr Charakter vollendet*', *Mienenzug*, modern, e.g. Meißner, *Sansara* 1,212, *Nationalzug*, since the 18th c.; cf. also *Nationalvorzug*, used by Goethe in *Don Ciccio*: '. . . *genoß der Verfasser des noch größeren Nationalvorzugs, einer lebendigen Welt-*

Anschauung', *Schmerzenszug*, 18th c., e.g. Goethe, *Iphig.* 2,1: '. . . *die blühenden Gesichter den Schmerzenszug langsamen Tods verrathen*', Goethe also used *Schreckenszug* (not listed in *DWb.*), *Trauerzug*, e.g. Jean Paul 2,24: '. . . *sah . . . im Glase dieses Portraits sein eigenes mit seinen Trauerzügen nachgespiegelt*' (much more frequently used is *Trauerzug* = 'funeral procession', which belongs to ~ (1).

der ~ (3) pull; in figur. sense = 'promptings, urge, attraction'; since the 16th c., mainly in ~ *zu etw.* or *jem.m*, including the notions of inclination towards sb. and desire for sth., e.g. Ziegler, *Banise* 488: '*ein innerlicher zug heißet mich lieben*', Goethe, 8,60 (W.): '. . . *fühlte einen neuen Zug nach Bamberg*', 21,94 (W.): '*durch einen unwiderstehlichen Zug hingeführt*', 23,271 (W.): '. . . *von Natur zur Religiosität geneigt, ihr Zustand, ihre Einsamkeit vermehrten diesen Zug*', Wieland 20,215: '. . . *Berg . . . wo sie mit durstigen weit ausgeholten Zügen den milden Strom des reinsten Himmels trinkt*'. There are several lit. compounds, such as *Herzenszug*, e.g. Willkomm, *Zeit.* 1,58: '. . . *diesem Herzenszuge sich hingeben*', though ~ *des Herzens* is preferred, e.g. Huch, *Pitt u. Fox* 109: '*laß ihn dem Zug seines Herzens folgen*' (also the example from Schiller quoted under *Schicksal*); cf. also Tiedge, *Werke* 2,183 [1823]: '*die Lüfte wehten still wie Blumenathemzüge*'. – For examples of early beginnings of ~ (3) in religious contexts in the language of the Mystics see *DWb.* 16,392.

in den letzten Zügen liegen to be breathing one's last; *Züge* here = *Atemzüge*; since Early NHG, e.g. Luther Bible transl. Mark 5,23, Goethe, *Faust I*, 2962; since the 18th c. extended to things and abstracts for 'to be near extinction, peter out', e.g. Gottsched, *Beytr.z.krit.H.* 1,310 on Low German: '*jetzo ist es ganz herunter gekommen und liegt in den letzten Zügen*'.

der ~ nach dem Westen (hist.) the move to the West, also attraction of the West; since the 2nd half of the 19th c., when inhabitants of East Prussia, Posen, Silesia and other Eastern areas flooded into Berlin and P.Lindau dealt with this in a cycle of novels of which the first bore the title *Der Zug nach Westen* [1886]. ~ here can be taken as ~ (1) and ~ (3).

der ~ (4) pain (which makes one feel a kind of pull); close to ~ (3), but only phys., belonging to *ziehen* (see *der Schmerz zieht jem.*, p. 2728); since the 17th c., e.g. Goethe IV,3,148 (W.): '. . . *der Zug aber in den Schenkeln und Seiten fatal*'.

← See also under *anziehen* (for *Anzug, anzüglich* and *Anzüglichkeit*), *Atem* (for *bis zum letzten Atemzug* and *mit einem Atemzug*), *aufziehen* (for *Aufzug*), *ausziehen* (for *Auszug*), *bemerken* (for *mit diesem Zuge bemerken wollen*), *best* (for *im besten Zug*), *beziehen* (for *Bezug, mit Bezug auf, Bezugnahme* and *bezüglich*), *blitzen* (for *Blitzzug*), *brechen* (for *durch sein Lächeln brach ein Zug von Mißmut*), *fehlen* (for *Fehlzug*), *gehen* (for *der Zug geht, ihre Züge sind soso* and *wunderbar geht durch jene Welt noch ein anderer schrecklicher Zug*), *grob* (for *in groben Zügen*), *Grund* (for *verlangte auf Grund dieses Vorzuges* and *auf den Vorzug der Gründlichkeit stolz zu werden*), *gut* (for *einen guten Zug aus der Flasche tun, ein Zug oder eine Scene*, where *er hat einen guten Zug am Leibe* should also have been listed), *klimmen* (for *Klimmzüge machen*), *Peitsche* (for *angstgepeitscht begann den irren Zug der Frevler*), *piepen* (for *eine gute Henne unter einem ganzen Zug Piepchen*), *rauben* (for *Raubzug*), *Reihe* (for *an den fröhlichen Zug mich zu reihen*), *Reue* (for *Reuezug*), *Schach* (for *Schach-zug*), *Schein* (for *wenn unter den besondern zufälligen Zügen das Allgemeine vorscheint*), *Schicksal* (for *der Zug des Herzens ist des Schicksals Stimme*), *schlüpfen* (for *mit vollen Zügen*), *schneiden* (for *edelgeschnittene Züge*), *schön* (for *das ist ein schöner Zug in seinem Charakter*), *Sieg* (for *Siegeszug*), *sprechen* (for *wenn der Geist die Züge bestimmt*), *streichen* (for *strich alle Vorzüge heraus*), *streifen* (for *Streifzug*), *sympathetisch* (for *ein geheimer sympathetischer Zug*), *überrollen* (for *Zug der Zeit*), *umwittern* (for *Zauberhauch, der euren Zug umwittert*), *Verzug, Winkelzug* and *ziehen* (for *in vollen Zügen*).

Zugabe
die ~ (1) (obs.) admission; derived from *etw. zugeben* = 'to admit to sth.'; used by Herder (edit. S.) 3,166 and still occasionally in the 19th c., but now obs., displaced by *Zugeständnis, Eingeständnis* or *das Zugeben*.

die ~ (2) additional item given as a gift; since MHG (*zuogâb*) for material gifts; figur. with abstracts since the 18th c., e.g. Goethe IV,1,259 (W.): '*die Zugabe, die uns das Schicksaal zu jeder Glückseligkeit drein wiegt*'; in the context of concerts, operas, etc. = 'encore'.

die ~ (3) (legal, a.) codicil, appended statement, postscript; since Early NHG, used by Luther 11,278 (Weimar); now a.

← See also under *geben* (for *hast du nur den Kern, die Schale gibt sich dann als eine Zugab*).

zugaffen: see *gaffen*.

Zugang
einen ~ *zu etw. haben* to have access to sth.; f.r.b. Frisius [1556], e.g. Luther Bible transl. Ephes. 2,18 (in A.V. 'access'); in wider sense = 'way leading to sth., entrance to sth.', as in Hutten [edit. Böcking] 1,380: '*öffene uns einen zugang zu der christenlichen warheit*', Nietzsche, *Werke* 4,369: '*er kennt keine kostspieligen Zugänge zum Vergnügen*'.

an ~ *gewinnen* to gain an increase in sth. (e.g. members, visitors, clients, etc.); since the 18th c., e.g. Goethe IV,27,298 (W.): '. . . *Jena an Celebrität und Zugang gewinnen werde*'; cf. also ~ *finden* = 'to find acceptance, be admitted', e.g. (DWb) Ranke, *Sämmtl. Werke* 38,16: '*in die . . . Alpen hatte der Protestantismus keinen Zugang gefunden*'.

zugänglich
zugänglich approachable, amenable; only since the 18th c., frequent in Goethe's writings, e.g. for 'easily reachable', but also for 'approachable' with ref. to persons, e.g. IV,10,283 (W.) in wider sense = 'willing to listen, responsive', which established itself in the 19th c.; hence *Zugänglichkeit*, since the 19th c.

zugeben
etw. ~ (1) to add sth.; f.r.b. Frisius [1556], used by Luther 28,542 (Weimar): '*zu der heiligen schrifft sol man nichts zugeben*', where *hinzugeben* or *hinzufügen* would now be preferred, but in comm. contexts it is still used for 'to add (as a gift)'; cf. *Zugabe*.

etw. ~ (2) to concede, admit to sth.; sometimes verging on 'to confess to sth.'; since Early NHG, e.g. Luther 18,63 (Weimar): '*wenn man noch heutigs tags den Juden zugebe, das Christus ein lauter mensch were*'; hence also the past participle in absolute construction *zugegeben, . . .* = 'admittedly, granted . . .' (for *wenn auch zugegeben werden würde, daß . . .*); modern.

etw. ~ (3) to permit sth., allow sth. to happen; since Early NHG, f.r.b. Frisius [1556], used by Luther Bible transl. Psalm 16,10 (where the A.V. has 'suffer'). This is still in use, e.g. Raabe, *Hungerpastor* 2,333, but *sich in etw.* ~ , as still used by Droste-Hülshoff (letter to Schücking 348), is obs.

← See also under *frei* (for *frei zugeben*) and *Fuchs* (for *gemessen eben hat sie der Fuchs und seinen Schwanz noch zugegeben*).

zugegen
~ *sein* (1) (obs.) to be opposed or in conflict; since Early NHG and still in the 18th c., e.g. Brockes, *Ird. Vergn.* 9,5,79 [1721]: '*der Natur widersprüchig und zugegen*'; now obs., displaced by *im Widerspruch mit, entgegengesetzt* (and in some contexts *dagegen*).

~ *sein* (2) to be present; of legal origin, since MHG, usual only with ref. to persons, e.g. Goethe, *Faust* 10106, rare with ref. to things.

← See also under *Herz* (for *das Herz ist hier des ganzen Volks, die Besten sind zugegen*).

zugehen

etw. geht jem.m zu sth. reaches sb., is sent or given to sb.; figur. since Early NHG, when at first it often referred to diseases befalling sb.; then in many contexts, e.g. Goethe 25,287 (W.): '*die seinem Bezirk . . . zugegangenen großen Vortheile*'; frequent with *Nachricht*.

etw. geht auf etw. zu things are moving towards sth.; with abstracts since Early NHG, e.g. Luther 34,2,9 (Weimar): '*es wyrdt nicht uff eyn ebentewer zugehen*'; often with ref. to the seasons, e.g. *es geht auf den Winter zu*.

dort geht es . . . (adverb) *. . . zu* things there are in a . . . state, there things happen in a . . . way; since MHG, used by Luther in his Apocr. transl. 2 Macc. 2,28 (in Engl. version 2,27); always with a modal or temporal adverb; recorded by Frisius [1556].

zugehen (intrans.) to help, assist; since Early NHG; hence the regional terms for 'domestic help' such as *Zugehefrau* or *Zugeherin* (where other areas use *Lauffrau* or *Putzfrau*, in modern standard *Hausgehilfin*). It is strange that *DWb.* [1956] does not list the meaning 'to help', although *Zugeherin* is recorded (without comment).

← See also under *bunt* (for *es geht bunt zu*), *Ding* (for *es geht nicht mit rechten Dingen zu*), *Flor* (2) (for *es gieng in floribus zu*), *Glas* (for *weil es in ihren Häusern wohl und galant zugehet*), *Jude* (for *es geht dort zu wie in einer Judenschule*), *katholisch* (for *da geht's nicht katholisch zu*), *knapp* (for *es geht bey ihm gar knapp zu*), *Kraut* (for *es ist mit Kräutern zugegangen*), *Kuckuck* (for *es müßte doch mit dem Kuckuck zugehen*), *richtig* (for *das geht nicht richtig zu*) and *spitz* (for *bei denen geht es spitz zu*). For tech.phys. *zugehen* see under *zulaufen*.

zugehören

etw. gehört jem.m zu sth. belongs to sb.; since Early NHG, same as *gehören* (for which see p. 954), which is now the preferred verb.

jem. gehört einem Verein zu sb. is a member of an association; since Early NHG, the same as *gehören zu* (see p. 954), but *angehören* is now the usual verb.

zugeknöpft *zugeknöpft* (coll.) buttoned-up, tight-lipped, reticent, reserved, uncommunicative; since the 19th c.

← See also under *Tasche* (for *Mann mit zugeknöpften Taschen*).

Zügel

See under *fallen* (for *jem.m in die Zügel fallen*),

gehen (for *Zügel zu frei lassen*, also *ungezügelt*), *hängen* (for *einem Pferd den Zügel hängen*), *harsch* (for *den Zügel schießen lassen*), *hemmen* (for *Hemmzügel anlegen*), *kurz* (for *ein Pferd im Zügel kurz halten*), *Sporn* (for *Gutartigkeit ihres Gemüts, das weder Sporns noch Zügels bedürfe*) and *straff* (for *etw./die Zügel straffer anziehen*).

zügellos

zügellos unbridled, uncontrolled; in figur. sense current since the 17th c., synonymous with *ungezügelt* (current since the 18th c., e.g. Wieland 23,403: '*ungezügelter Schwärmer*'), e.g. Goethe 10,21 (W.). Usually the notions of 'lack of self-control' and 'inclined to self-indulgence' are present so that it can border on 'licentious', 'wanton'. Hence *Zügellosigkeit*, since the 19th c., e.g. Goethe, *Gespr.* 5,145: '*. . . daß er an seiner Zügellosigkeit zu grunde gegangen ist*'.

zügeln

See under *bezügeln*, *entzügeln* and *gehen* (for *sich zügeln*).

zugenäht

See under *nähen* (for *verflucht und zugenäht*) and *Tasche* (for *zugenähte Taschen haben*).

Zugereister

ein ~ a newcomer (to a country or town); only since the 19th c.; occasionally *Zugewanderter* is used instead, also coll. *Reingeschmeckter*.

zugesellen: See *Geselle* (also for *Zugesellung*).

zugestehen: See *stehen* (for *Zugeständnis* see *Stand*).

zugetan

jem.m ~ sein (lit.) to be attached or devoted to sb., have great affection for sb.; *~* meant at first 'related', used like *verwandt* and often coupled with it; since Early NHG, f.r.b. Corvinus. Then it came to be used in a wider sense for 'keeping sb. company' and being devoted to that person (as a follower or friend), as in Schiller, *D.Carlos* 1,9: '*so treu und warm, wie heute dem Infanten, auch dermaleinst dem König zugetan?*', but also (since the 17th c.) expressing warm affection for sb. With ref. to abstracts it means 'being fond of sth., devoting oneself to sth.', e.g. *der Musik, den Künsten ~*, but also 'to incline towards sth.', f.r.b. Stieler, *Geh.Venus* (repr.) 147 [1660]: '*dem geize zugethan*'.

Zugewanderter: see *Zugereister*.

zügig

zügig speedy, rapid, brisk; only since the 20th c., derived from *Zug* (*der Feder, des Pinsels*) moving quickly and without apparent effort or delay; now in contexts far removed from drawing or painting, e.g. *ein zügiges Vorgehen, zügige Erledigung*.

zugkräftig

zugkräftig (1) popular, (capable of) attracting applause, customers, buyers; since the 19th c., coined in stage circles, but now also used in trade, e.g. *ein zugkräftiger Artikel*; cf. coll. *das zugkräftigste Pferd im Stall der Firma*, which can describe the best-selling article of the firm or the most successful person or department of a firm.

zugkräftig (2) powerful, effective; though referring to the noun *Zugkraft* which in phys. sense has been current for a long time, the adjective in this sense is recent, not yet listed in *DWb*. [1956].

zugleich See under *aber* (for *wenn das ja vnd aber zugleich vffziehen, so ist nicht viel dahinder*), *Fuchs* (for *er ist Fuchs und Hase zugleich*), *gesalzen* (for *eine etwas gesalzene und zugleich kummergewohnte Frau*) and *Schüssel* (for *aus zwei Schüsseln zugleich essen*).

Zugluft: see *Zug*.

zugreifen

zugreifen to grasp what is available, help oneself to what is offered; extended from phys. 'grasping' in Early NHG, e.g. Agricola [1528]: '*greyff zu, ehe dir die hende gebunden werden*', Petri [1605] and Henisch [1616]: '*greif zu, weil's zeit ist*', Goethe used it in *Zahme Xenien* III and in *Faust I*, 1764. Steinbach [1734] recorded '*zugreifflich = rapax*', but this is obs.

helfend ~ to assist, lend a hand; since the 18th c., when Steinbach, *Vollst. Dt. Wb.* [1734] recorded: '*man darff nicht viel sagen, er greifft bald zu*'; cf. also *jem. m unter die Arme greifen* (p.1133).

die Behörden sollten ~ the authorities should take measures, tackle what is amiss; derived from the sense 'to attack', 'take action' (beginnings in MHG), since 2nd half of 18th c., e.g. (DWb) Gervinus, *Gesch. d. dt. Dicht.* 4,424: '*Lessing erledigte, wo er ernsthaft zugriff*'. Cf. *zu Mitteln greifen* (p.1130) and *sicher vor den Griffen seiner Polizei* (p.1140).

← See also under *Hand* (for *mit beiden Händen zugreifen*).

Zugriff *etw. jem.s* ~ *entziehen* to prevent sb. from getting hold of sth.; modern, rather stilted; for figur. *entziehen* see p. 662.

Vieler ~ *hält ein Schiff* (prov.) if many people lend a hand, all goes well (literally: 'the ship stays afloat'); since Early NHG, f.r.b. Franck [1541], still listed in modern collections.

zugrunde-

See under *Grund* (for *zugrunde gehen, -legen, -liegen, -richten and -ziehen*), also under *Gewicht* and *Grund* (for *zugrunde sinken*).

Zugstück

das ~ box-office draw, popular play (opera, ballet, etc.); from the language of the stage; since the 18th c., e.g. Goethe 21,89 (W.). The dating under *Stück* (p.2406) is wrong.

zugute-

See under *gut* (for *zugute halten* and *zugute tun*) and *halten* (for *zu gut halten*).

Zugvogel

der ~ (coll.) sb. who does not settle down anywhere for any length of time, indefatigable traveller; since the 18th c., e.g. Goethe IV,8,77 (W.), sometimes in critical remarks, when it comes close to *Zigeuner*; in stud. sl. for 'girl of easy virtue'; also used with ref. to servants who will not stay long in their posts, hence *Zugvogelgeschlecht*, as used for servant girls by Bismarck, *Briefe a.s. Braut u. Gattin* 64.

zuhaften: see *kleben*.

zuhalten

mit einer Frau ~ (obs.) to cohabit with a woman; derived from the obs. meaning ~ = 'to live, pass one's time' (still used in some NW areas in the 19th c., e.g. by Droste-Hülshoff). Current since the 15th c., e.g. Luther 32,332 (Weimar): '. . . *bracht ir zu oren, wie ir man mit einer andern zuhielte*'; still used in the 18th c., now obs., as is *jem. m* ~ = 'to stand by sb.', still used early in the 19th c., displaced by *zu jem. m halten*.

etw. ~ to shut, cover, block sth.; frequent with ref. to parts of the body, e.g. Luther Apocr. transl. Ecclesiasticus 27,15: '*ir haddern macht, das man die ohren zuhalten mus*', but also with ref. to other objects, e.g. Lehman [1662]: '*den Säckel zuhalten*' = 'to keep one's purse closed'; occasionally in lit. with an abstract as the subject, as in Lessing [edit.M.] 2,8: '*du kannst sie nicht sehen, weil dir die Liebe die Augen zuhält*'.

← See also under *halten* (for *halten mit der erden zuo*) and *Ohr* (for *sich die Ohren zuhalten*).

zuhängen: see *hängen* (p. 1233).

zu Hause: see *Haus*

Zuhausesein: see *schlürfen*.

zuherrschen: see *herrschen*.

zuhören

fleißige Zuhörer machen fleißige Lehrer (prov.) diligent listeners make diligent teachers; modern prov., only recorded since the 19th c., e.g. by Simrock [1846].

zujauchzen: see *austrommeln*.

zukehren

See under *Rücken* (for *jem. m* or *einer Sache den Rücken zukehren*) and *Schwert* (for *feindselig eins dem andern zugekehrt*).

zukiffen

zugekifft sein (s.) to be doped, befuddled; from

kiffen (sl.) = 'to take drugs'; both simplex and compound are 20th c. sl.

zuklemmen: see *Klemme*.

zuknöpfen

See under *bescheren* (for *vergiß das Zuknöpfen nicht*), *oben* (for *bis oben zugeknöpft*) and *zugeknöpft*.

zukommen

zukommen (obs.) to arrive, come; since MHG as in the Lord's Prayer: '*zuo chome dîn rîche*' (in Mone, *Anzeiger* 8,41,88), even used sometimes by Luther, still in Adelung [1801] and Goethe, *Dicht.u.Wahrh.* 2,9 has '*Redouten des zukommenden Winters*'; now displaced by the simplex.

etw. kommt jem.m zu (1) sth. reaches sb., is received by sb., befalls sb.; with abstracts such as *Glück*, *Unglück*, *Krankheit*, *Überraschung*, *Nachricht* since Early NHG, e.g. *er ahnte nicht, was noch auf ihn zukommen würde*, Herder [edit. S.] 21,3: '*Verstand kommt dir nicht zu, er wohnet in dir*'. In philosophy since the 18th c. *etw. kommt einer Sache zu* = 'sth. possesses sth., is endowed with sth., belongs to sth.', e.g. Wolff, *Logik* [1725]: '*der Grund, warumb einem Dinge etwas zukommen kan oder nicht, ist entweder in ihm, und zwar in etwas zu suchen, was es beständig an sich hat, oder . . .*'.

etw. kommt jem.m zu (2) sb. is entitled to sth.; since the 17th c., but now displaced by *zustehen* (see second meaning of *zustehen* on p. 2349).

jem.m etw. ~ lassen to provide sth. for sb., grant or give sth. to sb., let sb. have sth.; natural extension of *etw. kommt jem.m zu* (1).

einer Sache kommt etw. zu (lit.) sth. possesses sth., can be credited with sth.; with abstracts such as *Bedeutung*, *Beachtung*, etc., e.g. *diesem Ereignis kommt große Bedeutung zu* = 'this event is of great significance'; since the 18th c., e.g. Goethe 42,2,258 (W.); essentially, this meaning of ~ denotes no more than 'to have'.

das kommt dir nicht zu (regional) that does not befit you; a negative off-spring from *etw. kommt jem.m zu* (2); recorded by Stieler [1691], still used in some regions, e.g. Anzengruber, *Schandfleck*, chapt. 14.

das lasse ich auf mich ~ (coll.) I'll let this take its course, I'll wait to see how (or if) it affects me, will deal with it when it happens; modern.

wir werden dann auf Sie ~ (comm.) we shall contact you in due course; modern.

zukriegen

du kriegst die Tür nicht zu! (sl.) dear me! what a silly thing! would you believe it! exclamation of surprise (sometimes expressing irritation at one's own behaviour); 20th c. sl.

Zukunft

die ~ (1) (obs.) arrival; from MHG to the 17th c.; later still occasionally in lit., e.g. Goethe, *Was wir bringen* (Forts. 1): '*Wundertöne, die mir der Parzen nahe Zukunft deuten*'; displaced by *Ankunft*.

die ~ (2) (ling.) future tense; only since 18th c. for *tempus futurum* replacing *zukünftige Zeit* (which was still used by Gottsched).

die ~ (3) (personified) the Future; in lit. sometimes seen as a person since the 18th c., e.g. *die ~ wird es lehren, zeigen, erweisen, die ~ wird unsere heutigen Vergehen richten*, Schiller, *Spr.d.Confuzius*: '*zögernd kommt die Zukunft hergezogen*', Haller, *Alfred* 191 [1773]: '*die Zukunft gebiert neue Erfordernüsse*'. See further examples among the cross-references.

etw. hat (eine) ~ sth. has a future, will develop strongly in times to come; general since the 19th c., often in the negative (as in Engl.): *es hat keine ~* (or *ist ohne ~*); cf. also the pronouncement by Emperor Wilhelm II (23.9.1898): '*unsere Zukunft liegt auf dem Wasser*', which became a slogan for advocates of a strong navy and expansion overseas. Hence also *zukunftsreich* and *zukunftsvoll*, both since the 19th c.

← See also under *blicken* (for *Ausblick in die Zukunft*), *blind* (for *schwach und für die Zukunft blind*), *enthüllen* (for *wenn sich die Zukunft unsern Augen enthüllen wird*), *glatt* (for *die Zukunft mit Brettern vernagelt zu sehen*), *Gold* (for *das Gold der Zukunft über sich selbst dahinrauschen fühlte*), *Gott* (for *Klotz, woraus die Zukunft noch ein Götterbild schaffen kann*), *Griff* (for *mit einem vertrauensvollen Griff in die Zukunft*), *hell* (for *eine helle Zukunft*), *Kreuz* (for *auf dem Kreuzwege seiner Zukunft stehen*), *Saat* (for *Saaten in die Zukunft streu'n*), *Schulter* (for *pygmäenhaft steigt die Zukunft auf die Schultern des Jetzt*), *schwarz* (for *nicht so schwarz in die Zukunft blicken*), *vorausnehmen* (for *ein thörichtes Vorausnehmen der Zukunft*) and *Windstille* (for *die Zukunft heller geworden schien*).

zukünftig

seine Zukünftige (ihr Zukünftiger) (coll.) his future wife (her future husband); an ellipsis, current since the 16th c. (cf. Engl. ellipsis 'his or her intended'); e.g. Fel. Platter (edit. Boos) 313.

← See also under *Nacht* (for *Nacht zieht ihre Decke vor das Zukünftige*).

Zukunftsmusik

das ist ~ that is pie in the sky, a castle in the air (or in Spain); beginnings as *Musik der Zukunft* and *zukünftige Musik*, used by Robert Schumann in 1833. Wagner in 1850 published an essay *Das Kunstwerk der Zukunft* and in 1861 an article entitled ~, accepting the term (which was also used sometimes for compositions by Liszt). The term was sometimes derided, e.g. Grillparzer, *Sämtl. Werke* [edit. Sauer] 3,204: '*habe die Hegelsche Philosophie überlebt, werd' auch die Zukunftsmusik überleben*', but adopted with pride by Wagner's followers. Later given its present derogatory meanings, to which *Zukunftsmusikant* and *Zukunftsmusiker* were added.

Zukunftsschloß
Zukunftsschlösser bauen to build castles in the air (or in Spain); since the 19th c., e.g. (T.) Zobeltitz, *Auf märk. Erde* 131 [1910]. *DWb.* [1956] does not list the noun.

Zukunftsstaat
der ~ (hist.,a.) the Socialist State; the term was first used by A.Meißner in 1849, but became current only ca. 1870 when Social Democrats used it frequently and Bismarck (in *Polit. Reden* 7,258) said on 17.9.1878: '. . . *daß ich endlich auch erführe, wie Herr Bebel und Genossen sich den Zukunftsstaat . . . eigentlich denken*'. Details in Ladendorf, *Histor. Schlagwb.* 354 [1906].

zulächeln
etw. lächelt jem.m zu (lit.) sth. smiles at sb.; since the 18th c. with abstracts as the subject, e.g. S.v.Laroche, *Frl. St.* 2,70 [1771]: '. . . *ohne daß Ihnen das Glück jemals zugelächelt hätte*', Goethe 49,1,111 (W.): '*der Berg freut sich sein und lächelt ihm zu*'.

zulachen
jem.m ~ (lit.) to laugh (with joy, relief, encouragement) at or towards sb.; since Early NHG, e.g. Luther 34,2,471 (Weimar), also with *Glück* as the subject as in the locution quoted under *zulächeln*; cf. also Wieland, *Werke* [Acad.edit.] 1,1,1390: '*die heitre Gegend lacht ihm Ruhe zu*'.

zulangen
es langt nicht zu it does not suffice, is not enough (for a certain purpose or one's needs); cf. *auslangen* (for *mit etw. auslangen*), also *ausreichen* (p.147); since the 17th c., recorded by Kramer [1702]; often with ref. to *Geld*, but also such abstracts as *Kraft*.

zulänglich
zulänglich sufficient; since the 17th c. in phys. and figur. contexts, e.g. Lessing [edit. M.] 4,68: '*die zulänglichste Antwort darauf ist, daß . . .*', Goethe IV,21,310 (W.): '*keine Vorschläge waren zulänglich, noch durchgreifend*'.

zulassen
zulassen to admit, allow; figur. extension from phys. 'to let in, grant admission' with ref. to abstracts since Early NHG, when 'admitting' became 'permitting', f.r.b. Frisius [1556]: '*eine klag zulassen*', e.g. Luther 12,684 (Weimar), also in his Bible transl. Mark 10,4: '*Moses hat zugelassen, einen scheidbrieff zu schreiben*' (where the A.V. used 'suffered'); hence *zugelassen* = 'permitted, allowed', f.r.b. Hulsius [1616] and *zulässig* = 'permissible', which appeared in the 16th c., only in modern period sometimes used for *zuverlässig* = 'reliable', e.g. by Goethe II,5,1,84 (W.), but this has disappeared again. The negation *unzulässig* has been current since the 16th c. When Campe [1813] suggested it as a replacement for *inadmissibel*, he maintained at the same time that *unzuläßlich*, also current since the 16th c. and recorded by Kramer [1700], would be the better form.

← See also under *Ehre* (for *dieß soll ime zugelassen sein*).

Zulauf
einen großen ~ *haben* to have much popular support, attract many followers; since Early NHG, f.r.b. Frisius [1556] with *machen*; Luther and Fischart used it with *haben*; figur. (where no actual movement of people is implied) since the 17th c.

zulaufen
jem.m ~ to join sb.; with ref. to crowds running towards and acclaiming sb. since Early NHG, only since modern period for 'to become sb's follower', e.g. Keller, *Werke* 4,10; often now in polit. contexts for 'to vote for sb.'; pejor. in such cases as *viele Dumme sind dem Demagogen zugelaufen*.

etw. läuft auf etw. zu sth. approaches sth., develops into (or towards) sth.; figur. when the subject is a thing which cannot run or an abstract; at least since the 17th c., e.g. Grimmelshausen [edit. K.] 2,527: '*die Zeit eben gegen dem Ende des Augusti zulieff*'; *zugehen* is preferred.

etw. läuft spitz zu (phys., tech.) sth. ends in a sharp point, tapers towards a pointed end; since Early NHG, but at first with *zugehen*, f.r.b. Corvinus [1646]: '*winckel, der spitz oder scharpff zugehet*'; with ~ in Olearius, *Pers. Reisebeschr.* 92 [1696]: '*kurtze stieffeln, so vorne spitz zulauffen*'.

zulegen
etw. ~ to add sth.; since Early NHG with abstracts, e.g. Luther 30,1,155, (Weimar), Goethe, *Faust I*, 990. Hence *Zulage* = 'additional pay or allowance', *Gehaltszulage*, etc.

jem.m etw. ~ to give sb. sth., endow (or saddle) sb. with sth.; since Early NHG, e.g. Luther 1,274 (Weimar), Fischart, *B.* 34a, Wieland, *Luc.* 1,328: '. . . *hat ihm der große Haufe den Beinamen Kanon zugelegt*'.

sich etw. ~ to acquire sth.; of phys. origin (con-

nected with *Beilager*); general since the 18th c.,
e.g. Wieland 12,85: '*der hat ein feines junges Weib
sich zugelegt für seinen Leib*', then extended to
things or abstracts, e.g. *er hat sich einen neuen
Anzug, einen Titel zugelegt*.

Geld ~ (comm.) to lose money in a transaction, end up with a deficit; modern.

zulegen (intran., coll.) to add, increase; in
many contexts, e.g. = 'to increase speed', 'step
on it' (cf. obs. *beilegen* on p. 127), e.g. *einen Zahn
~*, or = 'to win more votes', e.g. *bei den Wahlen
tüchtig ~*, or 'to gain in value', e.g. *gestern hat das
Pfund zugelegt*. All these coll. locutions are
recent, but are in essence mere extensions of *etw.
~* (see above).

← See also under *Fuchs* (for *Meilen, zu denen
der Fuchs seinen langen Schweif zugelegt hat*).

zuleide: see *leiden*.

zuletzt See under *glatt* (for *zuletzt belegert uns
. . . der tüfel*), *herrlich* (for *wie wir's dann zuletzt so
herrlich weit gebracht*), *hinauslaufen* (for *mußte es
zuletzt zu gewaltsamen Szenen hinauslaufen*) and
lachen (for *wer zuletzt lacht, lacht am besten*).

zulieb See under *leiden* (for *keinem zuliebe und
keinem zuleide*) and *Ohr* (for *einem etwas ze lieb
reden*).

zumachen

die Augen ~ (euphem.) to die; at least since the
18th c., e.g. Wieland, *Luc.* 3,368: '*sobald der Alte
die Augen zumacht*'; cf. *die Augen schließen*
(p.116).

kein Auge ~ (coll.) to get no sleep at all; modern coll.; quite different is the context in Lessing
1,509: '*ich mache kein Auge zu, so schlage ich mich
mit ihm herum*'.

mach zu! (coll.) hurry up, get a move on! modern, but Stieler (1691) recorded synon. '*mach
fort! = accelera gradum*'.

mach die Tür von außen zu (coll.) get out of
here; modern coll.

← See also under *Bude* (for *die Bude
zumachen*), *Fenster* (for *die Fensterläden
zumachen*), *Fuchs* (for *sich den eltern vnd schul-
meistern treflich zumachen*), *klappen* (for *die Klappe
zumachen*), *Loch* (for *ein Loch mit dem andern
zumachen*) and *Tür* (for *der Letzte macht die Türe
zu*).

zumal

zumal (1) (a.) together; since Early NHG,
both in temporal sense = 'at the same time' (still
used by Schiller) and in local sense, as in Keller,
Werke 4,223: '*als ob drei zumal im Bette lägen*';
both are now a.

zumal (2) especially, particularly; since Early
NHG, f.r.b. Corvinus, *Fons* [1623], Kramer

[1702]: '*ich gehe nicht gern aus dem Hause, zumal
im Winter*'.

← See also under *halten* (for *aber etliche sint
zemale grob als daz wazzer*). See also under *Mal*
(for *zu einem Mal*).

zumauern: see *Mauer*.

zumessen

See under *Glück* (for *Glücksblume, die der
Schöpfer ihnen zugemessen hat*) and *messen* (for
*damit auch ihm seine gebührende Portion des Ruhms
zugemessen werde*).

zumute

jem.m ist gut (wohl) ~ sb. feels cheerful, is in
good spirits; ~ , current since OHG (*ze muote*)
has remained in use only as an adverb describing
one's feelings; Kramer [1702] recorded: '*die
Reiche wissen nicht, wie einem Armen zu Mut ist*';
cf. also related *wohlgemut*. Wander [1880]
recorded as a coll. expression '*es ist ihm zumuthe,
wie dem Mops im Spucknapf*' for 'sb. feels
depressed or under painful restraint'.

jem.m ist nach etw. ~ sb. feels like wanting (or
wanting to do) sth., is in the mood for sth.; only
since modern period (but cf. Kramer [1702]:
'*keinen Mut zu etwas haben*'); cf. synon. *jem.m
steht der Sinn nach etw.* (p. 2347), which may
have influenced the locution with ~.

zumuten

jem.m etw. ~ (1) (obs.) to presume sth. of sb.,
impute sth. to sb.; since Early NHG, still in the
19th c. (Heine, G. Keller); now displaced by
zuschreiben, zutrauen, von jem.m erwarten; see also
the related *vermuten* (p. 2565).

jem.m etw. ~ (2) to demand or expect sth.
from sb.; first in Early NHG with ref. to sugges-
tions or advice, but since the 16th c. entailing an
exacting, even unreasonable demand, recorded
by Kramer [1702]; hence *die Zumutung*, f.r.b.
Kramer, e.g. Goethe IV,32,143 (W.) on a proposed visit: '*so ist doch auch diese Zumuthung bey
einer so weiten Entfernung . . . etwas stark*'; often in
welch eine Zumutung! = 'what a thing to ask for! a
tall order'.

sich zuviel ~ to overtask or overtax oneself,
bite off more than one can chew; cf. Goethe
IV,19,404 (W.): '*ich darf mir nichts zumuten*'.

zunächst: see *durchstechen*.

zunageln: see *Brett*.

zunähen

See under *nähen* (for *verflucht und zugenäht*),
Tasche (for *zugenähte Taschen haben*) and *zugenäht*.

zünden

etw. ~ to set sth. alight, cause sth. to burst out
in flames; since the 17th c., e.g. (DWb) Spee,

Güld.Tugendb. 305 [1649]: *'mein Hertz er zündet inniglich'*, Alexis, *Ruhe i.d.e.B.* 1,168: *'es war ein Funke, der viele Gedanken zündete'*, with figur. Mine in Goethe, *Lehrj.* 3,6: *'... ein Wunder, daß endlich der kleine Funke die Mine zündete?'*, F.Schlegel, *Luc.* 66: *'noch ehe der Blitz der Liebe in ihrem Schoß gezündet'*. Now largely displaced by compounds.

zündend stirring, rousing, electrifying, kindling enthusiasm; since the 18th c., e.g. Goedeke, *Grundriß* 1,717 [1862]: *'die Leiden des Jungen Werthers fielen zündend in die Gemüther'*; frequent in *zündende Rede*, also *zündende Gedanken*, as in Bismarck, *Ged.u.Erinn.* 2,75.

bei ihm hat es gezündet (1) (coll.) he has understood, seen the light, caught on, the penny has dropped; modern coll. (not yet recorded in *DWb.* [1956]).

bei ihm hat es gezündet (2) (coll.) he has fallen in love, caught fire; modern coll., also missing in *DWb.*

← See also under *anzünden*, *blitzen* (for *diese sogenannte Nation zu entzünden*), *entzünden* (also for *Entzündung*), *Feuer* (for *bis wir ihnen die Streu unter dem Steiß angezündet haben*), *Flamme* (for *sin herze wart enzündet*), *Gesinde* (for *des Himmels Lampen anzuzünden*) and *Licht* (for *dem Tag ein Licht anzünden* and *das Licht an beiden Enden anzünden*).

Zunder

der ~ (1) (lit.) tinder, fuel, sth. which sets persons or abstracts alight; frequent in lit. since MHG, e.g. *der minne ~* = 'the passion of love', used by several poets, Lohenstein, *Armin.* 2,10b [1689]: *'der Zunder dieses Unheils'*, Hagedorn 3,144: *'euch heißt der Wein der Unart Zunder'*, Musäus, *M.* 3,11: *'was ist Ehre als Zunder des Stolzes'*. Schiller in *M.Stuart* 1,7 used *den ~ zu etwas tragen*, and in *Braut v.M.* 2062 as well as in *Glocke* 355 he chose the compound *Feuerzunder*.

der ~ (2) (cant) the head; only in the language of the underworld.

der ~ (3) (sl.) nonsense, rubbish; belongs to the group which also contains *Zimt* and *Zinnober* used in this extended sense; 20th c. sl.

jem.m ~ geben (coll.) to hit (or cause trouble to) sb.; first in mil.sl. where it meant 'to put sb. (or sb.'s position) under fire', then in general coll. for 'to hit, lay into sb.'; hence also *~ kriegen* = 'to cop it, get it in the neck'; 20th c. coll.

dürr wie (ein) ~ tinder-dry, as dry as dust; since MHG, e.g. Wolfram v. Eschenbach, *Parz.* 256,27; later as the compound *zunderdürr* or *zündertrocken*; cf. Heine [edit. E.] 2,91: *'wie morscher Zunder'*.

etw. brennt (or *fängt Feuer) wie ~* sth burns like tinder; since MHG, e.g. Megenberg, *B.d.Natur* 405. Later in the opposite *es ist wie nasser* (or *feuchter) ~* = 'it will not catch fire', since the 18th c.

← See also under *fangen* (for *die jugent ein zundel ist, der seer bald fehet*).

Zündstoff

der ~ (lit.) dynamite, powder keg, sth. which is liable to cause an explosion, revolution, trouble; in this figur. sense since the 19th c.; cf. similar *Brennstoff*, as in Wieland 22,320: *'in einem mit lauter Zunder und Brennstoff augefüllten Gemüthe'*.

Zündung: see *fehlen* (for *Fehlzündung*).

zunehmen

See under *Gerste* (for *der knecht nimpt zu wie die reife gerste*), *gut* (for *also hett auch ... die Summ zugenommen*) and *Mond* (for *bei ihr ist zunehmender Mond*).

zuneigen: see *neigen*.

Zuneigung

die ~ (1) inclination; with ref. to leanings towards sth. or sb. general since the 17th c.; Kramer [1702] recorded *'wider seine Zuneigung etwas thun'* for 'to do sth. against one's inclination'.

die ~ (2) affection; in the sense of deep or cordial feeling towards sb. influenced by French *inclination*; in German general since the 18th c., e.g. *eine ~ zu jem.m fassen* = 'to become fond of sb.'.

Zunft

die ~ class, group, clique; out of the original meaning 'agreement, contract' arose the specialized sense 'guild, corporation', since Early NHG extended to groups of like-minded people or persons following a similar profession, e.g. H.Sachs, *Fab.* 2,92: *'... lebet in der schweinen zunft'*, Luther 23,113 (Weimar): *'der schwermer zunft'*, even with abstracts, e.g. Stoppe, *Parnaß* 5 [1735]: *'der düstern Sorgen schwarze Zunft'*; cf. also G.Keller, *Ges. Werke* 2,314 (*Seldw.II*): *'... der lachenden und stets zechenden Zunft der Seldwyler'*; frequent also in compounds, e.g. *Hexenzunft* in Goethe, *Faust I*, 4402, *Spitzbubenzunft* in Schiller, *Fiesco* 1,9, Bürger, 9a on the blessings of Bacchus: *'... weil besser wird durch seinen Lohn die Dichterzunft gedeihen'* (Goethe in a review of G.Hiller, *Gedichte* used *Dichtergilde*). For further details see *ZfMundartf* 17 [1941] and 22 [1954].

← See also under *stoßen* (for *einen aus der zunft stoßen*).

Zunftgeist

der ~ (lit.) corporate spirit, *esprit de corps*; since

the 18th c. when Heynatz listed it with the gloss *esprit de corps* and Herder [edit. S.] 17,96 used it in a neutral sense, but since the 19th c. predominantly pejor., e.g. F.Th. Vischer, *Ästhet.* 2,265 on universities: *'denn sie sind gegliederte Corporationen mit dem ganzen trotzigen Zunftgeiste des Mittelalters'*, where 'clannishness, desire to exclude all outsiders' becomes the predominant meaning.

← See also under *Geist* (p.962) (for *Zunftgeist*).

zünftig

zünftig competent, proper, acceptable; current since MHG, first for 'belonging to a guild', extended to 'acceptable to a guild (or one's peers)', since the 18th c., e.g. Klopstock, *Gelehrtenrep.* 14 [1774], and then since the 19th c. in many regions as a term of approval, e.g. (DWb) E.M. Arndt [edit. R.-M.] 5,331: *'nur wer Geheimniß schweigen kann, der ist der rechte, zünftige Mann'*.

zungbeißend: see *Kopf*.

Zunge

die ~ (1) (lit.) language; since OHG as a transl. of Lat. *lingua*, much used in relig. and courtly lit. in the Middle Ages, e.g. Walter v.d.V. 9,8: *'sô wê dir, tiuschiu zunge'*, still frequent in Baroque lit., listed, but called *'veraltet'* by Adelung, criticized because of its foreign origin by Campe, now a., but still used occasionally in poetry and in some locutions such as *alle Länder deutscher Zungen* = ' all German-speaking countries'.

die ~ (2) (lit.) the voice (esp. in emotion, particularly ecstasy); of bibl. origin, e.g. Psalm 51,16 (in A.V. 51,15, where 'my mouth' is used) and 66,17 (where A.V. has 'my tongue'); often in relig. lit., e.g. J.Mentzer's hymn: *'o daß ich tausend Zungen hätte'*; cf. also *mit Zungen reden*, first in the Bible (Mark 16,17) from Aramaic or Hebrew sources; for 'speaking when inspired or carried away by ecstasy', as in 1 Cor. 14,26: *'er hat eine lere, er hat zungen'*, still ocassionally in mod. lit., e.g. G.Hauptmann, *Weber* 62: '. . . fängt an, mit 'Zungen' zu reden', but also in nonrelig. contexts for 'to proclaim sth. in an elated condition', as in (DWb) P.Heyse 1,171: *'im Becher schäumt der Wein, in Zungen wird gesprochen'*.

die ~ (3) (tech.) tongue, flap, catch, pointer; with ref. to scales since Early NHG (cf. *Zünglein an der Wage* below), with ref. to the catch in a belt (also called *Dorn der Schnalle*) since Early NHG; more recent are ~ for the lower part of the trigger of a pistol or gun (e.g. Stifter 3,31: *'drücke an der eisernen Zung'*) and for the flap on

shoes (in standard German *Lasche*), and in the regions and in trades for many other things (see *DWb.* 16,606 [1956]).

die ~ (4) (mus.) reed, tongue; since Early NHG with ref. to organs and some wind instruments; hence also *Zungenpfeifen* and *Zungenregister*.

die ~ (5) (lit.) tongue, flame in movement; cf. phrases with *lecken* with ref. to flames (p. 1598); since the 18th c. mainly in the compounds *Feuerzungen* and *Flammenzungen*. Goethe used *Feuerzunge*, but in one instance at least with ref. to a passionate voice (*Iphig.* 3,1). Related *Zungen der Wellen* is modern.

die ~ (6) (personified) tongue, voice; since MHG, e.g. Walter v. d.Vogelweide 29,36: *'daz im diu zunge hinket von wîne'*, Bürger, *Lenore*: *'sie weiß nicht, was die Zunge spricht'*, Alexis, *Woldemar* 130: *'wenn ihm die Zunge faselt'*, Goethe, *Iphig* 1,3: *'so dringt auf sie vergebens der Überredung goldne Zunge los'*, Schiller, *Räuber* 1,2: *'mein Herz hörte nicht, was meine Zunge pralte'*; cf. also Goethe, *Lehrj.* 4,16: '. . . wird diese Zunge ihre Verräterin'.

die (7) (zool.) sole (*Pleuronectes solea*); since Early NHG, recorded in Diefenbach, 331b and Maaler [1561]. Usually called *Seezunge*, not in Adelung, but listed in Campe [1810] (cf. p. 2226 on zool. *See*-compounds); the less popular kind from the Baltic Sea is called *Rotzunge*.

die ~ (8) (geogr.) spit, projecting natural feature; first in comparisons, e.g. Carbach, *Livius* [1533]: *'zeucht eyn strich in das meer wie eyn zungen'* and still today, e.g. Frisch, *Homo faber* 20: *'dazwischen Zungen von Land, Sand'*; usually in compounds, e.g. *Gletscherzunge*= 'glacier tongue, snout', e.g. C.F.Meyer, *J.Jen.* 3, *Landzunge* = 'spit, headland', recorded by Adelung together with *Erdzunge* (which is now obs.), used by Goethe in *Reise an Rh.u.M. (St. Rochus)*. *Meerzunge* only since the 19th c., recorded by *DWb.* [1885].

böse Zungen malicious tongues or gossips; under influence of the Bible general since Early NHG (familiar through James 3,5-8 and Ecclesiasticus 28,22: *'böse zungen schneiden schärpffer dann ein schwert'*), e.g. Murner, *Schelmenz.* (repr.) 2: '. . . das böse zungen sindt so gemeyn', also Luther 18,464 (Weimar), where Karlstadt's use of *'boßhafftige zungen'* occurrs, and Goethe 2,227 (W.): *'du findest dort Tabak und böse Zungen'*.

etw. bindet jem.s ~ (lit.) sth. makes sb. tongue-tied; since the 18th c., e.g. Gökingk 3,89: *'nur Scham und Geifer band die Zunge ihm'*.

etw. liegt jem.m auf der ~ sth. is on the tip of sb.'s tongue; used with several verbs, e.g. Goethe, *Werther* (16.3.1772): '. . . *saß mir's auf der Zunge*'; see also under *schweben*.

das soll nicht über meine ~ (or *Lippen*) *kommen* that shall not pass my lips; since the 17th c., mainly used when promising not to reveal sth., but sometimes close to *das bringe ich nicht über die* ~ where it implies silence through reticence or shame. See also under *springen* among the cross-references.

laß dir die ~ *schaben* (coll.) you are too fussy about your food; f.r.b. Kramer [1702]. Older is *die* ~ *schaben müssen* = 'to have to choose one's words with care and speak correctly', as in Luther 6,68b (Jena), also *die* ~ *waschen*, as in Fischart, *Garg.* (repr.) 61. The entry on *die* ~ *schaben* on p. 2068 is wrong.

an diesem Wort zerbricht man sich die ~ that word is a tongue-twister; modern, e.g. E.Th.A. Hoffmann, *S.Werke* [edit. G.] 2,123: '. . . *gab ihm einen solchen Zähne und Zunge zerbrechenden Namen . . .*'; hence *zungenbrecherisch* (since the 19th c.); *abbrechen* can also be used; cf. also Goethe 43,265 (W.): '. . . *verwickelte sich mit gewissen brescianischen Redensarten die Zunge . . . im Munde*'.

er hat eine scharf geschliffene ~ his tongue is so sharp as if it had been honed; beginnings in the Bible, esp. Psalm 57,5: '. . . *und ihre zungen scharfe schwerdter*'. Luther 29,167 (Weimar) used '*die zunge schärfen*'; cf. G.Keller, *Werke* 7,26: '. . . *daß wir hier auch geschliffene Zungen haben*'.

er ist schnell von ~ (or *schnellzüngig*) he has a quick (or ready) tongue; modern.

etw. erfriert jem.m auf der ~ (lit.) sth. dies on sb.'s tongue; modern, e.g. Ebner-Eschenbach 2,305: '. . . *daß ein unschuldiges Späßchen ihm auf der Zunge erfror*'; cf. similar locution in Heine [edit. E.] 1,18: '*wie Blei lag meine Zung im Mund*'.

mit tausend Zungen predigen (a.) to make every possible appeal to sb., try all kinds of persuasion; hyperbolic *tausend Zungen* has been current since the 17th c., esp. with ref. to *Fama*, e.g. Goethe IV,13,190 (W.): '*da Fama tausend Zungen hat*', also Goethe 21,5 (W.): '*und hättest du tausend Zungen, du solltest mir meinen Vorsatz nicht ausreden*', Maler Müller, *Werke* 2,124: '*es heben sich tausend Zungen, wir haben geduldet die lange Nacht*'.

etw. auf der ~ *zergehen lassen* (lit.) to savour or taste sth. on one's tongue, enjoy the sound of what one is saying; modern, e.g. Th.Mann, *Zauberberg* 136: '. . . *sagte Settembrini mit äußerstem Genuß, indem er die heimatliche Silbe*

langsam auf der Zunge zergehen ließ'.

sich die ~ *aus dem Hals rennen* (coll.) to run until one's tongue is hanging out; similarly *sich die* ~ *aus dem Hals reden* = 'to talk till one is blue in the face'; both modern.

die ~ *im Zaum halten* to curb one's tongue, keep one's tongue in check; in many phrases with *bändigen, bezähmen, bezügeln, hüten* and *zügeln*, also with *Maul, Mund, Mundwerk* or *Sprache* instead of ~, many of these locutions since Early NHG. – The difficulty experienced when doing this was mentioned by Brant, *Narrenschyff* 19: '*keyn mensch synr zungen meister ist*' (in similar wording in some proverbs).

die Plapperzunge tongue that never stands still; since the 19th c. both for the organ and its owner when it means 'chatter-box'. See also under *Maul* (p.1672) for *Plappermaul*.

die ~ *ist* . . . the tongue is . . .; in some lit. comparisons but mainly in prov., e.g. Franck [1541]: '*die zung ist des hertzens dolmetsch*', *die* ~ *ist der falscheste Zeuge des Herzens*, since the 19th c., recorded by Eiselein [1839] and Simrock [1846]; cf. also Psalm 45,2: '*meine Zunge ist als der Griffel eines guten Schreibers*'.

← See also under *abbeißen* (for *sich eher die Zunge abbeißen als . . .* and *sich die Zunge abbeißen vor Lachen*), *Band* (for *der Zunge das Band lösen*), *Bein* (for *die Zunge ist kein Bein, schlägt aber manchem den Rücken ein*), *beißen* (for *sich auf die Zunge beißen*), *binden* (for *jem.m die Zunge binden*), *brauchen* (for *er weiß die Zunge zu gebrauchen*), *brennen* (for *es brannte Dankmarn auf der Zunge* and *die Frage brannte ihm auf der Zunge*), *Engel* (for *mit Engelzungen reden*), *falsch* (for *falsche Zungen*), *Feld* (for *gab ihrer Seele und Zunge freies Feld*), *fertig* (for *fertig und geschwind mit der zungen, vnd der stammelnden zunge wird fertig vnd reinlich reden* and *wenn er die Götter all auf fertger Zunge trägt*), *gesalzen* (for *daß es ihm bis morgen auf der Zunge brennte*), *Geißel* (for *er wird dich verbergen fur der geissel der zungen*), *Gewürz* (for *das Gewürtzgärtlein der Gelübden ist die Zung der Prediger*), *Gicht* (for *in deine Zunge dir die kalte Gicht*), *Gift* (for *diu boese zunge ist ein vergift* and *der Zungen Giftgeschoß*), *glatt* (for *er zischt mit glatter Zunge*), *Gold* (for *die Zungen singender Poeten, wenn ihm die Zunge einmal mit dem Herzen durchgeht* and *des gerechten zunge ist köstlich silber*), *greifen* (for *schwarze Fahnen, aus denen feurige Zungen griffen*), *Haar* (for *Haare auf der Zunge haben*), *herausstrecken* (for *jem.m die Zunge herausstrecken, herausstecken* or *herausrecken*), *Honig* (for *von dessen Zung der Honig floß*), *hüten* (for *seine Zunge hüten*), *Katze* (for *Katzenzunge*), *kleben* (for *die Zunge klebt jem.m am Gaumen*), *laufen* (for *ich ließ meiner Zunge freien Lauf*), *lösen* (for *jem.m die Zunge lösen*), *Luft* (for *so muß die Zung es thun, die macht den Helden Luft*), *Ochs* (for *einen Ochsen auf der Zunge haben*), *Otter* (for *Otternzunge*), *Rachen* (for *mir klebt die Zunge am Rachen*), *regen* (for *so lang ich Zung und Feder regen kann*), *rufen* (for *mit ehrner Zunge ruft die Glocke schon*), *schießen* (for *sie schießen mit jren zungen eitel lügen*), *Schiff* (for *diu reine zunge sî der sêle ruoder*), *Schlange* (for *sie scherffen jre zunge wie eine schlange* and *Schlangenzunge*), *schlüpfen* (for *Schlüpfrigkeit der Zunge*), *schweben* (for *etw. schwebt jem.m auf der zunge*), *schwer* (for *eine schwere Zunge haben/kriegen*), *Schwert* (for *Lästerzunge*), *Seele* (for *die Seele sitzt ihm auf der Zunge*), *Silber* (for *Silberzunge*), *spitz* (for *seiner spitzen Zunge Behendigkeit*), *Spott* (for *Spötterzunge*), *springen* (for *ein Wort über die Zunge springen lassen*), *Stahl* (for *mit ihrer Zunge scharfem Stahl*), *stechen* (for *stechende Lästerzungen*), *Stich* (for *ertrage nicht der Zunge Stich*), *tragen* (for *du trägst dein gutes Herz in den Augen und auf der Zunge*), *wetzen* (for *seine Zunge wetzen*) and *zähmen* (for *die Zunge zähmen*).

züngeln: see *lecken*.

Zungendrescher

der ~ (a.) wily, crafty lawyer (who perverts justice); term of contempt since ca. 1500; Luther used it in 24,639 (Weimar): '. . . *beschissen und versucht von solchen landstreichern und zungendreschern*', still in the 19th c., e.g. Fontane, *Werke* I,4,396: '*derlei Allotria sind gut für Professore, Advokaten und Zungendrescher*'; also since Early NHG for 'malicious talker', e.g. H.Sachs [edit. K.] 11,150. *Zungendrescherei* was still used in the 19th c., e.g. Heine [edit. E.] 6.61, but the whole group is now a.

zungenentfesselnd: see *Fessel*.

zungenfertig: see *fertig*.

Zungenfertigkeit: see *Grund*.

Zungengericht: see *Gericht*.

Zungenhonig: see *Gift*.

zungenlos: see *gehören*.

Zungenschlag

der ~ way of speaking, enunciation; with ref. to the human voice since the 17th c.; sometimes used for 'stammering, thick voice', but otherwise rarely on its own, mostly with a qualifying adjective, e.g. *ein falscher* ~ = 'a slip of the tongue' and *ein neuer* ~ = 'a statement never made or heard before', both modern. See also similar locutions under *Schlag* (6).

er hat einen ~ (coll.) he cannot speak properly, usually meaning 'he is too drunk to make sense';

modern, synonymous with older *er hat eine schwere Zunge*.

Zungensünde: see *gerade*.

züngig

See under *doppelt* (for *doppelzüngig*), *scharf* (for *scharfzüngig*), *Schlange* (for *schlangenzüngig*) and *spitz* (for *spitzzüngig*).

Zünglein

das ~ *an der Wage* the thing that tips the scale; ~ originally = 'the pointer on scales'; figur. use since Early NHG, e.g. Apocr. transl. Wisd. of Sol. 11,23: '*denn die welt ist fur dir wie das zünglin an der wage*' (not in this wording in modern Bible editions), f.r.b. Brack, *Voc.rerum* [1483], Stieler [1691] listed the compound *Wagzünglein*; Goethe 31,57 (W.): '*über meine sicilianische Reise halten die Götter noch die Wage in Händen; das Zünglein schlägt herüber und hinüber*', Herder [edit.S.] 18,85: '*das Zünglein der Waage menschlicher Handlungen*' (also Goethe 41,1,209 (W.)). Since the 19th c. often in political contexts for a small party which can help a large party to achieve a majority, hence *das* ~ *an der Wage sein* = 'to hold the balance of power'.

das ~ (also *Schamzünglein*) (med.) clitoris; in use at least since the 17th c., recorded by Hyrtl, *Anatom.* 172 [1889].

← See also under *hüten* (for *liegt auch dein Zünglein in peinlicher Hut*).

Züngler: see *Gesicht*.

zupaß

etw. kommt jem.m ~ sth. suits sb., is just what sb. wanted; this belongs to *Paß* (obs.) = 'appropriate condition'; cf. the entries under *passen* (p. 1835); first (in the 16th c.) with ref. to health, now only with *kommen*, e.g. Gutzkow, *Ges.W.* 2,139: '*da kam der Verkauf . . . dem jungen Bräutigam zupaß*'.

zupfen

jem. am Kragen ~ (coll.) to remind sb.; mainly in the context of making sb. realise the stupidity or wrongness of his behaviour, amounting therefore to an admonition (as in *jem. am Ärmel* ~); at least since the 18th c., e.g. Goethe, *Dicht.u.Wahrh.* 4,18 reporting on frivolous behaviour (i.e. smashing glasses): '*wir andern folgten, und ich bildete mir denn doch ein, als wenn mich Merck am Kragen zupfte*'. Hildebrand in *DWb.* 5 [1873] added in explanation: '*die Redensart mag an den großen Kragen des 17., 16. Jahrh. entstanden sein*'.

← See also under *Ärmel* (for *jem. am Ärmel zupfen*), *Löwe* (for *den toten Löwen kann jeder Hase am Bart zupfen*), *Nase* (for *jem. an/bei der Nase zupfen* and *sich bei der Nase zupfen/nehmen/ziehen*) and *verzupfen* (also *for zerzupfen*).

zupflastern

etw. ~ to cover sth. over, patch sth. up; figur. since Early NHG, e.g. Fischart, *Bienk.* 113a; usually derogatory meaning 'to hide the blemishes of sth.'.

← See also under *Pflaster*.

zuraten

jem.m ~ to advise sb. to do or accept sth., give encouragement; general since the 18th c. (not yet in Kramer [1702]); often in *ich will weder* ~ *noch abraten* = 'I do not wish to advise you for or against (or one way or another)'; hence also *auf sein Zuraten* = 'on his advice or encouragement'.

zurechnen

jem.m etw. ~ to attribute or impute sth. to sb., hold sb. responsible for sth.; since Early NHG, e.g. Luther 8,76b (Jena): '*den meineid wird euch Gott nicht "zurechen"* ', Kramer [1702] recorded: '*einem die Schuld eines Dinges zurechnen*'; hence *Zurechnung* = 'attribution, imputation', also 'responsibility', now little used, but still current in the legal adjectives *zurechnungsfähig* = 'of sound mind, sane' and *unzurechnungsfähig* = 'not responsible for his actions, of unsound mind', for which see p. 2540.

etw. einer Sache (or *jem.m*) ~ to class sth. as belonging to sth. (or sb.); synonymous with *hinzurechnen* or *hinzuzählen*; since Early NHG; Mentel used it in his preface to *Judith* in his Bible transl., Luther 16,378 (Weimar) with ref. to persons, Goethe 46,21 (W.) with ref. to things.

zurechtbiegen

etw. ~ to change or adapt sth. so that it becomes suitable for one's use or that one has in mind, lick sth. into shape. It is a member of a large group of *zurecht*-compounds which express the notion of 'putting sth. to rights, correcting sth. (or sb.) or arranging sth. in an orderly way'. Others are *zurechtbringen*, current since Early NHG, e.g. Luther Bible transl. Matth. 17,11: '*Elias sol . . . alles zu recht bringen*' (where the A.V. has 'restore all things'), *zurechtdrechseln*, *zurechtfeilen* (18th c.), *zurechtflicken*, at least since the 19th c., used by Bismarck in *Pol.Reden* 4,233, *zurechthämmern* (19th c.), *zurechthobeln* (19th c.), *zurechtkneten* (used by Nietzsche), *zurechtlenken*, since the 18th c., e.g. Herder [edit.S.] 12,13, *zurechtmachen*, since Early NHG, f.r.b. Frisius [1556], *zurechtordnen* (19th c.), *zurechtrücken*, used by Goethe III,10,121 (W.), *zurechtschmieden* (19th c.), *zurechtschneiden*, 18th c., e.g. Goethe 21,138 (W.), *zurechtschustern* (derogatory) (19th c.), *zurechtstellen*, since the 18th c., frequent in Goethe's writings, *zurecht-*

stutzen, 19th c., e.g. Bismarck, *Pol.Reden* 4,198, *zurechtweisen*, 18th c., e.g. Goethe II,11,23 (W.) and *zurechtzimmern*, 19th c., used by G.Keller.

← See also under *gerade* (for *Welt . . . die er nach Belieben zurechte rücken könnte*), *Gestell* (for *rück nur dein zart Gestell zurecht*), *Kopf* (for *jem.m den Kopf zurechtsetzen*, also under *gerade*), *lecken* (for *etw. zurechtlecken*) and *legen* (for *jem.m etw zurechtlegen* and *sich etw. zurechtlegen*).

zurechtfinden

sich ~ to find one's way about, get along, manage; not only in such local contexts as in *nach Hause finden* (see p. 787), but also synonymous with *sich (selbst) finden* (see p. 788) or indicating the arrival at a solution of sth. puzzling, find out what's what; since the 17th c., e.g. Stieler, *Geh. Venus* [repr.] 35, Goethe 30,42 (W.)

zurechtflicken: see *zurechtbiegen*.

zurechtführen

jem. ~ (rare) to put sb. on the right road, guide sb. towards the right conduct; since the 18th c.; *zurechthelfen* (rare), as in Herder [edit. S.] 19,173 can also be used.

zurechthämmern: see *zurechtbiegen*.

zurechthelfen

jem.m ~ to help sb. to regain his balance, sanity, clear state of mind; since Early NHG, e.g. Luther Bible transl. Gal. 6,1. See also under *zurechtführen*.

zurechthexen: see *Hexe*.

zurechthobeln: see *zurechtbiegen*.

zurechtkneten: see *zurechtbiegen*.

zurechtkommen

zurechtkommen to cope, manage; since the 17th c.; often in *er kommt gut zurecht* = 'he does very well'.

noch ~ to arrive just in time (or in good time); at least since the 18th c., e.g. Lessing [edit. M.] 10,60.

mit etw. ~ (1) to work sth. out, find a solution for sth., manage sth.; since the 18th c., e.g. Goethe 26,223 (W.) O.Stoeßl, *Morgenrot* 259 [1929]: '*wie konnte man wohl mit einer Sprache zurechtkommen, die sich gleich mehrerer Aoriste erfreute!*'.

mit etw. ~ (2) (financial) to manage or get along with sth. (money, income, assets); the same as *auskommen mit etw.*, which is much older (see p. 137); f.r.b. Kramer [1702], e.g. Goethe 21,162 (W.): '*der Entrepreneur zahlt uns und mag sehen, wie er zurechte kömmt*'.

mit jem.m ~ to get along with sb., hit it off with sb.; since the 17th c., also with ref. to countries with which one maintains good relations.

zurechtlegen

sich etw. ~ (1) (lit.) to have sth. ready, prepare oneself for sth. (with an answer, excuse, etc.); also with ref. to plans for a task in hand; since the 18th c., e.g. Goethe III,6,231 (W.).

sich etw. ~ (2) (lit.) to think sth. over, reflect on sth.; the same as *überlegen* (2) (see p. 2508); since the 18th c., e.g. Goethe 42,2,468 (W.), Raabe, *Sämtl. Werke* 3,1,327: '*ich lege mir jetzt oft mein Leben zurecht, wie es hätte geführt werden müssen*'.

← See also under *legen* (for *jem.m etw. zurechtlegen* and *sich etw. zurechtlegen*, where the dating should be corrected) and *Rätsel* (for *wie er sich das Räthsel seiner Tage zurechtlegen und ausbilden wollte*).

zurechtmachen

etw. für etw. ~ to make sth. suitable for some purpose; modern, e.g. (DWb) Brentano 2,459: '*nach den neuesten Methoden wird der Text zurechtgemacht*', also with ref. to disguises or masks, e.g. *er wurde* (or *hat sich*) *für den Maskenball als Pirat zurechtgemacht*.

sich etw. ~ to make up sth. to fit the case; modern, mainly with ref. to excuses for sth. reprehensible or faulty, e.g. (T.) Bismarck, *Ged.u. Erinn.* 1,217: '. . . *daß er* [i.e. Napoleon III] *sich nachträglich eine Rechtfertigung für das Ergebniß des Krieges zurecht machte*'. A stronger term is *sich etw. zurechtschwindeln* (modern), another is *sich etw. zurechtlügen*, which occurs in Fontane, *Werke* I,5,91.

← See also under *stramm* (for *sich stramm zurechtmachen*) and *zurechtbiegen*.

zurechtrücken

etw. ~ to correct or improve sth.; since the 18th c., recorded by Adelung (but not yet by Kramer), e.g. Goethe 8,223 and IV,23,48 (W.).

← See also under *rücken* (for *sich zurechtrücken*) and the cross-references under *zurechtbiegen*.

zurechtschneidern

etw. ~ (coll.) to make sth. fit for a certain purpose; cf. Engl. 'to tailor sth.'; 18th c., e.g. Goethe 21,138 (W.); cf. similar terms listed under *zurechtbiegen*.

zurechtsetzen

Dinge ~ to put (or arrange) things in their proper order; figur. since the 18th c.; also reflex. for ' to accommodate oneself to things', as in Goethe, *Gespr.* [edit. B.] 3,210: '. . . *müssen sehen, wie wir uns mit dem Leben wieder zurechtsetzen*'.

← See also under *gerade* and *Kopf* (for *jem.m den Kopf zurechtsetzen*).

zurechtstauchen

jem. ~ (coll.) to bring sb. to his senses; derived from phys. *stauchen* = 'to push, press, jolt, kick'; modern; figur. in such cases as *das Leben wird ihn schon* ~ . It can also be used for 'to give sb. a severe reprimand'.

zurechtstellen

jem. ~ (a.) to correct sb.; this can contain the notion of reproof; in the 18th c. used as a synonym for *zurechtsetzen*, but Campe [1810] no longer recorded *zurechtsetzen* and *zurechtstellen* in this sense.

sich einer Sache ~ (rare) to accede to sth.; the same as *befolgen* (or even *gehorchen*); modern, e.g. (T.) Rosegger, *Gottsucher* 274: '*sie stellten sich seinen Anordnungen zurecht*'. Not listed in *DWb*. [1956].

zurechtstuken

jem. ~ (regional coll.) to give sb. a strong reprimand; *stuken* is a regional variant of *stauchen* (see under *zurechtstauchen*); recent, recorded for Berlin; it appears as a simplex in Meyer, *D.richt. Berliner*[1925], where, however, the compound is not listed.

zurechtstutzen: see *zurechtbiegen*.

zurechtweisen

jem. ~ (1) to guide sb., show sb. a better way; figur. since the 18th c., when Goethe II,11,23 (W.) used it with *Leben* as the subject.

jem. ~ (2) to rebuke, reprimand, censure sb.; since the 18th c., recorded by Adelung, but not yet by Kramer [1702], e.g. Goethe 22,135 and IV,24,209 (W.).

Zurede

die ~ (a.) encouragement; the same as *Zuspruch*; recorded in this sense by Kramer [1702] and still used in the 19th c., but then displaced by the verbal noun *das Zureden* which is still current and used for 'kindly persuasion' (see *zureden* below).

← See also under *windelweich* (for *Zurede macht mich windelweich*).

zureden

jem.m ~ to persuade sb.; mainly with ref. to kind urging or well-meant advice, also consoling words. This meaning is the opposite of its first sense which implied rebuke, accusation, also abuse, f.r.b. Frisius [1556]. The present kindly meaning has been in use since the 17th c., recorded by Stieler [1691].

← See also under *Rede* (for *dem muß man wie einem kranken Roß zureden*).

zureichen

See under *Fuchs* (for *wann die löwenhaut nit zureicht, so muß man den fuchsbalg daran sezen*) and *reichen* (for *es reicht nicht zu* and the adjective *zureichend*).

zurichten

jem. übel ~ to injure sb. badly, beat sb. up; derived from *zurichten* = 'to inflict (sth.)' (see also the notes on *anrichten* on p. 55); since Early NHG, e.g. Luther 30,3,307 (Weimar): '. . . *jamer, so der bapst . . . zugericht hat*'; since the 16th c. with ref. to 'beating, mauling, ill-treating, injuring', e.g. H.Sachs [edit. K.] 9,67: '*hat dich ein weib so grichtet zu?*' Goethe 22,44 (W.); also with ref. to non-phys. injuries, e.g. Goethe, *Gespr.* [edit. B.] 6,68: '. . . *durch Hegelsche Philosophie so zurichtet worden*'.

← See also under *gehen* (for *mit Leimen, Hobeln und Zurichten . . . zu Werke gehen*).

zuriegeln: see *Riegel*.

zurück

nichts wie ~ ! (coll.) back – as fast as possible; modern; cf. the imperative ~ ! = 'go back, stop!', as in Schiller, *Bürgschaft* 106: '*Zurück! du rettest den Freund nicht mehr*'.

es muß ~ (coll.) it must be returned, taken or brought back; elliptical for *zurückgebracht werden*; modern.

← See also under *zurückmüssen*.

es gibt kein Zurück mehr a return to the former state (condition, life) is impossible; elliptical for *Zurückkehren*; modern; similarly *ich kann nicht mehr* ~ = 'I cannot reverse my decision, cannot give up what I have set out to do, retract what I have said'; cf. Goethe II,2,20 (W.): '. . . *in dieser Schlinge gefangen . . . nicht mehr weiß, wie er zurück soll*'.

← See also under *weit* (for *so weit zurück sein*).

zurückbeben: see *beben*.

zurückbehalten

etw. ~ (1) to retain or hold on to sth.; with abstracts only since the 19th c., e.g. Nietzsche 4,209: '. . . *eine kleine Skepsis gegen alles . . . zurückzubehalten*'.

etw. ~ (2) to continue to feel after-effects, to be left with sth.; mainly with ref. to illness, e.g. *von dieser Lungenentzündung hat er einige Beschwerden zurückbehalten*; modern.

zurückbilden

etw. ~ (lit.) to reform or reshape in one's mind sth. belonging to the past; since the 18th c., e.g. Goethe IV,8,241 (W.): '. . . *meine jetzige Denkart . . . nach meiner ersten zurückzubilden*'.

sich ~ to return to its former state or form; mainly in biol. contexts, where it can also mean 'to disappear', e.g. *die Schwellungen bilden sich zurück*; since the 19th c.

zurückbleiben

zurückbleiben (a.) to stay away, refuse or be unable to be present; since the 17th c., still used by Goethe 22,346 (W.), but *fernbleiben* or *wegbleiben* would now be used.

die Zurückgebliebenen the survivors; 19th c. and still used, although *die Hinterbliebenen* is now the preferred term.

etw. bleibt hinter etw. zurück sth. is inferior to sth. else; since the 18th c., e.g. (DWb) Bodmer, *V.d.Wund.* 5 [1740].

← See also under *bleiben* (for *er sah sie beschenkt von allen andern, er wollte nicht zurückbleiben*) and *Glied* (for *die Poesie der Sachen bleibt allemahl zurück*).

zurückblicken

zurückblicken to look back on past events, experiences, etc., reminisce; general since the 18th c., e.g. Goethe 24,181 (W.). See also *Rückblick* (p. 342) and *zurückschauen* (p. 2086).

← See also under *Gesicht* (for *bis wieder sein Licht ins versteinte Gesicht zurückblickt*).

zurückbringen

etw. ~ (1) to bring sth. back (to one's mind); with abstracts since the 18th c., e.g. Goethe 10,106 (W.): '. . . *bringt das Gefühl mir jener Zeit zurück*'.

etw. ~ (2) (coll.) to make sth. fall back, deteriorate or lose in value; modern, also used with ref. to persons, esp. their health, e.g. *die Krankheit hat ihn sehr zurückgebracht*.

zurückdämmen: See under *Damm* and *entzügeln* (for *Furcht, welche die That zurückdämmte*).

zurückdrängen

etw. ~ (lit.) to press or hold sth. back, Press sth.; figur. with abstracts since the 18th c., e.g. Goethe 41,1,135 (W.), often in *seine Gefühle* ~, recorded by Sanders [1860].

zurückfahren

zurückfahren to start back, recoil (in horror); since the 18th c., e.g. Goethe 49,295 (W.): '*Judas erschrickt, fährt zurück*', Schlegel, *Lucinde* 96: '. . . *so angeblickt, daß ich ordentlich zurückfuhr*'.

zurückfallen

jem. fällt zurück (1) sb. returns to his former ways or beliefs; since Early NHG, esp. with ref. to the relapse of a convert, e.g. Heine, *Rom.* 304: '*dieses Zurückfallen in den alten Aberglauben*', but also with ref. to illness = 'suffers a relapse'.

jem. fällt zurück (2) sb. falls behind, drops back; with ref. to intellectual decline, loss of energy or failure in competitions (in sport); modern, not yet recorded by Campe [1811]; cf. *Rückfall* (p. 2019).

etw. fällt auf jem. zurück sth. reflects on sb.; derived from phys. 'to fall back on sb.', figur. since the 17th c., f.r.b. Corvinus [1646], e.g. Schlegel's transl. of Shakespeare, *Hamlet* 5,2: '. . . von Planen, die verfehlt zurückgefallen auf der Erfinder Haupt'.

← See also under *halten* (p.1209) (for *fielen zurück und verachteten alles*).

zurückfinden: see *finden* (p. 787).

zurückfließen

etw. fließt zurück (lit.) sth. flows back; with abstracts since the 18th c., frequent in Schiller's writings; *zurückfluten* can also be used figur. in this sense (19th c.)

zurückführen

etw. ~ wollen (lit.) to strive to bring sth. back; figur. only since the 19th c.

etw. auf etw. ~ to trace sth. back to sth. else, explain sth. as having arisen from sth. else; since the 19th c., e.g. Rückert, *Morg.* 2,241: '. . . der seinen Ursprung . . . zurückführt auf die Tochter des Propheten*'.

← See also under *führen* (for *jemandes Behauptung aufs Ungereimte zurückführen*).

zurückgeben

etw. gibt etw. zurück sth. returns sth.; figur. since the 18th c., e.g. Schiller, *Resignation*: '*was man von der Minute ausgeschlagen, gibt keine Ewigkeit zurück*'.

zurückgeben to reply; at first with an object (18th c.), e.g. Goethe 10,95 (W.): '*gib ein holdes Wort des Abschieds uns zurück*', but later often without, e.g. *nein, gab er zurück* = 'no, he replied'.

jem.m. etw. ~ to reply in the same kind, retaliate; with ref. to insults, injuries or accusations; sometimes *mit Zinsen* = 'with interest' is added; cf. much older *jem. mit gleicher Münze bezahlen* (p. 1723).

jem.m sein Wort ~ to release sb. from his promise; sometimes with ref. to releasing sb. from an engagement, when it can also mean 'to break off an engagement'; modern, not yet listed in Campe [1811].

← See also under *leer* (for *einem leeren Bild, das weder Druck noch Kuß zurückgiebt*).

zurückgehen

etw. geht zurück (1) sth. is retracted, cancelled, annulled; since Early NHG with ref. to treaties, promises, engagements.

etw. geht zurück (2) sth. subsides, is diminished, recedes, grows weak, goes down (or goes wrong); since Early NHG, e.g. H.Sachs [edit. G.] 21,91; similarly *es geht zurück mit etw.* (used by Schiller) = 'sth. is in a state of decline'.

zurückgehen to think back, reconsider; in most cases like *zurückdenken*; since Early NHG, e.g. Luther 32,279 (Weimar), Goethe 22,51 (W.): '*zwingt mein Gemüth nicht, zurückzugehen und zu überdenken . . .!*

etw. geht auf etw. zurück sth. can be traced back to or has its origin in sth., has arisen from sth.; since the 18th c., also for 'to date back', as in Klopstock, *Gelehrtenrep.* 7 [1774]: '*der Ursprung dieser Benennung geht in alte Zeiten zurück*'.

zurückgeißeln: see *Geißel*.

Zurückgezogenheit

See under *Eiland* (for *selige Zurückgezogenheit*) and *fühlen* (for *Zustand gänzlicher Zurückgezogenheit*).

zurückgreifen

nach (or *zu*) *etw. ~* (lit.) to turn back to (or fall back on) sth. in the past; in wider sense = "to have recourse to sth.'; figur. since the 19th c., e.g. Gervinus, *Lit.* 5,78: '. . . daß sie . . . nach dem Alterthum zurückgriffen'; hence also *zurückgreifend* (lit.) = 'reaching back, having its roots in the past', as in Goethe 41,222 (W.): '*zurückgreifende Motive*'.

auf jem ~ to take up or reconsider sb. formerly set aside; modern, e.g. *bei der Besetzung der Stelle griff man schließlich auf ihn zurück*.

zurückhalten

etw. hält jem. zurück (1) sth. restrains sb. (from doing sth.); since the 17th c., e.g. Opitz, *Teutsche Poet.* [repr.] 16; also reflex. *sich ~* = 'to restrain oneself', also 'to keep aloof' and used with ref. to moderation, e.g. in eating, drinking, etc.

etw. (or *jem.*) *hält jem. zurück* (2) sth. (or sb.) keeps or detains sb.; modern, e.g. (Kl.-St.) St. Zweig, *Balzac* 303. Similarly *jem. von etw. ~* = 'to deter sb. from sth.'.

etw. nicht länger ~ to hold sth. back no longer; with abstracts since the 18th c., e.g. Goethe 22,79 (W.).

zurückhaltend reserved, restrained, cool; since the 18th c., sometimes in the reflex. sense = 'holding back, hesitating', as in Goethe IV,30,113 (W.), but usually describing reserved behaviour, general since the 19th c.

← See also under *halten* (p. 1211) (for *sich zurückhalten*), *kurz* (for *der Kaiser hielt das väterliche Erbe zurück*) and *Leib* (for *zurückhaltend, im Geben oder Bezahlen geizig*).

Zurückhaltung: see *Reserve*.

zurückhufen: see *Huf*.

zurückkehren

zurückkehren (bibl.) to give way, fall back, perish; only now in the Bible, e.g. Psalm 129,5 and

Isaiah 42,17 and 59,13, also as a trans. verb in Isaiah 44,25 and reflex. in Psalm 6,11.

etw. kehrt zurück sth. returns; with ref. to abstracts since the 18th c. (not yet listed in Kramer [1702]), e.g. Goethe 24,212 (W.). Hence the now obs. use in linguistic contexts of *zurückkehrend* = 'reflexive' (with ref. to verbs); recorded by Adelung, then listed but rejected as unsuitable by Campe [1811]. Cf. *Rückkehr* (p. 2020).

← See also under *Echo* (for *das Echo seiner Befehle kehrt zurück*), *gut* (p. 1175) (for *daß niemand zu jener alten Scheinwissenschaft zurückkehren werde*), *Schoß* (for *in den Schoß der alleinseligmachenden Kirche zurückkehren*), *Schütze* (for *die Lüge kehrt sich zurück und trifft den Schützen*) and *Wald* (for *in die Wälder zurückkehren*).

zurückkommen

auf etw. ~ (1) to return to sth., take sth. up again; modern (19th c.).

auf etw. ~ (2) to fall back on sth.; also 'to revert to sth. said earlier'; modern; hence also *immer wieder auf etw.* ~ = 'to harp on sth.'.

mit etw. ~ to get (or fall) behind with sth.; since the 17th c.; in earlier periods sometimes with ref. to declining resources or health; now hardly recorded.

von etw. ~ (1) (obs.) (1) to recover from sth.; with abstracts since the 18th c., e.g. Goethe 24,263 (W.), also sometimes = *sich erholen* or *bessern*; no longer listed in some recent dictionaries.

von etw. ~ (2) (obs.) to give sth. up; recorded by Campe [1811], but now obs., since shorter *von etw. abkommen* expresses the same notion.

mit leeren Händen ~ to return empty-handed, come back without having obtained what one wanted; modern.

unverrichteter Dinge (or *Sache*) ~ to return without having achieved anything; modern.

etw. kommt jem.m zurück sth. comes back, returns to sb.'s mind or memory; since the 18th c.

← See also under *Hammel* (for *um auf den besagten Hammel zurückzukommen*).

zurückkönnen

nicht mehr ~ to be unable to turn back, to retract a statement; ellipsis with *gehen, weichen* or *nehmen* left out; not before the 18th c. (not listed in Kramer [1700]).

zurückkriechen: see *Schale*.

zurücklassen

einen bitteren Geschmack (or *Nachgeschmack*) ~ to leave a bitter taste (or aftertaste) behind, modern.

jem. (or *etw.*) *läßt alles hinter sich zurück* sb. (or sth.) leaves all others behind, surpasses everybody (or everything); modern.

← See also under *hängen* (for *ließ ihr Plundern zurück*).

zurücklernen: see *Grund* (p. 1161).

zurückliegen

etw. liegt viele Jahre zurück sth. occurred many years ago, dates back many years; general since the 19th c.

zurückmüssen

zurückmüssen to have to turn back; ellipt. for *zurückgehen, – weichen müssen*; modern, e.g. Stifter 5.1.361: '*die Franzosen konnten nicht vor, sie mußten zurück*'; also with ref. to non-phys. retreats.

zurücknehmen

etw. ~ to take sth. back, withdraw sth. (a statement, promise); since the 17th c., e.g. Lehman 3,460 [1662]; it could be used reflex., e.g. Goethe 24,179 (W.), but that usage is obs.

zurückpressen

See under *Damm* (for *die Sprödigkeit der Schönen ist nur ein Damm, der einen Regenstrom zurückepreßt*) and *pressen*.

zurückrufen: see *rufen*.

zurückschauen: see *schauen*.

zurückscheuchen: see *scheuchen*.

zurückschicken: see *glatt*.

zurückschrecken: see *Schrecken*.

zurückschreiten: see *fortschreiten*.

zurücksehen: see *sehen*.

zurücksetzen: see *setzen*.

zurückspiegeln: see *Spiegel*.

zurückstecken

See under *Loch* (for *ein Loch zurückstecken müssen*) and *Pflock* (for *einen Pflock zurückstecken*).

zurückstehen

See under *frei* (for *wir Unterwaldner stehen frei zurück*) and *stehen*.

zurückstellen: see *stellen*.

zurücktreten

etw. im Geist ~ *lassen* (lit.) to let sth. occupy a less prominent place in one's mind; this belongs to ~ = 'to retreat', 'to return to sth. in the past', as in Lessing [edit. M.] 18,284: '*wie oft wünschte ich, mit eins in meinen alten isolirten Zustand zurückzutreten*'; modern.

← See also under *treten*.

zurückturnen: see *turnen*.

zurückweisen

etw. ~ to reject sth.; since the 17th c., recorded by Kramer [1702]; often close to *abweisen*.

auf etw. ~ to refer back to sth.; since the 18th c., e.g. Stifter, *Werke* [edit. S.] 3,349.

← See also under *brennen* (for *die Profanen von der Schwelle zurückweisen)* and *Schranke* (for *jem. in die Schranken zurückweisen).*

zurückwollen

zurückwollen to wish to return or to turn back (from some enterprise); since the 17th c., recorded by Kramer [1702].

← See also under *sauber* (for *wie er zurückwolle, wenn's sauber sei im Reich).*

zurückzahlen

See under *doppelt* (for *das habe ich ihm doppelt und dreifach zurückgezahlt)* and *Zinsen* (for *etw. mit Zins und Zinseszinsen zurückzahlen).*

zurückziehen

See under *Feuer* (for *jem. aus dem Feuer zurückziehen), Gehäuse* (for *dies Gehäuse von Manieren, in welches du Spröde dich zurückziehst), Getümmel* (for *die Muse hat sich zurückgezogen), Krebs* (for *ich zog mich von Valmy zurück), privat* (for *sich ins Privatleben zurückziehen), sagen* (for *wenn sie sich in einen einzigen Geist zurückzöge)* and *ziehen* (for *aus dem neuen Hause in das alte zurückziehen).*

zurufen: see *Gewalt.*

Zusage: see *binden.*

zusagen

See under *Kopf* (for *jem.m etw. auf den Kopf zusagen)* and *sagen* (pp. 2047/8).

zusammenballen: see *Ball.*

zusammenbeißen: see *beißen.*

zusammenbinden

See under *binden* (for *was viele Seelen zusammenbindet* and *zusammengebunden aus . . .)* and *Strauß* (1) (for *einen Strauß zusammenbinden).*

zusammenblasen: see *blasen.*

zusammenbrauen: see *brauen.*

zusammenbrechen

zusammenbrechen to break down, collapse, crumble; figur. since the 18th c.

zusammenbringen

Dinge or *Leute* ~ to bring things or people together, unite, collect; with ref. to persons since the 16th c., with abstracts since the 18th c. (Goethe used it with *Gedanken).*

Ideen or *Vorstellungen* ~ (rare) to reconcile ideas; since Early NHG, e.g. Luther 34,2,143 (Weimar); now *in Einklang bringen* is preferred.

etw. ~ to achieve or manage sth.; figur. when used for 'bringing together' non-phys. parts until they form a complete whole; Goethe used it in IV,29,50 (W.)

Zusammenbruch *der* ~ collapse, failure; only since the 19th c. in phys. and figur. use (not yet

listed by Campe [1811]).

zusammendrängen: see *Schaf.*

zusammenfahren

(vor Schreck) ~ to start back, be startled; since Early NHG; see the notes on *emporfahren* under *fahren* (p. 712).

zusammenfallen

etw. fällt zusammen sth. collapses, disintegrates; since Early NHG, e.g. Fischart, *Bienenk.* 257b [1588]; cf. the note on *zu Fall kommen* under *fallen* (p. 722).

Dinge fallen zusammen (1) things coincide; sometimes therefore also 'to clash', 'to occur at the same time'; since the 18th c.

Dinge fallen zusammen (2) things correspond, tally; since the 18th c., e.g. Goethe 46.43 (W.).

← See also under *Sack* (for *das alles fällt in einen Sack zusammen).*

zusammenfassen

Dinge ~ to combine, integrate, unite things; from phys. gathering or grasping together figur. since the 18th c., e.g. *seine Gedanken* ~ = 'to collect one's thoughts'.

etw. ~ to summarize, sum up, condense sth.; since the 17th c., but not yet in Kramer [1700]; hence *die Zusammenfassung* = 'summary, synopsis, résumé', also since the 17th c., recorded by Stieler [1691], from which the meaning 'condensation' followed naturally, as did the adj. *zusammenfassend* = 'summary, synoptic'.

sich ~ (rare) to pull oneself together, control oneself; Goethe used it in 24,147 (W.), but *sich zusammennehmen* has displaced it.

zusammenflechten *Dinge* ~ (lit.) to combine or intertwine things; figur. since Early NHG, e.g. Luther 16,246 (Weimar); not listed in Stieler or Kramer.

zusammenflicken: see *Scherbe.*

zusammenfließen See under *gießen* (for *unde daz zesamne flüsse)* and *Grenze* (for *die Grenze, wo jede Tugend mit dem verwandten Laster zusammenfließt).*

zusammenfluten: see *Flut.*

zusammengeben: see *Teufel* (p. 2450).

zusammengehen

zwei Dinge gehen zusammen two things match, go together; since the 17th c., recorded by Kramer but not yet in Stieler; usually now *zusammenpassen.*

zusammengehen (regional) to shrink; since the 17th c., recorded by Kramer [1702]; now *eingehen* or *schrumpfen* are preferred.

zusammengehören: see *gehören.*

zusammengeraten: see *geraten.*

Zusammenhalt: see *locker.*

zusammenhalten See under *halten* (for *drum haltet fest zusammen*), *Hanf* (for *zusammenhalten wie Hanf und Harz*) and *Pech* (for *zusammenhalten wie Pech und Schwefel*).

Zusammenhang

See under *halten* (for *daß man es aus seinem Zusammenhang herausreiße*) and *herausreißen* (for *aus dem Zusammenhang herausgerissen*).

zusammenhängen: see *Ende*.

zusammenhauen: see *hauen*.

zusammenhexen: see *hexen*.

zusammenjüdeln: see *Jude*.

zusammenketten: see *Kette*.

zusammenklauben: see *klauben*.

zusammenklauen

etw. ~ (coll.) to steal sth.; cf. the notes on the simplex on p. 1479; the compound current since the 18th c., later also in mil.sl.

zusammenkleben: see *Pech*.

zusammenkleckern: see *Klecks*.

zusammenklemmen: see *Klemme*.

zusammenkneifen

den Arsch ~ (vulg.) to kick the bucket; modern, probably derived from *kneifen* (coll.) = 'to run away', discussed on p. 1501.

zusammenknicken: see *knicken*.

zusammenknüpfen

See under *knüpfen*, *plan* (for *planlos mir zusammenknüpfen*) and *Sand* (for *Sand zusammenknüpfen*).

zusammenkochen: see *kochen*.

zusammenkommen

See under *Berg* (for *Berg und Tal kommen nicht zusammen*), *Bier* (for *beim sauren Bier zusammenkommen*) and *jung* (for *so jung kommen wir nicht wieder zusammen*).

zusammenkoppeln

Dinge ~ to yoke, bind, tie things together; belongs to *Koppel* = 'yoke (of animals)'; figur. since Early NHG, e.g. Luther 6,424 (Weimar). Luther used it also reflex. in his Bible transl. Isaiah 5,18 (where the A.V. has 'draw with cords').

zusammenkratzen: see *kratzen*.

zusammenkrümeln: see *krümeln*.

Zusammenkunft

See under *Gelegenheit* (for *Gelegenheitsmacherin unserer Zusammenkunft*) and *halten* (for *sich von den Zusammenkünften fern zu halten*).

zusammenlaufen

die Linien laufen zusammen the lines converge or meet; since Early NHG, used by Dürer in *4 Bücher . . . Prop.* Q4b.

alle Fäden laufen in seiner Hand zusammen he pulls all the strings in this affair; modern, Goethe used it in IV,15,8 (W.), G. Keller in *Werke* 2,52.

zusammengelaufenes Volk, Gesindel, Pack (pejor.) rabble, riff-raff; since the 17th c., e.g. Goethe IV,11,181 (W.): '. . . *Art und Weise zusammengelaufner und unsichrer Gesellschaften*';

see also similar pejor. *hergelaufen* (p. 1301) and the notes under *Pack*.

zusammenlaufen (tech.) to shrink (with ref. to textiles), to coagulate (with ref. to paints), to curdle (with ref. to milk); the meaning 'shrink' since the 18th c., the others since the 19th c.

← See also under *Wasser* (for *das Wasser läuft einem im Mund zusammen*).

zusammenleben: see *Kitt* (where *zusammenfügen* also occurs).

zusammenlegen

Termine ~ to arrange for events to occur at the same time; modern, e.g. *die Hochzeiten der Geschwister wurden zusammengelegt*.

Dinge ~ (econ.) to merge or amalgamate things (e.g. firms), to consolidate things (e.g. shares); modern.

zusammenleimen: see *Leim*.

zusammennähen: see *nähen*.

zusammennehmen

Dinge ~ to see or take things as a whole; with abstracts since the 18th c.; hence *zusammengenommen* = 'taken (seen, treated) together', e.g. Lessing [edit. L.] 5,408 or Goethe 23,216 (W.), and *alles zusammengenommen* = 'all things considered', modern.

etw. ~ to summon up sth.; since the 18th c. with such abstracts as *Mut, Kraft, Gedanken*, e.g. Immermann, *Münchh.* 4,54: '*ehe ich meine Gedanken zusammennehmen kann*', Uhland, *Ged.* 1,307: '*nimm alle Kraft zusammen, die Lust und auch den Schmerz*'.

sich ~ to pull oneself together, control oneself; since the 18th c., e.g. Bürger, 67a: '*nimm dich zusammen, sonst . . .*'; very frequent in Goethe's writings, although he occasionally also used *sich zusammenfassen* (see above); hence *zusammengenommen* (lit.) = 'calm, cool and collected', e.g. Goethe, *Lehrj.* 7,8: '*von einem würdigen, zusammengenommenen Betragen*', also in 41,2,117 (W.), even with ref. to a work of art in 47,228 (W.): '*in sich fest zusammengenommen*'.

sich wieder ~ (a.) to recover (from an illness); still in Goethe IV,3,40 (W.), but *sich erholen* would now be used.

← See also under *gehen* (for *mit fremden Menschen nimmt man sich zusammen*).

zusammennesteln

sich ~ (lit.) to form (or contract itself into) a tangled mass; since the 19th c., e.g. (DWb) Gutzkow, *Ges.Werke* 6,72; also sometimes used as an intrans. verb.

zusammenpacken

jem. ~ (coll., a.) to cause sb. trouble, give sb. a bad time; Goethe wrote in IV,3,108 (W.): '*ich bin . . . zusammengepackt von tausenderley Umständen*'; derived from ~ = 'to treat roughly'; no longer listed in late 20th c. dictionaries.

zusammenpassen: see *fett*.

zusammenplatzen: see *platzen*.

zusammenpressen

etw. ~ to condense sth.; since the 18th c., e.g. Lessing [edit. M.] 7,469 with ref. to a piece of writing.

Angst preßt jem.m das Herz zusammen (lit.) fear grips (or constricts) sb.'s heart; since the 18th c., e.g. (DWb) Heinse [edit. Sch.] 2,282.

zusammenraffen: see *raffen.*

zusammenraspeln: see *raspeln.*

zusammenraufen

sich ~ (coll.) to arrive at agreement in the course and at the end of a fight; 20th c. coll. There is also *sich zusammenstreiten* in this sense, and in some areas even *sich zusammentrinken*, all describing violent disputes which end in agreement or reconciliation. The entire group is so recent that *DWb.* [1954] did not record it.

zusammenreihen: see *Reihe.*

zusammenreimen: see *Reim.*

zusammenreißen

sich ~ (coll.) to pull oneself together; not recorded in *DWb.* [1954], which only lists *sich zusammennehmen* in this sense (for which see above); see also under *Riemen* for *sich am Riemen reißen.*

zusammenrinnen: see *Gesinde.*

zusammenrücken: see *rücken.*

zusammenrühren: see *rühren.*

zussammenrütteln: see *rütteln* (also under *Nuß*).

zusammensacken: see *einsacken.*

zusammenschachteln: see *Schachtel.*

Zusammenschau

die ~ (lit.) synopsis, synoptic view; modern, not yet listed in Sanders [1865]; *DWb.* [1954] calls it *'ein neueres Wort'.*

zusammenschicken: see *Kalb* (also under *schicken*).

zusammenschießen: see *schießen.*

zusammenschlagen

See under *Hand* (for *die Hände überm Kopf zusammenschlagen*), *hören* (for *er hat läuten hören, aber nicht zusammenschlagen*) and *Schlag* (for *Güter zusammenschlagen*).

zusammenschließen

See under *Kranz* (for *dem sich zusammenschließenden Menschenkranz*) and *schließen.*

zusammenschmelzen

etw. schmilzt zusammen sth. melt away, dwindles; figur. since the 18th c.; Goethe used it with *Kasse*; see also under the simplex (p. 2152) and under *Schnee* (p. 2162).

Dinge ~ to fuse, combine, bring together or unite things; since Early NHG, e.g. Luther 30,2,488 (Weimar): *'eine person aus gott und mensch zusamen geschmolzen'*, Herder [edit. J.M. 11,222: *'die Kunst . . . die . . . Menschen schmilzt zusammen'*, Wieland 18,52: *'in ein Ganzes zusammengeschmelzt'*, whereas Goethe always used *zusammengeschmolzen*; Wieland also used *Zusammenschmelzung.*

zusammenschmieden

Dinge ~ (lit.) to forge things together, unite things to form a lasting whole; with abstracts since the 18th c., sometimes with ref. to love or marriage, also with *Pläne* (as in the case of the simplex); cf. H.v.Kleist [edit. Schm.] 3,395: *'welch eine . . . Anklage wider mich zusammengeschmiedet worden ist'*; also used with ref. to the 'forging' of a work of literature.

zusammenschmieren: see *schmieren.*

zusammenschmoren: see *schmoren.*

zusammenschneien: see *schneien.*

zusammenschnüren: see *Schnur.*

zusammenschnurren: see *schnurren.*

zusammenschrauben: see *Schraube.*

zusammenschrumpfen: see *schrumpfen.*

zusammenschürzen: see *Schürze.*

zusammenschustern: see *Schuster.*

zusammenschweißen: see *Schweiß.*

zusammensetzen

See under *brennen* (for *Vorstellungen von jenem zusammengesetzten Ganzen*), *Happen* (for *aus feinen Häppchen Zusammengesetztes*) and *setzen* (for *sich mit jem.m zusammensetzen*).

zusammensinken: see *sinken.*

Zusammenspiel: see *Spiel* (also *for zusammenspielen*).

zusammenstauchen: see *stauchen.*

zusammenstecken

See under *Kopf* (for *die Köpfe zusammenstecken*) and *stecken* (for *die Zwei stecken immer zusammen*).

zusammenstellen: see *stellen.*

Zusammenstellung: see *Gift.*

zusammenstimmen

See under *halten* (for *das vollkommene Zusammenstimmen*) and *Stimme.*

Zusammenstimmung: see *produzieren.*

zusammenstoppeln: see *stoppeln.*

zusammenstoßen: see under *stoßen* (also for *Zusammenstoß*).

zusammenstürzen: see *stürzen.*

zusammentragen: see *tragen.*

zusammentreffen

See under *richtig* (for *kein Zusammentreffen der Massen*), *Tag* (for *mein erstes Zusammentreffen mit dem damaligen Tageshelden*) and *treffen* (for *seine Reime treffen in glücklichem Wohllaut zusammen*).

zusammentreten: see *treten.*

zusammentrommeln: see *Trommel.*

zusammentun: see *tun.*

zusammenwachsen

mit etw. ~ (lit.) to become firmly attached to sth., develop close ties with sth.; since the 18th c., e.g. Goethe 35,29 (W.): *'. . . Vaterstadt, mit der sie ja zusammengewachsen war'.*

zusammenwerfen

Dinge ~ to lump things together; since the 18th c.; it can also be used loosely for 'mixing things up' and for 'confusing things'; general in all three meanings since the 19th c.; cf. similar phrases under *Brühe, hundert, Tiegel* and *Topf*.

zusammenwürfeln: see *bunt*.

zusammenziehen

See under *dringen* (for *zu gedrungen, um zusammen gezogen zu werden*), *Gewitter* (for *Gewitter, das über seinem Haupte sich zusammenzog* and *seine Stirn hatte sich zusammengezogen*), *Leim* (for *wie ein leim, der zwei hölzer zusammen zeucht*), *Natur* (for *stolze Selbstgenügsamkeit zieht das Herz des Weltmanns zusammen*) and *Wetterecke* (for *als es sich in der Wetterecke gegen das arme Deutschland zusammenzieht*).

zusammenzimmern: see *Schraube*.

Zusatz: see *besudeln*.

zuschanden

etw. ~ machen to destroy sth., demolish or damage sth.; first with ref. to persons as in Luther's Bible transl. Romans 5,5: '*hoffnung aber leßt nicht zuschanden werden*', which means '. . . be brought to shame' (cf. the A.V. version 'hope maketh not ashamed'), but later the meaning 'to damage or destroy' came to predominate.

zuschanzen: see *Schanze* (2)

zuschauen

See under *schauen* (for *schau zu, daß . . .*) and *Seele* (for *seelenruhig zuschauen*).

Zuschauer

See under *jagen* (for *die dem Zuschauer Schamröthe abjagt* and *schauen* (for *der Zuschauer*).

Zuschauerkulisee

die ~ (lit.) background formed by rows of people in an auditorium; recent locution; cf. *Geräuschkulisse* (p. 1565).

zuschieben: see *Peter* (also under *Schuld*).

zuschießen: see *schießen*.

Zuschlag

der ~ additional charge, fee or payment; modern, but the verb *zuschlagen* = 'to increase the price, demand an additional payment' has been current since the 17th c.; cf. entry on *aufschlagen* (p. 99).

den ~ bekommen or *erhalten* (comm.) to get the contract or the order; derived from the language of auctioneering where the fall of the hammer signifies the success of a bid; in this locution only since the 20th c., but *jem.m etw. zuschlagen* with ref. to sales, auctions or awards has been current since the 17th c. (cf. Schirmer, *Wb. d.dt. Kaufmannssprache* 216 [1911]).

zuschlagen

See under *Nase* (for *jem.m die Tür vor der Nase zuschlagen*) and *Schlag* (for *zuschlagen und jem.m etw. zuschlagen*), also under *Zuschlag* (above) and under *Ball*.

zuschneiden

etw. ist auf etw. zugeschnitten sth. is made to fit sth. else or fulfil certain requirements; cf. Engl. 'tailor-made'; both derived from the appropriate 'cutting of the cloth' by a tailor; general since the 2nd half of the 18th c., e.g. Goethe 38,447 (W.); cf. under *Leib* (for *wie auf den Leib geschnitten*) and *Schneider* (for *sich etw. zurechtschneidern*).

← See also under *schneiden* (for *ich schnitt mein Leben nach meiner Pension zu*).

Zuschnitt

der ~ suitability, applicability; beginning in the 18th c. (see p. 2168), but modern in such locutions as *von internationalem ~*.

← See also under *Schnitt* (for *Zuschnitt* = 'pattern').

zuschnüren: see *Schnur*.

zuschreiben

See under *Leber* (for *einer Erhitzung der Leber zugeschrieben*) and *schreiben* (for *jem.m etw. zuschreiben*).

Zuschrift

die ~ (1) (a.) epigram; current in the 18th c., e.g. Herder [edit. S.] 15,351.

die ~ (2) (a.) dedication; since the 17th c., frequent in the 18th c. (Gottsched and Hagedorn used it), whereas Wieland preferred *Zueignungsschrift* (in *Werke* 5,249), which also appeared in the 17th c., recorded by Sperander; now *Widmung* and *Zueignung* are the usual terms.

zuschulden: see *Schuld*.

zuschulen

(*sich*) *jem.* (or *etw.*) *~* (rare) to train sb. (or prepare sth.) for one's own purposes; occasionally in lit. since the 19th c., e.g. Mörike, *Mozart* 23: '. . . *Kapelle, die er sich zugeschult*'; DWb. [1954] does not list the verb; *einschulen* is the preferred term.

zuschüren: see *schüren*.

Zuschuß: see *schießen*.

zusehen

See under *Gurgel* (for *wo in die lenge wirst zusehen*) and *sehen* (for *ich kann nicht länger zusehen, zusehen, daß . . .* and *sie hatten das Zusehen*).

zusehends: see *sehen*.

zusenden

See under *Glück* (for *das mir mein altes Glück vertraulich zugesendet*) and *Grube* (for *jem. der Grube zusenden*).

zusetzen

See under *Gewehr* (for *man ihnen ein einiges i . . . zuesetzet*), *setzen* (for *etw. zusetzen* (1) and (2) and *jem.m zusetzen*) and *Stock* (for *daß ich von dem Grundstock nichts zugesetzt habe*).

zusichern: see *sicher*.

zusperren: see *Sperre*.

zuspielen: see *Spiel*.

zuspitzen

See under *fein* (for *ein feiner Plan, fein zugespitzt*) and *spitz* (for *etw. spitzt sich zu* (1) and (2), also for *Zuspitzung*).

zusprechen

See under *kalt* (for *ungeachtet des frembden zusprechens*), *sprechen* (for *einer Sache zusprechen,*

etw. spricht jem.m zu and *jem.m etw. zusprechen)*
and *Thron* (for *mir zugesprochen von zwei großen
Thronen).*

zuspringen

jem.m ~ (a.) to come (or rush) to sb.'s assistance; since Early NHG, f.r.b. Frisius [1556],
e.g. Raabe, *Sämtl. W.* III,1,556; synonymous with
(but now less used than) *beispringen* (see p. 233).

Zuspruch: see *krabbeln.*

Zustand

das ist doch kein ~ (coll.) that's intolerable (not
right, fair), should not be allowed; since the 17th
c., e.g. Abr. a Sancta Clara, *Etwas f.A.* 2,100
[1711]: *'ist es nicht ein Zustand? Im neuen Jahr . . .
sitzest du im Wirthshaus!';* cf. Goethe 6,123 (W.):
'welch ein Zustand!'.

Zustände kriegen (or *bekommen*) (coll.) to have
a fit, be beside oneself (with anger, fright, impatience); modern coll. (not listed in *DWb.*
[1954]). Cf. the related *jem. in einen* ~ *versetzen*
(p. 2251).

← See also under *blicken* (for *Einblicke in diesen
Zustand*), *faul* (for *die Zustände sind oberfaul*),
gären (for *der seltsam gärende Zustand*), *Geist* (for
Geisteszustand), *Gewicht* (for *Gleichgewicht . . . ist
eigentlich der Zustand seiner Freiheit*), *Gott* (for *im
gottverlassensten Zustande*), *grob* (for *Personen und
Zustände mit groben Strichen gezeichnet*), *Himmel*
(for *hatte Ablaste wol den Himmel, aber nicht ihren
Zustand geändert*), *Kopf* (for *Zustand der Zerstreuung und Unthätigkeit*), *kosten* (for *kostet den Zustand mit süßer Hoffnung voraus*), *laufen* (for
rücksichtlich unserer öffentlichen Zustände), *mündig*
(for *den noch unmündigen Zustand der Kunst*),
Nacht (for *in solchem nachtwandlerischen Zustande*), *Natur* (for *im Naturzustand*), *nieder* (for
aus niedrem Zustand), *Rom* (for *Zustände wie im
alten Rom*), *schweben* (for *in so schwebenden
Zuständen*), *setzen* (for *jem. in einen Zustand versetzen*), *stagnieren* (for *meine Zustände stagnieren*)
and *versinken* (for *die traurige Versunkenheit jener
Zustände).*

zustande: see *Stand.*

zustatten: see *Statt.*

zustecken

See under *Satan* (for *muß der Satan es dem
alten Gauner zugesteckt haben*) and *stecken*
(p. 2342).

zustehen: see *stehen.*

zustellen: see *stellen.*

zusteuern

etw. ~ (coll.) to contribute sth.; mainly with
ref. to financial support towards a common
effort, collection, etc.; since Early NHG, f.r.b.
Frisius [1556]; the same as, but less used than
beisteuern (or *zu etw. beitragen*, p. 236).

← See also under *Steuer* for *auf etw. zu steuern*,
where *auf etw. zusteuern* can also be used.

zustimmen

mit etw. ~ (a.) to agree with sth., fit sth.; since

Early NHG, used by Luther (see the notes on
mit etw. stimmen on p. 2373 and under *überein* for
Übereinstimmung on p. 2505); still current in the
18th c., whereas *zu etw. stimmen* (or *passen*) is
now preferred.

jem.m ~ to agree with sb.; since Early NHG,
f.r.b. Calepinus [1598]; Kramer [1702] listed it
but referred to *beystimmen* and instanced there
'einem beystimmen in seiner Meinung'; hence also
einer Sache ~ = 'to consent to sth.'.

Zustimmung

See under *gewinnen* (for *die Zustimmung des
Kaisers zu gewinnen*) and *schweigen* (for *Schweigen
bedeutet Zustimmung).*

zustopfen: see *Loch.*

zustoßen: see *stoßen.*

zustreichen: see *Kleister.*

Zustrom

der ~ (1) inflow, influx, inrush; with ref. to
masses of people moving towards a place, im-
migrants arriving, countryfolk moving into towns
since the 19th c.; it can also occur with ref. to
abstracts, e.g. (DWb) Jean Paul [edit. H.] 15/18,
553: *'in einem solchen Zustrom neuer Begebenheiten'.*

der ~ (2) (econ.) influx (of money, subsidies,
dividends, etc.); as an econ. term modern, not
yet recorded by Schirmer [1911].

zuströmen

einem Platz (einer Partei) in Massen ~ to throng
towards a place, join a party in great numbers;
since the 18th c., e.g. Goethe IV,37,45 (W.).

viel Geld strömte zu much money came pouring
in, flowed in that direction; since the 2nd half of
the 18th c.

zustutzen: see *stutzen (2).*

zutage: see *Tag.*

zutragen

See under *heiß* (for *einem etw. (brüh)heiß zutragen*), *Holz* (for *zancke nicht mit einem schwetzer,
das du nicht holz zutragest zu seinem feur*) and *tragen* (for *sich zutragen*, also for *zuträglich* and
Zuträglichkeit).

zuträglich: see *tragen.*

zutrauen

dem trau ich alles zu (coll.) he is capable of
anything, I would not put anything (bad,
immoral, treacherous, etc.) past him; pejor.
extension of the neutral (or positive) belief in
sb.'s capabilities; beginnings in the 17th c., e.g.
Kramer [1702]: *'einem nichts gutes zutrauen'.*

er traut sich zuviel zu he takes too much on
himself; often with a note of criticism = 'he over-
rates himself'; since the 17th c., e.g. Butschky,
Pathmos 11 [1677]: *'. . . daß wir uns selbst mehr
zutrauen . . . als wir zu leisten vermögen'.* Similarly
ich traue ihm nicht viel zu (coll.) = 'I do not think
him up to much, he is no great shakes'.

ich hätte es ihm nie zugetraut I never thought
that he had it in him; since the 19th c.

← See also under *hinter* (for *indem Taubert der Cottaschen Buchhandlung eine Kollusion zutraut*).

zutreffen: see *treffen.*

Zutritt: see *vermitteln.*

zutröpfeln: see *Gift.*

zutun

See under *Auge* (for *man muß zuweilen auch ein Auge zutun* and *kein Auge zutun*), *Geld* (for *wenn Geld redet, soll man das Maul zuthun*) and *Gesicht* (for *die lieblichen Violen thun ihr Gesichte zu*).

zuunterst: see *kehren.*

zuverlässig

See under *Gesicht* (for *die so zuverlässige Unterscheidungskraft seines Geschmacks*) and *Gold* (for *zuverlässig wie Gold*).

Zuversicht

See under *Gewitter* (for *söllicher zuoversicht*), *Gewohnheit* (for *die gewonheit gebirt ein zuoversicht*) and *Sicht* (for *Zuversicht* and *zuversichtlich*).

zuviel

See under *Glas* (for *ein Glas zuviel trinken*), *gut* (for *des Guten zuviel tun*), *melken* (for *zuviel melken gibt Blut*), *Pferd* (for *ein willig Pferd soll man nicht zuviel reiten*), *Rippe* (for *er hat ein paar Rippen zuviel*), *Sack* (for *zuviel zerreißt den Sack*) and *zutrauen* (for *er traut sich zuviel zu*).

zuvor: see *greifen* (p. 1132).

zuvoreilen: see *brennen* (p. 391).

zuvorkommen

jem.m ~ to forestall sb., steal a march on sb.; since the 18th c. in figur. contexts, e.g. Goethe 24,160 (W.).

zuvorkommend obliging, helpful, courteous; belongs to = 'to anticipate sb.'s wishes or hopes by a friendly action'; current since Early NHG, e.g. Luther Bible transl. Romans 12,10: '*einer kome dem andern mit ehrerbietung zuvor*' (in A.V. 'in honour preferring one another'); the adjective was influenced by French *prévenant.*

zuvorrennen: see *rennen.*

zuvortun

es jem.m ~ (a.) to surpass sb., go one better than sb. else; since Early NHG, e.g. Luther Bible transl. Gen. 30,8, still used by Schiller, now a.

zuwachsen

etw. wächst zu sth. becomes overgrown or covered (and closed) by sth.; since Early NHG, e.g. Luther 1,560a (Jena): '*als wären euch die ohren zugewachsen*'; often with ref. zu healing wounds, also where 'wound' is taken in its figur. sense.

etw. wächst jem.m zu sth. accrues to sb., becomes sb.'s gain or property; first used with ref. to the harvest, with abstracts such as *Nutzen, Vorteil* or *Übel* since the 18th c., e.g. Lessing 8,232: '*so wenig Glaubwürdigkeit ihr auch durch mein Ansehn zuwachsen kann*'; hence *der Zuwachs* = 'increase, gain', since the 18th c., also with abstracts (earlier *ein Zuwachsen* was used).

← See also under *Pilz* for a doubtful example.

zuwege: see *Weg.*

zuwehen

etw. weht jem.m zu (poet.) sth. wafts, flows or floats towards sb.; since the 17th c., e.g. (DWb) Wieland (Akad.Edit.) 1,3,40: '*Genius der Liebe . . . wehe mir Trost und erquickende Hofnung zu*'. The verb belongs to the extensive (lit.) group which expresses the notion that sb. or sth. abstract 'sends, conveys, intimates or transmits' sth. abstract to a person; examples are *zublasen, zuflüstern, zujubeln, zumurmeln, zuraunen, zurufen, zuschicken, zuseufzen, zusingen, zuwallen* and *zuwispern.* Even *zutrinken* in some contexts such as *jem.m Gesundheit zutrinken* can be classed as a member of this group. Most of them appeared in the 18th c.

zuweisen

jem.m etw. ~ to assign, allot or grant sth. to sb.; since the 18th c., esp. in legal contexts or with ref. to official decisions.

zuwenden

See under *Gott* (for *so wandte sie sich andern Göttern zu*), *Hand* (for *weil des Schicksals karge Hand ihm nicht Hörner zugewandt*), *Licht* (for *daß ein Mann sich dem Licht zuwenden würde*), *Partie* (for *um dieser geliebten Pflegetochter eine so große Partie zuzuwenden*), *Schoß* (for *einem Schoßkinde, der dramatischen Kunst, zugewendet*) and *weltzugewandt.*

zuwerfen

jem.m etw. ~ (lit.) to throw sth. in sb.'s direction; figur. with abstracts since the 18th c., often with *Blick*, also with *Glück*, e.g. Wieland 22,148: '*da mir der Zufall Vermögen genug für meine Bedürfnisse zuwarf*'.

← See also under *Seil* (for *jem.m ein Haltseil zuwerfen*).

zuwider: see *Freiheit.*

zuwinken

etw. winkt jem.m zu (lit.) sth. beckons to sb.; with abstracts since the 18th c., e.g. Wieland 26,182: '*fromme Hoffnungen winkten mir zu*'; less used than the simplex, for which see p. 2675.

zuwispern

jem.m etw. ~ (lit.) to whisper sth. to sb.; occasionally with abstracts since the 18th c., e.g. (Sa.) F.L. Schröder, *Beitr.z.dt. Schaubühne* 3,1,51 [1786]: '*mein Herz wisperte mir immer ihre Wünsche zu*'. See also the note under *zuwehen.*

zuzählen

jem.m (or *einer Sache*) *etw.* ~ (a.) to allot, apportion or assign sth. to sb. (or sth.); since the 18th c., e.g. Wieland 27,10: '*da jede meiner Stunden eigenen Geschäften zugezählt ist*', where *zuteilen* would now be preferred; cf. a similar use of *zulegen* in Goethe, *Faust I*, 989/90: '*die Zahl der Tropfen, die er hegt, sei Euren Tagen zugelegt*'.

zuziehen

jem. ~ to call or bring in sb. (for a consultation, a meeting, etc.); since the 15th c., e.g.

Storm, *Werke* 4,148: '*ein Arzt wurde nicht zu-gezogen*'; *hinzuziehen* can also be used.

sich etw. ~ to incur, catch, get, contract sth.; with ref. to unwelcome acquisitions since the 15th c., since the 16th c. also to pleasant ones; e.g. Ranke, *Sämtl. Werke* 30,116: '*diese Erwerbung hat uns den Neid Europas zugezogen*'; often with *Unheil, Tadel, Verdruß, Händel*, very frequent with *eine Krankheit*. Sometimes the object can be a person, e.g. *er hat sich einen Feind zugezogen*.

← See also under *einlegen* (for *zog mir Er-kältungen zu*).

Zuzug

der ~ immigration, arrival of newcomers, new tenants, etc.; the earliest examples refer to troop reinforcements, in Early NHG in non-mil. con-texts, e.g. with ref. to newcomers to a town in S.Franck, *Chron.* 23b. Often = *Zuwachs*.

zwacken

etw. aus etw. ~ (a.) to tear or rip sth. out of sth.; since Early NHG, when Luther 18,69 (Weimar) used it for 'tearing sth. out of its con-text'. The meaning 'to steal' (cf. Engl. 'to pinch' in this sense) has become obs., but *abzwacken* = 'to take away', as in Goethe 2,74 (W.) is still alive.

etw. zwackt jem. (coll.) sth. plagues sb., causes pain or trouble; derived from ~ = 'to pinch', extended to abstracts such as illness or worry; cf. similar and etym. related *zwicken*.

Zwang

der ~ *einer Sache* the compulsion or pressure exerted by sth.; general with abstracts since the 18th c., e.g. Wieland 10,168: '*der leidige Zwang der Etikette*', and Adelung's recording: '*der Zwang des ältesten . . . Stiles in Bildwerken*'; frequent in *der* ~ *der Gesetze, der Mode, der Verhältnisse*. In earlier periods often combined with other nouns, such as ~ *und Drang*, f.r.b. Frisius [1556] who also recorded aus *Not und* ~, which Goethe still used, e.g. IV,10,83 (W.): '*ich bin indessen von Noth und Zwang umgeben*'. There are many (modern) compounds, e.g. *Gewissenszwang, Hofzwang, Regelzwang, Systemzwang, Zunft-zwang*.

tu dir keinen ~ *an* (coll.) don't stand on cere-mony, do as if you were at home; modern as a coll. locution, but there are beginnings in non-coll. instances, such as Bode, *Yoricks Reise* 2,162 [1768]: '*ich that mir keinen Zwang an, meinen Husten zurückzuhalten*'; derived from *sich einen* ~ *antun* = 'to force oneself to do sth., esp. to restrain oneself, keep oneself under control', recorded by Adelung, current in various locu-tions since Early NHG, e.g. Luther 24,402 (Weimar): '*das fleisch im zwang halten*'.

Zwang(s). . . compulsory . . . , enforced . . . , compulsive . . . ; in scores of compounds, the first of which appeared in the 17th c., when Stieler [1691] recorded *Zwangliebe*, but the

majority, both legal and psychol. are modern with the exception of *Zwangdienst* (recorded by Adelung). Campe [1811] listed about a score of them, of which *Zwangtrieb* is probably the earli-est psychol. one. He defined it: '*ein mit Zwang verbundener Trieb, der mit Zwang oder Gewalt wirkt (Instinct)* (Moerbeek)'. Other psychol. terms followed such as *Zwangsdenken* = 'com-pulsion' and *Zwangsgefühl* = 'obsessive compul-sion'. The adj. *zwangsläufig* = 'inevitable' followed late in the 19th c., recorded in tech. contexts.

das ist (ja) freiwilliger ~ (joc.coll.) obviously I must (since you twist my arm); joc. remark made when urged to do sth. which one had wanted to do anyhow; modern.

~ *währt nicht lang* (prov.) things done under duress will not last; ~ here not = 'compulsion' but = *Erzwungenes*, i.e. 'sth. done when under compulsion', as made clear by the wording used in other languages, e.g. Fr. *chose violente n'est pas permanente*, Ital. *cosa aforzata è di poca durata*; in German since the 16th c., e.g. Franck [1541] and still listed in modern prov. collections.

← See also under *Geist* (for *Geisteszwang*), *Glied* (for *wurde durch einen geheimen Zwang in Verborgenheit und Armut gehalten*), *stehen* (for *unter einem Zwang stehen*), *studieren* (for *Zwang einer studierten Anständigkeit*) and *verschulen* (for *durch Schulzwang verderben*).

zwängen

zwängen (intrans., lit.) to make strenuous efforts pressing and forcing things; since the 18th c., e.g. Goethe, *Zahme Xenien* 4: '*sie mühen und zwängen und kommen zu nichts*'.

sich ~ (lit.) to feel constricted or hemmed in; occasionally in lit. since the 18th c., e.g. Goethe, *Divan* 3,8: '*im starren Bande zwängen sich die freien Lieder*'.

← See also under *einzwängen* (also for *Einzwängung*) and *unfolgsam* (for *das unfolgsame, störrische Haar in die gewünschte Form zu zwän-gen*).

zwanglos

zwanglos unconstrained, unfettered, casual, informal; since the 18th c. (Kant, Herder), recorded by Adelung; also (sometimes with mild disapproval) used for 'unconventional'.

in zwangloser Folge at irregular intervals; mainly with ref. to the publication of journals or series of books; since the 18th c., recorded by Adelung.

Zwangsjacke

die ~ strait-jacket; from its original᾽use for restraining violent prisoners or patients extended in the 19th c. to describe 'restraining measures, restraint by force'; *Zwangswamms* also occurs in this sense (phys. and figur.).

Zwangsmittel: see *gut* (p. 1178).
Zwanziger: see *Gold*.

zwatzeln

verzwatzeln (regional coll.) to go hopping mad; belongs to *zwatzeln = zappeln*; since the 18th c., mainly in *ich bin fast verzwatzelt* or *es ist zum Verzwatzeln*.

Zweck

der ~ (1) (obs.) centre of the target, aim; used figur. since Early NHG, e.g. Fischart, *Bienenk.* 50b [1581]: '*disz ist der zweck, das maal, schießblatt und zil, dsrnach alle gute catholische christen ire pfeil und augenmerck richten müssen*', also Luther 6,315b (Jena), still in the 18th c., e.g. Wieland 25,46: '. . . *Pfeil, der stumpf zu Boden fällt, auch manchen abgedrückt, der seinen Zweck erhält*'; sometimes (since Early NHG) as *~ und Ziel*, recorded by Stieler [1691], e.g. Herder [edit. S.] 5,28. In modern times also in the negative *es ist ohne ~ und Ziel*, as in Stifter, *Werke* 1,190, or in reverse order *ohne Ziel und ~*, as in O. Ludwig, *Werke* [edit. B.] 5,90.

der ~ (2) goal, aim (in life); since the 18th c., e.g. Schiller, *Wall. Tod* 12: '*wer durchs Leben gehet ohne Wunsch, sich jeden Zweck versagen . . .*'. Close to this is *~ =* 'end or purpose in view, destination', e.g. *~ der Fahrt* = 'intended destination' in Gottsched, *Ged.* 1,244, Schiller, *Picc.* 1585: '*trau niemand hier als mir . . . sie haben einen Zweck*', Goethe 1,215 (W.): '*. . . daß zum Zwecke Wasser fließe*'. Hence *zu seinem ~ kommen*, since Early NHG, e.g. Lehman 1,139 [1662]; cf. Günther, *Ged.* 254 [1735]: '*frisch gewagt kommt bald zum Zwecke*'; similarly *zum ~ gelangen* and *den ~ erlangen* (since Early NHG).

nahe zum ~ schießen to get close to one's target, almost attain what one had aimed for; figur. since the 17th c., e.g. Lehman 1,239 [1662].

den ~ verfehlen to fail to attain one's purpose; since Early NHG, when it ran *des Zwecks fehlen*; with *verfehlen* since the 18th c., e.g. Knigge, *Umgang* 7,9; cf. *weit vom ~ schießen*, current since the 16th c. The opposite is *seinen Zweck erreichen*, as in Goethe, *Wahlverw.* 2,5; cf. also *etw. erfüllt seinen ~* = 'sth. serves its purpose', also *er hat den rechten ~ getroffen*, still current in the 19th c., now obs.

den ~ aus den Augen verlieren to lose sight of one's purpose; since the 18th c., e.g. Goethe IV,30,109 (W.).

das ist der ~ der Übung that is the point of the exercise; modern, not listed in Campe [1811], not even in *DWb.* [1954].

'*es wächst der Mensch mit seinen größern Zwecken*' people grow in stature as they strive for higher goals; quotation from Schiller, *Wall.*, *Prol.* 60.

← See also under *bestimmen* (for *etw. für einen gewissen Zweck bestimmen*), *breit* (for *seine Zwecke zu unabsehlich*), *gehen* (for *aller Zweck gehet dahin, daß man erlerne*), *gelangen* (for *aber daß wir wider zu dem zweck gelangen*), *Hand* (for *wenn sich der Kirchenglaube nur durch die Regierung zu ihren Zwecken gut handhaben läßt*), *heilig* (for *der Zweck heiligt die Mittel*), *Hinterlist* (for *für hinterlistige Zwecke*), *Mittel* (for *ein Mittel zum Zweck*), *richten* (for *das auge seiner intention nur allein gerade zu seinem zweck richte*), *unbehaust* (for *der Unmensch ohne Zweck und Ruh*) and *zwecklos* (for *es hat keinen Zweck*).

zweckbestimmt

zweckbestimmt functional (e.g. building, tool), purposive (e.g. undertaking), biased, tendentious (e.g. piece of writing); probably since the 19th c., because the noun *Zweckbestimmung* has been recorded since the beginning of the 19th c. *DWb.* [1954] does not record the adjective.

zweckbetont

zweckbetont purposive, with stress laid upon its usefulness, utilitarian; modern (not yet listed in *DWb.* [1954]); cf. the note on *betonen* (p. 291).

zweckbewußt

zweckbewußt (rare) determined, single-minded; since the 19th c. with ref. to persons, but much less used than *zielbewußt* and *zielstrebig*.

Zweckdenken

das ~ (lit.) thinking which puts usefulness foremost, utility thinking; 20th c. term, not yet listed in *DWb.* [1954].

zweckdienlich

zweckdienlich pertinent, relevant, suitable, useful; since late in the 18th c.; not yet recorded by Adelung, but listed by Campe [1811]; cf. *zu etw. dienen* (p. 479).

zweckentfremdet

zweckentfremdet misused, used for a purpose for which it was not intended; 20th c. compound, not yet listed in *DWb.* [1954]; cf. *entfremden* (p. 849).

zweckentsprechend

zweckentsprechend appropriate, suitable; since the middle of the 19th c.; cf. *entsprechen* (p. 659).

zweckgemäß

zweckgemäß, zweckmäßig appropriate, suitable; both appeared in the 18th c. (before then *sweckig/zweckicht* and *zweckhaft* were used); in Goethe II,4,319 (W.) *zweckgemäß* occurs, in 22,63 and 23,46 (W.) he used *zweckmäßig*. Lessing [edit. L.-M.] used *zweckmäßig*. Adelung and Campe did not record either word.

Zweckgerüste: see *Gerüst.*

zweckhaft

zweckhaft appropriate, useful, suitable; since the 17th c. (*Trübner* is wrong in stating that it was first used by Herder, since Stieler recorded it in 1691 along with *zweckicht*).

zwecklich

zwecklich (a.) appropriate, suitable; since the 18th c., used by Goethe in IV,24,286 (W.), but now rare if not obs.

zwecklos

es ist ~ , es hat keinen Zweck it is pointless, serves no purpose, is of no use; since the 18th c.; Goethe and Schiller used ~ and Campe [1811] listed it. He did not record *es hat keinen Zweck*, but it occurs in Goethe 19,14 (W.).

zweckmäßig: see *zweckgemäß*.

Zweckschuß

der ~ (obs.) hit, sth. that hits the target; in phys. sense since the 17th c., figur. since the 19th c., but now no longer recorded in the standard dictionaries.

zweckvoll

zweckvoll (a.) appropriate, suitable; since the 18th c., used by Schiller, now rare.

zweckwidrig

zweckwidrig inappropriate, harmful, wrong; since the 18th c., used by Kant and Goethe; still current in tech. and med. contexts.

zwei

die (sometimes *das*) *Zwei* (poet.) the two; in poet. contexts since the 17th c. mainly with ref. to a pair of lovers, e.g. Zesen, *Adr.Ros.* 1: '*dieses traute zwei*', Goethe 15,1,228 (W.): '*Liebe, menschlich zu beglücken, nähert sie ein edles Zwei . . .*'; cf. also Rückert, *Weish.d.Brah.* 1,19 [1836]: '*Die Zwei ist Zweifel, Zwist, ist Zwietracht, Zwiespalt, Zwitter; die Zwei ist Zwillingsfrucht am Zweige süß und bitter*'.

(nur) ~ only a few, just one or two; in vague statements about a short time, short distance or very few things, as in Engl. 'just one or two', since the 17th c., e.g. Gryphius, *T.Ged.* 1,862 [1698]: '*ich wollte gern zwey worte mit ihm reden*', G. Keller, *Ges. Werke* 4,46 (*Seldw.*): '*das Glück dauert nie länger als zwei Minuten*'.

eins, ~ , drei (coll.) in next to no time, in a jiffy; sometimes simply as *eins, ~* (e.g. in P. Rebhuhn [edit. Tittm.]), but usually in the fuller form, e.g. (DWb) Kotzebue, *S. dram.Werke* 2,33: '*ich eile nun auch an meine Geschäfte, und eins, zwey, drey ist der Mittag da*'.

ich und du und wir ~ (coll.) we both together, the two of us; in some regions also as *wir ~ beide*; modern.

alles, was ~ Beine hat, kam dorthin (coll.) everybody came to that place; in this form modern; cf. *er steht noch auf ~ Beinen* = 'he is still alive' and G. Hauptmann, *Weber* 54.

er arbeitet (schafft, schuftet) für ~ (coll.) he does two men's work, does as much work as would ordinarily be done by two people; modern.

da gehören ~ dazu (coll.) don't take me for granted; expresses a person's objection to sth. about which he has not been consulted; modern, in lit. contexts since the 19th c., e.g. Fontane, *Ges.Werke* 1,6,32: '*ich bin für Frieden, aber zum guten Frieden gehören zwei*'; cf. Engl. locutions (in a different context) such as 'it takes two to tango'.

'*zwei Seelen und ein Gedanke, zwei Herzen und ein Schlag*' two souls with but a single thought, two hearts with one heartbeat; quotation of the closing lines of the 2nd act of the drama *Der Sohn der Wildnis* by Friedrich Halms. Now often half-joc. used for 'how nice that we have both thought of the same idea'.

die ~ Brüder (vulg.) the testicles; see the entry on *die Brüder* on p. 408.

was zweien gerecht ist, ist einem zu eng, dreien zu weit (prov.) what burdens one, is right for two and too public for three; this refers to the possession of a secret; f.r.b. Franck [1541].

wenn ~ dasselbe tun, so ist es nicht dasselbe (prov.) what is permissible to one person is not necessarily allowable to another; of Classical origin, e.g. Terence, *Adelphoe* 5,3,37: '*duo dum idem faciunt . . . hoc licet impune facere huic, illi non licet*' and Terence, *Heauton Timorumenos* 4,5,49: '*aliis si licet, tibi non licet*'. In German circles with a Classical education *quod licet Jovi non licet bovi* is also used.

was ~ wissen, erfahren hundert (prov.) what two have learned is passed on to a hundred; modern in this wording, recorded by Simrock [1846], but cf. the entries under *drei* and *hundert* on *was drei wissen, erfahren (bald) dreißig*.

← See also under *Auge* (for *vier Augen sehen mehr als zwei, solange als zwei große Augen noch offen sind* and *alles steht auf zwei Augen*), *Bank* (for *zwischen zwei Bänken sitzen*), *Bein* (for *zwei Hunde an einem Bein kommen selten überein*), *dienen* (for *niemand kann zwei Herren dienen*), *Dotter* (for *seine Hühner legen Eier mit zwei Dottern*), *dritte* (for *wenn zwei sich streiten, lacht der Dritte*), *Ei* (for *dem frommen Schweppermann zwei*), *Finger* (for *sie sind wie zwei Finger an einer Hand*), *Fliege* (for *zwei Fliegen mit einem Schlage treffen*), *gehen* (for *es sind zwo welt*), *Gesicht* (for *Mancher zwei Gesichter hat*), *Gevatter* (for *zwei Gevatter zu einem Kind gewinnen*), *Gleis* (for *auf zwei Gleisen fahren*), *greifen* (for *Mittelding zwischen zwei ineinander greifenden Systemen*), *Hahn* (for *zwei Hähne vertragen sich nicht auf einem Mist*), *Hand* (for *zwei Dinge bieten einander die Hände*), *hängen* (for *in diesen zwei Geboten hanget das ganze Gesetz*), *Hose* (for *zwei Hosen eines Tuchs sein*), *Kissen* (for *besser zwei auf dem Kissen als eins auf dem Gewissen*), *Linse* (for *zwei Linsen auf einem Brett*), *Schuh* (for *das sind zwei verschiedene Schuhe*), *Seele* (for *zwei Seelen wohnen, ach! in meiner Brust*), *Seite* (for *alles hat seine zwei Seiten*), *Stuhl* (for *zwischen zwei Stühlen sitzen*, also under *fallen* for *wer auf zwei Stühlen sitzen will*), *suchen* (for *da haben sich zwei gesucht und gefunden*) and *Wurst* (for *das ist eine andere Wurst mit zwei Zipfeln*). For *entzwei* see *entzweigehen, entzweireißen, entzweisein* (p. 663) and under *brechen* for *entzweibrechen*.

zweideutig

See under *Blume* (for *die zweideutigen Worte, die heuchlerischen Blumen*), *Gefährte* (for *die Neigung eine sehr zweydeutige Gefährtin des Sittengefühls*), *Schale* (for *zweideutig schwankt die Wagschal ihrer Gunst*) and *schielen* (for *schielende und zweideutige Antworten*).

Zweideutigkeit

See under *hocken* (for *mit ihren Trivialwitzen und Zweideutigkeiten*) and *ungezogen* (for *die ungezogensten Zweydeutigkeiten*).

zweierlei

See under *anfangen* (for *Anfang und Ende ist zweierlei*), *geben* (for *es ist nur zweierlei möglich, ein drittes gibt es nicht*), *messen* (for *mit zweierlei Maß messen*), *Morgen* (for *Versprechen und Halten ist zweierlei*) and *Sprache* (for *zweierlei Sprachen reden*).

zweifach: see *drei*.

Zweifel

der ~ plagt (lit.) doubt tortures (sb.); at least since the 18th c., e.g. Goethe, *Urfaust* 15: '*mich plagen keine Skrupel noch Zweifel*'. Other cases where ~ is personified are *der ~ nagt*, e.g. Chamisso 4,185: '. . . *Schlangenbiß des Zweifels nicht langsam mir am kranken Herzen nage*', Gutzkow, *R.v.G.* 5,70: '. . . *einen so nagenden Zweifel über meine bisherigen Auffassungen*', *ein ~ steigt* (or *stößt*) *jem.m auf*, e.g. Wieland 18,57: '*ohne daß ihnen jemals ein Zweifel über ihre eigene Ehrlichkeit aufgestiegen wäre*', also B. Brecht, *Guter Mensch* (*Vorspiel*). Similarly, *ein ~ beschleicht jem.* (18th c.).

~ ist des Glaubens Feind (prov.) doubt is the enemy of faith; f.r.b. Petri 1,118 [1605].

← See also under *anfechten* (for *ein Zweifel ficht ihn an*), *auslösen* (for *Zweifel auslösen*), *außer* (for *außer allem Zweifel*), *dürr* (for *er hat uns nicht im zweifel gelassen*), *Gegengift* (for *des Zweifels Gegengift*), *gern* (for *Christen, welche ihren Zweifeln nachhängen*), *Gewicht* (for *es stehe noch im Gleichgewichte deß Zweifels*), *gut* (for *zwar zweifel tett noch nye chain guot*), *Haufen* (for *das sei on zweifel recht und gut*), *heben* (for *und hübe deine Rede jeden Zweifel*), *hegen* (for *Zweifel hegen*), *irre* (for *die Irrgärten des Zweifels*), *klein* (for *wer horchte da auf kleinlich dunkle Zweifel?*), *Luft* (for *nichts als Unvollendetes, Zweifel, Grundloses und Luftiges*), *Panzer* (for *das in Zweifel, Abwehr und Härte gepanzerte Leid*), *Schach* (for *zwivel hat mir sprochen schach und mat*), *schön* (for *den schweren Zweifel deines Vaters zu erschüttern*), *setzen* (for *Zweifel in etw. setzen*), *stellen* (for *etw. in Zweifel stellen*), *Träne* (for *wie Zweifel oft das Haupt hing*), *unterliegen* (for *unterliegt keinem Zweifel*), *verbannen* (for *die Zweifel aus meiner Brust zu verbannen*), *verkleistern* (for *die Zweifel nicht bloß zu verkleistern, sondern zu heben sucht*) and *ziehen* (for *jem. zieht jem. aus einem Zweifel*).

zweifelhaft

See under *beglücken* (for *das matte zweifelhafte Licht*) and *Grenze* (for *das zweifelhafte Licht, worin die Grenzen schwimmen*).

zweifeln

See under *Gegengift* (for *des Zweifels Gegengift durch Zweifeln zu erlangen*), *Grund* (for *eine frühere Grundlage des Gedichts ist also unbezweifelt*), *irre* (for *die Freunde zweifeln, werden irr an dir*), *kollidieren* (for *daß man an der Unendlichkeit unseres Raumes zweifeln kann*) and *lassen* (for *ich zweifle, ob . . .*).

Zweifelsknoten: see *gordisch*.

Zweifelsmeer: see *Meer*.

Zweifelsnebel: see *Nebel*.

zweifelsreich: see *reich*.

Zweifelsucht: see *blind*.

zweiflerisch: see *gegenüber*.

Zweig

der ~ branch; since etymologically ~ and *zwei* are closely related, MHG terms such as *zwîgebel* = 'having two tines' and *zwîen* = 'to form branches' can be taken as derived as much from *zwei* = 'two' as from *zwî* = 'branch'. Truly figur., however, and belonging to 'branch' is MHG *zwey* or *zwî* when applied to the Virgin Mary or to Jesus (influenced by Isaiah 11,1). This led to ~ = 'son', in use since the 16th c., e.g. Franck, *Chron.* 84 [1538], and the application to persons brought about ~ *der Familie* or *des Geschlechts*, extended in the 18th c. to abstracts such as ~ *einer Wissenschaft, Kunst, Literatur, Gesetzgebung, Verfassung* (the last two used by Schiller and Goethe). Only since the 19th c. in comm. contexts and in scores of compounds, e.g. *Erwerbszweig, Zweigunternehmen*.

← See also under *Baum* (for *ein Glied desselben mit einem Zweige zu vergleichen*), *grün* (for *auf keinen grünen Zweig kommen*), *packen* (for *ich habe den grünen Zweig der Gesundheit wieder fest zu packen gekriegt*) and *treiben* (for *mein alter Stamm treibt fürder keine Zweige*).

zweigen: see *abzweigen* and *verzweigen*.

Zweigespann

ein ~ (coll.) a twosome, duo; orginally = 'a team of two horses'; since the 19th c. in coll. use for people; cf. *Doppelgespann* (p. 1020).

Zweigestirn: see *doppelt*.

zweigleisig

~ fahren (coll.) to pursue a dual-track policy; usually containing the notion of indulging in double-dealing; 20th c.

Zweiheit: see *leuchten*.

Zweikampf: see *geben*.

zweimal

See under *fragen* (for *besser zweimal fragen als einmal irregehen*), *sagen* (for *das läßt er sich nicht zweimal sagen*) and *Sieg* (for *der sigt zweymal der sich selbs überwint*).

zweischenklig: see *Schenkel*.

zweischneidig

See under *Klinge* (for *es gibt zweischneidige Klingen*), *Messer* (for *des besagten A. Zunge ein zweyschneidiges Schwert*) and *Schwert* (for *ein zweischneidiges Schwert*).

zweiseitig

zweiseitig (a.) two-faced, trying to please both sides; current since the 18th c. and still used in the 19th c., but now no longer recorded.

zweit

mein zweites Ich (or *Selbst*) (lit.) my second self; usually with ref. to a close friend; frequent in Classical literature, used by Aristotle, Plutarch and Cicero with *ander*, in Seneca, *De moribus* with ~. For the attribution to other sources (Pythagoras, Zeno) see Büchmann, *Gefl. Worte* 363 [1994]; in German lit. since the 18th c.; *zweites Selbst* for 'a separate being alongside oneself' occurs in Goethe 24,50 (W.).

ein zweiter Tod (lit.) a life comparable to death (or not worth living); since the 18th c., e.g. Goethe 10,4 (W.): '*rette mich . . . von dem Leben hier, dem zweiten Tode*'.

wie kein Zweiter (coll.) like no one else, without an equal; with ref. to sb.'s unrivalled excellence; in use since the 19th c.

der zweite Sieger (joc. coll.) the loser (in a contest between two persons); first in stud.sl.; modern.

← See also under *Gesicht* (for *das zweite Gesicht*), *greifen* (for *Darstellungen aus zweiter Hand*), *Mal* (for *sich etw. nicht zum zweiten Mal sagen lassen*), *Natur* (for *etw. wird jem.m zur zweiten Natur*), *Ohr* (for *taub an dem zweiten Ohre*) and *Simson* (for *ein zweiter Simson*).

zweiunddreißigblättrig: see *Bibel*.

zweizüngig

zweizüngig (a.) two-faced, double-dealing; since Early NHG, used by Luther 26,591 (Weimar) and still current in the 19th c., but now a., displaced by *doppelzüngig*.

zwerch: see *blitzen*.

Zwerchfell

See under *kitzeln* (for *ein Schauspiel, wenn es dein Zwerchfell zum Gelächter kitzelt*) and *Kost* (for *die Zwerchfelle seiner Zuschauer zu erschüttern*).

Zwerg

ein ~ a tiny (miserable, dwarf-like) thing; as an offensive term for a small person since the 17th c., e.g. Dannhauer, *Catech.* 1,185 [1687]: '*auswendig bistu ein großer Mann, inwendig ein elender Zwerch*', Goethe, *Faust I*, 613: '*. . . daß ich mich recht als Zwerg empfinden sollte*'. Since the 18th c. applied to tiny things, e.g. J.G. Jacobi, *Sämtl. Werke* 3,124 [1807]: '*. . . den kleinsten Zwerg von Almanach*', also in comparisons, e.g. Wieland 11,259: '*. . . der Ätna selbst sei gegen ihn ein Zwerg*'. *Gezwerg* as a singular for ~ and as a collective noun can also occur, in derogatory sense as early as in MHG, e.g. Hugo v. Langen-

stein, *Martina* 116,20 and still used in the 20th c., though becoming a. (like many collectives with *Ge-*). In ordinary sense (not disparagingly) Goethe used *Gezwergvolk* in *Faust* 10745. A modern off-shoot from ~ is *Zwergling*, e.g. Radlof, *Trefflichkeiten* 291 [1811].

Zwerg(en)volk pygmies; also called *Pygmäen* (from Homer's use of the term in *Iliad* 3,6); since the 19th c., recorded by Sanders [1865], but not yet by Campe [1811]; Sanders indicated that *Pygmäenvolk* is the preferred term.

Zwerg-. . . (also *Zwergs-*. . .) dwarf . . . ; in compounds since Late MHG, mostly of a botanical nature, e.g. *Zwergapfel*, recorded since the 15th c. Stieler [1691] listed *Zwerkpferdlein* for 'tiny horse, hobby-horse', defining it as *Kinderpferdlein*, but also mentioning the zool. meaning '*equus pumilus*'. Some botanical compounds were listed by Frisch [1741] and by Adelung, but few of a more general kind, surprisingly since quite a few arose in the 18th c., including derogatory ones, such as *Zwergverstand* = 'very low intelligence', but the majority of the compounds now current joined the group in the 19th c., when Campe [1811] listed *Zwergfuß*, *-gestalt* and *-schritt*, apart from some fifty bot. and zool. terms.

zwergenhaft (also *zwerghaft*) dwarf-like, tiny; since the 18th c., when Goethe used *zwergenhaft* and Jean Paul *zwerghaft*. Lessing 11,715 used *zwergicht*, Alexis, *Hosen d.H.v.B.* 2,2,90 has *zwergisch*; in 19th c. lit. *zwergig* occurs with ref. to plants and people.

der Gartenzwerg (coll.) little runt; term of contempt for a small person compared to a garden gnome; modern (even for 'garden gnome' in its ordinary sense not yet recorded in *DWb.* [1878]).

verzwergen to shrink, become stunted; at least since the 17th c., since Kramer [1702] listed *verzwergt* for 'stunted', e.g. Meißner, *Alcib.* 3,293 [1781]; *sich verzwergen* occurs occasionally in modern lit., *Verzwergung* arose in the 19th c.

← See also under *Gift* (for *Giftzwerg*) and *verschaffen* (for *zum häßlichsten Zwerge verschafft dich mein Wort*).

Zwetsche

meine sieben Zwetschen (coll.) my few bits and pieces, my various belongings; since the 19th c.; see also under *sieben* for *seine Siebensachen* (p. 2258).

ein Gesicht wie eine verhutzelte (*vertrocknete, eingeschrumpfte*) ~ (coll.) a face like a shrivelled prune; since the 19th c., in various forms in different regions.

die ~ (also *Zwetschke* or *Quetsche*) (obscene) vagina; used in many regions, little recorded except in 19th c. dialect dictionaries (e.g. Fischer, Mensing), but certainly very much older. It can also (as can similar terms) be used for 'woman' and 'harlot'; cf. the entries on *Feige* (p. 752), *Feigenblatt* (p. 753), *Maus* (p. 1675), *Muschel* (p. 1725) and *Pflaume* (p. 1802), also Engl. (obscene) 'plum' for 'vagina'.

Zwickel

ein komischer ~ (regional coll.) a weird eccentric person, odd customer; ~ originally described a wedge of wood or iron (current since OHG), extended to mean 'gusset' in clothing or in a bag, a wedge-shaped piece of bread or part of a beard. Since the 17th c. in phrases relating to oddness or strangeness, even derangement, e.g. *er hat einen ~ zuviel* or *nicht jeder ~ sitzt bei ihm richtig, jeder hat seinen ~* = 'everybody has some queer moods or habits, some weakness', recorded by Pistorius, *Thes.* [1715]. Now in the regions applied to persons, e.g. *er ist ein komischer ~* , *er spielt den großen ~* = 'he fancies himself as an important person'.

Zwickelerlaß

ein ~ (coll., a.) a law or bill which is seen by its critics as interfering with personal liberty; derived from the Prussian regulation of 1932 introduced by Bracht, Minister for Home Affairs, that bathing costumes must have a gusset substantial enough to hide the genitals; later (from 1958 onward) applied to any law or bill which is considered to be either too restrictive or prudish; now a., no longer listed in late 20th c. dictionaries, apart from *Pons*.

zwicken

etw. zwickt jem. st. plagues, hurts or worries sb.; in figur. contexts with abstracts as the subject since the 16th c., e.g. H. Sachs [edit.K.] 3,387: '*die unruhig unruh die zwickt mich immerzu*' or in Lehman 2,547 [1662] with '*Narrheit mit ihrem Sporn*' as the subject, but diseases have more frequently been seen as the tormentors, often in the combination ~ *und zwacken*, current since the 16th c. (H. Sachs) and still in use. It has been suggested that ~ = 'to castrate (an animal)' and *gezwickt* = 'barren' might explain the development of *Zwickel* (see above) from 'wedge' to 'oddness' or 'weakness'. – Goethe 46,145 (W.) used *jem. ~* for 'to rob sb.'; this is obs., but *jem.m etw. abzwicken* still occurs for 'to deprive sb. of sth.'.

← See also under *Gewissen* (for *also zwickt das Gewissen noch manchen im Wohlleben*).

Zwickmühle: see *Mühle*.

Zwiebel

er hat an der ~ gerochen (coll.) he is in tears; refs. to the effect that onions have on our eyes and noses appeared as early as in the Middle Ages, e.g. Trimberg, *Renner* [edit. Ehr.] 9842; Franck [1541] listed: '*er hat zwibel geschelet oder gessen*' and Petri [1605] recorded: '*zwibeln schelen ohne augenthrenen ist nicht jedermann gegeben*'; similarly with *riechen*, as in Raabe, *Hungerpastor*

1,192 [1864] with ref. to leave-taking: '*nun hat der Junge auch wieder an der Zwiebel gerochen*'; cf. also Goethe 9,107 (W.): '*mir sind auch gar oft die Augen übergangen, und täglich ist mirs noch, als röch ich Zwiebeln*', Heine, *Lut.* 2,29: '. . . *hält sich die officielle Trauer schon etwelche Zwiebeln vor die Nase, um betrüglich zu flennen*'.

in Hüllen und Häute gewickelt wie eine ~ wrapped up in many skins; e.g. Wieland 10,200. Refs to the numerous skins of onions are old and still occur in modern period, e.g. Schiller, *Xenien* 56: '*ist denn die Wahrheit ein Zwiebel, an dem man die Häute nur abschält?*'.

die ~ (1) (coll.) turnip, thick old-fashioned pocket-watch; in lit. since the 19th c., but not yet in Campe [1811].

die ~ (2) (regional coll.) bun (hairstyle); only in some areas, in others *Krone* or *Krönchen* is used; in some parts of Germany ~ can stand for 'head'.

Zwiebeln trägt man hin, Knoblauch bringt man wieder (prov.) nothing is achieved or changed; with ref. to people it means 'people stay the same, remain unreformed'; Luther used it in a sermon on the 65th Psalm, it also occurs in (Wander) H. Sachs IV,cxi,1; it was still recorded as current in the 19th c.

die ~ hat sieben Häute, ein Weib neun (prov.) onions have seven skins, women nine; only in modern collections, e.g. Simrock [1846].

Zwiebelfish: see *Fisch*.

zwiebeln

jem. ~ (coll.) to give sb. a bad or hard time, keep at sb., plague or harrass sb.; since the 17th c., f.r.b. Stieler [1691]; origin is not clear, and the more obvious explanation that it refers to the effect of onions on one's eyes is not accepted by everybody. Weigand suggested that it might describe the taking away of things from sb. in the same way as one removes skins from an onion, therefore similar to *jem. schinden*. The term is current in many regions, also in mil. sl.; in lit. since the 17th c., e.g. Abr.a S. Clara, *Judas* 1,22 [1686].

Zwiebelturm

der ~ (arch.) onion tower; also sometimes referred to as *Turm mit Zwiebelkopf*; only since the 19th c., but not yet in Campe [1811].

Zwiegespräch

ein ~ mit sich selbst (lit.) an internal dialogue, a conversation with oneself; often in *ein ~* (or *Zwiesprache*) *mit sich selbst halten*; since early in the 19th c. with both nouns; figur. also when one partner in the dialogue is mute (e.g. a ghost or an object) or when both are objects, e.g. Hebbel, *Werke* [edit. Werner] 10,212: '*ich horchte auf Nußbaum und Brunnen und ihe seltsames Zwiegespräch*', Gutzkow, *Zauberer v.R.* 3,244 [1858]: '. . . *falls nicht das Gebet ein Zwiegespräch der Seele mit sich selbst ist*', similarly in Raabe, *Hungerpastor*

3,64 (and in 1,138 he also used *Zwiesprache hal-ten*); cf. Goethe, *Gespr.* [edit. B.] 6,314: '. . . *bin ich sodann im Freien und halte geistige Zwiesprache mit den Ranken der Weinrebe*'. In some cases *er hält Zwiesprache mit sich selbst* means no more than 'he is pondering on sth.'.

Zwielicht

ins ~ *geraten* to come under a cloud, lay one-self open to suspicion; modern.

← See also under *steigen*.

Zwiespalt

See under *husten* (for *sidmal der kindertouf, ie in zwispalt kumen ist*) and *Spalt* (for *Zwiespalt, Zwie-spalt stiften* and *innerer Zwiespalt*).

zwiespältig: see *Spalt*.

Zwiesprache: see *Zwiegespräch*.

Zwietracht

See under *Fackel* (for *die Fackel der Zwie-tracht*), *Fessel* (for *jeder Zwietracht Furien zu entfes-seln*), *Gebirge* (for *wo auf gebirgten Leichen die wilde Zwietracht steht*), *Gefecht* (for *ein zweitracht unter den ständen*), *Gegenstand* (for *ich bin ein Gegenstand der Zwietracht*), *Geschoß* (for *wo ihr Geschoß die Zwietracht spannt*), *klirren* (for *lösen irdscher Zwietracht Klirren auf*), *lodern* (for *wird die Zwietracht nicht in vollen Flammen lodern?*) and *los* (for *die alte Zwietracht ist los*).

Zwietrachtsapfel: see *Apfel*.

Zwillinge

. . . *und . . . sind* ~ (lit.) . . . and . . . are twins; with ref. to abstracts since the 17th c. in lit., e.g. Lehman 1,176 [1662]: '*ehr und hoffarth sind zwilling*', Klopstock, *Oden* [edit. M.-P.] 2,37: '*des Gedankens Zwilling, das Wort*'; cf. also Hebbel, *Tageb.* [edit. W.] 2,71: '*das Unglück gebiert nur Zwillinge*'. Sometimes *Zwillingsbrüder* is used, e.g. Fr.H. Jacobi, *Werke* 3,350 on materialism and idealism: '*durch die ganze philosophische Geschichte sehen wir diese Zwillingsbrüder . . . hadern*', simi-larly with *Zwillingsgeschwister*, as in Zschokke, *Ausgew. Schr.* 21,193: '*Schmerz und Freude sind ein zärtliches Zwillingsgeschwister*', Goethe 13,1,304 (W.): '*die Liebe und die Thorheit sind Zwillingsgeschwister von alter Zeit*' and *Zwillings-schwestern*, as in Wieland (Acad.Edit.) 2,19: '*die Zwillinge, Wahrheit und Liebe*'; also *Zwillingstöchter*, e.g. (DWb) v.Haller, *Staatswiss.* 1,385 [1816]: '*Gerechtigkeit und Liebe sind . . . . Zwillingstöchter des nemlichen göttlichen Gesezes*'.

Zwillinge (tech.) twins; in many trades for a couple of identical lines, beams, threads, pipes, crystals, etc.; beginnings in the 16th c., e.g. A. Dürer, *4 Bücher* Q4c [1520]: '*figur der zweier linien, die wil ich nennen den zwiling*'. See also the entry under *Zwillingsbuchstaben* (below). In medi-cine *Zwillingsmuskeln* is used tor 'twin muscle'.

die ~ (astron.) Gemini; a loan-translation from Latin, since MHG, *die Sonne* (or *der Mond*) *geht in die* ~ (or *steht in den Zwillingen*).

← See also under *Siam* (for *siamesische Zwill-inge*).

Zwillingsbuchstaben

die ~ (ling.) doubled letters; since the 18th c., usually with ref. to doubled consonants, used by Gottsched in a note on doubled *nn* at the end of female names (no longer used since the 19th c.); cf. also Fr. Branky in *ZfdW.* 5,275. *Zwillinge* suf-fices (and is older), and *Zwillinge* can also be used for two juxtaposed forms of a word, e.g. Luther 10,1,1,375 (Weimar): '*solch tzwillinge der wort odder spruch*'.

Zwillingsgemüse: see *Gemüse*.

Zwillingsgeschwister: see *Geschwister* (and *Zwillinge*).

Zwillingsgestirn

das ~ Castor and Pollux; since the 17th c., recorded by Kramer [1702]. In lit. often used with ref. to people sharing distinction in the same field, e.g. Jean Paul, *Werke* [edit.H.] 49/51,27 with ref. to Homer and Shakespeare.

Zwillingspaar

das ~ (lit.) the bosom; of bibl. origin from Song of Solomon 4,5: '*deine zwo brüste sind wie zwei junge rehzwillinge, die unter den rosen weiden*' (in A.V. '. . . like two young roes that are twins which feed among the lilies'); in lit. since the 18th c., J.E. Schlegel, *Werke* 6,93 [1761]: '*der Brust erhabner Schmuck, ein listig Zwillingspaar*' or Goethe 14,168 (W.): '*ich hab euch oft beneidet ums Zwillingspaar, das unter Rosen weidet*'.

Zwillingsschwester: see *Schwester* (and *Zwill-inge*).

Zwingburg

die ~ (lit.) citadel, fortress, stronghold; *Zwing-.* . . here indicates its purpose, i.e. domi-nation by force; figur. since the 19th c. for 'edi-fices' (even institutions) which stand for power which subjugates, e.g. Börne, *Schriften* 12,16 [1829]: '*die Zwingburgen der Gewalt*' or O. Lud-wig on Lessing's rôle in destroying old rules of dramatic writing calling him '*Zertrümmerer der Zwingburgen*'; hence with ref. to revolutionary activities: *die Zwingburgen stürmen* or *erstürmen*. *Zwingfeste* can be used in the same figur. con-texts, e.g. Goethe 36,339 (W.).

zwingen

See under *bezwingen*, *Decke* (for *zwing dich, krumm zu liegen*, also under *krumm*), *drängen* (for *einen trengen, zwingen*), *erzwingen*, *gehen* (for *die Achtung läßt sich nicht erzwingen*), *Geist* (for *Zauber, der zum Geist gewaltig zwingt den Geist*), *Getriebe* (for *aneinander zwingen*), *Gewand* (for *der verschämteste Begriff ist gezwungen, die mystische Gewänder fallen zu lassen*), *gewinnen* (for *dem jun-gen Mann Empfindung abzuzwingen*), *Grund* (for *daß sy die geschrift . . . zwingen*), *gut* (for *etw. wozu man gezwungen wird*), *Knie* (for *jem. in/auf die Knie zwingen*), *Kost* (for *kostbar und gezwungen*), *Schnur* (for *dîne snüere die twingent daz herze mîn* and *eine Art des gezwungenen Styl)* and *schwach* (for *nur der Starke wird das Schicksal zwingen*).

Zwingfeste: see *Zwingburg*.

Zwingherr

der ~ tyrant, despot; since early in the 19th c., when the term was often applied to Napoleon, e.g. by Börne in *Ges.Schr.* 1,117 [1829], but also used for despotic rulers of other periods; hence *zwingherrisch* = 'despotic', f.r.b. Campe [1811] (*zwingherrlich* also occurs, mainly in S. Germany and Switzerland), and *Zwingherrschaft*, since early in the 19th c., recorded by Campe.

zwinkern

zwinkern to wink, look at sb. with a wink; since late in the 19th c. as an unspoken message indicating (secret) agreement or understanding of the situation, also conveying satisfaction about the development of events as in Nietzsche, *Werke* 1,5,39 [1895]: '*sie zwinkern mit den Augen . . . und scheinen sagen zu wollen, es wird wohl irgend ein guter Vortheil dabei sein*'; hence also in compounds *mit einem Augenzwinkern* = 'with a (meaningful) wink' and *augenzwinkernd*, both modern, and *jem.m zuzwinkern*, since the 19th c., e.g. (DWb) Gaudy, *Sämtl.Werke* 13,78: '. . . *wobei er ihm zum Zeichen des Einverständnisses mit den Augen zuzwinkerte*'.

Zwirn

der ~ (1) (coll.) (alcoholic) spirit, hard liquor; since the 18th c., recorded by Campe [1811], but not yet by Adelung; this is connected with the etym. root of ~, which is *zwei*, since it describes a doubled thread. The term therefore denoted sth. of doubled strength, i.e. *doppeltgebrannt*; occasionally found in lit., e.g. Grabbe, *Sämtl. Werke* [edit. Bl.] 3,155, where the variant term *blauer ~* is used.

der ~ (2) (vulg.) semen, sperm; recorded since the 19th c. (though probably older), also called *weißer ~*; cf. French sl. *fil blanc*, also Engl. obs. vulg. 'to thread the needle'. Many regional vulg. phrases contain refs to ~ = 'sperm', e.g. *der ~ geht ihm aus* = 'he has become impotent', recorded in the 19th c. for East Prussian areas, *er hat den guten ~ früher in schlechte Säcke vernäht* = 'he remains childless because of his loose-living past', *er will seinen jungen ~ nicht in alte Lumpen vernähen* = 'he does not want to marry a much older woman', recorded by Wander [1880]. Rädlein [1711] recorded: '*er hat seinen Zwirn (beym Frauenzimmer) schon vernehet, er hat das seinige gethan, er kan nicht mehr*'. In zool. the sperm of lobsters has been called ~ since the 18th c., recorded by Nemnich [1796], sometimes called *Krebszwirn*.

der ~ (3) (cant) money; recorded since 1840, also called *schwarzer ~*. Wolff in his dictionary of *Rotwelsch* wants to connect this with Yiddish terms, but some scholars maintain that there is

no need for that assumption since many trades use the material they need and handle all day as a term for 'money' (see the entries under *Blech* (p. 337), *Draht* (p. 490), *Pulver* (p. 1917) and *Stoff* (p. 2377)).

schlechter ~ (regional coll.) a bad business, queer goings-on, poor show; ~ here = *Sache* = 'affair, business' (cf. entries under *Ding* (p. 479), *Geschichte* (p. 1001), *Kram* (p. 1539)); first recorded for mil. sl. in the 2nd half of the 19th c., now coll. in several regions.

~ spinnen to ponder, turn things over in one's mind; belongs to the group of phrases with figur. *Faden, Garn, Kunkel, Rocken, spinnen* and *Werg* (see p. 914); cf. *Gedankenzwirn abwickeln*, used by Goethe (*Briefw. Karl August* 1,2) and *Gedanken spinnen/fortspinnen* on p. 2304.

er hat seltsamen ~ im Kopf he has queer ideas, strange notions; belongs in essence to the previous entry; current since the 18th c., e.g. Gotter, *Schausp.* 296 [1795]: '*was machen Sie für Zwirn . . .*' = 'what has put this extraordinary idea into your head?', Musäus, *Ph.* 1,63: '*mag Gott wissen, was der Kerl für Zwirn im Kopf hat*' (he also used *Teufelszwirn im Kopf*); cf. *wirre Fäden spinnen* and *Hirngespinst* (p. 2304), *er spinnt einen seltsamen Faden* (p. 708) and *Gott verwirret sein Garn* (p. 914).

jem.m ist der ~ ausgegangen (coll.) sb. has no more to say, is lost for words; recorded for several areas since the 19th c. Here ~ is used in a positive sense which brings it near to the appreciative *sie hat ~ im Kopf* (coll.) = 'she is clever, nobody's fool', recorded by Sanders [1865] with an example from H. Grimm, *Novellen* 125 [1856].

das ist mit blauem ~ genäht (coll.) that is pure invention, a ludicrous assertion; f.r.b. Körte [1837]. This contains an accusation of alcoholic influence (cf. *Zwirn* (1) above) but also connects with *blau* = 'untrue' as in *blaues Märchen, blauer Dunst*, etc. (see p. 334).

sein ~ ist zu Ende (regional coll.) he is at the end of his tether financially; this refers to ~ (3) = 'money'; since the 19th c., recorded by Wander [1880].

der beste ~ (regional coll.) best suit, Sunday-best; only since the 2nd half of the 20th c.

(blauen) ~ wickeln (coll.) to be a wallflower, be without a partner at a dance; assumed to be a ref. to dances in the spinning-room, but only recorded since early in the 20th c.

Meister ~ (coll.) the tailor; this belongs to the group discussed on p. 1683 (*Meister Bakel, Pfriem*, etc.), which began to appear in the 16th c.; *Meister ~* has only been recorded since the 19th c.

sich an einem ~ lenken lassen (lit.) to be easily led or influenced; e.g. Rückert, *Mak.* 1,63; cf. also Platen, *Gasele* 16: '*wer hält das All an diesem*

Zwirne?'. See also similar phrases with *Faden* (*Leitfaden*), *Schnur*, *Seil* and *Strick*.

← See also under *Fuchs* (for *Fuchszwirn*).

zwirnen

etw. ~ (lit.) to weave or work sth. into a tissue or web; since the 18th c., e.g. Goethe, *Die Weisen und die Leute 51*: 'den rechten Lebensfaden spinnt Einer, der lebt und leben läßt, er drille zu und zwirne fest!', Jean Paul, *Leben Fibels 69*: 'Redefaden . . . zu spinnen und zu zwirnen'; now a., if not obs.

jem. ~ (sl.) to give sb. a hard time; from mil. sl. since the 2nd half of the 19th c., when intrans. ~ = 'to work hard, exert oneself' also occurred.

Dinge zusammenzwirnen (rare) to collect items and twist them into a package; f.r.b. Sanders [1865] with an example from Kürnberger, *Novellen 2,210* [1861]: 'das alles haben sie mir so zusammen gezwirnt' with ref. to producing a web of incriminating material.

Zwirnsfaden

See under *Faden* (for *zuletzt über Zwirnsfäden stolpert*) and *hinaussetzen* (for *doch an einer Ecke mit Zwirnsfäden angebunden*).

zwirnsfadendünn: see *dünn*.

zwischen

See under *Angel* (for *zwischen Tür und Angel*), *Bank* (for *zwischen zwei Bänken sitzen*), *Baum* (for *zwischen Baum und Borke sitzen/sein*), *Fell* (for *es sitzt mir zwischen Fell und Fleisch*), *Feuer* (for *zwischen zwei Feuer geraten*), *Gewächs* (for *hält die Mitte zwischen Leben und Tod*), *Himmel* (for *zwischen Himmel und Erde*), *Jahr* (for *zwischen den Jahren*), *Kegel* (for *zwischen Kugel und Kegel kommen*), *Lippe* (for *zwischen Lipp' und Kelchesrand*), *Meerrettich* (for *zwischen Rindfleisch und Meerrettich gemacht*), *mein* (for *er kann zwischen mein und dein nicht unterscheiden*), *Mittel* (for *Mitteldinger zwischen Sein und Nichtsein* and *Mittellinie zwischen zu wenig und zu viel*), *Ohr* (for *den Kopf zwischen die Ohren nehmen*), *Rheumatismus* (for *er hat Rheumatismus zwischen Daumen und Zeigefinger*) and *Stuhl* (for *zwischen zwei Stühlen sitzen*).

Zwischenfall

der ~ unforeseen event; only since the 2nd half of the 18th c., used by Goethe; at first mainly in pl with reference to repeated interruptions, then also in sg for an unexpected event; hence also *ohne* ~ = 'without a hitch', modern.

Zwischenglied

das ~ intermediate stage or link, transitional item; since the 18th c. for a phenomenon that appears between two stages of a development or sth. which is a variant form, as in Herder [edit. S.] 30,414: '. . . daß vom Atheisten bis zum . . . Schwärmer eine große Kette mit allen Zwischengliedern sich verbreitet'.

Zwischenhändler

der ~ intermediary, go-between; modern.

Zwischenlösung

die ~ temporary or provisional solution; modern.

Zwischenraum: see *Raum*.

Zwischensatz

der ~ (1) (ling.) parenthesis, inserted clause; since early in the 18th c., f.r.b. Wächtler [1703].

der ~ (2) (mus.) middle section of a composition, esp. one between two movements of the main theme; since the 18th c.

zwischenschalten: see *schalten*.

zwischenschieben: see *flicken*.

Zwischenträger

der ~ talebearer, telltale, informant; usually implying malicious intent since the 18th c. (the female kind is called *Zwitsche* in 20th c. sl.). In more recent times ~ has also been used in a positive sense for sb. who conveys messages between parties as go-between, even mediator (since 1st half of 19th c.).

Zwischenursache: see *Mittel*.

Zwischenzeit: see *Wurf*.

Zwist: see *nagen*.

Zwistigkeit: see *beugen*.

Zwitsche: see *Zwischenträger*.

zwitschern

zwitschern (lit.) to make a twittering noise; originally only for noises made by birds, figur. with ref. to things, e.g. (T.) Bergengruen, *Großtyrann 14* [1935]: 'das zwitschernde Morgenläuten', Carossa, *Schicksale D.B. 37* [1930]: 'über das Wasser surrte und zwitscherte das Drahtseil'; it can also be used with ref. to fast high-pitched women's voices; all only since the 20th c.

etw. . . . -zwitschern to sing, warble, twitter sth.; in compounds where ~ stands for 'uttering' sth. continuously, affectionately, secretly according to context; since the 18th c., e.g. Börne, *Schriften 4,118*: '. . . frische Zweige säuseln mich vom Pulte weg, tausend Vögel zwitschern mich hinaus', Heine, *Reis. 3,249*: 'das Lied von Byron'scher Zerrissenheit, das mir schon seit zehn Jahren . . . vorgepfiffen und vorgezwitschert wird', also in *jem.m etw. zuzwitschern* with such abstracts als *Liebesworte, Zärtlichkeiten, Trost,* etc.; missing in *DWb.* [1954].

einen ~ (coll.) to have a quick one, take a snifter; first recorded for Berlin in 1840 with the explanation that the verb referred to the sound made by the cork drawn from the bottle; hence in the 20th c. in compounds such as *Zwitscherecke* for an area, esp. a road-crossing where there are several public houses.

← See also under *alt* (for *wie die Alten sungen, so zwitschern die Jungen*) and *Schwalbe* (for *zwitschern wie eine Schwalbe*).

Zwitter

der ~ thing or creature which is a cross between two things; first in OHG for 'bastard', since MHG for 'hermaphrodite, bisexual person', f.r.b. Alberus [1504]; since the 18th c. extended to plants, animals, impure minerals, esp. in compounds, but also in wider sense to persons. It can denote a person who is in essence neither one thing nor another, as in Möser, *Phant.* 3,227 with ref. to persons who are not truly free but subjected to limitations: '... *sind keine wahre Freien, sondern Zwitter*', but more commonly in descriptions of persons with a mixture of characteristics, beliefs or attitudes, e.g. Wieland, *Gold. Spiegel* 1,6: '*diese gravitätischen Zwitter von Schwärmerei und Heuchelei*', C.F. Meyer, *A.Borgia* 107: '*ein wunderlicher Zwitter, gemengt aus geistiger Armuth und unerschöpflichem Erfindungstriebe*'; hence also for things since the 19th c., e.g. Freytag, *Soll u.H.* 1,71: '*ein Zwitter von Tasche und Mappe*'.

zwitterhaft, zwitterig ambiguous, not clearly defined; in both forms since the 18th c., first in biol. contexts for 'hermaphroditic', then extended, e.g. Goethe, *Gespr.* [edit. B.] 8,360: '*wodurch das Drama den zwitterhaften Charakter des Melodramas erhalte*', *Werke* 52,163 (W.): '*ein albernes zwitterhaftes Geschöpf*'; Wieland, *Sämtl. Werke* 12,205 used '*zwittrische Figur*' with ref. to centaurs.

der Zwitterschein (poet.) twilight, uncertain light; since the 18th c., only in poetry.

zwölf

von ~ bis Mittag arbeiten, denken, etc. to do, think, etc. not(hing) at all; in many contexts, e.g. *er arbeitet nur von ~ bis Mittag* = 'he does not do a stroke of work', *er denkt (nur) von ~ bis Mittage* = 'he is incredibly stupid', *er behält nichts von ~ bis Mittag* = 'he has a memory like a sieve', all recorded since ca. 1900. Different in origin is *das dauert von ~ bis Mittag* (in some regions *von ~ bis läut*) = 'that does not last', a development by substitution from *von elf bis Mittag*, a ref. to bell-ringing in the countryside at 11 o'clock so that farm workers could reach home in time for their midday meal; recorded since the 2nd half of the 19th c.; cf. the prov. *zwischen ~ und Mittag gar Vieles noch geschehen mag*, recorded by Simrock [1846].

sein Hut weist (steht, sitzt, zeigt) auf halb ~ (coll.) his hat is not sitting on straight; since the 18th c., recorded by Lichtenberg, *Verm.Schr.* 5,273 with '*weist*'.

jetzt schlägt's aber ~! (coll.) that's the limit, that puts the lid on it; expression of anger; recorded since late in the 19th c.; cf. *dreizehn* (for *jetzt schlägt's dreizehn*). In some regions there is also *es hat ~ geschlagen* = 'it is all over, that's the end of it' and *bei dem hat's ~ geschlagen* = 'he is near death', recorded for Swabia by Fischer.

in den Zwölfen (Zwölften or *den heiligen Zwölfen)* during the twelve days of Christmas; old superstitions are associated with this period, e.g. a belief in the appearance of ghosts, such as *der*

wilde Jäger; in lit. since the 18th c., e.g. Rötger, *Allg.Rep.* 2314 [1824]: '*in den sogannten Zwölfen sollen keine abergläubischen Dinge betrieben werden*', M. Claudius, *Sämtl.Werke* 1,115: '*der ewige Jäger, der übern Zwölften sein Thun so hat*'. In some regions superstitions remain, e.g. there must be no changing of the bed sheets during this period since this would bring about the death of a member of the family; cf. also Sandvoss, *Sprichwörterlese* 137: '*in den Zwölften soll man den Wolf nicht bei seinem Namen nennen. Ein alter Aberglaube, weil man meint, er falle sonst die Heerde an; man soll ihn nicht Wolf, sondern Ding, Unthier u.dgl. nennen. In der Regel braucht man es uneigentlich, wenn man sich scheut, den Namen von jemand, der uns schaden kann, zu nennen*'.

← See also under *Dutzend* (for *davon gehen zwölf aufs Dutzend*), *fünf* (for *fünf Minuten vor zwölf/Torschluß*) and *Minute* (for *bis fünf Minuten nach zwölf*).

Zwölfbote: see *Bote*.

zyklopisch

zyklopisch (1) (obs.) cruel, sadistic, barbaric; refers both to the Cyclops Polythemus, the one-eyed cruel giant of Greek mythology known to readers through Homer and to the tribe of that name alleged to have lived along the Sicilian coast and to be one-eyed, gigantic, cruel canibals; in German since the 16th c., e.g. (DWb) Menius, *Chron. Carionis* 3,241 [1564]; now obs.

zyklopisch (2) gigantic; mainly with ref. to structures, esp. walls, since the Cyclops were reputed to have built walls with huge untreated rocks not held together by any mortar; hence *zyklopische Mauer, zyklopische Felsenmauern* = 'cyclopean masonry' (as still extant in Tiryns, Mycene), e.g. Goethe 15,1,200 (W.): '... *plumpes Mauerwerk ... aufgewältzt, cyclopisch wie Cyclopen, rohen Stein sogleich auf rohe Steine stürzend*'; at the same time (ca. 1800) applied to anything huge, including abstracts, e.g. *zyklopische Arbeit* or *Kraft*; hence also since 2nd half of the 19th c. *zyklopenartig* and *-haft* = 'cyclopean'.

zyklopische Familie (psychol.) (extremely) patriarchal family; derived from a passage in Homer about life among Cyclops suggesting that the oldest or dominant male in the family had unlimited, including sexual rights over everybody; introduced into psychol. writings by Freud and his followers (ca. 1920).

Zylinder

den ~ nehmen (coll.) to retire (from one's post); since ca. 1870; a ref. to the wearing henceforth of the top hat of the middle classes (an Engl. fashion which arrived via France in the middle of the 19th c.) and abandoning one's professional headgear, helmet, cap, etc.; hence also *jem.m den ~ verleihen* = 'to dismiss sb. or to force sb. to request permission to retire', since the beginning of the 20th c.; cf. *den Hut nehmen* (p. 1390).

etw. aus dem ~ zaubern (coll.) to produce sth. as if by magic; since the 2nd half of the 20th c., e.g. (S.-B.) *Mannh. Morgen* of 22.5.1981: '*dieser Brief wurde von der Staatsanwaltschaft wie ein Kaninchen aus dem Zylinder gezaubert*'.

der ~ (1) (coll.) the head; mainly in *jem.m etw. auf den ~ geben* = 'to beat sb. on the head', but, as in the case of similar phrases with *Deckel* (see p. 460), *Hut* (see p. 1390) and *Kappe* (see p. 1437), referring not to a blow but some kind of reprimand or punishment.

der ~ (2) (mil. sl.) steel helmet; since 1st World War.

der ~ (3) (vulg.) lavatory seat; from mil. sl. of 2nd World War. Now obs.

KEY TO PRINCIPAL ABBREVIATIONS

jem.m	jemandem (dat.)
Kluge	F. Kluge, *Etymologisches Wörterbuch der deutschen Sprache*, 11th ed., Berlin und Leipzig 1934.
Lehman	C. Lehman, *Florilegium Politicum*, etc., Frankfurt 1640.
Lexer	M. Lexer, *Mittelhochdeutsches Handwörterbuch*, Leipzig 1872–8.
LG	Low German
Lipperheide	F. Freih. v. Lipperheide, *Spruchwörterbuch*, 2nd ed., München 1909.
MHG	Middle High German
mil.	military
M. Latin	medieval Latin
N.	Northern Germany
NED	*Oxford English Dictionary, A New English Dictionary on Historical Principles*, Edited by Sir James Murray, Henry Bradley, W. A. Craigie and C. T. Onions. Oxford 1884–1928.
NHG	New High German
NW	North-Western Germany
obs.	obsolete
OE	Old English
offic.	in civil service language
OHG	Old High German
ON	Old Norse
OS	Old Saxon
Oxf.	*The Oxford Dictionary of English Proverbs*, compiled by W. G. Smith, Oxford, 1935.
p.	page
poet.	used mainly in poetic language
pop.	popular
pop. etym.	popular etymology
prov.	proverb, proverbial
sb.	somebody
Schmeller	J. A. Schmeller, *Bayerisches Wörterbuch*, Stuttgart 1827–37.
Schulz-Basler	G. Schulz und O. Basler, *Deutsches Fremdwörterbuch*, Strassburg und Berlin 1913ff.
s.e.	self-explanatory
sl.	slang
S. Singer	S. Singer, *Sprichwörter des Mittelalters*, Bern 1944–7.
sth.	something
SW.	South-Western Germany
Trübner	*Trübners Deutsches Wörterbuch*, herausg. v. A. Götze, Berlin 1939ff.
v.	verse, verses
vulg.	in vulgar use (obscene terms are included under this heading, but specially marked as such)
Waag	A. Waag, *Die Bedeutungsentwicklung unseres Wortschatzes*, 5th ed., Lahr 1926.
Wb.	Wörterbuch
Weigand	F. L. K. Weigand, *Deutsches Wörterbuch*, 5th ed., Gießen 1909–10.
Weist.	Weistümer; usually the collection by J. Grimm, Göttingen 1840–69 is referred to; Österr, is appended to the Austrian collections.
Westph.	Westphalia, Westphalian
zool.	zoological term.

Where later editions than those cited above have been quoted (especially in the cases of Büchmann, Dornseiff and Kluge), details of the editions used are given in the text.

The abbreviations for journals mostly follow the accepted practice (*MLR for Modern Language Review, MLN for Modern Language Notes, IF for Indogermanische Forschungen*, etc.), only some long titles have been still further abbreviated though still left recognizable (e.g. *Z.f.d.W.* for *Zeitschrift für deutsche Wortforschung, Z.f.d.U.* for *Zeitschrift für den deutschen Unterricht, Z.f.r.P.* for *Zeitschrift für romanische Philologie*, etc.). Other works, referred to or quoted have been mentioned in abbreviated but recognizable form. It is intended to give a comprehensive list of them when the dictionary is completed. From Fasc. 9 Goethe (W.) = Weimar edition, Schiller (S.) = Säkularausgabe.

ISBN 0-631-20791-0